Business: Its Legal, Ethical, and Global Environment

4th Edition

Marianne Moody Jennings
Arizona State University

SOUTH-WESTERN College Publishing

An International Thomson Publishing Company

Acquisitions Editor: Rob Dewey
Team Director: Jack C. Calhoun
Developmental Editor: Kurt Gerdenich
Production Editors: Karen Truman and Sharon L. Smith
Production House: TSI Graphics
Cover and Interior Designer: Craig LaGesse Ramsdell
Cover Photo: (c) Sam Sargent/Photographic Resources
Photo Researcher: Jennifer Mayhall
Marketing Manager: Scott D. Person

 This book is printed on acid-free recycled paper.

Library of Congress Cataloging-in-Publication Data
Jennings, Marianne Moody.
    Business: its legal, ethical, and global environment / Marianne Moody Jennings.—4th ed.
          p.   cm.
    Includes bibliographical references and indexes.
    ISBN 0-538-85441-3
    1. Business law—United States.   2. Business ethics.   I. Title.
KF889.3.J46   1996
346.73'07—dc20
[347.3067]   96-9283
                                                             CIP

2 3 4 5 6 7 8 VH 3 2 1 0 9 8 7 6

Printed in the United States of America

I(T)P

International Thomson Publishing
South-Western College Publishing is an ITP Company.
The ITP trademark is used under license.

http://www.lawinfo.com/	**LawInfo** LawInfo is an online source for locating attorneys and legal resources.
http://www.lawlinks.com/	**Lawlinks.Com** Lawlinks.Com highlights Internet legal resource for both attorneys and consumers.
http://www.lectlaw.com/	**'Lectric Law Library** The 'Lectric Law Library provides legal information for people involved in the legal profession, and for people who have, or are starting, a business.
http://www.legal.net/	**Legal dot Net** Legal dot Net is for those who provide, regulate, support or are merely interested in knowing about legal services.
http://www.lcp.com/The-Legal-List/TLL-home.html	**Legal List** The Legal List, maintained by Erik J. Heels, compiles legal resources on the Internet and elsewhere.
http://www.lcsweb.com/lrroom.htm	**Legal Research Room** The Legal Research Room provides federal and state law links, as well as general legal resources.
http://www.pls.com:8001/	**U.S. House of Representatives Internet Law Library** The U.S. House of Representatives Internet Law Library provides access to over 1,600 law-related resources of the Internet.
http://www.law.indiana.edu/law/v-lib/lawindex.html	**WWW Virtual Law Library** Virtual law library maintained by the Indiana University School of Law—Bloomington.

STATE AND FEDERAL LEGISLATIVE AND JUDICIAL RESOURCES

http://law.house.gov/cfr.htm	**Code of Federal Regulations** The U.S. House of Representatives Internet Law Library maintains a searchable version of the Code of Federal Regulations.
http://www.law.cornell.edu/supct/supct.table.html	**Decisions Of The U.S. Supreme Court** The Legal Information Institute (LII), part of the Cornell University Law School, maintains hypertext and searchable court decisions for recent Supreme Court cases.
http://lawlib.wuacc.edu/washlaw/uslaw/statelaw.html	**StateLaw** StateLaw, maintained by the Washburn University School of Law, provides state government and legislative information.
http://www.law.emory.edu/FEDCTS/	**U.S. Federal Courts Finder** Emory Law School maintains links to recent court decisions from the U.S. circuit courts of appeals.
http://law.house.gov/17.htm	**U.S. House of Representatives Internet Law Library** The U.S. House of Representatives Internet Law Library maintains links to U.S. state and territorial law sites.
http://www.law.cornell.edu/ucc/ucc.table.html	**Uniform Commercial Code** The Legal Information Institute (LII), part of the Cornell University Law School, maintains a hypertext and searchable version of the Uniform Commercial Code.
http://www.law.cornell.edu/uscode/	**United States Code** The Legal Information Institute (LII), part of the Cornell University Law School, maintains a hyperlinked and searchable version of the U.S. Code.
http://www.law.emory.edu/FEDERAL/usconst.html	**United States Constitution** Emory Law School maintains a hypertext version of the U.S. Constitution.

To the core of my global environment:
Terry, Sarah, Claire, Sam, and John

Brief Contents

Contents

THIRD-PARTY RIGHTS IN
CONTRACTS 537

INTERNATIONAL ISSUES IN
CONTRACT PERFORMANCE 539
  Assuring Payment 539
  Assuring Performance—International
    Peculiarities 539

SUMMARY 540

QUESTIONS AND PROBLEMS 542

C H A P T E R   1 6

Financing of Sales and Leases:
Credit and Disclosure
Requirements 546

ESTABLISHING A CREDIT
CONTRACT 548

STATUTORY REQUIREMENTS FOR
CREDIT CONTRACTS 548
  State Usury Laws 548
  The Equal Credit Opportunity Act 549
  The Truth-in-Lending Act 554
  Fair Credit Billing Act 562
  Fair Credit Reporting Act 563
  Consumer Leasing Act 567

ENFORCEMENT OF CREDIT
TRANSACTIONS 568
  The Use of Collateral: The Security
    Interest 568
  Collection Rights of the Creditor 568
  Suits for Enforcement of Debts 572
  The End of the Line on Enforcement of
    Debts: Bankruptcy 573

SUMMARY 574

QUESTIONS AND PROBLEMS 574

PART IV

BUSINESS AND ITS
EMPLOYEES 579

C H A P T E R   1 7

Management of Employee
Conduct: Agency 580

NAMES AND ROLES—AGENCY
TERMINOLOGY 582
  Agency 582
  Principals 582
  Agents 582
  Masters-Servants 582
  Independent Contractors 582
  Agency Law 583

CREATION OF THE AGENCY
RELATIONSHIP 583
  Express Authority 583

  The Writing 583
  Capacity 584
  Implied Authority 584
  Apparent Authority 585
  Ratification 589

THE PRINCIPAL-AGENT RELATION-
SHIP 591
  The Agent's Responsibilities 591
  The Principal's Rights and
    Responsibilities 593

LIABILITY OF PRINCIPALS FOR
AGENTS' CONDUCT—THE RELA-
TIONSHIP WITH THIRD PARTIES 594
  Contract Liability 594
  Liability of Principals for Agents'
    Torts 596

TERMINATION OF THE AGENCY
RELATIONSHIP 600

TERMINATION OF AGENTS UNDER
EMPLOYMENT AT WILL 601
  The Implied Contract 601
  The Public Policy Exception 603
  The Antiretaliation Statutes: Protections
    for Whistle-Blowers 607

AGENCY RELATIONSHIPS IN INTER-
NATIONAL LAW 609

SUMMARY 610

QUESTIONS AND PROBLEMS 611

C H A P T E R   1 8

Management of Employee
Welfare 614

WAGES AND HOURS
PROTECTION 616
  The Fair Labor Standards Act 616
  Coverage of FLSA 616
  Penalties for FLSA Violation 617
  Liability for FLSA Violation 617
  Enforcement of FLSA 618
  FLSA Regulations 618
  The Equal Pay Act of 1963 620

WORKPLACE SAFETY 621
  Occupational Safety and Health Act 621
  OSHA Responsibilities 623
  State OSHA Programs 627
  Employee Impairment and Testing
    Issues 627

EMPLOYEE PENSIONS, RETIREMENT,
AND SOCIAL SECURITY 628
  Social Security 628
  Private Retirement Plans 629
  Unemployment Compensation 630

WORKER'S COMPENSATION LAWS 633
  Employee Injuries 633
  Fault Is Immaterial 636

Preface

BUSINESS: ITS LEGAL, ETHICAL,
AND GLOBAL ENVIRONMENT

Building the Bridge: Applying Legal and Ethical Reasoning to Business Analysis

As the capstone project for their business degree, our business school students at Arizona State University were assigned the Marriott International case study. Our students expertly discussed Marriott's core competencies. The students offered classic SWOT analysis: Strengths, Weaknesses, Opportunities, and Threats. Should Marriott spin off its real estate assets and focus on hotel management? In came the students' economic analysis, factoring in the nature and importance of economic swings and the resulting vulnerability of real estate ventures. Later, they discussed Marriott's marketing and its hotel management. In other words, we had very capable *business* students.

But with each presentation I found myself raising the same unanswered questions: What are the rights of the bondholders and the shareholders? Would a corporate resolution with shareholder approval be necessary for Marriott's strategy? Could the officers and directors be accused of insider trading for giving themselves as shareholders the most valuable portions of the company and spinning off the company's heavy debt obligations? What are the ethics of transferring all the risk and debt to the bondholders? Are shareholders and bondholders both stakeholders? Don't both have rights within the company? Our capable business students, adept at complex business analysis, stumbled over basic legal and ethical issues.

Why couldn't these students competently discuss legal issues? It was not for lack of exposure to the law. I taught my course "by the book," so to speak. Students could recite the components of a valid contract, rattle off the requirements for bankruptcy, recall from memory the antitrust statutes. Yet, I was coming to realize, this rote knowledge was not enough. One of my best former students, who had gone on to medical school, came to me perplexed about her office lease. She said that the complex in which she wanted to open her practice had a "no advertising" policy. In fact, she said that when she toured the premises with a leasing agent, the leasing agent turned to her and said, "You're not one of those doctors who advertises, are you? Because if you are, we can't lease to you. We have a policy against it." One of my best students, who knew the antitrust statutes well, could not apply them to her everyday business. Worse, perhaps, she could not *recognize* when to apply these statutes: She did not see the antitrust implications of the agent's statements nor the problems with the physicians in the complex taking such an approach to screening tenants.

I reached the conclusion that there were shortcomings in the standard approach to teaching business students law and ethics. Students were not ignorant to legal issues; rather, they simply lacked the necessary skills to recognize legal and ethical issues and to apply law and ethics to business decision-making. As instructors, we were not integrating legal and ethical reasoning with business analysis. My conclusion led me to develop my own materials for classroom use and eventually led to the publication of the first edition of this book. Now in its fourth edition, *Business: Its Legal, Ethical, and Global Environment* brings to the classroom the most integrated approach to learning law and ethics available in the market today. Throughout every chapter and in every feature, students and instructors are continually reminded of how various legal and ethical principles apply in business contexts. For all areas of law and ethics, this book answers the question: How does this concept affect a business?

Strengthening the Bridge: New Content, Business Applications, and Learnings Aids

For the fourth edition, *Business: Its Legal, Ethical, and Global Environment* has undergone a major revision. New content has been added, new business applications integrated into every chapter, and new learning aids developed to help students understand legal and ethical concepts.

NEW CONTENT
Parts and chapters in *Business: Its Legal, Ethical, and Global Environment* have been reorganized and redesigned to better facilitate student understanding of how law and ethics apply to the business world. In general, each part begins with an overview and ends with a series of integrative problems to help students combine the various aspects of law with business management and operations. Part I offers the student an overview of the legal, ethical, and judicial environments of business. Part II covers the regulatory environments of business. Part III covers the law and ethics of competition and sales. Part IV covers the legal and ethical issues of business and employees. Part V covers the law and ethical dilemmas of business organization and capitalization.

Ethics Business Ethics and Social Responsibility (Chapter 2) offers an increased focus on the application of ethics to business decision-making. Ethics coverage is also integrated throughout all chapters.

Property Business Property (Chapter 12) now offers a separate chapter on property law, including intellectual, tangible personal, and real property issues.

Alternative Dispute Resolution Managing Disputes: Alternative Dispute Resolution and Litigation Strategies (Chapter 4) now offers increased coverage of alternative dispute resolution (ADR) topics.

Bankruptcy Financing of Sales and Leases: Credit and Disclosure Requirements (Chapter 16) now includes coverage of bankruptcy.

NEW BUSINESS APPLICATIONS

Biography Each chapter contains at least one biography. Biographies (1- to 3-page features) provide students with business history through the study of individuals and companies involved with the area of law and ethics covered in the chapter. For example, Business and the Constitution (Chapter 5) discusses Time Warner's public relations battle and ethical dilemma over the release of its artist Ice-T's album with the song "Cop Killer" (pgs. 166–168). Students have the opportunity to see how the constitutional principle of free speech relates to business and how businesses face questions of social responsibility. In addition, they are given insights into issues such as shareholder power and the interaction of corporate managers with the powerful forces of an institutional investor such as a police pension fund.

For the Manager's Desk Each chapter also contains at least one For the Manager's Desk. These readings provide students with excerpts from various business publications including *Forbes*, *The Wall Street Journal*, *Fortune*, and *Business Week*, as well as other publications including the *National Law Journal*, *California Management Review*, *American Business Law Journal*, and the *Real Estate Law Journal*. These readings, some short and others in-depth, offer students the opportunity to see how business interrelates with ethics and law. See pages 34, 46, and 77.

Judg

Judgment Judgments open each chapter by presenting a legal and ethical problem relevant to the topics covered in the chapter. For example, Business and the Constitution (Chapter 5) presents students with the case facts from *United States* v. *Lopez* and questions why federal law, and not state law, applies to a high school in San Antonio, Texas. Students then find answers to these questions within the text of the chapter (in this situation, the *Lopez* case appears later in the chapter). Moreover, these answers are referenced in the text and clearly marked with a Judgment icon.

Integrative Problems Each Part closes with 1–5 substantive problems that require students to think critically about and apply the major issues from the preceding chapters. Integrative problems offer students the opportunity to apply legal and ethical reasoning to business analysis. Often these problems require students to prepare memoranda or other practical types of business writing. See pages 141–146.

LEARNING AIDS

Visit the Jennings
Legal Environment
Web Site:
http://www.
thomson.com/swcp/
bef/jennings/
jennings.html

Internet Margin Notes For further student exploration, every chapter integrates World Wide Web addresses highlighting links to legal and business resources. At their option, students can review unedited cases and full statutes, visit government departments and international organizations, and examine relevant business materials. The text includes over 150 Web addresses. See pages 83, 86, and 172.

Case Headlines Every court case has a case headline that summarizes what issues are involved in the case. In Business Torts (Chapter 9), students read *Page* v. *American National Bank & Trust Company* (pgs. 311–314), a case addressing the liability of banks for robberies of customers as they use or attempt to use the bank's ATMs. Although students likely won't remember the name *Page*, the headline, "Pummeled at the ATM," will keep the case and its holding fresh in their memories.

Chapter Openers Chapters begin with an opening problem, titled Judgment, which presents a legal dilemma, relevant to the chapter's discussion and similar to those business managers need to handle. These are revisited and answered in the body of the chapter. Next, opening statements discuss the major topics of the chapter and present the general goals for the chapter, in the form of questions to be answered. Finally, quotations, often humorous, pique students' interest and focus the chapter to the major issues.

Chapter Summary Each chapter concludes with a summary that reinforces the major concepts of the chapter. Each summary is constructed around the key questions introduced at the start of the chapter and key terms presented throughout the chapter.

Text Design *Business: Its Legal, Ethical, and Global Environment* now takes advantage of a full-color design. Each feature has a distinctive design and color for easy identification. All Judgments, and many of the Biographies and For the Manager's Desk readings, contain relevant photos to help students relate to the people and issues discussed.

Supporting the Bridge: Organization and Features

In addition to the new features added to this edition, the classic features have been updated and strengthened. As well, the organization has been revised to better meet student needs in the classroom.

ORGANIZATION

As noted above, there are five new parts in the book which serve to organize the materials around business operations. Every chapter integrates international (marked by a global icon) and ethical topics.

Part I In four chapters, Part 1 offers an introduction to law, an introduction to business ethics and the judicial system, and a discussion of litigation and alternative dispute resolution. Part 1 provides students with a foundation in law and ethics, as well as legal and ethical reasoning, necessary for the areas of law in the chapters that follow. By being brief (four chapters), Part 1 offers instructors an early and logical break for exams.

Part 2 In seven chapters, Part 2 covers the regulatory environment of business, including the following topics: constitutional law, administrative and international law, business crimes and business torts, product advertising and liability, and environmental regulation. With the completion of Parts 1 and 2, students have a grasp of the legal system, ethical boundaries, and the laws that affect business operational decisions.

Part 3 The five chapters in Part 3 present students with the legal and ethical issues surrounding competition and sales. Part 3 includes the following topics: real, tangible personal, and intellectual property; trade restraints and antitrust laws; contract and sales law; and financing of sales and leases, including credit disclosure and requirements. From the negotiation of price to the collection of a counts, this segment of the book covers all aspects of selling business products and services.

Part 4 The three chapters in Part Four discuss the contractual and regulatory aspects of employer and employee relationships. Topics include: agency law and employee conduct, management of employee welfare, and employment discrimination.

Part 5 In Part Five, students study the advantages and disadvantages of various business organizations and the regulation of the capital markets. The three chapters in Part 5 include the following topics: business organization, securities laws, and business combinations. The final chapter on business combinations has been reorganized, rewritten, and updated to reflect the new mergers of the 1990s.

FEATURES

Court Cases Edited court language cases provide in-depth points of law, and many cases include dissenting and concurring opinions. Case questions follow to help students understand the points of law in the case and think critically about the decision. See pages 153 and 159.

Consider . . . Consider problems, along with Ethical Issues boxes and Business Planning Tips, have been a part of every chapter since the first edition, and they are continued in greater numbers in this edition. Considers, often based on real court cases, ask students to evaluate and analyze the legal and ethical issues discussed in the preceding text. By being integrated into the text, students must address and think critically about these issues as they encounter them. Through interactive problems, students learn to judge case facts and determine the consequences. See pages 11 and 45.

Ethical Issues Ethical Issues boxes appear in every chapter and present students with real-world ethical problems for students to grapple with. Ethical Issues help integrate coverage of ethics into every chapter. See pages 20 and 63.

Business Planning Tips Students are given sound business and legal advice through Business Planning Tips. With these tips, students not only know the law, they know how to anticipate issues and ensure compliance. See pages 56, 60, and 162.

Exhibits Exhibits include charts, figures, and business and legal documents that help highlight or summarize legal and ethical issues from the chapter. See pages 39, 89, and 91.

End of Chapter Problems The end of the chapter problems have been updated and focus more on actual cases.

Crossing the Bridge: Who Should Use This Book?

With its comprehensive treatment of the law, integrated business applications, and new full-color design, *Business: Its Legal, Ethical, and Global Environment* is well-suited for both undergraduate and MBA students. The book is used extensively in undergraduate education programs around the country. In addition, this edition has been class-tested with MBA students, and it is appropriate for MBA and executive education programs.

A Note on AACSB Standards

The AACSB standards emphasize the need for students to have an understanding of ethical and global issues. The fourth edition continues with its separate chapter on ethics as well as ethical issues and dilemmas for student discussion and resolution in every chapter. The separate chapter on international law appears in expanded version in this edition and each chapter has a segment devoted to international law issues. An icon appears in each of the chapters when legal and ethical issues related to global business issues appears. The fourth edition includes readings on women as executives in other cultures, the role of lawyers in other countries, and the attitude outside the United States on insider trading.

This edition presents students with the legal foundation necessary for business operations and sales, but also affords the students the opportunities to analyze critically the social and political environments in which the laws are made and in which businesses must operate. Just an examination of the lists of the companies and individuals covered in the biographies and of the publications from which the For the Manager's Desk readings are taken demonstrate the depth of background the fourth edition offers in those areas noted as critical by the AACSB. The materials provide a balanced look at regulation, free enterprise, and the new global economy.

New to this edition are margin notes that direct the student to various tools and topics available on the Internet. These margin notes offer students the opportunity to browse for more information or undertake projects for additional research and class work.

Supplements

Business: Its Legal, Ethical, and Global Environment continues to offer a comprehensive and well-crafted supplement package for both students and instructors. Contact your ITP Sales Representative or South-Western College Publishing for more details. The following student supplements are available:
- Study Guide
- The Lighter Side of Law: Cases and Readings to Captivate our Imaginations and Memories about Business and Its Encounters with Law
- Legal Tutor software for contract law
- Legal Tutor software for sales law

The following instructor resources are available:
- Instructor's Manual with Transparency Masters
- Instructor's Manual MS-DOS 3.5"
- Test Bank
- MicroExam computerized test bank
- Cases on Disk 3.5"
- PowerPoint Masters and Disk
- Handbook of Statutes and Forms
- CNBC Video segments

ACKNOWLEDGMENTS

By its fourth edition, a book has evolved to a point of trademark characteristics. This book is known for its hands-on examples and readings for business managers. That trademark evolves because of the efforts of many. There are the reviewers and adopters of the text who provide ideas, cases, and suggestions for improvement and inclusion. For this edition, the following colleagues offered their seasoned advice:

William N. Bockanic
John Carroll University

Andrew Jackson Holliday
Washington and Lee University

Don Boren
Bowling Green State University

Henry E. Mallue, Jr.
College of William and Mary

Richard Coffinberger
George Mason University

Leo C. Moersen
George Washington University

Evelyn Boss Cogan
LaSalle University

Debi Moon
DeKalb College

Norman Hawker
Western Michigan University

John Norwood
University of Arkansas

Any edition of a book bears the mark of the editors who work to design, refine, market, and produce it. This book carries the insight of Rob Dewey, the steady hand of Kurt Gerdenich, the eye for detail of Karen Truman and Sharon Smith, and the design quality of Craig Ramsdell. This book also carries the unmistakable liveliness of an author who shares her life with four helpful children and one tolerant husband. Their vibrancy and inspiration is found in the color and charm of these pages.

Marianne Moody Jennings

ABOUT THE AUTHOR

Professor Marianne Jennings is a member of the Department of Business Administration in the College of Business at Arizona State University, a professor of legal and ethical studies in business and director of the Joan and David Lincoln Center for Applied Ethics. Professor Jennings earned her undergraduate degree in finance and her J.D. from Brigham Young University. She has worked with the Federal Public Defender and U.S. Attorney in Nevada and has done consulting work for law firms, businesses, and professional groups including the National Leadership Institute, Dial Corporation, Motorola, the National Association of Credit Managers, Mesa Community College, State Farm Insurance, Southern California Edison, the Arizona Auditor General, the city of Phoenix, Midwest Energy Supply, Bell Helicopter, and the Hispanic Women's Conference.

Professor Jennings joined the faculty at ASU in 1977 as an assistant professor. She was promoted to associate professor in 1980 and to full professor in 1983. At ASU, Jennings teaches graduate courses in business ethics, the legal environment of business, and strategic legal planning. She has authored more than 130 articles in academic, professional, and trade journals. Currently she has six textbooks and monographs in circulation. Jennings is a columnist for *The Arizona Republic*, and her work has appeared in *The Wall Street Journal*, *The Chicago Tribune*, *The Christian Science Monitor*, and other newspapers around the country. A collection of her essays, *Nobody Fixes Real Carrots Anymore*, was published in 1994. She was given the Arizona Press Club award in 1994 for her work as a feature columnist. Jennings is a weekly business commentator on "All Things Considered" for National Public Radio.

Jennings has conducted more than 200 workshops and seminars in the areas of business, personal and professional ethics, legal ethics, real estate, credit management, legal issues for academic administrators, law for the CPA, and legal and political strategic planning. She has twice been named professor of the year in the College of Business and was the recipient of a Burlington Northern teaching excellence award. Jennings was named a Wakonse Fellow in 1994 and was named Distinguished Faculty Researcher for the College of Business that same year. In 1995, she was appointed a Dean's Council of 100 Distinguished Scholar.

Jennings is a contributing editor for the *Real Estate Journal* and the *Journal of Corporate Finance*. In 1984, she served as then-Governor Bruce Babbitt's appointee to the Arizona Corporation Commission. During 1986–1988, she served as Associate Dean in the College of Business. From 1986–1987, she served as ASU's faculty representative to the NCAA and PAC-10. Jennings is a member of twelve professional organizations, including the state Bar of Arizona, and has served on four boards of directors. Currently she serves on the Board of Directors for Arizona Public Service, and the Center for Children with Chronic Illness and Disability at the University of Minnesota. Jennings is chair of the Bonneville International Advisory Board for KHTC/KIDR.

Jennings is married to Terry H. Jennings, and has four children: Sarah, Claire, Sam, and John.

List of *Exhibits*

Acknowledgments

Part One

Business: Its Legal, Ethical, and Judicial Environment

Every business and businessperson needs parameters for operation. What is legal? Where can I find the laws I need to know? How do I make decisions about legal conduct that, personally, is morally or ethically troublesome to me? What if a disagreement occurs with a customer, employee, or shareholder? How can I resolve our differences? What forums are available for airing disputes?

This portion of the book explains what law is, where it can be found, how it is applied, and how legal disputes are resolved. But beyond the legal environment of a business is its ethical posture. Beyond operating a business within the bounds of the law, is the manager making ethical choices and behaving honorably in the conduct of business? Law and ethics are inextricably intertwined. A commitment to both is necessary and helpful in ensuring smooth operations and successful business performance.

Judgment

John J. Marchica, 31 years old, a welder for the Long Island Railroad (LIRR), was assigned the task of repairing a metal grating set over a shaftway at LIRR's Hempstead station in Nassau County, Long Island, New York. When Marchica and his co-workers arrived to repair the grating, they discovered that vagrants had taken advantage of the broken grating latch. They had opened the grating, crawled through a four-foot shaftway, broken a window, gained access to a trainman's room, and used the trainman's room as an "operations center" for drugs, prostitution, and ID sales for illegal aliens.

When Marchica began welding the grate, sparks from his acetylene torch fell to the bottom of the shaft onto accumulated debris of leaves, paper, glass, crack vials and hypodermic instruments. The debris began to smolder. Marchica volunteered to clean out the debris. He had on his heavy-duty welding gloves and climbed down into the shaftway to move the debris. Unfortunately, a hypodermic needle lying hidden in the debris stabbed Marchica's right palm. Marchica, bleeding, was taken to the nearest hospital. He took the needle along in a bag. He was advised to have a tetanus and a hepatitis shot and to get a test for the human immunodeficiency virus (HIV). He then reported back to LIRR's medical department. He was told the HIV test advice was ridiculous and that he should just wash his hands with warm soapy water. The LIRR doctor threw away the needle and syringe without conducting tests.

Marchica had HIV tests conducted six times. The tests were negative. But Marchica lost 30 pounds, abstained from relations with his wife, began seeing a psychiatrist and taking antidepressants. Marchica filed suit against the LIRR under the Federal Employers' Liability Act (FELA) because of his fear of developing acquired immune deficiency syndrome (AIDS) and for negligent infliction of emotional distress.

The LIRR claims it is not liable under FELA for fear injuries. Should fear injuries be covered?

Introduction to Law

For most people, law is understood through what affects them directly. More often than not, people are exposed to law through some personal problem. Some are exposed to law through traffic tickets. Others encounter the law when a problem arises with a landlord or lease. Their understanding of the law may be limited by the anger they feel about a landlord or traffic ticket. However, if there were no traffic laws, the roads would be a study in survival of the fittest. And in the case of a troublesome landlord, the law provides a remedy when parties do not meet their agreed-upon obligations.

Types of laws and penalties for violating them vary from state to state and city to city. But however much they vary, laws exist everywhere and at every level of government. Indeed, law is a universal, necessary foundation of an orderly society; it helps maintain order and ensures that members of a society will meet minimum standards of conduct or risk penalties. Law is made up of rules that control people's conduct and their inter relationships. Traffic laws control not only our conduct when we are driving but also our relationships with other drivers using the roads. In some instances we owe them a right-of-way and will be liable to them for any injuries we cause by not following the traffic laws. What types of laws are there?

This chapter offers an introduction to law. How is law defined? What are the purposes and characteristics of law? Where are laws found and who enacts them?

Law, says the judge as he looks down his nose,

Speaking clearly and most severely,

Law is as I've told you before,

Law is as you know I suppose,

Law is but let me explain it once more,

Law is The Law.[1]

W. H. Auden

DEFINITION OF LAW

Philosophers and scholars throughout human history have offered definitions of law. Aristotle, the early Greek philosopher, wrote that "the law is reason unaffected by desire" and that "law is a form of order, and good law must necessarily mean good order." Oliver Wendell Holmes, Jr., a U.S. Supreme Court justice of the early twentieth century, said that "law embodies the story of a nation's development through many centuries." Sir William Blackstone, the English philosopher and legal scholar, observed that law was "that rule of action which is prescribed by some superior and which the inferior is bound to obey." *Black's Law Dictionary* defines law as "a body of rules of action or conduct prescribed by the controlling authority, and having legal binding force." Law has been defined at least once by every philosopher, statesman, politician, and police officer.

But law is simply the body of rules governing individuals and their relationships. A society enacts most of those rules through a recognized governmental authority. It gives us basic freedoms, rights, and protections. Law offers a consistent model of conduct for members of society in their business and personal lives and gives them certainty of expectations. Plans, businesses, contracts, and property ownership are based on the expectation of the law's consistent protection of rights. Without such a consistent framework of legal boundaries, ours would be a society of chaos and confusion.

CLASSIFICATIONS OF LAW

Public versus Private Law

Public law includes laws that are enacted by some authorized government body. State and federal constitutions and statutes are all examples of public laws, as are the federal securities laws, state incorporation and partnership procedures, and zoning laws.

Private law, on the other hand, is developed between two individuals. For example, landlords usually have regulations for their tenants and these regulations are private laws. The terms of a contract are a form of private law for the parties to that contract. Although the requirements for formation and the means for enforcing that contract may be a matter of public law, the terms for performance are the private law created by the parties to that rental contract. Employer rules in a corporation are also examples of private law; so long as those rules do not infringe any public rights or violate any statutory protections, those rules are a private law relationship between employer and employee that constitute part of the employee's performance standards.

Criminal versus Civil Law

A violation of a **criminal law** is a wrong against society. A violation of a **civil law** is a wrong against another person or persons. Criminal violations have penalties such as fines and imprisonment. Running a red light is an example of a criminal violation and generally carries a fine as punishment. Violations of civil laws require restitution: The party who violated the civil law must compensate the harmed party. If you do run a red light and strike and injure a pedestrian, you are also guilty of a civil wrong, and you may be required to pay for that pedestrian's damages.

If you drive while intoxicated, you have broken a criminal law and will be subject to a fine, jail, or license suspension. If you have an accident while driving intoxicated, you commit a civil wrong against anyone you injure. People who are injured as a result of your driving while intoxicated can file a civil suit against you in order to recover for injuries to their persons and property (cars).

There are other differences between civil and criminal laws and their enforcement. For example, there are different rights and procedures in the trials of criminal cases (see Chapter 8 for more details).

Substantive versus Procedural Law

Substantive laws are those that give rights and responsibilities. **Procedural laws** provide the means for enforcing substantive rights. For example, if Zeta Corporation has breached its contract to buy 3,000 microchips from Yerba Corporation, Yerba has the substantive right to expect performance and may be able to collect damages for breach of contract by bringing suit. The laws governing how Yerba's suit is brought and the trial process are procedural laws; the subject matter and issues of the litigation are the substantive law.

Common versus Statutory Law

The term **common law** has been in existence since 1066, when the Normans conquered England and William the Conqueror sought one common set of laws governing a then very divided England. The various customs of each locality were compromised and conglomerated so that each locality would then operate under a "common" system of law. This common law was developed by the judges in each locality as they settled disputes. They consulted their fellow judges before making decisions so that their body of common law achieved consistency. This principle of following other decisions is referred to as **stare decisis**, meaning "let the decision stand" (see Chapter 2), and as a process of legal reasoning it is still followed today. The courts use the judicial decisions of the past in making their judgments to provide for consistency or to serve as a basis for making a change in the law when circumstances are different.

As much of an improvement as it was, the common law was still just unwritten law. Because of increased trade, population, and complexities, the common law needed to be supplemented. Thus **statutory law**, which is passed by some governmental body and written in some form, was created.

Today in the United States there is both common law and statutory law. Some of our common law still consists of principles from the original English common law. There is, however, still a growing body of common law: The judicial system's decisions constitute a form of common law that is used in the process of stare decisis. Courts throughout the country look to other court decisions when confronted with similar cases. Statutory law exists at all levels of government—federal, state, county, city, and town.

Our statutory law varies throughout the country because of the cultural heritages of various regions of our nation. For example, the southwestern states have marital property rights statutes—often referred to as community property laws—that were influenced by the Spanish legal system implemented in Mexico. The northeastern states have very different marital property laws that were influenced by English laws on property ownership. Louisiana's contract laws are based on French principles because of the early French settlements there.

Law versus Equity

Equity is a body of law that attempts to do justice when the law does not provide a remedy, or when the remedy is inadequate, or when the application of the law is terribly unfair. Equity originated in England because the technicalities of the common law often resulted in unresolved disputes or unfair resolutions. The monarchy allowed its chancellor to hear those cases that could not be resolved in the common law courts, and eventually a separate set of equity courts developed that were not bound by rigid common law rules. These courts could get more easily to the heart of a dispute, and over time they developed remedies not available under common law. Common law, for example, usually permitted only the recovery of monetary damages. Courts of equity, on the other hand, could issue orders, known as **injunctions**, prohibiting certain conduct or ordering certain acts. The equitable remedies available in the courts of chancery were gradually combined with the legal remedies of the common law courts so that now parties can have both their legal and equitable remedies determined by the same court.

Today's courts award equitable remedies when the legal remedy of money damages would be inadequate. For example, Walt Disney often brings suit against companies and individuals for infringement of its copyrighted characters. Disney cannot be adequately compensated with money because the continued use of the characters will cost Disney its exclusive rights. The remedy it seeks and is given is an injunction that orders the infringing party to stop the unauthorized use.

PURPOSES OF LAW

Keeping Order

Laws carry some form of penalty for their violation. Traffic violations carry a fine or imprisonment or both. Violations of civil laws also carry sanctions. If your landlord breaches some part of your lease, you can seek money damages. A driver who injures another while driving intoxicated must pay for the damages and the costs of the injuries the other person experiences. These penalties for violations of laws prevent feuds and other primitive, unpeaceful methods of settling disputes.

Influencing Conduct

Laws also influence the conduct of society's members. For example, securities laws require certain disclosures to be made about securities before they can be sold to the public. The antitrust laws of the early twentieth century prohibited some methods of competition while they controlled others. In effect, these laws changed the way businesses operated.

Honoring Expectations

Businesses commit resources, people, and time with the expectation that the contracts for those commitments will be honored and enforced according to existing law. Investors buy stock with the knowledge that they will enjoy some protection in that investment through the laws that regulate both the securities themselves and the firms in which they have invested. Laws allow prior planning based on the protections inherent in the law.

Promoting Equality

Laws have been used to achieve equality in those aspects of life and portions of the country in which equality is not a reality. For example, the equal right to employment acts (see Chapter 19) were passed to bring equality to the job market. The social welfare programs of state and federal governments were created to further the cause of economic justice. The antitrust laws attempt to provide equal access to the free enterprise system.

Law as the Great Compromiser

A final and very important purpose of law is to act as the great compromiser. Few people, groups, or businesses agree philosophically on how society, businesses, or government should be run. Law serves to mesh views together into one united view so that all parties are at least partially satisfied. When disputes occur, the courts impose the law upon the parties in an attempt to compromise their two opposing views. Thus the U.S. Supreme Court has provided compromises for business and labor through its interpretation of the statutes relating to union organizations, strikes, and other economic weapons (see Chapter 18). In the relationship between labor and management, the law serves as the mediator.

CHARACTERISTICS OF LAW

Flexibility

As society changes, the law must change with it. When the United States was an agricultural nation, the issues of antitrust, employment discrimination, and securities fraud rarely arose. However, as the United States became an industrialized nation, those areas of law expanded and continue to expand. Today, as the United States is evolving toward a technological and information-based society, still more areas of law will be created and developed. The area of computer fraud, for example, was unknown 30 years ago; today most states have criminal statutes to cover such theft (see Chapter 8). The introduction of the fax machine has required courts to reexamine how offers and acceptances of contracts are made to take into account the speed with which contracts may now be formed (see Chapter 14).

Changing circumstances require courts to review and interpret laws. Circumstances change through technology, sociology, and even biology. The existence of the human immunodeficiency virus (HIV) has necessitated the review of many employment issues that have arisen because of the presence of the virus and those inflicted with it in the workplace. *Marchica* v. *Long Island Railroad Company* is an example of a case in which the court dealt with an HIV-related issue for an employee. Changing circumstances brought forward for judicial review a heretofore unaddressed issue. The case also provides an answer to the chapter's opening "Judgment."

Judgment

Marchica v. Long Island Railroad Company
31 F.3d 1197 (2d Cir. 1994)

CLEANING UP THE CRACK HOUSE: WHO PAYS FOR THE INJURIES?

FACTS

John J. Marchica (plaintiff), 31, a welder for the Long Island Railroad (LIRR) (defendant), was assigned the task of repairing a metal grating set over a shaftway at LIRR's Hempstead station in Nassau County, Long Island, New York. When Marchica and his co-workers arrived to repair the grating, they discovered that vagrants had taken advantage of the broken grating latch. Vagrants had opened the grating, crawled through a four-foot shaftway, broken a window, gained access to a trainman's room, and used the trainman's room as an "operations center" for drugs, prostitution, and ID sales for illegal aliens.

When Marchica began welding the grate, sparks from his acetylene torch fell to the bottom of the shaft onto accumulated debris of leaves, paper, glass, crack vials, and hypodermic instruments. The debris began to smolder. Marchica volunteered to clear out the debris. He had on his heavy-duty welding gloves and climbed down into the shaftway to move the debris. Unfortunately, a hypodermic needle lying hidden in the debris stabbed Marchica's right palm. Marchica, bleeding, was taken to the nearest hospital. He took the needle along in a bag. He was advised to have a tetanus and a hepatitis shot and to get a test for the human immunodeficiency virus (HIV). He then reported back to LIRR's medical department. He was told the HIV test advice was ridiculous and that he should just wash his hands with warm soapy water. The LIRR doctor threw away the needle and syringe without conducting tests.

Marchica visited a physician and was advised to abstain from relations with his wife and to be tested several times for HIV. Marchica had tests performed one month, six months, and one year from the date of the October 25, 1989, incident. In November 1989, Marchica began seeing a psychologist because he was having difficulty sleeping, was experiencing nightmares, and was suffering from irritability. His wife and co-workers said they often saw him crying and vomiting. Marchica lost 30 pounds following the injury. Marchica's psychologist referred him to a psychiatrist who prescribed several antidepressants for him. Marchica's final blood test in May 1990 was negative.

In June 1992, Marchica brought suit against the LIRR under the Federal Employers' Liability Act (FELA). Marchica alleged that the LIRR was negligent in failing to provide him with a safe place to work and for failing to maintain Hempstead Railroad Station in a reasonably safe condition. Marchica said his physical and psychological injuries resulted from LIRR's negligence.

The trial court held that FELA does provide for a cause of action for fear of contracting AIDS. The jury found Marchica 55 percent culpable and LIRR 45 percent culpable. The jury awarded Marchica $225,000 for past pain, suffering and emotional distress, and $55,000 for future damages. Of the $280,000 awarded, Marchica's share (45 percent) was $126,000. LIRR appealed.

JUDICIAL OPINION

CARDAMONE, Judge

Congress enacted FELA so that railroad employees who were injured due to the negligence of their employer or of a coworker would have a remedy. The remedy was intended to be broad and Congress prohibited employers subject to liability under the Act from limiting that liability through contract or otherwise. FELA provides in part:

Every common carrier by railroad while engaging in [interstate] commerce . . . shall be liable in damages to any person suffering injury while he is employed by such carrier in such commerce . . . resulting in whole or in part from the negligence of [the carrier]. . . .

The employment and negligence requirements of FELA need no discussion. We turn to whether plaintiff who failed to prove exposure to AIDS

Continued

suffered an actionable injury. Because the scope of FELA is a legal issue, our review of the district court's conclusion that emotional distress is a cognizable injury under that statute is **de novo** [i.e., anew or for the first time].

It has long been accepted by scholarly writers that if a negligent actor's conduct results in a physical injury for which there is liability, the actor is also liable for whatever emotional harm stems from the physical injury. Further, recovery for emotional harm does not depend on the seriousness or extent of the initial physical injury. A majority of states now recognize a separate cause of action for negligent infliction of emotional distress.

At first, common law cases in state courts permitted recovery for emotional harm only when the plaintiff suffered a physical injury or impact that led to the emotional distress. But, even in those states, it takes very little trauma to justify recovery for the tort of negligent infliction of emotional distress. And, in the majority of jurisdictions the physical injury or impact test has been discarded and recovery is now permitted in a broader range of circumstances.

In place of a physical injury requirement, some states apply a zone of danger test, allowing recovery where plaintiff has been threatened with physical injury by the defendant's conduct, and was in reasonable fear of injury, whether or not the plaintiff was actually impacted or suffered such physical injury.

The bystander test, a variation on the zone of danger test, is followed in some jurisdictions and permits a plaintiff witnessing the death or severe injury to a family member to recover, even though not in the zone of physical danger.

The common law of other states imposes a more expansive physical manifestation test, granting recovery when the plaintiff's emotional injury is severe enough to manifest itself in a physical injury.

A minority of states have done away with all formal tests and allow recovery for severe mental distress that was reasonably foreseeable.

The Supreme Court recently held that causes of action for negligent infliction of emotional distress are cognizable under FELA. But the Court limited recovery to those plaintiffs who meet the common law zone of danger test, that is, "those plaintiffs who sustain a physical impact as a result of a defendant's negligent conduct, or who are placed in immediate risk of physical harm by that conduct."

We believe Marchica's claim meets this test. He sustained a puncture wound from a discarded hypodermic needle as a result of LIRR's negligent conduct. Because he suffered a physical impact, Marchica is entitled to receive compensation for all injuries—physical and emotional—proximately caused by the physical impact. Further, his emotional distress manifested itself physically in post traumatic stress disorder, accompanied by sleeplessness, weight loss, vomiting, rashes and anxiety, shortly after he sustained the physical impact. And his emotional injury was reasonably foreseeable, as it was of the sort that a person in his circumstances would ordinarily experience.

In its first challenge to the judgment, the railroad asserts the traditional negligent infliction of emotional distress analysis is inappropriate, and urges us instead to follow the specific jurisprudence employed in fear-of-developing-disease cases. Those cases generally hold as a prerequisite to recovery for emotional distress that a plaintiff prove actual exposure to a disease and a reasonable medical probability of later developing it.

Yet, as is made clear in a case heavily relied upon by defendant, the fear-of-future-disease analysis applies only "[w]ith respect to infliction of emotional distress absent physical injury or contact."

Proof of exposure to a contaminated substance, or exposure plus manifestation of emotional distress or probable future injury, are [sic] substitute means for providing a guarantee of the merits of a plaintiff's claim, where no physical injury has been incurred.

Had Marchica merely touched the discarded needle and become concerned about the possibility of developing AIDS, the case would stand on a very different footing. But because Marchica's emotional distress was the direct result of a documented physical injury and was

Continued

reasonably foreseeable in light of the fact that he may have been exposed to HIV by way of the needle puncture, he was not required to prove actual exposure to the disease in order to state a viable cause of action.

We now pass to the fear-of-developing-AIDS cases. We recognize that in the recent wave of emotional distress cases based on a fear of developing AIDS, several courts have, as in other fear-of-developing-disease cases, required plaintiff to prove actual exposure to the disease as a prerequisite to recovery. Again, these cases are distinguishable primarily because plaintiffs did not suffer a physical injury.

Even where exposure was shown to exist, recovery was precluded in a number of cases because the actual likelihood of developing AIDS was remote. Again, in none of these cases did plaintiffs—unlike the instant plaintiff—suffer a precipitating physical injury.

After examining these cases, we are unable to agree with defendant that there is a common law rule in fear-of-developing-AIDS cases that proof of exposure and a medical likelihood of developing the disease is required in all circumstances. Rather, the common law rule to be gleaned is the same as it is with the other fear-of-developing-disease cases, that is to say, the exposure requirement—plus actual likelihood of developing the disease—simply is a means of ensuring the genuineness of the claim in situations where the plaintiff would not be able to satisfy the traditional tests of genuineness in negligent-infliction-of-emotional-distress cases. Because Marchica satisfies the traditional zone of danger test adopted by the Supreme Court in the FELA context, these fear-of-developing-AIDS cases are inapplicable.

The railroad points in addition to a handful of fear-of-developing-AIDS cases where recovery was denied even though plaintiff suffered a precipitating injury, because there was no proof of actual exposure to the HIV virus. These cases held that emotional distress was unreasonable as a matter of law.

But not all courts have applied so rigid an actual exposure test and we decline to do so. Some courts only require plaintiff to allege a specific incident of possible exposure that could lead to a reasonable fear of developing AIDS.

It is quite apparent from the recitation of the inconsistent decisional law that this area of the law is in a developing stage. We adopt the approach of those cases just discussed which take a more flexible view because they are most consistent with FELA's remedial nature. Thus, a FELA plaintiff who has suffered a physical impact may recover for a fear of developing AIDS if the impact caused by the defendant's negligence occurred under circumstances that would cause a reasonable person to develop a fear of AIDS. The circumstances surrounding Marchica's puncture would fulfill these requirements, and therefore his claim is cognizable.

The second point defendant makes is that where a claim of emotional distress is founded on the fear of developing a disease, the plaintiff must exercise due diligence to become familiar with the realities of the disease and defendant should not be held liable for emotional distress to the extent the plaintiff's fear is based on ignorance. Had Marchica educated himself about HIV and AIDS, defendant insists, he would not have had a rational basis for his fear.

Again, we agree with the general proposition that a plaintiff may only recover for damages proximately caused by a defendant's breach of duty. But we are unable to embrace the notion that a reasonable person, punctured by a discarded hypodermic needle with blood in it, in a location known to be frequented by drug users, exercising due diligence, would not fear developing AIDS. Just the opposite is true; any reasonable person would have such fear.

Evidence presented to the jury revealed that Marchica was advised to be tested for HIV, and even the LIRR medical department considered the needle that punctured Marchica's palm to be infectious. Plaintiff's medical expert on HIV and AIDS testified that the medical community was still exploring precisely how the virus is transmitted and, he added, that in his opinion the disease could be transmitted through a needle that has been used and discarded. From this evidence the jury was entitled to find there was a rational basis for plaintiff's fear of developing AIDS.

Continued

For the reasons stated therefore the judgment of the district court is affirmed.

CASE QUESTIONS
1. Describe Marchica's employment. Describe the task he was performing and where he was when his injury occurred.
2. What injury did Marchica experience?
3. What medical treatment did Marchica receive?
4. What medical advice was Marchica given?
5. What happened to Marchica after he was treated for his injury?
6. What is the basis for Marchica's lawsuit? What negligence on the part of the LIRR does he allege?
7. What did the trial court find? Were damages awarded? How much and why?
8. What is FELA and what is its purpose? Are Marchica's injuries covered under FELA?

C O N S I D E R . . . 1.1 Based on the language in the *Marchica* opinion, would the following injuries be covered under FELA?

1. A hospital employee who is bitten by a patient rumored to have AIDS experiences emotional distress. [*Hare* v. *State*, 570 N.Y.S.2d 125 (1990).]
2. A hospital employee is stuck by several discarded hypodermic needles and experiences emotional distress. [*Carroll* v. *Sisters of Saint Francis Health Service, Inc.*, 868 S.W.2d 585 (Tenn. 1993).]
3. A paramedic is pricked by a hypodermic needle and the user of the needle is unknown. The paramedic experiences emotional distress. [*Burk* v. *Sage Prods., Inc.*, 747 F. Supp. 285 (E.D. Pa. 1990).]
4. A mortician who touches an HIV-infected decedent experiences emotional distress. [*Funeral Services by Gregory, Inc.* v. *Bluefield Community Hosp.*, 413 S.E.2d 79 (W. Va. 1991).]

C O N S I D E R . . . 1.2 In 1933, Walt Disney Company entered into a contract with Irving Berlin, Inc., assigning musical copyrights in exchange for a share of Berlin revenues. The agreement exempted from copyright protection Disney's use of the assigned music in motion pictures. The music was used in several Disney feature-length cartoons (*Snow White* and *Pinocchio*) which later were made available for sale on videocassette. Berlin's heirs brought suit alleging infringement. Was this new technology an infringement? Could videocassettes have been anticipated? [*Bourne* v. *Walt Disney Co.*, 68 F.3d 621 (2d Cir. 1995).]

Consistency

Although the law must be flexible, it still must be predictable. Law cannot change so suddenly that parties cannot rely on its existence or protection. Being able to predict the outcome of a course of conduct allows a party to rely on and enter into a contract or dissuades a party from the commission of a crime. For a contract there is a judicial remedy for breach or nonperformance, and for a crime there is a prescribed punishment.

Pervasiveness

The law must be pervasive and cover all necessary areas, but at the same time it cannot infringe individual freedoms and/or become so complex that it is difficult to enforce. For example, laws cover the formation, operation, and dissolution of corporations. There are, however, no laws that will interfere with corporate management decisions on expanding, developing, and changing the nature of the corporation. So long as the shareholders' rights are protected, the corporation has great flexibility in management.

Analyzing and understanding case decisions is made easier through the use of case briefs. Lawyers, law students, and judges use this uniform system of case shorthand to help gain perspective about a case, recall facts and issues, and review the parties and case procedures. Exhibit 1.1 (pg. 13) demonstrates a case brief for the *Marchica* case.

The Theory of Law: Jurisprudence

Law is the compromise of conflicting ideas. Not only do people differ in their thinking on the types of specific laws, they also differ on the theory behind the law or the values a legal system should try to advance or encourage. Many can agree on the definition of law and its purposes but still differ on how those purposes are best accomplished. The incorporation of theories or values into the legal process is, perhaps, what makes each society's laws different and causes law to change as society changes its values. These different theories or value bases for law are found in an area of legal study called **jurisprudence**, a Latin term meaning "wisdom of the law."

Business Planning Tip

Keeping abreast of changing circumstances in technology, medicine, and sociology helps businesses plan ahead. In the Marchica case, the LIRR learned through expensive litigation that HIV carried implications for workplace safety.

In many contracts for copyrighted works or patented products, significant revenues have been lost because technological changes were not anticipated.

For example, in Sony Corporation of America v. Universal City Studios, 464 U.S. 417 (1984), the U.S. Supreme Court faced the copyright issues surrounding the use of videotape recorders (VTRs or VCRs). Universal Studios and Walt Disney Productions wanted royalties from VCR manufacturers because consumers were using their VCRs to tape Universal and Disney movies for free. The Supreme Court held that videotaping by consumers with their VCRs was exempt under copyright laws.

Many TV shows of the 1950s and 1960s are syndicated today at relatively low cost because actors and writers are not given royalties from the syndicated sales.

Contracts for protected products require a technology clause to cover future uses of the product through means not available at the time of contracting. For example, the following clause is one used in a cable TV contract:

COVENANTS: Subscriber covenants and agrees not to duplicate, reproduce, video-tape, or use the programming or equipment provided hereon for any purpose except home use on television sets converted to the movie club by the company.

Being informed and anticipating changes are all activities that provide businesses protection from changing circumstances.

Name of case:	Marchica v. Long Island Railroad Co.
Court:	Second Circuit; Federal Court of Appeals
Citation:	31 F.3d 1197 (2d Cir. 1994)
Parties and their roles:	John J. Marchica (plaintiff) Long Island Railroad Co. (defendant)
Facts:	Marchica was injured by a hypodermic needle discarded in trash he was cleaning up in order to weld a grate closed in a LIRR station. Marchica became physically and mentally ill because of his fear of exposure to AIDS.
Issues:	Is the LIRR liable to Marchica for his injuries? Is fear of AIDS an injury for which employees can be compensated?
Lower court decision:	The lower court found Marchica 55 percent responsible for his injury and LIRR 45 percent responsible. He was awarded 45 percent of $280,000 for his injuries, or $126,000.
Decision on appeal:	Marchica's verdict was affirmed.
Reasoning:	The injury was foreseeable. Marchica's fear resulted from physical injury. LIRR did not take reasonable precautions.

Exhibit 1.1
Sample Case Brief

FOR THE MANAGER'S DESK

A PRIMER ON JURISPRUDENCE

Legal Philosophy in a Nutshell
Five Minutes of Legal Philosophy

First Minute
"An order is an order," the soldier is told. "A law is a law," says the jurist. The soldier, however, is required neither by duty nor by law to obey an order that he knows to have been issued with a felony or misdemeanor in mind, while the jurists, since the last of the natural law theorists among them disappeared a hundred years ago, have recognized no such exceptions to the validity of a law or to the requirement of obedience by those subject to it. A law is valid because it is a law, and it is a law if in the general run of cases it has the power to prevail.

This view of the nature of a law and of its validity (we call the positivistic theory) has rendered the jurist as well as the people defenseless against laws, however arbitrary, cruel, or criminal they may be. In the end the positivistic theory equates the law with power; there is law only where there is power.

Second Minute
There have been attempts to supplement or replace this tenet with another: Law is what benefits the people. That is, arbitrariness, breach of contract, and illegality, provided only that they benefit the people, are law. Practically speaking, that means that every whim and caprice of the despot, punishment without laws or judgment, lawless killing of the sick—whatever the state authorities deem to benefit to the people—is law. That *can* mean that the private benefit of those in power is regarded as a public benefit. The equating of the law with supposed or ostensible benefits to the people thus transformed a *Rechtsstaat* into a state of lawlessness.

No, this tenet should not be read as: Whatever benefits the people is law. Rather, it is the other way around: Only what is law benefits the people.

Third Minute
Law is the will to justice, and justice means: To judge without regard to person, to treat everyone according to the same standard.

If one applauds the assassination of political opponents and orders the murder of those of another race while meting out the most cruel, degrading punishments for the same acts committed against those of one's own persuasion, that is neither justice nor law.

If laws consciously deny the will to justice, if, for example, they grant and deny human rights arbitrarily, then these laws lack validity, the people owe to them no obedience, and even the jurists must find the courage to deny their legal character.

Fourth Minute
Surely public benefit, along with justice, is an end of the law. Surely laws as such, even bad laws, have value nonetheless—the value of safety regarding the law against doubt. And surely, owing to human imperfection, the three values of law—public benefit, legal certainty, and justice—cannot always be united harmoniously in laws. It remains, then, only to consider whether validity is to be granted to bad, detrimental, or unjust laws for the sake of legal certainty or whether it is to be denied them because they are unjust or socially detrimental. One thing, however, must be indelibly impressed on the consciousness of the people and the jurists: there can be laws that are so unjust, so socially detrimental that their validity, indeed their very character as laws, must be denied.

Fifth Minute
There are, therefore, principles of law that are stronger than any statute, so that a law conflicting with these principles is devoid of validity. One calls these principles the natural law or the law of reason. To be sure, their details remain somewhat doubtful, but the work of the centuries has established a solid core of them and they have come to enjoy such a far-reaching consensus in the declaration of human and civil rights that only the deliberate skeptic can still entertain doubts about some of them.

In religious language the same thoughts have been recorded into biblical passages. On the one hand it is written that you are to obey the authorities who have power over you. But then on the other, it is also written that you are to obey God before man—and this is not simply a pious wish, but a valid proposition of law. The tension between these two directives cannot, however, be

Continued

relieved by appealing to a third—say, to the maxim: Render unto Caesar the things that are Caesar's and unto God the things that are God's. For this directive too, leaves the boundary in doubt. Rather, it leaves the solution to the voice of God, which speaks to the conscience of the individual only in the exceptional case.

Discussion Questions
1. What is the positivist's view of law? Does it matter to a positivist whether a law is just?
2. What type of law is stronger than any statute? What are its origins? Do you have an example of a principle today that would fit into this type of law?

3. If a law is unjust, is obedience to that law necessary? How should people respond or react to unjust laws? Is civil disobedience justified?
4. How does the author respond to the statement: Law is what benefits the people. Does he agree or disagree?

Source: "Fünf Minuten Rechtsphilosophie," by Gustav Radbruch, translated by Stanley L. Paulson, in *Rechtsphilosophie*, and edited by Erik Wolf and Hans-Peter Schneider (Stuttgart: K. F. Koehler Verlag, 1973), pp. 327–29. Reprinted with permission of K. F. Koehler Verlag.

Justice Oliver Wendell Holmes, in "The Common Law," had a different view of the theory of law than that expressed in "A Primer on Jurisprudence." In his famous essay written in 1918, at the height of World War I, Holmes rejected the notion of natural law. His essay began with the famous phrase, "The life of the law has not been logic; it has been experience." Holmes's opinion is that our interactions with each other constitute the foundation of law.

FOR THE MANAGER'S DESK

THE COMMON LAW

Ideas and Doubts: Oliver Wendell Holmes

It is not enough for the knights of romance that you agree that his lady is a very nice girl—if you do not admit that she is the best that God ever made or will make, you must fight. There is in all men a demand for the superlative, so much so that the poor devil who has no other way of reaching it attains by getting drunk. It seems to me that this demand is at the bottom of the philosopher's effort to prove that truth is absolute and of the jurist's search for criteria of the universal validity which he collects under the head of natural law.

The juries who believe in natural law seem to be in that naive state of mind that accepts what has been familiar

and accepted by them and their neighbors as something that must be accepted by all men everywhere. No doubt it is true that, so far as we can see

ahead, some arrangements and the rudiments of familiar institutions seem to be necessary elements in any society that may spring from our own and that would seem to us to be civilized—some form of permanent association between the sexes—some residue of property individually owned—some mode of binding oneself to a specified future conduct—at the bottom of it all, some protection for the person.

It is true that beliefs and wishes have a transcendental basis in the sense that their foundation is arbitrary. You cannot help entertaining and feeling them, and there is an end of it. As an arbitrary fact people wish to live, and we say with various degrees of

Continued

certainty that they can do so, only on certain conditions. To do it they must eat and drink. That necessity is absolute. It is a necessity of a lesser degree but practically general that they should live in society. If they live in society, so far as we can see, there are further conditions. If I do live with others they tell me what I must do if I wish to remain alive. If I do live with others they tell me that I must do and abstain from doing various things or they will put the screws to me.

Discussion Questions

1. According to Justice Holmes, what makes people obey certain laws and subscribe to certain standards?
2. Why does he see natural law as evidence of man's desire to deal in superlatives?
3. Does Justice Holmes feel that everyone's view of natural law is the same?
4. Another legal philosopher, John Austin, stated, "The matter of jurisprudence is positive law: law, simply and strictly so called: or law set by political superiors to political inferiors." Does Justice Holmes's philosophy agree or disagree with this position? Is there a different theory advanced with this statement?

Source: Essay by Oliver Wendell Holmes; reprinted with permission from 32 *Harvard Law Review* 40 (1918). Copyright © 1918 by The Harvard Law Review Association.

Roscoe Pound, another legal philosopher and dean of Harvard Law School for 20 years, had a very different view of jurisprudence than Justice Holmes. His view was that law exists as the result of those who happen to be in power. In 1941, Pound wrote his famous credo, called "My Philosophy of Law."

FOR THE MANAGER'S DESK

MY PHILOSOPHY OF LAW: ROSCOE POUND

I think of law as in one sense a highly specialized form of social control in a developed politically organized society—a social control through the systematic and orderly application of the force of such a society. In this sense it is a regime—the regime which we call the legal order. But that regime operates in a systematic and orderly fashion because of a body of authoritative grounds of or guides to determination which may serve as rules of decision, as rules of or guides to conduct, and as bases of prediction of official action, or may be regarded by the bad man, whose attitude is suggested by Mr. Justice Holmes as a test, as threats of official action which he must take into account of before he acts or refrains from action. Moreover, it operates through a judicial process and an administrative process, which also go by the name of law . . .

Discussion Questions

1. Would it be fair to consider Dean Pound's view of the law as merely the rules of those in charge?
2. What is Dean Pound's view on how Holmes's "bad man" is controlled by law?
3. Does Dean Pound discount the theory of natural law?
4. Do you agree with Dean Pound's views?

Source: Reprinted from *My Philosophy of Law*, Roscoe Pound, © 1941, with permission of the West Publishing Corporation.

There are many cases in which how the law should work is unclear. Conflicting philosophical views often come together in litigation. Judges and lawmakers must struggle to do the best good for the most members of society. The *Baby M* case is a classic conflict of laws and morals that involves the intense issue of surrogate motherhood.

In the Matter of Baby M
537 A.2d 1127 (N.J. 1988)

"YES, SIR, THAT'S MY BABY . . ."

FACTS

In February 1985, William Stern and Mary Beth Whitehead entered into a surrogacy contract, which stated that Elizabeth Stern was infertile and that the Sterns wanted a child.

The Sterns had met at the University of Michigan in 1974 while they were both completing their Phds. They married but decided to postpone having children until Mrs. Stern completed her medical degree. During her residency, Mrs. Stern learned that she suffered from multiple sclerosis; pregnancy thus posed a serious health risk for her. As a result, the Sterns decided to forgo having their own children. But Mr. Stern's family had been killed in the Holocaust and, as the only survivor, he had a strong desire to continue his bloodline. The couple considered adoption but discovered that their ages and different religious backgrounds would cause significant delays in that process.

Faced with few alternatives and anxious to have a child, the Sterns turned to Mrs. Whitehead as a surrogate mother. They were brought together by the Infertility Center of New York (ICNY), which afforded them legal counsel and gave them the form contract that they signed. Mr. Whitehead was also a party to the contract. Mrs. Stern, who had no physical part in the conception or birth of Baby M, was not made a party to the contract to avoid violation of the New York statute prohibiting the sale of babies. Mr. Stern was to pay Mrs. Whitehead $10,000 after the child's birth and $7,500 to ICNY.

Mrs. Whitehead was successfully artificially inseminated in 1985, and on March 27, 1986, Baby M was born. To avoid publicity at the hospital, Mr. and Mrs. Whitehead were listed as the parents, and they named the little girl Sara Elizabeth Whitehead. On March 30, 1986, Mrs. Whitehead turned the baby over to the Sterns at her home, and the Sterns renamed the baby Melissa.

Mrs. Whitehead experienced emotional despair to such an extent that she could neither eat nor sleep. The Sterns were so frightened by her conduct that when she came to their home and asked to have the baby for just one week, the Sterns agreed.

The baby was not returned, and for four months Mr. and Mrs. Whitehead traveled from New Jersey to Florida, staying in 20 different motels and homes. Authorities who came to apprehend them were confused because the child's name was still as it appeared on the birth records, not Melissa Stern. Florida authorities and courts eventually found the baby with Mrs. Whitehead's parents and returned her to the Sterns.

The Sterns brought suit seeking possession and custody of the child and termination of Mrs. Whitehead's parental rights. The trial court held that the surrogacy contract was valid, terminated Mrs. Whitehead's parental rights, awarded custody of the baby to Mr. Stern, and ordered adoption of Melissa by Mrs. Stern. Mrs. Whitehead appealed.

JUDICIAL OPINION
WILENTZ, *Chief Justice*

Mrs. Whitehead contends that the surrogacy contract, for a variety of reasons, is invalid. She contends that it conflicts with public policy since it guarantees that the child will not have the nurturing of both natural parents—presumably New Jersey's goal for families. She further argues that it deprives the mother of her constitutional right to the companionship of the child, and that it conflicts with statutes concerning termination of parental rights and adoption.

We have concluded that this surrogacy contract is invalid. One of the surrogacy contract's basic purposes, to achieve the adoption of a child through private placement, though permitted in New Jersey, "is very much disfavored." Its use of money for this purpose—and we have no doubt whatsoever that the money is being paid to obtain an adoption and not, as the Sterns argue, for the personal services of Mary Beth Whitehead—is illegal and perhaps criminal. In addition to the inducement of money, there is the coercion of

Continued

contract: the natural mother's irrevocable agreement, prior to birth, even prior to conception, to surrender the child to the adoptive couple. Such an agreement is totally unenforceable in private placement adoption.

The surrogacy contract conflicts with: (1) laws prohibiting the use of money in connection with adoptions; (2) laws requiring proof of parental unfitness or abandonment before termination of parental rights is ordered or an adoption granted; and (3) laws that make surrender of custody and consent to adoption revocable in private placement adoptions.

The evils inherent in baby-bartering are loathsome for a myriad of reasons. The child is sold without regard for whether the purchasers will be suitable parents. The natural mother does not receive the benefit of counseling and guidance to assist her in making a decision that may affect her for a lifetime. In fact, the monetary incentive to sell her child may, depending on her financial circumstances, make her decision less voluntary. Furthermore, the adoptive parents may not be fully informed of the natural parents' medical history.

Baby-selling results in the exploitation of all parties involved. The negative consequences of baby-buying are potentially present in the surrogacy context, especially the potential for placing and adopting a child without regard to the interest of the child or the natural mother.

As the trial court recognized, without a valid termination [of parental rights, which Mrs. Whitehead did not give], there can be no adoption. Our statutes, and the cases interpreting them, leave no doubt that where there has been no written surrender to an approved agency or to the Division of Youth and Family Services, termination of parental rights will not be granted in this state absent a very strong showing of abandonment or neglect.

In this case a termination of parental rights was obtained not by proving the statutory prerequisites but by claiming the benefit of contractual provisions. From all that has been stated above, it is clear that a contractual agreement to abandon one's parental rights, or not to contest a termination action, will not be enforced in our courts. The Legislature would not have so carefully, so consistently, and so substantially restricted termination of parental rights if it had intended to allow termination to be achieved by one short sentence in a contract.

Intimated, but disputed, is the assertion that surrogacy will be used for the benefit of the rich at the expense of the poor. . . . [I]t is clear to us that it is unlikely that surrogate mothers will be as proportionately numerous among those women in the top twenty percent income bracket as among those in the bottom twenty percent. Put differently, we doubt that infertile couples in the low-income bracket will find upper-income surrogates.

The long-term effects of surrogacy contracts are not known, but feared—the impact on the child who learns her life was bought, that she is the offspring of someone who gave birth to her only to obtain money.

In sum, the harmful consequences of this surrogacy agreement appear to us all too palpable. In New Jersey the surrogate mother's agreement to sell her child is void.

CASE QUESTIONS
1. Give the background of the Sterns and the reasons for the surrogacy contract.
2. What concerns does the court have about enforcing the surrogacy contract?
3. Technology today permits the implantation of a fertilized egg as opposed to insemination of a surrogate. In this situation the surrogate mother is not the biological mother, but only the "carrier" of the baby for the duration of gestation. Would a surrogate contract in these circumstances be different? Should contracts for these types of surrogacy arrangements be permitted?
4. Is this litigation a result of medical technology and new issues that did not exist before insemination was possible?
5. Is a surrogate contract a violation of natural law?

Aftermath: Custody of Baby M was awarded to the Sterns, and Mrs. Whitehead was given visitation rights. The court determined that the Sterns offered a better environment for Baby M because Mrs. Whitehead had exhibited reckless behavior while Baby M was with her.

In late 1992 and early 1993, Mr. Bill Clinton, the newly elected president of the United States, began working to fill cabinet positions for his new administration. His first choice for position of attorney general was Ms. Zoë Baird, general counsel for Aetna Life Insurance Company. Ms. Baird's nomination

The Women Who Would Be Attorney General
Zoë Baird and Kimba Wood

was eventually withdrawn when it was revealed that she and her husband, a professor at Yale Law School, had hired a nanny and a chauffeur in the United States illegally and had failed to pay wage taxes for the two.

Following Ms. Baird's failed nomination, Mr. Clinton began discussions with a federal judge, Kimba Wood. Judge Wood had also employed a nanny for the care of her child. The nanny was not an illegal alien, but Judge Wood and her husband, a writer for *Time* magazine, had also not paid wage taxes. Judge Wood's name, although appearing in news reports as a candidate for attorney general, was never formally sent forward as a nomination. Eventually, Janet Reno, a public attorney from Florida who had no children, was nominated and confirmed as attorney general.

After the issues surrounding household employee taxes in relation to Ms. Baird and Judge Wood arose, subsequent nominees and candidates for office were scrutinized for these wage tax problems.

Zoë Baird

If the candidates or nominees had not paid their taxes, they were categorized as "having a Zoë Baird problem." "Having a Zoë Baird problem" was the end of many nominations and candidacies.

Since the time of her failed nomination, Ms. Baird has continued her work with Aetna and given birth to a second child. Judge Wood continues her work on the federal bench; she fell victim recently to intense media scrutiny when the private diaries of a New York broker became public and revealed the judge's affair with him.

Issues

1. Would Judge Wood's and Ms. Baird's lives have been different if they had obeyed the law?

2. Did they limit their opportunities by not complying with the law?

3. At the time of their nominations, only 25 percent of all U.S. citizens with household help complied with the law. Shouldn't the two women have been given leniency since everybody else was doing what they were doing?

E T H I C A L ■ I S S U E S

1.1 A Japanese cable radio network, called Cable Radio Usen, offers a menu of stations to its listeners that are referred to as "alibi stations." The alibi stations provide background noises which include coffee shops, train stations, telephone booths, pachinko parlors, and mah-jongg games. Many bar patrons ask the bar owners to switch to an appropriate station while they call home or work. Thus, a bar patron can call home explaining that his train is late with authentic background mass transit rumblings and announcers' "Watch your feet" warnings.

Cable Radio Usen is completely legal. Is it ethical? Is everything that is legal also moral? Would you use Cable Radio Usen to deceive your supervisor? Do the background noise channels have any purpose beyond deception?

SOURCES OF LAW

Laws exist in different forms at every level of government. As discussed earlier, law exists in statutory form but also exists in its common law form through judicial decisions. Statutory law exists at all levels of government. Statutes are written laws that are enacted by some governmental body with the proper authority—legislatures, city governments, and counties—and that are published and made available for public use and knowledge. These written statutes are sometimes referred to as codified law, and their sources as well as constitutions are covered in the following sections.

Constitutional Law

Explore the U.S. Constitution: http://www.law. emory.edu/ FEDERAL/ usconst.html

The U.S. Constitution and the constitutions of the various states are unique forms of law. **Constitutions** are not statutes because they cannot be added to, amended, or repealed with the same ease as can a statute. Constitutions are the law of the people and are changed only by lengthier and more demanding procedures than those used to repeal statutes.

Constitutions also tend to protect general rights, such as speech, religion, and property (see Chapter 5 for a more complete discussion). They also are a framework for all other forms of laws. The basic rights and protections afforded in them cannot be abridged or denied by the other sources of law. In other words, a statute's boundaries are formed by constitutionally protected rights. Exhibit 1.2 (pg. 21) is an illustration of the sources of law; constitutional law is at the base of the pyramid diagram because of its inviolate status.

Statutory Law at the Federal Level

CONGRESSIONAL LAW

Explore the U.S. Code: http://www.law. cornell.edu/ uscode/ *or* http://ssdc.ucsd. edu/gpo/

Congress is responsible for statutory law at the federal level. The laws passed by Congress become part of the **United States Code (U.S.C.)**. Examples of such laws are the 1933 and 1934 Securities Acts (see Chapter 21), the Sherman Act and other antitrust laws (see Chapter 13), the Equal Employment Opportunity Act (see Chapter 19), the National Labor Relations Act (see Chapter 18), the Truth in Lending Act (see Chapter 16), and the Internal Revenue Code (see Chapter 20).

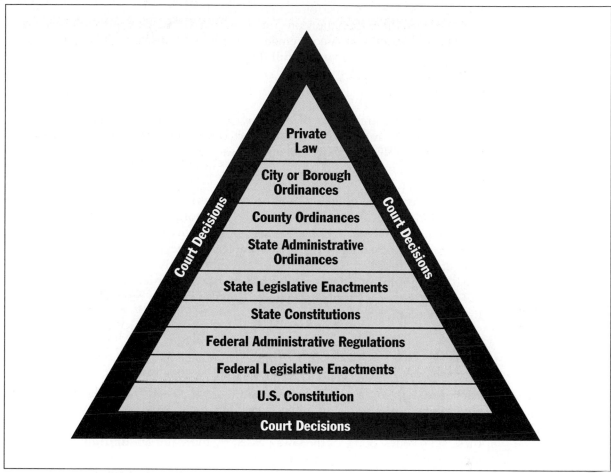

Exhibit 1.2
Sources of Law

Statutes from the U.S.C. are referenced or cited by a standard form of legal shorthand, often referred to as a **cite** or **citation**. The number of the title is put in front of "U.S.C." to tell which volume of the Code to go to. For example, "15 U.S.C." refers to Title 15 of the United States Code (Title 15 happens to cover securities). There may be more than one volume that is numbered "15," however. To enable you to find the volume you need, the reference or cite has a section (§) number following it. This section number is the particular statute referenced, and you must look for the volume of Title 15 that contains that section. For example, the first volume of Title 15 contains §§ 1–11. A full reference or cite to a United States Code statute looks like this: 15 U.S.C. § 77. When a U.S.C. cite is given, the law cited will be a federal law passed by Congress.

Explore the Code of Federal Regulations: http://law.house. gov/cfr.htm

ADMINISTRATIVE REGULATIONS

Another form of codified law exists at the federal level and consists of regulations passed by administrative agencies. Called the **Code of Federal Regulations (C.F.R.)**, the administrative regulations at the federal level are extensive and affect virtually every business. The details of compliance with federal statutes (found in the United States Code) are found in the C.F.R. For example, sample forms for disclosure of credit information are found in the C.F.R., as are the Security and Exchange Commission's requirements for financial disclosures in the periodic reports of a public company. A full discussion of regulation and administrative agencies is found in Chapter 6.

EXECUTIVE ORDERS

Explore executive orders: http://library.whitehouse.gov/?request=ExecutiveOrder

Executive orders are laws of the executive branch of the federal government and deal with those matters under the direct control of that branch. For example, when Richard Nixon was president, he issued an executive order governing the classification and release of "top secret" documents. And during his presidency, Jimmy Carter issued executive orders that required government contractors to employ a certain percentage of minority workers in their businesses in order to qualify for federal projects (see Chapter 19). George Bush issued one executive order requiring federal agencies to use alternative dispute resolution before going to court and another requiring them to implement recycling programs. On his second day as president, Bill Clinton issued an executive order reversing George Bush's "gag rule" on abortion counseling. The same order also reversed a previous executive order banning the use of federal funds for research involving fetal tissue obtained from abortions.

Statutory Law at the State Level

LEGISLATIVE LAW AND STATE CODES

Explore the Uniform Commercial Code: http://www.law.cornell.edu/ucc/ucc.table.html

Each state has its own code containing the laws passed by its legislature. **State codes** contain the states' criminal laws, laws for incorporation, laws governing partnerships, and contract laws. Much of the law that affects business is found in these state codes. Some of the laws passed by the states are **uniform laws**, which are drafted by groups of businesspeople, scholars, and lawyers in an effort to make interstate business less complicated. For example, the **Uniform Commercial Code** has been adopted in 49 states and governs contracts for the sale of goods, commercial paper, security interests, and other types of commercial transactions. Having this uniform law in the various states gives businesses the opportunity to deal across state lines with some certainty.

Other uniform acts passed by many state legislatures include the Uniform Partnership Act, the Uniform Residential Landlord Tenant Act, the Model Business Corporation Act, and the Uniform Probate Code.

STATE ADMINISTRATIVE LAW

Visit hyperlinks to state legislation: http://lawlib.wuacc.edu/washlaw/uslaw/statelaw.html *or* http://law.house.gov/17.htm

Just as at the federal level, state governments have administrative agencies with the power to pass regulations dealing with the statutes and powers given by the state legislatures. For example, most states have an agency to handle incorporations and the status of corporations in the state. Most states also have a tax agency to handle income or sales taxes in the state.

Local Laws of Cities, Counties, and Townships

In addition to federal and state statutes, local governments can pass **ordinances** or statutes within their areas of power or control. For example, cities and counties have the authority to handle zoning issues, and the municipal code will outline the zoning system and whatever means of enforcement and specified penalties apply. These local laws govern lesser issues, such as dog licensing, curfews, and loitering.

Private Laws

Private laws are a final source of written law and are found in contracts and the regulations agreed to, for example, by employers and employees. These are laws limited in their application to the parties involved in a contractual relationship. However, these private laws are just as enforceable through lawsuits for breach of contract (see Chapters 3 and 4).

C O N S I D E R . . . **1.3** Often, business people must read statutes, regulations, and ordinances to determine whether their business operations are legal, require licenses, or are otherwise regulated. Ticket brokers and scalpers would be affected by the following three New York statutes. Read them and then answer the questions that follow.

§ 25.07. Ticket prices
1. Every operator of a place of entertainment shall, if a price be charged for admission thereto, print or endorse on the face of each such ticket the established price. Such operator shall likewise be required to print or endorse on each ticket the maximum premium price at which such ticket or other evidence of the right of entry may be resold or offered for resale.
2. Maximum premium price. It shall be unlawful for any person, firm or corporation to resell or offer to resell any ticket to any place of entertainment for more than the maximum premium price.

§ 25.09. Ticket speculators
1. Any person who in violation of subdivision two of section 25.07 of this article unlawfully resells or offers to resell or solicits the purchase of any ticket to any place of entertainment shall be guilty of ticket speculation.
2. Any person, firm or corporation which in violation of subdivision two of section 25.07 of this article unlawfully resells, offers to resell, or purchases with the intent to resell five or more tickets to any place of entertainment shall be guilty of aggravated ticket speculation.

§ 25.11. Resales of tickets within one thousand feet of a place of entertainment having a permanent seating capacity in excess of five thousand persons
1. No person, firm, corporation or not-for-profit organization shall resell, offer to resell or solicit the resale of any ticket to any place of entertainment having a permanent seating capacity in excess of five thousand persons within one thousand feet from the physical structure of such place of entertainment unless such person, firm, or corporation is lawfully reselling tickets from a location licensed pursuant to section 25.13 of this article.
2. Notwithstanding subdivision one of this section, an operator may designate an area within the property line of such place of entertainment having a permanent seating capacity in excess of five thousand persons for the lawful resale of tickets only to events at such place of entertainment by any person, firm, corporation or not-for-profit organization which purchased the tickets for the purposes described in section 25.05 of this article and is no longer able to use them.

What is ticket speculation? Is it legal? Is it ethical? Are these statutes civil or criminal statutes? If you were a ticket broker, what would you need to do to be in compliance with the law?

ETHICAL ISSUES

1.2 Does ticket scalping serve a purpose for some people? At the NCAA Final Four Basketball Tournament in 1992, midcourt seats were selling for $2,500. The late concert promoter Bill Graham once said, "If I wanted to, I could make more money scalping tickets than producing a show." Mr. Graham led a crusade for anti-scalping legislation in California. Selling tickets at the event site is illegal in California, but ticket brokers are permitted to sell tickets at prices above the original cost so long as they operate away from the event.

Economist Steve Happel favors little or no regulation of scalping: "Look at the people on the Chicago Board of Trade. They buy wheat futures. Why are we so concerned about ticket scalpers?"

California state assemblyman Bill Lockyer, who has introduced antiscalping legislation, has stated, "The brokering of tickets confers an advantage to the wealthy and the well-connected that the fan of average means does not have. I still believe we need a law to stop the practice."

Does scalping encourage unethical behavior? For example, in exchange for alcohol, drugs, or money, homeless people in Texas are recruited to stand in ticket lines to buy tickets when there are limits on purchases. In California, a lawsuit was filed accusing a ticket broker of bribing ticket agency employees to obtain more and better seats to concert events that would later be sold for between 10 and 20 times their face value. Would you participate in scalping, either as a buyer or a seller? Why or why not?

INTRODUCTION TO INTERNATIONAL LAW

Governmental changes in Germany and the former U.S.S.R., the evolution of the European Union, and the competitive skills of Japan and other nations have caused a dramatic change in the business marketplace. Businesses now operate in a global market. Companies headquartered in Japan have factories in the United States, and U.S. firms have manufacturing plants in South America. Barriers to economic development that once existed because of governmental constraints in Germany and the former Soviet Union no longer exist. An international market requires businesses to understand laws beyond those of the United States.

International law is not a neat body of law like contract law or the Uniform Commercial Code. Rather, it is a combination of the laws of various countries, international trade customs, and international agreements. Article 38(1) of the Statute of the International Court of Justice (a court of the United Nations that countries consent to have resolve disputes) is a widely recognized statement of the sources of international law:

Explore the Statute of the International Court of Justice: http://www.un.org/ Overview/Statute/ contents.html

> *The Court, whose function is to decide in accordance with international law such disputes as are submitted to it, shall apply:*
> *(a) international conventions, whether general or particular, establishing rules expressly recognized by the contesting states;*
> *(b) international custom as evidence of a general practice accepted as law;*
> *(c) the general principles of law recognized by civilized nations;*
> *(d) judicial decisions and the teachings of the most highly qualified publicists of the various nations, as subsidiary means for the determination of rules of law.*

Custom

Every country has its boundaries for allowable behavior, and these boundaries are unwritten but recognized laws. The standards of behavior are reflected in statements made by government officials. Among countries that have the same standards of acceptable behavior, there exists an international code of custom. Custom develops over time and through repeated conduct. For example, the continental shelf sea territorial standard came into existence in 1945 when President Harry S. Truman, in the Truman Declaration, established mileage boundary lines. Most countries accepted the declaration because it reflected their customary operations. By 1958 the standard became a part of the Geneva Convention.

Another example of international custom, though one not yet accepted by all nations, is the granting of diplomatic asylum. Some nations grant it and others do not; it is an area of developing custom.

Each individual country will have its own customs peculiar to business trade. Businesses operating in various other countries must understand those customs in negotiating contracts and conducting operations within those countries. For example, unlike the United States most countries do not offer a warranty protection on goods and instead follow a philosophy of "caveat emptor," or "let the buyer beware." Other countries also do not recognize the extensive rules of insurance and risk followed here with respect to the shipment of goods. Multinational firms must make provisions for protection of shipments in those countries with different standards.

Recently, the customs of Mainland China with respect to intellectual property, most particularly computer software, lagged behind those of Europe and the United States. Chinese custom was to separate infringement into two categories: ordinary and serious acts. Ordinary infringement is not regarded as a legal issue and requires only that the party apologize, destroy the software and not engage in infringement again. Courts were rarely involved in ordinary infringement cases. However, the U.S. government demanded that more protection for its copyright holders or trade sanctions be imposed and China agreed to revise its customs and laws to afford protection. In this case, China's custom had to be changed to provide protection similar to that afforded in other countries.

Treaties

Examine various treaties: http://law.house.gov/89.htm

A **treaty** is an agreement between or among nations on a subject of international law signed by the leaders of the nations and ratified by the nations' governing bodies. In the United States, treaties are ratified by the Senate.

Treaties can be between two nations—**bilateral treaties**—or among several nations—**multilateral treaties**. There are also treaties that are recognized by almost all nations, which are called general or **universal treaties**. Universal treaties are a reflection of widely followed standards of behavior. For example, the Geneva Convention is a universal treaty covering the treatment of prisoners of war. The Vienna Convention is a universal treaty covering diplomatic relations. The Warsaw Convention is a treaty that provides international law on the issues of liability for injuries to passengers and property during international air travel.

Private Law in International Transactions

Those businesses involved in multinational trade and production rely heavily on private law to assure performance of contractual obligations. Even though each country has a different set of laws, all of them recognize the autonomy of parties in an international trade transaction and allow the parties to negotiate contract terms that suit their needs so long as none of the terms is illegal. **Party autonomy** allows firms to operate uniformly throughout the world if their contracts are recognized as valid in most countries. For example, most international trade contracts have a choice-of-law clause whereby the parties decide which country's law will apply to their disputes under the contract.

International Organizations

Some international organizations offer additions to international law. For example, the United Nations General Assembly has the authority to adopt resolutions to govern international relations and to censure companies that create difficulties in the international marketplace because of unfair dealings.

Act of State Doctrine

The **act of state doctrine** is a theory that protects governments from reviews of their actions by courts in other countries. In any action in which the government of a country has taken steps to condemn or confiscate property, the courts of other countries will not interfere. For example, in many cases foreign countries will engage in **expropriation** (also called **appropriation**), or the taking of private property. Also referred to as **confiscation** or **nationalization**, the process is really one of eminent domain, and courts of other countries will not interfere in this governmental process.

Trade Law and Policies

The importance of trade laws, tariffs, and policies has increased directly with increases in international business transactions. For example, the U.S. trade representative, once a dignitary position, has been upgraded to a cabinet-level position. Although Congress is responsible for enacting trade laws and various federal agencies are responsible for their administration, the U.S. trade representative assumes responsibility for negotiating trade agreements with foreign countries. The laws passed by Congress include import restrictions, tariffs, and enactments such as the Buy American Act (41 U.S.C. §§ l0a–10d (1987)), which requires federal agencies to give preference to U.S. suppliers in their procurement of goods and services. Additional details on trade laws, tariffs, restrictions, and trade agreements are found in Chapter 7.

The United States and China used a trade agreement as the means for requiring the Chinese to afford greater intellectual property protections (patent, copyright, trademark) for U.S. businesses.

Explore GATT:
http://ananse.irv.uit.
no/tradelaw/gatt/
nav/toc.html
Explore NAFTA:
gopher://wiretap.
spies.com/11/Gov/
NAFTA

Two important treaties to which the United States is a party will have a significant effect on our economy. The first is the Geneva-based General Agreement on Tariffs and Trade (GATT). GATT will establish uniform trade policies between the United States and the European Union nations. The goal of GATT has been called "borderless trade."

The second treaty is the North American Free Trade Agreement (NAFTA), which is a trade agreement among the United States, Canada, and Mexico. This lengthy agreement was signed by then-president George Bush in 1992 and has been approved by the legislative bodies of all three nations. The agreement is now in the implementation stage and is designed to permit the free flow of goods, services, and capital among the three nations.

E T H I C A L   I S S U E S

1.3 With NAFTA, 800,000 low-skill manufacturing jobs (such as those in the apparel, food-processing, and consumer-goods manufacturing industries) have been transferred to Mexico, where labor costs are lower. The effect of this transfer of labor is that U.S. blue-collar workers must retrain and retool. Economists also maintain that the agreement now permits efficient use of resources and may reduce costs. Some labor representatives in the United States refused to support NAFTA because of disparity in the wage levels in Mexico and the U.S. minimum wage levels. Does NAFTA take advantage of a poorer economy and its workers? Should companies transfer their plants to Mexico to take advantage of the lower wages there? Who should pay the costs of the retraining of the displaced U.S. workers?

The European Union

Learn more about the European Union: http://www.cec.lu/

Once referred to as the Common Market and the European Community (EC), the European Union (EU) is a tariff-free group of European countries that includes Austria, Belgium, Denmark, Finland, France, Germany, Greece, Ireland, Italy, Luxembourg, the Netherlands, Portugal, Spain, Sweden, and the United Kingdom. This group of 15 countries has joined together to enjoy the benefits of barrier-free trade. Formed on December 31, 1992, the single economic community requires member nations to subscribe to the same monetary standard, the elimination of immigration and customs controls, universal product and job safety standards, uniform licensing of professionals, and unified taxation schedules. Now that the EU exists officially, trade agreements will be negotiated on behalf of the 15 member countries as if they were one country. More details on the governance of the EU and its laws can be found in Chapter 7.

SUMMARY

How is law defined?
* Law is a form of order. Law is the body of rules of society governing individuals and their relationships.

What types of laws are there?
* Public law—codified law; statutes; law by government body
* Statutory law—codified law
* Criminal law—laws regulating wrongful conduct and carrying sentences and fines
* Civil law—laws regulating harms and carrying damage remedies
* Substantive laws—laws giving rights and responsibilities
* Procedural laws—laws that provide enforcement rights
* Common law—law developed historically and by judicial precedent
* Private law—rules created by individuals for their contracts, tenancy, and employment

Continued

What are the purposes of law?
- Keep order; influence conduct; honor expectations; promote equality; offer compromises

What are the characteristics of law?
- Flexibility; consistency; pervasiveness
- Jurisprudence—theory of law

Where are laws found and who enacts them?
- Constitution—document that establishes structure and authority of a government
- Federal statutes—laws passed by Congress; the United States Code
- State statutes—laws passed by state legislatures, including uniform laws on contracts and business organizations
- Ordinances—local laws passed by cities, counties, and townships

What are the sources of international law?
- Treaties—agreements between and among nations regarding their political and commercial relationships
- Act of state doctrine—immunity of governmental action from discipline by other countries; sanctity of government's right to govern
- European Union—group of 15 nations working collectively for uniform laws and barrier-free trade

QUESTIONS AND PROBLEMS

1. Bryant Gunderson is a sole proprietor with a successful bungee-jumping business. He is considering incorporating his business. What levels and sources of law would affect and govern the process of incorporation?
2. Jeffrey Stalwart has just been arrested for ticket scalping outside the Great Western Forum in Los Angeles. Jeffrey sold a ticket to a U2 concert to an intense fan for $1,200; the face value of the ticket was $48. Ticket scalping in Los Angeles is a misdemeanor. Will Jeffrey's court proceedings be civil or criminal? Suppose that the fan sued Jeffrey under a provision of the Consumer Protection Act that permits recovery of fees paid scalpers in excess of a ticket's face value. Would these court proceedings be civil or criminal?
3. Describe the types of business matters regulated by state law. Describe the types of business matters regulated by federal law.
4. Define and contrast the following:
   a. civil law and criminal law
   b. substantive law and procedural law
   c. common law and statutory law
   d. private law and public law
5. Why are there differences in types and extent of laws in various countries? How do countries reconcile their legal differences to facilitate international business?
6. Jane Pregulman leases a one-bedroom apartment at Desert Cove Apartments. One of the regulations listed in her lease prohibits tenants from parking bicycles on their balconies or patios. What type of law is this? Is it enforceable?
7. Randy Redmond is an engineer with a city utility. The city has adopted an employment policy that creates a smoke-free work environment. Randy has smoked for 15 years and

now can no longer smoke at his desk. Is this a form of law? What is it? Is it enforceable? (For more discussion of this issue, see Chapter 18.)

8. Classify the following subject matters as substantive or procedural laws.
   a. Taxation
   b. Corporation law
   c. Evidence
   d. Labor law
   e. Securities

9. Mercury Corporation manufactures solar panels for residential use. Mercury is experiencing some sales resistance because homeowners fear that trees and buildings will block the sunlight from their solar panels. At this time there is no law in Mercury's state protecting light for solar panels. What can Mercury do? What bodies in government could pass protective legislation?

10. Jose Camilo-Torres is a cacao farmer in Guyana. He has operated a large, successful business for 22 years and has sold his chocolate base product to U.S. companies such as M&M/Mars and Hershey's. After a change in government, Camilo-Torres's farm is taken over by the new government's agriculture department. Camilo-Torres will operate the farm and be paid a salary, but the profits will belong to the new government. Camilo-Torres has turned to his U.S. buyers and requested their assistance in stopping the actions of his government. Can anything be done? Could the government's actions be set aside in a U.S. court? What if the government's takeover is unfair and does not provide Camilo-Torres with adequate compensation? What label is given to the government's takeover of the farm?

NOTE

1 Excerpt from "Law Like Love" from W. H. Auden; *Collected Poems by W. H. Auden.* Copyright © 1940 and renewed 1968 by W. H. Auden. Reprinted by permission of Random House, Inc.

Judgment

"The most it will cost is $11 to $12 to fix it completely," Tom, the lead engineer, said. "But it will set us back timewise." The engineers working on the design of Ford Motor Company's new subcompact car, the Pinto, faced a dilemma. The gas tank on the Pinto was in a precarious spot. Any rear-end collision, regardless of speed, would result in a rupture and explosion. The explosion would occur on impact, leaving occupants only seconds to get out of the small two-door car. Those in the back seat would be severely burned or killed. Even the driver would have difficulty getting out in time to avoid burns. But the engineers faced a market deadline and a maximum price for the Pinto of $1,999. The design was sent forward without any changes. Why would a company manufacture and sell a car with such inherent dangers?

Business Ethics and Social Responsibility

Every business and every businessperson will at some time face an ethical dilemma. That dilemma may be having to decide whether to hire a top salesperson who has come to the job interview with sensitive data from a competitor and former employer. The dilemma may be having to decide whether to market in Third World countries a large inventory of a toy that has been banned in the United States by the Consumer Product Safety Commission. The dilemma may be one like the engineers face in the chapter's opening "Judgment": do I defy my employer because of safety issues? An ethical dilemma could be as simple as determining your company's level of quality or disclosing long-term exposure hazards to line employees. The old philosophy of "what's good for business is good for the country" is no longer adequate to ensure a business's long-term survival and earnings.

Businesses today must answer not only to their shareholders but also to a myriad of constituents, often referred to as stakeholders, who demand responsibility and integrity if companies are to win their patronage. For example, one consumer's expressed outrage about a company's sponsorship of a television program that did not meet family-hour viewing standards resulted in the withdrawal of that sponsorship. Time-Warner was forced to cope with strong public reaction to rapper artist Ice-T's song "Cop Killer." Both ethical and socially responsible behavior are demanded by shareholders to ensure long-term earnings growth, by customers in return for their loyalty, and by communities as a condition for incentives to locate and maintain business facilities in the area. In short, the shareholder is only one of many forces that work to shape the direction, goals, and conduct of a company. Other stakeholders, such as employees, customers, and communities, have an interest in the long-term success of a company. If a company is to win the marathon and overcome the temptation to sprint, a culture of ethical and socially responsible behavior must be ingrained in the attitudes of management and the responses of employees. This chapter answers the questions: What is business ethics? Why is business ethics important? What ethical standards should a business adopt? How do employees recognize ethical dilemmas? How are ethical dilemmas resolved? How does a business create an ethical atmosphere?

There is no pillow as soft as a clear conscience.
Kenneth Blanchard and Norman Vincent Peale
The Power of Ethical Management

Trust, but verify.
Ronald Reagan and Mikhail Gorbachev

The world is full of cactus, but we don't have to sit on it.
Will Foley

Goodness is the only investment that never fails.
Henry D. Thoreau
Walden: "Higher Laws"

WHY BUSINESS ETHICS?

Many people have referred to the term **business ethics** as an oxymoron: the words *business* and *ethics* seem to somehow contradict each other. Nonetheless, there are some compelling reasons for choosing ethical behavior. These reasons are discussed in the following sections.

✳ *Importance of Values in Business Success*

As you learn in other disciplines, from economics to management, business is driven by the bottom line. Profits control whether the firm can obtain loans or gain investors and serve as the sole indicator of the firm's and, in most cases, its employees' success. Indeed, business firms can be defined as groups of people working together to obtain maximum profits. The pursuit of the bottom line, however, can occasionally distort the perspective of even the most conscientious among us. The fear of losing business, and consequently losing profits and capital support, can persuade people to engage in conduct that, although not illegal, is unethical. But those who pursue only the bottom line fail to recognize that a successful business is more like a marathon than a sprint, requiring that ethical dilemmas be resolved with a long-term perspective in mind. Indeed, those firms that adhere to ethical standards perform better financially over the long run. For example, the Ethics Resource Center in Washington, D.C., compared the performance of 21 companies that had written codes of ethics with the performance of a Dow Jones composite company. The center's study found that if $30,000 had been invested in the composite company 30 years ago, the investment would be worth $134,000 today. If that same $30,000 had been invested in the 21 companies with codes of ethics, the investment would be worth $1,021,861 today. The U.S. corporations that have paid dividends for one hundred years or more are those firms that have codes of ethics or are known for their emphasis on ethical behavior. In a 1990 survey on ethics by the Ethics Resource Center, 85 percent of the 3,000 U.S. companies responding indicated that they had a code of ethics.

The Tylenol tampering incident of 1982 offers one of the most telling examples of the rewards of being ethical. When Tylenol capsules were discovered to have been tainted with deadly poison, Tylenol's manufacturer, McNeil Consumer Products Company, a subsidiary of Johnson & Johnson, followed its code of ethics, which required it to put the interests of the consumer first. In what many financial analysts and economists considered to be a disastrous decision and a dreadful mistake, McNeil recalled all Tylenol capsules from the market—31,000,000 bottles with a retail value of about $100 million. A new and safer form of a noncapsule Tylenol caplet was developed, and within a few months Tylenol regained its majority share of the market. The recall had turned out to be neither a poor decision nor a financial disaster. Rather, the company's actions enhanced its reputation and served to create a bond between Tylenol and its customers that was based largely on trust and respect for the integrity of the company and the product.

In contrast to the positive nature of ethical behavior is unethical behavior. For example, companies in the defense contracting business who were part of the spending and overcharging scandal several years ago are still reeling from the charges, struggling to regain credibility. Beech-Nut suffered tremendous earnings

Visit Beech-Nut:
http://www.
beechnut.com/

losses as a result of the discovery that its baby food "apple juice" did not in fact contain any real apple juice. Nestle has endured many consumer boycotts since the early 1970s as a result of its intense—and what came to be perceived by the public as exploitative and unethical—marketing of infant formula in Third World nations, where the lack of sanitation, refrigeration, and education led to serious health problems in infants given the formula (see Chapter 15). In 1989, nearly 20 years after the infant formula crisis, Nestle's new "Good Start" formula has been slow in market infiltration and, because of continuing consumer resistance, has not performed as well as its quality and innovativeness would predict. As the Nestle case illustrates, a firm's reputation for ethical behavior is the same as an individual's reputation; it takes a long time to gain but it can be lost instantly as the result of one bad choice.

In 1992, Sears experienced a reduction in earnings when an investigation of its auto repair centers by the California Consumer Affairs Department and officials in New Jersey resulted in official complaints against it for overcharging repair customers. This company crisis made national news and resulted in what might be termed an overhaul of Sears's compensation system for auto center employees. Sears also ran full-page ads in newspapers all over the country to assure potential customers that operations were now different at the auto centers and that they could continue to trust Sears. The fraud accusations against Sears resulted in national negative publicity, reductions in auto center customers, long-lasting effects on its reputation, and an immediate reduction in income.

Visit Salomon Brothers, Inc.: http://www.salomon.com

Salomon Brothers, Inc. became the target of an 11-month probe after it was discovered that Salomon bond traders were controlling the U.S. Treasury bond market through prearranged transactions using major customers' names. Almost immediately after the news of Salomon's cornering of the bond market appeared in national papers, there was a $29 million drop in earnings for one quarter. Further, Salomon paid $122 million in fines, was given a two-month suspension from bond trading, and was required to establish a $100 million fund to compensate other firms hurt by the cornering of the bond market.

Visit the U.S. Securities and Exchange Commission: http://www.sec.gov/

During the early 1990s, the financial returns on investments in derivative securities were enticing. Many firms, from Procter & Gamble through Gibson Greetings to Barings Bank, joined the bandwagon to invest in these risky ventures that offered high returns, but, if leveraged, could bring disaster if the high stakes turned against the firm (see Chapter 21). The risk and high exposure of these investment mechanisms were not disclosed to shareholders or the public. When the markets turned, the investments went bad, and the firms experienced large financial write-offs or even, in the case of Barings Bank, bankruptcy. The firms now face lawsuits from shareholders and customers, and the SEC has proposed strict regulation of derivatives through required, detailed disclosures (see Chapter 21 for more details).

Visit Orange County, California: http://www.oc.ca.gov/

Orange County, California, had invested heavily in derivatives and was heavily leveraged when the derivatives market turned the wrong way for its portfolio. The result was bankruptcy for the county. A financial newsletter commented, "It was the biggest orgy of bond speculation in world history." A professional surfer from Huntington Beach offered his views on the county's bankruptcy: "It all comes down to greed."

The poor value choices of the firms mentioned above resulted in tremendous financial setbacks and, in the case of Orange County, destruction. The core values of a firm give it long-standing profitability. "The Tony Bennett Factor" (pg. 34) offers some insight into longevity, profitability, and values.

FOR THE MANAGER'S DESK

THE TONY BENNETT FACTOR

I had blocked out the background noise offered courtesy of MTV and my teenager, but I glanced up and saw Tony Bennett. My parents raised me on Tony Bennett LPs back in the '50s. "I Left My Heart in San Francisco" enjoyed hours of play in Tyrone, Pa. And here he was back, "Tony Bennett Unplugged."

Mr. Bennett has not changed. Yet his success has spanned generations. Suddenly my work with a colleague, Prof. Louis Grossman, had new meaning. We had been studying business longevity, trying to determine what makes some businesses survive so successfully for so long.

Prof. Grossman and I began our study when we spotted a 1982 full-page ad in this newspaper placed by Diamond Match Co. The ad touted the company's 100 years of consistent dividend payments. Today's standards tell us that 100 quarters of dividend payments would be stellar. What kind of company was this? Were there others?

We discovered seven other industrial firms that could boast of making at least an annual dividend payment for a string of 100 years or more: Scovill, Inc.; Ludlow Corp.; Stanley Works; and Corning Glass Works. Pullman, Ludlow and Stanley had unbroken chains of a century of quarterly dividend payments as well.

Mr. Bennett and our eight companies have survival in common. These survivors' tools make management theories of today seem trite. They had no shifting paradigms. No buzzwords.

Mr. Bennett recognized his strength as a balladeer and stuck with it, through everything from the Beatles to Hootie and the Blowfish. Although each of our companies recognized the importance of diversification, they

all held fast to a WBAWI — or "what business are we in?" — philosophy. They knew their strengths, developed strong market presences based on those strengths and never forgot their roots. Mr. Bennett never performed without singing "I Wanna Be Around." Singer never left its sewing machines. Pullman never deserted its train cars. Diamond held on to its matches.

The firms diversified only when their strengths allowed. Scovill began as a brass button manufacturer and backed into brass manufacturing

because it knew brass. Scovill bought Hamilton Beach because Hamilton Beach was a major brass purchaser. Scovill understood this customer's business.

Other companies have forgotten the WBAWI lesson and paid the price. Sears abandoned its catalog, insurance and real estate businesses and now struggles to find a retail presence. IBM has suffered for not understanding its business was the workplace, not mainframe computers. Its Lotus takeover shows it may recognize the PC as the workplace.

All Mr. Bennett needs are a microphone and a pianist to make music. All eight of our companies were low-cost producers. All eight were cost conscious. Scovill executive vice presidents with worldwide responsibilities shared a secretary. Spartan company headquarters were the rule for these firms. There were barely six-figure salaries for executives. By contrast, IBM's Louis Gerstner hired an executive chef at $120,000 just last month.

Mr. Bennett has used the same musical arranger for nearly 30 years. Our eight companies' management team histories are in direct contrast to the executive recruiting practices in vogue today. Scovill, founded during the Jefferson administration in 1803, had only 12 CEOs during its 100-year dividend run. Three of the companies (Singer, Stanley and Diamond) had CEOs who served for

Continued

more than 40 years. Seven of the companies never had a CEO serve for fewer than 10 years. They were not afraid of home-grown management. Their officers and CEOs came up through the ranks. Management succession is found in all eight companies.

Perhaps this information demonstrates the importance of continuity and stability. The executives appreciated the tension between short-term results and long-term performance, but the short term did not control decision-making. Donald Davis, chairman and CEO of Stanley Works, put it this way: "The tension is always there. One of the top management's toughest jobs really is to mediate between the two view-points— short-term profit results now vs. investment for future development."

Mr. Bennett did and does spend time on the road in concert, in direct contact with audiences—no mega-tours, just constant gigs. And a full century before we heard of customer service, these firms sent their sales forces and vice presidents alike out on the road to talk directly with customers. They had interesting marketing studies: one-on-one feedback. Sales calls, follow-ups, replacements and refunds allowed them to remain in the customers' minds and good graces.

One officer said it best: "Anyone can read the monthly financial reports: What we need to do is to interpret them so we can spot trends. We call on customers, on suppliers, we look at the bottom line of course, but we know how that line reached the bottom."

Mr. Bennett has never made a bad recording or disappointed during a live performance. Our eight firms had strong commitments to integrity. Their mantra was: "If there's integrity, there will be quality and profits." Their integrity manifested itself in more than just quality. Frederick T. Stanley, founder of Stanley Works, spoke of the intricate balance between automation and employees: "Machines are no better than the skill, care, ingenuity and spirit of the men who operate them. We can achieve perfect harmony when shortening of an operation provides mutual advantages to the workman and the producers." Ethics before its time. Re-engineering done correctly in the 1800s. Nothing at the expense of the customer or the employee.

Our firms were no less remarkable than Mr. Bennett and his success with Generation X —his third generational conquest. The sad part of their stories is what happened following the takeover battles of the '80s. But that is a story for another time. For now, it is reassuring to realize that cost-consciousness, focus, customer service, home-grown management and integrity are keys to longevity. Today's management fads seem as shallow as Ice T and Madonna. There is a simple Tony Bennett factor in success that makes today's fads much easier to debunk and infinitely easier to question.

In 1989, the Exxon oil tanker *Valdez* ran aground in Alaska's Prince William Sound, and 11 million gallons of crude oil leaked into Alaska's waters and onto its shores. Evidence of cutbacks in crews and maintenance levels for tankers dogged Exxon as the cleanup litigation continued through 1996. Exxon settled with the federal government for $1.15 billion in the government's case against Exxon for violation of environmental laws. The Exxon name suffered because of its association with oil spills.

Visit NBC's Dateline: http://www.nbc. com/news/shows/ dateline/index.html *Visit General Motors:* http://www.gm. com/

Perhaps the most widely publicized ethical downfall of the past decade concerned the segment on the NBC News magazine *Dateline NBC* regarding the sidesaddle gas tanks on General Motors pickup trucks built between 1973 and 1987. In a very public apology issued on a *Dateline NBC* broadcast after GM had filed a libel suit against NBC, the anchors for the show stated that NBC had made a mistake in using detonators in staging a crash involving one of the GM pickups. NBC also acknowledged that the speed of the crash vehicle was greater than that reported. Commentators suggested that the credibility of *Dateline NBC* and other news magazine programs would suffer because of NBC's conduct and the apology. NBC also paid GM $1 million to settle the case.

You've Got to Know When to Fold Them, Know When to Walk Away, Know When to Run
Stephen Mirretti—Arizona Judge and Gambler

Stephen Mirretti served as the presiding judge for the municipal courts in Tempe, Arizona. As presiding judge, Mirretti was responsible for awarding contracts for public defender work in the city courts, traffic schools, and all other service and supply contracts for the courts. Mirretti was paid $93,239 per year as presiding judge.

Mirretti had a lavish lifestyle, with a large, custom-built home, expensive imported autos, and several cellular phones. Mirretti also ran investment companies and programs on the side. He had court employees and lawyers invest in the ventures that he developed.

Mirretti's secretary said that she spent about 20 percent of her time working on Mirretti's side businesses, typing documents such as promissory notes. Court employees began to notice that Mirretti spent a great deal of time in Las Vegas and that he hired private jets to fly him from Phoenix to Las Vegas. Mirretti, in fact, was a well-known figure at Las Vegas hotels and casinos, known as "the judge" and enjoying lines of credit.

Mirretti was gone about 75 percent of the time, but his time records indicated that he was at work. A routine review by city auditors in 1993 revealed some problems with mismanagement. The Supreme Court of Arizona, responsible for the supervision and administration of all Arizona courts, then sent in its own team of auditors.

The court auditors discovered a complicated web of kickbacks and payoffs. A defense lawyer had been awarded public defender contracts by Mirretti for 10 years but had never submitted a bid during that period as city ordinance and state law require. The same lawyer had purchased a home from Mirretti for $11,000 more than Mirretti paid seven months earlier (in a depressed real estate market).

Mirretti faxed lists of DUI (driving under the influence) defendants to lawyers in exchange for payments. Mirretti had awarded the city court's driving school contract to the Arizona Consortium for Traffic Safety (ACTS), owned by Steven Papp, who also ran the hearing officer program of the court for Mirretti. ACTS and Papp did not submit bids for their contracts. The hearing officer caseload decreased 36 percent from 1989 to 1993, but the fees paid to Papp increased from $70,000 to $160,000 in that same period.

After the investigation was concluded, Mirretti and three attorneys pleaded guilty to a kickback and money-laundering scheme that funneled $478,000 in city court funds to Mirretti from 1986–1994. Mirretti explained the scheme:

The secret payments to me were related to and contingent upon the fact that the contractors continued to be provided the lucrative contracts at the court. I received my public-money salary under false pretenses and false representation that I was properly performing my administrative and judicial duties as presiding judge, when, in fact, I was secretly using and corrupting the position to obtain kickbacks from the contractors for my gambling losses and personal benefit.

In August 1995, Stephen Mirretti noted that he was doing manual labor for $6 per hour. Sadly he noted, "I can't even afford to take my children to see [the Walt Disney movie] *Operation Dumbo Drop*." In February 1996, Mirretti was sentenced to eight years in prison.

Issues
1. Would Miretti make the same choices today?
2. Why did he go so far adrift?
3. What impact did his activities have on the justice system?

Ethics as a Strategy

Ethical behavior not only increases long-term earnings; it also enables businesses to plan ahead and anticipate social needs and cultural changes that require the firm or its product to evolve. One of the benefits of ethical behavior and a firm's participation in community concerns is the goodwill that such involvement fosters. Conversely, the absence of that goodwill and consequent trust can mean the destruction of the firm.

When methyl isocyanate gas leaked from the Union Carbide plant in Bhopal, India, in 1984, the deadly gas left over 2,500 dead and 200,000 injured. It was later discovered that there had been problems in the plant with some of the equipment designed to prevent such leaks. While actual liability issues were hotly debated in court, many ethical questions were raised regarding the plant and Union Carbide. For example, was it a wise decision to build such a plant in a country with little expertise in the relevant technology? Did the people in the town know of the potential dangers of the plant? Why was a city of shacks allowed to be erected so close to the plant?

According to the Indian government, the plant had been operated well within legal and regulatory requirements, and Union Carbide's management had been cooperative in installing any additional equipment needed. Should Union Carbide have done more than was legally required? Did the plant operators need more training for such emergencies? Finally, the Bhopal incident raises many questions about the relationship between U.S. businesses and their operations in Third World countries that may not be prepared to deal with the latest technologies and may not be fully informed about the associated risks.

C O N S I D E R . . . **2.1** After the Union Carbide incident in Bhopal, the city of Akron, Ohio, passed a right-to-know law. The law requires disclosure to employees of any toxic substance they may be working with. The Akron ordinance made the failure to disclose illegal; before, it had been simply unethical to not disclose. What about unknown substances? Is there a duty to disclose the unknown? For example, during the 1920s and 1930s no one knew of the danger of black lung for all coal miners. Likewise, no one knew of the danger of asbestosis until the disease began to develop. Is there an obligation to disclose the general danger of constant exposure? What about the dangers to employees who work at computer terminals all day? There is some evidence that pregnant women who work around terminals have a higher incidence of miscarriages. Should employees be warned that constant exposure may pose a health threat?

Business Ethics for Personal Reasons

It would be misleading to say that every ethical business is a profitable business. First, not all ethical people are good managers or possess the necessary skills for making a business a success. But there are many competent businesspeople who have suffered for being ethical and many others who seem to survive despite their lack of ethics. Columnist Dave Barry has noted that every time there is an oil spill, the oil companies ready themselves for the higher prices and profits that come because all that oil is lost at sea. Despite his conviction and jail term related to junk bond sales in the 1980s, Michael Milken recently earned a $50,000,000 fee for help-ing Ted Turner negotiate a merger with Time Warner. There are many whistle-blowers who, although respected by many, have been unable to find employment in their industries. If ethical behavior does not guarantee success, then why have ethics? The answer has to do with personal ethics applied in a business context. Ivan Boesky was once described as follows: "He beguiled everybody about his exhaustive research and canny stock analysis when he really made money the old-fashioned way. He stole it." Business ethics is really nothing more than a standard of personal behavior applied to a group of people working together to make a profit. Some people are ethical because it enables them to sleep better at night. Some people are ethical because of the fear of getting caught. But being personally ethical is a justification for business ethics—it is simply the correct thing to do.

The Value of a Good Reputation

A reputation, good or bad, stays with a business or individual for a long time. James Preston, the CEO of Avon, Inc. has said, "A bad reputation is like a hang-over. It takes a while to get rid of, and it makes everything else hurt." Another executive lamenting his chances to try again commented, "Would anybody let Roseanne sing the national anthem again?" Once a company makes poor ethical choices, it carries the baggage of those choices despite successful and sincere efforts to reform.

Salomon Brothers's experiences with the bond market and regulators occurred in 1991. By 1995, Salomon had still not recovered its top position among Wall Street firms and continued to experience losses. Its return on equity remains the lowest among the large Wall Street brokerage firms. There is no question that Salomon Brothers has changed—its management, attitude, and values—but it continues to suffer from the reputation it gained from illegally cornering the bond markets.

Leadership's Role in Ethical Choices

Leadership has been defined as the ability to see around corners. In other words, a leader sees a problem before it becomes a legal issue or liability and fixes it, thus saving company time and money. All social, regulatory, and litigation issues progress along a time line. As the issue is brought to the public's attention, either by stories or by the sheer magnitude of the problem, the momentum for remedies and reforms continues until behavior is changed and regulated. Ethical choices afford firms opportunities to take positions ahead of the curve. Firms can choose to go beyond the law and perhaps avoid regulation that might be costly or litiga-tion that can be devastating. For example, the issues relating to the problems with asbestos dust in the lungs of asbestos workers and installers were clear in the 1930s. More studies needed to be done, but there was sufficient evidence to justify lung protection for workers and the development of some alternative forms of in-sulation. However, the first litigation relating to asbestos and asbestos workers did not arise until 1968. For that 30-year period, those in the business of producing and selling asbestos insulation products had the opportunity to take preventive actions. They chose to wait out the cycle. The result was a ban of asbestos and liti-gation at levels that forced the largest producer, Johns-Manville (now Manville) into bankruptcy. Leadership choices were available in the 1930s for offering warn-ings, providing masks, and developing alternative insulators. Johns-Manville chose to continue its posture of controlling information releases and studies. The liability issue progressed to a point of no choices other than that of bankruptcy.

Every business regulation that exists today controls business conduct in an area where there was once no control but, rather, the opportunity for businesses to self-regulate by making good value choices. For credit disclosures (see Chapter 16) before there were requirements imposed by Congress and the Federal Trade Commission, lenders and creditors had the option of designing their own disclosure forms and providing full information to buyers and debtors. That option was not chosen, and the result is a full scheme of regulation, including forms and advertising requirements. More recently, the problems resulting from a lack of candor in auto-leasing agreements resulted in federal regulation of contracts in this consumer area. Ethical choices give businesses the freedom to make choices before regulators mandate them. Breaches of ethics bring about regulation and liability with few opportunities to choose and less flexibility. The notion of choices and leadership are diagrammed in Exhibit 2.1.

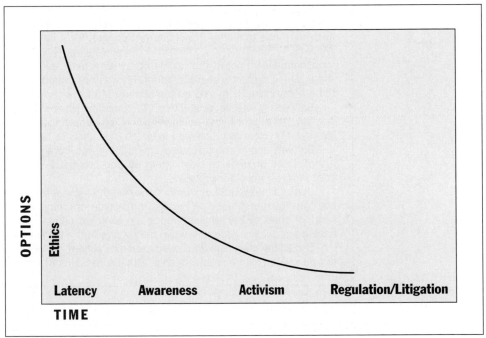

Source: Adapted from James Frierson's "Public Policy Forecasting: A New Approach," *SAM Advanced Management Journal,* Spring 1985, pp. 18–23.

Exhibit 2.1
Leadership and Ethics: Making Choices before Liability

Every issue progresses along a cycle that begins with a latency phase, in which the industry is aware of a problem. Derivatives were well known in the financial industry, but few investors were aware of their use by firms in which they held an interest. The awareness stage begins when the popular press reports on an issue and raises questions. Once the public has knowledge of a problem, it responds by either being assured that the problem is resolved or not really an issue or by calling for reform. The activism stage is one in which members of the public ask for either voluntary or regulatory reform. If voluntary reform is not forthcoming, those affected may sue or lobby for reform or both. For example, a group of parents, police officers, and shareholders protested Time Warner's production of

"Cop Killer," a song by the rap music artist Ice-T. The public outcry in the press and at Time Warner's shareholder meeting was strong. Congress was considering holding hearings on record labels and record content. Time Warner took the voluntary action of removing the song from the album. Time Warner eventually made a choice to withdraw the song, although later in the regulatory cycle when public outcry was strong, that choice averted regulation. It is important to understand that Time Warner could have made the choice not to publish the song of Ice-T initially. The following ethical issue entered the activism stage late in 1995.

ETHICAL ISSUES

2.1 "Women Who Marry Their Rapist." "My Daughter Is Living as a Boy." "Housewives vs. Strippers." "Is There Life after a Career in Porn?" These are themes from daytime TV talk shows. Former Education Secretary William Bennett used these titles to ask producers, sponsors, and viewers to refrain from participating in shows such as those of Maury Povich, Jerry Springer, Ricki Lake, Jenny Jones, and Montel Williams.

Bennett also noted that in March 1995 a male guest was set up on the *Jenny Jones Show* to meet a secret admirer. He was humiliated when his admirer turned out to be a gay man. He murdered the admirer after the show was taped.

Sally Jessy Raphael responded, "It's a real elitist view for a guy like this to stand up and say, 'I don't think four and one-half million people should watch this.' These people [her viewers] have as much right to watch their show as he has to watch *Nightline*."

Bennett and his group called on Time Warner, Paramount, and Fox—the producers of these shows—to clean them up and promised letter-writing campaigns, boycotts, and shareholder protests.

Oprah Winfrey, host of *Oprah*, once had the highest-rated talk show in the country. Ms. Winfrey has refused to engage in the type of theme show described earlier and was not cited by Bennett as among the targeted shows. However, Winfrey's ratings have been declining steadily while the ratings of the targeted shows have soared.

Should the producers and advertisers take action? Is Bennett infringing upon the right to free speech? What problems arise with the position of "just don't watch the shows!"?

WHAT IS BUSINESS ETHICS?

Many economists and professors of finance argue that insider trading actually makes the stock market more efficient and that such conduct should not be regulated. The purpose of ethics is to bring back into the purely quantitative models of business the elements of a fair playing field.

A business faces the special problem of having to develop moral standards for a group of people who will work together toward the common goal of profit for the firm. Each individual in the group will have his or her personal moral standards, but employees may find that the moral standards imposed by those at the top in a business may result in possible harm to those at the bottom or to others outside the firm. An employee may feel compelled to resolve the conflict between loyalty to an employer and the performance of an illegal or immoral act ordered by that employer by simply following the employer's direction. In other words, in developing standards of business ethics, an employee has personal economic interests in continuing employment that may compromise his or her personal moral standards.

Moral standards can be derived from different sources, and there is often much debate among ethicists about the origins of these standards. One theory is that our moral standards are simply the same as actual or **positive law**, that our ethical decisions are made simply upon the basis of whether an activity is legal. Positive law, or codified law, establishes the standard for ethical behavior.

Others believe that our moral standards are derived from a higher source and that they are universal. Often labeled **natural law**, this school of ethical thought supports the notion that some standards do not exist because of law (and, indeed, may exist in spite of laws). For example, there was a time when the United States permitted slavery. Even though the positive law would have allowed the activity and the standard of positive law would have considered slave ownership ethical, the natural laws would dictate that the deprivation of another's rights would be unethical.

Moral relativism (also called situational ethics) establishes moral standards according to the situation in which the dilemma is faced. Violation of the law, for example, is permitted if you are stealing to provide food for your starving family. Adultery is justified when you are caught in an unhappy marriage, as is the business situation in which you engage in lying to avoid offending a co-worker or a customer. Bribery is wrong in the United States, but a firm could develop a relativist approach and argue that to be competitive in international markets it may need to use bribery in countries where it is accepted.

A final source of moral standards is religious beliefs or divine revelation. The source of standards can be the Bible or the Koran or any inspired book or writing someone believes has resulted from divine revelation.

In some ethical dilemmas in business, there are conflicts among and between the interests of various stakeholders of the business. For example, shareholders are interested in earnings and dividends. The members of the community in which the business is located are interested in the jobs the business provides and are concerned about the environmental impact of the business. Suppose the business discovers that its air pollution-control equipment is not state-of-the-art technology and, although no laws are being violated, more pollution is being released than is necessary. To correct the problem, its factory must be shut down for a minimum of three months. The pollution will harm the air and the community, but the shutdown will harm the workers and the shareholders. The business must consider the needs and interests of all its stakeholders in resolving the ethical dilemma it faces. There has been much discussion and disagreement about this particular issue. In the following interview excerpt, economist Milton Friedman offers a different perspective on this ethical dilemma:

Q: Quite apart from emission standards and effluent taxes, shouldn't corporate officials take action to stop pollution out of a sense of social responsibility?

Milton Friedman: I wouldn't buy stock in a company that hired that kind of leadership. A corporate executive's responsibility is to make as much money for the shareholders as possible, as long as he operates within the rules of the game. When an executive decides to take action for reasons of social responsibility, he is taking money from someone else—from the stockholders, in the form of lower dividends; from the employees, in the form of lower wages; or from the consumer, in the form of higher prices. The responsibility of a corporate executive is to fulfill the terms of his contract. If he can't do that in good conscience, then he should quit his job and find another way to do good. He has the right to promote what he regards as desirable moral objectives only with his own money. If, on the other hand, the executives of U.S. Steel undertake to reduce pollution in Gary for the purpose of making the town attractive to employees and thus lowering labor costs, then they are doing the stockholders' bidding. And everyone benefits: The stockholders get higher dividends; the customer gets cheaper steel; the workers get more in return for their labor. That's the beauty of free enterprise. . . . To the extent that pollution caused by the U.S. Steel plant there is confined to that city and the people there are truly concerned about the problem, it's to the company's advantage to do something about it. Why? Because if it doesn't, workers will prefer to live where there is less pollution, and U.S. Steel will have to pay them more to live in Gary, Indiana.[1]

FOR THE MANAGER'S DESK

A CORPORATE OFFICER'S VIEW ON BUSINESS ETHICS

Richard S. Lombard served as vice president and general counsel for Exxon for 20 years. He also served as counsel with Baker & Botts in Dallas, Texas. These remarks were made by Lombard at the Andrew R. Cecil Lectures on Moral Values at the University of Texas at Dallas. In our country today, the chief social obligations of a business corporation are three: first, to provide goods or services that people want to buy at prices they are willing to pay; second, to reinvest in the business for the future; and third, to do all of this at a profit sufficient to give those who have financed the corporation an acceptable return on their investment.

These are not all; there are additional major obligations to obey the laws, to deal fairly with employees, and to carry on business in ways that protect the integrity of the environment and the safety of the public. In wartime, at least during popular wars, there is an obligation to cooperate with government policy in support of the war effort. And of course there is the important obligation to contribute to educational, cultural and charitable causes in the community.

The three principal obligations—to provide people with goods or services at prices they are willing to pay, to reinvest for the future, and to operate at a profit acceptable to investors—are so fundamental that a business cannot long survive if it fails to meet them.

The idea that business corporations have an obligation to society to operate at profit levels satisfactory to their investors is not self-evident, and some do not accept it. Some say that there is a tension between business morality and ethics, on the one hand, and business necessity on the other. In that view, the board of directors and officers of a corporation are thought to be constrained in their moral choices and ethical decision-making by a sordid desire to make profits. That is the view of those who criticize business for, as the critics put it, "valuing profits above principles." It assumes that the pursuit of profits is at best morally neutral. Other critics of business go further, and assert that the pursuit of profits not only lacks moral justification but is actively immoral in itself, and that those who engage in it are reprehensible.

Another perspective on that view is held by some businessmen and women themselves, who feel guilty about what they perceive as a subordination of their better moral natures to the imperatives of commerce, and are somewhat ashamed of their occupations.

There is a refreshing wind of understanding today of the social necessity of the pursuit of profit by corporate management. The sudden and dramatic collapse of communism in Europe and the former Soviet Union, and the brave efforts of the new leaders of former communist states to implement market economies in place of state socialism, have shown the world the social value of the profit motive. Even in some of the remaining communist countries, including China, the social utility of the profit motive has belatedly been recognized. A considerable amount of free enterprise is being permitted Chinese citizens and foreign investors, and its beneficial effects on the economy are already being appreciated.

The obligation of the corporation's directors and officers is to manage the business in the best long-term interests of all those who depend upon it: the owners, the lenders, the employees, the annuitants, their families, the suppliers, the customers, and the people in the communities where the corporation carries on its business. This is not a principle of economics devoid of moral underpinning: It is a moral obligation itself. To fail to meet it can bring heartbreak and misery to real people.

Source: Richard S. Lombard, "Corporate Social Responsibilities in the Nineties," *Individualism and Social Responsibility*, from the *Andrew R. Cecil Lectures on Moral Values in a Free Society*, Vol. XV, p. 143. University of Texas at Dallas, 1994.

ETHICAL POSTURES, SOCIAL RESPONSIBILITY, AND BUSINESS PRACTICE

The ethical perspective of a business often sets the tone for its operations and employees' choices. Historically, the philosophical debate over the role of business in society has evolved into four schools of thought on ethical behavior based on the responses to two questions: (1) Whose interest should a corporation serve? and (2) To whom should a corporation be responsive in order to best serve that interest? There are only two answers to these questions—"shareholders only" and "the larger society"—and the combination of those answers defines the school of thought. The following discussion is summarized in Exhibit 2.2.

	Moral question: Whose interest should corporation serve?	Policy question: Best way to serve interest is if the corporation is responsive to:
Inherence	Shareholders only	Shareholders only
Enlightened self-interest	Shareholders only	Larger society
Invisible hand	Larger society	Shareholders only
Social responsibility	Larger society	Larger society

Source: Adapted with permission of *American Business Law Journal,* from Daryl Hatano, "Should Corporations Exercise Their Freedom of Speech Rights?" 22 *A.B.L.J.* 165 (1984).

Exhibit 2.2
Social Responsibility of Corporations

Inherence

According to the **inherence** school of thought, managers answer only to shareholders and act only with shareholders' interests in mind. This type of manager would not become involved in any political or social issues unless it was in the shareholders' best interests to do so, and provided the involvement did not backfire and cost the firm sales. Milton Friedman's philosophy, as previously expressed, is an example of inherence. To illustrate how a business following the inherence school of thought would behave, consider the issue of a proposed increase in residential property taxes for school-funding purposes. A business that subscribes to the inherence school would support a school-tax increase only if the educational issue affected the company's performance and only if such a position did not offend those who opposed the tax increase.

Enlightened Self-Interest

According to this school of thought, the manager is responsible to the shareholders but serves them best by being responsive to the larger society. **Enlightened self-interest** is based on the view that, in the long run, business value is enhanced if business is responsive to the needs of society. In this school, managers are free to speak out on societal issues without the constraint of offending someone, as in inherence. Businesses would anticipate social changes and needs and be early advocates for change. For example, many corporations today have instituted job sharing, child-care facilities, and sick child care in response to the changing structure of the American family and workforce. This responsiveness to the needs of the larger society should also be beneficial to shareholders because it enables the business to retain a quality workforce.

The Invisible Hand

The **invisible hand** school of thought is the opposite of enlightened self-interest. According to this philosophy, managers believe that business ought to serve the larger society and that it does this best when it serves the shareholders only. Such businesses allow government to set the standards and boundaries for appropriate behavior and simply adhere to these governmental constraints as a way of maximizing benefits to their shareholders. They become involved in issues of social responsibility or in political issues only when society lacks sufficient information on an issue to make a decision. Even then, their involvement is limited to presenting data and does not extend to advocating a particular viewpoint or position. This school of thought holds that it is best for society to guide itself and that businesses work best when they serve shareholders within those constraints.

Social Responsibility

In the **social responsibility** school of thought, the role of business is to serve the larger society, and that is best accomplished by being responsive to the larger society. This view is simply a reflection of the idea that businesses profit by being responsive to society and its needs. A business following this school of thought would advocate full disclosure of product information to consumers in its advertising and would encourage political activism on the part of its managers and employees on all issues, not just those that affect the corporation. These businesses believe that this sense of social responsibility contributes to their long-term success.

C O N S I D E R . . . **2.2** Eclipse Enterprises, Inc. of Forestville, California, began in 1992 to produce its "True Crime" line of trading cards. The trading cards featured pictures of serial killers and mass murderers. On the back of the cards was information about the killers' crimes and victims. Among the card faces were: Charles Manson, Jeffrey Dahmer, Ted Bundy, John Wayne Gacy, and David Berkowitz (the Son of Sam killer). The line also includes some historical figures, such as Jack the Ripper, Lizzie Borden, and Al Capone. Would you produce or sell these cards?

Following substantial public outcry, Eclipse noted that it did not sell its $1 packets with only murderers in them: the card packets included other historical figures as well. In response to public concern, the county of Nassau, New York, passed an ordinance making it illegal to sell the cards to minors.

Eclipse claims the restriction violates its free speech rights. What problems do you see with enforcement?

If the ordinance is ruled to be unconstitutional, what role does ethics play in the marketing of this product? Would you market the product? Why or why not?

ETHICAL ISSUES

2.2 Actress Demi Moore starred in the 1995 movie entitled *The Scarlet Letter* that was based on Nathaniel Hawthorne's book of the same name. Hollywood Pictures ran the following quote from a *Time* magazine review: "'Scarlet Letter' Gets What It Always Needed: Demi Moore." The actual review by *Time* magazine read: "Stuffy old *Scarlet Letter* gets what it always needed: Demi Moore and a happier ending." A *Time* spokesman noted that the statement was clearly ironic.   In the same review, the *Time* critic, Richard Corliss, referred to the movie as "revisionist slog" and gave it an "F."

An ad for the 1995 movie *Seven* quoted *Entertainment Weekly* as calling it a "masterpiece." The actual review read, "The credits sequence . . . is a small masterpiece of dementia."

A movie industry observer stated in response to these examples, "The practice of fudging critics' quotes [in ads] is common."

Is the practice of fudging quotes ethical? Should Hollywood Pictures have pulled *The Scarlet Letter* ads?

 "Ford Motor Company and the Pinto" helps resolve the chapter's opening "Judgment."

FOR THE MANAGER'S DESK

FORD MOTOR COMPANY AND THE PINTO

Design of the Pinto Fuel System

In 1968, Ford began designing a new subcompact automobile that ultimately became the Pinto. Lee Iacocca, then a Ford vice president, conceived the project and was its moving force. Ford's objective was to build a car at or below two thousand pounds to sell for no more than $2,000.

Ordinarily, marketing surveys and preliminary engineering studies precede the styling of a new automobile line. Pinto, however, was a rush project, so styling preceded engineering and dictated engineering design to a greater degree than usual. Among the engineering decisions dictated by styling was the placement of the fuel tank. It was then the preferred practice in Europe and Japan to locate the gas tank over the rear axle in subcompacts because a small vehicle has less "crush space" between the rear axle and the bumper than larger cars. The Pinto's styling, however, required the tank to be placed behind the rear axle, leaving only 9 or 10 inches of "crush space"—far less than in any other American automobile or Ford overseas subcompacts. In addition, the Pinto was designed so that its bumper was little more than a chrome strip, less substantial than the bumper of any other American car produced then or later. The Pinto's rear structure also lacked reinforcing members known as "hat sections" (Two longitudinal side members) and horizontal cross members running between them, such as were found in cars of larger unitized construction and in all automobiles produced by Ford's overseas operations. The absence of the reinforcing members rendered the Pinto less crush-resistant than other vehicles. Finally, the differential housing selected for the Pinto had an exposed flange and a line of exposed bolt-heads. These protrusions were sufficient to puncture a gas tank driven forward against the differential upon rear impact.

Continued

Crash Tests

During the development of the Pinto, prototypes were built and tested. Some were "mechanical prototypes," which duplicated mechanical features of the design but not its appearance, while others, referred to as "engineering prototypes," were true duplicates of the design car. These prototypes, as well as two production Pintos, were crash-tested by Ford to determine, among other things, the integrity of the fuel system in rear-end accidents. Ford also conducted the tests to see if the Pinto as designed would meet a proposed federal regulation requiring all automobiles manufactured in 1972 to be able to withstand a 20-mile-per-hour fixed-barrier impact without significant fuel spillage and all automobiles manufactured after January 1, 1973, to withstand a 30-mile-per-hour fixed-barrier impact without significant fuel spillage.

The crash tests revealed that the Pinto's fuel system as designed could not meet the 20-mile-per-hour proposed standard. Mechanical prototypes struck from the rear with a moving barrier at 21 miles per hour caused the fuel tank to be driven forward and to be punctured, causing fuel leakage in excess of the standard prescribed by the proposed legislation. A production Pinto crash-tested at 21 miles per hour into a fixed barrier caused the fuel neck to be torn from the gas tank and the tank to be punctured by a bolt head on the differential housing. In at least one test, spilled fuel entered the driver's compartment through gaps resulting from the separation of the seams joining the rear wheel wells to the floor pan. The seam separation was occasioned by the lack of reinforcement in the rear structure and insufficient welds of the wheel wells to the floor pan.

Tests conducted by Ford on other vehicles, including modified or reinforced mechanical Pinto prototypes, proved safe at speeds at which the Pinto failed. Where rubber bladders had been installed in the tank, crash tests into fixed barriers at 21 miles per hour withstood leakage from punctures in the gas tank. Vehicles with fuel tanks installed above rather than behind the rear axle passed the fuel system integrity test at 31 miles per hour. A Pinto with two longitudinal hat sections added to firm up the rear structure passed a 20-mile-per-hour rear-impact, fixed-barrier test with no fuel leakage.

The Cost to Remedy
Design Deficiencies

When a prototype failed the fuel system integrity test, the standard of care for engineers in the industry was to redesign and retest it. The vulnerability of the production Pinto's fuel tank at speeds of 20- and 30-miles-per hour fixed-barrier tests could have been remedied by inexpensive "fixes," but Ford produced and sold the Pinto to the public without doing anything to remedy the defects. Design changes that would have enhanced the integrity of the fuel tank system at relatively little cost per car included the following: longitudinal side members and cross members for $2.40 and $1.80, respectively; a single shock-absorbent "flak suit" to protect the tank for $4.00; a tank within a tank and placement of the tank over the axle for $5.08 to $5.79; a nylon bladder within the tank for $5.25 to $8.00; placement of the tank over the axle surrounded with a protective barrier at a cost of $9.95; substitution of a rear axle with a smooth differential housing at a cost of $2.10; imposition of a protective shield between the differential housing and the tank at $2.35; improvement and reinforcement of the bumper at $2.60; addition of eight inches of crush space at a cost of $6.40. Equipping the car with a reinforced rear structure, smooth axle, improved bumper, and additional crush space for a total cost of $15.30 would have made the fuel tank safe in a 34- to 38-mile-per-hour rear-end collision by a vehicle the size of the Ford Galaxie. If, in addition to the foregoing, a bladder or tank within a tank were used or if the tank were protected with a shield, it would have been safe in a 40- to 45-mile-per hour rear impact. If the tank had been located over the rear axle, it would have been safe in a rear impact at 50 miles per hour or more.

Management's Decision
to Go Forward with
Knowledge of Defects

The idea for the Pinto, as noted, was conceived by Lee Iacocca, then executive vice president of Ford. The feasibility study was conducted under the supervision of Robert Alexander, vice president of car engineering. Ford's Product Planning Committee, whose members included Iacocca, Alexander, and Harold MacDonald, Ford's group vice president of

Continued

car engineering, approved the Pinto's concept and made the decision to go forward with the project. During the course of the project, regular product review meetings were held, chaired by MacDonald and attended by Alexander. As the project approached actual production, the engineers responsible for the components of the project "signed off" to their immediate supervisors, who in turn "signed off" to their superiors and so on up the chain of command until the entire project was approved for public release by Vice Presidents Alexander and MacDonald and ultimately by Iacocca. The Pinto crash test results had been forwarded up the chain of command to the ultimate decision makers and were known to the Ford officials, who decided to go forward with production. . . .

Harley Copp, a former Ford engineer and executive in charge of the crash testing program, testified that the highest level of Ford's management made the decision to go forward with the production of the Pinto, knowing that the gas tank was vulnerable to puncture and rupture at low rear-impact speeds, thus creating a significant risk of death or injury from fire, and knowing that fixes were feasible at nominal cost. He testified that management's decision was based on the cost savings that would inure from omitting or delaying the fixes. The figures that appeared in memos between and among Ford executives regarding the costs of fixing the gas tank's design are summarized in the following chart.

Benefits

Savings—180 burn deaths; 180 serious burn injuries; 2,100 burned vehicles
Unit cost—$200,000 per death; $67,000 per injury; $700 per vehicle
Total Benefits—(180 x $200,000) + (180 x $67,000) + (2,100 x $700) = $49.15 million

Costs

Sales—11 million cars; 1.5 million light trucks
Unit cost—$11 per car; $11 per truck
Total costs—(11,000,000 x $11) + (1,500,000 x $11) = $137 million

Ford's unit cost of $200,000 for one life was based on a National Highway Traffic Safety Administration calculation developed as follows:

Component	1971 Costs
Future productivity losses	
Direct	$132,000
Indirect	41,300
Medical costs	
Hospital	700
Other	425
Property damage	1,500
Insurance administration	4,700
Legal and court	3,000
Employer losses	1,000
Victim's pain and suffering	10,000
Funeral	900
Assets (lost consumption)	5,000
Miscellaneous accident cost	200
Total Per Fatality	$200,725

Copp's testimony concerning management's awareness of the crash test results and the vulnerability of the Pinto fuel system was corroborated by other evidence. At an April 1971 product review meeting chaired by MacDonald, those present received and discussed a report prepared by Ford engineers pertaining to the financial impact of a proposed federal standard on fuel system integrity and the cost savings that would accrue from deferring even minimal fixes. It is reasonable to infer that the report was prepared for and known to Ford officials in policy-making positions.

Finally, Copp testified to conversations in late 1968 or early 1969 with the chief assistant research engineer in charge of cost-weight evaluation of the Pinto, and to a later conversation with the chief chassis engineer, who was then in charge of crash testing the early prototype. In these conversations, both men expressed concern about the integrity of the Pinto's fuel system and complained about management's unwillingness to deviate from the design if the change would cost money.

The Accident

In November 1971, the Grays purchased a new 1972 Pinto hatchback manufactured by Ford in October 1971. The Grays had trouble with the car from the outset. During the first few months of ownership, they had to return the car to the dealer for repairs a number of times. Their car problems included excessive gas and oil consumption, downshifting of the automatic transmission, lack of power, and occasional stalling. It was later learned that the stalling and excessive fuel consumption were caused by a heavy carburetor float.

On May 28, 1972, Mrs. Gray, accompanied by 13-year-old Richard Grimshaw, set out in the Pinto from Anaheim, California, for Barstow to meet her husband. The Pinto was then six months old and had been driven approximately three thousand miles. Gray stopped in San Bernardino for gasoline, got back onto the freeway (Interstate 15), and proceeded toward her destination at 60–65 miles per hour. As she approached the Route 30 off-ramp, where traffic was congested, she moved from the outer fast lane to the middle lane of the freeway. Shortly after this lane change, the Pinto suddenly stalled and coasted to a halt in the middle lane. It was later established that the carburetor float had become so saturated with gasoline that it suddenly sank, opening the float chamber and causing the engine to flood and stall. A car traveling immediately behind the Pinto was able to swerve and pass it but the driver of a 1962 Ford Galaxie was unable to avoid colliding with the Pinto. The Galaxie had been traveling from 50 to 55 miles per hour but before the impact had been braked to a speed of from 28 to 37 miles per hour.

At the moment of impact, the Pinto caught fire and its interior was engulfed in flames. According to the plaintiff's expert, the impact of the Galaxie had driven the Pinto's gas tank forward and caused it to be punctured by the flange or one of the bolts on the differential housing so that fuel sprayed from the punctured tank and entered the passenger compartment through gaps resulting from the separation of the rear-wheel well sections from the floor pan. By the time the Pinto came to rest after the collision, both occupants had sustained serious burns. When they emerged from the vehicle, their clothing was almost completely burned off. Gray died a few days later of congestive heart failure as a result of the burns. Grimshaw managed to survive but only through heroic medical measures. He has undergone numerous and extensive surgeries and skin grafts and must undergo additional surgeries over the next 10 years. He lost portions of several fingers on his left hand and portions of his left ear, while his face required many skin grafts from various portions of his body.

The verdict in the case was for Grimshaw. The damages awarded: $3 million in compensatory and $125 million in punitive damages, which was later reduced to an unreported figure. Ford was indicted for negligent homicide in Indiana.

Discussion Questions

1. Give the total cost involved if all the fixes had been done.
2. What was management's position on the fixes? How do you view the cost-benefit analysis?
3. Who was responsible for Mrs. Gray's death and Grimshaw's injuries?
4. What school of thought was Ford subscribing to when it made the decision not to go with the fixes?
5. Was the Pinto design in violation of any laws?
6. Was Ford simply answering a public demand for a small, fuel-efficient, and inexpensive auto?
7. Ford was acquitted of the criminal charges in the Indiana case. Do you think there was criminal conduct?

Source: Excerpted from *Grimshaw v. Ford Motor Co.*, 174 Cal. Rptr. 348 (1981).

RECOGNIZING ETHICAL DILEMMAS

Despite a strong value system, an individual facing the complexities of business needs help in recognizing ethical dilemmas. There are two ways an ethical dilemma can be spotted: by language and by category.

The Language of Ethical Lapses

The first way to spot an ethical dilemma is by watching the language those involved use. There are key phrases of rationalization employed in ethical dilemmas. Those phrases are listed in Exhibit 2.3.

```
"Everybody else does it."

"If we don't do it, they'll get someone else to do it."

"That's the way it's always been done."

"We'll wait until the lawyers tell us it's wrong."

"It doesn't really hurt anyone."

"The system is unfair."

"I was just following orders."
```

Exhibit 2.3
The Language of Rationalization

ETHICAL ISSUES

2.3 Most criminals are caught when they are pulled over for traffic violations. For example, Timothy McVeigh, accused of producing and planting the bomb outside the federal building in Oklahoma City in 1995, was pulled over for speeding just outside of Oklahoma City. When asked why they speed, many people respond, "Nobody else goes the speed limit. Everybody does it." Isn't it still a violation of the law to speed? Is it ethical to speed? How do we factor in the German Autobahn experience on which there are no speed limits?

"EVERYBODY ELSE DOES IT."

Zoë Baird's nomination for attorney general in early 1993 met with opposition when investigations revealed that Baird and her husband had employed illegal immigrants as a chauffeur and as a nanny for their child and had failed to pay the Social Security, Medicare, and unemployment taxes required of household employers. The response of many to the issue was that only 25 percent of all household employers paid such taxes; fully 75 percent or "everybody else" did not. Statistical support is not a valid basis for making ethical choices. The law had been violated. "Everybody else does it" is a rationalization for a poor ethical choice. Everybody else was investing in those risky financial instruments, derivatives. The eventual and catastrophic losses from these instruments to Procter & Gamble, Orange County, Barings Bank, and Gibson Greetings show how "everybody else" is often wrong.

"IF WE DON'T DO IT, SOMEONE ELSE WILL."

The rationalization of competition. Since someone will do it and make money, it might as well be us. For Halloween 1994, there were O. J. Simpson masks and plastic knives and Nicole Brown Simpson masks and costumes complete with slashes and blood stains. When Nicole Simpson's family objected to this violation of the basic standard of decency, a costume-shop owner commented that if he didn't sell the items, someone down the street would. While nothing about the marketing of the costumes was illegal, the ethical issues that surround earning a profit from an event as heinous as the brutal murder of a young mother abound.

"THAT'S THE WAY IT HAS ALWAYS BEEN DONE."

Corporate or business history and business practices are not always sound. The fact that for years nothing has changed in a firm may indicate the need for change and an atmosphere that invites possible ethical violations. For example, until the Securities and Exchange Commission required corporate boards of directors compensation committees to make reports and to disclose the identities of their members, the sitting members of many of these committees had conflicts of interest. For example, a senior partner of a law firm who represented a given corporation often sat on that client's board and on its compensation committee. The result was that a lawyer whose firm was economically dependent on the corporation as a client was making salary determinations for the corporation's officers, who, of course, made the decisions about which law firm would represent them and their company. A conflict of interest existed, but everybody was doing it, and it was the way corporate governance had always been done. Again, unquestioning adherence to a pattern of practices or behavior often indicates an underlying ethical dilemma.

"WE'LL WAIT UNTIL THE LAWYERS TELL US IT'S WRONG."

Lawyers are trained to provide only the parameters of the law. In many situations, they offer an opinion that is correct in that it does not violate the law. Whether the conduct they have passed judgment on as legal is ethical is a different question. Allowing law and lawyers to control a firm's destiny ignores the opportunity to make wise and ethical choices. For example, Orange County, California, filed for bankruptcy in 1994 because its investment strategy, involving heavy investments in financial derivative instruments, had failed, and it had lost sums so large that it was rendered insolvent (see Chapter 21). Were the derivative investments legal? Absolutely. Were the derivative investments reviewed by lawyers? Yes, for both buyers and sellers. Legality is often not a sufficient standard for ethical behavior. Following the positive law does not always guarantee that a firm will avoid legal difficulties. Analyzing issues of fairness, risk, and disclosure requires input beyond just a legal opinion.

"IT DOESN'T REALLY HURT ANYONE."

When we are the sole rubberneckers on the freeway, traffic remains unaffected. But if everyone rubbernecks, we have a traffic jam. All of us making poor ethical choices would cause significant harm. A man interviewed after he was arrested for defrauding insurance companies through staged auto accidents remarked, "It didn't really hurt anyone. Insurance companies can afford it." The second part of his statement is accurate. The insurance companies can afford it—but not without cost to someone else. Such fraud harms all of us because we must pay higher premiums to allow insurers to absorb the costs of paying for and investigating fraudulent claims.

"THE SYSTEM IS UNFAIR."

Often touted by students as a justification for cheating on exams, this rationalization eases our consciences by telling us we are cheating only to make up for deficiencies in the system. Yet just one person cheating can send ripples through an entire system. The credibility of grades and the institution come into question as students obtain grades through means beyond the system's standards. As we see events unfold in China, Italy, and Brazil, with government employees awarding contracts and rights to do business on the basis of payments rather than on the merits of a given company or its proposal, we understand how such bribery only results in greater unfairness within and greater costs to those countries. Many economists have noted that a country's businesses and economy will not progress without some fundamental assurance of trust.

"I WAS JUST FOLLOWING ORDERS."

In many criminal trials and disputes over responsibility and liability, many managers will disclaim their responsibility by stating, "I was just following orders." There are times when individuals cannot follow the directions of supervisors for they have been asked to do something illegal or immoral. Judges who preside over the criminal trials of war criminals often remind defendants that an order is not necessarily legal or moral. Values require us to question or depart from orders when others will be harmed or wronged.

The Categories of Ethical Dilemmas

The second method for spotting an ethical dilemma is to understand the categories of ethical dilemmas. The following twelve categories were developed and listed in *Exchange,* the magazine of the Brigham Young University School of Business:

TAKING THINGS THAT DON'T BELONG TO YOU

Everything from the unauthorized use of the Pitney-Bowes postage meter at your office for mailing personal letters to exaggerations on travel expenses belongs in this category of ethical violations. Regardless of size, motivation, or the presence of any of the rationalizations discussed above, the unauthorized use of someone else's property or taking property under false pretenses still means taking something that does not belong to you. A chief financial officer of a large electric utility reported that after taking a cab from LaGuardia International Airport to his midtown Manhattan hotel, he asked for a receipt. The cab driver handed him a full book of blank receipts and drove away. Apparently the problem of accurately reporting travel expenses involves more than just employees.

SAYING THINGS YOU KNOW ARE NOT TRUE

Often in their quest for promotion and advancement, fellow employees discredit their co-workers. Assigning blame or inaccurately reporting conversations is lying. While "This is the way the game is played around here" is a common justification, saying things that are untrue is an ethical violation.

GIVING OR ALLOWING FALSE IMPRESSIONS

The salesman who permits a potential customer to believe that his cardboard boxes will hold the customer's tomatoes for long-distance shipping when he knows the boxes are not strong enough has given a false impression. A car dealer who fails to disclose that a car has been in an accident is misleading potential customers. A co-worker or supervisor who takes credit for another employee's idea has allowed a false impression.

BUYING INFLUENCE OR ENGAGING IN CONFLICT OF INTEREST

A company awards a construction contract to a firm owned by the father of the state attorney general while the state attorney general's office is investigating that company. A county administrator responsible for awarding the construction contract for a baseball stadium accepts from contractors interested in bidding on the project paid travel around the country to other stadiums that the contractors have built. The wife of a state attorney general accepts trading advice from the corporate attorney for a highly regulated company and subsequently earns, in her first attempt at the market, over $100,000 in the commodities market in cattle futures.

All of these examples illustrate conflicts of interest. Those involved in situations such as these often protest, "But I would never allow that to influence me." The ethical violation is the conflict. Whether the conflict can or will influence those it touches is not the issue, for neither party can prove conclusively that a quid pro quo was not intended. The possibility exists, and it creates discomfort. Hence, conflicts of interest are to be avoided.

HIDING OR DIVULGING INFORMATION

Taking your firm's product development or trade secrets to a new place of employment constitutes an ethical violation of divulging proprietary information. Failing to disclose the results of medical studies that indicate your firm's new drug has significant side effects is the ethical violation of hiding information that the product could be harmful to purchasers.

TAKING UNFAIR ADVANTAGE

Many current consumer protection laws were passed because so many businesses took unfair advantage of those who were not educated or were unable to discern the nuances of complex contracts. Credit disclosure requirements, truth-in-lending provisions, and new regulations on auto leasing all resulted because businesses misled consumers who could not easily follow the jargon of long and complex agreements.

COMMITTING PERSONAL DECADENCE

While many argue about the ethical notion of an employee's right to privacy, it has become increasingly clear that personal conduct outside the job can influence performance and company reputation. Thus, a company driver must abstain from substance abuse because of safety issues. Even the traditional company Christmas party and picnic have come under scrutiny as the behavior of employees at, and following, these events has brought harm to others in the form of alcohol-related accidents.

PERPETRATING INTERPERSONAL ABUSE

A manager sexually harasses an employee. Another manager is verbally abusive to an employee. Still another manager subjects employees to humiliating correction in the presence of customers. In some cases, laws protect employees. However, many situations are simply ethical violations that constitute interpersonal abuse.

PERMITTING ORGANIZATIONAL ABUSE

Many U.S. firms with operations overseas, such as Levi Strauss, The Gap, and Esprit, have faced issues of organizational abuse. The unfair treatment of workers in international operations appears in the form of child labor, demeaning wages, and too-long hours. While a business cannot change the culture of another country, it can perpetuate—or alleviate—abuse through its operations there.

VIOLATING RULES

Review Stanford University's "Code of Conduct for Business Activities":
http://www-portfolio.stanford.edu/200006

Many rules, particularly those in large organizations that tend toward bureaucracy from a need to maintain internal controls or follow lines of authority, seem burdensome to employees trying to serve customers and other employees. Stanford University experienced difficulties in this area of ethics as it used funds from federal grants for miscellaneous university purposes. Questions arose about the propriety of the expenditures, which quite possibly could have been approved through proper channels, but weren't. The rules for the administration of federal grant monies used for overhead were not followed. The result was not only an ethical violation but damage to Stanford's reputation and a new president for the university.

CONDONING UNETHICAL ACTIONS

In this breach of ethics, the wrong results from the failure to report the wrong. What if you witnessed a fellow employee embezzling company funds by forging her signature on a check that was to be voided? Would you report that violation? A winking tolerance of others' unethical behavior is in itself unethical. Suppose that as a product designer you were aware of a fundamental flaw in your company's new product; a product predicted to catapult your firm to record earnings. Would you pursue the problem to the point of halting the distribution of the product? Would you disclose what you know to the public if you could not get your company to act?

BALANCING ETHICAL DILEMMAS

Visit Levi Strauss & Co.:
http://www.levi.com/

In these types of situations, there are no right or wrong answers; rather, there are dilemmas to be resolved. For example, Levi Strauss struggled with its decision about whether to do business in the People's Republic of China because of known human rights violations by the government there. Other companies debated doing business in South Africa when that country's government followed a policy of apartheid. In some respects, the presence of these companies would help by advancing human rights and, certainly, by improving the standard of living for at least some international operations workers. On the other hand, their ability to recruit businesses could help such governments sustain themselves by enabling them to point to economic successes despite human rights violations.[2]

RESOLUTION OF BUSINESS ETHICAL DILEMMAS

The resolution of ethical dilemmas in business is often difficult, even in firms with a code of ethics and a culture committed to compliance with ethical models for decision making. Managers need guidelines for making ethical choices. Several prominent scholars in the field of business ethics have developed models for use in difficult situations.

Blanchard and Peale

The late Dr. Norman Vincent Peale and management expert Kenneth Blanchard offer three questions that managers should ponder in resolving ethical dilemmas: Is it legal? Is it balanced? How does it make me feel?

Browse antitrust cases at the U.S. Department of Justice: http://www.usdoj.gov

If the answer to the first question, "Is it legal?" is no, a manager should not proceed any further. An examination of the Justice Department's antitrust case against some of the country's best and largest universities demonstrates that managers still fail to ask the basic ethical question of whether they are in compliance with the law. In that case, 22 large private northeastern universities had agreed to offer the same financial aid packages to students, so that students' decisions on which institution to attend were based on factors other than the level of financial aid. This loan package arrangement was nothing more than an agreement on price; antitrust laws prohibit such agreements.

Answering the second question, "Is it balanced?" requires a manager to step back and view a problem from other perspectives—those of other parties, owners, shareholders, or the community. For example, an M&M/Mars cacao buyer was able to secure a very low price on cacao for his company because of pending government takeovers and political disruption. M&M/Mars officers decided to pay more for the cacao than the negotiated figure. Their reason was that some day their company would not have the upper hand, and then they would want to be treated fairly when the price became the seller's choice.

Answering "How does it make me feel?" requires a manager to do a self-examination of the comfort level of a decision. Some decisions, though they may be legal and may appear balanced, can still make a manager uncomfortable. For example, many managers feel uncomfortable about the "management" of earnings when inventory and shipments are controlled to maximize bonuses or to produce a particularly good result for a quarter. Although they've done nothing illegal, such practices often produce in managers such physical effects as insomnia and appetite problems.

The Front-Page-of-the-Newspaper Test

One very simple ethical model requires only that a decision maker envision how a reporter would describe a decision on the front page of a local or national newspaper. For example, with regard to the NBC News report on the sidesaddle gas tanks in GM pickup trucks, the *USA Today* headline read: "GM Suit Attacks NBC Report: Says show faked fiery truck crash." Would NBC have made the same decisions about its staging of the truck crash if that headline had been foreseen?

When Salomon Brothers's illegal cornering of the U.S. government's bond market was revealed, the *Business Week* headline read: "How Bad Will It Get?"; nearly two years later a follow-up story on Salomon's crisis strategy was headlined

"The Bomb Shelter That Salomon Built." During the aftermath of the bond market scandal, the interim chairman of Salomon, Warren Buffet, told employees, "Contemplating any business act, an employee should ask himself whether he would be willing to see it immediately described by an informed and critical reporter on the front page of his local paper, there to be read by his spouse, children, and friends. At Salomon we simply want no part of any activities that pass legal tests but that we, as citizens, would find offensive."

Dow Corning might have made different decisions about selling its silicone breast implants if it had envisioned such headlines as "Breast Implants: What Did the Industry Know, and When?" from *Business Week* shortly after a woman won a $4 million verdict for permanent injury resulting from her implants.

Laura Nash and Perspective

Visit the U.S. Consumer Product Safety Commission: gopher://cpsc.gov/ *Visit the American Medical Association:* http://www.ama-assn.org/

Business ethicist Laura Nash has developed a series of questions that business managers should ask themselves as they evaluate their ethical dilemmas. One of the questions is, "How would I view the issue if I stood on the other side of the fence?" For example, several large manufacturers produce a product called an infant baby walker. An infant as young as four months can be placed in the walker and enjoy upright movements long before motor skills have developed sufficiently to permit such movements unaided. The result is that many infants injure themselves; nearly 30,000 injuries were reported in 1992. The American Medical Association asked the federal Consumer Product Safety Commission to ban and recall the walkers because of the clear dangers they present; the commission refused. The AMA has also expressed concern about possible long-term skeletal damage because infants who are not yet ready to stand unaided are standing in the walkers.

The industry continued to sell the walkers up to the time of the ban, but what if you were a parent? Would you not want to have the information about the walker's safety? Would you bring suit against the company if there were an injury to your child while using the walker? Parents certainly see the walkers as something other than the high profit margins they offered.

Other questions in the Nash model include: "Am I able to discuss my decision with my family, friends, and those closest to me?" "What am I trying to accomplish with my decision?" "Will I feel as comfortable about my decision over time as I do today?" The Nash model forces managers to seek additional perspec-tives as decisions are evaluated and implemented. For example, when William Aramony served as the CEO of United Way, he enjoyed such perks as an annual salary of close to $400,000, flights on the Concorde, and limousine service. Even though these benefits were about the same as those of other CEOs managing comparable assets, it still would be difficult to justify such benefits to a contributor who earns $12,000 a year and has pledged 5 percent of it to United Way.

Business Planning Tip

Two simple practices help businesses and employees deal with ethical dilemmas. First, develop a code of ethics. Second, be certain all employees are given a copy. One company has placed its code of ethics on a laminated card. Employees are given $20 if they can show their card when an officer asks if they have it with them.

The Wall Street Journal Model

The Wall Street Journal model for resolution of ethical dilemmas consists of compliance, contribution, and consequences. Like the Blanchard-Peale model, any proposed conduct must first be in compliance with the law. The next step requires an evaluation of a decision's contributions to the shareholders, the employees, the community, and the customers. For example, furniture manufacturer Herman Miller decided to both invest in equipment that would exceed the requirements for compliance with the 1990 Clean Air Act and refrain from using rain forest woods in producing its signature Eames chair. The decision was costly to the shareholders at first, but ultimately they, the community, and customers enjoyed the benefits.

Finally, managers are asked to envision the consequences of a decision, such as whether headlines that are unfavorable to the firm may result. The initial consequences for Miller's decisions were a reduction in profits because of the costs of the changes. However, the long-term consequences were the respect of environmental regulators, a responsive public committed to rain forest preservation, and Miller's recognition by *Business Week* as an outstanding firm for 1992.

Explore the 1990 Clean Air Act: http://www.law.cornell.edu/uscode/42/ch85.html

Other Models

Of course, there are much simpler models for making ethical business decisions. One stems from Immanuel Kant's categorical imperative: "Do unto others as you would have them do unto you." Treating others or others' money as we would want to be treated is a powerful evaluation technique in ethical dilemmas.

CREATION OF AN ETHICAL ATMOSPHERE IN BUSINESS

The Tone at the Top

Ethics begins at the top of a company. A business must have from its board and its CEO a commitment to earning a profit *within ethical boundaries*. Employees work under the pressures of meeting quarterly and annual goals and can make poor choices if the company's priority with respect to values and ethics is not made clear. Evidence of that ethical commitment comes from a firm's adoption of a **code of ethics**. "Corning's Statement of Values" (pg. 59) provides an example from Corning Incorporated.

Top management must continue to emphasize that, above all, employees must perform within the ethical boundaries established by the company's code of ethics. When the state of California revealed that its undercover investigation of Sears Auto Centers found repeated patterns of unnecessary repairs, then-CEO Ed Brennan stated that employees had made mistakes by making poor choices. The pay incentive systems in the auto centers were tied to the receipts from repairs and sales of parts, and such an incentive system conflicted with the values established by Sears. Somehow the employees failed to grasp that the ethical standards were to take priority. Top management's continued emphasis on ethics can take the form of ongoing training and seminars in ethics for all employees.

Reporting Lines

Most companies have either an ombudsperson or a hot line, or both, to which employees can anonymously report ethical violations. Many firms have developed ethical news bulletins to offer employees examples of and guidelines on ethical dilemmas. Du Pont delivers an ethics bulletin to employees through its electronic mail system.

Developing an Ethics Stance

Both individuals and firms should decide up front what types of conduct they would never engage in and be certain that the rules are in writing, that everyone understands the rules, and that the rules will be enforced uniformly. Individuals can vary in their responses to various ethical dilemmas. For example, a woman who had taken $12,000 from her employer was terminated immediately upon the company's discovery of the embezzlement. At the company's next board meeting, the board members discussed the issue and had varying views. One director felt that taking something that does not belong to you is wrong and that termination was the appropriate action. Another director said that his remedy would be determined by whether the money was taken all at once or over a period of time. Another director said that his remedy would be determined according to why the employee took the money. Still another director noted that perhaps the employee did not understand that this type of action is wrong. The directors varied in their views on ethics. One is pragmatic—it is simply wrong. Another applies a relative approach—why did she take the money? The ethical stances of the directors are diagrammed in Exhibit 2.4.

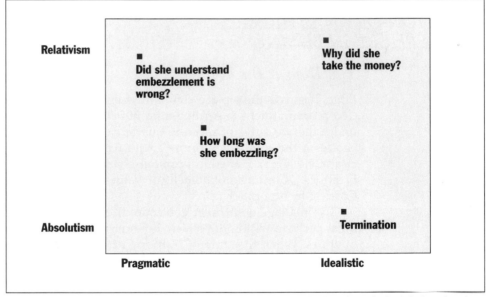

Source: Developed from Professor Patricia Pattison's presentation, "Teaching Ethics," Academy of Legal Studies in Business Annual Meeting, August 11–15, 1994, Dallas, Texas.

Exhibit 2.4
Your Ethics Stance: The Embezzling Employee

Knowing where you stand as a company sends clear signals to employees. Knowing where you stand as an individual sends clear signals for the behavior of those around you.

Ethical Culture

The methods of cultivating an ethical environment have become more crucial over the past year as new federal corporate sentencing guidelines have gone into effect.

Under the guidelines, officers of companies are able to mitigate the sentences for violations by employees under their supervision by documenting their own efforts to clarify for employees the importance of good legal and ethical choices.

Top management also needs to watch closely for practices and signals that are indications of a poor ethical environment. Here are a few signs and signals of an atmosphere that is ripe for unethical behavior:

1. Competition is so intense that business survival is threatened.

    Example: An employee steals drawings of a competitor's product.

2. Managers make poor judgments.

    Example: Chrysler executives had the odometers from their company cars disconnected so that the cars could later be sold as new.

3. Employees have few or no personal values.

    Example: Personal ethics are left at the company door because, as ethicist Albert Carr says, "Business is business," just as poker is poker.

4. Employees respond only to earnings demands. No constraints are placed on how the earnings are achieved.

    Example: E.F. Hutton's 1986 check-kiting scheme was perpetuated by branch managers as a way to maximize interest on accounts without regard to the risk involved, particularly for small banks.

FOR THE MANAGER'S DESK

CORNING'S STATEMENT OF VALUES: "VALORES, VALUES, VALEURS, VALORES, WERTE"

Who We Are

Our Purpose Our purpose is to deliver superior, long-range economic benefits to our customers, our employees, our shareholders, and to the communities in which we operate. We accomplish this by living our corporate values.

Our Strategy Corning is an evolving network of wholly owned businesses and joint ventures. Our strategy is to grow profitably by building upon our strengths and experiences. These include the markets we know, the specialty glass and ceramics technology in which we are preeminent, and our unique ability to make joint ventures work successfully.

We choose to compete in four global business sectors: *Specialty Materials, Consumer Housewares, Laboratory Sciences,* and *Telecommunications.* In these sectors, our combined market, technical, and management skills allow us to be worldwide leaders.

Within each sector we use varying organization and ownership structures, including partnerships with other companies, to best meet the requirements of our customers and to compete more effectively.

Our corporate network adds value beyond that created by its single parts. It is bound together by a dedication to total quality, a commitment to technology, shared financial resources, common values, and management links.

What We Value We have a set of enduring beliefs that are ingrained in the way we think and act. These values guide our

choices, defining for us the right course of action, the clearest directions, the preferred responses. Consistent with these values we set our objectives, formulate our strategies, and judge our results. Only by living these values will we achieve our purpose.

Quality We insist that Total Quality be the guiding principle of our business life. This means new ways of working together. It means knowing and meeting the requirements of our customers and our coworkers. It means doing it right the first time, on time, every time.

Integrity We demand honesty, decency, fairness. Respect must characterize all internal and external relationships.

Performance We hold ourselves and each other, as individuals and as an organization, accountable for our results.

Continued

Leadership We are a leader, not a follower. This extends to the markets we serve, our multiple technologies, our manufacturing processes, our management practices, and our financial performance. The goods and services we produce must never be ordinary and must always be truly useful.

Independence We cherish our corporate freedom. This condition has fostered the innovation and initiative that make our company great.

Technology We lead primarily by technical innovation. This belief in the power of technology is common to all our parts. It is the glue that binds us together. We are committed to translating our specific expertise into goods and services, to expanding the range of our scientific competence, and to linking these abilities with new market needs.

The Individual We know in the end that the commitment and contribution of all employees will determine our success. Open relationships with each other and with our customers are essential. Therefore, each employee must have the opportunity to participate fully, to grow professionally, and to develop to his or her highest potential.

Where We Want to Go

Our Financial Goals
Performance We will be consistently in the top 25 percent of the Fortune 500 in financial performance as measured by return on equity.

Growth We will grow at an annual rate in excess of 5 percent in real terms.

We will maintain a debt-to-capital ratio of approximately 25 percent and a long-term dividend payout of 33 percent.

We will issue new shares of stock on a limited basis in connection with employee ownership programs and acquisitions with a clear strategic fit.

Source: Reprinted with permission of Corning Inc.

ETHICAL ISSUES IN INTERNATIONAL BUSINESS

The global market presents firms with more complex ethical issues than they would experience when operations are limited to one country and one culture. Moral standards vary across cultures. In some cases, cultures change and evolve to accept conduct that was not previously acceptable. For example, it is permissible in India for donors to sell body organs for transplantation. Residents of India have sold their kidneys to buy televisions or just to increase their standard of living. In the United States, the buying and selling of organs by donors is not permitted, but recently experts have called for such a system as a means of resolving the supply and demand dilemma that exists because of limited availability of donors and a relative excess of needy recipients.

In many executive training seminars for international business, executives are taught to honor customs in other countries and "Do as the Romans do." Employees are often confused by this direction.

A manager for a U.S. title insurer provides a common example. He complained that if he tipped employees in the U.S. public-recording agencies for expediting property filings, the manager would not only be violating the company's code of ethics but could be charged with violations of the Real Estate Settlement Procedures Act and state and federal antibribery provisions. Yet that same type of practice is permitted, recognized, and encouraged in other countries as a cost of doing business. Paying a regulatory agency in the United States to expedite a licensing process would be bribery of a public official. Yet many businesses maintain that

Business Planning Tip

A new trend among international firms is to adopt international codes of ethics. For example, employees who are given gifts as part of cultural rituals must give them to the company. They are then donated to charity.

they cannot obtain such authorizations to do business in other countries unless such payments are made. So-called grease or facilitation payments are permitted under the Foreign Corrupt Practices Act (see Chapter 8), but it does not necessarily make such payments ethical.

An inevitable question arises when custom and culture clash with ethical standards and moral values adopted by a firm. Should the national culture or the company code of ethics control?

Typical business responses to the question of whether cultural norms or company codes of ethics should control in international business operations are: Who am I to question the culture of another country? Who am I to impose U.S. standards on all the other nations of the world? Isn't legality the equivalent of ethical behavior? The attitude of businesses is one that permits ethical deviations in the name of cultural sensitivity. Many businesses fear that the risk of offending is far too high to impose U.S. ethical standards into the conduct of business in other countries.

The successful operation of commerce is dependent upon the ethical roots of business. A look at the three major parties in business explains this point. These parties are the risk-takers, the employees, and the customers. Risk-takers—those furnishing the capital necessary for production—are willing to take risks on the assumption that their products will be judged by customers' assessment of their value. Employees are willing to offer production input, skills, and ideas in exchange for wages, rewards, and other incentives. Consumers/customers are willing to purchase products and services so long as they receive value in exchange for their furnishing, through payment, costs and profits to the risk-takers and employers. To the extent that the interdependency of the parties in the system is affected by factors outside of their perceived roles and control, the intended business system does not function on its underlying assumptions.

The business system is, in short, an economic system endorsed by society that allows risk-takers, employees, and customers to allocate scarce resources to competing ends.

Although the roots of business have been described as primarily economic, this economic system cannot survive without recognition of some fundamental values. Some of the inherent, indeed universal, values built into our capitalistic economic system, as described here, are as follows: (1) the consumer is given value in exchange for the funds expended; (2) employees are rewarded according to their contribution to production; and (3) the risk-takers are rewarded for their investment in the form of a return on that investment.

To a large extent, all business is based on trust. The tenets for doing business are dissolved as an economy moves toward a system in which one individual can control the market in order to maximize personal income.

Suppose, for example, that the sale of a firm's product is no longer determined by perceived consumer value but rather by access to consumers, which is controlled by government officials. That is, your company's product cannot be sold to consumers in a particular country unless and until you are licensed within that country. Suppose further that the licensing procedures are controlled by government officials, and those officials demand personal payment in exchange for your company's right to even apply for a business license. Payment size may be arbitrarily determined by officials who withhold portions for themselves. The basic values of the system have been changed. Consumers no longer directly determine the demand.

Beyond just the impact on the basic economic system, ethical breaches involving grease payments introduce an element beyond a now-recognized component in economic performance: consumer confidence in long-term economic performance.

Economist Douglas Brown has described the differences between the United States and other countries in explaining why capitalism works here and not in all nations. His theory is that capitalism is dependent upon an interdependent system of production. Consumers, risk-takers, and employees must all feel confident about the future, about the concept of a level playing field, and about the absence of corruption for economic growth to proceed. To the extent that consumers, risk-takers, and employees feel comfortable about a market driven by the basic assumptions, the investment and commitments necessary for economic growth via capitalism will be made. Significant monetary costs are incurred by business systems based on factors other than customer value discussed earlier.

In developing countries where there are "speed" or grease payments and resulting corruption by government officials, the actual money involved may not be significant in terms of the nation's culture. Such activities and payments introduce an element of demoralization and cynicism that thwarts entrepreneurial activity when these nations most need risk-takers to step forward.

China and Russia are recognized as economic growth successes over the last five years. Bribes and *guanxi* (or gifts) in China given to establish connections in the Chinese government are estimated at 3 to 5 percent of operating costs for companies, totaling $3 billion to $5 billion of 1993's foreign investment.

But China incurs costs from the choices government officials make in return for payments. For example, *guanxi* are often used to persuade government officials to transfer government assets to foreign investors for substantially less than their value. Chinese government assets have fallen over $50 billion in value over the same period of economic growth, primarily because of the large undervaluation by government officials in these transactions with foreign companies.

Perhaps Italy and Brazil provide the best examples of the long-term impact of foreign business corruption. While the United States, Japan, and Great Britain have scandals such as the savings and loan failures, political corruption, and insurance regulation, these forms of misconduct are not indicative of corruption that pervades entire economic systems. The same cannot be said about Italy. Elaborate connections between government officials, the Mafia, and business executives have been unearthed. As a result, half of Italy's cabinet has resigned and hundreds of business executives have been indicted. It has been estimated that the interconnections of these three groups have cost the Italian government $200 billion in addition to the inability to complete government projects.

In Brazil the level of corruption has led to a climate of murder and espionage. Many foreign firms have elected not to do business in Brazil because of so much uncertainty and risk—beyond the normal financial risks of international investment. Why send an executive to a country where officials may use force when soliciting huge bribes?

The Wall Street Journal offered an example of how Brazil's corruption has damaged the country's economy despite growth and opportunity in surrounding nations. The governor of the northeastern state of Paraiba in Brazil, Ronaldo Cunha Lima, was angry because his predecessor, Tarcisio Burity, had accused Lima's son of corruption. Lima shot Burity twice in the chest while Burity was having lunch at a restaurant. The speaker of Brazil's Senate praised Lima for his courage in doing the shooting himself as opposed to sending someone else. Lima was given a medal by the local city council and granted immunity from prosecution by Paraiba's state legislature. No one spoke for the victim, and the lack of support was reflective of a culture controlled by self-interest that benefits those in control. Unfortunately, these self-interests preclude economic development.

Paralleling such moral deterioration has been Brazil's lack of economic advancement despite growth in surrounding South American nations. Economists in Brazil document hyperinflation and systemic corruption. A Sao Paulo businessman observed, "The fundamental reason we can't get our act together is we're an amoral society." This business person probably understands capitalism. Privatization that has helped the economies of Chile, Argentina, and Mexico cannot take hold in Brazil because government officials enjoy the benefits of generous wages and returns from the businesses they control. The result is that workers are unable to earn enough even to clothe their families, 20 percent of the Brazilian population lives below the poverty line, and crime has reached levels of nightly firefights. Brazil's predicament has occurred over time as graft, collusion, and fraud have become entrenched in the government-controlled economy.[3]

E T H I C A L   I S S U E S

2.4 Burns & McCallister, an international management consulting firm, is listed by *Working Mother* magazine as one of the top 50 firms in the United States for employment of working mothers and is listed as one of the top 10 firms for women by *Working Woman* magazine. Burns & McCallister has earned this reputation for several reasons. First, nearly 50 percent of its partners are women. Second, the firm has a menu of employee benefits that include such things as flexible hours, sabbaticals, family leave, home-based work, and part-time partner-track positions.

However, Burns & McCallister has recently been the subject of a series of reports by both the *Los Angeles Times* and the *New York Times* because its policy on female executives in certain nations has become public. Burns & McCallister has learned, through its 50 years of consulting, that in certain countries in which they negotiate for contracts, women cannot be used in the negotiation process. The culture of many of these countries is such that women are not permitted to speak in a meeting of men. Burns & McCallister has thus implemented a policy prohibiting female partners from being assigned these potential account negotiations and later from the accounts themselves. Clerical help in the offices can be female, but any contact with the client must be through a male partner or account executive only.

For example, Japan still has a two-track hiring system, with only 3 percent of professional positions open to women. The remainder of the women in the workforce become office workers who file, wear uniforms, and serve tea. Dentsu, Inc., a large Japanese advertising firm, recently had a picture of the typical Dentsu "Working Girl" in its recruiting brochure. Surrounding the photo where comments primarily about her physical appearance: "Her breasts are 'pretty large'; her bottom is 'rather soft.'"

Burns & McCallister is being criticized for its posture. The head of Burns & McCallister's New York office has explained:

Look, we're about as progressive a firm as you'll find. But the reality of international business is that if we try to use women, we don't get the job. It's not a policy on all foreign accounts. We've just identified certain cultures in which women will not be able to successfully land or work on accounts. This restriction does not interfere with their career track. It does not apply in all countries.

The National Organization for Women (NOW) would like Burns & McCallister to take the position that its standards in the United States apply to all its operations. Because no restrictions are placed on women here, it contends that the other cultures should adapt to our standards; we should not change our standards to adapt to their culture. NOW maintains that without such a posture, change can never come

Continued

about. Do you agree with Burns & McCallister's policy for certain cultures with regard to female partners? Is Burns & McCallister doing anything that violates federal employment discrimination laws? Given Burns & McCallister's record with regard to women, is the issue really relevant to women's advancement in the firm? If the cultures in which the prohibition of women traditionally applies bring in the accounts with the highest dollar values, would your opinion regarding the posture be different? Do you agree with the NOW position that change can never come about if Burns & McCallister does not take a stand? Would Burns & McCallister be sacrificing revenues in changing its policies? Is this an appropriate sacrifice?

SUMMARY

What is business ethics?
- Moral standards—standards of behavior set by culture
- Moral obligations—standards of behavior set by natural law
- Moral relativism—moral standards by situation

Why is business ethics important?
- Profit
- Leadership
- Reputation
- Strategy

What ethical standard should a business adopt?
- Positive law—codified law
- Inherence—serves shareholders' interests
- Enlightened self-interest—serves shareholders' interest by serving larger society
- Invisible hand—serves larger society by serving shareholders' interests
- Social responsibility—serves larger society by serving larger society

How do employees recognize ethical dilemmas?
- Language
- Categories

How do employees resolve ethical dilemmas?
- Blanchard and Peale
- Front-page-of-the-newspaper test
- *Wall Street Journal* and stakeholders
- Laura Nash and perspective
- Categorical imperative

How does a business create an ethical atmosphere?
- Tone at the top
- Code of ethics
- Reporting lines
- Ethical posture

QUESTIONS AND PROBLEMS

1. E&J Gallo, the world's largest winery, has just announced that it will stop selling its Thunderbird and Night Train Express wines in the Tenderloin, the skid row of San Francisco, for six months. Gallo took the action after meeting with an activist group called Safe and Sober Streets, which has asked grocers to remove the high-alcohol wine from the district, where citizens say drunks create a menace. One retailer in the district said, "If I don't sell this, I will have to close my doors and go home."

   Discuss the actions of Gallo and the dilemma of the retailers in the district. Be sure to discuss the type of philosophy each of them holds with respect to social responsibility and ethical dilemmas.

2. Paul Backman is the head of the purchasing department for L. A. East, one of the "Baby Bells" that came into existence after the divestiture of AT&T. Backman and his department purchase everything for the company from napkins to wires for equipment lines.

   S.C. Rydman is an electronics firm and a supplier for L. A. East. L. A. East has used Rydman as a major supplier since 1984. Rydman is also the cosponsor of an exhibit at Wonder World, a theme park in Florida.

   Rydman's vice president and chief financial officer, Gunther Fromme, visited Backman in his office on April 3, 1993. Rydman had no bids pending at that time, and Fromme told Backman that he was there "for goodwill." Fromme explained that Rydman had a block of rooms at Wonder World because of its exhibit there and that Backman and his group could use the rooms at any time, free of charge.

   Should Backman and his employees use the block of rooms? Why or why not?

3. During the height of the Cold War, the United States, Japan, and members of what was then called the European Common Market had imposed restrictions on the sales of high-tech equipment and armored vehicles to the Soviet Union. During that time, Toshiba Machine Company, a subsidiary of Toshiba Corporation of Japan, sold eight robotized milling machines to the Soviet Union. The machines were used in the production of propellers for Soviet submarines. In spite of the propellers' military use, sales of the milling machines to the Soviets were continued because such sales were not specifically prohibited under the guidelines.

   Was Toshiba's choice to continue the sales ethical? Does it matter that the sales were legal under the multinational agreement? What if the end of the Cold War had come through combat? Would Toshiba have been responsible for aiding the Soviet Union?

4.* Old Joe Camel, originally a member of a circus that passed through Winston-Salem, North Carolina, each year, was adopted by R. J. Reynolds (RJR) marketers in 1913 as the symbol for a brand being changed from "Red Kamel" to "Camel." In the late 1980s, RJR revived Old Joe with a new look in the form of a cartoon. He became the camel with a "Top Gun" flier jacket, sunglasses, a smirk, and a lot of appeal to young people.

   In December 1991, the *Journal of the American Medical Association* (*JAMA*) published three surveys that found the cartoon character, Joe Camel, was very effective in reaching children. Children between the ages of 3 and 6 were surveyed and 51.1 percent of them recognized old Joe Camel as being associated with Camel cigarettes. The children in the study who were six years old were as familiar with Joe Camel as they were with the Mickey Mouse logo for the Disney Channel. The surveys also established that 97.7 percent of students between the ages of 12 and 19 have seen Old Joe and 58 percent of them think the ads are cool. Camel is identified by 33 percent of the students who smoke as their favorite brand.

   Before the studies appeared in the *JAMA*, the American Cancer Society, the American Heart Association, and the American Lung Association had petitioned the Federal Trade Commission (FTC) to ban the ads as "one of the most egregious examples in recent history of tobacco advertising that targets children."

   Michael Pertschuk, former head of the FTC and codirector of the Advocacy Institute, an antismoking group, has said, "These are the first studies to give us hard evidence, proving what everybody already knows is true: These ads target kids. I think this will add impetus to the movement to further limit tobacco advertising." Joe Tye, founder of Stop Teenage Addictions to Tobacco, has stated, "There is a growing body of evidence that teen smoking is increasing. And it's 100 percent related to Camel."

One researcher who worked on the study, Dr. Joseph R. DiFranza, stated, "We're hoping this information leads to a complete ban of cigarette advertising." Dr. John Richards summarized the study as follows, "The fact is that the ad is reaching kids, and it is changing their behavior."

An RJR spokeswoman responds that the average Camel smoker is 35 and "just because children can identify our logo doesn't mean they will use our product." However, since the introduction of Joe Camel, Camel's share of the under-18 market has climbed to 33 percent from 5 percent. In the 18 to 24 age bracket, market share has climbed to 7.9 percent from 4.4 percent.

In 1993, the FTC staff recommended a ban on the Joe Camel ads. In 1994, then-Surgeon General Joycelyn Elders blamed the $4 billion in smoking ads for increased smoking rates among teens. RJR's tobacco division chief, James W. Johnston responded, "I'll be damned if I'll pull the ads." But RJR has put together a team of lawyers and others it refers to as in-house censors to curb Joe's influence. A bandana campaign was nixed as was one for a punker Joe with pink hair.

In the fall of 1995, President Clinton announced his program to combat underage smoking, including proposals to ban certain forms of advertising.

In October 1995, RJR announced that Joe Camel will no longer appear on billboards. An RJR spokesman said, "The decision is based only on the market. When people see the same ad over and over and over again they begin to screen it out. We want to keep Joe fresh."

a. Diagram the events in the social/regulatory cycle for these ads.

b. Suppose you were the executive in charge of the R. J. Reynolds account at your advertising agency. The account represents nearly 20 percent of your firm's business. Would you recommend an alternative to the Joe Camel character? What if RJR threatened to withdraw its account if you did not continue with Joe Camel? Suppose you work with a pension fund that holds a large investment in RJR Would you consider selling your RJR holdings?

c. Do you agree with the statement that identification of the logo does not equate with smoking or smoking Camels? Do regulators agree? Is there market growth from Joe's ads?

d. What effect will the self-censorship have on the regulatory trend?

*Adapted with permission of West Publishing Company, from Marianne M. Jennings, *Case Studies in Business Ethics*, 2d ed. © 1996 West Publishing Company.

5. Nike ran a television ad for its hiking shoes using Samburu tribesmen on location in Kenya. In the ad, one tribesman speaks in his native Maa while the slogan "Just do it!" appears on the screen. When the ad was run on American television, an anthropologist from the University of Cincinnati said the man is really saying, "I don't want these. Give me big shoes." When asked about the ad, a Nike spokesperson said, "We thought nobody in America would know what he said."

Discuss the ethical commitment of Nike with regard to its ad content.

6. *TV Guide* magazine ran a cover photo showing Oprah Winfrey's head on the body of Ann-Margret for a story on Oprah. Neither women knew of the composite photo or gave permission.

How could this situation have been covered in a code of ethics? Was this a management decision?

7. Frank Kranack's station wagon was struck by a Domino's Pizza delivery car. The accident was just outside a Domino's store and when it happened, the Domino's manager appeared and said to the delivery person, "Let's get this pizza on the road." Kranack had neck and back injuries and his wife's right arm was permanently disabled because she absorbed most of the crash impact. Kranack filed suit, claiming the company's policy on quick delivery encourages dangerous driving. Last year, Domino's sold 230,000,000 pizzas nationwide and 90 percent of those sold were delivered. Kranack's

attorney says the 30-minute guarantee must be stopped to avoid dangerous driving and accidents.

Discuss the ethics of the 30-minute rule.

8. During a recession in the computer industry, Hewlett-Packard upped its philanthropic giving from $40 million to $60 million, most of it in the form of equipment to schools and universities. Is such an action prudent? What stakeholders are they satisfying?

9. During the past decade, the growth of demand for artificial fingernails has been nearly exponential. As a result, nearly all hair salons provide the service; in addition, there are nearly 150,000 nail salons across the country. The chemical products used for the various types of nails have evolved since 1935, when artificial nails were first used in Hollywood by movie cosmetologists. At that time, products with formaldehyde were used extensively. Other toxic substances have been part of the nail products over the years. Several studies (clinical and epidemiological) have offered the following conclusions:

- the affixture of artificial nails significantly deteriorates the natural nail;
- the affixture of artificial nails can result in the growth of fungus beneath the nail;
- inhalation of fumes from the product can cause light-headedness;
- several of the popular chemicals now used are known to cause birth defects;
- removal of the nails by technicians has resulted in a significant number of eye and face injuries as portions of the nail spring off.

Currently, a major university medical school is conducting a study of the effects of long-term exposure. The study will take two more years because the sample size of technicians who have had daily long-term exposure has just now become sufficiently large.

Sculpture Shelter, Inc., has developed a 3' x 2' x 2' plastic incubator device for use in the application and repair of artificial nails. The customer and the technician place their hands inside the unit. The plastic enclosure, which has an air circulator, then contains all fumes and particles. Each unit costs $2,800. The average cost for an original nail application is $50. Repairs cost $25. Technicians can do an original set in two hours and repairs in one and one-half hours. Sculpture Shelter's orders have been very limited.

Assume that you are the CEO of a firm that manufactures the nail product used in a majority of salons. What actions would you take?

10. "Shock Jock" Howard Stern's radio talk show, which originates at Infinity Broadcasting Corporation's flagship New York station, is number one in its time slot in New York, Philadelphia, Los Angeles, Boston, and several other cities. A total of 20 million listeners tune in each week. Stern is known for his banter that borders on, and occasionally is, indecent. His on-the-air routines involve such subjects as "Butt Bongo" and "Lesbian Dial-a-Date." Infinity has been fined $1.67 million by the Federal Communications Commission (FCC) for Stern's material, which allegedly violated federal on-the-air decency standards. Since the fines have not deterred the violations, one commissioner has cited ongoing complaints as the basis for conducting an FCC hearing into whether Infinity's licenses for its 11 stations should be revoked.

Stern's book, *Private Parts*, published by Simon & Schuster in October 1993, had such chapter titles as "Yes, I am Fartman"; Stern appears semiclothed on the cover. Twelve days after its release, the book was in its seventh printing, having sold more than one million copies. Does Infinity have an obligation to monitor and control Stern? Are shareholders of Infinity or Simon & Schuster concerned about standards of decency, given Stern's success? Would you publish Stern's book? Would you hire him as a radio talent?

NOTES

1 From "Interview: Milton Friedman," *Playboy*, February 1973. © 1973 *Playboy*.
2 Adapted from Marianne M. Jennings, *Case Studies in Business Ethics*, 2d ed. © 1996 West Publishing Company.
3 This material was adapted from an unpublished manuscript of Larry Smeltzer and Marianne Jennings.

Judgment

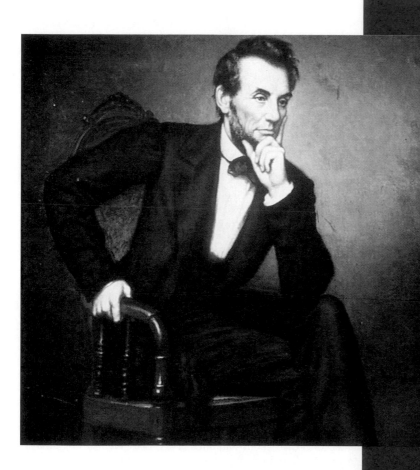

The following rule appears in State University's current catalog:

A course in which a grade of "C" or better has been earned may not be repeated. The second entry will not be counted in earned hours or grade point index for graduation.

Rod took his business math course and earned a "C." Not satisfied with his grade but unaware of the catalog regulation, Rod took the math course again and this time earned a "D." The registrar has entered the "D" grade in Rod's cumulative average. Rod objects based on the catalog rule but the registrar says the rule applies only if a higher grade is earned. What should Rod do? Should the grade count?

The Judicial System

Our introduction to law included discussions of statutory

law and common

law. With all of

the statutes at various levels, it may appear that statutory

law is a complete source of law. However, sometimes

statutes require interpretation, as does the hypothetical

school regulation above. Someone must determine

when, how, and to whom statutes apply. The law in

statutory form is not even half of all the law, the bulk of

which is found in judicial decisions. These contain both

statutory interpretations and common law. This chap-

ter covers the parties involved as well as the courts—

what they decide, when they can decide, and how those

decisions are made.

> *Abraham Lincoln . . . was an extremely clever man . . . and his disarming sense of humor helped him out of many a legal predicament. In one instance, Lincoln found himself in the peculiar position of having to plead two cases the same day before a judge. The same principle of law was involved in both cases, but in one case Lincoln represented the defendant and in the other he represented the plaintiff.*
>
> *In the morning, Lincoln . . . won a dismissal for his client. In the afternoon, he appeared as a prosecutor. . . . The judge. . . called Lincoln up to the bench and asked him to account for his change of attitude.*
>
> *"Your Honor," said Lincoln, "I may have been wrong this morning, but I know I'm right this afternoon."[1]*
>
> **Alex Ayres**
> *The Wit and Wisdom of Abraham Lincoln*

TYPES OF COURTS

In all U.S. court systems, there are two different types or levels of courts: trial courts and appellate courts.

Trial Courts

A **trial court** is the place in the judicial system where the facts of a case are presented. This court is where the jury will sit if the case is a jury trial. It is where the evidence and witnesses will be presented and where the first decision in the case is made, by either judge or jury. Courts at the trial level have the power to hear a case originally. The procedures for trials and trial courts are covered in Chapter 4.

Appellate Courts

There is always at least one other court, an **appellate court**, to review a trial court decision or to check the conduct of the judge, the trial, the lawyers, and the jury. This process of review helps assure a proper application of the law and proper use of procedural laws. Further, this system of review provides the legal system with uniformity. Reviews may result in published opinions, which can then be referred to and used for assistance in deciding future cases.

HOW COURTS MAKE DECISIONS

The Process of Judicial Review

Appellate courts do not hold trials. Rather, they review what has been done by trial courts to determine whether the trial court, often referred to as the lower court, made an error in applying the substantive or procedural law in the case. This is the process of **judicial review**.

The appellate court atmosphere is very different from that of the trial court. There is no jury, no witnesses, and no testimony. No new evidence is considered; only the evidence presented at trial is reviewed. The court reviews a transcript of the trial along with all the evidence presented at trial to determine whether an error has been made.

In addition to the transcript and evidence, each of the parties to a case can present the appellate court with a **brief**, which is a summary of the case and the legal issues being challenged on appeal. The appellate brief is each side's summary of why the trial court decision or procedures were correct or incorrect. The parties make their arguments for their positions in the brief and support them with statutes and decisions from other cases. The brief serves as a summary of the major points of error the parties allege occurred during the trial. This type of brief is called an **appellate brief** and is very detailed. In fact, many refer to lawyers' "briefs" as a misnomer because they are generally quite lengthy. Note that these briefs differ from the **case briefs** presented in Exhibit 1.1.

Many appellate courts permit the attorneys for the opposing parties to make timed **oral arguments** in their cases. Oral argument is a summary of the points that have been made in each party's brief. The judge can also ask questions of the attorneys at that time. At the trial level, there is one judge who makes all decisions. At the appellate level, there is more than one judge who reviews the actions

Listen to oral arguments made before the Supreme Court:
http://oyez.at.nwu.edu/oyez.html

Learn more about the Supreme Court Justices: http:// www.law.cornell. edu/supct/justices/ fullcourt.html

of the lower court in a case. The typical number is three, but in the case of state supreme courts and the U.S. Supreme Court, the full bench of judges on the court hears each case. For example, in U.S. Supreme Court decisions, all nine justices review the cases before the Court unless they have recused (disqualified) themselves because of some conflict.

The panel of appellate judges reviews the case and the briefs, hears the oral argument, and then renders a decision. The decision in the case could be unanimous or could be a split vote, such as 2 to 1. In the case of a split vote, the justice who is not in the majority will frequently draft a **dissenting opinion**, which is the judge's explanation for a vote different from that of the majority.

CHECKING FOR ERROR

A **reversible error** is one that might have affected the outcome of the case or would have influenced the decision made. Examples of reversible errors include the refusal to allow some evidence to be admitted that should have been admitted, the refusal to allow a particular witness to testify, and misapplication of the law.

When a reversible error is made, the appellate court **reverses** the lower court's decision. However, in some cases, the appellate court will also **remand** the case, which means the case is sent back to the trial court for further work. For example, if there is a reversal because some evidence should have been admitted that was not, the case is remanded for a new trial with that evidence admitted (i.e., allowed).

If there has not been an error, the appellate court simply **affirms** the decision of the lower court. An affirmed decision does not mean no mistakes were made; it means that none of the mistakes was a reversible error. The decision of the court will be written by a member of the court who has voted with the majority. The decision will explain the facts and the reasons for the court's reversal, remand, or affirmation.

In some appellate cases, the court will **modify** the decision of a lower court. The full case is neither reversed nor affirmed; instead, a portion or portions of the case are reversed or modified. For example, a trial court verdict finding a defendant negligent might be affirmed, but the appellate court could find that the damages awarded were excessive. In this type of decision, the case would be remanded for a redetermination of damages at the trial court level.

STATUTORY INTERPRETATION

In addition to checking for error, appellate courts render interpretations of statutes. Often, statutes seem perfectly clear until a new factual situation not covered by the statute arises.

C O N S I D E R . . .

3.1 In the chapter's opening "Judgment," the purpose of the university regulation was to prevent students from retaking courses to earn a higher grade point average (GPA). In the factual situation, the student earned a lower grade. The registrar entered the grade with the idea that entering a lower grade would be a deterrent for students retaking courses when they had a "C" or better. However, it is clear that a second grade, whether higher or lower, should not be entered.

Judgment

The Doctrine of Stare Decisis

Judicial review by appellate courts of lower court decisions provides the database for the doctrine of **stare decisis**. The decisions of the appellate courts are written and sometimes published so that they may be analyzed, reviewed, and perhaps applied in the future.

SETTING PRECEDENT

When a court reviews the decisions of lower courts, that court's previous decisions, along with decisions of other courts on the same topic, will be consulted. This process of examining other decisions for help in a new case uses case **precedent**, which is the doctrine of stare decisis, a Latin term meaning "let the decision stand." Such judicial thinking requires an examination of all related cases to determine whether the issue has already been decided and whether the same decision should apply again. Following case precedent does not mean similar cases will be decided identically; there are several factors that influence the weight given to precedent.

THE QUALITY OF THE PRECEDENT

Where the case originated is one of the factors that influences the application of precedent in a case. In federal courts, precedent from other federal courts is strongest when the case involves federal statutes.

In state courts, prior decisions within a particular state's own court system are given greater weight than decisions from courts of other states. There is no obligation of one state's courts to follow the precedent of another state's courts; they are free to examine it and use it, but, as with all precedent, there is no mandatory requirement to follow another state's decisions.

PURPOSES OF PRECEDENT

The purposes of precedent are the same as the purposes of law. Law offers some assurance of consistency and reliability. The judiciary recognizes these obligations in applying precedent. There must be stability and predictability in the way law functions. There is no exact formula for deciding a case, but consistency is a key element in applying precedent.

In addition to consistency, however, judges must incorporate into their legal thought the need for flexibility in the law. New twists in facts arise and new technology develops, and the judiciary must be receptive to the need for change. For example, in Chapter 1, the *Marchica* case illustrated the need for a reexamination of the scope of a law based on a newly evolved disease and its possible transmission in the workplace.

INTERPRETATION OF PRECEDENT

There is more to precedent than just finding similar cases. Every case decision has two parts. One is the actual rule of law, which technically is the precedential part. However, judges never offer just a rule of law in a case. Their rule of law is given at the end of the case decision after there has been a full discussion of their reasons and other precedent. This discussion is called the **dicta** of the case, in which case precedents may be cited to the benefit of each party. In some instances, the rule of law may benefit one party while the dicta benefits the other party.

A dissenting opinion is dicta and is often quoted in subsequent cases to urge a court to change existing precedent. Application of precedent is not a scientific process; there is much room for interpretation and variation.

WHEN PRECEDENT IS NOT FOLLOWED

Precedent may not be followed for several reasons. Some of those reasons have already been given: The precedent is from another state or the precedent is interpreted differently because of the dicta in that precedent. Precedent is also not followed when the facts of cases can be "distinguished," which means that the context of the facts in one case is sufficiently different so that the precedent cannot be applied. For example, suppose that a court decided that using roadblocks to stop motorists to check for drunk drivers is constitutional. A subsequent case regarding roadblocks used to check for drivers' licenses may not be decided the same way. The distinguishing factor in the first case is the nature of the roadblocks: to prevent a hazardous highway condition. The court may not see the same urgency or safety issue in checking for drivers' licenses. The precedent is distinguishable.

The theories of law discussed in Chapter 1 may also control whether precedent is applied. For example, a court may not follow a precedent because of a moral reason or because of the need to change law on the basis of what is moral or what is right. A precedent may also be abandoned on an economic theory, in which the court changes the law to do the most good for the most people. For example, a factory may be a nuisance because of the noise and pollution it creates. There is probably ample case law to support the shutdown of the factory as a nuisance. However, the factory may also be the town's only economic support, and shutting it down will mean unemployment for virtually the whole town. In balancing the economic factors, the nuisance precedent may not be followed or it may be followed in only a modified way.

C O N S I D E R . . .   3.2 In the chapter's opening "Judgment," suppose that the registrar has always counted the lower grades in the cumulative GPA. Does Rod still have an effective argument? Is the registrar using a strained interpretation of the regulation?

E T H I C A L   I S S U E S

3.1 In California, beer brewers and wholesalers are permitted to offer discount coupons to customers, and they have developed "cross-coupons." Brewers use the cross-coupons to copromote their beer with another product. Other products copromoted with beer include charcoal briquets, ice, and tortillas. The coupons are generally large in value, such as $2 off a bag of charcoal with the purchase of any Miller Beer product.

Wholesalers offer rolls of the cross-coupons to retailers in volumes that exceed what the store could actually sell. In some cases retailers who don't even sell the copromoted items are given rolls of coupons. Many retailers don't pass the coupons along to customers but, instead, redeem them for cash and then offer better in-store displays to the brewer and price discounts of up to $1 per 12-pack to customers as a way of paying back the brewer.

Continued

A Coors wholesaler says, "The retailer just takes a roll of coupons provided by the rep, then sells five hundred 12-packs at 50 cents less."

Donald Decious, business practices chief at the California Alcoholic Beverage Control department, says this activity is "essentially commercial bribery."

If a bribe is defined as paying money for a desired result, is the cross-coupon practice commercial bribery? Aren't retailers free to redeem coupons for cash?

Courts struggle with issues of fact and law, and with changes in society, as they apply precedent and consider modifications. The following case shows how a court follows the doctrine of stare decisis, while recognizing its limitations, purposes, and areas for refinement.

Flagiello v. Pennsylvania Hospital
208 A.2d 193 (Pa. 1965)

IMMUNITY FOR THE HOSPITAL: DOES CHARITY PAY?

FACTS

Mary C. Flagiello was injured in the Pennsylvania Hospital in Philadelphia when she fell and fractured her right ankle while she was hospitalized for a different ailment.

Flagiello and her husband (plaintiffs) brought suit against Pennsylvania Hospital (defendant) for trespass. Pennsylvania Hospital answered that it was an eleemosynary institution engaged in a charitable enterprise and was not responsible for Flagiello's injury. The court dismissed the action.

The Flagiellos then brought another suit against the hospital. Their suit maintained that they had a contract with the hospital whereby they were to pay $24.50 a day for hospital facilities and nursing, but the hospital did not fulfill its obligations because it failed to provide reasonably fit and adequate care for Mrs. Flagiello after she sustained "fresh injuries." The court dismissed this action too on the ground that Pennsylvania Hospital was an eleemosynary, or charitable, institution. The Flagiello's appealed.

JUDICIAL OPINION

MUSMANNO, Justice

The hospital has not denied that its negligence caused Mrs. Flagiello's injuries. It merely announces that it is an eleemosynary institution, and, therefore, owed no duty of care to its patient. It declares in effect that it can do wrong and still not be liable in damages to the person it has wronged. It thus urges a momentous exception to the generic proposition that in law there is no wrong without a remedy.

The defendant hospital here does not dispute, as it indeed cannot, this fundamental rule of law, but it says that if the plaintiffs are allowed to invoke a remedy for the wrong done them, the enactment of that remedy will impose a financial burden on the hospital. Is that an adequate defense in law?

The hospital in this case, together with the Hospital Association of Pennsylvania, which has filed a brief as amicus curiae, replies to that question with various answers, some of which are: it is an ancient rule that charitable

Continued

hospitals have never been required to recompense patients who have been injured through the negligence of their employees; the rule of stare decisis forbids that charitable hospitals be held liable in trespass cases; if the rule of charitable immunity is to be discarded, this must be done by the State Legislature; and that since hospitals serve the public, there is involved here a matter of public policy which is not within the jurisdiction of the courts.

Whatever Mrs. Flagiello received in the Pennsylvania Hospital was not bestowed on her gratuitously. She paid $24.50 a day for the services she was to receive. And she paid this amount not only for the period she was to remain in the hospital to be cured of the ailment with which she entered the hospital, but she had to continue to pay that rate for the period she was compelled to remain in the hospital as a result of injuries caused by the hospital itself.

In the early days of public accommodation for the ill and the maimed, charity was exercised in its pure and pristine sense. Many good men and women, liberal in purse and generous in soul, set up houses to heal the poor and homeless victims of disease and injury. They made no charge for this care. The benefactors felt themselves richly rewarded in the knowledge that they were befriending humanity. In that period of sociological history, the hospitals were havens mostly for the indigent. The wealthy and the so-called middle class were treated in their homes where usually there could be found better facilities than could be had in the hospitals. The hospital or infirmary was more often than not part of the village parish. Charity in the biblical sense prevailed.

Whatever the law may have been regarding charitable institutions in the past, it does not meet the conditions of today. Charitable enterprises are no longer housed in ramshackly wooden structures. They are not mere storm shelters to succor the traveler and temporarily refuse those stricken in a common disaster. Hospitals today are growing into mighty edifices in brick, stone, glass and marble. Many of them maintain large staffs, they use the best equipment that science can devise, they utilize the most modern methods in devoting themselves to the noblest purpose of man, that of helping one's stricken brother. But they do all this on a business basis, submitting invoices for services rendered—and properly so.

We have seen how originally charitable hospitals devoted all their energies, resources and time to caring for indigent patients. Later, they began to care for paying patients as well. In the case of *Gable* v. *Sisters of St. Francis*, 227 Pa. 254, this Court pointed out that in 1910, two-thirds of the space of the hospital there in controversy was used for charity patients, and that about 60% of the hospital's income came from charitable donations, while only about 40% of the hospital's income was derived from paying patients. Today this has changed almost completely. In 1963, the fees received from patients in the still designated charitable hospitals throughout Pennsylvania constituted 90.92% of the total income of the hospitals.

But, conceding that it could not operate without its paying patients (of which the wife-plaintiff is one), the defendant hospital still objects to being categorized with business establishments because, it says, the law of charitable immunity is so deeply imbedded in our law and is of such ancient origin that it can only be extirpated by legislative enactment.

If havoc and financial chaos were inevitably to follow the abrogation of the immunity doctrine, as the advocates for its retention insist, this would certainly have become apparent in the states where that doctrine is no longer a defense. But neither the defendant hospital nor the Hospital Association of Pennsylvania has submitted any evidence of catastrophe in the States where charitable hospitals are tortiously liable.

Stare decisis channels the law. It erects lighthouses and flies the signals of safety. The ships of jurisprudence must follow that well-defined channel which, over the years, has been proved to be secure and trustworthy. But it would not comport with wisdom to insist that, should

Continued

shoals rise in a heretofore safe course and rocks emerge to encumber the passage, the ship should nonetheless pursue the original course, merely because it presented no hazard in the past. The principle of stare decisis does not demand that we follow precedents which shipwreck justice.

Stare decisis is not an iron mold into which every utterance by a Court, regardless of circumstances, parties, economic barometer and sociological climate, must be poured, and, where, like wet concrete, it must acquire an unyielding rigidity which no other later can change.

The history of law through the ages records numerous inequities pronounced by courts because the society of the day sanctioned them. Reason revolts, humanity shudders, and justice recoils before much of what was done in the past under the name of law. Yet, we are urged to retain a forbidding incongruity in the law simply because it is old. That kind of reasoning would have retained prosecuting for witchcraft, imprisonment for debt and hanging for minor offenses which today are hardly regarded misdemeanors.

The charitable immunity rule proves itself an instrument of injustice and nothing presented by the defendant or by amicus curiae shows it to be otherwise. In fact, the longer the argument for its preservation the more convincing is the proof that it long ago outlived its purpose if, indeed, it ever had a purpose consonant with sound law. "Ordinarily, when a court decides to modify or abandon a court-made rule of long standing, it starts out by saying that 'the reason for the rule no longer exists.' In this case, it is correct to say that the 'reason' originally given for the rule of immunity never did exist."

A rule that has become insolvent has no place in the active market of current enterprise. When a rule offends against reason, when it is at odds with every precept of natural justice, and when it cannot be defended on its own merits, but has to depend alone on a discredited genealogy, courts not only possess the inherent power to repudiate, but, indeed, it is required, by the very nature of judicial function, to abolish such a rule.

Perhaps the most eloquent, potent and meaningful demonstration in modern times of a Court's power to saw away from the tree of the law a branch which not only was infirm and tainted, but which could in time contaminate the soil of liberty in which the tree itself grew, was the case of *Brown* v. *Board of Education*, 347 U.S. 483, which, in 1953, repudiated the "separate but equal doctrine" laid down in *Plessy* v. *Ferguson*, 163 U.S. 537, and declared that there must be no segregation in the public schools of America on the basis of race. As amazing as it must now sound that the law of a country founded on the proposition that all persons are born equal should have countenanced and enforced segregation, yet such was the law of the land until the historic Brown decision of May 17, 1954.

Of course, the precedents here recalled do not justify a light and casual treatment of the doctrine of stare decisis but they proclaim unequivocally that where justice demands, reason dictates, equality enjoins and fair play decrees a change in judge-made law, courts will not lack in determination to establish that change. We, therefore overrule, and hold that the hospital's liability must be governed by the same principles of law as apply to other employers.

The judgments of the Court below are reversed.

CASE QUESTIONS

1. Where was Flagiello injured and how?
2. From whom does she seek recovery?
3. What defense does the hospital allege? What is the name of the doctrine it is using?
4. What reasons are given by the hospital for following the doctrine?
5. What reasons does the court give for abandoning the doctrine?
6. Under what circumstances should a court forsake precedent?
7. What will be the law in Pennsylvania with respect to negligence by hospitals?

FOR THE MANAGER'S DESK

RESULTS, NOT HOURS

A New Business Attitude About Lawyers

In June a worried general counsel facing a patent infringement suit walked into Chicago law firm Bartlit Beck Herman Palenchar & Scott. Six weeks from trial, he knew he needed a good trial lawyer. Name partner Fred Bartlit Jr. (1994 income $2.5 million) had just beaten a similar suit, saving $100 million for Miles Inc.

"What'll it cost me?" the general counsel asked.

"A million dollars if we lose," Bartlit's partner Sidney (Skip) Herman told the man. "And $2 million if we win."

The general counsel swallowed hard, and signed. In August Bartlit negotiated a confidential settlement that Bartlit and the client considered "close to a win." Bartlit and the client split the win/lose difference. Bartlit Beck got $1.5 million.

This marked a considerable departure from traditional corporate practice. Trial lawyers have long worked on contingency fees, but corporate defense lawyers have traditionally billed by the hour. Win or lose they get paid.

The switch to more contingency defense work is long overdue. The prestigious law firms run the meter at about $400 per lawyer-hour for partners and about $125 an hour for junior associates. This by-the-hour billing offers no incentive to the lawyers to get things done. The slower the firm works, and the more associates it puts on the case, the more money it makes. It's rather like the old cost-plus defense contracts. And the customer often gets only the services of the firm's most junior associates.

With today's massive restructurings and cost-cutting drives, in-house counsels are looking for any way to get more out of their litigation dollar. For the past several years companies like Houston-based Tenneco Inc. have been insisting their outside firms stick to a budget. Anything over a set amount simply doesn't get paid without renegotiation.

DuPont corporate counsel Daniel Mahoney recently slashed to 35, from 315, the number of outside firms the company uses. Firms on DuPont's list are now asked to discount their hourlies, or to bill a fixed amount—in exchange for bonuses for better verdicts.

The chief casualties of DuPont's legal cost-cutting have been large, prestigious law firms. Of the 35 the giant company still uses, 20 are like Bartlit Beck: small, entrepreneurial spinoffs from huge firms that work for fixed fees. "We want to stop buying hours, and start buying results," says Mahoney.

Contingency fees can, of course, be a lot more profitable than hourly fees for a law firm, but it means betting on a win. That means the incentive is not to bill hours but to win verdicts.

Until 1993 Bartlit was a top litigator at Chicago's 400-lawyer Kirkland & Ellis. He wanted more freedom to bill clients based on results, but the firm balked. So Bartlit, at age 61, left Kirkland . . .

This year Bartlit will probably earn more than $3 million, almost twice his take at Kirkland. . . .

Bartlit got there from one direction. Stephen Susman, head of Houston-based Susman Godfrey, got to the same place from the opposite direction. Susman, a Yale-educated Texan, started in 1976 representing plaintiffs in commercial litigation. Now half his work is defending the big companies he used to sue. Susman and his partners often outearn partners in even the largest and most prestigious Texas firms. In 1994 the firm brought in $825,000 in profits per partner. By comparison, partners at the Houston office of Weil, Gotshal & Manges earned $532,000 each, according to *Texas Lawyer* magazine. . . .

Susman Godfrey, like Bartlit Beck, runs a lean shop, normally assigning only one or two lawyers to a case, whereas big Wall Street firms might assign 30. Susman goes out of his way to keep pretrial discovery and depositions—a major cost in most lawsuits— to a bare minimum.

American business is restructuring. Why should anyone be surprised that the American bar is restructuring, too?

Source: Bruce Upbin, "Results, Not Hours," *FORBES*, Nov. 6, 1995, p.172 and 174. Reprinted By Permission of FORBES Magazine © Forbes Inc., 1995.

PARTIES IN THE JUDICIAL SYSTEM (CIVIL CASES)

Plaintiffs

Plaintiffs are the parties who initiate a lawsuit and are seeking some type of recovery. In some types of cases they are called **petitioners** (such as in an action for divorce). The plaintiffs file their suit in the appropriate court, and this filing begins the process.

Defendants

Defendants are the ones from whom the plaintiffs want recovery. They are the ones charged with some violation of the civil rights of the plaintiff. In some cases they are referred to as respondents.

Lawyers

In most cases, each of the parties will be represented by a **lawyer**. Lawyers have other functions besides representing clients in a lawsuit. Many lawyers offer "preventive" services. Lawyers draft contracts, wills, and other documents to prevent legal problems from arising. Clients are advised in advance so that they can minimize legal problems and costs.

  The attorney-client relationship is a fiduciary one and one that carries privilege. The attorney is expected to act in the best interests of the client and can do so without the fear of having to disclose the client's thoughts and decisions. The **attorney-client privilege** keeps the relationship confidential and assures that others (even an adversary in a lawsuit) cannot have access to lawyer-client conversations.

  Under the American Bar Association's Model Rules for Professional Responsibility, attorneys are obligated to represent clients zealously. Once an attorney agrees to represent a client, that representation must be given to the best of the lawyer's ability. Because of the privilege, many lawyers know that their clients actually did commit a crime or breach a contract. However, the client's confession to an attorney cannot be revealed. Even with that knowledge, it is the attorney's

Visit the American Bar Association Center for Professional Responsibility: http://www.abanet.org/cpr/home.html

---

E T H I C A L   I S S U E S

3.2 Steven Holley, a partner in the law firm of Sullivan & Cromwell, received a call from Linda Himelstein, the legal affairs editor of *Business Week*, regarding the pending lawsuit by Procter & Gamble against Bankers Trust for the losses Procter & Gamble experienced with derivative investments handled by Bankers Trust. Sulliver & Cromwell represented Bankers Trust in the Procter & Gamble lawsuit. *Business Week* reporters had been unable to obtain a copy of the three-hundred-page complaint in the lawsuit because the documents were under court seal because of sensitive allegations by Procter & Gamble relating to federal criminal statutes. Himelstein asked Holley for a copy. Holley was not handling Bankers Trust's defense for the firm and sent a copy to Himelstein. The eventual result was a cover story by *Business Week* that was an unflattering portrait of Bankers Trust and its derivatives programs.

  Should Holley have discussed the case with Himelstein? Holley says he did not know that the documents were sealed. What should he have done? Did he breach the firm's duty of confidentiality?

obligation to represent the client and make certain that the client is given all rights and protections under the law. A criminal defense attorney may know that his or her client has committed a crime. But committing a crime and the required proof for conviction of that crime are two different things. It is the lawyer's job to see that the other side meets its burdens and responsibilities in proving a case against the client. Lawyers do represent guilty people. Their role is to make sure that the system operates fairly with guilty and innocent people alike.

Lawyers and their titles and roles vary from country to country. In Great Britain and most of Canada, there are solicitors and barristers. Solicitors prepare legal documents, give legal advice, and represent clients in some of the lesser courts. Barristers are the only "lawyers" who can practice before higher courts and administrative agencies. In Quebec and France, there are three types of lawyers: the advocate, who can practice before the higher courts and give legal advice; the notaire, who can handle real property transactions and estates and can prepare some legal documents; and the juridique (legal counselor), who can give advice and prepare legal documents. In Germany, a lawyer who litigates is called Rechtsanwalt, and a lawyer who advises clients but does not appear in court is called Rechtsbeistand. Japan has but one class of lawyers called bengoshi. In Italy, the two types of lawyers, whose roles are similar to the dual British system, are avocati and procuratori.

Business Planning Tip

Businesses and managers have a say in their lawyers' conduct. Bankers Trust should have issued an order to its law firm: No media interviews, on or off the record. Also, sealed documents should have procedures and processes for handling: Who can get them? Who controls access? Both lawyer and business client should exercise care and caution.

E T H I C A L   I S S U E S

3.3 The brokerage firm of E. F. Hutton was charged with federal criminal violations of interstate funds transfers. In reviewing the case to determine Hutton's best action and defense, the lawyers for Hutton discovered an internal memorandum from one branch manager that expressed concern about the conduct the government eventually uncovered.

What are the lawyer's obligations with respect to the document? What is the company's obligation? If you were a manager at Hutton, would you voluntarily disclose the document to the government?

Judges

Judges control the proceedings in a case and, in some instances, the outcome. Trial judges control the trial of a case from the selection of a jury to ruling on evidence questions. (See Chapter 4 for more details on trial procedures.) **Appellate** judges review the work of trial court judges. They do not actually hear evidence but, rather, review transcripts. Their job is one of determining error but does not include conducting a trial.

Judges are selected in various ways throughout the country. Some judges are elected to their offices. Some states have merit appointment systems wherein judges are appointed on the basis of their qualifications. In some states, judges are appointed by elected officials subject to the approval of the legislature. And in some states with appointed judges, the judges are put on the ballot every other year (or some other period) for retention; voters in these states do not decide whom they want as judges, but do decide whether they want to keep them once they are in office.

Name Changes on Appeal

The lawyers and the parties stay in the "game" even after a case is appealed. However, the names of the parties do change on appeal. The party appealing the case is called the **appellant**. Some courts also call the party appealing a case the **petitioner**. The other party (the one not appealing) is called the **appellee** or **respondent**.

Some states change the name of the case if the party appealing the case is the defendant. For example, suppose that Smith sues Jones for his damages in a car accident. The name of the case at trial is *Smith* v. *Jones*. Smith is the plaintiff and Jones is the defendant. If Smith wins the case at trial and Jones decides to appeal, Jones is the appellant and Smith is the appellee. In some courts, the name of the case on appeal becomes *Jones* v. *Smith*. Other courts leave the case name the same but still label Jones the appellant and Smith the appellee.

THE CONCEPT OF JURISDICTION

There are courts at every level of government, and every court handles a different type of case. In order for a court to decide or try a particular case, both parties to the case and the subject matter of the case must be within the established powers of the court. The established powers of a court make up the court's **jurisdiction**. "Juris" means law and "diction" means to speak.

Jurisdiction is the authority or power of a court to speak the law. Some courts can handle bankruptcies, where as others may be limited to traffic violations. Some courts handle violations of criminal laws, whereas others deal only with civil matters. The **subject matter** of a case controls which court has jurisdiction. For example, a case involving a federal statute will belong in a federal district court by its subject matter. However, there are federal district courts in every state, and jurisdiction also involves the issue of which court. In **personam jurisdiction**, or jurisdiction over the person, controls which of the federal district courts will decide the case. Determining which court can be used is a two-step process; subject matter and in personam jurisdiction must fit in the same court.

SUBJECT MATTER JURISDICTION OF COURTS: THE AUTHORITY OVER CONTENT

There are two general court systems in the United States: the federal court system (see Exhibit 3.1) and the state court system.

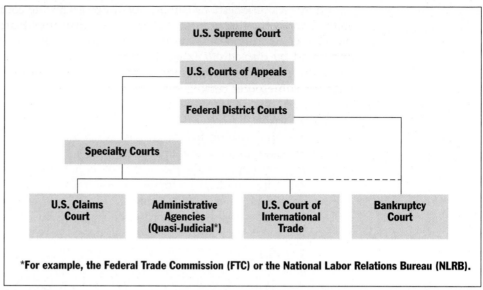

Exhibit 3.1
The Federal Court System

The Federal Court System

THE TRIAL COURT OF THE FEDERAL SYSTEM

Learn more about the U.S. Federal Court system: http://www.uscourts.gov/ *or* http://www.fjc.gov/

The **federal district court** is the general trial court of the federal system. However, federal district courts are limited in the types of cases they can hear; that is, their subject matter jurisdiction is limited. Federal district courts can hear three types of cases: those in which the United States is a party, those that involve a federal question, and those that involve diversity of citizenship.

JURISDICTION WHEN THE UNITED STATES IS A PARTY

Anytime the U.S. government is a party in a lawsuit, it will want to be tried in its own court system—the federal system. The United States is a party when it brings suit or when it is the defendant named in a suit. For example, if the Navy must bring an action to enforce a contract against a supplier, the United States is the plaintiff and the federal court system has subject matter jurisdiction. If a victim of a plane crash names the Federal Aviation Administration (FAA) in a suit, the United States is a defendant and the federal system again has jurisdiction.

FEDERAL JURISDICTION FOR A FEDERAL QUESTION

The federal district court has jurisdiction over cases involving federal questions. For example, if a business is suing for treble damages (a remedy of three times the amount of damages experienced) under the federal antitrust laws (see Chapter 13), there is a federal question and the case belongs in federal district court. A suit charging a violation of the Equal Protection Clause of the U.S. Constitution (see Chapter 5 for more details) also involves a federal question and can be brought in federal district court. Prosecutions for federal crimes also involve federal questions, and the United States will be a party as the prosecutor; these criminal cases are tried in federal district court. When the United States is a party in a case, the federal district court has exclusive jurisdiction.

Many federal questions can also be heard by a state court. For example, most state constitutions include the same Fifth Amendment protections included in the U.S. Constitution. A plaintiff often has a choice between federal and state court, and the decision to proceed in one forum as opposed to the other may be a strategic one based on the nature of the case, rules of procedure, and other factors related to differences between the two court systems.

JURISDICTION BY DIVERSITY

Most of the civil cases in federal district court are not there because they are federal questions or because the United States is a party. Most civil cases are in federal district court because the plaintiff and defendant are from different states and their case involves damage claims in excess of $50,000. Cases in which the parties are from different states qualify them for **diversity of citizenship** status, and federal district courts have the authority to hear these diversity cases. That authority is not exclusive; a state court can also hear diversity cases so long as neither party chooses to exercise the right to a federal district court trial. In diversity cases, state and federal courts have **concurrent jurisdiction**.

It is logical that federal courts should decide controversies among citizens of different states. If the case is held in one side's state court, that side may have an unfair advantage or built-in prejudice because of the location of the court.

When corporations are parties to suits, the diversity issue is more complex. The citizenship of a corporation can be its state of incorporation or the state in which its principal office is located. This citizenship test is used for subject matter jurisdiction. The citizenship test for in personam jurisdiction has been greatly expanded (pg. 91).

It is important to understand that when a federal court tries a case on the basis of diversity, it is simply trying the case under the same state laws but without the local prejudice that might exist in a state court. In other words, federal courts do not rule under a different set of laws; they simply apply the state law in a different setting.

LIMITED JURISDICTION—THE SPECIAL TRIAL COURTS OF THE FEDERAL SYSTEM

Not all cases in which the United States is a party or in which there is a federal question are decided in federal district courts. The federal system also has specialized trial courts to handle limited matters. For example, there is a Tax Court in the federal system, the jurisdiction of which is limited to tax issues. If you should decide to challenge the Internal Revenue Service because it would not allow one of your deductions, your case would be heard in Tax Court.

Bankruptcy Court is a well-used limited court in the federal system that has exclusive jurisdiction over all bankruptcies. Thus, no other court can handle a bankruptcy or bankruptcy issues. The Bankruptcy Court is limited to handling bankruptcies and does not handle any other type of trial or suit.

The U.S. Claims Court is another specialized federal court that handles the claims of government contractors against the U.S. government and vice versa. This court is experienced in government contracts and claims, and provides a faster forum for disposing of these issues without the longer process through federal district court.

Another court that is often discussed along with the federal system is the Indian Tribal Court. These are courts of the Native American nations that have exclusive jurisdiction over criminal and civil matters on the reservations. They are unique courts because of both their limited jurisdiction and their exclusivity rising from their sovereign nature.

THE STRUCTURE OF THE FEDERAL DISTRICT COURT SYSTEM

There is at least one federal district per state. The number of federal districts in each state is determined by the state's population and caseload. States such as Arizona and Nevada have only one federal district each, whereas states such as Illinois and New York have many. The number of courts and judges in each federal district is also determined by the district's population and caseload. Even in those states in which there is just one district, there are several judges and multiple courtrooms for federal trials. There are 96 federal districts in the 50 states plus 1 each in the District of Columbia and Puerto Rico.

THE IMPORTANCE OF FEDERAL DISTRICT COURT DECISIONS

Review online recent U.S. Courts of Appeals Decisions: http:// www.law.emory. edu/FEDCTS/

The subject matter of cases qualifying for federal district court is important. Such cases involve the interpretation of federal statutes and, in many cases, the resolution of constitutional issues. Because of the importance of these decisions, the opinions of federal district judges are published in a reporter series called the **Federal Supplement**, which reprints most opinions issued by federal district judges in every federal district. (Decisions of the Court of International Trade are also found in the *Federal Supplement*.) Cases in the *Federal Supplement* provide excellent precedent for interpretation and application of federal statutes. Just as there is a system for citing statutes (see Chapter 1), there is a system for citing case opinions. Such a system is necessary so that precedent can be found easily for use in future cases.

All case cites consist of three elements: an abbreviation for the reporter, the volume number, and the page number. The abbreviation for the *Federal Supplement* is "F. Supp." The volume number always appears in front of the abbreviation, and the page number appears after it. A formal cite will include in parentheses the federal district in which the case was decided and the year the case was decided. A sample federal district court cite of a case decided in the Northern District of Indiana looks like this:

Mathews v. *Lancaster General Hospital*
883 F. Supp. 1016 (E.D. Pa. 1995)

This method of uniform citation not only helps ease the burden of research; it is an automatic way of knowing where a case came from and how it can be used. A number of systems available on the Internet offer copies of court opinions for a fee.

THE APPELLATE LEVEL IN THE FEDERAL SYSTEM

Cases decided in federal district court and the specialized trial courts of the federal system can be appealed. These cases are appealed to the U.S. courts of appeals (formerly called the U.S. circuit courts of appeals).

Structure All of the federal district courts are grouped into **federal circuits** according to their geographic location. Exhibit 3.2 (pg. 84) is a map that shows the 13 federal circuits. Note that 11 of the circuits are geographic groupings of states; the twelfth is the District of Columbia, and the thirteenth is a nongeographic circuit created to handle special cases. A fourteenth circuit made by dividing the Ninth Circuit has been proposed.

Each circuit has its own court of appeals. The office of the court's clerk is located in the starred city shown in each of the federal circuits in Exhibit 3.2. The number of judges for each of the federal circuits varies according to caseload. However, most cases are heard by a panel of three of the circuit judges. It is rare for a case to be heard **en banc** (by the whole bench or all the judges in that circuit).

Procedures The U.S. courts of appeals are appellate courts and operate by the same general procedures discussed earlier in the chapter. An appeal consists of a record of the trial in the court below (here the federal district court), briefs, and possible oral argument. The standard for reversal is reversible error. Because the right of appeal is automatic, the appellate courts have tremendous caseloads. A full opinion is not given in every case. In the cases that are affirmed, the opinion may consist of that one word. Other decisions are issued as memorandum opinions for the benefit of the parties but not for publication.

Opinions The opinions of the U.S. courts of appeals are published in a series of reporters called the *Federal Reporter*. The system of citation for these cases is the same as for the federal district court opinions. The abbreviation for the *Federal Reporter* is "F." (Or sometimes "F.2d" or "F.3d"; the "2d" means the second series, which was started after the first "F." series reached volume 300, and now there is a

Exhibit 3.2
The Thirteen Federal Judicial Circuits

Source: Reprinted with permission and courtesy of West Publishing Company.

third series—"3d.") A formal cite will include in parentheses the federal circuit and date of the decision. A sample U.S. court of appeals cite would look like this:

Arrow Fastener Co. v. *Stanley Works*
59 F.3d 384 (2d. Cir. 1995)

THE U.S. SUPREME COURT

A decision by a U.S. court of appeals is not necessarily the end of a case. There is one more appellate court in the federal system—the **U.S. Supreme Court**. However, the Supreme Court's procedures and jurisdiction are slightly different from those of other appellate courts.

Appellate Jurisdiction and Process The Supreme Court handles appeals from the U.S. courts of appeals. This appeal process, however, is not an automatic right. The Supreme Court must first decide whether a particular case merits review. That decision is announced when the Court issues a **writ of certiorari** for those cases it will review in full. The Supreme Court, in its writ, actually makes a preliminary determination about the case and whether it should be decided. Only a small number of cases appealed to the Supreme Court are actually heard. For example, in 1995, 8,100 cases were on the Supreme Court's docket and only 97 opinions were issued. Cases are issued writs because there may be a conflict among the circuits about the law or because the case presents a major constitutional issue.

This writ of certiorari procedure also applies to other sources of appellate cases. Decisions from state supreme courts, for example, can be appealed to the U.S. Supreme Court. The Supreme Court also decides whether to review these cases.

Although the appellate workload of the U.S. Supreme Court is great, it is only part of the Court's jurisdictional burden. The Court also acts as a trial court or a court of **original jurisdiction** in certain cases. When one state is suing another state, the U.S. Supreme Court becomes the states' trial court. For example, the water dispute between California, Arizona, Colorado, and Nevada has been tried over a period of years by the U.S. Supreme Court. The Court also handles the trials (on an espionage charge, for example) of ambassadors and foreign consuls.

Structure The U.S. Supreme Court consists of nine judges who are nominated to the Court by the president and confirmed by the Senate. The appointment runs for a lifetime. A president who has the opportunity to appoint a Supreme Court justice is shaping the structure of the Court and the resulting decisions. For this reason, the U.S. Supreme Court is often labeled "conservative" or "liberal." The makeup of the bench controls the philosophy and decisions of the Court.

Review online
Supreme Court Cases:
http://www.law.
cornell.edu/supct/
supct.table.html

Opinions Because the Court is the highest in the land, its opinions are precedent for every other court in the country. The importance of these opinions has resulted in three different volumes of reporters for U.S. Supreme Court opinions. The first is the ***United States Reports*** (abbreviated "U.S."). These reports are put out by the U.S. Government Printing Office and are the official reports of the Court. Because these reports are often slow to be published, two private companies publish opinions in the ***Supreme Court Reporter*** (abbreviated "S. Ct.") and the ***Lawyer's Edition*** (abbreviated "L. Ed." or "L. Ed.2d").

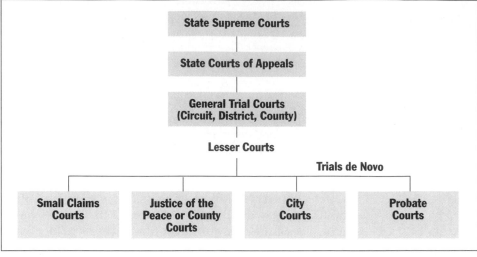

Exhibit 3.3
Typical State Court System

The State Court Systems

Although each state court has a different structure for its court system and the courts may have different names, there is a basic structure in each state that is similar to the federal system. Exhibit 3.3 is a diagram of a sample state court system.

STATE TRIAL COURTS

Each state has its own general trial court. This court is usually called a circuit, district, county, or superior court. It is the court in which nondiversity civil cases are heard and state criminal cases are tried.

In addition to its general trial court, each state also has its own group of "lesser courts." These are courts with **limited jurisdiction**; they are comparable to the specialty courts of the federal system. For example, most states have a **small claims court** in which civil cases with minimal damage claims are tried. In a true small claims court, there are no attorneys. Each party represents himself or herself before a judge. Such a setting offers parties the chance to have a judge arrive at a solution without the expense of attorneys. The amount recoverable in small claims court is indeed very small: $200–$5,000 are the typical limits.

Most states also have a lesser court that allows the participation of lawyers but limits the amount that can be recovered. The idea is to take the burden of lesser cases away from the usually overburdened general trial courts. These courts are called **justice of the peace courts** or **county courts**.

Most cities also have their own trial courts, which are limited in their jurisdiction to the trial of lesser crimes, such as a violation of a city ordinance. Many states call these courts **traffic courts** because city ordinances involve so many traffic regulations.

In addition to these courts, some states have very specialized courts to handle matters that are narrow in their application of law but frequent in occurrence. For example, although probating (processing) a will and an estate involves narrow issues of law, there is a constant supply of this type of case. Many states have a special court to handle this and such related matters as guardianships for incompetent persons.

Clarence Thomas was born to a poor family in Savannah, Georgia, in 1948. Through the work of his mother and grandparents, Mr. Thomas was able to attend college and go on to law school at Yale University. Mr. Thomas graduated from Yale Law School in 1974. After only six years of law practice, Mr. Thomas was appointed in 1981 by then-President Ronald Reagan to serve as head of the Civil Rights Division of the Department of Education.

Supreme Court Vetting— Justice Clarence Thomas

Anita Hill was born in 1955 in Morris, Oklahoma, the youngest of 13 children born to Albert and Erma Hill. Ms. Hill attended Oklahoma State University, where she majored in psychology and graduated in 1977 with honors. She attended Yale University Law School on an NAACP scholarship. Upon graduation from law school, she worked for a Washington, D.C., law firm from 1980 to 1981.

Mr. Thomas hired Ms. Hill in 1981 to work as a lawyer reporting to him in the Department of Education. In 1982, President Reagan appointed Mr. Thomas as head of the Equal Employment Opportunity Commission (EEOC—see Chapter 19 for more details). When Mr. Thomas asked Ms. Hill to work for him as a special assistant at the EEOC, Ms. Hill transferred to the EEOC in 1982. Mr. Thomas continued as head of the EEOC until 1990 when he was appointed by then-President Bush to the U.S. Court of Appeals for the District of Columbia. Ms. Hill left the EEOC in 1983 to take a position at the University of Oklahoma Law School as a professor of commercial law.

Justice Clarence Thomas

In 1991, Justice Thurgood Marshall retired from the U.S. Supreme Court, and President Bush nominated Mr. Thomas as Justice Marshall's replacement.

During Senate confirmation hearings, Ms. Hill alleged that Mr. Thomas had sexually harassed her by describing sexual acts and using sexual terms while they worked together in the Department of Education and at the EEOC. Her disclosures caused a great deal of public outcry and the Senate held televised hearings to listen to Ms. Hill's story. Mr. Thomas denied all of Ms. Hill's allegations. Although the hearings were divisive and contentious, the Senate confirmed Mr. Thomas's nomination by a vote of 52–48. Justice Thomas has served on the U.S. Supreme Court since 1991.

Issues

1. Mr. Thomas maintained that if he was engaging in the type of conduct Ms. Hill claimed, she would not have followed him to the EEOC from the Department of Education. Do you agree? Why or why not?
2. Was it ethical for Ms. Hill to wait to bring the charges?

Many of the lesser courts allow appeals to a general state trial court for a new trial (trial de novo) because not all judges in these lesser courts are lawyers, and constitutional protections require that an appeal is allowed.

STATE APPELLATE COURTS

State appellate courts serve the same function as the U.S. courts of appeals. There is an automatic right of review in these courts. Some states have two appellate-level courts to handle the number of cases being appealed. The opinions of these courts are reported in the state's individual reporter, which contains the state's name and some indication that an appellate court decided the case. For example, state appellate decisions in Colorado are reported in *Colorado Appeals Reports* (abbreviated "Colo. App."). These opinions are also reported in a **regional reporter**. All of the states are grouped into regions, and opinions of state appellate courts are grouped into the reporter for that region. Exhibit 3.4 presents the various regions and state groupings. For example, Nevada is part of the Pacific region, and its appellate reports are found in the *Pacific Reporter* (abbreviated "P." or "P.2d").

STATE SUPREME COURTS

State supreme courts are similar in their function and design to the U.S. Supreme Court. These courts do not hear every case because the right of appeal is not automatic. There is some discretion in what these supreme courts will hear. State supreme courts also act as trial courts in certain types of cases and are courts of original as well as appellate jurisdiction. For example, if two counties within a state have a dispute, the state supreme court would take the trial to ensure fairness. After a state supreme court decides an issue, it is important to remember that there is still a possibility of appeal to the U.S. Supreme Court if the case involves a federal question as a constitutional rights issue.

Exhibit 3.4
National Reporter System Regions

Pacific (P. or P.2d)	Northwestern (N.W. or N.W.2d)	Northeastern (N.E. or N.E.2d)	Southeastern (S.E. or S.E.2d)
Alaska	Iowa	Illinois	Georgia
Arizona	Michigan	Indiana	North Carolina
(California)	Minnesota	Massachusetts	South Carolina
Colorado	Nebraska	(New York)	Virginia
Hawaii	North Dakota	Ohio	West Virginia
Idaho	SouthDakota	**Atlantic (A. or A.2d)**	**Southern (So. or So.2d)**
Kansas	Wisconsin	Connecticut	Alabama
Montana	**Southwestern (S.W. or S.W.2d)**	Delaware	Florida
Nevada	Arkansas	District of Columbia	Louisiana
New Mexico	Kentucky	Maine	Mississippi
Oklahoma	Missouri	Maryland	
Oregon	Tennessee	New Hampshire	
Utah	Texas	New Jersey	
Washington		Pennsylvania	
Wyoming		Rhode Island	
		Vermont	

Note: California and New York each has its own reporter system. *Source:* The national reporter system was developed by West Publishing Company. Reprinted with permission of West Publishing Company.

The opinions of state supreme courts are significant and are reported in the regional reporters discussed earlier. Each state also has its own reporter for state supreme court opinions. For example, California has the *California Reporter*. The state supreme court reporters are easily recognized because their abbreviations are the abbreviation of each state's name. The following cite is one of a state supreme court: *Sims* v. *Gernandt Foreign Car Repair*, 459 S.E.2d 258 (N.C. 1995).

Exhibit 3.5
Sample Page of a National Reporter Case

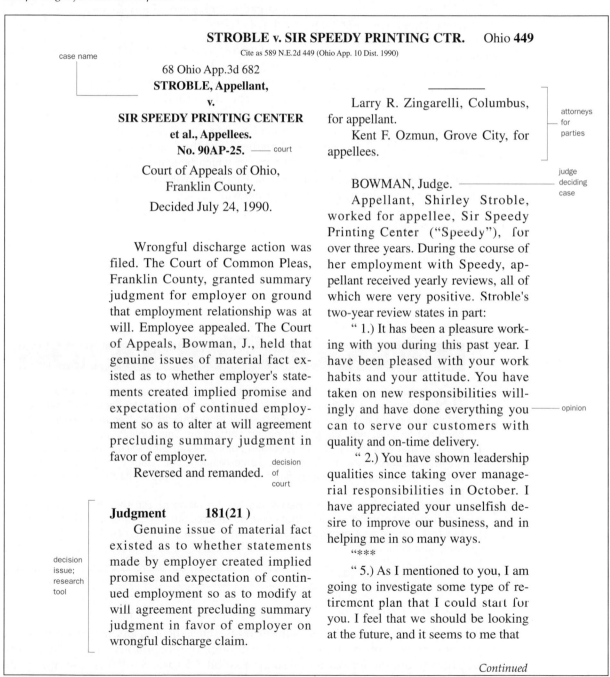

STROBLE v. SIR SPEEDY PRINTING CTR.   Ohio **449**

Cite as 589 N.E.2d 449 (Ohio App. 10 Dist. 1990)

case name

68 Ohio App.3d 682
STROBLE, Appellant,
v.
**SIR SPEEDY PRINTING CENTER
et al., Appellees.**
No. 90AP-25. —— *court*

Court of Appeals of Ohio,
Franklin County.

Decided July 24, 1990.

Wrongful discharge action was filed. The Court of Common Pleas, Franklin County, granted summary judgment for employer on ground that employment relationship was at will. Employee appealed. The Court of Appeals, Bowman, J., held that genuine issues of material fact existed as to whether employer's statements created implied promise and expectation of continued employment so as to alter at will agreement precluding summary judgment in favor of employer.

Reversed and remanded.   *decision of court*

Judgment   181(21)   *decision issue; research tool*

Genuine issue of material fact existed as to whether statements made by employer created implied promise and expectation of continued employment so as to modify at will agreement precluding summary judgment in favor of employer on wrongful discharge claim.

Larry R. Zingarelli, Columbus, for appellant.   *attorneys for parties*

Kent F. Ozmun, Grove City, for appellees.

BOWMAN, Judge.   *judge deciding case*

Appellant, Shirley Stroble, worked for appellee, Sir Speedy Printing Center ("Speedy"), for over three years. During the course of her employment with Speedy, appellant received yearly reviews, all of which were very positive. Stroble's two-year review states in part:

" 1.) It has been a pleasure working with you during this past year. I have been pleased with your work habits and your attitude. You have taken on new responsibilities willingly and have done everything you can to serve our customers with quality and on-time delivery.   *opinion*

" 2.) You have shown leadership qualities since taking over managerial responsibilities in October. I have appreciated your unselfish desire to improve our business, and in helping me in so many ways.

"***

" 5.) As I mentioned to you, I am going to investigate some type of retirement plan that I could start for you. I feel that we should be looking at the future, and it seems to me that

Continued

you are interested in a long term working relationship. Of course, this is what I would desire also, and am willing to help you with whatever considerations we can agree upon to satisfy your financial needs, along with professional growth."

Stroble's three-year review states, in part:

" 2.) You continue to maintain excellent work habits and produce excellent quality printing from your press. You have also taken on the managerial responsibilities with energy and determination.

***

" ***

" 4.) I would like to offer you a 5% raise effective today (Feb. 4), which would bring your hourly rate to $11.81. * * * I want to take this

opportunity to tell you again something I don't [*sic*] say often enough. That is: I appreciate you as a person and what you do for the business. I am glad that you work here and hope we will have many more years of working together."

On April 27, 1988, Stroble was charged by appellee, Barry Lowry ("Lowry").

On February 21, 1989, appellant filed a complaint against appellees for wrongful discharge. On October 3, 1989, appellees filed a motion for summary judgment, arguing that appellant was an employee at will. Appellees attached an affidavit of Lowry in which he states that, starting in February 1988, Stroble's relationship with

Source: Reprinted with permission and courtesy of West Publishing Company.

Exhibit 3.5 (*Continued*)

E T H I C A L   I S S U E S

3.4 Perhaps one of the most famous instances of a change of venue was the state criminal case that involved the trial of four Los Angeles police officers on charges of using excessive force on Rodney King. The officers' actions, which were captured on videotape, caught the nation's attention. The publicity was so extensive that the trial was moved to the suburban community of Simi Valley, far from the Los Angeles officers' base of operations. Some residents of South Central Los Angeles felt that the jurors in Simi Valley did not understand the problems they experience in police relations.

Was the change of venue necessary for the officers? Did the change of venue result in the selection of a jury that could not appreciate the nature of the community in which the incident occurred? Should a jury of your peers be composed of people from your community?

Judicial Opinions

Throughout the discussion of subject matter jurisdiction, published opinions of various courts have been mentioned. Although these opinions vary in their place of publication, the format is the same. Exhibit 3.5 (pgs. 89–90) is a sample page from a reporter, with each part of the excerpt identified. Opinions are reported consistently in this manner so that precedents can be found and used easily.

Venue

The concept of jurisdiction addresses the issue of which court system has the authority to try a case. The concept of **venue** addresses the issue of the location of the court in the system. For example, a criminal case in which a defendant is charged with a felony can be tried in any of a state's general trial courts. Heavy media coverage, however, may result in a judge's changing the venue of a case from the place where the crime was committed to another trial court where the publicity is less and it is easier to obtain an impartial jury.

IN PERSONAM JURISDICTION OF COURTS:
THE AUTHORITY OVER PERSONS

Once the proper court according to subject matter is determined, only half the job is done. For example, a case may involve a million-dollar claim between citizens of different states, in which case federal district court has subject matter jurisdiction over the parties. But there are 96 federal districts. So how is it decided which federal court will hear the case? The case will be heard by the federal district court with in personam jurisdiction over the parties. Subject matter jurisdiction only partly determines which trial court has jurisdiction; the other jurisdiction issue is power over the parties involved in the case.

The various criteria for determining in personam jurisdiction are examined here and are outlined in Exhibit 3.6.

Exhibit 3.6
Personal Jurisdiction

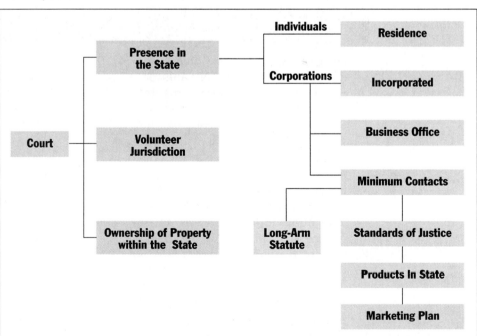

Ownership of Property Within the State

A party who owns real property in a state is subject to the jurisdiction of that state's courts for litigation related to that property. Actually, this type of jurisdiction gives the court authority over the person because the person owns a thing in the state. Technically, this type of jurisdiction is called **in rem jurisdiction**.

Volunteer Jurisdiction

A court has jurisdiction over a person who agrees to be subject to that court. In some contracts, for example, the parties agree that any lawsuits will be brought in the seller's state. The seller's state courts then have jurisdiction over that volunteer buyer.

Presence in the State

The third and final way a state court can take jurisdiction is by the "presence" of a party in the state, which is determined by different factors.

RESIDENCE

Individuals are present in a state if they have a residence in that state. There are different definitions of residency for tax and election laws, but the requirement here is simply that the person live in the state some time during any given year.

Corporations are residents of the states in which they are incorporated. A corporation is also a resident of any state in which it has a business office with employees.

"MINIMUM CONTACTS"

Review an uniform long-arm statute: http://www.law.vill.edu/vls/student_home/courses/civpro/unilonga.htm

Both corporations and residents can be subject to a state court's jurisdiction if they have "minimum contacts" in that state. The standard for **minimum contacts** is a fairness standard, which was established by the U.S. Supreme Court in *International Shoe* v. *Washington*, 326 U.S. 310 (1945). The Court basically required the states to notify out-of-state defendants of a suit and those defendants to have some contact with the state. Such contact can simply be the shipping of a product of the corporation into the state. Or the contact can be advertising the firm's product or service in a magazine with national circulation. Fairness does not require an office or an employee in the state. A business is present if its products or ads make their way into the state. These standards for in personam jurisdiction are more liberal than the citizenship requirements for diversity actions (see page 82).

Business Planning Tip

With national and international business transactions becoming so frequent, many contracts now include "forum selection" clauses. These portions of a contract to which the parties agree stipulate that if litigation is required, a particular court in a particular state or country will have jurisdiction over both parties. For example, a franchisor might have the forum-selection clause provide that all litigation by franchisees would be in the state and city where the franchisor's principal office is located. Checking a contract carefully for these clauses will enable you to decide, before signing, whether you want to agree to travel to another state or country if litigation becomes necessary.

LONG-ARM STATUTES: THE TOOLS OF MINIMUM CONTRACTS

In order to follow the Supreme Court's ruling on fairness, all of the states adopted **long-arm statutes**. These statutes are appropriately named: They give courts the power to extend their arms of jurisdiction into other states. For example, suppose that Zeta Corporation is incorporated in Ohio and has its manufacturing plant there. Zeta ships its glass baking dishes to every state in the country, although it has no offices anywhere except in Ohio. Joan Berferd, who lives in Alabama, is injured when one of Zeta's baking dishes explodes. Can the Alabama courts allow Berferd to file suit there and require Zeta to come to Alabama to defend the suit? Yes, because a long-arm statute is fair if it covers businesses shipping products to the state. Zeta entered the Alabama market voluntarily and must be subject to the Alabama courts. Long-arm statutes generally cover businesses with offices in the state, businesses shipping products into the state, and businesses that cause a **tort** to be committed in that state. The *Calder* v. *Jones* case involves an issue of whether a particular court had in personam jurisdiction over a business.

Calder v. *Jones*
465 U.S. 783 (1984)

"ENQUIRING" PEOPLE WANT TO KNOW: CAN I BE DRAGGED INTO COURT?

FACTS

Shirley Jones (respondent) is a professional entertainer who lives and works in California and whose television career is centered there. Ian Calder and John South (petitioners) wrote and edited an article about Jones and the article was published in the *National Enquirer* (a magazine with a circulation of 5,000,000 nationwide and 600,000 in California). The article contained certain items that Jones called libelous, and she brought suit against the petitioners in the California Superior Court for libel, invasion of privacy, and intentional infliction of emotional harm.

The petitioners were residents of Florida and had written and edited the article there. South was a reporter employed by the *Enquirer* and resided in Florida. A friend estimated that South traveled to California 6 to 12 times each year. Calder is editor and president of the *Enquirer*. He has been to California only twice—once for pleasure and once to testify in an unrelated trial. He reviewed South's article on Jones and approved it for publication. The petitioners were served with summons for the suit by mail.

The Superior Court dismissed the suit on grounds of First Amendment protection of freedom of the press. The California Court of Appeals reversed the holding and concluded California had jurisdiction because Calder and South had caused a tortious injury (libel) to Jones in California. Calder and South appealed to the U.S. Supreme Court.

JUDICIAL OPINION

REHNQUIST, Justice

In considering petitioners' motion to quash service of process, the Superior Court surmised that the actions of petitioners in Florida, causing injury to respondent in California, would ordinarily be sufficient to support an assertion of jurisdiction over them in California. But the court felt that special solicitude was necessary because of the potential "chilling effect" on reporters and editors which would result from requiring them to appear in remote jurisdictions to answer for the content of articles upon which they worked. The court also noted that respondent's rights could be

Continued

"fully satisfied" in her suit against the publisher without requiring petitioners to appear as parties. The superior court, therefore, granted the motion.

The California Court of Appeals reversed. The court agreed that neither of petitioner's contacts with California would be sufficient for an assertion of jurisdiction on a cause of action unrelated to those contacts. But the court concluded that a valid basis for jurisdiction existed on the theory that petitioners intended to, and did, cause tortious injury to respondent in California. The fact that the actions causing the effects in California were performed outside the state did not prevent the State from asserting jurisdiction over a cause of action arising out of those effects.

The Due Process Clause of the Fourteenth Amendment to the United States Constitution permits personal jurisdiction over a defendant in any state with which the defendant has "certain minimum contacts, such that the maintenance of the suit does not offend 'traditional notions of fair play and substantial justice.'" *International Shoe* v. *Washington*, 326 U.S. 310, 316 (1945). In judging minimum contacts, a court properly focuses on the "relationship among the defendant, the forum, and the litigation." (Citations omitted.)

The allegedly libelous story concerned the California activities of a California resident. It impugned the professionalism of an entertainer whose television career was centered in California (the article alleged that respondent drank so heavily as to prevent her from fulfilling her professional obligations). The article was drawn from California sources, and the brunt of the harm, in terms of both the respondent's emotional distress and the injury to her professional reputation, was suffered in California. In sum, California is the focal point of both the story and the harm suffered. Jurisdiction over petitioners is therefore proper in California based on the "effects" of their Florida conduct in California.

Petitioners argue that they are not responsible for the circulation of the article in California. A reporter and editor, they claim, have no direct economic stake in their employer's sales in a distant state. Nor are ordinary employees able to control their employer's marketing activity. The mere fact that they can "foresee" that the article will be circulated and have an effect in California is not sufficient for an assertion of jurisdiction. Petitioners liken themselves to a welder employed in Florida who works on a boiler that subsequently explodes in California.

Petitioners' analogy does not wash. Whatever the status of their hypothetical welder, petitioners are not charged with mere untargeted negligence. Rather their intentional, and alleged tortious, actions were expressly aimed at California. Petitioner South wrote and petitioner Calder edited an article they knew would have a potentially devastating impact upon respondent. And they knew that the brunt of that injury would be felt by respondent in the state in which she lives and works and in which the *National Enquirer* has its largest circulation. Under the circumstances, petitioners must "reasonably anticipate being haled into court there" to answer for the truth of the statements made in their article. An individual injured in California need not go to Florida to seek redress from persons who, though remaining in Florida, knowingly cause the injury in California.

We hold that jurisdiction over petitioners in California is proper because of their intentional conduct in Florida calculated to cause injury to respondent in California. The judgment of the California Court of Appeals is affirmed.

CASE QUESTIONS

1. Who is suing whom and for what?
2. Are the defendants residents of the same state (in which the suit is brought)?
3. Why do the defendants claim there is no in personam jurisdiction?
4. Do they have minimum contacts with California? Why?
5. What is the boiler analogy and why doesn't it work?

E T H I C A L   I S S U E S

3.5 The words "I've fallen and I can't get up!" were part of a TV commercial for a device whose marketing was directed at the elderly and whose appeal was that the device was hooked to communication links with emergency care providers. In fact, the device provided a link, but not a direct link, to a "911" number; there would be some interlink delay in getting notification to emergency personnel. The devices, worn around the neck, were in fact a means of effecting communication when the wearer could not get to a phone. However, the device was not directly linked to a "911" number.

Officials in Arizona brought charges against the company for deceptive advertising. Standards in Arizona require proof only that someone could be misled by the commercials; actions against advertisers do not require proof that someone was actually misled. The devices have been a help to many people, bringing assistance to those who would otherwise, because of temporary or permanent mobility impairment, be unable to call for help. Officials in other states did not find the ads misleading.

If you were an official for the company, would you change all of your ads, or modify only those in Arizona? Were the ads unethical?

THE INTERNATIONAL COURTS

Learn more about the International Court of Justice: http:// www.un.org/ Overview/ Organs/icj.html

The decisions of international courts provide precedent for parties involved in international trade. However, one of the restrictions on international court decisions is that the decision binds only the immediate parties to the suit on the basis of their factual situation. International courts do not carry the enforcement power or authority carried by courts in the U.S. federal and state systems. They are consensual courts and are only used when the parties agree to use them.

There are several courts of international jurisdiction. The **International Court of Justice** (ICJ) is the most widely known court. It was first established as the Permanent Court of International Justice (PCIJ) in 1920 by the League of Nations. In 1945, the United Nations (UN) changed the name and structure of the court. The ICJ is made up of 15 judges, no more than 2 of whom can be from the same nation, who are elected by the General Assembly of the UN. The court has been described as having **contentious jurisdiction**, which is to say that the court's jurisdiction is consensual: When there is a dispute, the parties can agree to submit the dispute to the ICJ.

There are other international courts in addition to the ICJ. The European Union has its **Court of Justice of European Communities** and the **European Court of Human Rights**. Jurisdiction in these courts is also consensual. Finally, there is the **Inter-American Court of Human Rights**.

The decisions of these courts and decisions from individual countries' courts dealing with international law issues can be found in *International Law Reports*.

In recent years London's Commercial Court, established over one hundred years ago, has become a popular forum for the resolution of international commercial disputes. Over half the cases in this court involve foreign enterprises. Some companies choose London's Commercial Court as the forum for their disputes for several reasons, even though neither they nor their transaction have any connection with England. First, the court has the advantage of being a neutral forum. Second, for U.S. firms, the use of the English language in the court is important.

Third, the court has a wide range of experience in international disputes, from shipping contracts to joint trading ventures. Fourth, the judges on the court were all once commercial litigators themselves and bring their depth of experience to the cases. Fifth, the court is known for its rapid calendar, moving cases along quickly. Major cases are heard within one year from the service of summons. Finally, the court has used a variety of creative remedies. The Commercial Court has issued pretrial injunctions to freeze assets, and its ties to the English government afford the injunctions international recognition. Perhaps the most famous of the Commercial Court's cases is its handling of the 20 class actions against Lloyd's of London.

Jurisdictional Issues in International Law

The jurisdiction of courts within a particular country over businesses from other countries is a critical issue in international law. A common subject in international disputes is whether courts in the United States, for example, can require foreign companies to defend lawsuits within the United States. The *Helicopteros Nacionales* case deals with the issue of a court's jurisdiction when the defendant is a foreign corporation.

Helicopteros Nacionales de Columbia, S.A. v. *Hall*
466 U.S. 408 (1984)

JURISDICTIONAL TAILSPIN: WHO GOES TO WHICH COURT?

FACTS

Helicopteros (Helicol) (petitioner) is a Colombian corporation with its principal place of business in Bogota. Its business is providing helicopter transportation for oil and construction companies in South America.

On January 4, 1976, a helicopter owned by Helicol crashed in Peru. Four U.S. citizens were killed in the crash, and their survivors (respondents) brought suit in Texas.

At the time of the crash, the four decedents were employed by Consorcio, a Peruvian consortium, and were working on a pipeline in Peru. Consorcio is the alter ego of a joint venture named Williams-Sedco-Horn (WSH), which had its headquarters in Houston, Texas. Consorcio was needed as the alter ego because Peruvian law prohibited the construction of the pipeline by an on-Peruvian entity.

Helicol negotiated its contract to supply helicopters on the Peru project through negotiations conducted in the Houston headquarters. Helicol sent its CEO to conduct the negotiations.

In the contract, which was in Spanish, the parties stated they were all residents of Peru and that any disputes would be submitted to Peruvian courts.

Helicol purchased helicopters and spare parts from Bell Helicopter in Fort Worth. Helicol pilots were also sent to Fort Worth for training, as were management and maintenance personnel.

The trial court awarded the respondents $1.14 million, and Helicol appealed on the grounds that the court lacked in personam jurisdiction. The court of appeals reversed and the respondents appealed to the Texas Supreme Court, where Texas courts were ruled to have jurisdiction; Helicol appealed.

JUDICIAL OPINION

BLACKMUN, Justice

The Due Process Clause of the Fourteenth Amendment operates to limit the power of a State to assert *in personam* jurisdiction over a nonresident defendant. Due process requirements are satisfied when *in personam* jurisdiction is asserted

Continued

over a nonresident corporate defendant that has certain minimum contacts with the forum such that the maintenance of the suit does not offend traditional notions of fair play and substantial justice. When a controversy is related to or "arises out of" a defendant's contacts with the forum, the Court has said that a relationship among the defendant, the forum, and the litigation is the essential foundation of *in personam* jurisdiction.

All parties to the present case concede that the respondents' claims against Helicol did not arise out of and are not related to Helicol's activities within Texas. We thus must explore the nature of Helicol's contacts with the State of Texas to determine whether they constitute the kind of continuous and systematic general business contacts the Court has found [necessary]. We hold that they do not.

It is undisputed that Helicol does not have a place of business in Texas and never has been licensed to do business in the State.

The one trip to Houston by Helicol's chief executive officer for the purpose of negotiating the contract with Consorcio/WSH cannot be described or regarded as a contact of a "continuous and systematic" nature and thus cannot support an assertion of *in personam* jurisdiction over Helicol by a Texas court. Similarly, Helicol's acceptance from Consorcio/WSH of checks drawn on a Texas bank is of negligible significance for purposes of determining whether Helicol had sufficient contacts in Texas. Common sense and everyday experience suggest that, absent unusual circumstances, the bank on which the check is drawn is generally of little consequence to the payee and is a matter left to the discretion of the drawer. Such unilateral activity of another party or third person is not an appropriate consideration when determining whether a defendant has sufficient contacts with a forum state to justify an assertion of jurisdiction. . . .

Accordingly, we reverse the judgment of the Supreme Court of Texas.

CASE QUESTIONS

1. List all the contacts Helicol had with the state of Texas.
2. What was the role of Consorcio in the pipeline operation in Peru?
3. Could Texas courts assert jurisdiction over Helicol?

Business Planning Tip

WSH probably intended Helicol to carry insurance to cover accidents involving the helicopters. However, this international contract neglected to provide for the rights of third parties injured as a result of their contract; a litigation clause for the protection of employees was necessary.

C O N S I D E R . . . **3.3** General Electric Capital Corporation (Gelco) owned Gelco Express United (Express) through Gelco's wholly owned subsidiary, International Couriers Corporation. Express is a Canadian corporation based in Canada that is in the retail overnight and same-day delivery courier business.

In 1987, Gelco executives met with representatives of Air Canada, a corporation owned by the Canadian government that provides passenger and freight air service in Canada and the United States. As a result of that meeting, a letter of intent was signed in which Air Canada agreed to purchase all outstanding shares of Express for 72,000,000 Canadian dollars. Air Canada would conduct due diligence and evaluate Gelco before closing the transaction. The meetings were held in Minnesota.

Continued

Air Canada hired Peat Marwick Thorne (Canadian partnership) to conduct its due diligence. Peat Marwick discovered significant irregularities in Express's financial statements, including an inadequate allowance for bad accounts and problems with accounts receivable. Deloitte and Touche (Canada) had audited Gelco's financial statements in 1985 and 1986.

Based on Peat Marwick's findings, Air Canada terminated its Letter of Intent with Gelco. However, negotiations continued and the purchase price was reduced. Peat Marwick continued to express concerns about Express's financial statements. Air Canada asked Gelco to waive the audit report requirement and accept a Peat Marwick finding of a positive net equity. Gelco agreed and the sale of Express to Air Canada was completed on September 17, 1987.

On October 2, 1987, General Electric (GE) and Gelco announced a merger agreement. On December 17, 1987, GE bought all outstanding Gelco shares for $35 a share. Two years later, Air Canada and Express sued Gelco for falsifying financial information. GE and Gelco sued Peat Marwick, Touche Canada, and Air Canada, claiming that they conspired to suppress information about Gelco's financial status in order to dupe GE into buying Gelco at an inflated price.

GE maintains that if Air Canada had halted negotiations, the true status of Express would have been disclosed publicly, thus depressing Gelco's stock. Air Canada could therefore not have expanded through acquisition.

The suit was brought in federal district court in Minnesota. Peat Marwick (Canada) and Touche (Canada) filed for a motion to dismiss for lack of in personam jurisdiction. Are these firms correct? Does the Minnesota federal court have jurisdiction over the two Canadian auditing firms? Of what importance is the fact that Express's books and records are in Canada? Would the place of negotiations be important? [*General Elec. Capital Corp.* v. *Grossman*, 991 F.2d 1376 (8th Cir. 1993).]

Conflicts of Law in International Disputes

The courts and judicial systems of countries around the globe vary, as do the procedural aspects of litigation. For example, in Japan there is no discovery process that permits the parties to examine each others' documents and witnesses prior to trial (see Chapter 4 for more details on discovery and the Japanese court system). And the United States permits lawyers to collect contingency fees and also permits broader tort recovery than would be available in most other countries.

Business Planning Tip

Due diligence, or the review and study of a company before its takeover, is a critical part of mergers and acquisitions. Contracts and letters of intent should spell out who will conduct the due diligence, where it will be done, how in-depth it will be, and the consequences of uncovering negative information.

Business Planning Tip

International mergers require resolution of issues such as what auditor will be used and where the audit work will be done. Decisions on this audit activity alone affect judicial jurisdiction.

Because of liberal discovery and recovery rules in the United States, many plaintiffs injured in other countries by products manufactured by U.S.-based firms want to bring suit in the United States to take advantage of our judicial system's processes and rules. However, the California Supreme Court has ruled in *Stangvik* v. *Shiley, Inc.*, 800 P.2d 858 (Cal. 1990), that if a plaintiff's home country provides an adequate forum for a dispute, the case cannot be brought in the United States. The suit involved family members of various patients who had died when their heart valves, manufactured by Shiley of Irvine, California, failed. The decision of the California Supreme Court required the plaintiffs to return to their home countries, where the recovery would be substantially less.

E T H I C A L   I S S U E S

3.6 Shiley sold 85,000 Bjork-Shiley Convexo-Concave heart valves before they were withdrawn from the market in 1986 because of a risk of structural failure. About half of the 85,000 valves were sold in foreign countries. Remedies available to patients and families in countries such as Ecuador and Chile, where the legal systems are not sophisticated, will be far less. Remedies available to patients in England, Australia, France, and Canada will be similar to those available in the United States.

Do all of the patients who had failed valves and their families experience the same level of harm? Is it ethical for a firm to pay out very little for a defective product simply because of the nature of the legal system in a particular country? Will the differences in recovery across nations lead companies to take quality and safety shortcuts when it comes to products sold in those countries? Could such differences lead to product dumping in countries where few remedies are available?

SUMMARY

What is the judicial process?
- Judicial review—review of a trial court's decisions and verdict to determine whether any reversible error was made
- Appellate court—court responsible for review of trial court's decisions and verdict
- Brief—written summary of basis for appeal of trial court's decisions and verdict
- Reversible error—mistake by trial court that requires a retrial or modification of a trial court's decision Options for appellate court:
    - Reverse—change trial court decision
    - Remand—return case to trial court for retrial or reexamination of issues
    - Affirm—uphold trial court's decisions and verdict
    - Modify—overturn a portion of the trial court's verdict
- Stare decisis—Latin for "let the decision stand"; doctrine of reviewing, applying, and/or distinguishing prior case decisions
- Case opinion—written court decision used as precedent; contains dicta or explanation of reasoning and, often, a minority view or dissenting opinion

Who are the parties in the judicial system?
- Plaintiffs/petitioners—initiators of litigation
- Defendants/respondents—parties named as those from whom plaintiff seeks relief

Continued

- Lawyers—officers of the court who speak for plaintiffs and defendants
- Attorney-client privilege—confidential protections for client conversations
- Appellant—party who appeals lower court's decision
- Appellee—party responding in an appeal

What courts can decide jurisdiction?—The power of the court to hear cases
- Subject matter jurisdiction—authority of court over subject matter
- Jurisdiction over the parties: in personam jurisdiction
  - Voluntary
  - Through property
  - Presence in the state: minimum contacts
  - Residence
  - Business office

The courts: Federal court system
- Federal district court—trial court in federal system; hears cases in which there is a federal question, the United States is a party, or the plaintiff and defendant are from different states (diversity of citizenship) and the case involves $50,000 or more; opinions reported in *Federal Supplement*
- Limited jurisdiction courts—bankruptcy court, court of claims
- U.S. Courts of Appeals—federal appellate courts in each of the circuits; opinions reported in *Federal Reporter*
- U.S. Supreme Court—highest court in United States; requires writ of certiorari for review; acts as trial court (original jurisdiction) for suits involving states and diplomats

The courts: State court system
- Lesser courts—small claims, traffic courts, justice of the peace courts
- State trial courts—general jurisdiction courts in each state
- State appellate courts—courts that review trial court decisions
- State supreme courts—courts that review appellate court decisions

International courts
- Voluntary jurisdiction
- International Court of Justice—UN court; contentious (consensual) jurisdiction; reported in *International Law Reports*
- London Commercial Court—voluntary court of arbitration

QUESTIONS AND PROBLEMS

1. Discuss the reasons for having judicial review. Give at least two reasons that a court could use for not following a previous decision, or precedent, on the same issue.
2. Compare the procedures at the trial and appellate levels of the court system. Is additional evidence presented at the appellate level? Will a jury be present at both the trial and the appeal of the case? How many judges will hear the case at the trial and appellate levels?
3. Rise to the Occasion, Inc. (RTTO) is a manufacturer of automatic breadmaking machines. RTTO is incorporated in Utah, runs its advertisements only in Utah newspapers and magazines, has two outlets for its product in Utah, and permits its sale by businesses that specialize in the bulk sale of grains. A number of RTTO owners have

purchased the machines for relatives in other states and shipped them as gifts. Faye Marvin, a resident of New Hampshire, received a RTTO breadmaker as a gift from her daughter in Utah. While using the RTTO breadmaker for the second time, Marvin was injured when the glass cover on the machine exploded. Marvin has filed suit in federal district court in New Hampshire. Can the New Hampshire court take in personam jurisdiction over RTTO?

4. Century Gas is a utility in Arizona. In 1989, Century applied to the Arizona Corporation Commission for a rate increase based on an expected increase in the price of natural gas during 1991. The commission ruled, and the appellate court affirmed, that rate decisions could not be based on future events. According to the judicial opinion, rate decisions and increases must be based on historical costs and financial information.

   In 1992, Century had a takeover offer from Norwest Utility, a large electric utility from the Pacific Northwest. Century filed an application with the commission to have the takeover approved. If the takeover occurred, Century's costs would decrease nearly 35 percent. In approving the merger, the commission wished also to decrease Century's rates based on the anticipated decrease in costs once the merger took place. Based on precedent, could the commission take this action?

5. Determine which court(s) would have jurisdiction over the following matters:
   a. Selling securities without first registering them with the Securities and Exchange Commission, as required under 15 U.S.C. § 77 et seq.;
   b. A suit between a Hawaiian purchaser of sunscreen lotion and its California manufacturer for severe sunburn that resulted in $65,000 in medical bills.

6. Jeffrey Dawes, the comptroller for Umbrellas Inc., a New York Stock Exchange company, has been charged with two violations of the federal Foreign Corrupt Practices Act. In which court will he be tried?

7. A Delaware banking corporation was named as trustee for the large estate of a wealthy individual in that individual's will. The beneficiaries of the trust are the deceased's two children, one of whom lives in Pennsylvania and the other in Florida. The bank does business in Delaware only. Can the beneficiary in Florida successfully require the bank to submit to the jurisdiction of Florida courts? [*Hanson* v. *Denckla*, 357 U.S. 235 (1958).]

8. Eulala Shute lived in Arlington, Washington, and through a local travel agent purchased a seven-day Carnival cruise. The cruise began in Los Angeles, went to Puerto Vallarta, Mexico, and then returned to Los Angeles. Carnival Cruise Lines, Inc., the owner of the ship and the firm responsible for the cruise, is a corporation based in Miami, Florida. While the cruise ship was in international waters off of Mexico, Shute tripped and fell on a deck mat during a guided tour of the ship's galley.

   Shute filed suit in federal district court in the state of Washington against Carnival to recover for her injuries. Could the Washington court take in personam jurisdiction over Carnival? [*Carnival Cruise Lines, Inc.* v. *Shute*, 499 U.S. 585 (1991).]

9. Hicklin Engineering, Inc. is a Minnesota corporation that manufactures transmission testing stands for worldwide sales. Hicklin's only place of business is Iowa. Aidco, Inc. is a Michigan corporation with its principal place of business in Michigan. Aidco also manufactures transmission testing stands for worldwide sales. Aidco sent letters to several of Hicklin's customers, raising questions about Hicklin's products and expertise, and offering a promotion of its transmission stands. Aidco is not licensed to do business in Iowa and has no offices, employees, or agents there. Hicklin has filed suit in Iowa against Aidco for the tort of intentional interference with contractual relations. Can Aidco be required to come to Iowa to defend the suit? [*Hicklin Engineering, Inc.* v. *Aidco, Inc.*, 959 F.2d 738 (8th Cir. 1992).]

10. Aerial Materials, an Oklahoma company that ships fabric nationwide, failed to deliver $500,000 worth of fabric to North Dakota Needles, a sewing factory. Would the case be tried in federal or state court and in which state would the trial be held?

NOTE

1 Alex Ayres, *The Wit and Wisdom of Abraham Lincoln*. Reprinted with permission of Penguin USA, © 1992 Penguin USA.

Judgment

In 1982, a planned merger between Gulf Oil Corporation and Cities Service Company failed. A small group of investors filed suit in 1984. By 1995, the suit had not yet gone to trial, but the parties involved had spent over $100 million in legal fees and costs. Thomas H. Moreland, the attorney for the investors, commented that the case could go on forever. Is there something Mr. Moreland and his clients could do to speed up the resolution of the case? Could you offer Mr. Moreland any advice or suggestions?

CHAPTER 4

The study of business regulation to this point has involved

an overview of

Managing Disputes: Alternative Dispute Resolution and Litigation Strategies

ethics, law and the courts responsible for enforcing,

interpreting, and applying the law. This chapter

focuses on disputes. This chapter answers the following

questions: How can businesses best resolve disputes?

What strategies should a business follow if litigation is

inevitable? How do courts proceed with litigation?

"Let's settle this now."

Doc Holliday
(just prior to the gun fight between the Earp brothers and the McLaurys and Billy Clanton at the O.K. Corral in Tombstone, Arizona, October 26, 1881)

WHAT IS ALTERNATIVE DISPUTE RESOLUTION?

Alternative dispute resolution (ADR) offers parties alternative means of resolving their differences outside actual courtroom litigation and the costly aspects of preparation for it. ADR ranges from very informal options, such as a negotiated settlement between the CEOs of companies, to the formal, written processes of the American Arbitration Association. These processes may be used along with litigation or in lieu of litigation.

TYPES OF ALTERNATIVE DISPUTE RESOLUTION

Arbitration

NATURE OF ARBITRATION

Arbitration is the oldest form of ADR and is the resolution of disputes in a less formal setting than a trial. Many contracts today have mandatory arbitration clauses in them that require, in the event of a dispute, that the parties submit to arbitration. Other contracts, including many consumer auto insurance contracts, offer voluntary arbitration for consumers involved in disputes over their coverage.

Arbitration can be binding or nonbinding. Binding arbitration means that the decision of the arbitrators is final. The parties cannot appeal the decision to any court. Nonbinding arbitration is a preliminary step to litigation. If one of the parties is not satisfied with the result in the arbitration, the case may still be litigated.

ARBITRATION PROCEDURES

Arbitration can be agreed upon well in advance. A contract may contain a future arbitration clause so that the parties agree at the time of contracting that any disputes will be submitted to arbitration. The parties may also agree to submit to arbitration after their dispute arises even though they do not have such a clause in their contract.

Visit the American Arbitration Association: http://www.adr.org/

Once the parties agree to arbitrate, they usually notify the American Arbitration Association (AAA), which for a fee will handle all the steps in the arbitration. The AAA is the largest ADR provider in the country with an annual case load of 60,000. A tribunal administrator is appointed for each case, and this administrator communicates with the parties and helps move the arbitration along. The fee charged by the AAA depends upon the amount of the claim. For example, a claim between $1 and $20,000 has a fee of 3 percent. Exhibit 4.1 (pg.105) is a sample AAA form of a demand for arbitration and the method for beginning arbitration. This document is the complaint form for arbitration.

Once a demand for arbitration is received, the tribunal administrator sends each of the parties a proposed list of arbitrators. Exhibit 4.2 (pg. 106) is a sample of such a notice. The parties are given seven days to reject any of the proposed arbitrators and to rank the remaining named possibilities in the order of their preference. The tribunal tries to make a mutually agreeable choice but can submit a new list if necessary. If the parties cannot agree, the AAA appoints an arbitrator but will never appoint anyone rejected by one of the parties.

The hearing date is set at a mutually agreeable time. Between the time the date is set and the actual hearing, the parties have the responsibility of gathering together the evidence and witnesses necessary for their cases. The parties are, in effect, doing their preparation. The parties can also request that the other party bring certain documents to the hearing. Some arbitrators are given subpoena power in

American Arbitration Association

MEDIATION   Please consult the Commercial Mediation Rules regarding mediation procedures. If you want the AAA to contact the other party and attempt to arrange a mediation, please check this box.   ☐

COMMERCIAL ARBITRATION RULES
DEMAND FOR ARBITRATION

DATE: _____

TO: Name _____
(of the party upon whom the demand is made)

Address _____

City and State _____ ZIP Code _____

Telephone (   ) _____ Fax _____

Name of Representative _____
(if known)

Representative's Address _____

City and State _____ ZIP Code _____

Telephone (   ) _____ Fax _____

The named claimant, a party to an arbitration agreement contained in a written contract, dated _____
_____, providing for arbitration under the
Commercial Arbitration Rules, hereby demands arbitration thereunder.

(Attach the arbitration clause or quote it hereunder.)

NATURE OF DISPUTE:

CLAIM OR RELIEF SOUGHT (amount, if any):

TYPE OF BUSINESS: Claimant _____ Respondent _____

HEARING LOCALE REQUESTED: _____
(City and State)

You are hereby notified that copies of our arbitration agreement and of this demand are being filed with the American Arbitration Association at its _____
office, with the request that it commence the administration of the arbitration. Under the rules, you may file an answering statement within ten days after notice from the administrator.

Signed _____ Title _____
(may be signed by a representative)

Name of Claimant _____

Address (to be used in connection with this case) _____

City and State _____ ZIP Code _____

Telephone (   ) _____ Fax _____

Name of Representative _____

Representative's Address _____

City and State _____ ZIP Code _____

Telephone (   ) _____ Fax _____

To institute proceedings, please send three copies of this demand with the administrative fee, as provided for in the rules, to the AAA. Send the original demand to the respondent.

Form C2–11/90

Source: Form appears courtesy of the American Arbitration Association.

Exhibit 4.1
Sample Demand for Arbitration

American Arbitration Association

Do not send this form to the other party.

CASE NUMBER: _____ DATE LIST SUBMITTED: _____

PARTIES: _____ AND _____

LIST FOR SELECTION OF ARBITRATOR(S)

After striking the name of any unacceptable arbitrator(s), please indicate your order of preference by number. We will try to appoint arbitrator(s) mutually acceptable who can hear your case promptly. Leave as many names as possible.

NOTE: Biographical information is attached. Unless your response is received by the Association by
_____, all names submitted may be deemed acceptable.

REQUEST FOR DATES

To enable the arbitrator(s) to avoid fixing an inconvenient hearing date, please cross off the dates that are not acceptable for a hearing, but leave as many days as possible so that the first mutually agreeable date for hearing may be set. If a mutually agreeable date is not available for these two months, the arbitrator(s) is/are empowered under the rules to fix the time and place for each hearing. If this form is not returned by _____, it will be assumed that any open date is satisfactory to you. The hearing will then be scheduled for a date preferred by the other party.

NOTE: Saturdays, Sundays, and other unavailable days have been marked off.

Month of _____						
1	2	3	4	5	6	7
8	9	10	11	12	13	14
15	16	17	18	19	20	21
22	23	24	25	26	27	28
29	30	31				

Month of _____						
1	2	3	4	5	6	7
8	9	10	11	12	13	14
15	16	17	18	19	20	21
22	23	24	25	26	27	28
29	30	31				

Please note that hearings generally commence at _____ a.m./p.m.

I anticipate that my case will require _____ hours/days of hearing.

PARTY: _____

BY: _____ TITLE: _____

Your telephone or fax response to this inquiry will be appreciated and will expedite administration. Please refer to the telephone and fax numbers on the enclosed letterhead.

Form G4–4/89

Source: Form appears courtesy of the American Arbitration Association.

Exhibit 4.2
Sample List for Selection of Arbitrators

certain states; that is, they have the power to require the production of documents or to have a witness testify.

The parties need not have lawyers but have the right to use one under AAA rules. A rule requires that the AAA and other parties be notified if an attorney will be used and that the attorney be identified.

Although the atmosphere is more relaxed, an arbitration hearing parallels a trial. The parties are permitted brief opening statements, after which they discuss the remedy that is sought. Each of the parties then has the opportunity to present evidence and witnesses. There is a right of cross-examination, and closing statements are also given. Some of the emotion of a trial is missing because, although emotional appeal influences juries, an expert arbitrator is not likely to be influenced by it. After the close of the hearing, the arbitrator has 30 days to make a decision.

In binding arbitration, the arbitrator's award is final. The award and decision cannot be changed, modified, or reversed. Only the parties can agree to have the case reopened; the arbitrator cannot do so.

Mediation

Visit a firm specializing in mediation, GAMA, Inc.: http://www.gama.com/

Arbitration can be complex and expensive in spite of its self-imposed procedural limitations. However, other forms of alternative dispute resolution are readily available and relatively inexpensive. **Mediation** is one such alternative. Mediation is a process in which both parties meet with a neutral mediator who listens to each side explain its position. The mediator is trained to get the parties to respond to each other and their concerns. The mediator helps break down impasses and works to have the parties arrive at a mutually agreeable solution. Unlike an arbitrator, the mediator does not issue a decision; the role of the mediator is to try to get the parties to agree on a solution. Mediation is completely confidential; what is said to the mediator cannot be used later by the parties or their lawyers in the event litigation becomes necessary. Mediation is less expensive than arbitration and does not require that the parties bring lawyers. Mediation is not binding unless the parties have agreed to be bound by the decision.

The Minitrial

In a **minitrial**, the parties have their lawyers present the strongest aspects of their cases to senior officials from both companies in the presence of a neutral advisor or a judge with experience in the field. At the end of the presentations by both parties, the neutral advisor can provide several forms of input, which are controlled by the parties. The advisor may be asked to provide what his or her judgment would be in the case, or the advisor may be asked to prepare a settlement proposal based on the concerns and issues presented by the parties. Minitrials are more adversarial than mediation but they are confidential, and the input from a neutral but respected advisor may help to bring the parties together. A minitrial is not binding.

Rent-a-Judge

Many companies and individuals are discovering that the time that elapses between the filing of a lawsuit and its resolution is too great to afford much relief. As a result, a kind of private court system, known as **rent-a-judge**, is developing in which parties may have their case heard before someone with judicial experience without waiting for the slower process of public justice. These private courts are like *The People's Court* without the television cameras. The parties pay filing fees and pay for the judges and courtrooms. These private courts also offer less expensive settlement conferences to afford the parties a chance at mediation prior to their private hearing. This and the other methods of alternative dispute resolution previously discussed offer parties the chance to obtain a final disposition of their cases more quickly and at less cost.

Summary Jury Trials

Under this relatively new method of alternative dispute resolution, the parties are given the opportunity to present summaries of their evidence to judge and jurors. The jurors then give an advisory verdict to start the settlement process. If the parties are unable to agree on a settlement, a formal trial proceeds. The benefit of this means of resolution is that the parties have an idea of a jury's perception so that they are assisted in their guidelines for settlement. This type of resolution occurs late in the litigation process, after the costs of discovery have been incurred. It can, however, save the expense of a trial.

Early Neutral Evaluation

Early neutral evaluation requires another attorney to meet with the parties, receive an assessment of the case by both sides, and then provide an evaluation of the merits of the case. The attorney, who is either a paid consultant or a volunteer through the state bar association, renders an opinion on the resolution of the case. The idea in this method of resolution is to encourage settlement. Because early neutral evaluation occurs before the discovery phase of the case, it can save time and money if the parties are able to settle.

FOR THE MANAGER'S DESK

SOUTHWEST AIRLINES AND CREATIVE DISPUTE RESOLUTION

In 1991, Dallas-based Southwest Airlines began a marketing campaign, using the slogan, "Just Plane Smart." Greenville-based Stevens Aviation had been using the slogan "Plane Smart" to market its airline service business. Following posturing by lawyers, Kurt Herwald, the chairman of Stevens Aviation, called Herb Kelleher, the chairman of Southwest Airlines (pictured here), and offered to arm wrestle for the rights to the slogan. Kelleher

rented a wrestling auditorium, sold tickets to the event, and offered the proceeds to charity. Kelleher, then 61, lost to Herwald, then 38, who is also a weight lifter. Herwald said, "Just to show sympathy for the elderly and that there's no hard feelings, we've decided to allow Southwest Airlines to continue using our slogan." After the event a commentator noted, "Not only did the companies save a court battle that would have taken years and cost several hundred thousand dollars, they gained loads of free publicity. They also made donations to charities."

C O N S I D E R . . .

Judgment

4.1 The parties in the chapter's opening "Judgment" hired a former judge, rented a courtroom, and agreed to take three weeks to present their cases to the judge. They forfeited any right to appeal the judge's decision. The investors were awarded $90 million. In effect, the parties selected a rent-a-judge option that was binding. The results were that the costs were greatly reduced, there was little public exposure of the facts in a sensitive investor case, and the matter was resolved in a short time. Any of the other forms of ADR would have worked well in the situation too. The case could have been submitted to arbitration, a mediator could have been hired, or the parties could have simply sat together and negotiated a settlement.

In the case of a dispute, regardless of its scope or complexity, businesses have choices for resolution that are flexible. All options should be pursued apart from litigation.

C O N S I D E R . . .

4.2 Peter and Theresa Lauer opened a retirement account with Merrill Lynch, Pierce, Fenner & Smith brokerage firm. The agreement they signed when they opened their account provided that any claims or disputes would be submitted to arbitration, and that the arbitration would be binding. The Lauers became convinced that their account was being mishandled. Mr. Lauer is fearful that if their dispute is taken to arbitration, the arbitrator will favor Merrill Lynch and that he and his wife will not be treated fairly. What information and advice can you give to Mr. Lauer to help him with his concern?

RESOLUTION OF INTERNATIONAL DISPUTES

Visit the International Chamber of Commerce: http://www1.usa1.com/~ibnet/icchp.html

Arbitration has been used in the international business arena since 1922. The **International Chamber of Commerce (ICC)** is a private organization that handles more than 250 arbitration cases each year. Most requests for ICC arbitration come from Western countries, and the typical subject matters are trade transactions, contracts, intellectual property, agency, and corporate law. International businesses can place in their contracts a clause that requires arbitration to be handled by the ICC. The process is very similar to that discussed earlier for the American Arbitration Association. A request for arbitration is submitted to the ICC Secretariat in Paris; the parties can nominate arbitrators and choose the location for the arbitration hearing. The award of the ICC is final, and payment must be made at the location of the hearing.

Visit the ICSID: http://www.worldbank.org/html/extdr/glance.html#icsid

In addition to the ICC, the World Bank has established the Center for Settlement of Investment Disputes (ICSID). The ICSID is an arbitral organization created specifically to hear disputes between investors and the nations in which they have made investments. This arbitration forum was created because of investors' fears that the courts of the nation in which they have invested may favor the government of that nation. Again, investment contracts can provide for the submission of disputes to the ICSID. Decisions of the ICSID are enforceable as if they were a court order and are final.

Pete Rose, a native of Cincinnati, Ohio, played 3,562 games for the Cincinnati Reds. He had 4,256 hits, 10 seasons with 200 or more hits, and 16 All-Star Game appearances. He retired as an active player in 1986 and became the manager of the Reds.

There's No Betting in Baseball
Pete E. Rose

For his 24 seasons with the Reds, he was known as "Charlie Hustle" and was baseball's first million-dollar player.

When Rose hit his 4,192nd hit, breaking Ty Cobb's record, he sold the bat he used. In 1989, an investigation conducted by the Office of the Baseball Commissioner revealed that Rose needed cash often. Between 1985 and 1987, the commissioner (A. Bartlett Giamatti) alleged that Rose bet on baseball, including bets on the Reds, the team for which he played and managed during that time.

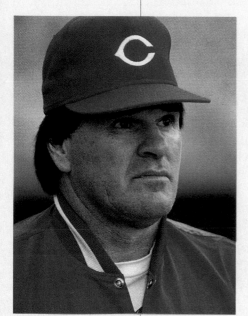

Giamatti charged Rose with a violation of major-league baseball's Rule 21, which prohibits a player from betting on his own team. Rule 21 also provides that players who engage in such betting can be banned from the sport for life.

Rose settled with the commissioner in 1988. In the settlement agreement, Rose neither admitted nor denied betting on baseball. But the remedy was his banishment with the right to apply for reinstatement after one year. On August 24, 1989, Giamatti reviewed Rose's reinstatement application and ruled that Rose was banished forever from baseball. Rose was thereby denied a place

Pete Rose

in the Baseball Hall of Fame.

Following the Rule 21 charges, the Internal Revenue Service conducted an investigation and charged Rose with tax evasion. Mr. Rose was sentenced to five months in federal prison in 1990, and was released in 1991 to a half-way house for three months. He paid a $50,000 fine and contributed one thousand hours of community service to five inner-city elementary schools.

Issues

1. Should Rose be permitted in the Baseball Hall of Fame?
2. What was so bad about Rose's betting?
3. Why did Rose settle? What issues were important to him in deciding to settle?

LITIGATION VS. ADR: THE ISSUES AND COSTS

Speed and Cost

Speed and cost are two compelling reasons businesses turn to ADR to resolve disputes. Costs of ADR are frequently one-tenth of the cost of litigating a dispute. For example, in 1993 Pacific Gas & Electric (PG&E) was facing six lawsuits that stemmed from the crash of a helicopter into one of the company's power lines. PG&E estimated that a lawsuit would take at least two years from the time of filing to finish with a cost of between $300,000 and $500,000. PG&E hired a mediator and the disputes were settled within 10 months from the time of the accident at a cost of about $20,000. The backlog in both state and federal court systems prevents timely disposition of cases. A civil case filed in federal district court today would likely not go to trial for at least two years.

The time and resulting backlogs and costs are issues not just for businesses but for the court systems as well. Today, 35 states have some form of mandatory ADR requirements. A typical state requirement is that judges refer disputes that involve less than $50,000 first to arbitration before the parties may go forward with a trial. Even though the arbitration is not binding, the parties are unlikely to appeal the arbitration decision. Arbitration, like other methods of ADR, offers the parties what they are seeking: an outsider's view of the case, the issues, and any resulting liability. The courts' workload is reduced when arbitration handles smaller cases.

Protection of Privacy

There are other reasons parties may choose ADR. Whatever matter is in dispute can be kept private if referred directly to ADR; there are then no public court documents available for examination. Even when a suit is filed, the negotiated settlement achieved through alternative means can be kept private to protect the interests of the parties. When Dillard's and Joseph Horne Company were litigating over Dillard's conduct in a Horne's takeover, the parties' dispute centered on whether Dillard's was conducting due diligence in obtaining access to Horne's facilities and records, or whether Dillard's was actually running the stores in an attempt to drive down the acquisition price. The business press reported on the litigation and the underlying dispute. The information was not flattering to either party. Dillard's was portrayed as a large firm taking advantage of a small chain and engaging in unethical conduct with respect to verifying financial information prior to acquisition. Horne's was portrayed as naive and inept. Dillard's and Horne settled the dispute, and both agreed to keep the terms of the settlement confidential. The result was that not only was the very public litigation ended, but the focus on alleged misconduct changed because of the settlement and its private nature.

Creative Remedies

Often, without the constraints of court jurisdiction and restraints of legal boundaries, a creative remedy can be crafted that helps both sides. For example, Intel, a computer chip manufacturer, experienced ongoing disputes with employees who left the company to begin their own businesses with products and in areas that would compete with Intel. The concern of Intel was whether

the employees were taking with them technology that had been developed at and belonged to Intel. Using only the courts, Intel would find itself in lengthy, expensive, and complex litigation over engineering and developmental issues. Such litigation is not only costly in a monetary sense but also for the morale of employees charged with product development. Constant legal battles with former employees is not healthy for a corporate image within a company or from the outside.

After filing suit against one group of employees, Intel agreed, along with the former employees, to have an expert oversee the former employees' work in their business. The expert would have knowledge of Intel's product development that the employees had been involved with and would agree to notify all sides if the new company of the former employees was infringing any of Intel's patents. The expert agreed to oversee the new company's work for one year, at which point technology would make anything developed by the former employees while they were still at Intel obsolete. This creative solution permitted the former employees to operate their business, but it also provided Intel with the reassurance that their intellectual property was not being taken.

Business Planning Tip

Intel took its former employee/property issue a step further. Recognizing that court battles were costly, not productive, and inevitable, given the fact that talented employees often leave to begin their own businesses, Intel developed a new program that proved to be a win-win solution to an ongoing legal issue. Intel established an incubator/venture capital program in which employees were encouraged to come to Intel with proposals for new products and other ideas that they wished to pursue on their own. An Intel committee would review the proposal and make a decision about whether Intel would invest. Intel would then provide funding for the start-up of the company in exchange for a portion of the returns on the sales of the products for a preestablished number of years. Eventually the employees would own their firms outright. With this solution, Intel encouraged employee creativity and entrepreneurship and solved the complex problem of employees departing with technology arguably developed while they were at Intel.

Judge and Jury Unknowns

While a good case and preparation are often offered as explanations for victory in a lawsuit, there are many good cases that, despite excellent preparation, are lost. There are unknowns in all forms of litigation. The unknowns are judges and juries and their perceptions and abilities. Research shows that 80 percent of all jurors have made up their minds about a case after only the opening statements in a trial are made. Further research has shown that juries use their predetermined ideas in reaching a verdict. Finally, research shows that juries employ hindsight bias in their deliberation processes; that is, juries view the outcome of a set of facts and conclude that one party should have done more. Knowing that someone was injured often clouds our ability to determine whether that person should have been able to prevent the injury.

Based on information about juries, many businesses will opt for a trial to a court in which a judge renders a decision. However, research with judges has demonstrated that even they are affected in their judgments in cases by predetermined ideas and hindsight bias, although to a lesser extent than jurors. "The Wild Card in Complex Business Litigation: The Jury" provides background information on the risks that juries pose for businesses in litigation.

FOR THE MANAGER'S DESK

THE WILD CARD IN COMPLEX BUSINESS LITIGATION: THE JURY

You have been behind them in the line in the grocery store that says "Cash Only" and they write a check. You have read about them in the surveys on literacy and know that some of them believe Latin is spoken in Latin America. These are typical citizens. If they are above the age of eighteen and can drive and/or vote, they can sit on juries. Juries determine who was at fault in an accident and whether there has been patent infringement in a computer program. We have the right to a jury when we are injured in a simple rear-end collision and bring suit for recovery and we also have the right to a jury trial on an antitrust suit involving the application of the Justice Department's Herfindahl-Hirschman index. While preparation, good witnesses and a good case are factors in whether you will win or lose, the fact is that the presence of a jury constitutes a wild card in litigation. Business cases seem to be most vulnerable to the jury unknowns because of the complexity of business cases. Complex cases seem to be on the increase for several reasons. First, causality becomes complex in product liability cases as in the DES suits when the causality of congenital damages to the daughters and granddaughters of DES mothers was an issue. Second, business is just more complex. For example, a shareholder suit against a board of directors for its actions in a hostile takeover will require reviews of market prices, discussion of market trends, and definitions of poison pills, shark repellants and leveraged buy-outs.

Former Chief Justice Warren Burger was one of the most vocal critics on the issue of mandatory jury trials in complex civil cases with his feelings that juries waste time and are often incapable of understanding the issues presented to them and the application of the law to the case. England and a good part of the third world nations have abandoned the jury system as an inadequate way of resolving civil disputes but the United States seems to hang on as a holdout because of the Constitutional aura surrounding the jury trial. This right is Jeffersonian in its origin and resulted from the complaints the colonists had against King George III for his trials without juries. Yet, it is important to note that most criticisms regarding the use of juries in complex suits is focused on civil cases and not on criminal prosecutions.

In the 1978 IBM antitrust case, a jury heard five months of testimony on IBM's alleged monopolization of various market segments in the computer industry. Again, there was a deadlocked jury and an interview with one of the jurors afterward gave some indication of the level of comprehension that resulted from the trial. The concept of "interface" was critical in the trial since the ability to interface would largely control whether there was ease of market entry and product compatibility. When a juror was asked what the term meant, the following reply was given:

Well, if you take a blivet, turn it off one thing and drop it down, it's an interface change, right?

In addition to the problems of complexity, there are additional difficulties with finding available jurors. Complex civil suits are quite lengthy, and this problem is only compounding. Trials are simply getting longer, as evidenced by the following statistics: in 1968, only 26 percent of the civil trials in federal district courts took one day; today that statistic is down to 14 percent; and in 1968, seventy-five cases lasted ten days or more and today that number is 359 cases. The question that arises about the jurors is: in cases like the five-month IBM trial, who were these people who were able to spend every day for five months sitting on a jury? Many critics noted that the result is an overabundance of retired individuals, housewives and the unemployed. There is an absence of professionals and business people who may have some experience with the issues. A cultural and financial gap is created when a jury has limited cross

Continued

sectional representation. The perceptions of individuals differ according to their circumstances. Peter Grace once noted that while he was working on the Grace Commission on government spending, he was dealing with billion dollar deficits and it was difficult for him to	return to his corporate life and get excited about million dollar losses. He had adapted the standard of the federal government as a means of evaluating dollars. The same thing happens inversely with jurors. For example, the American Bar Association's study of juror	deliberations indicated the verdict figures in a trade secret case ranged from $1.00 to $1.5 million and one juror commented as follows: "When you start talking millions, I can't relate to that. It doesn't mean anything to me. I have trouble paying $8.00 for parking everyday."

Absence of Technicalities

Under ADR, the parties have the opportunity to tell their stories. The strict procedural rules and evidentiary exclusions do not apply in these forums, and many companies feel more comfortable because ADR seems to be more of a search for the truth as opposed to a battle of processes. A mediator can serve as a communication link between the parties and help them to focus on issues and concerns. As one mediator expressed the benefit of ADR, "If you've done your job, . . . everyone goes home with big smiles."

Exhibit 4.3 provides a list of the benefits of ADR versus litigation.

Exhibit 4.3
Benefits of ADR versus Litigation

Litigation	Alternative Dispute Resolution
Technical discovery rules	Open lines of communication
Judicial constraints of precedent	Parties can agree to anything
Remedies limited (by law and precedent)	Creative remedies permitted
Backlog	Parties set timetable
Public proceeding	Privacy
Control by lawyers	Control by parties (or mediator/arbitrator)
Expensive	Cheaper
Strict procedures/timing	More flexibility
Judge/jury unknowns	Parties select mediator/arbitrator
Those who can afford to stay in win	Positions examined for validity
Benefit of enforcement	

FOR THE MANAGER'S DESK

A CHECKLIST FOR WHEN TO LITIGATE

Costs
Every lawsuit costs time and money. Costs of litigation include but by no means end with attorneys' fees, and other significant costs are often not considered before a business decides to become embroiled in a legal battle.

Legal Costs
The total legal fee must be considered in every case of possible litigation. A lawyer should be required to give an estimate of fees for any suit before the suit begins. The estimate should always include discovery costs. . . .

Time Costs (Hidden Downtime)
Litigation costs time as well as money. Indeed, in many cases, the loss of time can be more devastating to a firm than the financial loss. If a firm takes part in major litigation, chances are that its officers and possibly its directors will be involved in depositions, other forms of pretrial discovery and paperwork, and eventually in the trial itself. This involvement inevitably diverts the attention of the officers from their normal duties. . . .

Image Costs
If a lawsuit attracts the attention of the media, a firm may incur money and time costs stemming from public relations. Someone must be available to explain the firm's position to reporters and perhaps initiate an affirmative campaign to minimize negative publicity about the suit.

Capital Costs
Many auditors require that pending litigation be listed in the financial reports of the company. Ongoing litigation that carries the potential for great financial loss to a business can have a negative effect on the firm's financial rating and the ability to raise capital.

Costs of Alternatives to Litigation
The costs of litigation should be compared with the costs of alternatives to litigation. For example, it may not add much to potential litigation costs to submit a case to arbitration before pursuing full litigation. Such arbitration may produce a settlement that makes the trip to court unnecessary.

Costs of Not Litigating
There are costs for litigating, but there are also costs for not litigating. If the stakes are high enough, litigation may be worth pursuing regardless of the expense. For example, if a suit challenges the land records and thus the title to the land on which the business is located, the cost of not responding to the suit may be the loss of the property and the expense of reestablishing the business at another site. In a trademark or trade name suit the cost may be a product or company name or label. In a patent infringement case, the failure to sue an infringer may undermine a company's sales and its exclusivity in the marketplace.

Sometimes the price of not litigating or of not responding vigorously to litigation can

be a firm's very existence. For example, the product liability suits involving Johns-Manville and the other makers of asbestos threatened the lives of those firms because they involved the only product the firms made.

Public Relations Issues
Litigation is not a private matter. In every city, at least one reporter is assigned to the clerk's office in the state and federal courts for the purpose of checking on suits filed.

Many an electric bill goes unpaid simply because it is not good public relations for a utility company to appear in the newspapers and on television as the "bad guy" when a retired widow explains that the big power company has just filed suit because she has no money to pay her bill. . . .

Jury Appeal
When considering the effects of publicity on a case, a company should also consider the closely related matter of jury appeal. In some cases it will not matter how correct a business may be, how much of a remedy the law provides, or how wrong the other side is; the jury will simply side with the "little guy," and the business will have no chance of succeeding in the courtroom. For example, the Arthur Murray Dance Studios once fully litigated a case in which a man who had been severely injured in a car accident and was unable to complete the lessons in his contract with Arthur Murray (some 2,734 lessons, for which he had paid $24,812.40) sought to

Continued

recover his payments on the grounds that performance had become impossible. It is really very difficult to build jury appeal into such a case.

Discussion Questions
1. List the factors you should consider as you make a decision to litigate.

2. At the awards show for the Academy of Motion Picture Arts and Sciences (Academy), a character dressed as Snow White appeared in the opening musical number and sang with actor Rob Lowe. Walt Disney, Inc. had not given the Academy permission

to use the Snow White likeness, a trademarked Disney character. If you were the Walt Disney Corporation, would you sue the Academy?
3. List concerns you would have as an employer litigating a sexual harassment case.

Source: Frank Shipper and Marianne M. Jennings, *Avoiding and Surviving Lawsuits: The Executive Guide to Strategic Legal Planning for Business*, Jossey-Bass Publishing, Inc. © 1989. Excerpted and reprinted with permission with permission of the authors.

C O N S I D E R . . .

4.3 On its *Dateline NBC* news magazine program, NBC News broadcast a report on GM trucks manufactured between 1973 and 1987 and the safety issues surrounding the sidesaddle gas tanks on the trucks. The segment on the trucks and their gas tanks included a videotape of a staged crash conducted by NBC News and its consultants. When a car struck the side of a GM truck, the result was a fire, and the NBC correspondent reported that the gas tank had ruptured.

GM, having just had a $105 million verdict entered against it in a suit brought by parents for the death of their son in an accident involving one of the sidesaddle trucks, filed suit against NBC for defamation. GM had conducted its own investigation and had discovered that toy igniters had been used in the videotaped crash, that the speed reported in the segment was lower than the actual speed of the car, and that the gas tanks did not rupture as reported.

Within one day of the suit, NBC had its *Dateline NBC* anchors, Jane Pauley and Stone Phillips, read a lengthy on-air apology. In the apology, referred to by the *Wall Street Journal* as the most humiliating episode of crow-eating in NBC News's four decades, NBC admitted that it did not dispute the findings of the GM investigation.

Did GM make the correct decision to sue? Why didn't an NBC employee or consultant working on the segment raise the issue of the ethics of broadcasting a staged accident in a news program? Did NBC act appropriately in apologizing so quickly?

After the apology, NBC settled the suit by GM by agreeing to pay GM the $1 million cost of its investigation of the report.

E T H I C A L I S S U E S

4.1 The use of incendiary devices in the *Dateline* experiment was revealed when an employee's girlfriend turned over a videotape she made of the preparations. Many employees witnessed the use of the devices. Why didn't anyone object at the time?

WHEN YOU'RE IN LITIGATION. . .

There are times when a business must face litigation. In this portion of the chapter, the language, process, and strategies of civil litigation are explained.

How Does a Lawsuit Start?

A lawsuit begins because someone feels his or her rights have been violated. It is important to note that lawsuits are based on feelings. Whether rights have been violated and what damages were caused as a result of that violation are the issues that a trial will determine. The only restriction on the filing of a suit is that the plaintiff's claim of right is based on some law, either statutory law or common law.

People begin lawsuits. The judicial system does not unilaterally begin the enforcement of civil rights. This means that each individual has the responsibility of protecting his or her rights. The role of the judicial system is to determine whether those rights have been violated.

Although procedures vary from state to state, the following sections offer a general discussion of the procedures involved in a civil lawsuit. Exhibit 4.4 is a summary of the trial process.

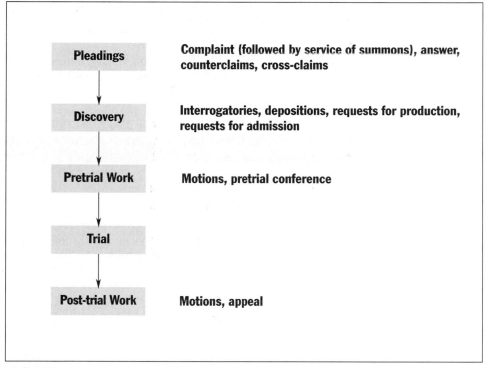

Exhibit 4.4
The Trial Process

THE COMPLAINT (PETITION)

The first step in a lawsuit is the filing of a document called a **complaint** or **petition**. The plaintiff must file the petition or complaint within certain time limits each state has for filing suit. These time limits are called statutes of limitations.

They vary depending upon the type of rights involved in a suit. The typical statute of limitations for personal injuries is two years; the typical limitation for contracts is usually four years.

A complaint is a general statement of the plaintiff's claim of rights. For example, if a plaintiff is suing for a breach of contract, the complaint must describe the contract, when it was entered into, and what the defendant did that the plaintiff says is a breach. Exhibit 4.5 (pg. 120) is a sample complaint in a suit over a car accident.

The complaint need not have every detail described in it. The standard for a valid complaint is that it must be definite enough in its description of what happened for the defendant to understand why the suit has been brought.

In addition to describing the violation of rights, the complaint must establish the subject matter jurisdiction of the court. For example, for a federal district court action, the complaint would either have to show that there was diversity and a damage claim of more than $50,000 or that a federal question was involved.

In some cases, the complaint is filed by a group of plaintiffs who have the same cause of action against one defendant. These types of suits are called **class action suits** and are typically filed in antitrust cases, shareholder actions against corporations, and employment discrimination cases. The class action suit enables a group of plaintiffs to share one lawyer and minimize litigation expenses while at the same time preserving their individual rights. Perhaps the most widely publicized type of class action lawsuit is the suit that results when a large jet airliner crashes and there are multiple deaths and injuries. All the plaintiffs were injured in the same event, and the defendant then litigates once with a group of plaintiffs.

Review current and concluded class action suits represented by The Alexander Law Firm: http://www.seamless.com/talf/class.html

---

FOR THE MANAGER'S DESK

COMPELLED INTO CLASS ACTION

Bradley A. Smith

I would like to introduce you to W. Pitts Carr, my attorney. I would like to, but I can't.

You see, I have never met Mr. Carr. I have never spoken to him on the phone. I have never written to him, nor has he ever written to me. I have never asked Mr. Carr to serve as my attorney, and he has never asked me if I wanted him to do so.

So how is it that Mr. Carr is my attorney? Well, awhile back (Mr. Carr has never told

me just when), a handful of the millions of people who have flown on airlines since 1988 decided that the airlines had engaged in illegal pricing and charged too much for their tickets. (I do not know much about the merits of this litigation, but if the airlines did these things, it doesn't seem to have worked out too well, what with all the bankruptcies and fare wars in the industry.) Anyway, Mr. Carr filed a class-action lawsuit. The class included me and literally millions of people who flew on major airlines between 1988 and mid-1992.

For those untutored in the American legal system, a class-action lawsuit is a method by which a very large number of people who have extremely similar or identical claims against the same defendant can sue in a single lawsuit. Originally, class actions were intended to conserve judicial resources by consolidating large numbers of claims into a single lawsuit, and to avoid the embarrassment of different juries reaching different verdicts for different plaintiffs on the basis of identical facts. At first, class actions were few.

Continued

However, as part of the "judicial reforms" in the 1960s, rules were changed making it much easier to file and maintain a class-action lawsuit. These reforms were based largely on the premise that it was good to encourage people to sue over small amounts.

Anyway, sometime in 1991 (or maybe earlier) W. Pitts Carr went into federal district court in Atlanta and, claiming to represent me, among others, sued most of America's major airlines.

As an attorney, I am familiar with class actions, and have even worked on class-action litigation. However, this was the first time I had ever been named a member of a class. When, in late August of 1992, I finally received notice of the suit, I got angry. I don't want to sue the airlines. I think the price I paid for my tickets was a fair price (lower, in fact, than in previous years), and I can't see how requiring the airlines to cough up millions in defense and settlement costs is going to do much to improve air travel, prevent industry bankruptcies or lower fares.

Furthermore, the court wasn't notifying me that the suit had begun. It was notifying me that the suit was, for all intents and purposes, over. In July 1992, Mr. Pitts reached a settlement with the airlines by which the airlines would set aside $408 million in flight certificates and $50 million in cash to settle the suit.

It gnawed at me that someone I don't know had, for two years, been claiming to represent me in order to sue someone I didn't want to sue, and no one had ever told me. I wondered briefly if I could sue Mr. Carr for invasion of privacy, but I realized I wouldn't get far—there are still a few restrictions left on frivolous litigation. So I calmed down and began to review the court's notice.

What struck me most was the way the form was skewed toward participation in the lawsuit. If I didn't do anything, I would automatically be considered a part of the class, as I had been for over a year. To get in on my share of the loot, all I had to do was put my name, address and Social Security number on a prepaid postcard, sign it, and drop it in the mail by Feb. 15, 1993. However, if I wanted to opt out of the class—if I wanted to state that W. Pitts Carr was speaking for me without my permission—then I had to write a letter to some post office box in New Jersey, pay my own postage, write in the lower left corner of the front of the envelope the words "class exclusion notice," and get it postmarked within two weeks.

I quickly realized that there was no chance that enough people would opt out to bring the suit to a halt. My dropping out would merely mean more for the remaining class members. Besides, the suit was already settled on the basis of my participation. By the time I was given the option to opt out, it was meaningless.

Then it dawned on me that all those class members were going to get only flight certificates, worth 10 percent or less off the cost of future airline tickets. What was going to happen to the $50 million in cash put up by the airlines? I scanned the court papers. Up to $20 million, I learned, was going to administer the settlement and provide notice to class members like me. The named plaintiffs who had actually had to respond to discovery requests would get between $2,500 and $5,000 each for their trouble. The way I figured it, this would probably leave a minimum of $29 million in cash. Who gets that? I found the fine print: "Plaintiffs' attorneys will apply to the court for an award of reasonable attorneys' fees . . . to be paid from the cash portion of the settlements." It seems that I was doing my part to make W. Pitts Carr a wealthy man.

Of course, it's not like the court refused to give me a chance to object to all this. Why, if I wanted to object to Mr. Carr's application for attorneys' fees, or to the settlement, all I had to do was file a motion with the clerk of the court within about two weeks of the date on which I received my notice. I thought about filing such a brief myself. But I was not in a position to drop my real clients to prepare one.

I decided to stay in the class and take my certificates. But they will not be used for travel. Rather, I will keep them as a reminder that in our legal system today not only can you be forced to defend a lawsuit you think is meritless—you can be forced to help prosecute one.

Another form of class action suit is the **derivative suit** in which shareholders sue a corporation to recover damages for actions taken by the corporation.

The final paragraphs of a complaint list the damages or remedies the plaintiff wants. The damages may be a **legal remedy** such as money, in which case a dollar amount is specified. The plaintiff may seek an **equitable remedy**, such as specific performance in the case of an action for breach of contract. **Specific performance** is an order of the court requiring a defendant to perform on a contract. In some cases, the plaintiff just wants the defendant to stop violating his or her rights. In those complaints, plaintiffs ask for **injunctions**, which are court orders requiring the defendant to stop doing the act complained of. In an action for nuisance, for example, an injunction orders the defendant to stop engaging in the conduct that causes the nuisance or orders the defendant to comply with a law or a previous decision. Or an injunction could order the construction of a fence to restrain animals that have become a nuisance.

Exhibit 4.5 is a sample complaint in an action involving a car accident.

Exhibit 4.5
Sample Complaint

Reed C. Tolman, Esq. (006502)
TOLMAN & OSBORNE, P.C.
4500 S. Lakeshore Drive, Suite 265
Tempe, Arizona 85282
Attorneys for Plaintiffs

SUPERIOR COURT OF ARIZONA

MARICOPA COUNTY

CRAIG CONNER and KATHY CONNER,) husband and wife, individually) and on behalf of their minor) son, CASEY CONNER,)) Plaintiffs,)) v.)) CARMEN A. CHENAL and THOMAS K.) CHENAL, wife and husband,)) Defendants,) _____)	**CV92-91319** COMPLAINT (Tort-Motor Vehicle)

For their complaint, plaintiffs allege:

1. Plaintiffs and defendants are residents of Maricopa County, Arizona.

2. This Court has jurisdiction over the subject matter under the Arizona Constitution, Art. 6, § 14.

3. Casey Conner is the minor son of Craig and Kathy Conner.

4. Carmen A. Chenal and Thomas K. Chenal are wife and husband. At all times relevant hereto, Carmen A. Chenal was acting for and on behalf of the marital community of which she is a member.

5. On or about July 20, 1990, defendant Carmen A. Chenal was driving her motor vehicle in the vicinity of Primrose Path and Cave Creek Road in Carefree, Arizona. At the time, Casey Conner was a

Continued

passenger in the back seat of defendants' vehicle, a 1976 Mercedes, ID No.11603312051326.

 6. At all times relevant hereto, defendant Carmen A. Chenal had a duty to care properly for the safety of Casey Conner. That duty included the responsibility to place Casey in an appropriate and functioning seatbelt.

 7. Prior to the accident that resulted in injuries to Casey Conner, Carmen A. Chenal knew that the right rear door of her vehicle was damaged and not functioning properly.

 8. Despite the duty Carmen A. Chenal had to care properly for the safety of Casey Conner, and despite her knowledge of a malfunctioning right rear door, Carmen A. Chenal negligently failed to place Casey in an appropriate and functioning seatbelt and negligently and carelessly operated her vehicle in such a way that the right rear door opened and allowed Casey to be ejected from the vehicle while the vehicle was in operation.

 9. Carmen A. Chenal's failure to exercise reasonable care for the safety of Casey and the failure to operate her vehicle in a careful and safe manner proximately caused Casey to suffer personal injuries.

 10. As a result of Casey Conner's injuries, he has experienced physical and psychological suffering, and his parents have incurred medical and other expenses, as well as lost earnings.

 WHEREFORE, plaintiffs request judgment against defendants for compensatory damages in an amount to be determined at trial.

 DATE this _____ day of July, 1992.
  TOLMAN & OSBORNE

By: _____
  Reed C. Tolman
  Southwest Business Center
  4500 S. Lakeshore Drive
  Suite 265
  Tempe, Arizona 85282

Source: Complaint appears courtesy of Tolman & Osborne, P.C., Tempe, AZ 85282.

Exhibit 4.5 *(Continued)*

THE SUMMONS

The complaint or petition of the plaintiffs filed with the clerk of the appropriate court—that is, the court with subject matter jurisdiction, inpersonam jurisdiction, and venue. The defendant, however, will not know of the suit just because it is filed. Thus the second step in a lawsuit is serving the defendant with a copy of the complaint and a **summons**, which is a legal document that tells the defendant of the suit and explains the defendant's rights under the law. Those rights include the opportunity to respond and the grant of a limited amount of time for responding. Exhibit 4.6 (pg. 122–123) is a sample summons.

A summons must be delivered to the defendant. Some states require that the defendant be given the papers personally. Other states allow the papers to be given to some member of the defendant's household or, in the case of a business, to an agent of that business (see Chapter 17 for a discussion of an agent's authority to receive lawsuit papers).

The summons is delivered by an officer of the court (such as a sheriff or magistrate) or by private firms licensed as **process servers**. Once the defendant is served, the server must file an affidavit with the court to indicate when and where the service was made. In rare circumstances, courts allow service of process by mail or by publishing the summons and complaint. These circumstances, however, are very limited and are carefully supervised by the courts.

Exhibit 4.6
Sample Summons

Name:
Address:
City, State, Zip:
Telephone:
State Bar Code:
Client:

ARIZONA SUPERIOR COURT, County of

ACTION NO:

SUMMONS

THE STATE OF ARIZONA TO THE DEFENDANTS:

YOU ARE HEREBY SUMMONED and required to appear and defend, within the time applicable, in this action in this court. If served within Arizona, you appear and defend within 20 days after the service of the Summons and Complaint upon you, exclusive of the day of service. If served out of the State of Arizona - whether by direct service, by registered or certified mail, or by publication—you shall appear and defend within 30 days after the service of the Summons and Complaint upon you is complete, exclusive of the day of service. Where process is served upon the Arizona Director of Insurance as an insurer's attorney to receive service of legal process against it in this state, the insurer shall not be required to appear, answer or plead until expiration of 40 days after date of such service upon the Director. Service by registered or certified mail without the State of Arizona is complete 30 days after the date of receipt by the party being served. Service by publication is complete 30 days after the date of first publication. Direct service is complete when made. Service upon the Arizona Motor Vehicle Superintendent is complete 30 days after filing the Affidavit of Compliance and return receipt or Officer's Return. RCP 4; ARS §§ 20-222, 28-502, 28-503.

Copies of the pleadings filed herein may be obtained by contacting the Clerk of Superior Court,
_____ County, located at _____,
Arizona. RCF 4.1(e).

SUMMONS
(Continued on Reverse Side)   1-1 °LawForms 10-92 1-93

YOU ARE HEREBY NOTIFIED that in case of your failure to appear and defend within the time applicable, judgment by default may be rendered against you for the relief demanded in the Complaint.

YOU ARE CAUTIONED that in order to appear and defend, you must file an Answer or proper response in writing with the Clerk of this Court, accompanied by the necessary filing fee, within the time required, and you are required to serve a copy of any Answer or response upon the Plaintiff's' attorney. RCP l0(D); ARS§12-311; RCP5.

The name and address of plaintiffs' attorney is:

SIGNED AND SEALED this date :_____

. . . .
Clerk

Method of Service:
☐ Private Process Service
☐ Sheriff or Marshall
☐ Personal Service
☐ Registered/Certified Mail (out of State)

By . . . .
Deputy Clerk

SUMMONS   1-1© LawForms 11-67, 3-84, 1-93

Source: Form appears courtesy of LawForms, Inc. Phoenix, AZ.

Exhibit 4.6 *(Continued)*

THE ANSWER

The parties' positions in a case are found in the **pleadings**. The complaint or petition is a pleading. The defendant's position is found in the **answer**, another part of the pleadings of a case. The defendant must file an answer within the time limits allowed by the court or risk default. The time limits are typically 20 days for in-state defendants and 30 days for out-of-state defendants. A failure to answer, or a **default**, is like a forfeit in sports: The plaintiff wins because the defendant failed to show up. The plaintiff can then proceed to a judgment to collect damages.

The defendant's answer can do any or all of several different things. The defendant may admit certain facts in the answer. While it is rare for a defendant to admit the wrong alleged by the plaintiff, the defendant might admit parts of the plaintiff's complaint, such as those that establish jurisdiction and venue. If the plaintiff already has correct venue, fighting that issue is costly and admitting jurisdiction is a way to move on with the case. If, however, the court lacked in personam jurisdiction over the defendant, the defendant could deny the jurisdiction.

A denial is a simple statement in the answer whereby the defendant indicates that the allegation is denied. An answer might also include a statement that the defendant does not know enough to admit or deny the allegations in the complaint and could include a demand for proof of those allegations.

An answer may also include a **counterclaim**, with which the defendant, in effect, countersues the plaintiff, alleging a violation of rights and damages against the plaintiff. The plaintiff must respond to the counterclaim using the same answer process of admitting and/or denying the alleged wrong. Exhibit 4.7 (pg. 125) is a sample answer.

The answer must be filed with the clerk of the court and a copy sent to the plaintiff. With the exception of amendments to these documents, the pleadings are now complete.

Seeking Timely Resolution of the Case

The fact that a suit has been filed does not mean that the case will go to trial. A great majority of suits are disposed of before trial because of successful motions to end them. **Motions** are requests to the court that it take certain action. They are usually made in writing and include citations to precedent that support granting the motion. Often the judge will have the attorney present oral arguments on the motion, after which the court then issues a ruling on the motion.

MOTION FOR JUDGMENT ON THE PLEADINGS

Either in the answer or by separate motion, a defendant can move for judgment on just the content of the pleadings. The theory behind a **motion for judgment on the pleadings** is that there is no cause of action even if everything the plaintiff alleges is true. For example, a plaintiff could file suit claiming the defendant is an annoying person. But unless the defendant is annoying to the extent of invading privacy or not honoring contracts, there is no right of recovery. The defendant in this case could win a motion for judgment on the pleadings because the law (perhaps unfortunately) does not provide a remedy for annoying people. A denial of a motion for judgment on the pleadings does not imply victory for the plaintiff. It simply means that the case will proceed with the next steps covered in this chapter.

MOTION TO DISMISS

A **motion to dismiss** can be filed any time during the proceedings but usually is part of the defendant's answer. Such a motion can be based on the court's lack of subject matter or in personam jurisdiction. Again, if the case is not dismissed it does not mean that the plaintiff wins; it just means that the case will proceed to the next steps and possibly trial.

MOTION FOR SUMMARY JUDGMENT

A **motion for summary judgment** has two requirements. Summary judgment is appropriate only when the moving party is entitled to a judgment under the law and when there are no issues of fact. Actions brought on the basis of motor vehicle accidents, for example, always involve different witnesses' testimonies and variations in facts. These types of cases cannot be decided by summary judgment. There are cases, however, in which the parties do not dispute the facts but differ on the applications of law. Consider, for example, a dispute involving a contract for the repair of a computer, including service and parts. Different laws govern contractual provisions for services and provisions for goods. The parties do not dispute the facts: they agree goods and services are covered in the contract. At issue is the question as to which law applies, and a summary judgment appropriately will resolve it. There may be other factual disputes about contract performance, but the partial summary judgment will determine which contract law will apply.

Grand, Canyon & Rafts
12222 W. Camelback
Phoenix, Arizona
555-5555
Attorneys for Defendant

SUPERIOR COURT OF ARIZONA

MARICOPA COUNTY

CRAIG CONNER and KATHY CONNER,)
husband and wife, individually)
and on behalf of their minor)
son, CASEY CONNER,)
)
       Plaintiffs,)
)
       v.)
)
CARMEN A. CHENAL and THOMAS K.)
CHENAL, wife and husband,)
)
       Defendants,)
_____)
	CV92-91319
	
	ANSWER

For their answer, defendants respond to plaintiffs' complaint as follows:

1. Admit paragraph one.
2. Admit paragraph two.
3. Have no knowledge to admit or deny paragraph three.
4. Have no knowledge to admit or deny paragraph four.
5. Admit paragraph five.
6. As for paragraphs 6 through 10, inclusive of plaintiffs' complaint, defendants have no knowledge of the statements alleged and deny all statements made therein.

Defendents deny any and all parts of plaintiffs' complaints not specifically mentioned herein.

DATED this _____ day of August, 1992.

      Grand, Canyon & Raft

By: _____

      Robert C. Canyon
      12222 W. Camelback
      Phoenix, Arizona

Exhibit 4.7
Sample Answer

Discovery

Trials in the United States are not conducted by ambush. Before the trial, the parties engage in a mandatory process of mutual disclosure of all relevant documents and other evidence. This court-supervised process of gathering evidence is called **discovery**. Under relatively recent changes to these procedural rules, the parties must offer to the other side lists of witnesses, all relevant documents, tangible evidence, and statements related to the case. Under the old discovery rules, the expense and difficulty of discovery techniques often meant the search for the truth was a cat-and-mouse game won by those with the most funds. Armed with the evidence in a case, the parties are more prepared, and perhaps more inclined, to negotiate a settlement.

The parties may still request documents from each other and some discovery tools remain a part of litigation.

REQUESTS FOR ADMISSIONS

A **request for admissions** asks the other side to admit a certain fact. There is some incentive to admit the facts requested if they are true because if these facts are denied and then proved at trial, attorney fees can be recovered for the costs of proving the facts that were denied. Requests for admissions sometimes merely request the other party to admit that a document is authentic. For example, the parties might have a dispute about the amount due under a contract but should be willing to admit that they signed the contract and that it is authentic. These requests for admission reduce the length of trials because an admission establishes a fact as true.

DEPOSITIONS

Depositions are the oral testimony of parties or witnesses that are taken under oath but outside the courtroom and before the trial. They can be taken long before a trial and help preserve a witness's or party's recollection. Depositions are also helpful in determining just how strong a case is. It is far better to discover damaging information in a deposition than it is to spend all the time and money to go to trial and discover the damaging testimony there.

LIMITATIONS ON DISCOVERY

Discovery has the general limitation of relevance. Only things that are evidence or could lead to the discovery of evidence are discoverable. However, discovery also has a specific limitation. Discovery cannot require the production of **work product**, which consists of the attorney's research, thoughts, analysis, and strategy. Discovery allows the other side the right to know all the evidence (if they ask for it), but it does not give them the right to know how that evidence will be used or what legal precedent supports a party's position. Discovery cannot request the production of legal research, trial strategy, or an attorney's comments or reactions to a witness.

REQUESTS FOR PRODUCTION

A **request for production** requires the other side to produce requested documents that have not already been given under the new discovery rules. For example, if a business is suing to recover lost profits, the defendant will probably want to request the income statements and perhaps income tax returns of that business so that he or she can prepare for damages issues. The new discovery rules provide for sanctions (penalties) for not turning over relevant documents at the start of a case.

C O N S I D E R . . . **4.4** Thomas D. Talcott was a Dow Corning materials engineer in 1976 when Dow was developing its silicone breast implant. Talcott had questions about the safety of the implants and raised his concerns, but product development, marketing, and sales went forward. In 1991 and 1992, concerns about the safety of the breast implants increased, and a number of lawsuits were filed by women who alleged that the implants had leaked and/or ruptured and caused cancer, lupus, and other autoimmune disorders. Lawyers for the women who have filed suit would like access to the company's records at the time Talcott was there to determine whether there is any documentation regarding his safety concerns. Can the lawyers get those documents? Can Talcott be required to testify in these cases? What kind of information can these plaintiffs obtain from the defendant companies in these product liability suits?

Source: Drawing by M. Stevens; © 1992 The New Yorker Magazine, Inc.

E T H I C A L   I S S U E S

4.2 If you had been Talcott and had strong feelings about the safety of a new product your employer was about to sell, what would you have done? Would it have done any good to bring it to the attention of all in the chain of command, from your supervisor up to the CEO? If you had been Talcott, would you have been able to continue to work for Dow Corning? Suppose that Talcott discussed his concerns about safety of the implants with everyone in the chain of command, but still the product was to enter the market. Would you notify a government agency or "leak" your information to the media? Why or why not?

Aftermath: Talcott left Dow Corning in 1976. He now serves as an expert witness for women who bring implant suits and is paid $400 per hour.

The Trial

If a case is not settled (and many are settled literally on the courthouse steps), the trial begins.

THE TYPE OF TRIAL—JURY OR NONJURY

Occasionally, the parties agree not to have a jury trial and instead have a trial to the court. In these cases, the judge acts as both judge and jury—both running the trial and determining its outcome. In highly technical cases it is sometimes better for both sides to have a knowledgeable judge involved than to try to explain the complexities of the case to a jury of laypersons.

If the parties do not agree on a nonjury trial, there are certain types of cases that carry a constitutional right to a trial by jury. The Seventh Amendment to the U.S. Constitution covers the jury requirement in civil trials:

In suits at common law, where the value in controversy shall exceed twenty dollars, the right of trial by jury shall be preserved, and no fact tried by a jury, shall be otherwise re-examined in any court of the United States other than according to the rules of common law.

Although this right is limited to what existed at common law at the time the U.S. Constitution was adopted, many states have expanded the right under their state constitutions. The absolute right to a jury trial exists only in criminal cases as covered in Article III and the Fifth and Sixth Amendments of the U.S. Constitution.

The pool of potential jurors and the selection of those jurors are resolved before trial. Usually, voting lists alone or combined with other lists (of driver's license holders, for example) are used as pools for potential jurors. People on these lists are randomly notified of a period of time during which they should report for jury duty. Many states excuse from jury duty certain individuals, like doctors and emergency workers, because of the needs they serve in society. Students are often excused if they are summoned for duty during the semester because of their peculiar obligations and time limitations on completing classes. Judges also usually have the power to excuse certain individuals who would experience hardship if they were required to serve. For example, a sole proprietor of a service business would have no income during the time of jury service and would probably be excused on a hardship basis.

Many more jurors than are needed are summoned to serve. These extra numbers are required because all the parties to a dispute participate in the selection of a jury.

Once a pool is available, the court begins the process of **voir dire**, which determines whether a potential juror is qualified to serve. Most states have jurors complete a questionnaire on general topics so that the selection process can move quickly. The questionnaire will cover such personal information as age, occupation, and so on. The questionnaire might also ask whether one has ever been a juror, a party to a lawsuit, or a witness. Exhibit 4.8 provides some sample voir dire questions.

1. Do you know any of the parties or lawyers in this case? (Asked after the judge introduces all parties and lawyers.)
2. What is your occupation?
3. Are you married?
4. What is your spouse's occupation?
5. Have you ever served on a jury?
6. Are you in favor of compensation for emotional injuries?
7. Do you believe in compensation for victims of police misconduct?
8. Do you support capital punishment?
9. What is your educational background?
10. Did you attend private or public school?
11. What is your spouse's educational background?
12. What seminars, courses, and workshops have you taken since you left school?
13. How old are you?
14. Do you have children? What are their ages and sexes?
15. How would people describe you?
16. Do you believe that people bring about their own misfortunes?
17. Do you do volunteer work? What type?
18. Do you have any relatives who are police officers?
19. Do you belong to a political party?
20. Did you serve in the armed forces?
21. Have you read about this case or heard TV/radio reports about it?
22. Have you formed an opinion about this case?
23. Do you equate laziness with black people?
24. Do you think there is any difference between black and white people?
25. Do you believe black people commit more crimes than white people?

Exhibit 4.8
Sample Voir Dire Questions

A juror can be removed from a jury panel for two reasons. First, a juror can be removed for cause, which means the juror is incapable of making an impartial decision in the case. If a juror is related to one of the attorneys in the case, for example, the juror would be excused for cause. Some jurors reveal their biases or prejudices, like racial prejudice, in the questionnaire they are required to complete. Others may express strong feelings of animosity toward the medical profession. Clearly, the removal of such jurors for cause in cases involving civil rights and malpractice suits is an important part of trial strategy.

Sometimes a juror cannot be excused for cause but an attorney feels uncomfortable about the juror or the juror's attitudes. In these circumstances, the lawyer issues a **peremptory challenge**, which excuses the juror. The peremptory challenge is the attorney's private tool. However, the use of peremptory challenges is limited. All states have a statute or court rule limiting the number of peremptory challenges an attorney may use in a trial. In recent years the U.S. Supreme Court has ruled that there are some limitations on the use of peremptory challenges. The Court has indicated that such a challenge cannot be based on either race or gender. If the trial judge suspects that either of these factors may have induced one of the lawyers to seek a preemptory challenge, the lawyer will be required to produce a plausible explanation for the use of the preemptory challenge that is unrelated to race or gender.

C O N S I D E R . . . **4.5** Jimmy Elem was convicted of second-degree robbery in a Missouri trial court. During voir dire, the prosecutor struck (dismissed) two black men, offering the following explanation:

I struck [juror] number twenty-two because of his long hair. He had long curly hair. He had the longest hair of anybody on the panel by far. He appeared to not be a good juror for that fact, the fact that he had long hair hanging down shoulder length, curly, unkempt hair. Also, he had a mustache and a goatee-type beard. And juror number twenty-four also has a mustache and goatee-type beard. Those are the only two people on the jury . . . with facial hair . . . . And I don't like the way they looked, with the way the hair is cut, both of them. And the mustaches and the beards look suspicious to me.

After his conviction, Elem challenged the prosecutor's use of the peremptory challenge on the two black men as racially motivated and demanded a new trial. Is the prosecutor's explanation race-neutral? [*Purkett* v. *Elem*, 115 S. Ct. 1769 (1995).]

Visit a jury consultant, Carolyn Robbins Jury Simulations, Inc.: http://www.crjury. com/

Jury selection is an art and a science. Jury consulting firms specialize in providing data to attorneys for jury selection. These firms do thorough checks of the potential jurors' backgrounds and offer statistics on the reactions of certain economic and social groups to trials and trial issues. There is much about a case at trial that is uncontrollable, but jury selection is a part of the process that, with thorough preparation, can increase the likelihood of favorable results by ensuring an optimally favorable jury panel. "The Science of Jury Selection" (pg. 131) provides some insight into the complexity of jury selection.

Jury or trial consultants perform jury profiles, find surrogate juries, and often conduct mock trials. The use of trial consultants has increased dramatically since the 1970s, and membership in the American Society of Trial Consultants has grown from 19 members in 1983 to 250 members today.

Jury consultants were used to assist in defense victories in the William Kennedy Smith rape trial and the O. J. Simpson double homicide trial.

TRIAL LANGUAGE

It is often difficult to piece together all the witnesses and evidence in a trial. A lengthy trial may leave the jurors confused. The attorney for each party, therefore, is permitted to make an **opening statement** that summarizes what that party hopes to prove and how it will be proved. Most attorneys also mention the issue of **burden of proof**, which controls who has the responsibility for proving what facts. Although the plaintiff has the burden of proving a case, the defendant has the burden of proving the existence of any valid defenses. There are various standards for meeting the burden of proof. In criminal cases, the standard is proof beyond a reasonable doubt. In civil cases the standard is proof by a preponderance of the evidence.

FOR THE MANAGER'S DESK

THE SCIENCE OF JURY SELECTION

Little known outside the legal world but a powerhouse within, Litigation Sciences, a unit of Saatchi & Saatchi PLC, employs more than 100 psychologists, sociologists, marketers, graphic artists and technicians. Twenty-one of its workers are Ph.D.s. Among other services, the firm provides pre-trial opinion polls, creates profiles of "ideal" jurors, sets up mock trials and "shadow" juries, coaches lawyers and witnesses, and designs courtroom graphics. . . .

Sophisticated trial consulting grew, ironically, from the radical political movements of the 1960s and 1970s before finding its more lucrative calling in big commercial cases. The Harrisburg 7 trial in 1972, in which Daniel Berrigan and others were charged with plotting anti-war-related violence, was a landmark.

In that case, a group of left-leaning sociologists interviewed 252 registered voters around Harrisburg. The researchers discovered that Episcopalians, Presbyterians, Methodists and fundamentalist Protestants were nearly always against the defendants; the lawyers resolved to try to keep them off the jury.

The defense also learned that college-educated people were uncharacteristically conservative about the Vietnam War. A more blue-collar panel became a second aim. Ultimately, that carefully picked jury deadlocked with a 10–2 vote to acquit, and the prosecution decided not to retry the case. Litigation consulting had arrived.

The fledgling science went corporate in 1977 when International Business Machines Corp. hired a marketing professor to help defend a complex antitrust case. The problem for IBM trial lawyers, Thomas Barr and David Boies, was how to make such a highly technical case understandable. As the trial progressed, they were eager to know if the jury was keeping up with them.

The solution devised by the professor was to hire six people who would mirror the actual jury demographically, sit in on the trial and report their reactions to him. He then briefed Messrs. Boies and Barr, who had the chance to tilt their next day's presentation accordingly. Thus, the "shadow" jury was born. Mr. Vinson, the professor, got the law bug and formed Litigation Sciences. (IBM won the case.) . . .

Influencing the Outcome
. . . Theoretically jurors are supposed to weigh the evidence in a case logically and objectively. Instead, Mr. Vinson says, interviews with thousands of jurors reveal that they start with firmly entrenched attitudes and try to shoe-horn the facts of the case to fit their views.

Pre-trial polling helps the consultants develop a profile of the right type of juror. If it is a case in which the client seeks punitive damages, for example, depressed, underemployed people are far more likely to grant them. Someone with a master's degree in classical arts who works in a deli would be ideal, Litigation Sciences advises. So would someone recently divorced or widowed. (Since Litigation Sciences generally represents the defense, its job is usually to help the lawyers identify and remove such people from the jury.)

For personal-injury cases, Litigation Sciences seeks defense jurors who believe that most people, including victims, get what they deserve. Such people also typically hold negative attitudes toward the physically handicapped, the poor, blacks and women. The consultants help the defense lawyers find such jurors by asking questions about potential jurors' attitudes toward volunteer work, or toward particular movies or books.

Lawyers remain divided about whether anything is wrong with all this. Supporters acknowledge that the process aims to manipulate, but they insist that the best trial lawyers have always employed similar tactics. "They have not have been able to articulate it all, if they did it," says Stephen Gillers, a legal ethics expert at New York University law school. "What you have here is intuition made manifest."

Because the plaintiff has the burden of proof, the plaintiff presents his or her case and evidence first. The attorney for the plaintiff decides the order of the witnesses, and questioning of these witnesses under oath is called **direct examination**. Although the defense cannot present witnesses during this part of the trial, it can question the plaintiff's witnesses after their direct examination is through. The defense questioning of plaintiff witnesses is called **cross-examination**, after which the plaintiff may again pose questions to clarify under **redirect examination**.

Once the plaintiff has finished his or her case, there must be enough evidence to establish a **prima facie case**, one in which the plaintiff has offered some evidence on all the elements required to be established for recovery. Although the evidence may be subject to credibility questions and be challenged by defense evidence, there must be some proof for each part of the claim. If the plaintiff does not meet this standard, the defendant can and may make a motion for a **directed verdict**. This motion for a directed verdict is made outside the jury's hearing and argued to the judge. If it is not granted, the trial proceeds with the defendant's case.

C O N S I D E R . . . **4.6** Racine Outdoor Signs, Inc. was named as a defendant in a lawsuit by Priscilla Bowlin. The lawsuit alleges that Grant Windsor, an employee of Racine, negligently ran into Bowlin's car and caused substantial injuries. Racine does indeed have an employee named Grant Windsor, but he was on vacation in Europe at the time of the accident, is 72 years old, and has not driven in three years. Would a motion to dismiss prior to trial be appropriate for Racine? What distinguishes this motion from a directed verdict?

If there is no directed verdict, the defendant has the same opportunity to present witnesses and evidence. Throughout the trial, the judge will apply the rules of evidence to determine what can and cannot be used as evidence. The typical evidence is a witness's testimony. However, there is also tangible evidence. In a contracts case, there is likely to be a great deal of paper evidence— letters, memos, and cost figures.

One of the evidentiary issues that has been debated and litigated over the past few years is the use of expert testimony in cases. The issue the courts face is determining whether the expert's testimony reflects scientific knowledge or whether the testimony is contrived for the trial (often called "junk science.") In *Daubert* v. *Merrell Dow Pharmaceuticals*, 113 S. Ct. 2786 (1993), the U.S. Supreme Court was faced with the issue of which experts and experiments should be allowed as evidence in a case brought by two children and their families against Merrell Dow for birth defects caused by their mothers' ingestion of Bendectin, an antinausea prescription drug marketed by Merrell Dow. The U.S. Supreme Court held that experts' testimony should be allowed only if the expert testimony reflects scientific knowledge derived by scientific method and it is relevant to the case. The Ninth Circuit has added an additional test since *Daubert:* The judge should determine whether the scientific tests were conducted previously or done only for purposes of preparing expert testimony.

C O N S I D E R . . .

4.7 Karsten Manufacturing Corporation filed suit against the Professional Golf Association (PGA) because the PGA had proposed a ban of Karsten's U-groove Ping brand clubs from professional play. Karsten hired Richard Smith, then an Arizona State University finance professor, to develop an economic model to correlate professional and cosumer usage. Smith's model showed that if pros play with Ping clubs, a proportionate number of duffers will play with them. If the pros can't use Ping clubs, Karsten is out of business because amateur golfers will not purchase Karsten products. Professor Smith said he conducted valid regression analysis. The attorney for the PGA, Larry Hammond, called it "junk science" that interferes with the real issues in the case. Should the Smith model be admitted? Does it make a difference that the model was developed only for the case? Does it make a difference that Professor Smith's consulting firm was paid over $1 million for the model?

Business Planning Tip

Dos and Don'ts of Litigation

DON'T:	DO:
Circulate memos after you've been sued trying to establish blame	Collect all data and information
Destroy documents or other evidence	Disclose everything to your lawyer
Discuss the case with anyone except with the approval of your attorney	Propose ADR
Threaten employees or suggest what their testimony should be	Correct any problems that may have contributed to the suit (such attorney correction is not admissible in the case)
Handle media inquiries without consulting your attorney	

There are restrictions on the forms and types of evidence that can be used at trial. Most people are familiar with the hearsay rule of evidence. **Hearsay** is evidence offered by a witness who does not have personal knowledge of the information being given but just heard it from someone else. For example, suppose that Arkansas Sewing and Fit Fabric are involved in contract litigation. Fit says there was no contract. Arkansas has a witness who overheard the president of Fit Fabric talking to someone on a plane saying he had a contract with Arkansas but had no intention of performing on it. The witness's testimony of the airplane conversation is hearsay and cannot be used to prove the contract existed. The reason for the hearsay rule is to keep evidence as reliable as possible. The person testifying about the hearsay may not know of the circumstances or background of the conversation and he or she is testifying only to what was said by another.

Once the evidence is presented and the parties are finished with their cases, there is one final "go" at the jury. The parties are permitted to make **closing arguments**, which review the evidence that was presented, highlight the important points for the jurors, and point out the defects in the other side's case.

After the cases and closing arguments are presented, the jurors are given their **instructions**. These instructions tell the jurors what the law is and how to apply the law to the facts presented. The instructions are developed by the judge and all the attorneys in the case.

Jury deliberations are done privately; they cannot be recorded and no one can attend the deliberations except the jurors. Jurors can, but are not required to, discuss what happened during the deliberations after they are ended and a decision is returned to the court.

The U.S. Supreme Court has ruled that jury verdicts need not be unanimous. A state can adopt a rule that requires only a simple majority or three-fourths of the jury to agree on a verdict. In those states requiring unanimous verdicts, it is not unusual for juries to be unable to agree on a verdict. The jurors have then reached a deadlock, which is called a **hung jury**. If a trial results in a hung jury, the case can be retried. There is, however, the additional expense of retrying the case.

The result of jury deliberations is the **verdict**. The verdict is given to the judge and is usually read by the judge's clerk.

Even after the verdict, the case is not over. The losing party can make several motions to get around the verdict. One such motion is for a new trial, wherein the attorney argues the need and reason for a new trial to the judge.

Another motion after the verdict, one that a judge is less likely to grant, is a motion for a **judgment NOV**. *NOV* stands for *non obstante veredicto,* which means "notwithstanding the verdict." In other words, the moving attorney is asking the trial judge to reverse the decision of the jury. The basis for granting a judgment NOV is that the jury's verdict is clearly against the weight of the evidence. Occasionally, juries are swayed by the emotion of a case and do not apply the law properly. It is, however, a strong show of judicial authority for a judge to issue a judgment NOV, and they are rare.

Even if no motions are granted, the case still may not be over; it can go to an appellate court for review. Such an appeal must be done within a specified time limit in each state. Here the trial has come full cycle to the principle of judicial review and stare decisis. Exhibit 4.9 (pg. 136) summarizes of steps in civil litigation.

ISSUES IN INTERNATIONAL LITIGATION

As noted earlier, international courts have no enforcement powers. They serve as avenues for voluntary mediation. However, courts in each nation in which a firm is doing business would have jurisdiction over that firm in the nation's court system. In a recent infringement dispute over Mattel's "Barbie" and the French doll "Sindy," the parties litigated in London, where both firms were doing business and the dolls were selling well.

Among the critical questions that arise in international litigation are which set of laws applies and what court is the appropriate forum for a lawsuit that involves citizens of different countries. For example, many non-U.S. citizens who are injured in their own countries by products made by U.S. firms will generally be able to recover more under the product liability and tort laws of the United States. In *Piper Aircraft Co.* v. *Reyno,* 454 U.S. 235 (1981), the pilot and five passengers were killed when a charter flight from Blackpool to Perth, Scotland, crashed in the Scottish highlands. The pilot and passengers were traveling in a twin-engine Piper Aztec, an aircraft manufactured in Pennsylvania by Piper Aircraft Co. The British Department of Trade conducted an investigation of the crash and determined that its cause was mechanical failure. The relatives and estates of the passengers brought suit in the United States against Piper Aircraft .Scottish law does not recognize strict tort liability (see Chapter10), and U.S. laws on liability and damages are far more favorable than those of Scotland. The Supreme Court held that the case was properly heard in

Scotland because the accident was in Scotland and all the parties in the case were either English or Scottish.

A similar ruling was made with respect to the 2,500 victims of the Union Carbide gas leak in Bhopal, India. Some of the victims filed suit in the United States because the law and damages provisions here afforded them much greater relief. Their suit was dismissed to India, and the court added that Union Carbide would be required to submit to the jurisdiction of Indian courts and be required to follow discovery rules of the United States.

Some businesspeople feel the United States has too many lawyers and that too much legal activity leads to higher costs and a loss of our competitive edge in the international market. "The United States and Its Lawyers" (pg. 137) offers some data on this issue.

Our legal system and its parties vary greatly from other countries' systems. "Following Japan in Reform" describes some of the limitations other countries use to control litigation.

FOR THE MANAGER'S DESK

FOLLOWING JAPAN IN REFORM

Japan's Reforms for Controlling Litigation

Many businesspeople have argued that too many lawyers and lawsuits hurt the United States in the competitive international market. The following curbs instituted in Japan have been cited as ways of controlling litigation:

Limits on the Number of Lawyers
To become a *bengoshi* (lawyer) in Japan, an individual must win a slot at the Legal Training & Research Institute. This government-run school accepts only 2 percent of the 35,000 annual applicants. Only 400 new *bengoshi* are added each year to Japan's 14,336 lawyers.

Limits on Recovery
No class actions or contingent fees are permitted in Japan.

Costs to Plaintiffs
Plaintiffs are required to pay money to their lawyers up front. The amount required is 8 percent of the recovery sought plus the nonrefundable filing fee.

Discovery Limitations
There is no discovery from either side. Parties go to trial not knowing the evidence the other side will present. The theory here is that plaintiffs must be certain about their evidence before a case goes to trial.

Limits on Damage Awards
Judges, not juries, determine damages, and even in wrongful death cases the damages do not exceed $150,000.

Encouragement of Settlement and Cultural Disdain for Confrontation
In Japan, a cultural pride exists in being able to resolve disputes outside the courtroom; those who must litigate are looked down upon.

Discussion Questions
1. If the United States adopted the Japanese litigation system, would you feel that your rights would be affected?
2. Is the United States beginning to adopt a cultural attitude to eliminate confrontation by embracing ADR?
3. In the English court system, the loser pays court costs and the costs of the other party involved in the litigation. Should such a rule be adopted in the United States? In all cases? Would you be less willing to pursue a case for yourself or your company if you knew that you would be required to pay if you lost the case?

Sources: Michele Galen et al., "Guilty," *Business Week*, April 13, 1992, pp. 60–66; and ABA Report on International Lawyers (1990).

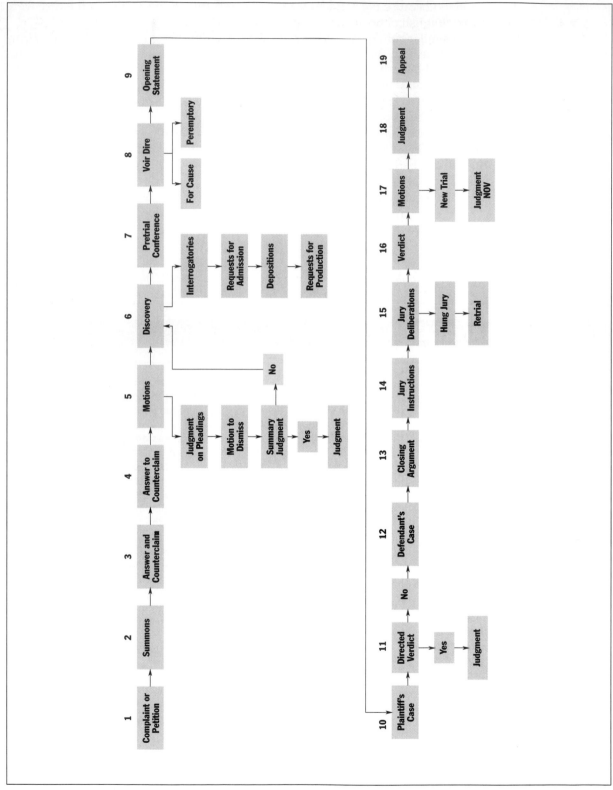

Exhibit 4.9
Steps in Civil Litigation

FOR THE MANAGER'S DESK

THE UNITED STATES AND ITS LAWYERS

Spending on legal services in the United States rose from $10 billion in 1972 to $100 billion in 1991. The Institute for Legal Studies at the University of Wisconsin compiled statistics on the numbers of lawyers in various countries throughout the world (see table).

In 1987, the U.S. insurance industry paid $117 billion in liability-loss payments, a figure that amounts to 2.5 percent of the U.S. gross national product (GNP). That percentage is three times higher than that of any other nation listed in the table presented here. Critics of lawyers argue that this "tort tax" deters innovation and research and development by U.S. businesses. Lawyers maintain that tort recovery encourages safety precautions and ensures that victims are adequately compensated and cared for after their injuries.

A survey of state court case filings in 24 states shows that 33 percent of all the cases filed were domestic relations and 14 percent involved contract disputes. Also, the argument is made that law without lawyers is not a system of justice but rather a system that leaves victims without representation and remedies.

Country	Lawyers	Lawyers per 100,000 population
Pakistan	46,000	508.4
Singapore	990	396.0
United States	780,000	312.0
Belgium	21,104	214.0
Finland	9,314	191.6
Germany	15,900	190.1
Israel	7,500	182.5
Argentina	50,000	169.4
Canada	42,710	168.5
Venezuela	31,400	159.1
Australia	3,000	145.7
New Zealand	4,700	144.6
England and Wales	68,067	134.0
Scotland	6,350	124.5
Chile	12,300	104.9
Japan	124,000	101.6
Spain	32,540	84.6
Italy	46,401	81.2
Costa Rica	1,959	80.3
Ireland	2,500	71.4
Brazil	85,716	69.1
Norway	4,412	68.7
Egypt	30,000	68.2
Nepal	1,000	63.2
Denmark	3,000	58.7
Switzerland	3,300	51.4
France	27,700	49.1
Panama	900	43.1
Turkey	22,395	42.1
Former U.S.S.R.	100,000	35.3
Holland	5,124	35.2
India	247,373	34.4
Others	66,399	—
WORLD TOTAL	2,024,054	

In their book *The Liability Maze*, Peter Huber and Robert Litan of the Brookings Institution in Washington, D.C., note:

But those who worry that overlawyering is eroding America's competitiveness say the problem is deeper. Would America not be better off, they ask, if it spent more time innovating instead of litigating? If more of its brightest young minds became engineers rather than lawyers?

Discussion Questions

1. Do you believe the United States is overlawyered?
2. Do you think that lawyers are necessary to cope with all the laws? For example, the Code of Federal Regulations has quadrupled in size since 1960. Are there too many regulations?
3. Do lawyers have a conflict of interest in cases in which they have an economic interest if the litigation is prolonged? What ethical obligations should they have with respect to settlement of a case?
4. If you were charged with a crime or faced with a civil suit, would you feel comfortable handling the case without a lawyer?

Sources: "A Survey of the Legal Profession," *The Economist*, July 18, 1992, p. 55; Peter Huber and Robert Litan, *The Liability Maze.*

SUMMARY

How can businesses resolve disputes?
- Alternative Dispute Resolution (ADR)—means of resolving disputes apart from court litigation

Types of ADR:
- Arbitration—hearing with relaxed rules of evidence
- Mediation—third party acts as go-between
- Minitrial—private judge and courtroom; shortened trial
- Rent-a-judge—hired judge resolves dispute
- Summary jury trial—advisory verdict by jurors in a mock trial
- Early neutral evaluation—third-party evaluation before litigation proceeds
- International Chamber of Commerce (ICC)—voluntary international court that offers arbitration in international disputes

What strategies should business follow if litigation is inevitable?
- Voir dire—jury selection method to screen bias
- Production—obtain and produce documents
- Deposition—questioning of witnesses under oath

How do courts proceed with litigation?
- Litigation—use of courts to resolve disputes
- Complaint—plaintiff's statement of a case
- Summons—document to serve defendant with lawsuit
- Answer—defendant's response in litigation
- Statute of limitations—time limit for filing suit
- Discovery—advance disclosure of evidence in case
- Deposition—testimony in advance of trial while under oath
- Reform—steps to limit suits and damage awards
- Trial—jury selection done through voir dire
- Opening statements
- Plaintiff's case
- Defendant's case
- Evidence consists of testimony, tangible evidence but not hearsay to prove the case

QUESTIONS AND PROBLEMS

1. Anna's Dresses, Inc., was delinquent in its payment to one of its suppliers. Anna's intended to pay them, but it had a cash flow problem and chose to pay rent to its landlord so as not to be evicted from its store rather than make a payment to the supplier. Anna's president is served with a complaint for breach of contract and a summons. The complaint lists the supplier as the plaintiff. What has happened? What must Anna's do now?
2. In the Johns-Manville asbestos litigation, Samuel Greenstone, an attorney for 11 asbestos workers, settled their claims for $30,000 and a promise that he would not "directly or indirectly participate in the bringing of new actions against the Corporation." The 1933 case settlement was documented in the minutes of Johns-Manville's board meeting. Could the information in the minutes be used in later litigation against Johns-Manville? How could a plaintiff's attorney obtain the information?

3. In question two, do you feel Greenstone made an ethical decision in his agreement? Wasn't his loyalty to his 11 clients and his obligation to obtain compensation for them? Would you have agreed to the no-further-participation-in-a-lawsuit clause? Would you, if you had been an executive at Johns-Manville, have supported the clause?

4. Whaler Manufacturing entered into a contract to buy seven lathes from Hooper, Inc. Hooper delivered the machines and Whaler was to pay for them over a period of one year. Detroit Second National Bank came to repossess the machines from Whaler because Hooper had failed to make payment. To stop the repossession, Whaler paid Detroit the $5,000 due on Hooper's loan from Detroit. Because Whaler had only agreed to pay $4,000 for the machines to Hooper, it stopped its payments. Hooper sued for breach of contract. In answering Hooper's lawsuit, what does Whaler need to include?

5. A discrimination suit by a former flight attendant against Atlantic East Airlines is going to trial. Jury selection has begun. An executive from Atlantic East notices that a member of the potential juror panel was a flight attendant responsible for pregnancy leave reforms among airline flight attendants during the early 1980s. This potential juror is no longer a flight attendant and is raising two small children at home. The executive informs Atlantic East's lawyer. Can the lawyer do anything to prevent the woman from sitting on the jury?

6. Applegate is in litigation with Magnifium over a contract breach. Applegate has been approached by a former janitor for Magnifium who can testify regarding conversations about the contract between Magnifium executives. The janitor heard them when the executives had stayed late at work and he was doing his cleaning. Can Applegate use the statements at trial?

7. What benefits exist in using alternative dispute resolution? Why would a business choose one method of alternative dispute resolution as opposed to another type?

8. Ralph Dewey has just brought an age discrimination suit against his employer, Waddle Walk, Inc., a manufacturer of baby walkers, jumpers, and other toddler equipment. Dewey alleges that his salary is much lower than the other, younger managers at the company. What information would Dewey need to establish his case? What discovery tool should he use to obtain that information?

9. The ABC news program, Day One, ran two reports on February 28 and March 7, 1995, that left viewers with the impression that Philip Morris Company spikes its cigarettes with nicotine to make them more addictive. Philip Morris filed a $10 billion defamation suit against Capital Cities/ABC Inc. for defamation on March 24, 1995. The suit alleged that the "spiking" report was untrue. An ABC News spokesman said in response to the suit, "ABC News stands by its reporting on this issue."

Philip Morris is based in New York, the suit was filed in Richmond, Virginia, and a news conference to announce the suit was held in Washington, D.C., on the day hearings were to begin to determine whether the FDA should regulate nicotine as a drug. Philip Morris was not the primary target of the *Day One* report, but it was mentioned by name in the broadcasts. Philip Morris did not ask ABC for a retraction prior to filing suit.

J. D. Lee, a Knoxville, Tennessee, plaintiff's attorney who has had experience litigating against tobacco companies noted that the prospect of getting his hands on Philip Morris's internal documents in such a suit made him gleeful: "I would have a field day with Philip Morris."

By September, 1995, ABC and Philip Morris had settled the suit. ABC issued the following public apology and agreed to pay attorneys' fees for Philip Morris:

> *It is the policy of ABC News to make corrections where they are warranted.*
>
> *On February 28 and March 7, 1994, the ABC program,* Day One, *aired segments dealing with the tobacco industry. Philip Morris filed a defamation lawsuit alleging that the segments wrongly reported that, through the introduction of significant amounts of nicotine from outside sources, Philip Morris "artificially spikes" and "fortifies" its cigarettes with nicotine, and "carefully controls" and "manipulates" nicotine for the purpose of "addicting" smokers.*
>
> *Philip Morris states that it does not add nicotine in any measurable amount from any outside source for any purpose in the course of its manufacturing process, and that its finished cigarettes contain less nicotine than is found in the natural tobacco from which they are made.*

ABC does not take issue with those two statements. We now agree that we should not have reported that Philip Morris adds significant amounts of nicotine from outside sources. That was a mistake that was not deliberate on the part of ABC, but for which we accept responsibility and which requires correction. We apologize to our audience and Philip Morris.

ABC and Philip Morris continue to disagree about whether the principal focus of the reports was on the use of nicotine from outside sources. Philip Morris believes that this was the main thrust of the programs. ABC believes that the principal focus of the reports was whether cigarette companies use the reconstituted tobacco process to control the levels of nicotine in cigarettes in order to keep people smoking. Philip Morris categorically denies that it does so. ABC thinks the reports speak for themselves on this issue and is prepared to have the issue resolved elsewhere.

ABC and Philip Morris have agreed to discontinue the defamation action.

What do you think of Philip Morris's decision to litigate? Would you have made the same decision? Was it a public relations tactic as well as an enforcement of rights? What motivation did both sides have for settling the case? Evaluate the ethics of ABC News in running the story. Evaluate the ethics of Philip Morris in filing suit without first approaching ABC for a retraction.

10. Jared Neil is a U.S. citizen. He flew from New York City to Stockholm, Sweden, on a flight of Transnational Airways, a British corporation. The plane crashed as it was landing in Stockholm. Although no passengers were killed, Neil and others were severely injured. The crash was caused by the pilot's negligence. Could Neil sue Transnational? In which country? Are there any restrictions on his recovery?

ETHICS, COURTS, AND LITIGATION

Many businesses, lawmakers, and legal experts feel that there is too much litigation. There are currently pending, at state and federal levels, reforms in the types of suits that may be filed as well as limits on damage awards. In the following materials, you will have the opportunity to review the issues of rights, damages, courts, litigation, and the role of ADR. The following case is one cited frequently for excesses in litigation against businesses.

Problem 1

Review the following case and answer the questions presented.

THE $4,000,000 PAINT JOB

BMW of North America, Inc. v. *Gore*   646 So. 2d 619 (Ala. 1994)

FACTS

Dr. Ira Gore, Jr., purchased a new 1990 BMW 535i automobile from German Auto, Inc., a Birmingham, Alabama, dealership. Dr. Gore, a graduate of Harvard and Duke Medical School, signed a "Retail Buyers Order" and "Acknowledgment of Disclosure" in which he acknowledged that the car might have sustained damage, that he had inspected it and agreed to accept it.

Gore drove the car for nine months before taking it to "Slick Finish," an auto detail shop. Gore took the car in to make it "snazzier." The auto detailer told Gore that the car had been partially refinished. Gore later determined that the refinishing had been done because of acid rain damage to the paint on the car during transit from Germany (BMW AG) to the North American vehicle preparation center in Brunswick, Georgia. The preparation center (BMW NA) did not disclose any damage to a dealer or customer if the damage was less than 3 percent of the manufacturer's suggested retail price (MSRP). The refinishing of Gore's auto cost $601.

Upon his discovery that the automobile had been refinished, Gore sued German Auto, BMW AG, and BMW NA, alleging that the failure to disclose the refinishing constituted fraud, suppression of a material fact, and breach of contract. With respect to the BMW defendants, only the suppression claim was submitted to the jury. The jury returned a verdict against all three defendants for $4,000 in compensatory damages, and it assessed $4,000,000 in punitive damages against the BMW defendants jointly, based on a determination that the BMW defendants had been guilty of gross, malicious, intentional, and wanton fraud. The trial court entered a judgment on that verdict and subsequently denied post-judgment motions filed by the BMW defendants.

The BMW defendants appealed.

JUDICIAL OPINION

Per curiam

BMW NA's chief argument is that the punitive damages award is excessive when measured by the factors stated in *Green Oil Co.* v. *Hornsby* because: (1) the award of punitive damages is 1,000 times the award of compensatory damages and bears no reasonable relationship to the risk of harm, which is purely economic; (2) BMW NA's conduct was much less reprehensible than that of defendants in other cases in which juries made much smaller damages awards; (3) it did not profit from its nondisclosure, because German Auto paid full price for the car; (4) the fact that it has a substantial net worth does not alone justify an exorbitant award; and (5) Gore never tried to resolve the matter without resorting to litigation.

This Court also stated in *Green Oil*:

The following could be taken into consideration by the trial court in determining whether the jury award of punitive damages is excessive or inadequate:

(1) Punitive damages should bear a reasonable relationship to the harm that is likely to occur from the defendant's conduct as well as to the harm that actually has occurred. If the actual or likely harm is slight, the damages should be relatively small. If grievous, the damages should be much greater.

(2) The degree of reprehensibility of the defendant's conduct should be considered. The duration of this conduct, the degree of the defendant's awareness of any hazard which his conduct has caused or is likely

to cause, any concealment or 'cover-up' of that hazard, and the existence and frequency of similar past conduct should all be relevant in determining this degree of reprehensibility.

(3) *If the wrongful conduct was profitable to the defendant, the punitive damages should remove the profit and should be in excess of the profit, so that the defendant recognizes a loss.*

(4) *The financial position of the defendant would be relevant.*

(5) *All the costs of litigation should be included, so as to encourage plaintiffs to bring wrongdoers to trial.*

(6) *If criminal sanctions have been imposed on the defendant for his conduct, this should be taken into account in mitigation of the punitive damages award.*

(7) *If there have been other civil actions against the same defendant, based on the same conduct, this should be taken into account in mitigation of the punitive damages award.*

BMW NA argues that there is no evidence that its adoption of the nondisclosure policy was "gross, oppressive, or malicious."

The evidence shows that BMW adopted the policy of nondisclosure in 1983 and that the policy applied to the sale of all automobiles in all states. Based on this evidence, we conclude that Gore satisfactorily proved that BMW NA engaged in a pattern and practice of knowingly failing to disclose damage to new cars, even though the damage affected their value, and that BMW NA followed this policy for several years. Based on that evidence, we conclude that Gore satisfied the burden placed on him to show that BMW NA's conduct was reprehensible.

Was the Conduct Profitable to BMW NA? The next issue we address is whether the conduct was profitable to BMW NA. The evidence shows that it was. In fact, the jury awarded Gore $4,000 in compensatory damages.

One of the purposes for assessing punitive damages is to remove the profit resulting from a fraud or misrepresentation. Punitive damages should be in excess of the profit, so that the wrongdoer recognizes a loss.

It is clear from the evidence that the $4 million judgment would not have a substantial impact upon BMW NA's financial position.

If there have been other civil actions against the same defendant, based on the same conduct, this fact should be taken into account in mitigation of the punitive damages award. BMW NA, in an appendix to its brief, states that Gore's counsel in this case has filed 24 other actions against BMW NA in Alabama and Georgia. In one of those actions, *Yates* v. *BMW of North America, Inc.*, 642 So.2d 937 (Ala.Civ.App.), cert. quashed, 642 So.2d 937, the case was tried by a jury in the same circuit in which this case was tried, but that jury, while awarding a similar amount of compensatory damages, awarded zero punitive damages.

In *Yates*, the purchaser was a doctor, as here. In *Yates*, the jury heard evidence of BMW NA's policy of nondisclosure and of the number of vehicles sold throughout the United States that had some repair work done on them before they were sold as new automobiles. However, in *Yates*, the jury, although it received similar instructions on the issue of punitive damages, awarded none. This Court views the disparity between the two jury verdicts— $4 million in punitive damages in this case, and $0 in the *Yates* case—as a reflection of the inherent uncertainty of the trial process and a result of the fact that the cases were tried differently to different juries and at different times. Despite similarities, the trial in *Yates* was not identical to the trial in the case before us. The conclusions reached by 12 different persons upon hearing different evidence that was argued differently cannot dictate the conclusion of the jury in this case.

It seems apparent from the record that the jury's punitive damages award is based upon a multiplication of $4,000 (the diminution in value of the Gore vehicle) times 1,000 (approximately the number of refinished vehicles sold in the United States).

Gore's counsel specifically argued the following during closing:

They've taken advantage of nine hundred other people on those cars that were worth more. . . . If what Mr. Cox said is true, they have profited some four million dollars on those automobiles. Four million dollars in profits that they have made that were wrongfully taken from people. That's wrong, ladies and gentlemen. They ought not be permitted to keep that. You ought to do something about it. . . .I urge each and every one of you and hope that each and every one of you has the courage to do something about it. Because, ladies and gentlemen, I ask you to return a verdict of four million dollars in this case to stop it.

In defending the jury's punitive damages award, Gore argues that the harm is "likely to occur" in the future if the substantial award is not upheld, because the policy of nondisclosure was not changed before the verdict in this case was returned, even though BMW NA had been faced with lawsuits and with requests by dealers that it change the policy. Gore contends that, because of the size of the award, "[f]ive days after this punitive damages verdict, BMW NA adopted a full disclosure policy."

We find no error in the admission of the evidence that showed how pervasive the nondisclosure policy was and the intent behind BMW NA's adoption of it. However, when applying the reasonable relationship test to the amount of punitive damages to be awarded in this case, we do not consider those acts that occurred in other jurisdictions.

After thoroughly and painstakingly reviewing this jury award in light of the factors discussed above, we hold that a constitutionally reasonable punitive damages award in this case is $2,000,000, and that a remittitur of the $4 million jury verdict

is appropriate. Therefore, the trial court's order denying BMW NA's motion for a new trial is affirmed on the condition that the plaintiff file with this Court within 21 days a remittitur of damages in the sum of $2,000,000; otherwise, the judgment will be reversed and this cause remanded for a new trial as to the defendant BMW NA.

CASE QUESTIONS
1. What was wrong with Dr. Gore's car and how did he discover the problem?
2. What basis did the jury use for awarding $4,000,000 in punitive damages?
3. What arguments do the various BMW corporations make in order to try to have the appellate court reduce the damages?
4. Would you have awarded the $4,000,000? Why or why not?
5. If you were BMW, would you change the disclosure policy?
6. What options does the appellate court give BMW?

INTEGRATIVE PROBLEMS

PART 1

Problem 2

Consider the history of the following cases

Agent Orange—250,000 Claims Herbicide used as a defoliant in the Vietnam war. Vietnam veterans allege a variety of injuries due to small amount of dioxin in Agent Orange. Despite wide spectrum of claims, class-action status is achieved—an important first. In 1985 a consortium led by Dow Chemical agrees to a $180 million settlement, despite plaintiffs' failure to prove link between dioxin and claimed injuries.

Asbestos—270,000 Claims Widely used insulation material. Litigation explodes when studies show that inhaling asbestos fibers can cause lung disease. Issue never gains class-action status; clogs up courts for years. Most manufacturers bankrupted, including Johns-Manville, the largest. Manville creates a $2.5 billion trust. Payments begin in 1989, stop a year later when the trust starts to run dry. Payments resume this year [1995] to 270,000 claimants.

Dalkon Shield—327,000 Claims Intrauterine birth control device. Government forces manufacturer A. H. Robins to suspend sales in 1974 after study links device to pelvic inflammatory disease, resulting in spontaneous abortions. Nine years later, company files for bankruptcy. Litigation settled in 1988 when plaintiffs force sale of Robins to American Home Products for $3.3 billion; $2.5 billion of proceeds goes into a trust for claimants.

Silicone Breast Implants—480,000 Claims Becomes mother of all mass torts in 1992 when in the wake of growing concerns that implants cause auto-immune disease, the government calls for a moratorium on use. Within two years, four major defendants, led by Dow Corning, face over 20,000 lawsuits. Defendants agree to $4.25 billion "global" settlement—which lures an astounding 480,000 claimants. Settlement craters; Dow Corning files for bankruptcy. Final outcome yet to be determined.

Source: Wilton Woods, "Mass Torts Come of Age," *FORTUNE*, October 16, 1995, p.76. © 1995 Time Inc. All rights reserved.

Is it better to have the companies file for Chapter 11 bankruptcy? What lessons should companies learn from these mass litigations?

Problem 3

The following op-ed piece was written by Pete Van De Putte, a small businessman:

A RED, WHITE AND BLUE MESS

Pete Van de Putte

What does it feel like as the owner of a small business to discover you have been hit with a frivolous lawsuit? Imagine that your doctor tells you, "I've got some bad news for you." Because, to get sued these days is a lot like contracting a terrible illness. At the very best, after a long, costly struggle, you just manage to survive. At the very worst, you (meaning your company) die. Either way, you keep asking yourself in outrage, "Why me?"

The U.S. Senate this week is debating legal reform, including extending limitations on punitive damages and joint and several product liability to include protections for all Americans. As the senators deliberate, let me share my personal lawsuit horror story—one that shows why legal reform is vital, and why it is only fair to expand it to include protections for all small businesses, nonprofits like the Girl Scouts or Little League, and municipalities.

My company, the Dixie Flag Manufacturing Co. of San Antonio, Texas, grew out of a family decorating business my mom and dad started in 1958. In 1974, my father sold the decorating firm, but continued the part he loved most—the flag business. In 1980, I joined Dixie Flag and now serve as president. We employ 63 people. We are proud to make and sell American flags for businesses and classrooms across the country ranging from small, hand-held wavers to a massive 55-foot-by-110-foot mounted edition of Old Glory.

In 1991, my firm and eight other businesses were named as defendants in a lawsuit over an incident that allegedly occurred in 1989. According to the plaintiff, he had been driving when he noticed a large flag being lowered in the parking lot of a local business. The plaintiff, claiming concern that a corner of this large flag would touch the ground, parked his car, got out and offered to help the employees of this business lower the flag. He then claimed that, as he was feeding the bottom corner of the flag into a container, a powerful gust of wind billowed the massive banner and yanked it into the air. According to the suit, the plaintiff was then thrown 70 feet into the air, and, of course, injured.

Two years later, he sued for unspecified damages claiming that the American flag was an "unreasonably dangerous product" that should be required to carry instruction and warning labels.

At first I was mystified. Although my company makes large flags, my best guess was that we didn't make that flag. We immediately had to stop everything we were doing—stop taking orders, checking inventory, working with the factory— just to get to the bottom of this story.

After devoting a week of several employees' time combing through ancient invoices, we confirmed that our company did not make or sell the flag cited in this incident—or the flagpole. In fact, we had no connection whatsoever to this bizarre flag injury except that, coincidentally, we happen to be a flag company. Relieved, I called my liability insurance agent to give him the good news.

His answer floored me. He told me that none of this mattered. I would have to settle in order to stay out of court.

I was livid with anger, not just for the way I was being treated by an unfair system, but for my employees who joined me in wasting a week of our lives on our knees, sifting through mountains of paper.

The company that actually sold the flag and the flagpole to the business was not even included in the suit. It was a one-man business operating out of the back of a pickup truck and had no insurance and little money. But Dixie Flag had insurance and money (a "deep pocket," in other words). So under something called the doctrine of "joint and several liability," we were a perfect target. There was no possibility of being dismissed from the case. I would have to prove in court that I had no connection to this incident.

Against my instructions, my insurance company settled for $6,000. Later the attorney called to tell me how "lucky" I was. He said it would have cost $10,000 in attorney fees to get the case thrown out in court. As he saw it, we saved $4,000.

Two other flag-makers were sued—neither of which sold the flag or the pole—and settled for $14,000 and $1,500, respectively. That means that the plaintiff in this case was able to extract at least $21,500 from three small businesses, none of which were involved in any way in the incident, without ever having to prove his claim in court— all because of the doctrine of joint and several liability.

Ending abusive lawsuits is a critical issue to small business. But it is also an issue of basic fairness for all Americans. The product liability reforms now before the Senate would protect small manufacturers like me from legal extortion masquerading under the doctrine of joint and several liability.

Yet unless strengthening amendments are passed, the bill won't protect the small service companies that constitute 70% of small business in this country from exposure to this litigation lottery. It won't protect volunteer organizations or municipalities that, as deep pockets, also are lucrative targets.

My experience proves that our legal system is seriously broken. It has to be fixed, but there is no sense in fixing it just for manufacturers like me.

Source: Pete van de Putte, " A Red, White and Blue Mess." *The Wall Street Journal*, April 1, 1995.

DISCUSSION QUESTIONS

1. Is it the intention of the U.S. legal system to punish those who are not responsible?
2. Would you feel comfortable recovering money from someone not responsible for your injury?
3. Does this qualify as an abusive lawsuit?
4. Is "joint and several liability" a fair doctrine for defendants?
5. What changes in litigation would you make to help individuals like Van De Putte?
6. Was Van de Putte correct to settle the suit?

INTEGRATIVE PROBLEMS

PART 1

A business is regulated by everything from the

United States Constitution to the guidelines of the

Part Two

Consumer Product Safety

Commission. Managers

must know codified law as well as the law that

develops as cases are litigated

and new issues of liability

arise. The regulatory environ-

Business: Its Regulatory Environment

ment of business includes penalties for criminal

conduct and punitive damages for knowing injuries

to customers. Part Two describes laws that regulate

businesses and business operations, the sanctions

that are imposed for violation of these laws, and the

manner by which businesses can make compliance

with the law a key part of their values.

Judgment

Alfonso Lopez, Jr., a 12th-grade student at Edison High School in San Antonio, Texas, arrived at school on March 10, 1992, carrying a concealed .38 caliber handgun and five bullets. School officials, acting on an anonymous tip, confronted Lopez. He admitted that he had the gun. Lopez was arrested and charged with a violation of a Texas law that prohibits firearm possession on school premises. The next day these state criminal charges were dismissed after federal agents charged Lopez with violating the federal law called the Gun-Free School Zones Act of 1990. A federal grand jury indicted Lopez for knowing possession of a firearm in a school zone, a felony violation of the Gun-Free School Zones Act. The penalties for violation of the state law were much less and Lopez would probably be tried as a minor whereas the federal law carried mandatory prison time. Lopez asked his lawyer, "How is it that federal law applies to a high school in San Antonio? Shouldn't Texas law apply? What authority does the federal government have to run schools in Texas?"

CHAPTER 5

Business and the Constitution

The U.S. Constitution is a remarkable document. It was drafted by a group of independent states two hundred years ago in an attempt to unify the states into one national government that could function smoothly and efficiently without depriving those independent states of their rights. The fact that it has survived so many years with so few changes is indicative of the flexibility and foresight built into the document.

This chapter covers the application of the U.S. Constitution to business. There are several questions answered in this chapter: What are the constitutional limitations on business regulation? Who has more power to regulate business—the states or the federal government? What individual freedoms granted under the Constitution apply to businesses?

> *Some men look at constitutions with sanctimonious reverence, and deem them like the ark of the covenant, too sacred to be touched. . . . I am certainly not an advocate for frequent and untried changes in laws and constitutions. . . . But . . . laws and institutions must go hand in hand with the progress of the human mind.*
>
> **Thomas Jefferson**

THE U.S. CONSTITUTION

An Overview of the U.S. Constitution

Review the U.S. Constitution: http:// www.law.emory. edu/FEDERAL/ usconst.html

Although virtually every constitutional issue and every court decision on a constitutional issue are complicated and detailed, the **U.S. Constitution** itself is a simple and short document. Contained within it is the entire structure of the federal government, its powers, the powers of the states, and the rights of all citizens. The exact language of the U.S. Constitution is presented in Appendix A.

Articles I, II, and III—The Framework for Separation of Powers

The first three articles of the U.S. Constitution set up the three branches of the federal government. Article I establishes the **legislative branch** of the federal government. The two houses of Congress—the House of Representatives and the Senate—are created, their method of election of members is specified, and their powers are listed.

Article II creates the **executive branch** of the federal government. The office of president along with its qualifications, manner of election, term, and powers are specified.

Article III establishes the **judicial branch** of the federal government. This article creates only the U.S. Supreme Court and establishes its jurisdiction. Congress, however, is authorized to establish inferior courts, which it has done in the form of federal district courts, specialized federal courts, and U.S. courts of appeals (see Chapter 3, Exhibit 3.2).

The first three articles establish the nature of the federal government as involving the **separation of powers**. Each of these branches is given unique functions that the other branches cannot perform, but each branch also has curbing powers on the other branches of government through the exercise of its unique powers. For example, the judicial branch cannot pass laws, but it can prevent a law passed by Congress from taking effect by judicially interpreting the law as unconstitutional. The executive branch does not pass legislation but has veto power over legislation passed by Congress. The executive branch has responsibility for foreign relations and negotiating treaties. However, those treaties do not take effect until they are ratified by the Senate. This system of different powers that can be used to curb the other branches' exercise of power is called a system of **checks and balances**.

The writers of the U.S. Constitution designed federal government this way to avoid the accumulation of too much power in any one branch of government. In *Nixon* v. *Administrator of General Services*, 433 U.S. 425 (1977), the Supreme Court held that former President Nixon was required to turn over to Congress any records and materials of the executive branch that were relevant to the congressional inquiry into the Watergate scandal, a break-in at the Democratic Party's national headquarters that was masterminded by members of the Nixon administration.

CONSIDER . . .   **5.1** During the time that Anne M. Burford served as administrator of the Environmental Protection Agency (EPA), the Congressional Subcommittee on Oversight and Investigations of the House Committee on Energy and Commerce sought documents from the EPA regarding the cleanup of hazardous wastes (known more commonly as the Superfund) (see Chapter 11 for more details). With the advice of the Department of Justice, Burford did not turn over the documents, arguing that certain of them were developed for the use of the Cabinet Council and that executive privilege extended to cover such materials.

Could the documents be withheld? Would release of the documents, as the *Nixon* case states, "prevent the Executive Branch from accomplishing its constitutionally assigned function"? Would the congressional subpoena of the documents result in congressional control of executive branch functions?

Other Articles

Article IV is the clause dealing with states' interrelationships. Article V provides the procedures for constitutional amendments. Article VI is the **Supremacy Clause** (discussed later in the chapter), and Article VII simply provides the method for state ratification of the Constitution.

The Bill of Rights

In addition to the three articles, the U.S. Constitution has 27 amendments, the first 10 of which are the **Bill of Rights**. Although these rights were originally applicable to federal procedures only, they were extended to apply to the states by the **Fourteenth Amendment**. These amendments cover rights from freedom of speech (First Amendment) to the right to a jury trial (Sixth Amendment) to protection of privacy from unlawful searches (Fourth Amendment) to due process before deprivation of property (Fifth Amendment). The amendments as they apply to businesses are covered later in this chapter and in Chapter 8.

THE ROLE OF JUDICIAL REVIEW AND THE CONSTITUTION

The Supreme Court and its decisions are often in the news because the cases decided by the Court are generally significant ones that provide interpretations of the U.S. Constitution and also define the extent of the rights we are afforded under it. The role of the U.S. Supreme Court is to decide what rights are provided by the general language of the U.S. Constitution. For example, the Fifth Amendment guarantees that we will not be deprived of our life, liberty, or property without "due process of law." Due process of law, interpreted by the courts many times now, includes such rights as the right to a hearing before a mortgage foreclosure or at least the right of notice before property is sold after repossession as a result of nonpayment of the debt on it.

The First Amendment protects the simple right to freedom of speech, but the Supreme Court has been faced with issues such as whether limits on campaign contributions are a violation of that right to be heard. The Fourth Amendment is the privacy amendment and protects us from warrantless searches. This general idea has been analyzed in the context of garbage taken from cans waiting for pickup on the street and unannounced inspections by OSHA regulators of company workplaces.

The U.S. Supreme Court has the responsibility of determining the extent and scope of the rights and protections afforded by the U.S. Constitution. In addition, the U.S. Supreme Court plays the unique role of reviewing the actions of the other branches of government. The Court is a crucial part of the checks and balances system set up in our Constitution. During World War II, the Court reviewed the action of Congress for the constitutionality of its authorization to intern Japanese-Americans. The U.S. Supreme Court also reviews the constitutionality of actions taken by the other branches of government.

CONSTITUTIONAL LIMITATIONS OF ECONOMIC REGULATIONS

The Commerce Clause

The **Commerce Clause** is found in Article 1, Section 8, Part 3 of the U.S. Constitution and provides Congress with the power "[t]o regulate Commerce with foreign Nations, and among the several States, . . ." Although the language is short and simple, the phrase *among the several states* has created much controversy. The clause limits Congress to the regulation of interstate commerce. Local commerce or intrastate commerce is left to the states for regulation. Defining interstate commerce has been the task of the courts. The standards are defined from two perspectives: federal regulation of state and local commerce, and state and local regulation of interstate commerce.

STANDARDS FOR CONGRESSIONAL REGULATION OF STATE AND LOCAL BUSINESS ACTIVITY

The issue as defined by the Court is whether there is sufficient interstate contact or effects for the application of federal standards. The Constitution gives Congress authority to regulate "interstate" matters and vests all the remaining regulatory authority in the states.

The U.S. Supreme Court has defined the extent of interstate commerce. The Court initially gave a very narrow interpretation to the scope of the Commerce Clause. For activity to be subject to federal regulation, there had to be a "direct and immediate effect" on interstate commerce. In 1918, the Court ruled that manufacturing was not "commerce" (was solely intrastate) and struck down an act of Congress that attempted to regulate goods manufactured in plants using child labor [*Hammer* v. *Dagenhart*, 247 U.S. 251 (1918)]. During the 1930s, Congress and President Roosevelt bumped heads with the Court many times in their attempts to legislate a recovery from the depression. The Court consistently refused to validate federal legislation of manufacturing, operations, and labor [*Schechter Poultry* v. *United States*, 295 U.S. 495 (1935); *Carter* v. *Carter Coal*, 298 U.S. 238 (1936)]. Roosevelt refused to accept the roadblock to his legislation and initiated his court-packing plan to increase the number of members of the court with Roosevelt appointees.

The Court responded in *NLRB* v. *Laughlin Steel*, 336 U.S. 460 (1940), by ruling that intrastate activities may be local in character but still affect interstate commerce and thus be subject to federal regulation. The "affectation" doctrine thus expanded the authority of the federal government in regulating commerce. In the words of the Court, " If it is interstate commerce that feels the pinch, it does not matter how local the squeeze" (336 U.S. at 464). Today, judicial review of congressional action based on the Commerce Clause is perfunctory. Typically, there is always some connection between the legislation and congressional authority.

The Commerce Clause has had a critical role in the elimination of discrimination because the Court's liberal definition of what constitutes interstate commerce has permitted the application of federal civil rights laws to local activities.

Judgment

The following case is one in which the U.S. Supreme Court, for the first time in nearly a century, limited the power of Congress in regulating local activities. The case provides the answers for the questions posed in the chapter's opening "Judgment."

United States v. *Lopez*
115 S. Ct. 1624 (1995)

ARMED AND REGULATED IN TEXAS

FACTS
Alfonso Lopez, Jr. (respondent), a 12th-grade student at Edison High School in San Antonio, Texas, arrived at school on March 10, 1992, carrying a concealed .38 caliber handgun and five bullets. School officials, acting on an anonymous tip, confronted Lopez. Lopez admitted that he had the gun. Lopez was arrested and charged with a violation of the Texas Penal Code that prohibits possession of a firearm on school premises.

The following day the state charges were dropped after federal officials charged Lopez with violation of federal law, the Gun-Free School Zones Act of 1990. A federal grand jury indicted Lopez for knowing possession of a firearm in a school zone. Lopez moved to dismiss his indictment on the grounds that the provision of the Gun-Free School Zone Act with which he was charged (Section 922(q)) is unconstitutional and beyond the power of Congress to legislate controls over public schools. The district court found the statute to be a constitutional exercise of congressional authority.

After Lopez waived a jury trial, there was a trial to the bench. Lopez was found guilty and sentenced to six months' imprisonment and two years' supervised release.

Lopez appealed and challenged his conviction on the basis of the Commerce Clause and the lack of authority for Congress to regulate public schools. The Fifth Circuit Court of Appeals agreed with Lopez, found the Gun-Free School Zones Act an unconstitutional exercise of congressional authority, and reversed the conviction. The U.S. Attorney appealed.

JUDICIAL OPINION
REHNQUIST, Chief Justice
[W]e have identified three broad categories of activity that Congress may regulate under its commerce power. First, Congress may regulate the use of the channels of interstate commerce. Second, Congress is empowered to regulate and protect the instrumentalities of interstate commerce, or persons or things in interstate commerce, even though the threat may come only from intrastate activities. Finally, Congress' commerce authority includes the power to regulate those activities having a substantial relation to interstate commerce.

Within this final category, admittedly, our case law has not been clear whether an activity must "affect" or "substantially affect" interstate commerce in order to be within Congress' power to regulate it under the Commerce Clause.

Continued

We now turn to consider the power of Congress, in the light of this framework, to enact § 922(q). The first two categories of authority may be quickly disposed of: § 922(q) is not a regulation of the use of the channels of interstate commerce, nor is it an attempt to prohibit the interstate transportation of a commodity through the channels of commerce; nor can § 922(q) be justified as a regulation by which Congress has sought to protect an instrumentality of interstate commerce or a thing in interstate commerce. Thus, if § 922(q) is to be sustained, it must be under the third category as a regulation of an activity that substantially affects interstate commerce.

First, we have upheld a wide variety of congressional Acts regulating intrastate economic activity where we have concluded that the activity substantially affected interstate commerce. Examples include the regulation of intrastate coal mining; intrastate extortionate credit transactions, restaurants utilizing substantial interstate supplies, inns and hotels catering to interstate guests, and production and consumption of home-grown wheat. Where economic activity substantially affects interstate commerce, legislation regulating that activity will be sustained.

Section 922(q) is a criminal statute that by its terms has nothing to do with "commerce" or any sort of economic enterprise, however broadly one might define those terms. Section 922(q) is not an essential part of a larger regulation of economic activity, in which the regulatory scheme could be undercut unless the intrastate activity were regulated. It cannot, therefore, be sustained under our cases upholding regulations of activities that arise out of or are connected with a commercial transaction, which viewed in the aggregate, substantially affects interstate commerce.

Second, § 922(q) contains no jurisdictional element which would ensure, through case-by-case inquiry, that the firearm possession in question affects interstate commerce. For example, in *United States v. Bass*, 404 U.S. 336, 92 S.Ct. 515, 30 L.Ed.2d 488 (1971), the Court interpreted former 18 U.S.C. § 1202(a), which made

it a crime for a felon to "receiv[e], posses[s], or transpor[t] in commerce or affecting commerce . . . any firearm." 404 U.S., at 337, 92 S.Ct., at 517. The Court interpreted the possession component of § 1202(a) to require an additional nexus to interstate commerce both because the statute was ambiguous and because "unless Congress conveys its purpose clearly, it will not be deemed to have significantly changed the federal-state balance." The *Bass* Court set aside the conviction because although the Government had demonstrated that Bass had possessed a firearm, it had failed "to show the requisite nexus with interstate commerce."

The Government argues that possession of a firearm in a school zone may result in violent crime and that violent crime can be expected to affect the functioning of the national economy in two ways. First, the costs of violent crime are substantial, and, through the mechanism of insurance, those costs are spread throughout the population. Second, violent crime reduces the willingness of individuals to travel to areas within the country that are perceived to be unsafe. The Government also argues that the presence of guns in schools poses a substantial threat to the educational process by threatening the learning environment. A handicapped educational process, in turn, will result in a less productive citizenry. That, in turn, would have an adverse effect on the Nation's economic well-being.

Admittedly, a determination whether on intrastate activity is commercial or noncommercial may in some cases result in legal uncertainty. But, so long as Congress' authority is limited to those powers enumerated in the Constitution, and so long as those enumerate powers are interpreted as having judicially enforceable outer limits, congressional legislation under the Commerce Clause always will engender "legal uncertainty."

For the foregoing reasons the judgment of the Court of Appeals is affirmed.

DISSENTING OPINIONS
Justice STEVENS, dissenting
Guns are both articles of commerce and articles that can be used to restrain commerce. Their

Continued

possession is the consequence, either directly or indirectly, of commercial activity. In my judgment, Congress' power to regulate commerce in firearms includes the power to prohibit possession of guns at any location because of their potentially harmful use; it necessarily follows that Congress may also prohibit their possession in particular markets. The market for the possession of handguns by school-age children is, distressingly, substantial. Whether or not the national interest in eliminating that market would have justified federal legislation in 1789, it surely does today.

BREYER, STEVENS, SOUTER and
GINSBURG, Justices

The issue in this case is whether the Commerce Clause authorizes Congress to enact a statute that makes it a crime to possess a gun in, or near, a school. 18 U.S.C. § 922(q)(1)(A) (1988 ed., Supp. V). In my view, the statute falls well within the scope of the commerce power as this Court has understood that power over the last half-century.

In reaching this conclusion, I apply three basic principles of Commerce Clause interpretation. First, the power to "regulate Commerce . . . among the several States," U.S. Const., Art. I, § 8, cl. 3, encompasses the power to regulate local activities insofar as they significantly affect interstate commerce. As the majority points out, at 1630, the Court, in describing how much of an effect the Clause requires, sometimes has used the word "substantial" and sometimes has not. And, as the majority also recognizes in quoting Justice Cardozo, the question of degree (how much effect) requires an estimate of the "size" of the effect that no verbal formulation can capture with precision. I use the word "significant" because the word "substantial" implies a somewhat narrower power than recent precedent suggests.

Second, in determining whether a local activity will likely have a significant effect upon interstate commerce, a court must consider, not the effect of an individual act (a single instance of gun possession), but rather the cumulative effect of all similar instances (i.e., the effect of all guns possessed in or near schools).

Third, the Constitution requires us to judge the connection between a regulated activity and interstate commerce, not directly, but at one remove. Courts must give Congress a degree of leeway in determining the existence of a significant factual connection between the regulated activity and interstate commerce—both because the Constitution delegates the commerce power directly to Congress and because the determination requires an empirical judgment of a kind that a legislature is more likely than a court to make with accuracy. Thus, the specific question before us, as the Court recognizes, is not whether the "regulated activity sufficiently affected interstate commerce," but, rather, whether Congress could have had "a rational basis" for so concluding.

Applying these principles to the case at hand, we must ask whether Congress could have had a *rational basis* for finding a significant (or substantial) connection between gun-related school violence and interstate commerce. Or, to put the question in the language of the explicit finding that Congress made when it amended this law in 1994: Could Congress rationally have found that "violent crime in school zones," through its effect on the "quality of education," significantly (or substantially) affects "interstate" or "foreign commerce"? As long as one views the commerce connection, not as a "technical legal conception," but as "a practical one," the answer to this question must be yes. Numerous reports and studies—generated both inside and outside government—make clear that Congress could reasonably have found the empirical connection that its law, implicitly or explicitly, asserts.

For one thing, reports, hearings, and other readily available literature make clear that the problem of guns in and around schools is widespread and extremely serious.

Having found that guns in schools significantly undermine the quality of education in our Nation's classrooms, Congress could also have found, given the effect of education upon interstate and foreign commerce, that gun-related violence in and around schools is a commercial, as well as a human, problem.

Continued

Education, although far more than a matter of economics, has long been inextricably intertwined with the Nation's economy.

In recent years the link between secondary education and business has strengthened, becoming both more direct and more important. Scholars on the subject report that technological changes and innovations in management techniques have altered the nature of the workplace so that more jobs now demand greater educational skills.

Finally, there is evidence that, today more than ever, many firms base their location decisions upon the presence, or absence, of a work force with a basic education.

The economic links I have just sketched seem fairly obvious. Why then is it not equally obvious, in light of those links, that a widespread, serious, and substantial physical threat to teaching and learning also substantially threatens the commerce to which that teaching and learning is inextricably tied? That is to say, guns in the hands of six percent of inner-city high school students and gun-related violence throughout a city's schools must threaten the trade and commerce that those schools support. The only question, then, is whether the latter threat is (to use the majority's terminology) "substantial." And, the evidence of (1) the extent of the gun-related violence problem, (2) the extent of the resulting negative effect on classroom learning, and (3) the extent of the consequent negative commercial effects, when taken together, indicate a threat to trade and commerce that is "substantial."

In sum, a holding that the particular statute before us falls within the commerce power would not expand the scope of that Clause. Rather, it simply would apply preexisting law to changing economic circumstances.

CASE QUESTIONS

1. Explain the judicial history of the Commerce Clause. Has the U.S. Supreme Court always had the same position with respect to local regulation by federal statute?
2. Describe the three categories of activity Congress is permitted to regulate.
3. What arguments does the U.S. government make in tying the Gun-Free School Zones legislation to commerce? How does it establish the economic impact of the presence of guns at school?
4. Is it clear to you when the Commerce Clause would restrict congressional activity and when it would not? Is the court certain that it has a test that all can follow and understand?
5. What points do the dissenting justices make in their opinions?
6. Suppose that Congress passed legislation that regulated the sale of produce to schools. Would that legislation be upheld under the commerce clause? Suppose Congress passed legislation that made it a crime for unlicensed vendors to sell soda pop on school campuses. Would that legislation be upheld under the commerce clause? What are the differences in these laws from the gun law?

E T H I C A L   I S S U E S

5.1 In his dissenting opinion, Justice Breyer notes that employers are heavily involved in their communities in improving the local school systems. These employers are expending funds, offering expertise and contributing to changes in curricula and structure of the schools. Is such involvement an appropriate use of shareholder funds and officer and employee time? Why would a business undertake such responsibilities in its local education system?

C O N S I D E R . . . **5.2** Ollie's Barbecue is a family-owned restaurant in Birmingham, Alabama, specializing in barbecued meats and homemade pies, with a seating capacity of 220 customers. It is located on a state highway eleven blocks from an interstate highway and a somewhat greater distance from railroad and bus stations. The restaurant caters to a family and white-collar trade, with a take-out service for Negroes. It employs thirty-six people, two-thirds of whom are Negroes.

In the twelve months preceding the passage of the Civil Rights Act, the restaurant purchased locally approximately $150,000 worth of food, $69,683 or 46 percent of which was meat that it bought from a local supplier who had procured it from outside the state.

The restaurant has refused to serve Negroes in its dining accommodations since its original opening in 1927, and since July 2, 1964, it has been operating in violation of the Civil Rights Act. A lower court concluded that if it were required to serve Negroes, it would lose a substantial amount of business.

The lower court found that the Civil Rights Act did not apply because Ollie's was not involved in "interstate commerce." The court held that there was no connection between food purchased in interstate commerce and then sold in a restaurant and the conclusion that discrimination would affect that commerce.

Is Ollie's subject to the Civil Rights Act? Is there sufficient intrastate commerce? [*Katzenbach v. McClung*, 379 U.S. 294 (1964).]

C O N S I D E R . . . **5.3** The Heart of Atlanta Motel is located in downtown Atlanta, Georgia, on Courtland Street, two blocks from Peachtree Street. The motel has 216 rooms for transient guests and is readily accessible to interstate highways 75 and 85 and state highways 23 and 41. The Heart of Atlanta Motel advertises in magazines with national circulation and maintains over fifty billboards and highway signs throughout Georgia. Approximately 75 percent of its guests are from out of state. The motel had a policy of refusing to "rent rooms to Negroes." The United States brought suit against the motel for violation of the Civil Rights Act. The motel maintains that it is not involved in interstate commerce and is not subject to the Civil Rights Act. Do you agree with the motel's assertion that it is not involved in interstate commerce? [*Heart of Atlanta Motel, Inc. v. United.States.*, 379 U.S. 241 (1964).]

STANDARDS FOR STATE REGULATION OF INTERSTATE COMMERCE
The Commerce Clause does not deal only with the issue of federal power. The interpretation of the clause also involves how much commerce the states can regulate without interfering in the congressional domain of interstate commerce. In answering this question the courts are concerned with two factors: (1) whether federal regulation supersedes state involvement and (2) whether the benefits achieved by the regulation outweigh the burden on interstate commerce. These two factors are meant to prevent states from passing laws that would give local industries and businesses an unfair advantage over interstate businesses. There are, however, some circumstances in which the states can regulate interstate commerce. Those circumstances occur when the state is properly exercising its **police power**.

What is the Police Power? The police power is the states' power to pass laws that promote the public welfare and protect public health and safety. Regulation of these primary concerns is within each state's domain. It is, however, inevitable that some of the laws dealing with public welfare and health and safety will burden interstate commerce. Many of the statutes that have been challenged constitutionally have regulated highway use. For example, there are cases that have tested a state's power to regulate the length of trucks on state highways [*Raymond Motor Transportation* v. *Rice*, 434 U.S. 429 (1978).] In *Bibb* v. *Navajo Freight Lines, Inc.*, 359 US. 520 (1959), the Supreme Court analyzed an Illinois statute requiring all trucks using Illinois roads to be equipped with contour mudguards. These types of mudguards were supposed to reduce the amount of mud splattering the windshields of other drivers and preventing them from seeing. Both cases revolved around the public safety purpose of each statute.

The Balancing Test A statute is not entitled to constitutional protection just because it deals with public health, safety, or welfare. Although the courts try to protect the police power, that protection is not automatic. The police power is upheld only so long as the benefit achieved by the statute does not outweigh the burden imposed on interstate commerce. Each case is decided on its own facts. States present evidence of the safety benefits involved, and the interstate commerce interests present evidence of the costs and effects for interstate commerce. The question courts must answer in these constitutional cases is whether the state interest in public health, welfare, or safety outweighs the federal interest in preventing interstate commerce from being unduly burdened.

In performing this balancing test, the courts will of course examine the safety, welfare, and health issues. However, the courts will also examine other factors, such as whether the regulation or law provides an unfair advantage to intrastate or local businesses. A prohibition on importing citrus into Florida would give instate growers an undue advantage.

Courts also examine the degree of the effect on interstate commerce. State statutes limiting the length of commercial vehicles would require commercial truck lines to buy different trucks for certain routes or in some cases stop at a state's border to remove one of the double trailers being pulled. These stops can have a substantial effect on interstate travel. On the other hand, a state law that requires travelers to stop at the border for a fruit and plant check is not as burdensome: only a stop is required, and the traveler would not be required to make any further adjustments. Also, the state's health interest is great; most fruit and plant checks are done to keep harmful insects from entering the state and destroying its crops. In the *Bibb* case, the courts found that the evidence of increased safety was not persuasive enough to outweigh the burden on interstate commerce.

Another question courts answer in their analysis is whether there is any way the state could accomplish its health, welfare, or safety goal with less of a burden on interstate commerce. Suppose a state has a health concern about having milk properly processed. One way to cover the concern is to require all milk to be processed in-state. Such a regulation clearly favors that state's businesses and imposes a great burden on out-of-state milk producers. The same result, however, could be produced by requiring all milk sellers to be licensed. The licensing procedure would allow the state to check the milk processing procedures of all firms and accomplish the goal without imposing such a burden on out-of-state firms.

In recent years the most compelling police power issue has involved the states' authority to regulate hazardous waste disposal. The following case focuses on this issue and provides insights on evolving waste disposal issues.

Fort Gratiot Sanitary Landfill, Inc. v. Michigan Dept. of Natural Resources
504 U.S. 353 (1992)

THIS LANDFILL IS OUR LANDFILL

FACTS
In 1978 Michigan enacted its Solid Waste Management Act (SWMA), which required all Michigan counties to estimate the solid waste they would generate over the next 20 years and to develop plans for providing for its disposal.

St. Clair County adopted such a plan and required permits for the operation of solid waste landfills. Fort Gratiot (petitioner) held such a permit for operation.

On December 28, 1988, the Michigan legislature amended the SWMA by adopting two provisions concerning the "acceptance of waste or ash generated outside the county of disposal area." Those amendments (Waste Import Restrictions), which became effective immediately, provide:

A person shall not accept for disposal solid waste . . . that is not generated in the county in which the disposal area is located unless the acceptance of solid waste . . . that is not generated in the county is explicitly authorized in the approved county solid waste management plan. In order for a disposal area to serve the disposal needs of another county, state, or country, the service . . . must be explicitly authorized in the approved solid waste management plan of the receiving county.

On February 1, 1989, Fort Gratiot was denied a permit for operation because it accepted up to 1,750 tons per day of out-of-state waste. Fort Gratiot filed suit seeking a declaration that the Waste Import Restrictions were unconstitutional. The district court dismissed the complaint and the court of appeals affirmed. Fort Gratiot appealed.

JUDICIAL OPINION
STEVENS, Justice
Before discussing the rather narrow issue that is contested, it is appropriate to identify certain matters that are not in dispute. Michigan's comprehensive program of regulating the collection, transportation, and disposal of solid waste, as it was enacted in 1978 and administered prior to the 1988 Waste Import Restrictions, is not challenged. No issue relating to hazardous waste is presented, and there is no claim that petitioner's operation violated any health, safety, or sanitation requirement. Nor does the case raise any question concerning policies that municipalities or other governmental agencies may pursue in the management of publicly owned facilities. The case involves only the validity of the Waste Import Restrictions as they apply to privately owned and operated landfills.

As we have long recognized, the "negative" or "dormant" aspect of the Commerce Clause prohibits States from "advanc[ing] their own commercial interests by curtailing the movement of articles of commerce, either into or out of the state." A state statute that clearly discriminates against interstate commerce is therefore unconstitutional "unless the discrimination is demonstrably justified by a valid factor unrelated to economic protectionism."

New Jersey's prohibition on the importation of solid waste failed this test. [T]he evil of protectionism can reside in legislative means as well as legislative ends. Thus, it does not matter whether that ultimate aim of [a law] is to reduce the waste disposal costs of New Jersey residents or to save remaining open lands from pollution, for we assume New Jersey has every right to protect its residents' pocketbooks as well as their environment. And it may be assumed as well that New Jersey may pursue those ends by slowing the flow of *all* waste into the State's remaining landfills, even though interstate commerce may incidentally be affected. But whatever New Jersey's ultimate purpose, it may not be accompanied by discriminating against articles of commerce coming from outside the State unless there is some reason, apart from their origin, to treat them differently. Both on its face and in its plain effect, [the law] violates this principle of nondiscrimination.
Continued

The Court has consistently found parochial legislation of this kind to be constitutionally invalid, . . .

The Waste Import Restrictions enacted by Michigan authorize each of its 83 counties to isolate itself from the national economy. Indeed, unless a county acts affirmatively to permit other waste to enter its jurisdiction, the statute affords local waste producers complete protection from competition from out-of-state waste producers who seek to use local waste disposal areas. In view of the fact that Michigan has not identified any reason, apart from its origin, why solid waste coming from outside the county should be treated differently from solid waste within the county, the foregoing reasoning would appear to control the disposition of this case.

Respondents Michigan and St. Clair County argue, however, that the Waste Import Restrictions—unlike the New Jersey prohibition on the importation of solid waste—do not discriminate against interstate commerce on their face or in effect because they treat waste from other Michigan counties no differently than waste from other States. Instead, respondents maintain, the statute regulates evenhandedly to effectuate local interests and should be upheld because the burden on interstate commerce is not clearly excessive in relation to the local benefits.

In *Dean Milk Co.* v. *Madison,* 340 U.S. 349, 71 S.Ct. 295, 95 L.Ed. 329 (1951), another Illinois litigant challenged a city ordinance that made it unlawful to sell any milk as pasteurized unless it had been processed at a plant "within a radius of five miles from the central square of Madison." We held the ordinance invalid, explaining:

[T]his regulation, like the provision invalidated in *Baldwin* v. *Seelig, Inc.,* [294 U.S. 511, 55 S.Ct. 497, 79 L.Ed. 1032 (1935)], in practical effect excludes from distribution in Madison wholesome milk produced and pasteurized in Illinois. "The importer . . . may keep his milk or drink it, but sell it he may not." In thus erecting an economic barrier protecting a major local industry against competition from

without the State, Madison plainly discriminates against interstate commerce.

The fact that the ordinance also discriminated against all Wisconsin producers whose facilities were more than five miles from the center of the city did not mitigate its burden on interstate commerce. As we noted, it was "immaterial that Wisconsin milk from outside the Madison area is subjected to the same proscription as that moving in interstate commerce."

In short, neither the fact that the Michigan statute purports to regulate intercounty commerce in waste nor the fact that some Michigan counties accept out-of-state waste provides an adequate basis for distinguishing this case.

For the foregoing reasons, the Waste Import Restrictions unambiguously discriminate against interstate commerce and are appropriately characterized as protectionist measures that cannot withstand scrutiny under the Commerce Clause. The judgment of the Court of Appeals is therefore reversed.

DISSENTING OPINION
REHNQUIST, Chief Justice, and
BLACKMUN, Justice
When confronted with a dormant Commerce Clause challenge "[t]he crucial inquiry . . . must be directed to determining whether [the challenged statute] is basically a protectionist measure, or whether it can fairly be viewed as a law directed to legitimate local concerns, with effects upon interstate commerce that are only incidental." Because I think the Michigan statute is at least arguably directed to legitimate local concerns, rather than improper economic protectionism, I would remand this case for further proceedings.

It is no secret why capacity is not expanding sufficiently to meet demand—the substantial risks attendant to waste sites make them extraordinarily unattractive neighbors. The result, of course, is that while many are willing to generate waste—indeed, it is a practical impossibility to solve the waste problem by banning waste production—few are willing to help dispose of it. Those locales that do provide disposal capacity to
Continued

serve foreign waste effectively are affording reduced environmental and safety risks to the States that will not take charge of their own waste.

In adopting this legislation, the Michigan Legislature also appears to have concluded that, like the State, counties should reap as they have sown—hardly a novel proposition. It has required counties within the State to be responsible for the waste created within the county. It has accomplished this by prohibiting waste facilities from accepting waste generated from outside the county, unless special permits are obtained. In the process, of course, this facially neutral restriction (i.e., it applies equally to both interstate and intrastate waste) also works to ban disposal from out-of-state sources unless appropriate permits are procured. But I cannot agree that such a requirement, when imposed as one part of a comprehensive approach to regulating in this difficult field, is the stuff of which economic protectionism is made.

CASE QUESTIONS

1. What type of restrictions has Michigan placed on solid waste disposal?
2. Of what significance is it that the restrictions apply both to outside counties and to other states?
3. Is economic protectionism involved?
4. Does this decision on the Michigan restrictions prevent states from assuming responsibility for hazardous waste?
5. Does the dissent support the restrictions? Why or why not?

C O N S I D E R . . . **5.4** Alabama has passed a statute that imposes an additional fee on hazardous wastes generated outside, but disposed of inside, the state. Seventy-two dollars per ton is the additional fee charged out-of-state users in addition to the base fee of $25.60. Will this Alabama statute survive the standards established by the Supreme Court in *Fort Gratiot*? [*Chemical Waste Management, Inc.* v. *Hunt*, 504 U.S. 334.]

E T H I C A L   I S S U E S

5.2 Alabama is one of only 16 states that have commercial hazardous waste landfills, and the Emelle facility is the largest of the 21 landfills of this kind located in these 16 states.

The wastes and substances being disposed of at the Emelle facility "include substances that are inherently dangerous to human health and safety and to the environment. Such waste consists of ignitable, corrosive, toxic and reactive wastes which contain poisonous and cancer-causing chemicals and which can cause birth defects, genetic damage, blindness, crippling and death." Increasing amounts of out-of-state hazardous wastes are shipped to the Emelle facility for permanent storage each year. From 1985 through 1989, the annual tonnage of hazardous waste received has more than doubled, increasing from 341,000 tons in 1985 to 788,000 tons by 1989. Of this, up to 90 percent of the tonnage permanently buried each year is shipped in from other states.

Is it ethical for states to enjoy the economic benefits of production and dispose of waste elsewhere? Are the extra fees charged unconscionable? Couldn't states monopolize the "dumping" market and enjoy a robust economy?

CONGRESSIONAL REGULATION OF FOREIGN COMMERCE

The Commerce Clause also grants Congress the power to regulate foreign commerce. The case of *Gibbons* v. *Ogden*, 9 Wheat. 1 (1824), defined foreign commerce as any "commercial intercourse between the United States and foreign nations." This power to regulate applies regardless of where the activity originates and where it ends. For example, many international trade transactions begin and end in the city of New York. Although the paperwork and delivery of the goods may be solely within one state (here within one city), the foreign commerce power is not restricted by the interstate standards. If there is foreign commerce, there can be congressional regulation regardless of the place of transaction.

Business Planning Tip

The problems surrounding solid waste disposal require cooperation and a utilitarian ethics. Many businesses, legislators, and governors have been meeting to collectively solve the problem of solid waste disposal. These meetings, some for information and others for discussion, help all parties avoid costly litigation, such as the Fort Gratiot case that still does not resolve the problem. More and more businesses are working proactively with government and regulators to solve problems in a win-win manner for both.

Constitutional Standards for Taxation of Business

Article 1, Section 8, Paragraph (1) gives Congress its powers of taxation: "The Congress shall have Power To lay and collect Taxes, Duties, Imposts and Excises, . . ." In addition, the Sixteenth Amendment to the Constitution gives this power: "The Congress shall have power to lay and collect taxes on income, from whatever source derived, without apportionment among the several States, and without regard to any census or enumeration."

Business Planning Tip

Know state taxation laws before you decide where to locate a plant, office, or warehouse. For example, Nevada does not have an inventory tax so many manufacturers have large warehouse facilities there, including Spiegel and Levi Strauss. Other states have no sales tax but have very high property tax rates. Still other states have high sales tax and low income tax rates. Structuring a nationwide business requires an understanding of intrastate as well as interstate taxes.

It has been said that taxes are the price we pay for a civilized society. The U.S. Supreme Court has consistently upheld the ability of Congress, and local governments as well, to impose taxes. However, there is one area in taxation that still results in considerable litigation. This area involves state and local taxation of interstate commerce. Interstate businesses are not generally exempt from state and local taxes just because they are interstate businesses. However, the taxes imposed on these businesses must meet certain standards.

First, the tax cannot discriminate against interstate commerce. A tax on milk could not be higher for milk that is shipped in from out of state than for milk produced within the state.

Second, the tax cannot unduly burden interstate commerce. For example, a tax on interstate transportation companies that is based upon the weight of their trucks as measured upon entering and leaving the states would be a burdensome tax.

Third, there must be some connection ("a sufficient **nexus**") between the state and the business being taxed. The business must have some activity in the state, such as offices, sales representatives, catalog purchasers, or distribution systems.

Finally, the tax must be apportioned fairly. This standard seeks to avoid having businesses taxed in all 50 states for their property. It also seeks to avoid having businesses pay state income tax on all their income in all 50 states. Their income and property taxes must be apportioned according to the amount of business revenues in each state and the amount of property located in that state. General Motors does not pay an inventory tax to all 50 states on all of its inventory, but it does pay an inventory tax on the inventory it holds in each state. Perhaps the most significant decision on state taxation in recent years is the following U.S. Supreme Court case on catalog sales.

Quill Corp. v. *North Dakota*
504 U.S. 298 (1992)

IS NORTH DAKOTA A TAXING STATE?

FACTS

Quill is a Delaware corporation with offices and warehouses in Illinois, California, and Georgia. None of its employees works or lives in North Dakota, and it owns no property in North Dakota.

Quill sells office equipment and supplies; it solicits business through catalogs and flyers, advertisements in national periodicals, and telephone calls. Its annual national sales exceed $200 million, of which almost $1 million are made to about three thousand customers in North Dakota. The sixth largest vendor of office supplies in the state, it delivers all of its merchandise to its North Dakota customers by mail or common carriers from out-of-state locations.

As a corollary to its sales tax, North Dakota imposes a use tax upon property purchased for storage, use, or consumption within the state. North Dakota requires every "retailer maintaining a place of business in" the state to collect the tax from the consumer and remit it to the state. In 1987, North Dakota amended its statutory definition of the term "retailer" to include "every person who engages in regular or systematic solicitation of a consumer market in th[e] state." State regulations in turn define

"regular or systematic solicitation" to mean three or more advertisements within a 12-month period. Thus, since 1987 mail-order companies that engage in such solicitation have been subject to the tax even if they maintain no property or personnel in North Dakota.

Quill has taken the position that North Dakota does not have the power to compel it to collect a use tax from its North Dakota customers. Consequently, the state, through its tax commissioner, filed this action to require Quill to pay taxes (as well as interest and penalties) on all such sales made after July 1, 1987. The trial court ruled in Quill's favor.

The North Dakota Supreme Court reversed, and Quill appealed.

JUDICIAL OPINION

STEVENS, Justice

This case, like *National Bellas Hess, Inc.* v. *Department of Revenue of Ill.*, 386 U.S. 753, 87 S.Ct. 1389, 18 L.Ed.2d 505 (1967), involves a State's attempt to require an out-of-state mail-order house that has neither outlets nor sales representatives in the State to collect and pay a use tax on goods purchased for use within the State. In *Bellas Hess* we held that a similar Illinois statute violated the Due Process Clause

Continued

of the Fourteenth Amendment and created an unconstitutional burden on interstate commerce. In particular, we ruled that a "seller whose only connection with customers in the State is by common carrier or the United States mail" lacked the requisite minimum contacts with the State.

In this case the Supreme Court of North Dakota declined to follow *Bellas Hess* because "the tremendous social, economic, commercial, and legal innovations" of the past quarter-century have rendered its holding "obsole[te]."

As in a number of other cases involving the application of state taxing statutes to out-of-state sellers, our holding in *Bellas Hess* relied on both the Due Process Clause and the Commerce Clause.

The Due Process Clause "requires some definite link, some minimum connection, between a state and the person, property or transaction it seeks to tax," and that the "income attributed to the State for tax purposes must be rationally related to 'values connected with the taxing State.' " Prior to *Bellas Hess,* we had held that that requirement was satisfied in a variety of circumstances involving use taxes. For example, the presence of sales personnel in the State, or the maintenance of local retail stores in the State, justified the exercise of that power because the seller's local activities were "plainly accorded the protection and services of the taxing State." We expressly declined to obliterate the "sharp distinction . . . between mail order sellers with retail outlets, solicitors, or property within a State, and those who do no more than communicate with customers in the State by mail or common carrier as a part of a general interstate business."

Our due process jurisprudence has evolved substantially in the 25 years since *Bellas Hess,* particularly in the area of judicial jurisdiction. Building on the seminal case of *International Shoe Co.* v. *Washington,* 326 U.S. 310, 66 S.Ct. 154, 90 L.Ed. 95 (1945), we have framed the relevant inquiry as whether a defendant had minimum contacts with the jurisdiction "such that the maintenance of the suit does not offend 'traditional notions of fair play and substantial justice.' "

Applying these principles, we have held that if a foreign corporation purposefully avails itself of the benefits of an economic market in the forum State, it may subject itself to the State's *in personam* jurisdiction even if it has no physical presence in the State.

Comparable reasoning justifies the imposition of the collection duty on a mail-order house that is engaged in continuous and widespread solicitation of business within a State. In "modern commercial life" it matters little that such solicitation is accomplished by a deluge of catalogs rather than a phalanx of drummers: the requirements of due process are met irrespective of a corporation's lack of physical presence in the taxing State. Thus, to the extent that our decisions have indicated that the Due Process Clause requires physical presence in a State for the imposition of duty to collect a use tax, we overrule those holdings as superseded by developments in the law of due process.

In this case, there is no question that Quill has purposefully directed its activities at North Dakota residents, that the magnitude of those contacts are more than sufficient for due process purposes, and that the use tax is related to the benefits Quill receives from access to the State. We therefore agree with the North Dakota Supreme Court's conclusion that the Due Process Clause does not bar enforcement of that State's use tax against Quill.

CASE QUESTIONS

1. Did Quill Corporation own any property in North Dakota?
2. Were any Quill offices or personnel located in North Dakota?
3. How did Quill come to have customers in North Dakota?
4. Will Quill be subject to North Dakota's use tax?
5. Is there a jurisdictional difference between pamphlets being present in a state and the presence of salespeople in that state?

5.5 You purchase a suit from Merg, a Florida-only clothing store, while visiting Fort Lauderdale. The clerk offers to ship your suit to you in Oregon so that you avoid Florida sales tax (and Oregon's sales tax as well). Is the transaction taxable by either state?

STATE VERSUS FEDERAL REGULATION OF BUSINESS—CONSTITUTIONAL CONFLICTS

Preemption—The Supremacy Clause

Although the Constitution has some specific sections dealing with the authority of the federal government and that of state and local governments, it is inevitable that there should be some crossovers in laws. For example, both state and federal governments regulate the sale of securities and have laws controlling the sale of real property. When there are crossover areas and those crossovers create conflicts, there is a constitutional issue of who has the power to regulate. This constitutional issue of conflict is governed by Article VI of the Constitution, sometimes called the **Supremacy Clause**, which provides: "This Constitution, and the Laws of the United States which shall be made in Pursuance thereof; and all Treaties made, or which shall be made, under the Authority of the United States, shall be the supreme Law of the Land; . . ."

This clause means that when state and local laws conflict with federal statutes or regulations or executive orders or treaties, the federal law, regulation, executive order, or treaty is superior to the state or local law. However, there are often cases in which a state law does not directly conflict with the federal law but the field to which the laws apply is largely regulated or preempted by the federal government. Occasionally, Congress actually specifies its intent in an act. For example, many credit laws on the federal level can be circumvented by state law so long as the state law is at least as protective as the federal law. In other words, Congress allows the states to regulate the field in some instances and sets the standards for doing so. Most statutes, however, do not specify congressional intent on **preemption**. Whether a field has been preempted is a question of fact, of interpretation, and of legislative history. The question of preemption is determined on a case-by-case basis. The questions examined in a preemption issue are:

1. What does the legislative history indicate? Some hearings offer clear statements of the effect and scope of a federal law.
2. How detailed is the federal regulation of the area? The more regulation there is, the more likely a court is to find preemption. Volume itself is indicative of congressional intent.
3. What benefits exist from having federal regulation of the area? Some matters are more easily regulated by one central government. Airlines fly across state lines, and if each state had different standards there would be no guarantee of uniform standards. The regulation of aircraft and their routes is clearly better handled by the federal government.
4. How much does a state law conflict with federal law? Is there any way that the two laws can coexist?

Time Warner, Inc., signed as a recording artist Mr. Tracy Marrow, known by his professional name of Ice-T. Mr. Morrow and Time Warner released an album in 1992 called *Body Count*. One song on the album was entitled "Cop Killer." Among other lyrics in the song were the following:

Time Warner, Free Speech and Questionable Taste: The Ice-T Cop Killer Song Controversy

"I've got my twelve-gauge sawed-off. . .
I'm 'bout to dust some cops off. . .
Die, pig, die."

When the album was released, it was shipped to radio stations in small replicas of body bags. The album initially enjoyed plentiful air play that resulted in protests from police officers and their spokesman, Charlton Heston. Nearly 1,100 shareholders appeared at Time Warner's annual meeting to protest. A police officer spoke at the meeting and said Time Warner had "lost its moral compass, or never had it."

A shareholder who spoke at the meeting said Time Warner always "pushed the envelope" and produced public outcry. The shareholder recalled recording artist Madonna's controversial video and her "sex" book as well as the release of the film *The Last Temptation of Christ*, which was largely boycotted.

Levin responded to the shareholders by announcing a four-for-one stock split and a 12 percent increase in Time Warner's dividend. He also maintained that the song "Cop Killer" was free speech and only depicted "the despair and anger that hang in the air of every American inner city." Levin maintained the song did not advocate "attacks on police."

Ice-T

After the shareholder meeting, the protests continued. The city of Philadelphia's municipal pension fund sold its $1.6 million in Time Warner shares. The following comments from corporate officers were published in the *Wall Street Journal*:

Roger Salquist, CEO of Calgene, Inc.:

"I'm outraged. I think the concept of free speech has been perverted. It's anti-American, it's anti-humanity, and there is no excuse for it. I hope it kills them. It's certainly not something I tolerate, and I find their behavior offensive as a corporation. If you can increase sales with controversy without harming people, that's one thing." But Time Warner's decision to support Ice-T *"is outside the bounds of what I consider acceptable behavior and decency in this country."*

David Geffen, chairmen of Geffen Records (who has refused to release Geto Boys records because of lyrics):

"The question is not about business, it is about responsibility. Should someone make money by advocating the murder of policemen? To say that this whole issue is not about profit is silly. It certainly is not about artistic freedom. If the album were

Continued

about language, sex or drugs, there are people on both sides of these issues. But when it comes down to murder, I don't think there is any part of society that approves of it. . . . I wish [Time Warner] would show some sensitivity by donating the profits to a fund for wounded policemen."

Jerry Greenfield, co-founder of Ben & Jerry's Homemade, Inc.:
"Songs like 'Cop Killer' aren't constructive, but we as a society need to look at what we've created. I don't condone cop killing. [But] to reach a more just and equitable society everyone's voice must be heard."

Neal Fox, CEO of A. Sulka & Co. (an apparel retailer owned by Luxco Investments):
"As a businessperson, my inclination is to say that Time Warner management has to be consistent. Once you've decided to get behind this product and support it, you can't express feelings of censorship. They didn't have recourse."

"Also, they are defending flag and country for the industry. If they bend to pressures regarding the material, it opens a Pandora's box for all creative work being done in the entertainment industry. On a personal basis, I abhor the concept, but on a corporate basis, I understand their reasoning."

John W. Hatsopoulos, Executive Vice President, Thermo Electron Corp.:
"I think the fact that a major U.S. corporation would almost encourage kids to attack the police force is horrible. Time Warner is a huge corporation. That they would encourage something like this for a few bucks. . . . You know about yelling fire in a crowded theater. I was so upset I was looking at [Thermo Electron's] pension plan to see if we owned any Time Warner stock" in order to sell it. *"But we don't own any."*

Bud Konheim, CEO, Nicole Miller, Ltd.:
"I don't think that people in the media can say that advertising influences consumers to buy cars or shirts, and then argue that violence on television or in music has no impact. The idea of media is to influence people's minds, and if you are inciting people to riot, it's very dangerous. It's also disappointing that they chose to defend themselves. It was a knee-jerk reaction instead of seizing the role to assert moral leadership. They had a great opportunity."

George Sanborn, CEO, Sanborn, Inc.:
"Would you release the album if it said, 'Kill a Jew or bash a fag'? I think we all know what the answer would be. They're doing it to make money."

Mark Nathanson, CEO, Falcon Cable Systems Co.:
"If you aren't happy with the product, you don't have to buy it. I might not like what [someone like Ice-T] has to say, but I would vigorously defend his right to express his viewpoint."

Continued

Stoney M. Stubbs, Jr., Chairman, Frozen Food Express Industries, Inc.:

"The more attention these types of things get, the better the products sell. I don't particularly approve of the way they play on people's emotions, but from a business standpoint [Time Warner is] probably going to make some money off it. They're protecting the people that make them the money . . . the artists."

Levin defended Time Warner's position in the *Wall Street Journal* as follows:

"Time Warner is determined to be a global force for encouraging the confrontation of ideas. We know that profits are the source of our strength and independence, of our ability to produce and distribute the work of our artists and writers, but we won't retreat in the face of threats of boycotts or political grandstanding. In the short run, cutting and running would be the surest and safest way to put this controversy behind us and get on with our business. But in the long run it would be a destructive precedent. It would be a signal to all the artists and journalists inside and outside Time Warner that if they wish to be heard, then they must tailor their minds and souls to fit the reigning orthodoxies."

"In the weeks and months ahead, Time Warner intends to use the debate engendered by the uproar over this one song to create a forum in which we can bring together the different sides in this controversy. We will invest in fostering the open discussion of the violent tensions that Ice-T's music has exposed. We believe that the future of our country—indeed, of our world—is contained in the commitment to truth and free expression, in the refusal to run away."

The album sales reached only 300,000. Some stores refused to sell it, and radio stations refused to air any cuts from the album. By August 1992, a new version of the album was released without the "Cop Killer" song. Willie D., a member of the Geto Boys said Ice-T's free speech rights were violated. "We're living in a communist country and everyone's afraid to say it."

Time Warner's board met to establish general standards for releases. In January 1993, Ice-T left the Time Warner label because of "creative differences."

In June 1995 Senator and presidential candidate Robert Dole pointed to Time Warner's records and artists as part of a moral decay. Public outcry resulted, and Time Warner's recording division was restructured. Michael Fuchs, the head of Warner Music Group, was fired by Levin.

Issues

1. Is Time Warner's concern truly artistic expression?
2. Did Ice-T's lyrics push too far?
3. Evaluate Time Warner's responses and actions.

The following case deals with a preemption issue involving airline advertising and states' rights to regulate.

American Airlines, Inc. v. Wolens
115 S. Ct. 817 (1995)

FREQUENT FLYER PROGRAMS: ADVANTAGE AIRLINES

FACTS

Wolens and others (plaintiffs) are participants in American Airlines's frequent flyer program, AAdvantage. AAdvantage members earn mileage credits when they fly on American. The members can exchange those credits for flight tickets or class-of-service upgrades. Wolens complained that AAdvantage program modifications, instituted by American in 1988, devalued credits that AAdvantage members had already earned. The examples Wolens gave were American's imposition of capacity controls (limiting the number of seats per flight available to AAdvantage members) and blackout dates (restrictions on dates AAdvantage members could use their credits). Wolens brought suit alleging that these changes and cutbacks violated the Illinois Consumer Fraud and Deceptive Business Practices Act.

American Airlines challenged the suit on the grounds that the regulation of airlines was preempted by the Airline Deregulation Act (ADA) of 1978, which deregulated domestic air transportation but also included the following clause on preemption: "[N]o State . . . shall enact or enforce any law, rule, regulation, standard, or other provision having the force and effect of law relating to rates, routes, or services of any air carrier. . . . " [49 U.S.C. App. § 1305(a).]

The Illinois Supreme Court found that the rules on the frequent flyer program were only tangentially related to rates, routes, and services and required American Airlines to defend the suit. American Airlines appealed.

JUDICIAL OPINION

GINSBURG, Justice

We need not dwell on the question whether plaintiffs' complaints state claims "relating to [air carrier] rates, routes, or services."

Plaintiffs' claims relate to "rates," i.e., American's charges in the form of mileage credits for free tickets and upgrades, and to "services," i.e., access to flights and class-of-service upgrades unlimited by retrospectively applied capacity controls and blackout dates. But the ADA's preemption clause contains other words in need of interpretation, specifically, the words "enact or enforce any law" in the instruction: "[N]o state. . . shall enact or enforce any law . . . relating to [air carrier] rates, routes, or services."

The Illinois Consumer Fraud Act declares unlawful "[u]nfair methods of competition and unfair or deceptive acts or practices, including but not limited to the use or employment of any deception, fraud, false pretense, false promise, misrepresentation or the concealment, suppression or omission of any material fact, with intent that others rely upon the concealment, suppression or omission of such material fact, or the use or employment of any practice described in Section 2 of the 'Uniform Deceptive Trade Practices Act' . . . in the conduct of any trade or commerce . . . whether any person has in fact been misled, deceived or damaged thereby."

The Act is prescriptive; it controls the primary conduct of those falling within its governance. This Illinois law, in fact, is paradigmatic of the consumer protection legislation underpinning the NAAG guidelines. The NAAG Task Force on the Air Travel Industry, on which the Attorneys General of California, Illinois, Texas, and Washington served, reported that the guidelines created no "new laws or regulations regarding the advertising practices or other business practices of the airline industry. They merely explain in detail how existing state laws apply to air fare advertising and frequent flyer programs."

Continued

The NAAG guidelines highlight the potential for intrusive regulation of airline business practices inherent in state consumer protection legislation typified by the Illinois Consumer Fraud Act. For example, the guidelines enforcing the legislation instruct airlines on language appropriate to reserve rights to alter frequent flyer programs, and they include transition rules for the fair institution of capacity controls.

As the NAAG guidelines illustrate, the Illinois Consumer Fraud Act serves as a means to guide and police the marketing practices of the airlines; the Act does not simply give effect to bargains offered by the airlines and accepted by airline customers. In light of the full text of the preemption clause, and of the ADA's purpose to leave largely to the airlines themselves, and not at all to States, the selection and design of marketing mechanisms appropriate to the furnishing of air transportation services, we conclude that § 1305(a)(1) preempts plaintiffs' claims under the Illinois Consumer Fraud Act.

American sees the DOT, however, as the exclusively competent monitor of the airline's undertaking. American points to the Department's authority to require any airline, in conjunction with its certification, to file a performance bond conditioned on the airline's "making appropriate compensation . . ., as prescribed by the [Department], for failure . . . to perform air transportation services in accordance with agreements therefor."

When Congress dismantled that regime, the United States emphasizes, the lawmakers indicated no intention to establish, simultaneously, a new administrative process for DOT adjudication of private contract disputes.

Nor is it plausible that Congress meant to channel into federal courts the business of resolving, pursuant to judicially fashioned federal common law, the range of contract claims relating to airline rates, routes, or services. The ADA contains no hint of such a role for the federal courts.

The conclusion that the ADA permits state-law-based court adjudication of routine breach of contract claims also makes sense of Congress'

retention of the FAA's saving clause, § 1106, 49 U.S.C. App. § 1506 (preserving "the remedies now existing at common law or by statute"). The ADA's preemption clause, § 1305(a)(1), read together with the FAA's saving clause, stops States from imposing their own substantive standards with respect to rates, routes, or services, but not from affording relief to a party who claims and proves that an airline dishonored a term the airline itself stipulated. This distinction between what the State dictates and what the airline itself undertakes confines courts, in breach of contract actions, to the parties' bargain, with no enlargement or enhancement based on state laws or policies external to the agreement.

American suggests that plaintiffs' breach of contract and Illinois Consumer Fraud Act claims differ only in their labels, so that if Fraud Act claims are preempted, contract claims must be preempted as well. But a breach of contract, without more, "does not amount to a cause of action cognizable under the [Consumer Fraud] Act and the Act should not apply to simple breach of contract claims." The basis for a contract action is the parties' agreement; to succeed under the consumer protection laws, one must show not necessarily an agreement, but in all cases, an unfair or deceptive practice.

For the reasons stated, the judgment of the Illinois Supreme Court is affirmed in part and reversed in part, and the case is remanded for proceedings not inconsistent with this opinion.

CASE QUESTIONS
1. What type of problem is alleged with respect to the AAdvantage program?
2. What two remedies does a frequent flyer have under state law?
3. Will the court permit either of these state remedies? What is the distinction between the two remedies? Why is one permitted and the other preempted?
4. What is the danger in statutory regulation of frequent flyer programs?
5. Do frequent flyers have contract rights? Can they enforce them? Where?

E T H I C A L   I S S U E S

5.3 Would you have changed the frequent flyer terms retroactively? Is it ethical to do so? What if, as American Airlines had, you had a clause that permitted you to change the terms of the frequent flyer rewards at any time? Does that clause make it more ethical to make the changes?

C O N S I D E R . . .

5.6 In 1987, the National Association of Attorneys General (NAAG), an organization whose membership includes the attorneys general of all 50 states, various territories, and the District of Columbia, adopted Air Travel Industry Enforcement Guidelines containing detailed standards governing the content and format of airline advertising, the awarding of premiums to regular customers (so-called frequent flyers), and the payment of compensation to passengers who voluntarily yield their seats on overbooked flights. These guidelines do not purport to "create any new laws or regulations" applying to the airline industry; rather, they claim to "explain in detail how existing state laws apply to air fare advertising and frequent flyer programs" [NAAG Guidelines, Introduction (1988)].

Despite objections to the guidelines by the Department of Transportation (DOT) and the Federal Trade Commission on preemption and policy grounds, the attorneys general of seven states sent a memorandum to the major airlines announcing that "it has come to our attention that although most airlines are making a concerted effort to bring their advertisements into compliance with the standards delineated in the . . . guidelines for fare advertising, many carriers are still [not disclosing all surcharges]" in violation of the guidelines. The memorandum said it was the signatories' "purpose . . . to clarify for the industry as a whole that [this practice] is a violation of our respective state laws on deceptive advertising and trade practices"; warned that this was an "advisory memorandum before [the] initiate[on of] any immediate enforcement actions"; and expressed the hope that "protracted litigation over this issue will not be necessary and that airlines will discontinue the practice . . . immediately."

Trans World Airlines and others then filed suit in federal district court claiming that state regulations of fare advertisements were preempted by federal law. The district court entered an injunction restraining enforcement of the NAAG guidelines. The court of appeals affirmed, and Dan Morales, the attorney general of Texas, appealed.

Is there preemption of the ad guidelines? [*Morales* v. *Trans World Airlines*, 504 U.S. 374 (1992).]

C O N S I D E R . . .

5.7 Karen Silkwood was an employee at the Cimarron, Oklahoma, plant of Kerr-McGee Corporation. Silkwood was involved in grinding and polishing plutonium samples. During a three-day period in 1974, Silkwood was contaminated by the plutonium. Her home and roommate were also found to be contaminated. She was killed in an unrelated auto accident approximately one week later.

Continued

Silkwood's father brought suit under Oklahoma tort law for the contamination injuries to his daughter and her property. The jury awarded $500,000 for personal injury, $5,000 for property damage, and $10,000,000 as punitive damages.

The Atomic Energy Act (passed by Congress) regulates the byproduct, source, and so forth of radioactive materials. States are precluded from regulating the safety aspects of hazardous materials.

Kerr-McGee contended that Oklahoma law cannot be used to allow recovery by Silkwood because the act has preempted state regulation. What questions should be considered? Has there been preemption? [*Silkwood* v. *Kerr-McGee Corp.* 464 U.S. 238 (1984).]

APPLICATION OF THE BILL OF RIGHTS TO BUSINESS

Certain of the amendments to the U.S. Constitution have particular significance for business. This is especially true for the First Amendment on freedom of speech and the Fourteenth Amendment for its issues of substantive and procedural due process and equal protection. The Fourth, Fifth, and Sixth Amendments on criminal procedures also have significance for business; those issues are covered in Chapter 8.

Commercial Speech and the First Amendment

Review recent legal actions taken by The Media Institute, a non-profit research foundation for the media's right to free speech: http://www.mediainst.org/

The area of First Amendment rights and freedom of speech is complicated and full of significant cases. The discussion here is limited to First Amendment rights as they apply to businesses. The speech of business is referred to as **commercial speech**, which is communication that is used to further the economic interests of the speaker. Advertising is clearly a form of commercial speech.

FIRST AMENDMENT PROTECTION FOR ADVERTISING

Until the early 1970s the U.S. Supreme Court held that commercial speech was different from the traditional speech afforded protection under the First Amendment. The result was that government regulation of commercial speech was virtually unlimited. The Court's position was refined in the 1970s, however, to a view that commercial speech was entitled to First Amendment protection but not on the same level as noncommercial speech. Commercial speech was not an absolute freedom; rather, the benefits of commercial speech were to be weighed against the benefits achieved by government regulation of that speech. Several factors are examined in performing this balancing test:

1. Is there a substantial government interest that is furthered by the restriction of the commercial speech?
2. Does the restriction directly accomplish the government interest?
3. Is there any other way of accomplishing the government interest? Can it be accomplished without regulating commercial speech? Are the restrictions no more extensive than necessary to serve that interest?

Under these standards, there is clearly authority for regulation of fraudulent advertising and advertising that violates the law. For example, if credit terms are advertised, Regulation Z requires full disclosure of all terms (see Chapter 16 for more details). This regulation is acceptable under the standards just listed. Further, restrictions on where and when advertisements are made are permissible. For example, cigarette ads are not permitted on television, and such a restriction is valid.

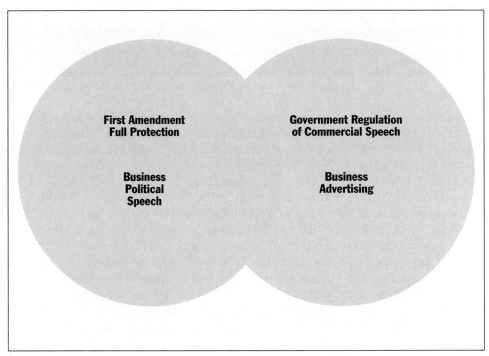

**First Amendment
Full Protection**

**Government Regulation
of Commercial Speech**

**Business
Political
Speech**

**Business
Advertising**

Exhibit 5.1
Commercial Speech Rights and Limitations

Exhibit 5.1 illustrates the degrees of protection afforded business speech. The gray area represents those cases in which the need for information dissemination conflicts with regulations on ad content or form.

The shaded-area cases in the 1970s that resulted in the reform of the commercial speech doctrine began with restrictions on professional advertising. In *Virginia State Board of Pharmacy* v. *Virginia Citizens Consumer Council, Inc.,* 425 U.S. 748 (1976), the Supreme Court dealt with the issue of the validity of a Virginia statute that made it a matter of "unprofessional conduct" for a pharmacist to advertise the price or any discount of prescription drugs. In holding the statute unconstitutional, the Court emphasized the need for the dissemination of information to the public. In a subsequent case, the Court applied the same reasoning to advertising by lawyers [*Bates* v. *State Bar of Arizona,* 433 U.S. 350 (1977).]

First Amendment Rights and Profits from Sensationalism

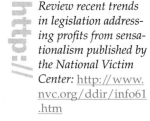

Browse essays discussing the impact of the Internet on free speech: http://www.hotwired.com/staff/userland/24/

Review recent trends in legislation addressing profits from sensationalism published by the National Victim Center: http://www.nvc.org/ddir/info61.htm

In the past few years a number of book publishers and movie producers have pursued criminal figures for the rights to tell the stories of their crimes in books, television programs, and movies. Many of the victims of the crimes and their families have opposed such money-making ventures as benefits that encourage the commission of crimes. The state of New York, for example, has passed a statute requiring that earnings from sales of such stories be used first to compensate victims of the crimes. Statutes such as the one in New York create dilemmas between First Amendment rights and public policy issues concerning criminal activities. The following case deals with this First Amendment dilemma.

Simon & Schuster, Inc. v. Members of the New York State Crime Victims Board
502 U.S. 105 (1991)

DO THE CRIME, MAKE A DIME: MURDERERS TURNED AUTHORS

FACTS

In the summer of 1977, New York City was terrorized by a serial killer popularly known as the Son of Sam. The hunt for the Son of Sam received considerable publicity, and by the time David Berkowitz was identified as the killer and apprehended, the rights to his story were worth a substantial amount of money. Berkowitz's chance to profit from his notoriety while his victims and their families remained uncompensated did not escape the notice of New York State's legislature.

The legislature enacted what came to be known as its Son of Sam law, which provides that monies received by criminals in cases of notoriety will first be made available to crime victims. The author of the statute, Senator Emanual R. Gold, said, "It is abhorrent to one's sense of justice and decency that an individual . . . can expect to receive large sums of money for his story once he is captured—while five people are dead, [and] other people were injured as a result of his conduct."

The law is as follows:

Every person, firm, corporation, partnership, association or other legal entity contracting with any person or the representative or assignee of any person, accused or convicted of a crime in this state, with respect to the reenactment of such crime, by way of a movie, book, magazine article, tape recording, phonograph record, radio or television presentation, live entertainment of any kind, or from the expression of such accused or convicted person's thoughts, feelings, opinions or emotions regarding such crime, shall submit a copy of such contract to the board and pay over to the board any moneys which would otherwise, by terms of such contract, be owing to the person so accused or convicted or his representatives. [N.Y. Exec. Law § 632-a(l) (McKinney 1982)]

The money is deposited in an escrow account and is payable to any victim of the crime who brings suit within five years from the establishment of the account.

Since its enactment in 1977, the Son of Sam law has been invoked only a handful of times. These include for Jean Harris, the convicted killer of "Scarsdale Diet" doctor Herman Tarnower; Mark David Chapman, the convicted assassin of John Lennon; and R. Foster Winans, the former *Wall Street Journal* columnist convicted of insider trading.

Simon & Schuster entered into a contract in 1981 with organized crime figure Henry Hill (who was arrested in 1980) and author Nicholas Pileggi for a book about Hill's life. Hill said, "At the age of twelve my ambition was to be a gangster. To be a wiseguy. To me being a wiseguy was better than being president of the United States." Hill admitted engineering some of the most daring crimes of his day, including the 1978–79 Boston College basketball point-shaving scandal and the theft of $6 million from Lufthansa Airlines in 1978, the largest successful cash robbery in U.S. history.

Hill and Pileggi produced *Wiseguy,* a book published in 1986. The book depicts, in colorful detail, the day-to-day workings of organized crime, primarily in Hill's first-person narrative. Throughout *Wiseguy,* Hill frankly admits to having participated in an astonishing variety of crimes.

The book was also a commercial success: Within 19 months of its publication, more than a million copies were in print. A few years later, the book was converted into a film called *Goodfellas,* which won a host of awards as the best film of 1990.

The Crime Victims Board requested that Simon & Schuster turn over all monies paid to Hill and that all future royalties be payable not to Hill but to the statutorily prescribed escrow account.

Simon & Schuster brought suit seeking both a declaration that the Son of Sam law violates the First Amendment and an injunction barring the statute's enforcement. The district court found the statute consistent with the First

Continued

Amendment. A divided court of appeals affirmed. Simon & Schuster appealed.

JUDICIAL OPINION
O'CONNOR, Justice

A statute is presumptively inconsistent with the First Amendment if it imposes a financial burden on speakers because of the content of their speech.

"Regulations which permit the Government to discriminate on the basis of the content of the message cannot be tolerated under the First Amendment."

The Son of Sam law is such a content-based statute. It singles out income derived from expressive activity for a burden the State places on no other income, and it is directed only at works with a specified content. Whether the First Amendment "speaker" is considered to be Henry Hill, whose income the statute places in escrow because of the story he has told, or Simon & Schuster, which can publish books about crime with the assistance of only those criminals willing to forgo remuneration for at least five years, the statute plainly imposes a financial disincentive only on speech of a particular content.

The Son of Sam law establishes a financial disincentive to create or publish works with a particular content. In order to justify such differential treatment, "the State must show that its regulation is necessary to serve a compelling state interest and is narrowly drawn to achieve that end."

There can be little doubt, on the other hand, that the State has a compelling interest in ensuring that victims of crime are compensated by those who harm them. Every State has a body of tort law serving exactly this interest. The State's interest in preventing wrongdoers from dissipating their assets before victims can recover explains the existence of the State's statutory provisions for prejudgment remedies and orders of restitution.

The State likewise has an undisputed compelling interest in ensuring that criminals do not profit from their crimes. Like most if not all States, New York has long recognized the "fundamental equitable principle," that "[n]o one shall be permitted to profit by his own fraud, or to take advantage of his own wrong, or to found any claim upon his own iniquity, or to acquire property by his own crime."

As a means of ensuring that victims are compensated from the proceeds of crime, the Son of Sam law is significantly over inclusive. As counsel for the Board conceded at oral argument, the statute applies to works on *any* subject, provided that they express the author's thoughts or recollections about his crime, however tangentially or incidentally. In addition, the statute's broad definition of "person convicted of a crime" enables the Board to escrow the income of any author who admits in his work to having committed a crime, whether or not the author was ever actually accused or convicted.

These two provisions combine to encompass a potentially very large number of works. Had the Son of Sam law been in effect at the time and place of publication, it would have escrowed payment for such works as *The Autobiography of Malcolm X*, which describes crimes committed by the civil rights leader before he became a public figure; *Civil Disobedience*, in which Thoreau acknowledges his refusal to pay taxes and recalls his experience in jail; and even the *Confessions of Saint Augustine*, in which the author laments "my past foulness and the carnal corruptions of my soul," one instance of which involved the theft of pears from a neighboring vineyard. The argument that a statute like the Son of Sam law would prevent publication of all of these works is hyperbole—some would have been written without compensation—but the Son of Sam law clearly reaches a wide range of literature that does not enable a criminal to profit from his crime while a victim remains uncompensated.

Should a prominent figure write his autobiography at the end of his career, and include in an early chapter a brief recollection of having stolen (in New York) a nearly worthless item as a youthful prank, the Board would control his entire income from the book for five years, and would make that income available to all of the

Continued

author's creditors, despite the fact that the statute of limitations for this minor incident had long since run.

The State's interest in compensating victims from the fruits of crime is a compelling one, but the Son of Sam law is not narrowly tailored to advance that objective. As a result, the statute is inconsistent with the First Amendment.

The judgment of the Court of Appeals is accordingly reversed.

CASE QUESTIONS

1. Why was the so-called Son of Sam law passed?
2. What happened to monies earned by criminals for "selling their stories"?
3. What book is at issue in this case?
4. Does the Son of Sam statute violate the First Amendment?
5. How can the statute be rewritten?
6. Does Hill keep his royalties?

ETHICAL ISSUES

5.4 Orenthal James (O. J.) Simpson was charged with murder in June 1994 in the double homicide of his ex-wife, Nicole Brown Simpson, and her friend, Ronald Goldman.

Because Mr. Simpson was charged with a capital crime, he was incarcerated upon being charged. California's version of the Son of Sam law only prevents profits from crimes after there has been a conviction. Mr. Simpson authored a book, *I Want to Tell You,* while he was incarcerated and his nine-month trial progressed. Mr. Simpson also signed autographs and sports memorabilia and sold them from the Los Angeles County jail. Mr. Simpson's cottage industry from jail netted him in excess of $3 million. Could a law that passes constitutional muster be passed to prevent profits from crime like Mr. Simpson was able to obtain?

Mr. Simpson was acquitted of the murders. Following his acquittal, prosecutors in the case, Christopher Darden, Marcia Clark, and Hank Goldberg signed multimillion dollar book contracts to write about their experiences during the trial. Alan Dershowitz, Johnnie Cochran, and Robert Shapiro, members of the Simpson defense team, signed six-figure contracts to write books about the trial from the defense perspective. Mr. Simpson has not yet signed for a new book but did make a video detailing his side of the story.

Is it moral to profit from a crime and a trial? Are these contracts a form of making money from the deaths of two people? Many TV stations have refused to carry advertisements for Mr. Simpson's video. Would you have declined this advertising revenue?

Corporate Political Speech

Not all commercial speech is advertising. Some businesses engage in **corporate political speech**. For example, many businesses will participate in advertising campaigns against certain propositions or resolutions—for example, tax resolutions going before the voters. However, many states once restricted the political advertising allowed corporations and other businesses. The rationale for such a restriction was that corporate assets and funds were great and that corporations might be able to exercise too much power in influencing voters.

In *First National Bank of Boston* v. *Bellotti*, the U.S. Supreme Court developed what has become known as the Bellotti doctrine, which gives corporations the same degree of First Amendment protection for their political speech that individuals enjoy in their political speech. Although commercial speech can be regulated, political speech enjoys full First Amendment rights.

First National Bank of Boston v. Bellotti
435 U.S. 765 (1978)

BANKS ARE PEOPLE TOO: FIRST AMENDMENT POLITICAL SPEECH

FACTS

Massachusetts had passed a statute that prohibited businesses and banks from making contributions or expenditures "for the purpose of . . . influencing or affecting the vote on any question submitted to the voters, other than one materially affecting any of the property, business or assets of the corporation." The statute also provided that "no question submitted to the voters solely concerning the taxation of the income, property or transactions of individuals shall be deemed materially to affect the property, business or assets of the corporation." The statute carried a fine of up to $50,000 for the corporation and $10,000 and/or one year imprisonment for corporate officers.

First National Bank and other banks and corporations (appellants) wanted to spend money to publicize their views on an upcoming ballot proposition that would permit the legislature the right to impose a graduated tax on individual income. Frances X. Bellotti, the attorney general for Massachusetts (appellee), told First National and the others that he intended to enforce the statute against them. First National and the others brought suit to have the statute declared unconstitutional. The lower courts held the statute constitutional and First National appealed.

JUDICIAL OPINION

POWELL, Justice

"There is practically universal agreement that a major purpose of [the First] Amendment was to protect the free discussion of governmental affairs." If the speakers here were not corporations, no one would suggest that the State could silence their proposed speech. It is the type of speech indispensable to decision-making in a democracy, and this is no less true because the speech comes from a corporation rather than an individual. The inherent worth of the speech in terms of its capacity for informing the public does not depend upon the identity of its source, whether corporation, association, union, or individual.

The court below nevertheless held that corporate speech is protected by the First Amendment only when it pertains directly to the corporation's interests. In deciding whether this novel and restrictive gloss on the First Amendment comports with the Constitution and the precedents of this Court, we need not survey the outer boundaries of the Amendment's protection of corporate speech, or address the abstract question whether corporations have the full measure of rights that individuals enjoy under the First Amendment. The question in this case, simply put, is whether the corporate identity of the speaker deprives this proposed speech of what otherwise would be its clear entitlement to protection.

Freedom of speech and the other freedoms encompassed by the First Amendment always have been viewed as fundamental components of the liberty safeguarded by the Due Process Clause, and the Court has not identified a separate source for the right when it has been asserted by corporations.

In the realm of protected speech, the legislature is constitutionally disqualified from dictating the subjects about which persons may

Continued

speak and the speakers who may address a public issue. If a legislature may direct business corporations to "stick to business," it may also limit other corporations—religious, charitable, or civic—to their respective "business" when addressing the public. Such power in government to channel the expression of views is unacceptable under the First Amendment. Especially where, as here, the legislature's suppression of speech suggests an attempt to give one side of a debatable public question an advantage in expressing its views to people, the First Amendment is plainly offended. Yet the State contends that its action is necessitated by governmental interests of the highest order. We next consider these asserted interests.

Appellee . . . advances two principal justifications for the prohibition of corporate speech. The first is the State's interest in sustaining the active role of the individual citizen in the electoral process and thereby preventing diminution of the citizen's confidence in government. The second is the interest in protecting the rights of shareholders whose views differ from those expressed by management on behalf of the corporation.

Preserving the integrity of the electoral process, preventing corruption and "sustaining the active, alert responsibility of the individual citizen in a democracy for the wise conduct of government" are interests of the highest importance. Preservation of the individual citizen's confidence in government is equally important.

To be sure, corporate advertising may influence the outcome of the vote; this would be its purpose. But the fact that advocacy may persuade the electorate is hardly a reason to suppress it: The Constitution "protects expression which is eloquent no less than that which is unconvincing." We noted only recently that "the concept that government may restrict speech of some elements of our society in order to enhance the relative voice of others is wholly foreign to the First Amendment. . . . " Moreover, the people in our democracy are entrusted with the responsibility for judging

and evaluating the relative merits of conflicting arguments. They may consider, in making their judgment, the source and credibility of the advocate. But if there be any danger that the people cannot evaluate the information and arguments advanced by appellants, it is a danger contemplated by the Framers of the First Amendment."

The statute is said to . . . prevent the use of corporate resources in furtherance of views with which some shareholders may disagree. This purpose is belied, however, by the provisions of the statute, which are both under- and over-inclusive.

The under-inclusiveness of the statute is self-evident. Corporate expenditures with respect to a referendum are prohibited, while corporate activity with respect to the passage or defeat of legislation is permitted, even though corporations may engage in lobbying more often than they take positions on ballot questions submitted to voters.

The over-inclusiveness of the statute is demonstrated by the fact that [it] would prohibit a corporation from supporting or opposing a referendum even if its shareholders unanimously authorized the contribution or expenditure.

Assuming, arguendo, that protection of shareholders is a "compelling" interest under the circumstances of this case, we find "no substantially relevant correlation between the governmental interest asserted and the State's effort" to prohibit appellants from speaking.

Reversed.

CASE QUESTIONS

1. What did the Massachusetts statute regulate?
2. What justification did Massachusetts offer for the statute? What were its concerns in passing the statute?
3. Why does the Court discuss under-inclusiveness and over-inclusiveness?
4. How does the Court respond to the fact that corporate speech might be more persuasive?
5. Is the statute constitutional?

FOR THE MANAGER'S DESK

THE MOST-CITED NAME IN LAW

Franklin Roosevelt? No way. U.S. Supreme Court Justice Oliver Wendell Holmes? Not even close. Abraham Lincoln, has to be, right? No.

The most-often-cited name in American jurisprudence is George Herman "Babe" Ruth. The Sultan of Swat, the Bambino, a man who rarely appeared in court, who didn't have a lawyer for most of his professional career and who was educated in a Baltimore orphanage.

Yet nearly 50 years after his death (1995 marks the 100th anniversary of his birth), more judges, scholars and attorneys have used his name as a reference, an analogy, a metaphor than they have any other figure, real or imagined. Consider:

U.S. District Judge Leonard P. Moore wrote in 1971 in the *Curt Flood* case, which challenged baseball's reserve clause, that "in this century alone, the names of such players, as Babe Ruth of home run fame, were probably better known to a greater number of our populace than many of our statesmen; and their exploits better remembered than the activities of our outstanding public figures."

In a *Harvard Law Review* reflection on the career of retiring Supreme Court Justice Harry A. Blackmun, Pamela Karlan, who once clerked for the judge, used a baseball metaphor to assess Justice Blackmun's legal career: "He was never a Babe Ruth, but a good everyday hitter and fielder" 108 *Harvard L. Rev.* 13 (1994).

Robert Jarvis, a professor of law at Nova University Shepard Broad Law Center in Florida, unearthed the predominance of Ruth citations and presented it in a paper at a Hofstra University conference, "Baseball and the Sultan of Swat," which celebrated the Bambino's 100th birthday.

"No one else is even close," says Professor Jarvis. "His name is mentioned at least 10 times more often than anyone else."

Professor Jarvis's search, which led to discovering Babe Ruth's omnipresence, started when he and a colleague were discussing their childhood heroes. Professor Jarvis's was Babe Ruth; his colleague's was Albert Einstein.

"Ruth is the greatest figure of the 20th century!" he told her. "What was Einstein's lifetime batting average?" To prove his point, Professor Jarvis bet that the Babe had a greater impact on the American legal system than Einstein.

He conducted searches through Westlaw and Lexis and, after discounting cases and citations involving Albert Einstein Hospital and Babe Ruth Little League, discovered that, indeed, Babe Ruth not only out-hit Einstein in legal circles, but he out-hit everyone else when it came to being mentioned.

When Professor Jarvis saw that Hofstra was calling for papers for its Babe Ruth conference, he submitted "Babe Ruth as Legal Hero." (His article was published in the Summer 1995 issue of the *Florida State University Law Review*.)

"As I researched this, the question I really wanted to find out was, 'Who was Babe Ruth's lawyer?'" he says. Despite numerous biographies and articles on the Babe, none of them mentions a lawyer by name. Before 1922, Professor Jarvis says, the baseball player didn't use a lawyer; he even negotiated his own contracts.

The Babe needed a lawyer in 1929, when he was briefly considered a suspect in his first wife's death (she died in a fire). Professor Jarvis says prominent Boston trial lawyer John P. Feeny, who happened to be a baseball fan and whom the Babe knew socially, served as his counsel. The next year, after marrying his second wife, Claire, the Bambino adopted a daughter, Julia. But again, says Professor Jarvis, there is no record of an attorney.

It's inconceivable today that a figure of Ruth's stature wouldn't use a lawyer—or that when he did use one, the attorney would vanish from the record. Professor Jarvis attributes this to the times: Unlike today's celebrities, the Babe was shielded from negative publicity by a friendly press. And when the Babe's behavior— which included speeding and public drunkenness—was cited, it was treated as a matter for organized baseball rather than the courts.

Continued

Babe Ruth was a party in only two reported cases. In the first, *Ruth D. Educational Films Inc.*, 185 N.Y.S. 952 (App. Div. 1920), he sought $1 million in damages and an injunction against the company. The suit charged that Educational Films Inc. had produced several newsreels and two shorts about Babe Ruth without compensating him. A New York trial court dismissed the action, however, on the ground that Mr. Ruth was a public figure and that his home runs were news; the dismissal was upheld on appeal.

The second case, according to Professor Jarvis, involved candy bars. The Curtis Candy Co., famed for its Baby Ruth bar, claimed the candy was named after the daughter of President Grover Cleveland.

The Babe was making his own candy bar, called Ruth's Homerun, and hired Washington, D.C., trademark lawyer Victor W. Cutting to procure a trademark for it. The Babe lost his suit when the government refused to grant him a trademark on his own confection, because of the likelihood of public confusion.

In all, Professor Jarvis says, Mr. Ruth used only four lawyers in his lifetime for advice and representation. One of them was his manager—Miller J. Huggins, who ran the New York Yankees from 1918 to 1929. Christy Walsh was a member of the California bar but didn't practice law; he handled Mr. Ruth's finances during his playing career. The Babe's second wife's

father, James Monroe Merritt, was a law professor at the University of Georgia.

But the attorney involved longest with Babe's affairs, says Professor Jarvis, was Melvyn Gordon Lowenstein, a New York lawyer who succeeded Mr. Walsh as the player's business manager. Mr. Lowenstein, who died in 1971, handled Mr. Ruth's finances and was executor of his estate.

So why has George Herman "Babe" Ruth made such an impression on American society, and the legal community, that he still occupies a part of the American psyche? "He's taken on a mythic proportion," says Professor Jarvis. "He was a noun; now he's an adjective— Ruthian. You can use him in so many kinds of comparisons."

Source: Jon Caroulis,"Babe Ruth: The Sultan of Legal Cites? Yup." *The National Law Journal*, May 22, 1995, p. A12. Reprinted with the permission of *The National Law Journal*, © 1995, The New York Law Publishing Company.

C O N S I D E R . . . **5.8** Mrs. Margaret Gilleo owns a single-family home in the area of Willow Hill in Ladue, Missouri. Mrs. Gilleo placed a 24-inch by 36-inch sign on her lawn that read, "SAY NO TO WAR IN THE PERSIAN GULF. CALL CONGRESS NOW." A Ladue ordinance prohibited such signs in residential areas and Mrs. Gilleo was asked to remove it. She filed suit claiming the ordinance violated her free speech rights. She said that other residents were permitted to put signs up advertising their homes for sale. Should Mrs. Gilleo's rights be protected? Does it make a difference that her speech was political and not commercial speech? [*City of Ladue* v. *Gilleo*, 114 S. Ct. 2038 (1994).]

Eminent Domain—The Takings Clause

The right of a governmental body to take title to property for a public use is called **eminent domain**. This right is established in the Fifth Amendment to the Constitution and may also be established in various state constitutions. Private individuals cannot require property owners to sell their property, but governmental entities can require property owners to transfer title for public projects for the public good. The Fifth Amendment provides that "property shall not be taken for a public use without just compensation." Thus, for a governmental entity to exercise properly the right of eminent domain, three factors must be present: public purpose, taking (as opposed to regulating), and just compensation.

PUBLIC PURPOSE

To exercise eminent domain, the exercising governmental authority must establish that the taking is necessary for the accomplishment of a government or **public purpose**. When eminent domain is mentioned, use of property for highways and schools is thought of most frequently. However, the right of the government to eminent domain extends much further. For example, the following uses have been held to constitute public purposes: the condemnation of slum housing (for purposes of improving city areas), the limitation of mining and excavation within city limits, the declaration of property as a historic landmark, and the taking of property to provide a firm that is a town's economic base with a large enough tract for expansion.

According to the U. S. Supreme Court, the public purpose requirement for eminent domain is to be interpreted broadly, and "the role of the judiciary in determining whether that power is being exercised for a public purpose is an extremely narrow one" [*United States ex rel. TVA* v. *Welch*, 327 U.S. 546 (1946)].

TAKING OR REGULATING

For a governmental entity to be required to pay a landowner compensation under the doctrine of eminent domain, that there has been a taking of the property must be established. Mere regulation of the property does not constitute a taking, as established by *Village of Euclid, Ohio* v. *Ambler Realty Co.*, 272 U.S. 365 (1926). Rather, a taking must go so far as to deprive the landowner of any use of the property. In the landmark case of *Pennsylvania Coal* v. *Mahon*, 260 U.S. 393 (1922), the Supreme Court established standards for determining a taking as opposed to mere regulation. At that time Pennsylvania had a statute that prohibited the mining of coal under any land surface where the result would be the subsidence of any structure used as a human habitation. The owners of the rights to mine subsurface coal brought suit challenging the regulation as a taking, and the Supreme Court ruled in their favor, holding that the statute was more than regulation and, in fact, was an actual taking of the subsurface property rights.

Because of the vast amount of technology that has developed since that case was decided, there are many new and subtly different issues in what constitutes a taking. For example, in some areas the regulation of cable television companies is an infringement on air rights. Such specialized areas of real estate rights are particularly difficult to resolve. In *Loretto* v. *Teleprompter Manhattan CATV Corp.*, 458 U.S. 100 (1982), the U.S. Supreme Court held that the small invasion of property by the placement of cable boxes and wires did constitute a taking, albeit very small, and required compensation of the property owners for this small, but permanent, occupation of their land. Recently, the courts have been faced with the issue of whether zoning or use regulations serve to limit the use of land so much that the result is a taking.

In recent years, the issue of taking has addressed local zoning restrictions on development. These restrictions focus on maintenance of beaches, wetlands, and other natural habitats. For example, in *Nollan* v. *California Coastal Commission*, 483 U.S. 825 (1987), the Nollans sought permission from the California Coastal Commission to construct a home on their coastal lot where they currently had only a small bungalow. The commission refused to grant permission to the Nollans for construction of their home unless they agreed to give a public easement across their lot for beach access. The Supreme Court held that the demand by the commission for an easement was a taking without compensation and, in effect, prevented the Nollans from using their property until they surrendered their exclusive use.

Yet another issue that arises in taking occurs when regulations take effect after owners have acquired land but before it is developed. In *Lucas* v. *South Carolina Coastal Council*, 505 U.S. 1003 (1992), the U.S. Supreme Court declared that ex post facto legislation that prevents development of previously purchased land is a taking. In *Lucas*, David Lucas purchased for $975,000 two residential lots on the Isle of Palms in Charleston County, South Carolina. In 1988 the South Carolina legislature enacted the Beachfront Management Act, which barred any permanent habitable structures on coastal properties. The court held South Carolina was required to compensate Mr. Lucas because his land was rendered useless.

JUST COMPENSATION

The final requirement for the proper exercise by a governmental entity of the right of eminent domain is that the party from whom the property is being taken be given **just compensation**. The issue of just compensation is difficult to determine and is always a question of fact. Basic to this determination is that the owner is to be compensated for loss and that the compensation is not measured by the governmental entity's gain. In *United States* v. *Miller*, 317 U.S. 369 (1943), the Supreme Court held that in cases where it can be determined, fair market value is the measure of compensation. And in *United States ex rel. TVA* v. *Powelson*, 319 U.S. 266 (1943), the Supreme Court defined fair market value to be "what a willing buyer would pay in cash to a willing seller."

Possible problems in applying these relatively simple standards include peculiar value to the owner, consequential damages, and greater value of the land because of the proposed governmental project. Basically, the issue of just compensation becomes an issue of appraisal, which is affected by all the various factors involved. Thus, in determining just compensation, the courts must consider such factors as surrounding property values and the owner's proposed use.

C O N S I D E R . . . **5.9** The Commonwealth of Massachusetts, in need of an interim facility for female prisoners released from state prison but not yet entitled to full release, condemned a motel located near the court complex for use as the necessary shelter. Several individuals are opposed to the taking of the property. The owner of the motel protests on the ground that a public purpose is not being served. The surrounding restaurant, business, and motel owners protest on the same grounds, as well as on grounds that the resulting devaluation of their property and loss of income constitute a taking of their properties for which they must be compensated. The motel owner objects further when the appraised value and compensation offer are reduced because of the resulting effects on surrounding properties. Discuss the issues of public purpose, the regulating versus taking of surrounding lands, and just compensation.

Procedural Due Process

Both the Fifth and the Fourteenth Amendments require state and federal governments to provide citizens (businesses included) due process under the law. **Procedural due process** is a right that requires notice and the opportunity to be heard before rights or properties are taken away from an individual or business. Most people are familiar with due process as it exists in the criminal justice system: the right to a lawyer, a trial, and so on (Chapter 8). However, procedural due process is also very much a part of civil law. Before an agency can take away a business license or suspend a license or impose a fine for a violation, there must be due process. This is true of both state and federal agencies.

Businesses encounter the constitutional protections of due process in their relationships with customers. For example, the eviction of a nonpaying tenant cannot be done unilaterally. The tenant has the right to be heard in the setting of a hearing. The landlord must file an action against the tenant, and the tenant will have the opportunity to present defenses for nonpayment of rent. The due process clause of the U.S. Constitution provides protection for individuals before their property is taken. Property includes land (as in the case of eminent domain, see pgs. 178–180), rights of possession (tenants and leases), and even intangible property rights. For example, students cannot be expelled from schools, colleges, or universities without the right to be heard. Students must have some hearing before their property rights with respect to education are taken away.

All proceedings designed to satisfy due process requirements must provide notice and the right to be heard and present evidence (see Chapter 6 for more details). If these rights are not afforded, the constitutional right of due process has been denied and the action taken is rescinded until due process requirements are met. Suppose that OSHA charged a company with safety violations in its plants. Before a fine or order could be imposed, procedural due process requires that the company have the right to be heard and present evidence on the violation. In court cases, a matter reduced to a judgment entitles the victorious side to collect on that judgment. However, under due process, even the proceedings for collection allow the losing party or debtor to be notified of the proceedings and to be heard.

C O N S I D E R . . . **5.10** When the Crafts moved into their residence in October 1972, they noticed that there were two separate gas and electric meters and only one water meter serving the premises. The residence had been used previously as a duplex. The Crafts assumed, based on information from the seller, that the second set of meters was inoperative.

In 1973, the Crafts began receiving two bills: their regular bill and another with an account number in the name of Willie C. Craft, as opposed to Willie S. Craft. In October 1973, after learning from a Memphis Light, Gas & Water (MLG&W,) meter reader that both sets of meters were running in their home, the Crafts hired a private plumber and electrical contractor to combine the meters into one gas and one electric meter. Because the contractor did not combine the meters properly, they continued to receive two bills until January 1974.

Continued

During this time period, the Crafts' utility service was terminated five times for nonpayment.

Mrs. Craft missed work several times to go to MLG&W offices to resolve the "double billing" problem. She sought explanations on each occasion but was never given an answer.

In February 1974, the Crafts and other MLG&W customers filed suit for violation of the Due Process Clause. The district court dismissed the case. The court of appeals reversed and MLG&W appealed.

Have the Crafts been given due process? [*Memphis Light, Gas & Water Div.* v. *Craft,* 436 U.S. 1 (1978).]

Substantive Due Process

Procedural rules deal with how things are done. All rules on the adjudication of agency charges are procedural rules. Similarly, all rules for the trial of a civil case, from discovery to jury instructions, are also procedural. These rules exist to make sure the substantive law is upheld. Substantive law consists of rights, obligations, and behavior standards. Criminal laws are substantive laws, and criminal procedure rules are procedural laws. **Substantive due process** is the right to have laws that do not deprive businesses or citizens of property or other rights without justification and reason.

Most of the early court cases dealing with substantive due process centered around economic issues. During the late nineteenth and early twentieth centuries, there was as much expansion of business regulation as there was expansion of business. Many of these regulations were challenged on grounds they were depriving businesses of economic rights without justification and unreasonably. In the landmark case of *Lochner* v. *New York,* 198 U.S. 45 (1905), the U.S. Supreme Court invalidated a New York statute that prohibited bakery employees from working more than 10 hours a day and 60 hours a week. The Court found that in balancing the economic rights of the business against the health of employees, there was not enough evidence to show that the law accomplished its purpose. In other words, the statute was an unjustified invasion of the rights of bakeries without some "substantial showing" of benefits achieved.

Since *Lochner* and other early twentieth-century cases, the Court has broadened its standards for substantive due process. Now the Court uses a test of "some (more or less) relation" to the achievement of a government goal. A substantial showing is not required, only a tenuous connection. So long as the law is reasonably designed to correct a harm, it is substantively valid.

CONSIDER . . . **5.11** Larry Collins was an employee in the sanitation department of Harker Heights, Texas (respondent). On October 21, 1988, he died of asphyxia after entering a manhole to unstop a sewer line. His widow, Myra Jo Collins (petitioner), brought suit alleging that Collins "had a constitutional right to be free from unreasonable risks of harm to his body, mind and emotions and a constitutional right to be protected from the city of Harker Heights's custom and policy of deliberate indifference

Continued

toward the safety of its employees." Her complaint alleged that the city violated that right by following a custom and policy of not training its employees about the dangers of working in sewer lines and manholes, not providing safety equipment at job sites, and not providing safety warnings. The complaint also alleged that a prior incident had given the city notice of the risks of entering the sewer lines and that the city had systematically and intentionally failed to provide the equipment and training required by a Texas statute.

The district court dismissed the complaint and the court of appeals affirmed. Collins appealed on the grounds that the city substantively deprived her husband of his life through its lack of training.

Did the city violate Collins's due process rights? [*Collins* v. *City of Harker Heights, Texas,* 503 U.S. 115 (1992).]

C O N S I D E R . . . **5.12** The Village of Hoffman passed an ordinance that requires a business to obtain a license if it sells any items that are "designed or marked for use with illegal cannabis or drugs." Guidelines define the items (such as "roach clips," "pipes," "paraphernalia"). Flipside is a merchant in the village selling, among other things, "roach clips" and pipes specially designed for smoking marijuana. Flipside filed suit challenging the ordinance as overly vague, broad, and violative of due process because of the inability to apply the ordinance consistently. Is the ordinance constitutional? [*Village of Hoffman Est.* v. *Flipside, Hoffman Est.,* 455 U.S. 191 (1982).]

E T H I C A L   I S S U E S

5.5 What ethical issues do you see in Flipside's sales of "roach clips" and pipes? While the items themselves are legal, do they encourage and facilitate illegal drug use?

Equal Protection Rights for Business

The Fourteenth Amendment grants citizens the right to the **equal protection** of the law. Lawmakers, however, are often required to make certain distinctions in legislating and regulating that result in classes of individuals being treated differently. Such different or **disparate treatment** is justified only if there is some rational basis for it. In other words, there must be a rational connection between the classifications and the achievement of some governmental objective. Most classifications survive the rational basis test. But an example of a classification that would not survive is one requiring the manufacturers of soft drinks to use only nonbreakable bottles for their product but allowing juice manufacturers to use glass bottles; this is irrational. If there is a public safety concern about the glass, it must apply equally to all beverage manufacturers.

THE ROLE OF CONSTITUTIONS
IN INTERNATIONAL LAW

Browse constitutions from around the world: http://www. uni-hamburg.de/ law/index.html

Although the U.S. Constitution is the basis for all law in the United States, not all countries follow a similar system of governance. The United States and England (and countries established through English colonization) tend to follow a pattern of establishing a general set of principles, as set forth in a constitution, and of reliance on custom, tradition, and precedent for the establishment of law in particular legal areas.

In countries such as France, Germany, and Spain (and nations colonized through their influences), a system of law that is dependent on code law exists. These countries have very specific codes of law that attempt to be all-inclusive and cover each circumstance that could arise under a particular provision. These nations do not depend on court decisions, and often there are inconsistent results in application of the law because of the lack of dependence on judicial precedent.

Approximately 27 countries follow Islamic law in some way. The incorporation of other systems (such as a constitution or code) depends upon a nation's history, including its colonization by other countries and those countries' forms of law. When Islamic law is the dominant force in a country, it governs all aspects of personal and business life. The constitutions in these lands are the tenets of the nation's religion.

SUMMARY

What is the Constitution?
- U.S. Constitution—document detailing authority of U.S. government and rights of its citizens

What are the constitutional limitations on business regulations?
- Commerce Clause—portion of the U.S. Constitution that controls federal regulation of business; limits Congress to regulating of interstate and international commerce
- Intrastate commerce—business within state borders
- Interstate commerce—business across state lines

Who has more power to regulate business—the states or the federal government?
- Supremacy Clause—portion of the U.S. Constitution that defines relationship between state and federal laws

What individual freedoms granted under the Constitution apply to businesses?
- Bill of Rights—first ten amendments to the U.S. Constitution that provides individual freedoms and protection of individual rights
- First Amendment—freedom of speech protection in U.S. Constitution
- Commercial speech—ads and other speech by businesses
- Corporate political speech—business ads or positions on candidates or referenda

- Due process—indicates constitutional guarantee against the taking of property or other governmental exercise of authority without an opportunity for a hearing
- Equal protection—indicates constitutional protection for U.S. citizens against disparate treatment
- Substantive due process—constitutional protection against taking of rights or property by statute

QUESTIONS AND PROBLEMS

1. Oklahoma statute Title 29, Section 4-115(B) provides in part: "No person may transport or ship minnows for sale outside the state which were seined or procured within the waters of this state." William Hughes holds a Texas license to operate a commercial minnow business near Wichita Falls, Texas. Hughes was arrested by an Oklahoma game warden for transporting minnows purchased from a licensed Oklahoma dealer from Oklahoma to Texas.

   He was charged with a violation of § 4-115 (B) and he challenged the charges on the grounds that the statute was repugnant to the Commerce Clause. The lower court convicted and fined him, and he appealed. Is the Oklahoma statute constitutional or an impermissible burden on interstate commerce? [*Hughes* v. *Oklahoma*, 441 U.S. 322 (1979).]

2. Mrs. Florence Dolan owned a plumbing and electric supply store on Main Street in Portland. Fanno Creek flows through the southeastern corner of Mrs. Dolan's lot on which her store is located. She applied to the city for a permit to redevelop her lot. Her plans included the addition of a second structure.

   The City Planning Commission granted Mrs. Dolan's permit but included the following requirement:

   Where landfill and/or development is allowed within and adjacent to the 100-year floodplain, the city shall require the dedication of sufficient open land area for greenway adjoining and within the floodplain. This area shall include portinos at a suitable elevation for the construction of a pedestrian/bicycle pathway within the floodplain in accordance with the adopted pedestrian/bicycle plan.

   Mrs. Dolan maintained that the requirements were a taking of her property because she would be required to reserve a portion of her property for the pedestrian/bike path, and her plans would have to be redone to accommodate the city's requirements. The city maintains that its requirements are all simply part of a redevelopment plan for the city and a means of working with the flood plain created by Fanno Creek. Mrs. Dolan says the city has imposed additional expense and forced her to dedicate a large portion of her lot to public use. Who is correct? Is Portland taking property from Mrs. Dolan? Is the city required to pay compensation to her? [*Dolan* v. *City of Tigard*, 114 S. Ct. 2309 (1994).]

3. The Public Utility Regulatory Policies Act of 1978 (PURPA) was part of the federal legislation of the 1970's energy crisis. PURPA gave the Federal Energy Regulatory Commission (FERC) the power to regulate the development of small and cogeneration power facilities. The state of Mississippi has brought suit in federal district court to have that portion of PURPA declared unconstitutional. Mississippi maintains the federal government is regulating purely intrastate matters and that because there is no commerce involved, there can be no reliance on the federal government's commerce power. Is PURPA unconstitutional? Is the regulation of utilities the regulation of commerce? [*Federal Energy Regulatory Commission* v. *Mississippi*, 456 U.S. 742 (1982).]

4. Bruce Church, Inc., is a company engaged in extensive commercial farming in Arizona and California. A provision of the Arizona Fruit and Vegetable Standardization Act requires that all cantaloupes grown in Arizona "be packed in regular compact arrangement in closed standard containers approved by the supervisor." Arizona, through its agent Pike, issued an order prohibiting Bruce Church, the appellee, from transporting uncrated cantaloupes from its ranch in Parker, Arizona, to nearby Blythe, California, for packing and processing.

   It would take many months and $200,000 for Bruce Church to construct a processing plant in Parker. Further, Church had $700,000 worth of cantaloupes ready for transportation. Church filed suit in federal district court challenging the constitutionality of the Arizona statutory provision on shipping cantaloupes. The court issued an injunction against the enforcement of the act on the grounds that it was an undue burden on interstate commerce. Will the regulation withstand Commerce Clause scrutiny? [*Pike* v. *Bruce Church*, Inc. 397 U.S. 137 (1970).]

5. The International Longshoremen's Union refused to unload cargo shipped from the Soviet Union as a way of protesting the Soviet invasion of Afghanistan. Allied International, an importer of Soviet wood products, could not get its wood unloaded when it arrived in Boston. Allied sued on the basis of the National Labor Relations Act, claiming the conduct was an unlawful boycott. The union claims no commerce is involved and that federal law does not apply. Is there commerce? Does the National Labor Relations Act apply? [*International Longshoremen's Association* v. *Allied International Inc.*, 456 U.S. 212 (1982).]

6. For the past 62 years, Pacific Gas & Electric (PG&E) has distributed a newsletter in its monthly billing envelopes. The newsletter, called Progress, reaches over three million customers and has contained tips on conservation, utility billing information, public interest information, and political editorials.

   A group called TURN (Toward Utility Rate Normalization) asked the Public Utility Commission (PUC) of California to declare that the envelope space belonged to the ratepayers and that TURN was entitled to use the Progress space four times each year. The PUC ordered TURN's request, and PG&E appealed the order to the California Supreme Court. When the California Supreme Court denied review, PG&E appealed to the U.S. Supreme Court, alleging a violation of its First Amendment rights. Is PG&E correct? [*Pacific Gas & Electric* v. *Public Utility Commission of California*, 475 U.S. 1 (1986).]

7. The Minnesota legislature enacted a 1977 statute banning the retail sale of milk in plastic nonreturnable, nonrefillable containers, but permitting such sale in other nonrefillable containers, such as paperboard milk cartons. Clover Leaf Creamery brought suit challenging the constitutionality of the statute under the Equal Protection Clause, alleging that there was no rational basis for the statute. The Minnesota legislature's purpose in passing the statute was to control solid waste, arguing that plastic containers take up more space in solid waste disposal dumps. The Minnesota Supreme Court found evidence to the contrary: The jugs took up less space and required less energy to produce. On appeal to the U.S. Supreme Court, can the statute survive a constitutional challenge? Is there a "rational basis" for the statute? What effect does the evidence to the contrary have on the statute's constitutionality? [*Minnesota* v. *Clover Leaf Creamery*, 449 U.S. 456 (1981).]

8. Iowa passed a statute restricting the length of vehicles that could use its highways. The length chosen was 55 feet. Semi trailers are generally 55 feet long; double or twin tracks (one cab pulling two trailers) are 65 feet long. Other states in the Midwest have adopted the 65-foot standard. Consolidated Freightways brought suit challenging the Iowa statute as an unconstitutional burden on interstate commerce. The Iowa statute meant Consolidated could not use its twins in Iowa. The Iowa legislature claims the 65-foot doubles are more dangerous than the 55-foot singles. However, the statute did provide a border exception: Towns and cities along Iowa borders could make an exception to the length requirement to allow trucks to use their city and town roads. Can Iowa's statute survive a constitutional challenge? Is the statute an impermissible burden

on interstate commerce? [*Kassel* v. *Consolidated Freightways Corp.*, 450 U.S. 662 (1981).]

9. In 1989, the city of Cincinnati authorized Discovery Network, Inc., to place 62 free-standing newsracks on public property for distributing free magazines that consisted primarily of advertising for Discovery Network's service. In 1990, the city became concerned about the safety and attractive appearance of its streets and sidewalks and revoked Discovery Network's permit on the ground that the magazines were commercial handbills whose distribution was prohibited on public property by a preexisting ordinance. Discovery Network says the prohibition is an excessive regulation of its commercial speech and a violation of its rights. The city maintains the elimination of the newsracks decreases litter and increases safety. Is the ban on newsracks constitutional? [*City of Cincinnati* v. *Discovery Network, Inc.*, 507 U.S. 410 (1993).]

10. In 1988 the voters of Escondido, California, approved Proposition K, an ordinance that set rents at their 1986 levels and prohibited increases without city council approval. John and Irene Yee own several mobile home parks in Escondido and have filed suit alleging that "the rent control law has had the effect of depriving [them] of all use and occupancy of [their] real property and granting to tenants the right to physically permanently occupy their land." Is the rent ordinance constitutional? [*Yee* v. *City of Escondido, California*, 503 U.S. 519 (1992).]

Judgment

A. Duda & Sons, Inc., has a plaque posted in the lobby of its company headquarters that reads: "But seek ye first the Kingdom of God, and his righteousness and all these things shall be added unto you." An employee complained to the Equal Employment Opportunity Commission (EEOC) about the plaque, stating that it constituted religious harassment in the workplace.

At the Montgomery County Middle School, the name of its December music event was changed from "Christmas Concert" to "Winter Concert" when a teacher complained that the use of the word "Christmas" constituted religious harassment.

Based on these complaints and others (a total of 538 religious harassment complaints), the EEOC proposed rules on religious harassment that prohibited verbal or physical contact that "denigrates or shows hostility or aversion toward an individual because of his/her religion . . . or that of his/her relatives, friends or associates."

An executive in a Florida hospital asked, "These rules could prevent an employee from wearing a necklace with a crucifix to work. Would I have to control Bible reading by my employees when they're having a break? The rules are unmanageable. Where do I turn? How can I raise my concerns about them?"

CHAPTER 6

The regulations of administrative agencies at the federal

Administrative Law

and state levels

affect the day-to-day operations of all businesses. From

permits to labor regulations, every business is affected.

Agencies are the enforcement arm of governments. Cre-

ated by one of the branches of government, they affect

the way businesses operate. The following questions

are answered in this chapter: What is an administrative

agency? What does it do? What laws govern the opera-

tion of administrative agencies? How do agencies pass

rules? How do agencies enforce the law?

Grade A Fancy ketchup must flow no more than 9 centimeters in 30 seconds at 69 degrees Fahrenheit.
Excerpt from a Food and Drug Administration regulation

Ninety percent of a 100-person panel, composed of people 50 to 70 years old, must be able to open and close the package within five minutes, then again within one minute.
Consumer Product Safety Commission rule on child-proof caps

WHAT ARE ADMINISTRATIVE AGENCIES?

An **administrative agency** is best defined by what it is not: It is not a legislative or judicial body. An administrative agency is a statutory creation within the executive branch with the power to make, interpret, and enforce laws. Such agencies exist at practically every level of government, and their names vary considerably. Exhibit 6.2 (pg. 193) is a list of all the federal administrative agencies and their acronyms.

States also have administrative agencies that are responsible for such things as the licensing of professions and occupations. Architects, contractors, attorneys, accountants, cosmetologists, doctors, dentists, real estate agents, and nurses are all professionals whose occupations are regulated in most states by some administrative agency. Utility and securities regulation are also handled by administrative agencies in each of the states.

All these agencies at every level of government derive their authority from the particular legislature responsible for their creation. Congress creates federal agencies; state legislatures create state agencies; and city governments create their cities' administrative agencies.

The structures of agencies may differ significantly but most will have an organizational chart to show how different departments operate. Exhibit 6.1 is a sample organizational chart of a state utility commission, and Exhibit 6.3 (pg. 194) is an organizational chart for the Securities and Exchange Commission.

Legislators begin the administrative process leading to the creation of an agency with the recognition of a problem and the passage of a law designed to remedy the problem. The enacted law gives the overview—what the legislature wants to accomplish and the penalties for noncompliance with the law. The law may also establish an administrative agency with the power to adopt rules to deal with the problems of enforcement of the statute. The law, referred to as an **enabling act**, gives the agency the power to deal with the issues and problems the act addresses.

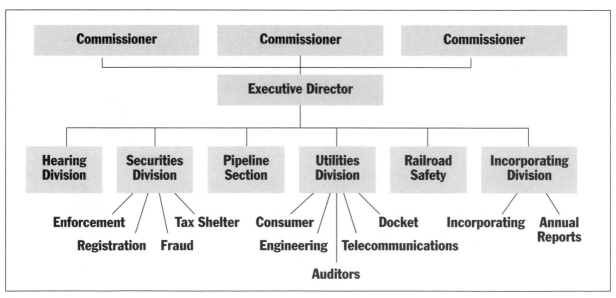

Exhibit 6.1
Organizational Chart of the Arizona Corporation Commission

Executive Office of the President

Executive Departments

Department of Agriculture

Department of Commerce

Department of Defense

  Office of the Secretary of Defense

  Department of the Air Force

  Department of the Army

  Department of the Navy

Department of Education

Department of Energy

Department of Health and Human Services

Department of Housing and Urban Development (HUD)

Department of the Interior

Department of Justice

Department of Labor

Department of State

Department of Transportation

Department of the Treasury

Independent Agencies

Action

Administrative Conference of the United States

Advisory Committee on Intergovernmental Relations

American Battle Monuments Commission

Appalachian Regional Council

Board for International Broadcasting

Civil Aeronautics Board (CAB)

Commission on Fine Arts (CFA)

Commodity Futures Trading Commission (CFTC)

Consumer Product Safety Commission (CPSC)

Delaware River Basin Commission

Environmental Protection Agency (EPA)

Equal Employment Opportunity Commission (EEOC)

Export-Import Bank of the United States

Farm Credit Administration (FCA)

Federal Communications Commission (FCC)

Federal Deposit Insurance Corporation (FDIC)

Federal Election Commission (FEC)

Federal Emergency Management Agency (FEMA)

Federal Home Loan Bank Board (FHLBB)

Federal Labor Relations Authority (FLRA)

Federal Maritime Commission (FMC)

Federal Mediation and Conciliation Service

Federal Mine Safety and Health Review Commission

Federal Reserve System

Federal Trade Commission (FTC)

General Services Administration (GSA)

Inter-American Foundation

International Communications Agency (ICA)

International Development Cooperation Agency (IDCA)

Interstate Commerce Commission (ICC)

Merit Systems Protection Board

National Aeronautics and Space Administration (NASA)

National Capital Planning Commission

National Credit Union Administration

National Foundation on the Arts and Humanities

National Labor Relations Board (NLRB)

National Mediation Board

National Science Foundation (NSF)

National Transportation Safety Board (NTSB)

Nuclear Regulatory Commission (NRC)

Occupational Safety and Health Administration (OSHA)

Office of Personnel Management (OPM)

Overseas Private Investment Corporation

Panama Canal Commission

Pennsylvania Avenue Development Corporation

Postal Rate Commission

Railroad Retirement Board (RRB)

Securities and Exchange Commission (SEC)

Selective Service System (SSS)

Small Business Administration (SBA)

Susquehanna River Basin Commission

Tennessee Valley Authority (TVA)

U.S. Arms Control and Disarmament Agency

U.S. Commission on Civil Rights

U.S. International Trade Commission

U.S. Metric Board

U.S. Postal Service

U.S. Water Resources Council

Veterans Administration

Exhibit 6.2
Federal Administrative Agencies

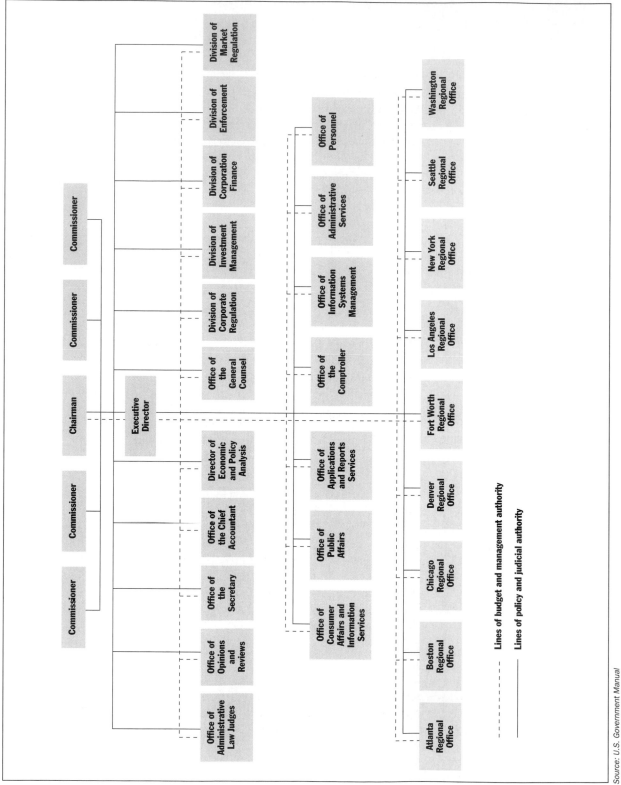

Exhibit 6.3
SEC Organizational Chart

Source: U.S. Government Manual

ROLES OF ADMINISTRATIVE AGENCIES

Specialization

Administrative agencies are specialists in their particular areas of law, and this type of specialization is needed not only because of the complexities of law but also because of the complexities of the regulated areas. For example, environmental regulation is complex because of both the chemical analyses involved in determining pollution levels and the types of equipment and technology needed for controlling pollution.

Visit the Federal Communication Commision: http://www.fcc.gov/
Visit the Commodity Futures Trading Commision: http://www.cftc.gov/cftc/

Similarly, neither Congress nor the judiciary has the necessary specialization or expertise to deal with the highly technical matters handled by administrative agencies, such as broadcast frequencies (Federal Communications Commission), commodities trading (Commodity Futures Trading Commission), and mining (Federal Mine Safety and Health Review Commission). The people staffing these agencies, therefore, can be chosen for their expertise, which helps ensure adequate protection for the public and the members of the regulated industries.

Protection for Small Business

Administrative agencies have traditionally been protectors of small interests. An individual or competitor who finds a false advertisement in a newspaper would probably not take the time or effort to bring a private suit to collect damages for the false advertisement. But an agency created to oversee truth in advertising would undertake routine enforcement against such advertisements, and so the small business competitor and the consumer are afforded protection and rights they might not otherwise have. An agency's enforcement authority has the effect of making others more aware of the need for compliance. Enforcement of one small claim creates an atmosphere of compliance.

Faster Relief

If enforcement of all government regulations were dependent upon court hearings, not only would there be a substantial increase in the caseload of the courts, but there would be a backlog for those hearings that would interfere with the goal of swift action and enforcement. Administrative agencies help to expedite the investigation and disposition of violations. In addition, administrative agencies serve as review boards for the granting of licenses. If such license applications required legislative hearings, license and permit applications would be delayed substantially and businesses would be left in limbo until a hearing could be held. An administrative agency provides an efficient way for fast licensing and timely enforcement.

Due Process

Administrative agencies provide the opportunity to be heard before any action to remove property, rights, or income can be taken. *Goldberg* v. *Kelly*, 397 U.S. 254 (1970), is often described as the judicial decision responsible for the creation of administrative agencies and procedures as we have them today. In *Goldberg*, the Supreme Court ruled that before a benefit (such as aid to dependent children) could be taken away, the agency must present its evidence and allow a response. Regulatory action thus requires due process, which includes the right to see the evidence and present your side of the story.

Social Goals

Visit the Environmental Protection Agency: http://www.epa.gov/

Some experts see administrative agencies as a means for accomplishing social goals that might otherwise be delayed or debated until no resolution can be reached. For example, the Environmental Protection Agency is assigned the goal of creating a cleaner environment. If every permit for a factory or rule on discharges were debated by Congress, the goal might be lost in the political arena. Further, having judicial review and determination of these issues would result in a delay that might make the goal moot. Administrative agencies can be created and then permitted to function independently of the judicial and legislative branches. Very often, these agencies are created in response to a pressing social issue. For example, the Federal Home Loan Bank Board was established to regulate home mortgages after all the difficulties with foreclosures in the Great Depression. The goal was a more equitable system for mortgage lending and mortgage foreclosure, and an agency was created to accomplish those goals.

E T H I C A L   I S S U E S

6.1 The Internal Revenue Service (IRS) is a federal administrative agency responsible for drafting the regulations on taxes, collecting tax dollars, and ensuring compliance with the tax laws. The following questions and data are routinely asked and collected by IRS agents in the course of tax audits or reviews of individual tax returns to ensure compliance with the tax laws:

1. Home phone number
2. Work phone number
3. Date of birth
4. Confirm that 1994 is an extension—please provide copy.
5. Either spouse previously married? Paying or receiving alimony or child support? If so, how much and paid to whom?
6. Educational background of both—highest level achieved—degree received, etc.
7. Mr. X's previous occupation, employer, and date
8. Date(s) of birth of children
9. Purchase documents—application, closing documents, etc., for home. Who is mortgage holder? [What is the] payment?
10. What other real estate owned and when acquired? Monthly rent? Do you manage or do you have a management company?
11. Did you make any improvements during 1993 to any of your real estate? What was done, how much was it, and how was it paid for?
12. How many autos do you own? What are they? What is the payment?
13. Do you own any large assets (over $10,000) besides auto and real estate? What is it, and where is it kept? Is it paid for—if not, what is the payment?
14. Did you sell any assets in 1993? If so, what, to whom, and how much?
15. Did you loan anyone any money during 1993? If so, who and how much?
16. Did you receive repayments of any loaned money in 1993?
17. What loans do you have besides auto and mortgage? How much? Monthly payment?
18. Do you ever take cash advances from credit cards or lines of credit? How much and how often?
19. What cash did you have on hand in 1993 usually, personally or for business, not in a bank—at your home, safe deposit box, hidden somewhere, etc.?
20. What is the largest amount of cash you had at any one time in 1993?

Continued

21. Did you transfer funds between your accounts? If so, how much and when?
22. Did Mrs. X deposit her paychecks into the bank? What account?
23. Did you ever redeposit funds previously withdrawn from your accounts?
24. Do you have a safe deposit box? Where? What is kept in it?
25. Were you involved in any cash transactions of $10,000 or more?
26. How long has business been at its current location? Where was it previously?
27. Employee business expenses—what meals are being deducted? Please provide appointment calendar, receipts, business purpose, business relationship for all expenses.

Have we sacrificed privacy in the interest of ensuring adequate tax collection? Is it ethical for the auditing agent to fish for information in this way? Would you be obligated to answer these questions if you were the subject of the audit? Do all the questions have a relationship to determining compliance?

LAWS GOVERNING ADMINISTRATIVE AGENCIES

Apart from their enabling acts, administrative agencies are also subject to some general laws on the functioning of agencies. This section covers those laws.

The Administrative Procedures Act

Review the Administrative Procedures Act:
http://www.law.cornell.edu./uscode/5/ch5.html

This act was the first to deal with administrative agency procedures. It was passed in 1946 after some agencies had been in existence long enough for some standard procedures to be established. The **Administrative Procedures Act (APA)** requires agencies to follow certain uniform procedures in making rules (those procedures are covered later in this chapter). The APA has been amended a number of times, including the Freedom of Information Act, the Federal Privacy Act, and the Government in the Sunshine Act.

The Freedom of Information Act

Review the Freeedom of Information Act:
http://www.law.cornell.edu/uscode/5/552a.html

The **Freedom of Information Act (FOIA)** is an APA amendment passed in 1966. It allows access to certain information federal agencies possess and requires that the agencies publicly disclose their procedures and decisions. The types of procedures that must be publicly disclosed relate to agencies' structures: Where the central and regional offices are located and which office or office division will respond to requests for information. Agencies must also publish their rules, regulations, procedures, policy statements, and reports.

Some agency information need not be published, but it must be available to the public upon request. This information includes the orders resulting from a hearing, any interpretations of unpublished rules the agency follows, and in-house management tools such as staff policies and manuals.

This information, not published but available to the public, can be obtained by an **FOIA request**, which must be written and must describe the documents sought. A general request for all the agency's research would not be a sufficient description, but a request, say, for the results of the Federal Trade Commission's study of coaching programs for college entrance exams would be allowable. The agency can charge for time and for copying costs in processing the request, although these charges must be published and applied uniformly to all requests. One exception allows an agency to waive fees for nonprofit public interest groups.

If an agency wrongfully refuses to supply the information requested, the party requesting it can bring a court action to enforce the request, with all costs paid by the agency.

Some information is exempt from FOIA requests. There are nine categories of exemptions, including requests that would reveal trade secrets or information about government workers' personnel records.

Agencies can refuse to release information that is exempt, but they can also decide to release that information if they wish to waive an exemption. Some requests have resulted in court cases brought by the parties protected by the exemptions. For example, suppose that one cola company requests the patented formula for another company's cola from the Department of Commerce. The company with the formula could bring suit to stop the disclosure. Such suits are called "reverse FOIA suits." However, the U.S. Supreme Court has held in *Chrysler Corp.* v. *Brown*, 441 U.S. 281 (1979), that the right to stop or grant disclosure rests with the agency and not with the party who supplied the information to the agency.

E T H I C A L   I S S U E S

6.2 Is the FOIA a means for legal industrial espionage? Could a competitor use a FOIA request as a means of gaining information about another firm that would not otherwise be available? For example, one firm could determine whether another is having product liability safety problems with its product and could alter its product to prevent such problems. Should any further controls be placed on FOIA requests?

Federal Privacy Act

By 1974, federal agencies had tremendous amounts of information about businesses and individuals. At least one, and usually more than one, agency could give an individual's name, occupation, address, Social Security number, and income. Furthermore, agencies were exchanging information among themselves to obtain more data for their files, all of which activity was going on without the knowledge of the individuals involved. In 1974, Congress passed the **Federal Privacy Act (FPA)** to reduce exchanges of information between agencies about individuals.

The FPA prohibits federal agencies from communicating any records to another agency or person without first obtaining the consent of the person whose record is being communicated. The FPA protects all records about

Review the Federal Privacy Act: http://www.law.cornell.edu/uscode/5/552a.html

---

E T H I C A L   I S S U E S

6.3 In the summer of 1993, the Internal Revenue Service (IRS) disciplined several employees who, out of curiosity, were looking up tax returns of famous people. The employees were not working on the taxpayers' returns; they were not obtaining information for investigations; they were simply checking to see who made how much income.

Is this practice so bad? What is wrong with just looking at data that are accessible at work?

individuals that might be in the possession of the agency, including medical and employment histories.

There are certain exemptions from the FPA. Because law enforcement agencies would have a difficult time trying to conduct investigations if they had to get permission from the individuals being investigated in order to obtain information, law enforcement agencies are exempt. Congress can also obtain information without consent. Routine agency tasks are also exempt from the prior permission requirement. For example, employees of the Securities and Exchange Commission (SEC) need constant access to information about stock sales by directors to perform their duties regarding the control of insider trading.

Government in the Sunshine Act

Review the Government in the Sunshine Act: http://www.law.cornell.edu/uscode/5/552b.html

The **Government in the Sunshine Act** is a 1976 amendment to the APA and is often called an **open meeting law**. Its purpose is to require prior public notice of meetings of those agencies with heads appointed by the president. All the agencies with the word *commission* in their names have agency heads appointed by the president.

This open meeting law applies only to meetings between or among agency heads. For example, when the commissioners of the FTC meet together, that meeting must be public and held only after there has been prior notice. Staff members can hold meetings in private without giving notice. Most states also have sunshine laws for state administrative government operations.

As with the other statutes, there are exemptions under the open meeting law. If an agency meeting will cover national defense, foreign policy, trade secrets, personnel, or law enforcement issues, the meetings need not be public. The SEC commissioners could meet privately to discuss an enforcement program designed to curb insider trading (see Chapter 21).

The Federal Register Act

Although the **Federal Register Act (FRA)** is not a part of the APA, its provisions are necessary for all the acts under the APA to work. The FRA created the **Federal Register System**, which oversees publication of federal agency information. This system provides the means for Sunshine Act notices and publication of agency rules and procedures.

Review the Code of Federal Regulations: http://law.house.gov/cfr.htm

Three publications make up the Federal Register System. The first is the *U.S. Government Manual*. This publication is reprinted each year and lists all federal agencies and their regional offices along with addresses. In addition, the *Manual* contains statistics about the agencies and their sizes.

The second publication of the Federal Register Act is the *Code of Federal Regulations* (covered in Chapter 1). The *Code of Federal Regulations* contains

Business Planning Tip

Managers should have access to either the *Federal Register* or a trade publication that offers summaries of what the agencies affecting their businesses are doing. For example, in late 1991, then-Transportation Secretary Samuel Skinner released data showing the noisiest airplane fleets in the country along with his proposal to outlaw the noisiest planes by the year 2000. In the *Federal Register* release by the Department of Transportation, airlines were ranked by the percentage of their fleets that included the types of noisy planes to be outlawed. The percentage of so-called Stage Two aircraft (those airplanes that would not meet federal guidelines) ranged from 63.4 percent of TWA's fleet, to 27.8 percent of American Airlines fleet.

This type of public information release has an impact on flyers and investors—managers must be prepared to respond.

all regulations of all the federal agencies. The volumes are in paperback, and the entire *Code* is republished each year because of tremendous changes in the regulations. Exhibit 6.4 is a sample excerpt from the *Code*.

Search the Federal Register *and the* U.S. Government Manual*:* http://www.lib.ncsu.edu/stacks/gpo/

The third publication under the Federal Register System serves to provide a daily update on changes in the regulations. This publication, called the **Federal Register**, is published every government working day and contains proposed regulations, notices of meetings (under the Government in the Sunshine Act), notices of hearings on proposed regulations, and the final versions of amended or new regulations. The *Federal Register* totals about 60,000 pages a year, or about 250 pages every working day. More than seven thousand regulations are published each year in the *Federal Register*.

Exhibit 6.4
Federal Regulations that Affect Pacifiers [Excerpted from 16 C.F.R. § 1511 and § 1511.2 Definitions (1995)]

(a) A <u>pacifier</u> is an article consisting of a nipple that is intended for a young child to suck upon, but is not designed to facilitate a baby's obtaining fluid, and usually includes a guard or shield and a handle or ring.

(b) <u>Guard</u> or <u>shield</u> means the structure located at the base of the nipple used to prevent the pacifier from being completely drawn into the child's mouth.

(c) <u>Handle</u> or <u>ring</u> means the structure usually located adjacent to the guard or shield used for holding or grasping the pacifier. A hinged handle or ring is one that is free to pivot about an axis parallel to the plane of the guard or shield.

§ 1511.3 Guard or shield requirements.

(a) <u>Performance requirements</u>. Place the pacifier in the opening of the fixture illustrated in Figure 1(a) of this part so that the nipple of the pacifier is centered in the opening and protrudes through the back of the fixture as shown in Figure 1(b). For pacifiers with non-circular guards or shields, align the major axis of the guard or shield with the major axis of the opening in the fixture. Apply a tensile force to the pacifier nipple in the direction shown. The force shall be applied gradually attaining but not exceeding 2.0 pounds (8.9 newtons) within a period of 5 seconds and maintained at 2.0 pounds for an additional 10 seconds. Any pacifier which can be completely drawn through an opening with dimensions no greater than those of Exhibit 1(a) by such a force shall fail the test in this part.

(b) <u>Ventilation holes</u>. The pacifier guard or shield shall contain at least two holes symmetrically located and each being at least 0.20 inches (5 millimeters) in minor dimension. The edge of any hold shall be no closer than 0.20 inches (5 millimeters) to the perimeter of the pacifier guard or shield.

Continued

---

§ 1511.5 Structural integrity tests.

(a) <u>Nipple</u>. Hold the pacifier by the shield or guard, grasp the nipple end of the pacifier and gradually apply a tensile force to the pacifier nipple in any possible direction. The force shall be applied gradually, attaining but not exceeding 10.0 pounds (44.5 newtons) within a period of 5 seconds and maintained at 10.0 pounds for an additional 10 seconds.

(b) <u>Handle</u> or <u>ring</u>. Hold the pacifier by the shield or guard or base of the nipple, and push or pull on the handle or ring in any possible direction. The force shall be applied gradually attaining but not exceeding 10.0 pounds (44.5 newtons) within a period of 5 seconds and maintained at 10.0 pounds for an additional 10 seconds.

(c) <u>Heat cycle deterioration</u>. After the testing prescribed in paragraphs (a) and (b) of this section, all pacifiers shall be subject to the following: submerge the pacifier in boiling water for 5 minutes and then remove the pacifier and allow it to cool for 5 minutes in room temperature air, 60º to 80º F. (16º to 27º C). After the cooling period, resubmerge the pacifier in the boiling water for 5 minutes. The process shall be repeated for a total of 6 boiling/cooling cycles. After the sixth cycle, the pacifier shall again be subjected to the structural tests in paragraphs (a) and (b) of this section and section 1511.3.

Exhibit 6.4 *(Continued)*

THE FUNCTIONS OF ADMINISTRATIVE AGENCIES AND BUSINESS INTERACTION

Administrative agencies have three functions: promulgating regulations, and enforcing and adjudicating rules. Businesses will find themselves interacting with agencies in all three areas of operation.

Providing Input on Regulations during Agency's Promulgation

Promulgating regulations is the legislative function of administrative agencies. It has two forms: **formal rulemaking** and **informal rulemaking**. Some agencies combine these into a rulemaking that is a cross between formal and informal—**hybrid rulemaking**.

FORMAL RULEMAKING
The steps involved in formal rulemaking are diagrammed in Exhibit 6.5 (pg. 202).

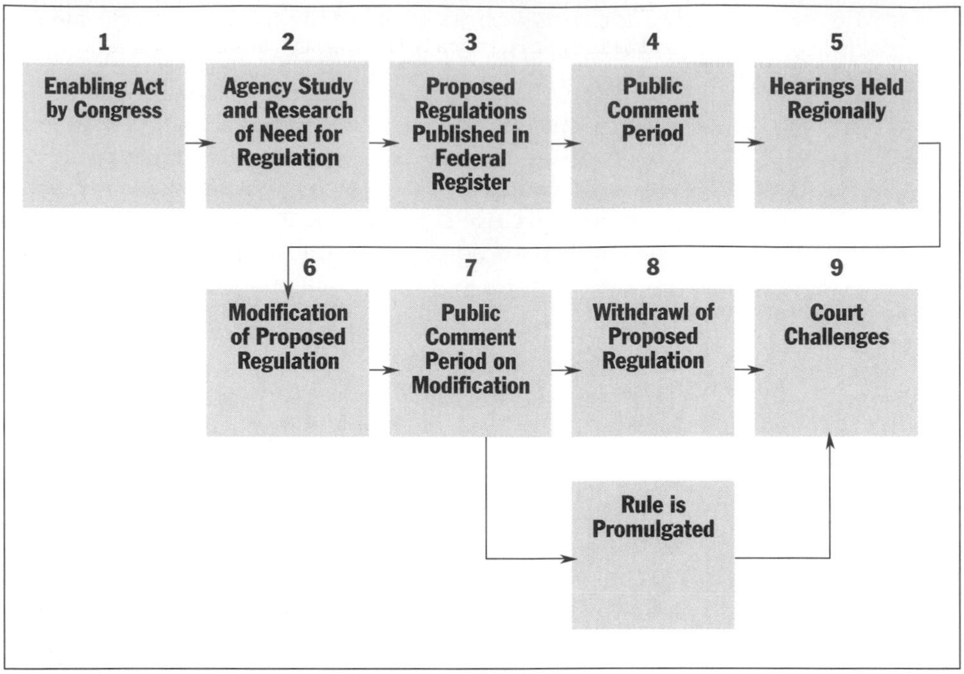

Exhibit 6.5
Steps in Formal Rulemaking by Administrative Agencies

Congressional Enabling Act Congress is responsible for passing statutes designed to remedy a perceived problem that is within federal jurisdiction. At the point of legislation, constituents have an opportunity to voice their views and concerns about problem areas. For example, many people saw a problem with the way credit transactions were being handled in the early 1970s. There were concerns about disclosures, billings, and advertisements. Congress passed the Consumer Credit Protection Act, or Truth in Lending Act, in response to these concerns and problems. In addition, Congress authorized the Federal Reserve Board to promulgate rules covering the specifics of disclosure and gave the board the responsibility to enforce this new credit regulation. The actual details of credit disclosures are found in the Federal Reserve Board's regulations (as a group called Regulation Z).

After the 1929 stock market crash, Congress perceived problems with the way securities were being sold and traded on the national exchanges. To correct some of the problems and abuses in the trading of securities, Congress passed the 1933 and 1934 Securities Acts (see Chapter 21 for more details), the first of which created the Securities and Exchange Commission (SEC) as the administrative agency responsible for the enforcement of the two acts. The following is an excerpt from the 1933 Securities Act, the enabling act for the SEC:

(a) There is hereby established a Securities and Exchange Commission (hereinafter referred to as the "Commission") to be composed of five commissioners to be appointed by the President by and with the advice and consent of the Senate. Not more than three of such commissioners shall be members of the same political party and in making appointments members of different political parties shall be appointed alternately as nearly as may be practicable. . . .

Browse a summary of Federal Reserve Board regulations: http://www.bog.frb.fed.us/frregs.htm
Review the Truth in Lending Act: http://www.law.cornell.edu/uscode/15/1601.html

Explore the 1933 and 1934 Securities Acts: http://www.law.uc.edu/CCL/

(b) The Commission is authorized to appoint and fix the compensation of such officers, attorneys, examiners, and other experts as may be necessary for carrying out its functions under this chapter. . . .

Agency Research of the Problem Any regulation passed by an administrative agency must have some purpose and evidence to show that the regulation will accomplish the purpose. Rules passed without some study and evidence supporting their need or effectiveness could be challenged by the persons or industries affected as arbitrary and capricious (discussed later in this chapter).

The study can be done by the agency staff, or the agency can hire outside experts to conduct the study for it. The study will examine issues such as whether the regulation will be cost effective. Some regulations may cost billions of dollars for industries to follow. Regulation Z, for example, requires lenders to send out a substantial amount of paperwork; the preparation of the paperwork and the cost of mailing, along with personnel costs for the work involved are tremendous. However, full knowledge of the cost of consumer debt is an important goal as specified by Congress in the Consumer Credit Protection Act. Although the study may reveal that the cost is great, it could also reveal that the cost outweighs the hazards to consumers. In other words, the study not only focuses on monetary costs but also on the problems the regulation is trying to correct and the cost of those problems to the individual and to society.

Proposed Regulations After the study, and based upon the needs and costs shown by the study, the agency will publish its proposed rules or rule changes in the *Federal Register*. The published form of the regulation by this time has been through many departments and many hands. Legal counsel for the agency will review the regulation for language problems. Other experts within the agency will also review its content for problems and inaccuracies. Economists, financial analysts, and scientists are examples of experts used within an agency to review a regulation before publication.

To be valid, the notice in the *Federal Register* must contain certain information. If notice is not given or is given improperly, a court can set aside the action taken by the agency and require the rulemaking process to be repeated with proper notice. Requirements for a *Federal Register* notice include the following:

1. The name of the agency proposing the rules
2. The statutory authority the agency has for promulgating the rules (citing the enabling act)
3. Either the language of the proposed rule or an accurate summary or description of the proposed rules

Review the Regulatory Flexibility Act: http://www.law.cornell.edu/uscode/5/601.html

Although not required to do so, some agencies provide background information in the notice so that some history and the function of the rule are given. In addition to publishing the notice of proposed rules in the *Federal Register*, an agency is required under the **Regulatory Flexibility Act** to publish a notice in the publications of those trades and industries that will be affected by the rule. For example, the regulation governing disclosures of sales of used vehicles was published in automobile dealers associations' publications. Exhibit 6.6 (pg. 204) is a sample of a proposed rule publication from the SEC on the disclosure of executive compensation in proxy statements to shareholders.

SECURITIES AND EXCHANGE COMMISSION
17 C.F.R. Parts 229 and 240
(Release No.33-6940; 34-30851; FIle No. S7-16-92)
RIN 3235-AF34
Executive Compensation Disclosure
AGENCY: Securities and Exchange Commission.
ACTION: Proposed rules.

SUMMARY: The Commission is publishing for comment proposed amendments to the executive compensation disclosure requirements applicable to proxy statements, periodic reports and other filings under the Securities Exchange Act of 1934, and to registration statements under the Securities Act of 1933. The proposed amendments are intended to make disclosure of compensation paid or awarded to executive officers clearer and more concise, and of greater utility to shareholders. New provisions would require a report by the Board Compensation Committee, or in its absence, the Board of Directors, on the bases for its compensation decisions in the last fiscal year with respect to the Chief Executive Officer and the other named executive officers, and the relationship of such compensation to company performance, together with a graph comparing the cumulative return on the company's common stock with the Standard and Poor's 500 Stock Index over at least the last five years, and with the return on either a nationally recognized industry index or a registrant-constructed peer group index. Additional disclosure is proposed, for certain registrants, regarding the relationships of the Compensation Committee members to the registrant.

DATES: Comments should be received on or before August 31,1992.

ADDRESSES: Comments should be submitted in triplicate to Jonathan G. Katz, Secretary, Securities and Exchange Commission, 450 Fifth Street, NW., Stop 6-9, Washington, DC 20549.

FOR FURTHER INFORMATION CONTACT: Catherine T. Dixon at (202) 272-2589, or Gregg W. Corso at (202) 272-3097, Division of Corporation Finance, Securities and Exchange Commission, 450 Fifth Street, NW., Washington, DC 20549.

I. Executive Summary

The Commission today is proposing substantial revisions to its rules governing disclosure of executive compensation. The proposed amendments are intended to provide shareholders with a clear and concise presentation of compensation paid or awarded to executive officers, and the directors' bases for making such compensation decisions.

The goals of the Commission initiative are to assure that shareholders are well informed and all the facts regarding the compensation that the shareholders are paying are out in the open, and to foster better accountability of the board of directors to the shareholders.

Exhibit 6.6
Sample Proposed Rule Notice from the Federal Register *(SEC Proposal on Executive Compensation Disclosure)*

The Public Comment Period One of the purposes for publication of proposed rules is to allow the public an opportunity to review and provide input on the proposed rules. The period during which the agency accepts comments on the rule is called the **public comment period**. Under the APA, the public comment period cannot be less than 30 days, but most agencies make the public comment period much longer.

Private citizens, government officials, industry representatives, business-people, and corporations can all send in their public comments. This is the opportunity business has to provide information and express concerns about proposals. There is no formal format for a public comment; most just appear in letter form. Because comments are generally made by those who do not like the rule, most comment letters are negative. Anyone who wishes later to challenge the validity of a federal regulation must participate in the comment period and voice his or her concerns at that time.

Some agencies allow members of the public (and others who would be entitled to make comments) to participate in public hearings. These hearings are not for the purpose of challenging the agency's study that resulted in the rule; they are not trial proceedings and are only informational in nature. The hearing officers or commissioners for the agency ask questions of witnesses, but no other parties can question those who appear to make comments. The purpose of the hearings is to take input on the proposals and consider additional evidence and factors relevant in promulgating the final version of the rule.

Exhibits 6.7 and 6.8 (pg. 206) are examples of letters sent to the SEC offering input on the proposed rules on disclosure of executive compensation in proxy statements (see proposal in Exhibit 6.6).

Exhibit 6.7
Letter to the SEC

Mr. John W. Andersen
927 Windward Ct.
Oshkosh, WI 54901

August 31,1992

Mr. Jonathan G. Katz
Secretary
Securities & Exchange Commission
Washington, D.C. 20013

RE: File No. F7-15-92
    Proposed Proxy Revisions for Compensation Disclosure

Mr. Katz:

I am chairman of the Compensation Committee of the Board of Directors of Oshkosh Truck Corporation. We have 1651 shareholders and are traded through NASDAQ.

Our committee and our directors are very concerned about our ability to comply at a reasonable expense with the proposed compensation disclosure proxy revisions. We think companies as small as ours are well beneath the level where your concerns are focused and should be excused through creation of a threshold of compensation visibility.

We are sensitive to the issues of shareholder abuse through excessive executive compensation, both actual and perceived. Our "outside" directors are independent and not drawn from the executive offices of other corporations. Our company is one in which executive hirings in recent years have been through the marketplace, rather than from within, so that we are very much aware of the forces of competition for compensation in companies such as ours.

Continued

Our highest paid executive currently receives an annual base cash compensation of $325,000.00. His maximum cash bonus potential is 50% of that base, determined upon performance. His expected bonus for this year will be materially less. However, his compensation as well as that of five vice presidents whom we have hired over the past few years, has been negotiated against our relevant background marketplace. Our business and our geographic location do not give us any advantage.

As we understand the proposed disclosure rules, we will be required to employ independent compensation advice to confirm what we already know to be the market compensation forces which drive our decisions. We will need this paid advice to help us prepare the proposed annual "very specific discussion, particularized both with respect to the company and to each of the individual named executives;" the cost does not relate to the benefit for our company.

While we have no objection to the concept behind the proposed rules, we think that if they are applied to every public company, without regard to the actual size of the particular compensation packages in effect, you will implement a monumental overkill and a full employment act for professional compensation consultants and lawyers.

Properly aim the requirements at those companies who choose to pay their executives like entertainers and athletes. Exempt companies who have no cash compensation in excess of, say, $750,000. Set some similiar threshold for non-cash compensation.

Companies like ours already find it difficult to recruit and retain qualified and competent outside directors. Other liability exposures added by other branches of federal and state governments in recent years are burdened enough. Please tailor disclosure rules to hit your real targets and let the market control the actions of smaller companies such as ours.

Sincerely,

John W Andersen

John W. Andersen

cc: Mr. John Clifford
    Mr. Mike Grebe
    Mr. R. Eugene Goodson

Exhibit 6.7 *(Continued)*

Exhibit 6.8
Letter to the SEC

August 26, 1992

Jonathan G. Katz
Secretary
Securities and Exchange Commission
450 Fifth St NW
Washington, D.C. 20549

RE: File No. S7-15-92 and S7-16-92

Dear Mr. Katz:

On behalf of the members of the District Council of Carpenters of Seattle, North Puget Sound & Vicinity I would like to comment on the Commission's proxy reform and executive compensation proposals. The District Council

Continued

represents thousands of working men and women whose retirement security is dependent in large measure on the effective performance of the corporations whose stock is held by our member's pension funds. It is our belief that the reforms embodied in the two proposals on which comment is sought will help advance the interests of the owners of corporations, including the working men and women whose pension funds own an increasingly significant portion of the stock of American companies.

The Commission's proposals on revising executive compensation disclosure represents [sic] a progressive effort to deal with the issue of excessive executive compensation. Providing shareholders with more comprehensive executive compensation information in an understandable format will enable shareholders to make more informed decisions relating to executive compensation and performance. Greater disclosure will provide shareholders with the information that will allow shareholders to provide for a closer alignment of executive pay and performance.

The full Commission, its staff, and the Chairman are to be commended for moving forward on important regulatory revisions that will help democratize the corporate governance process and enhance the financial performance of American corporations. I urge that after proper consideration of public comment on the proposals, that the Commission move promptly to adopt as proposed new proxy communication and executive compensation regulations.

Very truly yours,

Richard L. Hart
Executive Secretary
RLH/nlb
opeiu#8

Exhibit 6.8 *(Continued)*

C O N S I D E R . . . **6.1** The chapter's opening "Judgment" described the EEOC's proposed guidelines on religious harassment in the workplace and the business concerns about those guidelines.

The U.S. Senate passed a resolution 94–0 urging the EEOC to drop the guidelines. The general public became actively involved in the rulemaking. Religious and business groups flooded the EEOC with more than 100,000 letters of protest.

Attorneys who examined the proposed rules issued opinions for their business clients that concluded the only way to avoid religious harassment lawsuits by employees or customers under the proposed rules, was to ban all religious expression in the workplace, including the wearing or display of a yarmulke or a cross. The attorneys further concluded that banning such personal expression, a form of speech, would result in a flood of First Amendment suits.

The EEOC withdrew the proposed rules. EEOC spokesman Mike Widomski explained that "the public outcry and the number of comments that were received" triggered the reversal.

Public comments and input have an impact in the regulatory process. Is this a reasonable process? How do you feel about this particular rulemaking situation? Do you believe allowing comments is a fair process?

Judgment

Deciding What to Do with the Proposed Regulation After the comment period is over, the agency has three choices about what to do with the proposed rules. The first choice is simply to adopt the rules. The second choice is to modify the proposed rules and go through the process of public comment again. If the modification is minor, however, the APA allows the agency to adopt a modified version of the rule without going through the public comment period again. The final choice of the proposing agency would be to withdraw the rule. Some rules have so many comments pointing out their impracticability, inflexibility, or prematurity that they are withdrawn from the promulgation process. For example, the Federal Trade Commission withdrew its proposed rules on regulating advertisements during children's programming hours because of strong industry opposition, the existence of a private industry code already controlling the area, and complicated legal issues involved in the regulation of commercial speech. Subsequently, modified rules were proposed and adopted.

Court and Legislative Challenges to Proposed Rules Those parties who made comments on the rules during their proposal stage can challenge the validity of the rules in court. An administrative rule can be challenged on several different grounds.

The first ground on which to challenge an agency rule is that it is arbitrary, capricious, an abuse of discretion, or is in violation of some other law. This standard is generally applied to informal rulemaking and simply requires the agency to show that there is evidence to support the proposed rule. Without such evidence, the rule can be held to be **arbitrary** and **capricious**. The following case addresses the issue of whether an agency's action is arbitrary and capricious.

Motor Vehicles Manufacturers Ass'n v. *State Farm Mutual Insurance Co.*
463 U.S. 29 (1983)

FASTEN YOUR SEAT BELTS: RULEMAKING IS A ROUGH RIDE

FACTS

The Department of Transportation (DOT), charged with the enforcement of the National Traffic and Motor Vehicle Safety Act of 1966 and the task of reducing auto accidents, passed Standard 208 in 1967. Standard 208 is the seat belt requirement for motor vehicles, and its original form simply required that all cars be equipped with seat belts. It soon became clear to the DOT that people did not use the belts, so the department began a study of passive restraint systems, which do not require any action on the part of the occupant other than operating the vehicle. The two types considered were automatic seat belts and air bags. Studies showed that these devices could prevent approximately 12,000 deaths a year and over 100,000 serious injuries.

In 1972, after many hearings and comments, the Department of Transportation passed a regulation requiring some type of passive restraint system on all vehicles manufactured after 1975. The regulation allowed an ignition interlock system, which requires car occupants to have their seat belts fastened before a car could be started. Congress, however, revoked the requirement of the ignition interlock.

Because of changes in directors of the DOT and the unfavorable economic climate in the auto industry, the requirements for passive restraints were postponed. In 1981, the depart-

Continued

ment proposed a rescission of the passive restraint rule. After receiving written comments and holding public hearings, the agency concluded there was no longer a basis for reliably predicting that passive restraints increased safety levels or decreased accidents. Further, the agency found it would cost $1 billion to implement the rule, and they were unwilling to impose such substantial costs on auto manufacturers.

State Farm filed suit on the rescission of the rule on the basis that it was arbitrary and capricious. The court of appeals held the rescission was, in fact, arbitrary and capricious. Auto manufacturers appealed.

JUDICIAL OPINION

WHITE, Justice

The ultimate question before us is whether NHTSA's (National Highway Traffic Safety Administration) rescission of the passive restraint requirement of Standard 208 was arbitrary and capricious. We conclude, as did the Court of Appeals, that it was.

The first and most obvious reason for finding the rescission arbitrary and capricious is that NHTSA apparently gave no consideration whatever to modifying the Standard to require that airbag technology be utilized. Standard 208 sought to achieve automatic crash protection by requiring automobile manufacturers to install either of two passive restraint devices: airbags or automatic seatbelts. There was no suggestion in the long rulemaking process that led to Standard 208 that if only one of these options were feasible, no passive restraint standard should be promulgated. Indeed, the agency's original proposed standard contemplated the installation of inflatable restraints in all cars. Automatic belts were added as a means of complying with the standard because they were believed to be as effective as airbags in achieving the goal of occupant crash protection.

The agency has now determined that the detachable automatic belts will not attain anticipated safety benefits because so many individuals will detach the mechanism. Even if this conclusion were acceptable in its entirety,

standing alone it would not justify any more than an amendment of Standard 208 to disallow compliance by means of the only technology which will not provide effective passenger protection. It does not cast doubt on the need for a passive restraint standard or upon the efficacy of airbag technology. In its most recent rulemaking, the agency again acknowledged the life-saving potential of the airbag.

Given the effectiveness ascribed to airbag technology by the agency, the mandate of the Safety Act to achieve traffic safety would suggest that the logical response to the faults of detachable seatbelts would be to require the installation of airbags. At the very least this alternative way of achieving objectives of the Act should have been addressed and adequate reasons given for its abandonment. But the agency not only did not require compliance through airbags, it did not even consider the possibility in its 1981 rulemaking. Not one sentence of its rulemaking statement discusses the airbags-only option. We have frequently reiterated that an agency must cogently explain why it had exercised its discretion in a given manner.

For nearly a decade, the automobile industry waged the regulatory equivalent of war against the airbag and lost—the inflatable restraint was proven sufficiently effective. Now the automobile industry has decided to employ a seatbelt system which will not meet the safety objectives of Standard 208. This hardly constitutes cause to revoke the standard itself. Indeed the Motor Vehicle Safety Act was necessary because the industry was not sufficiently responsive to safety concerns. The Act intended that safety standards not depend on current technology and would be "technology-forcing" in the sense of inducing the development of superior safety design.

It is not infrequent that the available data does not settle a regulatory issue and the agency must then exercise its judgment in moving from the facts and probabilities on the record to a policy conclusion. Recognizing that policy making in a complex society must account for uncertainty, however, does not

Continued

imply that it is sufficient for an agency to merely recite the terms "substantial uncertainty" as a justification for its actions. The agency must explain the evidence which is available, and must offer a "rational connection between the facts found and the choice made."

In this case, the agency's explanation for rescission of the passive restraint requirement is not sufficient to enable us to conclude that the rescission was the product of reasoned decision making. We start with the accepted ground that if used, seatbelts unquestionably would save many thousands of lives and would prevent tens of thousands of crippling injuries. Unlike recent regulations we have reviewed, the safety benefits of wearing seatbelts are not in doubt and it is not challenged that were those benefits to accrue, the monetary costs of implementing the standard would be easily justified.

Since 20 to 50 percent of motorists currently wear seatbelts on some occasions, there would seem to be grounds to believe that seatbelt use by occasional users will be substantially increased by the detachable passive belts.

Whether this is the case is a matter for the agency to decide, but it must bring its expertise to bear on the question.

An agency's view of what is in the public interest may change, either with or without a change in circumstances. But an agency changing its course must supply a reasoned analysis. We do not accept all of the reasoning of the Court of Appeals but we do conclude that the agency has failed to supply the requisite "reasoned analysis" in this case. Accordingly, we remand the matter to the NHTSA for further consideration consistent with this opinion.

CASE QUESTIONS

1. What regulation is at issue in the case?
2. When was the regulation first adopted?
3. What changes has the regulation undergone over the years?
4. What was done with the regulation to result in this judicial decision?
5. Who challenged the agency's actions, and what were the reasons for this challenge?
6. Is the agency's action valid?

A second theory for challenging an agency's regulation is that the regulation is unsupported by **substantial evidence**. This **substantial evidence test** is applied in the review of formal and hybrid rulemaking. Where the arbitrary and capricious standard simply requires some proof or basis for the regulation, substantial evidence requires that more convincing evidence exist in support of the regulation than against it. The following case involves a business challenge to an administrative regulation based on the issue of whether substantial evidence was presented.

Business Planning Tip

In the State Farm case it is an insurer, not an auto manufacturer, who is challenging the proposed regulation (or lack thereof). Certainly the insurer does not carry the responsibility of implementing the safety designs or perfecting the technology. However, because the implementation of such safety features helps reduce claims for accident injuries and damages, the insurer has a business interest in seeing that the regulations are passed. Very often, businesses must become involved in regulatory proceedings for rules that might not regulate them directly but will benefit or cost them indirectly. Another example of insurance involvement in legislative or regulatory issues is in the area of anti-drunk-driving legislation. Insurers will not be regulated, but the resulting regulation can reduce payouts for them.

Corn Products Co. and Derby Foods, Inc. v. Department of Health, Education & Welfare and Food and Drug Administration
427 F.2d 511 (3d Cir. 1970)

SKIPPY AND PETER PAN TAKE ON THE FDA

FACTS

Corn Products Company (petitioner) manufactures peanut butter known as "Skippy" brand and holds 22 percent of the peanut butter market. Derby (also a petitioner) holds 14 percent of the market with its product, "Peter Pan."

Peanut butter originally was made of ground peanuts, salt, and sometimes sugar. This combination had the disadvantages of oil separation, short shelf life, and stickiness. These deficiencies have been diminished, if not eliminated, by the addition of stabilizing ingredients, mainly hydrogenated vegetable oils. Today peanut butter is made of peanuts, an oil component, the stabilizer, and seasonings.

The Food and Drug Administration (FDA) adopted a regulation limiting the percentage (by weight) of optional ingredients that may be added to the peanut ingredients to ten percent. The regulation allows for the addition or removal of peanut oil but limits the fat content to 55 percent.

Corn Products and Derby urged the adoption of a 13 percent as opposed to a ten percent standard and challenged the regulation as not being supported by substantial evidence.

JUDICIAL OPINION

STALEY, Circuit Judge

Using an affirmative approach to the order under consideration, the issue becomes whether the findings upon which the 90 percent standard is based are supported by substantial evidence. Corn Products' argument that the standard should have designated partially hydrogenated peanut oil as peanut ingredient must be directed at those findings which equate them.

Skippy fails to comply with the standard because it contains 8 1/2 percent of partially hydrogenated peanut oil and an amount of seasonings which together exceed the ten percent limit on optional ingredients. No distinction is made in the standard between hydrogenated peanut oil and other hydrogenated vegetable oils.

Four expert witnesses, all chemists, testified to the dissimilarity between vegetable oil and hydrogenated oil. There was testimony that there is no nutritional variation between these oils. The basic function of the hydrogenated oil, to prevent oil separation in the product, is said to be served regardless of the source oil. The use of hydrogenated peanut oil does not add flavor to the product. From the foregoing, it is quite clear that there is substantial evidence to support a conclusion which makes no distinction between hydrogenated vegetable oils.

The standard reflects the practice of a number of manufacturers and to those not in compliance there will be no economic hardship in complying. The fact of exclusion of the leading producers does not make the regulation unreasonable. Skippy and Peter Pan will not be banned; merely a change in product formula will be required.

CASE QUESTIONS

1. What standard did the FDA pass for peanut butter?
2. Why didn't Corn Products and Derby meet the standard?
3. What arguments do they make in appealing the regulation?
4. Does it matter that the regulation excluded their substantial shares of the market?
5. Was there substantial evidence to support the rule changes?

A third ground on which to challenge an agency's regulation involves the rule that a regulation can be set aside if the agency did not comply with the APA requirements of notice, publication, and public comment or input. The procedures for rulemaking must be followed in order for the regulatory process and resulting rules to be valid. Thus, an agency that seeks public comment for the purposes of drafting legislation cannot then turn the legislation into rules after the comment period. The notice must specify that promulgated rules will be the result of the proceedings. The following case addresses an agency's attempt to change a rule without following the APA requirements.

San Diego Air Sports Center, Inc. v. Federal Aviation Administration
887 F.2d 966 (9th Cir. 1989)

ARE PARACHUTES AIR TRAFFIC?

FACTS

San Diego Air Sports Center (SDAS) operates a sports parachuting business in Otay Mesa, California. SDAS offers training to beginning parachutists and facilitates recreational jumping for experienced parachutists. It indicates that the majority of SDAS jumps occur at altitudes in excess of 5,800 feet.

The jump zone used by SDAS overlaps the San Diego Traffic Control Area (TCA). Although the aircraft carrying the parachutists normally operate outside the TCA, the parachutists themselves are dropped through it. Thus, each jump must be approved by the air traffic controllers.

In July 1987, an air traffic controller in San Diego filed an Unsatisfactory Condition Report complaining of the strain that parachuting was putting on the controllers and raising safety concerns. The report led to a staff study of parachute jumping within the San Diego TCA. In October 1987, representatives of the San Diego Terminal Radar Approach Control (TRACON) facility met with SDAS operators. In December 1987, the San Diego TRACON sent to SDAS a draft letter of agreement outlining agreed-upon procedures and coordination requirements. Nonetheless, the San Diego TRACON conducted another study between January 14, 1988, and February 11, 1988, and about two months after the draft letter was sent, the San Diego TRACON withdrew it.

SDAS states that the air traffic manager of the San Diego TRACON assured SDAS that it would be invited to attend all meetings on parachuting in the San Diego TCA. However, SDAS was not informed of or invited to any meetings.

In March 1988, the FAA sent a letter to SDAS informing SDAS that "[e]ffective immediately parachute jumping within or into the San Diego TCA in the Otay Reservoir Jump Zone will not be authorized." The FAA stated that the letter was final and appealable.

SDAS challenged the letter in federal court on grounds that it constituted rulemaking without compliance with required APA procedures.

JUDICIAL OPINION

BEEZER, Circuit Judge

The Federal Aviation Act requires that rules affecting the use of navigable airspace be issued in accordance with the Administrative Procedure Act (APA). 49 U.S.C. App. § 1348(d). The "principal purpose" of section 553 of the APA is "to provide that the legislative functions of administrative agencies shall so far as possible be exercised only upon public participation." Section 553 of the APA requires agencies to adhere to three steps when promulgating rules: Notice of the proposed rule, opportunity to comment, and an explanation of the rule ultimately adopted. 5 U.S.C. § 553 (b),(c). These three requirements have been referred to as "the statutory *minima*" imposed by Congress.

Not every decision made by administrative agencies requires citizen participation. The APA lists four instances when the statutory *minima* do not apply: When the agency is promulgating (1) interpretive rules, (2) general statements of policy, or (3) rules of agency organization, procedure, or practice, or (4) when the requirement of notice and participation are impractical or contrary to public interest.

Continued

Congress was concerned that the exceptions to section 553, though necessary, might be used too broadly. The Senate noted that the courts have a "duty . . . to prevent avoidance of the requirements of the [Act] by any manner or form of indirection." We have stated that "[t]he exceptions to section 553 will be 'narrowly construed and only reluctantly countenanced.' "

The FAA letter does not come within either of the first two exceptions. The letter creates an immediate, substantive rule, i.e., that no parachuting will be allowed in the San Diego TCA.

The FAA argues that parachuting created an emergency to which it responded in the letter at issue. It is further argued that a response to an immediate emergency is covered by the fourth exception. This argument is not persuasive. The only accident known to the FAA occurred two years before it issued its letter. Furthermore, the FAA itself claims to have extensively studied the situation before issuing the letter. The FAA does not explain why public participation as required by the APA could not be included in its study.

Finally, the FAA argues that the letter is not a rule at all; rather, the FAA characterizes the letter as an order to which the requirements set forth in section 553 of the APA does [sic] not apply. We find this argument somewhat mystifying, as there are equally stringent participation requirements for orders. Furthermore, the FAA is wrong; the letter is a rule.

A time-honored principle of administrative law is that the label an agency puts on its actions "is not necessarily conclusive." Equally true, however, is the fact that agencies can issue rules through adjudication (the process by which orders are normally issued) and orders through rulemaking.

In this case no record was kept of the "process" that resulted in the FAA letter; we can only scrutinize the letter itself. The letter clearly promulgates a rule. It states that *all* parachuting by any party will be prohibited in the San Diego TCA from the time it is issued. This comports with this court's statement that "[s]ubstantive rules are those which effect a change in existing law or policy."

The Federal Aviation Act requires that rules affecting the use of navigable airspace be issued in accordance with the APA. 49 U.S.C.App. § 1348(d). In issuing this substantive rule, the FAA failed to do so. A substantive rule is invalid if the issuing agency fails to comply with the APA. Therefore, the petition for review is granted.

CASE QUESTIONS
1. What problem did the FAA have with SDAS?
2. How did the FAA attempt to control SDAS?
3. Was the letter an attempt to promulgate regulation?
4. Would the FAA letter shut down SDAS?
5. Was SDAS deprived of due process by the letter?

Another basis for challenging a regulation is that the regulation is unconstitutional. Many challenges based on constitutional grounds deal with regulations that give an agency authority to search records or that impose discriminatory requirements for licensing professionals. For example, a requirement of a minimum residency period before allowing an applicant to become licensed in a particular profession has been challenged successfully. Zoning board regulations that discriminate against certain classes or races as to the use of property have also been successfully challenged as unconstitutional. Further, broadcasters will often depend on freedom of speech—the First Amendment—to challenge new Federal Communication Commission (FCC) regulations.

In the following case, a business challenged a labeling rule on grounds that its First Amendment rights were violated and that the agency was exceeding its authority.

Rubin v. Coors Brewing Company
115 S.Ct. 1585 (1995)

ROCKY MOUNTAIN HIGH: ALCOHOL CONTENT ON THE LABEL

FACTS

Coors Brewing Company (respondent) brews beer. In 1987, it applied to the Bureau of Alcohol, Tobacco and Firearms (BATF) for approval of proposed labels and advertisements that disclosed the alcohol content of its beer. BATF refused to approve the disclosure under section 205(e)(2) of the Federal Alcohol Administration Act (FAAA), which prohibits the selling, shipping, or delivery of malt beverages, distilled spirits, or wines in bottles:

unless such products are bottled, packaged, and labeled in conformity with such regulations, to be prescribed by the Secretary of the Treasury, with respect to packaging, marking, branding, and labeling and size and fill of container . . . as will provide the consumer with adequate information as to the identity and quality of the products, the alcoholic content thereof (except that statements of, or statements likely to be considered as statements of, alcoholic content of malt beverages are prohibited unless required by State law and except that, in case of wines, statements of alcoholic content shall be required only for wines containing more than 14 per centum of alcohol by volume), the net contents of the package, and the manufacturer or bottler or importer of the product.

Regulations related to this statutory restriction (27 C.F.R. § 7.26(a)) prohibit the disclosure of alcohol content on beer labels.

In addition to prohibiting numerical indications of alcohol content, the labeling regulations proscribe descriptive terms that suggest high content, such as "strong," "full strength," "extra strength," "high test," "high proof," "pre-war strength," and "full oldtime alcoholic strength." (27 C.F.R. § 7.29(f)). The prohibitions do not preclude labels from identifying a beer as "low alcohol," "reduced alcohol," "non-alcoholic," or "alcohol-free."

When BATF refused to approve the labels, Coors filed suit in federal district court challenging the regulation as violative of the First Amendment. BATF (the government) argued that the ban on alcohol content in labels was needed to prevent "strength wars" among brewers who would then compete in the marketplace on the potency of their beers.

The district court found for Coors, but the U. S. Court of Appeals for the Tenth Circuit reversed, finding that the government's interest in suppressing strength wars was substantial. It remanded the case to the trial court for determining whether the ban was an appropriate means of avoiding strength wars. The lower court found there was no evidence of any relationship between the disclosure on labels of alcohol content and competition on the basis of conduct. The court of appeals (on the second appeal) concluded that BATF's regulation violated the First Amendment.

JUDICIAL OPINION

THOMAS, Justice

Both the lower courts and the parties agree that respondent seeks to disclose only truthful, verifiable, and nonmisleading factual information about alcohol content on its beer labels. Thus, our analysis focuses on the substantiality of the interest behind § 205(e)(2) and on whether the labeling ban bears an acceptable fit with the Government's goal. A careful consideration of these factors indicates that § 205(e)(2) violates the First Amendment's protection of commercial speech.

According to the Government, the FAAA's restriction prevents a particular type of beer drinker—one who selects a beverage because of its high potency—from choosing beers solely for their alcohol content. In the Government's view, restricting disclosure of information regarding a particular product characteristic will decrease the extent to which consumers will select the product on the basis of that characteristic.

Respondent counters that Congress actually intended the FAAA to achieve the far different purpose of preventing brewers from making inaccurate claims concerning alcohol content.

Continued

According to respondent, when Congress passed the FAAA in 1935, brewers did not have the technology to produce beer with alcohol levels within predictable tolerances—a skill that modern beer producers now possess. Further, respondent argues that the true policy guiding federal alcohol regulation is not aimed at suppressing strength wars. If such were the goal, the Government would not pursue the opposite policy with respect to wines and distilled spirits.

Rather than suppressing the free flow of factual information in the wine and spirits markets, the Government seeks to control competition on the basis of strength by monitoring distillers' promotions and marketing. The respondent quite correctly notes that the general thrust of federal alcohol policy appears to favor greater disclosure of information, rather than less. This also seems to be the trend in federal regulation of other consumer products as well. See, *e.g.*, Nutrition Labeling and Education Act of 1990, Pub. L. 101-535, 104 Stat. 2353, as amended (requiring labels of food products sold in the United States to display nutritional information).

The Government carries the burden of showing that the challenged regulation advances the Government's interest "in a direct and material way." That burden "is not satisfied by mere speculation and conjecture; rather, a governmental body seeking to sustain a restriction on commercial speech must demonstrate that the harms it recites are real and that its restriction will in fact alleviate them to a material degree."

The Government attempts to meet its burden by pointing to current developments in the consumer market. It claims that beer producers are already competing and advertising on the basis of alcohol strength in the "malt liquor" segment of the beer market. The Government attempts to show that this competition threatens to spread to the rest of the market by directing our attention to respondent's motives in bringing this litigation. Respondent allegedly suffers from consumer misperceptions that its beers contain less alcohol than other brands. According to the Government, once respondent gains relief from § 205(e)(2), it will use its labels to overcome this handicap.

Under the Government's theory, § 205(e)(2) suppresses the threat of such competition by preventing consumers from choosing beers on the basis of alcohol content. It is assuredly a matter of "common sense," that a restriction on the advertising of a product characteristic will decrease the extent to which consumers select a product on the basis of that trait. In addition to common sense, the Government urges us to turn to history as a guide. According to the Government, at the time Congress enacted the FAAA, the use of labels displaying alcohol content had helped produce a strength war. Section 205(e)(2) allegedly relieved competitive pressures to market beer on the basis of alcohol content, resulting over the long term in beers with lower alcohol levels.

We conclude that § 205(e)(2) cannot directly and materially advance its asserted interest because of the overall irrationality of the Government's regulatory scheme. While the laws governing labeling prohibit the disclosure of alcohol content unless required by state law, federal regulations apply a contrary policy to beer advertising. The failure to prohibit the disclosure of alcohol content in advertising, which would seem to constitute a more influential weapon in any strength war than labels, makes no rational sense if the government's true aim is to suppress strength wars.

While we are mindful that respondent only appealed the constitutionality of § 205(e)(2), these exemptions and inconsistencies bring into question the purpose of the labeling ban. To be sure, the Government's interest in combating strength wars remains a valid goal. But the irrationality of this unique and puzzling regulatory framework ensures that the labeling ban will fail to achieve that end. There is little chance that § 205(e)(2) can directly and materially advance its aim, while other provisions of the same act directly undermine and counteract its effects.

The Government argues that a sufficient "fit" exists here because the labeling ban applies to only one product characteristic and because the ban does not prohibit all disclosures of alcohol content—it applies only to those involving labeling and advertising. In

Continued

response, respondent suggests several alternatives, such as directly limiting the alcohol content of beers, prohibiting marketing efforts emphasizing high alcohol strength (which is apparently the policy in some other Western nations), or limiting the labeling ban only to malt liquors, which is the segment of the market that allegedly is threatened with a strength war. We agree that the availability of these options, all of which could advance the Government's asserted interest in a manner less intrusive to respondent's First Amendment rights, indicates that § 205(e)(2) is more extensive than necessary.

We affirm the decision of the court below.

CASE QUESTIONS

1. What inconsistencies exist in BATF's regulatory scheme?
2. To survive a First Amendment challenge, what must a regulation of commercial speech accomplish?
3. What market perception is Coors trying to correct with its labels?
4. In what ways could BATF accomplish its goals of preventing strength wars other than the § 205(e)(2) complete ban?
5. Did the label control prevent strength wars?
6. What are general government trends with respect to disclosure?

E T H I C A L   I S S U E S

6.4 What issues and dilemmas do you foresee if marketing of beer targets percentage of alcohol? What issues do you see in marketing beer with higher alcohol content?

Another theory for challenging a regulation in court is **ultra vires**, a Latin term meaning "beyond its powers." An ultra vires regulation is one that goes beyond the authority given to the agency in its enabling act. Although most agencies stay clearly within their authority, if an agency tries to change the substance and purpose of the enabling act through regulation, the regulations would be ultra vires. For example, the intent of the 1933 Securities Act was to provide full disclosure to investors about a securities sale. The SEC could not, on the basis of its authority, pass a rule that eliminated securities registration in favor of an unregulated securities market.

Business Planning Tip

The structure of a label or advertising campaign can be determined by regulations. Verify regulatory requirements before designs and content are final. The Coors labeling case began in 1987 and was not resolved until 1995. Early interaction is important in business relationships with regulators.

Proactive Business Strategies in Regulation

Some administrative regulations can be eliminated through the use of legislation. In an enabling act called a **sunset law**, Congress creates an agency for a limited period of time during which the agency must establish its benefits and other justification for its continuation. The enabling act may provide for an audit to determine effectiveness after the agency has been in existence for two years. Without renewal by Congress, the sun sets on the agency and it is terminated. Some businesses lobby for the creation of sunset agencies to better control the number of agencies and their effectiveness.

Some agencies' power is controlled through congressional purse strings. With **zero-based budgeting** the agency does not automatically receive a budget amount but rather starts with a zero budget each year and then is required to justify all its needs for funds. This type of control gives Congress some say each year in how the agency is operating. For example, the budget could be renewed only on the condition that the agency not promulgate certain regulations opposed by Congress.

Business Planning Tip

How to Respond to Proposed Rules

Some agencies propose rules on an "emergency" basis, which means the rules will go into effect in less than 30 days. Thirty days may not be enough time for businesses to react, study, and offer comments. Lawyers can bring a "good-cause" action in federal district court to require an agency to establish the need for expedited rulemaking. A court can, if it finds no good cause for emergency, require the agency to follow the normal rulemaking time frame.

Another tool for curbing regulation that has been used in recent years has been action by the executive branch. For example, former President Bush imposed a 90-day moratorium on all new regulations in 1992. During this period, regulators were not permitted to promulgate new regulations. Additionally, the *Negotiated Rulemaking Act of 1990* helps businesses work with regulators and permits agencies to develop new methods for resolving controversies outside of the traditional rulemaking process.

C O N S I D E R . . . **6.2** In August 1995, the Food and Drug Administration (FDA) announced the promulgation of rules to regulate tobacco advertisements. Two smokeless-tobacco firms have brought suit challenging the FDA's authority. The firms maintain the FDA regulates drug advertising, and tobacco is not classified as a drug. Further, they say Congress has reserved its authority through the Federal Cigarette Labeling and Advertising Act. The FDA maintains that agencies can assert authority such as when the FCC prohibited tobacco ads on radio and TV. Who is correct? Who should regulate the ads?

E T H I C A L   I S S U E S

6.5 In the above FDA litigation, convenience stores joined in the litigation. Why would they do so? Is marketing tobacco a moral dilemma?

INFORMAL RULEMAKING

The process for informal rulemaking is the same as that for formal rulemaking with the exception that no public hearings are held on the rule. The only input from the public comes in the form of comments using the same procedures discussed earlier.

BUSINESS RIGHTS IN AGENCY ENFORCEMENT ACTION

Administrative agencies not only make the rules; they enforce them. In so doing the agencies are also responsible for adjudicating disputes over the scope or interpretation of the rules. Exhibit 6.9 is a chart of the steps involved in agency enforcement and adjudication.

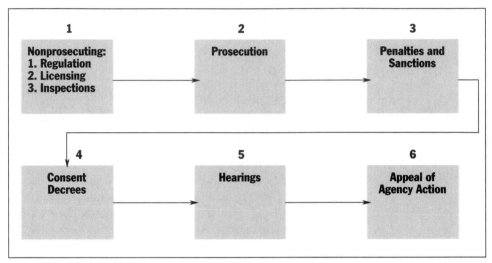

Exhibit 6.9
Steps for Administrative Agency Enforcement and Adjudication

Licensing and Inspections

Much of an administrative agency's role enforcement is carried out by requiring the submission of certain types of paperwork. Many agencies issue licenses or permits as a way of enforcing the law. For example, state administrative agencies may require building contractors to be licensed so that their dues can finance a recovery fund for the victims of bankrupt or negligent contractors. The Environmental Protection Agency (EPA) carries out its function of protecting the environment in part by requiring licenses or permits for the discharge of foreign substances into the air or water and by requiring advance approval for the construction of projects substantially affecting the environment (see Chapter 11 for more details). The idea behind the licensing and permit method of enforcement is to curtail illegal activity up front and also to have records in case problems arise.

Agencies also have the authority to conduct inspections, such as when an agency responsible for restaurant licenses inspects restaurant facilities to check for health code violations. The Occupational Safety and Health Administration (OSHA) at the federal level has the authority to inspect plants to check for violation of OSHA standards. This power of inspection at unannounced times is an enforcement tool by itself. There is strong incentive to comply with regulations when an inspection could happen at any time. A business can refuse an inspection, but an agency can obtain a warrant and return for a mandatory inspection.

Visit the Occupational Safety and Health Administration: http://www.osha.gov/

Prosecution of Businesses

Administrative agencies are also given the authority to prosecute violators. These agency prosecutions, however, are not traditional criminal prosecutions; the sanctions imposed for agency violations are not jail terms but rather are fines, penalties, and injunctions. The penalties required to be paid are not criminal penalties but rather civil penalties. For example, in the case of false advertising—a violation of Federal Trade Commission (FTC) rules—the agency could impose restitution as a sanction: The violator would have to reimburse all those individuals who bought the product based on false advertising. In some cases, an agency may merely want a violator to stop certain conduct and promise not to engage in that type of conduct again.

BEGINNING ENFORCEMENT STEPS

Regardless of the remedy an agency seeks, all action begins with the agency's issuing a **complaint** against the violating party. The complaint describes when and what the company did and why it is a violation. In "Regulatory Power Gone Amok?" author James Bovard expresses his concern about the role and power of administrative agencies—in this case, the Department of Agriculture. As well, columnist George Will in "Reasonable Explanations Won't Stop Bureaucrats," addresses the Department of Labor.

Once a complaint is filed, an agency can negotiate with a party for an order or proceed to a hearing to obtain an order from an administrative law judge. The remedies in an order vary according to the type of violation and whether it is ongoing. The FTC could, and typically does, order companies running deceptive ads to stop using the ads and promise not to use them again in the future. These sanctions usually come in the form of an **injunction**, which is a court order that prohibits specifically described conduct. Many statutes are unclear about the extent of authority an agency is given in enforcement proceedings and what types of sanctions an agency can impose for violations. The authority to assess civil penalties, for example, varies from agency to agency.

FOR THE MANAGER'S DESK

REGULATORY POWER GONE AMOK?

The Agriculture Department has placed a death sentence on as many as 500 million California peaches and nectarines.

Federal agencies have busied themselves in recent years lecturing the public on the need to eat more fresh fruits and vegetables.

Nowhere in the pronounce-ments of the surgeon general and other health officials has there been a warning: Do not eat small-sized fruit. Yet Agriculture Department officials seem to believe that small-sized nectarines and peaches are so dangerous that the entire force of the federal government must be marshaled to ban their sale.

The San Joaquin Valley is littered with piles of rotting fruit—a feast for the worms.

Once again, Agriculture Department marketing orders are seeking to achieve prosperity by mandating waste.

It is a federal crime for California farmers to sell nectarines less than $2\,^3/_8$ inches in diameter and peaches less than $2\,^7/_{16}$ inches in diameter. Because the San Joaquin Valley had good growing weather this year, the harvest has yielded a larger than usual number of slightly smaller

Continued

fruits. The federal size restrictions may be effectively condemning more nectarines and peaches than ever before.

The Agriculture Department issued a decree explaining its longstanding nectarine policy in the June 19 *Federal Register:* "The minimum size requirements established for California nectarines recognize that larger sized nectarines provide greater consumer satisfaction than those of smaller sizes." And, since many people prefer larger nectarines, the department made it a federal crime to sell smaller nectarines—and sent in the nectarine police to enforce its dictates. Agriculture Department bureaucrats appear to believe that if consumers see small nectarines in the grocery store, they may become spooked and never buy nectarines again.

Federal and state agricultural bureaucrats can be extremely condescending toward farmers, claiming to need dictatorial power over some of the nation's farmers to protect those farmers against themselves. The only catch is, the bureaucrats usually know as little as or less than the farmers. The California Tree Fruit Agreement administers federal and state farm marketing standards. Its John Field, when asked on July 27 about studies to justify restrictions on small nectarine sales, replied: "We don't have any empirical studies . . . but if you look at price quotes for plums, that would kind of

indicate intuitively that there is not a great demand for" small nectarines and peaches. Government officials are effectively imposing tens of thousands of dollars of penalties on growers based on bureaucrats' guesses about consumer preferences on fruit.

Dan Gerawan, California's largest nectarine and peach farmer and the leading opponent of the controls, observes: "Through the years, the CTFA has continuously raised the

minimum size regulations. While a certain small size may have been a quality, edible fruit one year, the following year it would be . . . no longer of edible quality."

On May 15 Mr. Gerawan's lawyer, Clifford Kemper, wrote Dan Haley, administrator of the Agriculture Department's Agricultural Marketing Service, asking for an emergency suspension of the minimum size restrictions on California nectarines and peaches. The Agriculture Department replied that it had requested the California Nectarine Administrative Committee to "undertake market research to determine the effect of fruit

size on consumer preferences for fresh California nectarines and peaches," and promised that information would be available by Dec. 31.

But, in the meantime, the U.S. attorney in Fresno, Calif., has filed to get a federal injunction against Mr. Gerawan and a $100 fine for every box of undersized fruit he sells. (The boxes were fetching less than $10 each.) Mr. Gerawan had been selling his small peaches and nectarines in South Los Angeles, providing fresh fruit for inner-city buyers. Federal regulators apparently feared that allowing poor blacks to pay lower prices for small fruit would make it more difficult for the Agriculture Department to force the rich to pay higher prices for large fruit. . . .

Rep. George Miller (D., Calif.) recently put a large number of illegal nectarines in the House members' private dining room. The fruits were avidly consumed—with no complaints about their size. Rep. Miller is gathering cosigners for a letter to Agriculture Secretary Edward Madigan demanding that the department end its ban on relatively small nectarines and peaches.

Discussion Questions
1. Is there too much regulation?
2. Do agencies need some checks and balances?
3. Could the growers have had more input? How?
4. What can growers do now?

Source: James Bovard, "A Fruitless Massacre in California," *The Wall Street Journal,* Aug. 11, 1992, p. A14. Reprinted with permission of *The Wall Street Journal* © 1992 Dow Jones & Company, Inc. All Rights Reserved Worldwide.

FOR THE MANAGER'S DESK

REASONABLE EXPLANATIONS WON'T STOP BUREAUCRATS

How KTOZ-AM suffered under the Department of Labor's attention

Autumn, season of mists and mellow fruitfulness, this year will also be a season of mayhem as congressional Republicans reach the climax of their attempt to get the government on a shorter leash. To get in the mood to enjoy this blood sport, consider the way the people at radio station KTOZ-AM in Springfield, Mo., spent their summer. They spent it suffering the attentions of the U.S. Department of Labor, which caught KTOZ's people committing the unspeakable faux pas of doing volunteer work.

Last year the little 500-watt daytime station, which covers an 80-mile radius, was bankrupt, but was cherished by a smattering of people fond of its music format of big bands, jazz and blues. Nineteen of them who fancied the chance to be amateur disc jockeys scraped together $35,000 to buy the station from a bankruptcy court, invested $60,000 in new equipment and began volunteering their time to keep it on the air.

This came to the attention of a commissar in the Labor Department's Kansas City outpost. He was gnawed by the fear that this volunteerism was a low and cunning dodge to evade the rigors of the Fair Labor Standards Act of 1938, thereby mocking justice and jeopardizing American prosperity. So he saddled his charger and rode to the rescue of the volunteers, undaunted by the fact that they, in their unregenerate state, did not want to be rescued.

They were having fun, and that was not even the worst of it. They were not being paid the minimum wage of $4.25, and the law is quite strict about the fact that all "employees" of a for-profit business must be paid at least that so America can be a land fit for heroes and so the government can collect its FICA taxes.

Speaking as if to a particularly dim 5-year-old—slowly and with precise enunciation—the people at KTOZ explained that they were not employees and the station was not making a profit and would the commissar enjoy hearing some Glenn Miller? But your tax dollars buy bureaucrats made of sterner stuff than the Springfield scofflaws supposed; the bureaucrats cannot be deflected from their duties merely by reasonable explanations.

The commissar told them that the government is large-spirited and latitudinarian, willing, when the spirit moves it, to give specific exemptions to the minimum wage requirement. But KTOZ's volunteers had not tugged their forelocks and said, "Mother may I?" to the government. Therefore the station might have to pay back wages and interest and maybe a fine. The implication was that they should thank their lucky stars that Alcatraz has been closed.

Because it is all so unfair, as an unrepentant Labor Department official in Washington stoutly insisted in a letter to the congressman from that district, explaining that the investigation of KTOZ has been discontinued but was virtuous:

"The Department's decision not to pursue this matter should not be viewed as condoning work for no pay. There are very good and strong policy reasons why for-profit companies are not allowed to employ people for no pay. First of all, those practices take wages out of workers' pockets and force everyone's wages down."

Amazing, is it not, how migraine-inducing the government's reasoning can be? You, Labor Department: What do you—what can you—mean by the phrase "employ people for no pay"? Let's take this slowly. They. Are. Not. Employees. (Are we going too fast?) Concentrate. V-o-l-u-n-t-e-e-r-s. And what wages are being taken out of whose pockets by people donating labor without which the station would be stone silent?

KTOZ's listeners burn with the spirit that chased the redcoats back to Boston from Concord bridge. One suggested organizing a KTOZ fan club. "To get the feds' attention, we could call it the 'KTOZ Militia.'" Many lawyers volunteered—that dread word again—to help defend KTOZ without pay. Can they be disbarred for that offense?

This week a congressional committee will consider changes to the 1938 law to make volunteerism less obnoxious in the squinty eyes of the government. And if in coming weeks you wonder whence springs the passion behind the grinding down of government, remember KTOZ's story, and imagine how many Americans have had comparable experiences.

CONSENT DECREES

Rather than go through a hearing and the expense of the administrative process, some companies will agree to penalties proposed by an agency. They do so in a document called a **consent decree**, which is comparable to a **nolo contendere** plea in the criminal system. The party does not admit or deny a violation but simply negotiates a settlement with the administrative agency. The negotiated settlement will include the same types of sanctions the agency would have the power to impose if the case went to hearing. The agency may be willing to give up a little in exchange for the violator's willingness to settle and save the agency time and costs of full prosecution. The consent decree is a contract between the charged party and the regulatory agency. Exhibit 6.10 provides an FTC consent decree.

Business Planning Tip

Businesses can take steps to alleviate the severity of a penalty by negotiating with the agency and by developing a good working relationship with the agency. Some businesses advocate a self-reporting policy: When a violation occurs, they report it to the agency. Such a relationship establishes the good faith of the business and credibility when it comes to regulatory issues.

Exhibit 6.10
Excerpts from an FTC Consent Decree

In the matter of the National Media Group, Inc. et al. Consent Order, etc., in regard to Alleged Violation of The Federal Trade Commission Act

This consent order, among other things, requires a King of Prussia, Pa. firm and a corporate officer, engaged in the advertising and sale of "Acne-Statin," an acne "treatment," to cease disseminating or causing the dissemination of advertisements that represent that Acne-Statin cures acne, eliminates or reduces the bacteria and fatty acids responsible for acne blemishes, and is superior to all other acne preparations and soap for the antibacterial treatment of acne. . . . Additionally, they are required to establish an independent, irrevocable trust account containing sixty thousand dollars ($60,000) to be used to pay half of all requests for restitution by Acne-Statin purchasers; and obligated to conduct and be totally responsible for the administration of the restitution program.

(The original complaint appeared here.)

Order

It is ordered, That respondents, The National Media Group, Inc. a corporation,...and the corporate respondent's officers, agents, representatives, and employees...do forthwith cease and desist from:

A. Disseminating or causing the dissemination of any advertisement by means of the United States mails or by any means in or affecting commerce,... which directly or indirectly:

Continued

1. Represents that use of Acne-Statin will cure acne or any skin condition associated with acne.

2. Represents that Acne-Statin will eliminate or reduce the bacteria responsible for pimples, blackheads, whiteheads, or other acne blemishes or any skin condition associated with acne.

3. Represents that Acne-Statin will eliminate or reduce the fatty acids responsible for pimples, blackheads, whiteheads, other acne blemishes or any skin condition associated with acne.

4. Represents that Acne-Statin is superior to prescription or over-the counter antibacterial acne preparations in the treatment of acne.

5. Represents that Acne-Statin is superior to soap in the antibacterial treatment of acne.

It is further ordered, That:

A. Within thirty (30) days of final acceptance of this consent order by the Federal Trade Commission (hereinafter the "Commission"), respondent, The National Media Group, Inc., shall establish an interest-bearing trust account containing the sum of sixty thousand dollars ($60,000), for the purpose of paying restitution to Acne-Statin purchasers. . . .

Exhibit 6.10 *(Continued)*

HEARINGS

If the parties cannot reach an agreement through a consent decree, then the question of violations and penalties will go to an administrative hearing, which is quite different from the litigation procedures described in Chapter 4. Here there is no jury. The plaintiff or prosecutor is the administrative agency, represented by one of its staff attorneys. The defendant is the person or company accused of violating an administrative regulation. The judge is called an **administrative law judge (ALJ)** at the federal level, and in some state-level agencies is called a **hearing examiner** or **hearing officer**. The defendant can be represented by an attorney.

An ALJ has all the powers of a judge. He or she conducts the hearing, rules on evidentiary and procedural questions, and administers oaths. The ALJ also has certain unique powers, such as the ability to hold settlement conferences between the parties. The ALJ also has the responsibility of making the decision in the case. That decision is cast in the form of a written opinion that consists of findings of facts, conclusions of law, and an order specifying the remedies and sanctions.

The ALJ also has the ethical responsibilities of a trial judge; that is, the judges are prohibited from having **ex parte contacts**, which are contacts with one side or one of the parties in the dispute without the knowledge of the others. Staff members of the agency are prohibited from supplying information to the ALJ except when they are witnesses or attorneys in the hearings.

Administrative hearings can have as participants more than just the agency and the party charged with a violation. Other parties with an interest in the case can intervene. These **intervenors** file motions to intervene and are usually

Mike Espy was elected to Congress as a representative from Missouri in 1988. Bright and young, he was welcomed to the House and given substantial responsibilities. When Bill Clinton was elected president, he tapped Mr. Espy (only 40 at the time) for his cabinet as secretary of agriculture. Mr. Espy was described as a fast-rising political star.

Tyson Foods, Inc., the world's largest producer of fresh and processed poultry product, soon developed a close relationship with Mr. Espy. At the time of Mr. Espy's appointment, Tyson and other regulators were fighting proposed Department of Agriculture guidelines (ultimately not promulgated) that would have imposed a "zero tolerance" on the presence of fecal matter during processing. The proposed regulations would have substantially increased costs for Tyson and other processors.

Tyson offered and Mr. Espy accepted numerous benefits from Tyson, including a ride on a Tyson corporate jet, free lodging at a lakeside cabin owned by Tyson, and seats in Tyson's skybox at a Dallas Cowboys game. Additionally, Mr. Espy's girlfriend received a $1,200 college scholarship from Tyson Foods. Mr. Espy went to the 1994 Super Bowl at government expense, saying he made the trip because Smokey the Bear was being honored in public service announcements at the game.

When information about these corporate gifts and government spending was reported, there was tremendous public outcry. Mr. Espy paid back Tyson Foods for the jet rides and the tickets. However, a special prosecutor was appointed to look into these issues and others, including Quaker Oats's furnishing Mr. Espy a ticket to a Chicago Bulls playoff game after he contacted the company and made the request. In addition, a lobbyist for Sun Diamond, a raisin and almond firm, sponsored a birthday party for Mr. Espy and 150 Department of Agriculture employees.

By December 1994, Mr. Espy, who had pledged that he would clean up the U.S. poultry business, resigned, saying, "It seemed as if I was just twisting in the wind."

Manley C. Molpus, president of the Grocery Manufacturers Association and a friend of Mr. Espy's said, "Clearly, there were some lapses of judgment in the administration of his affairs that should have been taken care of with greater sensitivity to the law as well as perception."

A former congressional colleague noted: "It seems as though he behaved as though he was still a member (of Congress). This is not a corrupt or venal guy."

Mike Espy

Issues

1. Was Mr. Espy's role at Agriculture different from his role in Congress?
2. Was paying Tyson back enough?

permitted to do so at any time before the start of a hearing. Typical intervenors are industry organizations: Should the FCC hold hearings on charges against a television station on the content of ads on the station, the National Association of Broadcasters would probably want to intervene in the hearing.

The rules of evidence and procedure are somewhat relaxed in administrative hearings. Agencies involved in the hearings can issue subpoenas for documents, but the subpoenas can only be enforced by the courts. All of the investigation and adjudication processes of administrative agencies are subject to the constitutional standards of due process, which include the following rights: right to notification of the charges; right to notification of the hearing day; right to present evidence; right to be represented by an attorney; right to an impartial judge; right to a decision based on the law or regulation; and right to cross-examine the witnesses of the agency or intervenors.

ADMINISTRATIVE LAW OF APPEALS

Once the ALJ has issued a decision, the decision can be appealed. However, the appellate process in administrative law is slightly different. The first step in an appeal of an ALJ decision is not to a court but to the agency itself. This gives the agency a chance to correct a bad decision before the courts become involved.

The appeal is to the next higher level in the agency. For example, in the FTC an appeal of an ALJ's decision goes to the commissioners of the FTC for reconsideration. In some agencies the structure is such that there may be appeals to more than one person in the structure. Those appealing an ALJ decision, however, must go through all the required lines of authority in the agency before they can go to court. This process is known as **exhausting administrative remedies**. If an appeal is made before administrative remedies are exhausted, the court will reject the case on those grounds.

There are some exceptions to the exhaustion rule. A decision by a zoning board to allow construction of a building project could go directly to court

---

E T H I C A L   I S S U E S

6.6 Some businesses take a backdoor approach to getting around administrative regulations. They go over an agency's head to its source of funding, namely Congress. After the Association of National Advertisers succeeded in having Michael Pertschuk removed from the development of regulations for children's TV advertising, its attention turned to Congress. As a result of strong lobbying efforts, Congress passed the FTC Improvements Act of 1980. In addition to cutting the FTC budget severely, one of the sections of the act provided that the FTC could not use section 5 (its general power in its enabling act to regulate "deceptive trade practices"; see Chapter 11) to regulate children's television advertising. Shortly after passage, the FTC withdrew all of its rulemaking procedures for children's TV advertising. The organizations and businesses lobbying for the FTC Improvements Act contributed PAC (political action committee) money to members of Congress. Does the ability of businesses to circumvent administrative agencies hinder the agencies' effectiveness? Was the lobbying just an exercise of the businesses' rights? Was the lobbying a way to curtail forever the FTC's power in this area? Is such lobbying an ethical business practice? Does this type of circumvention allow businesses to operate unregulated? *Note:* In 1990 the FTC was able to pass some rules on children's TV advertising and Congress held hearings in 1993 to determine whether more regulation of children's TV was needed.

because, if the building is started but the decision to allow construction later overruled, the builder is damaged. Alternatively, if the building is not started, other purchasers of the land and the builder are harmed. In other words, fast action is required to maintain all parties' positions.

If an agency has gone beyond its enabling act, a party can also go directly to court. This is more of a challenge to a regulation than it is to the agency's decision, and direct appeal is therefore permitted.

Finally, an agency decision can be appealed directly to court if exhaustion of administrative remedies would be futile, as evidenced by public statements of officials of the agency. When the FTC was trying to develop rules on children's TV advertising, for example, a group of interested parties brought a court action to have then-FTC chairman Michael Pertschuk removed from the rulemaking process because he had indicated strong feelings in the press about his position. It would have been futile to try administrative remedies because the appeal would have been taken to the party they were trying to remove.

A decision of a federal administrative agency is appealed to one of the U.S. courts of appeals (as indicated in Chapter 2). In most states, appeals from state administrative agencies also go to state courts of appeals. However, some states require a **trial de novo**, which means the case is appealed to the state's general trial court, where it is tried. In other words, the hearing is repeated but this time under strict rules of procedure and evidence.

An appellate court can simply affirm an agency action, find that an agency has exceeded its authority, find that an agency has violated the U.S. Constitution, or rule that an agency has acted arbitrarily or that an agency's decision or action is not supported by the evidence. The *State Farm* seat belt case is an example of a court's reversal of administrative agency action in the area of rulemaking.

Exhibit 6.11 (pg. 227) provides a summary of the roles of administrative agencies.

Business Planning Tip

<u>Howard Stern's Loophole</u>
In 1993, the Federal Communications Commission (FCC) fined "shock jock" Howard Stern and his employer, Infinity Broadcasting, $1.7 million for indecent broadcasts.

The fines were based on a 1991 FCC-published general guidelines on standardized structure for fines. Local phone companies challenged the guidelines in court for being "rules" rather than "policy." If the guidelines were indeed rules, the FCC had failed to follow rulemaking requirements under the APA.

In July 1994, a federal court of appeals found the policy to be rules. The court voided the guidelines as well as all post-1991 fines, including Stern's and Infinity's.

The court held the Stern fines could be assessed using only pre-1991 guidelines and would require all five commissioners to vote to reissue the fines. The fines were reissued and Infinity paid, but there was a two-year delay.

Following the process is required of all of us—even regulators. Always verify the rules, the process, and the fines.

THE ROLE OF ADMINISTRATIVE AGENCIES
IN THE INTERNATIONAL MARKET

The United States wins the award for the most administrative agencies and regulations. Some businesses have argued that the amount of regulation hinders them in the international marketplace. For example, just the readability level of regulations, as shown in Exhibit 6.12 (pg. 227), demands much time and energy as companies attempt to interpret and comply with the laws.

Many regulators, legislators, and businesses have advocated elimination and streamlining of existing regulations, as well as careful consideration before new regulations are promulgated.

Activity	Steps	Parties	Results
Passing Rules	Rule Proposed Comments Modification, Withdrawal, Promulgation	Agency Consumers Business Congress Agency	New Rules Modified Rule Withdrawn Rules
Enforcement	Licensing	Agency Business	
	Inspections	Agency Courts (if Warranty is Required) Business	Search and inspection
	Complaints	Agency	Fines Penalties Injunctions Consent decrees Hearings

Exhibit 6.11
The Roles of Administrative Agencies

Documents and Populations	Grade Level
1. *Love Story*	7.64
2. Reading Level of U.S. Population over Age 65	9.71
3. *Playboy*	11.46
4. Reading Level of General U.S. Population	11.68
5. *Sports Illustrated*	12.82
6. *Your Medicare Handbook*	14.94
7. *ERISA Summary Plan Description*	15.29
8. *Wall Street Journal*	16.34
9. *Social Security Handbook*	17.51
10. Reading Level of Lawyers	19.00
11. *Albermarle* (U.S. Supreme Court Ruling)	20.30
12. Occupational Safety and Health Act	30.79
13. Employment Retirement Income Safety Act	32.10
14. Section 18 of the Social Security Act	41.04

Sources: Warren S. Blumenfeld et al., "Readability of an ERISA Summary Plan Description vis-a-vis Intended Readership: An Empirical Test of Local Legal Compliance with a Federal Regulation." Paper presented at the Western American Institute for Decision Science Meeting, Reno, Nevada, March 1979. Warren S. Blumenfeld et al., "Readability of the Real Estate Settlement Procedures Act." Paper presented at the Southeastern Regional Business Law Association Meeting, Chapel Hill, North Carolina, October 1980.

Exhibit 6.12
Various Reading Levels of Documents and Populations

C O N S I D E R . . .   **6.3** While the private sector downsizes, the number of employees at federal regulatory agencies increased by 6.8 percent (about 8,000 people) between 1990 and mid-1992. During that same period, businesses eliminated almost 1.5 million jobs. According to government figures, the cost of running federal administrative agencies in 1991 was $562 billion, or twice the defense budget. Is there too much regulation? Is all the regulation necessary? If business is downsizing, shouldn't the need for regulators decrease?

SUMMARY

✓ **What is an administrative agency?**
- Administrative agency—statutory creature with the ability to make, interpret, and enforce laws

What laws govern the operation of administrative agencies?
- Administrative Procedure Act—general federal law governing agency process and operations
- Government in the Sunshine Act—federal law requiring public hearings by agencies (with limited exceptions)
- Federal Privacy Act—federal law protecting transfer of information among agencies unless done for enforcement reasons
- Freedom of Information Act—federal law providing individuals with access to information held by administrative agencies (with some exemptions such as for trade secrets)

What do administrative agencies do?
- Rulemaking—process of turning proposed regulations into actual regulations that requires public input
- *Federal Register*—daily publication that updates agency proposals, rules, hearing notices, and so forth
- *Code of Federal Regulations*—federal government publication of all agency rules
- Licensing—role in which an agency screens businesses before permitting operation
- Inspections—administrative agency role of checking businesses and business sites for compliance

How do agencies pass rules?
✓ - Public comment period—period in rulemaking process when any individual or business can provide input on proposed regulations
- Promulgation—approval of proposed rules by heads of agencies

How do agencies enforce the law?
✓ - Consent decree—settlement (nolo contendere plea) of charges brought by an administrative agency
- Administrative law judge (ALJ)—overseer of hearing on charges brought by administrative agency

QUESTIONS AND PROBLEMS

1. Residents of New York City who were receiving financial aid under the federally assisted program of Aid to Families with Dependent Children (AFDC) brought a class-action suit alleging that the New York officials responsible for the administration of the program were terminating aid to them without notice of the termination or without a hearing prior to the termination. The residents challenged the actions of the state officials as violative of their constitutional right to due process. The procedures for termination changed after the complaints of these residents, and notices and hearings were provided. What types of procedures would be necessary to protect the residents' due process rights? Must a court afford these procedures? [*Goldberg* v. *Kelly*, 397 U.S. 254 (1970).]

2. In 1979, Congress passed the Chrysler Corporation Loan Guarantee Act of 1979. The act was passed to keep the Chrysler Corporation in business and out of bankruptcy. The act established the Chrysler Corporation Loan Guarantee Board, made up of top federal officials, to oversee Chrysler's bailout. The meetings of this board necessarily involved sensitive discussions about Chrysler and its status. Would the meetings be covered under the Sunshine Act and thus open to the public? [*Symons* v. *Chrysler Corp. Loan Guarantee*, 670 F.2d 238 (D.C. 1981).]

3. Because of overcrowded conditions at the nation's airports during the late 1960s, the Federal Aviation Administration (FAA) promulgated a regulation to reduce takeoff and landing delays at airports by limiting the number of landing and takeoff slots at five major airports to 60 slots per hour. The airports were Kennedy, LaGuardia, O'Hare, Newark, and National. At National Airport (Washington), 40 of the 60 slots were given to commercial planes, and the commercial carriers allocated the slots among themselves until October 1980. In 1980, New York Air, a new airline, requested some of the 40 slots, but the existing airlines refused to give up any. The secretary of transportation, in response and "to avoid chaos in the skies" during the upcoming holidays, proposed a rule to allocate the slots at National. The allocation rule was proposed on October 16, 1980, and appeared in the *Federal Register* on October 20, 1980. The comment period was seven days starting from the October 16, 1980, proposal date. The airlines and others submitted a total of 37 comments to the secretary. However, Northwest Airlines filed suit on grounds that the APA required a minimum of 30 days for a public comment period. The secretary argued that the 30-day rule was being suspended for good cause (the holiday season was upon them). Who is correct? Should an exception be made, or should the FAA be required to follow the 30-day rule? [*Northwest Airlines, Inc.* v. *Goldschmidt*, 645 F.2d 1309 (8th Cir. 1981).]

4. Richardson-Vicks, Inc., is the manufacturer and seller of Vick's Pediatric Formula 44 (Pediatric 44), a cough medicine for children. In its ads for Pediatric 44, Vicks claims that the syrup contains active ingredients that enable it to begin working instantly. However, Pediatric 44 is considered to have only inactive ingredients, according to FDA regulations on "active" and "inactive" ingredients. A competitor has alleged that Vicks is "misbranding" its products. Can the FDA take any action? What steps could it take? Will the FDA be required to make an interpretation of the "active"/"inactive" regulation? [*Sandoz Pharmaceuticals* v. *Richardson-Vicks, Inc.*, 902 F.2d 222 (3rd Cir. 1990).]

5. Read the following excerpt from the *Wall Street Journal*:

   The smell of the greasepaint and the roar of the crowd, indeed.

   The circus of yesteryear, loved by children and fondly remembered by older folk, keeps running smack into the modern world. In 1992, tents must fall within local fire codes. If the clown isn't a U.S. citizen, he had better have a valid work visa along with his makeup kit and big false nose. And the kid who wants to run away from home and join the circus? Forget it. . . .

   Consider Carson & Barnes, the last of the five-ring road shows. The circus is traveling an 18-state route this year, from March 21 to Nov. 15, doing one-night stands. Each morning, about 200 performers and other employees, 150 animals, 80 trucks roll into town. Roustabouts race to erect the "Biggest Big Top On Earth." The circus performs two shows, packs, goes to sleep, rises at dawn and heads for the next stop.

With scheduling tight, satisfying the local tests is no mean feat. The 237 small towns where the circus is performing this year all usually require about half a dozen permits, with regulations varying from place to place.

This summer, the circus's soft-drink concession got shut down briefly because of bad water. An Illinois inspector found a high bacteria count and sent word to Wisconsin, so the water flunked inspection in Racine and Jefferson. . . .

If a sucker isn't born every minute, it is true that people are easily fooled and that can cause the circus trouble. While his circus was crossing Texas this year, someone complained about the stunt Argentine acrobat Sulliana Montes de Oca does with her French poodle. The dog sits on a platform as Ms. Montes de Oca appears to execute a handstand on the poor dog's head.

It's an illusion, of course, but a local inspector even came out to investigate an abuse complaint, circus officials say. They showed him the steel rod the circus crowd doesn't see that actually supports Ms. Montes de Oca when she does the trick. Dave Brandt, the show's press agent, says, "Who would ever think a nine-pound French poodle can hold up a 90-pound woman?" . . .

Local officials worry about the welfare of children as well as animals. About half a century ago, the Miller family circus actually did hire some young teenagers. And local kids willing to help set up the show got in free. But child-labor laws and insurance policy problems have put a stop to that. Applicants must be 18.

Nevertheless, Carson & Barnes has problems even with the only minors it does employ—those who perform in acts with their parents. Last year, California inspectors demanded that 14-year-old Dulce Vital quit holding target balloons for her father's archery act. Though the act is risky and Ms. Vital is young, she knew the routine. When she was replaced in Desert Hot Springs by a 19-year-old stand-in, Isabel Macias, the new girl caught an arrow in the forehead and today has a scar to show for it.

Then there is the foreign-performer problem. Carson & Barnes employs about 80 Latin Americans a year, and tangles for months with immigration officials to get papers for them. Last year, temporary-visa applications for the Chimals, a Mexican family of acrobats, got lost in the bureaucracy, say circus officials. The up-shot: For 10 days, the circus performed with an empty ring.

Certain towns make it harder on Carson & Barnes than others. "The fire marshal from hell is here today," reads the general manager's journal entry for Ojai, Calif. The fireman was concerned, among other things, that the inspector's ID number wasn't printed on fire extinguishers.

The hang-up forced the gathering afternoon audience to wait in the hot sun while circus officials jumped through hoops. Finally, at showtime, the fireman was willing to let the show go on if one fire extinguisher could be shown to function properly. One was tested, it worked, and the circus started half-an-hour late. . . .

Source: "Bunting & Red Tape: The Modern Circus Walks a High Wire," *The Wall Street Journal*, Aug. 31, 1992, pp. A1, A4. Reprinted by permission of *The Wall Street Journal*, © 1992 Dow Jones & Company, Inc. All Rights Reserved Worldwide.

Is too much regulation exerted upon the circus? Is all the regulation necessary?

6. Suppose that the SEC has proposed a new rule for the filing of registered companies' annual reports (see Chapter 21). One of the provisions of the rule requires the reports to be filed within three months after the close of the company's financial year. All of the companies commenting on the rule mentioned that the time for filing should be extended at least 30 days because most accounting firms require 90 days to complete their work for an annual report. After the comment period, the SEC changed the rule's time limit to 120 days. Is another public comment period required, or can the rule now be promulgated?

7. Hooked on Phonics is a reading program that departs from the current educational reading philosophy of "whole-language learning." The program emphasizes the more traditional reading process of having children sound out letters and combinations of

letters. The Federal Trade Commission (FTC) filed a false advertising complaint against Gateway Educational Products, Inc., the owner of the Hooked on Phonics program. The FTC claimed that Gateway's TV claim that those with reading disabilities would be helped "quickly and easily" and that Hooked on Phonics could "teach reading in a home setting without additional assistance" was misleading. Gateway does not feel the claims are false, but it does not want to have bad publicity. What advice can you give Gateway on handling the FTC charges?

8. In March 1992, the Federal Communications Commission (FCC) proposed rules that would increase the maximum number of radio stations a company could own from 12 AM stations and 12 FM stations to 30 of each. The FCC proposed the changes because more than half of the nation's 11,000 radio stations are unprofitable, and the larger ownership blocks would allow some economies of scale. Critics were vocal about domination and monopolization. As a result, the FCC changed the ownership maximums to 18 FM and 18 AM stations and issued its final rules on August 5, 1992. Describe the process the FCC employed to make these changes. Explain what public outcry accomplished.

9. The Food and Drug Administration (FDA) is concerned about laser eye surgery, noting that the industry concerned with correcting vision is spawning joint ventures, wine-and-cheese seminars to court potential investors, and databases of nearsighted consumers. There are 800-numbers and some dissatisfaction among the 700 patients who've had the surgery, including complaints of farsightedness. The corrective laser surgery costs $2,000 per eye and is not covered by insurance. Further, the only regulation the FDA has in the field covers granting permission to laser manufacturers, which has been given, to sell their machines to opthamologists. The FDA would like to know more and perhaps control some aspects of patients' care. Describe the steps the FDA must take.

10. Some administrative agencies have exemptions for their licensing requirements. For example, some state bars exempt lawyers licensed in other states from having to go through their licensing procedures. The Interstate Commerce Commission exempts some drivers and companies from its licensing requirements. Can agencies allow these exemptions? Are they unfair to others? [*American Trucking Ass'n* v. *ICC*, 697 F.2d 1146 (D.C. 1983).]

Judgment

Harry Carpenter, the CEO of W.S. Kirkpatrick & Company, Inc., a U.S. corporation, learned that the Republic of Nigeria was interested in contracting for the construction of an aeromedical center at Kaduna Air Force Base in Nigeria. Carpenter contacted Benson "Tunde" Akindele, a Nigerian citizen, for his help in getting the contract. Akindele arranged for Kirkpatrick to get the contract in exchange for Kirkpatrick's payments to two Panamanian companies owned by Akindele a "commission" of 20 percent of the construction and equipment contract price. Akindele would then give the 20 percent commission as a bribe to Nigerian officials.

Kirkpatrick was awarded the contract, and Environmental Tectonics, an unsuccessful bidder, learned of the commission and reported it to both the Nigerian Air Force and the U.S. Embassy in Lagos, Nigeria. Were any laws violated? If so, who committed the violations? Are the Nigerian officials immune because their award of the contract was an act of state?

International Law

Shakespeare was ahead of his time when he wrote that "the world is your oyster." Today's global business environment is the dream of economists who have fostered the notion of free trade since the publication of Adam Smith's *The Wealth of Nations* about two hundred years ago. Trade barriers are down, resources are flowing, and even the smallest of businesses are involved in international trade. Trade across borders still involves additional issues and laws, and carries risks that do not exist in transactions within nations. Businesses must understand the legal environment of international trade to enter into contracts and conduct operations in ways that minimize legal risks because, as noted in Chapter 4, litigation across borders can be difficult. This chapter covers the legal environment of international business. What laws affect businesses in international trade? What international agreements affect global businesses? What contract issues exist in international business?

If a foreign country can supply us with a commodity cheaper than we ourselves can make it, better buy it of them with some part of our own industry, employed in a way in which we have some advantage.
Adam Smith

I don't believe you can run a major U.S. company from abroad. George III tried to run the United States from Britain and look what happened to him.
Sir Gordon White
Chairman, Hanson Industries, Inc.

SOURCES OF INTERNATIONAL LAW

"When in Rome, do as the Romans do" is advice that can be modified for business: When in Rome, follow Roman law. In each country where a business has operations, it must comply with the laws of that nation. Just as every U.S. business must comply with all the tax, employment, safety, and environmental laws of each state in which it operates, every international business must comply with the laws of the countries in which it operates.

The various systems of laws can be quite different, and businesses are well advised to obtain local legal counsel for advice on the peculiarities of each nation's laws. Generally, a nation's laws are based on one of three types of systems. The United States has a **common law** system. Like England, our laws are built on tradition and precedent (see Chapter 1). Not every possible situation is codified; we rely on our courts to interpret and apply our more general statutes and, in many cases, to develop principles of law as cases are presented (as with the common law doctrine of negligence; see Chapter 9).

Other countries rely on civil law or **code law**. This form of law is found in European nations that are not tied to England, France, Germany, Spain, and countries influenced through their colonial activities. Countries with code law systems do not rely on court decisions but rely instead on statutes or codes that are intended to cover all types of circumstances and attempt to spell out the law so there is little need for interpretation.

A final system of law is **Islamic law**, which is followed in some form in 27 countries. Islamic legal systems are based on religious tenets and govern all aspects of life, from appropriate dress in public to remedies for contract breaches. Many of the Islamic countries have a combination of civil and Islamic systems that result from the influences of both colonization and Islam.

"How come a Mexican shop is selling Afghanistan rugs made in Japan?"

Source: © Goddard Sherman/Rothco. Reprinted with permission.

Before its collapse in the former Soviet Union and Eastern Europe, communism was also classified as a legal system. Now the former Communist nations struggle with evolving cultural, market, and governmental systems. In fact, much international work is being completed by U.S. lawyers, accountants, and other professionals, who are assisting in the development of constitutions, legislation, and even such issues as development of tax codes and collection systems.

Examine various bilateral and multilateral treaties: http://law. house.gov/89.htm *Visit NATO:* http:// www.nato.int/

Treaties are another source of international law. Treaties can be bilateral (between two nations) or multilateral (among more than two nations). Some treaties exist for purposes of security; one example is the North Atlantic Treaty Organization (NATO), a treaty among the United States and European nations that establishes a deployment of armed forces and a security system in Europe. Other treaties cover trade agreements (see pages 246–249). Exhibit 7.1 (pg. 248) provides a summary of the treaties and statutes of international law covered in this chapter.

PRINCIPLES OF INTERNATIONAL LAW

Visit the International Court of Justice: http://www.un. org./Overview/ Organs/icj.html

The sources of international law simply serve to govern businesses as they operate in a particular country, and the laws may vary from country to country. However, some principles of international law apply to all countries and people in the international marketplace. As was discussed in Chapters 1, 3, and 4, there really is no way to enforce international laws. The International Court of Justice established by the United Nations is a court of voluntary jurisdiction for disputes between
nations; it is not a court for the resolution of business disputes between nations. Nonetheless, the principles of international law do affect the decisions and operations of businesses, regardless of the availability of court resolution of rights.

Sovereign Immunity

The concept of **sovereign immunity** is based on the notion that each country is a sovereign nation. This status means that each country is an equal with other countries; each country has exclusive jurisdiction over its internal operations, laws, and people; and no country is subject to the jurisdiction of another country's court system unless it so consents. Our court system cannot be used to right injustices in other countries or subject other countries to penalties. For example, in *Schooner Exchange* v. *McFaddon*, 7 Cr. 116 (1812), a group of American citizens attempted to seize the vessel *Exchange* when it came into port at Philadelphia because the citizens believed the ship had been taken improperly on the high seas by the French emperor Napoleon and that the ship rightfully belonged to them. The U.S. Supreme Court held that the ship could not be seized because sovereign immunity applied and France could not involuntarily be subjected to the jurisdiction of U.S. courts.

Review the Foreign Sovereign Immunities Act of 1976: http:// www.law.cornell. edu/uscode/28/ 1602.html

The Foreign Sovereign Immunities Act of 1976 clarified the U.S. government's position on sovereign immunity and incorporates the *Schooner Exchange* doctrine. Not only are countries immune, but the act also adds a clarification to the concept of sovereign immunity of sovereign nations for illegal acts. For example, in *Argentine Republic* v. *Amerada Hess Shipping Co.*, 488 U.S. 428 (1989), the Supreme Court dismissed a suit brought in a U.S. federal court by a Liberian-chartered commercial ship company against the government of Argentina for its unprovoked and illegal attack on a company ship that was in neutral waters when the war between

Great Britain and Argentina broke out over the Falkland Islands. The attack by the Argentine navy was unprovoked and in clear violation of international law. However, the U.S. Supreme Court clarified that under the Sovereign Immunities Act and principles of international law, all sovereign nations are immune from suits in other countries, even for those acts, like that of Argentina's, that are clear violations of international law.

A distinction has been made, however, by both the Foreign Sovereign Immunities Act and the courts with respect to the commercial transactions of a sovereign nation. For example, the sale of services and goods, loan transactions, and contracts for marketing, public relations, and employment services contracts entered into by a country are, in essence, voluntary agreements that subject that country's government to civil suits in another nation's courts according to the terms of the agreement or according to the basic tenets of judicial jurisdiction (see Chapter 3).

Expropriation, or the Act of State Doctrine

Under this doctrine, the acts of governments of foreign nations are recognized as valid by U.S. courts, even though under our system of legal rights there may be some question whether the acts were legal or appropriate. This doctrine has been challenged most frequently in cases in which a foreign country has expropriated or nationalized private property in a country by an order of attachment. In effect, the foreign government has seized control of private property. Under our standards of due process, such a taking would be unconstitutional without just compensation (see Chapter 5 for a discussion of eminent domain and just compensation), but the **act of state** doctrine provides that "the courts of one country will not sit in judgment on . . . the acts of another done within its own territory." [*Underhill* v. *Hernandez*, 168 U.S. 250 (1897).]

The effect of the act of state doctrine is to leave foreign affairs in the hands of the legislative and executive branches of government and keep courts out of the "loop." There are many cases in which **expropriation** violates principles of international law. In most cases, expropriation or nationalization violates our notions of equity and justice. However, some protection exists for businesses and individuals who invest in foreign nations because the Sovereign Immunities Act exemption for commercial activity also applies in cases of expropriation. The following case clarifies the distinction between expropriation and commercial activity, one of which enjoys immunity and the other of which does not.

Riedel v. *Bancam*
792 F.2d 587 (6th Cir. 1986)

PESOS TO DOLLARS: EXCHANGE RATES CAN KILL INVESTMENTS

FACTS

W. Christian Riedel, a resident of Ohio, had an account with Unibanco, S.A. and asked that it transfer $100,000 to Banca Metropolitana, S.A. (Bamesa) (predecessor to Bancam) for investment in a certificate of deposit (CD). Bamesa merged with another bank to form Bancam, and Riedel's CD was renewed with the newly merged bank.

Shortly after Riedel's renewal, the government of Mexico issued new rules governing accounts from foreigners in Mexican banks. The rules required the banks to pay the CDs in pesos

Continued

at a rate that was substantially below exchange rates. A month after these rules were put into effect, Bancam was nationalized.

When Riedel's CD came due, the exchange rate was 74.34 pesos to the dollar. He was paid $53,276.23 for his $100,000 investment.

Riedel brought suit in a U.S. federal district court, alleging that Bancam had violated both federal and Ohio securities laws in selling the CDs in the United States without registration. Bancam filed a motion to dismiss the suit on grounds that the Sovereign Immunities Act of 1976 precluded U.S. courts from taking jurisdiction over the matter. Bancam also claimed protection under the act of state doctrine. Finally, Bancam claimed that the CD was not a security for purposes of U.S. securities laws.

The district court dismissed Riedel's suit on grounds that it lacked jurisdiction over the claims under Ohio laws and also on grounds of sovereign immunity and the act of state doctrine. Riedel appealed.

JUDICIAL OPINION

KENNEDY, Circuit Judge

In this appeal, Riedel does not challenge the District Court's conclusion that the certificates of deposit that Bancam issued are not "securities" under federal securities law. Instead, Riedel argues that the "act of state doctrine" does not bar his breach of contract and Ohio securities law claims. The District Court, however, did not refer to the "act of state doctrine" in denying Riedel's motion for a new trial. In addition to holding, as a matter of law, that the certificate of deposit involved in this case was not a "security" under federal securities law, the District Court ruled that it did not have jurisdiction over Riedel's breach of contract and Ohio securities law claims. The District Court concluded that: "Diversity jurisdiction pursuant to 28 U.S.C. Section 1332, does not permit a citizen of this state to sue a foreign government or agency thereof, in a federal district court."

We agree that the District Court did not have jurisdiction under 28 U.S.C. § 1332 over the breach of contract and Ohio securities law

claims. Title 28 U.S.C. § 1332(a)(4) confers original jurisdiction on the district courts over civil actions between a foreign state, as plaintiff, and a citizen of a State. Title 28 U.S.C. § 1332(a)(4), however, does not apply to suits between a citizen of a State and a foreign state, as defendant. A "foreign state," under 28 U.S.C. § 1603(a), "includes a political subdivision of a foreign state or an agency or instrumentality of a foreign state. . . ." Since the Government of Mexico nationalized Bancam on September 1, 1982, Bancam qualifies as an "agency or instrumentality of a foreign state" under 28 U.S.C. § 1603(b)(2). Therefore, this action involves an Ohio citizen and a "foreign state," as a defendant. Consequently, 28 U.S.C. § 1332(a)(4) does not apply. Accordingly, we hold that the District Court properly concluded that it did not have jurisdiction under 28 U.S.C. § 1332 over the breach of contract and Ohio securities law claims.

We conclude, however, that the District Court may have had jurisdiction over the breach of contract and Ohio securities law claims under the [Foreign Sovereign Immunities Act (FSIA) 28 U.S.C. § 1330.] Although the FSIA ordinarily entitles foreign states to immunity from federal jurisdiction, 28 U.S.C. § 1605(a)(2) creates a "commercial activity" exception to this immunity. Title 28 U.S.C. § 1605(a)(2) provides in pertinent part:

A foreign state shall not be immune from the jurisdiction of courts of the United States or of the States in any case . . . in which the action is based upon commercial activity carried on in the United States by the foreign state; or upon an act performed in the United States in connection with a commercial activity of the foreign state elsewhere or upon an act outside the territory of the United States in connection with a commercial activity of the foreign state elsewhere and that act causes a direct effect in the United States.

Accordingly, 28 U.S.C. § 1605(a)(2) applies only when a foreign state's "commercial activity" has the required jurisdictional nexus with the United States.

Continued

We hold that the sale of the certificates of deposit in this case was a "commercial activity." . . .

The "act of state doctrine" precludes courts in this country from questioning the validity and effect of a sovereign act of a foreign nation performed in its own territory. . . .

Under the "act of state doctrine," courts exercise jurisdiction but prudentially "decline to decide the merits of the case if in doing so we would need to judge the validity of the public acts of a sovereign state performed within its own territory."

Accordingly, we affirm the portion of the District Court's order denying Riedel's motion for a new trial on the breach of contract claim. The "act of state doctrine," however, does not bar the Ohio securities law claim. Riedel bases that claim on Bancam's failure to register the certificate of deposit with the Ohio Division of Securities and not on Bancam's failure to repay dollars at the certificate's maturity.

Since the District Court may have had the subject matter jurisdiction, we remand the Ohio securities law claim for further proceedings consistent with this opinion. We also note that even if the District Court concludes that it has subject matter jurisdiction, Bancam has also argued that the District Court does not have personal jurisdiction. Assuming that the District Court decides that it has subject matter jurisdiction under the FSIA, the District Court will also have to make findings of fact to determine whether Bancam has sufficient "contacts" with the United States to satisfy due process.

Reversed in part.

CASE QUESTIONS
1. Describe Riedel's investment.
2. What did he get back from his original investment?
3. What are the bases for his suit against Bancam in Ohio?
4. Does the act of state doctrine apply?
5. Does Mexico have sovereign immunity for its expropriation of the bank?
6. What issues will the court be determining when the case is remanded?

C   O   N   S   I   D   E   R   .   .   .   **7.1** Scott Nelson was employed at the Kingdom of Saudi Arabia, a hospital in Saudi Arabia. He had signed an employment contract to act as a monitoring systems engineer at the hospital. Mr. Nelson responded to an ad run in the United States, was hired, and began work in December 1983.

Mr. Nelson, in the course of his employment, discovered numerous safety violations. When, in March 1984, he brought them to the attention of hospital officials, they told him to ignore it.

On September 27, 1994, Mr. Nelson was summoned to the security office where he was arrested by agents of the Saudi government.

He was transported to a jail cell where he was shackled, tortured, and beaten. He was kept for four days with no food and confined to an overcrowded cell area infested with rats. When food was eventually provided, he was required to fight other prisoners for it.

After 39 days and U.S. intervention, Mr. Nelson was released from jail. He refused to return to the hospital and left to return to the United States.

Mr. Nelson and his wife brought a damages suit against his former employer for their failure to warn him about the government. The Saudi government sought to dismiss the suit under the Foreign Sovereign Immunities Act.

Was the activity commercial? Should the Nelsons be permitted to sue? [*Saudi Arabia* v. *Nelson*, 507 U.S. 349 (1993).]

The chapter's opening "Judgment" presented an interesting dilemma in which a U.S. firm brought suit against the successful bidder for a contract and its accomplices under the Racketeer Influenced and Corrupt Organizations Act (RICO) for violation of the Foreign Corrupt Practices Act. As noted in the decision that follows, the initial reaction to the case was to consider it one that must be dismissed under the act of state doctrine.

W. S. Kirkpatrick & Co., Inc. v. Environmental Tectonics Corp., Int'l.
493 U.S. 400 (1990)

TATTLE TALES, KICKBACKS, AND OTHER TALES OF INTERNATIONAL BUSINESS

FACTS

Harry Carpenter, the CEO of W.S. Kirkpatrick & Company, Inc., a U.S. corporation (petitioner), learned that the Republic of Nigeria was interested in contracting for the construction of an aeromedical center at Kaduna Air Force Base in Nigeria as well as supplying its equipment. Carpenter contacted Benson "Tunde" Akindele, a Nigerian citizen, to obtain his help in securing the contract. Tunde arranged for Kirkpatrick to be awarded the contract in exchange for Kirkpatrick's paying to two Panamanian companies owned by Akindele a "commission" of 20 percent of the construction and equipment contract price. Akindele would then give the 20 percent commission to Nigerian officials as a bribe.

Kirkpatrick was awarded the contract, and Environmental Tectonics, an unsuccessful bidder, learned of the commission and reported it to the Nigerian Air Force and the U.S. Embassy in Lagos, Nigeria.

Environmental Tectonics (respondent) brought civil suit in federal district court in New Jersey seeking damages under the RICO statute, the Robinson-Patman Act, and the New Jersey Anti-Racketeering Act.

Kirkpatrick filed a motion to dismiss the case on the ground that it was barred by the act of state doctrine. A legal advisor for the State Department wrote a letter to the district court regarding the department's views on the case and on the act of state doctrine, and the district court dismissed the suit. The court of appeals reversed, and Kirkpatrick appealed. The State Department filed an *amicus curiae* brief.

JUDICIAL OPINION

SCALIA, Justice

This Court's description of the jurisprudential foundation for the act of state doctrine has undergone some evolution over the years. We once viewed the doctrine as an expression of international law, resting upon "the highest considerations of international comity and expediency." We have more recently described it, however, as a consequence of domestic separation of powers, reflecting "the strong sense of the Judicial Branch that its engagement in the task of passing on the validity of foreign acts of state may hinder" the conduct of foreign affairs.

In every case in which we have held the act of state doctrine applicable, the relief sought or the defense interposed would have required a court in the United States to declare invalid the official act of a foreign sovereign performed within its own territory. . . . In the present case, by contrast, neither the claim nor any asserted defense requires a determination that Nigeria's contract with Kirkpatrick International was, or was not, effective.

Petitioners point out, however, that the facts necessary to establish respondent's claim will also establish that the contract was unlawful. Specifically, they note that in order to prevail respondent must prove that petitioner Kirkpatrick made, and Nigerian officials received, payments that violate Nigerian law, which would, they assert, support a finding that the contract is invalid under Nigerian law. Assuming that to be true, it still does not suffice. The act of state doctrine is not some vague doctrine of abstention but a *"principle of decision* binding

Continued

on federal and state courts alike." Act of state issues only arise when a court *must* decide— that is, when the outcome of the case turns upon—the effect of official action by a foreign sovereign. When that question is not the case, neither is the act of state doctrine. That is the situation here. Regardless of what the court's factual findings may suggest as to the legality of the Nigerian contract, its legality is simply not a question to be decided in the present suit, and there is thus no occasion to apply the rule of decision that the act of state doctrine requires. ("The issue in this litigation is not whether [the alleged] acts are valid, but whether they occurred.")

Petitioners insist, however, that the policies underlying our act of state cases—international comity, respect for the sovereignty of foreign nations on their own territory, and the avoidance of embarrassment to the Executive Branch in its conduct of foreign relations—are implicated in the present case because, as the District Court found, a determination that Nigerian officials demanded and accepted a bribe "would impugn or question the nobility of a foreign nation's motivations," and would "result in embarrassment to the sovereign or constitute interference in the conduct of foreign policy of the United States." The United States, as *amicus curiae*, favors the same approach to the act of state doctrine, though disagreeing with

petitioners as to the outcome it produces in the present case.

Even though the validity of the act of a foreign sovereign within its own territory is called into question, the policies underlying the act of state doctrine may not justify its application.

The short of the matter is this: Courts in the United States have the power, and ordinarily the obligation, to decide cases and controversies properly presented to them. The act of state doctrine does not establish an exception for cases and controversies that may embarrass foreign governments, but merely requires that, in the process of deciding, the acts of foreign sovereigns taken within their own jurisdictions shall be deemed valid. That doctrine has no application to the present case because the validity of no foreign sovereign act is at issue.

The judgment of the Court of Appeals for the Third Circuit is affirmed.

CASE QUESTIONS
1. Describe the transactions that led to the New Jersey litigation.
2. What is the concern about embarrassment to the Nigerian government?
3. What is the State Department's position in the case?
4. Does the suit ask that the acts of the Nigerian government be invalidated?
5. Will the suit be permitted to go forward?

Protections for U.S. Property and Investment Abroad

Review the Hickenlooper amendment: http://www.law.cornell.edu/uscode/22/2370.html

The effects of nationalization and expropriation combined with the act of state doctrine and sovereign immunity are to chill U.S. investments in foreign countries. To discourage expropriation, the Foreign Assistance Act of 1962 contained what has been called the Hickenlooper amendment, which requires the president to suspend all forms of assistance to countries that have expropriated the property of U.S. citizens or regulated the property in such a way as to effectively deprive a U.S. citizen of it (through taxation or limits on use).

Many trade treaties that have been negotiated or are being negotiated with other countries contain protections against expropriation. Some treaties provide U.S. companies and investors with the same levels of protection as the citizens of those countries. For example, if a country affords its citizens due process before taking over private property, U.S. citizens and companies must be afforded those same protections prior to expropriation.

Finally, Congress has created a federal insurer for U.S. investments abroad. The Overseas Private Investment Corporation (OPIC) is an insurer for U.S. investment in those countries in which the per capita income is $250 or less. OPIC will pay damages for expropriation, for inability to convert the currency of the country, or for losses from war or revolution.

Repatriation

Repatriation is the process of bringing back to your own country profits earned on investments in another country. In some nations there are limits on repatriation; businesses can remove only a certain amount of the profits earned from the operations of a business within a country. Repatriation limits are considered acts of state and are immune from litigation in the United States.

Business Planning Tip

Businesses should examine all aspects of a country's development before deciding to do business there. The following issues should be researched and deliberated prior to opening operations in another country:

1. What is the economic climate?
2. What is the government structure?
3. What are cultural attitudes about economic development? Are there any ill feelings by indigenous peoples toward other nations?
4. What is the legal structure of the country? What laws exist? How are they made? Are they changed easily?
5. How is the court system? Will it provide an appropriate and fair forum for resolution of disputes?
6. What experiences have other businesses had in dealing with this nation?

Forum Non Conveniens, *or You Have the Wrong Court*

Business Planning Tip

Limits on repatriation should be checked before an investment is made in a foreign country. Limits could be set strictly on amounts, or on amounts over certain time periods. Financial planning requires foreknowledge of these types of limits.

The doctrine of *forum non conveniens* is a principle of U.S. justice under which cases that are brought to the wrong court are dismissed. The doctrine allows judicial discretion whereby such issues as the location of the evidence, the location of the parties, and the location of the property that will be used to satisfy any judgment that is made are examined. For example, when the Union Carbide disaster occurred at its Bhopal, India, plant, victims and families brought suit against Union Carbide in New York City. A U.S. court of appeals dismissed the case and sent it back to India on the grounds of *forum non conveniens* [*In re Union Carbide Corp. Gas Plant Disaster*, 809 F.2d 195 (2d Cir. 1987).]

Conflicts of Law

No two countries match in terms of the structure of their legal system or in their laws. For example, the law in the United States, codified by the widely adopted Uniform Commercial Code (UCC), is that all contracts and contract relationships are subject to a standard of good faith. In Canada, the good faith exists only if the parties place such a provision in their agreement. Under German law, protections are given not on the basis of good faith but rather on the basis of who is the weaker party. Just among three major commercial powers, laws on contracts are significantly different. The rules on conflicts of law in international transactions are as follows: (1) if the parties choose which law applies, that law will apply; (2) if no provision is made, the law of the country where the contract is performed will be used. Agreeing to and understanding the set of laws to be applied in a contract is a critical part of international transactions.

FOR THE MANAGER'S DESK

COMPANIES USE CROSS-CULTURAL TRAINING TO HELP THEIR EMPLOYEES ADJUST ABROAD

Dale Pilger, **General Motors** Corp.'s new managing director for Kenya, wonders if he can keep his Kenyan employees from interrupting his paper work by raising his index finger.

"The finger itself will offend," warns Noah Midamba, a Kenyan. He urges that Mr. Pilger instead greet a worker with an effusive welcome, offer a chair and request that he wait. It can be even trickier to fire a Kenyan, Mr. Midamba says. The government asked one German auto executive to leave Kenya after he dismissed a man—whose brother was the East African country's vice president.

Mr. Pilger, his adventurous wife and their two teenagers, miserable about moving, have come to this Rocky Mountain college town for three days of cross-cultural training. The Cortland, Ohio, family learns to cope with being strangers in a strange land as consultants Moran, Stahl & Boyer International give them a crash immersion in African political history, business practices, social customs and nonverbal gestures. The training enables managers to grasp cultural differences and handle culture-shock symptoms such as self-pity.

Cross-cultural training is on the rise everywhere because more global-minded corporations moving fast-track executives overseas want to curb the cost of failed expatriate stints. "Probably between $2 billion and $2.5 billion a year is lost from failed assignments," says J. Stewart Black, an associate professor of business administration at Dartmouth's Tuck School. Nearly half of major U.S. companies now give executives cross-cultural training before foreign transfers, compared with about 10 percent a decade ago, consultants estimate. . . .

American businesses "are dumb if they don't use cross-cultural training," says Richard B. Jackson, personnel vice president of **Reynolds Metals** Co.'s overseas arm. The big aluminum maker's high rate of expatriate burnout fell "to almost zero," Mr. Jackson notes, after the company began using cross-cultural training in the late 1970s. Other concerns train U.S.-based executives as well because their global duties often take them abroad. . . .

"You don't need research" to prove that cross-cultural training works because so much money has been wasted on failed overseas assignments, counters Gary Wederspahn, director of design and development at Moran Stahl.

General Motors agrees. Despite massive cost cutting lately, the auto giant still spends nearly $500,000 a year on cross-cultural training for about 150 Americans and their families headed abroad. "We think this substantially contributes to the low [premature] return rate" of less than 1 percent among GM expatriates, says Richard Rachner, GM general director of international personnel. That compares with a 25 percent rate at concerns that don't properly select and coach expatriates, he adds.

The Pilgers' experience reveals the benefits and drawbacks of such training. Mr. Pilger, a 38-year-old engineer employed by GM for 20 years, sought an overseas post but never lived abroad before. He finds the sessions "worthwhile" in readying him to run a vehicle-assembly plant that is 51 percent owned by Kenya's government. . . .

The couple's instructors don't always know everything about preparing expatriates for Kenyan culture, either. Mr. Midamba, an adjunct international-relations professor at Kent State University and son of a Kenyan political leader, concedes that he neglected to caution Mr. Pilger's predecessor against holding business dinners at Nairobi restaurants.

As a result, the American manager "got his key people to the restaurant and expected their wives to be there," Mr. Midamba recalls. But "the wives didn't show up." Married women in Kenya view restaurants "as places where you find prostitutes and loose morals," notes Mungai Kimani, another Kenyan trainer.

The blunder partly explains why Mr. Midamba goes to great lengths to teach the Pilgers the art of entertaining at home. Among his tips: Don't be surprised if guests arrive an hour early, an hour late or announce their departure four times.

Source: Joann S. Lublin, "Companies Use Cross-Cultural Training to Help Their Employees Adjust Abroad," *The Wall Street Journal*, August 4, 1992, p. .B1. Reprinted by permission of *The Wall Street Journal*, © 1992 Dow Jones & Company, Inc. All Rights Reserved Worldwide.

PROTECTIONS IN INTERNATIONAL COMPETITION

Although trade barriers are coming down and a global marketplace seems to be a reality, there is still much regulation of international competition. Regulation can be found in the forms of antitrust laws, protections for intellectual property, and trade treaties.

Antitrust Laws in the International Marketplace

All U.S. firms are subject to the antitrust laws of the United States, regardless of where their operations and anticompetitive behavior may occur. Firms from other countries operating in the United States or engaging in trade that has a substantial impact in the United States are also subject to U.S. antitrust laws. These firms are not covered under the act of state doctrine because they are not governmental entities and are engaging in commercial activity. For example, Go Video, a U.S. firm from Arizona, brought a successful antitrust suit against Japanese manufacturers for their alleged refusal to deal with the company in its attempt to develop a dual-deck VCR. U.S. courts and antitrust laws had jurisdiction because of the substantial impact the actions of the Japanese manufacturers would have on the VCR market in the United States.

The converse is also true. Firms outside the United States may enjoy the protections and benefits of our antitrust laws and bring suit for violations if it can be established that the violations they are alleging had a substantial impact on trade in the United States.

Review the Export Trading Company Act of 1982: http://www.law.cornell.edu/uscode/15/4001.html
Visit the Department of Justice: http://www.usdoj.gov/

The Export Trading Company Act of 1982 carved an exception to the antitrust laws for U.S. firms that combine to do business in international markets. Large U.S. firms that would otherwise be prohibited from merging for anticompetitive reasons are permitted to form export trading companies (ETCs) for purposes of participating in international trade. The Justice Department approves applications for ETCs in advance, provided the applicants can demonstrate that the proposed joint venture will not reduce competition in the United States, increase U.S. prices, or cause unfair competition. Thus, companies like Mobil and Exxon are able to work together to explore Siberian oil fields in a combination that would otherwise be prohibited both under the antitrust laws and for purposes of ongoing operations. These combinations are necessary for effective negotiation of large foreign contracts.

Protections for Intellectual Property

Protections for intellectual property in the international marketplace are constantly undergoing refinements. Worldwide registration for patents, copyrights, and trademarks are goals that are within reach as the mechanisms for administration are being put into place. Details on international protections are found in Chapter 12.

Criminal Law Protections

All persons and businesses present within a country are subject to that nation's regulatory scheme for business as well as to the constraints of the country's criminal code. Compliance with the law is a universal principle of international business operations. Expulsion, fines, penalties, and imprisonment are all remedies available to governments when foreign businesses break the law in a particular nation.

Clark Clifford, a Washington, D.C., attorney, rose to political prominence early in his legal career. In 1947, he helped write the National Security Act, a piece of legislation that would affect U.S. world presence for decades. He served as Harry Truman's strategist when Truman came from behind to defeat Thomas E. Dewey in the 1948 presidential campaign.

Advisor to Presidents and International Banks—Clark Clifford and the BCCI Debacle

He played poker with Winston Churchill on the train to Fulton, Missouri, where Churchill gave his famous "iron curtain" speech about the Communist takeover of Eastern European nations.

Mr. Clifford was John F. Kennedy's personal lawyer, Lyndon B. Johnson's secretary of defense, and diplomatic advisor to Jimmy Carter. In 1989, when Speaker of the House Jim Wright was being investigated for ethics violations, he hired Clifford to represent him.

Mr. Clifford also represented large corporate clients, such as Standard Oil, AT&T, RCA, TWA, and ABC. Washington legend holds that he was the first Washington, D.C., lawyer to earn over $1 million a year, something he achieved in the 1960s.

Beginning in the late 1970s, the Bank of Credit & Commerce International (BCCI), an international bank, began to expand its operations into the United States. It hired some of the country's best lawyers to assist in its expansion, and the hand-picked team was headed by Clark Clifford.

BCCI created a corporation, First American Bankshares, to own and operate its U.S. bank holdings. First American was able to acquire banks throughout the country, from New York to California and deep into Georgia. Mr. Clifford served as chairman of First American, and his law firm, Clifford and Warnke (of which Clifford was the managing partner), served as outside legal counsel for First American. Robert Altman, a partner in Clifford & Warnke, served as president of First American.

Clark Clifford

In 1988, BCCI was charged with money-laundering in Florida, and Clifford & Warnke served as defense counsel for the company. The bank successfully defended against the charges.

In 1992, BCCI collapsed. The international web of financing was defunct, and thousands were left without their money. The state of New York and the Justice Department brought charges against Mr. Clifford and Mr. Altman. The indictments alleged they had created ownership fronts to keep from federal regulators the true owners of the BCCI holdings in the United States. The indictment also charged the two with sham loans and stock deals. The government sought $40 million from the pair as funds improperly obtained through the commission of crimes.

Mr. Clifford and Mr. Altman entered pleas of not guilty, responding that they did not know their clients were front men for Middle Eastern ownership interests. A federal district court judge determined that Mr. Clifford, then 85 years old, was too ill to stand trial. Mr. Altman, then 45, had a year-long trial in which he was acquitted of the charges.

Mr. Clifford, in testimony before Congress about the BCCI scandal, said he did not know BCCI was a house of cards built on fake deposits and phony loans. He said he had no knowledge of BCCI's money-laundering, drug money, arms deals, or bribery of public officials. "You have my word as a gentleman," he testified. He added, glancing toward Mr. Altman in the hearing room, "Our consciences are clear."

BCCI losses in the United States totaled $5 billion. The government insurance for deposits at the U.S. banks paid the losses BCCI customers experienced.

Issues

1. Do you think Mr. Clifford should have known of the BCCI activities?
2. Who pays for the BCCI losses?
3. Did Mr. Clifford behave as one who was above the law?
4. Would you want your career to end on this note?

ETHICAL ISSUES

7.1 "You can't be a global player without a presence in the U.S." The advice is from James McDermott, president of Keefe, Bruyette & Woods, a consulting firm, and he was speaking of international banking. Many agreed with Mr. McDermott's assessment, including Daiwa Bank of Japan. Daiwa was established in Japan in 1918, and as of November 2, 1995, was the 10th largest bank in Japan and the 21st largest bank in the world. Its 1994 assets were $183.5 billion and its earnings for 1994 were booked as $1.3 billion. Daiwa set up its U.S. offices with headquarters in New York under the name of Daiwa Bank Trust Company. There were branches and offices of Daiwa Bank Trust in 11 states in the largest U.S. cities. The U.S. division of the bank employed about 400 people.

Toshihide Iguchi was the executive responsible for running the U.S. bank's trading operations. It would be the trading operations that would result in the bank's downfall. The loss in the bank's trading operations began in 1983 but were not entered on the books. Between 1983 and 1995, more than $1 billion in trading losses were not reported. Indeed, the records of the bank were falsified to conceal the losses. Records were also falsified to conceal another $97 million in losses from 1984 to 1987 in bank operations for the Manhattan offices.

Throughout this period, federal regulators had warned Daiwa officials to separate its trading activities from its record-keeping and custody of funds. The functions were never separated.

In July 1995, Mr. Iguchi confessed his wrongdoing to senior management officials in Japan and urged them to buy back some of the Treasury bonds he had sold illegally to cover up the losses. His letter assured the senior management that there was "zero possibility" that federal regulators would discover what they were doing. In late July, an officer from Japan met with Iguchi in New York and told him to continue the cover-up until Daiwa issued its six-month financials for the period ending September 30, 1995.

But Daiwa officials reported the problems of the U.S. division and Iguchi's activities to Japanese regulators on August 8, 1995. The same report was made to U.S. regulators in Washington, D.C., on September 15, 1995.

In early November 1995 federal and state regulators "deported" Daiwa operations in the United States, requiring that all U.S. operations be shut down. In addition to deportation, the federal government issued a 24-count indictment charging the bank with deception of federal regulators and cover-ups of losses. Fines for the violations could be $1.3 billion.

Iguichi pleaded guilty to trying to conceal the losses. He converted $377 million in securities held by Daiwa for its customers to his own use and sold them to try to make up the losses. Masahiro Tsuda, the general manager of the New York office was also named in the indictments.

Takashi Kaiho, Daiwa's president, complained about the criminal charges and vowed to fight them, contending that "blaming Daiwa Bank for thievery and other un–authorized activities makes no sense."

Do you agree? Is it unfair to hold Daiwa accountable? If Daiwa is not responsible for what happened, who is? The term *rogue trader* has been used frequently in financial debacles. Barings Bank, the 200 year old international bank that collapsed because of derivative trading, claimed its bankruptcy was the result of one trader. What signals and atmosphere allow a rogue trader to operate?

Often, the complexities of international operations produce layers of business organizations throughout the world. These layers are often necessary for individual countries and proper business structure under the law. However, the layers of organizations may provide opportunities for laundering of money, concealment of transactions, and other complex transactions that can often escape regulatory detection for a time. However, the activities are eventually discovered, and countries are cooperating more to be certain the complexities of international business do not conceal illicit activities.

Trade and Tariff Protection

Whether supported or despised by economists, tariffs and restrictions on trade have existed for as long as trade itself. Duties, quotas, and tariffs have all been used to control the flow of goods over and across national boundaries. For most of history, these limits on trade have been imposed on a nation-by-nation basis. However, new forms of trade agreements are developing, and nations are organizing in larger groups in an attempt to eliminate many of the individually based barriers to trade.

Review GATT: http://ananse.irv.uit.no/trade_law/gatt/nav/toc.html

The General Agreement on Tariffs and Trade (GATT) is the most expansive attempt to negotiate free trade and boasts one hundred member countries. The GATT has been able to reduce tariffs nearly 70 percent through meetings of its members called "rounds." The president of the United States is authorized by Congress to participate in these rounds and agree to reductions in tariffs.

Visit the UNCITRAL http://www.un.or.at/uncitral/
Review the CISG: http://ananse.irv.uit.no/trade_law/sales/cisg/txt/cisg.complete.html

The United Nations Commission on International Trade Law (UNCITRAL) has as its goal the drafting and adoption of uniform trade laws that would help reduce trade barriers. The UNCITRAL has drafted the Contracts for the International Sale of Goods (CISG), which is a model statute for international sales contracts based on Article II of the Uniform Commercial Code. The CISG has had limited acceptance, but it can serve as a guideline for drafting international sales contracts (see Chapter 14).

The European Economic Community (EEC) was created by the Treaty of Rome and was formerly known as the Common Market; it is often referred to as the European Community (EC) and is now known as the European Union (EU). The EU members are: Austria, Belgium, Cyprus, Denmark, Finland, France, Germany, Greece, Ireland, Italy, Luxembourg, the Netherlands, Portugal, Spain, Sweden, and the United Kingdom. The goal of the EU is to create tariff-free trade among its members and maintain uniform tariffs for outsiders. In addition, the EU has undertaken the ambitious goals of uniformity in laws, with proposals on product liability and litigation for member countries to ensure uniform costs and results. The EU has progressed to the point of having some enforceable international law. For example, the EU has created the European Commission, which has the authority to issue regulations and decisions that are binding on all EU members. The goal of the EU is to build one market of 340 million consumers. In January 1999, the EU plans to introduce a single currency known as the Euro.

Visit the European Union: http://www.cec.lu/

The EU has in place 282 directives that govern everything from health and safety standards in the workplace to the sale of mutual funds across national boundaries. Pending is approval by at least 12 members of the Maastricht Treaty, an amendment to the Treaty of Rome that will create a single European currency, a central bank, and a uniform policy for all members on defense and foreign policy. Many issues still remain unresolved as the EU works toward that singular marketplace.

Review NAFTA: gopher://wiretap.spies.com/11/Gov/NAFTA

The United States has a free-trade agreement with Canada and recently signed the North American Free Trade Agreement (NAFTA), which eliminates 65 percent of the tariffs on U.S. industrial and agricultural exports to Mexico. Over a 15-year period all trade barriers on imports and exports will be eliminated, which would make North America the largest trading bloc in the world. The early stages of NAFTA's effects have involved job losses, labor cost disparities, and pricing.

CONTRACTING-PARTY AUTONOMY IN INTERNATIONAL BUSINESS

International contracts require additional precautions and steps because of the difficulties and expense in enforcement through either arbitration or litigation. Because of the nature of international law, contracting parties have great latitude in negotiating their agreements. They can specify the law that applies, the courts that will enforce, the use of mandatory arbitration, and the remedies in the event of breach. Autonomy of the parties is touted in the CISG and has proven to be a means of avoiding conflicts, even in contracts that do not involve international markets.

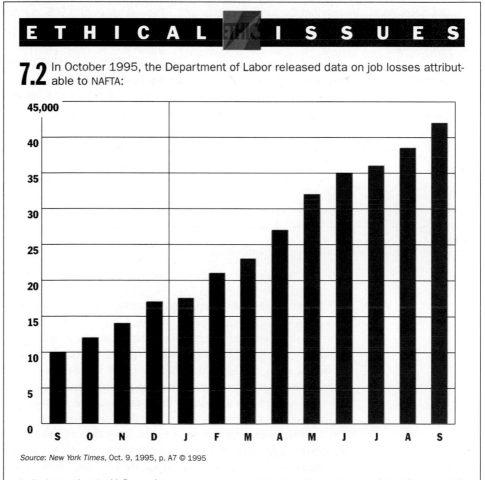

ETHICAL ISSUES

7.2 In October 1995, the Department of Labor released data on job losses attributable to NAFTA:

Source: *New York Times*, Oct. 9, 1995, p. A7 © 1995

Is it damaging to U.S. workers and the United States to have international free trade? Do tariffs afford more economic stability for individual nations? Because of wage disparities, will free trade ever be fair to U.S. workers?

Name	Purpose
North Atlantic Treaty North Atlantic Treaty Organization (NATO)	Treaty between U.S. and European nations that establishes a deployment of armed forces and security set-up in Europe
Foreign Sovereign Immunities Act of 1976	U.S. statute that clarifies the immunity of foreign countries and officials from prosecution for crimes in the U.S.
Act of state doctrine (Expropriation)	Recognition of foreign government's actions as valid; U.S. courts may not be used to challenge another country's actions, even toward U.S. citizens
Foreign Assistance Act of 1962 (Hickenlooper amendment)	Authorization given to president to cut off aid to countries where U.S. citizens' property has been taken by the government or regulated so as to deprive owner of use
Overseas Private Investment Corporation (OPIC)	Federal insurer for U.S. companies' investments in countries with low per capita income
Repatriation	Bringing back to your own country money earned on investments in other countries
Export Trading Company Act of 1982	Antitrust combination exemption for companies joining to compete in international markets
General Agreement on Tariffs and Trade (GATT)	Agreement among 100 countries to increase trade by reducing tariffs
North American Free Trade Agreement (NAFTA)	Agreement among U.S., Canada, and Mexico that eliminates 65 percent of the tariffs across borders now with the goal of tariff elimination by 2010.

Exhibit 7.1
The Treaties, Principles, and Statutes of International Law

In negotiating an international contract, parties should determine which country's laws will govern the transaction. Courts will not interfere with this decision so long as the law chosen has some relation to the transaction. The parties should also agree to submit to the jurisdiction of a particular court so that litigation does not begin with the issue of whether there is or is not jurisdiction in a particular court. If the parties wish to submit to arbitration prior to litigation, the terms and nature of arbitration should be delineated in the contract.

International contracts carry peculiar and additional risks. One of the lessons of the 1991 war in the Persian Gulf, for example, is that international contracts should have provisions for war, interruption of shipping lines, and other political acts. Often referred to as *force majeure* clauses, these provisions in international contracts allow the parties to agree what will happen in the event of sudden changes in government or in the global political climate rather than rely on a court to determine after the fact what rights, if any, the parties had. (See Chapters 14 and 15 for more details on contract issues.)

C O N S I D E R . . . **7.2** Terrorist acts, such as bombings, have become more frequent over the past few years. What happens when there is a substantial interruption in a business's operations because a bombing destroys or damages its leased facilities? Would you add provisions and protections to your lease? What terms would you want if you were the landlord?

In addition to the risks of political changes, international contracts have the risks of changing currency exchange rates, long distances in transportation, and difficulties with collection of payments. Most international contracts have built-in performance guarantees. For example, a seller ships goods with a **bill of lading** (a document of title that the carrier will have). To be able to pick up the goods from the carrier, the buyer must have a copy of the bill of lading. The seller can have a bank release the bill of lading to the buyer when the buyer has paid or when the buyer's bank issues a letter of credit (which is the bank's commitment to pay) to the seller for the amount due for the goods. The effect of these two documents is that the seller or carrier does not release the goods until payment is made or assured. The flow of goods is controlled across borders through documents that travel with the goods and through banks that will issue the payment. At the same time, the buyer is assured that the goods are there before payment is made or authorized.

SUMMARY

What laws affect businesses in international trade?
- Foreign Sovereign Immunities Act of 1976
- Foreign Assistance Act of 1962 (Hickenlooper amendment)
- Overseas Private Investment Corporation (OPIC)
- Export Trading Company Act of 1982

What principles of international law affect business?
- Sovereign immunity—freedom of one country from being subject to orders from another country
- Expropriation; act of state doctrine—recognition by U.S. courts of the actions of other governments as valid despite noncompliance with traditional U.S. rights and procedures
- Repatriation—returning profits earned in other countries to one's native land

What treaties or agreements or practices affect international business and trade?
- North Atlantic Treaty
- North Atlantic Treaty Organization (NATO)
- General Agreement on Tariffs and Trade (GATT)
- North American Free Trade Agreement (NAFTA)
- Duties, quotas, tariffs—controls on prices and quantities of goods by nations with the goal of balancing imports and exports

What contract issues exist in international trade?
- Contracting-party autonomy—principle in international law that permits contracting parties to choose their applicable law and forum and means for dispute resolution

Continued

- Conflict of laws—issue as to which country's law applies in international transactions
- *Forum non conveniens*—doctrine requiring dismissal of cases that should be heard in another country's courts
- *Force majeure*—a contract clause that excuses performance because of unanticipated events

QUESTIONS AND PROBLEMS

1. Describe the sources of international law.
2. Suppose that the government of Brazil took possession of the cacao farms of a chocolate factory owned by a U.S. firm. What rights would the U.S. factory have? What limits exist on those rights?
3. Lloyd Brasileiro was secretary of the Brazilian National Superintendency of Merchant Marine (now called the Brazilian National Department of Waterway Transportation). Mr. Brasileiro is a concurrent citizen of Brazil and the United States. Mr. Brasileiro hired Clara Zveiter in the United States to serve as his secretary for his U.S. operation. Zveiter was, however, a citizen of Brazil; and when she filed suit against Mr. Brasileiro for sexual harassment, he claimed he was exempt because the act of state doctrine protected him. Ms. Zveiter says Brasileiro was engaged in commercial activity. Does the act of state doctrine require dismissal of the suit? [*Zveiter v. Brazilian Nat'l Superintendency of Merchant Marine*, 841 F.Supp. 111 (S.D.N.Y. 1993).]
4. Suppose that a foreign country is shipping batteries to the United States and, in violation of our antitrust laws, has refused to sell its batteries to retailers who charge below their minimum price. Would the foreign country be subject to prosecution and civil suit for violation of the antitrust laws?
5. United Arab Shipping Company (UASC) is a corporation formed under the laws of Kuwait. Its capital stock is wholly owned by the governments of Kuwait, Saudi Arabia, the United Arab Emirates, Qatar, Iraq, and Bahrain. No single government owned more than 19.33 percent of UASC's shares and the corporation was created by a treaty among the owner nations.

   Three seamen who were injured while working for UASC brought suit against it in federal district court in the United States. UASC maintains it enjoys sovereign immunity. The seamen claim it is a commercial enterprise and not entitled to immunity. Who is correct? [*Mangattu v. M/V IBN Hayyan*, 35 F.3d 205 (5th Cir. 1994).]
6. Smith & Smith, a U.S. computer firm, contracted to install a computer system for Volkswagen, Germany, in the company's headquarters in Berlin. Smith's contract included the following liability limitation: "We are only liable for loss of data which is due to a deliberate action on our part. We are not responsible for lost profits in any event." The contract had no provisions on choice of law. A crash in the Smith & Smith system caused a loss of 92 days of financial data. Volkswagen was required to use its auditors to restructure the database at a substantial cost. Smith & Smith says it did nothing deliberate and is, therefore, not liable. Volkswagen cites German law that mandates protection by sellers against such losses and permits recovery of lost profits. U.S. law would honor the Smith & Smith clause. Which law applies? Why?
7. In 1995, the French passed a law known as *Loi Toubon* that requires contracts in which performance will occur in France to be written in French. What disadvantages for foreign firms do you see in this policy?
8. The United States has issued an executive order prohibiting any commerce with Iran that helps it to develop its energy resources. Is such a restriction possible and legal? What businesses would be affected?

9. Walid Azab Al-Uneizi was an employee of the Ministry of Defense of Kuwait. Liticia Guzel was an employee of the Willard Inter-Continental Hotel in Washington, D.C. One of her duties was restocking minibars in guest rooms. Al-Uneizi approached Miss Guzel outside Rooms 610 and 612 and conferred with her about restocking Room 612. After Miss Guzel had finished restocking Room 612, Al-Uneizi assaulted and raped her. After the rape, Al-Uneizi gave her a Kuwaiti flag pin. Miss Guzel has brought suit against both Al-Uneizi and the Kuwaiti government, who seek a dismissal under the act of state doctrine. Should the case be dismissed against both? [*Guzel* v. *State of Kuwait*, 818 F. Supp. 6 (1993).]

10. When the Barings Bank bankruptcy occurred in 1995, Mr. Nick Leeson, the trader responsible for the immense losses the bank experienced after heavy derivative investments, fled to Germany. He was brought back to Hong Kong, the site of his trades, for trial. He is a British citizen who was arrested in Germany. Describe all the principles and issues of international law involved in his arrest, return, and eventual trial in Hong Kong.

Judgment

John Park is the president of Acme Markets, a national retail food chain. Acme operated 16 warehouses that were subject to inspection by the Food and Drug Administration (FDA). During 1970 and 1971, FDA inspectors found rodents in Acme's Philadelphia and Baltimore warehouses. The FDA's chief of compliance wrote to Park and asked that he direct his attention to cleaning up the warehouses. Park directed a subordinate officer to take care of the problems. When the FDA inspected the warehouses again, rodent infestation was still evident. The FDA charged Acme and Park with criminal violations of the Federal Food, Drug, and Cosmetic Act. Park says he tried to clean up the warehouses but his subordinates failed, and that he should not be liable. Is Park correct?

Business Crime

Business and crime have jointly occupied the headlines of newspapers for much of the past decade. Since 1970, there have been 1,043 Fortune 500 corporations involved in at least one violation of a major criminal law. Violations include kickbacks, bribes, illegal political contributions, tax evasion, fraud, antitrust violations, and securities fraud. All the corporations either were tried for criminal charges or entered into consent decrees to settle the charges. Fifty executives from 15 different companies went to jail in these cases.

Many executives perceived that immediate economic benefits were worth the threat of the fines, imprisonment, and personal disgrace to the individuals and companies. Every business person needs a background in the nature of business crimes: why they happen, who is liable, what penalties exist, and the rights of corporate and individual defendants in the criminal justice system.

> *Did you ever expect a corporation to have a conscience, when it has no soul to be damned and no body to be kicked?*
> **Lord Chancellor Edward Thurlow, 1731–1806**
>
> *Your crimes show a pattern of skirting the law.*
> **Judge Kimba Wood,**
> on sentencing junk-bond king Michael Milken to prison
>
> *You don't put Michelangelo or da Vinci in jail. To lose that mind for even a day would be a tragedy.*
> **Charles Keating,**
> on the sentencing of junk-bond king Michael Milken

CORPORATE CRIME

Many business crimes are committed because the business world exerts pressure to produce results. Economic pressure is responsible for much business crime. It often can bear on individual employees whose personal financial situations are bleak enough to cause or contribute to attempted embezzlement from their employers. This type of crime is crime against a business. Exhibit 8.1 provides a summary of companies and business executives that have had encounters with laws, regulators, and courts.

Exhibit 8.1
A Roster of Wrongdoing

Name/Company	Allegations	Outcome
Robert Altman, attorney; officer in BCCI subsidiary (1992)	Conspiracy; fraud; commercial bribery; falsifying business records; filing false documents	Acquitted
BCCI (1992)	RICO violations; fraud; money-laundering; larceny falsification of documents	Guilty plea; $550 million fine
Ivan Boesky, arbitrager; worked with Michael Milken (1988)	Securities fraud	Guilty plea; three-year prison sentence; $100 million in fines and restitution
Brown, Columbia, Cornell, Harvard, Pennsylvania, Princeton, and Yale Universities and Dartmouth College (1992)	Monopolization in financial aid awards	Consent decrees agreeing to halt agreements on standard financial aid practices
Clark Clifford, officer in BCCI subsidiary; former secretary of defense (1992)	Conspiracy; fraud; commercial bribery	Too ill to stand trial
Dun & Bradstreet (1992)	Misleading customers into overpurchasing credit services in five suits	Settlement of $18 million
Drexel Burnham Lambert, Inc. (1990)	Securities fraud	Plea bargain; $650 million for criminal charges; $1.6 billion in settlement of investor lawsuits (9,000 investors); agreement to fire Michael Milken
E. F. Hutton (1985)	Check-kiting; mail and wire fraud	Guilty plea; $2 million fine
Exxon (1989)	Oil spill; felony pollution charges	$1 billion plus $100 million additional damages; cleanup
Ford (1980)	Negligent homicide (Pinto)	Indicted; civil suits nationally

Continued

Name/Company	Allegations	Outcome
General Electric (1991)	Fraud (defense contract); false billing	$70 million fine; guilty plea
Hertz Rent A Car (1988)	Criminal overcharging on repair of damaged rental cars	$13 million refund to consumers
Charles Keating, former CEO of Lincoln S&L (1991)	Securities fraud; federal charges of bankruptcy fraud pending	Convicted; serving 10-year term; partial reversal of case
Merril Lynch & Co., Inc. (1992)	SEC/congressional investigation into junk bonds	Settled with SEC
Michael Milken, head of bonds for Drexel Burnham (1990)	Securities fraud; income tax evasion	Guilty plea; $200 million in fines and penalties; $400 million to settle civil suits; 10-year prison sentence; permanent ban from securities industry; paroled
MiniScribe (1990)	SEC charges (fraud)	$550 million verdict in civil trial
MIT (1992)	Monopolization in financial aid awards	Barred from future combinations with other schools
Salomon Brothers (1992)	Cornering bond market; false bids; false records	$290 million fine; two-month suspension
Sears Roebuck (1992)	Consumer fraud in its auto repair shops	Settlement of $8 million (California); 933,000 coupons to repair shop customers ($50 each)
Kidder Peabody & Co. (1994)	Negligence in supervision of fraudulent bond trader	Firm sold by GE; SEC investigation
Phar-Mor, Inc. (1994)	Fraud; embezzlement	Bankruptcy (Chapter 11); SEC action pending
Honda USA (1995)	Bribes; kickbacks	Guilty pleas and convictions of 16 officers
U.S. Savings & Loans (1995)	Banking law violations; fraud	$45 million in fines; $2.9 billion in restitution; over 4,000 executives sentenced to prison.

Exhibit 8.1 *(Continued)*

Jim G. Locklear was a purchasing agent. His spectacular career as a buyer began in 1977 with Federated Stores in Dallas, Texas. Federated officers described him as a man with an eye for fashion and a keen ability to negotiate. In 1987, Locklear was

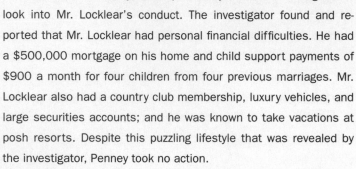

James Locklear: The J. C. Penney Buyer

offered a position with Jordan Marsh, in the Boston area, with an annual salary of $96,000.

Citing a desire to return to Dallas, Locklear left the Jordan Marsh position after only three months. He returned to Dallas as a buyer for J. C. Penney at an annual salary of $56,000. Mr. Locklear did a phenomenal job as the buyer for the

J. C. Penney

J. C. Penney Home Collection. Penney was the first department store to feature coordinated lines of dinnerware, flatware, and glasses. Under Mr. Locklear's purchasing, annual sales in Penney's tabletop line went from $25 million to $45 million.

Based on an anonymous tip, Penney hired an investigator to look into Mr. Locklear's conduct. The investigator found and reported that Mr. Locklear had personal financial difficulties. He had a $500,000 mortgage on his home and child support payments of $900 a month for four children from four previous marriages. Mr. Locklear also had a country club membership, luxury vehicles, and large securities accounts; and he was known to take vacations at posh resorts. Despite this puzzling lifestyle that was revealed by the investigator, Penney took no action.

In 1992, Penney received an anonymous letter disclosing a kickback situation between Mr. Locklear and a manufacturer's representative (rep). Penney investigated a second time, referred the case for criminal prosecution, and filed a civil suit against Mr. Locklear.

The investigation conducted by authorities found that Locklear received payments from vendors through several corporations he had established. During the five-year period from 1987 to 1992, Mr. Locklear had received $1.5 million from vendors, manufacturers' reps, and others.

Mr. Locklear was charged with commercial bribery and entered into a plea agreement that resulted in a five-year prison sentence. Mr. Locklear also served as a witness for the prosecution of those who paid him the bribes. A vendor described his payment of a $25,000 fee to Mr. Locklear as follows: "It was either pay it or go out of business." Mr. Locklear was sentenced to eighteen months and is now in federal prison.

Issues

1. Should Penney have known of the difficulties earlier?
2. Was Mr. Locklear's personal life responsible for his poor value choices at work?
3. Is anyone really harmed by Locklear's activity? Wasn't he a good buyer?

Another more general economic pressure brought to bear on a business is to continue operating and make a profit. This type of pressure is felt by upper- and middle-level managers and is passed along to employees. The drive to succeed or present a good earnings record can then lead many employees into crimes on behalf of the corporation. These crimes do not directly line employee pockets. The business benefits and employees benefit indirectly through profit sharing, salary increases, bonuses, or through just being able to keep their jobs.

Intrabusiness Crime

Estimates of losses from internal business thefts range from $4 billion to $44 billion a year. Law enforcement officials claim that 90 percent of all crime occurs inside businesses. They also estimate that the losses attributable to business crimes are 40 times greater than losses from crimes committed on the street. Losses from business crimes do not include the indirect costs businesses now have because of the amount of crime—the cost of security (estimated at $30 billion) and of insurance against internal thefts. A 1992 survey conducted for the National Retail Foundation found that 30 percent of employees interviewed admitted stealing from employers. Yet another 1992 study found that 38 percent of all inventory loss occurs because of employee theft. No one can document how many business failures have resulted from such in-house theft.

Small businesses have higher employee theft costs because they cannot afford the sophisticated monitoring measures larger corporations will adopt. Most employee theft is systematic. It goes on over a period of time and is well planned. For example, employees of an aircraft plant filled their pockets with nuts and bolts each day at the end of the shift. Over time, enough hardware was accumulated to fill kegs, which were then sold. Garment workers for apparel manufacturers have gone home with jeans in their purses. Nine out of every 10 purchasing agents take kickbacks. All of these acts can be prosecuted under some criminal statute.

Interbusiness Crime

Interbusiness crime occurs among competitors and results in one business's gaining a competitive advantage over others. For example, a federal grand jury indicted General Electric for allegedly defrauding the Air Force of more than $800,000 on defense contracts. The Defense Department asked Pratt & Whitney for a $40 million refund on profits made by the firm in supplying jet engine spare parts. And General Dynamics was investigated for overcharging in its defense contracts.

Banks and other financial institutions become involved in interbusiness crime through failure to carefully check their systems operations. Such was the failure of First National Bank of Boston, which facilitated the laundering of proceeds from racketeering and loan sharking by not giving the required notice to the Treasury Department of the conversion of large amounts of cash to cashier's checks.

Sophisticated forms of eavesdropping have become a means of obtaining information from competitors to gain an advantage. Such eavesdropping can take advantage of high-tech developments in electronic interception. More simply, eavesdropping can be carried out by using binoculars from across the street to read competitor's computer screens.

Other interbusiness crimes that provide a competitive edge are antitrust violations, securities fraud, excessive campaign contributions, and bid-rigging violations. From price-fixing to insider trading, all these violations serve at least temporarily to give a business a competitive edge.

WHO IS LIABLE FOR BUSINESS CRIME?

Judgment

One of the major differences between nonbusiness and business crimes is that more people can be convicted for business crimes. For nonbusiness crimes, only those actually involved can be convicted. For business crimes, on the other hand, those in the management of firms whose employees commit criminal acts can be held liable if they authorized the conduct, knew about the conduct but did nothing, or failed to act reasonably in their supervisory positions. The following case discusses the liability standards for those who are in charge but may not themselves commit a criminal act. It also provides an answer to the chapter's opening "Judgment."

United States v. *Park*
421 U.S. 658 (1975)

IS CHASING RATS FROM WAREHOUSES IN MY JOB DESCRIPTION?

FACTS

Acme Markets, Inc., was a national food retail chain headquartered in Philadelphia, Pennsylvania. At the time of the government action, John R. Park was president of Acme, which employed 36,000 people and operated 16 warehouses.

In 1970, the Food and Drug Administration (FDA) forwarded a letter to Mr. Park describing, in detail, problems with rodent infestation in Acme's Philadelphia warehouse facility. In December 1971, the FDA found the same types of conditions in Acme's Baltimore warehouse facility. In January 1972, the FDA's chief of compliance for its Baltimore office wrote to Mr. Park about the inspection. The letter included the following language:

We note with much concern that the old and new warehouse areas used for food storage were actively and extensively inhabited by live rodents. Of even more concern was the observation that such reprehensible conditions obviously existed for a prolonged period of time without any detection, or were completely ignored.

We trust this letter will serve to direct your attention to the seriousness of the problem and formally advise you of the urgent need to initiate whatever measures are necessary to prevent recurrence and ensure compliance with the law.

After Mr. Park received the letter, he met with the vice president for legal affairs for Acme and was assured that he was "investigating the situation immediately and would be taking corrective action."

When the FDA inspected the Baltimore warehouse in March 1972, there was some improvement in the facility, but there was still rodent infestation. Acme and Park were both charged with violations of the Federal Food, Drug, and Cosmetic Act. Acme pleaded guilty. Mr. Park was convicted and fined $500; he appealed based on error in the judge's instruction, given as follows:

The individual is or could be liable under the statute, even if he did not consciously do wrong. However, the fact that the Defendant is president and is a chief executive officer of the Acme Markets does not require a finding of guilt. Though he need not have personally participated in the situation, he must have had a responsible relationship to the issue. The issue is, in this case, whether the Defendant, John R. Park, by virtue of his position in the company, had a position of authority and responsibility in the situation out of which these charges arose.

The court of appeals reversed Mr. Park's conviction and the government appealed.

Continued

JUDICIAL OPINION

BURGER, Chief Justice

Central to the Court's conclusion [in *United States v. Dotterweich*], 320 U.S. 277 (1943), that individuals other than proprietors are subject to the criminal provisions of the Act was the reality that "the only way in which a corporation can act is through the individuals who act on its behalf."

At the same time, however, the Court was aware of the concern . . . that literal enforcement "might operate too harshly by sweeping within its condemnation any person however remotely entangled in the proscribed shipment." A limiting principle, in the form of "settled doctrines of criminal law" defining those who "are responsible for the commission of a misdemeanor," was available. In this context, the Court concluded, those doctrines dictated that the offense was committed "by all who have . . . a responsible share in the furtherance of the transaction which the statute outlaws."

The Act does not, as we observed in *Dotterweich*, make criminal liability turn on "awareness of some wrongdoing" or "conscious fraud." The duty imposed by Congress on responsible corporate agents is, we emphasize, one that requires the highest standard of foresight and vigilance, but the Act, in its criminal aspect, does not require that which is objectively impossible. The theory upon which responsible corporate agents are held criminally accountable for "causing" violations of the Act permits a claim that a defendant was "powerless" to prevent or correct the violation to "be raised defensively at a trial on the merits." *U.S. v. Wiesenfeld Warehouse Co.*, 376 U.S. 86 (1964). If such a claim is made, the defendant has the burden of coming forward with evidence, but this does not alter the Government's ultimate burden of proving beyond a reasonable doubt the defendant's guilt, including his power, in light of the duty imposed by the Act, to prevent or correct the prohibited condition.

Turning to the jury charge in this case, it is of course arguable that isolated parts can be read as intimating that a finding of guilt could be predicated solely on respondent's corporate position. . . . Viewed as a whole, the charge did not permit the jury to find guilt solely on the basis of respondent's position in the corporation; rather, it fairly advised the jury that to find guilt it must find respondent "had a responsible relation to the situation," and "by virtue of his position. . . had authority and responsibility" to deal with the situation. The situation referred to could only be "food . . . held in unsanitary conditions in a warehouse with the result that it consisted, in part, of filth or . . . may have been contaminated with filth."

Park testified in his defense that he had employed a system in which he relied upon his subordinates, and that he was ultimately responsible for this system. He testified further that he had found these subordinates to be "dependable" and had "great confidence" in them.

[The rebuttal] evidence was not offered to show that respondent had a propensity to commit criminal acts, that the crime charged had been committed; its purpose was to demonstrate that respondent was on notice that he could not rely on his system of delegation to subordinates to prevent or correct unsanitary conditions at Acme's warehouses, and that he must have been aware of the deficiencies of this system before the Baltimore violations were discovered. The evidence was therefore relevant since it served to rebut Park's defense that he had justifiably relied upon subordinates to handle sanitation matters.

Reversed.

CASE QUESTIONS

1. What problems did the FDA find in the Acme warehouses?
2. Over what period of time did the FDA find the problems?
3. Was Mr. Park warned about the problem?
4. What action did Mr. Park take?
5. What standard of liability did the instruction given by the judge impose?
6. Was the instruction correct?
7. Is Mr. Park guilty of a criminal violation?

In 1990, Congress enacted what has been called the "white-collar kingpin" law. A response to the 1980s savings and loan scandals, the law imposes minimum mandatory sentences (10 years in most instances) for corporate officers who mastermind financial crimes such as bank and securities fraud.

C O N S I D E R . . . **8.1** Virginia T. Morris was the chief executive officer and chairman of the board of directors of Northwest National Bank, a financial institution located in Fayetteville, Arkansas. She was indicted on several counts of bank fraud, money-laundering, making false entries in the books of a federally insured financial institution, and making false material statements to a federal bank examiner. Mrs. Morris was convicted and sentenced to prison. She appealed her case on grounds that all the paperwork for the loans, checks, and drafts involved in the case were completed and signed by employees at the bank and not by her. The government has responded by noting that all overdraft approvals were done orally by her. Can Mrs. Morris be held criminally responsible for conduct completed on paper exclusively by others? [*United States* v. *Morris*, 18 F.3d 562 (8th Cir. 1994).]

Browse the Law & Leading Attorneys (L&LA) web site addressing white collar crime: http://www. lawlead.com/florida/ business/chapters/ b18.html

Liability for crimes also extends to employees who participate with the company and its management in illegal acts. An employee who works with his or her employer in establishing fraudulent tax shelters for customers can be held liable along with the company and its officers. The key to liability is personal knowledge of wrongdoing.

C O N S I D E R . . . **8.2** Joseph Marren was employed as a doorman at Michael's Magic Touch, a massage parlor that also permitted its women masseuses to engage in sexual acts for a fee.

Mr. Marren was responsible for answering customer inquiries and for seeing that credit card charges were handled properly. Marren received a portion of the credit card proceeds for his referrals.

Michael Russo, owner of Magic Touch, was arrested, tried, and convicted of charges of prostitution and tax evasion. Marren was also charged with violations. Can Mr. Marren be held criminally liable? [*United States* v. *Marren*, 890 F.2d 924 (7th Cir. 1989).]

C O N S I D E R . . . **8.3** Rudolf G. "Butch" Stanko began the Cattle King Packing Company in Colorado in 1981. He was an officer and a shareholder of the corporation. Mr. Stanko hired Gary Waderich as general sales manager and operations manager.

Stanko, Waderich, and Cattle King were charged with violations of the Federal Meat Inspection Act for selling adulterated meat (meat mixed with inedible scraps to enhance poundage).

Mr. Stanko lived in Scotts Bluff, Nebraska, and claimed he could not be charged because he did not oversee day-to-day operations. He used the "I-was-in-Scotts Bluff " defense. Will this defense work? [*United States* v. *Cattle King Packing Co., Inc.*, 793 F.2d 232 (10th Cir. 1986).]

THE PENALTIES FOR BUSINESS CRIME

Statutes specify penalties for crimes. Some statutes have both business and individual penalties. Exhibit 8.2 provides a summary of the penalties under the major federal statutes.

Exhibit 8.2

Penalties for Business Crime under Federal Law

Agency	May complaint name individual?	Maximum individual penalty	Maximum corporate penalty
Internal Revenue Service	Yes	Willful failure to pay, $10,000/five years willful failure to file, $25,000/one year fraud, $100,000/three years	Willful failure to pay, $10,000, 50 percent assessment, prosecution costs; willful failure to file, $100,000; fraud, $500,000
Antitrust Division of the Justice Department	Yes	$100,000, three years, or both	$1 million, injunction, divestiture
Food and Drug Administration	Yes	$1,000, one year, or both for first offense; $10,000, three years, or both thereafter; illegal drug importation, $250,000/ten years	$1,000 for first offense, $10,000 thereafter; seizure of condemned products; illegal drug importation, $250,000
Federal Trade Commission	Yes	Restitution, injunction	Restitution, injunction, divestiture, $10,000 per day for violation of rules, orders
Securities and Exchange Commission	Yes	$10,000, five years, or injunction both (1933); $100,000, five years, or both (1934)	$2,000,000
Equal Employment Opportunity Commission	No	(some state liability possible)	Injunction, back pay award, reinstatement
Office of Federal Contract Compliance	No		Suspension, cancellation of contract
Environmental Protection Agency	Yes	Medical waste, $50,000/ two years; solid waste, $250,000/ two years $50,000 per day of violation penalty	Medical waste, $1,000,000; solid waste, $1,000,000; $50,000 per day of violation penalty

Continued

Agency	May complaint name individual?	Maximum individual penalty	Maximum corporate penalty
Occupational Safety and Health Administration	No	Willful, maximum of $70,000 per violation; minimum of $5,000 per violation; death, $10,000 and/or six months; false reports, $10,000 and/or six months; advance notice of inspection, $1,000 and/or six months	$70,000
Consumer Product Safety Commission	Yes	$50,000, one year, or both	$500,000 (civil)
Fair Labor Standards Act Department	Yes	$10,000 per employee, six months, or both	$100,000, reimbursement of wages

Exhibit 8.2 *(Continued)*

FOR THE MANAGER'S DESK

THE SAVINGS AND LOAN STATISTICS

From 1988 to June 30, 1995, the federal government, through the Office of the Special Counsel of the Justice Department, conducted investigations into failed savings and loans "to find and prosecute those who looted our financial institutions." When the Office of Special Counsel concluded its work, the following statistics were released:

Number of defendants charged: 6,405

Types of crimes:
4,297 bank crimes
1,852 S&L crimes
256 credit union crimes

Convictions:
5,506 defendants convicted (96.5 percent conviction rate)

Types of persons convicted:
Officers, directors or CEOs: 29 percent; accountants,

attorneys, and consultants: 71 percent

Types of persons charged:
Directors and officers—1,268 (97.5 percent) convicted

Presidents or CEOs—484 (95.1 percent) convicted

Prison time:
Of the 5,506 defendants convicted, 75.5 percent were sentenced to prison

Fines imposed:
$45,000,000

Restitution ordered:
$2.9 billion

James G. Richmond, who served as special counsel, noted that the 71 percent conviction rate of outsiders proves his point: "If you get an officer who goes bad, he isn't just going to do it with one guy. The most logical accomplice is the lawyer, accountant, or appraiser."

Reforming Criminal Penalties

Some regulators and legislators argue that the difficulty with most criminal law penalties is that they were instituted with "natural" persons in mind, as opposed to "artificial" corporate persons. Fines may be significant to individuals, but a $10,000 fine to a corporation with billions in assets and millions in income is simply a cost of doing business.

A recommendation advanced for the reformation of criminal penalties is that the penalties must cost the corporation as much as a bad business decision would cost. For example, if a company develops a bad product line, net earnings could decline 10–20 percent. Penalties expressed in terms of net earnings, as opposed to set dollar amounts, are more likely to have a deterrent effect on business criminal behavior.

Another recommendation advanced, and one that has been implemented to a certain extent, requires prison sentences for officers and directors. The human element of the corporation—the action element—is then punished for the acts done in the name of the business.

A third and final recommendation for reforming criminal penalties would require corporations to stand criminally responsible under traditional criminal statutes for corporate wrongs. For example, when Ford Motor Company manufactured the Pinto automobile with a design flaw involving the gas tank location, many civil suits were brought for deaths and injuries caused by the exploding gas tank. However, Ford was indicted for a criminal charge of homicide. A traditional common law crime was applied to the corporate conduct of using poor product design.

The following case involves a creative sentence imposed by a judge on a corporation.

United States v. Allegheny Bottling Co.
695 F. Supp. 856 (E. D. Va. 1988) *Cert. Den.*

THE COKE AND PEPSI WARS: CRIMINAL SANCTIONS FOR PRICE-FIXING

FACTS

Mid-Atlantic Coca-Cola Bottling Company and Allegheny Pepsi-Cola Bottling Company were charged with conspiracy to fix prices on Coke and Pepsi in order to avoid the ruinous competition that price wars were causing. Several officers pleaded guilty to the charges, and some were found guilty by a jury.

The trial evidence showed that in the Baltimore market, Coke sold from 6,200,000 to 7,000,000 cases of soft drinks a year. Prior to the price-fixing agreement, the price per case was $6.00 to $6.40. After the price-fixing agreement in 1982, the price was $6.80 per case, and it remained there for a full year. This additional 40 cents per case allowed the companies to earn over $1 million more. In pronouncing sentence on the corporate defendants, the judge used a creative solution (later affirmed by the appellate court).

Continued

JUDICIAL OPINION

DOUMAR, District Judge

The Lord Chancellor of England said some two hundred years ago, "Did you ever expect a corporation to have a conscience when it has no soul to be damned, and nobody to be kicked?" Two hundred years have passed since the Lord Chancellor espoused this view, and the whole area of what is and is not permitted or what is or is not prohibited, has changed both in design and application. Certainly, this Court does not expect a corporation to have a conscience, but it does expect it to be ethical and abide by the law. This Court will deal with this company no less severely than it will deal with any individual who similarly disregards the law.

. . . Allegheny Bottling Company [parent of Allegheny Pepsi] is sentenced to three (3) years imprisonment and a fine of One Million Dollars ($1,000,000). Execution of the sentence of imprisonment is suspended and all but $950,000 of said fine is suspended, and the defendant is placed on probation for a period of three years.

As special conditions of the probation, in addition to the normal terms of probation, the defendant, Allegheny Bottling Company, shall provide:

(a)   An officer or employee of Allegheny of comparable salary and stature to Jerry Polino (former vice president of sales who pled guilty to the conspiracy charges) to perform forty (40) hours of community service per week in the Baltimore, Maryland area for a two (2) year period without compensation to the defendant. [The court required 40 hours of community service from someone of equal stature for each of the four officers of Allegheny who had been convicted or pleaded guilty to the price fixing conspiracy charges.]

Corporate imprisonment requires only that the Court restrain or immobilize the corporation. Such restraint of individuals is accomplished by, for example, placing them in the custody of the United States Marshal. The United States Marshal would restrain the corporation by seizing the corporation's physical assets or part of the assets or restricting its actions or liberties in a particular manner.

Cases in the past have *assumed* that corporations cannot be imprisoned, without any cited authority for that proposition. This Court, however, has been unable to find any case which actually held that corporate imprisonment is illegal, unconstitutional, or impossible. Considerable confusion regarding the ability of courts to order a corporation imprisoned has been caused by courts mistakenly thinking that imprisonment necessarily involves incarceration in jail. But since imprisonment of a corporation does not necessarily involve incarceration, there is no reason to continue the assumption, which has lingered in the legal system unexamined and without support, that a corporation cannot be imprisoned. Since the Marshal can restrain the corporation's liberty and has done so in bankruptcy cases, there is no reason he cannot do so in this case as he himself has so stated prior to the imposition of this sentence.

Corporate imprisonment not only promotes the purposes of the Sherman Act, but also promotes the purposes of sentencing. The purposes of sentencing, according to the United States Sentencing Commission, include incapacitating the offender, deterring crime, rehabilitating the offender, and providing just punishment. The corporate imprisonment imposed today is specifically tailored to meet each of these purposes.

CASE QUESTIONS

1. Is corporate imprisonment illegal?
2. How will the corporation be imprisoned?
3. Is community service a sufficient punishment for the corporation?
4. Can the corporation's assets be imprisoned?

Corporate Sentencing Guidelines: An Ounce of Prevention Means a Reduced Sentence

Visit the U.S. Sentencing Commission http://www.ussc.gov/

The U.S. Sentencing Commission, established by Congress in 1984, has developed both federal sentencing guidelines and a carrot-and-stick approach to fighting white-collar crime. Under the commission's guidelines, companies that take substantial steps to prevent, investigate, and punish wrongdoing and cooperate with federal investigators can be treated less harshly in sentencing. The goal of the commission was to ensure that companies would establish internal crime prevention programs.

The guidelines apply to securities, antitrust, bribery, money-laundering, employment, and contract laws at the federal level. The sentencing guidelines permit judges to place guilty companies on probation for a period of up to five years if their offense or offenses occurred during a time when they had no crime prevention programs in place. The guidelines use a formula that takes into account the seriousness of the offense, the company's history of violations, its cooperation in the investigation, the effectiveness of its compliance program, and the role of senior management in the wrongdoing. The guidelines are a form of mandatory sentencing. If certain factors are present, the judge must order prison times. For example, corporate officers who are proven to have masterminded criminal activity must be sentenced to some prison time.

The federal sentencing guidelines provide for a score or a number that determines the extent of the sentence of the company and individual officers, managers, and employees. A company's "culpability multiplier" can range from 0.05 to 4.00, which is then used to convert a business's culpability score (a number that ranges from 0 to 10 or above). Every company begins with a score of 5, which can be added to or subtracted from depending upon various factors in the guidelines. The larger the organization, the greater the number of points that will be added. Involvement of top officers in criminal conduct also adds to the score. Prior violations increase a company's score as do attempts to cover up the conduct (obstruction of justice).

A company's score is decreased by the presence of effective compliance programs designed to prevent and detect violations. If a company comes forward and reports the violations voluntarily, the score is decreased. Cooperation with investigators and acceptance of responsibility also serve to reduce the score.

These multipliers are also used in the computation of fines for a business and its employees and officers. Restitution by a company reduces penalties and fines if restitution is made before sentencing.

Business Planning Tip

Businesses should learn the following from the basic principles of the sentencing guidelines:

1. Have a code of ethics in place
2. Conduct training on the code of ethics
3. Have a company hot line and ombudsperson for employees to utilize anonymously in reporting violations
4. Protect employees who report violations
5. Investigate all allegations regardless of their sources
6. Report all violations immediately and voluntarily
7. Offer restitution to affected parties
8. Cooperate and negotiate with regulators
9. Admit your mistakes and shortcomings
10. Don't ever try to withhold a violation or restructure paperwork to cover it up

ELEMENTS OF BUSINESS CRIME

The **elements**, or requirements for proof, of a business crime will vary according to type. Crimes are violations of written laws, such as statutes or ordinances. But all crimes' specific elements can be classified into two general elements: *mens rea* or *scienter* and *actus reus*.

Mens Rea

A **crime** implies some voluntary action, which is to say that a criminal wrong is calculated or intentional; this element of criminal intent is the ***mens rea*** of a crime. *Mens rea* is the required state of mind for a crime—the intent to commit the act that is a crime. A criminal wrong is not based on an accident unless there was forewarning about the accident or the accident arose from criminal conduct. Thus, driving while intoxicated is a crime, and an accident that happens while a driver is intoxicated will also be a criminal wrong. Concealing income is intentional conduct calculated to avoid paying taxes; it is willful and criminal conduct. An oversight in reporting income is not a crime. The following case discusses the issue of intent in income tax cases.

Cheek v. United States
498 U.S. 192 (1991)

STEERING AROUND TAXES: THE PILOT WHO AVOIDED INCOME

FACTS

John L. Cheek (petitioner) has been a pilot for American Airlines since 1973. He filed his federal income tax returns through 1979 but then stopped filing them (with the exception of a frivolous return in 1982). Each year, he claimed more withholding allowances; by mid-1980 he was claiming 60 allowances. From 1981 to 1984, he indicated on his W-4 forms that he was exempt from federal income taxes.

In 1983, Mr. Cheek filed, unsuccessfully, for a refund of all taxes his employer withheld in 1982. This request triggered an investigation by the Internal Revenue Service (IRS), and Mr.

Continued

Cheek was indicted for six counts of willfully failing to file income tax returns and three counts of evading income taxes.

Mr. Cheek admitted not filing his returns, but at his trial, in which he testified and represented himself, he explained that he had begun attending seminars sponsored by, and following the advice of, a group that believes, among other things, that the federal tax system is unconstitutional. Some of the speakers at these meetings were lawyers who purported to give professional opinions about the invalidity of the federal income tax laws. Mr. Cheek produced a letter from an attorney stating that the Sixteenth Amendment did not authorize a tax on wages and salaries but only on gain or profit. Mr. Cheek's defense was that, based on the indoctrination he received from this group and from his own study, he sincerely believed that the tax laws were being unconstitutionally enforced and that his actions during 1980–86 were lawful. He therefore argued that he had acted without the willfulness required for conviction of the various offenses with which he was charged.

The jury found Mr. Cheek guilty on all counts. He appealed. The Seventh Circuit affirmed, and Cheek appealed again.

JUDICIAL OPINION
WHITE, Justice

The general rule that ignorance of the law or a mistake of law is no defense to criminal prosecution is deeply rooted in the American legal system.

Based on the notion that the law is definite and knowable, the common law presumed that every person knew the law. This common-law rule has been applied by the Court in numerous cases construing criminal statutes.

The proliferation of statutes and regulations has sometimes made it difficult for the average citizen to know and comprehend the extent of the duties and obligations imposed by the tax laws. Congress has accordingly softened the impact of the common-law presumption by making specific intent to violate the law an element of certain federal criminal tax offenses. Thus, the Court almost 60 years ago interpreted the statutory term "willfully" as used in the federal criminal tax statutes as carving out an exception to the traditional rule.

This special treatment of criminal tax offenses is largely due to the complexity of the tax laws.

Willfulness, as construed by our prior decisions in criminal tax cases, requires the Government to prove that the law imposed a duty on the defendant, that the defendant knew of this duty, and that he voluntarily and intentionally violated that duty.

Cheek asserted in the trial court that he should be acquitted because he believed in good faith that the income tax law is unconstitutional as applied to him and thus could not legally impose any duty upon him of which he should have been aware. Such a submission is unsound . . . [I]n "our complex tax system, uncertainty often arises even among taxpayers who earnestly wish to follow the law" and "'[i]t is not the purpose of the law to penalize frank difference of opinion or innocent errors made despite the exercise of reasonable care.'"

Claims that some of the provisions of the tax code are unconstitutional are submissions of a different order. They do not arise from innocent mistakes caused by the complexity of the Internal Revenue Code. Rather, they reveal full knowledge of the provisions at issue and a studied conclusion, however wrong, that those provisions are invalid and unenforceable. Thus in this case, Cheek paid his taxes for years, but after attending various seminars and based on his own study, he concluded that the income tax laws could not constitutionally require him to pay a tax.

We do not believe that Congress contemplated that such a taxpayer, without risking criminal prosecution, could ignore the duties imposed upon him by the Internal Revenue Code and refuse to utilize the mechanisms provided by Congress to present his claims of invalidity to the courts and to abide by their decisions. There is no doubt that Cheek, from

Continued

year to year, was free to pay the tax that the law purported to require, file for a refund and, if denied, present his claims of invalidity, constitutional or otherwise, to the courts. Also, without paying the tax, he could have challenged claims of tax deficiencies in the Tax Court, with the right to appeal to a higher court if unsuccessful. Cheek took neither course in some years, and when he did was unwilling to accept the outcome. As we see it, he is in no position to claim that his good-faith belief about the validity of the Internal Revenue Code negates willfulness or provides a defense to criminal prosecution. Of course, Cheek was free in this very case to present his claims of invalidity and have them adjudicated, but like defendants in criminal cases in other contexts, who "willfully" refuse to comply with the duties placed upon them by the law, he must take the risk of being wrong.

Remanded for other reasons.

CASE QUESTIONS
1. Why did Cheek not pay taxes?
2. Did Cheek misunderstand the law?
3. Doesn't Cheek's legitimate belief that the tax laws are unconstitutional eliminate the element of willfulness from his conduct?
4. Did Cheek have an alternative path for pursuing his challenge without risking criminal prosecution?
5. Is ignorance of the law a defense?

Some crimes not only require "knowing" or "willful" conduct but also require a refined or specific intent in relation to the crime. Securities fraud, for example, requires proof of not just intentional conduct but of intentional conduct with the idea of defrauding another. An accountant who makes an error in preparing corporate financial statements, unintentionally defrauding stock purchasers, did not intend to defraud them, and his act is probably one of negligence or omission rather than a knowing or willful act. However, a deliberate overstatement of income to comply with a corporate management request would be an act showing intent to defraud.

Criminal intent has been a particularly significant issue in business crimes. The intent element is significant because there are actually two intents involved when a corporation is prosecuted for a crime: the intent of the corporation to commit the crime and the intent of those in charge of the corporation, officers, and directors, to direct the corporation to commit the wrong.

C O N S I D E R . . . **8.4** The Interstate Commerce Commission (ICC) has the following regulation on the shipping of hazardous materials: "Each shipper offering for transportation any hazardous material subject to the regulations in this chapter, shall describe that article on the shipping paper by the shipping name prescribed in Section 172.5 of this chapter and by the classification prescribed in Section 172.4 of this chapter, and may add a further description not inconsistent therewith. Abbreviations may not be used."

International Minerals & Chemicals shipped sulfuric acid but did not label the shipment "Corrosive Liquid," as required under the regulation on the shipping papers. International was charged with a knowing and criminal violation of the regulation but insisted that the failure to identify was simply an oversight in paperwork for the shipment. Can there be a valid criminal charge? What if International had other slip-ups in its paper work? [*United States* v. *International Minerals & Chemical Corp.*, 402 U.S. 558 (1971).]

Actus Reus

All crimes include, in addition to the mental intent, a requirement of some specific action or conduct, which is the *actus reus* of the crime. For example, in embezzlement the *actus reus* is the taking of an employer's money.

EXAMPLES OF BUSINESS CRIMES

Theft and Embezzlement

The action of employees who take their employers' property is **theft** or **embezzlement**. For theft the following elements are necessary: (1) intent to take the property, (2) an actual taking of the property for permanent use, and (3) no authorization to take the property. These three elements are the *actus reus* of the crime. The *mens rea* is the taking of the property with the intent of permanently depriving the owner of use and possession.

For embezzlement the elements are the same as for theft, with the addition of one more element: The person commits the crime while in the employ or position of trust of the property owner. In other words, embezzlement is theft from a specific type of person—an employer. Although it is usually limited to funds, embezzlement can cover such items as inventory and equipment of a business. The following case involves an issue of embezzlement.

State v. Rhine
773 P.2d 762 (Okla. 1989)

CAN ONE EMBEZZLE ROADKILL?

FACTS

While trying to avoid a deer on the Oklahoma Turnpike in Ottawa County, a livestock truck crashed and overturned. Several animals from the truck were on or near the road, some of them injured and some of them dead. During the cleanup process, Mr. Rhine and others (appellees), who were members of the Ottawa County Sheriff's office, slit the throats of several injured animals, took them to a rendering plant, and had the meat processed for the sheriff's office. The officers assisting in the cleanup agreed that this meat should be shared among them as compensation for their efforts. The remaining live animals were to be taken to Joplin and left at the stockyards. Before reaching Joplin, however, appellees dropped off another hog at the rendering plant because the hog was scaring the other livestock on the trailer. This hog was also processed for the sheriff's office. Some of the meat was served to prisoners in the county jail, some was eaten at a chili cook-off to raise money for the sheriff's office, and some was given to officers who had helped at the accident site.

The officers were all charged with "embezzlement by a bailee of a live hog." The charges were dismissed, and the state appealed to the Oklahoma Supreme Court.

JUDICIAL OPINION

BUSSEY, Judge

The evidence shows that appellees originally took the animal with the intent to deliver it to Joplin where it could be held at the owner's disposal, and decided only afterward to appropriate the property. Thus the original acquisition was lawful, and the animal could be

Continued

subsequently embezzled. Appellees, however, claim that the State failed to establish the fact of a bailment, thus precluding any prosecution under 21 O.S.1981, § 1455. The State relies upon 15 O.S.1981, § 443 to show that an involuntary bailment had been established.

The State's argument is well taken. In *Mitchell* v. *Oklahoma Cotton Growers' Ass'n*, 108 Okl. 200, 235 P. 597 (1925), the Oklahoma Supreme Court addressed a situation where cotton bales had been carried off by flood waters and deposited on Mitchell's land. The Court held that under those circumstances, Mitchell was an involuntary bailee under the statute. Appellees in this case are in a similar situation inasmuch as they came into lawful possession of the hog in the course of an extraordinary emergency.

Appellees also contend that they established an absolute defense under 21 O.S.1981, § 1459. This statute provides:

Upon any prosecution for embezzlement it is a sufficient defense that the property was appropriated openly and avowedly, and under a claim of title preferred in good faith even though such claim is untenable. But this provision shall not excuse the retention of the property of another, to offset or pay demand held against him.

The record, viewed in the light most favorable to the State, supports the position that appellees retained the animals because they felt entitled to compensation for their services. The statute specifically excludes the defense of retention of property to offset or pay a demand, and this argument must fail.

Finally, the magistrate ruled that the evidence "failed to establish by a preponderance that the property was converted to the personal use of these Defendants." The undisputed evidence showed that appellees appropriated the meat to a use not authorized by the true owner. Therefore, the evidence did establish the necessary elements of the crime and this argument must also fail.

For the foregoing reasons, the ruling of the magistrate is reversed, and the case is remanded for further proceedings consistent with this opinion.

CASE QUESTIONS
1. What was taken and under what circumstances?
2. Why did the officers feel they were entitled to the property?
3. Why were the officers bailees?
4. Had the officers committed the crime of embezzlement?
5. Does it matter that the officers used the property for a good cause?

CONSIDER . . . 8.5 Darrin James was the manager of Allsup's Store in Clovis, New Mexico. Jay Finnell, his immediate supervisor, found $2,400 in cash below the checkstand, behind some books and papers. Mr. Finnell later discovered irregularities in the records of the store maintained by Mr. James. The sales receipts for the store were greater than the bank deposits. Is there sufficient evidence to convict Mr. James of embezzlement? [*State* v. *James*, 784 P.2d 1021 (N.M. App. 1989).]

CONSIDER . . . 8.6 The New York City Department of Health is responsible for the inspection of Manhattan restaurants to determine whether they comply with the city's health code. Forty-six of the department's inspectors were inducing restaurateurs to pay money to them for permit approval or for a favorable inspection.

The inspectors' parlance for these activities were as follows:

"bite the bullet"—restaurant has paid; need not collect from them; "cup of coffee"—restaurant owner will pay more than the going rate; "good stop"—restaurant owner would pay anything for good inspection report; "open drawer policy"—all inspectors shared their take.

All 46 inspectors were indicted for bribery and extortion after a two-year undercover investigation. Could the inspectors be charged with bribery and extortion? Who is harmed by the inspection payoffs? Why did the restaurant owners go along with the payments? Should they have gone to the police? [*United States* v. *Tillem*, 906 F.2d 814 (2d Cir. 1990).]

Computer Crime

Review a summary of federal computer crimes: http:// rampages.onramp. net/~dgmccown/ tlfedcc.htm

The dependence of businesses upon computer technology is great today. Often, such technology evolves more rapidly than the means for developing internal controls on its use. The result is that the ability for the commission of crimes using computers exceeds the ability to control or detect those crimes. Computer crimes fit into four categories:

1. *The unauthorized use of a computer or computer-related equipment.* Even the use of computers for personal projects and the theft of computer hardware and software for nonoffice use have resulted in losses to businesses. Illegal software use cost the software industry $15.2 billion in 1995. That is $482 per second; $28,900 per minute, and $11.7 million per hour.

2. *The alteration or destruction of a computer, its files, its programs, or data.* One of the most difficult problems facing businesses is a computer virus, a program that damages computers and/or computer data. Beyond such damage, the costs to businesses in dealing with these viruses include the man-hours and perhaps man-years of work spent in attempting to prevent or detect them. For example, the 52,000 outside researchers hooked up to computers at NASA's Ames Center spent four to eight hours each month trying to determine whether their computers were infected with a virus. Their total time commitment in this task amounted to 142 man-years.

3. *The entering of fraudulent records or data into a computer system.* The alteration of an academic record or a credit report would fit into this category.

4. *The use of computer facilities to convert ownership of funds, financial instruments, property, services, or data.* The ability to transfer funds electronically has brought about new areas of criminal activity and necessitated the development of statutes to cover the peculiar aspects of crimes facilitated by computers.

SOME COMPUTER CRIME TERMINOLOGY

The previous list covers all the types of computer crimes, which may also be referred to by various lay terms. For example, a popular form of financial computer crime is called the "salami technique." In a bank computer system, changes can be made randomly to reduce accounts by a few cents and then transfer that money to one account from which the person who has changed the system can make a legitimate withdrawal. Because the reduction is so small and spread over so many accounts, those affected are unlikely to report any problems. The salami technique has also been used effectively in businesses with programs covering large amounts of inventory of various kinds. Small amounts of inventory are transferred out to warehouses or fictitious firms. The employee making these changes in the system is then able to embezzle these inventory items.

"Scavenging" is the name given to crimes perpetrated by collecting data from discarded materials. For example, the carbon sheets in credit card transactions, which contain the cardholder's name, credit card number, and expiration date, can be recovered from trash bins and that information then used to acquire goods and services.

For those computer systems hooked into communications systems, there is the potential for a more traditional type of crime: wiretapping. There are equipment costs associated with wiretapping, however, and it is not as popular as other forms of computer crime.

STATE STATUTES COVERING COMPUTER CRIME

Forty-nine states have some form of computer fraud or crime statutes but are still struggling with definitions and the application of existing laws to computer crimes. For example, if a government employee uses part of his or her computer database to keep personal or small business records, has the employee taken government property through use of the database for nongovernment purposes? Computer crime statutes are examples of laws being developed in response to changing technology. Recently, counterfeit check and document scandals have emerged as a result of the use of desktop publishing capabilities of many home computers. A counterfeit check scheme in Louisiana yielded a home computer operator over $10,000. Prosecution of the case involves the difficult issue of showing that the sophisticated check copies were forgeries. Forgeries in 1995 were so costly that banks have begun fingerprinting customers as part of new systems designed to catch counterfeit instruments.

Most state statutes that specifically address computer crime were written before the virus phenomenon. Provisions in computer crime statutes that address viruses first appeared in 1989; changes in the statutes involved designating the distribution of a computer virus as a criminal offense. The difficulty in many of the statutes and proposals is catching those who develop the virus.

A number of traditional criminal statutes do not properly apply to computer crime. For example, burglary requires entering a facility unlawfully, and although a burglary statute would apply to someone entering a building to take computer hardware, it would not apply to someone gaining access to customer lists, formulas, or trade secrets. As the *National Law Journal* notes, cyber-criminals thrive because the laws lag behind technology. Also, enforcement of computer crime laws is a low priority as prosecutors focus their efforts and resources on the violent and socially damaging crimes surrounding gang activity.

INTERNATIONAL CONVENTIONS ON COMPUTER CRIME

The Berne (copyright) and Paris Conventions have provisions that permit businesses in member countries to obtain international copyright protection for their software products. Fifty-nine nations are members of one or more of the conventions (see Chapter 12).

FEDERAL STATUTES COVERING COMPUTER CRIMES

The Copyright Act provides protection for certain computer programs. Once a program is copyrighted, its unauthorized use or reproduction can be prosecuted as a copyright violation.

Certain federal statutes offer individual privacy protections with respect to databases. For example, the Fair Credit Reporting Act (FCRA) limits access to individuals' financial and credit histories; unauthorized use or access carries penalties. Equifax and TRW recently settled cases involving charges that they released

Explore the Berne Convention for the Protection of Literary and Artistic Works (Paris text 1971): http://www.law. cornell.edu:80/ treaties/berne/ overview.html *Review of Copyright Act of 1976, as amended (1994):* http://www.law. cornell.edu/usc/17/ overview.html

credit lists to marketing firms, selling the grouped lists on the basis of income and buying histories.

In 1984, Congress passed the Counterfeit Access Device and Computer Fraud and Abuse Act (CADCFA). This act makes it a federal crime to use or access federal or private computers without authorization in several types of situations. The CADCFA was amended in 1994 to cover additional new technologies, such as scanners, hand-held computers, and laptops.

CADCFA prohibits unauthorized access to U.S. military or foreign policy information, FDIC financial institutions data, or to any government agency computer. For example, in *Sawyer* v. *Department of the Air Force,* 31 MPSR 193 (1986), a federal employee was terminated from his position for tampering with air force invoices and payments. Penalties under CADCFA range from 5 to 21 years imprisonment.

The federal Computer Fraud and Abuse Act (CFAA) classified unauthorized access to a government computer as a felony, and trespass into a federal government computer as a misdemeanor. CFAA covers "intentional" and "knowing" acts and includes a section that makes it a felony to cause more than $1,000 damage to a computer or its data through a virus program.

Review the Counterfeit Access Device and Computer Fraud and Abuse Act: http://www.law.cornell.edu/uscode/18/1001.html

---

E T H I C A L   I S S U E S

8.2 Borland International Inc. and Symantec Corporation are software manufacturers based in Silicon Valley in California. A Borland executive, Eugene Wang, was planning to depart Borland to work for Symantec, considered Borland's archrival. Other Borland executives and its board uncovered evidence, on the evening of Mr. Wang's departure, that Mr. Wang had communicated trade secrets to Gordon Eubanks, Symantec's chief executive. Those secrets included future product specifications, marketing plans through 1993, a confidential proposal for a business transaction, and a memo labeled "attorney/client confidential" summarizing questions asked by the Federal Trade Commission (FTC) in its probe of restraint of trade allegations by Microsoft Corporation.

Mr. Wang had allegedly used his computer to communicate the information to Mr. Eubanks. The local police and Borland executives worked through the night, using Symantec's own software that reconstructs computer files after they have been destroyed.

When Mr. Wang reported for his exit interview, he was detained and questioned by investigators. Searches authorized by warrant of Mr. Eubanks' two homes and his office uncovered evidence that he had received Mr. Wang's information. Borland filed a civil suit against the two men.

Later during the day of the exit interview, Mr. Wang's secretary, who was transferring with him to Symantec, returned to copy from her computer what she called "personal files." A personnel official watched as she copied the files from her computer but became suspicious and notified plainclothes officers in the Borland parking lot. The secretary, Lynn Georganes, was stopped, and the two disks onto which she had copied materials were taken. The disks contained scores of confidential Borland documents, including marketing plans and business forecasts.

Local authorities and the FBI continue to investigate the case, and criminal charges have been filed. Do the actions of Mr. Wang and Mr. Eubanks fit any computer crime statutes? Was there theft involved in their actions? Were Ms. Georganes' actions ethical? Can't a competitor always hire an executive away, and wouldn't Mr. Wang have had most of the information in his head anyway? Can Mr. Eubanks be certain Mr. Wang will not do the same thing to him?

Criminal Fraud

Business crimes against individuals usually result from sales transactions. **Criminal fraud** is an example of this type of crime, the elements of which are the same as those the person defrauded would use to establish a contract defense: There was a false statement; the statement was material—that is, it was the type of information that would affect the buying decision; and there was reliance on the statement. The only differences between contract fraud and criminal fraud is that criminal fraud requires proof of intent, that the seller intended to mislead the buyer for the purpose of effecting the transaction and making money. In most of the savings and loans cases in which charges were brought, fraud charges were included because often documents and appraisals were forged or falsified. Forgery provides proof of the level of intent needed for criminal fraud.

FOR THE MANAGER'S DESK

WHY GIGANTIC FRAUDS STILL WORK

Criminal fraud remains with us despite the universal principle that "houses of cards" and other scams eventually collapse, leaving investors and banks making up the losses. The following excerpt from *FORTUNE* magazine explains "why frauds have nine lives."

Ever since the savings and loan collapses of the 1980s, which will probably wind up costing taxpayers about $125 billion, the FBI and other federal agencies have tried to pay more attention to bank fraud, as well as other white-collar crimes. Health care fraud troubles Attorney General Janet Reno so much she has made it a top priority.

But when fraud has to compete for attention with violence, violence usually wins. Immediately after the bombing of Oklahoma City's federal building in April, for example, the Bureau assigned more than 1,000 agents to the investigation. The horror of that mass murder and the fear it stirred around the nation no doubt justified that extraordinary effort. But consider: FBI has only 9,742 agents in all, so more than 10 percent of the entire force was detailed to a single crime.

The size of the Oklahoma City task force has been reduced considerably over the weeks (the FBI won't be more specific). But violent crime in general—especially that involving drugs and, more recently, terrorism—has overwhelmed the resources not only of the Bureau, but also of the courts and the U.S. Attorneys' offices that prosecute federal crimes.

So, in the case of an economic crime such as check kiting, a U.S. Attorney's office probably won't prosecute if the bank and the swindler can reach an agreement. "Usually the perpetrator pays off and leaves town," says Susan Barnes, first assistant U.S. Attorney for Western Washington, "so the fraud division will see the threat to the local public gone." If you run a bank farther down the interstate, watch out.

Foreign Corrupt Practices Act

Perhaps the most widely known criminal statute affecting firms that operate internationally is the **Foreign Corrupt Practices Act (FCPA)**. The FCPA applies to business concerns that have their principal offices in the United States. It contains

Review the Foreign Corrupt Practices Act:
http://www.law.cornell.edu/uscode/15/78dd-2.html
Visit the SEC:
http://www.sec.gov/

antibribery provisions as well as accounting controls for these firms, and it is meant to curb the use of bribery in foreign operations of companies.

The general standard of the act is the prohibition of making, authorizing, or promising payments or gifts of money or anything of value with the intent to corrupt. The prohibition is against payments designed to influence the official acts of foreign officials, political parties, party officials, candidates for office, or any person who will transmit the gift or money to one of the other types of persons.

The FCPA is the result of an SEC investigation that uncovered questionable foreign payments by large stock issuers who were based in the United States. Approximately 435 U.S. corporations had made improper or questionable payments in Japan, the Netherlands, and Korea. The most common type of payment was made to foreign government officials. Most of the payments were made in relation to tax valuation or assessments. First passed in 1977, the act was most recently amended in 1988.

For a payment to a foreign official to constitute a violation of the FCPA, payment or something of value must have been given to a foreign official with discretionary authority, a foreign political candidate, or a foreign political party for the purpose of getting the recipient to act or refrain from acting to help business operations.

Payments to any foreign official for "facilitation," often referred to as grease payments, are not prohibited under FCPA so long as these payments are made only to get these officials to do their normal jobs that they might not do or would do slowly without some payment. These grease payments can be made only to (1) secure a permit or license; (2) obtain paper processing; (3) secure police protection; (4) provide phone, water, or power supply; or (5) any other similar actions. Penalties for violations of the FCPA can run up to $2 million and 10 years imprisonment for individuals. Corporate fines are up to $2.5 million per violation.

The following case deals with a violation of the FCPA.

United States v. *Liebo*
923 F.2d 1308 (8th Cir. 1991)

THE NIGER CONNECTION: INFLUENCE IN EXCHANGE FOR A NIAGARA FALLS HONEYMOON

FACTS

Between January 1983 and June 1987, Richard H. Liebo was vice president in charge of the Aerospace Division of NAPCO International, Inc., of Hopkins, Minnesota. NAPCO's primary business consisted of selling military equipment and supplies throughout the world.

In early 1983, the Niger government contracted with a West German company, Dornier Reparaturwerft, to service two Lockheed C-130 cargo planes. After the Niger Ministry of Defense ran into financial troubles, Dornier sought an American parts supplier in order to qualify the Ministry of Defense for financing through the U. S. Foreign Military Sales program. The Foreign Military Sales program is supervised by the Defense Security Assistance Agency of the U.S. Department of Defense. Under the program, loans are provided to foreign governments for the purchase of military equipment and supplies from U.S. contractors.

In June 1983, representatives from Dornier met with officials of NAPCO and agreed that NAPCO would become the prime contractor on

Continued

the C-130 maintenance contracts. Under this arrangement, NAPCO would supply parts to Niger and Dornier, and Dornier would perform the required maintenance at its facilities in Munich.

Once NAPCO and Dornier agreed to these terms, Mr. Liebo and Axel Kurth, a Dornier sales representative, flew to Niger to get the president of Niger's approval of the contract. In Niger they met with Captain Ali Tiemogo, chief of maintenance for the Niger Air Force. Captain Tiemogo testified that during the trip, Mr. Liebo and Mr. Kurth told him that they would make "some gestures" to him if he helped get the contract approved. When asked whether this promise played a role in deciding to recommend approval of the contract, Captain Tiemogo stated, "I can't say 'no,' I cannot say 'yes,' at that time," but "it encouraged me." Following Captain Tiemogo's recommendation that the contract be approved, the president of Niger signed the contract.

Tahirou Barke, Tiemogo's cousin and close friend, was the first consular for the Niger Embassy in Washington, D.C. Mr. Barke testified that he met Mr. Liebo in Washington sometime in 1983 or 1984. Mr. Barke stated that Mr. Liebo told him he wanted to make a "gesture" to Captain Tiemogo and asked Mr. Barke to set up a bank account in the United States. With Mr. Barke's assistance, Mr. Liebo opened a bank account in Minnesota in the name of "E. Dave," a variation of the name of Mr. Barke's then-girlfriend, Shirley Elaine Dave. NAPCO deposited about $30,000 in the account, and Mr. Barke used the money to pay bills and purchase personal items and also gave a portion of the money to Captain Tiemogo.

In August 1985, Mr. Barke returned to Niger to be married. After the wedding, he and his wife honeymooned in Paris, Stockholm, and London. Before leaving for Niger, he informed Mr. Liebo of his honeymoon plans, and Mr. Liebo offered to buy, as a gift, Mr. Barke's airline tickets

for both Mr. Barke's return to Niger and his honeymoon trip. Mr. Liebo made the flight arrangements and paid for the tickets, which cost $2,028, by charging them to NAPCO's Diners Club account. Mr. Barke considered the tickets a personal "gift" from Mr. Liebo.

Over a two-and-a-half-year period beginning in May 1984, NAPCO made payments totaling $130,000 to three "commission agents." The practice of using agents and paying them commissions on international contracts was acknowledged as a proper, legal, and accepted business practice in Third World countries. NAPCO issued commission checks to three "agents," identified as Amadou Mailele, Captain Tiemogo's brother-in-law; Fatouma Boube, Captain Tiemogo's sister-in-law; and Miss E. Dave, Mr. Barke's girlfriend. At Captain Tiemogo's request, both Mr. Mailele and Mr. Boube set up bank accounts in Paris. Neither Mr. Mailele, Ms. Boube, nor Miss Dave, however, received the commission checks or acted as NAPCO's agent. These individuals were merely intermediaries through whom NAPCO made payments to Captain Tiemogo and Mr. Barke. NAPCO's corporate president, Henri Jacob, or another superior of Mr. Liebo's approved these "commission payments." No one approved the payment for the honeymoon trip.

Following a three-week trial, the jury acquitted Mr. Liebo on all FCPA charges except for the count concerning NAPCO's purchase of Mr. Barke's honeymoon airline tickets and the related false statement count. Mr. Liebo appealed.

JUDICIAL OPINION
GIBSON, Circuit Judge
Liebo first argues that his conviction on Count VII for violating the bribery provisions of the Foreign Corrupt Practices Act by giving Barke airline tickets for his honeymoon should be reversed because insufficient evidence existed to establish two elements

Continued

of the offense. First, Liebo contends that there was insufficient evidence to show that the airline tickets were "given to obtain or retain business." Second, he argues that there was no evidence to show that his gift of honeymoon tickets was done "corruptly."

There is sufficient evidence that the airplane tickets were given to obtain or retain business. Tiemogo testified that the President of Niger would not approve the contracts without his recommendation. He also testified that Liebo promised to "make gestures" to him before the first contract was approved, and that Liebo promised to continue to "make gestures"if the second and third contracts were approved. There was testimony that Barke helped Liebo establish a bank account with a fictitious name, that Barke used money from that account, and that Barke sent some of the money from that account to Tiemogo. Barke testified that he understood Liebo deposited money in the account as "gestures" to Tiemogo for some "of the business that they do have together."

Although much of this evidence is directly related to those counts on which Liebo was acquitted, we believe it appropriate that we consider it indetermining the sufficiency of evidence as to the counts on which Liebo was convicted.

Moreover, sufficient independent evidence exists that the tickets were given to obtain or retain business. Evidence established that Tiemogo and Barke were cousins and best friends. The relationship between Barke and Tiemogo could have allowed a reasonable jury to infer that Liebo made the gift to Barke intending to buy Tiemogo's help in getting the contracts approved. Indeed, Tiemogo recommended approval of the third contract and the President of Niger approved that contract just a few weeks after Liebo gave the tickets to Barke. Accordingly, a reasonable jury could conclude that the gift was given to "obtain or retain business."

Liebo also contends that the evidence at trial failed to show that Lieboa cted "corruptly"

by buying Barke the airline tickets. In support of this argument, Liebo points to Barke's testimony that he considered the tickets a "gift" from Liebo personally. Liebo asserts that "corruptly"means that the offer, payment or gift "must be intended to induce the recipient to misuse his official position. . . ." Because Barke considered the tickets to be a personal gift from Liebo, Liebo reasons that no evidences howed that the tickets wrongfully influenced Barke's actions.

We are satisfied that sufficient evidence existed from which a reasonable jury could find that the airline tickets were given "corruptly." For example, Liebo gave the airline tickets to Barke shortly before the third contract was approved. In addition, there was undisputed evidence concerning the close relationship between Tiemogo and Barke and Tiemogo's important role in the contract approval process. There was also testimony that Liebo classified the airline tickets for accounting purposes as a "commission payment." This evidence could allow a reasonable jury to infer that Liebo gave the tickets to Barke intending to influence the Niger government's contract approval process. We coclude, therefore, that a reasonable jury could find that Liebo's gift to Barke was given "corruptly." Accordingly, sufficient evidence existed to support Liebo's conviction.

Remanded on other grounds.

CASE QUESTIONS

1. Describe the relationships of NAPCO, Messrs. Liebo, Jacob, Mailele, Barke, Ms. Fatouma Boube, Captain Tiemogo, and Miss Dave.
2. Was there a violation of the FCPA?
3. Were any of the payments bribes?
4. Would these types of payments be permitted to U.S. government officials?
5. If you were Mr. Liebo, would you have objected to the trip and payments?
6. Was NAPCO's conduct ethical?

C O N S I D E R . . .

8.7 A Philip Morris subsidiary, C. A. Tabacalera National, and a B.A.T. subsidiary known as C. A. Cigarrera Bigott entered into a contract with La Fundacion Del Nino (the Children's Foundation) of Caracas, Venezuela. The agreement was signed on behalf of the foundation by the foundation's president, who also was the wife of the then president of Venezuela. Under the terms of the agreement, these two tobacco firms were to make periodic donations to the Children's Foundation totaling $12.5 million. In exchange, the two firms would receive price controls on Venezuelan tobacco, elimination of controls on retail cigarette prices in Venezuela, tax deductions for donations, and assurances that the existing tax rates applicable to tobacco companies would not be increased.

Is the donation to the charity a violation of the FCPA? [*Lamb* v. *Philip Morris, Inc.*, 915 F.2d 1024 (6th Cir. 1990 *Cert. Denied*, 498 U.S. 1086 (1995)).]

International Business and the FCPA

Many businesses have been critical of the FCPA because of the lack of uniformity among various nations concerning the propriety of facilitating (grease) payments and the legality of bribes. A foreign agent can legally receive the payment, but a U.S. corporation cannot make the payment. However, a survey by the U.S. Government Accounting Office of the companies affected by the FCPA found that the ability of companies from other countries to bribe officials did not give them a competitive advantage. The survey found that U.S. trade increased in 51 of 56 foreign countries after the FCPA went into effect. The increase was attributed to the position adopted by U.S. companies with respect to their competitors—if they could not bribe government officials, they would disclose publicly any information about bribes made by any of the companies from other nations.

Business Planning Tip

Compliance with the FCPA requires great effort and diligence on the part of companies involved in international operations.

1. Use great caution on any payments to government officials, even for things as simple as getting the phone lines in your office connected. The task may be administrative or bureaucratic but the understanding of employees about what is and is not illegal is influenced by each choice to pay even so-called legal grease payments.

2. Do background checks on all your foreign employees and agents. Be certain that the propensity to commit these sorts of acts is not in their backgrounds. Obtain financial information and personal references for them.

3. Publish your complete and unambiguous policy on FCPA payments. Include details and examples for employees and post the policy in all offices.

4. Establish effective financial controls in all your offices and facilities. Send the outside auditors to your international offices to make surprise and spot-checks on the records.

5. Voluntarily report any slips or misunderstandings. Come forward with the information and disclose all relevant actions and records to the U.S. government.

RICO (Racketeer Influenced and Corrupt Organization Act) (18 U.S.C. Sections 1961–1968)

This complex federal statute was passed with the intent of curbing organized crime activity. The ease of proof and severity of penalties for RICO violations have made it a popular charge in criminal cases in which organized crime may not actually be involved.

Explore the Racketeer Influenced and Corrupt Organizations Act: http://www.law. cornell.edu/ uscode/18/1961. html

For RICO to apply, it must be established that there has been a "pattern of racketeering activity." That pattern is defined as the commission of at least two racketeering acts within a 10-year period. Racketeering acts are defined under the federal statute to include murder; kidnaping; gambling; arson; robbery; bribery; extortion; dealing in pornography or narcotics; counterfeiting; embezzlement of pension, union, or welfare funds; mail fraud; wire fraud; obstruction of justice or criminal investigation; interstate transportation of stolen goods; white slavery; fraud in the sale of securities; and other acts relating to the Currency and Foreign Transactions Reporting Act (an act passed to prevent money-laundering).

RICO provides for both criminal penalties and civil remedies. Under a RICO civil suit, injured parties can recover treble damages, the cost of their suit, and reasonable attorney fees. According to the *Journal of Accountancy*, 91 percent of all RICO civil actions have been based on the listed pattern crimes of mail fraud, wire fraud, or fraud in the sale of securities. The statute has been used frequently against corporations. For example, Northwestern Bell Telephone Company lobbyists, who took public utility commissioners to dinner and hired two of them as consultants after they left their commission jobs, were sued under RICO. A lawyer representing phone company customers brought a RICO suit based on an alleged pattern of bribing the utility regulators. [*H.J. Inc.* v. *Northwestern Bell Telephone Co.*, 492 U.S. 229 (1989).]

Another portion of the RICO statute permits prosecutors to freeze defendants' assets to prevent further crimes. When RICO charges are brought against corporations, the seizure of corporate assets can mean the termination of the business. Recently, the Justice Department issued guidelines requiring prosecutors to seek a forfeiture of assets in proportion to the crime rather than seize all of the business assets. A growing number of states have enacted their own versions of the RICO statute for application at the state level. Some state RICO laws are specifically directed at narcotics, but over 20 include securities fraud as one of the covered acts.

RICO violations have become added charges in many criminal cases. For example, if someone is charged with ongoing bribery of a state or local official, RICO charges can be added because of the pattern of corruption. Only one U.S. Supreme Court case has served to restrict RICO's application. In *Reves* v. *Ernst & Young*, 507 U.S. 170 (1993), the accounting firm of Arthur Young (later merged into Ernst & Young) was hired to conduct audits for the Farmer's Cooperative of Arkansas and Oklahoma. An investment by the co-op in a gasohol plant proved to be a financial disaster, and the farmers who held co-op notes that had served as the organization's means of financing over the years lost their investment when the co-op filed for bankruptcy. The investors filed suit against Arthur Young for violations of federal securities laws (see Chapter 21) and RICO. However, the Supreme Court exempted the accounting firm from RICO charges because it found that the firm did not participate in the management of the co-op. The auditor's participation was not that of directing the co-op's affairs, only that of offering its opinions on the financial statements of the firm. The case represents one of the few restrictions on RICO application.

Over the past few years, businesses have been lobbying very heavily for reforms to the broad civil and criminal liabilities created by RICO. It seems unlikely that Congress will change the rights of plaintiffs to bring treble damage suits under the act's protective and deterrent mechanisms. The following case involves an issue of RICO charges among competitors.

Bacchus Industries v. Arvin Industries, Inc.
939 F.2d 887 (10th Cir. 1991)

THE COMBUSTIBLE COOLER: FIRE AMONG COMPETITORS

FACTS

Arvin and Bacchus are competitors in the manufacture and sale of evaporative coolers, an economically efficient means of cooling homes in dry climates. A large difference between their two products is that the Bacchus cooler is round and constructed of fiberglass whereas the Arvin cooler is square and made of metal.

During 1983 and 1984, Bacchus received a great deal of negative publicity about its coolers because of an allegation that the fiberglass coolers were a fire hazard. Bacchus believes the negative publicity had its origins with Arvin. Bacchus based its beliefs and allegations on the following series of events.

On June 3, 1983, Bacchus suffered a major fire at its New Mexico plant. On June 7, 1983, Richard D. Fife, Arvin's vice president of marketing, sent a memo to Arvin's western area sales representatives informing them of the fire. Attached to the memo was a newspaper article describing the firefighters' difficulty in controlling the blaze and noting that "the fire spread fast because fiberglass is very flammable." Mr. Fife's memo transmitting the article stated: "The article identifies one of the major problems with fiberglass and/or plastic coolers. They are very flammable and emit toxic fumes which are deadly."

In August 1983, Arvin conducted a controlled burn test of evaporative coolers at Arvin's Phoenix plant ("the Phoenix Burn Test"). Evaporative coolers manufactured by Arvin, Bacchus, and a third manufacturer, Tradewinds, were ignited and then observed as they burned. A videotape of the Phoenix Burn Test shows that the Bacchus cooler burned more rapidly and more spectacularly than the Arvin cooler. Videotapes and still photographs of the Phoenix Burn Test were distributed to Arvin sales representatives and used on a limited basis as a sales tool.

On April 25, 1984, Mr. Fife sent another memo to Arvin's western area sales representatives advising them of a newspaper article from the El Paso Times entitled "Housing's coolers called fire hazards." The article reported that the Bacchus cooler could pose a fire hazard and detailed the results of the El Paso Housing Authority Board's own burn test of a Bacchus cooler and a Tradewinds cooler. The article noted "the toxicity of fumes from the blaze and the speed of the fire on the Bacchus model."

On May 3, 1984, Wayne Coggins, the Odessa, Texas, fire marshall, conducted an independent burn test of evaporative coolers manufactured by Arvin, Bacchus, and Tradewinds ("the Odessa Burn Test"). Mr. Coggins conducted the test to determine whether fiberglass and plastic coolers would create a fire hazard if they were involved in a fire or whether they were any danger to roofs once they caught on fire. An Arvin distributor supplied the evaporative coolers to Mr. Coggins, who directed his firemen to remove the coolers from the packing cartons and set them up on concrete blocks. Each cooler was ignited in the same manner and then observed as it burned. The videotape of the test shows that while all three coolers were inflammable, the nonmetallic coolers manufactured by Bacchus and Tradewinds burned more rapidly and more spectacularly than the metallic cooler manufactured by Arvin. The Odessa Burn Test was videotaped by three local television stations.

By letter dated May 10, 1984, Bacchus asked Arvin for permission to review the Phoenix Burn tape "to check its accuracy." Arvin's in-house counsel responded by letter dated June 12, 1984 as follows:

Please be advised that, in the regular course of its business, Arvin Air conducts tests of its products and those of its competitors, and in one instance, a test of inflammability was videotaped. In addition, we are advised that certain members of the electronic media have also videotaped such demonstrations.

Although I am assured that precautions were taken not to distort the characteristics of our competitors' products as well as our own, in order to
Continued

avoid any further misunderstanding in this regard, we have requested that any copies of our tape which may exist outside of the Arvin Air organization be returned to us. Henceforth, these test depictions will be used by my client solely for purposes of its own internal examination.

You will please understand that this retrieval does not, and cannot, extend to recordings of similar tests which may have been conducted by those outside of the employ of Arvin Industries, over whom my client has no control.

By memo dated June 11, 1984, Mr. Fife again contacted Arvin's western area sales representatives and informed them that Arvin had agreed to discontinue showing the Phoenix Burn Tape. Fife asked the representatives to discreetly recover any tapes from distributors without discussing the reason for the return.

Bacchus sued Arvin alleging violations of 18 U.S.C. §§ 1961–68 (RICO); 15 U.S.C. § 1 and § 2 (Sherman Antitrust Act); 15 U.S.C. § 13 (Clayton Antitrust Act); 15 U.S.C. § 1125 (Lanham Act); and state law claims for conspiracy to defraud and commercial disparagement.

The trial court granted summary judgment in favor of Arvin on all of Bacchus's claims except § 2 of the Sherman Antitrust Act.

Bacchus appealed.

JUDICIAL OPINION

ANDERSON, Senior District Judge

Bacchus' RICO claim fails because Bacchus has failed to properly allege a pattern of racketeering activity. A "pattern" by definition requires at least two acts of "racketeering activity" within a ten-year period. "Racketeering activity" is defined to include mail fraud (18 U.S.C. § 1341) and wire fraud (18 U.S.C. § 1343). 18 U.S.C. § 1961(1). These acts of racketeering activity are often referred to as "predicate acts" because they form the basis for liability under RICO.

However, a pattern of racketeering activity is not established merely by proving two predicate acts. Rather, "[t]o establish a RICO pattern it must also be shown that the predicates themselves amount to, or that they otherwise constitute a threat of, *continuing* racketeering activity."

Thus, to properly allege a pattern of racketeering activity as required by RICO, Bacchus must identify a minimum of two instances of racketeering activity as defined in § 1961(1) which amount to, or otherwise constitute a threat of continuing racketeering activity by the enterprise. Bacchus claims that Arvin committed numerous acts of mail fraud and wire fraud by communicating, through the mail and by telephone, with Arvin sales representatives and with Bacchus. Bacchus claims that Arvin intentionally misrepresented the Bacchus cooler as a fire hazard through its memoranda and by distributing the Phoenix Test Burn tape. Bacchus also claims that Arvin made fraudulent misrepresentations in Arvin's June 12, 1984 letter to Bacchus in which Arvin agreed to withdraw the Phoenix Test Burn tape.

In order to state a claim of mail fraud under 18 U.S.C. § 1341, Bacchus must allege (1) the existence of a scheme or artifice to defraud or obtain money or property by false pretenses, representations or promises, and (2) use of the United States mails for the purpose of executing the scheme. The elements of wire fraud under 18 U.S.C. § 1343 are similar but require that the defendant use interstate wire, radio or television communications in furtherance of the scheme to defraud.

Actionable fraud in turn consists of the misrepresentation of a fact, (2) known to be untrue by the maker, (3) made with an intent to deceive and to induce the other party to act in reliance thereon to his detriment.

We find that the district court properly granted summary judgment in favor of Arvin on the § 1962(d) claim because Bacchus failed to state adequately a claim for fraud, including mail fraud and wire fraud. We also find that the evidence suggests that Arvin sent the memoranda and the Phoenix Test Burn tape to its sales representatives in order to provide them with information on a competitor's product and not to deceive or to induce detrimental reliance. While Bacchus disputes the veracity of the claim that Bacchus coolers might pose a fire hazard, the mere transmittal of the information to the sales representatives was not fraudulent. Similarly, the June 12,

Continued

1984 letter from Arvin to Bacchus was not fraudulent. While Arvin agreed to withdraw the Phoenix Test Burn tape, Arvin also indicated that other tests may have been conducted over which Arvin had no control.

Because Bacchus presented no evidence in support of its § 1962(d) claim that Arvin employees and agents participated in a conspiracy to violate § 1962(a), (b), or (c), we find that the district court properly granted summary judgment on the RICO conspiracy claim.

CASE QUESTIONS

1. Why did Bacchus emphasize that Arvin had twice communicated to its sales force about the flammability issue?
2. What did the court examine for predicate offenses?
3. Was Arvin engaged in a pattern of racketeering?
4. Does Bacchus still have some cause of action against Arvin?
5. Is this a civil suit or a criminal suit?

ETHICAL ISSUES

8.3 What do you think of the decision of the Arvin marketing vice president to circulate the information about the fire? Do you believe Arvin was fair in its depiction of the Bacchus cooler as flammable? Is this ethical competition?

CONSIDER . . .

8.8 Odessa Mae French operated the Pines Motel as a house of prostitution for seven years. During that time, Ms. French avoided any local law enforcement action by allowing the sheriff to have free services at the Pines. Eventually, the federal government brought charges against the operation for tax evasion and RICO violations. Would the services to the sheriff constitute a form of bribe that would support a RICO charge? [*United States* v. *Tunnell*, 667 F.2d 1182 (5th Cir. 1982).]

Federal Crimes

A great deal of interbusiness crimes are found at the federal level. Violations of the Securities Exchange Acts (Chapter 21), the Sherman Act (Chapter 11), the Internal Revenue Act, the Pure Food and Drug Act, the environmental statutes (Chapter 13), the Occupational Safety and Health Act (Chapter 18), and Consumer Product Safety statutes (Chapter 10) carry criminal penalties. Most criminal convictions are obtained under the antitrust laws.

State Crimes

Similar criminal statutes at the state level cover such areas as criminal fraud and securities. In addition, states have particular regulations and laws for certain industries. The sale of liquor in most states is strictly regulated. The result is that there are many incidents of bribes and kickbacks in these highly regulated industries as businesses try to work around the regulatory restrictions.

PROCEDURAL RIGHTS FOR BUSINESS CRIMINALS

Business criminals are treated the same procedurally as other criminals. They have the same rights under the criminal justice system. The U.S. Constitution guarantees protection of certain rights. The **Fourth Amendment** protects the individual's privacy and is the basis for requiring warrants for searches of private property. The **Fifth Amendment** provides the protection against self-incrimination and is also the "due process" amendment, which guarantees that an accused individual will have the right to be heard. The **Sixth Amendment** is meant to ensure a speedy trial; it is the basis for the requirement that criminal proceedings and trials proceed in a timely fashion. These constitutional rights are discussed in the following sections.

Fourth Amendment Rights for Businesses

The Fourth Amendment to the U.S. Constitution provides that "the right of the people to be secure in their persons, houses, papers, and effects, against unreasonable searches and seizures, shall not be violated." This amendment protects individual privacy by preventing unreasonable searches and seizures. Before a government agency can seize the property of individuals or businesses, there must be a valid **search warrant**—or an applicable exception to the warrant requirement—which must be issued by a judge or magistrate and must be based on probable cause. In other words, there must be good reason to believe that instruments or evidence of a crime are present at the business location that is to be searched. The Fourth Amendment applies equally to individuals and corporations. In an unauthorized search, a corporation's property is given the same protection. If an improper search is conducted (without a warrant and without meeting an exception), then any evidence recovered is inadmissible at trial for the purposes of proving the crime.

Exceptions to the warrant requirement are based on emergency grounds. For example, if an office building with relevant records is burning, government agents could enter the property without a warrant to recover the papers. Similarly, if the records are being destroyed, the government need not wait for a warrant. Another exception to the warrant requirement is the "plain view" exception. This exception allows police officers to seize evidence that is within their view. No privacy rights are violated when evidence is exposed to the view of others. The following case deals with this Fourth Amendment exception.

Dow Chemical Co. v. United States
476 U.S. 1819 (1986)

LOW-FLYING FEDERAL AGENTS: PHOTOGRAPHIC SEARCHES

FACTS

Dow Chemical (petitioner) operates a two thousand-acre chemical plant at Midland, Michigan. The facility, with numerous buildings, conduits, and pipes, is visible from the air. Dow has maintained ground security at the facility and has investigated fly-overs by other, unauthorized aircraft. However, none of the buildings or manufacturing equipment is concealed.

In 1978, the Environmental Protection Agency (EPA) conducted an inspection of Dow. EPA requested a second inspection, but Dow denied the request. The EPA then employed a commercial aerial photographer to take photos of the plant from 12,000, 3,000, and 1,200 feet. The EPA

Continued

had no warrant, but the plane was always within navigable air space when the photos were taken.

When Dow became aware of the EPA photographer, it brought suit in federal district court and challenged the action as a violation of its Fourth Amendment rights. The district court found that the EPA had violated Dow's rights and issued an injunction prohibiting the further use of the aircraft. The court of appeals reversed and Dow appealed.

JUDICIAL OPINION

BURGER, Chief Justice

The photographs at issue in this case are essentially like those used in map-making. Any person with an airplane and an aerial camera could readily duplicate them. In common with much else, the technology of photography has changed in this century. These developments have enhanced industrial processes, and indeed all areas of life; they have also enhanced enforcement techniques. Whether they may be employed by competitors to penetrate trade secrets is not a question presented in this case. Governments do not generally seek to appropriate trade secrets of the private sector, and the right to be free of appropriation of trade secrets is protected by law.

That such photography might be barred by state law with regard to competitors, however, is irrelevant to the questions presented here. State tort law governing unfair competition does not define the limits of the Fourth Amendment. The Government is seeking these photographs in order to regulate, not compete with, Dow.

Dow claims first the EPA has no authority to use aerial photography to implement its statutory authority of "site inspection" under the Clean Air Act.

Congress has vested in EPA certain investigatory and enforcement authority, without spelling out precisely how this authority was to be exercised in all the myriad circumstances that might arise in monitoring matters relating to clean air and water standards.

Regulatory or enforcement authority generally carries with it all the modes of inquiry and investigation traditionally employed or useful to execute the authority granted.

Environmental standards cannot be enforced only in libraries and laboratories, helpful as those institutions may be.

The EPA, as a regulatory and enforcement agency, needs no explicit statutory provisions to employ methods of observation commonly available to the public at large; we hold that the use of aerial photography is within the EPA's statutory authority.

DISSENTING OPINION

POWELL, MARSHALL, BRENNAN,
AND BLACKMUN, Justices

The Fourth Amendment protects private citizens from arbitrary surveillance by their Government. Today, in the context of administrative aerial photography of commercial premises, the Court retreats from that standard. It holds that the photography was not a Fourth Amendment "search" because it was not accompanied by a physical trespass and because the equipment used was not the most highly sophisticated form of technology available to the Government. Under this holding the existence of an asserted privacy interest apparently will be decided solely by reference to the manner of surveillance used to intrude on that interest. Such an inquiry will not protect Fourth Amendment rights, but rather will permit their gradual decay as technology advances.

EPA's aerial photography penetrated into a private commercial enclave, an area in which society has recognized that privacy interests may legitimately be claimed. The photographs captured highly confidential information that Dow had taken reasonable and objective steps to preserve as private.

CASE QUESTIONS

1. Of what significance is the fact that Dow's plant could be seen from the air?
2. Did Dow take any steps to protect its privacy?
3. Is the EPA specifically given aerial surveillance authority?
4. Did the EPA need a warrant for taking its aerial photographs?
5. What objections does the dissent raise to the decision?

In many business crimes, the records used to prosecute the defendant are not in the possession of the defendant. The records are, instead, in the hands of a third party, such as an accountant or a bank. Does the Fourth Amendment afford the defendant protection in documents that discuss the defendant or reflect the defendant's finances and transactions when those documents are in the hands of another? In some cases, there is a privilege between the third party and the defendants, and certain documents are protected and need not be turned over. Notes on trial strategy, audit procedures, and other plans and thoughts are not discoverable because such communications are privileged between lawyers and clients. Some states recognize an accountant/client privilege. The priest/parishioner privilege generally exists; however, there are exceptions in which reporting is required, such as in cases of abuse.

C O N S I D E R . . . **8.9** The IRS attached levies to the property and other assets of G. M. Leasing Corp. for nonpayment of taxes. To satisfy the levy, the IRS seized several automobiles from the street in front of G. M.'s offices. Also, without a warrant, the IRS entered G. M.'s offices and seized business books and records. Has the Fourth Amendment been violated with the seizure of the cars? Of the books and records? [*G. M. Leasing Corp.* v. *United States*, 429 U.S. 338 (1977).]

Fifth Amendment Rights for Businesses

The Fifth Amendment extends several protections to those facing criminal charges.

SELF-INCRIMINATION

The statement "I take the Fifth" is used so often that it has made the Fifth Amendment well known for its protection against self-incrimination. For example, Charles Keating took the Fifth Amendment protection 80 times in his testimony before Congress on Lincoln Savings & Loan. No one can be compelled to be a witness against himself or herself. However, this protection applies only to natural persons; corporations are not given this privilege. A corporation cannot prevent the required disclosure of corporate books and records on grounds that they are incriminating.

Corporate officers cannot assert Fifth Amendment protection to prevent compulsory production of corporate records. Nor can corporate officers use the Fifth Amendment to prevent the production of corporate records on grounds that those records incriminate them personally. The rules applicable to corporate officers have been extended to apply to those involved in labor unions, close corporations, and even unincorporated associations. The same rule is applicable to sole shareholders of small corporations as well.

MIRANDA *RIGHTS*

The famous *Miranda* doctrine resulted from an interpretation of the Fifth Amendment by the U.S. Supreme Court in *Miranda* v. *Arizona*, 384 U.S. 436 (1966). *Miranda* **warnings** must be given to all people who are subjected to custodial interrogation. Custody does not necessarily mean "locked in jail," but it is generally based on an individual's perceptions of a situation. If a person feels he or she is without freedom to leave a place by choice, the level of custody at which *Miranda* rights must be issued has been reached. The warnings tell those in custody of their Fifth Amendment right to say nothing, as well as their right to an attorney. The failure to give *Miranda* warnings is not fatal to a case so long as the crime can be proved through evidence other than the statement of the defendant; the prosecution can still proceed based on other evidence.

DUE PROCESS RIGHTS

The Fifth Amendment also contains due process language. The same language is found in the Fourteenth Amendment and made applicable to the states. **Due process**, as Chapters 5 and 6 discuss, means that no one can be convicted of a crime without the opportunity to be heard, to question witnesses, and to present evidence.

Due process in criminal proceedings guarantees certain procedural protections as a case is investigated, charged, and taken to trial. The Sixth Amendment complements due process rights by requiring that all these procedures be completed in a timely fashion. The following subsections discuss the basic steps in a criminal proceeding as diagrammed in Exhibit 8.3 (pg. 287).

Warrant and/or Arrest A criminal proceeding can begin when a crime is witnessed, as when a police officer attempts to apprehend a person who just robbed a convenience store. When the convenience store is robbed but the robber escapes, and if the police can establish that a certain individual was probably responsible for the robbery, a **warrant** can be issued and the individual then arrested. Whether with or without a warrant, the due process steps begin with the arrest.

Initial Appearance Once an arrest has been made, the defendant must have an opportunity to appear before a judicial figure within a short time period (usually 24 hours) to be informed of his or her charges, rights, and so on. This proceeding is generally referred to as an **initial appearance**. Dates for other proceedings are set at this time and, if the individual can be released, the terms of the release are also established. The individual may be required to post a bond to be released; others are held without release terms (release terms are generally dependent upon the nature of the crime and the defendant). The term *released on his own recognizance* or *released OR* means the defendant is released without having to post a bond.

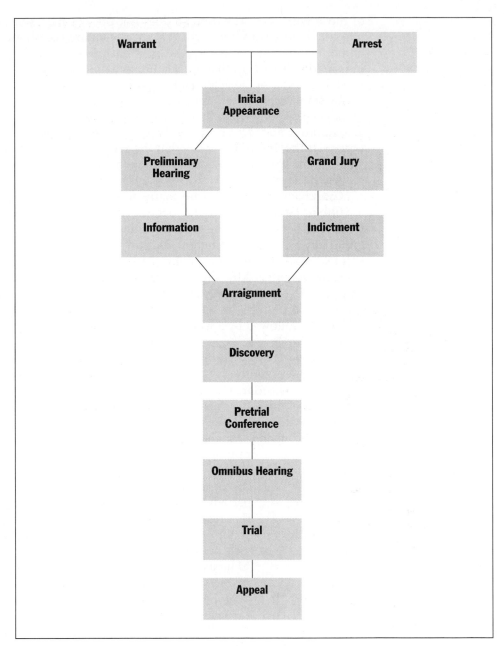

Exhibit 8.3
Steps in Criminal Proceedings

Preliminary Hearing or Grand Jury Up to this step in the criminal proceedings, the defendant's charges are based on the word of a police officer; there has not yet been any proof brought forth linking the crime and the defendant. The purpose of a preliminary hearing or grand jury proceeding is to require the prosecution to establish that there is some evidence that the defendant committed the crime.

In a **preliminary hearing**, the prosecution presents evidence to a judge to indicate that the accused committed the crime. The prosecution presents witnesses, and the defendant and the defendant's attorney are present for cross-examination of those witnesses. The defense does not present its case at this time but could make an offer of proof to show that the defendant could not have committed the crime. If the judge finds there is sufficient proof, an **information** is issued. The information is to a criminal proceeding what a complaint is to a civil proceeding: It establishes what the defendant did and when and what crimes were committed.

In some crimes, the evidence of the crime is presented to a **grand jury**, which is a panel of citizens who serve for a designated period of time (usually six months) and act as the body responsible for the review of evidence of crimes. If the grand jury finds that there is sufficient evidence that a crime was committed, it issues an **indictment**, which is similar to an information and serves the same function.

Grand jury proceedings are conducted secretly, whereas preliminary hearings are public. Grand juries also have the authority to conduct investigations to determine whether crimes were committed and who did so. Perhaps the most famous grand jury was the Washington, D.C., area grand jury that was investigating President Clinton and his wife, Hillary, for their involvement in a failed savings and loan, and its assets. Mrs. Clinton is the only first lady to testify before a grand jury. Despite her public figure status, Mrs. Clinton's testimony remained a secret. In cases that are taken before a grand jury, the criminal process begins with an indictment followed by a warrant to arrest those charged.

The Arraignment An **arraignment** is the proceeding at which the defendant enters a plea of guilty, not guilty, or no contest (nolo contendere). If a not guilty plea is entered, a date for trial is set. If the defendant enters a guilty or no contest plea, chances are the plea is the result of a **plea bargain**, which is the term used in criminal proceedings for a settlement. The defendant may plead guilty to a lesser offense in exchange for the prosecution's promise to support a lesser sentence, such as probation or minimum jail time.

Discovery If a case is going to trial, there is a discovery period. Many states have mandatory criminal discovery laws that require each side to turn over certain types of information to the other side, including lists of witnesses they will call and lists of exhibits that will be used at trial. Exhibits include documents, murder weapons, and pictures.

Omnibus Hearing In some cases, the defense attorney wishes to challenge the prosecution evidence on grounds that it was obtained in violation of any of the constitutional protections discussed earlier. Some documents, for example, may have been seized without a warrant. The **omnibus hearing** is the forum wherein all of these challenges can be presented for the judge's ruling as to the admissibility of evidence. It is held before the trial so the jury is not exposed to evidence that should not have been admitted. In the O. J. Simpson double-homicide trial, an omnibus hearing was held on the admissibility of evidence gathered at Mr. Simpson's estate without a warrant.

Trial If no plea agreement is reached before trial, the case then proceeds to trial.

Business Planning Tip

Homicide is the second leading cause of death in the workplace. Robbery is responsible for most on-the-job deaths. In 1994, 73 percent of all workplace homicides were committed at the hands of a robber. Only 9 percent of all workplace homicides were the result of the actions of a co-worker. The leading cause of death in the workplace for men is traffic accidents; for women, homicide. The jobs at greatest risk for employee homicides: security guards, taxi drivers, and convenience store clerks. As a result of these statistics, employers are taking extra precautions: keeping limited cash on hand, arming and training employees, monitoring by camera, and maintaining two-person shifts around the clock.

SUMMARY

Who is liable for business crimes?
- Vicarious liability—holding companies accountable for criminal conduct of their officers
- Elements—requirements of proof for crimes
- *Mens rea*—requisite mental state for commission of a crime
- *Actus reus*—physical act of commission of a crime

What penalties exist for business crimes?
- Penalties—punishments for commission of crimes; includes fines and imprisonment
- Corporate sentencing guidelines—federal rules used to determine level of penalties for companies and officers; a system that decreases penalties for effort and increases penalties for lack of effort and other problems in company operations

What is the nature of business crime?
- Computer crime—crimes committed while using computer technology; includes such activities as transferring funds (salami technique) and collecting data without authorization (scavenging)
- Counterfeit Access Device and Computer Fraud and Abuse Act—federal law making it a crime to access computers without authorization
- Criminal fraud—misrepresentation with the intent to take something from another without his/her knowledge; to mislead to obtain funds or property
- Foreign Corrupt Practices Act—federal law that regulates financial reports of international firms and prohibits bribes to influence government actions and officials in other countries
- Racketeer Influenced and Corrupt Organizations Act (RICO)—federal law designed to prevent racketeering by making it a crime to engage in certain criminal activities more than once

What are the rights of corporate and individual defendants in the criminal justice system?
- Fourth Amendment—provision in U.S. Constitution that protects against invasions of privacy; the search warrant amendment
- Fifth Amendment—the self-incrimination protection of the U.S. Constitution
- Sixth Amendment—the right-to-trial protection of the U.S. Constitution
- Search warrant—judicially issued right to examine home, business, and papers in any area in which there is an expectation of privacy
- *Miranda* warnings—advice required to be given those taken into custody; details right to remain silent and the right to have counsel
- Due process—right to trial before conviction
- Warrant—public document authorizing detention of an individual for criminal charges; for searches, a judicial authorization
- Initial appearance—defendant's first appearance in court to have charges explained, bail set, lawyer appointed, and future dates set
- Preliminary hearing—presentation of abbreviated case by prosecution to establish sufficient basis to bind defendant over for trial

Continued

- Information—document issued after preliminary hearing requiring defendant to stand trial
- Grand jury—secret body that hears evidence to determine whether charges should be brought and whether defendant should be held for trial
- Indictment—document grand jury issues in requiring defendant to stand trial
- Arraignment—hearing at which trial date is set and plea is entered
- Plea bargain—settlement of criminal charges
- Omnibus hearing—evidentiary hearing outside the presence of the jury

QUESTIONS AND PROBLEMS

1. In the summer of 1993, the United States experienced the great, but temporary, Pepsi syringe scare. In several areas throughout the country, "consumers" came forward and claimed they found medication syringes in cans of Pepsi. The Food and Drug Administration (FDA) and officers of PepsiCo reeled for several days as they attempted to cope with the allegations. Within a short period of time from when the stories on the syringes first appeared, a film taken by a hidden store camera showed one of the "consumers" actually inserting a syringe into a Pepsi drink product prior to purchase.

   Assume that a criminal charge of adulteration requires proof of an intentional act. Would the hidden camera film establish the intent element of the crime?

2. Allan Welsh was the manager of Sam's Self-Service Restaurant in Council Bluffs, Iowa. Sam's Self-Service was owned by McBluffs, Inc. Welsh's duties included hiring and firing employees, purchasing food and supplies, limited bookkeeping, and depositing daily receipts.

   In the summer of 1974, Donald Mangan and Bernard Menard, employees of McBluffs, talked with Mr. Welsh and expressed dissatisfaction with his work. He was told his services would be terminated in 30 days unless his performance improved.

   On October 3, 1974, the restaurant had gross receipts of $1,276.46 and a bank deposit entry of $1,274.00 These figures were called in by Mr. Welsh to Mr. Menard. Mr. Welsh told Mr. Menard that he would deposit the money.

   Mr. Welsh left the restaurant with the bank deposit sack but never returned to work. He returned the keys to the restaurant and collected his vacation pay on October 8. On November 1, Mr. Mangan and Mr. Menard received the bank statements and discovered that the $1,274 deposit had never been made. What crime(s) has been committed? [*State* v. *Welsh*, 245 N.W. 2d 290 (Iowa 1976).]

3. Mr. Wittman is a vice president of West Valley Estates, Inc. Under Mr. Wittman's direction, West Valley violated the terms of its dredging permit by dredging and filling land beyond the permit limits. The state of Florida brought criminal charges against West Valley for violation of the permit laws. West Valley said Mr. Wittman did this on his own and that the board never authorized him to go beyond the permit limits, and thus the corporation could not be held liable. Is this a correct analysis? [*West Valley Estates, Inc.* v. *Florida*, 286 So. 2d 208 (Fla. 1973).]

4. The state of Ohio had a statute that provided criminal penalties for anyone who "with intent to defraud . . . make[s] a check . . . or, with like intent, utter[s] or publish[es] as true and genuine such false . . . matter, knowing it to be false. . . ." Could a violation be established by showing that an individual wrote a check drawn on a bank at which he had no checking account? Is the proper intent established? [*In re Clemons*, 151 N.E.2d 553 (Ohio 1958).]

5. Reuben Sturman was charged with income tax evasion based largely on evidence the Internal Revenue Service and the Justice Department gathered through records of a Swiss bank in which Mr. Sturman had made substantial deposits over the past five years. The U.S. officials obtained the records from the Swiss bank pursuant to a treaty arrangement the U.S. government has with the Swiss government regarding the exchange of bank and bank record information. Mr. Sturman challenged the charges and the evidence on grounds that he had an expectation of privacy in his Swiss bank account and that U.S. officials were required to have a warrant before obtaining information about specific accounts in the Swiss banking system. Is Mr. Sturman correct? [*United States* v. *Sturman,* 951 F.2d 1466 (6th Cir. 1991).]

6. Bernard Saul was a salesperson for A. P. Walter Company, a wholesale auto parts business, assigned to the D&S Auto Parts account. Mr. Saul took inventory at D&S each week and phoned in an order to Walter to cover the needed inventory replacements. Between 1976 and 1982, Mr. Saul ordered parts from Walter and invoiced D&S, but actually kept a portion of the parts for himself and sold them to other dealers and pocketed the money himself. Through an audit, D&S discovered that it had paid for $155,445.20 of parts that were not received. Can Mr. Saul be charged with any crimes? Can Walter be charged with any crimes? [*D&S Auto Parts, Inc.* v. *Schwartz,* 838 F.2d 965 (7th Cir. 1988).]

7. The SEC has issued several subpoenas to some third parties with records relevant to the investigation of Jerry T. O'Brien. Mr. O'Brien was not notified of the subpoenas and claims he should have been so that he could assert his Fifth Amendment rights. Can the records be used in the criminal case? Does he have a Fifth Amendment right to the papers? [*SEC* v. *O'Brien,* 467 U.S. 735 (1984).]

8. The Department of Agriculture conducts warrantless searches of produce packing plants on an unannounced basis. Is this a violation of the Fourth Amendment? [*Wayne Cusimano, Inc.* v. *Block,* 692 F.2d 1025 (11th Cir. 1982).]

9. John Blondek and Vernon Tull were employees of Eagle Bus Company, a company based in the United States. Both Mr. Blondek and Mr. Tull were indicted for violations of the FCPA for paying a $50,000 bribe to Donald Castle and Darrell Lowry, officials of the Saskatchewan (Canada) provincial government to ensure that their bid to provide buses to Saskatchewan would be accepted. Messrs. Castle and Lowry were also indicted. Can they, as foreign officials, be prosecuted under the FCPA? [*United States* v. *Blondek,* 741 F. Supp. 116 (N.D. Tex. 1990).]

10. Harlan Nolte and others invested in IFC Leasing Company, a master music recording leasing program. The company was created to acquire and lease master music recordings. Jerry Denby, the executive vice president of IFC, contacted Stephen Weiss, a partner in the law firm of Rosenbaum, Wise, Lerman, Katz & Weiss, to draft the prospectus for investors. Mr. Weiss drafted four documents used in the recruitment of investors for IFC. The complex structure of the investments, according to the documents, would have substantial tax consequences (to their benefit) for the investors.

    After Mr. Nolte and others had made their investments, the IRS issued an opinion that the deductions explained in the prospectus and other documents would not be allowed. Criminal fraud actions were brought against IFC and its officers as well as Stephen Weiss. The Justice Department also indicted both Mr. Weiss's law firm and his partners. Mr. Weiss's partners and the firm, through its management committee, maintain they cannot be held criminally liable for the actions of one partner. The Justice Department maintains that the firm and the partners were negligent in their supervision of Mr. Weiss and should, therefore, be held criminally liable. Do you agree with the Justice Department's position? Why or why not? [*Nolte* v. *Pearson,* 994 F.2d 1311 (8th Cir. 1993).]

Judgment

At 9:30 P.M. on December 7, 1988, JoKatherine Page went to the Brainerd Road branch of the American National Bank & Trust Company of Hamilton County, Tennessee. Mrs. Page frequented the Brainerd branch for using the 24-hour automated teller machine (ATM) located there. She parked her car near the ATMs and walked to the machine, leaving her 14-year-old son, Jason, in the car. There were two other patrons near the ATM. One was a Mrs. Kurtz, a friend of Mrs. Page. The two were exchanging pleasantries when they were approached by a group of four to six young black males. One of them pushed Mrs. Page to the machine, holding a gun to her back, and demanded that she withdraw $300 from the ATM. Two others stood at her car pointing a gun at Jason, threatening to kill him if she did not cooperate.

Mrs. Page turned to tell Jason to stay in the car, and the man behind her struck her in the face with a solid object, severely injuring her face. The young thugs departed. Mrs. Page has sued American National Bank & Trust Company to recover for her injuries. Should she recover from the bank? How was the bank to blame for injuries from a third party, a thief?

CHAPTER 9

Criminal wrongs require guilty parties to pay a debt to

Business Torts

society through a

fine, imprisonment, and/or community service. However,

criminal wrongs and other types of actions may harm

individuals. The harm to an individual or a firm is a

civil wrong that entitles those who experience that

harm to recover their damages. Torts are civil wrongs

that provide a remedy for individuals who are harmed.

This chapter answers these questions: What are the

types of civil wrongs that create a right of recovery for

harm? What are the types and elements of torts? What are

the business costs and issues surrounding torts?

The desire for safety stands against every great and noble enterprise.
Tacitus

Gentlemen:
You have undertaken to cheat me. I will not sue you for the law takes too long. I will ruin you.
Cornelius Vanderbilt

WHAT IS A TORT?

Tort originates from the Latin term *tortus*, which means "crooked, dubious, twisted." Torts are civil wrongs, actions that are not straight but twisted. A **tort** is an interference with someone's person or with someone's property that results in injury to them or to their property. For example, using someone else's land is an interference with that person's property rights and is the tort of trespass. Damage could result if you held a concert on someone else's land and the concert crowds destroyed the property's vegetation or left litter that had to be removed. The law provides protection for us and our property through the law of torts, which is a way to recover for the damages done to us.

Tort Versus Crimes

A tort is a private wrong. When a tort is committed, the party who was injured is entitled to collect compensation for damages from the wrongdoer for the private wrong. A crime, on the other hand, is a public wrong and requires the wrongdoer to pay a debt to society through a fine or by going to prison. For example, the crime of assault will result in imprisonment, probation, and/or a fine. However, the victim could bring suit against the charged assailant to recover damages, such as medical bills, lost wages, and pain and suffering. The suit would be for the tort of assault.

Types of Torts

There are three types of tort liability: **intentional torts**, **negligence**, and **strict tort liability**. Intentional torts are the harms that result when parties commit intentional acts. For example, battery, or the striking of another person, is an intentional tort. A person is injured because you chose to hit him. However, suppose that you are stretching your arms in a crowd and you strike a man in the nose and hurt him. You have not committed the tort of battery, but you may have committed the tort of negligence. You did not intentionally strike the man as you would if you were having an argument, but you were carelessly swinging your arms in a crowd of people. These careless actions, or actions done without thinking through the consequences, are torts and constitute negligence. Such accidental harms also impose liabilities on the parties. The key difference between intentional torts and negligence is state of mind. Under the intentional tort standard, the party intended to commit the act. Under negligence, the party may have been careless or may not have thought carefully through his actions, but the actions taken were not done with the intent to cause harm. Strict tort liability is generally used in product liability and is discussed extensively in Chapter 10.

Torts are also classified as property torts and personal torts. The example of trespassing given earlier is a property tort because the injury is done to someone's property. The tort of defamation is an example of a personal tort because it involves publishing untrue statements about a person, resulting in harm to that person. The tort of negligence can involve injury to person or property. For example, if someone runs a red light and bumps into your car, he has been careless and the tort of negligence has occurred. If you are injured and your car is damaged, you have experienced both personal and property damage. Regardless of the tort classification, the remedy for the tort is recovery for the damage done to you or your property. Exhibit 9.1 (pg. 295) illustrates the types of tort actions.

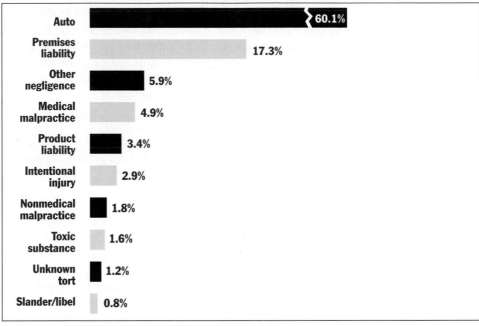

Exhibit 9.1
Types of Torts

THE INTENTIONAL TORTS

Defamation

Defamation is an untrue statement by one party to another about a third party. It consists of either slander or libel; **slander** is oral or spoken defamation and **libel** is written (and in some cases broadcast) defamation. The elements for defamation are:

1. a statement about a person's reputation, honesty, or integrity that is untrue;
2. publication;
3. a statement that is directed at a person and is made with malice and the intent to injure that person; and
4. damages.

PUBLICATION

For defamation to occur, the statement must be communicated to a third party. An accountant who addresses a group of lawyers at a luncheon meeting and untruthfully states that another accounting firm has been involved in a securities fraud has met the publication element. So has a supplier who notifies other suppliers that a certain business is insolvent when it is not. Technically, the statement is published if it is communicated to one other person. The more publication, however, the greater the damages.

MALICE

Malice requires that the statements be made or printed with the knowledge they are false or with reckless disregard for whether they are true or false. For example, a newspaper that prints a story on the basis of an unconfirmed source who has been shown to be unreliable in the past would be acting with malice. Malice is required in defamation cases in which the victim is a public figure.

STATEMENT ABOUT A PARTICULAR PERSON

The general statement "All accountants are frauds" is not sufficiently narrow to be defamatory. The defamatory statement must either be about a particular person or be narrow enough in scope to include only a small group of businesses. For example, the statement "All the accountants in Parkland office complex are dishonest" is specific enough to meet this element.

DAMAGES

The person who is defamed must be able to establish damages such as lost business, lost profits, lost advertising, lost reputation, or some economic effect resulting from the defamatory statements.

THE DEFENSES TO DEFAMATION

There are certain times when defamatory statements are made or printed but the tort of defamation is not established because there is a valid defense. For example, a statement may be defamatory but if it is the truth, it is not defamation. For example, you could publicly disclose that your boss took LSD during the late 1960s when he was in college. The remark might hurt your employer's reputation, but if it is the truth, it is not the tort of defamation despite the harm it may do to him.

Some speech is privileged; that is, there is a strong public interest in protecting the speech regardless of whether it is true. For example, members of Congress enjoy an **absolute privilege** when they are speaking on the floor of the Senate or House because there is a strong public policy to encourage free debate of issues. The same is true of judicial proceedings; in order to encourage people to come forward with the truth, witnesses enjoy an absolute privilege when testifying about the matters at hand. The media enjoy a **qualified privilege**, which is freedom to publish information even though it may be inaccurate so long as it is not published with malice or with reckless disregard for whether the information published is true or false. Perhaps one of the most famous libel cases addressing the defense of the media privilege involved Carol Burnett and a story about her printed by the *National Enquirer*. The case decision about this incident follows.

Burnett v. National Enquirer, Inc.
144 Cal. App. 3d 991 (1983)

ONLY THE *ENQUIRER* DIDN'T KNOW FOR SURE: CAROL BURNETT, HENRY KISSINGER, AND DEFAMATION

FACTS
On March 2, 1976, the *National Enquirer* (appellant) published in its weekly publication a "gossip column" headlined "Carol Burnett and Henry K. in Row" that included the following four-sentence item:

In a Washington restaurant, a boisterous Carol Burnett had a loud argument with another diner, Henry Kissinger. Then she traipsed around the place offering

everyone a bite of her dessert. But Carol really raised eyebrows when she accidentally knocked a glass of wine over one diner and started giggling instead of apologizing. The guy wasn't amused and "accidentally" spilled a glass of water over Carol's dress.

Ms. Burnett (respondent) filed suit against the *Enquirer* alleging that the item was entirely false and libelous after the *Enquirer* printed the following retraction:

Continued

An item in this column on March 2 erroneously reported that Carol Burnett had an argument with Henry Kissinger at a Washington restaurant and became boisterous, disturbing other guests. We understand these events did not occur and we are sorry for any embarrassment our report may have caused Miss Burnett.

After a jury trial, Ms. Burnett was awarded $300,000 compensatory damages and $1,300,000 punitive damages. The trial court reduced the amounts to $50,000 compensatory and $750,000 punitive damages. The *Enquirer* appealed.

JUDICIAL OPINION

ROTH, Presiding Justice

Prior to addressing the merits of appellant's contentions and in aid of our disposition, we set out the following further facts pertaining to the publication complained of . . . .

On the occasion giving rise to the gossip column item hereinabove quoted, respondent, her husband and three friends were having dinner at the Rive Gauche restaurant in the Georgetown section of Washington, D.C. The date was January 29, 1976. Respondent was in the area as a result of being invited to be a performing guest at the White House. In the course of the dinner, respondent had two or three glasses of wine. She was not inebriated. She engaged in banter with a young couple seated at a table next to hers, who had just become engaged or were otherwise celebrating. When curiosity was expressed about respondent's dessert, apparently a chocolate souffle, respondent saw to it the couple were provided with small amounts of it on plates they had passed to her table for the purpose. Perhaps from having witnessed the gesture, a family behind respondent then offered to exchange some of their baked alaska for a portion of the souffle, and they, too, were similarly accommodated. As respondent was later leaving the restaurant, she was introduced by a friend to Henry Kissinger, who was dining at another table, and after a brief conversation, respondent left with her party.

There was no "row" with Mr. Kissinger, nor any argument between the two, and what

conversation they had was not loud or boisterous. Respondent never "traipsed around the place offering everyone a bite of her dessert," nor was she otherwise boisterous, nor did she spill wine on anyone, nor did anyone spill water on her and there was no factual basis for the comment she " . . . started giggling instead of apologizing."

The impetus for what was printed about the dinner was provided to the writer of the item, Brian Walker, by Couri Hays, a freelance tipster paid by the National Enquirer on an ad hoc basis for information supplied by him which was ultimately published by it, who advised Walker he had been informed respondent had taken her Grand Marnier souffle around the restaurant in a boisterous or flamboyant manner and given bites of it to various other people; that he had further but unverified information respondent had been involved in the wine-water spilling incident; but that, according to his sources, respondent was "specifically, emphatically" not drunk. No mention was made by Hays of anything involving respondent and Henry Kissinger.

Having received this report, Walker spoke with Steve Tinney, whose name appears at the top of the National Enquirer gossip column, expressing doubts whether Hays could be trusted. Tinney voiced his accord with those doubts. Walker then asked Gregory Lyon, a National Enquirer reporter, to verify what Walker had been told by Hays. Lyon's inquiry resulted only in his verifying respondent had shared dessert with other patrons and that she and Kissinger had carried on a good-natured conversation at the restaurant.

In spite of the fact no one had told him respondent and Henry Kissinger had engaged in an argument, that the wine-water spilling story remained as totally unverified hearsay, that the dessert sharing incident was only partially bolstered, and that respondent was not under any view of the question inebriated, Walker composed the quoted item and approved the "row" headline.

The National Enquirer is a publication whose masthead claims the "Largest Circulation Of Any Paper in America." It is a member of the

Continued

American Newspaper Publishers Association. It subscribes to the Reuters News Service. Its staff call themselves newspaper reporters.

By the same token the National Enquirer is designated as a magazine or periodical in eight mass media directories and upon the request and written representation of its general manager in 1960 that "In view of the feature content and general appearance [of the publication], which differ markedly from those of a newspaper . . ." its classification as a newspaper was changed to that of magazine by the Audit Bureau of Circulation. It does not subscribe to the Associated Press or United Press International news services. According to a statement by its Senior Editor it is not a newspaper and its content is based on a consistent formula of "how to" stories, celebrity or medical or personal improvement stories, gossip items, and TV column items, together with material from certain other subjects. It provides little or no current coverage of subjects such as politics, sports, or crime, does not attribute content to wire services, and in general does not make reference to time. Normal "lead time" for its subject matter is one to three weeks. Its owner allowed it did not generate stories "day to day as a daily newspaper does."

At appellant's request, the trial court herein made its determination after hearing and based on extensive evidence that the *National Enquirer* was not a newspaper for purposes of the application of Civil Code section 48a.

Seen in this light, the essential question is not then whether any publication is properly denominated a magazine or by some other designation, but simply whether it ought to be characterized as a newspaper or not within the contemplation of § 48a.

Having so decided, we are also satisfied to conclude without extensive recitation of the evidence that the trial court consistently with the foregoing rationale correctly determined the *National Enquirer* should not be deemed a newspaper for the purposes of the instant litigation.

Nearly twenty years ago, it was announced in *New York Times Co. v. Sullivan*, 376 U.S. 254 (1964) that:

The constitutional guarantees [relating to protected speech] require, we think, a federal rule that prohibits a public official from recovering damages for a defamatory falsehood relating to his official conduct unless he proves that the statement was made with "actual malice"—that is, with knowledge that it was false or with reckless disregard of whether it was false or not.

[W]e are of the opinion the award to respondent of $750,000 in order to punish and deter appellant was not justified.

In so concluding, we are persuaded the evidence fairly showed that while appellant's representatives knew that part of the publication complained of was probably false and that the remainder of it in substance might very well be, appellant was nevertheless determined to present to a vast national audience in printed form statements which in their precise import and clear implication were defamatory, thereby exposing respondent to contempt, ridicule and obloquy, and tending to injure her in her occupation. We are also satisfied that even when it was thought necessary to alleviate the wrong resulting from the false statements it had placed before the public, the retraction proffered was evasive, incomplete and by any standard, legally insufficient. In other words, we have no doubt the conduct of appellant respecting the libel was reprehensible and was undertaken with the kind of improper motive which supports the imposition of punitive damages.

Nevertheless, evidence on the point of appellant's wealth adequately established appellant's net worth to be some $2.6 million and its net income for the period under consideration to be about $1.56 million, such that the penalty award, even when substantially reduced by the trial court based on its conclusion the jury's compensatory verdict was "clearly excessive and . . . not supported by substantial evidence," continued to constitute about 35% of the former and nearly half the latter.

The judgment is affirmed except that the punitive damage award herein is vacated and the matter is remanded for a new trial on that

Continued

issue only, provided that if respondent shall, within 30 days from the date of our remittitur, file with the clerk of this court and serve upon appellant a written consent to a reduction of the punitive damage award to the sum of $150,000, the judgment will be modified to award respondent punitive damages in that amount, and so as modified affirmed in its entirety. . . .

CASE QUESTIONS

1. Was malice established in the case? Why was it necessary to establish malice?
2. Is the *National Enquirer* a newspaper for purposes of the protection of the privilege?
3. Are the damages reduced? To what? Why?
4. Should tabloids like the *National Enquirer* enjoy the protection of the privilege?

E T H I C A L   I S S U E S

9.1 Douglas Electric and Mike Grace, d/b/a MG Electric, were working together as subcontractors on a project for Wheel Construction, Inc. They were assisting each other in the electrical subcontract work, sharing workers and materials. Neal Hastings, owner of Douglas Electric, handled the paperwork for the job.

James Snyder, owner of Wheel Construction, received the following letter, which Hastings later admitted he wrote:

```
April 15, 1988

Wheel Construction Inc.
J. W. Snyder, Owner
111 Ogden Road
Springfield, Ohio 45503

Dear Sirs:

    I write to you so that you may be informed of fraud and
"kick-backs" that are presently undermining your operations.
    In August of 1987, Jeff Hurley approached Mike Grace, MG
Electric, concerning a grave personal problem. Jeff's brother
was in big trouble with the law and needed cash to pay attor-
ney fees in an attempt to keep him from going to prison.
    A deal was cut and MG was given four jobs (Wilmington Speed-
way, Beavercreek Pro Care, Blue Ash Marathon, and Stuckeys gas
canopy) in return for several thousand dollars directly to Jeff.
    I recommend you take these allegations and look at these job
files for confirmation of facts. I would assume that extras have
been added to all of these jobs and would question the validity of
each considering the pact between these two people. I would note
the lack of bids from MG as an indicator of the above allegation.
    You have a lot at stake to have someone within your company
working for themselves instead of you at your risk.
```

Mr. Snyder terminated Mr. Grace from the project because of the letter. Mr. Grace then sued Mr. Hastings and Douglas Electric for libel.

Can Mr. Grace establish a successful libel claim? Why did Mr. Hastings write the letter? Even if the content of the letter were accurate, would you have written it? [*Douglas Electric Corp.* v. *Grace*, 590 N.E. 2d 363 (Ohio 1990).]

C O N S I D E R . . . **9.1** Clint Eastwood, an Oscar-winning actor and director, brought suit against the *Star* tabloid newspaper for its reports on his relationship with his newborn child. The story was written in an interview format. Mr. Eastwood was never interviewed for the story. What torts have been committed? Was there malice on the part of the *Star*?

FOR THE MANAGER'S DESK

REFERENCES, RISK, AND DEFAMATION

Paul Calden, a 33-year-old low-level manager was fired from his job at Allstate Insurance Company in St. Petersburg, Florida, for carrying a gun to his job. His supervisors at Allstate would later describe him as a "total lunatic."

Mr. Calden applied for a job with Firemen's Fund Insurance in Tampa, Florida. Firemen's Fund contacted the Allstate offices for a reference. Allstate sent a letter signed by a vice president that was neutral in its description of Mr. Calden and did not disclose the true reasons for his termination. Mr. Calden had threatened litigation; there was some fear among the employees about him and Allstate agreed to a four-month severance package despite his only having worked at Allstate for nine months. Allstate also agreed to draft and send the neutral letter.

After Mr. Calden was terminated by Firemen's Fund, he shot and killed three executives of the company while they were having lunch at a

cafe. One of the executive's wives filed suit against Firemen's Fund and Allstate. The suit against Allstate was based on its failure to disclose Mr. Calden's bizarre behavior and the risk that he was in the workplace.

Allstate defended its actions on the grounds that the average verdict in a defamation

suit by a former employee against his/her former employer for a job reference is $57,000. In one Florida case, a former employee was awarded $25 million in damages.

About 15 states now have some form of law that creates a privilege for employers in providing references. The presence of the privilege is

designed to free managers in their discussions of former employees and their performances. A survey indicates that without such protection, disclosures about violent tendencies will not be made and the risk to employees at a new firm is high. Fifty-four percent of all employers indicate they would not disclose violent behavior when asked for a reference.

The statutory protections are proposed in most every state. The issues in adoption of the statutes are whether the standard should be intentionally false information or recklessly false information for assigning liability.

In some states there is a qualified privilege for those who have a moral obligation to speak. These types of privilege statutes provide protection for whistle-blowers (see Chapter 17) in that a controlled (limited) disclosure of information made in good faith will not subject a businessperson to liability for defamation. However, verification of the truth of such statements is critical.

Contract Interference

The tort of **contract interference** or **tortious interference with contracts** or **tortious interference** occurs when parties are not allowed the freedom to contract without interference from third parties. The tort developed in England before the twentieth century and still exists today.

While the elements required to be established for tortious interference are complex, a basic definition is that the law affords a remedy when someone intentionally persuades another to break a contract already in existence with a third party. Bryan A. Garner, the author of *Tortious Interference*, explains tortious interference in the following simple examples: "Say you had a contract with Joe Blow, and I for some reason tried to get you to break that contract. Or say that Pepsi has an exclusive contract with a hotel chain to carry Pepsi products, and Coke tries to get the hotel to carry Coke despite that contract. That's tortious interference."

Perhaps one of the most famous cases involving the question of tortious interference was that of *Texaco, Inc.* v. *Pennzoil, Co.*, 729 S.W.2d 768 (Tex. 1987). The board of directors of Getty Oil had agreed to sell a substantial portion of its oil to Pennzoil. While Getty and Pennzoil were drafting their agreement, Texaco stepped in and made a competing bid. The Getty board then accepted the Texaco offer. Pennzoil filed suit against Texaco for tortious interference of contract. The trial court awarded Pennzoil $7.53 billion in actual damages and $3 billion in punitive damages. While the appellate court reduced the punitive damages by $2 billion, it did find that Texaco interfered with the Pennzoil contract because its officers described their conduct as "stop[ping] the train."

"Let me refresh your memory. It was the night before Christmas and all through the house not a creature was stirring until you landed a sled, drawn by reindeer, on the plaintiff's home, causing extensive damage to the roof and chimney."

FOR THE MANAGER'S DESK

A NEW TWIST ON THE TORT OF INTERFERENCE

Recently, the CBS news show *Sixty Minutes* pulled from a scheduled airing an interview with a former tobacco executive in a news story about the industry when threats of both libel and tortious interference with contract suits arose. The former executive of Brown & Williamson, Jeffrey S. Wigand, agreed to have the interview

run only if CBS News would indemnify him against the suits. Brown & Williamson lawyers notified CBS News that Wigand had signed a confidentiality agreement and that the company would sue CBS News for interference with that contract if the interview were run. *Sixty Minutes* ran a story on tobacco companies without the interview. CBS correspondents Mike Wallace and Morley Safer protested the decision of CBS

News executives. However, the *Wall Street Journal* ran a story describing CBS News's unusual arrangements with Wigand, including the payment of a consulting fee of $12,000 and the promise of full indemnification. Many lawyers commented that the promises CBS made to Wigand could be depicted as inducements for Wigand to breach his contract agreement of confidentiality with Brown & Williamson.

False Imprisonment

Review "Eddie Bauer Accused of 'Consumer Racism'" regarding false imprisonment: http://utahonline.sltrib.com/95/DEC/12/twr/02505136.htm

False imprisonment is often referred to as "the shopkeeper's tort" because it generally occurs as a result of a shoplifting accusation in a store. **False imprisonment** is the detention of a person for any period of time (even a few minutes) against his or her will. No physical harm need result; the imprisoned party can collect minimal damages simply for being imprisoned without consent. Because shopkeepers need the opportunity to investigate matters when someone is suspected of shoplifting, the tort of false imprisonment does carry the defense of the **shopkeeper's privilege**. This privilege allows a shopkeeper to detain a suspected shoplifter for a reasonable period of time while the matter or incident is investigated. In most states, the shopkeeper must have a reasonable basis for keeping the person; that is, the shopkeeper must have reason to suspect the individual even if it turns out later that the individual has an explanation or did not do what the shopkeeper suspected. The following case deals with the issue of a shopkeeper's detention of a shopper for suspicion of shoplifting.

Canto v. J. B. Ivey and Co.
595 So. 2d 1025 (Fla. 1992)

DETAINED AS DELINQUENTS: MISGUIDED SECURITY

FACTS

On November 16, 1986, Joseph Canto, Jr., then 11-years-old, and Samantha Canto, then 16, went shopping at the Ivey department store in Gainesville, Florida. After entering the store, they stopped at a display table to look at metallic chain-link belts. A videotape taken by a security

camera shows the children stopping at the display table, handling the items and exchanging conversation while looking around, and Samantha handing something to Joseph, which he placed in his pocket. Jo Ann Williams stopped the children as they were leaving the store and told them she had reason to believe

Continued

that they had stolen something and to follow her to the security office. The sheriff's report discloses that Ms. Williams called the sheriff's office soon thereafter, but that an officer did not arrive for another hour. Another employee, managing agent Kirsten Aalto, arrived at the security office and aided Ms. Williams. The children were released by the officer about two hours after they were initially detained by Ms. Williams. No merchandise was found on the children.

Joseph and Samantha said they were questioned in an intimidating manner, were not allowed to use the bathroom or call their parents, and were called "delinquents" and "shoplifters."

Through their parents, Joseph and Samantha (appellants) filed suit for damages incurred for their psychological counseling and treatment and for punitive damages.

The trial court dismissed counts II, IV, and V of their complaint on a directed verdict. The jury found for Ivey on counts I and III. The Cantos appealed.

JUDICIAL OPINION

Per Curiam

Ivey had raised the defense at trial that it was immune from liability for false imprisonment pursuant to Section 812.015, Florida Statutes (1989). Subsection (3)(a) thereof provides:

A law enforcement officer, a merchant, a merchant's employee, or a farmer who has probable cause to believe that retail or farm theft has been committed by a person and that he can recover the property by taking the person into custody may, for the purpose of attempting to effect such recovery or for prosecution, take the person into custody and detain him in a reasonable manner for a reasonable length of time. . . . In the event the merchant, merchant's employee, or farmer takes the person into custody, a law enforcement officer shall be called to the scene immediately after the person has been taken into custody.

Appellants first claim that the verdict form submitted to the jurors was an improper statement of the law and could have confused them, because it asked whether Ivey employees detained the children "in an unreasonable manner *and* without probable cause to believe that they

had committed retail theft." (Emphasis added.) Appellants contend that liability could be imposed if the merchant's employees failed to comply with any of the requirements of subsection (3), and that the jury should have been asked whether Ivey's employees restrained the children "without probable cause or in an unreasonable manner or for an unreasonable length of time." We disagree that the verdict form's failure to include this language constitutes reversible error.

Section 812.015(5) provides:

A merchant, merchant's employee, or farmer who takes a person into custody, as provided in subsection (3) . . . shall not be criminally or civilly liable for false arrest or false imprisonment when the merchant, merchant's employee, or farmer has probable cause to believe that the person committed retail theft or farm theft.

Thus, Ivey could not be liable under count I for false imprisonment if the jury determined there *was* probable cause for the detention. The judge instructed the jurors that if they found at any time during the detention there was no longer probable cause to detain the children, they should find for the plaintiffs. We consider that this instruction clarified any possible confusion the verdict form may have engendered.

As to appellants' second issue, the Cantos contend the trial court erred in directing a verdict against them on their claims for intentional infliction of emotional distress and defamation. We agree that the trial court erred in concluding that a corporate employer cannot be held vicariously liable for an intentional act of its employee.

Ivey claimed that the conduct of its employees was privileged. A privilege exists as a matter of law to engage in reckless or even outrageous conduct if there is sufficient evidence that shows the defendant "did no more than assert legal rights in a legally permissible way." Therefore, if the evidence discloses that Ivey's employees acted within their legal rights in detaining the Canto children, then Ivey cannot be vicariously liable for intentional infliction of emotional distress. We find no evidence in the record suggesting that the conduct of either employee even approached the limits of this privilege.

Continued

Regarding counts IV and V, pertaining to the tort of defamation, Joseph Canto testified that Aalto and Williams referred to him as a "shoplifter." Nevertheless, a communication is privileged, even though defamatory, "when made in good faith upon any subject in which the party communicating has an interest, or in reference to which he has a right or duty, and made upon an occasion to properly serve such right, interest, or duty." This privilege can be overcome only if the plaintiff shows the defendant was motivated by malice, defined as ill will and a desire to harm the plaintiff. Aalto's deposition testimony indicates that she was acting in good faith in detaining the children, and any allegedly defamatory references to the children were made while she was fulfilling her duties as managing agent on the evening in question. There is not a scintilla of evidence which would point to any ill will on the part of Aalto or a desire to harm the children. Again, because appellants have not provided this court with a transcript of Williams' testimony, we have insufficient evidence from which to conclude that the trial court erred.

Affirmed.

CASE QUESTIONS
1. Why were the children detained?
2. Describe what happened when they were detained.
3. Did the children take anything?
4. What happened at the trial court with their suit?
5. Does the shopkeeper's privilege protect Ivey?
6. If you were the security officer, would you have done anything differently?

Forty-three states now permit store owners to collect civil fines from shoplifters. The fines range from the value of the stolen items to up to $5,000 in addition to the value of the stolen items.

Intentional Infliction of Emotional Distress

This tort imposes liability for conduct that goes beyond all bounds of decency and results in emotional distress in the harmed individual. One of the difficulties with this tort is that the only damage the plaintiff is required to prove is that of emotional distress. Although "pain and suffering" damages have been awarded for some time in negligence actions in which the plaintiff recovers damages for physical and property injuries, the awarding of damages for mental distress alone is a relatively new phenomenon. However, the tort of **intentional infliction of emotional distress** has been used quite often by debtors who are harassed by creditors and collection agencies in their attempts to collect funds.

Invasion of Privacy

The intentional tort of invasion of privacy is actually three different torts: (1) intrusion into the plaintiff's private affairs, (2) the public disclosure of private facts, and (3) the appropriation of another's name for commercial advantage. The appropriation tort is discussed subsequently under competition torts. The two other components of the privacy tort represent a right to be left alone and not have personal matters publicly disclosed. Intrusion simply requires proof that the defendant was present when the plaintiff was doing something normally considered private.

One of the most famous invasion of privacy cases was *Galella* v. *Onassis*, 353 F. Supp. 196 (S.D.N.Y. 1972). In the case, Mrs. Jacqueline Kennedy Onassis brought suit against Ron Galella, a photo journalist, for invasion of her privacy. As a result of the case, Mr. Galella was ordered to remain at least 50 yards from Mrs. Onassis and 100 yards from her children.

COMPETITION TORTS

Appropriation

The appropriation of someone's name, likeness, or voice for commercial advantage without his or her permission constitutes the tort of **unauthorized appropriation**. For example, if a gas station used your picture in its window to show you as a satisfied customer, you might not be harmed greatly, but your privacy is invaded because you have the right to decide when, how, and where your name, face, image, or voice will be used. The fact that you do use the gas station and are a satisfied customer is not the issue in appropriation—it is the use without your permission that constitutes the tort. The following case addresses the unauthorized appropriation of a singer's voice.

Midler v. Ford Motor Co.
849 F.2d 460 (9th Cir. 1988)

FORD TO BETTE: LET'S DANCE; BETTE TO FORD: ONLY IF I SAY SO

FACTS

In 1985, Ford Motor Company and its advertising agency, Young & Rubicam, Inc., advertised the Ford Lincoln Mercury with a series of nineteen 30-or-60-second television commercials in what the agency referred to as "The Yuppie Campaign." The aim was to make an emotional connection with Yuppies, bringing back memories of when they were in college. The agency tried to get the "original people," that is, the singers who had popularized the songs, to sing them. When those efforts failed, the agency decided to go with "sound-alikes."

When Young & Rubicam was preparing the Yuppie Campaign it presented the commercial to its client by playing an edited version of Bette Midler (plaintiff/appellant) singing "Do You Want to Dance?" taken from the 1973 Midler album, *The Divine Miss M.*

After Ford accepted the idea and the commercial, Young & Rubicam contacted Midler's manager, Jerry Edelstein. The conversation went as follows: "Hello, I am Craig Hazen from Young & Rubicam. I am calling you to find out if Bette

Midler would be interested in doing . . . ?" Mr. Edelstein: "Is it a commercial?" "Yes." "We are not interested."

Undeterred, Young & Rubicam sought out Ula Hedwig, who had been one of the "Harlettes," backup singers for Midler for 10 years. Hedwig was told by Young & Rubicam that "they wanted someone who could sound like Bette Midler's recording of ['Do You Want to Dance?']." She was asked to make a demo tape. She made an a cappella demo and got the job. At the direction of Young & Rubicam, Ms. Hedwig made a record for the commercial. She first had to listen to Miss Midler's recording of it and was then told to "sound as much as possible like the Bette Midler record."

After the commercial aired, Miss Midler was told by a number of people that it sounded exactly like her. Ms. Hedwig was told by friends that they thought it was Miss Midler.

Miss Midler, a nationally known actress and singer, won a Grammy in 1973 as Best New Artist of the Year. She has had both gold and platinum records. She was nominated in 1979
Continued

for an Academy Award for Best Female Actress in *The Rose*, in which she portrayed a pop singer. *Newsweek* described her as an "outrageously original singer/comedienne." *Time* hailed her as "a legend" and "the most dynamic and poignant singer-actress of her time."

Miss Midler filed suit against Ford and Young & Rubicam for appropriation. Young & Rubicam had a license from the song's copyright holder to use it. Neither the name nor the picture of Miss Midler was used in the commercial. The district court entered judgment for Ford and Young & Rubicam, and Miss Midler appealed.

JUDICIAL OPINION

NOONAN, Circuit Judge

At issue in this case is only the protection of Midler's voice. The district court described the defendant's conduct as that "of the average thief." They decided, "If we can't buy it, we'll take it." The court nonetheless believed there was no legal principle preventing imitation of Midler's voice and so gave summary judgment for the defendants.

The First Amendment protects much of what the media do in the reproduction of likenesses or sounds. A primary value is freedom of speech and press. The purpose of the media's use of a person's identity is central. If the purpose is "informative or cultural" the use is immune; "if it serves no such function but merely exploits the individual portrayed, immunity will not be granted." It is in the context of these First Amendment and federal copyright distinctions that we address the present appeal.

Nancy Sinatra once sued Goodyear Tire and Rubber Company on the basis of an advertising campaign by Young & Rubicam featuring "These Boots Are Made for Walkin'," a song closely identified with her; the female singers of the commercial were alleged to have imitated her voice and style and to have dressed and looked like her. The basis of Nancy Sinatra's complaint was unfair competition; she claimed that the song and the arrangement had acquired "a secondary meaning" which, under California law, was protectible. This court noted that the defendants "had paid a very

substantial sum to the copyright proprietor to obtain the license for the use of the song and all of its arrangements." To give Sinatra damages for their use of the song would clash with federal copyright law. Summary judgment for the defendants was affirmed. If Midler were claiming a secondary meaning to "Do You Want to Dance" or seeking to prevent the defendants from using that song, she would fail like Sinatra. But that is not this case. Midler does not seek damages for Ford's use of "Do You Want to Dance," and thus her claim is not preempted by federal copyright law. What is put forward as protectible here is more personal than any work of authorship.

Bert Lahr once sued Adell Chemical Co. for selling Lestoil by means of a commercial in which an imitation of Lahr's voice accompanied a cartoon of a duck. Lahr alleged that his style of vocal delivery was distinctive in pitch, accent, inflection, and sounds. The First Circuit held that Lahr had stated a cause of action for unfair competition, that it could be found "that defendant's conduct saturated plaintiff's audience, curtailing his market." That case is more like this one.

A voice is as distinctive and personal as a face. The human voice is one of the most palpable ways identity is manifested. We are all aware that a friend is at once known by a few words on the phone. At a philosophical level it has been observed that with the sound of a voice, "the other stands before me." A fortiori, these observations hold true of singing, especially singing by a singer of renown. The singer manifests herself in the song. To impersonate her voice is to pirate her identity.

We need not and do not go so far as to hold that every imitation of a voice to advertise merchandise is actionable. We hold only that when a distinctive voice of a professional singer that is widely known is deliberately imitated in order to sell a product, the sellers have appropriated what is not theirs and have committed a tort in California. Midler has made a showing, sufficient to defeat summary judgment, that the defendants here for their own profit in selling their products did appropriate part of her identity.

Continued

CASE QUESTIONS

1. In what context was Miss Midler's voice sought?
2. Did Miss Midler agree to allow her voice to be used?
3. Was there some confusion about who was singing in the commercial?
4. What is the difference between this case and the Nancy Sinatra case?
5. What is the difference between this case and the Bert Lahr case?
6. Was the use of Miss Midler's voice unfair competition?
7. Was the use of Miss Midler's voice appropriation?

Aftermath: Miss Midler's case was tried and she recovered $400,000 from the defendants in October 1989.

C O N S I D E R . . . **9.2** George "Spanky" McFarland was once a child actor in the popular *Our Gang* series. *Our Gang* was a short-subject comedy series shown in movie theaters from the 1920s to the 1940s. The series was later revived as *Little Rascals* for television. McFarland's character in the series was named "Spanky." Joseph Miller opened his new restaurant in Ocean Township, New Jersey, calling it "Spanky McFarland's." Mr. McFarland filed suit against the restaurant owners for invasion of privacy, unjust enrichment, and trademark violations. He died before the lawsuit was completed. Should Mr. McFarland's name be entitled to protection from appropriation? Should that right survive him? [*McFarland* v. *Miller*, 14 F.3d 912 (1994).]

Business Planning Tip

Do not use photos, voices, songs, images, or trademarks without permission. There is civil liability, particularly when commercial advertising or activity is involved.

NEGLIGENCE

The tort of negligence is one that applies in a variety of circumstances, but it is always used when the conduct of one party did not live up to a certain minimum standard of care we are all expected to use in driving, in our work, and in the care of our property. Negligence imposes liability on us when we are careless. The elements of and defenses to negligence are covered next.

Element One: The Duty

Each of us has the duty to act as an **ordinary and reasonably prudent person** in all circumstances. The standard of the ordinary and reasonably prudent person is not a standard we always live up to; when we do not, we are negligent. The standard of the ordinary and reasonably prudent person is not always what everyone else does or what the law provides. For example, suppose you are driving on a curvy highway late at night and it is raining quite heavily. The posted speed limit is 45 mph. However, the ordinary and reasonably prudent person will not drive 45 mph because the road and the weather conditions dictate that slower driving is more appropriate. The level of care imposed on us by the ordinary and reasonably prudent person standard is one that requires an examination of all conditions and circumstances surrounding an event that leads to an injury. Many negligence cases struggle with the difficult task of determining whether a duty exists.

Duties, for purposes of negligence actions, can arise because of an underlying statute. Every traffic law carries a criminal penalty (fine and/or imprisonment) for violations of it. However, that law imposes a duty of obedience. A violation of that law is also a breach of duty for purposes of a civil or negligence action. When you run a red light, you have not only committed a crime; you have also breached a duty and are liable for injuries and damages resulting from that breach.

Professionals such as doctors, lawyers, and dentists have the duty of practicing their professions at the level of a reasonable professional. Failure to do so is a breach of duty and a basis for malpractice (negligence by professionals) lawsuits.

Landowners owe duties to people who enter their property. For example, the duty to trespassers, such as thieves, is not to intentionally injure them. Placing man traps would be a breach of this duty.

The following case involves the issue of whether a duty exists.

Crinkley v. Holiday Inns, Inc.
844 F.2d 156 (4th Cir. 1988)

TO CATCH A THIEF: GUESTS AS BAIT

FACTS

Sarah and James Crinkley decided to attend a function at the Charlotte (North Carolina) Civic Center on February 27 and 28, 1981. They consulted a Holiday Inn directory obtained during a previous Holiday Inn stay and chose the Holiday Inn-Concord.

During the approximately two weeks preceding the weekend of February 27–28, guests at several Charlotte area motels had been assaulted and robbed on the premises by a group the media later dubbed the "Motel Bandits." The motels involved were located throughout the metropolitan Charlotte area. The assistant manager of the Holiday Inn-Concord, Brian McRorie, was aware of the Motel Bandits from various news media reports. He was contacted by several unidentified members of the local county sheriff's office who wanted to know if he was aware of the Motel Bandits and what motel security plans he had while they remained at large. Some of these officers also offered to serve, for a fee, as security guards during their off-duty hours.

As a result of this information, Mr. McRorie contacted Jim Van Over about the possibility of hiring security guards to patrol the motel.

Mr. Van Over was the Holiday Inn-Charlotte manager and supervised the Holiday Inn-Concord as an employee of TRAVCO, the company responsible for managing the Concord site; he was also the president of the Metrolina Innkeepers Association and had been interviewed for news stories on the Motel Bandits. Mr. Van Over told Mr. McRorie that security was not needed, although he had said in his interviews that he had added security personnel at his own facility. Mr. McRorie instructed his employees to be particularly alert for anything suspicious, and he periodically patrolled the premises on February 27, the last time being sometime between 8:00 and 8:30 P.M. The motel also continued its program of encouraging local law enforcement personnel to frequent the premises by offering a free snack tray and discount meals in the restaurant, although it did not employ any of those personnel as security guards.

Continued

At approximately 8:00 P.M. on February 27, the Crinkleys arrived at the Holiday Inn–Concord. After spending a short time checking in, they parked their car in front of their room and began unloading their baggage. As James Crinkley was bringing in the last of their items, Sarah Crinkley, who was standing in the doorway to their room, noticed a man come around the corner of the motel and begin walking toward them. When the man reached the Crinkley's room, he stopped and asked to speak with James Crinkley. Almost immediately, the man began trying to push the Crinkleys into their room. Despite James Crinkley's efforts to resist him, the man succeeded in getting the Crinkleys into their room. The man was armed with a gun, and once inside he beat James Crinkley, turned on the television, and called for his accomplices. He was joined in the room by two men who again beat James Crinkley, bound and gagged him, and put a mattress on top of him. After going through the Crinkleys' possessions, the men approached Sarah Crinkley. They pushed her down and demanded her money and her engagement ring. When she told them that the ring would not come off, one of the men put a gun to her head and told her that if she did not take it off, he would "blow her brains out." She got the ring off and gave it to the men. They then bound and gagged her before fleeing. After freeing herself after a short time, she removed the mattress and gags from her husband and called the front desk for help. The desk clerk notified the Cabarras County Sheriff's Office, and a deputy arrived at the Crinkleys' room within minutes. The Crinkleys were taken to an area hospital for emergency medical care. James Crinkley sustained multiple bruises to his head and upper body region, as well as a severely broken jaw. His broken jaw was wired, a condition which lasted approximately six weeks. Sarah Crinkley's subsequent condition was more complicated. Before the assault she was under a physician's care for hypertension and obesity. In April 1982—approximately 14 months after the assault—she suffered a heart attack. A balloon angioplasty was performed in an effort to clear the

blockage in her arteries but was unsuccessful. After consulting with her doctors, she opted for heart bypass surgery to treat her condition. In addition to her cardiac problems, friends and family noted that Sarah Crinkley's personality changed drastically after the assault. She became fearful, anxious, and withdrawn. Her activities also were observed to be much more restricted. In early 1984, she began seeing a psychiatrist, who diagnosed her as suffering from posttraumatic stress disorder and major affective disorder.

The Crinkleys filed suit for negligence. The jury found TRAVCO negligent for not providing security and held Holiday Inns liable because TRAVCO was its agent. Sarah Crinkley was awarded $400,000 and James Crinkley $100,000 in compensatory damages.

Holiday Inns appealed.

JUDICIAL OPINION
PHILLIPS, Circuit Judge
In North Carolina, as generally, the elements of the prima facie negligence claim are the familiar ones: (1) a duty by defendant to conform his conduct to a particular standard of care, (2) breach of that duty, (3) proximate causation, and (4) injury.

The duty here in issue is that of a landowner or lessee to business invitees on his premises. In North Carolina, as generally, there is no duty on such a person's part to insure the safety of his invitees. Rather, such a person owes only the general duty of exercising reasonable or ordinary care for their safety. While this duty does not ordinarily extend to protecting invitees from the intentional, criminal acts of third persons, it may in appropriate circumstances. Specifically, such a duty of care may in appropriate circumstances be found owed by the operators of places of public accommodation to their guests.

Foreseeability determines "whether a duty to protect [his] business invitees against criminal acts of third persons will be imposed upon a particular landowner in a particular case." Foreseeability may be shown by all relevant evidence, including that of prior criminal activity on the
Continued

premises involved, or in the general area in which the premises is situated. Defendants contend that the evidence of prior criminal activity here was insufficient in and of itself to make it reasonably foreseeable that "Motel Bandits" operating in Charlotte would threaten the Holiday Inn-Concord, thereby giving rise to a duty to protect against that particular risk. We disagree.

While the evidence of prior criminal activity at the Holiday Inn-Concord might alone be insufficient to establish the foreseeability of criminal activity on the premises, we think that the evidence in its totality sufficed here to permit a jury finding of duty to take reasonable precautions.

In the two weeks just before the attack on the Crinkleys, seven motels within the general area had been victimized by what the police and press had identified as the same group of assailants. At times, the group struck at more than one motel in a single night. The systematic nature of the attacks, their apparent perpetration by a single group, and the fact that the group continued to operate even after law enforcement efforts had focused on them and Charlotte motels were alerted to their presence make it reasonably foreseeable that the attacks would continue.

Finally, the evidence is sufficient to establish that it was reasonably foreseeable that the Holiday Inn-Concord might be a target. The premises was a motel near a major highway, making it similar to several of the motels victimized in Charlotte. Evidence at trial indicated that motels with relatively more affluent clienteles, judged by reference to room rates, were the preferred targets. The Holiday Inn-Concord was in this category. That relatively lax security measures necessarily enhance the attractiveness of a particular motel as a potential target is manifest. ("[D]efendant . . . should have reasonably foreseen that the conditions on its motel premises were such that its guests might be exposed to injury by the criminal acts of third persons. . . .")

In addition to the circumstantial evidence of foreseeability, there was evidence of actual notice of the specific threat. McRorie, the motel's assistant manager, testified that he was aware of the "Motel Bandits" depradations. He also testified that he was contacted by local law enforcement officers who wanted to make sure that he was aware of the situation and would make adequate security arrangements. Some of these officers offered their services as security guards for hire, on the specific basis of this particular threat. McRorie himself took the threat seriously enough to ask his superiors about the possibility of hiring patrol guards. And though he was told that the threat did not justify taking such action, he warned his employees to be alert to suspicious circumstances and patrolled the premises the night the Crinkleys were attacked.

To prove that the special duty of care created by the circumstances was breached, the Crinkleys relied primarily on the testimony of an expert in hotel-motel security, Kenneth Prestia.

Prestia testified that security at the Holiday Inn-Concord was inadequate in several respects. The motel had widespread access from several directions, a security problem exacerbated by the fact that the front desk did not provide employees with a view of all points of access. Existing fencing was of inadequate height adequately to deter access to the premises and there were no "no trespassing" signs around the perimeter. He opined that these obvious physical measures have a deterrent effect on crime by conveying the impression that the motel maintained a heightened security posture, and that their absence therefore increased the risk of criminal activity on the premises.

Prestia also opined that there were inadequacies apart from these physical measures. The motel had not instituted a formal security plan specifically tailored to the premises and did not employ security patrols. Prestia testified that security patrols are again particularly important where there is widespread access to the motel and limited observation from the employees. On this same point, he noted that more security patrols could be added during a period of higher crime activity or an increased threat of crime, a measure that could be taken by hiring off-duty law enforcement personnel.

We think there was enough evidence for the jury reasonably to conclude that the defendants

Continued

breached their duty to provide adequate security to protect their guests against the specific, known foreseeable risk created by the circumstances.
Affirmed.

CASE QUESTIONS

1. Describe the activity of the Motel Bandits.
2. Describe what happened to the Crinkleys.
3. Describe the relationships between Holiday Inns, Holiday Inn-Concord, and TRAVCO.
4. Why is Holiday Inns, Inc., liable if it didn't make the operations decisions?
5. Do negligence duties arise because of employment and franchise relationships?

Business Planning Tip

Businesses that have the public on their premises have the duty of taking appropriate precautions for their guests. Shopping malls must provide security for customers in parking lot/garage areas. Adequate lighting is important, as are frequent patrols. Total quality management requires managers to note issues and details and commit resources to solving problems. In the Crinkley case, a few inexpensive changes might have avoided the harm and the liability.

Element Two: Breach of Duty

Once the standard of care and the duty are established under element one, there must be a determination that the defendant fell short of that standard or breached that duty in order for the plaintiff to recover on the basis of negligence. For example, an accountant owes a duty to his client to perform an audit in a competent and professional manner and to conform the audit to the standards and rules established by the American Institute of Certified Public Accounts (AICPA). Failure to comply with these standards would be a breach of duty and would satisfy this second element of negligence.

In many cases, courts try to determine whether the duty was breached in order to determine whether the defendant's action satisfied the standard of care established in element one.

The following case focuses on the issues of safety and the liability of businesses and property owners for injuries that result from the acts of third parties. The focus of this case and others similar to it is whether there were sufficient precautions taken to prevent the criminal activity. This case provides the answer to the chapter's opening "Judgment."

Judgment

Page v. American National Bank & Trust Co.
850 S.W.2d 133 (Tenn. 1991)

PUMMELED AT THE ATM: LIABILITY OF BANKS FOR HIGHWAY ROBBERY

FACTS

At 9:30 P.M. on December 7, 1988, JoKatherine Page (plaintiff/appellee) went to the Brainerd Road branch of the American National Bank & Trust Company of Hamilton County, Tennessee. Mrs. Page frequented the Brainerd branch to use the 24-hour automated teller machine (ATM) located there. Mrs. Page parked her car near the ATM and walked to the machine, leaving her 14-year old son, Jason, in

the car. There were two other patrons near the ATM, one of them a Mrs. Kurtz, a friend of Mrs. Page. As the two were exchanging pleasantries, they were approached by a group of four to six young black males. One of them pushed Mrs. Page to the machine, held a gun to her back, and demanded that she withdraw $300 from the ATM. Two others stood at her car pointing a gun at Jason, threatening to kill him if she did not cooperate.

Continued

Mrs. Page turned to tell Jason to stay in the car, and the man behind her struck her in the face with a solid object, severely injuring her face. The young thugs departed. Mrs. Page and her son sued American National Bank & Trust Company (ANB) to recover for their injuries. The suit was based on the following allegations:

(a) The lighting at and about the ATM was completely inadequate to deter crime.

(b) The defendant knew that the area in which it placed the ATM was unsafe and failed to warn plaintiffs.

(c) The defendant failed to exercise reasonable care to protect its customers, including plaintiffs, from assaults when such assaults were or should have been reasonably foreseeable.

(d) The machine was designed by the defendant or its agents in such a way that Mrs. Page was required to leave the safety of her automobile to use the machine.

(e) The defendant knew that this machine was located in an area of potential risk to its customers and was aware of prior similar incidents at other branches of ANB and at branches of other banks in the same area in which it's Brainerd branch is located.

Despite such knowledge, the defendant failed to take necessary and reasonable steps to correct the deficiencies of which it was aware, all in a conscious and callous disregard of the welfare of its customers, including the plaintiffs.

(f) The defendant failed to place a guard at the ATM or to take such other security precautions as were reasonably necessary to protect its customers, including the plaintiffs.

(g) The defendant failed to conform to the actions of a reasonably prudent bank operator in similar situations.

(h) The defendant failed to provide its customers, including the plaintiffs, a safe place in which to conduct their business with the defendant.

(i) The defendant failed to establish or follow standards of safety recognized in the banking industry.

The jury found for the Pages and awarded Mrs. Page $125,000 in damages and Jason $10,000. The bank appealed.

JUDICIAL OPINION

SANDERS, Presiding Judge

The Bank argues this case is controlled by the holdings of our supreme court in the case of *Cornpropst v. Sloan*, 528 S.W.2d 188 (Tenn. 1975).

In *Cornpropst* the plaintiff had gone to a shopping center after dark. After doing her shopping she was returning to her car to leave when a man she had never seen before suddenly drove up beside her car and grabbed her and inflicted injuries to her while trying to force her into his car. Plaintiff filed suit for personal injuries against the merchants and owners who comprised the shopping center association. She alleged they were negligent in failing to furnish her a safe place to shop. Prior to this attack upon the plaintiff there had been committed various crimes, assaults, and other acts of violence either on the premises or in the vicinity. She said defendants failed to furnish security guards for the area; they knew or should have known the parking lot was dangerous, especially for a woman after dark; they were negligent in failing to warn of the potential dangers of the area. In doing so the majority of the [supreme] court [denied recovery as follows]:

At common law, a private person or corporation, as distinguished from governmental units, had no duty whatsoever to protect others from the criminal acts of third parties. That general rule has remained steadfast in the tort law of this country, despite the exceptions that have appeared from time-to-time, where special relationships and special circumstances have combined to impose liability.

We are dealing with an act of nonfeasance, the failure to take steps to protect another from harm, as distinguished from misfeasance, or active misconduct causing positive injury to others.

The cases involving liability for the criminal acts of third persons are most numerous involving the innkeeper guest relationship and the patron public amusement owners and operators, including lounges, beer parlors, rock and roll concerts, bowling alleys, etc. In the great majority of cases involving these relationship the offender that perpetrates the criminal act giving rise to the litigation is identified in advance, and

Continued

liability is predicated on some action or course of conduct of the particular offender that gave notice of the imminent probability of danger.

In the instant case the offender was not, and under the allegations of the bill, could not have been identified in advance of the perpetration of the action. The complaint relies entirely upon the vague allegation that various crimes, assaults and other acts of violence had been committed either on the premises or in the immediate area.

Vagueness is only one of the factors that have perplexed the courts in dealing with tort liability for criminal acts of third persons.

It is an easy matter to know whether a stairway is defective and what repairs will put it in order. Again, it is fairly simple to decide how many ushers or guards suffice at a skating rink or a railroad platform to deal with the crush of a crowd and the risks of unintentional injury which the nature of the business creates, but how can one know what measures will protect against the thug, the narcotic addict, the degenerate, the psychopath and the psychotic? Must the owner prevent all crime? We doubt that any police force in the friendliest community has achieved that end.

. . . We assume that advocates of liability do not intend an absolute obligation to prevent all crime, but rather have in mind some unarticulated level of effectiveness short of that goal. Whatever may be that degree of safety, is there any standard of performance to which the owner may look for guidance? We know of none, and the record does not suggest one, and we are at a loss to understand what standard the jurors here employed.

In our opinion the appropriate rule applicable to this case is as follows: There is no duty upon the owners or operators of a shopping center, individually or collectively, or upon merchants and shopkeepers generally, whose mode of operation of their premises does not attract or provide a climate for crime, to guard against the criminal acts of a third party, unless they know or have reason to know that acts are occurring or about to occur on the premises that pose imminent probability of harm to an invitee; whereupon a duty of reasonable care to protect against such act arises.

The Appellees argue in their brief that the rule pronounced by the supreme court has no application to the case at bar in that it is applicable only to owners and operators of a shopping center.

A fair reading of *Cornpropst* makes it abundantly clear that the supreme court intended for the rule therein stated to be applicable to merchants and shopkeepers except where a different standard has been adopted for institutions such as carriers, utilities, innkeepers, etc., as recognized in the opinion of the court. The court made it clear also that it was not its purpose to make an all-inclusive rule. It said:

We are not called upon, in this case, to draft a rule applicable to all of the many types of business and entertainment and service establishments or of every premises liability, or special relationship situation wherein a duty of protection of invitees might be asserted, and we do not propose to do so.

Appellees also insist the Bank does not fall within the class of businesses governed by the *Cornpropst* rule because its mode of operation attracts and provides a climate for crime. The plaintiffs provided ample evidence to support this claim by showing:

1. Five similar previous crimes at the very same branch's ATM.
2. Two letters from the Chattanooga Crime Prevention Bureau specifically addressing the fact that the drive-in area adjacent to the Brainerd Branch ATM provided thieves with a "good place to hide and grab money."
3. A previous warning from a customer who was assaulted and shot at the exact same ATM about the dangerous situation at that location.
4. The ATM at the Brainerd Branch is on the side of the building, shielded from the line of sight of east-bound traffic by a sharp curve away from the building, and largely obstructed from the west by the large American National Bank sign, a tall retaining wall, and other obstacles.
5. On the night of the assault, the area about the ATM was not well lighted as required by federal regulations. In fact, the area where the

Continued

assailants hid was not lighted at all and provided the exact hiding place warned of by the Chattanooga Crime Prevention Bureau.

6. The ATM was located in a high-crime area.

In light of our holding in this case, we must concede the Plaintiffs proved each of these allegations to the complete satisfaction of the jury but, even so, that does not take the Bank out of the rule of *Cornpropst*. Let us conclude that the jury found the Bank was careless or negligent based on the proof in support of these allegations. The court in *Cornpropst* said: "In our opinion it is a mistake to equate the duty of a shopkeeper with respect to criminal acts with the duty of shopkeepers with respect to careless acts." The proof did show there had been five robberies at the ATM over a four-year period; two of them occurred in 1984, one in 1986, one in 1987, and one in 1988. It is interesting to note that three of the five occurred during the day and two occurred at night.

The evidence relating to item No. 2 above is that in 1985 the Bank requested the Crime Prevention Bureau of Chattanooga to make a survey and recommendations concerning security of all its ATM locations (Teller-24). After making the survey the director of the Bureau wrote the Bank a letter which, as pertinent here, stated: "Sam Morris of our office did surveys on all Teller-24 locations. We found the locations well secure as far as lights and visibility. . . . The drive-in at 3535 Brainerd Road, the extension at 4614 Highway 58 and the slope of the building at 8191 E. Brainerd Road are good places for someone to hide and grab money."

There is no proof the unknown assailants had been hiding in the vicinity of the ATM prior to the assault.

In No. 6 above, the Plaintiffs say "The ATM was located in a high-crime area." We assume it is their contention it is negligence per se to do business in a high-crime area.

We are unable to see that an employer has a general duty to protect his employees from the assaults of criminals. We are likewise unable to see that there are any exceptional circumstances in this case which would give rise to such a duty. We would be saying, in legal effect, that those who live there and those who engage in business there are not exercising the prudence and judgment of ordinary people.

In the case at bar we hold, as the supreme court held in *Cornpropst*, that the sudden intentional criminal acts of the unidentified assailants, which could not have been prevented or deterred by the exercise of reasonable care by the Bank, was the whole proximate cause of harm to the Plaintiffs. We hold the trial court was in error.

The judgment of the trial court is reversed and the complaint dismissed.

CASE QUESTIONS

1. What mistakes do the Pages allege the bank made in terms of the nature and location of the Brainerd ATM?
2. Why is the fact that third parties, and not bank employees, were responsible for the injuries so important in the analysis?
3. Why is it significant that the injuries resulted from criminal activity?
4. Is there a flaw in the court's analysis about the prior report indicating that the area around the Brainerd ATM provided a place for thieves to hide? Why does the court comment that there was no evidence that the thieves were hiding in the bushes prior to the attack on the Pages?
5. Could it ever be negligence on the part of a business just to decide to open operations in a high-crime area? Why or why not?

Element Three: Causation

After establishing that a duty existed and that there was a breach of duty, the plaintiff in a negligence suit must also establish that the breach of the duty was the cause of his or her damages. A test that is often used to determine **causation** is the **"but for" test**—"but for the action or lack of action of the defendant, the plaintiff would

There are several safety tips that all businesses should follow with respect to safety of their customers, especially with respect to criminal acts. The list follows:

1. Good lighting
2. Access to public phones
3. Security patrols
4. Locked gates to parking lots; gate or security access
5. Escorts provided for customers and employees to their vehicles after closing hours
6. Camera security
7. Assigned parking spaces for tenants and employees
8. Warning signs to use caution and be alert

Many hotels change key access codes with each guest and post security personnel near guest elevators at night so that there is no access to the elevators unless you can show your room key. Some hotels have floors for women who are traveling alone, and extra security is provided on those floors.

not have been injured." For example, suppose that a guest is enjoying a scenic view of the ocean from a cliff near his hotel. At the edge of the cliff there is a fence that had been installed by the hotel but that the hotel does not keep in good repair. When the guest leans against the fence to take a picture, the fence breaks and the guest falls over the cliff. The hotel breached its duty to keep its premises in reasonably safe condition, and its failure to do so caused the injury to the guest. The "but for" test is limited by the so-called zone of danger rule, which requires that the plaintiff be in the zone of danger when the injury occurs. The zone of danger includes all those people who could foreseeably be injured if a duty is breached. For example, the hotel would also be liable to those injured by the guest as he fell through the weak fence because they are in the zone of danger.

Element Four: Proximate Cause

Some cut-off line must be drawn between the "but for" causation and events that contribute to the injury of the plaintiff—an element of a negligence case called proximate cause. Suppose that you have a tire replaced at a tire store and the technician fails to tighten the wheel sufficiently. As you drive down the street, the tire comes loose, rolls off, and strikes another car. Did the tire store cause the damage to the other car? Yes. Any accidents caused by that car? Yes. Suppose the tire comes off, rolls to the sidewalk, and strikes a pedestrian. Did the tire store cause that injury? Yes. Suppose the pedestrian sees the tire coming and jumps out of the way, but in so doing injures another pedestrian. Did the tire store cause that injury? Yes. In all these accidents the following statement can be made: "But for the failure to tighten the wheel the accident would not have occurred." Suppose that the tire injures a pedestrian, although not fatally, but a doctor treating the pedestrian, through malpractice, causes the pedestrian's death. Did the tire store cause the death? No; another's negligence intervened.

The following is a landmark case on the element of proximate cause.

Palsgraf v. *Long Island Ry. Co.*
162 N.E. 99 (N.Y. 1928)

FIREWORKS IN THE PASSENGER'S PACKAGE AND NEGLIGENCE IN THE AIR

FACTS
Helen Palsgraf (plaintiff) had purchased a ticket to travel to Rockaway Beach on the Long Island Railway (defendant). While she was standing on a platform at the defendant's station waiting for the train, another train stopped at the station.

Two men ran to catch the train, which began moving as they were running. One of the men made it onto the train without difficulty, but the other man, who was carrying a package, was unsteady as he tried to jump aboard. Employees of the defendant helped pull the man in and push

Continued

him onto the train car, but in the process the package was dropped. The package contained fireworks, and when it was dropped, it exploded. The vibrations from the explosion caused some scales (located at the end of the platform on which Palsgraf was standing) to fall. As they fell, they hit Palsgraf, who was injured. Palsgraf filed suit against the railroad for negligence.

JUDICIAL OPINION
CARDOZO, Chief Justice
The conduct of the defendant's guard, if a wrong in its relation to the holder of the package, was not a wrong in its relation to the plaintiff, standing far away. Nothing in the situation gave notice that the falling package had in it the potency of peril to persons thus removed. Negligence is not actionable unless it involves the invasion of a legally protected interest, the violation of a right. "Proof of negligence in the air, so to speak, will not do." The plaintiff, as she stood upon the platform of the station, might claim to be protected against intentional invasion of her bodily security. Such invasion is not charged. She might claim to be protected against unintentional invasion by conduct involving in the thought of reasonable men an unreasonable hazard that such invasion would ensue. These, from the point of view of the law, were the bounds of her immunity, with perhaps some rare exceptions, survivals for the most part of ancient forms of liability, where conduct is held to be at the peril of the actor. If no hazard was apparent to the eye of ordinary vigilance, an act innocent and harmless, at least to outward seeming, with reference to her, did not take to itself the quality of a tort because it happened to be a wrong, though apparently not one involving the risk of bodily insecurity, with reference to some one else.

A different conclusion will involve us, and swiftly too, in a maze of contradictions. A guard stumbles over a package which has been left upon a platform. It seems to be a bundle of newspapers. It turns out to be a can of dynamite. To the eye of ordinary vigilance, the bundle is abandoned waste, which may be kicked or trod on with impunity. Is a passenger at the other end of the platform protected by the law against the unsuspected hazard concealed beneath the waste? If not, is the result to be any different, so far as the distant passenger is concerned, when the guard stumbles over a valise which a truckman or a porter has left upon the walk? The passenger far away, if the victim of a wrong at all, has a cause of action, not derivative, but original and primary. His claim to be protected against invasion of his bodily security is neither greater nor less because the act resulting in the invasion is a wrong to another far removed. In this case, the rights that are said to have been violated, the interests said to have been invaded, are not even of the same order. The man was not injured in his person or even put in danger. The purpose of the act, as well as its effect, was to make his person safe. If there was a wrong to him at all, which may very well be doubted, it was a wrong to a property interest only, the safety of his package. Out of this wrong to property, which threatened injury to nothing else, there has passed, we are told, to the plaintiff by derivation or succession a right of action for the invasion of an interest of another order, the right to bodily security. The diversity of interests emphasizes the futility of the effort to build the plaintiff's right upon the basis of a wrong to some one else. The gain is one of emphasis, for a like result would follow if the interests were the same. Even then, the orbit of the danger as disclosed to the eye of reasonable vigilance would be the orbit of the duty. One who jostles one's neighbor in a crowd does not invade the rights of others standing at the outer fringe when the unintended contact casts a bomb upon the ground. The wrongdoer as to them is the man who carries the bomb, not the one who explodes it without suspicion of the danger. Life will have to be made over, and human nature transformed, before prevision so extravagant can be accepted as the norm of conduct, the customary standard to which behavior must conform.

The risk reasonably to be perceived defines the duty to be obeyed, and risk imports relation; it is risk to another or to others within the

Continued

range of apprehension. Here, by concession, there was nothing in the situation to suggest to the most cautious mind that the parcel wrapped in newspaper would spread wreckage through the station. If the guard had thrown it down knowingly and willfully, he would not have threatened the plaintiff's safety, so far as appearances could warn him. His conduct would not have involved, even then, an unreasonable probability of invasion of her bodily security. Liability can be no greater where the act is inadvertent.

DISSENTING OPINION
ANDREWS, Justice

Assisting a passenger to board a train, the defendant's servant negligently knocked a package from his arms. It fell between the platform and the cars. Of its contents the servant knew and could know nothing. A violent explosion followed. The concussion broke some scales standing a considerable distance away. In falling, they injured the plaintiff, an intending passenger.

Upon these facts, may she recover the damages she has suffered in an action brought against the master? The result we shall reach depends upon our theory as to the nature of negligence. Is it a relative concept—the breach of some duty owing to a particular person or to particular persons? Or, where there is an act which unreasonably threatens the safety of others, is the doer liable for all its proximate consequences, even where they result in injury to one who would generally be thought to be outside the radius of danger? This is not a mere dispute as to words. We might not believe that to the average mind the dropping of the bundle would seem to involve the probability of harm to the plaintiff standing many feet away whatever might be the case as to the owner or to one so near as to be likely to be struck by its fall. If, however, we adopt the second hypothesis, we have to inquire only as to the relation between cause and effect. We deal in terms of proximate cause, not of negligence.

Negligence may be defined roughly as an act or omission which unreasonably does or may affect the rights of others, or which unreasonably fails to protect one's self from the dangers resulting from such acts.

Where there is the unreasonable act, and some right that may be affected there is negligence whether damage does or does not result. That is immaterial. Should we drive down Broadway at a reckless speed, we are negligent whether we strike an approaching car or miss it by an inch. The act itself is wrongful. It is a wrong not only to those who happen to be within the radius of danger, but to all who might have been there—a wrong to the public at large.

Negligence does involve a relationship between man and his fellows, but not merely a relationship between man and those whom he might reasonably expect his act would injure; rather, a relationship between him and those whom he does in fact injure. If his act has a tendency to harm some one, it harms him a mile away as surely as it does those on the scene.

The proposition is this: Every one owes to the world at large the duty of refraining from those acts that may unreasonably threaten the safety of others. Such an act occurs. Not only is he wronged to whom harm might reasonably be expected to result, but he also who is in fact injured, even if he be outside what would generally be thought the danger zone.

As we have said, we cannot trace the effect of an act to the end, if end there is. Again, however, we may trace it part of the way. An overturned lantern may burn all Chicago. We may follow the fire from the shed to the last building. We rightly say the fire started by the lantern caused its destruction. A cause, but not the proximate cause. What we do mean by the word "proximate" is that, because of convenience, of public policy, of a rough sense of justice, the law arbitrarily declines to trace a series of events beyond a certain point. This is not logic. It is practical politics.

This last suggestion is the factor which must determine the case before us. The act upon which defendant's liability rests is knocking an apparently harmless package onto the platform. The act was negligent. For its proximate consequences the defendant is liable. If its contents

Continued

were broken, to the owner; if it fell upon and crushed a passenger's foot, then to him; if it exploded and injured one in the immediate vicinity, to him. Mrs. Palsgraf was standing some distance away. How far cannot be told from the record—apparently 25 to 30 feet, perhaps less. Except for the explosion, she would not have been injured. . . . The only intervening cause was that, instead of blowing her to the ground, the concussion smashed the weighing machine which in turn fell upon her. There was no remoteness in time, little in space. And surely, given such an explosion as here, it needed no great foresight to predict that the natural result would be to injure one on the platform at no greater distance from its scene

than was the plaintiff. Just how no one might be able to predict. Whether by flying fragments, by broken glass, by wreckage of machines or structures no one could say. But injury in some form was most probable.

Under these circumstances I cannot say as a matter of law that the plaintiff's injuries were not the proximate result of the negligence.

CASE QUESTIONS
1. Who was carrying the package?
2. How far away from the incident was Mrs. Palsgraf?
3. What does Justice Cardozo find?
4. What points does the dissent make?

Element Five: Damages

The plaintiff in a negligence case must be able to establish damages that resulted from the defendant's negligence. Such damages could include compensation for damages such as medical bills, lost wages, and pain and suffering, as well as any property damages. In many of the cases in this chapter, plaintiffs have also recovered punitive damages. Often referred to as "smart money," punitive damages are similar to civil penalties that are paid to plaintiffs because of the high level of carelessness involved on the defendant's part.   *Loss of consortium*

Defenses to Negligence

CONTRIBUTORY NEGLIGENCE

In some cases, an accident results from the combined negligence of two or more people. A plaintiff who is also negligent gives the defendant the opportunity to raise the defense of **contributory negligence**. Contributory negligence is simply negligence by the plaintiff that is part of the cause of an accident. For example, suppose that a boat owner is operating his boat late at night on a lake in which the water is choppy and when he is intoxicated. An intoxicated friend is sitting at the bow of the boat trying to put her feet into the water when the owner takes the boat up to high speed. She falls in and is injured. The issue of causation becomes complicated here because there were breaches of duties by both parties. Did he cause the accident by driving at high speed late at night on a choppy lake while intoxicated? Or did she cause the accident by sitting without protection or restraint on the bow of the boat when the boat was being driven like that? The effect of the defense of contributory negligence is a complete bar to both from recovery.

COMPARATIVE NEGLIGENCE

Some states, in order to eliminate the harsh effect of contributory negligence, have adopted a defense of **comparative negligence**. Under this defense, the jury simply determines the level of fault for both the plaintiff and the defendant and, based on this assessment of fault, determines how much each of the parties will be awarded. For example, using our boat example, the jury could find that the boat owner was 75 percent at fault and the passenger was 25 percent at fault. Under comparative negligence, the passenger could recover for her injuries, but the amount recovered would be 25 percent less because of her fault in causing the accident. If the jury finds that the plaintiff was more at fault than the defendant in causing the accident, the plaintiff would recover nothing.

The defense of comparative negligence was developed largely because of the perceived unfairness of contributory negligence, which was a complete bar to recovery. The concept of comparative negligence has resulted in more litigation and more verdicts for plaintiffs permitted to use the defense.

ASSUMPTION OF RISK

The **assumption of risk** defense requires the defendant to prove that the plaintiff knew there was a risk of injury in the conduct he or she undertook but decided to go forward with it anyway. For example, there are some inherent dangers in activities such as skydiving, skiing, and roller skating. You assume the inherent risks in these activities, but you do not assume the risks caused by the owners of the premises or equipment. For example, when you ski, you assume the natural risks that exist in skiing, but you do not assume the risk of faulty equipment you rent. If the failure of that equipment causes your injuries, the rental company would be responsible for that injury. To assume the risk, you must be completely aware of the risk and you must assume the risk voluntarily.

TORT REFORM

As noted in Chapter 3, the United States has a sizeable court system equipped with sufficient lawyers for the support of litigation. The United States permits greater recovery for torts while requiring less in terms of proof than other nations. Over the past decade a number of reforms have been proposed, particularly with respect to tort litigation, to limit recovery or place other limitations on the amount of increasing tort litigation. For example, some reform proposals would limit damages. Those limitations may be general limitations on damage awards or limitations like the Canadian system of $200,000 for pain and suffering. Although nearly all states have adopted some form of limitations in tort recovery, these reforms are a maze of laws differing from state to state, have been subject to judicial challenges (in many cases successful), and have provided little hope for insurers as they try to forecast their risks in insuring businesses and their properties and agents.

Discover more about Peter Huber's Views on Tort Reform:
http://khht.com/ huber/home.html

Peter W. Huber, a senior fellow at the Manhattan Institute, a conservative New York think tank, maintains that judges should defuse confrontations in tort cases by encouraging the litigants to settle and by establishing rules that would hold defendants liable only in those cases in which they are at fault and a large recovery will deter future accidents that would not otherwise be deterred.

Judge Richard Neeley of the West Virginia Supreme Court understands Mr. Huber's point but suggests that judges will never undertake such reforms:

[T]ort law is local law. The typical high-stakes liability suit pits a plaintiff from the same state as the judge and jury against an out-of-state company. As long as I am allowed to redistribute wealth from out-of-state companies to injured in-state plaintiffs, I shall continue to do so. Not only is my sleep enhanced when I give someone else's money away, but so is my job security, because the in-state plaintiffs, their families and their friends will re-elect me.[1]

Judge Neeley says that the U.S. Supreme Court should undertake the responsibility of making uniform limitations and laws for recovery, as they have done with libel and slander, so that he and other judges can be stopped.

Proposals for reform continue from doctors, insurers, manufacturers, and property owners. In many cases, ballot propositions allow voters to determine whether there should be limitations in tort recovery.

E T H I C A L   I S S U E S

9.2 How do you feel about Judge Neeley's statement? Is it fair to allow recovery just because it helps you and your state? Should tort liability be decided on these economic bases, or on the basis of whether someone is at fault?

FOR THE MANAGER'S DESK

A TRIAL JUDGE'S VIEW OF TORT REFORM

When we permit unlimited awards for pain and suffering and when we permit large awards for punitive damages in actions against health plans, we overlook the harm we may be causing countless persons who depend upon those plans for payment of their medical and hospital bills.

Our system for awarding damages is not the only rational system. I just completed another products liability case in which Dutch substantive law was applicable. The product involved was zirconium metal powder. It was shipped from a German company to an American company which sold it to the plaintiff, a distributor of metal products in Amsterdam. The product exploded into flames when the plaintiff mixed a portion for resale.

The plaintiff's home was burned to the ground; he was horribly burned over most of his body; his wife was badly burned; he spent three months in a burn unit and many more months in rehabilitation. He remains forever terribly scarred in face and body. He sued the German seller and the American reseller, charging a lack of an adequate warning.

The parties agreed that Dutch law as it existed in 1988, the date of the explosion, was applicable. The law on liability was similar to American products liability law. The law on damages was quite different.

The medical expenses must have been enormous, but no doctor testified for either side and no medical expenses were proven. The plaintiff and his wife provided eloquent testimony about his

treatment, pain and suffering. There was no medical recovery because every cent of the plaintiff's medical care had been provided without cost to plaintiff under the Dutch health care system. Unlike the law in the United States, double recovery of medical expenses is not allowed under Dutch law. You cannot recover both from a medical plan and from a defendant.

Plaintiff's claim for property damage was limited to $25,000, because his fire insurance had paid $175,000 of his $200,000 fire loss. Loss of income, to the extent not covered by the Dutch social security system, was recoverable.

As for pain and suffering, referred to in the Dutch law as immaterial damages, Dutch courts generally consider the same factors as American courts consider. No maximum

Continued

amount was established under the Dutch code, but as a matter of practice, degrees of severity have been established, with monetary amounts being associated with each degree. The largest award in the most severe category of immaterial damages was a 1992 award of 300,000 Netherlands guilders—or about $150,000.

As for punitive damages, there are none. As the expert legal opinion submitted in evidence in the case stated, "Under Netherlands law the function of tort law is to compensate injured plaintiffs. It is not a function of Netherlands tort law to regulate the behavior of potential tort feasors or to mete out punishment to actual tort feasors."

It would be interesting to study how quickly and completely the Dutch system compensates injured victims and the amount of court and attorney time and expense it spends in delivering this compensation. It would be interesting to compare the Dutch experience in this regard with the American experience.

American jurisdictions are beginning to face up to the problems to which I have referred. The Oregon Basic Health Service Act adopted a rational approach to providing medical coverage to 120,000 persons who were not qualified for Medicaid but who fell below the federal poverty level. The proposed plan recognized that medical resources are limited; it established, in a descending order of priority, a schedule of medical conditions and treatments; it established the cost of providing the treatments and left it to the legislature to

determine how far down the list coverage could go—it all depended upon how much the legislature was willing to appropriate. This was a clear recognition that we can only provide those medical services which we are willing to pay for. I see no room in that system for a court to enter the picture and order that treatment be provided to a greater degree than that authorized by the plan. An autologous bone marrow transplant for any given condition would either be provided or not provided, depending upon the decision of the legislature.

Georgia has addressed the problem of punitive damages in products liability cases. The legislature recognized that if punitive damages are simply to deter, the punishment should be imposed once. To impose multiple punitive damage awards in mass tort situations goes beyond deterrence and serves only to reward some plaintiffs and their attorneys unduly and to deprive other plaintiffs of the ability to recover anything.

The Georgia statute contains no ceiling on the amount of the punitive damages award. But it allows but one recovery, regardless of the number of cases against a particular defendant. The plaintiff who collects the punitive damages award must pay 75% of the award to the state treasury.

Numerous other proposals are surfacing—for example, extending genuine no fault concepts, removing some kinds of claims from the courts. Some of the proposals are unsound; some look interesting.

Whatever the proposals are, the organized bar seems unreceptive. Last February I received the following notice: "Emergency Meeting To Alert Members To Radical Legislative Proposals To Drastically Limit If Not Totally Eliminate New Jersey Citizens' Access To The Courts"—all in capital letters, no less. In fact, although the proposals may have been unwise, they were far from radical. They merely nibbled around the edges of the problem.

Much serious work is being done in tort reform. Better it would be if the organized bar joined these efforts—not to sabotage them but to find fairer, more efficient ways of distributing limited resources among injured people.

At the beginning of these remarks I referred to a sentence in an opinion authored by Chief Justice Vanderbilt which has remained with me through the years. In *State v. Culver*, written three months before his death, Chief Justice Vanderbilt stated: "The nature of the common law requires that each time a rule of law is applied it be carefully scrutinized to make sure that the conditions and needs of the times have not so changed as to make further application of it the instrument of injustice."

I would suggest that the conditions and needs of the times have changed, requiring that we carefully scrutinize facets of our tort law, particularly as it relates to awards for pain and suffering and for punitive damages. We should not permit rules which were appropriate when formulated to become instruments of injustice.

Source: the Honorable Dickinson R. Debevoise, "A Trial Judge's View of Tort Reform," 25 *Seton Hall Law Review* 853, pp. 859-862, 1994. Reprinted with permission.

In early 1994, Capital Cities/ABC Inc. ran a story on its news program *Day One* that accused the tobacco industry of "spiking" cigarettes with nicotine to increase the addiction level. Philip Morris Co. filed a $10 billion libel suit against ABC.

ABC and Philip Morris— The Spiked Tobacco Apology

ABC ran stories about the libel suit and added that it stood by its news story about "spiking." Walt Bogdanich, the producer of *Day One*, and correspondent John Martin, who handled the story, also steadfastly maintained their report was accurate.

As discovery in the case unfolded, lawyers for ABC found that while the tobacco companies manipulated nicotine levels, there was not evidence to support the *Day One* report that the industry manipulated nicotine levels to keep smokers hooked.

There was disagreement among ABC camps about what to do once the information in the documents was revealed. The outside lawyers continued to prepare for trial, even to the point of drafting their opening statement to the jury. However, the outside attorneys had warned ABC that a jury in a trial deep in the heart of tobacco-growing country, where Philip Morris had filed its suit, might not be disposed to find against Philip Morris. Lawyers within ABC felt that the suit should be settled. Both Mr. Bogdanich and Mr. Martin hired their own lawyers and opposed any settlement by the network.

For nearly a year, between summer 1994 and summer 1995, draft language of a settlement and apology was faxed between ABC and Philip Morris. Mr. Bogdanich and Mr. Martin were not permitted to see the discovery documents and were not told of nor given copies of proposed settlements.

Finally, in August 1995, ABC and Philip Morris reached a settlement agreement that Mr. Bogdanich and Mr. Martin did not sign. ABC would pay $15 million to Philip Morris for its legal fees. ABC would announce its "mistake" and apologize both during *World News Tonight* and *Monday Night Football* on August 21, 1995. The following is the apology:

Continued

It is the policy of ABC News to make corrections where they are warranted.

On February 28 and March 7, 1994, the ABC program, Day One, *aired segments dealing with the tobacco industry. Philip Morris filed a defamation lawsuit alleging that the segments wrongly reported that, through the introduction of significant amounts of nicotine from outside sources, Philip Morris "artificially spikes" and "fortifies" its cigarettes with nicotine, and "carefully controls" and "manipulates" nicotine for the purpose of "addicting" smokers.*

Philip Morris states that it does not add nicotine in any measurable amount from any outside source for any purpose in the course of its manufacturing process, and that its finished cigarettes contain less nicotine than is found in the natural tobacco from which they are made.

ABC does not take issue with those two statements. We now agree that we should not have reported that Philip Morris adds significant amounts of nicotine from outside sources. That was a mistake that was not deliberate on the part of ABC, but for which we accept responsibility and which requires correction. We apologize to our audience and Philip Morris.

ABC and Philip Morris continue to disagree about whether the principal focus of the reports was on the use of nicotine from outside sources. Philip Morris believes that this was the main thrust of the programs. ABC believes that the principal focus of the reports was whether cigarette companies use the reconstituted tobacco process to control the levels of nicotine in cigarettes in order to keep people smoking. Philip Morris categorically denies that it does so. ABC thinks the reports speak for themselves on this issue and is prepared to have the issue resolved elsewhere.

ABC and Philip Morris have agreed to discontinue the defamation action.

Philip Morris ran full-page ads in *The Wall Street Journal* and other papers and magazines with a copy of the ABC apology and the words "Apology Accepted" in large letters above it.

Issues

1. Why did ABC run the story initially?
2. Why did ABC agree to the retraction?
3. Did ABC do enough to compensate the parties?

SUMMARY

What are the types of civil wrongs that create a right of recovery for harm?
- Tort—a civil wrong; action by another that results in damages that are recoverable
- Intentional tort—civilly wrong conduct that is done deliberately
- Negligence—conduct of omission or neglect that results in damages
- Strict tort liability—imposition of liability because harm results

What are the types and elements of torts?
- Defamation—publication of untrue and damaging statements about an individual or company
- Product disparagement—the tort of defamation for products
- Malice—publication of information knowing it is false or with reckless disregard for whether it is false
- Privilege—a defense to defamation that protects certain statements because of a public interest in having information such as testimony in a trial or media coverage protected from suit
- Interference—the wrong of asking a party to breach a contract with a third party
- False imprisonment—wrongful detention of individual; shopkeepers have a privilege to reasonably detain those they have good cause to believe have taken merchandise
- Shopkeeper's privilege—defense to torts of defamation, invasion of privacy and false imprisonment for merchants to detain shoppers when shopkeepers have reasonable cause to believe merchandise has been taken without payment
- Intentional infliction of emotional distress—bizarre and outrageous conduct that inflicts mental and possible physical harm on another
- Invasion of privacy—disclosing private information, intruding upon another's affairs or appropriating someone's image or likeness
- Appropriation—the use of another's likeness, image, voice, or trademark for commercial gain and without permission
- Reasonable and prudent person—the standard by which the conduct of others is measured; a hypothetical person who behaves with full knowledge and alertness
- Causation—the "but for" reason for an accident
- Proximate cause—the foreseeability requirement of causation
- Contributory negligence—negligence on the part of a plaintiff that was partially responsible for causing his/her injuries
- Comparative negligence—newer negligence defense that assigns liability and damages in accidents on a percentage basis and thus reduces a plaintiff's recovery by the amount his/her negligence contributed to the cause of the accident
- Assumption of risk—plaintiff's voluntary subjection to a risk that caused his/her injuries

What is the business issue surrounding torts?
- Tort reform—political and legislative process of limiting damages and changing methods of recovery for civil wrongs

QUESTIONS AND PROBLEMS

1. Sylvia Salek is a teacher at Passaic Collegiate School. The yearbook contained a section entitled "The Funny Pages," consisting of pictures of students and faculty accompanied by purportedly humorous captions. One of the pages in this section contained a picture of Ms. Salek sitting next to and facing another teacher, John DeVita, who had his right hand raised to his forehead. The photograph is captioned "Not tonight, Ms. Salek. I have a headache." Another page in the yearbook contains a picture of Mr. DeVita eating with the caption "What are you really thinking about, Mr. DeVita?"

   Ms. Salek brought suit against the school on grounds that the photographs and captions made it seem that Mr. DeVita was refusing to engage in a sexual relationship with her. What tort(s) is Ms. Salek alleging? [*Salek* v. *Passaic Collegiate School*, 605 A.2d 276 (N.J. 1992).]

2. Douglas Margreiter was severely injured in New Orleans on the night of April 6, 1976. He was the chief of the pharmacy section of the Colorado Department of Social Services and was in New Orleans to attend the annual meeting of the American Pharmaceutical Association.

   On Tuesday evening, April 6, Mr. Margreiter had dinner at the Royal Sonesta Hotel with two associates from Colorado who were attending the meeting and were staying in rooms adjacent to Mr. Margreiter's in the New Hotel Monteleone. Margreiter returned to his room between 10:30 P.M. and 11:00 P.M.; one of his friends returned to his adjoining room at the same time. Another friend was to come by Mr. Margreiter's room later to discuss what sessions of the meetings each would attend the next day.

   About three hours later, Mr. Margreiter was found severely beaten and unconscious in a parking lot three blocks from the Monteleone. The police who found him said they thought he was highly intoxicated, and they took him to Charity Hospital. His friends later had him moved to the Hotel Dieu.

   Mr. Margreiter said two men had unlocked his hotel room door and entered his room. He was beaten about the head and shoulders and had only the recollection of being carried to a dark alley. He required a craniotomy and other medical treatment and suffered permanent effects from the incident.

   Mr. Margreiter sued the hotel on grounds that the hotel was negligent in not controlling access to elevators and hence to the guests' rooms. The hotel says Mr. Margreiter was intoxicated and met his fate outside the hotel. [*Margreiter* v. *New Hotel Monteleone* 640 F.2d 508 (5th Cir. 1981).]

3. Carolyn Dolph was shopping at the Dumas, Arkansas, Wal-Mart at 3:00 P.M. on Friday, June 16, 1989. She had just gone through the check-out line and was attempting to leave the store when she was accosted near the exit by the loss-prevention officer for the store, Loretta McNeely. Ms. Dolph testified that Ms. McNeely told her that she knew that Ms. Dolph had been apprehended for shoplifting in the McGehee Wal-Mart the week before, and because of that she was not allowed to shop at any Wal-Mart store. According to Ms. Dolph, Ms. McNeely made the accusation four times. Ms. Dolph countered that Ms. McNeely was mistaken. Ms. McNeely did not believe her; instead, she thought Ms. Dolph was going through typical shoplifter's denial. They were arguing the point, according to Ms. Dolph, where people could overhear, and she felt as if she were on display "right in front of the store."

   To resolve the matter, Ms. Dolph and Ms. McNeely moved to a nearby service area, and Ms. McNeely went into a mezzanine office to call the McGehee store. After telephoning McGehee, Ms. McNeely then "hollered down" questions to Ms. Dolph from the office, according to Ms. Dolph. During the time that Ms. McNeely was calling, Ms. Dolph believed that she was being watched by Wal-Mart employees and that she was not free to leave. Ms. McNeely then requested that Ms. Dolph come up to the office, but she refused and asked to see the manager. It turned out that Ms. McNeely was in error and that Ms. Dolph's sister—not Ms. Dolph—had been apprehended in McGehee for shoplifting.

Ms. Dolph sued Wal-Mart for slander and was awarded $25,000. Wal-Mart has appealed because Ms. Dolph did not produce anyone at the trial who could testify of hearing the "hollered" exchange. Why is this evidence important? Should Wal-Mart win the appeal? [*Wal-Mart Stores, Inc.* v. *Dolph*, 825 S.W.2d 810 (Ark. 1992).]

4. A woman used the women's restroom at a roller-skating rink run by Abate. She discovered that the restroom had see-through panels in the ceiling that allowed observation of those in the restroom. Is this an invasion of privacy? [*Harkey* v. *Abate*, 346 N.W.2d 74 (Mich. 1983).]

5. Mr. Wesson is a plumbing subcontractor who works for Shalimar Development. He and Shalimar have had many disagreements, and Shalimar has decided not to use Mr. Wesson on any future projects. When Mr. Wesson discovered this decision, he drove to the various job sites of Shalimar and told other subcontractors that Shalimar was insolvent, difficult to work with, and generally slow in paying. Several of the subcontractors have asked for meetings with Shalimar's president to discuss termination of work. List any possible torts committed by Mr. Wesson.

6. Mae Tom went to Kresge's store on November 15, 1977, slipped, and fell on a clear substance on the floor. No one ever determined what the substance was, but Kresge's did sell soft drinks in the store, and customers could walk around with their drinks. Mae Tom wishes to recover for her injuries. Can she do so? [*Tom* v. *S.S. Kresge Co., Inc.*, 633 P.2d 439 (Ariz. App. 1981).]

7. Peoples Bank and Trust Company is the conservator of the estate of Nellie Mitchell, a 96-year-old resident of Mountain Home, Arkansas, who has operated a newsstand on the town square since 1963. Before that, she delivered newspapers on a paper route and, according to the evidence, still makes deliveries to certain "downtown" business establishments and select customers.

It appears that Nellie, as she is known to almost everyone in this small Ozark Mountain town, is a town "landmark" or "treasure." She has cared for herself and raised a family as a single parent for all these years on what must have been the meager earnings of a "paper girl."

Her newspaper stand was in a short, dead-end alley between two commercial buildings on the town square. She received permission to put a roof over the alley, and this newsstand was her sole means of support. Her tenacity was evident at trial when she was asked whether she lived with her adult daughter, Betty. She replied, "No, Betty lives with me."

In the October 2, 1990, edition of the *Sun*, published by Globe International, Inc., there was a photograph of Nellie with a story entitled:

SPECIAL DELIVERY

World's oldest newspaper carrier, 101, quits because she's pregnant! I guess walking all those miles kept me young.

The "story" purports to be about a "paper-gal Audrey Wiles" in Stirling, Australia, who had been delivering papers for 94 years. Readers are told that Miss Wiles became pregnant by "Will," a "reclusive millionaire" she met on her newspaper route. "I used to put Will's paper in the door when it rained, and one thing just kind of led to another."

In words that could certainly have described Nellie Mitchell, the article, which was in the form and style of a factual newspaper account, in part said:

"[S]he's become like a city landmark because nearly everyone at one time or another has seen her trudging down the road with a large stack of papers under her arm."

The photograph used in the October 2 edition of the *Sun*, of Nellie apparently "trudging down the road with a large stack of papers under her arm," had been used by the defendant in a reasonably factual and accurate article about Nellie published in another of the defendant's publications, the *Examiner* in 1980.

Peoples Bank, on behalf of Nellie, filed suit against Globe for invasion of privacy and intentional infliction of emotional distress. The jury awarded Nellie $650,000 in compensatory damages and $850,000 in punitive damages. Globe asked the court to reverse the verdict or, in the alternative, reduce the damages. Have any torts been committed? Describe them. [*Peoples Bank & Trust Co.* v. *Globe Int'l*, Inc. 786 F. Supp. 791 (W.D. Ark. 1992).]

8. Benjamin VonBehren, then two-years old, and his mother paid a visit to their neighbors, Edward and Diane Bradley. Mr. and Mrs. Bradley were not home, but Benjamin and his mother were invited into the Bradley home by the Bradley's sixteen-year old daughter, who was at home babysitting her nine-year old brother, Andy. Andy and Benjamin went to the backyard to play with the Bradley's dog, a labrador retriever. The Bradley's dog had a bird in its mouth, which was disturbing to Benjamin. Benjamin hit the dog and pulled its ears and tail to get it to spit out the bird. The dog instead bit Benjamin, who had severe lacerations on his face.

The VonBehrens sued the Bradleys, and the trial court dismissed the case because Benjamin had provoked the dog. The VonBehrens have appealed. What should the appellate court do? Should the Bradleys be held liable? [*VonBehren* v. *Bradley*, 640 N.E.2d 664 (Ill. 1994).]

9. KSL Recreation Corp. and Boca Partnership signed an agreement on February 23, 1994 to form a joint venture to renovate and expand the 356-acre Boca Raton Hotel & Club resort in Palm Beach County, Florida. The joint venture did not go through because KSL demanded an additional $3.5 million in expenses and fees. Boca then negotiated a loan with Olympus Real Estate Corporation. Boca was about to close on the financing of the renovation with Olympus when KSL faxed a copy of a lawsuit against Boca to Olympus. The lawsuit was not yet filed. Boca had a litigation clause in its agreement with Olympus and it was required to pay more fees and a higher interest rate. Did KSL interfere with Boca's contract with Olympus?

10. Suppose that a maintenance man hired by the manager of an apartment complex sexually assaults a tenant one morning. The maintenance man was able to gain access to his victim's apartment through use of his pass key. Would the apartment owner be liable to the tenant for her damages? What additional information would help her case?

NOTE

1 Paul M. Barrett, "Court May Have to Lead Product-Liability Reform," *The Wall Street Journal*, October 7, 1988, p. B6.

Judgment

Stella Liebeck, 81, suffered third-degree burns when coffee spilled on her lap inside her car after she went through a McDonald's drive-through in Albuquerque, New Mexico. The temperature of the coffee, according to corporate guidelines, is 180 to 190 degrees. Mrs. Liebeck has sued McDonald's to recover for her injuries resulting from the coffee spill.

Should Mrs. Liebeck be allowed to recover? What theories could she use to recover?

Jack Clark ordered a chicken enchilada at the Mexicali Rose restaurant. There was a one-inch-long chicken bone in the enchilada, and Mr. Clark received severe throat injuries when he swallowed and choked on the bone. Mr. Clark wants to know if he has any right to recover from Mexicali Rose.

C H A P T E R 1 0

Product Advertising and Liability

The first jury verdict over $1,000,000 in a product liability suit occurred in 1962. Today there are more than 400 multimillion-dollar verdicts a year. Business payments to claimants are estimated to be $100 billion a year. In 1994, the median award in product liability cases was $509,000.

Product liability cases today are common, the judgments and settlements are large, and insurance coverage costs are now a major expense to businesses. Buyers seem increasingly willing to have matters concerning defective products settled in court.

Product liability is a unique area of law. It has social roots in that it attempts to lessen the burden of losses by requiring a manufacturer or manufacturer's insurer to pay for a defective product. It also has contract roots in that if a product does not do what it is supposed to do, a breach of contract has occurred. It also has its roots in tort law insofar as there is an injury resulting from someone else's carelessness. In these senses, product liability is a combination of contract law, tort law, and social responsibility.

This chapter answers the following questions: How did product liability law develop? What are the contract theories for recovery? What is required for a tort-based recovery on a defective product? How does advertising create liability for a business? What is strict tort liability for products? What reforms are proposed for cutting back liability? Are international product liability standards different?

> *Advertising may be described as the science of arresting the human intelligence long enough to get money.*
>
> **Edmund Leach**

DEVELOPMENT OF PRODUCT LIABILITY

For some time, courts followed the principle of **caveat emptor**, which means "let the buyer beware." This theory meant that sellers were not liable for defects in their products and that it was the buyer's responsibility to be on the alert for defects and take the appropriate precautions.

The doctrine of caveat emptor was eliminated in *Henningsen* v. *Bloomfield Motors, Inc.*, 161 A.2d 69 (N.J. 1960). In that case, a woman who was injured while driving an auto purchased by her husband was permitted to recover without any finding of negligence on the part of the manufacturer.

Following the *Henningsen* decision, the *Restatement Second of Torts* adopted its now famous Section 402A on strict tort liability (discussed later in this chapter). With this adoption, the area of product liability had gone full swing from no liability (caveat emptor) to an almost per se standard of liability for defective products.

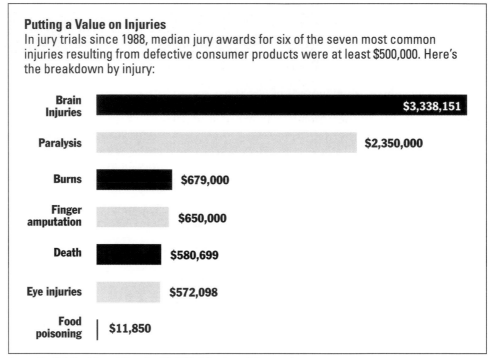

Putting a Value on Injuries
In jury trials since 1988, median jury awards for six of the seven most common injuries resulting from defective consumer products were at least $500,000. Here's the breakdown by injury:

Brain Injuries	$3,338,151
Paralysis	$2,350,000
Burns	$679,000
Finger amputation	$650,000
Death	$580,699
Eye injuries	$572,098
Food poisoning	$11,850

Source: *The Wall Street Journal*, November 20, 1995. © Dow Jones & Company, Inc.

Exhibit 10.1
The Types of Product Liability Injuries and Recovery Amounts

ADVERTISING AS A CONTRACT BASIS FOR PRODUCT LIABILITY

Express Warranties

An **express** warranty as provided in the Uniform Commercial Code (UCC) is an express promise by the seller as to the quality, abilities, or performance of a product

Review UCC § 2-313:
http://www.law.
cornell.edu/ucc/2/
2%2d313%2ehtml

Business Planning Tip

Always review the language used in ads for products. Determine whether express warranties are being made. Make sure that warranties, statements of fact, and promises of performance are accurate. Remember that samples are also warranties.

(UCC § 2-313). The seller need not use the words *promise* or *guarantee* to make an express warranty. Such a warranty is made when a seller uses a sample or model or provides a description of the goods. Promises of how the goods will perform are also express warranties. Examples of express warranties are: "These goods are 100 percent wool"; "This tire cannot be punctured"; "These jeans will not shrink."

Any statements made by the seller to the buyer before the sale is made that are part of the basis of the sale or bargain are express warranties. Opinions, however, are not considered a basis for transactions and are therefore not express warranties. For example, the statement "These jeans are the best on the market" is sales-puffing and not an express warranty. Exhibit 10.2 gives some examples of statements of fact versus opinions.

Statement	Fact	Opinion
"This car gets twenty miles per gallon."	x	
"This car gets great gas mileage."		x
"These goods are 100 percent wool."	x	
"This is the finest wool around."		x
"This truck has never been in an accident."	x	
"This truck is solid."		x
"This mace stops assailants in their tracks."	x	
"This mace is very effective."		x
"This makeup is hypoallergenic."	x	
"This makeup is good for your skin."		x
"This ink will not stain clothes."	x	
"This ink is safe to use."		x
"This computer is IBM-compatible."	x	
"This computer is as good as any IBM."		x
"This watch is waterproof."	x	
"This watch is durable."		x

Exhibit 10.2
Statements of Fact versus Opinion

CONSIDER... **10.1** John R. Klages was employed as a night auditor at Conley's Motel on Route 8 in Hampton Township. He worked from 11 P.M. until 7 A.M., five days a week. On March 30, 1968, at approximately 1:30 A.M., two individuals entered the motel and announced, "This is a stickup. Open the safe." Mr. Klages indicated that he was unable to open the safe because he did not know the combination. One of the individuals then pointed a gun at his head and pulled the trigger. Fortunately for Mr. Klages, the gun was a starter pistol and he was not seriously injured.

Continued

The next day Mr. Klages and a fellow employee, Bob McVay, decided that they needed something to protect themselves against the possibility of future holdups. After reading an article concerning the effects of mace, Mr. McVay suggested that they consider using mace for their protection and secured from the Mark1 Supply Company four leaflets describing certain mace weapons.

After reading and discussing the literature with their employer, Mr. McVay purchased an MK-II mace weapon from Mark1 Supply Company, which described the mace as follows:

Rapidly vaporizes on face of assailant effecting instantaneous incapacitation. . . .*It will* instantly stop and subdue *entire groups*. . . instantly stops assailants in their tracks. . . . *[A]n attacker is* subdued instantly, *for a period of 15 to 20 minutes. . . . Time Magazine stated the Chemical Mace is "for police the first, if not the final, answer to a nationwide need—a weapon that* disables as effectively *as a gun and yet does no permanent injury." . . . The effectiveness is the result of a unique,* incapacitating formulation (*patent pending*), *projected in a shotgun-like pattern of heavy liquid droplets that, upon contact with the face, cause extreme tearing, and a* stunned, *winded condition, often accompanied by dizziness and apathy.*

At approximately 1:40 A.M. on September 22, 1968, while Mr. Klages was on duty, two unknown individuals entered the motel office, requested a room, and announced a stickup. One of the intruders took out a gun and directed Mr. Klages to open the safe. Using the cash register as a shield, Mr. Klages squirted the mace, hitting the intruder "right beside the nose." Mr. Klages immediately ducked below the register, but the intruder followed him down and shot him in the head. The intruders immediately departed, and Mr. Klages called the police. The bullet wound caused complete loss of sight in Mr. Klages's right eye. He claims a breach of an express warranty. Is he right? [*Klages* v. *General Ordnance Equipment Corp.*, 19 UCC Rep. Serv. (Callaghan) 22 (Pa. 1976).]

CONSIDER . . . **10.2** Custom Concepts, Inc., was retained by McDonald's to develop a Magic Crystal Ball toy for McDonald's Happy Meals. The Magic Crystal Ball was a plastic ball enclosing a paper cube. A child could ask the ball a question and then turn the cube upside down, and an answer would appear on one of the faces of the cube.

Custom entered into a contract with Plastic Products Company, Inc., to produce the balls. Their contract was for the sale of 1,785,500 crystal balls "per U.S. Testing Approved prototype." The prototype, as developed by Custom, met McDonald's safety standards. However, when the first crystal balls arrived, they failed the safety tests. Custom ended its contract with Plastic Products on the grounds that an express warranty had been breached. Is Custom correct in its analysis? [*Beck* v. *Plastic Products Co., Inc.*, 412 N.W.2d 315 (Minn. 1987).]

Federal Regulation of Warranties and Advertising

Express warranties are advertisements for goods. Advertising is crucial to both business success and consumers. Because accurate advertising is necessary to ensure full information to support a competitive environment, it is important that advertising be policed for its fairness and accuracy.

C O N S I D E R . . . **10.3** The following is ad copy for Firestone tires:

When you buy a Firestone tire—no matter how much or how little you pay—you get a safe tire.

Firestone tires are custom-built one by one. By skilled craftsmen. And they're personally inspected for an extra margin of safety. If these tires don't pass all of the exacting Firestone inspections, they don't get out.

Every new Firestone design goes through rugged tests of safety and strength far exceeding any driving condition you'll ever encounter. We prove them in our test lab. On our test track. And in rigorous day-to-day driving conditions. All Firestone tires meet or exceed the new Federal Government testing requirements. (They have for some time.)

Firestone—The Safe Tire. At 60,000 Firestone Safe Tire Centers. At no more cost than ordinary tires.

Does Firestone make any express warranties in this ad? [*Firestone Tire & Rubber Co.* v. *FTC*, 481 F.2d 246 (6th Cir. 1973).]

Visit the Federal Trade Commission:
http://www.ftc.gov/
Review the Federal Trade Commission Act and the Wheeler-Lea Act: http://www.law.cornell.edu/uscode/15/ch2.html#s45

In 1914 Congress passed the **Federal Trade Commission Act**, which authorized the **Federal Trade Commission (FTC)** to prevent "unfair and deceptive trade practices." Initially the FTC used its power to regulate all forms of deceptive advertising. However, the Supreme Court, in interpreting the 1914 act, severely restricted the FTC to the regulation of false advertising that adversely affected competition. In reaction to this Court ruling, Congress passed the **Wheeler-Lea Act** of 1938, giving the FTC the power to regulate "unfair and deceptive acts or practices" whenever the public is being deceived regardless of any effects on competition.

With the Wheeler-Lea Act, the FTC has expanded its authority over the years. Unsubstantiated or ambiguous advertising claims have been challenged, and deceptive techniques in TV ads have also been reviewed by the FTC. The only restriction the FTC has experienced since the Wheeler-Lea Act was passed came after attempts by the agency to regulate the content and number of ads on children's television programming. In that case, the FTC ran into powerful opposition by broadcaster, advertising, and producer groups. These groups brought court actions in an attempt to halt the proceedings and at one point disqualified the FTC chairman from the proceedings. This struggle ended with congressional passage of the **FTC Improvements Act of 1980**. The act actually terminated the FTC's authority in the children's TV case and put general restrictions on the FTC. In 1990 some children's TV regulations were passed.

E T H I C A L   I S S U E S

10.1 In the children's TV case, the FTC was stopped by strong congressional lobbying on the part of the affected businesses. Does this put business above the law? Is this right to turn to Congress intended as a protection? Could the powers of administrative agencies be curtailed by such action? Should the businesses involved in the children's TV case attempt some form of self-regulation in lieu of formal regulation? Is business recognition of a societal harm important? Should business propose responses to these social movements?

CONTENT CONTROL AND ACCURACY

The FTC has regulated the accuracy of ads in several ways. First, the FTC has challenged certain types of price claims. If an ad announces "50% off," the prices must actually be half the original prices; the original price cannot be inflated to cover the markdown. If an ad quotes a "normal" price, that price must reflect what most sellers in the area are charging.

The FTC has also challenged the accuracy of ads. Claims that goods are "100% wool" are not only the basis for express warranty recovery but are also the basis for an FTC challenge. Also, the FTC challenges advertising methods. For example, using "marbles" in soup to make it look thicker as it pours is deceptive. The FTC has used its powers to ensure that ads accurately depict the product as it exists.

FTC CONTROL OF PERFORMANCE CLAIMS

Any claims of the ability or efficacy of a product must be supportable. If a sunburn relief product claims to "anesthetize nerves," the advertiser must be able to prove that claim. The Firestone ad in Consider 10.3 was held to be deceptive for its excessive claims.

Where an advertising claim cannot be substantiated, the FTC has used **corrective advertising** as a remedy. Corrective advertising requires a seller to correct the unsubstantiated claims made in previous ads. The following case involves an issue of corrective advertising.

Warner-Lambert Co. v. FTC
562 F.2d 749 (D.C. Cir. 1977)

DOES LISTERINE PREVENT COLDS?

FACTS
Listerine, a product of the Warner-Lambert Corporation, has been on the market since 1879 and has been represented through advertising to be beneficial for colds, cold symptoms, and sore throats. After a 1972 complaint about Warner-Lambert advertising for Listerine, the FTC held four months of hearings on the ad issues and then ordered Warner-Lambert (petitioner) to do the following:

1. Cease and desist representing that Listerine will cure colds or sore throats, prevent colds or sore throats, or that users of Listerine will have fewer colds than nonusers;

2. Cease and desist representing that Listerine is a treatment for, or will lessen the severity of, colds or sore throats; that it will have any significant beneficial effect on the symptoms of sore throats or any beneficial effect on symptoms of

colds; or that the ability of Listerine to kill germs is of medical significance in the treatment of colds or sore throats or their symptoms;

3. Cease and desist disseminating any advertisement for Listerine unless it is clearly and conspicuously disclosed in each advertisement, in the exact language below, that "Contrary to prior advertising, Listerine will not help prevent colds or sore throats or lessen their severity." This requirement extends only to the next 10 million dollars of Listerine advertising.

Warner-Lambert appealed the order.

JUDICIAL OPINION
WRIGHT, Circuit Judge
The first issue on appeal is whether the Commission's conclusion that Listerine is not beneficial for colds or sore throats is supported by the evidence.

Continued

First, the Commission found that the ingredients of Listerine are not present in sufficient quantities to have any therapeutic effect.

Second, the Commission found that in the process of gargling it is impossible for Listerine to reach critical areas of the body in medically significant concentration.

Third, the Commission found that even if significant quantities of the active ingredients of Listerine were to reach critical sites where cold viruses enter and infect the body, they could not interfere with the activities of the virus because they could not penetrate the tissue cells.

. . . [T]he Commission found that the ability of Listerine to kill germs by millions on contact is of no medical significance in the treatment of colds or sore throats.

. . . [T]he Commission found that Listerine has no significant beneficial effect on the symptoms of sore throat. The Commission recognized that gargling with Listerine could provide temporary relief from a sore throat by removing accumulated debris irritating the throat. But this type of relief can also be obtained by gargling with salt water or even warm water.

Petitioner contends that even if its advertising claims in the past were false, the portion of the Commission's order requiring "corrective advertising" exceeds the Commission's statutory power. The Commission's position is that the affirmative disclosure that Listerine will not prevent colds or lessen their severity is absolutely necessary to give effect to the prospective cease and desist order; a hundred years of false cold claims have built up a large reservoir of erroneous consumer belief that would persist, unless corrected, long after petitioner ceased making the claims.

If the Commission is to attain the objectives Congress envisioned, it cannot be required to confine its road block to the narrow lane the transgressor has traveled; it must be allowed effectively to close all roads to the prohibited goal, so that its order may not be bypassed with impunity.

We turn next to the specific disclosure required: "Contrary to prior advertising, Listerine

will not help prevent colds or sore throats or lessen their severity." Petitioner is ordered to include this statement in every future advertisement for Listerine for a defined period. In printed advertisements it must be displayed in type size at least as large as that in which the principal portion of the text of the advertisement appears and it must be separated from the text so that it can be readily noticed. In television commercials the disclosure must be presented simultaneously in both audio and visual portions. During the audio portion of the disclosure in television and radio advertisements, no other sounds, including music, may occur.

These specifications are well calculated to assure that the disclosure will reach the public. It will necessarily attract the notice of readers, viewers and listeners, and be plainly conveyed. Given these safeguards, we believe the preamble "Contrary to prior advertising" is not necessary. It can serve only two purposes: either to attract attention that a correction follows or to humiliate the advertiser. The Commission claims only the first purpose for it, and this we think is obviated by other terms of the order. The second purpose, if it were intended, might be called for in an egregious case of deliberate deception, but this is not one. While we do not decide whether petitioner proffered its cold claims in good faith or bad, the record compiled could support a finding of good faith. On these facts, the confessional preamble to the disclosure is not warranted.

Accordingly, the order, as modified, is affirmed.

CASE QUESTIONS

1. What claims does the FTC make about Listerine?
2. What proposals for corrective advertising are made in the order?
3. What modifications in the order does the court make?
4. What happens to the preamble, "Contrary to prior advertising"?
5. Is Listerine still required to make disclosures in future ads? For how long?

On January 28, 1986, NASA launched the space shuttle *Challenger* in 30°F weather. Seventy-four seconds into the launch, the low temperature caused the O-ring seals on the *Challenger*'s booster rockets to fail. The *Challenger* exploded, killing all seven persons aboard (six astronauts and Ms. Christa McAuliffe, a school teacher chosen and trained for the mission).

The Space Shuttle *Challenger* Explosion, Engineers, and O-Rings

Morton Thiokol was the NASA subcontractor responsible for the booster rocket assembly. Roger Boisjoly was an engineer at Morton Thiokol who had raised concerns about the O-rings. Boisjoly had given a presentation on the O-ring issue at a conference, but Thiokol took no action. Boisjoly noted the problems in his activity report and finally, in July 1985, wrote a confidential memo to R. K. Lund, Thiokol's vice president for engineering. Excerpts appear below:

This letter is written to insure that management is fully aware of the seriousness of the current O-ring erosion problem . . . The mistakenly accepted position on the joint problem was to fly without fear of failure. . . [This position] is now drastically changed as a result of the SRM [shuttle recovery mission] 16A nozzle joint erosion which eroded a secondary O-ring with the primary O-ring never sealing. If the same scenario should occur in a field joint (and it could), then it is a jump ball as to the success or failure of the joint . . . The result would be a catastrophe of the highest order—loss of human life. . .

It is my honest and real fear that if we do not take immediate action to dedicate a team to solve the problem, with the field joint having the number one priority, then we stand in jeopardy of losing a flight along with all the launch pad facilities.

Space Shuttle
Challenger

In October of 1985, Boisjoly presented the O-ring issue at a conference of the Society of Automotive Engineers and requested suggestions for resolution.

On January 27, 1986, the day before the launch, Boisjoly attempted to halt the launch. However, four Thiokol managers, including Lund, voted unanimously to recommend the launch. One manager urged Lund to "take off his engineering hat and put on his management hat." The managers then developed the following revised recommendations. Engineers were excluded from the development of these findings and the final launch decision.

* Calculations show that SRM-25 [the designation for the <u>Challenger</u>'s January 28 flight] O-rings will be 20° colder than SRM-15 O-rings
* Temperature data not conclusive on predicting primary O-ring blow-by
* Engineering assessment is that:

    —Colder O-rings will have increased effective durometer [that is, they will be harder]

```
—"Harder" O-rings will take longer to seat
  More gas may pass primary [SRM-25] O-ring before the primary
  seal seats (relative to SRM-15)
—If the primary seal does not seat, the secondary seal will seat
  Pressure will get to secondary seal before the metal parts rotate
  O-ring pressure leak check places secondary seal in outboard
  position which minimizes sealing time
—MTI recommends STS-51L launch proceed on 28 January 1986
  SRM-25 will not be significantly different from SRM-15
```

After the decision was made, Boisjoly returned to his office and wrote in his journal:

```
    I sincerely hope this launch does not result in a catastrophe.
I personally do not agree with some of the statements made in Joe
Kilminster's [Kilminster was one of the four Thiokol managers who voted to rec-
ommend the launch] written summary stating that SRM-25 is okay to fly.
```

The subsequent investigation by the presidential commission placed the blame for the faulty O-rings squarely with Thiokol. Charles S. Locke, Thiokol's CEO, maintained, "I take the position that we never agreed to the launch at the temperature at the time of the launch. The *Challenger* incident resulted more from human error than mechanical error. The decision to launch should have been referred to headquarters. If we'd been consulted here, we'd never have given clearance, because the temperature was not within the contracted specs."

Boisjoly testified before the presidential panel regarding his opposition to the launch and the decision of his managers (who were also engineers) to override his recommendation. Boisjoly, who took medical leave for post-traumatic stress disorder, has left Thiokol, but he does receive disability pay from the company. Currently, Mr. Boisjoly operates a consulting firm in Mesa, Arizona. He speaks frequently on business ethics to professional organizations and companies.

In May 1986, then-CEO Locke stated, in an interview with *The Wall Street Journal,* "This shuttle thing will cost us this year 10¢ a share." Locke later protested that his statement was taken out of context.

Roger Boisjoly offers the following advice on whistle-blowing:

a. *You owe your organization an opportunity to respond. Speak to them first VERBALLY. Memos are not appropriate for the first step.*
b. *Gather collegial support for your position. If you cannot get the support then make sure you are correct.*
c. *Then spell out the problem in a letter.*

Source: Adapted by permission from Marianne M. Jennings; *Case Studies in Business Ethics,* 2d ed. © 1995 by West Publishing Company. All rights reserved.

Issues
1. Do you think Mr. Boisjoly feels some responsibility for the *Challenger* accident?
2. Would you have done anything differently?
3. What can companies do to be certain they listen to a Roger Boisjoly?

FTC CONTROL OF CELEBRITY ENDORSEMENTS

In the past 10 years, the FTC has entered a new aspect of ad content control—namely, the use of **celebrity endorsements** for products. At the time the FTC became involved, its director of consumer protection stated:

The effectiveness of having a product touted by a well-known movie star or sports figure is apparent from the increasing use of celebrity endorsements in advertising. A sales pitch by a celebrity may be more believable than the same message delivered by an unknown spokesperson. The endorsement can be an important part of sales strategy, and is often quite handsomely rewarded. The endorser may profit from a false advertisement just as much as the manufacturer, and thus it is not unreasonable to obligate him to ascertain the truthfulness of the claims he is being paid to make.[1]

With a celebrity endorsement, the FTC requires several steps. First, as the quote indicates, the celebrity must ascertain the truth of the ad claims. Second, the celebrity cannot make any claims about product use unless the celebrity has actually used and experienced the product. Finally, if any claims are being made that are not the celebrity's, the source of the information must be disclosed as part of the ad.

Business Planning Tip

Use caution in ad language and comparisons. The biggest companies are in litigation over ads:

- PepsiCo filed suit against Procter & Gamble claiming P&G portrayed its Pringles Right Crisps potato chips as better nutritionally than Frito-Lay chips. Frito-Lay seeks corrective ads, damages and side-by-side accurate comparisons.
- Scott Paper of Canada sued Procter & Gamble after P&G launched its first Bounty paper towel ad campaign in Canada using its famous "Bounty: the quicker-picker-upper." Scott maintains the slogan is deceptive about absorption power.
- SmithKline Beecham and Johnson & Johnson*Merck have sued each other over antacid claims for their Tagamet HB and Pepcid AC products.

FTC CONTROL OF BAIT AND SWITCH

One of the better-known FTC ad regulations prohibits the use of **bait and switch**, which is a sales tactic in which a cheaper product than the one in stock is advertised to get customers into a store. The seller has no intention of selling the product and in some cases might not even have the product in stock. But the ad is used as "bait" to get the customers in and present them with a "better," more expensive product. Such ad tactics are considered deceptive and subject to FTC remedy.

FTC CONTROL OF PRODUCT COMPARISONS

Visit the Better Business Bureau: http://www.bbb.org/bbb/

Another aspect of active enforcement by the FTC is in the area of product comparisons. The FTC permits and even welcomes comparisons of products, but such comparisons must be accurate. Results of surveys must be supportable, and product preference tests must be done fairly. In the past few years, the FTC has taken a laissez-faire approach in ad regulation. Other agencies, such as state attorneys' general offices, the Better Business Bureau, and private companies and individuals, have undertaken public and private enforcement of deceptive ad claims.

A 1989 change in the federal trademark law has increased the amount of litigation over comparative ads. Under the law as it existed before, a company could be held liable only for misrepresentations regarding its own products. Now, companies can be held liable for misrepresentations regarding other products. Additional changes in the law make litigation over comparative ads somewhat more rewarding because plaintiffs will be able to recover treble damages, the defendant company's profits, and, in some cases, attorney fees. Suits pending under the revised law include an action by MCI against AT&T for claims that AT&T is cheaper than MCI and a suit by Gillette against Wilkinson for claims that men preferred Wilkinson's Ultra Glide razor to Gillette's Ultra Plus.

FTC REMEDIES

The FTC has a wide range of remedies available in the event of deceptive advertising. Corrective ads can be mandated. The FTC can also obtain injunctions to prevent the running of deceptive ads. Companies and endorsers can be required to reimburse purchasers misled by ads.

One of the most frequently used FTC remedies is the consent decree. A **consent decree** is a negotiated settlement between the FTC and the advertiser. It is the equivalent of a no-contest plea. The FTC and the advertiser agree to remedies, and the case is disposed of through the decree without further action.

Business Planning Tip

Checklist for ads:
1. Did legal counsel review the ads?
2. Do product designers know the claims made in ads? Do they agree?
3. Are pictures and samples accurate?
4. If comparisons are made to other products, are the claims verifiable? Is the other product depicted fairly and accurately?
5. Can all claims be verified factually?

AD REGULATION BY THE FDA

The Food and Drug Administration (FDA) also has authority over some forms of advertising. For example, the FDA has control over direct advertising to the public of prescription medications. Products such as Retin A have had direct ads and news releases subject to FDA regulation. For example, in the case of Retin A, the FDA warned Ortho, its manufacturer, that Retin A had been approved as an anti-acne cream, not as an anti-aging cream, and that it could not be advertised to the public as such.

When the 1992 hearings on the safety of silicone breast implants were held, Dow Corning, a manufacturer of the implants, established a telephone information hot line for implant users. The FDA issued a warning to Dow about the accuracy of the information it was disseminating through the hot line.

Visit the Food and Drug Administration:
http://www.fda.gov/

ETHICAL ISSUES

10.2 Ortho sponsored research on the anti-aging effects of Retin A. For example, the University of Pennsylvania Medical School, which received 3 percent of the royalties on sales from Retin A, released a study concluding that Retin A was an age combatant. Other physicians accepted honoraria to hold or participate in symposia on the anti-aging effects of Retin A. Is there a conflict of interest in these forms of advertising?

FOR THE MANAGER'S DESK

UNRESTRAINED PROMOTION

The Ethics of Promoting Potentially Harmful Products

To understand the significance of the "World Health Organization Code of Marketing for Breastmilk Substitutes," it is important to understand what occurred before the Code's adoption in 1981 and, indeed, before the controversy began in the early 1970s. As early as the 1930s, physicians working in tropical environments recognized that bottle feeding of infants posed a risk of disease to the infant. Sanitation and refrigeration are not generally available to the population in many such countries. Water supplies are unpurified, thereby increasing the probability that a formula mixed with local water will produce diarrhea and disease in the bottlefed child. Poverty encourages the over-dilution of powdered formula, thereby reducing the amount of nutrition the child receives from each bottle. Once a mother's ability to breast-feed "lets down," the baby must be fed in an alternative way. If the mother is too poor to afford formula, which is an expensive product, there is a temptation and need to place other products in the baby bottle. These products may

range from powdered whole milk (which is unsatisfactory for a baby's digestive system) to white powders such as corn starch.

By the late 1960s, medical authorities from the developing world were reporting increased bottle feeding, a decline in breast feeding, and a dramatic increase in the number of malnourished and sick babies being brought to hospi-

tals and clinics too late for a "cure." Some pediatricians and experts in tropical medicine were calling bottle feeding a major public health problem in the developing world. Their professional concern was for the babies, but their anger was directed at the infant formula companies whose promotional activities were encouraging mothers of all economic and social strata to bottle-feed.

Exacerbating the problems confronting the mother in a risky environment were the promotional efforts of the infant formula companies. Promotion of bottle feeding

and infant formula products was rampant and unchecked before 1970. No organized complaints about commercial promotion and sale had been raised, and the industry operated in carte blanche and caveat emptor fashion. Mass media promotion was frequent and intense, featuring billboards, radio jingles, and other devices. To further persuade mothers, the companies promoted their products through posters, baby books, and samples distributed through the health care system itself. The advertising images of robust, smiling children contrasted sharply with the reality of malnourished babies. The advertising created an idealized image of what infants should look like and a clear concept of how that ideal could be achieved by even the most destitute of families. By making these images visible with posters in health clinics and hospitals, companies also implied the endorsement of the health profession for their products and their technology.

The most insidious commercial practice involved "milk nurses." These were women employed by the companies on a sales commission basis. They dressed in nurses' uniforms and literally prowled the halls of maternity wards encouraging mothers of newborns to allow

Continued

those babies to be fed with formula. A commitment from the mother started the baby on the formula path which, if not quickly reversed, resulted in the mother having a lactation "let down" that made it impossible for her to breast-feed. When this occurred, the baby was ef-

fectively "hooked" on bottle feeding, the industry had a new customer, and the milk nurse had another sales commission.

Discussion Questions
1. What types of marketing techniques were used?
2. Would any of the tech-

niques used be a basis for recovery under any of the theories discussed earlier in the chapter?
3. What ethical observations can be made about the foreign operations of these infant formula companies?

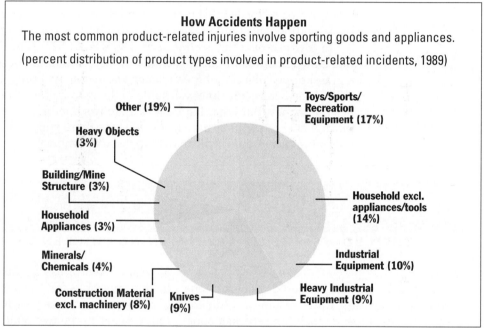

Exhibit 10.3
Types of Product-Related Accidents

PROFESSIONAL ADS

Most states have limitations on the types of ads professionals (such as doctors, lawyers, dentists, and accountants) can use in reaching the public. At one time, states had complete bans on ads by professionals. However, the U.S. Supreme Court held such bans to be too restrictive and violative of First Amendment protections on commercial speech. Restrictions may include requirements on fee disclosures or caveats on distinctions in individual cases and needs. The extent and validity of the restrictions continue to be refined through judicial application of First Amendment rights.

CONTRACT PRODUCT LIABILITY THEORIES: IMPLIED WARRANTIES

The UCC's Article II governs contracts for the sale of goods and includes several provisions for implied warranties. The requirements for each of the implied, in addition to coverage of express, warranties are discussed in the following sections.

The Implied Warranty of Merchantability

The **implied warranty of merchantability** (UCC § 2-314) is given in every sale of goods by a merchant seller. This warranty is a promise that the goods are fit for their ordinary purposes. The warranty is not given by all sellers, only by merchant sellers. Briefly defined, merchants are those sellers who are engaged in the business of selling the good(s) that are the subject of the contract. The warranty means the goods are of fair or average quality and are fit for ordinary purposes. Under this warranty, basketballs must bounce, food items must be free of foreign objects, and book bindings must hold together. See Exhibit 10.3 (pg. 341) for types of injuries.

In *Metty* v. *Shurfine Central Corp.*, 736 S.W.2d 527 (Mo. 1987), the court found that a breach of the implied warranty of merchantability occurred because part of a grasshopper in a can of green beans was eaten by a pregnant woman who purchased the beans. Shurfine was liable to the woman for resulting complications to her pregnancy. But what happens if there is something natural, such as a cherry pit in a cherry pie, that harms someone? Is there still a breach of warranty? The following case provides an answer to these questions.

Mexicali Rose v. *Superior Court*
16 U.C.C.2d Rep. Serv. (Callaghan) 607 (Cal. 1992)

THEM BONES: THE LIFE-THREATENING CHICKEN ENCHILADA

FACTS

Jack A. Clark (plaintiff) ordered a chicken enchilada at Mexicali Rose restaurant (defendants). Because of a one-inch-long chicken bone in the enchilada, Mr. Clark choked and received throat injuries. He brought suit for breach of implied warranty, negligence, and strict liability. The trial court dismissed the case because the bone was natural and not foreign. The court of appeals affirmed, and Clark appealed.

JUDICIAL OPINION

LUCAS, Chief Justice

On appeal, plaintiff asserts the foreign-natural test draws an arbitrary line of liability, focusing on the substance itself, and unfairly exonerates the restaurateur from all liability simply because the injury-producing substance happens to be "natural" to the food served. Pointing to changes in technology that have occurred during the past

55 years, plaintiff asserts defendants should be held responsible for the failure to remove all bones from its chicken enchiladas because it is today easier to remove bones from food than it was in 1936. Plaintiff contends we should abandon the foreign-natural test and adopt a test developed in other jurisdictions based on the "reasonable expectations" of the customer.

Under the foregoing proposed test, according to plaintiff, defendants could be held (i) liable in negligence for their failure to exercise reasonable care in the preparation of the food, (ii) liable for violating California's statutory implied warranty because a chicken bone in a chicken enchilada renders the latter unfit for human consumption under the implied warranty of merchantability and fitness of California Uniform Commercial Code §§ 2314 and 2315.

The question we address, therefore, is whether a restaurant keeper may be held liable for serving

Continued

food containing substances natural to the product that, when consumed by the patron, cause injury.

In *Mix* v. *Ingersoll Candy Co.*, 6 Cal.2d 674, the plaintiff swallowed a fragment of chicken bone contained in a chicken pot pie he consumed in the defendant's restaurant. *Mix* affirmed the trial court order dismissing the plaintiff's complaint for negligence and breach of implied warranty. We held there could be no liability under either an implied warranty or negligence theory, explaining that the statutory implied warranty of fitness of food does not make the purveyor an insurer, but merely requires that food be reasonably fit for human consumption. Although we conceded that it is frequently a question for the jury to determine whether an injury-producing substance present in food makes the food unfit for consumption, we maintained that a court in appropriate cases may find *as a matter of law* that an alleged harmful substance in food does not make the food defective or unfit for consumption.

More recently, however, courts addressing the foreign-natural distinction have deviated from strict application of *Mix* to conclude that the ultimate issue of liability should not be based on a determination whether the object causing injury was either foreign or natural, but instead should be based on whether the consumer reasonably should have anticipated the natural injury-producing substance in the food.

As adopted in most of the preceding decisions, the "reasonable expectation" test differs from the foreign-natural rule of *Mix* in two important respects. First, whether bones or other injurious substances ought to be anticipated in a particular dish becomes a question for the trier of fact, unless as a matter of law the food was fit for consumption because the substance was natural to the food served. Second, and more important, this reasonable expectation test focuses not on the components of the dish, but on the final item sold to the consumer and the expectations that are engendered by the type of dish and the type of preparation used in making the dish. Thus, courts rejecting the exclusive application of the *Mix* foreign-natural test, which by definition bars a negligence claim, have frequently identified the failure to focus on food *preparation*

and the consumer expectation that is created by processing or by the nature of the dish sold as the principal analytical defect of the *Mix* rule.

Defendants assert that "public policy and good common sense support the *Mix* rule." They contend that allowing a plaintiff to recover even in negligence for an injury caused by a natural substance is unreasonable because, they assert, this would place a burden on all restaurants to remove all bones. Defendants claim the better policy is "to encourage consumers to be careful."

As noted above, we agree with defendants to the extent they reason that a restaurant patron cannot expect a chicken pie to be free of all bones. Such an expectation would be unreasonable and unrealistic to the ordinary consumer and would not conform to either federal or state health and safety standards.

On the other hand, we disagree with defendants that we should continue to preclude a plaintiff from attempting to state a cause of action in negligence when a substance natural to the preparation of the food product has caused injury.

Such a new rule, expanding a restaurateur's potential liability and allowing an action in negligence for injuries caused by both natural and foreign substances in food, corresponds to modern development in tort law. . . .

It is reasonably foreseeable that a sizable bone could cause the unsuspecting patron substantial injury if swallowed. Under these principles, we believe it is a question for the trier of fact to determine whether the presence of the injury-producing substance was caused by the failure of the defendants to exercise reasonable care in the preparation of food, and whether the breach of duty to exercise such care caused the consumer's injury. In so concluding, we emphasize that restaurateurs have available all the traditional defenses to a negligence cause of action, including comparative negligence.

CASE QUESTIONS
1. What happened to Mr. Clark?
2. What is the "foreign-natural" test?
3. What is the "reasonable expectation" test?
4. Which test will California follow?
5. Will Mr. Clark recover for breach of warranty?

C O N S I D E R . . . **10.4** On September 6, 1986, Floyd Simeon, 63, and his son, Edward Simeon, 38, went to the Sweet Pepper Grill, a restaurant at the River Walk in New Orleans. They ordered a dozen and a half raw oysters. Floyd ate six oysters and Edward ate nine or ten. The men had eaten raw oysters before, and these looked and smelled "good."

Two days later, Mr. Simeon began running a fever and complained of pain in his ankle. Several physicians were consulted and it was determined that Mr. Simon was suffering from vibrio vulnificus septicemia, an infection resulting from eating raw oysters with vibrio vulnificus bacteria. As the disease progressed, Mr. Simeon developed severe blisters on his legs and began to lose subcutaneous tissue. Plastic surgeons and other physicians tried to stop the spread of the disease, but they were unsuccessful and Mr. Simeon died on September 23, 1986.

Mrs. Simeon brought a suit against Sweet Pepper Grill for breach of the warranty of merchantability. Should the restaurant be held liable? [*Simeon* v. *Doe*, 618 So. 2d 848 (La. 1993).]

C O N S I D E R . . . **10.5** Mrs. Hubbs, 80, suffered from arthritis and osteoporosis. She purchased "The Clapper," a device designed to turn electrical appliances on by responding to sound, namely, the clapping of hands.

Mrs. Hubbs did not follow the instructions in the product to adjust its sensitivity. As a result of continual hard clapping, Mrs. Hubbs broke her wrists. She has sued the Clapper's manufacturer for breach of the warranty of merchantability. Should she recover? [*Hubbs* v. *Joseph Enterprises*, 604 N.Y.S.2d 292 (1993).]

Judgment   In the chapter's opening "Judgment," the issue of the liability for spilled coffee is raised. In this famous case, the jury originally awarded Mrs. Liebeck $2.8 million in damages. Mrs. Liebeck's attorney, Ken Wagner, said he asked the jury to consider that restaurant chains sell one billion cups of coffee each day with revenues of $1.34 million a day. Mr. Wagner asked for two days of revenue as punitive damages. The award was later reduced to $640,000.

C O N S I D E R . . . **10.6** George Morgan, 58, purchased coffee at a Burger King drive-through. He suffered third-degree burns when the bottom of his coffee cup collapsed, spilling hot coffee over his legs and groin. What is different about Mr. Morgan's accident from Mrs. Liebeck's accident? Are there different liability issues?

The Implied Warranty of Fitness for a Particular Purpose

The **implied warranty of fitness for a particular purpose** (U.S.S. § 2-315) arises when the seller promises a buyer that the goods will be suitable for a use the buyer has proposed. For example, the owner of a nursery makes an implied warranty for a particular purpose when telling a buyer that a weed killer will work in the buyer's rose garden without harming the roses. An exercise enthusiast is

Business Planning Tip

After the two coffee-spill lawsuits, fast food restaurants made the following operational changes:

(1) No hot chocolate sold at drive-throughs; hot chocolate is generally for children and spill risk is high;

(2) Coffee temperatures reduced from 180° to 140°

(3) Drink carrier given with all coffee orders;

(4) Warning signs at window: "coffee is hot, use caution."

given this warranty when the seller recommends a particular shoe as appropriate for aerobics.

The requirements for this warranty are as follows:

1. The seller has skill or judgment in use of the goods.
2. The buyer is relying on that skill or judgment.
3. The seller knew or had reason to know of the buyer's reliance.
4. The seller makes a recommendation for the buyer's use and purpose.

The following case involves an issue of the implied warranty of fitness for a particular purpose.

Rubin v. Marshall Field & Co.
597 N.E.2d 688 (Ill. 1992)

THE EYE MAKEUP REMOVER THAT HAS YOU SEEING RED

FACTS

Cynthia Rubin (plaintiff) went to Marshall Field's department store (one of two defendants) on April 5, 1986. While browsing, she got into a conversation with Julianna Reiner, a sales clerk, and she told Ms. Reiner that she used Vaseline to remove her eye makeup. Ms. Reiner said Vaseline could clog her eye ducts and cause cataracts or other permanent eye damage, and recommended Princess Marcella Borghese Instant Eye Make-Up Remover manufactured by Princess Marcella Borghese, Inc., the other defendant. Ms. Rubin asked if the product was safe. Ms. Reiner showed her the box, which said "recommended for all skin types." Ms. Reiner said, "If it wouldn't be safe for you, it wouldn't say this on the box." Relying on Ms. Reiner's representations, Ms. Rubin purchased the product.

That night she used the product to remove her eye makeup. Her eyelids and the skin around her eyes turned red, became taut and rough, and started to sting. She washed her skin repeatedly and kept a cold washrag on her eyes all night. Two days later, when the burning did not subside, she called an ophthalmologist and went to

see him the next day. He told her that she had contact dermatitis and prescribed an ointment.

A few weeks later, because the burning and roughness of her eyelids persisted, Ms. Rubin decided to see Dr. Katherine Wier, a dermatologist. Dr. Wier prescribed a similar ointment and told Ms. Rubin that the chemical causing the burning would remain in her system for three or four months. The stinging subsided, but Ms. Rubin could not wear eye makeup again regularly until summer of 1987. When she tried to wear makeup again before that, her eyelids turned bright red and began swelling upon removal of the makeup.

Ms. Rubin filed suit for breach of implied warranty of fitness for a particular purpose. The jury found for her awarding her $1,250 in damages and $14,500 in attorney fees; Marshall Field's appealed.

JUDICIAL OPINION

McCORMICK, Justice

Defendants admit that Reiner was an agent for both defendants when she sold plaintiff the product. Reiner testified that she had no

Continued

specific recollection of the transaction, but she never said anything about adverse effects of other products, and she "never use[d] the word [V]aseline, ever."

Dr. Wier testified that eyelid skin and genital skin is the most sensitive skin on the body, and very fair skin, like plaintiff's, is easily irritated. Dr. Wier could say with medical certainty that the makeup remover caused plaintiff's reaction, which was probably a primary irritant reaction compounded by an allergic reaction. She classified plaintiff's reaction as a primary irritant reaction because of the speed with which the reaction occurred. The detergent in the makeup remover was probably the irritant, opening the pores and allowing other chemicals, to which plaintiff was allergic, to penetrate the skin. She believed that some other people whose skin was as fair as plaintiff's would react adversely to the product, and "a few might have a similar disastrous reaction."

On cross-examination, Dr. Wier admitted that the detergent in the eye makeup remover was also used in at least three other products, including baby shampoo. She considered the eye makeup remover fairly safe.

Revlon, Inc., which owns Princess Marcella, manufactured the eye makeup remover. Dr. Earl Brauer, vice-president of medical affairs for Revlon Research, testified that he tested the product plaintiff returned to defendants and found that it included only the proper chemicals with nothing extraneous added. He monitors personal injury complaints for Revlon products, and with more than 50,000 units of the eye makeup remover manufactured since 1978, plaintiff is the first consumer to complain of adverse effects. He said that she must have had an idiosyncratic allergic reaction because the product does not contain any irritants.

Defendants argue that this court should reverse the judgment for plaintiff on the cause of action for breach of implied warranty because plaintiff did not prove that there was any defect in the makeup remover, and because the evidence showed that her reaction to the product was idiosyncratic.

The Uniform Commercial Code, Ill. Rev. Stat. 1985, ch. 26, para. 2-315, provides:

"Where the seller at the time of contracting has reason to know any particular purpose for which the goods are required and that the buyer is relying on the seller's skill or judgment to select or furnish suitable goods, there is unless excluded or modified under the next section, an implied warranty that the goods shall be fit for such purpose."

Therefore, under the statute, plaintiff needed to prove (1) a sale of goods; (2) before the sale the seller had reason to know (a) a particular purpose for which plaintiff bought the goods, and (b) that she was relying on the seller's skill to select goods suitable for that purpose; and (3) the goods were not suitable for that particular purpose. The action is in contract, not tort.

Some cases have added a requirement that plaintiff prove the product was defective. None of these cases makes reference to the UCC. The reasoning of these cases has been criticized. Anderson, in his commentary to the UCC, said:

"It is unfortunate that the warranty law has been so influenced by the tort law. With respect to negligence and strict tort, it is logical to require that there be a defect in the goods. In the case of warranty, it should be sufficient to impose liability that there has been a breach of warranty. In many cases, the breach of warranty consists of the presence of a defect that prevents the goods from being used. In other cases, the breach consists merely of failing to conform to the contract's standard. For example, when the seller delivers a red table instead of the green table required by the contract there is clearly a breach of warranty. Yet the red table was not defective in any intelligent sense of the word merely because it did not conform to the contract. . . .

"The need for defining a defect becomes unnecessary insofar as warranty law is concerned if the matter is approached from the aspect of conformity or nonconformity, rather than in terms of whether there is a defect. The presence of a defect should be regarded as merely evidence of the fact that the goods are in such a condition that some warranty has been broken. If all the circumstances lead to the conclusion that the

Continued

goods do not conform, there is a breach of warranty. It is unnecessary to determine whether what made them not conform is to be labeled a 'defect.'"

Plaintiff's proof of breach of implied warranty was complete when she showed that defendants' agent implicitly warranted that the product would be safe for her skin in particular, and it was not suitable for that particular use. She did not need to prove in addition that the product was defective.

Defendants contend that they proved that plaintiff's reaction was idiosyncratic, and this provides an absolute defense to the implied warranty action.

Plaintiff has presented considerable evidence beyond the sale itself to show that the warranty implied by defendants' acts in this case was far more specific. Plaintiff testified that after defendants' agent, Reiner, recommended the product, she asked whether the product would be safe for her. Reiner pointed to the box, which said "recommended for all skin types," and said "if it wouldn't be safe for you, it wouldn't say this on the box." Reiner could see plaintiff's skin and she knew of plaintiff's concern about the safety of the product for use on that skin. Under these specific factual circumstances, it is reasonable to infer a warranty that the product would not harm plaintiff's skin. While an idiosyncratic reaction may provide a defense in most implied warranty cases, in which the warranty is only that most people could use the product for the general purpose for which it was made, idiosyncrasy is not a defense when the warranty implied by the circumstances of the transaction is more specific, as it was in this case. Therefore, we affirm the finding of liability.

CASE QUESTIONS
1. What warranty is at issue?
2. What distinction does the court make in proving a defect exists in the product?
3. Does Ms. Rubin's idiosyncratic reaction affect her warranty protection?
4. Was the product defective?
5. Why is recovery permitted?

Eliminating Warranty Liability by Disclaimers

Warranties can be eliminated by the use of **disclaimers**. The proper method for disclaiming a warranty depends on the type of warranty. Express warranties, however, cannot be given and then taken back. Basically, an express warranty cannot be disclaimed.

The implied warranty of merchantability and the implied warranty of fitness for a particular purpose can be disclaimed by using a phrase such as "WITH ALL FAULTS," or "AS IS." Either warranty alone can be disclaimed by using the name of the warranty: "There is no warranty of merchantability given" or "There is no implied warranty of fitness for a particular purpose."

Even though the UCC is clear on the language to be used for warranty disclaimers and the process seems to be easy, even the warranty disclaimers are subject to the general UCC constraint of good faith. Unconscionable disclaimers of warranties or waiver of warranties when one party has no bargaining power may not be valid. For example, a disclaimer of liability for personal injury resulting from a breach of the warranty of merchantability would be unconscionable. The following case deals with a warranty disclaimer and whether it is valid.

Business Planning Tip

The statements of employees count in warranty protections. Employees should be cautioned about making absolute guarantees or offering promises of performance or suitability.

Ressallat v. Burglar & Fire Alarms, Inc.
606 N.E.2d 1001 (Ohio 1992)

CONSPICUOUS BURGLARS: DISCLAIMING LIABILITY FOR ALARMS

FACTS

On October 7, 1974, the Ressallats (appellants) purchased a burglar alarm system from Burglar & Fire Alarms, Inc. (BFA). The system was designed to alert the Ressallats, both via warning lights and the sounding of a horn, when an unauthorized person had entered the house. The burglar alarm system was linked with the telephone system so that, simultaneously with the sounding of the alarm, a call was placed through the telephone lines to BFA's "central monitoring station." The Ressallats paid a monthly fee for these services.

On the advice of BFA's salesperson, the Ressallats arranged with the telephone company to have the phone cable, from the pole to the house, buried. However, in 1985 the Ressallats began having problems with the telephone lines. Although General Telephone Company (GTE) resolved the difficulties with the phone lines, the cable was not reburied. Instead, it was strung directly from the pole to the Ressallats' house, suspended just a few feet above the ground. Although Dr. Ressallat contacted GTE several times about reburying the phone cable, the company took no action.

In September 1986, the Ressallats' home was burglarized. The burglar apparently obtained unimpeded access to the house by cutting the exposed telephone wires so as to prevent transmission of the alarm. Inside the house, wires to the burglar alarm horn were severed at the electric service box. Jewelry and coins worth over $100,000 were stolen from the house. The Ressallats' insurance company, Physicians' Insurance Company of Ohio (PICO), reimbursed the Ressallats in the amount of $17,125.37, the maximum payable on their homeowners' policy.

The Ressallats filed suit for breach of warranty. BFA defended on grounds that it has disclaimed warranties beyond the cost of the system. The trial court found the warranty disclaimers to be conspicuous and valid and dismissed the suit.

JUDICIAL OPINION

EVANS, Justice

Under R.C. 1302.29 [UCC Rep Serv § 2-316], unless exclusions or disclaimers of warranty are part of the parties' "bargain in fact," a purchaser of goods in Ohio receives, in addition to any express warranty (which generally only provides for repair or replacement of defective goods), an implied warranty that the goods shall be merchantable and "fit" for their intended purpose. Although courts generally uphold disclaimers of implied warranties between parties who have equal bargaining power, they are reluctant to afford validity to such disclaimers when a purchaser is simply a consumer, rather than a commercial entity. As stated by the Supreme Court:

> *. . . [D]isclaimers of implied warranties . . . must be a part of the parties' bargain in fact. If it is contained in a printed clause which was not conspicuous or brought to the buyer's attention, the seller had no reasonable expectation that the buyer understood that his remedies were being restricted to repair and replacement.*

Further, R.C. 1302.29(B) requires compliance with the following:

> *. . . Subject to division (C) of this section, to exclude or modify the implied warranty of merchantability or any part of it the language must mention merchantability and in case of a writing must be conspicuous, and to exclude or modify any implied warranty of fitness the exclusion must be by a writing and conspicuous. . . .*

The code itself defines "conspicuous," and provides that a determination of conspicuousness is a matter of law for the court to decide.

> *(J) 'Conspicuous.' A term or clause is conspicuous when it is so written that a reasonable person against whom it is to operate ought to have noticed it. A printed heading in capitals (as: NONNEGOTIABLE BILL OF LADING) is conspicuous. Language in the body of a form is 'conspicuous' if it is*

Continued

in larger or other contrasting type or color. . . . Whether a term is 'conspicuous' or not is for decision by the court.

The disclaimer of warranties at issue herein appears on the back page of the sales contract, which was signed on the front by both parties. The disclaimer is buried in the middle of a full page of small type, in a style identical to the rest of the text on the page. There are no outstanding headings alerting a purchaser to the disclaimer, and there is no mention of "merchantability" as required by R.C. 1302.29. Furthermore, Dr. Ressallat testified in his deposition that the disclaimer was not mentioned by the salesman at the time of the sale of the burglar alarm system, nor was it brought to his attention that anything was printed on the back page of the contract.

We believe the court erred in concluding that the disclaimer of warranties in these parties' contract was conspicuous. First, the disclaimer fails to mention "merchantability," a requirement of the code which must be fulfilled if a disclaimer of the implied warranty of merchantability is to be found valid. Additionally, we find that the trial court ignored the statutory language and applied an improper standard in determining that the disclaimer was conspicuous. In making that determination, the court stated:

These warranties and conditions are not hidden, but clearly spelled out in common understandable language which leaves no doubt as to what is and what is not covered, and when.

While we agree that the common, ordinary definition of "conspicuous" can be "not hidden," or "clearly spelled out," the code explicitly sets forth what the term means under the circumstances of this case. One's understanding of the terminology bears no relation to conspicuousness under the code. In the disclaimer at issue, there are no prominent headings, and there is not print of a different style or color that would draw one's attention. The disclaimer wording blends in with the surrounding "terms" and "conditions" and is in no way more noticeable. We find that the disclaimer in the contract is, as a matter of law, inconspicuous.

Absent evidence or testimony supporting the breach of warranty claims, the disclaimers are irrelevant, and thus provide no ground for reversal of the court's judgment.

Judgment affirmed.

CASE QUESTIONS
1. Why did the Ressallats turn to someone other than their insurer?
2. Why was the disclaimer inconspicuous?
3. Did it matter that the disclaimer is inconspicuous?
4. Will the Ressallats recover?

C O N S I D E R . . .

10.7 Nunes Turfgrass, Inc., was the largest independent sod grower in California. Based in Modesto with outlets in seven other California cities, it had been in business since 1962. Vaughan-Jacklin Seed Company was a corporate grower, developer, and commercial retailer of grass seed and was based in Post Falls, Idaho. At the time of the dispute, Vaughan-Jacklin had been in business for 50 years and was one of the largest seed companies in the world.

Nunes sold its sod fields and seed mixes under the Nunes name to landscapers, golf courses, and the general public. In 1980, Nunes began to notice that its customers wanted a hardier, more drought-resistant type of grass (bluegrass-perennial ryegrass blend). Nunes contacted Doyle Jacklin, the sales and marketing manager for Vaughan-Jacklin, and discussed its needs. Mr. Jacklin researched the needs and recommended to Nunes the Jackpot perennial ryegrass. Nunes relied on the recommendation and ordered 8,000 pounds of Jackpot in September 1981.

Continued

Before the seed was shipped, Vaughan-Jacklin sent a written confirmation of sale with this warranty and disclaimer:

JACKLIN SEED COMPANY, DIVISION OF VAUGHAN-JACKLIN CORPORATION, warrants that seed it sells conforms to the label description as required by State and Federal Seed Laws. IT MAKES NO OTHER WARRANTIES, EXPRESS OR IMPLIED, OF MERCHANTABILITY, FITNESS FOR PURPOSE, OR OTHERWISE, AND IN ANY EVENT ITS LIABILITY FOR BREACH OF ANY WARRANTY OR CONTRACT WITH RESPECT TO SUCH SEEDS IS LIMITED TO THE PURCHASE PRICE OF SUCH SEEDS. JACKLIN SEED COMPANY FURTHER LIMITS TO SUCH PURCHASE PRICE ITS LIABILITY OF ANY KIND ON ACCOUNT OF ANY NEGLIGENCE WHATSOEVER ON ITS PART WITH RESPECT TO SUCH SEEEDS.

The seed bags had the same language, to which was added the following:

LIABILITY for damages for any cause, including breach of contract or breach of warranty, with respect to this sale of seeds IS LIMITED TO A REFUND OF THE PURCHASE PRICE OF THE SEEDS. THIS REMEDY IS EXCLUSIVE. IN NO EVENT SHALL THE LABELER BE LIABLE FOR ANY INCIDENTAL OR CONSEQUENTIAL DAMAGES, INCLUDING LOSS OF PROFIT.

In September and October 1981, Nunes overseeded 56 acres with the Jackpot seed. Within weeks of overseeding, large clumps of off-colored ryegrass appeared in the fields, rendering them unfit for sod production. The result was that Nunes could not make sod sales and was forced to liquidate its business in 1984.

Can Nunes recover for breach of warranty? [*Nunes Turfgrass, Inc.* v. *Vaughan-Jacklin Seed Co.*, 246 Cal. Rptr. 823 (1988).]

Privity Standards for UCC Recovery

If you have a contract to buy a car and the seller breaches the contract by refusing to deliver, you can bring suit for breach of contract. There is privity between you and the seller. The people in your car pool, however, could not sue the seller for breach if you no longer have a car to use (even though they are affected) because they have no privity of contract with the seller. Traditionally, a recovery for a breach of contract requires privity of contract. A breach of warranty is a breach of contract, and until the time of the UCC, privity was required to be able to recover on a breach of warranty theory.

Section 2-318 of the UCC establishes requirements for breach of warranty recovery. The section has three alternatives that states can adopt, each of which provides warranty protections for *more* than the buyer. For example, Alternative A covers the buyer and members of the buyer's household and guests. Alternative B covers any natural person who is reasonably expected to use the goods and suffers personal injury. Alternative C extends the warranty protection to any person who may be expected to use the goods and is injured. Alternative C also prohibits the disclaimer of liability for personal injury to those covered by the warranty.

Business Planning Tip

To disclaim a warranty:
1. Use LARGE type.
2. Use different color type.
3. Place the disclaimer on the front of the contract.
4. Use proper statutory language.
5. Have buyers initial the disclaimer.

C O N S I D E R . . . **10.8** Nikolas Ruiz suffered third-degree lacerations to his left hand when he was caught in an escalator at a department store (J. C. Penney). Nikolas, a four-year-old boy, and his mother were not negligent in any way. Who would have liability for the injuries if West-inghouse manufactured and installed the escalator? Is privity an issue?

Exhibit 10.4 summarizes the UCC warranty protections and disclaimers.

Type	Creation	Restriction	Disclaimer
Express	Affirmation of fact or promise of performance (samples, model, descriptions)	Must be part of the basis of the bargain	Cannot make a disclaimer inconsistent with an express warranty.
Implied Warranty of Merchantability	Given in every sale of goods by a merchant ("fit for ordinary purposes")	Only given by merchants	(1) Must use "merchantability" or general disclaimer of "as is" or "with all faults" (2) if written—must be conspicuous
Implied Warranty of Fitness for a Particular Purpose	Seller knows of buyers reliance for a particular use (buyer is ignorant)	Seller must have knowledge; buyer must rely on that knowledge	
Title	Given in every sale	Does not apply in circumstances where apparent warranty is not given	
Magnuson-Moss (Federal Consumer Product Warranty Law)	Only consumer products of $15 or more	Must label "Full" or "Limited"	

Exhibit 10.4
UCC Warranties: Creation, Restrictions, and Disclaimers

STRICT TORT LIABILITY—PRODUCT LIABILITY UNDER SECTION 402A

Visit the American Law Institute: http://www.ali.org/

The first tort theory for recovery for defective products is **strict liability** in tort. This tort was created and defined by Section 402A of the *Restatement (Second) of Torts*. Restatements of the law are developed by the American Law Institute, an educational group of professors and practicing attorneys. Restatements are not the law, even though they are adopted and recognized in many states as the controlling statement of law in that state. The adoption of a restatement generally comes in the form of judicial acceptance of the doctrines provided.

Restatement § 402A:

402A. Special Liability of Seller of Product for Physical Harm to User or Consumer

(1) One who sells any product in a defective condition unreasonably dangerous to the user or consumer or to his property is subject to liability for physical harm thereby caused to the ultimate user or consumer, or to his property if

    (a) the seller is engaged in the business of selling such a product, and

    (b) it is expected to and does reach the user or consumer without substantial change in the condition in which it is sold.

(2) The rule stated in Subsection (1) applies although

    (a) the seller has exercised all possible care in the preparation and sale of his product, and

    (b) the user or consumer has not bought the product from or entered into any contractual relations with the seller.

Section 402A has no privity requirements and is not subject to the disclaimers that can eliminate warranty liability. Negligence requires proof of some knowledge of a defect. Section 402A applies if a product is defective, regardless of whether knowledge of a defect existed.

Unreasonably Dangerous Defective Condition

This part of 402A requires that a product be in a condition of danger such that an ordinary person would not contemplate its use. Eggs are not unreasonably dangerous because of their effects on body cholesterol levels. However, eggs that contain a harmful disease or that were injected with a virus would be unreasonably dangerous.

A product can be unreasonably dangerous because it contains a foreign substance. Most product liability cases relating to food are based on this tenet. Rats in pop bottles, moldy bananas in cereal, parts of a snake in frozen vegetables, and stones in soup are all factual circumstances that have been recognized as 402A defective conditions.

Section 402A applies to defective conditions regardless of the precautions taken by the manufacturer. Manufacturers or food processors who take great precautions in their procedures could overcome a charge of negligence; however, strict liability focuses on the fact that a defect exists, not whether the manufacturer could or could not have prevented the problem. In other words, strict liability does not require a showing of a breach of duty; it only requires a showing of a defective product.

The most common types of product liability cases are based on the following:

1. Design defects
2. Dangers of use that were not warned about or dangers because unclear use instructions were given
3. Errors in manufacturing, handling, or packaging of the product

DESIGN DEFECT

A product with a faulty design exposes its users to unnecessary risks. And products must be designed with all foreseeable uses in mind. Thus, cars must be designed in view of the probability of accidents. A design that creates an otherwise unnecessary explosion upon a rear-end collision is a faulty design.

To make the best possible case in the event of a product liability suit, it is helpful for the manufacturer to have complied with all federal and state regulations on the product. It is also helpful if the manufacturer has used the latest technology and designs available within the industry and has met industry standards in designing its product.

PROPER WARNINGS AND INSTRUCTIONS

Manufacturers have a duty to warn buyers when there is a foreseeably dangerous use of a product that buyers are not likely to realize is dangerous. They also have a duty to supplement the warnings. For example, as defects are discovered in autos, the manufacturers send recall notices to buyers. Similarly, manufacturers of airplanes have sent warnings on problems and proper repair procedures to airlines throughout the life of a particular plane design's use.

Manufacturers must also give adequate instructions to buyers on the proper use of the product. Over-the-counter drugs carry instructions about proper dosages and the limitations on dosages.

MANUFACTURING, HANDLING, OR PACKAGING ERRORS

This breach of duty is the most difficult form of negligence to prove. There are usually so many handlers in the process of manufacturing and packaging a product that it becomes difficult to prove when and how the manufacturer was negligent. One of the issues in drug manufacturing cases is whether the packaging for the materials is sufficient. Does it protect against tampering? Is it child-proof? These types of dangers are foreseeable and require special duties with regard to packaging drugs.

The following case deals with a manufacturing defect.

Crossley v. General Motors Corp.
33 F.3d 818 (7th Cir. 1994)

THE FLYING CHEVY BLAZER: WAS IT INTACT AS IT FLEW?

FACTS

On July 23, 1988, Richard Crossley was driving his 1987 Chevrolet S-10 Blazer on a banked, curved, two-lane connector ramp linking two interstate freeways near Ontario, California. He was traveling at approximately 70 miles an hour in a 55-mile-per-hour zone and passing other vehicles when he lost control of his Blazer. The Blazer rotated 360 degrees and flew off the side of the connector ramp, passenger side first.

After the Blazer flew off the connector, it sailed 40 to 50 feet in the air at approximately 60 miles an hour before hitting the ground. The Blazer landed on its right rear tire and rolled over several times before coming to rest 287 feet away. Mr. Crossley was ejected from the Blazer when it was 50 feet in the air. He

suffered a closed head injury and is now a spastic quadriplegic.

Experts for both sides agreed that Mr. Crossley's tires were in poor condition: they were mismatched in both size and brand; worn; and had nails, screws, and plugs in them. All three eyewitnesses noticed generally that the tires looked substandard, and specifically that the left rear tire was low on air pressure.

Officer Trinidad Gonzales of the California Highway Patrol investigated the accident. He found the right rear wheel and axle stub resting 10 feet from where the Blazer stopped. Officer Gonzales began inspecting the pavement on the highway where Mr. Crossley lost control for gouges, abrasions, or any other marks that would indicate that the tire came

Continued

off while the Blazer was on the roadway. After 30 minutes of investigation, neither Officer Gonzales, who previously had investigated over one hundred rollover accidents, nor Officer Ellen Conley, who assisted in investigating the accident, found any irregular marks on the highway.

Mr. Crossley filed suit against GM and contended that the axle shaft cracked before he lost control of his Blazer, and that the crack occurred because of a manufacturing defect for which he sought to hold GM strictly liable.

The jury deliberated and returned the following signed special verdict form:

> Question No. 1: Was there a defect in manufacture of the product involved?
> Answer: YES
>
> Question No. 2: Did the defect exist when it left the possession of the defendant?
> Answer: YES
>
> Question No. 3: Was the defect a cause of injury to plaintiff?
> Answer: NO

The district court therefore entered judgment on the verdict in favor of General Motors. Mr. Crossley appealed.

JUDICIAL OPINION

HARLINGTONWOOD, Circuit Judge

As part of its defense, General Motors intended to call as a witness Kenneth Orlowski, an expert in assessing rollover accidents, to explain the dynamics of rollovers to the jury. To assist Orlowski in explaining those concepts to the jury, General Motors sought to introduce a videotape of a study of rollover sequences that involved a 1982 Malibu (the Malibu tape). Crossley objected to the presentation of the Malibu tape because it depicted a different model vehicle, the test was conducted in a controlled setting during which the automobile was propelled from a dolly at 31 miles per hour, and the road surfaces were different. The district court allowed General Motors to play the Malibu tape for the purpose of demonstrating "general scientific and engineering principles."

Professor David Flebeck, Crossley's metallurgy expert, testified that General Motors was supposed to heat treat the axle so that the outer case had high hardness and the inner core was softer, or ductile. Flebeck further stated that the individual grains of metal in the axle of Crossley's Blazer were damaged during the hardening process, causing the outer case and inner core of the axle to become brittle. The brittle nature of the axle could cause the axle to fracture under even normal operating loads. Flebeck opined that the axle embrittlement caused Crossley to lose control of his vehicle and therefore caused his injuries. Professor Roland Ruhl, Crossley's accident reconstruction expert, concurred in Flebeck's assessment of what caused the accident, and added that there was no substantial damage to the right rear quarter of the Blazer, as would be consistent with the vehicle hitting the ground with sufficient force to break the axle.

General Motors elicited the testimony of three eyewitnesses to the accident, a metallurgist, and an accident reconstructionist, among others, all of whom presented ample evidence suggesting that Crossley's negligence caused his accident, not a cracked axle shaft.

Crossley also argues that the special verdict form reveals an inconsistency in the jury verdict. The supposed inconsistency is based on the jury concluding that there was a manufacturing defect in the Blazer, but that the defect did not cause Crossley's accident. Our duty is to attempt to reconcile an apparently inconsistent jury verdict, if doing so is possible.

Reconciling the jury verdict in this instance is an easy task. Causation clearly is a distinct element under California law, which controls in this diversity action. The mere existence of a defect does not prove that the defect was responsible for subsequent injuries—if a person intentionally drives a defective Blazer off a cliff, the driver's estate cannot recover against General Motors because the vehicle in which the injuries occurred was defective. In this case, the jury concluded that although Crossley's Blazer was improperly manufactured, Crossley's negligence caused him to lose control of his vehicle and crash, and it was not until the impact of the crash that the already brittle axle broke.

Continued

That assessment of events, whether accurate or not, certainly is internally consistent.

The judgment of the district court therefore is affirmed.

CASE QUESTIONS

1. Did the jury find that Mr. Crossley's Blazer had a manufacturing defect?

2. What is the impact of Mr. Crossley's excessive speed in the case?

3. Why does the court discuss causation?

4. Do you agree with the decision? Do you think the defect made Mr. Crossley's injuries worse?

5. Why is the jury's special verdict not inconsistent?

C O N S I D E R . . . **10.9** Classify the following as design, manufacture, or warning defects:

- Failure to disclose changes in fuel and operations for a helicopter in hot weather and higher altitudes
- A polio vaccine that produces not immunity, but polio in a child
- Teflon-induced autoimmune system disease caused by Teflon used in the manufacturer of an implanted TMJ jaw device
- Diamond represented as a grade V.V.S. is actually a lower grade
- Infant swing that causes infants to fall out backwards if they fall asleep and their weight shifts
- Tobacco-causing lung cancer
- Fondue pot tipping over and burning two-year-old child
- Bleeding of pizza-box ink onto pizza

Reaching the Buyer in the Same Condition

The requirement that a product reach the buyer without "substantial change" is a protection for the seller. A seller will not be liable for a product that has been modified or changed. The reason for this requirement is that once a product is modified or changed, it becomes unclear whether the original product or the modifications caused the unreasonably dangerous condition. Volkswagen would not be held liable for a dune buggy accident just because the builder and owner of the dune buggy happened to use a Volkswagen engine in building the vehicle. Because Volkswagen's product had been taken apart and modified, its liability has ended. One issue that arises in airplane crash cases is whether the air carrier followed the manufacturer's repair procedures. The failure to follow these procedures could eliminate the manufacturer's liability because the aircraft may have been altered.

The Requirement of a Seller Engaged in a Business

Section 402A requires the seller to be "engaged in the business of selling the product." This requirement sounds like the merchant requirement for the UCC warranty of merchantability. However, the meaning of "selling the product" is slightly broader under 402A than the UCC meaning of merchant. For example, a baseball club is not a merchant of beer, but if the club sells beer at its games, it is a seller for purposes of 402A. Section 402A covers manufacturers, wholesalers, retailers, food sellers, and even those who sell products out of their homes.

In recent years, some courts have allowed recovery from groups of sellers. For example, in the controversy over diethylstilbestrol (DES, a drug taken by pregnant women), the plaintiffs could show that their harms resulted from DES but could not show exactly who manufactured the drug their mothers took. The courts permitted recovery against the group of manufacturers of DES during that time period. [*Sindell* v. *Abbott Lab.*, 607 P.2d 924 (Cal. 1980).]

C O N S I D E R . . .   **10.10** Craig and Karen Foster received a prescription from their infant twins' pediatrician to help the twins, who were suffering from colic. The drug prescribed is Phenergan, a drug manufactured and sold by American Home Products/Wyeth. The Fosters' pharmacy substituted Promethazine Syrup Plain, a generic of Phenergan manufactured and sold by My-K Laboratories, Inc.

The twins were given the syrup several times over a few days with the last dose given on the evening of September 10, 1988. Six-week-old Brandy was found dead in her crib the next morning. Her cause of death was listed as Sudden Infant Death Syndrome (SIDS). A physician expert at the SIDS Center at the University of Maryland said the death was caused by promethazine.

The Fosters sued My-K and Wyeth. Wyeth was sued because it developed the drug although it did not manufacture the prescription actually given to Brandy. Should Wyeth be held liable? [*Foster* v. *American Home Prods. Corp.*, 29 F. 3d. 165 (4th Cir. 1994).]

NEGLIGENCE—A SECOND TORT
FOR PRODUCT LIABILITY

A suit for product defects can also be based in negligence. The elements for establishing a negligence case are the same as those for a Section 402A case with one addition: establishing that the product seller or manufacturer either knew of the defect before the product was sold or allowed sales to continue with the knowledge that the product had a defect. Establishing this knowledge is difficult in an evidentiary sense in court, but a plaintiff in a product liability suit who shows that the defendant-seller knew of the problem and sold or continued to sell the product will be able to collect punitive damages in addition to damages for personal injury and property damage. Establishing knowledge in a product liability case usually produces a multimillion-dollar verdict because punitive damages are awarded in addition to compensatory ones.

Examples of cases in which establishing knowledge has been an issue include the Ford Pinto exploding gas tank cases (in which the plaintiffs used internal memos from engineers) and the Dow Corning breast implant suits (in which an engineer, Thomas Talcott, who worked for Dow Corning in 1976, testified for the plaintiffs regarding his feelings during the product's development that leakage was possible).

Comparisons of the various product liability theories are found in Exhibits 10.5 and 10.6 (pg. 357).

Type	Privity required?	Knowledge of problem required?	Warranty promise required?
Negligence	No	Yes	No
Section 402A/ strict tort liability	No	No	No
Express warranty	Yes	No	Yes
Implied warranty of merchantability	Yes	No	No
Implied warranty of fitness for a particular purpose	Yes	No	Yes

Exhibit 10.5
Comparison of Product Liability Theories

Contract	Tort
Express Warranty	Tort
Implied Warranty of Merchantability	402A—Strict Tort Liability*
Implied Warranty of Fitness for Particular Purpose	Negligence**

*Elements

1) Defective condition unreasonably dangerous:
   design;
   manufacturing defect; or
   inadequate warning

2) Defendant in business of using, selling, or manufacturing product

3) Condition of product is the same

**Add 4) Knowledge of defect

Exhibit 10.6
Legal Basis for Product Liability

PRIVITY ISSUES IN TORT THEORIES OF PRODUCT LIABILITY

Privity is not the standard for recovery in negligence actions. The standard for recovery in negligence actions is whether the injury that resulted was foreseeable and foreseeable to that particular party. For example, a manufacturer of toasters can foresee use by children of the equipment and would have a duty to warn that they should not use it unless supervised by adults. A manufacturer of a weed killer could foresee the presence of dogs, cats, and other pets in a yard sprayed with the killer and should either make the product not harmful to them or warn of the need to keep them away from the sprayed area for a certain period of time. Children, dogs, and other pets certainly have no privity with the manufacturers, but they can recover from the manufacturer (or their parents and owners can) on the basis of their foreseeability and the foreseeability of the danger causing their injuries.

Likewise, parties other than the product manufacturer may be responsible for defective conditions in the products and can be held liable for their participation. For example, parts manufacturers may be held liable if it can be shown that defects in their parts resulted in a product's defect and the injury to the plaintiff.

C O N S I D E R . . .   **10.11** John Evraets underwent eye surgery in September 1983 at a hospital in Long Beach, California. He had a cataract removed and an artificial lens implanted. The lens was manufactured, designed, tested, distributed, and sold by Intermedics Intraocular, Inc., and Pharmacia Opthalmics, Inc.

After the operation Mr. Evraets suffered pain; irritation; decreased vision; light sensitivity; deterioration of his eye structures, including macular, retinal, and corneal damage; edema; and a detached retina and vitreous humor. He was ultimately obliged to undergo another surgery to replace the lens. In addition to his physical suffering, Mr. Evraets experienced emotional distress, shock, and fright.

In August 1991, Mr. Evraets read a published article in which he learned that defects in Intermedic's and Opthalmic's lens implants were the source of his injuries. Could Mr. Evraets recover from these companies? On what basis? [*Evraets* v. *Intermedics Intraocular, Inc.*, 34 Cal. Rptr. 2d 852 (1994).]

E T H I C A L   I S S U E S

10.3 In the early 1960s, Dow Corning and other manufacturers began marketing silicone-filled implants for use in breast enlargement procedures. The silicone implants are breast-shaped bags filled with silicone gel. The bag itself is made of another form of silicone that is like a heavy plastic; this latter material is the same substance used in sealant and the children's toy, Silly Putty.

In the course of conducting its research, Dow Corning found that laboratory animals exposed to silicone gels developed tumors. A panel of research experts examined the Dow Corning studies and concluded that 80 percent of the exposed animals had developed tumors. The figure was so high that the panel deemed the research suspect and labeled the study "inconclusive." A 1975 study, which was eventually discovered during litigation in 1994, explained that silicone implants harmed the immune systems of mice. A lawyer representing women in a class action suit against Dow found the study among Dow documents.

Outside Dow Corning, other companies expressed their own concerns about silicone implants. James Rudy, then-president of Heyer-Schulte Corporation, wrote a "Dear Doctor" letter in 1976 to inform physicians about the risk of the implants rupturing. Between 1976 and 1978, Congress gave the FDA its first authority to regulate

Continued

medical "devices" such as implants. Nevertheless, despite the studies and warnings, the implants continued to be sold to approximately 150,000 women a year. It was also at this time that a two-year Dow Corning study found malignant tumors in 80 percent of the laboratory animals exposed to silicone gels.

The study concluded: "As you will see, the conclusion of this report is that silicone can cause cancers in rats; there is no direct proof that silicone causes cancer in humans; however, there is considerable reason to suspect that silicone can do so."

In a 1984 landmark case, a federal district court, in awarding Maria Stern of Nevada $1.5 million in punitive damages, held that Dow Corning had committed fraud in marketing the implants as safe. In ruling on a posttrial motion, U.S. District Judge Marilyn Hall Palel wrote that although Dow Corning's own studies cast considerable doubt on the safety of the product, the company had not disclosed those studies to patients, including Stern, an act that she labeled "highly reprehensible."

Dow Corning's litigation forced it into Chapter 11 bankruptcy. Dow Chemical has been held liable in one case. List possible product liability theories for recovery. Was it ethical to sell the implants without disclosure of the possible harms?

DEFENSES TO PRODUCT LIABILITY TORTS

Three defenses are available to a defendant in a product liability tort:

1. Misuse or abnormal use of a product
2. Contributory negligence
3. Assumption of risk

Misuse or Abnormal Use of a Product

Any use of a product that the manufacturer has specifically warned against in its instructions is a **misuse**. Using a forklift to lift 25,000 pounds when the instructions limit its capacity to 15,000 pounds is a misuse of the product, and any injuries resulting from such misuse will not be the liability of the manufacturer. Product misuse also occurs when a plaintiff has used the product in a manner that the defendant could not anticipate and warn against.

Contributory Negligence

Contributory negligence is traditionally a complete defense to a product liability suit in negligence. For example, although a front loader might have a design failure of no protective netting around the driver, a driver who is injured while using the front loader for recreational purposes is contributorily negligent. Contributory negligence overlaps greatly with product misuse.

Some states, as discussed previously, have adopted a standard of **comparative negligence**, under which the plaintiff's negligence is not a complete defense: The negligence of the plaintiff merely serves to reduce the amount the plaintiff is entitled to recover. For example, a jury might find that the defendant is 60 percent at fault and the plaintiff is 40 percent at fault. The plaintiff recovers, but the amount of that recovery is reduced by 40 percent.

The following case involves an issue of negligence and misuse.

Abbott v. American Honda Motor Co.
682 S.W.2d 206 (Tenn. 1984)

HOTDOGGING: THE ATC AND STRICT LIABILITY

FACTS

On June 12, 1981, Scott Abbott (plaintiff-appellant), age 11, was riding a Honda ATC-70, three-wheel, all-terrain motorcycle on his father's property near his home. As he was going up a hill, the ATC lost its speed and power and he applied the brakes. He released the brakes and began to ease the motorcycle backwards down the hill. The ATC then picked up speed, and he applied the brakes again. As a result of these events, the front wheel came off and Abbott was thrown off the vehicle and onto the ground. The ATC then passed over Abbott and seriously burned him when the unshielded underside of the exhaust pipe came into contact with him. He experienced permanent scarring, and he and his parents sued Honda for their damages under theories of negligence, strict liability, breach of implied warranty of merchantability, and breach of fitness for a particular purpose.

The jury found for Honda, and the Abbotts appealed.

JUDICIAL OPINION

SANDERS, Judge

As their first assignment of error, the Appellants assert that the trial judge, at best, issued confusing instructions relative to the doctrine of contributory negligence and, at worst, issued incorrect instructions relative to the doctrine.

The courts do recognize, however, that plaintiffs can conduct themselves in such a way as to defeat recovery. Regardless of which label is used, "contributory negligence" or "assumption of risk," the courts have generally held that ordinary lack of care is not a defense, while "voluntarily and unreasonably proceeding to encounter a known danger" is a defense.

. . . [W]hen a plaintiff, with knowledge of the defect, uses the product in such a manner as to voluntarily and unreasonably encounter a known danger, the act may be plead as a defense to an action based on strict liability in tort. *We do not deem it determinative of the availability of this defense whether it be called negligence, contributory negligence or assumption of risk. It is more a matter of the unreasonableness of permitting a plaintiff to deliberately put in motion a known danger and attempt to profit thereby.*

The Appellants also contend the jury charge on the issue of intervening negligence was in error. Pertinent to this matter, the judge charged:

Ladies and gentlemen of the jury, in this case the defendants have interposed the plea of intervening cause or action. They say in this case that the parent, that is to say young Scott's father, failed to advise him and warn him of the instructions in that book, and therefore that was an intervening cause of his accident.

The law is that the chain of causation is not broken by the occurrence of an intervening act or event if that act or event might reasonably have been anticipated. . . .

If you find, therefore, that the parent of the minor plaintiff did not properly instruct and supervise the minor plaintiff in the use of the motorcycle, and that such failure itself caused the injury sustained, then the acts and omissions of the parent are an intervening cause sufficient to relieve the defendants of liability.

The Appellants first contend the trial court erred in giving the charge of intervening negligence since the charge "was not substantiated by the weight of the evidence."

We disagree. In this case, there was a question of whether or not the father of the injured minor plaintiff properly instructed the youngster as to the correct operation of the motorcycle, and was pled as an affirmative defense by the Defendants.

The judgment of the trial court is affirmed.

CASE QUESTIONS

1. What misuse is alleged?
2. Is the misuse a complete defense?
3. Was there negligence? If so, whose?

Assumption of Risk

When a plaintiff is aware of a danger in the product but goes ahead and uses it anyway, **assumption of risk** occurs. If a car manufacturer recalled your car for repair and you failed to have it done, despite full opportunity to do so, you have assumed the risk of driving with that problem.

PRODUCT LIABILITY REFORM

Visit FMC Corporation: http://fmcweb. ncsa.uiuc.edu/home. html

"Our product-liability system discourages innovation because of unforeseeable potential liability," says Robert Malcott, CEO of FMC Corporation. Mr. Malcott issued this statement as the chair of the Business Roundtable's task force on product liability. This task force and others have proposed several changes, including limiting punitive damages; meeting government standards as a defense; instituting liability shields for drugs, medical devices, and aircraft; and requiring higher standards of proof for recovery of punitive damages.

Visit THOMAS, a service of the U.S. Congress, for the status of current Congressional bills: http://thomas. loc.gov/

In each session since 1977, a bill on product liability reform has been introduced in Congress. However, such a bill faces significant opposition from consumer groups and trial lawyers. As trade barriers fall, the ability of the United States to compete with nations with limits on product liability will be hindered. The Business Roundtable and other business groups continue to work for reform at the federal and state levels. Further, businesses continue to emphasize total quality management as a tool for minimizing product liability. See "A Checklist for Preventing Product Liability" (pg. 364).

The American Law Institute (ALI) has proposed the *Restatement (Third) of Torts*, which would change the current strict liability standard to a negligence standard for defective design and informational defect cases. In other words, plaintiffs who bring product liability cases based on defective design and instruction would have to establish negligence to recover. The strict liability standard would be eliminated under this new proposal. Strict liability would still be the standard for manufacturing defects.

FEDERAL STANDARDS FOR PRODUCT LIABILITY

Consumer Product Safety Commission

Visit the Consumer Product Safety Commission: http://www. cpsc.gov/

The federal level of government generally is not involved in product liability issues. However, the **Consumer Product Safety Commission (CPSC)** is a regulatory agency set up under the Consumer Product Safety Act to regulate safety standards for consumer products. The commission has several responsibilities in carrying out its purposes:

1. *To protect the public against unreasonable risks of injury from consumer products*
   To perform this function, the commission has been given the authority to recall products and order their repair or correction. The commission also has the power to ban products completely. This ban can apply only if a product cannot be made less dangerous. The ban on asbestos is an example of the commission's powers. For example, in 1994, the CPSC recalled nearly all types of metal bunk beds.
2. *To develop standards for consumer product safety*
   These standards take the form of regulations and minimum requirements for certain products.

3. *To help consumers become more informed about evaluating safety*
   Certain regulations require disclosure of the limits of performance and hazards associated with using a particular product.
4. *To fund research in matters of product safety design and in product-caused injuries and illnesses*

The act carries civil penalties of $2,000 for each violation, up to a maximum of $500,000. Knowing or willful violations carry a criminal fine of up to $50,000 and/or one year imprisonment. In addition, consumers have a right to sue in federal district court for any damages they sustain because of a violation of a regulation or law.

Uniform Product Liability Act

Visit the Department of Commerce: http://www.doc.gov/

In a number of different attempts, the Department of Commerce has tried to issue drafts and recommendations to the states on a set of uniform product liability laws. The proposed act would change the law substantially by establishing several defenses, such as state-of-the-art manufacturing or design. In addition, the proposed law establishes how a product can be defective. In view of the confusion as to standards in product liability, the high awards for damages, and the high insurance premiums paid by businesses, a change seems necessary but has been slow in coming (see "Litigation Thwarts Innovation in the U.S."). Tort reform efforts continue at both federal and state levels.

FOR THE MANAGER'S DESK

LITIGATION THWARTS INNOVATION IN THE U.S.

American innovation is in trouble in the courts. Burt Rutan, the pioneering designer of the *Voyager,* used to sell construction plans for novel airplanes to do-it-yourselfers. In 1985, concerned about the lawsuits that would follow if a home-built plane crashed, he took the plans off the market.

The Monsanto Company decided in 1987 not to market a promising new filler and insulator made of calcium sodium metaphosphate. The material is almost certainly safer than asbestos, which it could help to replace in brakes and gaskets. But safer is not good enough in today's climate of infectious litigation.

Liability fears have caused the withdrawal of exotic drugs that the Food and Drug Administration consider safe and effective, including some for which no close substitute is known.

In the past 15 years most companies have halted U.S. research on contraceptives and drugs to combat infertility and morning sickness. "Who in his right mind," the president of one pharmaceutical company asked in 1986, "would work on a product today that would be used by pregnant women?"

Liability is supposed to fall on "defective," unduly dangerous products and services. What has gone wrong?

The old rules of negligence, which lasted until the 1960s in most states, looked closely at the human actors on the scene. Were they careful? Had they been well trained? Thus tested, engineers, surgeons, chemists and pharmacologists at the leading edge of their professions fared well.

The new rules of "strict liability," invented by U.S. courts in the 1960s and 1970s, place technology itself in the dock. After an accident jurors are given a few days to evaluate the design of a mass-vaccination program, a power plant or an advanced military aircraft. Sympathy for the victims clouds the analysis, and if finding a design defect is what it takes to help out the unfortunate claimant, then that is what many juries find.

Moreover, human nature is predisposed to accept the
Continued

old and familiar risk while rejecting the novel and the exotic. Cigarette makers usually win before the jury, whereas pioneers in gene splicing or laser surgery are at constant peril. By the same token, consulting engineers favor older design options in their specifications, fearing that new ones will carry greater risk—not physical risk but legal.

The various elements of liability in the courts today all join to thwart innovation. Take the duty to warn of hazards, great and small, common and bizarre, in staggering detail. It is a game that sellers master only by playing for a long time. The warnings on birth-control pills have been honed for 30 years and now run on for several pages of dense detail. No equivalent warning can be offered for a next-generation mode of contraception, even if on balance it is safer.

Modern law also demands that risky products come, in effect, with their own insurance contract attached, underwritten by some producer's liability insurer. Insurance, by design, spreads costs broadly and somewhat indiscriminately; when one product comes under intense liability attack, an entire industry may lose its coverage. For the prudent business no insurance usually means no product.

The most regressive effects are felt precisely where fruitful innovation is most urgently needed. Liability today is highly—and often indiscriminately—contagious. Progress is undercut the most in the markets already battered by a hurricane of litigation: contraceptives, vaccines, obstetrical services and light aircraft, for example.

More often than not the best anticipatory defense in the modern legal environment is to sit still. Age, familiarity and ubiquity provide the surest legal protection. When it encourages improvement at all, today's liability system promotes the trivial and marginal change. The drug manufacturer endlessly fine-tunes the warning or microscopically adjusts the dosage in the capsule. The doctor orders more tests and X-rays in order to pile up a protective paper trail. Companies hire squadrons of risk managers, industrial hygienists and consumer psychologists. Liability-driven safety management becomes a mirror image of the legal process itself—fussy, cumulative, bureaucratic and preoccupied with paper.

Meanwhile the threat of liability impedes or prevents the sharp break with technological tradition, the profound change in method or material, design or manufacture. Over the long term, however, the bold leap forward is all-important in the quest for safety, and it is precisely in the riskiest areas of life, where the litigation climate is worst, that such change is most urgently needed.

Today's U.S. liability system, unique in the world in its reach and impact, is all too adept at condemning services and technologies deemed unacceptable for one reason or another. What it lacks is a reliable way to say yes.

What is the solution? When we deal with essentially private risks (in transportation or personal consumption, for example), fair warning and conscious choice by the

consumer must be made to count for much more than they do today—not because individual choices will always be wise (they surely will not be) but because such a system at least allows positive choice and the acceptance of change.

Informed consent by the individual is not, however, going to take care of such complex or far-reaching safety issues as chemical-waste disposal, mass vaccination or central power generation. Those are, and obviously must continue to be, delegated to expert agencies acting for the collective good. But if they are to be useful at all, agents must be able to buy as well as sell. For safety agencies this means not only rejecting bad safety choices but also embracing good ones. Yet the long-standing rule, vigorously applied by our courts, is that even the most complete conformity to applicable regulations is no shield against liability.

The courts should be strongly encouraged, instead, to respect the risk and safety choices made by expert agencies. It may be politically unrealistic to propose that liability should be entirely foreclosed even in cases where activities are conducted with the express approval of qualified regulatory agencies, but surely it could be firmly curtailed in such circumstances. At the very least, full compliance with a comprehensive licensing order should provide liability protection against punitive, if not compensatory, damages. It has always been true that ignorance of the law is no excuse. Today knowledge of the law is no excuse either. It should be.

Source: Reprinted courtesy of Peter Huber and *Scientific American,* March 1989. Mr. Huber is a fellow at the Manhattan Institute.

FOR THE MANAGER'S DESK

A CHECKLIST FOR PREVENTING PRODUCT LIABILITY

Questions to Ask When Setting Up a Complaint-Reporting System

1. Are customer complaints forwarded to someone outside the complaint department?
2. Are we keeping track of the types and frequency of repairs on our products?
3. Are retailers and other product users and handlers surveyed for comments on product use and results?
4. Is there an incentive system for finding design and production defects?
5. Is product information given to the marketing and legal departments?
6. Has the philosophy of product liability prevention been made clear to employees?

Questions to Ask About Testing Facilities

1. Have testing facilities been established? If so, what type? Who tests the products?
2. Is there a program for testing products in the home?
3. Are products changed as a result of testing program discoveries?
4. Are warnings and instructions rewritten to reflect problems arising during testing?
5. Are products ever withdrawn because of defects revealed during testing?
6. Are employees, including executives, encouraged to test products?
7. Are customers at all levels (wholesale, retail) surveyed to determine any problems or misuses?

Questions to Ask About Quality Control

1. Is an appropriate level of worker on the production line?
2. Are production workers pretested to determine psychological difficulties?
3. Do executives conduct random quality control tests?
4. Are employees encouraged to do quality work of their own by checking products in retail stores?
5. Is there an incentive program for quality control?

Questions to Ask About Instructions and Warnings

1. Are instructions and warnings checked frequently for clarity and warning quality?
2. Is the attention of customers adequately drawn to warnings?

3. Do warnings cover a range of possible misuses?
4. Are users warned about possible long-term health hazards presented by the product, if such hazards exist?
5. Are users warned about the dangers of activities involving the product?

Questions to Ask About Advertisements and Claims

1. Are advertisements reviewed by legal counsel? Are warranties cleared with legal counsel?
2. Do product designers know what claims are made in advertising or by salespeople?
3. Are salespeople made aware that their oral statements to customers constitute warranties? Are they checked regularly to detect inappropriate promises?
4. Is adequate information about products and product limitations provided to salespeople?
5. Are rewards for salespeople tied to customer satisfaction as well as to sales volume?
6. Are pictures and demonstration models checked for express warranties?
7. Do written contracts and warnings make products' limitations clear?

Source: Frank Shipper and Marianne M. Jennings, *Avoiding and Surviving Lawsuits: The Executive Guide to Strategic Legal Planning for Business* Jossey-Bass Inc., Publishers, © 1989. Excerpted and reprinted with permission of authors.

INTERNATIONAL ISSUES IN PRODUCT LIABILITY

In 1985, the European Community Council of Ministers adopted a directive on product liability. The directive limits liability to "producers"; this is not as inclusive as U.S. law, which holds all sellers liable. There is a 10-year limit on liability,

and the "state-of-the-art" defense applies to most member countries: If a product upon its release was as good as any available, there is no product liability.

In addition to the council's guidelines are the International Standards Organization's 9000 Guidelines for Quality Assurance and Quality Management. These directives require products to carry a stamp of compliance with standards and procedures as a means of limiting product defects.

E T H I C A L   I S S U E S

10.4 In some cases, products outlawed in the United States are sold outside the United States. Referred to as dumping, the products are sold without mention of the U.S. litigation pending. What can be done about firms that sell defective products in Third World countries? For example, IUDs and non-flame-retardant pajamas were dumped after problems developed in the United States. Discuss the ethical issues.

SUMMARY

How does advertising create liability for a business?
- Express warranty—contractual promise about nature or potential of product that gives right of recovery if product falls short of a promise that was a basis of the bargain
- Bait and switch—using cheaper, unavailable product to lure customers to store with a more expensive one then substituted or offered instead
- Federal Trade Commission (FTC)—federal agency responsible for regulating deceptive ads
- Wheeler-Lea Act—federal law that allows FTC to regulate "unfair and deceptive acts or practices"
- Celebrity endorsements—FTC area of regulation wherein products are touted by easily recognized public figures
- Consent decree—voluntary settlement of FTC complaint

What are the contract theories of product liability?
- Implied warranty of merchantability—warranty of average quality, purity and adequate packaging given in every sale by a merchant
- Implied warranty of fitness for a particular purpose—warranty given in circumstances in which the buyer relies on the seller's expertise and acts to purchase according to that advice
- Disclaimer—act of negating warranty coverage
- Privity—direct contractual relationship between parties

What is required for tort-based recovery on defective product?

What is strict tort liability for products?
- Strict liability—standard of liability that requires compensation for an injury regardless of fault or prior knowledge
- Restatement § 402A—American Law Institute's standards for imposing strict liability for defective products

- Negligence—standard of liability that requires compensation for an injury only if the party responsible knew or should have known of its potential to cause such injury
- Punitive damages—damages beyond compensation for knowledge that conduct was wrongful
- Misuse—product liability defense for plaintiff using a product incorrectly

What defenses exist in product liability?
- Contributory negligence—conduct by plaintiff that contributed to his/her injury; serves as a bar to recovery
- Comparative negligence—negligent conduct by plaintiff serves as a partial defense by reducing liability by percentage of fault
- Assumption of risk—defense to negligence available when plaintiff is told of product risk and voluntarily uses it

What reforms are proposed in product liability?
- Consumer Product Safety Commission—federal agency that regulates product safety and has recall power
- Uniform Product Liability Act—proposed federal statute that would limit product liability suits and recovery

QUESTIONS AND PROBLEMS

1. Roger Gonzales purchased a Volvo station wagon for himself and his family. While the Volvo was pulling a U-Haul trailer and Mrs. Gonzalez was driving, there was an accident in which the Volvo rolled over. Mrs. Gonzalez was killed and the Gonzalez daughter was severely injured. The trailer hitch used on the Volvo was unsuitable for the Volvo's bumper. Mr. Gonzalez brought suit against Volvo for its failure to warn him not to use certain trailer hitches on the bumper that could cause accidents. Is Volvo liable? What is U-Haul's liability? [*Gonzalez* v. *Volvo of America Corp.*, 752 F.2d 295 (7th Cir. 1985).]

2. Joyce Payne got a permanent wave from a beautician, Mrs. Thrower. Mrs. Thrower used a permanent wave product called Soft Sheen, and she carefully read and followed all instructions on the wave kit. While Mrs. Thrower applied one step ("rearranger") in the process, Ms. Payne complained of a burning sensation in her back. The wave was completed, but two days later Ms. Payne was diagnosed in a hospital emergency room as having second degree burns on her back. She brought suit against the manufacturer of the wave and Mrs. Thrower. Mrs. Thrower says there were no warnings about the rearranger possibly burning skin. Who is liable? [*Payne* v. *Soft Sheen Products, Inc.*, 486 A.2d 712 (D.C. 1985).]

3. A patient with a cardiac pacemaker, who has experienced difficulty with it and as a result incurred medical bills, brought suit against the manufacturer for product liability. Does the manufacturer have a duty to warn the patient about the risks involved with a pacemaker? Is this the physician's responsibility? [*Brooks* v. *Medtronic, Inc.*, 750 F.2d 1227 (3rd Cir. 1984).]

4. The Woelfels were driving their car when their tire had a blowout. The tire had been used for 37,000 miles without a problem. The Woelfels have brought a suit under strict tort liability against the manufacturer of the tire. Will they win? What defenses can the manufacturer allege? [*Woelfel* v. *Murphy Ford Co.*, 487 A.2d 23 (Pa. 1985).]

5. Cuthbertson purchased from Martin-Marietta a front loader that had been manufactured by Clark Equipment. The front loader did not have a Roll Over Protection System (ROPS), a safety device that other manufacturers had. Eventually the ROPS was required by OSHA, and Martin-Marietta ordered one for Cuthbertson's loader, but it did

not arrive before he was injured in a roll-over accident. Who is liable? Why? [*Cuthbertson v. Clark Equipment*, 34 UCC Rep. Serv. (Callaghan) 71 (Maine 1982).]

6. William Bernick played hockey for Georgia Tech. In a game against Wake Forest, he was struck in the face by a hockey stick swung by Craig Jurden, a Wake Forest player. Mr. Bernick's upper jaw was fractured, three teeth were knocked out, and a fourth tooth was broken. He was wearing a mouthguard, but it shattered. Can Mr. Bernick recover? Why? [*Bernick v. Jurden*, 293 S.E.2d 405 (N.C. 1982).]

7. Roy E. Farrar Produce Co. (Farrar) ordered a shipment of boxes from International Paper Company (International) that were to be suitable for the packing and storage of tomatoes. The dimensions of the two sizes of boxes were to be such that either 20 or 30 pounds of tomatoes could be packed without the necessity of weighing each box. Mr. Farrar requested that boxes be the same type as those supplied to Florida packers for shipping tomatoes. Mr. Farrar told Mr. Wilson, an agent for International, to obtain the correct specifications for the Florida-type box.

   International shipped Mr. Farrar 21,500 unassembled boxes at a unit price of 64 cents per box. The boxes were not tomato boxes, were not Florida boxes, did not have adequate stacking strength, and would not hold up during shipping. Mr. Farrar had to repack 3,624 boxes (at a cost of $1.92 per box). Substitute boxes were purchased for 10 cents above the International price. The replacement boxes were Florida boxes and did not collapse. Mr. Farrar was also forced to pay growers $6 a box for tomatoes damaged during shipping. He could not use 6,100 boxes, and his sales dropped off, resulting in financial deficiencies in his operation. Can Mr. Farrar recover for his damages? Why? [*International Paper Co. v. Farrar*, 700 P.2d 642 (N.M. 1985).]

8. Cindi Cott, her husband Charles Price, and her father, John Cott, joined friends for an evening at the Peppermint Twist bar nightclub in Topeka, Kansas, on September 23, 1989. That evening, Peppermint Twist advertised watermelon shots for one dollar by posting it on a portable sign in the nightclub's parking lot. A watermelon shot contains Southern Comfort, Creme de Noyaux, and orange juice. Mary Cottrell was the Peppermint Twist waitress assigned to the table where Cindi, Charles, John, and their friends were sitting. Three shots were ordered. Mary poured the watermelon shots from a pour-and-serve container on her tray.

   Unbeknownst to Mary, the bar staff had confused a pour-and-serve container with Eco-Klene—a heavy-duty commercial dishwasher detergent with lye. Eco-Klene is red in color like the watermelon shots, and the bartenders had been using Eco-Klene near their sinks because they had run out of the normal dishwashing liquid they used. Eco-Klene contains sodium hydroxide, a cause of severe chemical burns that can be fatal.

   Cindi took a drink of the Eco-Klene, became very ill, and went to the restroom. John, curious, then tasted his Eco-Klene. Both were rushed to the hospital, experienced permanent physical damage, lost work time, and endured extensive rehabilitation. Cindi and John have sued Peppermint Twist. Can they recover? Are the manufacturers of Eco-Klene liable? [*Cott v. Peppermint Twist Management Co., Inc.*, 856 P.2d 906 (Kan. 1993).]

9. Morris and others are residents of Vermont who participated in the Nutri/System Weight Loss Program. They developed saturation of the bile with cholesterol, which contributed to gallstone and gallbladder disease. They brought suit alleging that the injuries were caused by Nutri/System foods. Can they recover? [*Morris v. Nutri/System, Inc.*, 774 F. Supp. 889 (D.C. Vt. 1991).]

10. Lori Yuzwak attended a horse auction with her two young daughters, Melissa and Mara. She explained to Barbara Dygert, the owner of a horse named Handy Deposit, that she wanted to buy a horse for her children. Ms. Dygert said the horse was quiet and gentle, did not have any vices, and would make a fine show horse for children. Mrs. Yuzwak bought Handy Deposit. The next day he kicked Mara in the face and seriously injured her. Mrs. Yuzwak has sued for breach of warranty. What warranties would she allege? Will she recover? [*Yuzwak v. Dygert*, 534 N.Y.S.2d 35 (1988).]

NOTE

1 *FTC News Summary*, May 19, 1978, pp. 1–2.

Judgment

In 1990, the U.S. Fish and Wildlife Service listed the northern spotted owl as an endangered species. Further, the service concluded that logging in the Northwest threatened the owl's continued existence. Lumber companies and trade associations protested, "Is it owls or is it jobs?" As the economies of the Northwest states suffered, the lumberjacks and lumber companies took their issue to Congress. A temporary measure allows continued harvesting through legislation overriding the U.S. Fish and Wildlife order. The battle continues in the pages of newspapers and over the airways. How much environmental regulation do we need? When can development be curtailed through regulation?

Environmental Regulation

When producing its products or providing its services, a

firm has an oblig-

ation to do so in a manner that does not illegally affect the

environment. Apart from the damage claims and penal-

ties that can result from the unlawful pollution of the

environment, social responsibility is a major issue.

Keeping a clean environment is a long-range goal not

only for society but for the businesses that hope to con-

tinue operating in that society. This chapter answers the

following questions: What are the public and private

environmental laws? What protections and require-

ments are there in environmental laws? Who enforces envi-

ronmental laws? What are the penalties for violations?

By the shores of Gitche Gumee,

By the shining Big-Sea-Water,
. . .

How they built their nests in summer,

Where they hid themselves in winter,

How the beavers built their lodges,

Where the squirrels hid their acorns,

How the reindeer ran so swiftly,

Why the rabbit was so timid . . .

Henry Wadsworth Longfellow
"Hiawatha's Childhood"

COMMON LAW REMEDIES
AND THE ENVIRONMENT

From earliest times, landowners have enjoyed the protections of the courts and various doctrines to prevent bad smells, noises, and emissions. Common law affords relief to adjoining landowners and communities when activities rise to the level of a **nuisance**. A nuisance exists when the activities of one landowner interfere with the use and enjoyment of their properties by other landowners or by members of the community in which the nuisance occurs. Bad smells, ongoing damage to paint on buildings, excessive noise, polluted air, and the operation of facilities that present health problems can all be enjoined as nuisances. In the following case, the New Jersey Supreme Court was faced with an issue of contamination of property and the liability of the transferors and transferees for the hazard that was created.

T&E Industries, Inc. v. Safety Light Corp.
587 A.2d 1249 (N.J. 1991)

YOU CAN'T BURY RADIUM OR LIABILITY

FACTS

United States Radium Corporation (USRC) owned an industrial site on Alden Street in Orange, New Jersey, where it processed radium from 1917 until 1926. USRC sold the radium for medical purposes and also used it to manufacture luminous paint for instrument dials, watches, and other products. Radium processing permitted recovery of only 80 percent of the radium from the carnotite ore transported to the plant from Colorado and Utah. The unextracted radium was contained in "tailings" that USRC discarded unto unimproved portions of the Alden Street site.

Through a complex series of chemical processes, the discarded radium emits radon, which can cause lung cancer when inhaled. Epidemiological studies had not been done at the time the tailings were discarded, and the federal government did not regulate the disposal of the tailings until 1978. However, many people had suspicions about handling radium, and as early as 1917 USRC employees measured the radioactivity of radium. One story told of how Dr. Van Sochocky, the president of USRC, "hacked" off his fingertip when radium lodged beneath his fingernail because he feared the effects of radium.

Radium processing ceased at the Alden site in 1926, and the site was leased to various commercial tenants until it was sold in 1943 to Arpin, a plastics manufacturer. The tailings were not removed from the site in spite of continually developing evidence about the danger. In fact, Arpin constructed a new portion of plant that rested on the discarded tailings. The property changed hands several times. T&E (plaintiff), a manufacturer of electronic components, leased the premises in 1969 and purchased it in 1974.

The Uranium Mill Tailings Radiation Control Act (1978) calls for the evaluation of inactive mill-tailing sites. New Jersey's Department of Environmental Protection (DEP) inspected the plaintiff's site and found radon levels exceeding state and federal standards. In spite of soil removal and other actions, the site could not be brought into compliance; T&E was forced to move its operations. The site could not be sold until cleanup of the tailings was complete.

In 1981, T&E sued Safety Light Corporation (a successor corporation to USRC) (defendant) and others (all corporations that bought from USRC or its transferees) based on nuisance, negligence, misrepresentation, fraud, and strict liability for abnormally dangerous activity. The

Continued

trial court dismissed the strict liability claim and found that USRC had no knowledge of the dangers when the tailings were disposed of. The jury found for T&E, but the trial court entered a judgment NOV for Safety Light. T&E appealed. The appellate court reversed the trial court's decision and Safety Light appealed.

JUDICIAL OPINION

CLIFFORD, Justice

The abnormally dangerous-activity doctrine emphasizes the dangerousness and inappropriateness of the activity. Despite the social utility of the activity, that doctrine imposes liability on those who, for their own benefit, introduce an extraordinary risk of harm into the community.

Because some conditions and activities can be so hazardous and of "such relative infrequent occurrence," the risk of loss is justifiably allocated as a cost of business to the enterpriser who engages in such conduct. Although the law will tolerate the hazardous activity, the enterpriser must pay its way.

Because the former owner of the property whose activities caused the hazard might have been in the best position to bear or spread the loss, liability for the harm caused by abnormally dangerous activities does not necessarily cease with the transfer of property.

A real-estate contract that does not disclose the abnormally dangerous condition or activity does not shield from liability the seller who created that condition or engaged in that activity.

The *Restatement* sets forth six factors that a court should consider in determining whether an activity is "abnormally dangerous."

(a) existence of a high degree of risk of some harm to the person, land, or chattels of others;

(b) likelihood that the harm that results from it will be great;

(c) inability to eliminate the risk by the exercise of reasonable care;

(d) extent to which the activity is not a matter of common usage;

(e) inappropriateness of the activity to place where it is carried on; and

(f) extent to which its value to the community is outweighed by its dangerous attributes.

Defendant does not dispute that liability can be imposed on enterprisers who engage in abnormally dangerous activities that harm others; but it contends that such liability is contingent on proof that the enterpriser knew or should have known of the "abnormally dangerous character of the activity." According to defendant, absent such knowledge that enterpriser "is in no position to make the cost-benefit calculations that will enable him to spread the risk and engage in the optimal level of activity." Defendant argues that absent such an opportunity, the policy basis for imposing strict liability on those who engage in abnormally dangerous activities, namely, cost spreading, cannot be realized.

We need not, however, determine whether knowledge is a requirement in the context of a strict-liability claim predicated on an abnormally dangerous activity. Even if the law imposes such a requirement, we are convinced, for the reasons set forth more fully below, that defendant should have known about the risks of its activity, and that its constructive knowledge would fully satisfy any such requirement.

Radium has always been and continues to be an extraordinarily dangerous substance. Although radium processing has never been a common activity, the injudicious handling, processing, and disposal of radium has for decades caused concern; it has long been suspected of posing a serious threat to the health of those who are exposed to it.

Furthermore, although the risks involved in the processing and disposal of radium might be curtailed, one cannot safely dispose of radium by dumping it onto the vacant portions of an urban lot. Because of the extraordinarily hazardous nature of radium, the processing and disposal of that substance is particularly inappropriate in an urban setting. We conclude that despite the usefulness of radium, defendant's processing, handling, and disposal of that substance under the facts of this case constituted an abnormally dangerous activity, Plaintiff's property is befouled with radium because of defendant's abnormally dangerous activity. Radiation levels at the site

Continued

exceed those permitted under governmental health regulations. Moreover, the property has been earmarked as a Superfund site. Because plaintiff vacated the premises in response to the health concern posed by the radium-contaminated site and because the danger to health is "the kind of harm, the possibility of which [made defendant's] activity abnormally dangerous," defendant is strictly liable for the resulting harm.

Here defendant knew that it was processing radium, a substance concededly fraught with hazardous potential. It knew that its employees who handled radium should wear protective clothing; it knew that some employees who had digested radium had developed cancer, and prior to the sale of the property, it knew that the inhalation of radon could cause lung cancer. Despite that wealth of knowledge concerning the harmful effects of radium exposure, defendant contends that it could not have known that disposal of the radium-saturated by-products behind the plant would produce a hazard. That contention appears to rest on the idea that somehow the radium's potential for harm miraculously disappeared once the material had been deposited in a vacant corner of an urban lot, or at the least that one might reasonably reach that conclusion—a proposition that we do not accept.

Surely someone engaged in a business as riddled with hazards as defendant's demonstrably was should realize the potential for harm in every aspect of that dangerous business. If knowledge be a requirement, defendant knew enough about the abnormally dangerous character of radium processing to be charged with knowledge of the dangers of disposal.

Finally, we reflect on the "parade of horribles" argument, namely, that our decision will create such uncertainty as to render it impossible for today's business community to regulate its affairs effectively. We have already noted the limited scope of our holding in that it extends only to that rare form of conduct that meets the criteria of an abnormally dangerous activity. Second, we note that almost without exception any conveyance of industrial property today would be made not in a vacuum but in full appreciation of regulatory requirements that would surely embrace a condition such as the one on the Alden Street property.

Affirmed.

CASE QUESTIONS
1. Who originally owned the property?
2. How was the property originally used?
3. How did the original owners feel about handling radium?
4. What was disposed of on the site?
5. Who will be held liable under CERCLA?
6. What made the disposal an abnormally dangerous activity?
7. What does the court say about the "parade of horribles" argument?

In many environmental problems, concerned parties do not want money for damages as much as they want the harmful activity halted. The courts have the power to issue injunctions against those who are harming either land, individuals, or the environment. Injunctions are granted in those cases in which the party (or parties) requesting the injunctive relief is able to establish ongoing harm as a result of the defendant's activities.

C O N S I D E R . . .

11.1 Spur Industries has operated a feedlot in an area about 20 miles from the city of Phoenix since 1956. Del E. Webb began the development of Sun City, a retirement community, in 1959. Spur expanded its operations in 1960 from 35 acres to 115 acres. Spur was feeding between 20,000 and 30,000 head of cattle. Each head produced 35 to 40 pounds of wet manure each day. Residents of Sun City are complaining about the odors and

Continued

flies. Webb has been unable to sell 1,300 lots located next to the feedlot. Could the residents win a nuisance suit against Spur? Does it matter that Spur was there first? [*Spur Industries, Inc. v. Del E. Webb Dev. Co., 494 P.2d 700 (Ariz. 1972).*]

STATUTORY ENVIRONMENTAL LAWS

At the federal level, most environmental laws can be placed in one of three categories: those regulating air pollution, those regulating water pollution, and those regulating solid waste disposal on land. In addition, the federal regulatory scheme has several laws affecting property rights that do not fit into these categories but are discussed in this subsection nonetheless.

Air Pollution Regulation

EARLY LEGISLATION

The first legislation dealing with the problem of air pollution passed in 1955 and was the **Air Pollution Control Act**. However, the 1955 act did very little to control or even to take steps to control the problem of air pollution.

Little action was taken to encourage greater involvement in the air pollution issue until Congress passed the **Air Quality Act** in 1967. Under this act, the Department of Health, Education and Welfare (HEW) was authorized to oversee the states' adoption of air quality standards and the implementation of those plans. Again, this legislation proved ineffective, for by 1970 no state had adopted a comprehensive plan.

E T H I C A L   I S S U E S

11.1 Do businesses have an obligation to sponsor research concerning pollution control? How could this be done? Could a joint business effort be used?

Review the Clean Air Act and Amendments: http://www.law. cornell.edu/ uscode/42/ch85. html#s7401
Visit the Environmental Protection Agency: http://www.epa. gov/

1970 AMENDMENTS TO THE CLEAN AIR ACT—NEW STANDARDS

Because the states did not take action concerning air pollution, Congress passed the 1970 amendments to the original but ineffective 1963 **Clean Air Act** (42 U.S.C. § 7401); these amendments constituted the first federal legislation with any real authority for enforcement. Under the act, the **Environmental Protection Agency (EPA)** was authorized to establish air quality standards, and once those standards were developed, states were required to adopt implementation plans to achieve the federally developed standards. These **state implementation plans (SIPs)** had to be approved by the EPA, and adoption and enforcement of the plans were no longer discretionary but mandatory. To obtain EPA approval, the implementation plans had to meet deadlines for compliance with the EPA air quality standards, and thus the Clean Air Act established time periods for achieving air quality.

The air quality standards set by the EPA specify how much of a particular substance in the air is permissible. It was up to each state to devise methods for meeting those standards. The first step taken by the states was to measure existing air content of substances such as sulfur dioxide, carbon monoxide, and hydro–carbons. Based on the results, the states then took appropriate steps to reduce the amounts of any substances that exceeded federal standards. The EPA required those state standards to mandate the development of air pollution devices. The lack of technology could not be used as a defense to air pollution.

1977 AMENDMENTS

With the 1977 amendments came authority for the EPA to regulate business growth in an attempt to achieve air quality standards. With this authority, the EPA classified two types of areas in which business growth could be contained. One type of area was called a **nonattainment area** and included those areas with existing, significant air quality problems, the so-called dirty areas. The second classification was for clean areas and was called **prevention of significant deterioration (PSD) areas**.

EPA ECONOMIC CONTROLS FOR NONATTAINMENT AREAS

For nonattainment areas, the EPA developed its **emissions offset policy** that requires three elements before a new facility can begin operation in a nonattainment area: (1) The new plant must have the greatest possible emissions controls; (2) the proposed plant operator must have all other operations in compliance with standards; and (3) the new plant's emissions must be offset by reductions from other facilities in the area.

In applying these elements, the EPA follows the **bubble concept**, which examines all the air pollutants in the area as if they came from a single source. If it can be shown that a new plant will have no net effect on the air in the area (after offsets from other plants), then the new facility will not be subject to a veto. Basically, the purpose of PSD regulations is to permit the EPA to have the right to review proposed plants before their construction.

NEW FORMS OF CONTROL—THE 1990 AMENDMENTS TO THE CLEAN AIR ACT

The Clean Air Act was revised substantially in 1990 with the **Clean Air Act Amendments of 1990**. These amendments focus on issues such as acid rain, urban smog, airborne toxins, ozone-depleting chemicals, and the various regional economic concerns and political problems attendant to these issues.

As of 1990, 96 cities were already three years late in achieving the attainment levels mandated by their SIPs in 1977, and 41 cities had carbon monoxide levels exceeding the goals in their SIPs. Under the 1990 amendments, the EPA is required to establish a **federal implementation plan (FIP)** within two years of a state's failure to submit to the EPA an adequate SIP. New deadlines were established for polluted areas according to current levels of pollution. Except for Los Angeles, Baltimore, and New York, compliance deadlines are set for the year 2000, with annual pollution-reduction goals for cities set at 3 to 4 percent a year.

The amendments have a substantial impact on smaller businesses, such as dry cleaners, paint shops, and bakeries, because the definition of a major source of pollution was changed from those businesses emitting 100 tons or more a year to those emitting 50 tons or more per year.

Motor vehicle manufacturers will experience substantial effects from the changes, as will gasoline producers. The nine worst nonattainment areas will be required to use reformulated gasolines that will reduce emissions by 15 percent by 1995 and 25 percent by 2000. More restrictive tailpipe emissions standards for autos to be phased in between 1994 and 1998 will require emissions reductions ranging from 30 to 60 percent for various pollutants. Gauges will be required in cars to alert drivers to problems with pollution control equipment. Car warranties must cover pollution control equipment for eight years or 80,000 miles.

Business Planning Tip

One of the effects of the Clean Air Act of 1990 has been the buying and selling of EPA sulfur dioxide emissions permits. If, for example, a utility has an EPA permit to discharge one ton of sulfur dioxide per year, but its equipment permits it to run "cleaner," the utility can sell the permit to another utility. In fact, the Chicago Board of Trade conducted a national auction for the sale of such permits. The price for a permit for one ton of sulfur dioxide ranged from $122–$450. The first day of trading these permits, March 30, 1993, produced sales of 150,000 permits worth $21.4 million. One percent of the bids were from environmental groups seeking to prevent use of the permits.

Plants that are major sources of toxic emissions will be required to use **maximum achievable control technology (MACT)**, although they can earn six-year extensions if they reduce emissions voluntarily by 90 percent by the time MACT standards are proposed by the EPA.

Utilities are affected substantially by the new amendments. A cap imposed on sulfur dioxide emissions is designed to address acid rain issues. Scrubber-installation incentives for utilities mean that putting in scrubbers now will result in a deadline extension for meeting the maximum sulfur dioxide emissions standards.

Administratively, the act contains the new requirement that all major polluting plants have operating permits that cite all of their Clean Air Act requirements. Furthermore, the penalties under the act were increased to allow field citations and civil penalties of up to $5,000 a day in addition to the $25,000 a day in general fines. The $5,000 per-day penalty applies to even minor violations, including recordkeeping. The EPA is also authorized under the amendments to pay $10,000 rewards to people who provide information leading to criminal convictions or civil penalties. Stiffer criminal penalties were added, with a possibility of up to two years imprisonment for false statements or failures to report violations. Willful violations carry penalties of up to five years and/or $1,000,000 in fines. The act specifically holds as criminally liable any responsible corporate officers.

C O N S I D E R . . . **11.2** Union Electric Company is an electric utility serving St. Louis and large portions of Illinois and Iowa. It operates three coal-fired generating plants in metropolitan St. Louis that are subject to sulfur dioxide restrictions under Missouri's SIP. Union Electric did not seek review of the implementation plan but applied for and obtained variances from the emissions limitations. When an extension for the variances was denied, Union Electric challenged the implementation plan on the grounds that it was technologically and economically infeasible and should therefore be amended. Will Union Electric succeed in having the plan amended? Consider the question in light of the 1990 Clean Air Act Amendments. [*Union Electric Co.* v. *EPA*, 427 U.S. 246 (1976).]

Water Pollution Regulation

EARLY LEGISLATION

In 1965, the first federal legislation on water quality standards was passed: the **Water Quality Act**. The act established a separate enforcement agency—the **Federal Water Pollution Control Administration (FWPCA)**—and required states to establish quality levels for the waters within their boundaries. Because the act contained few expeditious enforcement procedures, only about half of the states had developed their zones and standards by 1970, and none of the states was engaged in active enforcement of those standards with their implementation plans.

The **Rivers and Harbors Act of 1899**, which prohibits the discharge into navigable rivers and harbors of refuse that causes interference with navigation was used for a time to enforce water standards since state action was minimal. Specifically, the act prohibited the release of "any refuse matter of any kind or description" into navigable waters in the United States without a permit from the Army Corps of Engineers. For a time, the act was used to prosecute those industrial polluters that were discharging without permit.

PRESENT LEGISLATION

Review the Clean Water Act: http:// www.law.cornell. edu/uscode/33/ ch26.html

It was not until 1972 that meaningful and enforceable federal legislation was enacted with the passage of the **Federal Water Pollution Control Act of 1972** (33 U.S.C. § 1401). Under this act, two goals were set: (1) swimmable and fishable waters by 1983 and (2) zero discharge of pollutants by 1985. The act was amended in 1977 to allow extensions and flexibility in meeting the goals and was renamed the **Clean Water Act**. One of the major changes brought about by the act was the move of water pollution regulation from local to federal control. Federal standards for water discharges were established on an industry-wide basis, and all industries, regardless of state location, are required to comply.

Under the act, all direct industrial dischargers are placed into 27 groups, and the Environmental Protection Agency (EPA) (now responsible for water pollution control since the FWPCA was merged into it) establishes ranges of discharge allowed for each industrial group. The ranges for pulp mills, for example, differ from those for textile manufacturers, but all plants in the same industry must comply with the same ranges.

The ranges of discharges permitted per industrial group are referred to as **effluent guidelines**. In addition, the EPA has established within each industrial group a specific amount of discharge for each plant, which is the effluent limitation. Finally, for a plant to be able to discharge wastes into waterways it must obtain from the EPA a **National Pollution Discharge Elimination System (NPDES)** permit. This type of permit is required only for direct dischargers, or **point sources**, and is not required of plants that discharge into sewer systems (although these secondary dischargers may still be required to pretreat their discharges). Obtaining a permit is a complicated process that not only requires EPA approval but also state approval, public hearings, and an opportunity for the proposed plant owners to obtain judicial review of a permit decision.

In issuing permits, the EPA may still prescribe standards for release. Generally, the standards that are set depend upon the type of substance the discharger proposes to release. For setting standards, the EPA has developed three categories of pollutants: **conventional**, **nonconventional**, and **toxic pollutants**. If a discharger is going to release a conventional pollutant, the EPA can require it to pretreat the

FOR THE MANAGER'S DESK

THE EXXON VALDEZ

On March 24, 1989, the oil tanker *Exxon Valdez* ran aground on Bligh Reef, south of Valdez, Alaska, and spilled approximately 10.8 million gallons of oil into Prince William Sound. The captain of the tanker was Joseph Hazelwood.

Captain Hazelwood had a history of drinking problems and had lost his New York driver's license after two drunk-driving convictions. In 1985, with the knowledge of Exxon officials, Captain Hazelwood joined a 28-day alcohol rehabilitation program. Almost a week after the Prince William Sound accident, Exxon revealed that Captain Hazelwood's blood-alcohol reading was 0.061 in a test taken 10½ hours after the spill occurred. When announcing the test results, Exxon also announced Captain Hazelwood's termination.

Then-U.S. Interior Secretary Manual Lujan called the spill the oil industry's "Three Mile Island." After 10 days the spill covered a thousand square miles and leaked out of Prince William Sound onto beaches along the Gulf of Alaska and Cook Inlet. A cleanup army of 12,000 was sent in with hot water and oil-eating microbes. The workers found more than 1,000 dead otters among a local otter population of 15,000 to 22,000. Approximately 34,400 sea birds died, as did 151 bald eagles that ate

the oil-infested remains of the sea birds.

Joseph Hazelwood was indicted by the state of Alaska on several charges, including criminal mischief, operating a watercraft while intoxicated, reckless endangerment, and

negligent discharge of oil. He was found innocent of all charges except the negligent discharge of oil, was fined $50,000, and was required to spend a thousand hours helping in the cleanup of the Alaskan beaches.

Following the spill, critics of Exxon maintained that the company's huge personnel cutbacks during the 1980s affected the safety and maintenance levels aboard the tankers. Subsequent hearings revealed that the crew of the *Valdez* was overburdened with demands of speed and efficiency. The crew was working 10- to 12-hour days and often had interrupted sleep. Lookouts were often improperly posted, and junior officers were permitted control on the bridge without the required supervision. Robert

LeResche, oil-spill coordinator for the state of Alaska, said, "It wasn't Captain Ahab on the bridge. It was Larry and Curly in the Exxon boardroom." In response to Exxon's critics, then-CEO Lawrence Rawl stated, "And we say, 'We're sorry, and we're doing all we can.' There were 30 million birds that went through the sound last summer, and only 30,000 carcasses have been recovered. Just look at how many ducks were killed in the Mississippi Delta in one hunting day in December! People have come up to me and said, 'This is worse than Bhopal.' I say, 'Hell, Bhopal killed more than 3,000 people and injured 200,000 others!' Then they say, 'Well, if you leave the people out, it was worse than Bhopal.'"

Late in February 1990, Exxon was indicted by a grand jury in Anchorage on federal felony charges of violations of maritime safety and antipollution laws. The charges were brought after negotiations between Exxon and the Justice Department had been terminated. Both the state of Alaska and the Justice Department also brought civil suits against Exxon for the costs associated with cleaning up the spill.

By May 1990, Exxon had resumed its cleanup efforts using 110 employees at targeted sites. In 1991, Exxon reached plea agreements with the federal government and the state of Alaska on the

Continued

criminal charges. In the agreements, Exxon consented to plead guilty to three misdemeanors and pay a $1.15 billion fine. At the end of 1991, an Alaska jury awarded 16 fishermen more than $2.5 million in	damages and established a payout formula for similar plaintiffs in future litigation against Exxon. Eight hundred other civil cases remained pending at the time of the verdict. What was Exxon's "attitude" with regard to the spill?	What was the company's purpose in cutting back on staff and maintenance expenditures? Was Captain Hazelwood morally responsible for the spill? Was Exxon management morally responsible for the spill?

substance with the **best conventional treatment (BCT)**. If the pollutant to be discharged is either toxic or nonconventional, then the EPA can require the **best available treatment (BAT)**, which is the highest standard imposed. In issuing permits and requiring these various levels of treatment, the EPA need only consider environmental effects, and not the economic effects, on the applicant discharger.

C O N S I D E R . . . **11.3** Inland Steel Company applied for a permit from the EPA under the Federal Water Pollution Control Act of 1972. Although Inland was granted the permit, the EPA made the permit modifiable as new standards for toxic releases and treatment being were developed. Inland claimed the modification restriction on the permit was invalid because the EPA did not have such authority and also because Inland would be subject to every technological change or discovery made during the course of the permit. Inland filed suit. Was the restriction invalid? [*Inland Steel Co.* v. *EPA*, 547 F.2d 367 (7th Cir. 1978).]

Review the Safe Water Drinking Act: http://www.law.cornell.edu/uscode/42/300g-1.html
Review the Oil Pollution Act: http://www.law.cornell.edu/uscode/33/ch40.html

In 1986 Congress passed the **Safe Drinking Water Act**, which provides for the EPA to establish national standards for contaminant levels in drinking water. The states are primarily responsible for enforcement and can have higher standards than the federal standards, but they must at least enforce the federal standards for their drinking water systems.

In 1990 Congress passed the **Oil Pollution Act (OPA)** of 1990. The act was passed in response to large oil tanker spills, such as the one resulting from the grounding of the *Exxon Valdez* in Prince William Sound, Alaska, that resulted in a spill of 11 million gallons of crude oil that coated one thousand miles of Alaskan coastline. Another example was the 1990 explosion aboard the *Mega Borg* in Galveston Bay that resulted in a four million gallon spill and a fire that burned for more than a week.

The OPA applies to all navigable waters up to two hundred miles offshore and places the federal government in charge of all oil spills. Once full liability for cleanup is imposed on the company responsible for the spill, the federal government may step in and clean up a spill and then demand compensation for the costs incurred. The Oil Spill Liability Trust Fund, established by a five-cent-per-barrel tax, covers cleanup costs when the party responsible is financially unable to do the cleanup.

Those responsible for spills are liable for penalties of $25,000 a day or $1,000 a barrel spilled. If the spill is the result of negligence or willful misconduct, the penalties are $3,000 per barrel spilled. Failure to report a spill can bring a $250,000 fine for an individual (sole proprietor or officer, according to agency and criminal liability principles) and up to five years imprisonment or $500,000 for a corporation.

Solid Waste Disposal Regulation

EARLY REGULATION

Review the Toxic Substances Control Act: http://www.law.cornell.edu/uscode/15/ch53.html

Review the Resource Conservation and Recovery Act of 1976: http://www.law.cornell.edu/uscode/42/ch82.html

After several major open-dumping problems, such as the Love Canal chemical dumping near Buffalo, New York, two federal acts were passed that provided some enforcement power to the federal government for solid waste disposal. The **Toxic Substances Control Act (TOSCA)** (15 U.S.C. § 601) was passed in 1976 and authorized the EPA to control the manufacture, use, and disposal of toxic substances. Under the act, the EPA is authorized to prevent the manufacture of dangerous substances and stop the manufacture of substances subsequently found to be dangerous.

Also passed by Congress in reaction to dangerous dumping practices was the **Resource Conservation and Recovery Act of 1976 (RCRA)** (42 U.S.C. § 6901). The two goals of the act are to control the disposal of potentially harmful substances and to encourage resource conservation and recovery. A critical part of the act's control is a manifest or permit system that requires manufacturers to obtain a permit for the storage or transfer of hazardous wastes so that the location of such wastes can be traced through an examination of the permits issued.

THE SUPERFUND

Review the Comprehensive Environmental Response, Compensation, and Liability Act and Amendments: http://www.law.cornell.edu/uscode/42/ch103/html

In 1980 Congress passed the **Comprehensive Environmental Response, Compensation, and Liability Act (CERCLA)** (42 U.S.C. § 9601), which authorized the president to issue funds for the cleanup of areas that were once disposal sites for hazardous wastes. Under the act, a **Hazardous Substance Response Trust Fund** is set up to provide funding for cleanup. If funds are expended in such a cleanup, then, under the provisions of the act, the company responsible for the disposal of the hazardous wastes can be sued by the federal government and required to repay the amounts expended from the trust fund. Often called the **Superfund**, the funds are available for governmental use but cannot be obtained through suit by private citizens affected by the hazardous disposals.

In 1986 CERCLA was amended by the **Superfund Amendment and Reauthorization Act**. Under the amendments in that act, liability provisions were included, and the EPA is now permitted to recover cleanup funds from those responsible for the release of hazardous substances. Approximately seven hundred hazardous substances are now covered. (They are listed at 40 C.F.R. § 302.) Since the passage of the 1986 amendments, there has been judicial expansion of the concept of "responsibility." Clearly, those who release the substances are liable, but that liability has been expanded to include those who purchase the property and did not perform adequate checks on the property's history; and, as *Fleet Factors* (pg. 380) illustrates, even lenders can be included as responsible parties.

C O N S I D E R . . . 11.4 Grand Auto Parts Stores receives used automotive batteries from customers as trade-ins. Grand Auto drives a screwdriver through spent batteries and then sells them to Morris Kirk & Sons, a battery-cracking plant that extracts and smelts lead. Tons of crushed battery casings were found on Kirk's land. The EPA sought to hold Grand Auto liable for cleanup. Can Grand Auto be held liable? [*Catellus Dev. Corp.* v. *United States*, 34 F.3d 748 (9th Cir. 1994).]

United States v. Fleet Factors Corp.
901 F.2d 1550 (11th Cir. 1990)

THE LENDER LEFT HOLDING THE BAG (AND BARRELS OF TOXIC STUFF)

FACTS

In 1976, Swainsboro Print Works (SPW), a cloth-printing facility, entered into a "factoring" agreement with Fleet Factors Corporation (Fleet) in which Fleet agreed to advance funds against the assignmen to SPW'saccounts receivable. As collateral for these advances, Fleet obtained a security interesti n SPW's textile facility and all of its equipment, inventory, and fixtures.

In August 1979, SPW filed for bankruptcy under Chapter 11 (the corporate reorganization chapter). The Fleet factoring agreement continued until early 1981, when Fleet ceased advancing funds because SPW's debt to Fleet exceeded Fleet's estimate of the value of SPW's accounts receivable. On February 27, 1981, SPW ceased operations and began to liquidate its inventory. Fleet continued to collect the accounts receivable assigned to it under Chapter 11. In December 1981, SPW was adjudicated a bankrupt under Chapter 7, and the bankruptcy trustee assumed title and control of SPW's facility.

On August 31, 1982, Fleet contracted with Nix Riggers (Nix) to remove the unsold equipment in consideration for leaving the premises "broom clean." Nix had performed its work in the facility by the end of December 1983.

On January 20, 1984, the Environmental Protection Agency (EPA) inspected the facility and found seven hundred 55-gallon drums containing toxic chemicals and 44 truckloads of material containing asbestos. The EPA incurred costs of $400,000 in cleaning up the SPW facility. On July 7, 1987, the facility was conveyed to Emanuel County, Georgia, at a foreclosure sale from SPW's failure to pay state and county taxes.

The government sued Fleet and the two principal officers and stockholders of SPW to recover the costs of cleaning up the hazardous waste. The district court granted the government a motion for summary judgment with respect to the two principal officers and shareholders for the cost of removing the hazardous waste in drums. The district court denied the government's motion for holding Fleet liable for the asbestos-removal costs. Fleet moved to have the case dismissed. The court denied Fleet's motion, and Fleet appealed.

JUDICIAL OPINION

KRAVUITCH, Circuit Judge

The essential policy underlying CERCLA is to place the ultimate responsibility for cleaning up hazardous wastes on "those responsible for problems caused by the disposal of chemical poison." Accordingly, CERCLA authorizes the federal government to clean up hazardous waste dump sites and recover the cost of the effort from certain categories of responsible parties.

The parties liable for costs incurred by the government in responding to an environmental hazard are: (1) the present owners and operators of a facility where hazardous wastes were released or are in danger of being released; (2) the owners or operators of a facility at the time the hazardous wastes were disposed; (3) the person or entity that arranged for the treatment or disposal of substances at the facility; and (4) the person or entity that transported the substances to the facility. The government contends that Fleet is liable for the response costs associated with the waste at the SPW facility as either a present owner and operator of the facility, see 42 U.S.C. § 9607(a)(1), or the owner or operator of the facility at the time the wastes were disposed.

The district court reasoned that Fleet could not be liable under section 9607(a)(1) because it had never foreclosed on its security interest in the facility and its agents had not been on the premises since December 1983. The government contends that the statute should be interpreted to refer liability "back to the last time that someone controlled the facility however long ago." Thus, according to the government, the period of effective abandonment of the site by the

Continued

trustee in bankruptcy (from December 1983 to the July 1987 foreclosure sale) should be ignored and liability would remain with Fleet since it was the last entity to "control" the facility.

We agree Fleet cannot be held liable under section 9607(a)(1) because it neither owned, operated, or controlled SPW immediately prior to Emanuel County's acquisition of the facility. To reach back to Fleet's involvement with the facility prior to December 1983 in order to impose liability would torture the plain statutory meaning of "immediately beforehand."

There is no dispute that Fleet held an "indicia of ownership" in the facility through its deed of trust to SPW, and that this interest was held primarily to protect its security interest in the facility. The critical issue is whether Fleet participated in management sufficiently to incur liability under the statute.

The construction of the secured creditor exemption is an issue of first impression in the federal appellate courts. The government urges us to adopt a narrow and strictly literal interpretation of the exemption that excludes from its protection any secured creditor that participates in any manner in the management of a facility. We decline the government's suggestion because it would largely eviscerate the exemption Congress intended to afford to secured creditors. Secured lenders frequently have some involvement in the financial affairs of their debtors in order to insure that their interests are being adequately protected. To adopt the government's interpretation of the secured creditor exemption could expose all such lenders to CERCLA liability for engaging in their normal course of business.

Fleet, in turn, suggests that we adopt the distinction delineated by some district courts between permissible participation in the financial management of the facility and impermissible participation in the day-to-day or operational management of a facility.

Although we agree with the district court's resolution of the summary judgment motion, we find its construction of the statutory exemption too permissive towards secured creditors who are involved with toxic waste facilities. In order to achieve the "overwhelmingly remedial" goal of the CERCLA statutory scheme, ambiguous statutory terms should be construed to favor liability for the costs incurred by the government in responding to the hazards at such facilities. The district court's broad interpretation of the exemption would essentially require a secured creditor to be involved in the operations of a facility in order to incur liability. This construction ignores the plain language of the exemption and essentially renders it meaningless. Had Congress intended to absolve secured creditors from ownership liability, it would have done so. Instead, the statutory language chosen by Congress explicitly holds secured creditors liable if they participate in the management of a facility.

Our interpretation of the exemption may be challenged as creating disincentives for lenders to extend financial assistance to businesses with potential hazardous waste problems and encouraging secured creditors to distance themselves from the management actions, particularly those related to hazardous wastes, of their debtors.

Our ruling today should encourage potential creditors to investigate thoroughly the waste treatment systems and policies of potential debtors. If the treatment systems seem inadequate, the risk of CERCLA liability will be weighed into the terms of the loan agreement. Creditors, therefore, will incur no greater risk than they bargained for and debtors, aware that inadequate hazardous waste treatment will have a significant adverse impact on their loan terms will have powerful incentives to improve their handling of hazardous wastes.

Similarly, creditors' awareness that they are potentially liable under CERCLA will encourage them to monitor the hazardous waste treatment systems and policies of their debtors and insist upon compliance with acceptable treatment standards as a prerequisite to continued and future financial support.

Although the Court erred in construing the secured creditor exemption to insulate Fleet from CERCLA liability for its conduct prior to June 22, 1982, it correctly ruled that Fleet was liable for its subsequent activities if the government

Continued

could establish its allegations. Because there remain disputed issues of material fact, the case is remanded for further proceedings consistent with this opinion.

Affirmed and remanded.

CASE QUESTIONS

1. Describe Fleet's role as a creditor.

2. Who does the government wish to hold responsible for cleanup?

3. Is the lower court's decision affirmed?

4. What effect does the decision have on lenders' liability for cleanup?

5. Once property is taken back for foreclosure, what should a lender or creditor do? Conduct a cleanup?

FOR THE MANAGER'S DESK

FLEET FACTORS—WHAT LIABILITY DOES A LENDER HAVE FOR BAD PROPERTY?

When the *Fleet Factors* decision was handed down, lenders joined together in a resounding "What does this mean?" that registered 2.4 on the Richter Scale and actually damaged some of their collateral. Lenders were so distraught and confused that they were: (1) turning down loans; and (2) abandoning collateral rather than risk indicia of ownership. Recognizing that these behaviors (1) were abnormal for lenders; (2) detrimental to Alan Greenspan; and (3) had no prescriptive treatment currently approved by the FDA, the EPA instituted rulemaking to help. Rules were promulgated that exempted holders of mortgages, and deeds of trust, and lease financing transactions and any other relationships in which the land is or could serve as security for payment. The rule also offered details on conduct by lenders that was acceptable in repossession but would not rise

to the level of "owner/operator" conduct. Further, the EPA was kind enough to provide a how-to manual on foreclosure: How To Foreclose Without Demonstrating Indicia of Ownership. There were really simple rules for lenders: Foreclose and get rid of it. And do it fast. To the extent the property is not a mover, the lender must, under the rules as once promulgated, establish good faith efforts to sell.

Once the EPA rules on owner/operator exemptions for lenders were promulgated, the chemical folks and state attorneys general joined forces in *Kelley v. EPA*, 15 F.3d 1100 (D.C. 1994), to challenge the rules because lenders got better treatment than chemical manufacturers and state attorneys general had no one to tag for liability. Once you remove lenders from the picture, it's not much fun. Chasing after defaulting debtors for clean ups is fairly non-productive activity.

The D.C. Circuit held that although the EPA has the authority to determine what cleanup will be done, it is not given the authority under

CERCLA to determine who will do it. The court held that issues as to who is liable belong in the courts.

At the close of the case, the court conceded that the vacated regulations could be used by the EPA as policy statements to guide enforcement, but the EPA's intention to use it as such was unclear. Hence we have returned to our post-*Fleet Factors* confusion: no one knows when lenders will be held liable.

We are back to conflicts in the circuits and uncertainty as to the imposition of CERCLA liability on lenders. Lenders are left with the same advice given to land purchasers: check before you buy. Given the confusion on potential lender liability, similar advice is needed: check that collateral for barrels, tanks, puddles, things that go bump in the night, and other indicia of waste, hazardous and otherwise, before you extend the loan. For lenders with debtors in default: watch your workout language, limit your involvement, and sell, sell, sell, quickly, quickly.

Source: Excerpted from Marianne M. Jennings, "Lender Liability, CERCLA and Other Things that Go Bump in the Night," *Real Estate Law Journal* (Telephone: 1-800-950-1216), Winter 1996, pp. 372–375.

Environmental Quality Regulation

Review the National Environmental Policy Act: http://www.law.cornell.edu/uscode/42/ch55.html

Environmental controls of air, water, and waste are directed at private parties in the use of their land. However, as part of the environment control scheme, Congress also passed an act that regulates what governmental entities can do in the use of their properties. The **National Environmental Policy Act of 1969 (NEPA)** (42 U.S. § 4321) was passed to require federal agencies to take into account the environmental impact of their proposed actions and to prepare an **environmental impact statement (EIS)** before taking any proposed action.

An EIS must be prepared and filed with the EPA whenever an agency sends a proposed law to Congress and whenever an agency will take major federal action significantly affecting the quality of the environment. The information required in an EIS is as follows:

1. The proposed action's environmental impact
2. Adverse environmental effects (if any)
3. Alternative methods
4. Short-term effects vs. long-term maintenance, enhancement, and productivity
5. Irreversible and irretrievable resource uses

Examples of federal agency actions that have faced the issue of preparation of EISs include the Alaska oil pipeline, the extermination of wild horses on federal lands, the construction of government buildings, the NAFTA treaty, and highway construction.

The following case involves the question of whether an EIS was required to be prepared.

Sierra Club v. United States Dep't of Transportation
753 F.2d 120 (D.C. 1985)

SKIING AND LANDING AT JACKSON HOLE

FACTS

In 1983, the Federal Aviation Administration (FAA) issued two orders amending the operations specifications for Frontier Airlines, Inc., and Western Airlines, Inc. These amendments gave the airlines permanent authorizations to operate Boeing 737 jet airplanes (B-737s) out of Jackson Hole Airport, which is located within the Grand Teton National Park in Wyoming. These two airlines are the only major commercial carriers that schedule flights to and from Jackson Hole.

Private jets have flown into the airport since 1960; and Western Airlines has been flying into Jackson Hole since 1941. The airport is the only one in the country located in a national park, and Congress has continually funded expansions and improvements of the once single dirt-runway airport.

In 1978 Frontier applied for permission to fly B-737s into the Jackson Hole Airport. The FAA released its EIS on the application in 1980, which found that B-737s were comparable with C-580 propeller aircraft (the type then being used by Western and Frontier) for noise intrusion but were substantially quieter than the private jets using the airport. The study also showed that fewer flights would be necessary because the B-737 could carry more passengers and that different flight paths could reduce noise. Based on this EIS, Frontier was given the right to use B-737s for two years. When Frontier applied for permanent approval, the FAA used the 1980 EIS statement and found that with flight time restrictions, the impact would not harm the environment.

The Sierra Club, a national conservation organization, brought suit for the FAA's failure

Continued

to file an EIS for the 1983 amendments and for the use of national park facilities for commercial air traffic without considering alternatives.

JUDICIAL OPINION
Bork, Circuit Judge
We do not think the FAA violated NEPA by failing to prepare an additional EIS. Under NEPA, an EIS must be prepared before approval of any major federal action that will "significantly affect the quality of the human environment." The purpose of the Act is to require agencies to consider environmental issues before taking any major action. Under the statute, agencies have the initial and primary responsibility to determine the extent of the impact and whether it is significant enough to warrant preparation of an EIS. This is accomplished by preparing an Environmental Assessment (EA). An EA allows the agency to consider environmental concerns, while reserving agency resources to prepare full EIS's for appropriate cases. If a finding of no significant impact is made after analyzing the EA, then preparation of an EIS is unnecessary. An agency has broad discretion in making this determination, and the decision is reviewable only if it was arbitrary, capricious or an abuse of discretion.

This court has established four criteria for reviewing an agency's decision to forego preparation of an EIS. First, the agency must have accurately identified the relevant environmental concern. Second, once the agency has identified the problem, it must take a "hard look" at the problem in preparing the EA. Third, if a finding of no significant impact is made, the agency must be able to make a convincing case for its finding. Last, if the agency does find an impact of true significance, preparation of an EIS can be avoided only if the agency finds that changes or safeguards in the project sufficiently reduce the impact to a minimum.

The first test is not at issue here. Both the FAA and Sierra Club have identified the relevant environmental concern as noise by jet aircraft within Grand Teton National Park. The real issues raised by Sierra Club are whether the FAA took a "hard look" at the problem, and whether the methodology used by the agency in its alleged hard look was proper.

We find that the FAA did take a hard look at the problem. The FAA properly prepared an EA to examine the additional impact on the environment of the plan. The EA went forward from the 1980 EIS. The 1980 EIS, which was based on extensive research by Dr. Hakes of the University of Wyoming, noise testing by the FAA, and data derived from manufacturer information, showed that noise intrusions of B-737 jets over the level caused by C-580 propeller aircraft amounted to only 1 dbl near the Airport and decreased in proportion to the distance from the Airport. The agency, exercising its expertise, has found that an increase this minute is not significant for any environment. In addition, the EIS and Hakes studies were based on a worst case scenario, and it was determined that if certain precautions were taken the actual noise levels could be diminished greatly.

Petitioner (Sierra Club) argues that because Jackson Hole Airport is located within national parkland and a different standard—i.e., individual event noise level analysis—is mandated. Both individual event and cumulative data were amassed in preparing the 1980 EIS on which the EAs were based. The fact that the agency in exercising its expertise relied on the cumulative impact levels as being more indicative of the actual environmental disturbance is well within the area of discretion given to the agency. We agree with petitioner that although noise is a problem in any setting, "airplane noise is fundamentally inconsistent with the type of recreational experience Park visitors are seeking" and should be minimized. Here the FAA found that a cumulative noise increase of 1 dbl or less is not significant—even for the pristine environment in which Jackson Hole Airport is located.

Given all of these facts, we think the FAA was not required to prepare yet another EIS before granting permanent authorizations for the use of B-737s.

The orders of the FAA are hereby affirmed.

CASE QUESTIONS
1. What airport noise is at issue?
2. Who is involved in the case?
3. Was an EIS prepared?
4. What is the basis for the appeal?
5. What has the FAA allowed? Will the authorizations stand?

E T H I C A L   I S S U E S

11.2 The Superfund has been used quite frequently since its inception. As a result, more funds are needed to keep it going. Congress has proposed expanding the tax used to acquire funds to include all manufacturers. Whenever expansion of the funding sources for the Superfund has been proposed in Congress, the businesses not currently subject to the Superfund tax have opposed additional impositions on them. Do these firms have an obligation to assist in the cleanup? Can all firms claim that they do not affect the environment? Is cleanup a general business obligation?

Other Federal Environmental Regulations

In addition to the previously discussed major environmental laws, many other specific federal statutes protect the environment.

PESTICIDE CONTROL

Review the Environmental Pesticide Control Act: http://www.law.cornell.edu/uscode/7/ch6.html

Review the Asbestos Hazard Emergency Response Act: http://www.law.cornell.edu/uscode/15/2641.html

Under the **Federal Environmental Pesticide Control Act**, the use of pesticides is controlled. All pesticides must be registered with the EPA before they can be sold, shipped, distributed, or received. Also under the act, the EPA administrator is given the authority to classify pesticides according to their effects and dangers.

ASBESTOS CONTROL

The **Asbestos Hazard Emergency Response Act (AHERA)** passed in 1986 requires all public and private schools to arrange for the inspection of their facilities to determine whether their buildings have asbestos-containing materials (ACMs). Under the act, schools are required to develop plans for containment. The Clean Air Act also regulates asbestos by listing it as a toxic pollutant, and liability may result from the release of fibers from this known carcinogen. An amendment to the Superfund Act classified asbestos as a **Community Right-to-Know substance**, which means that there is a duty to disclose the presence of asbestos to potential buyers, tenants, and employees.

ENDANGERED SPECIES

Review the Endangered Species Act: http://www.law.cornell.edu/uscode/22/2151q.html

In 1973, Congress passed the **Endangered Species Act (ESA)**, a law that has proven to be a powerful tool for environmentalists in protecting species that are in danger of or threatened with extinction. Under the act, the secretary of the interior is responsible for identifying endangered terrestrial species, and the secretary of commerce identifies endangered marine species. In addition, these cabinet members must designate habitats considered crucial for these species if they are to thrive. In many instances, there is litigation concerning what species should or should not be on the list. Once a species is on the list, its critical habitat cannot be disturbed by development, noise, or destruction. The following case is a recent one that gives federal agencies broadsweeping authority in protecting endangered species. It provides the answer for the chapter's opening "Judgment."

Judgment

Babbitt v. *Sweet Home Chapter of Communities for a Great Oregon*
115 S. Ct. 2407 (1995)

OWLS VS. JOBS: LUMBER VS. ENDANGERED SPECIES

FACTS

Two U.S. agencies halted logging in the Pacific Northwest because it endangered the habitat of the northern spotted owl and the red cockaded woodpecker, both endangered species. Sweet Home Chapter (respondents) is a group of landowners, logging companies, and families dependent on the forest products industries in the Pacific Northwest. They brought suit seeking clarification of the authority of the secretary of the interior and the director of the Fish and Wildlife Service (petitioners) to include habitation modification as a harm covered by the Endangered Species Act (ESA).

The federal district court found for the secretary and director and held that they had the authority to protect the northern spotted owl through a halt to logging. The court of appeals reversed. Babbitt, the secretary of the interior, appealed.

JUDICIAL OPINION

STEVENS, Justice

Section 9(a)(1) of the Endangered Species Act provides the following protection for endangered species:

Except as provided in sections 1535(g)(2) and 1539 of this title, with respect to any endangered species of fish or wildlife listed pursuant to section 1533 of this title it is unlawful for any person subject to the jurisdiction of the United States to—(B) take any such species within the United States or the territorial sea of the United States[.] 16 U.S.C. § 1538(a)(1).

Section 3(19) of the Act defines the statutory term "take":

The term 'take' means to harass, harm, pursue, hunt, shoot, wound, kill, trap, capture, or collect, or to attempt to engage in any such conduct. 16 U.S.C. § 1532(19).

The Act does not further define the terms it uses to define "take." The Interior Department regulations that implement the statute, however, define the statutory term "harm":

Harm in the definition of 'take' in the Act means an act which actually kills or injures wildlife. Such act may include significant habitat modification or degradation where it actually kills or injures wildlife by significantly impairing essential behavioral patterns, including breeding, feeding, or sheltering. 50 CFR § 17.3 (1994).

We assume respondents have no desire to harm either the red-cockaded woodpecker or the spotted owl; they merely wish to continue logging activities that would be entirely proper if not prohibited by the ESA. On the other hand, we must assume *arguendo* that those activities will have the effect, even though unintended, of detrimentally changing the natural habitat of both listed species and that, as a consequence, members of those species will be killed or injured. Under respondents' view of the law, the Secretary's only means of forestalling that grave result—even when the actor knows it is certain to occur—is to use his § 5 authority to purchase the lands on which the survival of the species depends. The Secretary, on the other hand, submits that the § 9 prohibition on takings, which Congress defined to include "harm," places on respondents a duty to avoid harm that habitat alteration will cause the birds unless respondents first obtain a permit pursuant to § 10.

The text of the Act provides three reasons for concluding that the Secretary's interpretation is reasonable. First, an ordinary understanding of the word "harm" supports it. The dictionary definition of the verb form of "harm" is "to cause hurt or damage to: injure." Webster's Third New International Dictionary 1034 (1966). In the context of the ESA, that definition naturally encompasses habitat modification that results in actual injury or death to members of an endangered or threatened species.

Continued

Respondents argue that the Secretary should have limited the purview of "harm" to direct applications of force against protected species, but the dictionary definition does not include the word "directly" or suggest in any way that only direct or willful action that leads to injury constitutes "harm." Moreover, unless the statutory term "harm" encompasses indirect as well as direct injuries, the word has no meaning that does not duplicate the meaning of other words that § 3 uses to define "take." A reluctance to treat statutory terms as surplusage supports the reasonableness of the Secretary's interpretation.

Second, the broad purpose of the ESA supports the Secretary's decision to extend protection against activities that cause the precise harms Congress enacted the statute to avoid. As stated in § 2 of the Act, among its central purposes is "to provide a means whereby the ecosystems upon which endangered species and threatened species depend may be conserved."

Third, the fact that Congress in 1982 authorized the Secretary to issue permits for takings that § 9(a)(1)(B) would otherwise prohibit, "if such taking is incidental to, and not the purpose of, the carrying out of an otherwise lawful activity," 16 U.S.C. § 1539(a)(1)(B), strongly suggests that Congress understood § 9(a)(1)(B) to prohibit indirect as well as deliberate takings. The permit process requires the applicant to prepare a "conservation plan" that specifies how he intends to "minimize and mitigate" the "impact" of his activity on endangered and threatened species, 16 U.S.C. § 1539(a)(2)(A), making clear that Congress had in mind foreseeable rather than merely accidental effects on listed species.

The Court of Appeals made three errors in asserting that "harm" must refer to a direct application of force because the words around it do. First, the court's premise was flawed. Several of the words that accompany "harm" in the § 3 definition of "take," especially "harass," "pursue," "wound," and "kill," refer to actions or effects that do not require direct applications of force. Second, to the extent the court read a requirement of intent or purpose into the words used to define "take," it ignored § 9's express provision that a "knowing" action is enough to violate the Act. Third, the court employed *noscitur a sociis* to give "harm" essentially the same function as other words in the definition, thereby denying it independent meaning. The canon, to the contrary, counsels that a word "gathers meaning from the words around it." The statutory context of "harm" suggests that Congress meant that term to serve a particular function in the ESA, consistent with but distinct from the functions of the other verbs used to define "take." The Secretary's interpretation of "harm" to include indirectly injuring endangered animals through habitat modification permissibly interprets "harm" to have "a character of its own not to be submerged by its association."

When it enacted the ESA, Congress delegated broad administrative and interpretive power to the Secretary. See 16 U.S.C. §§ 1533, 1540(f). The task of defining and listing endangered and threatened species requires an expertise and attention to detail that exceeds the normal province of Congress. Fashioning appropriate standards for issuing permits under § 10 for takings that would otherwise violate § 9 necessarily requires the exercise of broad discretion. The proper interpretation of a term such as "harm" involves a complex policy choice. When Congress has entrusted the Secretary with broad discretion, we are especially reluctant to substitute our views of wise policy for his. In this case, that reluctance accords with our conclusion, based on the text, structure, and legislative history of the ESA, that the Secretary reasonably construed the intent of Congress when he defined "harm" to include "significant habitat modification or degradation that actually kills or injures wildlife."

In the elaboration and enforcement of the ESA, the Secretary and all persons who must comply with the law will confront difficult questions of proximity and degree; for, as all recognize, the Act encompasses a vast range of economic and social enterprises and endeavors. These questions must be addressed in the usual course of the law, through case-by-case resolution and adjudication.

      The judgment of the Court of Appeals is reversed.

CASE QUESTIONS

1. Is habitat modification harming endangered species?
2. Does the Court's interpretation mean no intent is required to violate ESA?
3. Did Congress intend to give the secretary authority to shut down an industry?
4. Is logging prevented now?
5. What ethical issues arise from this case?

Aftermath: In August 1995, Congress passed, as a rider to a budget-reduction bill, a provision that suspends environmental laws in some national forest areas in Washington and Oregon through 1996.

STATE ENVIRONMENTAL LAWS

In addition to federal enactments, all the states have enacted some form of environmental law and have established their own environmental policies and agencies. Some states may require new industrial businesses to obtain a state permit along with the required federal permits for the operation of their plants. Some states regulate the types of fuels that can be used in vehicles and offer incentives for carpooling.

ENFORCEMENT OF ENVIRONMENTAL LAWS

Federal environmental laws can be enforced through criminal sanctions, penalties, injunctions, and suits by private citizens. In addition to federal enforcement rights, certain common law remedies, such as nuisance or trespass, exist for the protection of property rights. This portion of the chapter discusses the various remedies available for environmental violations.

Parties Responsible for Enforcement

Although many federal agencies are involved with environmental issues, the Environmental Protection Agency (EPA), established in 1970, is the agency

E T H I C A L   I S S U E S

11.3 The environmental statutes and regulations provide for minimum standards of conduct. Does business have an obligation to perform above those minimum standards? For example, could businesses involved in surface mining work with communities and environmental groups to alleviate tension? Does such cooperation prevent more stringent regulations in the future? Are there long-term benefits to such cooperation?

Act	Penalties	Private suit
Clean Air Act	$25,000 per day, up to one year in prison, or both; five years/$1 million for knowing violations; $50,000 for field citations; $10,000 rewards for reporting violations	Citizen suits authorized; EPA suit for injunctive relief
Clean Water Act	$25,000 per day, up to one year in prison, or both	Citizen suits authorized; EPA suit for injunctive relief
Resource Conservation and Recovery Act	$25,000 per day, up to one year in prison, or both	No private suits; Hazardous Substance Response Trust Fund for cleanup; EPA suit for injunctive relief and reimbursement of trust funds

Exhibit 11.1
Penalties for Violation of Federal Environmental Laws

responsible for the major environmental problems of air and water pollution, solid waste disposal, toxic substance management, and noise pollution. The EPA is responsible for the promulgation of specific standards and the enforcement of those standards with the use of the remedies discussed in the following subsections. The federal EPA may work in conjunction with state EPAs in the development and enforcement of state programs.

The **Council on Environmental Quality (CEQ)** was established in 1966 under the National Environment Act and is part of the executive branch of government. Its role in the environment regulatory scheme is that of policymaker. The CEQ is responsible for formulating national policies on the quality of the environment and then making recommendations to lawmakers regarding its policy statements.

In addition to these major environmental agencies, other federal agencies are involved in enforcement of environmental issues, such as the Atomic Energy Commission, the Federal Power Commission, the Department of Housing and Urban Development, the Department of the Interior, the Forest Service, the Bureau of Land Management, and the Department of Commerce. Basically, all federal agencies that deal with the use of land, water, and air are involved in compliance with and enforcement of environmental laws.

Criminal Sanctions for Violations

Most of the federal statutes previously discussed carry criminal sanctions for violations. Exhibit 11.1 summarizes the various penalties provided under each of the discussed acts. In exercising its enforcement power, the epa may require businesses to maintain records or to install equipment necessary for monitoring the amounts of pollutants being released into the air or water.

The following case deals with the issue of criminal liability for environmental law violations.

United States v. Johnson & Towers, Inc.
741 F.2d 662 (3d Cir. 1984)

CHANGING YOUR OIL: IT CAN BE CRIMINAL

FACTS

Johnson & Towers (Johnson) repairs and overhauls large motor vehicles. In its operations, Johnson uses degreasers and other industrial chemicals that contain methylene chloride and trichlorethylene, classified as "hazardous wastes" under the Resource Conservation and Recovery Act (RCRA) and as pollutants under the Clean Water Act.

The waste chemicals from Johnson's cleaning operations were drained into a holding tank and, when the tank was full, pumped into a trench. The trench flowed from the plant's property into Parker's Creek, a tributary of the Delaware River. Under RCRA, generators of such wastes must obtain a permit from the EPA, but Johnson had not received or even applied for such a permit.

Jack Hopkins, a foreman, and Peter Angel, the service manager for Johnson, were charged with criminal violations of the RCRA and the Clean Water Act. Johnson was also charged and pled guilty. Messrs. Hopkins and Angel pled not guilty on grounds that they were not "owners" or "operators" as required for RCRA violations. The trial court agreed and dismissed all charges against Messrs. Hopkins and Angel except for the criminal conspiracy charges.

The government appealed the dismissal.

JUDICIAL OPINION

SLOVITER, Circuit Judge

The single issue in this appeal is whether the individual defendants are subject to prosecution under RCRA's criminal provision, which applies to:

any person who— . . . (2) knowingly treats, stores, or disposes of any hazardous waste identified or listed under this subchapter either — (A) without having obtained a permit under Section 6925 of this title . . . or (B) in knowing violation of any material condition or requirement of such permit.

If we view the statutory language in its totality, the congressional plan becomes . . . apparent. First, "person" is defined in the statute as "an individual, trust, firm, joint stock company, corporation (including a government corporation), partnership, association, State, municipality, commission, political subdivision of a State, or any interstate body." Had Congress meant to take aim more narrowly, it could have used more narrow language.

Second, under the plain language of the statute, the only explicit basis for exoneration is the existence of a permit covering the action. Nothing in the language of the statute suggests that we should infer another provision exonerating persons who knowingly treat, store or dispose of hazardous waste but are not owners or operators.

Finally, though the result may appear harsh, it is well established that criminal penalties attached to regulatory statutes intended to protect public health, in contrast to statutes based on common law crimes, are to be construed to effectuate the regulatory purpose.

In summary, we conclude that the individual defendants are "persons" within the RCRA, that all elements of that offense must be shown to have been knowing, but that such knowledge, including that of the permit requirement, may be inferred by the jury as to those individuals who hold the requisite responsible positions with the corporate defendant. For the foregoing reasons, we will reverse the district court's dismissal and we will remand for further proceedings consistent with this opinion.

CASE QUESTIONS

1. Who is charged with criminal violations?
2. What violations are charged?
3. What violations did the lower court dismiss?
4. Did Congress intend to prosecute corporate employees?
5. Does the appellate court reinstate the charges?
6. What proof is required to show violations by the "persons" involved?

Hazel O'Leary, an attorney, rose to the rank of vice president at Northern States Power Company in Minnesota. One of the highest ranking female utility executives in the country, Mrs. O'Leary caught the attention of President Clinton, who in 1993 asked her to serve as secretary of the Department of Energy (DOE). She was the first woman and first utility executive to serve in that post.

Hazel O'Leary, U.S. Energy Secretary

Early in her prominent role, Mrs. O'Leary earned praise and respect from many groups when she released previously classified documents that revealed the role of U.S. government officials and agencies in radioactive experimentation on citizens. She also worked to obtain compensation for the victims of these experiments.

Mrs. O'Leary proved to be a powerful force in the battle with Nevada legislators and business people over the proposed site for a high-level nuclear waste dump at Yucca Mountain. She raised issues about the site's impact on the state and surrounding communities.

In 1994, members of Congress released to the press copies of Mrs. O'Leary's overseas travel expenses showing she had spent more than any other cabinet official on overseas travel, including the secretary of state.

Hazel O'Leary

In 1995, a media report disclosed that the DOE had spent $43,000 of federal funds to pay for Carma International, a private company, to provide monthly evaluations of news coverage for the Energy Department. The reports from the company included lists of journalists with rankings based on whether their stories were positive or negative toward the department. The report concluded:

Unfavorable coverage from the federal and state level could have been devastating for the DOE this quarter. However, agency officials rose to the occasion, with Secretary O'Leary aggressively defending her organization and finding ways to streamline it.

Mrs. O'Leary said she was unaware of the list. Members of Congress called for her resignation. White House Chief of Staff, Leon Panetta, ordered a full report. White House spokesman Mike McCurry summarized, "It is simply unacceptable."

Representative Steve Chabot said, "It's outrageous Secretary O'Leary would use tax dollars to put together essentially an enemies list of reporters." The White House ordered Mrs. O'Leary to pay $43,000 to the Treasury from her office account.

Members of Congress asked Mrs. O'Leary to resign, but she stood firm and refused. Daniel Schorr of National Public Radio summarized the contract with Carma and press monitoring as follows, "It's dumb. It's so dumb."

Issues

1. How did Mrs. O'Leary make such a poor ethical choice?
2. Has Mrs. O'Leary limited her future?

Group Suits—The Effect of Environmentalists

In many circumstances, private suits have had the most effect either in terms of obtaining compliance with environmental regulations or in terms of abating existing nuisances affecting environmental quality. The reason for the success of these suits may be the ultimate outcome of the litigation—possible business shutdowns and, at the least, the payment of tremendous amounts of damages and costs.

Visit the Sierra Club:
http://www.
sierraclub.org/

Private suits have been brought by environmental groups that have both the organizational structure and sufficient funding for the initiation and completion of such suits. In some cases, the environmental groups are formed to protest one specific action, as is the case of Citizens Against the Squaw Peak Parkway; other groups are national organizations that take on environmental issues and litigation in all parts of the country. Examples of these national groups include the Sierra Club, the Environmental Defense Fund, Inc., the National Resources Defense Council, and the League of Conservation Voters. Some environmental groups represent business interests in environmental issues, as does the Mountain States Legal Foundation, which becomes involved in presenting business issues when private organizations and individuals bring environmental suits.

These environmental groups have not only been successful in bringing private damage and injunctive relief suits but have also been able to force agencies to promulgate regulations and to enjoin projects when EISs should have been filed but were not.

INTERNATIONAL ENVIRONMENTAL ISSUES

*Visit the European
Environment Agency:*
http://www.eea.dk/
*Visit the International
Organization for
Standardization:*
http://www.iso.ch/

By the end of 1992, the European Union (EU) had passed more than two hundred environmental directives that focus on noise restrictions; protection of endangered species; energy efficiency; recycling; and air, land, and water quality. The view of the EU is that environmental planning is to be conducted by member states as part of their economic development plans and processes. In 1990, the EU created the European Environment Agency to serve as a clearinghouse for environmental information; eventually the agency will operate for members in a manner similar to the EPA.

Many EU directives are designed to eliminate the need for regulation by encouraging different business choices and educating consumers. One directive requires manufacturers to make 90 percent of all packaging materials recyclable by the year 2000. Another directive will award companies the use of an "eco-audit" sticker on their labels and stationeries if they comply with an annual environmental audit of their manufacturing, waste management, materials use, and energy choices. The audits can be done in-house or conducted by registered eco-auditors, but results must be released to the public. An innovative directive of the EU has created an EU-wide "eco-label" to be placed on all consumer goods to provide information about the environmental impact of a product's production, distribution, life, and disposal. Germany has had such a label, called the "Blue Angel," for a number of years, and the EU has adopted the concept for its continental marketplace.

The International Organization for Standardization (ISO) (pronounced ICE-O, derived from the Greek *isos* meaning "equal") a private organization formed to promote the adoption and use of uniform standards of international trade, has developed ISO 14000, a series of standards for environmental management that would cover product labeling and company disclosure requirements.

E T H I C A L   I S S U E S

11.4 Environmental concerns have prompted voluntary actions on the part of the U.S. business community. Consider the following programs initiated by some companies:

Company	Program
Amana	Initiated companywide recycling program for newspapers, plastic jugs, and motor oil; proceeds donated to nonprofit environmental groups
Arco Chemical	Promotes the antifreeze agent propylene glycol over the more toxic ethylene glycol
AT&T	Publishes annual environmental report
Chevron	Publishes annual environmental report
Conoco	Ordered two double-hulled tankers and plans to add more to fleet
Du Pont	Will reduce air emissions by 60 percent over the next three years (through 1994); publishes annual environmental report
General Mills	Requires use of recycled paper in all cereal boxes; banned use of metals in heavy printing ink
H. J. Heinz	Developed easy recycling ketchup bottles; will not buy tuna caught with dolphins in nets
Johnson & Johnson	Eliminated use of Styrofoam cups in the workplace; started companywide recycling program at employee desks
Kodak	Established camera recycling program
McDonald's	Shortened straws; uses recycled paper for napkins and trays
Polaroid	Publishes annual environmental report
Procter & Gamble	Is developing recycling of disposable diapers
Scott Paper	Sponsors tree-planting programs
Union Carbide	Will spend $310 million over four years on environmental and recycling programs; publishes annual environmental report
Herman Miller	Stopped using rain forest mahogany in Eames signature chair; gave employees mugs and stopped using Styrofoam cups

None of the programs initiated by these companies is mandated by law. Why are the companies taking such steps? Discuss the benefits each company derives from its programs. Do some of the benefits meet Milton Friedman's test for social responsibility?

E T H I C A L   I S S U E S

11.5 In 1989, the Coalition for Environmentally Responsible Economies (CERES) issued its code of conduct for corporate governance. The coalition is a group that hopes to influence investment decisions on the basis of a corporation's environmental commitment. The code, called the Valdez Principles, is presented here in edited form.

The Valdez Principles
1. *Protection of the Biosphere.* We will minimize and strive to eliminate the release of any pollutant that may cause environmental damage to the air, water, or earth or its inhabitants. We will safeguard habitats in rivers, lakes, wetlands, coastal zones and oceans and will minimize contributing to the greenhouse effect, depletion of the ozone layer, acid rain, or smog.
2. *Sustainable Use of Natural Resources.* We will make sustainable use of renewable natural resources, such as water, soils and forests. We will conserve non-renewable natural resources through efficient use and careful planning. We will protect wildlife habitat, open spaces and wilderness, while preserving biodiversity.
3. *Reduction and Disposal of Waste.* We will minimize the creation of waste, especially hazardous waste, and wherever possible recycle materials. We will dispose of all wastes through safe and responsible methods.
4. *Wise Use of Energy.* We will make every effort to use environmentally safe and sustainable energy sources to meet our needs. We will invest in improved energy efficiency and conservation in our operations. We will maximize the energy efficiency of products we produce and sell.
5. *Risk Reduction.* We will minimize the environmental, health and safety risks to our employees and the communities in which we operate by employing safe technologies and operating procedures and by being constantly prepared for emergencies.
6. *Marketing of Safe Products and Services.* We will sell products or services that minimize adverse environmental impacts and that are safe as consumers commonly use them. We will inform consumers of the environmental impacts of our products or services.
7. *Damage Compensation.* We will take responsibility for any harm we cause to the environment by making every effort to fully restore the environment and to compensate those persons who are adversely affected.
8. *Disclosure.* We will disclose to our employees and to the public incidents relating to our operations that cause environmental harm or pose health or safety hazards. We will disclose potential environmental, health or safety hazards posed by our operations, and we will not take any action against employees who report any condition that creates a danger to the environment or poses health and safety hazards.
9. *Environmental Directors and Managers.* We will commit management resources to implement the Valdez Principles, to monitor and report upon our implementation efforts, and to sustain a process to ensure that the Board of Directors and Chief Executive Officer are kept informed of and are fully responsible for all environmental matters. . . .
10. *Assessment and Annual Audit.* We will conduct and make public an annual self-evaluation of our progress in implementing these Principles and in complying with applicable laws and regulations throughout our worldwide operations. . . .

The following chart lists the companies in which Valdez shareholder resolutions have either come to votes or were withdrawn after agreements in 1992. Where available, percentages of shareholder votes in favor of the resolutions are provided; votes in parentheses are from 1991.

Continued

Resolutions to sign the principles

American Cyanamid—10.8% (12.1%)
Amoco—withdrawn
Browning-Ferris—withdrawn
Champion International—5.7% (7.7%)
Chrysler—10.1% (9.6%)
Corning—7.1%
Exxon—7.9% (6.3%)
General Motors—10.7% (9.0%)
International Paper—6.0% (5.0%)
Kimberly-Clark—7.4% (5.6%)
Louisiana Pacific—8.8% (8.5%)
McDonald's—withdrawn
Mobil—6.7% (8.3%)
Occidental Petroleum—12.2% (14.9%)
PepsiCo—9.7% (7.9%)
Phillips Petroleum—11.4%
Safety-Kleen—7.5% (10.4%)
Southern—withdrawn
Sun Co.—6.5%
Union Carbide—5.5%
USX—6.9%

Waste Management—8.4% (9.5%)
Westinghouse—withdrawn
Wheelabrator—4.1%

Resolutions to report on the principles

American Electric Power—withdrawn
Atlantic Richfield—12.2% (9.5%)
Bristol-Myers Squibb—withdrawn
Burlington Resources—22.2%
Chevron—7.8%
Coastal—8.8%
Cooper Industries—12.4%
Emerson Electric—withdrawn
Great Lakes Chemical—17.0%
GTE—14.7% (10.3%)
Kerr-McGee—15.4% (16.8%)
Oregon Steel—6.2%
Raytheon—withdrawn
Tenneco—11.1%
Texaco—withdrawn
Union Pacific—12.4% (10.1%)

Does the set of principles reflect sound social responsibility? Would you have your company sign the principles? Is it sound corporate governance to do so?

Source: Investor Responsibility Research Center

SUMMARY

What are the public and private environmental laws? What protections and requirements are there in environmental laws?

- Nuisance—bad smells, noises, or dirt from one property that interferes with another's use and enjoyment of their property
- Nonattainment areas—areas with significant air pollution problems
- Emissions offset policy—new plants are not built until new emissions are offset by reductions elsewhere
- Bubble concept—EPA policy of maximum air emissions in one area
- Clean Air Act—federal law that controls air emissions
- Maximum Achievable Control Technology (MACT)—best means for controlling emissions
- Clean Water Act—federal law that regulates emissions in various water sources
- Effluent guidelines—EPA maximum allowances for discharges into water
- Safe Drinking Water Act—federal law establishing standards for contaminants
- Oil Pollution Act—federal law imposing civil and criminal liability for oil spills
- Resource Conservation and Recovery Act—federal law controlling disposal of hazardous waste through a permit system

- Superfund—funds available for government to use to clean up toxic waste sites
- Comprehensive Environmental Response, Compensation and Liability Act (CERCLA)—federal law providing funds and authority for hazardous waste site clean-ups
- Endangered Species Act—powerful federal law that can curb economic activity if it presents harm to endangered species or their habitat

Who enforces environmental laws?
- Environmental Protection Agency (EPA)—federal agency responsible
- Coalition for Environmentally Responsible Economies (CERES)—international environmental organization
- National Environmental Policy Act (NEPA)—federal law that requires federal agencies to assess environmental issues before taking actions
- Environmental Impact Statement (EIS)—report by federal agency on study of proposed action's effect on the environment

What are the penalties for violations?
- Injunction—judicial order halting an activity

QUESTIONS AND PROBLEMS

1. Philip Carey Company owned a tract of land in Plymouth Township, Pennsylvania, on which it deposited a large pile of manufacturing waste containing asbestos. Carey sold the land to Celotex, and Celotex sold the land to Smith Land & Improvement Corporation. The EPA notified Smith in July 1984 that unless the plaintiff took steps to eliminate the asbestos hazard, the EPA would do the work and pursue reimbursement. Smith proceeded with the cleanup to the EPA's satisfaction at a total cost of $218,945.44. Smith then turned to Celotex and Carey, as previous owners of the property, for reimbursement. These firms say they have no liability under CERCLA. Which firms are liable? [*Smith Land & Improvement Corp.* v. *Celotex*, 851 F.2d 86 (3rd Cir. 1988).]

2. A group of landowners situated near the Sanders Lead Company brought suit to recover for damages to their agricultural property from accumulations of lead particulates and sulfur oxide deposits released in Sanders' production process. The landowners' property had increased in value because of its commercial potential in being close to the plant. Sanders employs most of the town's residents in its operations. What common law and statutory rights do the landowners have, and what relief can be obtained? [*Borland* v. *Sanders Lead Co., Inc.*, 369 So. 2d 523 (Ala. 1979).]

3. In 1985, Manufacturers National Bank of Detroit issued a letter of credit for Z&Z Leasing, Inc., an industrial firm, in order to enable Z&Z to obtain bond financing from Canton Township, Michigan.

   After six years of operation, Z&Z was not doing well and had defaulted on its bond obligations. A consultant for the Bank found underground storage tanks on Z&Z's site. The tanks contained a yellowish liquid that was found to be a solvent and a hazardous substance. The bank paid off the Canton township bond obligation and foreclosed on the Z&Z property. By 1993, Z&Z had still not sold the property, and the EPA sought to hold the bank liable as an operator for the costs of cleaning up the tanks.

   Can the bank be held liable? [*Z&Z Leasing, Inc.* v. *Graying Reel, Inc.*, 873 F. Supp. 51 (E.D. Mich. 1995).]

4. Reynolds Metal has been held to the same technological standards in its pollution control for can-manufacturing plants as those applied to aluminum manufacturers. Reynolds claims the processes are different and that the technology is not yet available for can manufacturing. Does Reynolds have a point? [*Reynolds Metals Co.* v. *EPA*, 760 F.2d 549 (D.C. 1985).]

5. The Mitchells lived in a residential section of Beverly Hills, Michigan, and sought to enjoin the operation of a nearby piggery. The pigs were fed in an open field, and any garbage not eaten by the pigs was plowed under by tractors. The odors from the operation, particularly in the spring and summer, were such that the use and enjoyment of the Mitchells' property was impaired. Could the Mitchells file a suit? On what basis? Could they win? Are any federal statutory violations involved? [*Mitchell* v. *Hines*, 9 N.W. 2d 547 (Mich. 1943).]

6. Peabody Mine No. 47 was located one-fourth mile from Walter Patterson's land. Mr. Patterson used his land for farming and operated on a low maintenance schedule. His house had never been painted. Mr. Patterson said that gas, smoke, fumes, and dust traveled to his property, and he complained his clothes turned black, his bed clothes were dusty, his food was covered in coal dust, and his throat and nostrils were affected. Mr. Patterson said he was forced to sleep with the windows closed, even in the summer, to avoid blowing coal dust. The coal mine facilities operated 24 hours a day, six days each week. Does Mr. Patterson have any remedy? [*Patterson* v. *Peabody Coal Co.*, 122 N.E.2d 48 (Ill. 1954).]

7. Brad Bennett and Mario Giordano operate ranches in Oregon. Each has a reservoir used for water sources for their cattle. The U.S. Fish and Wildlife Service has issued an opinion that the water level in the reservoirs must be maintained at a specific level in order to preserve the habitat of two species of fish, the shortnose sucker and the Lost River. Bennett and Giordano protest, saying that in dry spells if their cattle can't drink, they'll lose their herds. Can the government order the maintenance of a water level? [*Bennett* v. *Plenert*, 63 F. 3d 915 (9th Cir. 1995).]

8. The Nuclear Regulatory Commission (NRC) was responsible for the decision to allow the once-crippled Three Mile Island Unit I nuclear plant to resume operation. Pursuant to the NEPA, the NRC considered the impact on the surrounding community and determined that there would be no adverse impact. A group, People Against Nuclear Energy (PANE), intervened in the action by the NRC and asked that the court require the NRC to consider whether the risk of a nuclear accident (as had been experienced with the original shutdown of the plant) might harm the community in a psychological sense. The NRC says the risk of an accident is not an effect on the environment. Is psychological health a factor in EIS evaluations? [*Metropolitan Edison Co.* v. *People Against Nuclear Energy*, 460 U.S. 766 (1983).]

9. The Tennessee Valley Authority (TVA) proposed the construction of Tellico Dam. If the dam is constructed, the known population of snail darters would be eradicated. A snail darter is a three-inch-long fish that is protected by the Endangered Species Act, which requires all federal agencies (like the TVA) not to fund, authorize, or carry out projects that would jeopardize the continued existence of an endangered species. At the time an environmental group brought the issue to light, the TVA had already expended $100 million in the construction of the dam, which would bring great economic benefits to the area. What factors are important in resolving such a dispute? Is it a matter of the significance of the species? Should an EIS have discussed this problem? [*Tennessee Valley Authority* v. *Hill*, 437 U.S. 153 (1978).]

10. Albert J. Hubenthal operated a 55-acre worm-farming operation in Winona County, Minnesota. Mr. Hubenthal maintained that large amounts of scrap materials, such as tires, wood, metal, leather, and solid waste, were necessary for a successful worm operation. The 55 acres were "messy, smelly and germy," as described by the neighbors. The county attorney called the farm a nuisance and warned Mr. Hubenthal that he had 30 days to clean up the farm. He refused and the county removed all materials from the worm farm. Could the county do this? Was the farm a nuisance? [*Hubenthal* v. *County of Winona*, 751 F.2d 243 (8th Cir. 1984).]

Problem 1

During the past decade, the growth of demand for artificial fingernails has been nearly exponential. As a result, nearly all hair salons provide the service and there are nearly 150,000 nail salons across the country. The chemical products used for the various types of nails have been in an evolutionary process since 1935, when artificial nails were first used in Hollywood by movie cosmetologists. At that time, products with formaldehyde were used extensively. Other toxic substances have been part of the nail products over the years.

Dust from shaping the acrylic nails spreads from the technicians' tables to other areas. The fumes from the nail products are obvious upon entry into any salon.

Several studies (clinical and epidemiological) have offered the following conclusions:

- the affixture of artificial nails significantly deteriorates the natural nail;
- the affixture of artificial nails can result in the growth of fungus beneath the nail that can result in more extensive infection and loss of the natural nail;
- inhalation of fumes from the product can cause light headedness;
- several popular chemicals now used are birth defect agents;
- removal of the nails by technicians has resulted in a significant number of eye and face injuries as portions of the nail spring off.

Currently, a major university medical school is conducting a study of the effects of long-term exposure. The study will take two more years because the number of technicians who have had daily long-term exposure has just now become a sufficient sample size.

Sculpture Shelter, Inc. has developed a 3'x 2'x 2' plastic incubator device for use in the application and repair of artificial nails. The customer and technician place their hands inside the units, which have an air circulator. The plastic enclosure then contains all fumes and particles. Each unit costs $2,800.00. The average cost for original nail applications is $45; repairs cost $20. Technicians can do an original set in two hours and repairs in one and a half hours. Sculpture Shelter's orders have been very limited.

Currently the political and legal environments are reeling from the effects of worker suits for long-term effects from asbestos exposure. Congress has proposed a bill called the High Risk Occupational Disease Notification and Prevention Act. The bill would establish an extensive federal program of identification, notification, and treatment of employees who are at risk of disease from exposure to health hazards in the workplace. Much of the program's cost would be borne by employers. An appointed board would designate occupational hazards and notify employees of the risks and their right to medical monitoring. Employers would pay for the medical monitoring.

Nail salons are regulated by state agencies through licensing nail technicians and periodic inspections of salon operations. All equipment used in nail salons must appear on the responsible state agency's list of authorized equipment.

a. What potential liability issues do you see for the nail salon owners?
b. What potential liability issues do you see for Sculpture Shelter?
c. What regulatory process must Sculpture Shelter go through to obtain approval for use of its device in salons?
d. What possible violations of environmental laws do you see? What remedies would be available?
e. Develop an accurate and legally defensible ad campaign for Sculpture Shelters.
f. Can each state regulate the Sculpture Shelter differently? Could each state agency impose different requirements on Sculpture Shelters?
g. What concerns should Sculpture Shelter have if it chooses to take its product into the international markets? What checklist of advice would you give this company?

Problem 2

From 1982 to 1988, the FCC was under the direction of a Reagan appointee, Mark Fowler, a 43-year-old communications lawyer who is described as a "visceral opponent of government interference in the marketplace." Upon his appointment as chairman, Mr. Fowler described his mission as one of "pruning, chopping, slashing, eliminating, burning and deep-sixing" a half century of regulation.

The following is a summary of Fowler's major actions with regard to broadcasting:

CHILDREN'S PROGRAMS Relaxed rules requiring broadcasters to air "informative" children's programming, rejected restrictions on cartoon shows based on toys (1983)

PUBLIC SERVICE Loosened guidelines requiring nonentertainment programming and coverage of community issues (1984)

COMMERCIALS Eliminated time and frequency limits on TV commercials allowing more commercials per hour and program-length ads (1984)

STATION OWNERSHIP Raised limit on group ownership of TV, AM, and FM stations from 7 each to 12 each (1984)

STATION TRANSFER Rescinded rule prohibiting buyer from reselling a station for three years after purchase, speeded consideration of license transfers (1982–85)

You are the CEO of the cartoon division of Universal Studios and you have been approached by Mattel Toys to develop a cartoon show to be used as a marketing tool for its He-Man action figures. In the past, a parent's group, Action for Children's Television (ACT), has been successful in stopping such joint productions and has consistently proposed elimination of advertising during children's TV programs.

a. Discuss the regulatory issues in this situation, Mr. Fowler's authority, and how ACT can have input.

b. What constitutional issues can be raised to counter ACT's objections?

c. What would be station owners' liability if a child injured another child based on what the child saw a cartoon character do?

d. What disclaimers are needed in childrens' advertising because of age and understanding problems?

e. Describe a plan for ACT to challenge Mr. Fowler's changes.

Problem 3

In 1990, the Boeing Company retained the services of Nomar Acuna, an executive at Boeing de Havilland, Inc., a Canadian-based manufacturer of small jetliners. Boeing was a part owner of de Havilland from 1986–1992. Acuna was hired as a consultant to assist Boeing and de Havilland with the possible sale of five airplanes to Bahamasair, the government-owned airlines of the Bahamas.

The Bahamian government had decided to buy five airplanes from Fokker N.V. of the Netherlands. Aviaco International Leasing had signed a contract to furnish the financing for the airplane purchases. Acuna then hired Duncan Rapier, a Canadian citizen, who contacted officials in the Bahamas about the possibility of purchasing planes from de Havilland. Rapier and Acuna were able to successfully negotiate a sale of five Dash 8 turboprop planes from de Havilland to Bahamasair for $64 million.

Aviaco filed suit in Miami against Boeing stating that it was cut out of the deal once Acuna stepped in to persuade the government officials to buy from de Havilland. Aviaco maintains that it was put out of business because it was forced out of the deal by Acuna.

A Bahamian government commission has issued a report on the transaction which concludes that Acuna funneled funds to Bahamian officials through Rapier and was paid $90,000 for his work. The report issues a finding that Acuna and de Havilland gave Rapier $1.14 million, and Rapier gave $786,000 of that amount to two businessmen who were close to two government ministers responsible for running Bahamasair. The commission report theorizes that Acuna was forced out as the party doing the financing because its presence prevented Acuna and Rapier from paying the fees to the government officials.

What legal issues do you see in these transactions and interactions? Have any criminal laws been violated? What would be the basis for Aviaco's lawsuit against Boeing?

Part Three

Business Competition and Sales

This section of the book covers the laws and regulations that apply to what a business sells, how it sells its product, and how the sales transaction for the product is set up and financed. Do you have the right to sell a product or have you appropriated someone else's idea? What can you say and write in your advertising? What kinds of comparisons can you make between your product and those of your competitors? What's fair and legal in competition? When do you have a contract and what kinds of terms do you need to have in it? What constitutes performance on a contract and what is a breach? Can you be compensated if the other side fails to perform? How can transactions be financed and what forms do you need? What are your rights as a seller for collecting payments under a contract?

This portion of the text covers all the preliminary aspects of contracts as well as the performance and collection issues in contract relations. The materials walk through the heart of business operations: sales; competition; property rights; advertising; contract formation and performance; and receivable collection.

Judgment

2 Live Crew, a popular rap musical group, recorded and performed a rap music version of Roy Orbison's famed 1964 "Oh, Pretty Woman" rock ballad. The song was written by Mr. Orbison and William Dees, and the rights to the song were assigned to Acuff-Ross Music, Inc. The rap version was called "Pretty Woman." Rap music is a "style of black American popular music consisting of improvised rhymes performed to rhythmic accompaniment." 2 Live Crew's manager had written to Acuff-Rose requesting permission to do the parody and offered to pay for rights to do so. Acuff-Rose responded by saying, "I am aware of the success enjoyed by the '2 Live Crew,' but I must inform you that we cannot permit the use of a parody of 'Oh, Pretty Woman.'"

2 Live Crew recorded the parody anyway. Acuff-Rose maintains the 2 Live Crew parody is infringement. Is it?

CHAPTER 12

The Vatican Library. The House of Windsor. Spuds

McKenzie. The common thread? They all have lucrative

arrangements for

the licensing of

Business Property

their images and symbols. The law affords protection

for these images and symbols even though the property

right is a bundle of images and feelings about a person,

business, or logo. According to a 1995 survey by the

National Law Journal, intellectual property is the

fastest-growing legal speciality.

This chapter covers the rights of businesses and

their intellectual property. What does a business own?

What are the types of business property? What are the

rights and issues in personal property owned by a busi-

ness? What statutory protections exist for intellectual

property? What issues of property protection exist in

international business operations? What are real prop-

erty interests and what rights are included? Making certain

the goodwill that symbols, names, and motifs

provide for a business is preserved and protected is an

important part of the ongoing success of a business.

*Possession is nine points
of the law. No, it's not.
Paperwork is.*

Harvard Business Review
September/October 1995

WHAT CAN A BUSINESS OWN? PERSONAL PROPERTY: THE TANGIBLE KIND

When we see a Dreyer's Ice Cream truck driving along beside us, we understand that Dreyer's Ice Cream owns that truck; it is a part of the Dreyer's fleet and is carried as business equipment on the books of the Dreyer's corporation. If someone took that truck, it would be theft and Dreyer's would be entitled to compensation if the truck were damaged or destroyed by theft. Dreyer's would also be entitled to compensation if someone hit the truck in an accident and damaged it. Because the truck is Dreyer's property, Dreyer's enjoys certain rights of ownership in it. The delivery truck is **tangible property**. Tangible property is the type of property we can see and touch. Delivery trucks, desks, computers, inventory, and the building and land in which a business is located are all forms of tangible property. We have specific laws governing real and personal property rights for tangible property. We have laws to protect us against theft of our property and laws that provide remedies if someone harms or destroys that property.

Types of Personal Property

The Dreyer's truck would be an example of one form of personal property that businesses own—equipment. Everything from the laser printer in the office to the Thermos brand water cooler construction crews have attached to their company trucks is included as a form of business equipment. Businesses also have personal property interests in the form of inventory or the goods that they hold for sale to customers.

Transfer of Personal Property

Business property that is equipment or inventory may or may not have **documents of title** associated with them. Vehicles in a company's fleet have the standard title documents for motor vehicles. Other types of tangible personal property that would have title documents include airplanes, helicopters, and even pure-bred animals. Title to these forms of personal property is transferred by the transfer of the document of title.

Many other forms of business property will not have any formal documents of title. Computers, desks, and file cabinets are typical forms of business property that would not have any title documents. These forms of personal property are transferred by a **bill of sale**. A bill of sale is simply a contract that reflects the sale of personal property and provides all the proof necessary to establish ownership.

Leases and Bailments of Personal Property

Many businesses choose to lease their equipment. A **lease** is a right of use and possession of property for a fixed or open-end period of time. The key difference between a lease of personal property and ownership is that in a lease the ownership of the property will revert back to the lessor.

In some circumstances personal property is rented for a short period of time. A temporary transfer of possession of personal property is called a **bailment**. If you rent an extra bed for company, you are the **bailee** in the bailment relationship. The rental store is the **bailor**. If you check your coat at the coat room in a Broadway theater, a bailment is created. The coat check person as an agent for the theater is the bailee, and you are the bailor. If you leave your watch at a jeweler's for repair, you are the bailor and the jeweler is the bailee.

The bailment relationship is created with very simple requirements: The bailor turns possession over to the bailee with the understanding that the personal property will be returned, and both parties intend to create a bailment relationship. The intention to create a bailment distinguishes the bailment relationship from a **license**. For example, if you park your car yourself in a parking lot and will pay for parking upon entry or departure, you have been given a license, the right to park on a lot that is owned by another. If you drive to a lot and a valet takes your keys and car and parks it for you, a bailment is created because possession of your car has been turned over to another. In those circumstances, you are the bailor and the parking lot owner is the bailee.

The bailment relationship carries duties and responsibilities. The bailee has the duty to return the bailment at the end of the agreed-upon period of possession. The bailee also has the duty of using reasonable care to protect the bailor's property while it is in his possession. In a parking valet situation, the bailee has a duty to take reasonable care to protect your car. A bailee cannot eliminate its liability for damage to the bailor's property. Often, parking stubs issued by valets will read: "RESTAURANT ASSUMES NO LIABILITY FOR DAMAGE TO PROPERTY." Such a disclaimer of liability is called an **exculpatory clause**, but it is not valid because it is against public policy to allow someone to hold himself harmless for his negligent acts. It is, however, valid for the restaurant to limit its liability. A parking stub from a valet that reads, ""RESTAURANT NOT LIABLE FOR ITEMS VALUED AT OVER $50 LEFT IN VEHICLE." The bailee is not disclaiming all liability but is rather letting the bailor know in advance not to leave valuable items in the car. Many parking valet stubs now disclaim liability for theft of cellular phones and stereo systems. Such disclaimers are valid because they limit, but do not eliminate, liability.

In rental bailments, the bailor has the duty of checking the rented equipment to be certain it is in working order and has no defects that could injure the bailee. For example, if you leased a snowblower from a rental equipment franchise and a loose belt on the snowblower caused it to injure you, the franchise would have liability for your injuries because of its failure to maintain the equipment. The franchise that rents equipment, however, is not responsible for injuries that you experience because an activity for which you use their equipment is dangerous. If you rent in-line skates from a rental franchise, the franchise is not responsible for any injuries you experience because of the inherent dangers in in-line skating. They would, however, be responsible if a defective buckle caused your skate to come loose and you fell and were injured as a result.

Creditors' Rights and Personal Property

Often a business may not have the cash available for the purchase of equipment or inventory. Many businesses rely on the extension of credit to purchase both these forms of business personal property. Creditors, on the other hand, are concerned about the ability of a business to pay for property, particularly in those

Business Planning Tip

Businesses that rent equipment should follow a regular maintenance schedule for their equipment. Also, their rental forms should include disclosures about the nature of activities for which their equipment is used. For example, businesses that rent ski equipment have disclosures on their rental forms about the risks that are inherent in skiing.

situations where the business is new and the capitalization is small. To provide more security for a creditor, a business can provide a **lien** or **security interest** to the creditor in the property that is purchased. Sometimes called a **chattel mortgage**, this form of security is created under Article 9 of the **Uniform Commercial Code (UCC)**. The UCC is a near-universal uniform law in the United States that governs commercial transactions, including contracts (see Chapters 14 and 15) and financial transactions such as notes, checks, and drafts.

Review Article 9 of the UCC: http://www.law.cornell.edu/ucc/9/overview.html

Article 9 of the UCC allows creditors to take a security interest in debtors' personal property. That security interest is created when a debtor signs a **security agreement** in exchange for the extension of credit or as security for an underlying debt. Once the creditor has a security interest in the personal property, that creditor has priority above other creditors in the event of the debtor's bankruptcy as well as the right of repossession of the secured property, often referred to as the **collateral**, if the debtor fails to make the necessary payments. Repossession under Article 9 is a nonjudicial process. The creditor is permitted to take back the property from the debtor without first going to court to obtain a foreclosure. The only restrictions on creditors' repossession of debtors' property when there has been a **default**, or nonpayment of the debt, is that the creditor cannot "breach the peace." A breach of the peace is a violation of the law. A creditor cannot trespass or use physical force to repossess the property. Perhaps the most common example of repossession is taking back cars for which payment has not been made. Those responsible for the actual repossession may take the car from a public place, but they cannot enter the debtor's private property to repossess the car because that would be a trespass, a violation of the law, and thus a breach of the peace.

One additional protection that an Article 9 creditor can obtain is through the filing of a **financing statement**. A financing statement is filed with a public agency (generally either the secretary of state or county recorder or clerk) to provide public notice that the creditor has an interest in the debtor's property. The filing is important because it often gives the creditor priority over subsequent creditors who might take a security interest in the same equipment or inventory.

WHAT CAN A BUSINESS OWN? PERSONAL PROPERTY: THE INTANGIBLE OR INTELLECTUAL KIND

In addition to the Dreyer's truck itself, referred to earlier, you will also see painted on the truck the signature brown and white stripes that are part of the ice cream's packing. You see the distinctive writing, "Dreyer's Grand Ice Cream." You recognize the truck from its distinctive paint and writing probably before you even read the name "Dreyer's." That distinctive color scheme, name, and writing are also business property that belongs to Dreyer's. The recognition and goodwill that come from those brown stripes and the name are forms of **intangible property** that also enjoy statutory protections, which include Dreyer's right to prevent others from using their distinctive name and colors and taking from it the goodwill those items have come to symbolize. The symbols represent a bundle of very valuable rights for the business.

Forms of intangible property include patents, copyrights, trademarks, trade names, and trade dress. Protections include federal rights, international protections, and common law rights of action for the damage to or taking of these forms of intangible property.

Protection for Business Intellectual Property

Federal law provides competitive protection for ideas, formulas, and trademarks. This section of the chapter covers these statutory protections of competition.

PATENTS

Visit the U.S. Patent and Trademark Office (PTO): http://www. uspto.gov/

Patents are a 17-year legal monopoly on products, processes, machines, and any combination of these three. During that 17-year period, the patent holder has the exclusive right to profits on the sales of the patented idea. An idea is patentable only if it is nonobvious, novel, and useful. And the idea must be reduced to some tangible form. For example, a discovery of a reproductive hormone in the male body is not patentable, but a product to stop production of that hormone for birth control purposes can be patented.

Anyone who sells or uses a patented product or process without the consent of the patent holder has committed patent **infringement**. Infringement entitles the patent holder to a statutory action for damages. The patent holder (the plaintiff) in such a case need only show that a patent was held and that the defendant infringed that patent. A Patent Office registration for a product or process, however, is not a guarantee of recovery. A court must still agree with the Patent Office determination that the product or process is nonobvious, useful, and novel.

C O N S I D E R . . .   **12.1** Procter & Gamble (P&G) was issued patent #4,455,333 on June 19, 1984, for an invention entitled "Doughs and Cookies Providing Storage-Stable Texture Variety." The patent covers a method of manufacturing ready-to-serve cookies that remain crispy on the outside and chewy on the inside for an extended shelf life. P&G markets these cookies under the Duncan Hines label.

P&G brought a patent infringement action against Nabisco Brands, Inc., which markets its own line of dual-textured cookies called "Almost Home" and "Chewy Chips Ahoy." P&G also sued Keebler Company for its dual-textured cookie called "Soft Batch" and Frito-Lay, Inc., for its "Grandma's Rich and Chewy." Each of the defendants denies infringement. They have moved for dismissal of the case on grounds that the patent is invalid because baking cookies is not patentable. Do you agree? Would you protect P&G's process? [*Procter & Gamble Co.* v. *Nabisco Brands, Inc.*, 604 F. Supp. 1485 (D.C. Del. 1985).]

COPYRIGHTS

Visit "The Copyright Web Site" for more information on copyrights: http:// www.benedict.com/

Patents protect inventors. **Copyrights** protect authors of books, magazine articles, plays, movies, songs, dances, and so on. Photographs are also entitled to copyright protection. A copyright gives the holder the exclusive right to sell, control, or license the copyrighted work. A copyright runs for the lifetime of the author plus fifty years.

Copyright protection is automatic; it exists from the time of creation. However, the creation must carry the appropriate copyright symbol: ©. Also, the creator is not entitled to bring an infringement suit on the work unless copies have been filed with the copyright office. Damages for infringement include the profits made by the infringer, actual costs, attorney fees, and any other expenses associated with the infringement action. All illegal copies can be obtained through court injunction and any distribution of the illegal copies halted by the same court order.

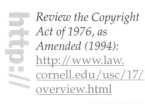

Review the Copyright Act of 1976, as Amended (1994): http://www.law. cornell.edu/usc/17/ overview.html

Judgment

The copyright laws were amended in 1976 to allow fair use of copyrighted materials. **Fair use** is occasional and spontaneous use of copyrighted materials for limited purposes—for example, a short quote from a copyrighted work. Fair use also allows instructors to reproduce a page or chart from a copyrighted work to use in the classroom; and copies of book pages can be made for research purposes. The following case involves an issue of a parody of copyrighted material being used for commercial gain. The case provides the answer for the chapter's opening "Judgment."

Campbell v. *Acuff-Rose Music, Inc.*
114 S. Ct. 1164 (1994)

THE "PRETTY WOMAN" RAP BY 2 LIVE CREW

FACTS

2 Live Crew, a popular rap musical group, recorded and performed a rap music version called "Pretty Woman" of Roy Orbison's famed 1964 "Oh, Pretty Woman" rock ballad. The song was written by Mr. Orbison and William Dees, and the rights to the song were assigned to Acuff-Rose Music, Inc. (respondent). Rap music is a style of black American popular music that consists of often-improvised rhymes performed to rhythmic accompaniment. 2 Live Crew's manager had written to Acuff-Rose to request permission to do the parody and offered to pay for rights to do so. Acuff-Rose's response: "I am aware of the success enjoyed by the '2 Live Crew,' but I must inform you that we cannot permit the use of a parody of 'Oh, Pretty Woman.'"

2 Live Crew recorded the parody anyway and named Messrs. Orbison and Dees as the songwriters and Acuff-Rose as the publisher on the CD cover. After over 250,000 copies of the CD had been sold and over one year later, Acuff-Rose Music, Inc., filed suit against Luther Campbell (also known as Luke Skywalker), Christopher Wongwon, Mark Ross, and David Hobbs, members of the 2 Live Crew group for infringement. 2 Live Crew maintained that its song was a parody and thus protected under the fair use exceptions of the copyright laws. The district court granted summary judgment for 2 Live Crew. The court of appeals held that the commercial nature of the parody rendered it presumptively unfair. 2 Live Crew (petitioners) appealed.

JUDICIAL OPINION

SOUTER, Justice

We are called upon to decide whether 2 Live Crew's commercial parody of Roy Orbison's song, "Oh, Pretty Woman," may be a fair use within the meaning of the Copyright Act of 1976, 17 U.S.C. § 107 (1988 ed. and Supp. IV).

It is uncontested here that 2 Live Crew's song would be an infringement of Acuff-Rose's rights in "Oh, Pretty Woman," under the Copyright Act of 1976, 17 U.S.C. § 106 (1988 ed. and Supp. IV), but for a finding of fair use through parody.

The first factor in a fair use enquiry is "the purpose and character of the use, including whether such use is of a commercial nature or is for nonprofit educational purposes." The central purpose of this investigation is to see whether the new work merely "supersede[s] the objects" of the original creation, or instead adds something new, with a further purpose or different character, altering the first with new expression, meaning, or message; it asks, in other words, whether and to what extent the new work is "transformative." Although such transformative use is not absolutely necessary for a finding of fair use, *Sony Corp. of America* v. *Universal City Studios, Inc.,* 464 U.S. 417 (1984), the goal of copyright, to promote science and the arts, is generally furthered by the creation of transformative works. Such works thus lie at the heart of the fair use doctrine's guarantee of breathing space within the confines of copyright and the more transformative the new work,

Continued

the less will be the significance of other factors, like commercialism, that may weigh against a finding of fair use.

Suffice it to say now that parody has an obvious claim to transformative value, as Acuff-Rose itself does not deny. Like less ostensibly humorous forms of criticism, it can provide social benefit, by shedding light on an earlier work, and, in the process, creating a new one. We thus line up with the courts that have held that parody, like other comment or criticism, may claim fair use under § 107.

Parody needs to mimic an original to make its point, and so has some claim to use the creation of its victim's (or collective victims') imagination, whereas satire can stand on its own two feet and so requires justification for the very act of borrowing.

The fact that parody can claim legitimacy for some appropriation does not, of course, tell either parodist or judge much about where to draw the line. Like a book review quoting the copyrighted material criticized, parody may or may not be fair use, and petitioner's suggestion that any periodic use is presumptively fair has no more justification in law or fact than the equally hopeful claim that any use for news reporting should be presumed fair.

As the District Court remarked, the words of 2 Live Crew's song copy the original's first line, but then "quickly degenerate[e] into a play on words, substituting predictable lyrics with shocking ones . . . [that] derisively demonstrate[e] how bland and banal the Orbison song seems to them." Judge Nelson, dissenting below, came to the same conclusion, that the 2 Live Crew song "was clearly intended to ridicule the white-bread original" and "reminds us that sexual congress with nameless streetwalkers is not necessarily the stuff of romance and is not necessarily without its consequences. The singers (there are several) have the same thing on their minds as did the lonely man with the nasal voice, but here there is no hint of wine and roses." Although the majority below had difficulty discerning any criticism of the original in 2 Live Crew's song, it assumed for purposes of its opinion that there was some.

We have less difficulty in finding that critical element in 2 Live Crew's song than the Court of Appeals did, although having found it we will not take the further step of evaluating its quality. The threshold question when fair use is raised in defense of parody is whether a periodic character may reasonably be perceived. Whether, going beyond that, parody is in good taste or bad does not and should not matter to fair use. As Justice Holmes explained, "[i]t would be a dangerous undertaking for persons trained only to the law to constitute themselves final judges of the worth of [a work], outside of the narrowest and most obvious limits. At the one extreme some works of genius would be sure to miss appreciation. Their very novelty would make them repulsive until the public had learned the new language in which their author spoke."

While we might not assign a high rank to the periodic element here, we think it fair to say that 2 Live Crew's song reasonably could be perceived as commenting on the original or criticizing it, to some degree. 2 Live Crew juxtaposes the romantic musings of a man whose fantasy comes true, with degrading taunts, a bawdy demand for sex, and a sigh of relief from paternal responsibility. The later words can be taken as a comment on the naivete of the original of an earlier day, as a rejection of its sentiment that ignores the ugliness of street life and the debasement that it signifies. It is this joinder of reference and ridicule that marks off the author's choice of parody from the other types of comment and criticism that traditionally have had a claim to fair use protection as transformative works.

The use, for example, of a copyrighted work to advertise a product, even in a parody, will be entitled to less indulgence under the first factor of the fair use enquiry, than the sale of a parody for its own sake, let alone one performed a single time by students in school.

We agree with both the District Court and the Court of Appeals that the Orbison original's creative expression for public dissemination falls within the core of the copyright's protective purposes. This fact, however, is not much help in this

Continued

case, or ever likely to help much in separating the fair use sheep from the infringing goats in a parody case, since parodies almost invariably copy publicly known, expressive works.

We think the Court of Appeals was insufficiently appreciative of parody's need for the recognizable sight or sound when it ruled 2 Live Crew's use unreasonable as a matter of law. It is true, of course, that 2 Live Crew copied the characteristic opening bass riff (or musical phrase) of the original, and true that the words of the first line copy the Orbison lyrics. But if quotation of the opening riff and the first line may be said to go to the "heart" of the original, the heart is also what most readily conjures up the song for parody, and it is the heart at which parody takes aim. Copying does not become excessive in relation to periodic purpose merely because the portion taken was the original's heart. If 2 Live Crew had copied a significantly less memorable part of the original, it is difficult to see how its periodic character would have come through.

This is not, of course, to say that anyone who calls himself a parodist can skim the cream and get away scot free. In parody, as in news reporting, context is everything, and the question of fairness asks what else the parodist did besides go to the heart of the original. It is significant that 2 Live Crew not only copied the first line of the original, but thereafter departed markedly from the Orbison lyrics for its own ends. 2 Live Crew not only copied the bass riff and repeated it, but also produced otherwise distinctive sounds, interposing "scraper" noise, overlaying the music with solos in different keys, and altering the drum beat. This is not a case, then, where "a substantial portion" of the parody itself is composed of a "verbatim" copying of the original. It is not, that is, a case where the parody is so insubstantial, as compared to the copying, that the third factor must be resolved as a matter of law against the parodists.

It was error for the Court of Appeals to conclude that the commercial nature of 2 Live Crew's parody of "Oh, Pretty Woman" rendered it presumptively unfair. No such evidentiary presumption is available to address either the first factor, the character and purpose of the use, or the fourth, market harm, in determining whether a transformative use, such as parody, is a fair one. The court also erred in holding that 2 Live Crew had necessarily copied excessively from the Orbison original, considering the periodic purpose of the use. We therefore reverse the judgment of the Court of Appeals.

The case was remanded for trial.

APPENDIX A
"Oh, Pretty Woman" by Roy Orbison and William Dees

Pretty Woman, walking down the street,
Pretty Woman, the kind I like to meet,
Pretty Woman, I don't believe you,
you're not the truth,
No one could look as good as you
Mercy
Pretty Woman, won't you pardon me,
Pretty Woman, I couldn't help but see,
Pretty Woman, that you look lovely as can be
Are you lonely just like me?
Pretty Woman, stop a while,
Pretty Woman, talk a while,
Pretty Woman give your smile to me
Pretty Woman, yeah, yeah, yeah
Pretty Woman, look my way,
Pretty Woman, say you'll stay with me
'Cause I need you, I'll treat you right
Come to me baby, Be mine tonight
Pretty Woman, don't walk on by,
Pretty Woman, don't make me cry,
Pretty Woman, don't walk away,
Hey, O.K.
If that's the way it must be, O.K.
I guess I'll go on home, it's late
There'll be tomorrow night, but wait!
What do I see
Is she walking back to me!
Oh, Pretty Woman.

APPENDIX B
"Pretty Woman" as Recorded by 2 Live Crew

Pretty woman walkin' down the street
Pretty woman girl you look so sweet
Pretty woman you bring me down to that knee
Pretty woman you make me wanna beg please
Oh, pretty woman
Big hairy woman you need to shave that stuff
Big hairy woman you know I bet it's tough

Continued

Big hairy woman all that hair it ain't legit
'Cause you look like 'Cousin It'
Big hairy woman
Bald headed woman girl your hair won't grow
Bald headed woman you got a teeny
    weeny afro
Bald headed woman you know your
    hair could look nice
Bald headed woman first you got to roll
    it with rice
Bald headed woman here, let me get this
    hunk of biz for ya
Ya know what I'm saying you look better
    than rice a roni
Oh bald headed woman
Big hairy woman come on in
And don't forget your bald headed friend
Hey pretty woman let the boys
Jump in
Two timin' woman girl you know you ain't right
Two timin' woman you's out with my

boy last night
Two timin' woman that takes a load off
    my mind
Two timin' woman now I know the baby
    ain't mine
Oh, two timin' woman
Oh pretty woman

CASE QUESTIONS
1. What constitutes fair use?
2. What is the significance of 2 Live Crew's commercial gain from the parody?
3. Why is the *Sony* case cited?
4. Why did 2 Live Crew's manager seek permission first?
5. Do you agree with the court's decision? Was it a fair use? Should the owner of the rights be allowed to decide how a song will be parodied for commercial gain?
6. Does the court comment on bad taste and parody quality? Why?

C O N S I D E R . . . **12.2** Cornell Woolrich wrote the story, "It Had to Be Murder," which was first published in February 1942 in *Dime Detective* magazine. The magazine's publisher, Popular Publications, Inc., obtained the rights to magazine publication of the story and Mr. Woolrich retained all other rights.

In 1945 Mr. Woolrich sold the motion picture rights to six of his stories, including "It Had to Be Murder," to B. G. De Sylva Productions for $9,250. He agreed to renew the copyrights at the appropriate time and assign them to Mr. De Sylva.

In 1953 actor Jimmy Stewart and director Alfred Hitchcock formed a production company called Patron, Inc., and bought the motion picture rights for "It Had to Be Murder" from De Sylva for $10,000. In 1954, Patron (along with Paramount) produced and distributed *Rear Window*, the motion picture based on the Woolrich story "It Had to Be Murder."

Mr. Woolrich died in 1968, before he could get the renewal rights for "It Had to Be Murder." He had no spouse or children and left his property in trust to Columbia University, with Chase Manhattan Bank as executor. Chase renewed the copyright to "It Had to Be Murder" and sold it to Sheldon Abend for $650 plus 10 percent of all proceeds from use of the story. *Rear Window* was rebroadcast in 1971 on ABC-TV, and Mr. Abend filed suit against Mr. Stewart and Mr. Hitchcock but withdrew his suit after he was paid $25,000.

Rear Window was later re-released in motion picture theaters and sold on videocassette and enjoyed a tremendous response. Mr. Abend brought suit again for copyright infringement. Mr. Stewart defended by arguing that he held the copyright interest in the movie and the original story owner had no rights. Who is correct? [*Stewart* v. *Abend*, 495 U.S. 207 (1990).]

E T H I C A L   I S S U E S

12.1 Computer technology affords the opportunity to take existing photographs and enhance, alter, and magnify them to create new images. The end result can look just like a real photograph, and the results are achieved from copyrighted photos. However, the copyright holders of those photos are not paid for such use since the photograph itself was not used as the final product. This is a situation in which the law has not yet caught up with technology. Where do ethics enter the picture? It may be legal to use a photograph as a basis for a new creation, but is it ethical to do so without compensation to the original photographer?

TRADEMARKS

Review the Lanham Act: http://www. law.cornell.edu/usc/ 15/22/overview. html

Trademarks are words, pictures, designs, or symbols that businesses place on goods to identify those goods as their product. "Xerox," the Mercedes-Benz triangle, and "M&M's" are all examples of trademarks. The Lanham Act of 1946 is a federal law passed to afford businesses protection of their trademarks. This law is really a protection of a company's goodwill. A trademark becomes associated with that company and is used as a means of identifying that company's goods or services. The **Lanham Act** assures the right to retain that unique identification.

To obtain protection, goods must move in interstate commerce. When this requirement is met, a trademark is registered on the Principal Register. The trademark must be unique and nongeneric. For example, "cola" is a generic term; "Coca-Cola" is a trademark. Before recent changes in the law, a trademark must have been in use before registration, but recent amendment to the Lanham Act allows preregistration, a practice followed in Europe for many years.

Business Planning Tip

Before you pay for a copyright or a trademark, be sure the seller owns the intellectual property and has the authority to sell it. The Lyons Group, owner and developer of "Barney," the large, child-like purple dinosaur of PBS, purchased the rights to Barney's "I Love You" theme song from Lee Bernstein. Jean Warren, a music publisher from Everett, Washington, surfaced in 1995 and told the Lyons Group that Ms. Bernstein had sold her the rights in 1983. The result was litigation involving all the parties.

Once a trademark is registered, the holder has the obligation of maintaining the unique nature of that trademark. To do so, there must be a generic term that can be associated with the trademark so the public does not turn the trademark itself into a generic term. For example, there are "Band-Aid brand adhesive strips" instead of "Band-Aids." There is "Jell-O brand gelatin dessert" instead of "Jell-O." There is "Formica brand kitchen countertops" instead of "Formica." Parker Brothers recently lost its "Monopoly" trademark because there is no generic term for the type of board game it was.

In *San Francisco Arts & Athletics, Inc.* v. *United States Olympic Committee,* 483 U.S. 522 (1987), the Supreme Court held that the term *Olympic* belongs to the U.S. Olympic Committee and could not be used by San Francisco Arts & Athletics, Inc. (SFAA) in promoting its "Gay Olympic Games."

The SFAA did not have permission to use the term Olympic. Use of a **trade name** without the registered owner's permission is infringement. Suit can be brought for injunctive relief to stop the use of the trademark. The plaintiff owner can also recover all damages and attorneys' fees. If the plaintiff can show a willful infringement, the Lanham Act allows the plaintiff to recover treble damages. Relief is also available for using a trademark without authorization in advertising.

In 1946, director Frank Capra produced *It's a Wonderful Life*, a movie based on a short story by Philip Van Doren Stern called "The Greatest Gift." The movie starring Mr. Jimmy Stewart, did not perform well at the

The History of *It's A Wonderful Life*

box office, and although it received five Academy Award nominations, it won none. The movie's copyright was allowed to lapse. Television stations showed the classic without paying fees since the copyright had lapsed.

However, the U.S. Supreme Court decision in *Stewart* v. *Abend* (pg. 411) offering an extension of the copyright protection of the underlying story to the movie affected Jimmy Stewart's life once again. The original story owner, Mr. Stern, had the rights to the story since the movie rights had lapsed. With a copyright in place, royalties had to be paid. The owners of *It's a Wonderful Life* began charging fees, and the result was costly access. *It's a Wonderful Life* was seen on television day and night during the holiday season when the copyright on the movie had lapsed. Now, with the copyright clarification, the movie rights have been reprotected. The story's continuing protection and the high royalty fees make *It's a Wonderful Life* a singular holiday event.

It's a Wonderful Life

Issues

1. Would the rights to a movie entitle the holder to royalties from a video game based on the movie?

2. What type of clause for protection of rights should a copyright holder place in the royalty/transfer agreement?

Recent changes in the law allow a competitor to seek treble damages when its product is used deceptively in a comparative ad.

A more recent and critical aspect of the Lanham Act is the concept of **trade dress**. Trade dress consists of the colors, designs and shapes associated with a product. If someone copies the color schemes and shapes, they are likely to benefit from the goodwill of the owner and developer of the trade dress. The following case is a landmark one on the extent of federal protection for trade dress.

Two Pesos, Inc. v. Taco Cabana, Inc.
505 U. S. 763 (1992)

TWO PESOS, TWO CABANAS, AND INFRINGEMENT

FACTS

Taco Cabana, Inc. (respondent), operates a chain of fast-food restaurants in Texas that serve Mexican food. The first Taco Cabana restaurant opened in 1978 in San Antonio, and five more opened by 1985. Taco Cabana's theme or trade dress is self-described as follows:

A festive eating atmosphere having interior dining and patio areas decorated with artifacts, bright colors, paintings and murals. The patio includes interior and exterior areas with the interior patio capable of being sealed off from the outside patio by overhead garage doors. The stepped exterior of the building is a festive and vivid color scheme using top border paint and neon stripes. Bright awnings and umbrellas continue the theme.

In December 1985, Two Pesos (petitioner) opened its first restaurant in Houston. Its motif was very similar to Taco Cabana's self-described motif above. Two Pesos expanded rapidly in Houston but did not enter the San Antonio market. Taco Cabana entered the Houston and Austin markets in 1986 and expanded into Dallas and El Paso, where Two Pesos was doing business.

In 1987, Taco Cabana sued Two Pesos in federal district court for trade dress infringement under the Lanham Act. The jury found that Taco Cabana has a trade dress; taken as a whole, the trade dress is nonfunctional; the trade dress is inherently distinctive; the trade dress has not acquired a secondary meaning

(which means that people associate the colors, configurations, and designs of the trade dress with Taco Cabana) in the Texas market; and the alleged infringement creates a likelihood of confusion on the part of ordinary customers about the source or association of the restaurant's goods or services. The trial court held that Two Pesos had infringed Taco Cabana's trade dress.

The court of appeals affirmed and Two Pesos appealed maintaining that without a finding of secondary meaning, there was no infringement.

JUDICIAL OPINION
WHITE, Justice
The Lanham Act was intended to make "actionable the deceptive and misleading use of marks" and "to protect persons engaged in . . . commerce against unfair competition."

A trademark is defined in 15 U.S.C. § 1127 as including "any word, name, symbol, or device or any combination thereof" used by any person "to identify and distinguish his or her goods, including a unique product, from those manufactured or sold by others and to indicate the source of the goods, even if that source is unknown." In order to be registered, a mark must be capable of distinguishing the applicant's goods from those of others. Marks are often classified in categories of generally increasing distinctiveness; following the classic formulation set out by Judge Friendly,

Continued

they may be (1) generic; (2) descriptive; (3) suggestive; (4) arbitrary; or (5) fanciful. The latter three categories of marks, because their intrinsic nature serves to identify a particular source of a product, are deemed inherently distinctive and are entitled to protection. In contrast, generic marks—those that "refe[r] to the genus of which the particular product is a species", are not registrable as trademarks.

The general rule regarding distinctiveness is clear: An identifying mark is distinctive and capable of being protected if it *either* (1) is inherently distinctive *or* (2) has acquired distinctiveness through secondary meaning.

Petitioner argues that the jury's finding that the trade dress has not acquired a secondary meaning shows conclusively that the trade dress is not inherently distinctive.

Engrafting onto § 43(a) a requirement of secondary meaning for inherently distinctive trade dress also would undermine the purposes of the Lanham Act. Protection of trade dress, no less than of trademarks, serves the Act's purpose to "secure to the owner of the mark the goodwill of his business and to protect the ability of consumers to distinguish among competing producers. National protection of trademarks is desirable, Congress concluded, because trademarks foster competition and the maintenance of quality by securing to the producer the benefits of good reputation."

[A]dding a secondary meaning requirement could have anticompetitive effects, creating particular burdens on the start-up of small companies. It would present special difficulties for a business, such as respondent, that seeks to start a new product in a limited area and then expand into new markets. Denying protection for inherently distinctive nonfunctional trade dress until after secondary meaning has been established would allow a competitor, which has not adopted a distinctive trade dress of his own, to appropriate the originator's dress in other markets and to deter the originator from expanding into and competing in these areas.

We agree with the Court of Appeals that proof of secondary meaning is not required to prevail on a claim under § 43(a) of the Lanham Act where the trade dress at issue is inherently distinctive, and accordingly the judgment of that court is affirmed.

CASE QUESTIONS

1. Does the court make a distinction between trade name and trade dress? Why not?
2. Does the Lanham Act require a showing of secondary meaning to acquire protection for trade dress?
3. What would happen to a new business if the secondary meaning requirement were imposed?
4. How could this suit have been resolved alternatively?
5. Evaluate the ethics of Two Pesos.

C O N S I D E R . . . **12.3** They can be spotted from a distance. The classic Ferrari design with its lined side panels and hidden headlights is unique. Although the Ferrari name is a registered trademark, the design of the Ferrari is not. Roberts Motor Company designed a car with a look similar to the Ferrari, but the Roberts car would sell for a much lower price. Ferrari brought suit against Roberts alleging infringement. Is Ferrari correct? Can a nonpatented, noncopyrighted design belong exclusively to Ferrari? [*Ferrari* v. *Roberts Motor Co.*, 944 F.2d 1235 (6th Cir. 1991), *cert. denied*, 112 S. Ct. 3028 (1992).]

C O N S I D E R . . **12.4** Fashion Victim, Ltd., sells a T-shirt called Skeleton Woopee with a fanciful design depicting skeletons engaged in sexual activity in seven different positions. Skeleton Woopee is Fashion's number one seller, 55,000 shirts having been sold since its introduction in 1990.

One of Fashion's customers found at a 1992 trade show a shirt that was featured in a catalog by Sunrise and was, in effect, Skeleto Woopee. The shirts by Sunrise were being sold for $36.00 a dozen, $4.50 less a dozen than Fashion's price. Four of the types of sexual activity depicted on the Sunrise shirt are different. Has there been an infringement, or is the idea too general? [*Fashion Victim, Ltd.* v. *Sunrise Turquoise, Inc.*, 785 F.. Supp. 1302 (N.D. Ill. 1992).]

Business Planning Tip

To protect their product configurations and trade dress, many companies are registering their product packaging as 3-D trademarks. The Black & Decker Dustbuster, Hershey's chocolate Kisses and chocolate and vanilla Hugs, and the Nintendo hand-held electronic game, Game Boy, are examples.

E T H I C A L   I S S U E S

12.2 Mr. Orenthal James Simpson has applied for trademark registration for his widely used nicknames of O. J. and Juice. Joseph J. Gleason, vice president and general counsel of Florida Citrus Mutual, a trade group, responded, "I'd question if he could copyright something that generic."

Are the nicknames entitled to trademark and trade name protection? The trade names and trademarks will be used for the merchandising of Simpson products. Mr. Simpson was acquitted of the double homicide charges against him for the killing of his ex-wife, Nicole Brown, and her friend Ronald Goldman. His name and nicknames are household words because of the notoriety of the trial. Evaluate the ethics of capitalizing on name recognition acquired because of a criminal trial.

C O N S I D E R . . . **12.5** Jim Henson Productions created a new character, Spa'am, a high priest of the wild boars, which is a group of boars that worship Miss Piggy, another Henson creation and a pig puppet. The movie, *Muppet Treasure Island*, introduced Spa'am as a character and also as a stuffed animal toy for children to purchase. Spa'am acts childish.

Continued

Hormel Foods Corporation brought suit against Henson Productions, alleging that the new character will cause the public to spurn Spam, Hormel's popular luncheon meat. Hormel's suit asked for an injunction against Henson Productions to prohibit it from releasing the movie until the character's name was changed. Hormel spokesman Alan Krejci notes, "Henson Productions is seeking to use our trademark . . . for monetary gain." Should the injunction be granted? Is the puppet and its name an infringement of the Spam trademark?

Business Planning Tip

When a business is in litigation over its trademark or trade name, the issue of consumer perceptions and receptions of the real trademark and knock-off goods is a central focus. The business must be able to establish confusion from imitations of its trademark or trade name. On the other side of the litigation, those charged with infringement want consumer feedback to establish the generic, and therefore unprotected, nature of the trademark or trade name.

Consumer surveys have become a critical part of infringement trials. Where the issue is whether the public has been misled by a trademark infringement, the responses of a representative sample are critical evidence in a case. One such case involved a survey of consumers in 24 shopping malls nationwide. The Baltimore Colts had become the Indianapolis Colts, and the Canadian Football League proposed calling one of its teams the Baltimore CFL Colts. The survey showed consumers were confused, and the data carried the case for the former Baltimore Colts's owners.

FOR THE MANAGER'S DESK

CAN A HARLEY'S VROOM BE TRADEMARKED?

Now that the U.S. Supreme Court has decided that colors can be trademarked a new question may arise: the extent to which sounds can function as trademarks. The use of sounds as trademarks is not new; well-known ones include the NBC chimes, the roar of the MGM lion and the Beneficial Insurance jingle.

A sound mark identifies and distinguishes services through audio rather than

visual means The U.S. Patent and Trademark Office has allowed the registration of a sound so long as it met the statutory requirement of a trademark. The National Broadcasting Co. Inc. was the first to register a sound when, in 1950, it registered "the musical notes G, E, and C played on chimes" for its radio broadcasting services.

According to the PTO, only 22 of the approximately 850,000 registered trademarks are sound marks, although interest in such registrations has grown. Since

1992, 11 sound trademarks have been registered and 29 new applications have been filed in the PTO, including 26 in 1995 alone. These new applications include those for the Mister Softee ice cream jingle, the sound of an AT&T modem and the theme from the Lone Ranger radio, film and television series.

But one recent application has sparked controversy. Last year, Harley-Davidson Inc. filed a trademark application to register the sound of its motorcycles. According to the application, the mark
Continued

consists of "the exhaust sound of applicant's motorcycles, produced by V-twin, common crankpin motorcycle engines when the goods are in use." Harley-Davidson claims that this "syncopated rumbling exhaust sound" is distinctive of its motorcycles and that its motorcycles have produced this sound since 1930.

The Harley-Davidson application could be one of the most controversial filed with the PTO. According to the PTO's records, since the application was filed on Feb. 1, 1994, eight oppositions have been lodged against registration of the mark. The opposing parties include Harley-Davidson's major competitors, such as Honda, Kawasaki and Suzuki, as well as individual motorcycle dealers and service shops.

These parties contend that the sound emitted by Harley-Davidson's motorcycles is purely functional, dictated by utilitarian considerations, and that any V-twin, common crankpin engine can produce a similar sound. These companies argue that the sound of Harley-Davidson's engine is not distinctive and registering the mark will hinder legitimate competition. In papers filed with the PTO, Harley-Davidson claims that relative to today's technology, its V-twin engine configuration lacks any functional benefits and that the company still uses it solely for the sound the engine produces.

The PTO set forth the criteria for registering a sound as a trademark in 1978, in deciding whether General Electric Broadcasting Co. could register the sound made by a ship's bell clock. In the application, the mark was described as "a series of bells tolled during four hour sequences beginning with one ring at approximately the first half hour and increasing in number by one ring at approximately every half hour thereafter."

The application was eventually refused on the ground that the applicant failed to prove the ship's bell sounds had become distinctive of applicant's broadcasting services. The opinion by the: TTAB, or Trademark Trial and Appeal Board, nonetheless provides guidance in determining when a sound is capable of registration.

In the case of the Harley-Davidson application, the TTAB must first decide whether the sound of a Harley-Davidson motorcycle is merely a function of the design of its V-twin, common crankpin engine. If the TTAB determines that it is, then registration must be denied since other manufactures must have the right to use V-twin, common crankpin engines.

If it decides that the sound is not functional, the TTAB must next examine whether the sound is nonetheless "inherently distinctive," as Harley-Davidson contends. It will undoubtedly be a difficult task for Harley-Davidson to demonstrate that the noise generated by a motorcycle engine is inherently distinctive, particularly since other manufacturers use V-twin, common crankpin engines.

Harley-Davidson may be able to demonstrate that the sound of its motorcycles has attained secondary meaning so that the public recognizes the sound and associates it with the company. If all Harley-Davidson motorcycles manufactured since 1930 produce a similar sound, as claimed, then it is possible that secondary meaning has developed because of long-term use and public exposure.

In order to prove secondary meaning, Harley-Davidson may choose to conduct a survey to attempt to demonstrate that an appreciable number of consumers recognize the exhaust sound alone as that of a Harley-Davidson motorcycle. If secondary meaning is proven, the mark would then be entitled to registration under the TTAB's decision in *General Electric Broadcasting*.

The Harley-Davidson application is raising eyebrows because, unlike arbitrary marks like the NBC chimes and the Beneficial insurance jingle, the exhaust sound of a motorcycle engine clearly originated as a result of purely utilitarian considerations—the design and engineering of a V-twin, common crankpin engine. This functional aspect does not mean that the sound is not capable of acting as a trademark as well. Other marks that began as utilitarian products have become protectable trademarks through long use and public recognition.

Registration of the sound of Harley-Davidson's motorcycles could have far reaching implications for U.S. commerce.

Source: Exerpted from *The National Law Journal*; "If Harley-Davidson has its way, the resounding roar that its motorcycles make could become a registered, protected sound under the U.S. Trademark Act," Nov. 6, 1995, p. B5 with permission.

12.6 Dreyer's Grand Ice Cream, Inc., began in Oakland, California. When it began nationwide expansion in the 1970s, it ran up against Breyer's Ice Cream in the eastern states. Would there be confusion between the brands? How could the confusion be eliminated?

PENALTIES FOR INFRINGEMENT

In addition to the civil suits that can be brought for infringement and resulting damages to a business owner, there are federal criminal penalties for copyright infringement. Currently, criminal penalties are available only when infringement is willful and for "commercial advantage or private financial gain." The criminal copyright laws are under review for possible change to criminal prosecution for willful violation regardless of financial gain. The review and proposed changes resulted from a case in which an MIT student uploaded and downloaded copyrighted software programs and then gave fellow students passwords for access. The result was that students at MIT enjoyed free access to the Internet at a cost of $1 million to the system's owners. However, the student did not charge for the access and thus realized no personal financial gain from the project. Revisions to the copyright law would allow prosecution for such copying regardless of personal financial gain.

Business Planning Tip

Be certain your employees understand the copyrighted nature of computer software and the protections afforded the owners of those programs. Be sure they understand that both criminal and civil penalties exist for infringement of the software programs.

Most employers acquire site licenses for computer software programs so that they enjoy a type of discount by not being required to purchase a full program for each employee. Have appropriate controls in place for the master disks and access to the programs so that the site license is not violated. Be certain employees understand the content of and reasons for the site license agreements.

E T H I C A L   I S S U E S

12.3 Evaluate the MIT student's conduct in providing free access to a paid computer service. It was not illegal under current laws, but was it unethical?

Yet another issue in the protection of software copyrights is whether employers should be held responsible for employees who pirate software for home and, perhaps, consulting use. While the copyright laws do not impose vicarious liability, courts have long held employers responsible for infringement by employees in other types of cases. Currently there are proposals to modify the law and hold employers accountable for infringement of software acquired in the course of employment by employees.

BUSINESS PROPERTY PROTECTION IN INTERNATIONAL BUSINESS

Patent Protection

A patent in the United States affords protection for inventors only in the United States. To ensure international protection, the inventor needs to register the patent in each country where he or she will be selling the product or idea.

The Story of the Devil and Procter & Gamble

Even the best-laid plans of Fortune 500 companies can be waylaid by the simplest of problems. Procter & Gamble's trademark of the moon and the stars evolved from 1851 through 1882 when it was patented with its thirteen stars (in honor of the 13 original colonies) and the man in the moon. In 1980, rumors circulated among tabloids, and urbanites maintained that Procter & Gamble's moon-and-stars trademark was linked to witchcraft. An additional rumor was that the trademark symbolized control of Procter & Gamble by Reverend Sun Myung Moon, a cult leader. The rumors came from different sources and appeared in different forms. One rumor held that the president of P&G had made a deal with Satan to ensure P&G's profitability. In exchange for the symbol (which, it was alleged, could form the number 666 if the stars were connected together [666 is a Biblical reference to the AntiChrist]) on all P&G products, P&G would enjoy great profitability. Another rumor had P&G's president on the *Merv Griffin, Donahue* and *60 Minutes* television shows confessing to his deal with Satan. Christian groups circulated pamphlets urging boycotts of P&G products.

Procter & Gamble's Moon-and-Stars Trademark

In 1982, Procter & Gamble filed suit against an Amway Corporation distributor for statements that a Procter & Gamble executive had confirmed Procter & Gamble's satanic ties. Amway's products, such as SA8 laundry detergent and Glister toothpaste, compete directly with Procter & Gamble products.

By 1985, the controversy surrounding the trademark and satanic influences was still swirling despite Procter & Gamble's aggressive litigation against those making the allegations. P&G received 9,000 calls per month about the rumors. As a result, Procter & Gamble withdrew its moon and stars trademark from all products.

In 1991, P&G won the suit against the Amway distributor (a Kansas couple). Procter & Gamble won a $15,000 defamation suit for the rumors the couple spread about Procter & Gamble and satanic influence.

In 1991, Procter & Gamble used its trademark again but eliminated certain elements of the symbol tied to the rumors that the symbol attempted to represent the satanic number 666.

In 1995, Procter & Gamble was given a tape of a message that had gone out over Amway voice mail to its distributors. The tape repeated the allegations of the '80s and named 43 Procter & Gamble products. Procter & Gamble has filed its 15th suit over its trademark.

Ann Landers responded to a reader's question about the trademark as follows:

Is that old turkey of a story still making the rounds? There isn't a shread of truth in it. Funny, how a lie can get halfway around the world in less time than it takes the truth to tie its shoelaces.

Issues

1. Did competitors benefit from the rumor?
2. Should P&G just adopt a different symbol?

The period for patent protection varies from country to country. The United States does not permit patent protection for products until the patent is granted, whereas other countries afford protection from the time application

is made. Procedures for obtaining patents also vary significantly from country to country. For example, many countries hold **opposition proceedings** as part of the patent process. Much like the federal regulatory promulgation steps (see Chapter 6), the description of the patent is published and the public is invited to study the description and possibly oppose the granting of a patent.

Some countries impose **working requirements** on the patent holder, which means that the idea or product must be produced commercially within a certain period of time or the patent protection is revoked.

Trademark Protection

In the United States, trademarks are registered to afford protection. However, like patents, the U.S. registration is effective only in the United States. For protection in other countries, a trademark must be registered (if the country affords the protection of registration). In some countries, known as common law countries, trademark protection is established through use in that country and through the recognition by others of the use and distinction provided by the trademark. In a recent change in the United States, protection for trademarks is afforded without actu-

Business Planning Tip

The Internet is used currently by approximately 20 million people. The World Wide Web offers businesses Web sites that they can use to advertise products. Internet users can simply point and click for access to these sites, but legal issues with these sites abound. For example, much of the material that appears in the Web sites involves trademarks, trade names, and copyrighted materials. Do users of Web sites agree to abide by the terms and conditions Web-site sponsors impose?

One of the difficulties is that copyright, trademark, and trade name restrictions on the use of Web-site materials are not brought on-screen for users to view and agree to. Most sponsors use a "Web-wrap" agreement that includes limitations on use and copying, liability disclaimers, and waivers of copyrights for those who participate in Web sites. All the user will see is a copyright notice, not the terms and conditions of the Web-site use.

Proposed revisions to the Uniform Commercial Code would require Web-site sponsors to disclose all conditions of use prior to use for the protections to be available. In other words, a Web-site user is not bound by the restrictions and conditions of the Web-site sponsor unless the user sees those restrictions when clicking in. Without those disclosures up front, Web-site sponsors stand to lose their intellectual property right protections.

ally introducing the product on the market. Beginning on November 16, 1989, companies could register trademarks without first marketing the product. This change has been perceived as one that will help the United States in its efforts to compete in the international market because European protection is afforded from the time of application, which can be before the product is used or marketed.

Visit the World Intellectual Property Organization: http://www.unicc.org/wipo/

Several international registries attempt to offer international protection. For example, the 1891 **Madrid Agreement Concerning the International Registration of Trademarks** provides a central form of registration through the International Bureau, which is part of the World Intellectual Property Organization (WIPO) in Geneva, Switzerland. Registrations with the bureau are effective for five years in all member countries unless one of the members objects to the trademark registration, in which case the registration is not effective in that country. In addition, the United States is a party to the 1929 **Pan American Convention**, which includes a provision affording trademark protection in all member countries.

In 1989, a diplomatic convention in Madrid resulted in the adoption of the Madrid Protocol Concerning the International Registration of Marks, which created WIPO. WIPO would serve, for those countries participating in the Madrid Protocol System established in 1891, as a central clearinghouse for all trademarks. National or local application would also result in WIPO application for participating nations. The system is designed to simplify, streamline, and reduce the costs of international trademark protection.

In 1996, the European Union will begin its one-stop trademark registration known as Community Trademark (CTM). Under the provisions of this program, U.S. companies can register their trademarks once and enjoy protection in all countries (15) that are part of the European Union. The trademark and backup materials are filed with the Office of Harmonization of the Internal Market (OHIM), which opened on April 1, 1996. The OHIM will then notify the trademark offices in each of the member states of the European Union.

Many countries have permitted the unauthorized use of trademarks in an effort to develop local economies. These countries permit the production of **knock-off goods**, which are goods that carry the trademark or trade name of a firm's product but are not actually produced by that firm. A costly problem for trademark holders is the **gray market**. Manufacturers in foreign countries are authorized to produce a certain amount of goods, but many foreign manufacturers exceed their licensed quota and dump the goods into the market at a much lower price and thereby reduce the trademark owner's market. Such excessive use is an infringement.

Visit BUFETE AF, a Spanish intellectual property law firm, to learn more about the Community Trademark: http://www.bufeteaf.es/eeum1.html

C O N S I D E R . . . **12.7** Congoleum Corporation holds the American patents for the manufacture of chemically embossed vinyl floor covering and owns corresponding patents in 26 foreign countries. Mannington is also involved in the manufacture of vinyl flooring and is authorized to use Congoleum patents in the United States. However, Mannington has just expanded its operations to other countries and is using its license rights in them. Congoleum claims that the patent license for the other countries must be obtained in those countries as well as in the United States. Is Congoleum correct? [*Mannington Mills, Inc.* v. *Congoleum Corp.*, 595 F.2d 1287 (3d Cir. 1979).]

ETHICAL ISSUES

12.4 At your hair salon you notice collections of Gucci, Louis Vuitton, and Fendi handbags, wallets, and briefcases in several glass display cases. As you examine them, you find that no article is priced over $68. You know that no item in any of the genuine collections is priced at or below $68 (key chains and small change purses excluded). Would you buy any of the items for yourself? For gifts? Would you report the salon to anyone? Is it fair to those foreign manufacturers to have these sales of knock-off goods?

C O N S I D E R . . . **12.8** Illia Lekach and Simon Falic are brothers-in-law who founded Perfumania, Inc. Perfumania is a chain of no-frills stores that sells 170 brands of upscale perfumes, such as Estée Lauder, Calvin Klein, and Chanel, at prices 20 to 70 percent below department store prices. LeKach referred to the company as the Toys "Я" Us of perfume sales.

Manufacturers of the expensive perfumes like to sell only to their full-price department store customers. Perfumania must get its supplies from the gray market—unauthorized and authorized distributors in other countries where manufacturers charge less than in the United States.

Givenchy, Boucheron, and Cosmair have sued Perfumania for copyright infringement and patent violations. The manufacturers maintain that they must pay the promotion fees on the perfumes and Perfumania enjoys the benefits of the expensive promotions without paying costs. One manufacturer notes, "I don't want to sell to the gray market. It's not a strategy. You kill your name."

Evaluate the legalities and ethics of Perfumania's gray market purchases and discount sales.

Copyrights in International Business

Review the Berne Convention for the Protection of Literary and Artistic Works (Paris Text 1971): http://www.law.cornell.edu:80/treaties/berne/overview.html

The United States was a party to the 1986 Berne Convention agreement and made it a part of U.S. copyright law through the **Berne Convention Implementation Act of 1988**. Under the convention and the act, a collective work can bear its own notice of copyright and still afford protection for the individual contributions within the work. Under prior copyright law, each contribution had to carry its own notice to be afforded full protection. These new provisions apply to books, magazines, and records. The purpose of the Berne Convention, called the Convention for the Protection of Literary and Artistic Works, was to establish international uniformity in copyright protection. The convention was signed on September 9, 1986, and became effective in the United States on March 1, 1989. Twenty-four countries are members of Berne, which is administered by WIPO. However, the Berne Convention gives backdoor copyright protection to works originating in non-Berne member countries if the work is simultaneously published in a Berne member country. Presently, some copyright holders are governed under previous U.S. copyright laws, which required separate and collective copyrights for full protection.

Business Planning Tip

To be certain federal protection for your intangible property rights is maximized, put either the "ⓔ" by the trade name or trademark or on the packaging or product, or place the words "Registered in U.S. Patent and Trademark Office" or "Reg. U.S. Pat. & Tm. Off." Once you are registered with the U.S. Patent and Trademark Office, obtaining registrations in other countries becomes much easier. Also, a registered product enjoys protection at the borders of the United States. Customs officials can exclude products that are being imported if they infringe a registered property right.

Differing International Standards

The protection of intellectual property in other countries is a difficult task, particularly when the standards of those countries do not recognize computer software as a property right.

China has led the world with software piracy. In 1994, the U.S. Trade Representative placed China on its Special 301 Priority Watch List. By February of 1995, the United States threatened to impose more than $1 billion in trade sanctions if China did not take action to curb software pirating. In August 1995, the United States and China reached an agreement to prevent the sanctions. China agreed to immediate action against known software pirates and to confiscate software packages without seals that U.S. companies would place on their software packages and materials. China remains on the trade watch list as the cultural change for appreciation of ownership rights with respect to computer programs takes place.

E T H I C A L ISSUES

12.5 The United States is the world's largest personal computer software market. The rate of software piracy in the United States in 1994 was 25 percent. In Asia, the average piracy rate is 70 percent, that is, 70 percent of all users of the software have pirated copies. China and Thailand have become known as "one copy" countries. There is only one legitimate copy of the personal computer software in the country, and the remaining copies are all pirated. Evaluate the costs and who is harmed by such widespread pirating.

ENFORCING BUSINESS PROPERTY RIGHTS

Product Disparagement

When an untrue statement is made about a business product or service, the defamation is referred to as **disparagement** and is either **trade libel** (written) or **slander of title** (oral). These business torts occur when one business makes untrue statements about another business, its product, or its abilities. The elements for disparagement are

1. false statement about a business product or about its reputation, honesty, or integrity that is untrue;
2. publication;
3. statement that is directed at a business and is made with malice and the intent to injure that business; and
4. damages.

These elements are the same as those discussed in Chapter 9 for the personal tort of defamation (see pgs. 295–300). The *Bose* case deals with the tort of disparagement.

Palming Off

Palming off, one of the oldest unfair methods of competition, occurs when one company sells its product by leading buyers to believe it is really another company's product. For example, there were many cases of palming off during the early 1980s when the Cabbage Patch dolls were popular, in demand, and scarce. Many replicas were made and called "Cabbage Patch dolls" even though they were not manufactured by Coleco, the original creator.

Establishing palming off requires proof that there is likely to be confusion because of the appearance or name of the competing product. For example, labeling a diamond DeBiers instead of DeBeers is likely to cause confusion. Competitors' packaging with the same colors and design as an original product creates confusion. Potential buyers are likely to be confused as to who actually made the product and who has what market and quality reputation.

Bose Corporation v. Consumers Union of United States, Inc.
466 U.S. 485 (1984)

WOOFERS, TWEETERS, AND DISPARAGEMENT

FACTS

Bose Corporation is the manufacturer of the Bose 901, a stereo loudspeaker. In May 1970, the Consumers Union publication, *Consumer Reports*, analyzed and evaluated loudspeaker systems. The middle-range price group was analyzed, and the Bose 901 was included. It was described in a two-page boxed-off section as "unique and unconventional," but the description also pointed out that a listener could "pinpoint the location of various instruments much more easily with a standard speaker than with the Bose system." The following is an excerpt from the boxed description:

Worse, individual instruments heard through the Bose system seemed to grow to gigantic proportions and tended to wander about the room. For instance, a violin appeared to be ten feet wide and a piano stretched from wall to wall. With orchestral music, such effects seemed inconsequential. But we think they might become annoying when listening to soloists. . . .

We think the Bose system is so unusual that a prospective buyer must listen to it and judge it for himself. We would suggest delaying so big an investment until you were sure the system would please you after the novelty value had worn off.

The article was not written by the same people who made the observation of the speakers. The observers described the sound as moving around the room and the article described the sounds as wandering back and forth.

Bose Corporation took exception to many of the statements made and asked *Consumer Reports* to publish a retraction. *Consumer Reports* would not retract the statements, and Bose sued for disparagement. The district court found that Bose was a public figure and, as such, was required to prove that the statements were made with knowledge they were false (malice). However, the court did find that some of the remarks constituted disparagement and held for Bose (petitioner). The court of appeals reversed on the grounds that the statements were not made with malice, that the article did not accurately reflect what evaluators heard but was written for a mass audience and not with reckless disregard for the truth. Bose appealed.

JUDICIAL OPINION

STEVENS, Justice

Respondent (Consumers Union) correctly reminds us that in cases raising First Amendment issues we have repeatedly held that an appellate court has an obligation to "make an independent examination of the whole record" in order to make sure "that the judgment does not constitute a forbidden intrusion on the field of free expression."

. . . There are categories of communication and certain special utterances to which the majestic protection of the First Amendment does not extend because they "are no essential part of any exposition of ideas, and are of such slight social value as a step to truth that any benefit that may be derived from them is clearly outweighed by the social interest in order and morality." Libelous speech has been held to constitute one such category. . . .

We agree with the Court of Appeals that the difference between hearing violin sounds move around the room and hearing them wander back and forth fits easily within the breathing space that gives life to the First Amendment. We may accept all of the purely factual findings of the District Court and nevertheless hold as a matter of law that the record does not contain clear and convincing evidence that [Consumers Union] prepared the loudspeaker article with knowledge that it contained a false statement, or with reckless disregard for the truth.

The judgment of the Court of Appeals is affirmed.

CASE QUESTIONS

1. Who prepared the *Consumer Reports* article?
2. Why is malice an important part of the case?
3. What classes of speech are exceptions to First Amendment protection?
4. Is disparagement a difficult tort to prove?

E T H I C A L   I S S U E S

12.6 Suppose that one of your research people discovers that a major competitor of yours in the fast food business uses soy filler in its hamburgers even though the hamburgers are advertised as "100% beef." Would you undertake an ad campaign based on that information? Is it fair competition if it is true? Suppose you only have a taste test in which people were asked whether the hamburgers tasted like they had filler. Would you run an ad campaign based on the taste test without knowing whether fillers were used?

The following case deals with the tort of palming off.

Bristol-Myers Squibb Co. v. McNeil-PCC, Inc.
786 F.Supp. 1982 (E.D.N.Y. 1992)

IS IT TYLENOL OR IS IT EXCEDRIN?

FACTS
Bristol-Myers develops, produces, and markets over-the-counter ("OTC") medicines, including Excedrin PM. Excedrin PM is an analgesic/sleep aid that is the largest seller in the United States. Extensive advertising and promotional campaigns by Bristol-Myers have resulted in Excedrin PM's excellent reputation and public acceptance.

McNeil (defendant) markets the leading line of analgesics in the United States under the Tylenol trademark. In 1991, McNeil filed for trademark protection for a new analgesic/sleep aid, Tylenol PM.

Both Excedrin PM and Tylenol PM contain essentially the same ingredients—namely, 500 mg of acetaminophen. The outer cartons of both Tylenol PM caplets and Excedrin PM caplets are predominantly dark blue. The trademarks "Tylenol" and "Excedrin" appear in white capital letters immediately followed by the yellow letters "PM." Below the products' name line appears the phrase "For pain with sleeplessness" for Tylenol and "For pain with accompanying sleeplessness" for Excedrin. At the lower right portion of the carton, McNeil has depicted the two light blue caplets imprinted with the Tylenol PM product name. Bristol-Myers has depicted two light blue tablets imprinted with the letters "PM."

Bristol-Myers filed suit alleging, among other things, product confusion, misappropriation, and infringement. Bristol-Myers asked for an injunction to halt McNeil's use of the Tylenol PM name and the trade dress of the product.

JUDICIAL OPINION
SPATT, District Judge
The Court finds the color scheme of Tylenol PM's trade dress to be a major departure from the traditional red, white and yellow schematic of the Tylenol analgesic line. McNeil chose blue as a result of the Cheskin color study on pill form conducted in 1983. However, the contemporaneous notes of McNeil's own package designer, Gerstman & Meyers, show that in August 1989, Carol Kahrs (product director for Tylenol) told the design firm that the color of the Tylenol PM pill "will be light blue like Excedrin PM."

A review of the approximately sixty separate package mockups reveals that multiple options were presented to McNeil in terms of color and design. The Court finds a number of these mockups particularly enlightening. . . . For some unknown reason, McNeil rejected all these possible designs, along with many others which would have moved its final product much
Continued

further along the spectrum away from the Excedrin PM trade dress.

Based on this evidence, the Court finds that McNeil had every opportunity, not to mention resources, to exercise good faith in selecting a trade dress that truly reflected the adult Tylenol line. Instead, every choice it made brought it closer to the Excedrin PM trade dress. This is not a case where designers and manufacturers had no options. Rather, McNeil consciously chose to assemble the elements of the Excedrin PM trade dress, a fact corroborated by the following startling admission of Donald Casey, the product manager:

Q: After you get by the mark could you pick out the package from exhibits 6, 7, 8 and 9 which look the most like this one? This one being Excedrin PM. . . .
A: 8B.

Q: 8B. Okay. Let me now ask you the question in kind of reverse. Looking at the Tylenol PM package, blue package, would you agree that it has some similarity to the Excedrin PM package?
A: Yes. . . .

Q: Is there any package you see on here which has a greater similarity to Excedrin PM than the Tylenol PM package you marketed. . . .
A: Not really.

Q: So if I'm understanding you then you spent about four hundred thousand dollars to have Gerstman & Meyers create about 60 or 70 of these package markups, right?
A: Yes.

Q: And in the end what you brought to market was the one package markup that looked—that had the greatest similarity to Excedrin PM, right?
A: As we phrased it, yes.

Bristol-Myers acknowledges that it has no monopoly, but it contends, and the Court agrees, that "the multiplicity of the similarities is objective evidence of defendant's conscious imitation of plaintiff's product." The Second Circuit has noted that

[i]n this circuit and others, numerous decisions have recognized that the second comer has a duty to so name and dress his product as to avoid all *likelihood of consumers confusing it with the product of the first comer.*

The Court finds the above evidence to be compelling on the issue of intentional copying. An analysis of the logotype, graphic devices and color configuration of the Excedrin PM and Tylenol PM packages leads to the inescapable conclusion that the defendant intentionally copied Bristol-Myers' analgesic-with-sleep-aid trade dress.

Where we can perceive freedom of choice with full knowledge of a senior user's mark, we can readily read into defendant's choice of a confusingly similar mark the intent to get a free ride upon the reputation of a well-known mark.

The focus of this particular factor is whether consumers spend much time evaluating the product before making a purchase or whether it is considered a "grab off the shelf."

Purchases such as microwave ovens, electric ranges and hi-fi loudspeakers are expensive items and ordinary consumers exercise much more discriminating care before buying. Consumers who spend $100 an ounce on perfume exercise care before parting with their money.

On the other hand, consumers buying sour cream or cookies often take little notice of a maker's name which is plainly evident to the purchaser's eye. Common sense dictates that price is the crucial factor in ascertaining the depth of attention the ordinary purchaser is likely to apply to a given purchase. The products sold by both the plaintiff and defendant are inexpensive OTC analgesics with a sleep aid, which are not major expenditures for most purchasers when buying the 24 caplet or tablet size. Where a product costs less than $5, purchasers have been characterized as casual buyers, likely to devote less time and attention to making a decision to purchase the item.

The Court finds that an OTC analgesic with sleep aid is more of a "grab-off-the-shelf" product, although with an admitted increase in the degree of care exercised by the general consuming public. Although far from overwhelming, the Court finds the evidence of "sophistication of the buyer" as support for a finding of likelihood of confusion to favor Bristol-Myers.

The Court finds that the defendant's use of the Tylenol PM trade dress does create a likelihood of confusion for an appreciable number of consumers. In reaching this decision, the Court places primary importance on the strength of the Excedrin PM trade dress, the similarity of the two trade dresses, the directly competitive nature of the products offered, the established fact of intentional copying by McNeil, and the lack of "deliberate and measured product selection by consumers" in a supermarket or pharmacy environment. Accordingly, the Court grants the plaintiff's motion for a preliminary injunction.

CASE QUESTIONS
1. Who had the market for analgesic/sleep aids? Who first entered the market?
2. Explain the factors that would probably create confusion between Excedrin PM and Tylenol PM.
3. Why was the price of the product important in determining confusion?
4. Does the court find that Tylenol PM was getting a free ride on Excedrin PMs success?

E T H I C A L   I S S U E S

12.7 A portion of the testimony of Donald Casey, the product manager for Tylenol PM, appears in the court opinion. Why is his testimony important? Could you, as a product manager, have made the same decision to pick the product package that most looked like Excedrin PM? Is it ethical to copy a product to create confusion?

Misappropriation

Some businesses have a **trade secret**—chemical formula, procedure, customer list, data, or device that only that business has. Generally, these types of secrets should be given patent or copyright protection. However, those that do not qualify for these federal statutory protections (discussed later in this chapter) have only the tort of misappropriation as protection. **Misappropriation** occurs when a competitor figures out the formula for a product or takes a customer list or other data and puts the product or information to use competitively. Misappropriation is conversion of a trade secret, and proof of misappropriation requires that there be some theft, industrial espionage, or bribery as the means used for obtaining the trade secret.

C O N S I D E R . . . **12.9** John McGhan has been involved in the radio and music industry for over a decade. He created "The Source," a youth radio network owned by NBC, and served as a director for Rolling Stone Magazine Productions.

Dick Ebersol, the owner of No Sleep Productions, Ltd., first approached Brandon Tartikoff (NBC's president of entertainment) to try the idea of *Friday Night Videos*, a music show to be broadcast on NBC to replace the failing SCTV comedy show. Mr. Tartikoff was not prepared to take action at that time, but in late 1982,

Continued

after the success of Music Television Video (MTV), he was more receptive to Mr. Ebersol's idea and asked Mr. Ebersol to come up with a proposal that would distinguish NBC's production from MTV's.

Mr. Ebersol then contacted Mr. McGhan and asked him to put together ideas for the show. He did and eventually Mr. Ebersol asked Mr. McGhan to produce the new show.

Mr. McGhan participated with Mr. Ebersol in discussions with NBC, and both agreed they would make more profit if they, as opposed to NBC, owned the show. Mr. McGhan began work on the production, was phased out of Rolling Stone, and turned down other offers of employment to do FNV. Troubles developed between Mr. McGhan and Mr. Ebersol, and before he was paid, Mr. McGhan's participation was ended. He claims misappropriation of the following ideas he contributed:

1. The Reel Rock Awards (video awards)
2. Where They Are Now (interviews with rock stars of yesteryear)
3. The Video-Vote (a 900 call-in number for viewers to vote on videos)
4. Private reels
5. Stereo simulcasts
6. Hall of Famers
7. A highly stylized announcer rather than an on-screen host

[*McGhan* v. *Ebersol*, 608 F.Supp. 277 (S.D.N.Y. 1985).]

WHAT CAN A BUSINESS OWN? REAL PROPERTY

The Nature of Real Property

LAND

Real property consists of more than just land itself; it is a bundle of rights. An old saying in property law is "The owner of the soil owns also to the sky and to the depths." When you own real property, you own the surface that we actually see and upon which buildings are placed, but you also own **air rights** and **mineral rights**.

AIR RIGHTS

Air rights in real property consist of the right to use the air above the surface land that is described as your real property interest. Your land interest can actually be separated into two interests so that you can keep the surface rights and transfer the air rights. The ownership of air rights is important in large cities because building up is the only way to expand available space in cities limited in expansion on the ground. For example, in New York City, the Met Life building is built in the air rights above Grand Central Station. This 59-story

Business Planning Tip

Before purchasing property, check the area for noise and other activity. Determine flight paths and plans for construction of airports, runways, and possible expansion of airport capacity and facilities.

building occupies the air rights above the station. The foundation of the building rests on the surface of the land through an **easement**, or a right to use the land of another for a limited purpose.

The sale of the air space above one's surface land can be profitable. In cities in which horizontal growth is limited, the only means of expansion for businesses is to build vertically. Excessive demand coupled with a finite supply make air space rights extremely valuable. In Los Angeles, the air space above the owned surface rights has its own value for which property taxes are assessed. Some businesses purchase air rights for possible future expansion and simply hold the rights until their expansion occurs.

There are limitations on air rights. All property owners take their air rights subject to the right of flight. Airplanes may use the air lots over your property in travel without committing trespass and without being required to pay compensation.

MINERAL RIGHTS

Mineral rights are rights to what rests below the surface of land. Examples of valuable commodities that a landowner can own beneath a property's surface include oil, gas, coal, geothermal energy pockets, and water. Just as with air rights, these subsurface rights can be transferred separately. The right to drill for oil and gas can be conveyed to another (possibly in exchange for royalty payments) and the surface rights retained. Those who purchase the mineral rights are again given an easement for access to the property for drilling.

FIXTURES

There is yet another form of real property rights that crosses personal property with real property. **Fixtures** are a part of the property that were once personal property but have become a part of the land or a structure on the land. For example, a microwave oven is personal property when it is purchased from a store. But if that oven is installed in a home in a place built especially for it and it is bolted to the walls or cabinets in the kitchen, it becomes a part of the real property. Fixtures often create confusion in the transfer of real property as the parties disagree over whether the personal property was intended to become a part of the real property. Questions that are important in determining whether an item is a fixture and part of the real property or personal property are as follows:

1. What did the parties intend? If the parties have agreed that an item is a fixture, it will be treated as such. For example, draperies in a home are a frequent source of disagreement among buyers and sellers over whether they stay with the home or go with the seller. If their contract includes draperies, then they are treated as fixtures and will transfer with the home to the buyer.
2. How is the item attached to the real property? The greater the degree of attachment and the more the item has become a part of the real property, the greater the likelihood that it will be classified as a fixture. One exception to this general rule is the classification of **trade fixtures**. Many forms of personal property that a business uses will be attached to the real property, but they are a part of the business and are not intended to remain a part of the real property. Retail stores have counters bolted to the floor. These counters are an integral part of the store, but they are trade fixtures and would be classified as personal property and not a part of the real property.
3. What is the relationship between the attacher and the property? Who attached the fixture to the real property and is the attacher a tenant or a landowner? Shelves attached by a tenant are probably not intended to

remain as part of the real property. Those same shelves attached by a home-owner would probably be classified as a fixture. A commercial tenant is different from a residential tenant because of the rules about trade fixtures being personal property.

4. Who wants to know? Courts vary in their classifications of fixtures according to who is asking whether an item is a fixture. If an insurer is seeking classification of an item as personal property so that an insurance claim for damage to the real property is less, the courts will probably find in favor of the insured and classify the item as a fixture. For purposes of tax valuation for property tax purposes, the courts label items as fixtures more frequently because of the increased value of the property they bring.

C O N S I D E R . . . **12.10** Consider the following items and determine whether the items would be fixtures or personal property. Assume that the parties have not reached an agreement on the nature of the fixtures.

a. A pipe organ installed in a building owned and operated by Organ Stop Pizza. Organ Stop Pizza features an organist each night who works with the patrons to play appropriate music and offer entertainment to children. What additional information would help you in determining whether the organ would be a fixture and real property or simply just personal property?

b. Refrigerators, washers, and dryers found in the apartments of a 20-unit complex a buyer has just purchased.

c. The garage-door opener and keys to a house just purchased.

d. A neon sign purchased by a tattoo parlor and installed above the door of its leased premises in a strip mall.

e. The color-coordinated bedspreads and curtains in a hotel just sold.

Interests in Real Property

There are various forms of ownership interests in real property. The highest degree of land ownership is call a **fee simple** interest. If a company or individual has a fee simple interest in property, it owns full rights to the property and has the freedom to mortgage the property, sell the property, and, in the case of individuals, transfer the property by will.

A lesser degree of real property ownership is the **life estate**. In this form of real property interest, one person is given the right to use and occupy the property for life. When that person, the **life tenant**, dies, the property either goes back to the grantor (the person who originally transferred it) or, in most cases, to another person (called the **remainderman**). Generally, the remainderman receives a fee simple interest. The life estate is used often in estate planning. A surviving spouse is given a life estate in the family residence with the couple's children (remaindermen) receiving the fee simple interest when the spouse passes away.

Another real property interest is the **easement**, which is a right to use another's property. There are access easements that permit the owner of the easement to use a path or road on another's property in order to gain access to his or her own real property. There are negative easements where the easement holder is promised by another property holder that the latter won't, for example, plant trees that will block the solar panels on the easement holder's property from the sun. There are easements in gross that run through most properties that are given to utility companies for the right to run wires and pipes through segments of property so individual property owners and the surrounding community can enjoy utility service.

FOR THE MANAGER'S DESK

THE SOLAR EASEMENT AND RIGHT TO LIGHT

One form of an easement that is negotiated in more and more sales contracts today is the solar easement. Under common law, there is no "right to light"; someone can build a building next to your property that blocks all of your light and not be liable for any damages. In the case of *Fontainebleau Hotel Corp.* v. *Forty-Five Twenty-Five, Inc.*, 114 So.2d 357 (Fla. 1959), a Miami hotel could not obtain relief from a court when the neighboring property owner constructed a 14-story addition to its existing hotel which blocked the afternoon sun from the plaintiff hotel's swimming pool and sunbathing areas. The court held that absent an agreement, there were no restrictions on the blockage of light.

However, with a properly negotiated contract, the right to light can be obtained and protected. The contract can specify that the seller gives a solar easement or right of light to the buyer. Or neighbors can agree to a solar easement among themselves. Even residential property owners can benefit from solar easement clauses, particularly when they have a solar heating system that requires the panels of the system to be near direct sunlight to maximize efficiency.

Some cities have passed ordinaces that prevent solar panel obstruction. often a part of zoning laws, these ordinaces give the solar system owner a statutory right of light. In these cities, title insurance companies physically inspect neighboring properties for solar systems so that they can exclude solar easements from their policy or offer additional insurance for increased "solar premium."

A final form of real property interest is the **lease**, which is temporary possession of real property. A lease can be a fixed lease in which there is a beginning and ending date. Or the lease can be a **periodic tenancy** in which the landlord and tenant go from period to period renewing the lease. For example, a month-to-month tenancy is a form of a periodic tenancy in which a tenant pays rent on a given day each month and thereby renews the lease. In order to end a periodic tenancy, the other party must be given a full period's notice of termination. If the rent in a periodic tenancy is paid on the first day of each month and the tenant wishes to end the lease, notice must be given on the first of the month. If, for example, a tenant notified the landlord on October 15 that the tenant wished to terminate the lease, the tenant's obligation to pay rent continues through November because the tenant will not have given a full period's notice until the end of November.

A lease for a fixed period has the benefit of fixed rent that cannot be changed until the lease is over. A periodic tenant's rent can be raised at any time once a full period's notice is given.

Most states have full statutory provisions on residential leases and many have requirements on commercial leases. These statutory provisions cover such issues as the condition of the property when the lease begins, maintenance, security deposits, and when lease agreements must be in writing to be enforceable. The following case deals with one state's ruling on the landlord's obligations with respect to the condition of leased property.

Lemle v. *Breeden*
462 P.2d 470 (Haw. 1969)

LEASING HAWAIIAN LUXURY: SIX BEDROOMS, SIX BATHS, AND SIXTY RATS

FACTS

Mrs. V. E. Breeden (defendant/appellant) owned a house in the Diamond Head area of Honolulu, which she rented to Mr. Henry C. Lemle (plaintiff/appellee) for $800 a month for the periods from September 22, 1964, to March 20, 1965, and from April 17, 1965, to June 12, 1965. The terms were agreed to on September 21, 1964, and that day Mr. Lemle paid Mrs. Breeden's agent $1,900 for a deposit and prepaid rent.

The dwelling consists of several structures containing six bedrooms, six baths, a living room, kitchen, dining room, garage, and saltwater swimming pool. The main dwelling is constructed in Tahitian style with a corrugated metal roof over which coconut leaves have been woven together for a grass shack effect. The house is relatively open without screening on windows or doorways.

Mr. Lemle, his wife, and four children moved into the home on September 22, 1964. That evening it became abundantly evident to Mr. Lemle that there were rats within the main dwelling and on the roof. During the night and the next two nights, he and his family were sufficiently apprehensive of the rats that they slept together in the downstairs living room. They saw and heard rats on all three nights.

On September 23, 1964, Mrs. Breeden's agent hired a firm to exterminate the dwelling and Mr. Lemle himself set traps, but the next two nights were no better. After three nights, the family left the dwelling and sought the refund of their $1,900. Upon Mrs .Breeden's refusal to return the money, Mr. Lemle brought suit. The trial judge found there was an implied warranty of habitability and ordered Mrs. Breeden to return the money plus interest. Mrs. Breeden appealed.

JUDICIAL OPINION

LEVINSON, Justice

The rule of caveat emptor in lease transactions at one time may have had some basis in social practice as well as in historical doctrine. . . . Yet in urban society where the vast majority of tenants do not reap the rent directly from the land but bargain primarily for the right to enjoy the premises for living purposes, often signing standardized leases, as in this case, common law conceptions of a lease and the tenant's liability for rent are no longer applicable.

In the law of sales of chattels, the trend is markedly in favor of implying warranties of fitness and merchantability. The reasoning has been (1) that the public interest in safety and consumer protection requires it, and (2) that the burden ought to be shifted to the manufacturer, who, by placing the goods on the market, represents their suitability and fitness. The manufacturer is also the one who knows more about the product and is in a better position to alleviate problems or bear the brunt of any losses. The same reasoning is equally persuasive in leases of real property.

The application of an implied warranty of habitability in leases gives recognition to the changes in leasing transactions today. It affirms the fact that a lease is, in essence, a sale as well as a transfer of an estate in land and is, more importantly, a contractual relationship. From that contractual relationship an implied warranty of habitability and fitness for the purposes intended is a just and necessary implication. Legal fictions and artificial exceptions to wooden rules of property law aside, we hold that in the lease of a dwelling, such as in this case, there is an implied warranty of habitability and fitness intended.

Here the facts demonstrate the uninhabitability and unfitness of the premises for residential purposes. For three sleepless nights the plaintiff and his family literally camped in the living room. They were unable to sleep in the proper quarters or make use of the other facilities in the house due to the natural apprehension of the rats which made noise scurrying about on the roof and invaded the house through the unscreened openings. *Continued*

The defendant makes much of the point that the source of the rats was the beach rocks and surrounding foliage. She contended that this exonerated her from the duty to keep the house free of rats. While it is not clear where the rats came from, assuming that they did originate from outside the premises, the defendant had it within her power to keep them out by proper and timely screening and extermination procedures. But to begin such procedures after the plaintiff had occupied the dwelling and to expect that he have the requisite patience and fortitude in the face of trial and error methods of extermination was too much to ask.

When the premises were vacated, they were not fit for use as a residence. Nor was there any assurance that the residence would become habitable within a reasonable time.

Affirmed.

CASE QUESTIONS
1. Who is the landlord? Who are the tenants?
2. Describe the property being leased.
3. What are the terms of the rental agreement?
4. How much was paid initially?
5. What problem did the tenants experience?
6. How long did the tenants stay on the property?
7. Why did the tenants leave?
8. Can the tenants have their money returned and be excused from the lease?
9. What theory is applied and what precedent is used for its application?

Transferring Real Property

The transfer of real property is more complex than the transfer of personal property. Real property is transferred through a document called a **deed**. A deed must be in writing, it must be signed by the owner (grantor) of the property, and it must contain a full legal description of the property in order to transfer title to real property.

There are several different types of deeds. The type of deed determines the degree of title protection the transferee is given by the transfer or grantor. A **warranty deed** or **general warranty deed** provides the highest degree of title protection from the grantor. When the grantor gives the grantee a warranty deed, he promises that he has good title, that he has the authority to transfer title, and that there are no liens or title problems other than anything noted on the deed. A deed may include a qualification, "subject to public utility easements," which means that the grantee takes the title subject to the utility easements through the property.

A **special warranty deed** or **bargain and sale deed** is one in which the grantor makes the same promises as under a warranty deed but does so only for the time during which he held title to the property. In this form of deed the grantor is simply saying that he did nothing during his ownership of the property to cloud the title. Most buyers will elect to purchase **title insurance**, which is a policy that affords reimbursement to the buyer in the event a title defect arises after the purchase. Title insurance is protection in addition to the grantor's promises, but it covers only defects in title that are of record, such as tax liens and easements.

A **quitclaim deed** is a deed that carries no warranties about the title to the land. In effect, the grantor in a quitclaim deed is saying, "I hereby transfer whatever interest I have in this real property, but there is no guarantee that I hold any interest in this property." The quitclaim deed is often used in situations where someone is trying to clear title to property and obtains quitclaim deeds from many individuals who might or might not have a claim on title.

While the delivery of a complete and signed deed is all that is necessary to transfer title to real property, the process of **recording** is done in nearly all property transfers. Recording is the filing of the deed with a government agency, usually a county recorder or county clerk, so that public notice is given of the transfer and ownership. The risk of not recording a deed is that the grantor could make a subsequent transfer of the land, and, depending upon particular state statutes, the original grantee could lose title to the land to that subsequent transferee.

Title to real property can be transferred in other ways. Real property can be transferred by will, and heirs obtain title through the probate of the estate (still by use of a deed). Title to land can also be transferred through **adverse possession**. Adverse possession is use of another's land for a statutory period of time (generally ranging from 10 to 20 years) in an open manner. In effect, what begins as a trespass can ripen into title if the owner of land takes no action to remove a trespasser from the land. Often called squatter's rights, adverse possession can occur in situations as simple as placing a fence incorrectly along a property's border. If the fence encroaches on a neighbor's land by six inches, and the fence remains there for 20 years, the fence builder acquires title to those extra six inches by adverse possession.

Financing Real Property Purchases

The purchase of real property is a major transaction for individuals and businesses. Most property buyers are unable to pay cash for their property. Financing arrangements that allow the creditor to take a lien on the purchased property have existed since English common law. The most common form of property security for a creditor is the **mortgage**. In this form of security, a borrower pledges property to the lender as security for the debt that arises because the lender advances the money for purchase of the property. In the event the buyer/borrower does not make the necessary payments to the lender, the lender can **foreclose** on the mortgage. **Foreclosure** is a judicial process in which the lender takes possession and title of mortgaged property and then sells it to satisfy the unpaid debt.

Another form of creditor security for real property purchases is the **deed of trust**. Popular in the western states, this form of security places title to property in the hands of a trustee who holds title until a debtor repays the creditor the full amount of the debt. If the debtor defaults on payments, the trustee may then proceed to sell the property to satisfy the debt. The deed of trust financing arrangement is beneficial to lenders because judicial foreclosure is not required in order to hold a property sale.

Because of the importance of these interests and the need to have priority over subsequent real property creditors, mortgages, and deed of trusts are also recorded in the public offices where deeds and other land interests are recorded.

SUMMARY

What does a business own? What are the types of business property?
- Tangible property—physical: real and personal property
- Intangible property—bundles of rights with respect to goodwill
- Real property—bundles of rights with respect to land, attachments, air space, and subsurface materials

What are the rights and issues in personal property owned by a business?
- Documents of title—formal legal document that serves to prove and transfer title to tangible personal property
- Bill of sale—informal document or contract that serves to prove and transfer title to tangible personal property
- Lease—right of use and possession of property for fixed or open-end period
- Bailment—temporary transfer of possession of personal property
- Bailor—party who owns property and surrenders possession
- Bailee—party who has temporary possession of the property of another
- License—right granted of access; generally oral; personal right that is in transferrable
- Exculpatory clause—clause that attempts to hold a party harmless in the event of damage or injury to another or another's property
- Lien—creditor's right in property to secure debt
- Security interest—UCC lien on personal property
- Chattel mortgage—term for lien on personal property
- Uniform Commercial Code—uniform statute governing commercial transactions adopted in 49 states
- Security agreement—contract that creates a security interest
- Collateral—property subject to lien, security interest, or chattel mortgage
- Financing statement—publicly-filed document reflecting security interest

What statutory protections exist for intellectual property?
- Patents—statutory protection for products and processes
- Copyrights—statutory protection for words, thoughts, ideas, music
- Trademarks—statutory protection for product symbols
- Trade names—statutory protection for unique product labels and names
- Trade dress—statutory protection for product colors and motifs

What issues of intellectual property protection exist in international operations?
- OPTH—European Community trademark registration

What private remedies exist for property protections?
- Product disparagement—false and damaging statements
- Misappropriation—use of another's ideas or trade secrets
- Palming off—causing deception about the maker or source of a product

What are real property interests and what rights are included?
- Air rights—rights of surface owner to air above land surface
- Mineral rights—rights of surface owner to materials beneath the land surface

- Easement—right or privilege in the land of another
- Fixtures—property that was once personal in nature that is affixed to real property and becomes a part of it
- Trade fixtures—personal property used in a trade or business that is attached to real property but is considered personal property
- Fee simple—highest degree of land ownership; full rights of mortgage and transferability
- Life estate—right to use and occupy property for life
- Remainderman—interest in third party following a life estate
- Lease—temporary possession and use of real property
- Periodic tenancy—lease that runs from period to period such as month-to-month
- Warranty deed—highest level of title protection in real property transfer
- Special warranty deed—promises of title protection only for grantor's period of ownership
- Bargain and sale deed—a special warranty deed
- Title insurance—insurance purchased for buyer's benefit of land title
- Quitclaim deed—transfer of title with no warranties
- Recording—public filing of land documents
- Adverse possession—acquisition of land title through use for statutory period
- Mortgage—lien on real property
- Foreclosure—process of creditor's acquiring mortgaged land for resale
- Deed of trust—alternative form of creditor security in land purchase

QUESTIONS AND PROBLEMS

1. Lotus 1-2-3 is a spreadsheet program that enables users to perform accounting functions electronically on a computer. Users manipulate and control the program with a series of menu commands such as "Copy," "Print," and "Quit." Lotus 1-2-3 has 469 commands arranged into more than 50 menus and submenus and includes what is known as a "macro" feature. Users can write a series of command choices that can then be executed with a single keystroke.

   Borland introduced its Quattro spreadsheet program in 1987, after three years of development work by its engineers. Borland's objective was to build a superior spreadsheet program and take over the market, but its product contains an identical copy of the entire Lotus 1-2-3 menu tree. Borland does not dispute its inclusion; it simply notes that the Quattro system builds on the Lotus commands.

   Lotus filed suit against Borland for infringement. Borland removed the interface part of its program, but Lotus contends the commands in the Quattro program are virtually the same as the Lotus program—the first letters are just different. Borland maintains the menus are not protected by copyright. Should they be protected? [*Lotus Dev. Corp.* v. *Borland Int'l, Inc.*, 49 F.3d 807 (1st Cir. 1995); cert. granted, 116 S. Ct. 39 (1995).]

2. Storck Candy manufactures Werther's Original Butter Toffee Candy. The toffee is sold in an eight-ounce bag with a brown background, a picture of a mound of unwrapped candy, an Alpine village, and an old-fashioned container pouring white liquid.

   Farley Candy Company introduced its butter toffee candy in a bag the same size and shape as Werther's with a pair of containers pouring liquid.

Storck says that Farley is using its trade dress in trying to sell its candy. Has Farley done anything that is a tort? Do federal laws offer protection? [*Storck USA, L.P* v. *Farley Candy Co., Inc.,* 785 F. Supp. 730 (N.D. Ill. 1992).]

3. Moe's Pizza, a restaurant located on Watts Street in New York City, leased its premises from Manhattan Mansions. Water from the bathroom of the residential apartment located above Moe's has been leaking into the kitchen at Moe's. On many occasions, the water leaked directly onto the grill and Moe's was forced to close in order to clean up the water. Additionally, many customers would leave when they saw the water dripping from the ceiling into the cooking area. Moe's withheld its rent of $3,418.76 for the month of February after repeated requests for repairs of the floor and leak were made. Manhattan Mansions has filled suit for nonpayment of rent and eviction. Moe's claims a breach of the implied warranty of habitability. Does the warranty apply here? [*Manhattan Mansions* v. *Moe's Pizza,* 561 N.Y.S. 2d 331 (1990).]

4. Robert Conroy invented and holds the patent for "inflatable bladders use in athletic footgear." The patent is called "Athletic Armor and Inflatable Bag Assembly." The "Bladders" can be inflated with air to cushion and protect the feet of the athletic shoe wearer.

   Reebok International, Ltd. manufactures a basketball shoe with inflatable bladders that it sells under the name of the PUMP. Conroy brought suit claiming Reebok infringed his patent. Reebok says the design and method of inflation is different from Mr. Conroy's patented system. Mr. Conroy says the idea of an inflatable shoe is his and he is entitled to royalties from Reebok. Is Mr. Conroy correct? [*Conroy* v. *Reebok International,* Ltd, 29 U.S. P. Q.2d 1373 (Mass. 1994).]

5. Roger Burten submitted his "Triumph" electronic game to Milton Bradley for possible mass production, but it was rejected twice after review. One year later, however, Milton Bradley began marketing a new electronic board game under the name of "Dark Tower." There were structural and design similarities between "Triumph" and "Dark Tower." Mr. Burten brought suit for fraud, breach of contract, and trade secret misappropriation. Can Burten recover under any of these theories? [*Burten* v. *Milton Bradley Co.,* 763 F.2d 461 (1st Cir. 1985).]

6. Vanna White is the hostess of *Wheel of Fortune,* one of the most popular game shows in television history. An estimated 40 million people watch the program daily. Capitalizing on the fame that her participation in the show has bestowed on her, Miss White markets her identity to various advertisers.

   Samsung Electronics ran a series of ads in at least half-a-dozen publications with widespread, and in some cases national, circulation. Each of the advertisements in the series followed the same theme: Each depicted a current item from popular culture and a Samsung electronic product. Each was set in the twenty-first century and conveyed the message that the Samsung product would still be in use by that time. By hypothesizing outrageous future outcomes for the cultural items, the ads created humorous effects. For example, one lampooned current popular notions of an unhealthy diet by depicting a raw steak with the caption: "Revealed to be health food. 2010 A.D." Another depicted irreverent "news"-show host Morton Downey Jr. in front of an American flag with the caption: "Presidential candidate. 2008 A.D."

   The advertisement that prompted the current dispute was for Samsung video cassette recorders (VCRs). The ad depicted a robot dressed in a wig, gown, and jewelry that was consciously selected to resemble Vanna White's hair and dresses. The robot was posed next to a game board instantly recognizable as the *Wheel of Fortune* game show set in a stance for which Miss White is famous. The caption of the ad read: "Longest-running game show. 2012 A.D." Defendants referred to the ad as the "Vanna White ad." Unlike the other celebrities used in the campaign, Miss White neither consented to the ads nor was she paid. Have Vanna White's rights been violated? Did Samsung violate federal law? [*White* v. *Samsung Elect. Am., Inc.,* 971 F.2d 1395 (9th Cir. 1992).]

7. Spuds MacKenzie is a ring-eyed dog known as the mascot/trademark for Bud Light beer. Beneath Spuds' picture, the following line appears: "The original Party Animal."

Another company has begun using the slogan. Anheuser-Busch claims the slogan is a trademark for Bud. Is Anheuser-Busch correct? [*In Re Anheuser-Busch*, No. 17,939, slip op. (May 16, 1990).]

8. Freddie Fuddruckers, Inc., uses glass-enclosed bakeries and butcher areas exposed to the public to emphasize its freshness as a decor theme in all its Fuddruckers restaurants. Fuddruckers floors are checkered, walls tiled, and lighting bright to communicate cleanliness and quality. Ridgeline opened its restaurants with nearly identical decor. Does Fuddruckers have any rights? [*Freddie Fuddruckers, Inc.* v. *Ridgeline, Inc.*, 589 F. Supp. 72 (1984).]

9. Do the following slogans constitute protectable business properties?
   MetLife: "Get Met, It Pays"
   General Electric: "GE Brings Good Things to Life"
   Nike: "Just Do It"

10. Would a new women's jean manufacturer adopting the name Lardashe be infringing the Jordache Jean's name? [*Jordache Enterprises* v. *Hogg Wyld*, 828 F.2d 1482 (10th Cir. 1987).]

Judgment

Microsoft Corporation virtually controls the software market for personal computers. Over 80 percent of the operating systems used in personal computers have Microsoft software. Rival Novell CEO Robert J. Frankenberg says, "There is no doubt Microsoft is out to kill us. This is not paranoia. They really are out to get us."

Bill Gates, CEO of Microsoft, has responded, "This is a fiercely competitive business."

Microsoft requires its customers who manufacture computers to pay a fee for each computer they ship, even if the computer contains another software maker's operating system. These manufacturers thus have an incentive to use Microsoft because they must pay double royalties if they don't.

"There are certainly grounds for an antitrust suit," says Mr. Frankenberg. Are there grounds for antitrust violations? Isn't Microsoft simply competing?

CHAPTER 13

Economic power is an inevitable result of the free

enterprise system. Building a better mousetrap should

result in attracting

Trade Practices: Antitrust Laws

more customers and developing economic power. But

gaining economic power through other means destroys the

free enterprise system and often precludes purchasers

from buying the better mouse trap. They are stuck with

a mousetrap that may be mediocre but is built by a firm

with perhaps ill-gained economic power and resulting

market control.

Antitrust law exists to regulate the growth of

economic or market power; it does so in part by

ensuring that competition remains a part of the free

enterprise system. This chapter answers the following

questions: What restraints of trade are permissible?

What antitrust laws exist? What penalties can be

imposed for violations? What are the forms of horizontal

trade restraints and defenses? What are the forms of

vertical trade restraints and defenses?

> *People of the same trade seldom meet together, even for merriment and diversion, but the conversation ends in some contrivance to raise prices. It is impossible indeed to prevent such meetings, by any law which would be consistent with liberty and justice. But though the law cannot hinder people of the same trade from sometimes assembling together, it ought to do nothing to facilitate such assemblies.*
> **Adam Smith**
> The Wealth of Nations

> *While the law of competition may be sometimes hard for the individual, it is best for the race, because it ensures the survival of the fittest in every department.*
> **Andrew Carnegie**

COMMON LAW PROTECTIONS
AGAINST RESTRAINT OF TRADE

Early Common Law of Trade Restraints

In the sixteenth century, the earliest trade restraint cases held that it was void per se for parties to agree that one party would not engage in a lawful trade or profession. Oddly enough, the void per se rule was not followed with the intent of encouraging competition; rather, it was followed out of fear that those not able to practice their trade would become a burden to society.

In the seventeenth and eighteenth centuries, the courts began to recognize that certain circumstances required some form of trade restraint. The first permissible type of restraint was allowed in the sale of a business: In the sale provisions, the seller agreed not to open a competing business. This trade restraint, called a **covenant not to compete**, was valid so long as it was reasonable in its length and scope. For example, in *Mitchell* v. *Reynolds,* 24 Eng. Rep. 347 (1711), a baker who sold his bakery agreed not to compete in the immediate area for five years, and a court held the covenant valid because it was limited in time and geographic scope.

Modern Common Law of Trade Restraints

Under common law, contracts and covenants that restrain trade are not illegal per se. Such contracts are enforceable so long as they are not unreasonable—that is, they go no further than necessary for protection. Exceeding reasonable time and geographic limits would be examples of unreasonable trade restraints. For example, a covenant in a contract for the sale of a dry cleaning business that prohibits the seller from opening another dry cleaning business anywhere in the state is unreasonably broad, but a similar covenant limited to the town where the business is located is probably reasonable. The reasonable restraint is related to the sale of a business and preservation of its goodwill.

Restraints in leases are also related to a business transaction and are valid. For example, a restriction in a shopping center lease that prohibits a lessee from operating a business that competes with other tenants is appropriate so long as the purpose of the restriction is to obtain a proper mix in the shopping center with the idea of attracting more business. Partners' and employees' restrictions that prevent them from competing for a certain time period after they leave a partnership or corporation are also reasonable so long as they are not excessive.

In the following case the court addresses the issue of a shopping center lease covenant and its reasonableness under common law standards.

Business Planning Tip

When negotiating valid covenants not to compete:
1. Be certain the covenant is necessary.
2. Be certain the covenant is reasonable.
   a. Covers only the geographic scope necessary (a five-mile radius for the sale of a dry cleaning business is reasonable; a worldwide prohibition is not)
   b. Covers only the time necessary (five years is reasonable; a lifetime prohibition is not)
3. Make the covenant part of the agreement of sale, lease, or employment. Separate agreements not to compete arouse suspicions.
4. Be certain the noncompete clause or paragraph is initialed by both parties.
5. Legal representation helps ensure validity by assumed understanding.

Child World, Inc. v. South Towne Centre, Ltd.
634 F. Supp. 1121 (S.D. Ohio 1986)

TOYS "Я" US ONLY

FACTS

Child World, Inc. (plaintiff), operates large retail toy stores throughout Ohio and other states called Children's Palace. South Towne Centre, Ltd. (defendant), is a limited partnership in Ohio that leases space in its South Towne Centre shopping complex to a Children's Palace store. Section 43(A) of the lease, executed in February 1976, provided as follows:

Except insofar as the following shall be unlawful, the parties mutually agree as follows:

A. Landlord shall not use or permit or suffer any other person, firm, corporation or other entity to use any portion of the Shopping Center or any other property located within six (6) miles from the Shopping Center and owned, leased, or otherwise controlled by the landlord (meaning thereby the real property or parties in interest and not a "straw" person or entity) or any person or entity having a substantial identity of interest, for the operation of a toys and games store principally for the sale at retail of toys and games, juvenile furniture and sporting goods such as is exemplified by the Child World and Children's Palace stores operated by Tenant's parent company, Child World, Inc. at the demised premises and elsewhere.

The lease was for 20 years and was signed by Barbara Beerman Weprin, the sole general partner of South Towne. Mad River Ltd. is another limited partnership in which Ms. Weprin is the sole general partner. Mad River owns another parcel of land approximately one-half mile from the South Towne Centre. On December 24, 1985, Mad River entered into an agreement to sell the parcel of land to Toys "Я" Us, Inc. Toys "Я" Us intends to construct a retail facility similar to the description in the above-noted lease clause. When Children's Palace was informed of the sale, they brought suit seeking to enforce the covenant not to lease or sell to a competitor of Children's Palace.

JUDICIAL OPINION

RICE, Circuit Judge

The consensus of the federal courts which have considered covenants in shopping center leases is one with which this Court can agree; namely, that the varying terms, conditions, and economic justifications for such restrictions render them inappropriate subjects for application of the *per se* rule. Defendants have not alleged nor proven anything about Section 43(A) of the lease which would indicate that it has only anticompetitive consequences. Indeed, in Finding of Fact #9, Defendants agree that Section 43(A) was negotiated as an inducement for Plaintiff to erect a Children's Palace store on Defendants' premises and to enter into a 20-year lease. This economic justification for exclusivity clauses is among the primary reasons that clauses such as Section 43(A) have not been found to be *per se* illegal, but rather have been found consistent with the public interest in economic development. Such laws can induce tenants to establish stores and to enter into a particular marketplace, often then encouraging the entry of other, often smaller, merchants.

A number of factors have been considered by the courts which have excluded restrictive covenants in shopping center leases: (1) the relevant product and geographic markets, together with the showing of unreasonable impact upon competition in these markets, due to the restrictive covenant; (2) the availability of alternate sites for the entity excluded by the operation of such a covenant; (3) the significance of the competition eliminated by the exclusivity clause, and whether present or future competitors were the parties excluded; (4) the scope of the restrictive covenant and whether it varied depending on particular circumstances; and (5) the economic justifications for the inclusion of the restrictive covenant in the lease.

Continued

Due to the particular facts of this case, however, the Court needs not, and specifically does not, reach the validity of the six-mile limitation contained in Section 43(A). Regardless of possible overbreadth, a restrictive covenant challenged as unreasonable . . . will be upheld to the extent that a breach of the covenant has occurred or is threatened to occur within a reasonable geographic area and time period. The parties have agreed, in Finding of Fact #12, that the parcel which Defendants seek to convey to Toys "Я" Us is approximately one-half mile from the Children's Palace store covered by the Lease. The Court finds that Section 43(A) is lawful and enforceable to the extent of one-half mile, as required by the facts of this case.

Turning to the impact which enforcement of Section 43(A), as applied in this case, would have upon the Defendants, the burdens of enforcement are not unduly great. As noted *supra,* Section 43(A) does not appear to preclude rental or sale, even within a one-half mile radius, to any number of stores which can compete with a Children's Palace toy and game store but which are not "copycat" stores. On the financial level, there is testimony from a representative of Defendants in the record to the effect that the value of the parcel in question increases almost daily. Moreover, Defendants believe that they will have no difficulty in finding another purchaser, should Section 43(A) preclude their sale of the parcel to Toys "Я" Us.

Enforcement of Section 43(A) to the extent of one-half mile would also not appear to foreclose the entry of Toys "Я" Us into competition with Plaintiff's store in the environs of the South Towne Centre shopping center. In his deposition, J. Tim Logan indicated that, even were Section 43(A) upheld, presumably in its entirety, Toys "Я" Us would still establish a store in the vicinity of Plaintiff's store.

Other courts have believed that restrictive covenants of a scope of one-half mile or more, albeit less than six miles, are legitimate lures by landlords in order for shopping center tenants to enter particular marketplaces and to thereby enhance the economic development of the community. The public has surely benefitted from the development of South Towne Centre. As a restriction of six miles appeared reasonable to Defendants' predecessors at the time of bargaining, enforcement of Section 43(A) of the Lease to the extent of one-half mile is consistent with that original calculation of value, and certainly reasonable.

CASE QUESTIONS

1. Who leased what from whom?
2. What restrictions were there in the lease agreement?
3. How did Toys "Я" Us become involved?
4. Is the sale a violation of the anticompetition clause?
5. Is the same shopping center involved?

C O N S I D E R . . . **13.1** In April 1965, Berkeley Heights Shopping Center leased 11,514 square feet of space to A&P Supermarkets. Under the terms of the lease, Berkeley agreed not to lease any other shopping center space to another grocery store. On April 16, 1977, A&P informed Berkeley that it was ceasing operations and subleasing the premises to Drug Fair, a modern drug store chain that sells food stuffs. In 1985, Berkeley sought to lease other space in the center to another grocery store and Drug Fair objected on the grounds of the covenant not to compete. Berkeley maintains the covenant only applies when the premises Drug Fair occupies are used as a grocery store operation. Who is correct? [*Berkeley Dev. Co.* v. *Great Atlantic & Pacific Tea Co.,* 518 A.2d 790 (N.J. 1986).]

FEDERAL STATUTORY SCHEME ON RESTRAINT OF TRADE

During the last half of the nineteenth century, the United States experienced a tremendous change in its economy. A primarily agricultural economy changed to an industrial economy. Law on business combinations was largely undeveloped and unsuitable for the types of predatory business practices this new industrial age brought. Furthermore, because common law was the only source of law for dealing with these business problems, those laws that did exist were nonuniform. In reaction to the lack of laws and the public outcry over business abuses, Congress became involved by passing federal statutes on antitrust issues in the late nineteenth and early twentieth century. With some amendments and changes, this scheme still exists and applies today. Exhibit 13.1 summarizes the general federal statutory antitrust statutes covered in detail in the following topic sections.

Jurisdiction of Federal Antitrust Laws

Federal laws cannot apply to business conduct unless interstate commerce is involved (see Chapter 5 for a complete discussion of interstate commerce). All federal antitrust statutes define interstate commerce for purposes of applying the statutes to businesses and are discussed in the following subsections.

Exhibit 13.1
Federal Antitrust Statutes

Statute	Original date	Jurisdiction	Coverage	Penalties
Sherman Act 15 U.S.C. § 1	1890	Commerce Clause	Monopolies; attempts to monopolize; boycotts; refusals to deal; price-fixing; resale price maintenance; division of markets	Criminal; $100,000 for individuals; $1 million for corps.; private suits
Clayton Act 1914 15 U.S.C. § 12	1914	Persons engaged in commerce	Tying; treble damages; mergers; interlocking directorates	Private suits
Federal Trade Commission Act 15 U.S.C. § 41	1914	Commerce Clause	Unfair methods of FTC competition	
Robinson-Patman Act 15 U.S.C. § 13	1936	Persons engaged in commerce and selling goods across state lines	Price discrimination	Private suits and criminal for international acts
Celler-Kefauver (part of Clayton Act) 15 U.S.C. § 18	1950		Asset acquisitions	
Hart-Scott-Rodino Antitrust Improvements Act 15 U.S.C. § 1311	1976 amended 1980, 1994	Gives greater authority to Justice Department for prosecution; requires premerger notification to Justice Department		

SHERMAN ACT JURISDICTION

The standards for Sherman Act jurisdiction are the same as the standards established under the Commerce Clause (see Chapter 5). Even if an activity is purely intrastate, it is subject to Sherman Act jurisdiction if the activity has a substantial economic effect on interstate commerce. Even if the activity of a business is purely local in nature, its economic impact and resources are examined to determine whether interstate commerce has been affected. There are very few times when interstate commerce is not found under the Sherman Act standard.

In *McClain* v. *Real Estate Board of New Orleans*, 441 U.S. 942 (1980), for example, an antitrust action against real estate brokers who worked only in the New Orleans area was permitted under the Sherman Act because the U.S. Supreme Court found that the brokers facilitated the loans and insurance for the properties they sold. The loans and insurance were provided by national firms, and funding came from outside the state. This involvement of interstate commerce, even in an indirect fashion, is sufficient for Sherman Act jurisdiction.

Review the Sherman Antitrust Act and the Clayton Antitrust Act: http://www.stolaf. edu/people/becker/ antitrust/statues. html

CLAYTON ACT JURISDICTION

The jurisdictional standard for the Clayton Act is narrower than that for the Sherman Act. The Clayton Act can be applied *only* to persons engaged in interstate commerce or in activities affecting interstate commerce.

ROBINSON-PATMAN ACT JURISDICTION

The Robinson-Patman Act has the most stringent jurisdictional requirements. The seller accused of price discrimination must be engaged in interstate commerce, and at least one of two claimed discrimination sales must be across state lines. A firm that sells only to in-state customers is not subject to Robinson-Patman jurisdiction.

Antitrust Penalties and Remedies

The federal antitrust laws have powerful incentives for compliance that include substantial penalties and remedies. The following subsections discuss these provisions and a summary appears in Exhibit 13.2 (pg. 447).

CRIMINAL PENALTIES

The Sherman Act carries felony criminal penalties. For individuals, the penalties are fines of up to $350,000 and/or up to three years in prison. For corporations, there are fines of up to $10 million. These criminal penalties require proof that the violator intended the anticompetitive conduct and realized the consequences of the action taken.

The FTC and Clayton Acts do not carry criminal penalties. However, certain forms of intentional price discrimination are made criminal under Section 4 of the Robinson-Patman Act. It is important to note that officers and directors of violating corporations can also be held criminally liable for antitrust violations.

The Antitrust Division of the Department of Justice or the local U.S. attorney's office is responsible for bringing criminal action under the antitrust laws.

EQUITABLE REMEDIES

Equitable remedies can be obtained by either the government or private parties. Equitable relief is an order from a court that restrains or prevents anticompetitive conduct. An injunction is a frequent form of antitrust relief; it is a court order prohibiting a violating party from engaging in anticompetitive conduct.

	Sherman Act	**Clayton Act**	**Robinson-Patman Act**	**FTC Act**
Criminal	$350,000 and/or three years in prison for individuals; $10 million for corporations; directors and officers also liable as to intent and knowledge	None	Section 4 for intentional price discrimination	None
Civil	Treble damages plus cost and attorney fees	Same	Same	None
Equitable	Injunctions, divestitures, asset distributions, sales	Same	Same	Same
Enforcers	Justice Department; U.S. attorney; state attorneys general; private persons	Same	Same	FTC

Exhibit 13.2
Antitrust Remedies

Equitable remedies are also affirmative in nature. They can require parties to take appropriate steps to eliminate the results of anticompetitive behavior. A firm can be ordered to divest itself of an acquired firm, for example; or in an unlawful asset acquisition, a court order can require that the assets be divided with a competing firm. Contracts whose terms violate the antitrust laws can be canceled by court order.

Equitable remedies give the courts discretion to fashion remedies that will eliminate the results of anticompetitive behavior.

PRIVATE ACTIONS FOR DAMAGES

Section 4 of the Clayton Act allows any person whose business or property is injured as a result of an antitrust violation to recover "threefold the damages by him sustained" (commonly referred to as **treble damages**) along with the costs of the suit and reasonable attorney fees. This section, with its substantial recovery provisions, is strong incentive for private enforcement of antitrust laws. Consumers, businesses, and state attorneys general can all bring private damage actions under Section 4.

The types of damages that can be recovered include lost profits, increased costs, and decreased value in property. These damage suits have a four-year statute of limitations; that is, suit must be brought within four years of the alleged violation. Those who bring private damage suits enjoy a proof benefit: If the government has brought suit and a violation is found, that judgment can be used in a private suit as prima facie evidence against the violating defendant. A prima facie case allows a plaintiff to survive a directed verdict and entitles the plaintiff to a judgment if the defendant offers no contradictory evidence (see Chapter 4 for more discussion).

Exhibit 13.1 (pg. 445) provides a summary of the federal antitrust laws, the jurisdictional requirements for their application, the types of activities covered under each statute, and the applicable penalties. Exhibit 13.2 provides a summary of penalties and remedies under the federal antitrust laws.

HORIZONTAL RESTRAINTS OF TRADE

Horizontal restraints of trade are designed to lessen competition among a firm's competitors. For example, Ford's and GM's fixing prices to drive Chrysler out of business would be a horizontal restraint. The Sherman Act covers the horizontal restraints of **price-fixing**, market division, **group boycotts** and refusals to deal, **joint ventures**, and monopolization. The Clayton Act also covers the problem of anticompetitive horizontal mergers or mergers with competitors.

Sherman Act Restraints

MONOPOLIZATION

Section 2 of the Sherman Act prohibits the act of **monopolizing**. Notice that the Sherman Act does not prohibit monopolies; there are certain types of monopolies recognized as exceptions to Section 2. For example, in a small town there is usually only enough economic base to support one newspaper; such an operation is not a Section 2 violation. Some businesses simply produce a product that is superior or unique; this type of monopoly is not a violation. When a business has obtained a large market share by **superior skill, foresight,** and **industry**, it has simply put its product in the market in a superior way and is entitled to its market share.

Acquiring a large market share through methods other than legitimate competition is prohibited under Section 2. To prove such monopolization, the following elements must be established:

1. The possession of **monopoly power** in the **relevant market**.
2. The willful acquisition or maintenance of that power.

Monopoly Power Judicial decisions have defined monopoly power under Section 2 as the power to control prices or exclude competition in a relevant market. To determine whether a firm has this ability, or monopoly power, the courts have examined the firm's **market power**, which is an economic term that means the firm has a relatively inelastic demand curve. An elastic demand curve means that the firm's products have competition from other firms or from firms with substitute products. For example, cosmetic firms have an elastic demand; buyers can switch to other products when there are price increases in one line or can even give up the use of cosmetics. On the other hand, the demand curve for gasoline is less elastic. Although there are substitute means of transportation, most drivers need to use their cars and hence need gasoline.

At some point, ever-increasing market power will turn into monopoly power. High profits and the lack of substitute goods are an indication that market power has made this transition. Some courts examine the firm's market share to determine whether it has monopoly power. There is, however, no set percentage figure used to make this determination. Most of the cases dealing with the percentage-of-market approach have involved firms with market shares greater than 50 percent.

Relevant Market In determining market share, a court must first determine a firm's market. The context in which market share is measured is called the **relevant market**. And each product has a relevant **geographic market**. For example, a beer producer may have 50 percent of all nationwide beer sales, but in a suit involving a local competitor, the producer's share might be only 20 percent because of the local beer's popularity. This local or **submarket** could be used as the relevant geographic market.

Each firm also has its own relevant **product market**, which is determined by consumers' preferences and their willingness to substitute other products for the product at issue. For example, a market could be defined as plastic wrapping materials, or it could be defined as food storage materials and include such wraps as wax paper, aluminum foil, and plastic storage bags. The product market is determined by the **cross-elasticity** of demand. Cross-elastic demand means consumers are willing to substitute other products in the event of unavailability or price changes.

The definition of relevant market is one of the key elements in monopolization cases. There will always be contradictory testimony from expert economists. As a result, the decisions on relevant market vary widely.

Purposeful Act Requirement Proving that a firm has monopoly power is only half of an antitrust monopolization case. The second element requires a showing that the firm acquired or is maintaining monopoly power by some purposeful or deliberate act that is not "superior skill, foresight, and industry" (which in short is the ability to build a better mousetrap). Some examples of prohibited purposeful conduct are **predatory pricing** and **exclusionary conduct**. Predatory pricing is pricing below actual cost for a temporary period to drive a potential competitor out of business. Exclusionary conduct is conduct that prevents a potential competitor from entering the market. For example, interfering with the purchase of a factory by a competitor would be improper exclusionary conduct.

The following case and problems illustrate purposeful conduct that violates Section 2 of the Sherman Act.

Syufy Enterprises v. *American Multicinema, Inc.*
793 F.2d 990 (9th Cir. 1986)

MOVIE MONOPOLIZATION: FIRST-AND-ONLY-RUN THEATERS

FACTS

Syufy Enterprises (Syufy) owned all four drive-in theater complexes in the San Jose market. Syufy also operated 15 screens in large-domed hardtop theaters, each with a seating capacity of 680–900 people. Syufy's hardtop theaters were called "event" theaters because of their wide screens, state-of-the-art sound, high ceilings and rocking chair seats.

American Multicinema, Inc. (AMC), owned and operated four theater complexes in the San Jose area, each of which housed six auditoriums with seating capacities of approximately 250 people. AMC's theaters were generally located within shopping malls and lacked many of the amenities found in Syufy's hardtop theaters. But AMC's theaters were conveniently located, offered a greater selection of movies than Syufy's, and charged, on average, a lower admission price.

AMC filed suit against Syufy alleging monopolization under the Sherman Act. It maintained that Syufy used its dominant position in the ownership of both hardtop and drive-in theaters to monopolize the exhibition of major films in the San Jose area. After a jury found Syufy monopolized and attempted to monopolize the hardtop film market in the San Jose area, Syufy appealed.

JUDICIAL OPINION
NORRIS, Circuit Judge
To establish monopolization under Section 2 of the Sherman Act, "a plaintiff must prove:

Continued

(1) possession of monopoly power in the relevant market; (2) willful acquisition or maintenance of that power; and (3) causal 'antitrust' injury."

Monopoly power—the first element of monopolization—is the power to control prices or exclude competition. We begin our analysis of the issue of market power with a discussion of market definition and then turn to the question whether there is substantial evidence that Syufy had monopoly power within the relevant market.

We begin by considering the definition of the relevant market within which Syufy allegedly possessed monopoly power.

AMC defined the relevant market as the market for exhibition of industry-anticipated top-grossing motion pictures in the San Jose area. Syufy does not dispute the geographic component of this definition—the San Jose area. Nor does it dispute limiting the product market definition to hardtop theaters. The only aspect of AMC's market definition that Syufy disputes is the limitation of the relevant product market to the exhibition of major films, more specifically to industry-anticipated top-grossing films. Syufy argues that this market definition is ex post facto and ad hoc, and that all first run films are in substantial competition with each other.

In economic terms, we might recharacterize Syufy's argument as follows: all first run films are interchangeable in use and the price and availability of any one film will affect the demand for all other films. Top-grossing films, Syufy argues, are simply those films that prove to be highly successful in the market place, but they possess no special characteristics that differentiate them from less successful films from an ex ante perspective. Syufy also argues that limiting the product definition to top-grossing films has the effect of irrationally and unfairly penalizing the exhibitor with the prescience to book films that later prove to be big hits with the movie-going public.

AMC's rejoinder is that Syufy's argument mischaracterizes the product market definition. AMC points out that it did not define the market as simply top-grossing films, but as *industry anticipated* top-grossing films. AMC argues that these films can be differentiated from other first run films from an ex ante perspective because they have larger budgets, "name" stars and directors, larger advertising budgets, command large guarantees, and possess other distinctive characteristics which can be identified before the film is released. In economic terms, the viability of AMC's product market definition depends on the proposition that anticipated top-grossing films are not interchangeable with other films in the eyes of consumers and that price increases or supply constrictions for such films do not result in a shift in consumption patterns to other films. In legal terms, the question is whether the films excluded from the definition are "interchangeab[le] in use" with those included in the market and whether there is "cross-elasticity of demand" between excluded and included products. In more colloquial terms, the viability of the proposed definition depends on the argument that if the price for admission to *E.T.* goes up, audiences will not flock to *My Dinner with André*.

We conclude that there is sufficient evidence in the record to permit a rational jury to conclude that industry-anticipated top-grossing films constitute a distinct product market. The evidence indicates that approximately thirty pictures a year are identifiable as "anticipated top-grossing films" on the basis of such criteria as national advertising support, longer playtimes, guaranteed rentals, famous stars, directors and producers, booking in first class theaters, and lucrative terms offered for the pictures by exhibitors. AMC compiled a list of the industry-anticipated top-grossing films based on bidding materials submitted by both Syufy and AMC. Although AMC did not present direct evidence going to the "cross-elasticity of demand" between this limited class of pictures and other films, the jury could reasonably have concluded from the evidence presented that the industry-anticipated top-grossing films were not in substantial competition with other films.

Syufy contends that even if AMC's market definition is valid, AMC failed to prove that Syufy possessed monopoly power within that market. Syufy argues that the only evidence probative of its market power is that it had a 60–69 percent share of the market, which Syufy

Continued

claims is insufficient, standing alone, to establish that it had monopoly power. As far as we know, neither the Supreme Court nor any other court has ever decided whether a market share as low as 60–69 percent is sufficient, standing alone, to sustain such a finding.

AMC argues that we need not decide that abstract question because the record contains evidence other than Syufy's market share that is probative of Syufy's power to control prices or exclude competition in the San Jose market.

In the case before us, Syufy's 60–69 percent market share is accompanied by a fragmentation of competition. One of AMC's expert witnesses computed market shares for both first run films and the 100 top-grossing films for the period 1975 through 1980. These calculations indicated that while Syufy's share ranged from 71.8 percent to 54.7 percent, no competing exhibitor in the San Jose area ever had a greater share than 24.7 percent and in some years the top competitor's share was below 12 percent.

In addition to the factors of Syufy's market share and the fragmentation of competition, there is evidence of a third factor that the jury could have considered in finding that Syufy had monopoly power in the relevant market— barriers to prospective competitors seeking entry to the market. There was testimony, for example, that while exclusive runs were becoming less and less common in other parts of the country, they persisted in the San Jose market, and that exclusive runs were probably a deterrent to the establishment of more theaters in the area. Still another indicator of barriers to entry was the evidence that Syufy extracted excessive clearances from distributors of certain films. Viewed in the light most favorable to AMC, the evidence would permit a rational jury to find that barriers to entry existed in the San Jose market.

We have no difficulty finding substantial evidence in the record that Syufy willfully maintained its monopoly power in the San Jose area. Daniel Marks, AMC's film buyer, testified that, in his opinion, Syufy had been engaging in buying clearances which were excessive, defined as clearances that encompass a greater geographical area than is justified for legitimate competitive reasons. The clearance for a particular theater is excessive if it reaches beyond the geographic zone within which the theater draws significant numbers of customers. Marks's testimony—that Syufy had submitted bids with large guarantees and lucrative terms in order to obtain clearances that were excessive—is probative of the willful maintenance of monopoly power. Although Syufy can point to evidence in the record indicating that its clearances were not excessive, it is for the jury, not this court, to resolve such evidentiary conflicts.

AMC's second theory of attempted monopolization is more straightforward: that Syufy attempted to monopolize the hardtop market. It is clear that a case of attempted monopolization cannot be sustained in the absence of any of the following elements: (1) specific intent to monopolize, (2) predatory or anticompetitive conduct directed to accomplishing the unlawful purpose, and (3) causal antitrust injury.

A. Specific Intent

As evidence of specific intent to monopolize, AMC cites the testimony of its chief executive officer, Mr. Durwood, concerning a conversation he had with Mr. Syufy, the chief executive officer of Syufy. The relevant portions of the testimony follow:

Q. And can you tell us what Mr. Syufy told you and what you told Mr. Syufy?

A. Well, we had—we had met in Los Angeles when we discussed trying to buy—making us an offer of the depreciated book value, and so on, which didn't excite me too much.

Q. That's what you told us about this morning, correct?

A. Yes.

Q. Can you concentrate on this phone call that you just identified?

A. On the phone call he said—his voice hit a crescendo. He got pretty high decibel count. He threatened to sue. He's going to start a massive building program against us if we didn't sell out.

Continued

San Jose is his town. He said he had 20 million dollars in cash and he was going to use it to build theaters against us.

Q. *Is that something that appears in your notebook, which is exhibit No. 50, sir?*

A. *Yes, sir.*

Q. *Did you write those notes down on or about the time of the phone call?*

A. *As soon as I cold get calmed down after hearing this conversation.*

Q. *Is there anything else you can recall of this conversation with Mr. Syufy?*

A. *No. He reiterated he wanted the eight domes exclusive, he wasn't going to share any product with us. If we didn't get out of San Jose, he was going to run us out. And he had 20 million dollars he could do it with.*

Although Mr. Syufy's remarks to Mr. Durwood are arguably consistent with a simple desire to succeed in free and open competition, the jury could reasonably have inferred a specific intent to monopolize from the threat to run AMC out of town.

B. Anticompetitive Conduct

If Syufy did indeed buy more clearance than needed for legitimate competitive reasons, then it engaged in conduct that would have been indisputably anticompetitive.

C. Causal Antitrust Injury

We agree with AMC that there was adequate evidence before the jury to support a finding that antitrust injury was caused by Syufy's anticompetitive conduct in obtaining excessive clearances. The Marks testimony offered with respect to causal antitrust injury on the hardtop monopolization claim is also substantial evidence of causal antitrust injury with respect to the attempted monopolization claim.

Affirmed on monopolization and attempts to monopolize charges.

CASE QUESTIONS

1. What distinction does AMC make between top-grossing films and industry-anticipated top-grossing films? Why is this distinction important for purposes of establishing monopoly power?

2. What is the significance of the statement, "If the price for admission to *E.T.* goes up, audiences will not flock to *My Dinner With André*"?

3. What analysis is offered to show Syufy's 60–69 percent of the market is monopoly power?

4. Why are exclusive run rights important in analyzing market share?

5. What evidence was there of Syufy's willful acquisition of monopoly power?

6. Does the conversation between Mr. Syufy and Mr. Durwood establish intent to monopolize?

C O N S I D E R . . . **13.2** In the chapter's opening "Judgment," the issue of the legalities of Microsoft's strategies of distribution were presented. Under the terms of a consent decree with the Justice Department, Microsoft has agreed to halt its mandatory royalty policy. What if Microsoft's products are truly superior? What if 90 percent of all computer users prefer Microsoft? Do the royalty agreements violate the law if market results would be the same? Does Microsoft have market power? Does Microsoft have monopoly power? What is Microsoft's geographic market?

Judgment

Microsoft has been charged with antitrust violations for its practice of "marketing vaporware." Marketing vaporware is the practice of announcing a product before it is ready for market, knowing it is not ready, to prevent consumers from buying a competitor's existing product. Is this practice anticompetitive? [*United States* v. *Microsoft*, 56 F.3d 1448 (D.C. 1995).]

E T H I C A L   I S S U E S

13.1 The Running Fox is a small running-shoe manufacturer well known among professional runners for its high-quality, highly protective shoe. Athletic Feet is a manufacturer of a full line of running shoes, from track to long-distance running. Athletic Feet also publishes *Runner's Monthly*, a top magazine in the field of running with an almost exclusively runner circulation. For the past three years, *Runner's Monthly* has published its "annual shoe survey" in which all the running shoes on the market are rated. Athletic Feet's shoes have been ranked as the top three in every category. Running Fox did not perform well in the ratings and has brought a monopolization suit against Athletic Feet. Athletic Feet says the relevant market is athletic shoewear because it not only manufactures running shoes but also tennis, basketball, baseball, and other types of sport shoes. In the athletic shoe market, Athletic Feet holds a 20 percent share of the market; but in the running-shoe market, it holds an 80 percent share. Obviously, Running Fox wants to argue that running shoes are the relevant market. Who is correct? What is the relevant market? Does *Runner's Monthly* have a conflict of interest?

C O N S I D E R . . . **13.3** Wal-Mart Stores, Inc., and many other discount retailers employ a successful marketing tool known as a "loss leader." The loss-leader strategy is to price one or several items below cost or at a "meet or beat the competition regardless of cost" in order to attract a disproportionate number of customers into the store with the idea that they will purchase other items while there.

Is this practice predatory pricing? Do loss leaders violate federal antitrust laws? [*Wal-Mart Stores, Inc. v. American Drugs, Inc.*, 891 S.W. 2d 30 (Ark. 1995).]

C O N S I D E R . . . **13.4** Amanda Reiss had completed her residency in ophthalmology in Portland, Oregon, and was moving to Phoenix, Arizona, to start her practice. She began looking for office space and met with a leasing agent who showed her several complexes of medical suites. Dr. Reiss was ready to sign for one of them when the leasing agent turned to her and said, "Oh, by the way, you're not one of those advertising doctors are you? Because they don't want that kind in any of my complexes." Has there been a violation of the antitrust laws?

ATTEMPTS TO MONOPOLIZE

Section 2 of the Sherman Act can be violated even though actual monopolization might not be the result. In other words, attempts at monopolization are also part of Section 2. There need not be an actual successful effort so long as it can be shown that the conduct created a "dangerous probability" of monopolization.

CONSIDER...   **13.5** Aluminum Company of America (Alcoa) has a 91 percent share of the market for virgin aluminum ingot, a product sold to manufacturers for use in producing aluminum tools, siding for homes, and other aluminum products. Alcoa has undertaken a massive production-facility expansion to meet expected increased demand. It has so much production space available for expansion that market entry for a competitor would likely be too costly and nearly fruitless. Is there a good case for a monopolization violation? Evaluate the monopoly power issue in light of the market share. Is overcapacity a purposeful or deliberate act? [*United States* v. *Aluminum Co. of Am.*, 148 F.2d 416 (2d Cir. 1945).]

PRICE-FIXING

Any agreement or collaboration among competitors "for the purpose and with the effect of raising, depressing, fixing, pegging, or stabilizing the price of a commodity" is the Supreme Court's definition of price-fixing. Under Section 1 of the Sherman Act, price-fixing is a **per se** violation, which means that the conduct is illegal and unreasonable as a matter of law. The effect of a per se violation of the antitrust laws is to shorten trials substantially because a per se violator has no defenses to present in the case. Some antitrust scholars feel the Supreme Court is moving away from its per se standard for price-fixing. Price-fixing can result from several different activities, covered in the following subsections.

Minimum Prices A minimum fee or price schedule discourages competition, puts an artificial restriction on the market, and provides a shield from market forces. There is no defense to this type of agreement. Even proof that the minimum price is a reasonable price is irrelevant once there is proof of an agreement.

Maximum Prices Although maximum prices sound like an excellent benefit for consumers, the effect is to stabilize prices, which translates into a restriction on free-market forces.

List Prices An agreement among competitors to use list prices as a guideline in sale prices is also a per se violation. There is still a violation even though the agreement was not mandatory and even though the list price was just a starting point in price negotiations. Just the exchange of price information has an effect on the market and interferes with the ability to price in relation to demand, supply, and competition.

Production Limitations An agreement to limit production is an agreement to fix prices because the parties are controlling the supply, which in turn controls the right to demand the resulting price.

Limitations on Competitive Bidding Some competitors have tried to avoid "ruinous competition" by eliminating bidding. In *National Soc'y of Professional Engineers* v. *United States*, 435 U.S. 679 (1978), a professional society agreed that there should not be bidding on engineering projects because the bidding process encouraged cost-cutting and posed possible safety risks in the construction of the projects bid. Although its motives were well intentioned, it was still found to have committed a violation because the agreement was price-fixing and a per se violation of the Sherman Act.

Credit Arrangement Agreements The cost of credit is part of the price of goods and services. Any agreement among creditor-competitors to limit credit terms or to charge a universal credit fee is an agreement relating to price and a per se violation.

| C O N S I D E R . . . | **13.6** Visx of Santa Clara, California, and Summit Technology of Waltham, Massachusetts, have formed a joint venture (to be called Pillar Point Partners), pooling their resources for a new surgical technique called refractive keratectomy, which corrects vision by removing corneal tissue with lasers. The process is an advancement over popular radial keratotomy, which requires a scalpel. |

Pillar Point Partners was created to resolve patent disputes and FDA-approval issues. Visx holds patents for the lasers but does not have regulatory approval. Summit has FDA approval for the sale of its laser. Pillar Point will license laser users and require licensees to pay a $250 royalty per procedure.

Dr. Frank O'Donnell, chairman of a competitor, Laser Sight of St. Louis, notes, "I've always thought this sounds like price-fixing." Is the fixed royalty fee price-fixing?

FOR THE MANAGER'S DESK

WHY DO COMPANIES SUCCUMB TO PRICE FIXING?

Down through the centuries social analysts have frequently charged, "Laws are like spiderwebs, which may catch small flies but let wasps and hornets break through." As more and more corporations have been caught in the web of price-fixing laws, however, this charge has lost its punch. Senior business managers in industries that have never before known these problems, as well as previous offenders, are probably more concerned now about their corporate exposure to being indicted and convicted of price-fixing than they were in any other recent period.

The costs of violating price-fixing laws are very high: lawyers' fees, government fines, poor morale, damaged public image, civil suits, and now prison terms. Justice

Department statistics indicate that 60 percent of antitrust felons are sentenced to prison terms. Thus, for very pragmatic reasons as well as for personal convictions, America's top executives are searching

for fail-safe ways of meeting legal requirements.

One CEO well expressed the frustration common to executives in convicted companies:

We've tried hard to stress that collusion is illegal. We point out that anticompetitive practices hurt the company's ethical standards, public image, internal morale, and earnings. Yet we wind up in trouble continually. When we try to find out why employees got involved, they have the gall to say that they 'were only looking out for the best interests of the company.' They seem to think that the company message is for everyone else but them. You begin to wonder about the intelligence of these people. Either they don't listen or they're just plain stupid.

Continued

General Management Signals

Some executives talked very explicitly about the problem of changing the culture of a problem division. Having been burned in the past, the financial vice president of a convicted company has adopted an inventive approach. He has communicated new acquisition criteria to his investment brokers. He is now at least as interested in information about a company's ethical practices as in its financial performance. One chief executive officer said that he and his top managers learned the hard way from troubles soon after making an acquisition. He felt that retraining management is helpful.

Some managers have been reviewing their practices and making tighter definitions of who can legitimately take part in pricing decisions. It takes careful analysis of the multiple sources of relevant information concerning prices as well as an explicit commitment procedure to make such rules both workable and prudent.

Attempts to move beyond top-level role modeling have led some executives to prepare codes of ethics on company business practices. In some companies this document circulates only at top levels and, again, the word seems to have trouble getting down the line. Even those documents that were sent to all employees seemed to have been broadly written, toothless versions of the golden rule. One company tried to get more commitment by requiring employees to sign and return a pledge.

For codes to really work, substantial specificity is important. One executive said his company's method was successful because the code was tied in with an employee's daily routine:

There is a code of business conduct here. To really make it meaningful, you have to get past the stage of endorsing motherhood and deal with the specific problems of policy in the different functional areas.

We wrote up 20 pages on just purchasing issues.

Auditing for Compliance

Once these more specific codes of business conduct are distributed, top managers may want more than a signed statement in return. Individuals can be held responsible if they have been informed on how to act in certain gray areas. The company can show its commitment to the code of checking to see that it is respected and by then disciplining violators.

Several companies are developing ways to implement internal policing. Some executives think that audits could hold people responsible for unusual pricing successes as well as for failures. Market conditions, product specifications, and factory scheduling could be coded, put on tables, and compared to prices. High variations could be investigated. One division vice president also plans to audit expense accounts to see that competitor contact is minimized.

Source: Jeffrey Sonnenfeld and Paul R. Lawrence, "Why Do Companies Succumb to Price Fixing?" *Harvard Business Review*, July 1978, pp. 37–49. Reprinted by permission of *Harvard Business Review*. Copyright © 1978 by the President and Fellows of Harvard College; all rights reserved.

DIVISION OF MARKETS

Any agreement between competitors to divide up an available market is a per se violation under the Sherman Act. The result of such an agreement is to give the participants monopolies in their particular area. Such a market division introduces an unnatural force into the competitive market. For example, office-product supply companies agreeing to operate only in certain cities throughout a state would be a division of markets and a per se violation.

C O N S I D E R . . . **13.7** BRG of Georgia, Inc. (BRG), and Harcourt Brace Jovanovich Legal and Professional Publications (HJB) are the nation's two largest providers of bar review materials and lectures. HJB began offering a Georgia bar review course on a limited basis in 1976 and was in direct, and often intense, competition with BRG from 1977 to 1979. BRG and HJB were the two main providers of bar review courses in Georgia during this period. In early 1980, they entered into an agreement that gave BRG an exclusive license to

Continued

market HJB's materials in Georgia and to use its trade name "Bar/Bri." The parties agreed that HJB would not compete with BRG in Georgia and that BRG would not compete with HJB outside of Georgia.

Under the agreement, HJB received $100 per student enrolled by BRG and 40 percent of all revenues over $350. Immediately after the 1980 agreement, the price of BRG's course was increased from $150 to over $400.

Is this an illegal division of markets? [*Palmer* v. BRG *of Georgia, Inc.*, 498 U.S. 46 (1990).]

GROUP BOYCOTTS AND REFUSALS TO DEAL

Visit the American Medical Association: http://www. ama-assn.org/

A group of competitors that agrees not to deal with buyers unless those buyers agree to standard credit or arbitration clauses have committed a per se violation.

Some group boycotts appear to have the best intentions. Many garment manufacturers once agreed not to sell to buyers who sold discount or pirated designer clothing. Certainly their intentions were good, but the result still has the anticompetitive effect of controlling the marketplace. Competitors cannot enforce the law through boycotts; other avenues of relief area available. The American Medical Association's rules that prohibited salaried medical practices and prepaid medical plans are illegal boycotts in spite of the protection motivations behind the restrictions.

The following case involves an issue of a well-intentioned but still illegal boycott.

FTC v. Superior Court Trial Lawyers Ass'n
493 U.S. 411 (1990)

A LEGAL BOYCOTT: LEGAL AID AND LEGAL FEES

FACTS

The U.S. Constitution requires that legal counsel be provided to indigent defendants. The District of Columbia, like other local governments, fulfills this responsibility through a program that hires private lawyers at a rate of $30 per hour. In 1982 these lawyers handled 25,000 indigent defendant cases at a cost of $4,579,572 to the District. Over 1,200 lawyers were registered for the indigent defendant program, with 100 lawyers classified as "regulars." Three of these 100 lawyers derived all of their income from indigent representation cases.

The Superior Court Trial Lawyers Association (SCTLA) had been concerned about the low fees paid in the program and had met with the mayor to encourage higher fees to ensure quality representation. The mayor was sympathetic but indicated that no funds were available for an increase.

In 1983 SCTLA formed a strike committee that recommended, as the only way to increase

fees, encouraging members to stop signing indigent representation agreements until a rate schedule of $45 for out-of-court time and $55 for in-court time was achieved. About 100 lawyers signed a petition to this effect and agreed not to accept new cases. The result was that 90 percent of the regulars refused to accept new cases.

Within 10 days of the September 6, 1983, petition, the criminal justice system in the District of Columbia was in chaos; the mayor met with the SCTLA strike committee and, declaring a crisis, increased the fees to the $45–$55 per hour rates. The agreement was approved by the city council on September 21, 1983.

The Federal Trade Commission (FTC) filed a complaint against SCTLA alleging that SCTLA's conduct was a conspiracy to fix prices and conduct a boycott, and it violated Section 5 of the FTC Act as an unfair method of competition. The administrative law judge (AJL) found for the FTC, the FTC found that a boycott had

Continued

occurred that caused harm, and the court of appeals remanded the case for a determination of whether SCTLA (respondents) had market power. The FTC appealed.

JUDICIAL OPINION

STEVENS, Justice

Respondents' boycott may well have served a cause that was worthwhile and unpopular. We may assume that the preboycott rates were unreasonably low, and that the increase has produced better legal representation for indigent defendants. Moreover, given that neither indigent criminal defendants nor the lawyers who represent them command any special appeal with the electorate, we may also assume that without the boycott there would have been no increase in District fees at least until Congress [acted]. These assumptions do not control the case, for it is not our task to pass upon the social utility or political wisdom of price-fixing agreements.

It is of course true that the city purchases respondents' services because it has a constitutional duty to provide representation to indigent defendants. It is likewise true that the quality of representation may improve when rates are increased. Yet neither of these facts is an acceptable justification for an otherwise unlawful restraint of trade. As we have remarked before, the "Sherman Act reflects a legislative judgment that ultimately competition will produce not only lower prices, but also better goods and services." *National Society of Professional Engineers* v. *United States*, 435 U.S. 679 (1978). This judgment recognizes that all elements of a bargain—quality, service, safety, and durability—and not just the immediate cost, are favorably affected by the free opportunity to select among alternative offers. That is equally so when the quality of legal advocacy, rather than engineering design, is at issue.

The social justifications proffered for respondents' restraint of trade thus do not make it any less unlawful. The statutory policy underlying the Sherman Act "precludes inquiry into the question whether competition is good or bad." Respondents' argument, like that made by petitioners in *Professional Engineers*,

ultimately asks us to find that their boycott is permissible because the price it seeks to set is reasonable. But it was settled shortly after the Sherman Act was passed that it "is no excuse that the prices fixed are themselves reasonable." Respondents' agreement is not outside the coverage of the Sherman Act simply because its objective was enactment of favorable legislation.

The lawyers' association argues that if its conduct would otherwise be prohibited by the Sherman Act and the Federal Trade Act, it is nonetheless protected by the First Amendment rights.

The activity the FTC order prohibits is a concerted refusal by [the] lawyers to accept any further assignments until they receive an increase in their compensation; the undenied objective of their boycott was an economic advantage for those who agreed to participate. No matter how altruistic the motives of respondents may have been, it is undisputed that their immediate objective was to increase the price that they would be paid for their services.

Respondents' concerted action in refusing to accept further assignments until their fees were increased was thus a plain violation of the antitrust laws.

Affirmed as to the finding of a violation. Reversed for further proceedings on the issue of market power.

CASE QUESTIONS

1. Explain the District of Columbia system for providing legal representation for indigent defendants.
2. What was the rate of compensation for lawyers in the program?
3. What fees did the lawyers want?
4. What was the effect of the refusal to take new cases?
5. How long did the boycott last?
6. Did the lawyers get the fees they desired?
7. Of what relevance is the motivation of the lawyers in staging the boycott?
8. Was the boycott a violation of antitrust laws?
9. Was the violation per se?

JOINT VENTURES

A **joint venture** is an undertaking by two or more businesses for a limited purpose. An oil corporation working with an engineering firm for the development of a new drill would be a joint venture; they would be business partners for that limited purpose and project.

Competitors who become involved in joint ventures are a natural concern. These combinations are subject, not to a per se violation standard, but to the **rule-of-reason** violation standard, which allows a court to consider the various benefits and detriments involved in a joint venture. For example, in one case all coal producers formed a joint venture sales agency during a time of a depressed coal market to increase sales and save selling costs. This joint venture was held reasonable under the Sherman Act. [*United States* v. *Appalachian Coal*, 228 U.S. 334 (1933).]

In another case, a joint venture between movie producers and movie theaters was held unreasonable because it gave the theaters exclusive showing rights to the producers' movies. [*United States* v. *Paramount Pictures*, 334 U.S. 131 (1948).]

EXCEPTIONS TO SHERMAN ACT VIOLATIONS

Some activities by competitors are protected even though the competitors are acting as a group and even though the effect may be to reduce competition. One such exception is the ***Noerr-Pennington* doctrine**, under which competitors are permitted to work together for the purpose of governmental lobbying and other political action.[1] Their conduct cannot be restrained under the Sherman Act because their activity enjoys the protection of the First Amendment. Competitors who work together to influence legislators and administrative agencies are protected even though they may be working for competitive benefits. For example, competitors can make appearances at new licensee hearings and oppose the granting of a license. The resulting reduction in competition is done within the confines of the First Amendment and is not subject to Sherman Act jurisdiction.

The Noerr-Pennington doctrine strikes a delicate balance between anticompetitive behavior and First Amendment rights. That balance often fluctuates as new issues in regulation, lobbying, and licensing arise. In some instances, market domination is at issue in regulatory proceedings. In *City of Columbia* v. *Omni Outdoor Advertising*, 499 U.S. 365 (1991), a company that was controlling the outdoor advertising market in one city attempted to use its lobbying First Amendment rights to protect its market control. An objection and suit by a competitor still resulted in the protection of Noerr-Pennington and First Amendment rights. Courts are hesitant to intervene in a business's right to lobby and petition government agencies even if the purpose is preservation of market superiority.

C O N S I D E R . . . **13.8** In Arizona, fees for title insurance searches and policies were established by rating bureaus established by the title companies. The bureaus recommended rates to the state and the state adopted those rates unless some specific objection was made. The result was that title search and insurance fees were the same for all companies within the state. The FTC filed a complaint against the title companies, alleging that they were engaged in price-fixing. The companies responded that government regulation of prices is not price-fixing. Do you agree? [*FTC* v. *Ticor Title Ins. Co.*, 504 U.S. 621 (1992).]

Review the Local Government Antitrust Act of 1984: http:// www.law.cornell. edu/ucode/15/34. html

There are additional exceptions to the antitrust laws. The Local Government Antitrust Act of 1984 was passed to eliminate the effects of several Supreme Court decisions that would not allow state and local governments to be exempted from the application of federal antitrust laws unless there was a state policy that specifically exempted such activities. The Local Government Antitrust Act has provided an exemption for these localities, which were facing over three hundred antitrust lawsuits at the time the act was passed.

In order to compete effectively in the international market, U.S. businesses have been permitted to form selling cooperatives or joint ventures with prior approval from the Justice Department. The Joint Venture Trading Act of 1983 allows joint ventures of competitors for the purpose of competing with foreign competitors (with Justice Department approval).The Shipping Act of 1984 allows carriers to enter into joint venture shipping arrangements so shippers can more effectively compete in the international market, where rates are set and routes and shipments are divided among competitors.

> **Business Planning Tip**
>
> Trade associations are very common today. They may provide continuing education or networks for business as well as contracts; however, the federal antitrust laws do apply to them so they cannot be used to stop market-place entries or control prices.
>
> While trade associations offer information, lobbying support, and strength of numbers, they cannot be used as a front for horizontal restraints of trade through price-fixing or market allocations.
>
> The following are tips for keeping trade associations free of anticompetitive behavior.
>
> 1. Don't exchange price information, including disclosures about credit terms, shipping fees, etc.
> 2. Don't reveal future plans with respect to customers (e.g., "I'm not going to deal with that company anymore").
> 3. Don't define or reveal territories (e.g., "I'm not interested in the Yuma region anymore").
> 4. Don't agree to uniform pricing, commissions, or refusals to deal.

Clayton Act Restraints

INTERLOCKING DIRECTORATES

The first Clayton Act horizontal restraint concerns the use of directors on the boards of competitive firms to lessen the effects of competition (**interlocking directorates**). Section 8 prohibits a director of a firm with $1 million or more in capital from being a director of a competing company. The intent of this prohibition is to lessen the likelihood of the exchange of anticompetitive information about price, markets, and other competitors.

HORIZONTAL MERGERS

Horizontal mergers are mergers between competitors. To determine when they have taken place, courts have applied a test of "presumptive illegality": Any merger that produces an undue percentage share of the market or significantly increases market concentration is a violation. In these cases, the courts examine market share and the relevant markets to determine whether there is undue concentration.

There are some defenses that justify a horizontal merger. One is the **failing company doctrine**, which allows the acquisition of a competitor that is clearly failing if it is an asset or inventory acquisition. Another defense is the small-company defense, which applies when two small companies merge with the hope of being better able to compete with the larger businesses in that market.

In *United States* v. *Von's Grocery Co.*, 384 U.S. 270 (1966), the Supreme Court held that a merger between Von's Grocery Company and Shopping Bag Food Stores, which would have given the two companies together a 7.5 percent share of the retail grocery market in Los Angeles, was violative of the Clayton Act because its effect would be to substantially lessen competition. In 1988, the Justice Department approved the merger of Von's and Safeway in southern California. The merger made the new Von's the largest competitor in terms of market percentage as well as in the number of stores. Justice Department attitudes and guidelines on mergers have changed largely because geographic markets have changed. Geographic markets are now defined in light of international trade. Some domestic combinations that would have been illegal in 1966 are now permissible because of size requirements for companies in international competition. For more details on mergers and antitrust issues, see Chapter 22.

VERTICAL TRADE RESTRAINTS

Various steps are involved in getting a product from its creation to its ultimate consumer. For example, producing packaged sandwich meats requires the manufacturer to obtain bulk-butchered meat (originally from a ranch) through a distributor and turn it into packaged sandwich meat that is sold to another distributor. This distributor sells to a grocery wholesaler, who sells to grocery stores, where consumers buy the packaged meat. This entire process has different levels of production and distribution but there is one vertical chain from start to finish.

The types of vertical restraints, which will be discussed in the following subsections, are:

- Resale price maintenance;
- Sole outlets and exclusive distributorships;
- Customer and territorial restrictions;
- Tying arrangements;
- Exclusive dealing or requirements contracts; and
- Price discrimination.

Resale Price Maintenance

Resale price maintenance is an attempt by a manufacturer to control the price retailers charge for the manufacturer's product. Resale price maintenance is a per se violation of Section 1 of the Sherman Act. Resale price maintenance includes either minimum or maximum prices, or both. A minimum price encourages a retailer to carry a certain product because its profit margin will be higher. One explanation offered to justify minimum prices is that without them dealers who advertise and offer service may be used by consumers for information only while these consumers actually buy at discount houses. Because resale price maintenance is a per se violation, however, this justification is irrelevant.

A manufacturer who attempts to set a maximum price is trying to prevent retailers with market power from charging a price higher than that set for the manufacturer's goods, thereby reducing the number of sales. The economic theory is that fewer goods would be sold under such circumstances than if there were open competition.

Resale price maintenance can also occur in ways other than actual price controls—for example, through the use of consignments. If the packaged-sandwich-meat manufacturer required all grocery stores to act as agents for the sale of its meats and paid a commission on each sale, there would be a consignment. The manufacturer could control the price through such an arrangement, but such price-controlled consignments are violations of Section 1 of the Sherman Act.

Manufacturers can offer a "suggested retail price" without violating Section 1, although, any attempt to enforce that suggested price would be a violation. For example, a manufacturer who refuses to sell to a retailer who does not use the suggested price is engaging in resale price maintenance.

At one time, states were permitted to allow resale price maintenance by statute. That power was taken away in 1975, and states cannot, by statute, allow minimum price schedules or require dealers to adhere to **fair trade contracts**, which are agreements on maximum or minimum prices.

Sole Outlets and Exclusive Distributorships

A **sole outlet** or **exclusive distributorship** agreement is one in which a manufacturer appoints a distributor or retailer as the sole or exclusive outlet for the manufacturer's product. This type of arrangement can be a violation of Section 1 but is subject to a rule-of-reason analysis. When the rule-of-reason is applied to alleged antitrust violators, the alleged violators have an opportunity to present justifications for their conduct.

In a rule-of-reason analysis of sole outlets or exclusive distributorships, courts examine several factors. One factor is a manufacturer's freedom to pick and choose certain buyers to deal with. However, the extent of the manufacturer's freedom is limited by the amount of **interbrand competition**, which is the competition available for the manufacturer's product. For example, in the case of the sandwich-meat manufacturer, so long as there are other manufacturers selling their products in the area, the manufacturer could agree to sell to only one chain of grocery stores. But if there is little interbrand competition, the antitrust laws require that **intrabrand competition** be more available. Thus, if the manufacturer were the only one distributing sandwich meats in the area, dealing with only one grocery chain might not be reasonable and could not survive an antitrust challenge.

The rule of reason also allows a court to consider other factors involved in a manufacturer's arrangements. For example, if the manufacturer agrees to limit outlets merely to benefit one of the outlets, there may be a violation.

C O N S I D E R . . .   **13.9** Department 56 is a company that manufactures and sells collectible Christmas village houses and other replica items to allow collectors to create the whimsical "Snow Village" town or "Dickens Christmas." Department 56 has only authorized dealers. Sam's Club, a division of Wal-Mart Stores, Inc., began selling Department 56 pieces from The Heritage Village Collection.

Susan Engel, president and CEO of Department 56, attempted to contact Wal-Mart because it is not an authorized Department 56 dealer. Wal-Mart did not respond, and Ms. Engel sent by Federal Express to National Collector clubs a letter that contained the following language:

Sam's Club should not have any Department 56 merchandise. In a marketing environment where most companies are fighting to get their merchandise into the Wal-Marts of
Continued

the world, we are fighting to get our merchandise out. While we recognize there is surely a place for mass market and warehouse stores, Department 56 Villages enjoy a strong heritage of dealer sales and service support. Our products simply do not fit the warehouse-style selling environment of Sam's Club.

Of strong importance to us—and we hope to you too—is the tradition of selling our villages through an exclusive dealer network made up almost entirely of independent retailers. Wal-Mart Stores, Inc. and its subsidiaries are predators on these hard working individuals. Sales of our products mean virtually nothing to the bottom line of a company the size of Wal-Mart. But to many of our loyal dealers, healthy Department 56 product sales mean survival.

Do you really need to shop at Sam's Club or Wal-Mart? Let's refuse to purchase villages or any other products from local Wal-Mart owned stores.

The letter asked collector club members to write Wal-Mart executives and local store managers. Names, mailing addresses, and telephone and fax numbers were offered.

Has Ms. Engel violated any laws? How do you think Sam's Club obtained the Department 56 products?

E T H I C A L   I S S U E S

13.2 Evaluate the conduct of Ms. Engel in sending out the letter. Were her statements about Wal-Mart and calls to action fair? Should Wal-Mart respond? How?

Customer and Territorial Restrictions

Sole outlets allow manufacturers to decide (within limitations) to whom they will sell goods. However, manufacturers are not given the right to control what the buyer does with goods and how those goods are sold. Under Section 1 of the Sherman Act, restricting to whom and where a buyer of a manufacturer's goods can sell is a rule-of-reason violation. The restrictions are subject to the rule of reason because interbrand competition may be increased even though intrabrand competition is reduced.

In applying the rule of reason to **customer and territorial restrictions**, there are several issues to be considered. The first is whether there is an increase in interbrand competition because of decreased intrabrand competition. A second consideration is whether the manufacturer imposing the restriction has market power. The more market power the manufacturer has, the fewer substitute goods consumers have, resulting in less interbrand competition.

Vertical restrictions are likely to be judged reasonable when the manufacturer is new to the market or is having financial or sales difficulties. If the restrictions will help the manufacturer get started or keep going, the objective of interbrand competition is met by the restrictions on intrabrand competition.

Tying Arrangements

Tying sales are those that require buyers to take an additional product in order to buy a needed product. For example, requiring the buyer of a copier machine to buy the seller's paper when there are other brands of paper suitable for use in the machine is a tying arrangement. The copier machine is the tying product or the desired product and the paper is the tied product or the required product.

Tying is usually an illegal per se violation of Section 3 of the Clayton Act (for goods contracts) and Section 1 of the Sherman Act (for services, real property, and intangibles). Both acts prohibit tying but cover different subject matters. Whether there is a violation depends on whether market power results from the tying arrangement and whether there are any defenses.

Market power is established if the tying product is unique. For example, requiring the purchase of inferior movie films in order to buy copyrighted quality films is an example of the presence of market power. Because the seller is the only one with the copyrighted films, there is market power that is being used to sell another unnecessary, low-demand product.

Two defenses have been recognized in tying cases. The first is the new-industry defense. Under this defense, the manufacturer of the tying product is permitted to have a tied product to protect initially the quality control in the start-up of a business. For example, a cable TV antenna manufacturer required purchasers to take a service contract also. The tying was upheld during the outset of the business so that the system could begin functioning properly and this new cable TV industry could catch hold.

A second defense is quality control for the protection of goodwill. This defense is rarely supportable. The only time it would apply is if the specifications for the tied goods were so detailed that they could not possibly be supplied by anyone other than the manufacturer of the tying product.

The following case involves an issue of whether a tying arrangement was valid.

Jefferson Parish Hosp. Dist. No. 2 v. Hyde
466 U.S. 2 (1984)

B.Y.O. ANESTHESIOLOGIST: HOSPITAL TYING ARRANGEMENTS

FACTS
Dr. Edwin G. Hyde, a board-certified anesthesiologist, applied for permission to practice at East Jefferson Hospital (petitioners) in Louisiana. An approval was recommended for his hiring, but the hospital's board denied him employment on grounds that the hospital had a contract with Roux & Associates for Roux to provide all anesthesiological services required by the hospital's patients. Dr. Hyde filed suit, which the district court dismissed. The court of appeals reversed that decision and held that the contract for the services with Roux was illegal per se. The hospital appealed.

JUDICIAL OPINION
STEVENS, Justice
The exclusive contract had an impact on two different segments of the economy: consumers

of medical services, and providers of anesthesiological services. Any consumer of medical services who elects to have an operation performed at East Jefferson Hospital may not employ any anesthesiologist not associated with Roux. No anesthesiologists except those employed by Roux may practice at East Jefferson.

There are at least twenty hospitals in the New Orleans metropolitan area and about 70 percent of the patients living in Jefferson Parish go to hospitals other than East Jefferson. Because it regarded the entire New Orleans metropolitan area as the relevant geographic market in which hospitals compete, this evidence convinced the District Court that East Jefferson does not possess any significant "market power"; therefore it concluded that petitioners could not use the Roux contract to anticompetitive ends. The same evidence led the Court of Appeals to

Continued

draw a different conclusion. Noting that 30 percent of the residents of the Parish go to East Jefferson Hospital, and that, in fact, "patients tend to choose hospitals by location rather than price or quality," the Court of Appeals concluded that the relevant market was the East Bank of Jefferson Parish. The conclusion that East Jefferson Hospital possessed market power in that area was buttressed by the facts that the prevalence of health insurance eliminates a patient's incentive to compare costs, that the patient is not sufficiently informed to compare quality, and that family convenience tends to magnify the importance of location.

The Court of Appeals held that the case involves a "tying arrangement" because the "users of the hospital's operating rooms (the tying product) are also compelled to purchase the hospital's chosen anesthesia service (the tied product)."

It is clear, however, that every refusal to sell two products separately cannot be said to restrain competition. For example, we have written that "if one of a dozen food stores in a community were to refuse to sell flour unless the buyer also took sugar it would hardly tend to restrain competition if its competitors were ready and able to sell flour by itself." Buyers often find package sales attractive; a seller's decision to offer such packages can merely be an attempt to compete effectively — conduct that is entirely consistent with the Sherman Act.

Accordingly, we have condemned tying arrangements when the seller has some special ability — usually called "market power" — to force a purchaser to do something that he would not do in a competitive market. When "forcing" occurs, our cases have found the tying arrangement to be unlawful.

The hospital has provided its patients with a package that includes a range of facilities and services required for a variety of surgical operations. At East Jefferson Hospital the package includes the services of the anesthesiologist. Petitioners argue that the package does not involve a tying arrangement at all — that they are merely providing a functionally integrated package of services.

Unquestionably, the anesthesiological component of the package offered by the hospital could be provided separately and could be selected either by the individual patient or by one of the patient's doctors if the hospital did not insist on including anesthesiological services in the package it offers to its customers. As a matter of actual practice, anesthesiological services are billed separately from the hospital services petitioners provide. There was ample and uncontroverted testimony that patients or surgeons often request specific anesthesiologists to come to a hospital and provide anesthesia, and that the choice of a hospital is particularly frequent in respondent's specialty, obstetric anesthesiology.

Thus, the hospital's requirement that its patients obtain necessary anesthesiological services from Roux combined the purchase of two distinguishable services in a single transaction. As noted above, there is nothing inherently anticompetitive about packaged sales. Only if patients are forced to purchase Roux's services as a result of the hospital's market power would the arrangement have anticompetitive consequences.

It is safe to assume that every patient undergoing a surgical operation needs the services of an anesthesiologist; at least this record contains no evidence that the hospital "forced" any such services on unwilling patients. The record therefore does not provide a basis for applying the *per se* rule against tying to this arrangement.

In order to prevail in the absence of *per se* liability, respondent has the burden of proving that the Roux contract violated the Sherman Act because it unreasonably restrained competition.

All the record establishes is that the choice of anesthesiologists at East Jefferson has been limited to one of the four doctors who are associated with Roux and therefore have staff privileges. Even if Roux did not have an exclusive contract, the range of alternatives open to the patient would be severely limited by the nature of the transaction and the hospital's unquestioned right to exercise some control over the identity and number of doctors to whom it accords staff privileges.

Petitioner's closed policy may raise questions of medical ethics, and may have inconvenienced

Continued

some patients who would prefer to have their anesthesia administered by someone other than a member of Roux & Associates, but it does not have the obviously unreasonable impact on purchasers that has characterized the tying arrangements that this Court has branded unlawful.

    Reversed.

CASE QUESTIONS

1. What is East Jefferson's share of the medical care market?
2. Do patients ever indicate any choice or knowledge regarding anesthesiologists?
3. Is the arrangement illegal per se?
4. Is the arrangement unreasonable?
5. Why was the issue of "force" important?

ETHICAL ISSUES

13.3 Why does the Court make the point that the practices of East Jefferson Hospital may involve ethical questions? What ethical problems exist with the exclusive Roux & Associates contract?

C O N S I D E R . . . **13.10** David Ungar holds a Dunkin' Donuts franchise. The terms of his franchise agreement require him to use only those ingredients furnished by Dunkin' Donuts. He is also required to buy their napkins, cups, and so on with the Dunkin' Donuts trademark on them. Is this an illegal tying arrangement? What if Dunkin' Donuts maintains that it needs these requirements to maintain its quality levels on a nationwide basis? [*Ungar* v. *Dunkin' Donuts of Am., Inc.*, 531 F.2d 1211 (3d Cir. 1976).]

Exclusive Dealing or Requirements Contracts

Under **exclusive dealing** or **requirements contracts**, a buyer agrees to handle only one manufacturer's goods and will not carry any competitors' brands. These contracts also exist when a buyer agrees to purchase all of its requirements from one seller, such as when the sandwich-meat manufacturer agrees to buy meat from only one slaughterhouse.

    These types of agreements are treated as tying arrangements because the buyer has, in effect, agreed not to use another's products; but they are treated more leniently. The contracts must cover a substantial dollar amount of the market, and a substantial share of the market must be foreclosed by the agreement. For example, if the sandwich-meat manufacturer is a national manufacturer, the agreement to buy from one slaughterhouse is substantial. However, if the manufacturer is a local one with limited distribution, the agreement will probably not foreclose much of the market from other slaughterhouses.

Price Discrimination

The Robinson-Patman Act prohibits **price discrimination**, which is selling goods at prices that have different ratios to the marginal cost of producing them. If two goods have the same marginal cost and are sold to different people at different prices, there is price discrimination. Four elements are required in a price discrimination case:

1. A seller engaged in commerce;
2. Discrimination in price among purchasers;
3. Commodities sold are of like grade or quality; and
4. A substantial lessening of competition in any line of commerce or a tendency to create a monopoly; or competition is injured, destroyed, or prevented.

If all the elements are established, both the buyer and the seller have violated the Robinson-Patman Act.

PRICE DISCRIMINATION AMONG PURCHASERS

For price discrimination to occur, there must actually be a purchase; Robinson-Patman does not cover leases and consignments. Also, the purchases must be made at about the same time. The discrimination can come in the form of the actual price charged but can also come from indirect charges. For example, offering different credit terms to equally qualified buyers can constitute price discrimination.

COMMODITIES OF LIKE GRADE OR QUALITY

For the Robinson-Patman Act to apply, the products sold must be of **like grade or quality**, which means that there are no physical differences in the product. Label differences do not make the products different. For example, the sandwich-meat manufacturer who makes a private label meat cannot discriminate in price for the sale of that meat if the contents are the same as the manufacturer's advertised label meat and only the label is different. However, if the private-label meat has lesser quality meat in it, there can be a price difference because the products are not the same.

LESSENING OR INJURING COMPETITION

Generally, injury to competition can be demonstrated by showing that there is a substantial price cut in a certain area by a large manufacturer with the effect of injuring or destroying a smaller competitor. Price discrimination is an example of the use of vertical restraints to lessen horizontal competition. Predatory pricing or pricing below cost is an example of conduct that will injure or destroy competition.

The following case involves an issue of competition injury through price discrimination.

Utah Pie Co. v. Continental Baking Co.
386 U.S. 685 (1967)

PIE IN THE SKY: FREE MARKET COMPETITION AND PRICING

FACTS

Utah Pie Company (petitioner) is a Utah corporation that for 30 years has been baking pies in its plant in Salt Lake City and selling them in Utah and surrounding states. It entered the frozen pie business in 1957 and was immediately successful with its new line of frozen dessert pies—apple, cherry, boysenberry, peach, pumpkin, and mince.

Continental Baking Company, Pet Milk, and Carnation (respondents), based in California, sell pies in Utah primarily on a delivered-price basis.

The major competitive weapon in the Utah pie market was price. Between 1958 and 1961,
Continued

there was a deteriorating price structure for pies in the Utah market. Utah Pie was selling pies for $4.15 per dozen at the beginning of the period; at the time it filed suit for price discrimination, it was selling the same pies for $2.75 per dozen. Continental's price went from $5.00 per dozen in 1958 to $2.85 at the time suit was filed. Pet's prices went from $4.92 per dozen to $3.46, and Carnation's from $4.82 per dozen to $3.30.

Utah Pie filed suit charging price discrimination by respondents based on allegations outlined in the opinion that follows. The district court found for Utah Pie. The court of appeals reversed, and Utah Pie appealed.

JUDICIAL OPINION

WHITE, Justice

We deal first with petitioner's case against the Pet Milk Company. . . . Pet's initial emphasis was on quality, but in the face of competition from regional and local companies and in an expanding market where price proved to be a crucial factor, Pet was forced to take steps to reduce the price of its pies to the ultimate consumer. These developments had consequences in the Salt Lake City market which are the substance of petitioner's case against Pet.

First, Pet successfully concluded an arrangement with Safeway, which is one of the three largest customers for frozen pies in the Salt Lake market, whereby it would sell frozen pies to Safeway under the latter's own "Bel-air" label at a price significantly lower than it was selling its comparable "Pet-Ritz" brand in the same Salt Lake market and elsewhere. . . .

Second, it introduced a 20-ounce economy pie under the "Swiss Miss" label and began selling the new pie in the Salt Lake market in August 1960 at prices ranging from $3.25 to $3.30 for the remainder of the period. This pie was at times sold at a lower price in the Salt Lake City market than it was sold in other markets.

Third, Pet became more competitive with respect to the prices for its "Pet-Ritz" proprietary label. . . . According to the Court of Appeals, in seven of the 44 months Pet's prices in Salt Lake were lower than prices charged in the California

markets. This was true although selling in Salt Lake involved a 30- to 35-cent freight cost.

The burden of proving cost justification was on Pet and, in our view, reasonable men could have found that Pet's lower priced "Bel-air" sales to Safeway were not cost justified in their entirety. Pet introduced cost data for 1961 indicating a cost saving on the Safeway business greater than the price advantage extended to that customer. These statistics were not particularized for the Salt Lake market, but assuming that they were adequate to justify the 1961 sales, they related to only 24 percent of the Safeway sales over the relevant period. The evidence concerning the remaining 76 percent was at best incomplete and inferential. It was insufficient to take the defense of cost justification from the jury, which reasonably could have found a greater incidence of unjustified price discrimination than that allowed by the Court of Appeals' view of the evidence.

The Court of Appeals almost entirely ignored other evidence which provides material support of the jury's conclusion that Pet's behavior satisfied the statutory test regarding competitive injury. This evidence bore on the issue of Pet's predatory intent to injure Utah Pie. As an initial matter, the jury could have concluded that Pet's discriminatory pricing was aimed at Utah Pie; Pet's own management, as early as 1959, identified Utah Pie as an "unfavorable factor," one which "d[u]g holes in our operation" and posed a constant "check" on Pet's performance in the Salt Lake City market. Moreover, Pet candidly admitted that during the period when it was establishing its relationship with Safeway, it sent into Utah Pie's plant an industrial spy to seek information that would be of use to Pet in convincing Safeway that Utah Pie was not worthy of its custom. . . . Finally, Pet does not deny that the evidence showed it suffered substantial losses on its frozen pie sales during the greater part of time involved in this suit, and there was evidence from which the jury could have concluded that the losses Pet sustained in Salt Lake City were greater than those incurred elsewhere. It would not have been an irrational step if the jury

Continued

concluded that there was a relationship between the price and the losses.

It seems clear to us that the jury heard adequate evidence from which it could have concluded that Pet had engaged in predatory tactics in waging competitive warfare in the Salt Lake City market. Coupled with the incidence of price discrimination attributable to Pet, the evidence as a whole established, rather than negated, the reasonable possibility that Pet's behavior produced a lessening of competition proscribed by the Act.

Petitioner's case against Continental is not complicated. Continental was a substantial factor in the market in 1957. But its sales of frozen 22-ounce dessert pies, sold under the "Morton" brand, amounted to only 1.3 percent of the market in 1958, 2.9 percent in 1959, and 1.8 percent in 1960. Its problems were primarily that of cost and in turn that of price, the controlling factor in the market. In late 1960 it worked out a co-packing arrangement in California by which fruit would be processed directly from the trees into the finished pies without large intermediate packing, storing, and shipping expenses. Having improved its position, it attempted to increase its share of the Salt Lake City market by utilizing a local broker and offering short-term price concessions in varying amounts. Its efforts for seven months were not spectacularly successful. Then in June 1961, it took the steps which are the heart of petitioner's complaint against it. Effective for the last two weeks of June it offered its 22-ounce frozen apple pies in the Utah area at $2.85 per dozen. It was then selling the same pies at substantially higher prices in other markets. The Salt Lake City price was less than its direct cost plus an allocation for overhead. . . . Utah's response was immediate. It reduced its price on all of its apple pies to $2.75 per dozen. . . . Continental's total sales of frozen pies increased from 3,350 dozen in 1960 to 18,800 dozen in 1961. Its market share increased from 1.8 percent in 1960 to 8.3 percent in 1961. The Court of Appeals concluded that Continental's conduct had had only minimal effect, that it had not injured or weakened Utah Pies as a competitor, that it had not substantially lessened competition and that there was no reasonable possibility that it would do so in the future.

We again differ with the Court of Appeals. Its opinion that Utah was not damaged as a competitive force apparently rested on the fact that Utah's sales volume continued to climb in 1961 and on the court's own factual conclusion that Utah was not deprived of any pie business which it otherwise might have had. But this retrospective assessment fails to note that Continental's discriminatory below-cost price caused Utah Pie to reduce its price to $2.75.

Even if the impact on Utah Pie as a competitor was negligible, there remain the consequences to others in the market who had to compete not only with Continental's 22-ounce pie at $2.85 but with Utah's even lower price of $2.75 per dozen for both its proprietary and controlled labels. . . . The evidence was that there were nine other sellers in 1960 who sold 23,473 dozen pies, 12.7 percent of the total market. In 1961 there were eight other sellers who sold less than the year before—18,565 dozen or 8.2 percent of the total—although the total market had expanded from 184,569 dozen to 226,908 dozen. We think there was sufficient evidence from which the jury could find a violation of § 2(a) by Continental.

Section 2(a) does not forbid price competition which will probably injure or lessen competition by eliminating competitors, discouraging entry into the market or enhancing the market shares of the dominant sellers. But Congress has established some ground rules for the game. Sellers may not sell like goods to different purchasers at different prices if the result may be to injure competition to either the sellers' or the buyers' market unless such discriminations are justified as permitted by the Act. In this case there was some evidence of predatory intent with respect to each of these respondents. There was also other evidence upon which the jury could rationally find the requisite injury to competition. The frozen pie market in Salt Lake City was highly competitive. At times Utah Pie was a leader in moving the general level of prices down, and at other times each of the respondents also bore responsibility

Continued

for the downward pressure on the price structure. We believe that the Act reaches price discrimination that erodes competition as much as it does price discrimination that is intended to have immediate destructive impact. In this case, the evidence shows a drastically declining price structure which the jury could rationally attribute to continued or sporadic price discrimination.

    Reversed.

CASE QUESTIONS

1. Describe the competitors in the Utah Pie frozen pie market.
2. Is it significant that the national competitors were selling their pies at different prices in Utah?
3. Does it matter that the size of the pie market (i.e., number of pies sold) increased during the period examined?

C O N S I D E R . . .   **13.11** Would the following conduct constitute price discrimination?

    Mead Johnson, Bristol-Myers Squibb, and Wyeth Ayerst Laboratories charged higher prices for formula sold to the U.S. Agriculture Department for its subsidy programs for welfare families than those charged to grocery retailers.

C O N S I D E R . . .   **13.12** A&P Grocery Stores decided to sell its own brand of canned milk (referred to as "private label" milk). A&P asked its longtime supplier, Borden, to submit an offer to produce the private label milk. Bowman Dairy also submitted a bid, which was lower than Borden's. A&P's Chicago buyer then contacted Borden and said, "I have a bid in my pocket. You people are so far out of line it is not even funny. You are not even in the ballpark." The Borden representative asked for more details but was told only that a $50,000 improvement in Borden's bid "would not be a drop in the bucket."

    A&P was one of Borden's largest customers in the Chicago area. Furthermore, Borden had just invested more than $5 million in a new dairy facility in Illinois. The loss of the A&P account would result in underutilization of the plant. Borden lowered its bid by more than $400,000. The Federal Trade Commission has charged Borden with price discrimination, but Borden maintains it was simply meeting the competition. Has Borden violated the Robinson-Patman Act? Does it matter that the milk was a private label milk and not its normal trade name Borden milk? Are the ethics of the A&P representative troublesome? [*Great Atlantic & Pacific Tea Co., Inc.* v. *FTC*, 440 U.S. 69 (1979).]

DEFENSES TO PRICE DISCRIMINATION

If there are legitimate cost differences in the manufacture or handling of a product, there cannot be price discrimination. Additional costs of delivery or of adding specifications to a product can increase the price without violating the Robinson-Patman Act. For example, if a sandwich-meat manufacturer produces a special low-fat bologna, the price for that product can be different. If the manufacturer uses different shipping companies for its customers, there again may be a price differential.

Quantity discounts are permitted so long as the seller can show that there are actual cost savings in the sale of increased quantities and not just an assumption that larger sales are more economical. Limiting the number of buyers who qualify for quantity discounts is some proof that the actual cost savings are not present.

Prices for products also can change according to market, inflation, material costs, and other variable factors. The seller must simply establish that a price change was initiated in response to one of these factors.

Another defense to a charge of price discrimination is **meeting the competition**. This defense must establish that a price change was made in a certain market to meet the competition there. Also, the seller must charge the same as its competitors and not a lower price. Finally, the price differences must be limited to an area or individuals. For example, a national firm may have a different price in one state because of more competition within that particular state.

Visit "Antitrust Policy" for more about mergers, price fixing, and vertical restraints:
http://www. vanderbilt.edu/ Owen/froeb/ antitrust/antitrust. html

Vertical Mergers

Vertical mergers are between firms that have a buyer-seller relationship. For example, if a sandwich-meat manufacturer merged with its meat supplier, there would be a vertical merger. In determining whether a vertical merger violates the Clayton Act, the courts determine the relevant geographic and product markets and then determine whether the effect of the merger will be to foreclose or lessen competition. For more details on vertical mergers, see Chapter 22.

ANTITRUST ISSUES IN INTERNATIONAL COMPETITION

As the level of international trade has increased, so also has the number of competitors. For example, three domestic manufacturers produce cars in the United States. However, the availability of international trade markets has resulted in the importing of cars from Japan, Great Britain, Germany, Sweden, and Yugoslavia; and international competition changes the market perspective because the relevant market is not the United States, but the world.

As a result of increased levels of international competition, more joint ventures of competitors and large companies that once would have seemed unthinkable under antitrust protections will be permitted. For example, American Telephone and Telegraph (AT&T) has entered into a joint venture agreement with the Economic Ministry of Taiwan to improve that nation's telecommunications systems. General Mills, Inc. was permitted to acquire RJR Nabisco's cold-cereal business in both the United Kingdom and the United States so that it could compete more effectively in the large North American and European markets.

Not all countries have adopted a complex set of antitrust laws like those of the United States. For example, although England has antitrust laws, treble damage provisions do not exist there. In addition, many countries that conduct their international trade via cartels have refused to respond to document requests by U.S. courts and have instructed their citizens to refuse as well. Furthermore, governments of foreign countries foster or sponsor many cartels. Under the doctrine of sovereign immunity (see Chapter 7), the United States would not be permitted to prosecute one of these cartels because of the governmental shield of immunity.

The U.S. Supreme Court has held that companies from other countries that engage in commerce in the United States will be subject to U.S. antitrust laws.

BIOGRAPHY

Old, Onerous, and Still on the Books:
Are dusty consent decrees hobbling Corporate America?

As anniversaries go, Oct. 12 was an odd one for General Electric Co. It was on that day 83 years ago that GE signed an agreement with the government designed to weaken the company's dominance of the lighting industry. Among other measures, the consent decree banned GE from manufacturing private-label or generic lighting products and required the company to disclose its ownership of several lighting businesses that had been thought to be independent.

The Stories of the Longest Antitrust Cases and the Companies Involved

Today, GE and a growing number of other companies constrained by decades-old consent decrees say it's time to remove the shackles. GE is negotiating with the Justice Dept.'s Antitrust Div. to lift the order, arguing that its provisions are hindering the company's ability to compete in a global economy. "By lifting this order, we would be able to do exactly what our competitors are doing," says company spokesman John J. Betchkal.

GE has plenty of company in its crusade against what many executives believe to be antiquated—and anticompetitive—orders. IBM and Eastman Kodak Co. have joined the fight, too. The argument is simple: How can antitrust agreements written decades ago be relevant in today's economy?

What has suddenly spurred these challenges, after years of little or no activity? Part of the answer, say experts, is that global competition has greatly intensified over the past decade. IBM, for instance, has been hit particularly hard and has been frustrated watching competitors flourish under practices it is barred from using.

General Electric Company

Slacking Off

Another factor has been a change in the government's attitude. It used to be almost impossible to persuade regulators and courts to abandon or modify consent decrees. But in July, the Federal Trade Commission announced that its antitrust decrees would lapse after 20 years. The agency also invited companies to seek reviews of old decrees. The average life span of the Justice Dept.'s antitrust orders is now 10 years. Experts say regulators finally realize that some decrees can impede competition if left unchecked too long. "The problem with these decrees is that they don't learn with society," says Daniel M. Wall, an antitrust lawyer in San Francisco.

GE, for example, wants to begin offering private-label lightbulbs to retailers—a business segment that global competitors such as Philips Lighting and Osram Sylvania Inc. already have. In addition, the company wants to sell generic products to compete in the lower-priced end of the lighting market. The company won't say how much these endeavors would be worth but is concerned that rivals are profiting from its predicament. The government is weighing GE's request.

Experts estimate that more than 100 of these decades-old decrees are still controlling some corporate behavior. Most antitrust agreements entered into today aren't open-ended. For example, the settlement reached recently between the government and Microsoft Corp. Is due to expire in just $6\frac{1}{2}$ years.

Re-lease?

Yet for all the sentiment that has been expressed in favor of updating outmoded enforcement measures, companies are encountering stiff opposition. Critics say it's because even with the passage of time and a more global marketplace, many companies still retain too much control over their industries to be freed from certain restraints. IBM is butting heads with a number of its competitors over a 1956 consent decree that, among other things, forced it to offer computer services separately from its manufacturing and sales business. It also required IBM, which had previously only leased its equipment, to sell outright its computers and equipment to competitors.

Such provisions created what are now multibillion-dollar aftermarkets composed of independent leasing and service businesses and dealers of used IBM computer equipment. The 265 independent lessors alone earn more than $15 billion. These companies argue that such revenues would plummet without the decree. "If you don't regulate IBM, it will put handcuffs on companies like ours to compete effectively. And that will cause consumers to suffer," argues Philip A. Hewes, a senior vice-president at ComDisco Inc., the largest independent computer-leasing company.

Independent service organizations (ISOs) agree, arguing that the court should draw a distinction between IBM's diminished strength in manufacturing and its continued dominance of the computer-service business. "There is a superficial appeal to IBM's argument that we need to reassess things after 40 years," says Ronald S. Katz, a San Francisco lawyer who represents the ISOs. "But IBM could hobble or get rid of its competition" if the decree were to be lifted. IBM, which has said it must be free to match such competitors as Electronic Data Systems Inc., declines to comment.

Ironic

Thus far, the Justice Dept. has remained silent on the IBM case, which is pending in federal court. Not so with respect to Kodak, which in May persuaded a court to overturn two consent decrees. Kodak successfully argued that it no longer possessed enough power to control prices or hinder competition. Consequently, Kodak claimed it should be allowed to sell private-label film and to bundle its film and photo finishing businesses. Robert B. Bell, Kodak's antitrust counsel in Washington, says his client would have come out with a number of innovative products if it weren't for the decrees from 1920 and 1954.

The government has appealed the Kodak case, arguing that the company still wields too much market control. The appeal, which is expected to be heard in January, is deemed so important that Assistant Attorney General Anne K. Bingaman is expected to make a rare court appearance to argue the case herself. That Bingaman would be battling the case so hard strikes some critics as ironic. "It's really baffling to companies to have the government fight decrees that are 80 years old when current policy allows them to expire in 10 years," says Bell.

Baffling, maybe. But the Kodak decision could affect dozens of other decrees on the books by creating a new legal standard for overturning them. That's a feat in antitrust law that hasn't been accomplished since 1932—the time of prohibition and the kidnapping of Charles Lindbergh, Jr.

Source: Linda Himelstein, "Old, Onerous, and Still on the Books," *Business Week*, November 7, 1994, pp. 58–59. Reprinted from the November 7, 1994 issue of *Business Week* by special permission, copyright © 1994 by The McGraw-Hill Companies.

Issues
1. Why are the older decrees still in effect?
2. Why do the companies feel the decrees should be lifted?

C O N S I D E R . . . **13.13** Laker Airways, Ltd., was founded as a charter airline in 1966. It began charter operations between the United States and the United Kingdom in 1970. In 1971 Laker sought to expand its transatlantic air service, hoping to gain a sizeable share of the transatlantic market by offering only basic air passage with little or no in-flight amenities and nonessential services. Flying at a reduced cost would enable Laker to set rates much lower than those charged by existing transatlantic carriers.

Laker's applications to the British and American governments for the start of such service was delayed by the other airlines' interference. However, by 1977 Laker had obtained the necessary authorizations.

Transatlantic air service prices are substantially controlled by the International Air Transport Association (IATA), a trade organization of the world's largest air carriers. The IATA meets annually to establish fixed fares, which are then implemented by the governments of the carriers. Because Laker's fares were approximately one-third of the competing fares offered by other carriers, Laker's new service jeopardized all the carriers' established markets. In 1977, the IATA agreed to set rates at a predatory level to drive Laker out of business.

Laker managed to stay in business until 1981 because it was carrying one out of every seven passengers scheduled for flights between the United States and England. During 1981 the devaluation of the pound resulted in severe financial constraints on Laker because its fleet of DC-10s had been financed in the United States and it was required to pay in U.S. dollars, although most of its revenues were in pounds.

The IATA lowered prices again, paid travel agents commissions to divert customers from Laker, and agreed that once Laker was out of business, they would return to "normal" fares.

Laker was forced into liquidation in February 1982. Through its liquidator, Laker filed an antitrust suit in the U.S. District Court for the District of Columbia. The suit alleged predatory pricing and the tort of unlawful interference with business relations.

Is Laker correct? Does it have a case? [*Laker Airways* v. *Sabena, Belgian World Airlines*, 731 F.2d 909 (D.C. 1984).]

C O N S I D E R . . . **13.14** A group of international reinsurers provides underwriting services for 19 U.S. insurers, including Hartford Fire Insurance, Allstate Insurance Company, CIGNA Corporation, and Aetna Casualty and Surety Company. Together, the group of international reinsurers decided to change their terms of coverage including the elimination of "sudden and accidental pollution damage" coverage. The international reinsurers refused to continue to do business with the U.S. companies unless they agreed to the new coverage terms.

The 19 U.S. insurance companies filed suit alleging a group boycott by the international reinsurers. The international firms filed a motion to dismiss, claiming they were not located in the United States and were not subject to U.S. antitrust laws.

Are the international insurance firms correct? Recalling the issues of jurisdiction from Chapter 3, do the international firms have sufficient presence in the United States to be subject to suit in federal district court? Is there an antitrust violation? [*Hartford Fire Ins.* v. *California*, 113 S. Ct. 2891 (1993).]

SUMMARY

What restraints of trade are permissible?
- Covenant not to compete—clause in employment or business sale contracts that restricts competition by one of the parties; must be reasonable in scope and time

What antitrust laws exist?
- Sherman Act—first federal antitrust law; prohibits monopolization and horizontal trade restraints such as price fixing, boycotts, and refusals to deal
- Clayton Act—federal antitrust statute that prohibits tying and interlocking directorates; controls mergers
- Federal Trade Commission Act—federal law that allows the FTC to regulate unfair competition
- Robinson-Patman Act—anti-price discrimination federal statute
- Celler-Kefauver Act—regulates asset acquisitions
- Hart-Scott-Rodino Antitrust Improvements Act—antitrust law that broadened Justice Department authority and provided new merger guidelines

What penalties can be imposed for restraints of trade?
- Equitable remedies—nonmonetary remedies such as injunctions
- Treble damages—three times actual damages available in antitrust cases

What are the forms of horizontal trade restraint and defenses?
- Horizontal restraints of trade—anticompetitive behavior among a firm's competitors
- Price-fixing—controlling price of goods through agreement, limiting supply, controlling credit
- Group boycotts—agreement among competitors to exclude competition
- Joint ventures—temporary combinations that may restrain trade
- Per se violation—violation of antitrust laws that has no defense or justification
- Monopolization—possession of monopoly power in the relevant market by willful acquisition
- Market power—power to control prices or exclude competition
- Relevant market—geographic and product market used to determine market power
- Predatory pricing—pricing below actual cost to monopolize
- Noerr-Pennington doctrine—protection of First Amendment activities from antitrust laws

What are the forms of vertical trade restraints and defenses?
- Resale price maintenance—requiring prices be set in vertical distribution
- Exclusive distributorship—limited dealership rights; not an antitrust violation so long as horizontal competition exists
- Tying—requiring buyers to take an additional product in order to purchase the product they wish
- Price discrimination—selling goods across state lines at prices that have different ratios to marginal costs

QUESTIONS AND PROBLEMS

1. Harold Vogel, an experienced gem appraiser, is a member of the American Society of Appraisers. Vogel's fee for his work is based on a percentage of the value of the appraised item. The society expelled him under the authority of a bylaw that provides: "It is unprofessional and unethical for the appraiser to do work for a fixed percentage of the amount of value." Mr. Vogel brought suit under Section 1 of the Sherman Act alleging that his expulsion was a boycott and that he no longer had referrals from the society. Mr. Vogel also claims the bylaw is a means of fixing prices. Is he right? [*Harold Vogel* v. *American Society of Appraisers*, 744 F.2d 598 (7th Cir. 1984).]

2. Denny's is a full-service marine dealer located near Peru, Indiana, that sells fishing boats, motors, trailers, and marine accessories in the central Indiana market. Renfro Productions and others are marine dealers in the same market area who compete with Denny's to sell boats to Indiana consumers. CIMDA is a trade association of marine dealers in that area. Renfro and others are producers of two boat shows held annually at the Indiana State Fairgrounds (the "Fairgrounds Shows"). The February Fairgounds Show (the "Spring Show") originated over 30 years ago. It is one of the top three boats shows in the United States, attracting between 160,000 and 191,000 consumers annually. The October show (the "Fall Show") is smaller and began in 1987.

   Denny's participated in the Fall Show in 1988, 1989, and 1990; it participated in the Spring Show in 1989 and 1990. At all of these shows Denny's was very successful, apparently because it encouraged its customers to shop the other dealers and then come to Denny's for a lower price. During and after the 1989 Spring Show, some of the other dealers began to complain about Denny's sales methods. After the 1990 Spring Show, these dealers apparently spent a good part of one CIMDA meeting "vent[ing] their . . . frustration" about Denny's. The complaints escalated. As a result, Renfro informed Denny's that after the 1990 Fall Show (in which Denny's was contractually entitled to participate) it could no longer participate in the Fairgrounds Shows. Is this an antitrust violation? [*Denny's Marina, Inc.* v. *Renfro Productions, Inc.*, 8 F.3d 1217 (7th Cir. 1993).]

3. Professional Real Estate Investors, Inc. (PRE), operated LaMancha Private Club and Villas, a resort in Palm Springs, California. PRE installed videodisc players in the resort's hotel rooms and assembled a library of more than two hundred motion pictures for guests to rent for in-room viewing. PRE was working to develop a market for the sale of similar systems to other hotels.

   Columbia Pictures Industries, Inc., and seven other motion picture studios held copyrights on the films PRE was renting. Columbia also licensed transmission of copyrighted motion pictures to hotel rooms through a wired cable system called Spectradyne.

   Columbia sued PRE for copyright infringement. PRE countersued, claiming Columbia's suit was a sham that cloaked underlying acts of monopolization and restraint of trade and that Columbia was simply tying up PRE in litigation while it expanded its Spectradyne service in hotels.

   Under the law PRE could sell or lease lawfully purchased videodiscs under the "first sale" doctrine of the Copyright Act. The only issue that remained was whether in-room viewing was a performance that required PRE to pay royalties.

   Is Columbia's activity subject to antitrust regulation or is it protected under the Noerr-Pennington doctrine? [*Professional Real Estate Investors, Inc.* v. *Columbia Pictures, Inc.*, 508 U.S. 49 (1993).]

4. Budget Rent-a-Car and Aloha Airlines have developed a "fly-drive" program. Under their agreement, customers of Aloha receive a $7 first-day rental rate for car rentals (the usual rate is $14). Robert's Waikiki U-Drive has brought suit challenging the agreement as a tying arrangement and unlawful. Is Robert's correct? [*Robert's Waikiki U-Drive* v. *Budget Rent-a-Car*, 732 F.2d 1403 (9th Cir. 1984).]

5. Eastman Kodak Company introduced its new "pocket 110 cameras" to the market in 1972. The cameras used special film that only Kodak manufactured. Also, only Kodak labs had the technology for developing the 110 film. Foremost Color Lab, a film processor, has brought suit on the basis that the 110 system creates a monopoly and is unlawful tying. Is Foremost correct? [*Foremost Pro Color* v. *Eastman Kodak Co.*, 703 F.2d 534 (9th Cir. 1984).]

6. Gardner-Denver, the largest manufacturer of ratchet wrenches and their replacement parts in the United States, has a dual pricing system for wrench parts and components. Its blue list had parts that, if purchased in quantities of five or more, were available for substantially less than its white list prices. Has Gardner-Denver engaged in price discrimination with its two price lists? [*D. E. Rogers Assoc., Inc.* v. *Gardner-Denver Co.*, 718 F.2d 1431 (6th Cir. 1983).]

7. Russell Stover is a candy manufacturer that ships its products to 18,000 retailers nationwide. Stover designates resale prices for its dealers, but does not request assurances from them that they are honoring the prices. It has, however, refused to sell to those retailers it believes will sell below the prices suggested. Is there an antitrust violation in this conduct? [*Russell Stover Candies, Inc.* v. FTC, 718 F.2d 256 (8th Cir. 1982).]

8. William Inglis & Sons is a family-owned wholesale bakery with production facilities in Stockton, California, that manufactured and distributed bread and rolls in northern California. ITT Continental is one of the nation's largest wholesale bakeries and was a competitor of Inglis in the northern California market. Both Inglis and Continental sold their bread under a private label and an advertised label. Continental's advertised bread was "Wonder" bread, whereas Inglis's advertised bread was "Sunbeam." The private label bread is sold at a lower price than advertised brand, but the principal difference between the two is the profit. Inglis filed a complaint stating that Continental was selling its private label bread at below-cost prices in a predatory price scheme designed to drive Inglis out of the market. Inglis also says the lower price on private bread earned Continental more grocery-shelf space for its "Wonder" bread. Is such conduct illegal under the Sherman Act? Is predatory pricing a per se violation? [*William Inglis* v. ITT *Continental Baking Co.*, 668 F.2d 1014 (9th Cir. 1980).]

9. On August 1, 1957, Procter & Gamble, the nation's leading manufacturer of soaps, detergents, and other high-turnover household products, acquired Clorox Chemical Company, the nation's leading producer of liquid bleach. Purex Corporation, the second leading producer of liquid bleach, brought suit challenging the acquisition as violative of the Clayton Act. At the time of the acquisition, Clorox held 48.8 percent of sales and Purex held 15.7 percent of sales. Purex says the enormous financial strength, advertising budget, and marketing skills of P&G would make it nearly impossible for any bleach manufacturer to compete. What factors are important in determining whether the merger is a valid one? [*Purex Corp.* v. *Procter & Gamble Co.*, 596 F.2d 881 (9th Cir. 1979).]

10. MacDonald Group, Ltd., owned and operated the Fresno Fashion Fair Mall and leased space to Edmond's, a California retail jeweler. The lease contained a covenant that limited MacDonald to one additional jewelry store as a tenant in the mall. The lease was entered into in 1969. In 1978, MacDonald was involved in the construction of an expansion to the mall and began negotiations to include a retail jeweler in the new space. Edmond's objected and brought suit. The covenant provides that only two jewelry stores would be tenants in the Fresno Fashion Fair Mall. The expansion would still be part of the Fresno Fashion Fair Mall and would not have a separate name. Would the covenant apply to the new addition to the mall? [*Edmond's of Fesno* v. *MacDonald Group, Ltd.*, 217 Cal. Rptr. 375 (1985).]

NOTE

1 The doctrine is named after the two U.S. Supreme Court cases in which it was developed: *Eastern R.R. President's Conference v. Noerr Motor Freight, Inc.*, 365 U.S. 127 (1961) and *United Mine Workers v. Pennington*, 381 U.S. 657 (1965).

Judgment

Schulze and Burch Biscuit Company purchased apple powder from Tree Top, Inc. Schulze manufactures Toastettes and uses the apple powder in making the fruit filling for these breakfast pastries. Edward Park, Schulze's director of procurement sent Ralph Brady, Tree Top's broker, a purchase order with the following language:

Important: The fulfillment of this order or any part of it obligates the Seller to abide by the terms, conditions and instructions on both sides of this order. Additional or substitute terms will not become part of this contract unless expressly accepted by Buyer; Seller's acceptance is limited to the terms of this order, and no contract will be formed except on these terms.

Mr. Brady sent a confirmation back to Mr. Park with the following language:

Seller guarantees goods to conform to the national pure food laws. All disputes under this transaction shall be arbitrated in the usual manner. This confirmation shall be subordinate to more formal contract, when and if such contract is executed. In the absence of such contract, this confirmation represents the contract of the parties. If incorrect, please advise immediately.

The apple powder Tree Top sent to Schulze had stem and wood splinters, and it caused Schulze's pastry machinery to clog and its line to shut down.

Schulze filed suit. Tree Top said that the powder complied with federal law, all that it was required to do. Schulze said those terms were not part of their contract. Who is right?

CHAPTER 14

Contracts have been necessary in business since business

began. They allow

Contracts and Sales: Introduction and Formation

businesses to count

on money, supplies, and services. Contracts are the

private law of business; the parties develop their own

A verbal contract isn't worth the paper it's written on.
Samuel Goldwyn

private set of laws through their contracts. These

private laws have the benefit of judicial enforcement

in all states. This chapter covers contract basics: What

is a contract? What laws govern contracts? What are

the types of contracts? How are contracts formed?

What contracts must be in writing?

WHAT IS A CONTRACT?

Businesses cannot expand and grow without being able to rely on commitments; resources are wasted if promises are not fulfilled. For example, suppose that Wonder Bread Company constructs a new wing and buys new equipment to expand production, but when the wing is ready to operate, the wheat supplier backs out of the supply contract with Wonder Bread. Wonder Bread has wasted resources and will lose the desire to expand because of the problems created by unenforceable agreements. These strong economic considerations brought about the involvement of the courts in enforcing contractual promises.

"A **contract** is a promise or set of promises for breach of which the law gives a remedy, or the performance of which the law in some way recognizes as a duty." This definition comes from the *Restatement of Contracts*, a statement of contract law by the American Law Institute (ALI), which recognizes a contract as a set of voluntary promises that the law will enforce for private parties. The remainder of this chapter focuses on the creation, performance, and enforcement of those promises.

SOURCES OF CONTRACT LAW

There are two general sources of contract law: common law and the Uniform Commercial Code.

Common Law

Common law was the first law of contracts. As discussed in Chapter 1, common law consists today of those traditional notions of law and that body of law developed by judicial decisions dealing with contract issues. Although it is not statutory law, the traditional English common law of contracts has been modified by statute in some states. Thus, certain types of contracts have unique and specific content requirements—for example, listing agreements for real estate agents, insurance policies, and consumer credit contracts (see Chapter 16 for a more complete discussion of the statutory requirements in consumer credit contracts). But however much specific language and statutory requirements these contracts have, their formation and enforcement are still governed by common law.

A general treatment of common law can be found in the ***Restatement (Second) of Contracts*** which is a general summary of the nature of common law contracts in the United States. A group of legal scholars wrote the *Restatement*, and changes have been made to reflect the changes in contract law over the years.

Common law applies to contracts that have land or services as their subject matter. A rental agreement for an apartment may be covered by common law or specific landlord-tenant statutes, but a contract for the construction of a home or an employment contract is governed by common law.

The Uniform Commercial Code

One of the problems with common law is its lack of uniformity. The states do not follow the same case decisions on contract law, and some states do not follow the *Restatement*; the result is that different rules apply to contracts in different states. Consequently, businesses once had great difficulty and expense when they contracted across state lines because of differences in state contract common law.

Review Article 2 of the UCC: http://www.law.cornell.edu/ucc/2/overview.html
Examine drafts of proposed changes to the UCC, published by the National Conference of Commissioners on Uniform State Laws: http://www.kentlaw.edu/ulc/

To address the need for uniformity, the National Conference of Commissioners on Uniform State Laws and the American Law Institute worked to draft a set of commercial laws appropriate for businesspeople, lawyers, and lawmakers. The result of their efforts was the **Uniform Commercial Code (UCC)**. The final draft of the UCC first appeared in the 1940s. With several revisions and much time and effort, the Code was adopted, at least in part, in all the states.

Article II of the UCC governs contracts for the sale of goods and has been adopted in all states except Louisiana. Although sections of Article II may have various forms throughout the states, the basic requirements for contracts remain consistent; businesses now have uniform requirements that have expedited interstate contracts. Article II is more liberal than common law, and contracts are more easily formed and performed and remedies are easier to determine under Article II. Specific differences are covered in the remaining sections of the chapter. Excerpts of Article II are reproduced in Appendix G. Article II is being revised and will add sections on software, formation issues under EDI (electronic data interchange) agreements, licenses, and leases.

Determining which contracts are UCC contracts and which are common law contracts is often difficult. The following case addresses this issue.

Kline Iron & Steel Co., Inc. v. Gray Communications Consultants, Inc.
715 F. Supp 135 (D. S.C. 1989)

SOME ASSEMBLY REQUIRED: IS IT A GOOD OR A SERVICE?

FACTS

In 1986, Gray Communications Consultants, Inc. (defendant), contacted various television-tower builders, including Kline Iron & Steel, Inc. (plaintiff), about manufacturing and erecting a television tower near Huttig, Arkansas.

No writing ever materialized to evidence the oral negotiations of the parties. Nonetheless, Kline Iron & Steel manufactured a tower. Gray refused to pay because the UCC required the contract ($297,072) to be in writing. Kline says the contract is for a service and is not covered under the UCC.

JUDICIAL OPINION

HENDERSON, Judge

First, the plaintiff asserts that the alleged oral contract is not subject to the writing requirement in § 36-2-201 (1) because it is a contract for services rather than for the sale of goods. The court disagrees and finds the contract is one "for the sale of goods" within the purview of § 36-2-201.

The UCC definition of "goods" is very broad. Section 36-2-105(l) provides:

"Goods" means all things (including specially manufactured goods) which are movable at the time of identification to the contract for sale other than the money in which the price is to be paid, investment securities (Title 36, Chapter 8) and things in action. "Goods" also includes the unborn young of animals and growing crops and other identified things attached to realty as described in the section on goods to be severed from realty (§ 36-2-107).

Construing this language, the South Carolina Supreme Court has held that a contract for the sale of a mobile home was a transaction in goods because the mobile home was "movable at the time of sale." This court perceives no reason not to characterize the television tower and other items to be provided under the contract as goods under § 36-2-105(l) since they would be movable at the time of identification to the contract. Nevertheless, the plaintiff asserts this particular contract is an agreement to provide

Continued

services rather than to sell goods. In support of its argument, the plaintiff stresses the "importance of the specialized knowledge and skill required to design, fabricate and erect such a product" and relies on the affidavit of David E. Monts, attached to its supplemental memorandum, which purports to segregate and value the service components of the alleged contract. Monts's affidavit asserts that the contract price reflects the following charges for services to be performed:

a.	Engineering, design, fabrication, and inspection	$353,502.00
b.	Erection services	$257,692.00
c.	Overhead costs	$59,856.00
d.	All-risk insurance premium	$39,873.00
e.	Cost for machined parts	$768.00
f.	General liability insurance premium	$93,137.00
Total		$804,828.00

The court concludes that while the agreement alleged to exist here is a hybrid contract, calling for both delivery of goods and performance of services, it is nevertheless a "contract for the sale of goods" within the ambit of § 36-2-201(1).

In considering whether a hybrid contract is for the sale of goods under the UCC, courts generally employ the "predominant thrust" or "predominant factor" test. Under this test, particular transactions are "For the sale of goods" if "their predominant factor, their thrust, their purpose, reasonably stated, is the rendition of service, with goods incidentally involved (e.g., contract with artist for painting) or is a transaction of sale, with labor incidentally involved (e.g., installation of a water heater in a bathroom)." The court finds that the primary thrust of the alleged contract is for the sale of goods.

The court holds these services are merely incidental to the sale of the tower and that the contract therefore is one for the sale of goods. The court reaches this conclusion on the basis of the following uncontested facts.

First, the transaction by its very nature appears to be one for the sale of a television tower. The plaintiff itself admits that "[t]he contract between Plaintiff and Defendant was to furnish a tower for a fixed price."

Second, the terms and language of the proposal show that the alleged agreement is predominantly for the sale of goods. Throughout the proposal, the defendant is referred to as the "Buyer," a term indicative of a transaction for the sale of goods. Further, more than two of the proposal's five typewritten pages are taken up with a detailed description of the tower and various accessories to be provided by the plaintiff and shipped "F.O.B. jobsite." By contrast, the erection services to be provided are listed in summary fashion in approximately one page. Finally, the proposal cites only the total contract price without allocating a particular amount to services.

The price of the assembly and erection services is at most $390,702 or approximately 26 percent of the total contract price. This price allocation is consistent with the proposal's requirement that 75 percent of the total price be paid "when tower materials are ready for shipment." That so little of the total contract price is attributable to the services to be performed demonstrates that those services are merely incidental to the sale of the tower and accessory products.

In light of these facts, the court concludes that the predominant thrust of the alleged agreement is to provide goods for the defendant and the contract is one for the sale of goods subject to the writing requirement of § 36-2-201.

CASE QUESTIONS

1. What is the subject matter of the contract?
2. Was the contract in writing?
3. If the contract is a UCC contract, is it required to be in writing?
4. What factors does the court examine to determine whether the contract is one for goods or services?
5. Is the contract a UCC contract?

The UCC has added a new section called "Article II Leases," which applies to leases of goods. Over the past 10 years, many new forms of goods transactions have developed, such as the long-term auto lease, which appears to be more of a sale than a lease. Because of the nature of these agreements, leases did not fit well under common law or traditional Article II. Article II Leases, drafted for these types of contracts, covers such issues as the statute of frauds (leases in which payments exceed $1,000, for example, must be in writing), contract formation, and warranties associated with a lease. This new section of the UCC has been adopted in approximately 10 states.

C O N S I D E R . . . **14.1** Determine which of the following would be covered by the UCC and which would be covered by common law:

a. Sale of mobile home by manufacturer [*Duffee* v. *Judson*, 389 A.2d 843 (Pa. 1977).]
b. A subcontractor's completion of a steel frame in an office building (the "sub" furnished the steel used) [*Belmont Industries, Inc.* v. *Bechtel Corp.*, 425 F. Supp. 524 (E.D. Pa. 1974).]
c. The sale of a yacht [*Peoria Harbor Marina* v. *McGlasson*, 434 N.E.2d 786 (Ill. 1982).]
d. The sale of a computer system to handle billing, provide financial data, and contain patient files for a physician's office for $19,940. The contract called for the design of the system, installation of the system, and provision for 16 hours of training. [*Delorise Brown, M.D., Inc.* v. *Allio*, 620 N.E.2d 1020 (Ohio 1993).]

TYPES OF CONTRACTS

Contracts exist in many different forms, and these forms can control many of the parties' rights and remedies with respect to the relationship. The following sections cover the various types of contracts and offer an introduction to contract terminology.

Bilateral versus Unilateral Contracts

A contract can result from two parties exchanging promises to perform, or one party exchanging a promise for the other party's actions. A **bilateral contract** is one in which both parties promise to perform certain things. For example, if you sign a contract to buy a used pink Cadillac for $2,000, you have entered into a bilateral contract with the seller. The seller has promised not to sell the car to anyone else and will give you the title to the car when you pay the $2,000. You have promised to buy that pink Cadillac and will turn over the $2,000 to the seller in exchange for the title. The contract consists of two promises: your promise to buy and the seller's promise to sell.

Some contracts have one party issuing a promise and the other party simply performing. This type of contract is called a **unilateral contract**. For example, suppose that your uncle said, "I will pay you $500 if you will drive my new Mercedes to San Francisco for me within the next five days." Your uncle has promised to pay but you have not promised to do anything. Nonetheless, you can hold your uncle to his promise if you drive his car to San Francisco. Your agreement is a promise in exchange for performance. If you drive the car to San Francisco, your uncle's promise will be enforceable as a unilateral contract.

Express versus Implied Contracts (Quasi Contracts)

Some contracts are written, signed (even notarized), and very formal in appearance. Others are simply verbal agreements between the parties (see page 501 for a discussion of the types of contracts that can be oral). A contract that is written or orally agreed to is an **express contract**. In still other situations, the parties do not discuss the terms of the contract but nonetheless understand that they have some form of contractual relationship. A contract that arises from circumstances and not from the express agreement of the parties is called an **implied contract**, as when you go to a doctor for treatment of an illness. You and the doctor do not sit down and negotiate the terms of treatment or the manner in which the doctor will conduct the examination or how much you will pay. You understand that the doctor will do whatever examinations are appropriate to determine the cause of your illness and that there is a fee associated with the doctor's work. The payment and treatment terms are implied from general professional customs. You have an **implied-in-fact** contract.

A second type of implied or enforceable agreement is called an **implied-in-law contract** or a **quasi contract**. The term *quasi* means "as if " and describes the action of a court when it treats parties who do not have a contract "as if" they did. The courts enforce a quasi contract right if one party has conferred a benefit on another, both are aware of the benefit, and the retention of the benefit would be an enrichment of one party at the unjust expense of the other.

It is important to understand that the theory of quasi contract does not apply to what has been referred to as "the officious meddler." The officious meddler is someone who performs unrequested work or services and then, based on a quasi contract theory, seeks recovery. For example, you could not be required to compensate a painting contractor who came by and painted your house without your permission because the contractor acted both without your knowledge and without your consent. However, if you are aware the painting is going on and you do nothing to stop it, you would be held liable in quasi contract.

C O N S I D E R . . . 14.2 Vance Hartke was a member of the U.S. Senate running for reelection and had appointed Jacques LeRoy as his campaign manager. Mr. LeRoy ordered printed campaign materials from Moore-Langen. After the campaign, no money was available in Hartke's campaign fund to pay Moore-Langen. Moore-Langen sued both Mr. Hartke and the campaign committee for payment. Could they both be held liable even though it was Mr. LeRoy who actually contracted for the materials? [*Hartke* v. *Moore-Langen Printing and Publishing Co., Inc.*, 459 N.E.2d 430 (Ind. 1984).]

Void and Voidable Contracts

A **void contract** is an agreement to do something that is illegal or against public policy. For example, a contract to sell weapons to a country on which a weapons ban exists is a void contract. Neither side can enforce the contract, even if the weapons have already been delivered, because allowing the seller to

Chapter 14 Contracts and Sales: Introduction and Formation

collect payment would encourage further violations of the law banning the weapons sales. A contract may be partially void; that is, only a portion of the contract violates a statute or public policy and is therefore unenforceable. For example, in many states it is illegal to charge excessive rates of interest (known as usury; see Chapter 16 for more discussion). In a usurious loan contract, the loan repayment would be enforceable but the interest terms would not be. As another example, suppose that an owner has sold her business and in the contract has agreed never to start another such business. Although the buyer deserves some protection for the payment of good will, the complete elimination of the seller's right to start a business is an excessive restraint of trade that is against public policy and would not be enforced, even though the actual sale of the business would be enforced.

A **voidable contract** is a contract that can be unenforceable at the election of one of the parties. For example, if there has been misrepresentation, the party who is the victim can elect to void the contract. Likewise, a minor who signs a contract can choose to be bound by the agreement or can choose to void the contract. These types of contracts are voidable at the option of one of the parties.

Unenforceable Contracts

An **unenforceable contract** is a contract that cannot be enforced because of some procedural problem. A contract that should be in writing to comply with the statute of frauds but is not is unenforceable. When suit to enforce a contract is not brought within the statute of limitations, the contract becomes unenforceable.

Executed versus Executory Contracts

Contracts are **executed contracts** when the parties have performed according to their promises or required actions (under unilateral agreements). Contracts are **executory contracts** when the promise to perform is made but the actual performance has not been done. A contract could be wholly executed, wholly executory, or partially executed. For example, referring to the offer your uncle made about the Mercedes trip to California, the contract is wholly executory at the time your uncle makes the offer. If you drive the car to San Francisco, your performance is complete but your uncle's is not; hence, the contract is partially executed. When your uncle pays you, the contract is wholly executed because both of you have performed your responsibilities under this unilateral contract. Courts often distinguish between executed and executory contracts in determining both the rights of the parties (particularly with respect to issues of public policy and capacity) and the remedies available to the parties.

FORMATION OF CONTRACTS

A contract is formed when two parties with the correct mental intent, under the correct circumstances, within the boundaries of the law, and with some detriment to each of them agree to do certain acts in exchange for the other's acts. This formation requires the presence of all of these elements; the lack of one element or the presence of a problem, such as illegality, can result in the invalidity of the contract. The elements necessary for the formation of a valid contract are outlined in Exhibit 14.1 (pg. 486).

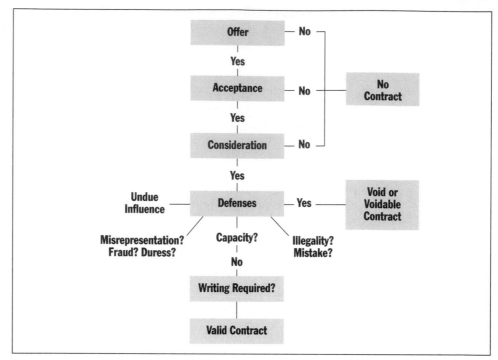

Exhibit 14.1
Overview of Contracts

Offer

The **offer** is the first part of a contract. The person who makes the offer is called the **offeror**, and the person to whom the offer is made is called the **offeree**. The requirements for a valid offer are covered in the following sections.

INTENT TO CONTRACT VERSUS NEGOTIATION

The offeror must intend to contract at the time the offer language is used. This requirement distinguishes offers from negotiations. For example, a letter from a business person may contain the following: "I am interested in investing in a franchise. I have heard about your opportunities. Please send me all necessary information." The letter expresses an interest in possibly contracting in the future, but there is no present intention to enter into a contract expressed in the language. But suppose the above letter of inquiry was followed by another letter with the following language: "I have decided to invest in one of your franchises. Enclosed are the necessary documents, signatures, and a deposit check." Here the parties have passed the negotiation stage and entered into part one of the contract—there is an offer.

Courts use an objective standard in determining the intent of the parties, which means that courts look at how a reasonable person would perceive the language, the surrounding circumstances, and the actions of the parties in determining whether a contract was formed. For example, a businessperson who is exasperated with the poor financial performance of his or her firm may say jokingly to someone over lunch, "I'd sell this company to anyone willing to take it." If that statement is made in the context of a series of complaints about the firm and the workload, it would not be an offer. That same language used in a luncheon meeting with a prospective buyer would create a different result.

In many situations, one party has simply requested bids or is inviting offers. The frustrated business owner could say, "I am interested in selling my firm. If you run into anyone who is interested, have them call me." The owner has not made an offer to sell but, rather, has made an invitation for an offer.

CONSIDER . . . 14.3 Review the following language and determine whether an offer has been made.

TO: Brit Ripley
FROM: Yachts International
RE: Sailing Vessel *Infinity*

We are prepared to make an offer to purchase the U.S. Coast Guard Documented Vessel *Infinity* for the price of $600,000 on the following terms and conditions:

> Price: $600,000
> Terms: Cash $300,000 at close of escrow
> Note: $300,000 (unsecured) due in one year
> Interest: 0.5% per month on unpaid balance vs. 100,000 shares of stock of a public company. Will guarantee $3.00 per share in one year. Buyer reserves the right to repurchase shares at $3.00 in one year if guarantee given.
> Escrow: ASAP
> Conditions:
> 1. All insurance to remain in effect until close.
> 2. Seller to deliver to Port of San Francisco in seaworthy and sailable condition.

> /s./J. P. Morgan
> YACHTS INTERNATIONAL

CERTAIN AND DEFINITE TERMS

One of the ways to determine whether there is intent to contract is also the second requirement for a valid offer. The offer must contain certain and definite language and cover all the terms necessary for a valid contract, which include the following:

- Parties
- Subject matter of the contract
- Price
- Payment terms
- Delivery terms
- Performance times

Under the UCC, the requirements for an offer are not as stringent as the requirements under common law. So long as the offer identifies the parties and the subject matter, the Code sections can cover the details of price, payment, delivery, and performance (see § 2-204 in Appendix G).

Also under the UCC, courts give great weight to industry custom and the previous dealings of the parties in determining whether the terms are certain and definite enough to constitute an offer (see § 2-208 in Appendix G). For example, the parties may have done business with each other for 10 years and their agreement simply contains a quantity and a price. Whatever payment and delivery terms have been used in their relationship in the past (their **course of dealing**) will be the terms for their ongoing relationship. The following case involves an interesting issue of course of dealing and the certainty and definiteness of terms.

Smith-Scharff Paper Co. v. P.N. Hirsch & Co. Stores, Inc.
754 S.W.2d 928 (Mo. 1988)

LEFT HOLDING THE BAG: 40 YEARS OF SALES

FACTS

Smith-Scharff is a Missouri corporation in business as a distributor of paper products. P.N. Hirsch is a division of INTERCO Inc., a Delaware corporation, and was a privately held company prior to 1964.

Smith-Scharff began selling paper products to Hirsch in 1947. Their business relationship was very nearly continuous until 1983, except for a one-year interruption sometime in the 1950s or 1960s during which Hirsch bought its paper bags from another company. At the time this interruption occurred, Hirsch bought all the bags with its logo imprinted on them that Smith-Scharff had in its possession.

Smith-Scharff had kept a supply of these bags in stock so that when a purchase order was received from Hirsch, Smith-Scharff could fill it in a timely fashion. Smith-Scharff ordered these bags from the manufacturer based on its own historical sales record to Hirsch. Hirsch was aware of this arrangement and periodically provided a generalized profile of its business forecasts to Smith-Scharff.

Hirsch was liquidated and its retail outlets sold to Dollar General. When Smith-Scharff discovered this, its president, Arthur L. Scharff, wrote a letter to the president of Hirsch, Bernard Mayer, and subsequently spoke with him. Smith-Scharff was looking for assurance that the Hirsch bags they had in stock would be bought. Mr. Mayer told Mr. Scharff that Hirsch would honor all commitments and that the integrity of Hirsch should not be questioned.

Thereafter, Smith-Scharff sent Hirsch a bill for $65,000, representing the cost of all the Hirsch bags in stock. Between October 1983 and May 1984, Hirsch purchased approximately $45,000 worth of these bags, but Smith-Scharff was left with an inventory totaling $20,679.46.

Smith-Scharff filed suit alleging breach of contract. The jury found for Smith-Scharff and awarded damages of $27,000. Hirsch appealed.

JUDICIAL OPINION

STEPHAN, Presiding Judge

Course of dealing is defined as:

. . . a sequence of previous conduct between the parties to a particular transaction which is fairly to be regarded as establishing a common basis of understanding for interpreting their expressions and other conduct.

After reviewing the record, we find that there was sufficient evidence to support the existence of a contract. Smith-Scharff and P.N. Hirsch had been engaged in business together for thirty-six years. In that time, Smith-Scharff discovered that the best way to service P.N. Hirsch and stay competitive in the market was to keep a supply of bags with the P.N. Hirsch logo in stock. P.N. Hirsch was aware of the way its account was handled by Smith-Scharff. While it is true that P.N. Hirsch did not specifically request Smith-Scharff to conduct business in this fashion, P.N. Hirsch accepted the benefits of the practice which avoided the delays involved in ordering the bags from the manufacturer. P.N. Hirsch could have told Smith-Scharff to stop stockpiling bags, but chose not to because the situation, as it stood, suited its business purposes. Under the Uniform Commercial Code, P.N. Hirsch is under an obligation of good faith. It is, therefore, estopped from denying the existence of a contract.

Having found that there was an agreement, we now look to whether it included disposition of merchandise upon termination of the relation. This contingency was never discussed by the parties, but there was a previous termination of relations which lasted approximately one year. At that time, P.N. Hirsch bought the remaining bags left in the possession of Smith-Scharff. It was, therefore, not unreasonable for Smith-Scharff to expect the same treatment again. It makes no difference that this time the termination was permanent because P.N. Hirsch was going out of business under that name.

Continued

It is clear that the bags were made specially for the benefit of P.N. Hirsch. P.N. Hirsch was aware of Smith-Scharff's business practice of pre-ordering bags, therefore, P.N. Hirsch is estopped from denying its responsibility to pay for them. It was reasonable for Smith-Scharff to expect P.N. Hirsch to purchase the remaining inventory. We, therefore, deny [the appeal] on all grounds.

The judgment of the trial court is affirmed.

CASE QUESTIONS

1. How long was the parties' relationship?

2. What practice was followed with regard to the bag inventory?

3. Was the final situation different from the parties' previous course of dealing?

4. Will Smith-Scharff recover?

5. Do you think P.N. Hirsch had an ethical obligation to pay for the bags, regardless of its legal obligation? Is there an element of ethics in the legal principle of reliance? Isn't the UCC's course of dealing just a way of injecting fairness into contract relations?

ETHICAL ISSUES

14.1 David Pelzman owns a restaurant called "David's on the Main" in Columbus, Ohio. It is a trendy and popular restaurant that is always fully booked for New Year's Eve. Jeff Burrey of Columbus called and made a reservation for New Year's Eve at David's, but did not go to David's as he had planned.

Mr. Pelzman sued Mr. Burrey for breach of contract. Mr. Pelzman says he paid for food and scheduled staff based on the number of reservations he had received. In his suit, Mr. Pelzman asked for $440 in damages or the price of the two-person package for New Year's Eve that parties who wish to participate pay.

Mr. Burrey, upon being served with the suit for his failure to arrive said, "Never in a million years did I think it was a contract. If they can sue a customer for not showing up for a reservation, then a customer can sue the restaurant for having to wait 15 minutes to be seated when they have a reservation."

Do you think that Mr. Burrey and David's had a contract? Was it fair of Mr. Burrey to make a reservation and then not show up? Was it ethical for Mr. Burrey to do so? Is it a proper use of the courts to have Mr. Pelzman filing this type of suit?

COMMUNICATION OF THE OFFER

An offer must be communicated to the offeree before it is valid. A letter in which an offer is made is not an offer until the letter reaches the offeree. For example, suppose Office Max had prepared an offer letter that included a substantial price discount for computers that was about to be mailed to Renco Rental Equipment so that Renco might buy the computers at the substantial discount. Before the letter is mailed, the machines offered in the letter are in high demand, and Office Max decides that rather than make its discount offer, it will just sell the machines easily in the retail market. The letter to Renco and other Office Max customers is never mailed. Renco, realizing the value of the computers and learning of the unmailed letter, cannot accept the discount computer offer because it was never communicated to them.

Some forms of communication are not treated as offers. For example, newspaper and television ads are considered invitations for offers. The ads are communicated to too many people for them to be considered part of an offer and are treated as preliminary negotiations only.

TERMINATION OF AN OFFER BY REVOCATION

Because an offer is one-sided, it can be revoked anytime before acceptance by the offeree. **Revocation** occurs when the offeror notifies the offeree that the offer is no longer good.

There are some limitations on revocation. One such limitation has already been mentioned: Acceptance by the offeree cuts off the right to revoke. Also, under common law, **options** cannot be revoked. An option is a contract in which the offeree pays the offeror for the time needed to consider the offer. For example, suppose that Yolanda's Yogurt is contemplating opening a new restaurant, and Yolanda has a property location in mind but is uncertain about the market potential. Yolanda does not want the property to be sold to someone else until she can complete a market study. Yolanda could pay the seller (offeror) a sum of money to hold the offer open for 30 days. During that 30-day period, the offeror can neither revoke the offer nor sell to anyone else.

Under the UCC, there is a form of an option that, without the offeree's payment, makes an offer irrevocable. Under a **merchant's firm offer** (see § 2-205 in Appendix G) the offer must be made by a merchant, put in writing, and signed by the merchant; moreover, the merchant must hold the offer open for a definite time period (but no longer than three months). A merchant is someone who is in the business of selling the goods that are the subject matter of the contract or holds particular skills or expertise in dealing with the goods. A rain check for sale merchandise from a store is an example of this type of offer. The firm offer cannot be revoked if the requirements are met, and money or consideration is not one of those requirements.

TERMINATION OF AN OFFER BY REJECTION

An offer carries no legally binding obligation for the offeree, who is free to accept or reject the offer. Once the offeree rejects the offer, the offer is ended and cannot later be accepted without the offeror renewing the offer.

Rejection by Counteroffer under Common Law An offer also ends when the offeree does not fully reject the offer but rejects some portion of the offer or modifies it before acceptance. These changes and rejections are called **counteroffers**. The effect of a counteroffer is that the original offer is no longer valid, and the offeree now becomes the offeror as the counteroffer becomes the new offer. Consider the following dialogue as an example:

> Alice: I will pay you $50 to paint the trim on my house.
> Brad: I will do it for $75.

Alice made the first offer. Brad's language is a counteroffer and a rejection at the same time. Alice is now free to accept or reject the $75 offer. If Alice declines the $75 counteroffer, Brad cannot then force Alice to contract for the original $50 because the offer ended. The following "Consider" deals with an issue of offers and counteroffers.

C O N S I D E R . . .   **14.4** December 30, 1977: John Hancock Insurance Company sends a commitment letter to Houston Dairy offering to loan Houston $800,000 at 9.25 percent interest; acceptance must be in writing within seven days and must be accompanied by a $16,000 letter of credit or cashier's check.

Continued

January 17, 1978: President of Houston Dairy sends letter of acceptance to Hancock along with cashier's check.

January 23, 1978: Hancock cashes the check (check went through standard company processing).

Hancock claims there is no contract because the acceptance occurred after the offer had expired. Houston Dairy maintains that its letter of acceptance was a new offer that was accepted by Hancock with the cashing of the check. Who is correct? Is there a contract?

Business Planning Tip

Docketing deadlines is important for businesses. Also, checks that a company receives should be reconciled with the purpose of payment to be certain that accidental overpayments (or, as in the Hancock case, acceptances) do not occur through oversight.

Rejection by Counteroffer under the UCC Under the UCC, modification by offerees was seen as a necessary part of doing business, and Section 2-207 (see Appendix G) allows flexibility for such modifications. Section 2-207 has two separate rules for modifications; one governs merchants and the other governs nonmerchant transactions. Exhibit 14.2 provides a visual overview of the UCC's rules for additional terms in acceptance.

For nonmerchants, the addition of terms in the counteroffer does not result in a rejection; there will still be a contract if there is a clear intent to contract, but the additional terms will not be a part of the contract. For example, consider the following dialogue:

Joe: I will sell you my pinball machine for $250.
Jan: I'll take it. Include $10 in dimes.

Joe and Jan have a contract, but the $10 in dimes is not a part of the contract. If Jan wanted the dimes, she should have negotiated before formally accepting the offer.

Exhibit 14.2
UCC Rules for Additional Terms in Acceptance

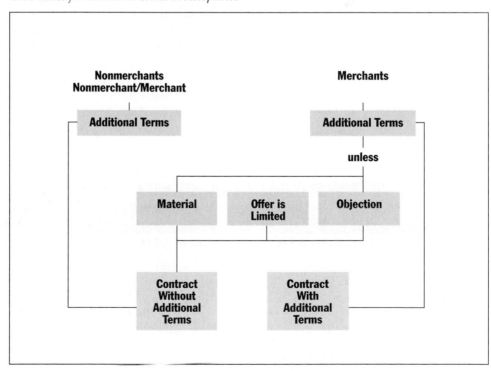

For merchants (both parties must be merchants), Section 2-207 has more complicated rules and details on additional terms in acceptance. Sometimes called the **battle of the forms**, Section 2-207 covers situations in which offerors and offerees send purchase orders and invoices back and forth with the understanding that they have a contract. Under Section 2-207, if the parties reach a basic agreement but the offeree has added terms, there will be an enforceable contract; the added terms are not a rejection under Section 2-207. Whether the added terms will become a part of the contract depends on the following questions:

1. Are the terms material?
2. Was the offer limited?
3. Does one side object?

If the terms the offeree adds to the original offer terms are *material*, they do not become a part of the contract. For example, suppose that Alfie sent a purchase order to Bob for 12 dozen red four-inch balloons at 4 cents each. Bob sends back an invoice that reflects the quantity and price, but Bob's invoice also has a section that states, "There are no warranties express or implied on these goods." Do Alfie and Bob have a contract with or without warranties? The waiver of warranties is a material change in what Alfie gets: now a contract without warranties. Because it is material, Section 2-207 protects Alfie and the warranty waiver is not part of the contract.

Terms that can be added but are not considered material are such payment terms as "30 days same as cash." Shipment terms are generally immaterial unless the method of shipment is unusually costly.

An offeror can avoid the problems of form battles and Section 2-207 by simply *limiting* the offer to the terms stated. Language that could be used would be: "This offer is limited to these terms." If the offeree attempts to add terms in the acceptance, there will be a contract, but the added terms will not be part of the contract. For example, suppose Alfie's offer on the balloons was limited and Bob accepted but added that the payment terms were "30 days same as cash." They would still have a contract but without the additional payment term.

A final portion of Section 2-207 allows the parties to take action to eliminate additional terms. They can do so by *objecting* to any added terms within a reasonable time. For example, if Alfie's offer was not limited and Bob accepted the payment terms, Alfie could object to the payment terms and they would then not be a part of the contract. Exhibit 14.2 summarizes the UCC's Section 2-207 rules.

The *Schulze* case is an example of one involving a 2-207 issue. It provides an answer for the chapter's opening "Judgment."

Schulze and Burch Biscuit Co. v. Tree Top, Inc.
831 F.2d 709 (7th Cir. 1987)

CHUNKY APPLE POWDER, CLOGGED MACHINES, AND PURCHASE ORDERS

FACTS

In the transaction that gave rise to the dispute in this case, Schulze and Burch Biscuit Company (Schulze) purchased low-moisture 16-mesh dehydrated apple powder from Tree Top, Inc. (Tree Top) to use in making strawberry and blueberry "Toastettes," which it sells to Nabisco, Inc.

On April 27, 1984, E. Edward Park, Schulze's director of procurement, telephoned Rudolph

Continued

Brady, a broker for Tree Top, and ordered 40,000 pounds of Tree Top's apple powder. Mr. Park told Mr. Brady that the purchase was subject to a Schulze purchase order and gave Mr. Brady the number of the purchase order, but Mr. Park did not send the purchase order or a copy of it to Mr. Brady or to Tree Top. On the front of the purchase order was the following clause:

Important: The fulfillment of this order or any part of it obligates the Seller to abide by the terms, conditions and instructions on both sides of this order. Additional or substitute terms will not become part of this contract unless expressly accepted by Buyer; Seller's acceptance is limited to the terms of this order, and no contract will be formed except on these terms.

Shortly after the telephone conversation, Mr. Brady sent Schulze a form entitled simply "Confirmation" that listed Mr. Brady as broker, Schulze as buyer, and Tree Top as seller as well as the quantity, price, shipping arrangements, and payment terms. It also showed the purchase order number that Mr. Park had given to Mr. Brady. Several preprinted provisions, including an arbitration clause, stood on the lower portion of the form:

Seller guarantees goods to conform to the national pure food laws. All disputes under this transaction shall be arbitrated in the usual manner. This confirmation shall be subordinate to more formal contract, when and if such contract is executed. In the absence of such contract, this confirmation represents the contract of the parties. If incorrect, please advise immediately.

Mr. Brady had sent a similar confirmation form to Schulze in each of at least 10 previous transactions between Tree Top and Schulze. Schulze had never objected to any of the preprinted provisions. Schulze had sent Mr. Brady a purchase order in two of those transactions; in each of the other transactions, as in the present case, Schulze simply informed Mr. Brady of the number of the appropriate purchase order.

Subsequently, Schulze brought suit seeking damages for breach of contract, alleging that the dehydrated apple powder had been so full of apple stems and wood splinters that it clogged the machinery of Schulze's Toastette assembly line, causing the line to shut down, with various financial losses. Schulze alleged that the powder thus failed to meet Schulze's specifications, which had governed the previous sales of apple powder. Tree Top alleged that the dispute was subject to arbitration because of the arbitration clause in the confirmation sent by Mr. Brady to Schulze.

The trial court ordered Schulze to submit to arbitration. Schulze appealed.

JUDICIAL OPINION
ESCHBACH, Senior Circuit Judge
The resolution of this case depends upon UCC § 2-207.

In this case, Brady, acting as Tree Top's agent, sent a confirmation that contained terms additional to those discussed by Brady and Schulze. Schulze did not object to the additional terms. Whether the contract was formed orally by the telephone call or by the confirmation acting as an acceptance, the arbitration clause was a term "additional to or different from those offered or agreed upon." The parties have proceeded on the assumption that they are both "merchants" for the purposes of § 2-207. The principal issue is thus whether the addition of the arbitration term would "materially alter" the contract. If so. . . . it would not become part of the contract.

Illinois courts, in deciding whether particular clauses are material alterations, have looked to the [UCC] Comment's formulation that a material alteration is one that would "result in surprise or hardship if incorporated without express awareness by the other party." Under Illinois law, the test for whether an additional term would be a material alteration in the contract is "whether the addition constitutes an unreasonable surprise to one of the bargaining parties."

Continued

No Illinois court has addressed the question whether addition of a clause providing for arbitration of disputes between the contracting parties is a material alteration. Some courts in other jurisdictions have held that to be a question that depends on the circumstances of each case. Other courts have followed the "New York rule" that addition of an arbitration clause is a material alteration.

But even in New York, courts have held that addition of an arbitration clause is not a material alteration if the party had reason to know that such a clause would be included in a confirmation.

In the present case, Tree Top did not offer proof of a trade usage of using arbitration to resolve disputes. But Tree Top did offer evidence of a prior course of dealing between the parties that would give notice to Schulze that an arbitration clause would likely be included in the confirmation.

In the present case, Tree Top's agent Brady had sent a confirmation form containing the same arbitration provision to Schulze in each of the previous nine transactions he brokered between the two parties. Schulze had ample notice that the tenth confirmation would be likely to include an arbitration clause. To prevent the clause from becoming part of the contract, Schulze needed only to give notice of objection within a reasonable time. As a matter of law, inclusion of such a clause in the tenth confirmation was not "unfair surprise." Therefore the addition of the arbitration clause was not a material addition to the contract, under the test used in Illinois law.

The next issue is whether Schulze's offer was one that "expressly limits acceptance to the terms of the offer" under § 2-207(2)(a). If so, under § 2-207(2)(a), additional terms in the acceptance do not become part of the contract. During the telephone conversation in which Park placed the order for the apple powder, he informed Brady that the transaction was "subject to" Schulze purchase order 11621. Schulze never sent the purchase order to Brady or to Tree Top. . . . In two of the previous ten transactions between Schulze and Tree Top that Brady

had brokered, Schulze had sent the purchase order to Brady.

Even assuming that the purchase order became part of the parties' contract, we hold that it was not, for the purposes of UCC § 2-207, an offer that *"expressly* limits acceptance to the terms of the offer" (emphasis added). In this case, neither Brady nor Tree Top could have seen the purchasing offer with the limiting language. Although Schulze had sent a purchase order in two of the previous nine transactions, that is insufficient to give notice that mere reference to the number of a purchase order is intended "expressly" to make the order acceptable only on the terms in a purchase order that remains unseen. That indirect incorporation falls short of an "express" limitation.

Because the offer did not expressly limit acceptance to its terms and because, as discussed above, the addition of the arbitration clause was not a material addition to the contract, the arbitration clause became part of the contract under § 2-207(2).

For the reasons stated, the judgment of the district court is affirmed.

CASE QUESTIONS

1. What was the problem with the powder?
2. In which document did the arbitration clause appear?
3. Is arbitration a material change?
4. Was the offer limited to the terms of the offer?
5. Did Tree Top have an ethical obligation to furnish apple powder that did not clog the machinery of Schulze and Burch? Does industry custom require that the apple powder be free of nonpowder items? Did Tree Top know of Schulze and Burch's planned use? Does that make a difference in your view of the ethics in the case?

Aftermath: Schulze and Burch still manufactures "Toastettes" and its name can be found on the box.

C O N S I D E R . . . 14.5 In the following three dialogues, determine whether there would be a contract if two nonmerchants were having the dialogue and then whether there would be a contract if two merchants were having the dialogue. If there is a contract, determine for both merchants and nonmerchants whether the additional terms mentioned during the dialogue would be part of their contract.

1. A: "I'll sell you my Peugot bicycle for $100."
    B: "I'll take it. Include your tire pump."
    Result:
    Nonmerchants _____
    Merchants _____

2. A: "I'll sell you my white 1974 Ford Torino for $358. This offer is limited to these terms."
    B: "I'll take it. Furnish a history of repairs."
    Result:
    Nonmerchants _____
    Merchants _____

3. A: "I'll sell you my antique Coca-Cola sign."
    B: "I'll take it if you will deliver it."
    Result:
    Nonmerchants _____
    Merchants _____

TERMINATION BY OFFER EXPIRATION

An offer can end by expiring, and once expired can no longer be accepted by the offeree. For example, if an offer states that it will remain open until November 1, it automatically terminates on November 1 and no one has the power to accept the offer after that time. The death of the offeror also ends the offer unless the offeree holds an option. Even offers without time limits expire after a reasonable time has passed. For example, an offer to buy a home is probably only good for one or two weeks because the offeror needs to know whether to try for another house. The offeror's offer terminates naturally if the offeree fails to accept within that time frame.

Acceptance: The Offeree's Response

An **acceptance** is the offeree's positive response to the offeror's proposed contract, and only persons to whom the offer is made have the power of acceptance. That acceptance must be communicated to the offeror using the proper method of communication, which can be controlled by the offeror or left to the offeree. In either case, the method of communication controls the effective time of the acceptance.

Business Planning Tip

Many businesses are relying on fax machines for offers and acceptances. These machines offer the benefit of quick, written documents. However, clarity is often sacrificed, and fax paper can fade. Further, in several recent cases signatures had been taped onto faxed copies. There was no authentic signature, and the taped signature could not be detected on the fax. Always follow up your faxes with actual documents for signature.

ACCEPTANCE BY STIPULATED MEANS

Some offerors give a required means of acceptance that is called a **stipulated means**. If the offeree uses the stipulated means of acceptance, the acceptance is effective sooner than the offeror's receipt; the acceptance is effective when it is properly sent. For example, if the offeror has required the acceptance to be mailed and the offeree properly mails the letter of acceptance, the acceptance is effective when it is sent. This timing rule for acceptance is called the **mailbox rule** and it applies in stipulated means offers so long as the offeree uses the stipulated means to communicate acceptance.

ACCEPTANCE WITH NO STIPULATED MEANS

If the offeror does not stipulate a means of acceptance, the offeree is free to use any method for communication of the acceptance. If the offeree uses the same method of communication or a faster one than that used by the offeror, the mailbox rule will also apply. If the offeree uses a slower method of acceptance, the acceptance is not effective until it is received. Exhibit 14.3 summarizes the timing of acceptance rules.

Type of Offer	Method of Acceptance	Acceptance Effective?
No means given	Same or faster method of communication	When properly mailed, dispatched (mailbox rule)
No means given	Slower method of communication	When received if offer still open
Means specified (Stipulated means)	Stipulated means used	Mailbox rule
Means stipulated (Specified means)	Stipulated means not used	Counteroffer and rejection

Exhibit 14.3
Timing Rules for Acceptance

C O N S I D E R . . .   **14.6** Under the following sequence of events, determine if a contract has been formed and, if so, when.

DAY 1: Oscar offers to sell his car to Ethan in a letter offer.
DAY 2: Ethan receives Oscar's offer.
DAY 3: Ethan mails an acceptance to Oscar.
DAY 4: Oscar calls to revoke the offer.

Consideration

Consideration is what distinguishes gifts from contracts and is what each party—offeror and offeree—gives up under the contract; it is sometimes called **bargained-for exchange**. If you sign a contract to buy a 1980 Mercedes for $17,000, your consideration is the $17,000 and is given in exchange for the car. The seller's consideration is giving up the car and is given in exchange for your $17,000. On the other hand, if your grandmother tells you that she will give you her Mercedes, there is no consideration, and your grandmother's promise (unfortunately) is not a contract and is not enforceable.

The courts are not concerned with the amount or nature of consideration so long as it is actually passed from one party to the other. A contract is not unenforceable because a court feels you paid too little under the contract terms. The amount of consideration is left to the discretion of the parties.

The following case deals with nearly all the issues involved in consideration.

Hayes v. Plantations Steel Co.
438 A.2d 1091 (R.I. 1982)

IS RETIREMENT WORTH IT? GIFT VS. PENSION

FACTS

Plantations is a closely held Rhode Island corporation that manufactures steel reinforcing rods for use in concrete construction. The company was founded by Hugo R. Mainelli, Sr., and Alexander A. DiMartino. A dispute between their two families in 1976 and 1977 left the DiMartinos in full control of the corporation. Edward J. Hayes had been an employee of the corporation for 25 years. He began with Plantations in 1947 as an estimator and draftsman and retired in 1972 at 65 as general manager, a position of considerable responsibility.

In January 1972, Mr. Hayes announced his intention to retire in July of that year because he had worked continuously for 51 years. He stated that he would not have retired, however, had he not expected to receive a pension.

Approximately one week before his actual retirement, Mr. Hayes spoke with Hugo R. Mainelli, Jr., who was then an officer and a stockholder of Plantations. This conversation was the first and only one concerning payments of a pension to Mr. Hayes during retirement. Mr. Mainelli said that the company "would take care" of him. There was no mention, however, of a sum of money or a percentage of salary that Hayes would receive, nor was there a formal authorization for payments by Plantations' shareholders and/or board of

directors. Starting in January 1973 and continuing until January 1976, Hayes received an annual sum of $5,000 from Plantations. After he stopped working for Plantations, he sought no other employment.

Mr. Mainelli said that his father, Hugo R. Mainelli, Sr., had authorized the first payment "as a token of appreciation for the many years of [Hayes'] service." Furthermore, "it was implied that that check would continue on an annual basis." Mr. Mainelli also testified that it was his "personal intention" that the payments would continue for "as long as I was around."

Mr. Mainelli said that after Mr. Hayes' retirement, he visited the premises each year to say hello and renew old acquaintances. During the course of his visits, Mr. Hayes would thank Mr. Mainelli for the previous check and ask how long it would continue so that he could plan an orderly retirement.

The payments were discontinued after 1976. At that time a succession of several poor business years plus the stockholders' dispute, which resulted in the takeover by the DiMartino family, contributed to the decision to stop the payments.

Mr. Hayes brought suit in 1977 after the company refused to make payments. The trial court found that Mr. Hayes had retired in reliance on Mr. Mainelli's promise and the court enforced the agreement. Plantations appealed.

Continued

JUDICIAL OPINION

SHEA, Justice

We turn first to the problem of consideration. The facts at bar do not present the case of an express contract. As the trial justice stated, the existence of a contract in this case must be determined from all the circumstances of the parties' conduct and words. Although words were expressed initially in the remark that Hayes "would be taken care of," any contract in this case would be more in the nature of an implied contract. Certainly the statement of Hugo Mainelli, Jr., standing alone is not an expression of a direct and definite promise to pay Hayes a pension. Though we are analyzing an implied contract, nevertheless we must address the question of consideration.

Contracts implied in fact require the element of consideration to support them as is required in express contracts. The only difference between the two is the manner in which the parties manifest their assent. In this jurisdiction, consideration consists either in some right, interest, or benefit accruing to one party or some forbearance, detriment, or responsibility given, suffered, or undertaken by the other. Valid consideration furthermore must be bargained for. It must induce the return act or promise. To be valid, therefore, the purported consideration must not have been delivered before a promise is executed, that is, given without reference to the promise. Consideration is therefore a test of the enforceability of executory promises and has no legal effect when rendered in the past and apart from an alleged exchange in the present.

In the case before us, Plantations's promise to pay Hayes a pension is quite clearly not supported by any consideration supplied by Hayes. Hayes had announced his intent to retire well in advance of any promise, and therefore the intention to retire was arrived at without regard to any promise by Plantations. Although Hayes may have had in mind the receipt of a pension when he first informed Plantations, his expectation was not based on any statement made to him or on any conduct of the company officer relative to him in January 1972. In deciding to retire, Hayes acted on his own initiative. Hayes's long years of dedicated service also is legally insufficient because his service too was rendered without being induced by Plantations's promise.

Clearly then this is not a case in which Plantations's promise was meant to induce Hayes to refrain from retiring when he could have chosen to do so in return for further service. Nor was the promise made to encourage long service from the start of his employment. Instead, the testimony establishes that Plantations's promise was intended "as a token of appreciation for [Hayes'] many years of service." As such it was in the nature of a gratuity paid to Hayes for as long as the company chose.

Hayes also argues that the work he performed during the week between the promise and the date of his retirement constituted sufficient consideration to support the promise.

Hayes left his employment because he no longer desired to work. He was not contemplating other job offers or considering going into competition with Plantations. Although Plantations did not want Hayes to leave, it did not try to deter him, nor did it seek to prevent Hayes from engaging in other activity.

Hayes argues in the alternative that even if Plantations's promise was not the product of an exchange, its duty is grounded properly in the theory of promissory estoppel.

Hayes urges that in the absence of a bargained-for promise the facts require application of the doctrine of promissory estoppel. He stresses that he retired voluntarily while expecting to receive a pension. He would not have otherwise retired. Nor did he seek other employment.

We disagree with this contention largely for the reasons already stated. One of the essential elements of the doctrine of promissory estoppel is that the promise must *induce* the promisee's action or forbearance. The particular act in this regard is plaintiff's decision whether or not to retire. As we stated earlier, the record indicates that he made the decision on his own initiative. In other words, the conversation between Hayes and Mainelli which occurred a week before Hayes left his employment cannot be said to have induced his decision to leave. He had reached that decision long before.

Continued

The underlying assumption of Hayes's initial decision to retire was that upon leaving the defendant's employ, he would no longer work. It is impossible to say that he changed his position any more so because of what Mainelli had told him in light of his own initial decision. These circumstances do not lead to a conclusion that injustice can be avoided only by enforcement of Plantations's promise. Hayes received $20,000 over the course of four years. He inquired each year about whether he could expect a check for the following year. Obviously, there was no absolute certainty on his part that the pension would continue. Furthermore, in the face of his uncertainty, the mere fact that payment for several years did occur is insufficient by itself to meet the requirements of reliance under the doctrine of promissory estoppel.

For the foregoing reasons, the defendant's appeal is sustained and the judgment of the Superior Court is reversed.

CASE QUESTIONS
1. Did Mr. Hayes retire in reliance on Mr. Mainelli's promise?
2. What did Mr. Hayes maintain about the week he remained employed prior to retirement?
3. Did the promise induce the detriment?
4. Is the promise to pay the funds supported by consideration?
5. Is there an ethical obligation to continue the payments?

FOR THE MANAGER'S DESK

THE ETHICS OF SCANNERS

Maybe they should call them 'scammers': Electronic checkout systems may be ripping you off

Hercule Poirot has nothing on Inspector Robert W. Alviene. It's just after Christmas, and Alviene, an official with the Morris County Office of Weights & Measures, is walking the aisles of a Bradlees Inc. Store in East Hanover, N.J., dropping items into his shopping cart. He isn't looking for post-Christmas bargains. He wants to know if Bradlees' electronic checkout scanning system is overcharging customers.

Sure enough, for the third time in three months at this store, Alviene finds mistakes at the checkout. A $21.99 set

of bedsheets scans at $29.99, and a $3.99 rawhide dog bone costs 50¢ more than it should. In all, six of the 17 items in his cart have the wrong price in the scanner, resulting in an overcharge of $12.30 on a $161.85 total purchase. A Bradlees spokesman calls the results "troubling" but denies that the company intentionally bilks anyone. All the same, says Alviene, "the customer is really getting burned in there."

Alviene's shopping trip, expected to produce a fine for the store, is the latest in a nationwide crackdown on scanner overcharges. A Dec. 14 survey by Vermont's attorney general found that local outlets

Continued

of Ames Department Stores Inc. and Rich's Department Stores had serious errors in their scanning systems. Two days later, Michigan Attorney General Frank J.Kelley announced similar findings at Sears, Roebuck & Co. and Wal-Mart Stores Inc. And J. C. Penney Co. is in settlement talks with San Diego County over its alleged mispricing. The Federal Trade Commission is now working to coordinate the proliferating state and local probes.

Authorities and the retailers say mistakes are a result of human error, not fraud. They say the lapses occur when store clerks fail to enter correct data into scanner computers, especially when prices change. Still, experts believe that the impact, which no one has tallied, is enormous. "It's a serious national problem," says Ken Butcher, weights and measure coordinator at the National Institute of Standards & Technology.

To Err Is Common
Investigators are focusing on nonfood retailers—such as discounters and department stores—which recently started using scanning technology. Although the technology is capable of 100 percent accuracy, some stores average as low as 85 percent, says Butcher. And the mistakes often favor retailers.A California survey of 9,000 items from 300 stores found overcharges on 2 percent of the products and undercharges on 1.3

percent. A Michigan study found a 4-to-1 ratio of overpricing to underpricing. "It's one of the few places you can be negligent and make money," says Michigan Assistant Attorney General Frederick Hoffecker.

Retailers staunchly defend the systems, noting that scanners are more accurate than clerks—who punch in the wrong prices about 10 percent of the time, according to NIST estimates. Some companies also say the issue is being blown out of proportion. "There are a number of individuals around the country who are always looking for ways to achieve instant press, and scanning accuracy seems to be a hot button right now," says a Wal-Mart spokesman.

True, regulators' sampling methods may be skewing their results: By relying heavily on sale items that have frequent price changes, the surveys suggest an inflated error rate, retailers say. Yet consumer advocates argue that high-volume sale items are where most rip-offs are likely to occur. "If a customer shoplifts, it's called a crime," gripes Pennsylvania consumer advocate Mary Bach. "But a store can 'shopper-lift,' and it's called a mistake."

To complicate matters, scanners' speed and the disappearance of price tags make it hard to detect errors. "I keep my eye on the prices when they light up after they get scanned," says Carol Hennessey, a 53-year-old office-supply-store employee as

she waits in line at a supermarket in Morris Plains, N.J. Hennessey says she has caught several stores mischarging her, "but you've got to wonder how many times you don't catch it."

To combat pressure from law enforcement agencies, some retailers have launched programs to improve their scanning systems. As part of a $985,000 settlement in May with San Diego County, Kmart Corp. designated a manager in each store nationwide to make sure prices in scanning computers match those advertised. Rich's Department Stores is mulling a similar move. Bradlees charges the correct amount when a mistake is brought to its attention. Some stores go further. Sears, which says it has a 95 percent accuracy rate, rebates $5 or 5 percent off mischarged items, whichever is more. And Wal-Mart gives a $3 refund per item.

That's scant comfort, however, for customers who think they've been had but can't prove it. For now, keep track of shelf prices, and hold on to your receipts. Inspector Alviene and his cohorts could be coming to a store near you soon.

Discussion Questions

1. Is a contract formed at the grocery store? When?
2. What is the price to be paid for the goods? The advertised price? The price at the shelf? The scanned price?
3. Could customers obtain a refund?

UNIQUE CONSIDERATION ISSUES

The concept of consideration and its requirement for contract formation has presented courts with some unique problems. Often an element of fairness and reliance exists in circumstances in which there is an offer and acceptance but no consideration. For example, many nonprofit organizations raise funds through pledges. Such pledges are not supported by consideration, but the nonprofit organizations rely on those pledges. Called **charitable subscriptions**, the courts enforce these agreements despite the lack of consideration.

The doctrine of **promissory estoppel** is also used as a substitute for consideration in those cases in which someone acts in reliance on a promise that is not supported by consideration. For example, suppose an employer said, "Move to Denver and I'll hire you." There is no detriment on your part until you begin work. The employer has no detriment either. However, if you sold your home in Phoenix and incurred the expense of moving to Denver, it would be unfair to allow the employer to claim the contract did not exist because of no consideration. You have acted in reliance on a promise, and that reliance serves as a consideration substitute.

CONSIDER... **14.7** Florence I. Kauth (formerly Florence I. Graber) sold seven and a half acres of a 10-acre parcel to Mabel St. Clair Schenley. The price was $325 per acre, and as part of the same transaction, Mrs. Kauth wrote the following:

June 17, 1941

Mabel St. Clair Schenley:

As a consideration of your purchase of 7^1/$_2$ acre tract belonging to me, located in Franklin Township, Summit County, Ohio, I hereby give you the option to purchase the remaining 2^1/$_2$ acres belonging to me, which joins your 7^1/$_2$ acre tract to the north, at the same price per acre as you are paying for the 7^1/$_2$ acre tract; namely, $325 per acre.

This option is granted to you only in the event I desire to sell the 2^1/$_2$ acre tract.

Very truly yours,
Florence I. Graber

Several years after this transaction, Mrs. Kauth traveled to California but told Mrs. Schenley that she would decide when she returned whether to sell the remaining two and a half acres.

When she returned, Mrs. Kauth told Mrs. Schenley that she would sell the property but only at a price far in excess of the amount of $325 per acre specified in the memorandum.

Mrs. Schenley refused to pay the higher price, and Mrs. Kauth sold the property to a third party. Mrs. Schenley would like to know her rights. Was there a contract? Did Mrs. Kauth breach the contract? [*Schenley* v. *Kauth*, 122 N.E.2d 189 (1953).]

Contract Form: When Writing Is Required

Some contracts can exist just on the basis of an oral promise. Others, however, are required to be in writing to be enforceable, and these contracts are covered under each state's **statute of frauds**.

Business Planning Tip

Electronic Contracts
The fax, the phone, and EDI (electronic
data interchange) allow businesses to do
business rapidly. Often transactions are
completed electronically with little or no
paperwork. Managers should follow these
tips in using these technological methods
of communication:
1. Follow up and verify to be certain
   someone with authority entered the
   transaction or sent the transmission.
2. Keep a hard copy for your records—
   "delete" OFTEN works too well.
3. Meet once each year to update your
   understanding of terms and your
   relationship.
4. Have your computer network
   checked for access and possible
   espionage.

COMMON LAW STATUTE OF FRAUDS

The term *statute of frauds* originated in 1677 when England passed the first rule dealing with written contracts: the Statute for the Prevention of Frauds and Perjuries. The purpose of the first statute and the descendant statutes today is to have written agreements for the types of contracts that might encourage conflicting claims and possible perjury if oral agreements were allowed. The following is a partial list of the types of contracts required to be in writing under most state laws:

1. Contracts for the sale of real property. This requirement includes sales, certain leases, liens, mortgages, and easements.
2. Contracts that cannot be performed within one year. These contracts run for long periods and require the benefit of written terms.
3. Contracts to pay the debt of another Cosigners' agreements to pay if a debtor defaults must be in writing. A corporate officer's personal guarantee of a corporate note must be in writing to be enforceable.

UCC STATUTE OF FRAUDS

Under the UCC, there is a separate statute of frauds for contracts covering the sale of goods. Contracts for the sale of goods costing $500 or more are required to be in writing to be enforceable.

C O N S I D E R . . .   **14.8** Which of the following contracts must be in writing to be enforceable?

1. A contract for the sale of an acre of land for $400
2. A contract for management consulting for six months for $353,000
3. A contract for the sale of a car for $358
4. A contract for a loan consigned by a corporation's vice president
5. A contract for the sale of a mobile home for $12,000

EXCEPTIONS TO THE STATUTE OF FRAUDS

There are some exceptions to the UCC and common law statute of frauds provisions that were created for situations in which the parties have partially or fully performed their unwritten contract. Under both the UCC and common law, if the parties go ahead and perform the oral contract, courts will enforce the contract for what has already been done. For example, if Alan agreed to sell land to Bertha under an oral contract and Bertha has paid, has the deed, and has moved in, Alan cannot use the statute of frauds to remove Bertha and get the land back.

WHAT FORM OF WRITING IS REQUIRED?

The form of writing required under the statute of frauds is not formal. Evidence of a written agreement can be pieced together from memos and letters. Under the UCC, merchants can meet the statute of frauds by sending confirmation memos (see § 2-201 in Appendix G). These **merchants' confirmation memoranda** summarize the oral agreement and are signed by only one party, but they can be used to satisfy the statute of frauds so long as the memo has been sent to the nonsigning party for review and there is no objection upon review.

Figure 14.4 provides a summary of UCC and common law formation provisions.

Area	UCC	Common Law
Application	Sales of goods	Services, real estate, employment contracts
Offers	Need subject matter (quantity), Code gives details	Need subject matter, price, terms, full details agreed upon
Options	Merchant's firm offer—no consideration needed	Need consideration
Acceptance	Can have additional terms	Mirror image rule followed
	Mailbox rule works for reasonable means of acceptance	Must use same/faster method for mailbox rule to get mailbox rule (old rule: same method)*
Consideration	Required for contracts but not for modification or firm offers	Always required
Writing Requirement	Sale of goods $500 or more	Real estate, contracts not to be performed in one year; paying the debt of another
Defenses*	Must be free of all defenses for valid contract	Must be free of all defenses for valid contract

*See Chapter 15

Exhibit 14.4
Common Law vs. UCC Rules on Formation

C O N S I D E R . . . **14.9** H.K.A. Enterprises, Inc., owned a houseboat that it rented to large corporations for entertaining customers and clients on Mississippi River cruises. H.K.A. wished to sell the houseboat and there were a series of telephone conversations between H.K.A. executives and those of Northport Marine for the purchase of the boat for $38,000. Northport sailed the boat from H.K.A.'s facility in La Crosse, Wisconsin, to its marina in Alma.

H.K.A. called Northport's president and asked him to have an appraisal done since H.K.A. was going to take legal action against a former lessee for damage to the boat. Several weeks later H.K.A. wrote to Northport "to reconfirm our agreement . . . to sell you our houseboat . . . for the sum of $38,000."

Northport responded and said it would purchase the boat for $20,000. H.K.A. sued for breach of contract.

Was there a contract formed? Was there a sufficient writing? [*First Bank (N.A.) v. H.K.A. Enterprises, Inc.,* 515 N.W.2d 343 (Wis. 1994).]

Boxing promoter Don King is responsible for negotiating contracts for some of the biggest names and title fights in modern boxing. For example, he negotiates all fights for world heavyweight champion Mike Tyson.

Don King—Altering Contracts?

Mr. King is known as a ruthless promoter who focuses on the "showmanship" of the fight and never signs an agreement that won't make money for him and everyone involved. From the time a contract is signed, Mr. King creates tension between the fighters and uses the sports press to generate public interest in the fight, which translates to box office ticket sales. Those in the boxing field have said that all Mr. King needs is two fighters, and he stages the rest. He has been credited with bringing boxing to mainstream television and to the forefront of sports coverage.

Don King

Mr. King always insures with Lloyd's of London for his fights because of the promotional costs involved, which are often incurred before a fighter cancels. Without insurance, Mr. King must bear those costs.

In 1991, Mr. King negotiated a contract between Julio Cesar Chavez and Harold Brazier for a boxing match, but the fight was canceled. The cancellation, however, occurred before any significant expenditures by Mr. King.

Joseph Maffia, the accountant for Don King Productions, Inc., said that Mr. King asked him to alter the contract terms to show that Mr. Chavez had received $350,000 in training fees. Mr. Chavez says he never received $350,000, but Mr. King submitted the contract to Lloyd's and received reimbursement.

A criminal trial of Mr. King for wire fraud and falsification of documents resulted in a hung jury with him facing a retrial.

Lloyd's of London has filed a civil suit against Mr. King to collect the $350,000 plus expenses.

Issues

1. Would parol evidence be admissible to prove the $350,000 was not paid?

2. Why are there both criminal and civil suits?

3. Have Mr. King's tactics helped or hurt professional boxing?

THE EFFECT OF THE WRITTEN CONTRACT— PAROL EVIDENCE

Once a contract is reduced to its final written form and is complete and unambiguous, the parties to the contract are not permitted to contradict the contract terms with evidence of their negotiations or verbal agreement sat the time the contractwas executed. This prohibition on extrinsic evidence for fully integrated contracts is called the **parol evidence** rule and is a means for stoppingongoing contradictions to contracts that have been entered into and finalized. It is a protection for the application of the document to the parties' rights as well as a reminder of the need to put the true nature of the agreement into the contract.

There are some exceptions to the parol evidence rule. If a contract is incomplete or the terms are ambiguous, extrinsic evidence can be used to clarify or complete the contract, as in the case of UCC contracts in which price, delivery, and payment terms can be added (see § 2-202 in Appendix G). Also, if one of the parties to the contract is alleging a defense to the contract's formation, then evidence of the circumstances creating that defense can be used as evidence. Evidence of lack of capacity or fraud do not violate the parol evidence rule. The following case involves an issue of parol evidence.

Intershoe, Inc. v. Bankers Trust
569 N.Y.S.2d 33 (1991)

LIRA, SHOES, AND EXCHANGE RATES

FACTS

Intershoe, Inc. (plaintiff), is a shoe importer that uses various foreign currencies, including Italian lira, in its business.

On March 3, 1985, Intershoe phoned Bankers Trust (defendant) and entered into several foreign currency transactions, one being a futures transaction involving lira. On March 13, Bankers Trust sent Intershoe a confirmation slip with the following terms: "WE [Bankers] HAVE BOUGHT FROM YOU [Intershoe] ITL 537,750,000" and "WE HAVE SOLD TO YOU USD 250,000.00."

The confirmation slip specified a rate of 2,151 lira per dollar and called for delivery of the lira approximately seven and a half months later, between October 1 and October 31, 1985. Intershoe's treasurer signed the slip and returned it to Bankers Trust on March 18, 1985.

By letter dated October 11, 1985, Bankers Trust notified Intershoe that it was awaiting instructions as to Intershoe's delivery of the lira. Bankers Trust responded in a letter dated October 25, 1985, that the transaction was a mistake and that it would not go through with it.

Continued

To cover commitments in other currency transactions, Bankers Trust was forced to purchase lira on the open market at a higher price than that on March 13, 1985, resulting in a loss of $55,014.85.

Intershoe filed suit claiming that it had purchased, not sold, lira and that it had sustained damages of $59,336.40. Bankers Trust counterclaimed for its damages.

The trial court held that there were issues of fact. Bankers Trust maintained that the case should be decided in its favor by summary judgment because of the parol evidence rule and appealed.

JUDICIAL OPINION

HANCOCK, JR., Justice

We turn to defendant's argument that UCC § 2-202 bars the parol evidence submitted in opposition to its motion.

There seems to be no question that the UCC applies to foreign currency transactions. Plaintiff does not dispute this point. Instead, plaintiff simply asserts that UCC § 2-202 has no application because defendant has not made a sufficient showing that the confirmation slip was "intended by the parties as a final expression of their agreement with respect to such terms as are included therein." Something more is required, plaintiff says, either language in the confirmation slip indicating that it was intended to be the final expression of the parties' agreement or uncontroverted evidence that the writing was so intended. Otherwise, according to plaintiff, there are factual issues as to the effect the parties intended the confirmation slip to have and summary judgment must be denied. We disagree.

Here, the essential terms of the transaction are plainly set forth in the confirmation slip: that plaintiff had sold lira to defendant, the amount of the lira it sold, the exchange rate, the amount of dollars to be paid by defendant for the lira, and the maturity date of the transaction. The signature of plaintiff's agent who signed and returned the confirmation slip five days later on March 18, 1985 signifies plaintiff's acceptance of these terms. Nothing in the confirmation slip suggests that it was to be a memorandum of some preliminary or tentative understanding with respect to these

terms. On the contrary, it is difficult to imagine words which could more clearly demonstrate the final expression of the parties' agreement than "WE HAVE BOUGHT FROM YOU ITL 537,750,000" and "WE HAVE SOLD TO YOU USD 250,000.00."

The confirmation is not of some bargain to be made in the future but expresses the parties' meeting of the minds as to a completed bargain's essential terms—a sale of 537,750 lira at a rate of 2151 for 250,000 dollars—made in a telephone conversation on March 13, 1985. The only evidence plaintiff has tendered does no more than contradict the stated terms of the confirmation slip—the very evidence which UCC § 2-202 precludes. It does not address the critical question of whether the terms in the confirmation slip were intended to represent the parties' final agreement on those matters. We conclude that where, as here, the form and content of the confirmation slip suggest nothing other than that it was intended to be the final expression of the parties' agreement as to the terms set forth and where there is no evidence indicating that this was not so, UCC § 2-202 bars parol evidence of contradictory terms.

We reject plaintiff's contentions that UCC § 2-202 requires that there be some express indication in the writing itself or some other evidence that the parties intended it to be the final expression of their agreement. . . . To require that the record include specific extraneous evidence that the writing constitutes the parties' final agreement as to its stated terms would in many instances impose a virtually insurmountable obstacle for parties seeking to invoke UCC § 2-202, particularly in cases involving large commercial banks and other financial institutions which typically close hundreds of transactions over the telephone during a business day. As a practical matter, a confirmation slip or similar writing is usually the only reliable evidence of such transactions, given the unlikely prospect that one who makes scores of similar deals each day will remember the details of any one particular agreement. Indeed, this case is illustrative inasmuch as neither of the participants had a specific recollection of the March 13, 1985 telephone conversation.

Continued

Plaintiff also argues that UCC § 2-202 does not bar the parol evidence submitted in opposition to defendant's motion because it is offered to show that there was never a contract between the parties. This argument is unavailing. Plaintiff does not dispute that it entered into a foreign currency transaction with defendant; its only contention is that the transaction called for it to purchase and not sell lira. Hence, the parol evidence is being used to contradict a term of the contract, not to show that there was no contract, and UCC § 2-202 applies.

Reversed.

CASE QUESTIONS
1. Describe the transaction.
2. Who sold according to the memo?
3. Who sold according to Intershoe?
4. Is the memo a final writing?
5. What dangers would the court introduce if orders such as this were contradicted by oral testimony?
6. Did someone fail to read a document carefully before signing? Does the parol evidence rule allow "failure to read" as a defense?

C O N S I D E R . . .

14.10 In 1985 Antonio Mastrobuono, an assistant professor of medieval literature, and his wife, Diana Mastrobuono, an artist, opened a securities trading account with Shearson Lehman Hutton, Inc. (Shearson).

The Mastrobuonos signed Shearson's standard form client's agreement that contained a paragraph (paragraph 3) in which all clients of Shearson's agreed to submit disputes to arbitration. The arbitration clause provided that the arbitration panel could award punitive damages. The same paragraph specified that the parties agreed their contract would be governed by the laws of New York, but New York state law prohibits the award of punitive damages.

The Mastrobuonos closed their account in 1987 because they alleged it had been mishandled. The arbitration panel awarded $159,327 in compensatory damages and $400,000 in punitive damages to the Mastrobuonos. Shearson paid the compensatory damages but challenged the punitive damage award as violative of New York law.

Should the punitive damages be allowed? How should the court interpret this contract when it contradicts itself? [*Mastrobuono* v. *Shearson Lehman Hutton, Inc.*, 115 S. Ct. 1212 (1995).]

FOR THE MANAGER'S DESK

STRATEGIC SUPPLIER PARTNERING

As one views the complex rules of contract formation with all of its timing and wording issues, it seems that the relationships between buyers and sellers must be adversarial. Under traditional notions of contract law, this perception of distrust between buyers and sellers was probably correct. With international competition and business's recognition that partnerships allow more effective world-wide competition, a new form of business relationship has been evolving. Referred to as strategic supplier partnering, buyers and sellers develop contract relationships that are by legal standards very casual.

Continued

These relationships are based on the parties' needs. For example, Wal-Mart needs its shelves stocked with jeans for its customers to buy, and those jeans must be in the correct sizes. VFI Corporation, manufacturers of Lee jeans, needs to sell its product and get it out in the marketplace. Wal-Mart and VFI have a strategic partner relationship. The two are linked by computer. When someone in Holbrook, Arizona, buys that one pair of 48 W 28 L Lee jeans, VFI knows at its headquarters not only what is selling at the Holbrook Wal-Mart, it knows what to send to replenish the Wal-Mart inventory. VFI undertakes the electronic work necessary to get the jeans to Wal-Mart. In some cases, the jeans are back on the Wal-Mart shelves within two days.

These types of relationships are far beyond the traditional contracts of "I'll buy 400 pairs of jeans in these sizes for $10 each." The buyer and seller are partners in reaching the market and providing those in the market with what they need.

These SPPS, as they are called, are based in large part on trust. Both sides must be willing to work with the other in a straightforward manner. There is access to sales data on both sides. An ethical posture is critical for these relationships to survive.

Traditional contract rules are nearly abandoned as the parties work together. Many update their agreements only once annually. Many have no formal contract and simply rely on EDI transfers and print-outs. The phone, the fax, and the computer are at the heart of successful SPPS. In a way, these relationships move toward the Japanese model of contracts. In Japan if one side proposes a price increase, the other side will accept it with the understanding that it is done in good faith, and that the same accommodation on price would be made for them at some future time if their costs and financial position warranted a good faith request for a price reduction. These types of takings and givings are different from the rigid concepts of consideration. However,

these are the trends for both national and international business.

For these SPPS to be successful, because there is not the traditional legal fall-back on contracts and litigation, those involved in successful SPPS offered the following advice in a 1994 survey:

1. There must be absolute honesty and integrity so that trust and credibility develop.
2. There should be a long-term commitment between the parties.
3. SPP should satisfy a strategic need for both parties.
4. There should be ongoing monitoring of the relationship so that both sides are satisfied and that needs are being met.
5. Both sides should be committed to continual improvement; both sides have the best interests of the other side at heart with the understanding that they will both benefit from satisfaction in their relationship and among their ultimate customers.

Source: Adapted from Marianne M. Jennings "The True Meaning of Relational Contracts," Vol. 73 *University of Denver Law Review* 3–21 (1995).

ISSUES IN FORMATION OF INTERNATIONAL CONTRACTS

The international business contract is very similar to domestic contracts. However, the unique aspect of international contracts is that additional risks and questions arise over the choice of currency, the impact of culture on contract interpretation and performance, and the stability of the governments of the parties involved in the contract. In other words, international contracts carry certain risks that are not part of contracts between businesses in the same country. Over the past few years the increased number of international transactions has resulted in recognition of the need for a more uniform law on international contract formation and performance. The

United Nations has developed such a set of laws, called the **United Nations Convention on Contracts for the International Sale of Goods (CISG)**. The CISG was adopted in 1980 by 11 countries (including the United States) and became effective on January 1, 1988. As of the end of 1995, 35 countries had adopted it.

Visit the Institute of Commercial Law, sponsored by the Pace University School of Law, to review the CISG: http://cisgw3. law.pace.edu/cisg/ text/database.html

The CISG, which applies to those contracts in which buyer and seller have their businesses in different countries (unless the parties agree otherwise), has four parts: Part I: Application; Part II: Formation; Park III: Sale of Goods; and Part IV: Final Provisions. Part II includes provisions for the requirements for offers and acceptance, including a merchant's firm offer provision. Acceptance is effective only upon receipt, and whenever forms do not match there is no contract unless the nonmatching terms are immaterial.

Party autonomy continues to remain a priority. The parties can always choose the applicable law, the nation for the location of courts for resolving disputes, and remedies. Details on global contracts are found in Chapter 7.

There are several significant differences between the UCC and the CISG. For example, the CISG follows the common law mirror image rule and not the more liberal UCC "battle of the forms" modification exception. The CISG also requires the presence of a price for an offer to be definite enough to be valid. Merchants' firm offers exist under the CISG, but there are no time limitations on their validity, as with the UCC three-month limit. Parties in international trade need to be familiar with the hybrid nature of the CISG in order to protect their contract rights.

Business Planning Tip

Avoiding Legal Pitfalls in International Transactions

1. Use short, simple contracts. The tendency to place all possibilities in a contract is a U.S. tradition. In Germany, for example, the parties have a one-page agreement that references and incorporates terms and conditions of one of the parties.

2. Watch unconscionability protections. While the United States focuses its unfairness protections on consumers, other countries afford these same protections to commercial transactions.

3. Some disclaimers are void in other countries. For example, the clause, "We are only liable for loss of data which is due to a deliberate act on our part. We are not responsible for lost profits in any event," would be valid in the United States but void in Germany. In Germany, sellers of software must assume liability for at least gross negligence.

4. One party's attempt to limit liability would be void in Germany. Any liability limitation must be specifically addressed and negotiated for such a clause to be valid.

5. Unusually long periods for performance are typical in the United States but void in Germany.

6. Price increase limitations are typical in non-U.S. contracts.

7. In other countries, parties can refuse to pay on a current contract if performance on an earlier contract was less than satisfying and damages are owed.

Those firms and countries not relying on the CISC should be familiar with the nuances of commercial law in the countries in which they are doing business. The tendency of many U.S. businesses is to draft a form contract using the home country legal concepts and carry them over to other countries. As the planning tips above indicate, such a practice and reliance on form contracts can be dangerous.

SUMMARY

What are contracts?
- Contract—promise or set of promises for breach of which the law gives a remedy, or the performance of which the law in some way recognizes as a duty

What laws govern contracts?
- Common law—traditional notions of law and the body of law developed in judicial decisions
- Restatement of (Second) Contracts—general summary of the common law of contracts
- Uniform Commercial Code (UCC)—set of uniform laws (49 states) governing commercial transactions

What are the types of contracts?
- Bilateral contract—contract of two promises; one from each party
- Unilateral contract—contract made up of a promise for performance
- Express contract—written or verbally agreed-to contract
- Implied contract—contract that arises from parties' voluntary conduct
- Quasi contract—theory for enforcing a contract even though there is no formal contract because the parties behaved as if there were a contract
- Implied-in-fact contract—contract that arises from factual circumstances, professional circumstances, or custom
- Implied-in-law contract—legally implied contract to prevent unjust enrichment
- Void contract—contract with illegal subject matter or against public policy
- Voidable contract—contract that can be avoided legally by one side
- Unenforceable contract—agreement for which the law affords no remedy
- Executed contract—contract that has been performed
- Executory contract—contract not yet performed

How are contracts formed?
- Offer—preliminary to contract; first step in formation
- Offeror—person making the offer
- Offeree—recipient of offer
- Course of dealing—UCC provision that examines the way parties have behaved in the past to determine present performance standards
- Revocation—offeror canceling offer
- Options—offers with considerations; promises to keep offer open
- Merchant's firm offer—written offer signed by a merchant that states it will be kept open
- Counteroffer—counterproposal to offer
- Battle of the forms—UCC description of merchants' tendency to exchange purchase orders, invoices, confirmations, etc.
- Acceptance—offeree's positive response to offer
- Mailbox rule—timing rule for acceptance
- Consideration—something of value exchanged by the parties that distinguishes gifts from contracts
- Charitable subscriptions—enforceable promises to make gifts
- Promissory estoppel—reliance element used to enforce otherwise unenforceable contracts

When must contracts be in writing?
- Statute of frauds—state statutes governing the types of contracts that must be in writing to be enforceable
- Merchants' confirmation memorandum—UCC provision that allows one merchant to bind another based on an oral agreement with one signature
- Parol evidence—extrinsic evidence that is not admissible to dispute an integrated unambiguous contract

What issues for contracting exist in international business?
- CISG—Contracts for the International Sale of Goods; a proposed uniform law for international commercial transactions

QUESTIONS AND PROBLEMS

1. L. A. Becker Co., Inc., sent D. A. Clardy a $100 down payment along with a merchandise order. Clardy deposited the check, as was its usual daily practice for payments. After examining the offer, Clardy sent a rejection letter along with a check for $100 to Becker, who claims Clardy accepted by cashing the check. Is Becker correct? [*L. A. Becker Co.* v. *Clardy*, 51 So. 211 (Miss. 1910).]

2. Consider the following proposal description:

> Attached are an original and two (2) carbon copies of our Proposal No. 620-M-86R covering the subject as agreed upon in your office last Friday, June 20, 1986. Please sign the original and one (1) copy on the lower left corner of page 9 and return to us for our execution. We will return one (1) executed copy for your files.
>
> Again we thank you for selecting us for this project. We assure you it is receiving our best attention. Our Engineering Department is proceeding with the designs, fabrication drawings, and material orders.
>
> We look forward to your receiving the necessary permits.

The "proposal" consists of five pages of typewritten terms, setting forth specifications for the manufacture, assembly, and erection of a television tower and related items, and four pages of preprinted "Terms and Conditions of Sale." The printed portion includes the following relevant terms:

> **Acceptance of Proposal**
>
> This proposal is for immediate acceptance and prior to such acceptance is subject to modification or withdrawal without notice.
>
> Acceptance of this proposal will evidence Buyer's intent that the sale be governed solely by the terms and conditions of this proposal.
>
> Any modifying, inconsistent or additional terms and conditions of Buyer's acceptance shall not become a part of any contract resulting from this proposal unless agreed to in writing by Kline.
>
> Any order or offer by Buyer as a result of this proposal shall not be binding upon Kline until accepted by Kline in writing by an officer of Kline. If accepted by Kline, this proposal shall constitute the agreement between the Buyer and Kline.

At the bottom of the final page are the following signature spaces:

KLINE IRON & STEEL CO., INC.

By _____

Its   (Seller)

GRAY COMMUNICATIONS, INC.

By _____

Its   (Buyer)

Is there an offer? When would the earliest acceptance be? [*Kline Iron & Steel Co., Inc.* v. *Gray Communications Consultants, Inc.*, 715 F. Supp. 135 (D. S.C. 1989).]

3. Would an arbitration clause added to the reverse side of a buyer's purchase order be a material change for purposes of the merchant's battle of the forms under Section 2-207 of the UCC? [*Berquist Co.* v. *Sunroc Corp.*, 777 F. Supp. 1236 (E.D. Pa. 1991).]

4. Mace Industries, Inc., sent a quotation to Paddock Pools for water treatment equipment. Paddock responded with a purchase order that had the following written on its reverse side:

    "THE SELLER AGREES TO ALL OF THE FOLLOWING TERMS AND CONDITIONS"

    The clause was then followed by language stating that acceptance was expressly conditional upon Mace's acceptance of the terms.

    Problems between the parties developed. Paddock says there is no contract because of its conditional acceptance. Mace maintains that Section 2-207 applies and that there was a contract, with the only issues being the additional terms Paddock wrote on its purchase order and whether they are part of the contract. Who is correct? [*Mace Industries, Inc.* v. *Paddock Pool Equipment Co., Inc.*, 339 S.E.2d 527 (S.C. 1986).]

5. Consider the following sequences of offers and acceptances and determine whether in each case there would be a contract.

    a.   September 1, 1996: A mails an offer to B
         September 2, 1996: B receives the offer
         September 3, 1996: A mails a revocation
         September 4, 1996: B mails an acceptance
         September 5, 1996: B receives the revocation
         September 6, 1996: A receives the acceptance
    RESULT: _____

    b.   September 1, 1996: A mails an offer to B
         September 2, 1996: B receives the offer
         September 3, 1996: B wires an acceptance
         September 4, 1996: B wires a rejection
         September 4, 1996 (later): A receives the acceptance
         September 5, 1996: A receives the rejection
    RESULT: _____

    c.   September 1, 1996: A mails an offer to B
         September 2, 1996: B receives the offer
         September 3, 1996: A wires a revocation
         September 3, 1996: B wires an acceptance
         September 4, 1996: B receives the revocation
         September 5, 1996: A receives the acceptance
    RESULT: _____

    d.   September 1, 1996: A "overnight expresses" an offer to B
         September 2, 1996: B receives the offer (before 10:30 A.M., no less)
         September 3, 1996: A "overnight expresses" revocation to B
         September 4, 1996: B phones acceptance
                            A maintains offer was revoked
         September 5, 1996: B receives A's revocation (a major slip-up in overnight delivery)
    RESULT: _____

    e.   September 1, 1996: A mails an offer to B
         September 2, 1996: B receives the offer
         September 3, 1996: B mails an acceptance
         September 4, 1996: B wires a rejection
                            A receives the acceptance
         September 4, 1996 (later): A receives the rejection
    RESULT: _____

    Would your answers be different under the UCC from those under common law?

6. Corinthian Pharmaceuticals Systems, Inc. placed a telephone order with Lederle Laboratories for one thousand vials of vaccine. Corinthian then followed the telephonic/computer order with two written confirmations. Neither the phone order nor the confirmations mentioned a price. Is there a valid offer? [*Corinthian Pharmaceuticals Systems, Inc.* v. *Lederle Lab.*, 724 F. Supp. 605 (S.D. Ind. 1989).]

7. Hillcrest Country Club contacted N. D. Judds Company about replacement of the roof on its clubhouse. Rick Langill served as Judds's representative in negotiating the contract. Hillcrest managers were in possession of a brochure that described the RS-18 roofing manufactured by Roof Systems made of galvanized steel laminated with acrylic film called Korad.

   Judds maintains Hillcrest received the brochure by calling Roof Systems. Hillcrest managers maintain Langill gave them the brochures. Mr. Langill generally stamps brochures and attaches a cover letter before mailing them out, but Hillcrest's brochure was not stamped although it was used as a basis for Hillcrest's specification sheet. The brochure touted a 20-year warranty and promised no chalking, fading, chipping, peeling, or other forms of coating deterioration.

   Judds submitted a bid with language that waived all warranties once final payment was made. Hillcrest accepted Judds's bid; and the roof was installed in July 1982.

   By September 1984, the roof panels on the Hillcrest clubhouse were flaking and required replacement. Judds cited the warranty waiver. Hillcrest replaced the roof at a cost of $80,000 and filed suit against Judds and Roof Systems.

   Did Roof Systems's warranty extend to Hillcrest? Was there privity of contract? Is this a UCC Section 2-207 problem? Was a contract formed? Does Hillcrest have a warranty? [*Hillcrest Country Club* v. *N.D. Judds Co.*, 12 U.C.C.2d Rep. Serv. (Callaghan) 990, 236 Neb. 233 (1990).]

8. Ben Diskin, a clothing manufacturer, placed an order with J. P. Stevens for 290 pieces of all-wool flannel material. Mr. Diskin issued a check to Stevens for $151,380. On the reverse side of the check, Mr. Diskin wrote:

   "In full payment for 290 pcs. of flannel as per contract, less anti. to be figured upon billing. Final total subject to adjustment."

   Stevens sent to Mr. Diskin its standard sales contract that was initialed as approved by the sales and credit departments, but there were no signatures. Do the parties have a contract? [*Diskin* v. *J. P. Stevens & Co.*, 652 F. Supp. 553 (D. Mass. 1987).]

9. Thomas Koenen signed a car-purchase order form to buy a limited edition Buick Regal. GM would manufacture only five hundred of these Regals. The order form was also signed by the car dealer's salesman and sales manager. Mr. Koenen gave Royal Buick Company (the dealer) a check for $500. No price is mentioned on the order form. Is there a contract? [*Koenen* v. *Royal Buick Co.*, 783 P.2d 822 (Ariz. 1989).]

10. Nation Enterprises, Inc., purchased a large (36 by 3 feet) gas-fired convection oven from Enersyst, Inc., to make its pizza crusts. There were problems with the oven that the parties were working to resolve, but Nation needed a second oven. It was going to purchase one from someone else, but Enersyst orally promised to fix the first oven if Nation bought the second oven from it. (Oven 1 was beyond its 60-day warranty.) Nation bought the second oven, but Enersyst did not fix the first one. Nation sued, but Enersyst claims its promise on the first oven is inadmissible under the parol evidence rule. Is this correct? [*Nation Enterprises, Inc.* v. *Enersyst, Inc.*, 749 F. Supp. 1506 (N.D. Ill. 1990).]

NOTE

1 Frank Shipper and Marianne M. Jennings, *Avoiding and Surviving Lawsuits: The Executive Guide to Strategic Legal Planning for Business*, Jossey-Bass Inc., Publishers. © 1989. Excerpted and reprinted with permission of the authors.

Judgment

Dorris Reed purchased a home from Robert King for $76,000. After Mrs. Reed moved in, she learned that the house had been the site of the murders of a mother and her four children. King and the real estate agents were aware of these events but did not disclose them to Mrs. Reed prior to the sale. The neighbors told Mrs. Reed of the murders after she moved into her home.

Is Mrs. Reed stuck with the house? Is there any way she can get out of the contract?

Contracts and Sales: Performance and Remedies

Once the parties have reached the point of forming a contract with an offer, acceptance, and consideration (as discussed in Chapter 14), it would seem that their troubles are over and that all they need to do is carry through with performance. However, their agreement may be subject to challenge because new information arises. Or perhaps what is considered sufficient performance to one party may not be sufficient to another. This chapter focuses on contract problems and answers the following questions: What if the assumptions made in formation turn out to be untrue? Must the parties go through with the contract? If one party does not perform, is the other excused? When is performance required, and when is it sufficient? What remedies exist? Do third parties have rights in a contract?

For want of a nail the shoe was lost;

For want of a shoe the horse was lost;

And for want of a horse the rider was lost;

For the want of a rider the battle was lost;

For the want of the battle the kingdom was lost

And all for the want of a horseshoe-nail.

Poor Richard's Almanac (1758)

DEFENSES IN CONTRACT FORMATION

Even though a contract may have been formed with the three elements of offer, acceptance, and consideration, one of the elements may be flawed. The result is a contract that may be void, voidable, or unenforceable. When one of the required elements of formation is flawed, the contract is subject to a defense. A **contract defense** is a situation, term, or event that makes an otherwise valid contract invalid. These defenses ensure that the parties enter into contracts voluntarily and on the basis of accurate information. The defenses are displayed in Exhibit 15.1 and are discussed in the following sections.

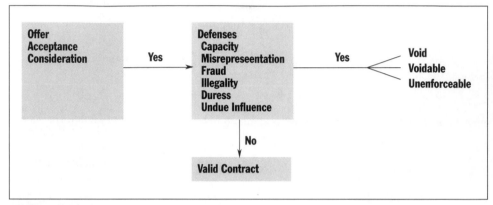

Exhibit 15.1
Defenses in Contract Formation

Capacity

Both parties to a valid contract must have **capacity**, which includes both age and mental capacity.

AGE CAPACITY

Age capacity means the parties must have reached the age of majority. In most states, that age is 18, but in some states the age of contractual capacity is 21. Before the time a party reaches the age of capacity, his or her contracts are voidable: A **voidable contract** of a minor allows the party lacking the necessary age (**minor** or **infant**) to choose not to honor the contract, in which case the other party to the contract will have no remedy. Because minors' contracts are voidable, they are not enforced by the courts. But there are some exceptions to the minors' contracts rules. Some statutes make such contracts enforceable; for example, student loan agreements are enforceable against minors. Minors' contracts for such necessities as food and clothing are still voidable, but courts do hold minors liable for the reasonable value of those necessities.

MENTAL CAPACITY

Contracting parties must also have mental capacity, which is the ability to understand that contracts are enforceable, that legal documents have significance, and that contracts involve costs and obligations. Contracts of those lacking mental capacity are also voidable. Moreover, if a party to a contract has been declared legally incompetent, that person's contracts are void. A **void contract** is one the courts will not honor, and neither party is obligated to perform under that agreement.

C O N S I D E R . . . **15.1** Because of a domestic relations problem, on May 9, 1983, John D. Gilbert canceled, on the advice of counsel, a Visa card held jointly with his wife. Mr. Gilbert made a new application, and a new credit card was issued to him.

The card was mailed to Mr. Gilbert at his business address. After a month, he received a Visa bill for $1,341.54 in purchases. Mr. Gilbert acknowledges that his married daughter Christine charged $85.44 and that he charged $89.88. The remaining $1,166.22 was charged by Ann Gilbert, Mr. Gilbert's minor daughter.

Mr. Gilbert refused to pay Ann's share of the bill, and Visa brought suit. Can Visa recover from Ann? Can Visa recover from Mr. Gilbert? [*Fifth Third Bank/Visa* v. *Gilbert*, 478 N.E. 2d 1324 (Ohio 1981).]

Misrepresentation

When one party to a contract is not given full or accurate information by the other party about the contract subject matter, **misrepresentation** occurs. Misrepresentation allows a **rescission** of the contract, which means the contract is rescinded or set aside. Misrepresentation occurs when a seller makes inaccurate statements about its product or fails to disclose pertinent information about its product that should be disclosed. For example, failing to disclose that a deluxe model car has a standard car engine is misrepresentation. The elements required for innocent misrepresentation are as follows:

1. Misstatement of a material fact (or the failure to disclose a material fact)
2. Reliance by the buyer on that material misstatement or omission
3. Resulting damages to the buyer

To be a basis for rescission, the misrepresentation must have been one regarding a **material fact**. A material fact is the type of information that would affect someone's decision to enter into the contract. For example, if a buyer for your stock in XYZ Corporation failed to disclose that a takeover was pending, there would be misrepresentation of a material fact. A takeover affects the price of stock, and the price of stock in the future affects your decision to buy and sell in the present.

Misrepresentation cannot be based on sales **puffing**, which is opinion about the subject matter of a contract. For example, suppose that a real estate agent told you a house you were considering buying was located in the "best area in town." Such a statement is an opinion and cannot be a basis for misrepresentation.

C O N S I D E R . . . **15.2** Analyze the following statements. Are they opinion, or could they be the basis for misrepresentation?

"This lightbulb will last two hundred hours."

"These suits are 100 percent wool."

"This fabric is the finest money can buy."

Continued

"This sweater is 50 percent cashmere."
"This toothpaste reduces cavities by 20 percent."
"This car gets 22 miles to the gallon."
"This stock has never decreased in value."
"This house has no easements running through the backyard."
"This car has not been in an accident."
"These bicycle locks are theft-proof."
"This carpet cleaning machine will remove every type of spot on your rugs."

The buyer must have reliance on (that is, attach some importance to) the statement that was made. For a buyer of stock to claim financial misrepresentation, the buyer must have actually examined the false financial statements of the company selling the stock and based the buying decision on the company's financial condition. A buyer who is buying cars only to take them apart for their used parts does not rely on a misrepresentation that the car has not been in an accident. Whatever information is given must be part of the reason the buyer has agreed to enter into the contract.

C O N S I D E R . . . **15.3** The Honda Motor Company ran an advertising campaign based on the following phrase, "You meet the nicest people on a Honda." The parents of Bradley Baughn and Douglas Bratz brought suit against Honda because their children were seriously injured while riding a Honda minitrail bike. The parents alleged the slogan misrepresented the danger of these bikes. Is the slogan a basis for recovery? [*Baughn* v. *Honda Motor Co.*, 727 P.2d 655 (Wash. 1986).]

C O N S I D E R . . . **15.4** Would it be misrepresentation to tout the health benefits of a product by calling it "Jogging in a Jug"?

Fraud

Although misrepresentation can result simply because of inaccurate information, **fraud** is the knowing and intentional disclosure of false information or the knowing failure to disclose relevant information. Fraud has the same elements of proof as misrepresentation, with the added element of **scienter**, or knowledge that the information given is false. An example of the distinction could be in a situation in which the seller of a home obtains an exterminator's report that says the house is clear of termites and passes it along to the buyer. Because the house actually has termites, there has been misrepresentation, but not fraud, because the seller was simply passing along the information without the knowledge of its accuracy. If, however, that same seller received a report from an exterminator that indicated there were termites and then found another exterminator to report there were no termites and passed that report along to the buyer, there would be fraud because there was knowledge of the false report and the intent to defraud the buyer. The following case includes a discussion of the elements of misrepresentation and provides the answer for the chapter's opening "Judgment."

Judgment

Reed v. King
193 Cal. App. 3d 130 (1983)

BUYING PROPERTY FROM THE ADDAMS FAMILY: HOW SCARY MUST IT BE?

FACTS

Dorris Reed purchased a home from Robert King for $76,000. Mr. King and his real estate agents did not disclose to Mrs. Reed that 10 years before, the house had been the site of the murders of a mother and her four children. After Mrs. Reed moved into the home, neighbors disclosed to her the story of the murders and the fact that the house carried a stigma. Because of its history, appraisers evaluated the true worth of the house to be $65,000. Mrs. Reed filed suit on the basis of misrepresentation and sought rescission and damages. Her complaint was dismissed by the trial court, and she appealed.

JUDICIAL OPINION

BLEASE, Associate Justice

In the sale of a house, must the seller disclose it was the site of a multiple murder?

Does Reed's pleading state a cause of action? Concealed within this question is the nettlesome problem of the duty of disclosure of blemishes on real property which are not physical defects or legal impairments to use.

Reed seeks to state a cause of action sounding in contract, i.e. rescission, or in tort, i.e. deceit. In either event her allegations must reveal a fraud. "The elements of actual fraud, whether as the basis of the remedy in contract or tort, may be stated as follows: There must be (1) a *false representation* or concealment of a material fact (or, in some cases, an opinion) susceptible of knowledge, (2) made with *knowledge* of its falsity or without sufficient knowledge on the subject to warrant a representation, (3) with the *intent* to induce the person to whom it is made to act upon it; and such person must (4) act in *reliance* upon the representation (5) to his *damage*."

The trial court perceived the defect in Reed's complaint to be a failure to allege concealment of a material fact. "Concealment" and "material" are legal conclusions concerning the effect of the issuable facts pled. As appears, the analytic pathways to these conclusions are intertwined.

Reed's complaint reveals only nondisclosure despite the allegation King asked a neighbor to hold his peace. There is no allegation the attempt at suppression was a cause in fact of Reed's ignorance. Accordingly, the critical question is: does the seller have duty to disclose here? Resolution of this question depends on the materiality of the fact of the murders.

In general, a seller of real property has a duty to disclose: "where the seller knows of facts *materially* affecting the value or desirability of the property which are known or accessible only to him and also knows that such facts are not known to, or within the reach of the diligent attention and observation of the buyer, the seller is under a duty to disclose them to the buyer.

Whether information "is of sufficient materiality to affect the value or desirability of the property . . . depends on the facts of the particular case." Materiality "is a question of law, and is part of the concept of right to rely or justifiable reliance." Accordingly, the term is essentially a label affixed to a normative conclusion. Three considerations bear on this legal conclusion: the gravity of the harm inflicted by nondisclosure; the fairness of imposing a duty of discovery on the buyer as an alternative to compelling disclosure, and its impact on the stability of contracts if rescission is permitted.

Numerous cases have found nondisclosure of physical defects and legal impediments to use of real property are material. However, to our knowledge, no prior real estate sale case has faced an issue of nondisclosure of the kind presented here. Should this variety of ill-repute be required to be disclosed? Is this a circumstance where "nondisclosure of the fact amounts to a failure to act in good faith and in accordance with reasonable standards of fair dealing[?]"

The paramount argument against an affirmative conclusion is it permits the camel's nose of unrestrained irrationality admission to the tent. If such an "irrational" consideration is permitted as a basis of rescission the stability of

Continued

all conveyances will be seriously undermined. Any fact that might disquiet the enjoyment of some segment of the buying public may be seized upon by a disgruntled purchaser to void a bargain. In our view, keeping this genie in the bottle is not as difficult a task as these arguments assume. We do not view a decision allowing Reed to survive a demurrer in these unusual circumstances as endorsing the materiality of facts predicating peripheral, insubstantial, or fancied harms.

The murder of innocents is highly unusual in its potential for so disturbing buyers they may be unable to reside in a home where it has occurred. This fact may foreseeably deprive a buyer of the intended use of the purchase. Murder is not such a common occurrence that *buyers* should be charged with anticipating and discovering this disquieting possibility. Accordingly, the fact is not one for which a duty of inquiry and discovery can sensibly be imposed upon the buyer.

Reed alleges the fact of the murders has a quantifiable effect on the market value of the premises. We cannot say this allegation is inherently wrong and, in the pleading posture of the case, we assume it to be true.

Reputation and history can have a significant effect on the value of realty. "George Washington slept here" is worth something, however physically inconsequential that consideration may be. Ill-repute or "bad will" conversely may depress the value of property. Failure to disclose such a negative fact where it will have a foreseeably depressing effect on income expected to be generated by a business is tortious. Some cases have held that *unreasonable* fears of the potential buying public that a gas or oil pipeline may rupture may depress the market value of land and entitle the owner to incremental compensation in eminent domain.

Whether Reed will be able to prove her allegation, the decade-old multiple murder has a significant effect on market value we cannot determine. If she is able to do so by competent evidence she is entitled to a favorable ruling on the issues of materiality and duty to disclose. Her demonstration of objective tangible harm would still the concern that permitting her to go forward will open the floodgates to rescission on subjective and idiosyncratic grounds.

CASE QUESTIONS

1. What information about the house was not disclosed to Mrs. Reed before she purchased it?
2. How did she discover the information and when?
3. Is the information material?
4. What does Mrs. Reed need to establish to be entitled to rescission and damages?
5. Is Mrs. Reed's case dismissed, or will she be permitted to go forward with the suit?
6. Would the information about the house make a difference to you in making a buying decision?
7. Should Mr. King and the real estate agents have disclosed the information to Mrs. Reed? Was there an ethical obligation to do so?

The failure to disclose material information about the subject matter of a contract can also constitute fraud. For example, a car dealership that fails to disclose to a customer that the car he is buying was in an accident is misrepresentation. If the car dealership performed the body work on the car in its own body shop, the failure to disclose the accident and repairs would be fraud.

With respect to real estate transactions, most states have passed some form of disclosure statutes. In some states, the history of criminal activity on a property must be disclosed. In other states, there are prohibitions on disclosure. Some of these states prohibit disclosure of information such as whether an occupant of the

FOR THE MANAGER'S DESK

THE DO'S AND DON'TS OF SELLING CARS

The car industry has its own language:

A CAR LOT GLOSSARY

Some of the ways auto sales-people talk about customers, and deals when customers are not within earshot.

be-back (bē'bak) *n.* A customer who promises to return but undoubtedly won't.
get-me-done (get'mē dun) *n.* A customer with bad credit who will take whatever vehicle the dealer can get a bank to finance.
high-gross (hī'grōs) *v.* Drive up the gross profit on a sale.—syn: **bump.**
lay-down (la'doun) *n.* A customer who walks in ready to sign any deal offered, without a fight.
roach (rōch) *n.* A customer with terrible credit.—syn: **flake** or **stroker.**
tire-kick•er (tir kik' r) *n.* A customer who pretends expertise but has none.
would-ya-take (wood'zh tāk) *v.* To pressure a customer to buy today: *"If I offered you this, would you take it today?"*

The car industry has its own rules:

SELLING CARS CHARMINGLY

Some dos and don'ts for sales-people suggested by the National Association of Auto Dealers.

Don't

- Swear, or use expressions like "you know," "yeah," and "uh-huh."
- Tell jokes you would not tell a schoolchild.
- Refer to female customers as "babe," "honey," or "sweetheart."
- Wear revealing clothes, evening attire, heavy

makeup or a lot of jewelry.
- Display cartoons that could be offensive.
- Treat men and women differently.
- Return from lunch with alcohol on your breath.
- Overpraise a vehicle or misrepresent its condition.
  - Use high-pressure tactics.
  - Recommend a competitor's product.

Do

- Tell the truth.
- Keep shoes polished and nails manicured.
- Men should wear a navy blazer or dark jacket with dark pants; women, a tan, blue or gray business suit.
- Display a picture of your family, because it conveys stability.
- Promise to find the answer to a customer's question if you do not know it; never invent an answer.
- Answer questions asked by customers' children.

Source: James Bennet, "A Charm School for Selling Cars," *The New York Times*, Mar. 29, 1995, pp. C1, C5. Copyright © 1995 by The New York Times Company. Reprinted by permission.

Business Planning Tip

When employees and agents are working for commissions as well as salary (or are on commission alone), there is great temptation to engage in misrepresentation. For example, in the Sears Roebuck & Company controversy over the allegations that its auto repair centers overcharged customers, Sears CEO Edward Brennan issued a statement indicating that the presence of incentives for selling parts and services may have contributed to poor decisions by employees in handling customers. Incentive-based pay systems must also have ethical guidelines.

property died of AIDS. However, even in these states, the truth must be revealed if the buyer asks specifically about the occupants and their health.

Duress

Duress occurs when a party is physically forced into a contract or deprived of a meaningful choice when deciding whether to enter into a contract.

FOR THE MANAGER'S DESK

INTERNATIONAL FRAUD

It was inevitable that the creative and devious would develop a scheme to capitalize on businesses anxious to enter international markets. Referred to as export diversion, U.S. firms sell premium-brand products at deep discounts because the firms buying them have promised penetration into untapped markets. The goods are shipped but then turned around at their ports of destination, shipped back to the United States duty-free as "American goods returned," and then resold to U.S. detailers and retailers at a large profit but still below what the manufacturer sells for. The result is that the manufacturer not only has no foreign markets, but is facing competition in U.S. markets from itself. Victims of this scam include LifeScan, Inc., a Johnson & Johnson subsidiary; ALPO dog foods; Glad plastic bags; Quaker Oats; Procter & Gamble; Duracell; and Hormel Foods.

Prevention techniques include marking products. For example, LifeScan includes a particular type of coupon in each shipment for international markets. If the coupons show up in U.S. stores, diversion has occurred and customs agents can step in to help.

Requiring employees to sell company stock holdings in order to keep their jobs is an example of duress because of a lack of choice. If there has been duress, the contract is voidable. The party who experienced the duress has the right to rescind the agreement, but rescission is a choice; the law does not make the contract illegal or unenforceable because duress was present. The choice of enforcement or rescission is left to the party who experienced the duress.

ETHICAL ISSUES

15.1 Dana Plumbing, Inc., was awarded a contract by Tennesco Homes, Inc., to perform all the plumbing work on a subdivision of 42 homes that Tennesco was building. Dana's contract provided that Tennesco would pay $4,200 per house for the plumbing work. The contract also provided that Dana would receive the contract price as follows: $2,200 to be paid after the trenches for the plumbing were dug; $1,000 after the pipes were installed prior to the foundation's being poured, and $1,000 when the inside fixtures were installed. It is customary in construction to pay the plumbing contractor 50 percent of the contract price after the first phase (digging) of the work is done. Dana dug all the trenches for the 42 homes and was paid the agreed-upon $2,200 for each home. Dana then refused to complete the last two phases of plumbing work unless Tennesco agreed to an additional $800 per house. Tennesco could hire another contractor, but it would then be required to pay almost $3000 per house for completion of the plumbing work because the new contractor had not performed the initial phase of work in which plumbing contractors earn the bulk of their profit. Dana indicated it would place mechanics' liens on the homes if Dana did not pay and Dana would not be able to clear title in order to close sales to home buyers. Evaluate the ethics of those running Dana Plumbing. Does Tennesco have any legal defenses? What should Tennesco do?

Undue Influence

Undue influence occurs when one party uses a close personal relationship with another party to gain contractual benefits. Before undue influence can be established, a **confidential relationship** of trust and reliance must exist between the parties. Attorneys and clients have a confidential relationship. Elderly parents who rely on a child or children for their care have a confidential relationship with those children. To establish undue influence, there must be an abuse of this confidential relationship. For example, conditioning an elderly parent's care upon the signing over of his or her land to a child is an abuse of the relationship. An attorney who offers advice on property disposition to his or her benefit is abusing the confidential relationship. Again, contracts subject to undue influence defenses are voidable. They can be honored if the party who experienced the influence desires to honor the contract.

Illegality and Public Policy

A contract that violates a statute or the general standards of public policy is void and cannot be enforced by either party. To enforce contracts that violate statutes or public conscience would encourage the commission of these illegal acts, and so contract law is controlled by the statutory prohibitions and public policy concerns of other areas of law.

CONTRACTS IN VIOLATION OF CRIMINAL STATUTES

Contracts that are agreements to commit criminal wrongs are void. For example, the old saying that "there is a contract out on his life" may be descriptive, but it is not accurate in the legal sense. There could never be a valid contract to kill someone because the agreement is one to commit a criminal wrong and is therefore void. No one is permitted to benefit from contracts to commit illegal acts. For example, a beneficiary for a life insurance policy will not collect the proceeds from the insured's policy if the beneficiary arranged for the death of the insured (contract for murder). The following "Consider" deals with the issue of benefits from an illegal contract.

C O N S I D E R . . . **15.5** Robert Hackett (plaintiff) was made a substitute fireman for the city of New Britain, Connecticut, in 1949. In 1950 he was made a full-time fireman, and in 1968 became a lieutenant. After earning the highest mark on the captain's examination, he was promoted to captain in 1974. He then scored the highest score on the deputy chief exam and was promoted to that rank in 1977.

Mr. Hackett had paid an employee in the city department responsible for administering the exams to ensure that he earned the highest grades (which he did). He had, in effect, purchased his last two promotions. When these acts were discovered (after Mr. Hackett had retired), criminal charges were brought against him and the city employee. Both were convicted of felonies.

The pension board of New Britain (defendant) then met and voted to reduce Mr. Hackett's pension by $5,483.97 a year because that reduction placed his pension at the level it would have been without the last two promotions. The board said the reduction was necessary because the last two promotions were obtained through illegal conduct. Mr. Hackett filed suit. Is illegality a defense to the pension? [*Hackett* v. *City of New Britain*, 477 A.2d 148 (Conn. 1984).]

CONTRACTS IN VIOLATION OF LICENSING STATUTES

In some cases, contracts are not contracts to commit illegal acts but are simply contracts for a legal act to be done by one not authorized to perform such services. Every state requires some professionals or technicians to be licensed before they can perform work for the public. For example, a lawyer must be admitted to the bar before representing clients. A lawyer who contracts to represent a client before having been admitted to the practice of law has entered into a void contract. Even if the lawyer successfully represents the client, no fee could be collected because the agreement violated the licensing statute, and to allow the lawyer to collect the fee, even in quasi contract, would encourage others to violate the licensing requirements. In some cases, licensing requirements are in place not for competency reasons but rather to raise revenues. For example, an architect may be required to pass a competency screening to be initially licensed in a state, and after that the license may be renewed simply by paying an annual fee. Suppose that the architect forgot to pay the annual renewal fee and, after the license had lapsed, entered into a $300,000 contract with a developer. The developer discovers the renewal problems after the work is completed and wants to get out of paying the architect. In this case, the issue is not one of competency screening but of financial oversight, and the architect would be permitted to collect the fee.

CONTRACTS IN VIOLATION OF USURY LAWS

These contracts are credit or loan contracts that charge interest in excess of the state's limits for interest or finance charges. These statutes are discussed in detail in Chapter 16.

CONTRACTS IN VIOLATION OF PUBLIC POLICY

Some contracts do not violate any criminal laws or statutory provisions but do violate certain standards of fairness or encourage conduct in violation of public policy. For example, many firms will include **exculpatory clauses** in their contracts that purport to hold the firms completely blameless for any accidents occurring on their premises. Most courts consider a firm's trying to hold itself completely blameless for all accidents regardless of the degree of care or level of fault against public policy, and will not, therefore, enforce, such clauses.

Also grouped into the public policy prohibition are contracts that restrict trade or employment. For example, when a business is sold, part of the purchase price is paid for the business's goodwill. The benefit of that payment is lost if the seller moves down the street and starts another similar business. Hence, the courts have permitted **covenants not to compete** to be included in these contracts so long as they are reasonable in time and geographic scope. These covenants and their legality are discussed in detail in Chapter 13.

Some contracts are not actually contracts for criminal or illegal activities, but the terms of the contract are grossly unfair to one party. A contract that gives all the benefits to one side and all the burdens to the other is an **unconscionable** contract. The standards for determining whether a contract is unconscionable are the public policy standards for fairness that cover all types of contract provisions and negotiations. Many consumer rental contracts have been declared unconscionable because the consumers were paying more in rent than it would cost to buy the rented appliance outright. Although the consumer might agree to the lease, public policy requires a fair agreement rather than one that gives all rights and benefits to the rental company.

The standards for unconscionability are set on a case-by-case basis. The courts have not given a firm definition of unconscionability. Even the UCC does not specifically define unconscionability, although one section (2-302) prohibits the enforcement of unconscionable contracts.

The *Water* v. *Min Ltd.* case on page 526 deals with a contract that involves several different defenses.

FOR THE MANAGER'S DESK

KILLER PERFORMANCE REQUIREMENTS IN RETAIL

It's called "the Squeeze." The Squeeze refers to the increasingly onerous logistical demands retailers place on clothing suppliers. The logistical demands add tremendous costs to suppliers, they are rigid, they are complex (some retailers' rules run 50 pages) and they carry penalties. Noncompliance with logistical requirements allows the retailer to take a "chargeback," or a deduction from its payment.

Here are some sample logistical requirements:

SHIPPING AND PACKING GUIDELINES FROM RETAILERS TO VENDORS

Packing Hanging Garments
You must have written authorization from Federated to ship GOH. All ready-to-wear merchandise should be shipped in conveyable cartons in order to maximize the use of UCC-128 shipping container label . . .
—*Lazarus, unit of Federated Department Stores*

Routing Instructions
Determine your RPS Zone number on the Zone Chart . . . determine your LTL [less than truckload] Zone number from the Zone Chart and follow the LTL Routing for that zone.
—*Kaufmann's, unit of May Department Stores*

Paperwork Documentation
Provide a separate packing list for each store and for each purchase order, detailed as to purchase order #, department #, store # and two letter code, style #, color (when ordered by color), size (when ordered by size), number of cartons and total units shipped.
—*Hecht's, unit of May Department Stores*

Charges include $300 for incorrect labels, $500 for incorrect packing materials and a 5 percent penalty if a shipment arrives late.

Schwab Co., the manufacturer of "Little Me" infants clothes, was charged $400 for late delivery of a $500 shipment.

A buyer for Federated Department Stores says, ". . . it's not our responsibility to keep vendors afloat. We have a separate philanthropy program." Small vendors complain they must hire extra people to handle special boxing and that retailers' chargebacks are reversed if they offer proof of compliance.

Smaller vendors are taking their products to specialty stores and boutiques. Large retailers say, "This is all still negotiable."

Discussion Questions
1. Is there a problem with unconscionability?
2. Would you deal with large retailers?
3. Is this kind of behavior anticompetitive?
4. Do you feel the guidelines and chargeback fees are truly negotiable?

Water v. *Min Ltd.*
587 N.E.2d 231 (Mass. 1992)

YOUNG, DRUGGED, AND WEALTHY: CAPABLE OF CONTRACTING?

FACTS

Gail A. Waters (plaintiff) was injured in an accident when she was 12 years old. At age 18 she settled a negligence claim with Commercial Union Insurance Company and purchased an annuity contract, the income from which was her support.

At age 21, Gail became romantically involved with Thomas Beauchemin (defendant), an ex-convict who introduced her to drugs and to Min Ltd., a partnership consisting of David and Robert DeVito and Michael D. Steamer (defendants), and suggested that she sell her annuity contract to them.

Gail signed a contract to sell her policy, with a cash value of $189,000, to the defendants for $50,000. The contract was signed on the hood of a car in the parking lot of a restaurant. The guaranteed return to the owner of the policy over its 25-year life was $694,000.

Gail filed suit to rescind the contract. The trial court found, among other things, that the contract was unconscionable. The DeVitos, Mr. Steamer, and Mr. Beauchemin appealed.

JUDICIAL OPINION

LYNCH, Justice

The defendants contend that the judge erred by (1) finding the contract unconscionable (and by concluding the defendants assumed no risks and therefore finding the contract oppressive); (2) refusing them specific performance; and (3) failing to require the plaintiff to return all the funds received from them.

Unconscionability. The defendants argue that the evidence does not support the finding that the contract was unconscionable or that they assumed no risks and therefore that the contract was oppressive.

The doctrine of unconscionability has long been recognized by common law courts in this country and in England. "Historically, a [contract] was considered unconscionable if it was 'such as no man in his senses and not under delusion would make on the one hand, and as no honest and fair man would accept on the other.' Later, a contract was determined unenforceable because unconscionable when 'the sum total of its provisions drives too hard a bargain for a court of conscience to assist.'"

The doctrine of unconscionability has also been codified in the Uniform Commercial Code (code), G.L.C. 106, § 2-302 (1990 ed.), and, by analogy, it has been applied in situations outside the ambit of the code.

Unconscionability must be determined on a case-by-case basis, with particular attention to whether the challenged provision could result in oppression and unfair surprise to the disadvantaged party and not to allocation of risk because of "superior bargaining power." Courts have identified other elements of the unconscionable contract. For example, gross disparity in the consideration alone "may be sufficient to sustain [a finding that the contract is unconscionable]," since the disparity "itself leads inevitably to the felt conclusion that knowing advantage was taken of [one party]." High pressure sales tactics and misrepresentation have been recognized as factors rendering a contract unconscionable. If the sum total of the provisions of a contract drive too hard a bargain, a court of conscience will not assist its enforcement.

The judge found that Beauchemin introduced the plaintiff to drugs, exhausted her credit card accounts to the sum of $6,000, unduly influenced her, suggested that the plaintiff sell her annuity contract, initiated the contract negotiations, was the agent of the defendants, and benefited from the contract between the plaintiff and the defendants. The defendants were represented by legal counsel; the plaintiff was not. The cash value of the annuity policy at the time the contract was executed was approximately four times greater than the price to be

Continued

paid by the defendants. For payment of not more than $50,000 the defendants were to receive an asset that could be immediately exchanged for $189,000, or they could elect to hold it for its guaranteed term and receive $694,000. In these circumstances the judge could correctly conclude the contract was unconscionable.

The defendants assumed no risk and the plaintiff gained no advantage. Gross disparity in the values exchanged is an important factor to be considered in determining whether a contract is unconscionable. "[C]ourts [may] avoid enforcement of a bargain that is shown to be unconscionable by reason of gross inadequacy of consideration accompanied by other relevant factors."

We are satisfied that the disparity of interests in this contract is "so gross that the court cannot resist the inference that it was improperly obtained and is unconscionable."

Amount of repayment order. The defendants also argue that the judge erred in failing to require the plaintiff to return the full amount paid by them for the annuity.

The defendants paid $18,000 cash after deducting $7,000 for a debt which was owed to them by Beauchemin. The remaining $25,000 due on the contract was never paid.

The judge's order was consistent with his findings that Beauchemin was the agent of the defendants, and that the plaintiff only received $18,000 for her interest in the annuity.

Judgment affirmed.

CASE QUESTIONS
1. List the possible defenses to this contract.
2. What made the contract unconscionable?
3. What protections for Gail could have been built into the annuity contract?
4. Is there any criminal conduct here?

CONTRACT PERFORMANCE

Once parties have contracted, they have the obligation of performance. The following subsections cover when performance is due, what constitutes performance, and when performance is excused.

When Performance Is Due

Performance is due according to the times provided in the contract. In some contracts, however, prescribed events must occur before there is an obligation of performance. These events are called **conditions**. **Conditions precedent** are events that give rise to performance. Suppose that Zelda has agreed to buy Scott's house and their contract provides that Zelda does not have to pay until she is able to obtain a reasonable loan to finance the purchase. This financing clause is a condition precedent to contract performance. If Zelda is denied financing, she is not required to perform under the contract. Another example of a condition precedent is in a contract for construction of jackets out of a material to be furnished by the seller. Unless the seller gives the manufacturer the fabric to work with, the manufacturer has no obligation to perform. **Conditions concurrent,** or **conditions contemporaneous**, exist in every contract; there is an exchange of benefits at the same time. One is willing to perform because the other side does.

Standards for Performance

The contract details what the parties are required to do for complete performance. In some contracts, performance is easily determined. If there is a contract between an employment agency and a potential employee to find work for the employee, performance is complete once the work is found.

But in some contracts, performance is complicated, and there may be errors in its execution. For example, construction contracts are long-term, complicated agreements. During the construction of a building, it is possible that some mistakes might be made. Is an owner allowed to not pay a contractor because there is a mistake or two? The doctrine of **substantial performance** applies in construction contracts, and it means that the constructed building is for practical purposes just as good as the one contracted for. For example, a builder might have substituted a type of pipe when the brand name specified in the contract was not available. The substitution is a technical breach of contract, but it is a substitute that is just as good. The builder will be paid for the construction, but the owner will be entitled to damages.

C O N S I D E R . . . **15.6** Philip and Kathleen Lester purchased a membership in Stateline Camping Club, Inc. The sales and membership agreement entitled them to use Stateline's facilities on a first-come, first-served basis, as set forth in club rules. The sales and membership agreement further provided that Stateline "will sell no more than six memberships for each Club campsite at any time . . . and that [this agreement] is subject to the terms of said Retail Installment Note (if any) and Rules of the Club, which may be amended or modified at any time. No oral representations have been made to the Buyer as to what amendment or modifications will or will not be made in the future." In addition, the membership and sales agreement stated that the Lesters acknowledged that "[i]f the facilities are renovated and until renovations are completed, the utility of my membership may be impaired."

In the handbook was a 14-day rule, which provided that "[n]o member may camp in excess of fourteen (14) consecutive days on the same resort-site or area." The rules defined "resort-site" as "[a] physical site consisting of parking space for one recreational vehicle, a service outlet for electricity and water, if so present, and sufficient ground space to provide for one tent." The club rules further provided that "[t]hese rules are subject to change at any time by the board of directors of Resort Camplands International, Inc."

Prior to the execution of the agreement, the sales representative, Michael Taylor, discussed these and other contractual provisions with the Lesters. Mr. Taylor explained that the Lesters would have unlimited use of Stateline's two hundred campsites on a first-come, first-served basis. He assured the Lesters that there would "always be a place for [them] at Stateline" because memberships were being sold on a six to one ratio.

In addition to explaining the contract documents to the Lesters, Mr. Taylor showed them promotional brochures claiming that various facilities and amenities existed at Stateline. In fact, however, many of these amenities did not exist at Stateline.

After the Lesters had purchased their membership, Resort Camplands sold "universal" memberships on a ten to one ratio. In April 1984, the board of directors of Resort Camplands, through their general counsel and vice president,

Continued

Kenneth Lenz, informed the members' advisory board that it intended to modify the 14-day rule.

Resort Camplands' board of directors, via a newsletter, added an *additional rule that requires that 7 days must elapse before the members staying 14 days can stay again*. This rule required campers to leave Stateline after they had camped for 14 consecutive days and did not permit them to return until 7 days later, regardless of whether there was space available.

In 1988, the Lesters spent 14 consecutive days in a Stateline campground. Resort Camplands ordered them to leave and not return until 7 days had elapsed, and did not give them the option of storing their trailer on-site or nearby. Resort did, however, offer the Lesters the opportunity to purchase a new gold card membership that would allow them to remain at a Stateline site for more than 14 days at a time if they paid an additional charge per season. Also, the gold card membership would double their maintenance fee and remove the existing cap on maintenance fees that limited their increase to the equivalent of the increase in the cost of living. At the time the Lesters left Stateline's campground, the campground had approximately one hundred campsites available for use.

The Lesters filed suit for breach of contract. Is there a breach? [*Lester* v. *Resort Camplands Internat'l, Inc.*, 605 A.2d 550 (Conn. 1992).]

When Performance Is Excused

There are times when all conditions of a valid contract are met but performance of the contract is excused. Under common law, the parties are excused from performance if performance has become impossible. **Impossibility** means that the contract cannot be performed by the parties or anyone else. For example, performance under a contract for the purchase and sale of land that has been washed away into a lake is impossible. Completing a year of dance lessons is impossible for someone who has had a paralyzing accident.

Under the UCC (and under the *Restatement)*, performance can be excused if there is commercial impracticability. **Commercial impracticability** (see § 2-615 in Appendix G) excuses performance if the basic assumptions the parties made when they entered into the contract have changed. Although this definition makes it seem that the UCC excuses performance when wars, embargoes, and unusually high price increases occur, courts have been reluctant to apply the excuse of commercial impracticability. The standard of commercial impracticability has been interpreted to mean nothing more or less than the common law standard of impossibility.

Parties can protect themselves from unusual events by putting in their contracts *force majeure* clauses, which excuse the parties from performance in the event of such problems as wars, depression, or embargoes.

C O N S I D E R . . . **15.7** Trans World Airlines (TWA) had a sales/leaseback arrangement on 10 aircraft with Connecticut National Bank. TWA was experiencing difficulty making payments, attributing the difficulties to the Gulf War, which resulted in decreased air travel because of terrorism and decreased oil flow. Is this an example of commercial impracticability? [*Connecticut Nat'l. Bank* v. *Trans World Airlines, Inc.*, 762 F. Supp. 76 (S.D.N.Y. 1991).]

Beech-Nut Nutrition Corporation was a division of Squibb Corporation. Its chewing gum segment was profitable but was sold in 1973. The baby food division of Beech-Nut, which had 15 percent of the baby food market, had never been profitable, and by 1978 creditors were increasingly anxious.

Beech-Nut had entered into a contract in 1977 with Interjuice Trading Corporation for Interjuice to furnish apple juice concentrate to Beech-Nut at a price that was 20 percent below market prices. This contract was a huge break for Beech-Nut since it used apple concentrate in 30 percent of its baby food products. The Interjuice contract attracted enough attention that Nestlé purchased Beech-Nut in 1979.

If It Ain't Apple Juice, It's Fraud

Jerome J. LiCari was the director of research and development for Beech-Nut. Mr. LiCari and the chemists in his department were concerned about the Interjuice contract for two reasons: (1) rumors of adulteration (substituted product or inferior product) in the apple juice concentrate market were rampant, and (2) the price was simply too good to be true.

At that time there were no tests to determine adulteration, but Mr. LiCari sent two of his employees to the Interjuice plant in Queens, New York. Interjuice officials refused to allow them to see processing operations but did provide them access to the plant storage tanks.

Mr. LiCari then tried, in 1981, to develop a test for adulteration. He could not, but he took his circumstantial evidence and concerns for Beech-Nut's reputation to John F. Lavery, Beech-Nut's head of operations. Mr. LiCari suggested Beech-Nut adopt Gerber's policy requiring suppliers to establish authenticity or lose their contracts. Mr. Lavery called Mr. LiCari "Chicken Little" and told him he had no proof.

In late 1981, Mr. LiCari, feeling that his tests showed the Interjuice concentrate had no apple juice, wrote a memo to Mr. Lavery suggesting Beech-Nut switch suppliers. Mr. Lavery did not respond.

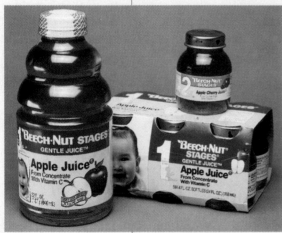

Beech-Nut Apple Juice

Mr. LiCari then took his cost and chemical analysis to Neils Hoyvald, the president and CEO of Beech-Nut, who told LiCari, "I'll look into it." He did nothing and told Mr. LiCari he had great technical ability but that his judgment was "colored by naivete and impractical ideals."

Mr. LiCari resigned from Beech-Nut and wrote a letter to the FDA disclosing the Interjuice adulteration and signing it, "Johnny Appleseed."

Mr. LiCari's letter started an FDA inquiry and the eventual discovery that Interjuice concentrate was a chemical concoction with no apple juice at all. After what the FDA called a cat-and-mouse game of shipping juice lots to avoid regulatory testing, the FDA found and tested a lot with no juice.

Messrs. Hoyvald and Lavery were indicted. Mr. LiCari, located as a witness through company files, testified at both trials that, "I thought apple juice should be made from apples."

Beech-Nut still struggles with market share and consumer loyalty.

Issues

1. Is there misrepresentation in the sale of Beech-Nut baby food?
2. Is there fraud?
3. Was Mr. LiCari harmed by his conduct?
4. Was Beech-Nut's conduct with respect to the Interjuice contract ethical?
5. Was Beech-Nut's conduct with respect to Mr. LiCari ethical?

C O N S I D E R . . . **15.8** In the early 1970s Westinghouse contracted to sell uranium to 22 utilities at contract prices of $7 to $10 per pound. After the 1974 energy crunch, Westinghouse had to pay $45 to $75 per pound in order to get the uranium and supplies were limited. Could Westinghouse be excused under commercial impracticability? [*In re Westinghouse Contract Litigation*, 429 F. Supp. 940 (E.D. Va. 1977).]

Often the obligation to perform is discharged by agreement of the parties. In some cases the parties agree to substitute someone else for the obligation in an agreement called a **novation**. For example, suppose that before forming a corporation, a business owner had signed a lease for store premises and then incorporates the business. The landlord agrees to substitute the new corporation as the tenant. All three parties (landlord, owner, and corporation) sign a novation. The owner is excused from individual liability and performance, and the corporation is substituted. Note that the landlord must agree; the owner cannot discharge his or her performance obligations by unilaterally substituting the corporation.

In other situations the parties reach an agreement for payment in full on a contract; such an agreement is called an **accord and satisfaction**. The amount they agree to pay may be less than the original contract amount, but disputes over warranties, repairs, and other issues change the value of the contract. The accord and satisfaction serves to discharge the performance of both parties.

CONTRACT REMEDIES

If performance is not excused and there is a valid contract, the nonbreaching party can recover for damages from the nonperforming party. The purpose of such **compensatory damages** is to put the nonbreaching party in the same position he or she would have been in had there not been a breach. The law has formulas to calculate the amount of compensatory damages for breach of every type of contract. For example, if a seller has agreed to sell a buyer a car for $5,000 and the seller breaches, the buyer could collect the extra $1,000 it would cost to buy a substitute car priced at $6,000.

In addition to compensatory damages, nonbreaching parties are entitled to collect the extra damages or **incidental damages** involved because of the breach. If a seller must run an ad in a newspaper to sell a car a buyer has refused to buy, the costs of the ad are incidental damages.

Some parties agree in their contracts on the amounts they will pay in the case of nonperformance. Damages agreed upon in advance are **liquidated damages**, and the contractual clauses containing them are enforceable so long as they are not excessive and compensatory damages are not awarded in addition to the liquidated damages.

In some cases, the nonbreaching party may be able to collect **consequential damages**. Consequential damages are damages that result because of the breach and generally involve such damages as lost business, lost profit, or late penalties. For example, if a contractor must pay a penalty of $200 per day for each day a building is late after the completion date stipulated in the contract and the contractor is late because the steel supplier did not meet its deadline, the $200-per-day penalty would be a consequential damage that the steel supplier would be required to pay. Whether a party will be able to collect consequential damages depends on whether the breaching party knew or should have known what the consequences of the breach would be. The following case involves an issue of consequential damages.

Lininger v. Dine Out Corp.
639 P.2d 350 (Ariz. 1981)

HOW MANY MEALS CAN ONE "DINE" OUT?

FACTS

Schuyler Lininger (plaintiff) is the operator of the Lodge on the Desert restaurant in Tucson. He contracted with Dine Out Corporation (defendant) to participate in a program in which Dine Out sells coupon booklets entitling purchasers to two meals for the price of one at participating establishments. Mr. Lininger had participated in the coupon program the previous year and had served 3,901 coupon customers. However, during the second year Dine Out did not advertise as promised and Mr. Lininger served only six coupon customers. Mr. Lininger filed suit for breach of contract; the trial court awarded him $4,298.58 in lost profits, and Dine Out appealed.

JUDICIAL OPINION

HATHAWAY, Chief Judge

Plaintiff claimed $23,342 in damages. Half of this sum represented the expected profit from the program, based on the number of customers and profit-per-customer during the previous year's program. Defendant contends that the award of $4,298.58 (minus $31.71 for the three coupons redeemed by Dine Out) was unsupported by the evidence. Defendant's contention is that the evidence of loss was speculative because the previous year's contract was not in evidence; there is no way to gauge the accuracy of the plaintiff's expert witness, according to Dine Out, because the terms of the previous contract may have been different.

Courts will award damages for loss of profits in an established business if they are proved with certainty. Such certainty is provided where the plaintiff devises some reasonable method of computing his net loss. Plaintiff testified that the two contracts were the same except for the difference in the dates of performance and the provision for approval by Dine Out. Thus, there was a sufficient basis for a comparison of the expected profit from the new contract and what was realized by plaintiff after defendant's breach. In addition, there was extensive testimony by an expert witness, a certified public accountant, as to his method of arriving at the estimate of lost profit. The testimony shows that the witness used conservative accounting procedures to arrive at a reasonable estimate of the loss. Since loss-of-profit damages for established businesses are not speculative as a matter of law and since plaintiff proved his particular damages with reasonable certainty, we hold there was no abuse of discretion in awarding the $4,298.58 for lost profits.

Dine Out's last argument is that plaintiff had a "duty to mitigate" his damages. One provision of the agreement was that plaintiff's restaurant could not participate in any similar program at the same time. Plaintiff testified that he was approached by two organizations offering a program similar to Dine Out's but declined because he was barred by his obligation to Dine Out. He presented an estimate in his trial memorandum that this cost him an additional $11,671 in damages.

Dine Out's position is that the rule of avoidable consequences required plaintiff to join one of these programs in order to minimize the amount of his damages, and that plaintiff's own testimony proves his failure to do so.

The doctrine of avoidable consequences is well established in Arizona. Plaintiff does not quarrel with this proposition but rather chal-

Continued

lenges Dine Out's right to assert it, having failed to plead it as an affirmative defense. We cannot grant Dine Out's request to amend the pleadings to assert the defense at this time pursuant to rule 15(b) of the Rules of Civil Procedure, as we do not believe the issue of avoidable consequences was "tried" to the court either expressly or impliedly.

Affirmed.

CASE QUESTIONS

1. What type of service did Dine Out provide?
2. What was the difference between the current year's contract and the former contract?
3. Was there a difference in revenue for Mr. Lininger?
4. How much is awarded to Mr. Lininger and why?

E T H I C A L   I S S U E S

15.2 Jan and Jeff Bennett were married on January 21, 1996. Their honeymoon was a 10-day cruise. They flew from Seattle to Puerto Rico where they were to begin their cruise, but their luggage did not arrive in Puerto Rico. They were assured by American Airlines that it was on its way. As each day passed, they were notified that their luggage would be waiting for them at the next port, but their luggage never arrived and they spent their 10-day cruise and honeymoon in the same clothes. They had no clothes for swimming, tennis, exercise, or other activities that were part of the cruise.

The Bennetts, who still do not have their luggage, returned home and filed suit against American Airlines for $500,000. They based the damages on their honeymoon's being ruined and their inability to take time from work for another year to take a similar cruise.

Is their demand for damages reasonable? What about the airlines' liability limitations for loss of passenger luggage? Is it fair to allow the Bennetts to recover so much for their lost luggage?

FOR THE MANAGER'S DESK

JUST-IN-TIME SUPPLY CONTRACTS— HIGH BENEFITS/ HIGH RISK

A manufacturing and business trend of the late 1980s is just-in-time management or just-in-time purchasing (JIT). Toyota Motor Company of Japan developed JIT techniques that emphasize reduction of inventory, limited production runs, short set-up times for product runs, and elimination of excesses in production. JIT allows a company to carry hours or minutes worth of parts or supplies near the production line rather than days or months of these parts or supplies.

These supply contracts, often SPPS (see Chapter 14), work well to save money for both buyer and seller. However, if there is the slightest glitch in delivery of parts or supplies, consequential damages are significant.

Continued

For example, in the old English case of *Hadley* v. *Baxendale,* 156 Eng. Rep. 145 (1854), the lack of timely delivery of a crankshift to a flour mill cost the mill customers, contracts, operations, and profit.	To help both sides, JIT contracts should have the parties cover the following: 1. Disclosures of the high risk of nondelivery 2. Discussion of damages in the event of nondelivery	3. Provision for risk premium—price paid for seller assuming risk of JIT failure 4. Limitations on consequential damages 5. Alternative inventory plans

E T H I C A L   I S S U E S

15.3 George Michael, an English recording artist, rocketed to international fame in the 1980s as the lead singer with the pop group Wham! Mr. Michael was signed in 1988 by Sony Music Entertainment for a 15-year exclusive recording contract. His first solo album with Sony was "Faith," which sold 14 million copies worldwide. Mr. Michael conducted a year-long world tour to promote the "Faith" album. After the tour, he became dissatisfied with his lack of privacy. Sony wanted him to do more tours, but he felt the tours would only create more privacy problems for him.

Mr. Michael also became dissatisfied with the image Sony had created for him. Mr. Michael said Sony had created a "sex-saturated" image of him and that his music and the quality of his songs were lost in the promotion of him as a sex symbol.

Mr. Michael brought suit alleging Sony had breached its contract with him through its insistence on the cultivated image. At the trial of the case in London, Sony barristers introduced evidence that Mr. Michael's agent had sought more money from Sony between 1988 and 1990. Sony barristers also established that Mr. Michael did not complain to Sony about his marketing during the 1988 "Faith" tour, nor did Mr. Michael's agents express any concerns.

Was Mr. Michael's suit about artistic freedom? Was there any breach of contract by Sony? Did Mr. Michael want more money than the original contract provided? Why can't he just be paid more? Didn't Sony make Mr. Michael a star? Is it ethical for him to leave Sony after its investment in his debut album?

NOTE: Mr. Michael lost his suit. But Dreamworks SKG and Virgin Records purchased his record contract from Sony for $40 million. [*Panayiotou* v. *Sony Music Entertainment(UK) Ltd.,* 8711 (1993).]

C O N S I D E R . . . **15.9** Boeing Company was scheduled to deliver several of its 747-400 jumbo jetliners to Northwest Airlines by December 31, 1988. Northwest set that deadline because it needed the $16 million in investment tax credits the planes would bring. Boeing missed the December 31 deadline, and Northwest wants to recover compensation from Boeing for the lost tax credits. Could Northwest recover for these lost credits?

CONTRACT PERSPECTIVES

Contracts, if properly performed and enforced, are the key to successful operation of any business. Contracts that are enforced give businesses the ability to plan and rely on future events and performances. However, as "Are Contracts Obsolete?" indicates, the enforceability of contracts may be an issue of concern to business.

FOR THE MANAGER'S DESK

ARE CONTRACTS OBSOLETE?

On the strength of 12-year contracts signed in 1978 to supply utilities with uranium at $38 a pound and up, International Minerals & Chemicals Corp. spent $180 million building plants to produce uranium. Now it sells for $15, and three utilities that had agreed to buy 20 percent of production from two of the plants are suing to get out of their contracts.

Unusual? Not at all. IMC President George Kennedy isn't the only executive whose contracts are under assault. In the past yeaz

- The Arkansas Public Service Commission moved to void an Arkansas Power & Light contract with a sister company supporting a contingent liability of $500 million.
- An act of Congress allowed more than a dozen forest products companies to welsh on $2 billion in timber contracts after prices had fallen to a fourth of the contractual level.
- Dow Chemical and Consumers Power began

slugging it out in court in a $520 million contractual dispute that arose when the utility said it wouldn't finish its nuclear power project on time.
- Nourse Auditorium in San Francisco was remodeled as a courtroom complete with carpeting, a $200,000 computer and tables for 100 lawyers. The reason: trying to determine which insurance contracts apply in lawsuits against five asbestos manufacturers and nearly 75 insurers.

Isn't anyone's word any good anymore?

Since 1970 the number of private contract disputes brought annually to federal courts has tripled, to 35,400. The plain fact is that for a number of companies, doing business by traditional contracts doesn't work anymore. More disturbing, courts are pressuring companies to compromise on contract claims or else are rewriting the contracts themselves.

Are contracts a thing of the past?

Unusually severe price fluctuation is partly to blame for the erosion of the contract

in recent years. When a company enters into a contract, it assumes the risk that prices will change. But prices in the last decade have often gyrated much more wildly than anyone expected. The classic example, of course, is Westinghouse, which discovered in 1975 that prices for the uranium it had agreed to supply utilities had risen so high that it would lose as much as $2 billion, more than the company's net worth at the time. Westinghouse decided, simply, that it would not abide by its contracts.

There have been sharp price swings in other eras, of course, and the contract has survived unscathed. But this time there are new forces at work.

Deregulation has aggravated price instability and triggered numerous attempts to get out from under painful contracts.

Also, outright government interference has voided contracts. The Arkansas PSC's attempt last year to force Arkansas Power & Light to break a contract failed in federal court. But in Washington a state court simply voided the WPPSS contracts underlying the biggest municipal

Continued

bond issue at that time. As for the $7 billion due bondholders, too bad.

Another new element eroding contract sanctity is the increasing pace of technological change. Contract law is rooted in English common law cases like the 1647 *Paradine* v. *Jane,* in which a tenant asked to be excused from back rent because he had been evicted by an invading German prince. (He had to pay anyway.) Such precedents aren't much help to a court trying to pinpoint the start of liability, when modern medicine can demonstrate that asbestosis traces back to products installed two decades before the disease was widely recognized.

Under these pressures, the few common law precedents allowing contracts to be broken are being broadened, not narrowed. For example, it has long been possible to be excused from a contract if performing it has become impossible—if, say, the music hall you wanted to rent burned down. Now, first in the Uniform Commercial Code adopted in the Sixties and more recently in the 1981 *Restatement (Second) of Contracts,* a review of common law, the word "impossible" has been changed, significantly, to "impracticable."

A key to using the *impracticability* excuse [emphasis added] is to show that it was impossible to foresee OPEC, inflation, disinflation or whatever. For example, the interstate pipeline companies expected endlessly rising demand for natural gas. So they were willing to sign contracts obligating them to pay escalating prices

for gas. Then came deregulation and energy glut, and some gas companies decided to renege. Says Tenneco general counsel Walter Sapp, "The Natural Gas Policy Act [which deregulated gas prices] was in effect an intervention of a *force majeure* nature." In other words, it's the government's fault, not ours.

Yet how unforeseeable was the drop in demand? Clearly, some gas pipeline companies did foresee it. Some pipeline companies knew enough to put "market out" clauses in their contracts, giving them an out in case demand fell off and high-priced gas went begging. "We like to think we were a little smarter," says Jim Walzel, president of Houston Natural Gas. MidCon Corp., who saw the gathering storm and sold much of its high-priced gas off-system to other lines. MidCon then was able to buy gas under better contracts after prices fell.

Another traditional way of being excused from a contract is "mutual mistake"— i.e., both parties misunderstood a crucial element in the deal at signing. A 1980 federal court case, *Alcoa* v. *Essex,* takes this legal principle into new territory. Alcoa's pricing formula, drawn up with the help of economist Alan Greenspan, failed to provide for rising energy costs on a contract to sell molten aluminum to Essex Group. Faced with a $75 million loss, Alcoa went to court. The judge agreed there had been a mutual mistake since both parties thought the pricing formula would reflect

Alcoa's true costs, so he rewrote the pricing clause.

The Alcoa decision could open the floodgates for contract dodgers. Already others are trying to use the Alcoa excuse. The Lower Colorado River Authority and the city of Austin, Tex. hauled Decker Coal, a joint venture of Nerco and Peter Kiewit Sons, into court over a $1 billion contract to supply coal. Austin wants out of the contract because the pricing was allegedly a "mutual mistake."

How can companies protect themselves against contract busting?

Writing better contracts is certainly one way, as a few pipeline companies demonstrated.

Writing shorter-term contracts may help also. A lot of companies that used to write 20-year contracts—Virginia Power, Rohm & Haas and Alcoa, to name only a few— have learned the hard way to look upon a five-year contract as long term.

Persuading your customers to shoulder future risks helps, too. The North American Coal Corp., a $500 million (sales) mining company, sells coal to utilities on cost-plus, narrow-margin contracts. In return the utilities take on the debt to finance the mining. North American's slimmer margins looked dumb when other mining companies were signing long-term contracts at fixed prices far above their costs. But now, with lower demand and prices, utilities are cutting back to the contractual minimum, or even suing to get out of the contracts. North American's lower prices still look attractive. Result: Although the coal industry's

Continued

return on equity has shrunk to about 11 percent, North American earned more than 20 percent last year.

New dispute-resolving techniques are also emerging that keep the discussion outside the courtroom. Some 22 insurance companies and 33 asbestos manufacturers are trying to set up a pool to settle contractual disputes.

There are also organizations, like New York City's new Center for Public Resources, that stage mock minitrials to help companies focus their dispute-resolving negotiations. CPR has lawyers present abbreviated versions of both sides of the dispute and then lets top executives of the companies resolve the matter themselves, with an impartial observer mediating. Texaco and Borden, who had been battling each other for two years over a $200 million gas contract, were able to resolve their dispute in a few weeks, thanks to such a minitrial.

"Some people are saying that it's very important for the courts to come in on these contract disputes," says University of Chicago law professor Douglas Baird. "I think that's crazy. Lots of businessmen make stupid mistakes.

But it's nonsense to think that a court will do any better."

Are contracts dead?

As business struggles to adapt to the increasing pace of change, so must the legal instruments in which business deals are articulated. Contracts aren't dead, they're just growing up.

Discussion Questions
1. What examples of major contracts that were unenforceable are given?
2. What suggestions are given for businesses in drafting their contracts?
3. What suggestions for legal reform are offered?

Source: Robert McGough, "Are Contracts Obsolete?" *FORBES*, April 29, 1985, p. 101. Reprinted By Permission of *FORBES* Magazine © Forbes, Inc., 1985.

C O N S I D E R . . . **15.10** Dan O'Connor paid $125 to have Notre Dame University's leprechaun mascot tattooed on his upper arm with the words "Fighting Irish" inscribed above the little gnome. The tattoo parlor inscribed the chosen leprechaun and "Fighting Irish."

Mr. O'Connor's girlfriend pointed out the spelling error, and Mr. O'Connor filed suit against the Tattoo Shoppe in Carlstadt, New Jersey, seeking unspecified damages.

Mr. O'Connor noted, "I was irate, and for a minute or two after I cooled down I kind of giggled. But I can't just live with this. You're not talking about a dented car where you can get another one . . . you're talking about flesh."

What damages should Mr. O'Connor receive? Would a refund of $125 be enough? What if the Tattoo Shoppe had a clause in its contract limiting damages to a refund? Would it be valid?

THIRD-PARTY RIGHTS IN CONTRACTS

Generally, a contract is a relationship between or among the contracting parties and is not enforceable by others who happen to benefit. For example, suppose a landowner and a commercial developer enter into an agreement for the construction of a shopping mall. Such a project means jobs for the area and additional business for restaurants, hotels, and transportation companies, but these businesses would not have the right to enforce the contract or collect damages for breach if the developer pulled out of the project. However, certain groups of people do have rights in contracts even though they may not have been parties to the contracts. A good example would be a beneficiary of a life insurance policy.

The beneficiary does not contract with the insurance company and does not pay the premiums, but the purchaser of the policy allows the beneficiary contract rights because the benefits of the contract are to go to that beneficiary.

In other types of third-party contract rights, the third parties are not part of the original contract, as is the life insurance beneficiary, but are brought in after the fact. For example, suppose that a plumbing contractor is owed $5,000 by a homebuilder for work done on homes in the builder's subdivision. In the sales contracts for the homes, the homebuilder is the seller, and the buyer's purchase monies will go to the homebuilder. However, the homebuilder could assign payment rights to the plumber as a means of satisfying the debt. This process, called **assignment**, gives the plumber the right to collect the contract amount from the buyer. The plumber takes the place of the homebuilder in terms of contract rights.

In some cases, the duty or obligation to perform under a contract is transferred to another party. The transfer of contractual duties and obligation is called a **delegation**. Generally, a delegation of duties carries with it an assignment of benefits. For example, suppose that Neptune Fisheries, Inc., has a contract with Tom Tuna, Inc., to sell 30 fresh lobsters each day. Neptune is stopping its lobster line and delegates its duties under the Tom Tuna contract to Louie's Lobsters, Inc. Louie's takes over Neptune's obligation to furnish the 30 lobsters and is assigned the right to benefits (payment for the lobsters) under the contract. Both Louie's and Neptune are liable to Tom Tuna for performance. A delegation, unlike a novation, does not release the original contracting party.

FOR THE MANAGER'S DESK

THE ETHICS OF BANKRUPTCY

The music group TLC (T-Boz, Left-Eye, and Chili), a three-woman group based in Atlanta, rose to the top of the music charts in 1993 and has since had two multiplatinum albums along with six top singles.

At the end of 1995, all three women filed for bankruptcy. If the bankruptcy judge grants their petition, the three women will be excused from the record contracts they signed five years ago with independent producers. When groups are unknown, as TLC was five years ago, the major record producers will not sign them. These groups rely on independent producers. The contracts negotiated with "new kids" are extremely

lopsided in the producer's favor. For example, a producer has the right to drop an artist at any time, but the artist has no right to leave the contract relationship. However, when groups' music takes off and they begin selling records, the stars want renegotiated contracts or contracts with other producers. They want more than the customary industry figure of 12 percent royalties for new artists.

From 1995 to 1996, three other groups filed for bankruptcy after achieving success in the pop music charts. Section 365 of the Federal Bankruptcy Code permits the bankruptcy court to release a debtor from contracts that are burdensome or oner-ous or impair the ability of the debtor to make a fresh start.

The lawyer for TLC maintains that the women have debts and meet the test for bankruptcy. The lawyer for their producer says the women face only a cash-flow problem and that $2.2 million in royalties is in the system for them. He also adds, "I think they wanted to be bankrupt because they think they can get out of their contract on the basis of bankruptcy."

Discussion Questions
1. Is it ethical to run up debts in order to declare bankruptcy to get out of a contract?
2. Is it ethical to declare bankruptcy to obtain a higher royalty percentage on your sales through another contract?

INTERNATIONAL ISSUES IN CONTRACT PERFORMANCE

Assuring Payment

International contract transactions for goods necessarily involve shipment. To control access to the goods and, hence, payment for the goods, many sellers use a **bill of lading** for transacting business. The bill of lading is a receipt for shipment issued by the carrier to the seller. It is also a contract for the shipment of the goods and evidence of who has title to the goods listed on the bill of lading. If a bill of lading is used, the buyer will not gain access to the goods unless and until the seller provides the necessary documents for release of the goods. Once the seller has the bill of lading, the seller can choose to transfer title to the goods by transferring the bill of lading. The seller could also pledge the bill of lading as security for the payment of a debt. A bill of lading can be made directly to the buyer, or it can be a negotiable bill of lading that can be transferred to anyone.

Review bills of lading:
http:// www.
showtrans.com/
bl.htm

The bill of lading is often used in conjunction with a line of credit in international transactions because the two together offer the seller assurance of payment and the buyer assurance of arrival of the goods. In international transactions, in which resolution of disputes over great distances can be difficult, this means of controlling access to goods and payment is very helpful.

In this type of transaction, the seller delivers goods to a carrier for transportation and receives a bill of lading. The seller then sends the bill of lading through his or her bank to the buyer's bank to give the buyer's bank title to the goods, which will be turned over to the buyer once the funds are deducted from the line of credit established by the bank for the buyer.

The buyer may also arrange for a **letter of credit** to be used in conjunction with the bill of lading. The letter of credit is issued by the buyer's bank and is sent to a corresponding bank where the seller is located. The letter of credit lists the terms and conditions under which the seller can draw on the letter of credit or be paid. For example, turning the bill of lading over to the corresponding bank may be the condition of drawing on the letter of credit; the bill of lading is then used by the corresponding bank and the buyer's bank to allow the buyer to take possession of the goods. Because banks are involved in these transactions through credit assurances, the seller enjoys more of an assurance of payment prior to shipment because a letter of credit is actually a confirmation of payment.

Assuring Performance—International Peculiarities

International contracts have a particular need for a *force majeure* clause. Wars, revolutions, and coups are often included in international contracts as justification for noncompletion of the contract. The *force majeure* clauses are summaries of potential international events that could hamper production or trade.

One other risk of international contracts is the stability of various currencies and their possible devaluation. The method and means of payment should be specified in the contract, and a clause covering devaluation may also be included so that full payment is ensured.

The following case illustrates what can happen between the negotiation of an international contract and the time for contract payment.

Lakeway Co. v. Bravos
576 S.W.2d 926 (Tex. 1979)

FALLING PESOS: NEGOTIATING AN EXCHANGE RATE

FACTS

Lakeway and Bravos (in a contract drawn and executed in both English and Spanish) agreed that Bravos would buy a certain Lakeway lot in Travis County, Texas. The purchase price was $25,820, with payment by Bravos to be in pesos. The agreement was executed July 31, 1976.

By the time the check was presented for final payment, it was August 30, 1976. The Mexican government devalued the peso on August 31, 1976, and the result was that Lakeway received $8,188.45 less than it would have had the transaction not been subject to an interim devaluation. Lakeway brought suit. Summary judgment was granted for Bravos, and Lakeway appealed.

JUDICIAL OPINION

SUMMERS, Chief Justice

Appellant (Lakeway) contends that the intention of the parties, as set forth in the contract, was for a total purchase price of $25,820.00; that how it was paid, whether in dollars or in pesos, was immaterial so long as the result to the seller was the required number of dollars; and that the peso figure in parenthesis was simply for the convenience of the buyer to let him know how many pesos would be required to buy the property. It urges that this intention is supported by the fact that the contract provides that "Seller agrees to notify Buyers in writing of the total amount due in Mexican pesos if a change in the official exchange rate occurs prior to such payment." We agree with these contentions.

However, in the instant case a check payable in the correct amount of pesos for final payment under the contract was delivered to Lakeway by the Bravos on August 18, 1976; such check was received by Lakeway without objection; said check was honored and cleared appellees' bank account on August 30, 1976, prior to the devaluation of the peso which occurred on August 31, 1976; and when honored and paid in due course, the payment became absolute and related back to the date of delivery of the check on August 18, 1976; and as of said date of delivery it produced the specified value in dollars and satisfied the terms of the contract.

The judgment of the trial court is affirmed.

CASE QUESTIONS

1. What was the land purchase price?
2. How much did Lakeway lose once there was devaluation?
3. Will Lakeway get more money?
4. How did the contract address the issue of devaluation?

SUMMARY

What if the assumptions made and the information given turn out to be untrue? Must the parties still go forward with the contract?

- Contract defense—situation, term, or event that excuses performance
- Capacity—mental and age threshold for valid contracts
- Voidable contract—one party can choose not to honor the contract
- Puffing—statements of opinion

- Material fact—basis of the bargain
- Void contract—contract that courts will not honor
- Misrepresentation—incomplete or inaccurate information prior to contract execution
- Rescission—setting aside of contract as a remedy
- Fraud—intentional misrepresentation
- Scienter—knowledge that information given is false
- Duress—physical or mental force that deprives party of a meaningful choice with respect to a proposed contract
- Undue influence—exerting control over another party for purposes of gain
- Confidential relationship—trust, confidence, reliance in a relationship
- Public policy—standards of decency
- Exculpatory clauses—attempt to hold oneself harmless for one's own conduct
- Unconscionable contract—contract that is grossly unfair

If one party does not perform, is the other side excused? When is performance required and when is it excused?
- Conditions precedent—advance events that must occur before performance is due, i.e., obtaining financing
- Substantial performance—performance that, for practical purposes, is just as good as full performance
- Commercial impracticability—defense to performance of sales contract based on objective impracticability
- Novation—agreement to change contract among all affected, i.e., agreement to substitute parties
- Accord and satisfaction—agreement entered into as settlement of a disputed debt

What remedies exist?
- Compensatory damages—amount required to place party in as good a position as before breach
- Incidental damages—costs of collecting compensatory damages
- Liquidated damages—agreement clause in contract that preestablishes and limits damages
- Consequential damages—damages owed to third parties from a breach

What are the contract performance issues in international business?
- Bill of lading—title document used to control transfer of goods
- Letter of credit—pledge by bank of availability of funds for a transaction

Do third parties have rights in a contract?
- Incidental beneficiary—an indirect beneficiary
- Donee beneficiary—a beneficiary designated in the contract; third party intended to benefit from the contract, e.g., life insurance
- Creditor beneficiary—a beneficiary designated in one contract who will compensate him for services given pursuant to a separate contract, e.g., health insurance

QUESTIONS AND PROBLEMS

1. Robert G. Rawlinson was employed by Germantown Manufacturing in Marple Township as its assistant controller. He embezzled $372,113.21 from the company, which discovered the theft, though not the exact amount, on May 21, 1982. Mr. Rawlinson admitted his wrongdoing and was fired. He did not tell his wife, and it was not until she eavesdropped on a telephone conversation between her husband and Peter Kulaski that she discovered something was amiss. Mr. Rawlinson told her (after his phone conversation) that he had taken $20,000 from the company and was fired. Mrs. Rawlinson testified that her "whole world fell apart" upon hearing the news. She was already depressed and tired because of a miscarriage she had suffered in late April.

    The following day Mr. Kulaski came to the Rawlinson home and asked them to sign two judgment notes. The first note was for $160,000, the amount Mr. Rawlinson admitted taking from the company. The second note was for any amounts above and beyond the $160,000 that would be established by the company president as having been taken by Mr. Rawlinson. Mrs. Rawlinson's name was on the documents, and she asked if they should not have an attorney. Mr. Kulaski told them they did not need an attorney because the company was acting in good faith and that no criminal charges would be brought if the Rawlinsons would cooperate. Mrs. Rawlinson felt that if she signed the notes, her husband would not go to jail.

    Mrs. Rawlinson had never before seen a judgment note and cried while trying to read these. She thought she was signing only for $160,000 and, because her husband had a check for $150,000 ready to turn over, that they could easily come up with the remaining $10,000.

    In August 1982, the president of the company verified that the total amount taken was $212,113.21 more than the $160,000 already paid. When demand for payment was made, Mrs. Rawlinson requested that the confession of judgment be opened and disallowed on the basis of misrepresentation. The lower court found for Mrs. Rawlinson, and German Manufacturing appealed. Give a list of defenses Mrs. Rawlinson could use. [*Germantown Mfrg. Co.* v. *Rawlinson*, 491 A.2d 138 (Pa. 1985).]

2. Tony Curtis, a respected actor, entered into a contract to write a novel for Doubleday & Company, publishers. Because of complex divorce proceedings and other personal factors, Mr. Curtis was unable to submit a satisfactory manuscript. Doubleday demanded a return of the $50,000 advance Mr. Curtis had received. Are they entitled to it? [*Doubleday & Co.*, v. *Curtis*, 763 F.2d 495 (2d Cir. 1985).]

3. Bernina Sewing Machines imports sewing machines and parts for U.S. distribution. Its contract prices are in francs. Because of the devaluation of the U.S. dollar, Bernina wants to be excused from its contracts. Can it be excused under any contract doctrine? [*Bernina Distributors, Inc.* v. *Bernina Sewing Machines*, 646 F.2d 434 (10th Cir. 1981).]

4. Would failure to disclose a delinquency on your mortgage on a loan application be a misrepresentation? [*Barrer* v. *Women's National Bank*, 761 F.2d 752 (D.C. 1985).]

5. Orkin investigated Helen M. Clarkson's home for termites and found none, but continued routine inspections. After one monthly inspection, Ms. Clarkson hired another firm to inspect for termites. The firm found termite tunnels and damage. Ms. Clarkson had to spend approximately $1,200 for repairs. Could she recover that amount from Orkin? [*Clarkson* v. *Orkin Exterminating Co., Inc.*, 761 F.2d 189 (4th Cir. 1985).]

6. List the possible consequences for an air traveler bumped due to overbooking of a flight. How much should a traveler be permitted to recover? [*West* v. *Northwest Airlines, Inc.*, 995 F.2d 148 (9th Cir. 1993).]

7. Amy was a 78-year-old widow who lived alone. She drove an hour each day to take care of her disabled sister, Mary. When Mary died, Amy drove to take care of Mary's husband, Bill. Bill left Amy a fourth of his estate when he died. Was there undue influence? [*Totman* v. *Vernon*, 494 A.2d 97 (R.I. 1985).]

Retail Buyers Order

ESTATE MOTORS LTD.
464 S. Woodward Telephone 644-8400
BIRMINGHAM, MICHIGAN 48011

Purchasers
Name _____ Robert Barto _____   Date __Feb. 21, 1990__

— NEW — CAR

PLEASE ENTER MY ORDER FOR ONE Mercedes Benz   — USED — TRUCK
AS FOLLOWS

Year	Make	Model or Series	Body Type	Color	Trim
1991	Mercedes Benz 500SL		2 Door	199 Black Pearl	Gray Leather

MVI or Serial No.	Stock No.	To Be Delivered
		On or About 19

CASH PRICE OF VEHICLE _____

_____

_____

199	BLACK PEARL—
	Gray Leather—
740	Black Soft Top

TOTAL _____

TAX _____

TOTAL CASH DELIVERED PRICE

CASH DEPOSIT SUBMITTED WITH ORDER   500—

SALESMAN /s/ (Doug MacFarlane)   SIGNED /s/ (Robert Barto)

PURCHASER

PURCHASER'S
NAME _____ Robert Barto _____

STREET
THIS ORDER IS NOT VALID UN-   ADDRESS _1 Winward Place_
LESS SIGNED BY DEALER OR
CITY &
HIS AUTHORIZED REPRESEN-   STATE _Gross Pointe Farms_   ZIP _48236_
TATIVE.

APPROVED_____   BUS. PHONE_____

Dealer or Authorized   RES. PHONE _886-2277_
Representative

THIS ORDER IS NOT A BINDING CONTRACT

CASH OR CASHIER'S CHECK UPON DELIVERY

---

8. On February 21, 1990, Robert Barto and his wife signed an agreement with Estate Motors, Ltd., of Birmingham, Michigan, to purchase a Mercedes Benz 500 SL automobile. They signed the above agreement.

   Doug MacFarlane, their salesman, told the Bartos that because of high demand, their car might not be delivered for 18 months.

   In mid-August 1991, Mr. MacFarlane telephoned Mr. Barto and informed him that his Mercedes would be at the dealership and ready for pickup on August 30. Mr.

MacFarlane also informed Mr. Barto in that telephone conversation for the first time that he would have to pay a luxury tax on his new car (in addition to the purchase price, state sales tax, and license/title fees) when he came to pick it up.

Mr. Barto was angry about having to pay the luxury tax because he believed that his car fell within the scope of the preexisting binding contract exception as his order for the car had been placed before September 30, 1990. During the ensuing weeks before his car arrived at Estate Motors, Mr. Barto telephoned the Mercedes-Benz district sales representatives and legal counsel and was informed that Mercedes-Benz was advising their dealers that the new luxury tax was not to be assessed on cars ordered before September 30, 1990. Mr. Barto also learned that of the 114 Mercedes-Benz dealers within the midwest region, only Estate Motors was assessing the tax on cars ordered before September 30, 1990.

Mr. Barto attempted to negotiate a manner of payment of the tax with Estate Motors. He first proposed that he bring with him two checks when he picked up his car—one check payable to Estate Motors for everything but the amount of the luxury tax, and one check for the luxury tax payable to the IRS. The dealer refused this arrangement. Mr. Barto then suggested that he pay the luxury tax into an escrow account. Again the dealer refused. Because Mr. Barto wanted his new car, he ultimately agreed to pay Estate Motors the full purchase price, including the luxury tax assessment.

On August 30, 1991, when Mr. Barto went to Estate Motors to pick up his Mercedes-Benz, he tendered to the dealer his check for $111,446 to cover the $99,950 purchase price of the car, the sales tax/license/title fees of $4,501, and the 10 percent luxury tax amounting to $6,995. Mr. Barto and the dealer also executed on August 30 Estate Motors' "Statement of Vehicle Sale," which reflected the breakdown of his $111,946 total purchase price, license/title transfer and proof of insurance information, and the odometer disclosure.

Mr. Barto continued to protest having to pay the $6,995 luxury tax on his new Mercedes after picking the car up. The dealer provided Mr. Barto with a blank IRS 843 form for a tax refund. When the IRS denied Mr. Barto's claim for refund, he filed suit against Estate.

Mr. Barto wished to rescind the agreement. He wanted his $500 back. Is Mr. Barto entitled to it? Is there a contract at all? [*Barto v. United States*, 823 F. Supp. 1369 (E.D. Mich. 1993).]

9. Betty Lobianco had a burglar alarm system installed in her home by Property Protection, Inc. The contract for installing the system provided:

> Alarm system equipment installed by Property Protection, Inc. is guaranteed against improper function due to manufacturing defects of workmanship for a period of 12 months. The installation of the above equipment carries a 90-day warranty. The liability of Property Protection, Inc. is limited to repair or replacement of security alarm equipment and does not include loss or damage to possessions, persons or property.

> On November 22, 1975, Ms. Lobianco's home was burglarized and $35,815 in jewelry was taken. The alarm system, which had been installed less than 90 days earlier, included a standby source of power in case the regular source of power failed. On the day of the fateful burglary, the alarm did not go off because the batteries installed in the system had no power.

> Ms. Lobianco brought suit to recover the $35,815. She claimed that the liability limitation was unconscionable and unenforceable under the UCC. Property Protection claimed that the UCC did not apply to the installation of a burglar alarm system. Who is correct? [*Lobianco v. Property Protection, Inc.*, 437 A.2d 417 (Pa. 1981).]

10. Northrup King Company produces and sells seeds to farmers and others throughout the United States. Northrup placed the following disclaimer on its product:

NOTICE: Northrup King Co. warrants that seeds sold have been labeled as required under State and Federal Seed Laws and that they conform to the label description. No liability hereunder shall be asserted unless the buyer or user reports to the warrantor within a reasonable period after discovery (not to exceed 30 days), any condition that might lead to a complaint. <u>Our liability on this warranty is limited in amount to the purchase price of the seeds. This warranty is in lieu of all other warranties, express or implied, including warranties of merchantability and fitness for a particular purpose. There are no warranties which extend beyond the face hereof.</u>

The underlined language was in red print on containers. Northrup sold pepper seeds to Floyd Ammons, whose pepper crop developed bacterial rust-spotting disease. Mr. Ammons brought suit for damages (loss of his crop), saying the disclaimer is unconscionable and void. It he right? [*Northrup King Co.* v. *Ammons*, 9 U.C.C.2d Rep. Serv. (Callaghan) 836 (4th Cir. 1989).]

Judgment

Albert and Marianne Driscoll of El Paso, Texas, owed $2,000 in credit card debt.

Household Credit Services, Inc., of Salinas, Kansas, was hired to collect the debt. A collector called Mrs. Driscoll's office 36 times in one hour, tying up the office phones. Another collector called the Driscolls at home and threatened a contract on their lives if they didn't pay up. Still another called Mrs. Driscoll's office and disrupted the office with a bomb threat.

The Driscolls went to see Noel Gage, an El Paso attorney, with one question, "Can they do this to us?"

CHAPTER 16

The English refer to credit sales as "buying on the never

never" because

Financing of Sales and Leases: Credit and Disclosure Requirements

you never really

pay for everything; there is always some outstanding

credit. Credit sales are a way of life in the United States.

Nearly all sellers advertise not only their products but

also the availability of credit terms for buyers. Credit is

used so often that both Congress and state legislatures

have enacted statutes regulating credit contracts. This

chapter covers those regulations and credit contracts.

How is a credit contract set up? What are the require-

ments? What statutes affect the credit contract? How are

credit contracts enforced?

Neither a borrower nor a lender be,

For a loan oft loses both itself and friend

And borrowing dulls the edge of

husbandry.

**Hamlet
Act I, Scene 3**

ESTABLISHING A CREDIT CONTRACT

A credit contract needs not only the usual elements of a contract (as covered in Chapter 14), including offer, acceptance, and consideration, but it requires additional information for the credit agreement to be valid. The following list covers the extra details needed in a credit contract:

1. How much the buyer/debtor is actually carrying on credit or financing;
2. The rate of interest the buyer/debtor will pay;
3. How many payments will be made, when they will be made, and for how long;
4. Penalties and actions for late payments;
5. Whether the creditor will have collateral; and
6. The necessary statutory disclosures on credit transactions

STATUTORY REQUIREMENTS FOR CREDIT CONTRACTS

The following statutes affect and, in some cases, control the terms in a credit contract.

State Usury Laws

Usury is charging an interest rate higher than the maximum permitted by law. If the maximum rate of interest permitted by statute is 21 percent, a creditor charging 24 percent has violated a statute and created a void contract.

The usury rate varies from state to state, and many states have different usury rates for the various types of transactions. For example, the usury rate for real estate loans may be lower than the usury rate for credit cards or installment credit transactions. Some states' usury rates are just a percentage figure, whereas other states include loan origination charges, finders' fees, service charges, and other fees paid by the debtor in determining the actual rate of interest charged.

Penalties for charging a usurious rate also vary. Some states treat the usurious agreement as completely void, and the penalty for the creditor is forfeiture of interest and principal. Other states allow the creditor to recoup the principal but deny any interest. Some states simply require the creditor to forfeit any interest above the maximum; others also impose a penalty on the creditor by allowing the debtor to collect two or three times the amount of excess interest charged as damages.

C O N S I D E R . . . **16.1** Tombstone Terrace (a mining joint venture) needed a loan for operations. It had approached several local and national lenders but was unable to secure a loan. Tombstone finally secured a loan for $300,000 from a group of foreign investors. The terms of the loan were as follows:

- $50,000 to be paid in six equal installments
- $30,000 in interest to be paid in two installments
- $20,000 in financier's fees to be paid in two installments
- 2 percent per-month charge for late payments

Continued

The usurious rate in the state at the time of the loan was 10 percent. Tombstone has defaulted on the loan. Is the loan usurious? Is it void? [*LaBarr* v. *Tombstone Terrace Mint*, 582 P.2d 639 (Ariz. 1978).]

E T H I C A L   I S S U E S

16.1 A popular banking and credit practice is to charge annual fees for credit cards as well as late penalties in addition to finance charges. For example, many cards have an annual $25 renewal fee. Many cards also have a $15–$25 late fee assessed on the account in addition to the finance charges on the account balance. The National Bank Act permits such charges, but consumers have brought suit challenging the fees as violating state usury laws since they are fees in addition to the maximum interest rates already assessed by the companies on the card balances. Is it fair for the creditors to assess such fees? Do you think it is usury? Is it good business to charge such fees? [*Spellman* v. *Meridian Bank*, 825 F. Supp. 1239 (E.D. Pa. 1995).]

The Equal Credit Opportunity Act

Review the Equal Credit Opportunity Act: http://www.law.cornell.edu/uscode/15/1691.html

Visit the Federal Trade Commission: http://www.ftc.gov/

The **Equal Credit Opportunity Act (ECOA)** was passed to ensure that credit was denied or awarded on the applicant's merits—the ability to pay—and not on such extraneous factors as sex, race, color, religion, national origin, or age. (See Exhibit 16.1 on pg. 550.) Questions regarding these matters can be asked of applicants for recordkeeping purposes, but the decision to extend or deny credit must be based on factors other than these. The following types of information also cannot be considered in making the credit decision:

1. Marital status of the applicant;
2. Applicant's receipt of public assistance income;
3. Applicant's receipt of alimony or child support payments; and
4. Applicant's plans for having children

The ECOA also provides married persons the right to have individual credit applications, lines, and ratings. Credit applications must specify that a spouse's income need not be disclosed unless the applicant is relying on that income to qualify for credit. Further, even on joint accounts, debtors can require creditors to report credit ratings individually for the spouses.

Violations of the ECOA carry statutory penalties. The ECOA is enforceable by the Federal Trade Commission (FTC), by the U.S. attorney general, and by private actions by debtors. Debtors can sue for their actual damages for embarrassment and emotional distress and also for punitive damages of up to $10,000. If a group of debtors brings a class action against a creditor, they can collect punitive damages of up to the lesser of $500,000 or 1 percent of the creditor's net worth. Punitive damages are recoverable even when there are no actual damages. The *Barber* case involves an issue of an ECOA violation.

Credit Statute (Federal))	Purpose and Scope
Equal Credit Opportunity Act 15 U.S.C. § 1691 (1974)	Prohibits discrimination on the basis of sex, race, age or national origin in credit extension decision
Consumer Credit Protection Act (CCPA) 15 U.S.C. § 1601 (1968)	Umbrella statute passed to deal with fairness of consumer credit transactions
Truth-in-Lending Act 15 U.S.C. § 1601 (1968)	Part of CCPA that governs disclosure of credit terms
Fair Credit and Charge Card Disclosure Act 15 U.S.C. § 1646 (1988)	Provides for disclosure requirements in the solicitation of credit cards
Regulation Z 12 C.F.R. § 226 (1981)	Federal Reserve Board regulations providing details for all disclosure statutes
Home Equity Loan Consumer Protection Act 15 U.S.C. § 1647 (1988)	Disclosure requirements for home equity loans and a rescission period
Fair Credit Billing Act 15 U.S.C. § 1637 (1974)	Rights of debtors on open-end credit billing disputes
Fair Credit Reporting Act 15 U.S.C. § 1681 (1970)	Right of debtors with respect to reports of their credit histories
Consumer Leasing Act 15 U.S.C. § 1667 (1976)	Disclosure requirements for leases of goods by consumers
Fair Debt Collections Practices Act 15 U.S.C. § 1692 (1977)	Regulation of conduct of third-party bill collectors and attorneys

Exhibit 16.1
Summary of Federal Laws on Consumer Credit

Barber v. *Rancho Mortgage & Investment Corp.*
32 Cal. Rptr. 2d 906 (1994)

THE LENDER WHO MAKES THINGS UP: DISCRIMINATORY DENIAL

FACTS

In March 1988, Forecast Mortgage (defendant) offered houses for sale in Victorville, California, at a project called Meadowood. The selling prices were less than the appraised values for the homes and they were thus in great demand. Florence and Joe Barber (the Barbers), who are black and live in Gardena, California, a suburb of Los Angeles, learned about these homes from their son, who then lived in the Victorville area. On March 18, 1988, after viewing the model homes, the Barbers placed their name on a waiting list. The next day their name was called and, with the assistance of one Ron Chapman, an employee of Great Western Real Estate, they viewed the homes remaining for sale. Finding one that they liked, they filled out a purchase and sale agreement, as well as other related documentation. This offer was accepted by Forecast subject to the contingency that the Barbers obtain financing for the purchase price, and an escrow was opened.

Continued

As a first step in obtaining the required financing, the Barbers also spoke with one Glen Wilson, a "loan application taker" employed by Rancho Mortgage and Investment Corporation, who was working at the store where Forecast was selling the homes. He looked at their financial documents and pre-qualified them for an FHA loan from Rancho. At Mr. Chapman's suggestion, the Barbers decided to formally apply for an FHA loan to finance their purchase. Such a loan required a low 5 percent down payment but was available *only* to borrowers who intended to live in the purchased home. This is the so-called owner-occupied rule that is very much at the heart of the dispute in this matter. On March 20, 1988, the Barbers completed and submitted a residential loan application to Rancho.

Subsequently, on March 24, 1988, Rancho requested additional documentation, which the Barbers supplied. On May 9, 1988, they had a meeting with one of Rancho's loan processors. Both Mr. and Mrs. Barber testified that the processor treated them with rudeness and belligerence. Documents and information that had previously been supplied were requested again. The processor asked them a lot of questions about whether they really intended to live in Victorville and commute to work in Los Angeles. The Barbers insisted that it was their intent to make such a commute; indeed, they intended to carpool with their son and daughter-in-law, who also worked in Los Angeles. They very much wanted to get out of the crowded and crime-ridden urban area in which they lived. They also responded to every demand made upon them by Rancho for additional documents and information, including those which were duplicative.

The Barbers heard nothing more about their loan application until May 22, 1988, when Mrs. Barber received a telephone call from Anne Merryfield, a loan officer at Rancho, who advised her that Rancho had not approved the Barbers for an "owner-occupied" loan because it appeared they were really investors who had no intention of living in the home as required. The decision to deny a loan to the Barbers was made by Darlene Tennent, one of Rancho's underwriters, who had the sole responsibility for deciding whether to qualify the Barbers for an owner-occupied loan. Her decision to deny the Barbers' application was based on FHA guidelines, which indicated that applicants who (1) already had a primary residence that was reasonably close to their long-standing places of employment, (2) owned other rental units, and (3) would be required to engage in a long commute to work were more likely to be investors rather than persons who would really occupy the home for which the FHA loan was being sought. Mrs. Tennent said that when she discussed these circumstances with an official at FHA, she was advised to reject the application. An FHA official stated that the FHA did not make recommendations or give direction to lenders regarding the acceptance or rejection of loan applications.

Neither Ms. Tennent nor anyone else at Rancho gave the Barbers any *written* confirmation or explanation for the rejection of their loan. After the Barbers were informed on May 22, 1988, that their loan application had been rejected, they made several attempts to obtain more information but neither anyone at Rancho nor anyone at the FHA would ever return their calls, except for one FHA official who promised to set up a meeting with a representative from Rancho but never did. It was never explained to them why their expressed intention to immediately occupy the home was not accepted as true; nor were they ever told by any of the defendants that they could have (1) applied for a non-FHA loan, (2) obtained a loan from a source other than Rancho, or (3) simply paid cash for the home, which, the Barbers testified, they were capable of doing.

On or about July 20, 1988, the Barbers were notified that the escrow, which had previously been opened to handle their purchase of the home, had been canceled as of that date. The escrow officer testified that she had been instructed by Forecast to cancel the escrow and return the Barbers' cash down payment that had accompanied their original offer. Since

Continued

Forecast had a backup offer for the home, it was promptly sold to another buyer.

The Barbers filed suit alleging violations of the ECOA. The trial court found for the Barbers and imposed $10,000 in punitive damages.

JUDICIAL OPINION

CROSKEY, Associate Justice

The Barbers concede that their evidence against all of the defendants is circumstantial. They correctly note that, "[v]ery seldom, if ever, is there direct evidence of discrimination,. . . ." The evidence presented by the Barbers against Rancho may be summarized as follows: (1) they are a black couple; (2) their loan was suspended in early May 1988, but they were never notified of that suspension although they were orally advised on May 22 that their loan application had been rejected; (3) over a month earlier, on April 11, 1988, Forecast was notified that the loan may not go "owner-occupied," but no such notification was given to the Barbers; (4) the Barbers never received a specific explanation as to why their loan was denied until after they filed this action and they were never given such notice and explanation in writing as required by the provisions of the Credit Act; (5) even though Rancho was in the business of making loans, it made no effort to preserve the Barbers' financing request by offering them a non-FHA loan which would not include an "owner-occupied" restriction; (6) the Barbers were treated rudely by Rancho employees, given the "run around" when they sought information about the status and progress of their loan application and they were repeatedly asked to supply information and documentation previously delivered; and (7) Rancho, while claiming to apply FHA guidelines which suggested that the Barbers might actually be "investors," never attempted to interrogate the Barbers as to whether they really intended to live in Victorville (as the jury ultimately believed) or why they were willing to make the 75 mile daily commute to Los Angeles from Victorville; Rancho simply disapproved the loan based on the information in the Barbers' application without making any effort to actually investigate and determine if the inference which they had chosen to draw from such information was the correct one.

The question we must resolve is whether such evidence is sufficient to support the jury's conclusion that Rancho unlawfully discriminated against the Barbers in violation of the Credit Act which provides, "It shall be unlawful for any creditor to discriminate against any applicant, with respect to any credit transaction—(1) on the basis of race, . . ." (15 U.S.C. § 1691(a)(1).)

Clearly, the evidence offered by the Barbers established prima facie discriminatory conduct (15 U.S.C. § 1691(a); 42 U.S.C. § 1982). Rancho tendered the explanation, which it claimed was non-discriminatory, that the information available to it indicated that the Barbers did not qualify for FHA financing so their application was rejected. In other words, the loan application was rejected not because the Barbers were black but because the information in their application caused Rancho to believe that they could not meet the "owner-occupied" requirement.

The jury was entitled to disbelieve this explanation, given the context of all of the evidence presented. Such rejection, taken together with the prima facie case presented by the Barbers, was sufficient to establish a case of unlawful discrimination.

However, such conclusion does not necessarily establish that the imposition of $10,000 in punitive damages was proper. The Credit Act has specific provisions relating to the award of damages. "(a) Any creditor who fails to comply with any requirement imposed under this subchapter shall be liable to the aggrieved applicant for any actual damages sustained by such applicant. . . . [and also] (b) . . . shall be liable to the aggrieved applicant for punitive damages in an amount not greater than $10,000, in addition to any actual damages provided in subsection (a)." (15 U.S.C. §§ 1691e(a) & (b).) The statute also spells out the standards which the court shall apply in fixing the amount of punitive damages. "In determining the amount of such damages in any action, the court shall

Continued

consider, among other relevant factors, the amount of any actual damages awarded, the frequency and persistence of failures of compliance by the creditor, the resources of the credit, the number of persons adversely affected, and the extent to which the creditor's failure of compliance was intentional."

Under this statutory provision, punitive damages can be imposed against any creditor who fails to comply with any requirement of the subchapter. While the use of the word "shall" does not require a punitive award for every violation of the Act, it would seem clear, given the statutory standards to be applied, that malicious or oppressive conduct is *not* required.

Although the traditional word "punitive" is used, one of the factors to be considered is whether the creditor's non-compliance was intentional. *This suggests that punitive damages could be awarded even though the creditor's actions were not wanton, malicious or oppressive. Thus, courts are allowed to award punitive damages under § 1691e(b) even though the creditor's conduct is not wanton, malicious, or oppressive, in order to increase the incentive for creditor compliance.* This incentive is particularly appropriate when actual damages are difficult to prove. However, since punitive damages are awarded to punish the defendant and to serve as an example or warning to others not to engage in similar conduct, they are only justified when the defendant has committed a particularly blameworthy act. Consequently, we hold that punitive damages may be awarded pursuant to § 1691e(b) if (1) the creditor wantonly, maliciously or oppressively discriminates against an applicant, *or (2) the creditor acts in 'reckless disregard of the requirements of the law,' even though there was no specific intention to discriminate on unlawful grounds.*

Rancho does not dispute that (1) there was no substantial evidence to demonstrate a basis for punitive damages and (2) the trial court erred in making the award without first making the necessary findings.

Rancho is also incorrect when it argues that there was no evidence of a violation of the Credit Act. It is undisputed that Rancho did not comply with the statute when it failed to provide the Barbers with a *written* explanation of the reasons for rejection of their loan application. (15 U.S.C. § 1691(d).) A timely and complete written explanation might have enabled the Barbers to provide additional information which would have allayed Rancho's suspicions as to their "investor" status or, at least, have given the Barbers an opportunity to make alternative financing arrangements. On this record, the trial court could reasonably conclude that Rancho had acted in a "reckless disregard of the requirements of the law." Such a conclusion would satisfy one of the alternative requirements for award of punitive damages under 15 U.S.C. § 1691e.

As the Barbers point out, the record reflects the following evidence that Forecast had discriminated against them. The Barbers had sufficient assets to finance or, if necessary, purchase for cash the home described in their sale contract. However, at no time after the opening of escrow did anyone at Forecast contact them and demand funds by a certain date or advise them that their failure to provide funds would result in cancellation of the escrow. Although Forecast (but not the Barbers) was advised by Rancho on April 11, 1988, that the Barbers' FHA loan application was in trouble, no effort was made to save the transaction with other financing means, including the payment of cash. The escrow was unilaterally canceled by Forecast on July 20 on the stated ground (which was not true) that the Barbers had never signed the escrow instructions. While the Barber escrow was still pending, Forecast entered into two other ("backup") purchase and sale agreements with potential buyers for the same home. One of those buyers ended up closing escrow on the home and moving in even *before* the Barber escrow was canceled. Finally, Forecast presented no evidence that any of the other Meadowood homes had been sold to blacks although there was evidence that Forecast had made sales in the past to "minorities" generally.

We thus have no trouble concluding that the jury properly found that Forecast had engaged in prohibited discriminatory conduct.

Continued

CASE QUESTIONS
1. What was suspicious about the owner-occupied reason for rejection?
2. Were other alternatives for the Barbers explored?

3. Why was it important that the non-FHA option be offered to the Barbers?
4. Evaluate the ethics of the lender's conduct after the Barbers were rejected.
5. Was there a breach of contract by the lender?

C O N S I D E R . . .

16.2 Ann Stone runs a $15-million direct-mail solicitation business in Virginia. Her clients include ITT Corporation and the National Republican Senatorial Committee. When she filed an application for a $25,000 loan, she was denied the loan unless her husband would sign for the loan as well. Has the ECOA been violated?

The Truth-in-Lending Act

Business Planning Tip

The following questions of credit applicants are prohibited under ECOA.

1. Are you receiving public assistance income?
   COMMENT: Applicant may voluntarily disclose income if relying on it to obtain credit, but need not disclose it.

2. Are you planning on starting a family?
   COMMENT: Questions about family and marital status are prohibited.

3. Are you pregnant?
   COMMENT: Questions about family and marital status are prohibited.

4. Are you married?
   COMMENT: Applicant can voluntarily disclose marriage if he/she is relying on spouse's income

5. Please circle: Miss, Ms. Mrs., Mr.
   COMMENT: Would reveal marital status

6. Will your spouse serve as a guarantor?
   COMMENT: Would reveal marital status

7. Do you have alimony or child support income?
   COMMENT: Can't require disclosure; applicant could reveal if relying on income to qualify.

The **Truth-in-Lending Act (TILA)** is actually part of the **Consumer Credit Protection Act** passed in 1968 by Congress (15 U.S.C. § 1601), which was the first federal statute to deal with credit issues. Its purpose was to make sure debtors were treated fairly through adequate disclosure of credit terms. The Federal Reserve Board was delegated the responsibility for enforcement of TILA and has promulgated various regulations to carry out the details of the act. One of them, **Regulation Z**, is perhaps better known than the statute which gave rise to it (12 C.F.R. § 226).

TILA APPLICATIONS

TILA does not apply to all credit transactions; it is limited to consumer credit transactions, which are contracts for goods or services for personal or home use. Thus, a computer purchased for a law office is not covered by TILA, but a computer purchased for the home is.

Wherever consumer credit is extended, TILA applies regardless of the type of credit transaction. **Open-end credit transactions**, like the use of a credit card, are covered under TILA. **Closed-end transactions**, also covered under TILA, are those in which the debtor is buying a certain amount and repaying it. A loan to buy a car that will be paid back over a fixed time, such as four years, is a closed-end transaction.

OPEN-END DISCLOSURE REQUIREMENTS

In charge-card credit arrangements, the creditor has several responsibilities at different stages in the transaction. When a debtor is first sent the credit card, the creditor must include the following information: what the interest (finance) charges and annual percentage rate are for charges on the credit card; when bills will be sent; what to do about questions on the bills; and when payments are due.

The monthly bill that the creditor is required to send must contain the balance from the last statement, payments and credits made during the billing period, new charges made during the billing period, and computation of finance charges.

Other required information on credit card bills includes the following: the dates of the billing period, the free-ride period or the time the debtor has to pay the balance to avoid any finance charges, and where to inquire about billing errors. Any changes in credit terms, billing, or charges must be sent to the debtor at least one month in advance of the change. Exhibit 16.2 is a sample billing statement.

In 1988 the Board of Governors of the Federal Reserve promulgated new rules pursuant to the **Fair Credit and Charge Card Disclosure Act of 1988** for the solicitation of credit card customers. The rules require the disclosure up front of certain information to these potential customers, such as the fees for issuing the card, the annual percentage rate for the card, any finance or transaction charges, and whether a grace period for payment exists.

In addition, potential customers must be told how the average daily balance is computed, when payments are due, whether there is a late payment fee, and whether there are charges for going over the credit limit.

Exhibit 16.2

Sample Billing Statement

↓ DETACH HERE AND KEEP LOWER PART FOR YOUR RECORDS ↓

DATE	STORE	REFERENCE #	DEPT. #	MERCHANDISE AND TRANSACTION DESCRIPTION	PURCHASES	PAYMENTS/CREDITS
AUG 2	RE	0810014	21	MISSES SUITS	217.19	
AUG 2	RE	0840051	146	GIRLS ACCESS./LINGERIE &		
AUG 2	RE	0840051	61	TODDLERS CLOTHING	121.16	
AUG 2	RE	0930042	404	LANCOME	23.32	
AUG 2	RE	1580015	110	CLUBHOUSE	96.99	

CLOSING DATE	PREVIOUS BALANCE	PLUS: FINANCE CHARGE	PLUS: TOTAL PURCHASES	LESS TOTAL PAYMENTS AND CREDITS	NEW BALANCE	ACCOUNT NUMBER	
AUG 22 89	0.00	0.00	458.66	0.00	458.66	PAYMENT FOR CURRENT BILLING CYCLE	45.00
						PLUS PAST DUE AMOUNT	0.00

Periodic Rate	Applied to following portion of Previous Balance	ANNUAL PERCENTAGE RATE
1.65	0.00	19.8

EQUALS TOTAL MINIMUM PAYMENT DUE	45.00
DUE DATE	SEP 17

PLANNING A MAJOR PURCHASE? ASK ABOUT OUR TIME OPTION PLAN (TOP) ACCOUNT. SUBJECT TO APPROVAL, THIS PLAN OFFERS LOWER MONTHLY PAYMENTS ON PURCHASES EXCEEDING $300 IN SELECTED DEPARTMENTS.

NOTICE: See Reverse Side for Important Information. Purchases or credits not shown will appear on your next statement.

To avoid **FINANCE CHARGE** on next statement, full payment of New Balance must be received by due date shown above.

macy's CALIFORNIA NC

Fleet Financial Group Inc. is the corporate parent of Fleet Finance Inc., a financing company and the largest bank in New England.

Fleet experienced negative publicity from all media sources over several lending practices. One was Fleet's program for home equity loans and second mortgages in which extremely high interests rates were charged and defaults or late payments brought rapid foreclosure proceedings. Another problem was discrimination in lending practices.

Fleet Financial: A Company with a Bad Credit History

Fleet's High Interest Mortgages for Minorities

As a result of Fleet's lending practices, many low-income residents who obtained second mortgages through Fleet lost their homes when they failed to make a payment.

The Union Neighborhood Assistance Corporation, a Boston-based community organization outraged by Fleet's lending practices, began a campaign to stop Fleet's expansion efforts. For example, in December 1994, Fleet's proposal to purchase 29 branches for Chemical Banking Corporation was eventually approved, but not without delay and only with a dissent by one of the Federal Reserve Board governors.

In early 1994 Fleet paid $115 million to settle two lawsuits and an investigation by the Georgia Attorney General's Office of alleged lending discrimination. Fleet settled similar charges in Boston in 1991 for $111 million and $38 million in 1994. Fleet did not admit wrongdoing in any of the settlements.

Finally, in February, 1994, Fleet agreed to an $8.5 billion loan program for poor and working class borrowers. Union Neighborhood Assistance will have a say in how the $8.5 billion is assigned in terms of parties, properties, and locations.

Issues

1. Even if Fleet did nothing wrong, what has public perception done?

2. Were Fleet's actions costly?

3. What do you think of Union Neighborhood's strategy of lobbying against approval of Fleet's acquisition?

FOR THE MANAGER'S DESK

THE RISK OF COMPUTER-EVALUATED CREDIT APPLICATIONS

Lawrence B. Lindsey, 41, who earns $123,100 a year, applied for a Toys "Я" Us credit card through the Delaware division of the Bank of New York. He pays his mortgage on time each month, has a clean credit record, and job security. Mr Lindsey's application was rejected; the letter from the bank explained as follows: "We have received your new account application. We regret that we are not able to approve it at this time."

The bank used a computerized scoring system to evaluate credit applications and Mr. Lindsey's was rejected, according to his letter, because "Multiple companies requested your credit report in the past six months."

Mr. Lindsey is also a member of the Federal Reserve Board, the federal agency that sets interest rates and regulates banks. He has expressed concerns about computerized credit scoring and has said:

"I would expect credit-scoring type procedures to be overwhelmingly dominant by the end of the decade. We will obtain the fairness of the machine, but lose the judgments, talents, and sense of justice that only humans can bring to decision making."

Discussion Questions

1. How is computer scoring more fair in credit applications?
2. What are the advantages of credit scoring?
3. Are lenders using computer screening to ensure compliance with the ECOA?
4. Are people unfairly affected by that use?
5. What problems does it create?
6. Do you foresee a time when computer scoring is regulated?
7. Would you use computer scoring for credit extension in your business?

The federal law focuses on the need for disclosure of all possible charges that can occur if a customer accepts the card, charges that may entail much more than the finance charges on the balance. Model forms are available for these disclosures and must be given in writing to a customer at the time of application or solicitation.

CLOSED-END DISCLOSURE REQUIREMENTS

In a closed-end contract, in which the amount to be paid is definite from the beginning, the creditor must include in the credit contract the following terms:

1. The amount the debtor is financing;
2. The **finance charges**; that is, the rate of interest charged for repayment;
3. The **annual percentage rate (APR)**, which is the finance charge reflected in a percentage figure;
4. The number and amount of payments and when they are due;
5. The total cost of financing (This figure is a total of the actual price of the goods or services along with all interest charges that will be paid over the scheduled repayment time.);
6. Whether there are any additional penalties such as prepayment penalties or late payment penalties;
7. Any security interest (lien or collateral) the creditor has in the goods sold by credit; and
8. The cost of credit insurance if the debtor is paying for credit insurance

Big Wheel Auto				Alice Green
ANNUAL PERCENTAGE RATE The cost of your credit as a yearly rate.	**FINANCE CHARGE** The dollar amount the credit will cost you.	**Amount Financed** The amount of credit provided to you or on your behalf.	**Total of Payments** The amount you will have paid after you made all payments as requested.	**Total Sales Price** The total cost of your purchase on credit including your down payment of
14.84%	$ *1496.80*	$ *6107.50*	$ *7604.30*	$ *1500—* _____ *9129.30*

You have the right to receive at this time an itemization of the Amount Financed.
☐ I want an itemization. ☒ I do not want an itemization.

Your payment schedule will be:

Number of Payments	Amount of Payments	When Payments are Due
36	*$ 211.23*	*Monthly beginning 6-1-95*

Insurance
Credit life insurance and credit disability insurance are not required to obtain credit, and will not be provided unless you sign and agree to pay the additional cost.

Type	Premium*	Signature
Credit Life	*$ 120—*	I want credit life insurance. *Alice Green* _____ Signature
Credit Disability		I want credit disability insurance. _____ Signature
Credit Life and Credit Disability		I want credit life and disability insurance. _____ Signature

Security: You are giving a security interest in: ☒ the goods being purchased.
☐ _____.

Filing fee $ *12.50*   **Non-filing insurance** $_____
Late charge: If a payment is late you will be charged $10.00

Prepayment: If you pay early, you
☐ may   ☐ will not   have to pay a penalty.
☒ may   ☐ will not   be entitled to a refund of part of the finance charge.

See your contract documents for any additional information about nonpayment, default, any required repayment in full before the scheduled date, and prepayment refunds and penalties.

I have received a copy of this document.

Alice Green _____   *5-1-95*
Signature   Date

*Means an estimate

Exhibit 16.3
Sample Closed-end Credit Contract

Exhibit 16.3 is an example of a closed-end credit contract.

The disclosure requirements of Regulation Z are enforced strictly. Failure to disclose even one of the items can cost the creditor a penalty under TILA.

C O N S I D E R . . . **16.3** Would the failure to disclose a $1 fee required for the filing of a lien document on a car loan be a violation of Regulation Z? [*Lewis* v. *Award Dodge, Inc.*, 620 F. Supp. 135 (D. Conn. 1985).]

Business Planning Tip

Standard form agreements should be checked for compliance with federal and state disclosure requirements. Periodic reviews should be done to determine whether the forms are in compliance with recent changes.

In addition to ensuring adequate disclosures in credit contracts, Regulation Z covers advertising that includes credit terms. If any part of the credit arrangement is mentioned in an advertisement, all terms must be disclosed. For example, if a creditor advertises payments "as low as $15 per month," the ad must also disclose the APR, the down payment required, and the number of payments.

The following case deals with credit advertising.

State v. Terry Buick, Inc.
520 N.Y.S.2d 497 (1987)

$99 PER MONTH PLUS FINE PRINT

FACTS

Terry Buick, Inc., is an automobile retailer that displayed across the street-side face of its building large yellow signs in block letters that read:

NO MONEY DOWN INSTANT CREDIT! $99/MO.

Terry Buick was located on Route 9, a very busy public highway in Poughkeepsie, New York. The actual credit terms of the sales were printed on 2 1/4" x 3 5/8" stickers, which could be read only by close inspection and were attached to the windshields of cars that were for sale. These small stickers showed the price of the car, the down payment, the term in months, and the average interest rate applied to installment payments. Suit was brought by the state of New York for violation of the credit advertisement regulations of TILA.

JUDICIAL OPINION

BENSON, Justice

This action for an injunction under 15 U.S.C. § 1664 (Truth in Lending Act), General Business Law Article 22-A and CPLR § 6301 enjoining Terry Buick, Inc. from continuing to advertise the terms for credit on vehicles it is selling in an

illegal, false and deceptive manner is determined as follows:

The Court viewed the defendant's place of business with the attorneys and examined a number of the windshield stickers. They were legible only upon inspection from a distance of a few feet and set forth the financial details of each offer. Examination of the stickers showed that almost every offering required a down payment to obtain $99 per month financing. Other used cars had only "99/MO" painted on their windshields. According to the testimony of one witness, the salesman did not know the price of several of such cars. He testified that no cars were offered for sale for $2,000 down and $99 per month.

The plaintiff relied heavily upon the testimony of an undercover agent, a woman in the employ of the Attorney General who went to the defendant's place of business in the guise of a prospective purchaser and engaged a salesman in conversation about the cars. She recorded the conversation secretly and offered the tape, which the Court admitted into evidence. The plaintiff emphasized in argument a statement which the salesman made to the

Continued

plaintiff's agent in which he admitted that the purpose of the advertising was to capture people's attention as they drove by and get them into the dealership.

The Truth in Lending statutes which govern the defendant's conduct are 15 U.S.C. § 1664(d) and New York General Business Laws §§ 350 and 350-a. The Federal statute is amplified by Regulation Z, 12 C.F.R. § 226.24. State courts have concurrent jurisdiction to enforce the Federal statute.

§ 1664(d) reads as follows:

If any advertisement . . . states the amount of the downpayment, if any, the amount of any installment payment, the dollar amount of any finance charge, or the number of installments or the period of repayment, then the advertisement shall state all of the following items . . .

1. the downpayment, if any;

2. the terms of repayment;

3. the rate of the finance charge expressed as an annual percentage rate.

The regulation adopted pursuant to the statute requires that "The creditor shall make the disclosures required by this subpart clearly and conspicuously."

The Court's inspection of the defendant's place of business and its advertising material showed beyond question that the announcement signs were a "come on" designed to lure the eager seeker of a good deal. It also showed that "what you see is not what you get." We have not given the testimony of the undercover agent much weight. It was a contrived tactic practiced upon a relatively guileless salesman by a young woman who pretended to be a purchaser. Her testimony is not necessary, however, to convince the Court that defendant's public announcement of its deals fell far short of the candid display which the law requires. The law requires full disclosure described in the plain language of the statute.

A look at the defendant's advertising scheme leads directly to the conclusion that it was designed to attract customers by half truths or falsity. No customer could buy a car on the terms boldly announced on the face of the building. The defendant's intentions did not have to be explained by testimony. No undercover agent was needed to obtain admissions. The message spoke for itself and could not be misread. It was "misleading in a material respect."

Truth in lending laws were not adopted for the canny shopper. They were made for the gullible and those easily led. . . . "In weighing a statement's capacity, tendency or effect in deceiving or misleading customers, we do not look to the average customer but to the vast multitude which the statutes were enacted to safeguard, including the ignorant, the unthinking and the credulous who, in making purchases, do not stop to analyze but are governed by appearances and general impressions." The plaintiff was not required to show that anyone had been deceived or that the advertising had injured anyone. It met its burden by showing its misleading effect.

The defendant's violation of Federal and New York State truth in lending laws has been demonstrated.

The motion for an order granting a preliminary injunction enjoining the defendant Terry Buick, Inc. from continuing to advertise the terms for credit on vehicles it is selling in an illegal, false and deceptive manner is granted.

CASE QUESTIONS

1. Describe the location of the large credit terms.
2. Where were the details of the credit transaction explained?
3. Did the court need the testimony concerning the salesman's words?
4. Did it matter that no one was deceived by the ads?
5. What will the court order Terry to do?

CREDIT CARD LIABILITIES

Regulation Z provides additional protection for credit card holders in addition to the required open-end disclosures. These additional protections are designed to limit the liability of a debtor for unauthorized use of a credit card.

First, a creditor cannot send an unsolicited credit card to a debtor. The debtor must have applied for the card or consented to have one sent. This protection is necessary so that debtors will be aware of what cards are coming and will know when to report losses or thefts.

Second, even if a credit card is stolen, Regulation Z provides dollar limitations for debtor liability. The maximum amount of liability a debtor can have for the misuse of a credit card is $50. This liability applies only if the debtor takes the appropriate steps for notifying the creditor of the theft or loss. The procedures for notification are given when the credit card is first sent to the debtor.

C O N S I D E R . . . **16.4** Suppose an employee of a firm forged a credit application for his company and then used the card for personal purchases. Would the credit card issuer be liable? Should the issuer verify the request and check references? [*Transamerica Ins. Co.* v. *Standard Oil Co.*, 325 N.W.2d 210 (N.D. 1981).]

CANCELING CREDIT CONTRACTS: REGULATION Z PROTECTIONS

In addition to all the usual disclosures for a closed-end contract, certain types of credit contracts must include a **three-day cooling off period** for the debtor, which is a buyer's protection for "cold feet." The buyer has the right to rescind certain types of credit contracts anytime during the 72 hours immediately following execution of a credit contract.

The types of credit contracts covered by the cooling-off period are those in which the creditor takes a security interest in the debtor's home. For example, if Alfie is installing a solar hot water system in his home, has purchased it on credit, and is giving the solar company a lien on his house, the three-day period applies; Alfie has three days to change his mind after he signs the contract. The three-day period also applies to **home solicitation sales**, which are those in which the buyer is first approached in his or her home by the seller/creditor. The protection here allows the buyer to recoup from any sales pressure that might have been used.

Where the three-day rescission period applies, the creditor must include both a description of the rights in the contract and a full explanation of the procedures the debtor should follow to rescind the contract during the three-day period.

Under the **Home Equity Loan Consumer Protection Act of 1988**, additional disclosures are required for those transactions in which consumers use their homes as security for the credit. These additional disclosures must explain that in the event the consumer does not pay the debt, he or she could lose the dwelling because it could be sold to pay the debt. The three-day rescission period also applies to home equity credit lines. If notice of this three-day rescission right is not given to the homeowner/debtor, the right of rescission will continue for three years. Variable rate loans require specific disclosures on maximum increases in interest rates and the impact on payments.

Exhibit 16.4 (pg. 562) is an example of a three-day cancellation provision.

TILA PENALTIES

TILA provides specific penalties for violations of disclosure provisions. A creditor is liable to an individual for twice the amount of finance charges and for attorney fees of the debtor. The minimum recovery for an individual is $100 and the maximum $1,000. A group of debtors bringing a class action against a creditor can collect the lesser of $500,000 or 1 percent of the creditor's net worth as damages

H-9 Rescission Model Form (Refinancing)

NOTICE OF RIGHT TO CANCEL

Your Right to Cancel

You are entering into a new transaction to increase the amount of credit provided to you. We acquired a [mortgage/lien/security interest] [on/in] your home under the original transaction and will retain that [mortgage/lien/security interest] in the new transaction. You have a legal right under federal law to cancel the new transaction, without cost, within three business days from whichever of the following events occurs last:

(1) the date of the new transaction, which is _____; or

(2) the date you received your new Truth-in-Lending disclosures; or

(3) the date you received this notice of your right of cancel.

If you cancel the new transaction, your cancellation will apply only to the increase in the amount of credit. It will not affect the amount that you presently owe or the [mortgage/lien/security interest] we already have [on/in] your home. If you cancel, the [mortgage/lien/security interest] as it applies to the increased amount is also cancelled. Within 20 calendar days after we receive your notice of cancellation of the new transaction, we must take the steps necessary to reflect the fact that our [mortgage/lien/security interest] [on/in] your home no longer applies to the increase of credit. We must also return any money you have given to us or anyone else in connection with the new transaction.

You may keep any money we have given you in the new transaction until we have done the things mentioned above, but you must then offer to return the money at the address below. If we do not take possession of the money within 20 calendar days of your offer, you may keep it without further obligation.

How to Cancel

If you decide to cancel the new transaction, you may do so by notifying us in writing, at
                            (creditor's name and business address).

You may use any written statement that is signed and dated by you and states your intention to cancel, or you may use this notice by dating and signing below. Keep one copy of this notice because it contains important information about your rights.

If you cancel by mail or telegram, you must send the notice no later than midnight of   (date)   (or midnight of the third business day following the latest of the three events listed above.) If you send or deliver your written notice to cancel some other way, it must be delivered to the above address no later than that time.

I WISH TO CANCEL

_____   _____
Consumer's Signature   Date

Exhibit 16.4
Three-day Cancellation Notice

Fair Credit Billing Act

The **Fair Credit Billing Act** affords debtors the opportunity to challenge the figures on an open-end transaction monthly statement. Errors on credit card accounts are covered by this act and, to a lesser degree, by Regulation Z. Creditors are required to supply on the monthly statement an address or phone number to write or call in the event a debtor has questions or challenges regarding the bill. The language must read: "IN CASE OF ERRORS, CALL OR WRITE . . . "

Under the act, debtors can collect damages if they comply with all the act's procedural requirements. First, a debtor must notify the creditor of any errors within 60 days from the receipt of the statement. The notification must be in writing for the damage sections to apply. If a creditor supplies a phone number for inquiries, the notice must explain that oral protests do not preserve all Regulation Z rights. The written protest of the debtor must include the debtor's name, the account number, and a brief explanation of the claimed error.

Once the creditor has received the written protest, 30 days are allotted for the creditor to acknowledge to the debtor receipt of the protest. The creditor has 90 days from receipt of the protest to take final action, either giving the debtor's account a credit or reaffirming that the charges are valid.

During the time the creditor is considering the debtor's protest, the debtor is not required to pay the questioned amount or any finance charges on that amount. If the charges are in fact accurate, the debtor will be charged for the finance charges during this time period. If the creditor fails to comply with any of the requirements or deadlines on bill protests, the debtor can be excused from payment even if the charges disputed were actually accurate.

Fair Credit Reporting Act

Review the Fair Credit Reporting Act:
http://www.avert. com/ref/FCRA/ fcrahead.html

The **Fair Credit Reporting Act (FCRA)** is designed to provide debtors some rights and protections regarding the credit information held by third parties about them. Before the passage of the FCRA, many debtors were denied the right to see their credit reports and were often victims of inaccurate reports. The FCRA brought credit reports out in the open.

WHEN THE FCRA APPLIES

The FCRA applies to consumer reporting agencies, which are third parties (not creditors or debtors) that compile, evaluate, and sell credit information about **consumer debt** and debtors. Commercial credit reporting agencies and commercial debtors are not subject to FCRA standards.

LIMITATIONS ON FCRA DISCLOSURES

Under the FCRA, consumer reporting agencies can disclose information only to the following:

1. A debtor who asks for his own report;
2. A creditor who has the debtor's signed application for credit;
3. A potential employer; and
4. A court pursuant to a subpoena

When a debtor files for credit, he or she has the right to know where a credit report came from. However, the creditor cannot show the report to the debtor, who must get the report through a credit reporting agency.

Not only are consumer agencies limited as to whom disclosures can be made, but they are also limited as to what can be disclosed. The following are the general limitations on debtor disclosures:

1. No disclosure of bankruptcies that occurred more than 10 years ago
2. No disclosure of lawsuits finalized more than 7 years ago
3. No disclosure of criminal convictions and arrests that have been disposed of more than 7 years ago

When a debtor applies for a loan of more than $50,000 or a job that pays more than $20,000, these limitations on disclosures do not apply.

Under the FCRA, debtors not only have the right to see reports; they have the right to make corrections of inaccurate information included in those reports. A debtor simply notifies the reporting agency of the alleged error. If the agency acknowledges the error, the debtor's report must be corrected, and anyone who has received a report on that debtor during the previous two years must be notified.

If the agency still stands by the information challenged by the debtor, the debtor has the right to have included in the credit report a hundred-word statement explaining his or her position on the matter. This statement is then included with the actual credit report in all future reports sent to third parties.

The following case deals with a problem of an inaccurate credit report.

Stevenson v. TRW, Inc.
987 F.2d 288 (5th Cir. 1993)

THE FATHER WITH THE PRODIGAL SON'S CREDIT RATING

FACTS

TRW Inc. is one of the nation's largest credit reporting agencies. Subscribing companies report to TRW both the credit information they obtain when they grant credit to a consumer and the payment history of the consumer. TRW then compiles a credit report on that consumer to distribute to other subscribers from whom the consumer has requested credit.

John M. Stevenson is a 78-year-old real estate and securities investor. In late 1988 or early 1989, Mr. Stevenson began receiving numerous phone calls from bill collectors regarding arrearages in accounts that were not his. Stevenson first spoke with TRW's predecessor, Chilton's, to try to correct the problem. When TRW purchased Chilton's, Mr. Stevenson began calling TRW's office in Irving, Texas. In August 1989, he wrote TRW and obtained a copy of his credit report dated September 6, 1989. He discovered many errors in the report. Some accounts belonged to another John Stevenson living in Arlington, Texas, and some appeared to belong to his estranged son, John Stevenson, Jr. In all, Mr. Stevenson disputed approximately 16 accounts, seven inquiries, and much of the identifying information.

The reverse side of the credit report contained a printed notice describing how consumers could send a written dispute of the accuracy of their credit reports to the local TRW office. Mr. Stevenson, however, called TRW to register his complaint and then wrote TRW's president and CEO on October 6, 1989, requesting that his credit report be corrected. His letter worked its way to TRW's consumer relations department by October 20, 1989, and on November 1, 1989, that office began its reinvestigation by sending consumer dispute verification forms (CDVs) to subscribers that had reported the disputed accounts. The CDVs ask subscribers to check whether the information they have about a consumer matches the information in TRW's credit report. Subscribers who receive CDVs typically have 20 to 25 working days to respond. If a subscriber fails to respond or indicates that TRW's account information is incorrect, TRW deletes the disputed information. Mr. Stevenson understood from TRW that the entire process should take from three to six weeks.

As a result of its initial investigation, TRW removed several of the disputed accounts from Mr. Stevenson's report by November 30, 1989. TRW retained one of the remaining accounts on the report because the subscriber insisted that the account was Mr. Stevenson's. The others were still either pending or contained what

Continued

TRW called "positive information." It also began to appear that Mr. Stevenson's estranged son had fraudulently obtained some of the disputed accounts by using his father's Social Security number. This information led TRW to add a warning statement in December 1989, advising subscribers that Mr. Stevenson's identifying information had been used without his consent to obtain credit. Meanwhile, Mr. Stevenson paid TRW a fee and joined its Credentials Service, which allowed him to monitor his credit report as each entry was made. TRW finally completed its investigation on February 9, 1990. By then, TRW claimed that all disputed accounts containing "negative" credit information had been removed. Inaccurate information, however, either continued to appear on Stevenson's reports or was reentered after TRW had deleted it.

Mr. Stevenson filed suit in Texas state court alleging both common law libel and violations of the Fair Credit Reporting Act (FCRA). TRW removed the case to federal court, and on October 2, 1991, the case was tried before a federal court without a jury. The district court granted judgment for Mr. Stevenson on both the libel and FCRA claims, and TRW appealed.

JUDICIAL OPINION

WILLIAMS, Circuit Judge

Congress enacted FCRA "to require that consumer reporting agencies adopt reasonable procedures for meeting the needs of commerce for consumer credit, personnel, insurance, and other information in a manner which is fair and equitable to the consumer, with regard to the confidentiality, accuracy, relevancy, and proper utilization of such information. . . ." To guard against the use of inaccurate or arbitrary information in evaluating an individual for credit, insurance, or employment, Congress further required that consumer reporting agencies "follow reasonable procedures to assure maximum possible accuracy of the information concerning the individual about whom" a credit report relates.

Consumers have the right to see their credit information and to dispute the accuracy or completeness of their credit reports. 15 U.S.C. §§ 1681g and 1681h. When it receives a complaint, a consumer reporting agency must reinvestigate the disputed information "within a reasonable period of time" and "promptly delete" credit information that has been found to be inaccurate or unverifiable. (15 U.S.C. § 1681i(a).) The parties here stipulated that TRW began its reinvestigation within a reasonable period of time after receiving Stevenson's written dispute. Nevertheless, the court found that TRW had negligently and willfully violated § 1681i(a) by not deleting inaccurate and unverifiable information promptly and by allowing deleted information to reappear.

The record, however, contains evidence from which the district court could find that TRW did not delete unverifiable or inaccurate information promptly. First, TRW did not complete its reinvestigation until February 9, 1990, although TRW's subscribers were supposed to return the CDVs by December 4, 1989. Second, § 1681i(a) requires prompt deletion if the disputed information is inaccurate or unverifiable. If a subscriber did not return a CDV, TRW claims that it deleted the disputed information as unverifiable. Yet, some disputed accounts continued to appear on Stevenson's credit report for several weeks. One subscriber failed to return the CDV, but its account appeared on the report issued on February 9, 1990. Another subscriber returned its CDV by December 4, 1989, indicating that TRW's information was inaccurate, yet the information was not deleted until after February 9, 1990.

Allowing inaccurate information back onto a credit report after deleting it because it is inaccurate is negligent. Additionally, in spite of the complexity of Stevenson's dispute, TRW contacted the subscribers only through the CDVs. Although testimony at trial revealed that TRW sometimes calls subscribers to verify information, it made no calls in Stevenson's case. TRW relied solely on the CDVs despite the number of disputed accounts and the allegations of fraud. TRW also relied on the subscribers to tell TRW whether to delete information from Stevenson's report. In a reinvestigation of the

Continued

accuracy of credit reports, a credit bureau must bear some responsibility for evaluating the accuracy of information obtained from subscribers.

The bureau had exhibited no ill will toward the plaintiff and had acted to fix the problem. Likewise, TRW provided Stevenson's credit report on request, did not conceal information about his report, investigated the disputed accounts, and attempted to resolve the complaints.

TRW moved slowly in completing its investigation and was negligent in its compliance with the prompt deletion requirement. The record does not reveal, however, any intention to thwart consciously Stevenson's right to have inaccurate information removed promptly from his report.

TRW maintains that most of Stevenson's distress was the result of the many calls he received from creditors of the fraudulently obtained accounts. TRW correctly questions the relevance of these creditors' calls to violations of FCRA. Nearly all of these calls occurred before Stevenson filed his written dispute and TRW began its reinvestigation. Only after that did the FCRA violations occur. Stevenson's distress because of creditors' calls arose before TRW's FCRA violations.

The record reveals evidence, however, that Stevenson suffered mental anguish over his lengthy dealings with TRW after he disputed his credit report. First, Stevenson testified that it was a "terrific shock" to him to discover his bad credit rating after maintaining a good credit reputation since 1932. Second, Stevenson was denied credit three times during TRW's reinvestigation: by Bloomingdale's, by Bank One, and by Gabbert's Furniture Company. Stevenson testified that he had to go "hat in hand" to the president of Bank One, who was a business associate and friend, to explain his problems with TRW. As a result, he obtained credit at Bank One. Third, Stevenson had to explain his credit woes to the president of the First City Bank Colleyville when he opened an account there. With a new president at First City Bank, Stevenson had to explain his situation again. Despite the fact that he was ultimately able to obtain credit, Stevenson testified to experiencing "considerable embarrassment" from having to detail to business associates and creditors his problems with TRW. Finally, Stevenson spent a considerable amount of time since he first disputed his credit report trying to resolve his problems with TRW.

The district court properly found that Stevenson had suffered humiliation and embarrassment from TRW's violations of FCRA. We affirm the award of $30,000 in actual damages based upon the finding of mental anguish. We also affirm the award of $20,700 in attorney's fees.

CASE QUESTIONS

1. What caused Mr. Stevenson's anguish? Was it the correction process?
2. What suggestions could you offer to TRW to prevent the problems with Mr. Stevenson's credit report?
3. What would you do differently if you were trying to correct your report?
4. Are the damages reasonable?

CONSIDER . . . **16.5** William Daniel Thompson, Jr., opened a credit account with Gordon's Jewelers and then failed to pay off a $77.25 balance. The failure to pay was recorded with the computerized credit reporting agency of the San Antonio Retail Merchants Association (SARMA). When William Douglas Thompson III applied for credit, it was denied because of the unfavorable report from Gordon's. Mr. Thompson III notified SARMA of the error but was still denied credit. Is SARMA liable if Mr. Thompson III files suit? [*Thompson* v. *San Antonio Retail Merchants Ass'n*, 682 F.2d 509 (5th Cir. 1982).]

E T H I C A L   I S S U E S

16.2 Recently it was discovered that credit reporting agencies were operating a second line of business by selling marketing lists of customers classified according to their spending habits and levels. Merchandisers would pay for the refined lists because the lists enabled them to reach a specific group of likely customers. Is this line of business appropriate for the credit agencies?

C O N S I D E R . .   **16.6** Clarence Landrum, Jr., was employed as a police major of the Levee Board Police Department. On August 31, 1989, while on duty, Mr. Landrum was involved in an auto accident. Pursuant to department policy, he was required to provide urine and blood samples at Methodist Health System Foundation. Mr. Landrum gave the samples to Methodist, which were transmitted to Laboratory Specialists, Inc. (LSI), for screening. LSI sent a report to the police department stating the urine sample indicated marijuana use.

Mr. Landrum offered a second sample, which also indicated marijuana use. He was suspended and, after a hearing, discharged for use of a controlled substance. Mr. Landrum claims his third test was clean and LSI should have included that information pursuant to his request under the FCRA. Is LSI covered under FCRA? [*Landrum v. Board of Comm'rs of Orleans Levee Dist.*, 758 F. Supp. 387 (E.D. La. 1991).]

E T H I C A L   I S S U E S

16.3 Lindsey Appliances follows a policy of reporting any and all late payments to a credit reporting agency. Lindsey includes a disclosure in its contracts that "late payments, even those late by one day, are reported to credit monitoring agencies." Is Lindsey's policy a fair one?

Consumer Leasing Act

Review the Consumer Leasing Act: http://www.law.cornell.edu/uscode/15/1667.html
Examine Article 2A of the UCC: http://www.law.cornell.edu/ucc/2A/overview.html

The **Consumer Leasing Act** is an amendment to TILA that provides disclosure protection for consumers who lease goods. Under this act, the lessor must disclose how much will be paid over the life of the lease, whether any money will be owed at the end of the lease, and whether the lease can be terminated.

Consumer leasing has become an important part of our economy. Recently, Article 2A was added to the Uniform Commercial Code. In this article, which immediately follows the sales article, all aspects on consumer leases are recovered. The topics in Article 2A include information about lease contracts, warranties, and remedies.

Business Planning Tip

When there is any question as to whether a consumer credit transaction is involved or whether a protective statute applies, the question is resolved in favor of the credit applicant. Many businesses treat all credit applications as consumer credit applications and apply the statutes (even though they are not required to do so) so that they can avoid any issues and questions on consumer credit.

ENFORCEMENT OF CREDIT TRANSACTIONS

Although a debtor has the benefit of paying over time, a creditor has the worry of trying to ensure payment. A creditor may be able to increase sales by extending credit, but risks of nonpayment also increase with each extension of credit. Fortunately, the law affords creditors some additional protections that can be used to guarantee repayment.

The Use of Collateral: The Security Interest

One way a creditor can have additional assurances of repayment is to obtain a pledge of collateral from the debtor. For goods, this collateral pledge is called a **security interest**. The creation of security interests is governed by Article IX of the Uniform Commercial Code.

A security interest is created by a written agreement called a security agreement. Once a security interest is created, the creditor is given the right to repossess the pledged goods in the event the debtor defaults on repayment. Thus, when a debtor purchases a car on credit, there is nearly always a security interest in that car that allows the lender the right to repossess the car and sell it to satisfy the loan in the event the debtor defaults. This right to sell gives the creditor some additional assurances that the debt will be repaid. For more information on security interests, see Chapter 12, page 405.

Collection Rights of the Creditor

Review the Fair Debt Collection Practices Act: http://www. member.com/ newaca/fdcpa.html

If a debtor falls behind on payments, the creditor has the right to proceed with collection tactics. Many creditors refer or sell their delinquent credit accounts to collection agencies. There was a time when some of these agencies engaged in questionable conduct in the collection of debts, including harassing debtors with phone calls and embarrassing them by contacting their friends and relatives. To control abuses in the collection process, Congress passed the **Fair Debt Collections Practices Act (FDCPA)** in 1977. The FDCPA became effective in 1978 and controls a great deal of debt collection. About two-thirds of the states have adopted some form of debt collection statutes. If state law, relative to the federal act, provides the same or greater protection for debtors in the collection process, the state law governs. In states without a collection law, the FDCPA applies.

WHEN THE FDCPA APPLIES

The FDCPA applies to consumer debts and debt collectors. Consumer debts are defined here as they are under TILA: debts for personal, home, or family purposes. Debt collectors are third-party collectors. The FDCPA does not apply to original creditors collecting their own debts; for example, Sears collecting Sears debts is not governed by the FDCPA. However, if Sears referred its collection accounts to Central Credit Collection Agency, Central Credit would be under the FDCPA. If Sears created its own collection agency with a name other than Sears, the FDCPA would apply to that agency as well.

The FDCPA does not apply to the collection of commercial accounts or to banks and the Internal Revenue Service. In a rule revision, attorneys collecting debts for clients were made subject to coverage of the FDCPA.

<table>
<tr><td>C O N S I D E R . . .</td></tr>
</table>

16.7 Telecredit Service Corporation's business is the collection of dishonored checks. Telecredit purchases these checks and then contacts the drawers to collect the funds.

Stanley Holmes wrote a $315 check to Union Park Pontiac that was dishonored. Union Park sold the check to Telecredit, and Telecredit sent letters and made contacts to collect the check. Some contacts would be violations of FDCPA, but Telecredit says it is not covered by FDCPA because it is not collecting the debts of another. Is this correct? [*Holmes* v. *Telecredit Service Corp.*, 736 F. Supp. 1289 (D. Del. 1990).]

COLLECTOR REQUIREMENTS UNDER THE FDCPA

One of the requirements for collectors under the FDCPA is written verification of debt. A collector must provide such verification if a debtor asks. The collector must also automatically provide written verification within five days after contacting the debtor. Written verifications must include the following information:

1. The amount of the debt;
2. The name of the creditor; and
3. The debtor's right to dispute the debt and the procedures for doing so
   If a debtor disputes a debt, the collector has 30 days to verify the debt and its amount before any collection contact can continue.

COLLECTOR RESTRICTIONS UNDER THE FDCPA

In addition to affirmative disclosure requirements, collectors are subject to certain prohibitions under the FDCPA. The following subsections cover the prohibitions.

Debtor Contact One of the most frequent abuses of collectors prior to the FDCPA was constant debtor contact and harassment. The FDCPA curbs the amount of contact: Debtors cannot be contacted before 8:00 A.M. or after 9:00 P.M. and debtors who work night shifts cannot be disturbed during their sleeping hours in the daytime.

The place of contact is also controlled by the FDCPA: Collectors must avoid contact at inconvenient places. Home contact is permitted, but contact in club, church, or school meetings is prohibited. Collectors can approach debtors at their places of employment unless employers object or have a policy against such contact.

To prevent harassment, the FDCPA gives debtors a chance to "call off" a collector. If a debtor tells the collector that he or she wants no more contact, the collector must stop and take other steps, such as legal action, to collect the debt. If the debtor is represented by an attorney and gives the name of the attorney to the collector, the collector can contact only the attorney from that point.

Third-Party Contact The FDCPA also prohibits notifying other parties of the debtor's debts and collection problems. However, the debtor's spouse and parents can be contacted regarding the debt. Other parties can be contacted for information, but the collector cannot disclose the reason for the contact. Further, the only information that can be obtained from these third parties is the address, phone number, and place of employment of the debtor.

These third parties cannot be told about the debt, the amount, delinquencies, or any other information about the debtor. The collector must even be careful to use appropriate stationery when writing for information so that the letterhead does not disclose the nature of the collector's business. Postcard contact with the debtor or third parties is prohibited because of the likelihood that others will see the information about the debtor.

Prohibited Acts Collectors have certain other restrictions on their conduct under the FDCPA. The general prohibition in the FDCPA is that collectors cannot "harass, oppress or abuse" the debtor. Using abusive language or physical force is prohibited. Misrepresenting the authority of a collector is also prohibited, as is posing as a law enforcement official or producing false legal documents. Debtors cannot be threatened with prison or other actions not authorized by law.

The following case involves an issue of FDCPA violations. Use the discussion of the FDCPA and this case to answer the chapter's opening "Judgment."

Judgment

Bentley v. Great Lakes Collection Bureau
6 F.3d 60 (2d Cir. 1993)

THE LANGUAGE OF COLLECTION: PAY UP

FACTS

Diane Bentley (plaintiff/appellant) owed $483.43 to Citicorp. Great Lakes is a debt collection agency that was retained by Citicorp Retail Services, Inc. (CRSI) to provide debt collection services. The contract entered into by CRSI and Great Lakes provided that Great Lakes "must have CRSI's prior written authorization to bring legal action to affect [sic] collection of any Referred Account." The service contract further provided that Great Lakes "shall at no time state or imply in any communication to a Referred Account that CRSI will sue the debtor without [prior] written authorization" from CRSI.

Great Lakes sent Ms.Bentley two computer-generated collection letters ("dunning letters") dated November 30, 1990, and December 18, 1990. The November 30 dunning letter included the following language:

> YOUR CREDITOR IS NOW TAKING THE NECESSARY STEPS TO RECOVER THE OUTSTANDING AMOUNT OF $483.43. THEY HAVE INSTRUCTED US TO PROCEED WITH WHATEVER LEGAL MEANS IS NECESSARY TO ENFORCE COLLECTION.
>
> ENCLOSE YOUR PAYMENT IN THE ENVELOPE PROVIDED AND MAKE YOUR CHECK OR MONEY ORDER PAYABLE TO GREAT LAKES BUREAU, INC.
>
> THIS IS AN ATTEMPT TO COLLECT A DEBT AND ANY INFORMATION OBTAINED WILL BE USED FOR THAT PURPOSE.

Great Lakes's computer is programmed to generate this form letter whenever the agency receives a new account.

The December 18 letter, a follow-up form letter, stated in relevant part:

> THIS OFFICE HAS BEEN UNABLE TO CONTACT YOU BY TELEPHONE, THEREFORE YOUR DELINQUENT ACCOUNT HAS BEEN REFERRED TO MY DESK WHERE A DECISION MUST BE MADE AS TO WHAT DIRECTION MUST BE TAKEN TO ENFORCE COLLECTION.
>
> WERE OUR CLIENT TO RETAIN LEGAL COUNSEL IN YOUR AREA, AND IT WAS DETERMINED THAT SUIT SHOULD BE FILED AGAINST YOU, IT COULD RESULT IN A JUDGMENT. SUCH JUDGMENT MIGHT, DEPENDING UPON THE LAW IN YOUR STATE, INCLUDE NOT ONLY THE AMOUNT OF YOUR INDEBTEDNESS, BUT THE AMOUNT OF ANY STATUTORY COSTS, LEGAL INTEREST, AND WHERE APPLICABLE, REASONABLE ATTORNEY'S FEES.
>
> AGAIN, DEPENDING UPON THE LAW IN YOUR STATE, IF SUCH JUDGMENT WERE NOT THEREUPON SATISFIED, IT MIGHT BE COLLECTED BY ATTACHMENT OF AN EXECUTION UPON YOUR REAL AND PERSONAL PROPERTY. GARNISHMENT MAY ALSO BE AN AVAILABLE REMEDY TO SATISFY AN UNSATISFIED JUDGMENT, IF APPLICABLE IN THE STATE IN WHICH YOU RESIDE.
>
> WE THEREFORE SUGGEST YOU CALL OUR OFFICE IMMEDIATELY TOLL FREE AT 1-800-874-7080 TO DISCUSS PAYMENT ARRANGEMENTS OR MAIL PAYMENT IN FULL IN THE ENCLOSED ENVELOPE.
>
> NO LEGAL ACTION HAS BEEN OR IS NOW BEING TAKEN AGAINST YOU.

Continued

In fact, CRSI had not authorized Great Lakes "to proceed with whatever legal means is necessary to enforce collection" as represented in the first letter, and Great Lakes had made no effort to telephone Ms. Bentley prior to December 18, had not referred her account to anyone's desk and was not about to make any decisions regarding her account as represented in the second letter. Great Lakes does not make the decision whether to initiate legal proceedings in matters involving CRSI; never recommends legal proceedings unless its advice is solicited from its clients; does not employ attorneys admitted to practice in the state of Connecticut; has no procedure by which to refer accounts to attorneys in Connecticut or other states to commence litigation; and is not informed when any of its clients ultimately sues a debtor. Moreover, even in cases in which its advice is solicited, Great Lakes recommends legal proceedings to its clients only for approximately 1 percent of the collection accounts referred to it.

Ms. Bentley filed suit in federal district court alleging that the two collection letters violated the FDCPA. The district court granted summary judgment for Great Lakes, and Ms. Bentley appealed.

JUDICIAL OPINION

MINER, Circuit Judge

The FDCPA prohibits the use of "any false, deceptive, or misleading representation or means in connection with the collection of any debt." 15 U.S.C. § 1692e (1988). We apply an objective test based on the understanding of the "least sophisticated consumer" in determining whether a collection letter violates section 1692e. *Clomon* v. *Jackson*, 988 F.2d 1314, 1318 (2d Cir. 1993). The sixteen subsections of section 1692e provide a nonexhaustive list of practices that fall within the statute's ban. These practices include "[t]he threat to take any action that cannot legally be taken or that is not *intended to be taken*." (emphasis added). A debt collection practice may violate the FDCPA even if it does not fall within any of the subsections, and a single violation of section 1692e is sufficient to establish civil liability under the FDCPA.

Here, the two dunning letters contained several admittedly false statements. First the November 30 dunning letter falsely stated that CRSI had given Great Lakes the authority to initiate legal proceedings against Bentley. It implied that the commencement of legal proceedings was imminent when, in fact, this was not the case. The district court concluded that these statements "were not misleading or deceptive within the meaning of [the FDCPA]," because "accepting the plaintiffs [arguments] would cause serious question on what, if anything, a creditor could say in its attempt to collect a lawful debt." But, although the court felt that the language was not violative of the statute, the FDCPA specifically prohibits the threat to take any action "that is not intended to be taken," and the "least sophisticated consumer" would interpret this language to mean that legal action was authorized, likely and imminent. Therefore, these statements are "false, deceptive, [and] misleading" within the meaning of the FDCPA.

Second, the December 18 dunning letter falsely stated that Great Lakes had attempted to contact Bentley prior to December 18 and that Bentley's account had been referred to someone's desk, where a decision would be made regarding her account. The reference to the status of Bentley's account is deceptive, implying "personal attention" to her account, when, in fact, no such "desk" existed. The letter therefore violates the FDCPA's strict prohibition against deceptive practices. The district court found that these inaccuracies in the December 18 letter were non-actionable violations of the FDCPA. We disagree. The FDCPA is a strict liability statute, and the degree of a defendant's culpability may only be considered in computing damages.

Moreover, the later letter's references to the various proceedings supplementary to judgment available to enforce collection (e.g., garnishment) also violated section 1692d(5)'s prohibition of threats to take action "that [are] not intended to be taken." These references to legal remedies, when read in conjunction with the first paragraph of that letter, which advised that the account was being reviewed by Great Lakes to determine "what direction must be

Continued

taken to enforce collection," would mislead the least sophisticated consumer. The quoted language conveys to the consumer that Great Lakes was authorized to make the decision to institute the legal action that could lead to the supplementary proceedings described. In the context of the letter, the threat of a lawsuit instigated by Great Lakes is strengthened by the statement: "No legal action *has been or is now being* taken against you." (emphasis added) In fact, CRSI retained the authority to decide whether legal proceedings of any kind would be instituted, and the likelihood of such proceedings on a claim for $483.43 was almost nonexistent.

The judgment of the district court is reversed and the case remanded for further proceedings consistent with the foregoing.

CASE QUESTIONS

1. What statements in the letters sent to Ms. Bentley were false?
2. Is it unethical to make false statements in collection letters? Hasn't the debtor been unethical in not paying?
3. What is the "least sophisticated consumer" standard?
4. What is the importance of a "likelihood of legal proceedings"?

PENALTIES FOR FDCPA VIOLATIONS

The Federal Trade Commission (FTC) is responsible for enforcement of the FDCPA. The FTC can use its cease and desist orders to stop collectors from violating the FDCPA and can also assess penalties for violations. However, the greatest power of enforcement under the FDCPA lies with individual debtors. Debtors who can prove collector violations can collect for actual injuries and mental distress. Debtors can also collect up to $1,000 in addition to actual damages for actions by collectors that are extreme, outrageous, malicious, or repeated. Attorney fees incurred by debtors in bringing their suits are also recoverable.

> *Business Planning Tip*
>
> *Generating form collection letters by computer must be carefully monitored. The FDCPA imposes notice and content requirements that must flow in sequence. Threatened actions must be taken or the threat is a violation.*

Suits for Enforcement of Debts

Occasionally, collection is ineffective and there is no collateral to repossess. The creditor has few options left but to bring suit to enforce collection of the debt. In bringing a successful suit, the creditor will obtain a **judgment**, which is the court's official document stating that the debtor owes the money and the collector is entitled to that money. However, in debt cases, the judgment is only the beginning. Once the creditor has the judgment, it must be executed to obtain funds.

A judgment is executed by having it attach to various forms of the debtor's property. For example, a judgment can attach to real property. A judgment can also attach to funds by **garnishment**, which is the attachment of a judgment to an account, paycheck, or receivables. Once there is attachment, the creditor is entitled to those funds. The third party holding the funds must comply with the terms of the garnishment and release the appropriate amount of funds to the creditor.

Employees are given some protection under the Consumer Credit Protection Act with respect to garnishments. One such protection is the limitation on the employer's ability to fire employees who have their wages garnisheed by a single creditor.

C O N S I D E R . . . **16.8** Clarence J. Ellis was employed by Glover & Gardner as a laborer/carpenter from August 1979 until June 18, 1980. On June 18, 1980, Charles Gardner, the president and owner of Glover & Gardner, received a notice of garnishment of Mr. Ellis's wages and fired Mr. Ellis that day. It was Mr. Ellis's first garnishment. Gardner said he fired Mr. Ellis because of alcoholism, poor job performance, insubordination, and dishonesty. However, Mr. Ellis's separation notice, which was sent to the Tennessee Department of Employment Security, gave as the reason for termination the garnishment. Did Mr. Gardner violate the law? [*Ellis* v. *Glover & Gardner Construction Co.,* 562 F. Supp. 1054 (M.D. Tenn. 1983).]

Under the Consumer Credit Protection Act, the amount that consumer creditors can garnishee on debtor wages is limited to 25 percent of the net wages. Garnishment for past-due child support is limited to 50 percent of net wages.

The End of the Line on Enforcement of Debts: Bankruptcy

Visit the American Bankruptcy Institute for more about bankruptcy: http://www.abiworld.org/home.html

Federal laws afford debtors shelter when their obligations cannot be paid. *Bankruptcy* is the legal process of having a debtor—individual, partnership, corporation, LLC (see Chapter 20)—turn over all non-exempt assets in exchange for a release from debts following the distribution of those assets to creditors. There are three forms of bankruptcy. Chapter 7 bankruptcy is the liquidation form in which the entity is dissolved or the individuals debts are discharged. Chapter 11 is the reorganization form in which a business enjoys protection from collection and creditors until a new plan for satisfying the business obligations is approved. Chapter 13 is the consumer debt adjustment plan under which consumers can be given a new repayment plan for their debts.

Once an individual or business voluntarily declares bankruptcy, all collection efforts must stop. A voluntary petition in bankruptcy provides the debtor with immediate relief from creditors. A debtor can be involuntarily petitioned into bankruptcy by creditors. In an involuntary petition case, the debtor has the opportunity for a hearing. The standard for declaring voluntary bankruptcy is that the individual or business has debts. The standard for creditors petitioning a debtor into involuntary bankruptcy is that the debtor is unable to pay debts as they become due.

Not all debts are discharged in bankruptcy. Alimony, child support, student loans and taxes are examples of debts that survive bankruptcy.

SUMMARY

What are the statutes that affect credit contracts?
- Usury—charging interest in excess of the statutory maximum
- Equal Credit Opportunity Act—federal law prohibiting denial of credit on the basis of sex, race, color, religion, national origin, age, marital status, public assistance income, alimony, or child support income and plans for additional family
- Truth-in-Lending Act—federal law governing disclosures in credit contracts
- Consumer Credit Protection Act—first federal statute on credit disclosure requirements
- Open-end transactions—credit card transactions
- Closed-end transactions—preestablished-amount finance contract, as in the financing of a television purchase
- Fair Credit and Charge Card Disclosure Act of 1988—federal law governing solicitation of credit card customers
- Regulation Z—federal regulation governing credit disclosures
- Three-day cooling off period—right of rescission on credit contracts initiated in the home
- Home Equity Loan Consumer Protection Act of 1988—federal law requiring disclosures for home equity consumer loans
- Fair Credit Billing Act—federal law governing rights of debtors to dispute credit card charge
- Fair Credit Reporting Act—federal law regulating disclosure of credit information to and by third parties
- Consumer Leasing Act — federal law governing consumer lease transactions

How are credit contracts enforced?
- Security interest — pledge of collateral for credit
- Fair Debt Collections Practices Act—federal law regulating collection of consumer debt by third parties
- Judgment—court order authorizing collection of money from party
- Garnishment—attachment of account, paycheck, or receivables to collect judgment
- Bankruptcy—federal process of collecting assets to pay creditors and discharge debts.
- Chapter 7—liquidation bankruptcy
- Chapter 11—reorganization bankruptcy
- Chapter 13—consumer debt adjustment plan

QUESTIONS AND PROBLEMS

1. In May 1976, TRW, (a credit reporting agency) issued a consumer report on Bennie E. Bryant in connection with his application for a federally insured home loan under the Veterans Administration. The consumer report had several inaccuracies, and Mr. Bryant went to TRW to point out the matters needing correction. The mortgage did not close for unrelated reasons.

In August 1976, Mr. Bryant applied for another mortgage. On September 28, TRW called the mortgage company to let them know his credit report would be unfavorable. When the mortgage company notified Mr. Bryant, he again went to TRW offices and explained that the September report contained new inaccuracies in addition to those that were part of the May report. After this meeting, a memo about possible inaccuracies was placed in Mr. Bryant's file. However, the credit report without corrections was issued to the mortgage company on September 30. No follow-through had been done on the file memo.

Mr. Bryant's August mortgage application was originally denied. After personal efforts on his part, however, the credit report was corrected and the mortgage was eventually given.

Does Mr. Bryant have any rights and protections? [*Bryant* v. *TRW, Inc.*, 689 F.2d 72 (6th Cir. 1982).]

2. Would a rental agreement with an option to purchase for a TV at a rate of $17 per week be covered under TILA? [*Clark* v. *Rent-It Corp.*, 685 F.2d 245 (8th Cir. 1982).]

3. Maurice Miller obtained an American Express credit card in 1966, and his wife, Virginia, was given a supplementary card. Her card had a different number, was issued in her name, and had a separate annual fee. When Mr. Miller died in 1979, American Express canceled both credit cards. Mrs. Miller sued for violation of the ECOA. Has there been a violation? [*Miller* v. *American Express Co.*, 688 F.2d 1235 (9th Cir. 1982).]

4. In community property states, signatures of both spouses are required on real property transactions. Would a mortgagee that requires both spouses' signatures on a mortgage application be violating the ECOA? [*McKenzie* v. *U.S. Home Corp.*, 704 F.2d 778 (5th Cir. 1983).]

5. Would the failure to disclose credit insurance premiums be a violation of TILA? [*Stewart* v. *Abraham Lincoln Mercury, Inc.*, 698 F.2d 1289 (5th Cir. 1983).]

6. James A. Swanson received a letter from a collection agency, the Southern Oregon Credit Service, indicating that if payment in full or definite arrangements for payment of his account were not made within 48 hours, the agency would begin a complete investigation into his employment and assets. Is the agency's threat a violation of the FDCPA? [*Swanson* v. *Southern Oregon Credit Service, Inc.*, 869 F.2d 1222 (9th Cir. 1988).]

7. Michele Lachman had her Visa card stolen and reported the theft to the issuer. Charges amounting to $1,431.72 were made after her notification of theft. The issuer tried to collect those amounts from Ms. Lachman over her protests about the stolen card. Have any federal laws been violated? [*Lachman* v. *Bank of Louisiana in New Orleans*, 510 F. Supp. 753 (N.D. Ohio 1981).]

8. A loan agreement provided for total number of payments as "one x $128.00 and 24 x $128.00." Is this sufficient disclosure of the total number of payments? Is it too confusing to be disclosure? Would it make any difference if the agreement showed how much would be paid in total? [*Sunamerica Finance Corp.* v. *Williams*, 442 N.E.2d 83 (Ohio 1982).]

9. American Future Systems, Inc. (AFS), sells china, cookware, crystal, and tableware, and extends credit to its customers for such purchases. Sales on a credit basis amount to over 95 percent of AFS sales. First National Acceptance Corporation (FNAC) is AFS's credit company and is wholly owned by AFS. AFS affords young people and minorities a chance to obtain credit in spite of their lack of prior credit histories.

Its general standards for credit are (1) a telephone in the residence, (2) positive credit experience of at least $100, and (3) employment with regular income. AFS has three specific marketing programs: a summer program, a winter program for single white females, and a winter program for minorities, married persons, and males.

Under the summer program, target customers are single white females living at home with a parent who could cosign for the credit. AFS does not always require the parent's signatures and might ship goods to this group without checking credit histories. This market is reached by salespeople who are sent only to white neighborhoods and instructed to avoid neighborhoods where there might be a racial mix.

If salespeople encounter a minority customer in their presentations, AFS will sell the goods and extend credit to them, but a credit check is done on both the applicant and cosigner before goods are shipped. About 20 percent of the applications of minority applicants are denied.

The winter program has two parts. The preferred part of the winter program consists of sales to single white women who are sophomores, juniors, or seniors in four-year colleges or nursing schools. The other part of the program focuses on minorities, males, and married persons attending college or vocational schools. Shipment to preferred customers is immediate, with automatic credit approval. Shipment to the nonpreferred winter group is deferred until the applicant makes three timely monthly payments.

AFS presented evidence that minority customers are, as a group, less creditworthy than their white counterparts. However, the statistics presented did not account for AFS's failure to solicit in minority neighborhoods.

The U.S. government brought suit for violation of the ECOA. Is the AFS program a violation of ECOA? [*United States* v. *American Future Systems, Inc.*, 743, F.2d 169 (3d Cir. 1984).]

10. In 1984, Jean Mayes purchased Albert L. Silva, d/b/a Rainbow Motors, a Nantucket car dealership. In May 1985, Jean Mayes entered into financing arrangements with Chrysler Credit Corporation to finance his car inventory. The borrower was Rainbow Motors, Jean Mayes as president and sole shareholder.

Chrysler demanded that Mr. Mayes and his wife, Michele Mayes, sign a "continuing guaranty" before it would extend credit. Mrs. Mayes, a well-compensated corporate attorney, was listed as a director and officer of Rainbow, but she did not participate in managing it.

Rainbow defaulted and Chrysler brought suit against Michele Mayes, seeking $750,126.41. Mrs. Mayes said Chrysler was stopped from collecting the debt because of the ECOA. Is she correct? [*Mayes* v. *Chrysler Credit Corp.*, 37 F.3d 9 (1st Cir. 1994).]

Problem 1

Karr Preventative Medical Products manufactured Acne-Statin, a skin cream. Karr hired Charles (Pat) Boone, a singer, and his family to serve as celebrity spokespersons for Acne-Statin.

Boone and his family appeared in television ads and stated the following:

(1) Acne-Statin provided a cure;
(2) Acne-Statin was superior to other anti-acne creams; and
(3) Acne-Statin was a "real help" to their family.

There is no cure for acne, so the FTC asked for substantiation of the claims. Its investigation revealed that not all members of the Boone family used the product, but all appeared in the ads endorsing the product.

What legal effect do the Boone family promises have on Karr? For those who have already purchased Acne-Statin, is there any remedy? Drawing on your knowledge about administrative agencies, what action can the FTC take against Karr and Pat Boone? What options do they have?

Problem 2

The attorney general of the state of New York has filed a complaint against Sears, the retailing giant, for deceptive advertising. The complaint focuses on ads Sears has run in New York newspapers featuring its kitchen cabinet replacement sales. The ads offer a 15 percent discount on the cabinets for a stated limited time, such as "Offer good through October 15 only." However, 2–3 days following the termination date in this example, yet another ad for a 15 percent discount appeared and read, "Offer good through Oct. 31 only."

The attorney general claims the ads are deceptive because they create a false sense of urgency. Sears's legal counsel has responded, "This is a ridiculous allegation. Overzealous bureaucrats have brought these charges. Sears intends to litigate the matter fully."

Evaluate Sears's ads and their legality. What would happen to those people who had already signed contracts thinking the special would end? Are they still bound to their agreements? Is Sears competing unfairly?

Drawing on the knowledge from Part I of the text, evaluate Sears's decision to fight the claim and litigate with the attorney general.

Problem 3

Socrates, Inc., is the manufacturer of a television tutorial system called Socrates, which is a compact unit with a one-wire connection to the television set and a small laptop keyboard. Socrates offers children's math and reading games as well as several informational art and music games.

The Socrates system has controls identical to those in the Nintendo game system and its math and reading tutorial programs are nearly identical to the Apple II Plus tutorials. However, the Socrates system requires only a television and is priced around $150. Apple's software requires an Apple II Plus (priced at $1,500) with software priced from $20 to $30 a program.

Socrates's system hit the market just before Christmas. Because of limited supply and very little advertising, the system had limited sales, but since Christmas many educators have begun to tout its benefits. Some teachers are recommending the system to parents and some school districts are seeking bulk purchases of the system because of cost.

Nintendo video systems are also self-contained systems that connect to television sets using one wire. Nintendo offers only games and the National Association of Educators (NAE) has decried the $100 system (with games running $20 to $30 each) as a "deterrent to the development of grade school children" and "responsible for neglecting home assignments."

Nintendo and Apple have aggressive litigation policies in pursuing full legal claims against the slightest infringements, and are considering filing suits for infringement against Socrates, Inc. Nintendo's infringement claim is described by its attorney as "tenuous" but Nintendo's CEO is concerned about the NAE position. To date, Nintendo has not suffered any decline in sales. However, the next Christmas sales period will be the only true measure of any decline.

In Apple's case, figures indicate a decline in sales to school districts with some sales representatives complaining of 50 percent sales reductions. The "ease, convenience, availability and cost" of Socrates are cited by the sales reps as nearly "insurmountable sales arguments." Apple's infringement case is described as "strong" by its lawyers. In the past, Apple has enjoyed a 90 percent success rate in winning infringement cases.

Drawing on your knowledge from Part I about litigation, discuss the wisdom of suits by Nintendo and Apple against Socrates. Be sure to consider all factors. Also, provide contrasts between the two cases and reasons for pursuing litigation.

Problem 4

(NOTE: Not all information about Sears here is factually correct. Some events occurred at other companies.)

On April 24, 1994, Arthur C. Martinez, chairman and CEO of the Sears Merchandise Group, announced that Pierre Rogers would be leaving Lancôme, a French cosmetics firm, to develop and market a cosmetics line for Sears. The makeup line would be sold in Sears stores and through direct marketing. Mr. Rogers indicated that he hoped to have Annette Golden of Revlon join his team. Sears referred to Mr. Rogers' departure from Lancôme as the beginning of a joint venture. Sears, had been experiencing difficulties in coaxing major cosmetic firms to sell their cosmetics to Sears. Lancôme has written to Sears about a noncompete clause signed by Mr. Rogers affirming he will not work for a competitor worldwide for five years. Mr. Rogers is recruiting Ms. Golden over Revlon's protests, and she also has a noncompete clause for five years in North America.

Sears only recently reinstated its cosmetic counters in stores after a 10-year hiatus. In the first quarter of 1994, 26 stores opened cosmetics counters. For the remainder of 1994, Sears had planned to open such counters in 99 more stores. By October 1995, Sears expected to have cosmetic counters in 200 stores.

Sears has been negotiating with Wilford Bottomley to purchase a new skin cream he has developed that moisturizes and removes age spots. Their negotiations have proceeded as follows:

Oct. 1, 1993: Sears's wire:
"Would be interested in buying patent for your anti-age skin cream."

Oct. 3, 1993: Bottomley letter:
"Have several offers, but am willing to talk."

Oct. 5, 1993: Sears's certified letter via overnight mail:
"Will purchase patent for Bottomley's Skin Cream for $1.2 million plus 10 percent royalties. This offer to remain open until October 31, 1993."

Oct. 7, 1993: Bottomley wire:
"Will need name to remain on product. Deal."

a. Do Sears and Pierre Rogers have a contract? Why or why not?
b. Do Bottomley and Sears have a contract?
c. Discuss the recruitment of Ms. Golden and her noncompete clause.
d. Do any of Sears's actions violate federal antitrust laws?

Part Four

Business and Its Employees

This portion of the book covers the rights and duties of employers and employees as they work together to operate a business. What are the regulations and restrictions relating to the hiring and firing of employees? How much authority do employees have to make decisions and take actions with respect to their work? How are safety regulations enforced in the workplace? What legal limits exist with respect to work hours? What role do unions play in employee and employer relations? What do federal and state antidiscrimination statutes provide? What are their effects on hiring, firing, promoting, and rewarding?

Judgment

Jerome Lange was the manager of a small grocery store that carried Nabisco products. Ronnell Lynch had been hired by Nabisco as a cookie salesman-trainee in October 1968. On March 1, 1969, Mr. Lynch was assigned his own territory, which included Lange's store.

On May 1, 1969, Mr. Lynch came to Mr. Lange's store to place previously delivered merchandise on the shelves. An argument developed between the two over Mr. Lynch's service to the store. Mr. Lynch became very angry and started swearing. Mr. Lange told him to either stop swearing or leave the store because children were present. Mr. Lynch then became uncontrollably angry and said, "I ought to break your neck." He then went behind the counter and dared Mr. Lange to fight. When Mr. Lange refused, Mr. Lynch viciously assaulted him after which he threw merchandise around the store and left.

Is Nabisco liable for Mr. Lynch's actions?

CHAPTER 17

All businesses have a common thread: employees. They

Management of Employee Conduct: Agency

need them, rely

on them, pay them, and give them authority to perform

certain business tasks. This delegation of authority is

the focus of this chapter. When is an employee acting

on behalf of an employer? How much authority does an

employee have? What duties and obligations do

employees owe employers? When is a business liable

for an employee's acts? These questions are a preview

of the topics covered in this chapter.

> At a time of grave crisis during the Civil War, Abe Lincoln was awakened late one night by an opportunist who reported that the head of customs had just died.
>
> "Mr. President, would it be all right if I took his place?"
>
> "Well," said Lincoln, "if it be all right with the undertaker, it's all right with me."
>
> **Morris Udall**
> *Too Funny to Be President*

581

NAMES AND ROLES—AGENCY TERMINOLOGY

Although some terms are used interchangeably, there are exact labels and definitions for the parties in an agency relationship. This section outlines and defines the terminology used to cover that relationship.

Agency

In an agency relationship, one party agrees to act on behalf of another party according to directions. It is a relationship that exists by common consent—both sides agree to it—and a relationship that is fiduciary—there are duties and responsibilities on both sides. The general term *agency* can be used to refer to many different types of relationships. A real estate agent who is hired to help market your house is an agent of yours; a sales clerk in a department store is an agent for that store; talent agents are agents for many actors at the same time.

Principals

In the employer-employee relationship, the employers are referred to as the **principals**. The term *principal* is used because some agents are not truly employees. A literary agent, for example, represents many authors who are the agent's principals, but the principals are not "employers," in the usual sense, of the agent.

Agents

Agents are people hired by a principal to do a task on behalf of the principal. The agent represents the principal in such a way that if the agent negotiates a contract, the principal but not the agent is bound by and a party to the contract. A president of a corporation is an agent of the corporation. When the president negotiates a contract, the corporation, not the president, is bound to perform that contract.

All employees are agents of the principal employer, but not all agents are employees. A corporation might hire an architect to design a new office building and obtain bids for the construction of the building. The architect would be an agent for very limited purposes but not an employee of the company.

Masters-Servants

A **master-servant relationship** is one in which the principal (master) exercises a great deal of control over the agent (servant). An employer-employee relationship for a production line worker is an example of a master-servant relationship. The employee works regular hours, is paid a regular wage, and is subject to complete supervision and control by the employer during work hours. The factors used to determine whether a master-servant relationship exists are as follows:
- Level of supervision of agent
- Level of control of agent
- Nature of agent's work
- Regularity of hours and pay
- Length of employment

Independent Contractors

An **independent contractor** is a person who is hired by another to perform a task but who is not controlled directly by the hiring party. For example, a corporation's attorney is an agent of the corporation only for purposes of legal representation and court appearances. However, the attorney is not a corporate employee and the corporation would have no control over the attorney's office operations. The attorney is an independent contractor. A subcontractor hired for performing partial work on a construction site is also an example of an independent contractor.

Principals have less responsibility for independent contractors than for servants because they have little control over a contractor's conduct. The distinction between master-servant relationships and independent contractor relationships is important because a principal's liability for an agent's actions varies depending upon the agent's status as servant or contractor.

Agency Law

Agency law is not statutory; rather, its source is common law. The reflection of common law regarding agency is found in the *Restatement of Agency*, which is a summary of the majority view of agency law in the United States that is followed by many courts in handling agency cases.

Studying agency law actually involves examining three different components. The first component is the creation of the agency relationship. The second component involves the examination of the relationship between principals and agents. The third component examines the relationship of the agent and principal to third parties. In this third component, the areas of contracts *and* torts are covered because principals have both contractual and tort liability for the acts of their agents.

CREATION OF THE AGENCY RELATIONSHIP

In most cases, determining whether an agency relationship exists is a simple task: A business hires an employee and that employee is an agent of the business. Agency relationships, however, are created in other ways and the requirements vary.

Express Authority

An employee who is hired by agreement (oral or written) is an agent and has been given **express authority** to act on behalf of the business. That authority, however, may be limited. A driver employee, for example, may only have the authority to deliver packages; a sales employee may have the authority to represent the company but is required to obtain another employee's signature to finalize sales contracts. An express contract specifies the limitations of an employee/agent's authority.

The Writing

An agency relationship is created by agreement, which need not be in writing, although it is best for both employer and employee if it is. A written contract specifying the agent's authority is required only if the agent will enter into contracts required to be in writing or if a state statute requires an agent's authority to be in writing. For example, many states require that real estate agents' commission contracts be in writing. An agent who will be negotiating contracts for a principal for longer than a year should have a written agreement.

Capacity

Because agents will enter into contracts for their principals, the principals must have the capacity to contract. Capacity here means capacity in the traditional contract sense: age and mental capacity (as covered in Chapter 15).

One of the most controversial issues in agency law concerns the **unincorporated association**, which is a group that acts as an entity but has no legal existence. Some charitable organizations—churches for example—have an ongoing existence and have probably built buildings, had fund-raising drives, and entered into many contracts. Because these organizations are not incorporated and do not have any legal existence, however, those who sign these contracts are not agents. Moreover, they are liable under contract terms because the organizations are not principals with capacity. For example, suppose that a Little League coach signs a credit contract for the purchase of Little League equipment. The Little League organization is nonprofit and is not incorporated. In the event the league does not raise enough money to pay for the sporting equipment, the signing coach will be liable because the league is not a principal with capacity.

The capacity of the agent is not an issue in the agency relationship for purposes of the agent's authority to enter into contracts. However, the capacity of the agent to drive, operate equipment, or work with the public is an issue that affects the employer's liability to third parties. Because of this liability, many employers conduct polygraph and psychological tests and drug screening as a precondition to hiring employees. Many firms also have ongoing drug-testing programs to ensure that employees are not reporting for work or working under the influence of drugs or alcohol.

Business Planning Tip

Before you sign on behalf of an organization, be sure you understand your liability. For example, if you sign a contract with a hotel for a group's meeting, you will have personal liability if your group is not incorporated and if the hotel is not paid. If your group is incorporated, be sure to sign so that the corporation, not you, is personally liable. You can use the following format:

(Your Group Name)

By: (Your Name)

(Your Title)

An example:

Pacific Southwest Academy of Legal Studies in Business, a nonprofit corporation

By: Marianne M. Jennings

Executive Secretary

Implied Authority

An agent under contract not only has the authority given expressly but also has certain **implied authority**. Implied authority is the extension of express authority by custom. For example, a person who is hired as president of a corporation probably does not have his or her exact duties specified in the contract. However, this president will likely have the same type of authority customarily held by corporate presidents: to sign contracts, to authorize personnel changes, to conduct salary reviews and changes, and to institute operational changes. The law gives the president customary authority unless the president's contract specifies otherwise. This implied authority can be limited by agreement between the parties if they do not want custom and practice to control their relationship.

Apparent Authority

In many cases an agency relationship arises, not by express or implied contracts, but because of the way a principal presents himself or herself to third parties. This theory of agency law, called **apparent authority** or **agency by estoppel**, holds a principal liable if the principal makes someone else think he or she has an agent.

Apparent authority exists by appearance. A third party is led to believe that an agent, although not actually holding express and accompanying implied authority, had the proper authority to deal with the third party. The third party is led to believe that certain promises will be fulfilled. For example, a mobile home dealer who has brochures, note pads, and other materials from a mobile home manufacturer has the appearance of having the authority to sell those homes even if there is no actual authority. The following case deals with issues of apparent authority that arose because of an agent's position.

Romero v. *Mervyn's*
784 P.2d 992 (N.M. 1989)

BEWARE OF WANDERING STORE MANAGERS OFFERING COMPENSATION

FACTS

On November 23, 1984, Lucy Romero and two of her adult daughters were shopping in Mervyn's Department Store in Albuquerque the day after Thanksgiving when the store was crowded with Christmas shoppers. As Mrs. Romero and her daughters were descending on an escalator, another customer either intentionally or accidentally pushed her. She fell to her hands and knees, hitting her jaw as she fell. A commotion ensued, and when Mrs. Romero reached the bottom of the escalator, a salesperson at a temporary station helped her to her feet and out of the path of other shoppers. Either this employee or a security guard watching from a two-way mirror summoned the store manager to the scene.

Dennis Wolf, the acting store manager, came in response to this call. His usual job as operations manager of the store entailed responsibility for directing and training employees. It was also his duty to investigate and gather information about incidents involving customer injuries on the premises. Mr. Wolf asked Mrs.

Romero whether she needed a wheelchair or an ambulance, and she replied that she did not. Her daughters were "very upset, a little bit hysterical" and kept asking who would pay for their mother's medical expenses. Mr. Wolf himself was nervous and in a hurry because the store was busy. According to Mrs. Romero and her daughters, Mr. Wolf told them that Mervyn's would pay any medical expenses. Mr. Wolf contended he told Mrs. Romero only that Mervyn's would submit the claim to its insurer and the insurer would decide whether to pay any claims arising from the incident.

Immediately following this conversation, Mrs. Romero's daughters helped their mother out of the store, brought the car around, and returned to their home in Santa Fe. The following Monday, Mrs. Romero was still in pain and decided she should seek medical attention. She had another of her daughters, who lived in Albuquerque, call Mervyn's and confirm with Mr. Wolf his promise that Mervyn's would pay the expenses. She also asked him if any forms needed to be completed when her mother went

Continued

to the doctor. He told her to come down to the store and pick up the necessary forms. When she did so, however, Mr. Wolf told her that he was out of the forms. Then, according to her testimony, he told her to go ahead and have her mother go to the doctor and that Mervyn's would pay the expenses.

After that, Mrs. Romero consulted a physician and underwent physical therapy that cost $2,041. Mervyn's, however, refused to pay the bills, and Mrs. Romero filed suit against the store. After the jury awarded her $2,041 in compensatory damages and $25,000 in punitive damages, Mervyn's appealed.

JUDICIAL OPINION

RANSOM, Justice

Besides being liable for acts within the actual authority of an agent, a principal also is responsible for the acts of the agent when the principal has clothed the agent with the appearance of authority. Romero's claim of apparent authority was based on Mervyn's alleged placement of Wolf in a position that would lead a reasonably prudent third party to believe Wolf possessed authority to bind Mervyn's in a contract to pay medical bills. While actual authority is determined in light of the principal's "manifestations of consent" to the agent, apparent authority arises from the principal's manifestations to third parties and can be created by appointing a person to a position that carries with it generally recognized duties.

We believe substantial evidence was presented on the issue of Wolf's actual authority. When Romero was hurt, Mervyn's other employees called for the "manager." Wolf was both acting manager and operations manager. When he appeared on the scene, the employees already present deferred to his handling of the situation. Mervyn's presented testimony that it was indeed part of Wolf's job to deal with customer injuries, that no one else at the store other than Wolf had such authority, and indeed that there was no one else to whom an injured customer could go. Pursuant to his duties, Wolf inquired whether Romero was hurt and

gathered information concerning the accident. It was at this point, according to testimony, that the first promises were made.

Mervyn's argues there was no testimony from Wolf or another agent of Mervyn's to suggest that it lay within Wolf's actual authority to bind Mervyn's. Moreover, Mervyn's argues, the evidence supported Mervyn's allegation that store policy in fact prohibited employees from admitting responsibility for customer injuries. Neither of these points mandated a different verdict. An agent's actual authority need not be proved by direct testimony; it can be inferred from attending circumstances.

Mervyn's also argues that Wolf's statements at the time of the accident should not be considered as evidence of his actual authority. Mervyn's theory is that the extrajudicial statements of an agent cannot be used to prove agency, and the admissions of an agent are not binding on the principal unless made within the scope of authority. True, but here it is uncontroverted that Wolf was the acting manager of the store. After prima facie proof of managerial agency, extrajudicial declarations of the agent are admissible and may be considered in determining the scope of the agent's authority. The fact that Wolf made an offer to pay Romero's medical expenses could be considered as evidence of authority to make a contract.

We believe substantial evidence also supported an instruction on apparent authority. Mervyn's alleged policy prohibiting employees from admitting responsibility for customer injuries is not controlling because the existence of such a policy was not public knowledge. A third person who deals with an agent is not bound by any secret or private instructions given to the agent by the principal.

The focus of our inquiry, rather, is the existence of substantial evidence from which the jury could find that Mervyn's placed Wolf in such a position and clothed him with such indicia of authority as would lead a third party, such as Romero, reasonably to conclude Wolf had the authority to make the promise at issue. Given the circumstances surrounding the

Continued

accident itself and the role Wolf played as an employee of Mervyn's upon arriving at the scene, the jury could have concluded that Mervyn's had placed Wolf in such a position.

Affirmed.

CASE QUESTIONS

1. What happened to Mrs. Romero, and where?
2. What promise did Mr. Wolf make?
3. Did Mrs. Romero attempt to verify the promise?
4. Is it reasonable to assume that a store manager would have the authority to make such a promise?
5. Does it matter that Mervyn's policy was that store managers should not make these promises?
6. Did Mervyn's have an ethical obligation to pay because there was, at a minimum, a misunderstanding? What policy would you institute with respect to customer injuries if you were managing the store?

C O N S I D E R . . .

17.1 On September 20, 1973, a Beech Model 18 Aircraft carrying singer Jim Croce and his entourage (the group) crashed shortly after takeoff from Natchitoches, Louisiana. All were killed.

At the time of the crash, the plane was being flown by Robert N. Elliott, an employee of Roberts Airways. Roberts had been asked by Mustang Aviation to fly the entourage according to a prepared itinerary. Mustang originally had entered into a contract with Lloyd St. Martin of Variety Artists International, a booking agent for popular singers, to fly the group itself. The agreement was entered into on September 18, 1973. Later that same day Mustang learned that its aircraft was disabled, and it was then that Mustang's director of operations called Roberts and asked it to substitute.

Relatives of Mr. Croce and the others killed in the crash brought suit against Mustang for the crash. What, if any, agency relationships existed in this case? How did they arise? Is Mustang liable for the crash? [*Croce* v. *Bromely Corp.*, 623 F.2d 1084 (5th Cir. 1980).]

FOR THE MANAGER'S DESK

A LOOK AT AN OLD CASE TO REVIEW AN ONGOING PROBLEM

The following case from 1919 tells us that the issues of agency law have always been with us. We also learn that if we're not minding the store, we don't dare leave it unattended, for apparent agents can cost us.

Kanelles v. *Locke*
12 Ohio App. 210 (1919)

VICKERY, Justice
It seems that Mrs. Locke was running the Hotel Ohio, in 1627 Prospect Avenue, Cleveland; that on the 23rd of December, 1918, at the hour of one o'clock in the morning, Mr. Kanelles applied, with a friend, and was received as a guest in said hotel, and paid the sum of $2 for a room, to which they were assigned; that in the hotel were notices posted as is required of innkeepers under the law of

Continued

Ohio; that after they were shown to a room Kanelles told the man who appeared to be in charge, and who showed them to the room, that he desired to leave his money and valuables with the hotel proprietor for the night, whereupon they all returned to the office and the man in charge wrote out a receipt describing $484 in currency, a diamond stickpin and two checks for $5 each; that the man signed this receipt with the name of the proprietress of the hotel, Mrs. Locke, by him, and gave it to Kanelles, after which he, Kanelles, retired; that in the morning he presented the receipt to Mrs. Locke and requested the return of his money and valuables, whereupon he learned that this man who apparently was in charge of the office was not in the employ of Mrs. Locke at all, and, as she claimed, had no authority to receive the money or valuables; that upon going to the room of this man Mrs. Locke found that he had absconded, taking the money and valuables with him; and that Mrs. Locke refused to make good the loss to her guest.

This man who signed the receipt, J. C. Clemens, was and had been for some time a roomer in this hotel. The hotel was open to receive visitors at this time in the morning, or night, and that no one was in the office to take charge of guests who might arrive except this person Clemens and a young lady who was also a boarder or lodger in the hotel; that when the plaintiff entered with his friend and asked for a room,

Clemens, who appeared to be in charge, got up and went behind the counter, had them register, got the key from its proper place, assigned them to a room, and took them to their room; and that after they had gone to the room, when the plaintiff requested that the hotel take charge of his valuables, they went down to the office, and with the help of the young lady wrote a receipt which at first was not satisfactory, and then wrote the receipt of which the following is a copy:

"Mr. D. Kanelles, Man in Room 111 Gave me 1 Diamond pin and $484.00 in bills and 2 $5.00 checks.

       "Mrs. Locke
       "Hotel Ohio
       "Per J. C. Clemens."

During this time the only person who appeared in charge of the office was this man Clemens. Whether Mrs. Locke had turned over the office to him to do these things we are not able to determine; but the fact remains that he was the only person there, apparently in charge of a public office that was receiving guests at that time in the morning or night, and that plaintiff became a guest and had a right to turn his valuables over to the hotel for safe-keeping, in accordance with the notices published in the hotel. We think the plaintiff was warranted in believing that this man in charge was the duly authorized agent for the purpose of receiving guests and receiving for safe-keeping valuables of the guests.

It is claimed by the defendant that this man was not

her agent and had no authority to receive valuables or do anything around the hotel, and that therefore she was not responsible for any money or valuables that might be deposited with him. We can not acquiesce in this doctrine. An agency may be created by estoppel, and that estoppel may be allowed on the ground of negligence or fault on the part of the principal, *upon the principle that when one of two innocent parties must suffer loss, the loss will fall on him whose conduct brought about the situation.*

Here the proprietress of this hotel left this man in the office either designedly or negligently, clothed with apparent authority to do what hotel clerks usually do, anyone who came in for the purpose of becoming a guest, and did become a guest, might reasonably conclude that he had *apparent* authority to do what clerks under similar circumstances would have a right to do.

Mrs. Locke, the defendant, had complied with all the requirements of the statute to relieve innkeepers from liability by posting the notices required by law, and we think that she was an innkeeper within the meaning of the law; we think that she by her voluntary act, or by her negligent act, had placed someone in a position where it would appear to anyone coming in to become a guest at the hotel that he was properly in charge, and that therefore she made herself by her conduct responsible for his acts, acting within the apparent scope of a clerk or employee in a hotel, to receive property of her guests;

Continued

and we think the court was clearly wrong in holding that there was no responsibility and in rendering a judgment against the plaintiff for costs. For these reasons the case will be reversed and

remanded to the municipal court for further proceedings in accordance with law.

Discussion Questions
1. What happened to allow Mr. Clemens's involvement?

2. What do we learn about the importance of "minding the store"?
3. Give an example of how something similar might happen today in a business.

Ratification

There are times when an agent without proper authority enters into a contract that the principal later ratifies. **Ratification** occurs when the principal reviews a contract and voluntarily decides that, even though the agent did not have proper authority, the contract will be honored as if the agent had full authority. Once a contract is ratified, it is effective from the time the agent entered into it even though the agent had no authority until after the fact. Ratification is a way for a principal to give an agent authority retroactively. The following case deals with the issues and requirements of ratification.

Perkins v. Rich
415 N.E.2d 895 (Mass. 1980)

THE COLLECTION PLATE REACHES BEYOND SUNDAY

FACTS

In 1962, the First Parish Unitarian Church of East Bridgewater hired Paul Rich (defendant) to be its minister at a small salary. During the mid-1960s, Mr. Rich's personality and his role in the Church changed dramatically. The change was attributed to "psychological traumatization by the Vietnam War." Mr. Rich initiated a highly publicized antiwar ministry and also expanded the church from 12 families and a budget of $5,000 to over 400 families.

In 1965, Mr. Rich assumed financial responsibilities for the church without formal authorization from the members of the parish committee. By 1969, Mr. Rich had taken over all business and financial affairs of the church.

The committee stopped meeting, and no annual meeting of church members was held after 1969.

At that point Mr. Rich began a project to develop a community that would feature museums, galleries, and exhibits. The community was to be funded from the profits of a large-scale housing development for the elderly, which was to be financed primarily with government funds. Mr. Rich and his family contributed over $100,000 to the church, but most of the planned project was financed by three mortgage notes.

All did not go well with the development, and by 1977 the church members became involved again when they discovered there were defaults on the mortgage notes. When the

Continued

mortgage holders (Jane Perkins, et al.) brought suit to foreclose, the church members claimed the mortgages were invalid because they were given without authorization from the committee. The lower court found for the mortgage holders, and the church appealed.

JUDICIAL OPINION
BROWN, Judge

Similar to most of the other transactions negotiated during Rich's tenure, the mortgages given to Bay State and Shawmut were signed by Rich on behalf of the Church in his capacity as president and treasurer. Each bank was given a previously recorded document which purportedly established his authority to act on behalf of the "Church corporation." Although the Church was found to be a de facto corporation, and Rich its de facto president and treasurer, Rich's lack of authority should have been apparent to the banks due to the irregularities on the face of each document. These irregularities created a duty upon the banks to inquire further as to Rich's authority, an investigation which would have revealed the true Church structure. The master further found that this would have saved the day for the Church but for the fact that reasonable and prudent inquiry by the Church would have brought about discovery of the mortgages. The Church's failure to assert its rights, once put on notice of unusually large expenditures, constituted ratification of Rich's actions.

The Committee claims that it did not know of the existence of the mortgages and thus that its failure to repudiate the mortgages resulted not from a ratification of the transactions, but from ignorance of essential facts. Generally, in order to establish ratification of unauthorized acts of an agent, a principal must have "full knowledge of all material facts." Ignorance of such facts will not lead to liability. However, a qualification to this rule is that one cannot "purposefully shut his eyes to means of information within his own possession and control." This is especially true of the Committee which functioned as

the "business center" of the Church and had a duty to keep itself informed of Church business.

Further, the Committee was not totally ignorant of Rich's actions. From the many indicia of the radical physical and structural changes to the Church and its surroundings, it should have been obvious to the Church that "something was afoot." The very nature of the construction and renovation indicated that large expenditures were being made. Although Rich was far from candid in his disclosures, he did inform Church members of various projects at Church events and through annual reports and publications. The Committee, whose responsibility was to approve payment of all bills, and Church members in general, deliberately ignored these facts. By not asking the simple question—"What is going on?," the Committee assumed the risk of what its investigation might have disclosed.

We thus conclude that the Committee's knowledge of substantial and costly physical changes at the Church should have provoked an investigation by the Committee which would have led to the discovery of the mortgages. In these circumstances the Committee's failure to act "will be deemed to constitute actual knowledge." By failing to disavow the mortgages, the Church ratified the transactions, a ratification which may be inferred without a vote by the Committee.

Accordingly the mortgages are valid.

Affirmed.

CASE QUESTIONS

1. What was the committee's responsibility in the church?
2. Did Mr. Rich have actual authority to negotiate the mortgages?
3. Did Mr. Rich have implied authority for the mortgages?
4. What is the significance of the extent of changes in the church's physical structure?
5. Did the committee have actual knowledge of what was going on?
6. Does the court impose a duty on principals to ask what is going on?

C O N S I D E R . . . **17.2** Benjamin Chavez served as executive director of the National Association for the Advancement of Colored People (NAACP). Mary Stansee, former employee of the NAACP executive offices charged Mr. Chavez with sexual harassment, and he settled the claim for $332,400. The NAACP was financially troubled at the time of the settlement, with a deficit of $2.7 million in 1973, and Mr. Chavez did not disclose the settlement to the board until after it was completed. Did Mr. Chavez have implied authority to make the settlement? Did he have apparent authority?

THE PRINCIPAL-AGENT RELATIONSHIP

To this point the focus has been on the relationship between the agent and principal, on the one hand, and third parties, on the other. However, it is important to realize that a contractual relationship exists between the agent and principal, so that each has certain obligations and rights. This section of the chapter covers that relationship.

The Agent's Responsibilities

Principals and agents have a **fiduciary** relationship, which is characterized by loyalty, trust, care, and obedience. An agent in the role of fiduciary must act in the principal's best interests.

DUTY OF LOYALTY

An agent is required to act only for the benefit of the principal, and an agent cannot represent both parties in a transaction unless each knows about and consent's to the agent's representation of the other. Further, an agent cannot use the information gained or the offers available to or by the principal to profit personally. For example, an agent who is hired to find a buyer for a new invention could not interfere with the principal's possible sale by demonstrating his or her own product. Neither can an agent, hired to find a piece of property, buy the property and then sell it (secretly of course) back to the principal. The following case involves an issue of an agent's fiduciary duty in a sale transaction.

Silva v. *Bisbee*
628 P.2d 214 (Haw. 1981)

DID I FORGET TO TELL YOU I'M A BUYER TOO?

FACTS

Bernice Bisbee (defendant/appellant) is a real estate broker employed by Midkiff Realty, Inc. In September 1972, she obtained from Richard and Marian Silva (plaintiffs/appellees) an exclusive listing agreement for the sale of their property in Kaleheo, Kauai. The land, which fronted on the Kaumualii highway, consisted of 34,392 square feet and one two-bedroom house and one four-bedroom house. The Silvas told Ms. Bisbee that they wanted $100,000 for the property.

Some time later, Ms. Bisbee obtained an offer for the property from David Larsen. The down payment was set at $35,000, with payments of $2,000 a month at 8 percent a year, but Mr. Larsen backed out before closing.

Continued

After that, a joint venture of six members formed the Pacific Equity Associates to buy the property. Ms. Bisbee was to manage the joint venture and would receive 10 percent of the profits for her services. One of the joint venture members, Toshio Morikawa, appeared as the buyer at the July 1973 closing of the property sale. Ms. Bisbee did not tell the Silvas of the venture nor of her pecuniary interest in it.

In August 1973, Ms. Bisbee prepared for the venture a financial statement that listed the market value of the Silva property at $149,424. Several times the venture was late making payments, which Ms. Bisbee covered. Mr. Silva and his wife were emotionally distressed about the late payments and told Ms. Bisbee. Eventually, because of defaults on the payments, the Silvas brought suit to cancel the contract and for damages for fraud by Ms. Bisbee, naming Midkiff Realty in the suit as well.

The jury returned a verdict for $29,000 in general damages for the Silvas and $50,000 in punitive damages. Ms. Bisbee and Midkiff appealed.

JUDICIAL OPINION

PADGETT, Judge

Bisbee and Midkiff concede that as brokers under a listing contract, they stood in a fiduciary relationship to the Silvas. It is axiomatic that a fiduciary cannot have a pecuniary interest in the purchase of property from the cestui que [beneficiary of the] trust without full disclosure. No such disclosure was made here. Bisbee's conduct in causing the purchase of the property by a joint venture in which she had a pecuniary interest constituted constructive fraud as a matter of law.

As to the issue of emotional distress, the appellants' motion for a directed verdict below was expressly based on the decision of the Supreme Court of Hawaii in *Rodrigues* v. *State*. Appellants here argue, however, that the emotional distress grew out of the failure to make the payments on time, not out of the fiduciary relationship, and that, therefore, the case is one sounding in contract.

It is well-settled that a party cannot complain on appeal that the motion for a directed verdict should have been granted on a ground not specified.

We read *Rodrigues* to say that given some evidence of emotional distress in the record, the question of whether such distress amounted to serious mental distress which a reasonable man normally constituted could not adequately cope with is one for the jury. Since there was testimony that Bisbee was informed of the fact of emotional upset arising out of the late payments, the test of foreseeability was met.

What we have said disposes of the contention that Midkiff's motion for a new trial was improperly denied. Bisbee was Midkiff's agent and Midkiff is equally liable with her for the damages arising out of her breach of fiduciary duty as well as the damages arising out of the claimed emotional distress.

The last points raised are that the evidence was insufficient to justify the award of punitive damages and that those damages are excessive. There was ample evidence from which the jury could have concluded that what Bisbee did was done willfully, wantonly or maliciously or characterized by some aggravating circumstances. Certainly the jury could have concluded that Bisbee's failure to advise the Silvas that their property was worth more than $100,000 was willful and that Bisbee's failure to advise them of her pecuniary interest in the purchaser was also willful. We cannot say in the circumstances of this case that the award of $50,000 punitive damages shocks the conscience of the court.

Affirmed.

CASE QUESTIONS

1. What did agent Bisbee fail to disclose?
2. Was Ms. Bisbee representing both sides in a transaction?
3. Can the Silvas recover for their emotional distress?
4. Do you think the jury awarded the difference between the listed value of the property and the actual value as punitive damages?
5. Why is Midkiff also liable?

<table>
<tr><td>

E T H I C A L   I S S U E S

17.1 Kate is an employee of a firm that works with nonprofit organizations to help them arrange financing for construction projects and other long-term goals. One of the firm's clients, a hospital, is interested in hiring a consultant to work with it on acquiring some property. Four firms have submitted bids for the hospital's work, and one bid is clearly the best and lowest of the four. Kate sees her supervisor's administrative assistant place a copy of the top proposal in an envelope and mail it to another firm that has not yet submitted its bid proposal. Has Kate's firm breached its fiduciary duty? Has the administrative assistant breached his fiduciary duty to his employer? Is the sending of the copy ethical?

</td></tr>
</table>

DUTY OF OBEDIENCE

An agent has the duty to obey reasonable instructions from the principal. The agent is not required to do anything criminally wrong or commit torts, of course; but he or she is required to operate according to the principal's standards and instructions. Failure to do so could mean the agent has gone beyond the authority given and is then personally liable for the conduct.

DUTY OF CARE

Agents have a duty to use as much care and act as prudently as they would if managing their own affairs. Agents must take the time and effort to perform their principals' assigned tasks. For example, officers of corporations must base their decisions on information, not guesses, and must ensure that their decisions are carried out by employees.

An agent who does not use reasonable care will be liable to the principal for any damages resulting from a lack of care. Thus, when an agent does not make adequate travel arrangements for a speaker, the agent is liable to the speaker for damages that resulted from the speaker's nonappearance at an engagement.

The Principal's Rights and Responsibilities

A principal has the right to expect that an agent will perform within the standards described above. In exchange, the principal has certain obligations. The first obligation is that of compensation, which can take various forms. Some agents work for a fee on a contingency basis. A real estate agent, for example, may have an arrangement in which he or she receives compensation only if a buyer for the property is found. Other types of agency relationships hold an agent partially responsible for the transaction. In a ***del credere* agency**, the agent sells the principal's goods and agrees to pay the principal if the buyer does not pay for those goods.

There can be a **gratuitous agency**, in which the agent has authority to act for the principal but will not be compensated. For example, some charitable organizations have agents act in fund-raising capacities, but these agents do not expect compensation.

Principals also have an obligation to indemnify agents for expenses the agents incur in carrying out the principal's orders. Corporate officers, for example, are entitled to travel compensation; sales agents are entitled to compensation for ads to sell goods, realty, or services.

E T H I C A L   I S S U E S

17.2 The Dilemma of Team Doctors: Agents of Players or Agents of Management? In a 1989 baseball game against the Toronto Blue Jays, Marty Barrett, a second baseman for the Boston Red Sox, "popped" his right knee while running to first base. Mr. Barrett had ruptured his anterior cruciate ligament (ACL). Two days after the game, Dr. Arthur Pappas, the Red Sox team doctor and chair of the University of Massachusetts Medical Center's orthopedic department performed surgery and removed most of Mr. Barrett's ACL. Dr. Pappas is also a part owner of the Red Sox and at a press conference described the injury as "torn cartilage" and "a stretched ligament."

Sports Illustrated asks the following questions about team doctors:

Team doctors face torturous ethical dilemmas. Are they supposed to be getting players ready to play, or are they supposed to be seeing to it that they heal completely? Should the doctors be more concerned with the immediate needs of the team or with the long-term health of players whose careers will be over while they are still young men? How does a doctor keep from feeling like a member of the team, which, as former Los Angeles Raider team internist Robert Huizenga says, "invariably has a subtle effect on a doctor's decision-making process"? What does a doctor do when a coach or an owner is pressuring a player to get back in the lineup—and the player says he's not ready? More to the point, what does a doctor do in this situation when he knows that the player is not ready?

Is there a conflict of interest? Is there a greater conflict if the physician is a part owner?

LIABILITY OF PRINCIPALS FOR AGENTS' CONDUCT— THE RELATIONSHIP WITH THIRD PARTIES

Contract Liability

Although the types of authority an agent has and the terms of the agency agreement define the authority of the agent, the contract liability of a principal is not determined by either what he or she intended or by the limitations agreed to privately by the agent and the principal. In other words, third parties have certain contract enforcement rights depending on the nature of the agent's work and the authority given by the principal. The liability of the principal for contracts made by an agent is controlled by the perceptions created for and observed by the third party to the contract. Those perceptions vary, and so the liability of the principal varies depending on the way in which the agent does business. For example, an officer of a corporation has the authority to bind the corporation, but what if the officer does not disclose that there is a principal? This section deals with those issues.

THE DISCLOSED PRINCIPAL

In a situation in which a third party is aware there is a principal involved and also knows who the principal is, the principal is liable to the third party but the agent is not. This is true whether the agent has express, implied, or apparent authority. If the agent has no authority, however, then the agent, not the principal, is liable. For example, suppose that Paula Abbaduhla is the vice president of Video Television, Inc., and she signs for a line of credit for the corporation at First Bank. So long as she signed the documents "Paula Abbaduhla, VP, Video Television, Inc.," Video would be solely responsible for the line of credit. If, however, she signed that same way but had no authority, she would be liable to Video if it had to honor the agreement. As another example, corporations cannot sell or buy property without board authorization in the form of a resolution. If Paula signed to buy land and did not have a resolution, she would have no express, implied, or apparent authority, and she would be liable for the land contract. (See Chapter 20 for a more thorough discussion of board resolutions and officers' authority.)

THE PARTIALLY DISCLOSED PRINCIPAL

In this situation, the third party knows that the agent is acting for someone else, but the identity of the principal is not disclosed. For example, an agent might be used to purchase land for development purposes when the developer does not want to be disclosed because disclosure of a major developer's involvement might drive up land prices. In this situation, the third-party seller of the land can hold either the principal or the agent liable on the contract. The agent thus assumes some risk of personal liability by not disclosing the identity of the principal.

THE UNDISCLOSED PRINCIPAL

In this situation, an agent acts without disclosing either the existence of a principal or the principal's identity. Again, such an arrangement might be undertaken to avoid speculation, or it could be undertaken simply to protect someone's privacy, such as when a famous person purchases a home and does not want any advance disclosure of the purchase or its location. Here, the agent stands alone for liability to the third party. If the principal decides to come forward, however, the third party could hold either liable. Exhibits 17.1 and 17.2 (pg. 596) provide summaries of the liability of agents and principals under the three forms of disclosure of the relationship.

Exhibit 17.1
Contract Liability of Disclosed Principal

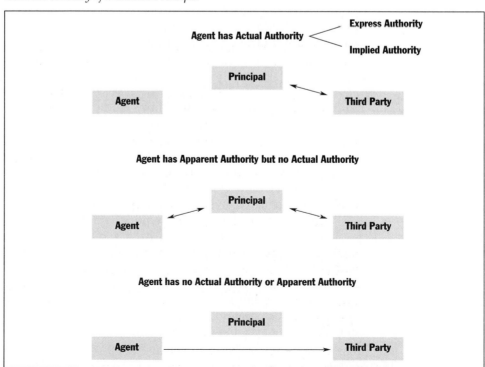

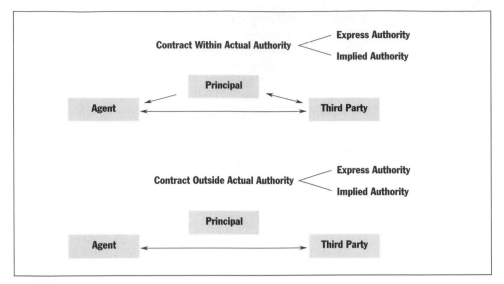

Exhibit 17.2
Contract Liability of Undisclosed or Partially Disclosed Principal

Liability of Principals for Agents' Torts

As for the liability of principals for torts committed by agents, two types of agents must be reconsidered: servants and independent contractors. The amount of liability a principal will have for an agent's torts depends first upon the status of the agent.

MASTER-SERVANT RELATIONSHIP

As discussed earlier in the chapter, there is a distinction between the liability of a principal for the acts of a servant and for those of an independent contractor. The principal is liable for the torts of the servant—an agent whose work, assignments, and time are controlled by the principal.

C O N S I D E R . . . **17.3** For the past 50 years, the Ladies Guild of the Trinity Lutheran Church in Indiana has run a Christmas program for the sick and infirm members of the church who are confined to hospitals or nursing homes. During the Christmas holidays, guild members bake cookies, place them in baskets made of Christmas cards, and deliver the baskets to the shut-ins. On December 15, 1980, William Goodman, accompanied by his wife Valeda, a guild member, was driving his automobile while delivering cookies. He turned his vehicle into Bernard Miller's motorcycle and, as a result of the accident, Mr. Miller's left leg required amputation just above the knee.

The guild always prepared a list of shut-in members who were to receive cookies, designated which members would deliver them to specified recipients, and checked to see whether the shut-ins actually received them; the guild also picked the delivery date. Mr. Goodman had participated as a driver in the program for the previous four or five years, and the guild knew he would be driving his wife. Mr. Goodman's only purpose in driving on the day of the accident was to deliver the cookies; the guild told him where to go, and he would have gone to any address it directed. He said that "he was doing it for the church—doing it
Continued

for everyone" and that he would not have delivered the cookies if he had not been so instructed.

Mr. Miller filed suit against the church. Is the church liable? [*Trinity Lutheran Church, Inc.* v. *Miller*, 451 N.E.2d 1099 (Ind. 1983).]

C O N S I D E R . . . 17.4 Reverend John Fisher is the pastor of St. James Episcopal Church in Ohio. Catherine Davis served there as parish secretary from 1978 until six months after Father Fisher arrived at St. James in January 1988. She was fired by Father Fisher after she went to the bishop of the diocese to complain about sexual harassment by Father Fisher. The bishop promised an investigation, which was not conducted because Father Fisher denied the allegations. Ms. Davis then brought suit against the Episcopal Diocese. The diocese denied liability, claiming it was not in control of Father Fisher's actions because he was an independent contractor. Do you agree? [*Davis* v. *Black*, 591 N.E.2d 11 (Ohio 1991).]

SCOPE OF EMPLOYMENT

Principals are liable for the conduct of servants while those servants are acting in the **scope of employment**. Scope of employment means that an agent is doing work for a principal at the time a tort occurs. Suppose a florist delivery driver has an auto accident while delivering flowers that is the delivery driver's fault. The florist will be liable to injured parties for this negligence on the part of the driver under the doctrine of **respondeat superior**.

Scope of employment has been defined broadly by the courts. Negligent torts committed while an employee is driving to a sales call or delivery are clearly within the scope of employment.

An employee who takes the afternoon off is not within the scope of employment, and the principal is not liable if an accident occurs during that time. An employee who uses the lunch hour to shop is not within the scope of employment. When an employee is acting on personal business, the scope of employment ends. The following case deals with the issue of scope of employment and answers the chapter's opening "Judgment."

Judgment

Lange v. National Biscuit Co.
211 N.W.2d 783 (Minn. 1973)

SHELF SPACE IS MY LIFE: FLIPPING OUT OVER OREOS

FACTS

Jerome Lange (plaintiff) was the manager of a small grocery store in Minnesota that carried Nabisco (defendant) products. Ronnell Lynch had been hired by Nabisco as a cookie salesman-trainee in October 1968. On March 1, 1969, Mr. Lynch was assigned his own territory, which included Mr. Lange's store.

Between March 1 and May 1, 1969, Nabisco received numerous complaints from grocers about Mr. Lynch's being overly aggressive and taking shelf space in the stores reserved for competing cookie companies.

On May 1, 1969, Mr. Lynch came to Mr. Lange's store to place previously delivered merchandise on the shelves. An argument
Continued

developed between the two over Mr. Lynch's service to the store. Mr. Lynch became very angry and started swearing. Mr. Lange told him to either stop swearing or leave the store because children were present. Mr. Lynch then became uncontrollably angry and said, "I ought to break your neck." He then went behind the counter and dared Mr. Lange to fight. When Mr. Lange refused, Mr. Lynch viciously assaulted him after which he threw merchandise around the store and left.

Mr. Lange filed suit against Nabisco and was awarded damages based on the jury's finding that although the acts of Mr. Lynch were outside the scope of employment, Nabisco was negligent in hiring and retaining him. The judge granted Nabisco's motion for judgment notwithstanding the verdict, and Mr. Lange appealed.

JUDICIAL OPINION

TODD, Justice

There is no dispute with the general principle that in order to impose liability on the employer under the doctrine of respondeat superior it is necessary to show that the employee was acting within the scope of his employment. Unfortunately, there is a wide disparity in the case law in the application of the "scope of employment" test to those factual situations involving intentional torts. The majority rule as set out in Annotation, 34 A.L.R.2d 372, 402, includes a twofold test: (a) Whether the assault was motivated by business or personal considerations; or (b) whether the assault was contemplated by the employer or incident to the employment.

Under the present Minnesota rule, liability is imposed where it is shown that the employee's acts were motivated by a desire to further the employer's business. Therefore, a master could only be held liable for an employee's assault in those rare instances where the master actually requested the servant to so perform, or the servant's duties were such that that motivation was implied in law.

The fallacy of this reasoning was that it made a certain mental condition of the servant the test by which to determine whether he was acting about his master's business or not. Moreover, with respect of all intentional acts done by a servant in the supposed furtherance of his master's business, it clothed the master with immunity if the act was right, because it was right, and, if it was wrong, it clothed him with a like immunity, because it was wrong. He thus got the benefit of all his servant's acts done for him, whether right or wrong, and escaped the burden of all intentional acts done for him which were wrong. Under the operation of such a rule, it would always be more safe and profitable for a man to conduct his business vicariously than in his own person. He would escape liability for the consequences of many acts connected with his business springing from the imperfection of human nature, because done by another, for which he would be responsible if done by himself. Meanwhile, the public, obliged to deal or come in contact with his agents, for intentional injuries done by them, might be left wholly without redress. . . . A doctrine so fruitful of mischief could not long stand unshaken in an enlightened system of jurisprudence.

In developing a test for the application of respondeat superior when an employee assaults a third person, we believe that the focus should be on the basis of the assault rather than the motivation of the employee. We reject as the basis for imposing liability the arbitrary determination of when, and at what point, the argument and assault leave the sphere of the employer's business and become motivated by personal animosity. Rather, we believe the better approach is to view both the argument and assault as an indistinguishable event for purposes of vicarious liability.

We hold that an employer is liable for an assault by his employee when the source of the attack is related to the duties of the employee and the assault occurs within work-related limits of time and place. The assault in this case obviously occurred within work-related limits of time and place, since it took place on authorized premises during working hours. The precipitating cause of the initial argument concerned the employee's conduct of his work.

Continued

In addition, the employee originally was motivated to become argumentative in furtherance of his employer's business. Consequently, under the facts of this case we hold as a matter of law that the employee was acting within the scope of employment at the time of the aggression and that plaintiff's posttrial motion for judgment notwithstanding the verdict on that ground should have been granted under the rule we herein adopt. To the extent that our former decisions are inconsistent with the rule now adopted, they are overruled.

Plaintiff may recover damages under either the theory of respondeat superior or negligence. Having disposed of the matter on the former issue, we need not undertake the questions raised by defendant's asserted negligence in the hiring or retention of the employee.

Reversed and remanded.

CASE QUESTIONS
1. What previous indications did Nabisco have that Lynch might cause some problems?
2. Was the attack of Lange within the scope of employment?
3. What test does the court give for determining scope of employment?
4. What is the "motivation test"?
5. Does this court adopt or reject the "motivation test"?

C O N S I D E R . . .

17.5 Dean Ray Von Aspern was a troop leader in the Boy Scouts of America (BSA) in southern California. Von Aspern had been discharged from the Air Force for improper sexual conduct and had been convicted of child abuse. BSA did not know of Von Aspern's background at the time he became a troop leader.

Sandra Cordts's (plaintiff) two sons were members of Von Aspern's troop. In December 1984, Mrs. Cordts learned that Von Aspern had sexually molested both her sons by engaging them in acts of sodomy and oral copulation while they were participating in scouting activities.

Mrs. Cordts filed suit against BSA under the doctrine of respondeat superior. Should Mrs. Cordts recover from BSA for Von Aspern's conduct? [*Cordts* v. *Boy Scouts of Am., Inc.,* 252 Cal. Rptr. 629 (1988).]

The liability of principals for the torts of agents has become a costly part of doing business. Many firms are undertaking various forms of testing to prevent employees who could cause injuries from driving, operating machinery, or otherwise working in situations in which human safety is an issue.

In *Skinner* v. *Railway Labor Executives Association,* 489 U.S. 602 (1989), the U.S. Supreme Court dealt with the issue of the validity of drug testing in the railroad industry. Under the Federal Railroad Safety Act of 1979, railroads were authorized to administer breath and urine tests to employees who had violated certain safety rules. A union brought suit against the secretary of transportation, alleging that railroad employees' rights to privacy under the Fourth Amendment (see Chapter 8) were violated by the law and the testing. However, the Supreme Court held that the need for safety and the government's responsibility for ensuring railroad safety permitted the testing. Although the court ruled that the tests did violate individual privacy, they were also held to be necessary for the greater interest of public safety.

C O N S I D E R . . . **17.6** The FAA announced required drug testing by all airlines for the following employees: flight crew members, flight attendants, flight or ground instructors, flight testing personnel, aircraft dispatchers, maintenance personnel, aviation security or screening personnel, and air traffic controllers. The tests required included screening for marijuana, cocaine, opiates, phencyclidine (PCP), and amphetamines.

Is this testing appropriate? Is it an unnecessary invasion of privacy? Should all employees be tested? [*Bluestein* v. *Skinner*, 908 F.2d 451 (9th Cir. 1990).]

INDEPENDENT CONTRACTORS

Principals are not generally liable for the torts of independent contractors, but there are two exceptions to this general no-liability rule. The first exception covers **inherently dangerous activities**, which are those that cannot be made safe. For example, using dynamite to demolish old buildings is an inherently dangerous activity. Without this liability exception, a principal could hire an independent contractor to perform the task and then assume no responsibility for the damages or injuries that might result.

The second exception to the no-liability rule occurs when a principal negligently hires an independent contractor. A landlord who hires a security guard, therefore, must check that guard's background because if a tenant's property is stolen by a guard with a criminal record, the landlord is responsible. Similarly, if a principal hires independent contractors knowing of their past employment history, the principal is liable for the conduct of those independent contractors. Thus a business that hires a collection agency to collect past due accounts, knowing that agency's reputation for violence, will be liable for the agency's torts even though they are independent contractors.

TERMINATION OF THE AGENCY RELATIONSHIP

An agency relationship can end in several different ways. First, the parties can have a definite duration for the agency relationship. A listing agreement for the sale of real property usually ends after 90 days. An agency can also end because the agent quits or the principal fires the agent. When the principal dies or is incapacitated, an agency ends automatically because the agent no longer has anyone to contract on behalf of.

Although the agency ends easily when an agent is fired or quits, the authority of the agent does not end so abruptly or easily. An agent can still have **lingering apparent authority** that exists beyond the termination of the agency in relation to third parties who are unaware of the agency termination. For example, if the purchasing agent for a corporation retires after 25 years, the agency between the agent and corporation has ended. However, many customers are used to dealing with the agent and may not be aware of the end of the agency. That purchasing agent could still bind the principal corporation even though actual authority has ended. The principal corporation can end lingering apparent authority by giving public **(constructive) notice** and private **(actual) notice**. Public notice is publication of the resignation. In many trade magazines and business newspapers, there are announcements and personal columns about business associate changes and other personnel news. These are public notices, and even though not everyone dealing with the agent may see the notice, they are deemed to have been given constructive notice. However, the principal must also give private notice to those firms that have dealt with the agent or have been creditors in the past. This notice is accomplished by letter sent to each firm or individual who has dealt with the agent. Without this notice, the agent's apparent authority lingers with respect to those third parties who have not received notice.

TERMINATION OF AGENTS UNDER EMPLOYMENT AT WILL

Most employees do not have a written contract that specifies the start and duration of their employment. Rather, most employees work at the discretion of their employers, which is to say that they have **employment at will**. Recent cases have restricted this employer freedom to hire and fire at will as courts have been giving employees/agents the benefit of their reliance. Employees can still be fired but not without some cause and documentation on the employer's part. Employees have based their protection rights on several theories. Exhibit 17.3 summarizes the "do's" and "don'ts" of terminating employees.

Do	Don't
Conduct regular reviews of employees, using objective, uniform measures of performance.	Don't make oral promises of job security to employees who might later be laid off. **Danger: breach-of-contract suit.**
Give clear, business-related reasons for any dismissal, backed by written documentation when possible.	Don't put pressure on an employee to resign in order to avoid getting fired. **Danger: coercion suit.**
Seek legal waivers from older workers who agree to leave under an early-retirement plan, and make sure they understand the waiver terms in advance.	Don't make derogatory remarks about any dismissed worker, even if asked for a reference by a prospective employer. **Danger: defamation suit.**
Follow any written company guidelines for termination, or be prepared to show in court why they're not binding in any particular instance.	Don't offer a fired employee a face-saving reason for the dismissal that's unrelated to poor performance. **Danger: wrongful-discharge suit**

Source: Arthur S. Hayes, "Layoffs Take Careful Planning to Avoid Losing the Suits that Are Apt to Follow," *The Wall Street Journal*, November 2, 1990, p. 131. Reprinted by permission of *The Wall Street Journal*, © 1990 Dow Jones & Company, Inc. All Rights Reserved Worldwide.

Exhibit 17.3
The Do's and Don'ts of Laying People Off

The Implied Contract

Many courts have implied the existence of a contract because of the presence of promises, procedures, and policies in an employee personnel manual. Personnel manuals have been held to constitute employee contracts or to become part of the employee

Business Planning Tip

If You Must Have a Manual . . .
Businesses should carefully draft personnel manuals and then follow all the procedures outlined in them. The obligations in a manual could be treated as contractual obligations. The manual's terms should be workable and followed to avoid litigation (or at least successful litigation) by employees who are terminated.

contracts when they are given to employees at the outset. One of the factors that will determine whether a personnel manual and its terms constitute a contract is the reliance of an employee on its procedures and terms.

C O N S I D E R . . . **17.7** Richard Woolley (plaintiff) was hired by Hoffman-LaRoche (HL, defendant) in October 1969 as an Engineering Section Head in HL's Central Engineering Department at Nutley, New Jersey. There was no written employment contract. Mr. Woolley began work in 1969 and had his first promotion in 1976 and a second promotion to Group Leader for Civil Engineering in 1977. In 1978 he was asked to write a report for his supervisors about piping problems in a building at Nutley.

Mr. Woolley submitted the report a month later, and one month after that he was told that the general manager had lost confidence in him. Mr. Woolley's immediate supervisors asked him to resign, but he refused. A formal letter asking for his resignation followed and he again refused. He was fired two months after he was asked for his resignation.

Mr. Woolley filed suit based on the express and implied promises in the employment manual, which he had first read in 1969. He maintained that he could not be fired at will and could only be terminated for cause according to the terms of the manual. Is Mr. Woolley correct? [*Woolley* v. *Hoffman-LaRoche, Inc.*, 491 A.2d 1257 (N.J. 1985).]

C O N S I D E R . . . **17.8** Joan Leikvold was hired by Valley View Community Hospital in 1972 as its operating room supervisor. In 1978, she became director of nursing. In 1979, she asked to return to her supervisor position. Carl Nusbaum, the director of Valley View, indicated that it was inadvisable for her to go from a managerial position to a subordinate position. In November 1979, Leikvold was fired.

Valley View's personnel manual provided as follows:

Every effort is made to help an employee to adjust himself to his work. If the employee's work, however, should be considered unsatisfactory during the first three months of employment, the hospital reserves the right to discontinue his services without notice. If an employee is discharged for unsatisfactory service after the three-month probationary period is completed, two weeks notice of such discharge will be given. Gross violations of conduct and hospital rules are grounds for immediate dismissal and will cause an employee to forfeit the usual two weeks notice. On such occasion, the employee will be paid in full only to the time of discharge. No notice or terminal pay is given for the following:

1. *Frequent tardiness*
2. *Sleeping on the job*
3. *Insubordination*
4. *Intoxication*
5. *Malicious gossip*
6. *Excessive garnishments*
7. *Conviction of a felony*
8. *Gambling on hospital premises*
9. *Unexcused absences*
10. *Soliciting tips or other serious misconduct*

The discharged employee who feels himself aggrieved by the terms of the discharge may appeal to Administration and will be granted a hearing.

Continued

Leikvold claims this section limits Valley View's right to discharge a nonprobationary employee to those cases in which the employee's work has been unsatisfactory or in which the employee has committed a gross violation of conduct or hospital rules. Is she correct? [*Leikvold* v. *Valley View Community Hosp.*, 688 P.2d 170 (Ariz. 1984).]

The Public Policy Exception

For more about whistle-blowers, visit Phillips & Cohen, a law firm that specializes in defending whistle-blowers: http://www. whistleblowers.com/

In a second group of employment-at-will cases, the courts have afforded protection to those employees, called *whistle-blowers*, who report illegal conduct or refuse to participate in conduct that is illegal or that is violative of public policy. For example, an employee was found to be wrongfully discharged when fired after supplying information to police who were investigating alleged criminal violations by a co-employee [*Palmateer* v. *International Harvester Co.*, 421 N.E.2d 876 (Ill. 1981)]. Other cases in which courts have found a wrongful discharge involve a refusal by an employee to commit perjury, a refusal by an employee to participate in price-fixing, and an employee-reported violation of the Food, Drug and Cosmetic Act. The *Wagenseller* case deals with the application of public policy protection to an employee at will.

In "A New View on Manuals, Employees, and Legalities," an expert on bureaucracies discusses his proposals for changing the way employees are evaluated and the way they work.

FOR THE MANAGER'S DESK

A NEW VIEW ON MANUALS, EMPLOYEES, AND LEGALITIES

Misguided Quest for Fairness Frequently Begets Bureaucracy

In 1988, when the Soviet Union was still the Soviet Union, Vladimir Kabaidze, the head of a major factory near Moscow, told attendees at a Communist Party conference, "I can't stand this proliferation of paperwork. It's useless to fight the forms. You've got to kill the people producing them."

Kabaidze's charming suggestion popped into my mind as I listened to Craig Cantoni describe one corporate policy manual as "something straight out of the old Soviet Union."

Craig "Does This Make Sense?" Cantoni is a human-resources executive who left corporate life to become a professional bureaucracy buster (at Capstone Consulting in Scottsdale).

I invite you to put your feet up, to kick off your stereotypes and to come along on a tour of the most interesting human-resources mind in the country.

What do you think of corporate dress codes?
They're insulting.

How about job descriptions?
If you want to limit people, that's a good way to start.

How about corporate policies in general?
Let's start by understanding how they come about. Start-up companies rarely have policies—no bureaucracy of any kind. They're chaotic. They have real customers. The customers aren't an abstraction, they're real people. No job boundaries. And instead of a policy manual, they have the example of the entrepreneur who runs the place. The company is growing, and everybody is energized. But then, as the business matures, at some point, the bureaucracy grows faster than the company. So just when things are going great, unbeknownst to anyone, the company has begun to die.

Continued

Any warning signs?
Fairness. Consistency.

Fairness?
Nobody sets out to make a company bureaucratic; they set out to make it fair. Here's an example: A company begins to move in employees from other cities. It occurs to someone that these "relocations" ought to be thought through. So someone is put in charge. And before long, that person is going to relocation conferences and getting the relocation newsletter.

Suddenly, this is a *big* job. And the person wants the title: relocation director. And a staff.

And for what? Is it cheaper? No. Is it more fair to the people coming in? Only if consistency is your idea of fairness.

So what's the solution?
In that example, the best policy is no policy. Each manager negotiates with the newly hired employees. It works. And, yes, somebody in Department X at some point will get a better deal than somebody in Department Y. That's not particularly fair, but so what? You want to hire adult employees, the sort who don't devote themselves to worrying about what somebody else got.

And how do you find these "adult" employees?
That's easy. You don't hire from big, bureaucratic companies. You hire from small, entrepreneurial ones. You get people who are self-motivated and self-managing. What's hard is, after they arrive, to remember that they are adults.

Reflect for a minute on how we treat employees like children—we give them report cards, we give them an increase in their allowance if they're good, we give them a lot of rules to follow, and we provide a nanny called Human Resources.

But isn't that attitude really a defense against lawsuits?
I've been wanting to do a study of this: I believe that the more a company tries to be fair and consistent and the more policy manuals it has, the more lawsuits it gets. You draw enough lines, and some manager is going to cross one.

So where does that leave Human Resources?
I want Human Resources to be devoted to helping grow the business—to helping big companies be less bureaucratic and entrepreneurial companies stay entrepreneurial.

Human Resources shouldn't be part of the bureaucracy, it should be the anti-bureaucracy.

Discussion Questions

1. What legal issues and implications do you see from the elimination of performance evaluations?
2. Employers note that one of their biggest HR problems is absenteeism of their employees. How can employers treat employees like these as adults?
3. Do you believe a business should have detailed policies in a manual or general policies that are simple to follow? What are the legal risks of both approaches?

Source: Dale Dauten, "Misguided Quest for Fairness Frequently Begets Bureaucracy," *Arizona Republic,* November 12, 1995. p. F6. Reprinted with special permission of King Features Syndicate.

Wagenseller v. Scottsdale Memorial Hosp.
710 P.2d 1025 (Ariz. 1985)

MOON RIVER: NOT EVERYONE ENJOYS IT

FACTS
Catherine Wagenseller was hired as a staff nurse by Scottsdale Memorial Hospital in March 1975. Kay Smith, her supervisor, had recruited her. An at-will employee, Ms. Wagenseller received several promotions, the latest in August 1979. In November 1979, she was fired.

Ms. Wagenseller and Ms. Smith had been friends for four years and maintained a good working relationship. In May 1979, they joined a group of personnel from other hospitals on an eight-day camping and rafting trip down the Colorado River. During the course of the trip, Ms. Wagenseller described an uncomfortable

Continued

feeling developing between the two because of Ms. Smith's and the others' conduct, which included heavy drinking, public urination, and a parody of the song "Moon River" in which listeners were "mooned" as a finale. Ms. Wagenseller refused to engage in these activities.

After the river trip, Ms. Smith treated Ms. Wagenseller differently, harassing her and using abusive language. Other staff members noted a marked change in Ms. Smith's behavior. Ms. Wagenseller also refused to participate in the "Moon River" skit when it was performed at the hospital upon their return. Five months after the river trip, Ms. Wagenseller was fired after she refused to quit.

She filed suit for violation of the at-will doctrine, and the trial court dismissed all claims. Ms. Wagenseller appealed on several grounds, including the public policy exception.

JUDICIAL OPINION

FELDMAN, Justice

Before deciding whether to adopt the public policy exception, we first consider what kind of discharge would violate the rule. The majority of the courts require "a clear mandate" of public policy. Other courts have allowed a cause of action where an employee was fired for refusing to violate a specific statute. Similarly, courts have found terminations improper where to do otherwise would have impinged on the employee's exercise of statutory rights or duties. A division of our court of appeals recently adopted the public policy exception, ruling that the discharge of an at-will employee who refused to conceal a violation of Arizona's theft statute was contrary to public policy.

We therefore adopt the public policy exception to the at-will termination rule. We hold that an employer may fire for good cause or for no cause. He may not fire for bad cause—that which violates public policy.

As the expressions of our founders and those we have elected to our legislature, our state's constitution and statutes embody the public conscience of the people of this state. It is thus in furtherance of their interests to hold that an employer may not with impunity violate the dictates of public policy found in the provisions of our statutory and constitutional law.

In the case before us, Wagenseller refused to participate in activities which arguably would have violated our indecent exposure statute. She claims she was fired because of this refusal.

While this statute may not embody a policy which strikes at the heart of a citizen's social right, duties and responsibilities as clearly and forcefully as a statute prohibiting perjury, we believe that it was enacted to preserve and protect the commonly recognized sense of public privacy and decency. The nature of the act, and not its magnitude, is the issue. The legislature has already concluded that acts fitting the statutory description contravene the public policy of this state. We thus uphold this state's public policy by holding that termination for refusal to commit an act which might violate the statute may provide the basis of a claim for wrongful discharge. The relevant inquiry here is not whether the alleged "mooning" incidents were either felonies or misdemeanors or constituted purely technical violations of the statute, but whether they contravened the important public policy interests embodied in the law. We are compelled to conclude that termination of employment for refusal to participate in public exposure of one's buttocks is a termination contrary to the policy of this state, even if, for instance, the employer might have grounds to believe that all of the onlookers were voyeurs and would not be offended. In this situation, there might be no crime, but there would be a violation of public policy to compel the employee to do an act ordinarily proscribed by law.

Reversed.

CASE QUESTIONS

1. According to the court's application of public policy, does it matter what type of statute is violated?
2. Does the willingness of participants affect the court's position on what conduct violates public policy?
3. Did Ms. Wagenseller's termination fit within the public policy exception?

C O N S I D E R . . .   **17.9** Arthur Suchodolski was a senior auditor for Michigan Consolidated Gas Company. While conducting a routine internal audit, he discovered several items that indicated poor internal management and the shifting of costs to ratepayers. He believed that accounts receivable were not being collected aggressively and that used office equipment was being sold to employees for very low prices. Suchodolski reported his findings to the regulatory rate-making body in the state and was fired. Would Suchodolski's termination violate public policy? [*Suchodolski* v. *Michigan Consol. Gas Co.*, 316 N.W.2d 710 (Mich. 1982).]

There has been a tremendous increase in suits brought by employees for improper discharge. Many companies, in the interest of maintaining fairness and saving expenses, have adopted a peer review policy. Peer review is a formal grievance procedure for nonunion employees. Employees who feel that they cannot get an adequate response from their supervisors or by following the lines of authority have the opportunity to present their cases to a panel of fellow employees and managers (three employees, two managers in the general configuration).

Panel members listen to the presentation, can ask for more information, vote on the issue, and issue a written opinion with an explanation.

Many companies (including Coors and GTE) are avoiding lawsuits through what seems to be a mutually satisfactory resolution of wrongful termination and other grievance cases. Some employers say this

Business Planning Tip

Encourage whistle-blowing. Publicize your hot line for disclosing illegal activity and encourage employees to come forward. Eliminate employee fears by directing the investigation of complaints to someone outside a reporting employee's chain of command. Be certain that all complaints are investigated and that investigations are done promptly. Whenever possible, publicize the investigation and its outcome to encourage other employees to come forward.

For the employee, the following suggestions should be followed:

1. Consult family and close friends for perspective and support.

2. Work within your system and through its chain of command before going public. Go through the various layers of management, even to the board of directors.

3. Voice/write your concerns; don't make accusations.

4. Maintain records of your internal contacts and their objections.

5. Find other employees who also know about this potentially volatile situation.

6. Keep a record of your information and carefully document your complaints. Eliminate speculation, personal opinion, and anger. Be objective.

7. Maintain copies of records.

8. Find support groups in your community (and nationwide, if necessary).

process encourages both managers and employees to make better decisions. The peer review process should be in the employee handbook, should be required prior to court action, and should be widely publicized.

The Antiretaliation Statutes: Protections for Whistle-Blowers

Many state and federal agencies are covered by statutes that protect employees at will who report misconduct of their employers. These statutes prohibit retaliatory action in the form of firing, demotion, reprimands, and pay cuts, and they permit employees to bring suit for violations. For example, at the federal level the Employee Protection Section (EPS) of the Energy Reorganization Act provides protection for employees of nuclear facilities who report violations of federal regulations. The federal False Claims Act permits employees of government contractors whose tips to the federal government result in fines or assessments to recover 25 percent of a fine. In a recent case in which General Electric paid a $70 million fine, an employee who reported the underlying incident collected $17.5 million.

Source: Reprinted with permission of Patrick McDonnell © 1988

Jeffrey Wigand is a chemist with a doctorate in endocrinology and biochemistry. He spent the bulk of his career at Union Carbide and six medical-equipment companies working in research and development

In 1989, Mr. Wigand was hired by Brown & Williamson, the makers of Kool brand cigarettes, to work at the company's Louisville headquarters as vice president of research and development. He was described by colleagues and friends as highly committed to the company. Mr. Wigand began smoking cigarettes just before he began his job in Louisville, but after six months of research work at Brown & Williamson, he stopped smoking.

Tobacco's Whistle-Blower: Jeffrey Wigand

Mr. Wigand's focus was on developing a safer cigarette. He was well liked by his colleagues and employees. In 1993, his research cohorts at Brown & Williamson gave him a Quality Leadership Award that was inscribed with the following, "To our mentor, coach, and friend."

Shortly afterward, Mr. Wigand was fired from his $300,000 a year position at Brown & Williamson. The reason given for the termination was the shut-down of Mr. Wigand's alternative cigarette research. Mr. Wigand battled Brown & Williamson over his severance package. Brown & Williamson sued Mr. Wigand for disclosing the terms of his severance to a friend. The suit was settled when Brown & Williamson agreed to continue health benefits for a family member and Mr. Wigand agreed to a broader confidentiality restriction.

Mr. Wigand was then interviewed by a staff member of the CBS television show *60 Minutes* for a segment on the tobacco industry. The segment was not aired, however, when Brown & Williamson told CBS of Mr. Wigand's confidentiality agreement and that Brown & Williamson would sue CBS for intentional interference with their contract mandating Mr. Wigand's silence.

Jeffrey Wigand

A Louisville court has ordered Mr. Wigand to remain silent under a temporary restraining order obtained by Brown & Williamson. However, Mr. Wigand has been subpoenaed to testify in several tobacco product liability suits in other states. Mr. Wigand's hair has turned gray in the last two years. He teaches chemistry and Japanese at a Louisville area high school for $30,000 a year.

A former colleague of Mr. Wigand's at Techicon Instruments described him as follows: "He's not a politician at all. He'd point out what people were thinking but wouldn't say."

The CEO of Biosonics where Wigand had also worked said, "I would never hire Jeff Wigand again under any circumstances." Mr. Wigand had sent a letter of protest regarding insider trading allegations when he reported his new treatment for dry mouth syndrome to Biosonics management.

On February 4, 1996, Mr. Wigand did appear on the television program *60 Minutes* and discussed his concerns about tobacco companies and his work at Brown & Williamson.

Issues

1. Isn't whistle-blowing always devastating for the whistle-blower?
2. Should the courts enforce Mr. Wigand's confidentiality agreement? Does a subpoena for Mr. Wigand make a difference?
3. Why do you think Mr. Wigand was fired?

FOR THE MANAGER'S DESK

LISTEN TO EMPLOYEES

Douglas P. Keeth, the former vice president of finance at United Technologies, discovered overbilling by United Technologies in its Sikorsky Aircraft division on Pentagon contracts for helicopters.

Mr. Keeth told his superiors of the problem, but no action was taken. He resigned

and disclosed the problem to the Defense Department.

United Technologies agreed to pay $150 million for uncovered accounting regularities, and under federal law, Mr. Keeth gets 15 percent of any fines or $22.5 million.

Under the federal 15 percent program, the government has collected $738 million based on employee tips. Another $500 million was collected in 1995 alone.

AGENCY RELATIONSHIPS IN INTERNATIONAL LAW

One of the complexities in law that has developed because of complex global organizations is the liability of various subsidiaries, officers, and owners of multinational organizations when the interrelationships and operations may not be clear or even known to them. Perhaps the best example of the pitfalls of complex, global structure is the multinational bank BCCI. Just a small portion of its structure is diagramed in Exhibit 17.4 (pg. 610).

BCCI was a complex, multinational organization with banks in 70 countries, including the United States (First American Bankshares headed by Clark Clifford and Robert Altman). The banks and businesses in the different countries were staffed by residents of those countries, and the full global network of BCCI was not disclosed to these subsidiaries and the individuals operating them. Regulations of operations were limited to the entities located in each of the various nations. Jurisdiction over other operations was limited. The layers of the organization made it difficult for anyone, even those in the subsidiaries, to be certain of the roles and activities of the full organization or of other subsidiaries.

BCCI collapsed and surrendered its U.S. assets to U.S. regulators in settlement of various charges. Clark Clifford and Robert Altman (see Exhibit 17.4 on page 610) were indicted for activities involving BCCI, although they were affiliated with U.S. operations only. Mr. Altman was acquitted of the charges, but Mr. Clifford was determined to be too ill to stand trial. (See Chapter 8 "Biography" for more details on Mr. Clifford and BCCI.) England, the United States, and other countries have been working together to determine who was responsible for the bank's collapse and how such tangled and evasive structures can be avoided in the future. One of the proposals considered is to require filing and full disclosure of all principal-agent and parent subsidiary relationships in all countries in which a bank conducts business.

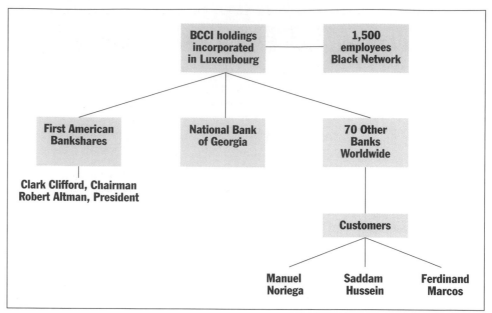

Exhibit 17.4
Overview of BCCI

SUMMARY

When is an employee acting on behalf of an employer?
- Principal—employer; responsible party
- Agent—party hired to act on another's behalf
- *Restatement of Agency*—common law view of agent-principal relationship
- Unincorporated association—nonlegal entity; no legal existence as natural or fictitious person

How much authority does an employee hold?
- Express authority—written or stated authority
- Implied authority—authority by custom
- Apparent authority—authority by perceptions of third parties
- Lingering apparent authority—authority left with terminated agent because others are not told of termination
- Actual notice—receipt of notice of termination
- Constructive notice—publication of notice of termination
- Ratification—after-the-fact recognition of agent's authority by principal
- *Del credere* agency—agent acts as guarantor for buyer
- Disclosed principal—existence and identity of principal is known
- Partially disclosed principal—existence but not identity of principal is known
- Undisclosed principal—neither existence nor identity of principal is known
- Gratuitous agency—agent works without compensation

When is a business liable for an employee's acts?
- Master-servant relationship—principal-agent relationship in which principal exercises great degree of control
- Independent contractor—principal-agent relationship in which principal exercises little day-to-day control over agent
- Scope of employment—time when agent is doing work for the principal
- Inherently dangerous activities—activities for which, even if performed by independent contractor, principal is liable

What duties and obligations do employees owe employers?
- Fiduciary—one who has utmost duty of trust, care, loyalty, and obedience to another

How is an agency relationship terminated?
- Employment at will—right of employer to terminate noncontract employees at any time

QUESTIONS AND PROBLEMS

1. Dr. Warren Lesch had a leak in his car's gas tank that had been repaired by Malcolm Weeks, an employee of Walker's Chevron, Inc., in Bel Air, Maryland. The tank was not repaired properly, and Dr. Lesch's home and garage were destroyed when the gas tank exploded. Dr. Lesch and his wife were severely burned as a result.

   Walker's Chevron is a "branded" station: It displays only Chevron signs and colors and sells only Chevron gas and oil. The Lesches have sued Mr. Weeks, Walker's Chevron, and Chevron USA. Who is liable for the explosion? [*Chevron USA, Inc.* v. *Lesch*, 570 A.2d 840 (Md. 1990).]

2. On September 29, 1984, Wilton Whitlow was taken to Good Samaritan Hospital's emergency room in Montgomery County, Ohio, because he had suffered a seizure and a blackout. He was examined by Dr. Dennis Aumentado, who prescribed the anti-epileptic medication Dilantin. Mr. Whitlow experienced no further seizures and was monitored as an outpatient at Good Samaritan over the next few weeks.

   Mr. Whitlow complained to Dr. Aumentado of warm and dry eyes, and his Dilantin dose was reduced. On October 20, 1984, he was again admitted to the emergency room with symptoms that were eventually determined to be from Stevens-Johnson syndrome, a condition believed to be caused by a variety of medications. Mr. Whitlow sued Dr. Aumentado and Good Samaritan for malpractice and Parke-Davis, the manufacturer of Dilantin, for breach of warranty.

   The hospital maintains it is not liable because Dr. Aumentado was an independent contractor. Is the hospital correct? [*Whitlow* v. *Good Samaritan Hosp.*, 536 N.E.2d 659 (Ohio 1987).]

3. On March 29, 1983, Barry Mapp was observed in the J. C. Penney department store in Upper Darby, Pennsylvania, by security personnel, who suspected that he might be a shoplifter. Michael DiDomenico, a security guard employed by J. C. Penney, followed Mr. Mapp when he left the store and proceeded to Gimbels department store. There, Mr. DiDomenico notified Rosemary Federchok, a Gimbels security guard, about his suspicions. Even though his assistance was not requested, Mr. DiDomenico decided to remain to assist in case Ms. Federchok, a short woman of slight build, required help in dealing with Mr. Mapp if he committed an offense in Gimbels. It came as no surprise when Mr. Mapp was observed taking items from the men's department of the store;

and when he attempted to escape, he was pursued. Although Ms. Federchok was unable to keep up, Mr. DiDomenico continued to pursue Mr. Mapp and ultimately apprehend him in the lower level of the Gimbels parking lot. When Ms. Federchok arrived with Upper Darby police, merchandise that had been taken from Gimbels was recovered. Mr. Mapp, who had been injured when he jumped from one level of the parking lot to another, was taken to the Delaware County Memorial Hospital, where he was treated for a broken ankle.

Mr. Mapp filed suit against Gimbels for injuries sustained while being chased and apprehended by Mr. DiDomenico. He alleged in his complaint that Mr. DiDomenico, while acting as an agent of Gimbels, had chased him, had struck him with a nightstick, and had beaten him with his fists. Gimbels says it is not liable because Mr. DiDomenico was not its agent. Is Gimbels correct? [*Mapp* v. *Gimbels Dep't Store*, 540 A.2d 941 (Pa. 1988).]

4. Nineteen-year-old Lee J. Norris was employed by Burger Chef Systems as an assistant manager of one of its restaurants. On a day when he was in charge and change was needed, Mr. Norris left to get change but also decided to get Kentucky Fried Chicken at a nearby store for his lunch to take back to Burger Chef. The bank where Mr. Norris usually got change is 1.6 miles from Burger Chef and the Kentucky Fried Chicken outlet is 2.5 miles from Burger Chef. After Mr. Norris left the bank and was on his way to the Kentucky Fried Chicken restaurant, he negligently injured Lee J. Govro in an accident. Is Burger Chef liable for the accident? [*Burger Chef Systems* v. *Govro*, 407 F.2d 921 (8th Cir. 1969).]

5. Dewey Nabors operates a real estate brokerage under the trade name Nabors & Company, which shares an office, telephone, and secretary with Midtown, a real estate management corporation that had hired Robert Keaton to oversee the completion of a shopping center. Mr. Nabors asked Mr. Keaton to order siding, pipes, and flooring for his personal residence and directed him to order these materials in the name of Nabors & Company. Mr. Keaton contracted with Richardson, Inc., for the flooring. Richardson understood that Mr. Keaton was working for Midtown and billed Midtown for Mr. Nabors's materials. Mr. Nabors refused to pay for the materials because he was dissatisfied. Is Midtown liable? What theory is Richardson using? [*Midtown Properties, Inc.* v. *Richardson, Inc.*, 228 S.E.2d 303 (Ga. 1976).]

6. Dale McGraw hired Jay L. Poyzer to do some work on a farm owned by Mr. McGraw and his partners. Mr. Poyzer was furnished a home to live in while doing the work. The heater in the home exploded, Mr. McGraw was injured, and he sued the partners and the partnership for damages. Can he recover from the partners? Did they authorize Mr. Poyzer's residence on the farm? Do they have to? [*Poyzer* v. *McGraw*, 360 N.W.2d 748 (Iowa 1985).]

7. Lennen & Newell, Inc., (L&N) is an advertising agency hired by Stokely-Van Camp to do its advertising. L&N contracted for the purchase of ad time from CBS, but no Stokely representative's signature is on the contract. If L&N does not pay for the ad time, is Stokely liable? [*CBS Inc.* v. *Stokely-Van Camp, Inc.*, 456 F. Supp. 539 (E.D.N.Y. 1977).]

8. Although James A. Schoenberger was promised a raise by his immediate supervisor, company policy was that the personnel department made all decisions on raises. The supervisor was in charge of a full department. Did the supervisor have the authority to give the raise? [*Schoenberger* v. *Chicago Transit Auth.*, 405 N.E.2d 1076 (Ill. 1980).]

9. Steve Conn, a musician and song writer, signed a contract to record at the Sound Doctor recording studio, which was authorized to market, sell, and distribute Mr. Conn's music in exchange. The studio ran ads to promote the music, but Mr. Conn claims it had no such authority and that there was a violation of copyright law. Did the studio have authority? [*Sound Doctor Recording Studio, Inc.* v. *Conn*, 391 So. 2d 520 (3d Cir. 1980).]

10. The physician for the Philadelphia Eagles football team examined Don Chuy, a player, and determined that because of a medical condition, Mr. Chuy should not

play football. The team's general manager then reported to a sports columnist that Mr. Chuy had a fatal blood disease. A report of the illness appeared in print and was picked up by other sources. Mr. Chuy's personal physician never diagnosed the disease. Mr. Chuy sued the football club for defamation. Is the club liable for the remarks made by the general manager? [*Chuy* v. *Philadelphia Eagles Football Club*, 595 F.2d 1265 (3d Cir. 1979).]

Judgment

Casimer Gacioch was a long-time Stroh Brewery worker who enjoyed the benefits of Stroh's no-limit, free beer policy. He also became an alcoholic, drank 12 bottles of beer each workday, and eventually was unable to perform his job. When he was fired, he applied for disability under workers' compensation on grounds that his alcoholism was caused by the workplace. Is Mr. Gacioch entitled to benefits?

Management of Employee Welfare

The employer-employee relationship has evolved from one of a paternal nature in the 1600s and 1700s, when the lives of employer and employee were intertwined, to one of a contractual nature. In the earlier period, employees usually were friends of their employers and continued as friends throughout the course of the employment (which usually lasted a lifetime). Employers often assumed responsibility for the well-being of their employees, a personal relationship made possible because of the less complex nature of business at the time. With the industrial revolution, however, more employees were needed and the personal relationship factor was lost. So also was the idea of a lifetime employee. The employer-employee relationship became thoroughly contractual.

The result of this contractual relationship was that each party became interested in maximizing his or her own economic benefit. Employers wanted the most work for the least amount of money. Employees wanted maximum pay, safe working conditions, and some type of insurance for retirement, unemployment, and disability. Because employers had the upper hand—they controlled the jobs—their bargaining positions were better than those of employees. As a result, workers organized to give themselves more bargaining power, and the federal government passed legislation to assure workers that some of their needs would be met.

This chapter discusses the work and safety standards covered in federal legislation. The questions answered by the materials in this chapter are: What wage and work hour protections exist for employees? Are there restrictions on children's work? What protections exist for safety in the workplace? What happens when an employee is injured in the workplace? Are workers entitled to pensions and are they regulated? What is the social security system and what benefits does it provide? What rights do unemployed workers have? How are labor unions formed and what is their relationship with employees?

Forget that a United States worker is five times more likely to die than a Swede. . . . Forget that a U.S. worker is three times more likely to die than a Japanese. The sad reality is that blue-collar blood pours too easily. OSHA's fines amount to mere traffic tickets for those who run our companies. The small fines are simply buried in the cost of production. Blood can be cash accounted, given a number and factored with other costs.
Joseph Kinney
Founder and Executive Director of National Safe Workplace Institute

*"The game begins in the spring. . . .
And it blossoms in the summer. . . .
You count on it, you rely on it. . . .
when you need it most, it stops."*
A. Bartlett Giamatti
Former Commissioner of Baseball

The series of laws affecting employee rights over the past 50 years is summarized in Exhibit 18.1.

Statute	Date	Provisions
Worker's Compensation	1900	Absolute liability of employers for employee injury; no common law tort suits by employees against employers.
Social Security Act 42 U.S.C. § 301	1935	FICA contributions, Unemployment compensation, Retirement benefits
Fair Labor Standards Act 29 U.S.C. § 201	1938	Minimum wages, Child labor restrictions, Equal pay
Equal Pay Act 29 U.S.C § 206	1963	Amendment to FLSA: equal pay for equal work.
Occupational Safety and Health Act 29 U.S.C. § 651	1970	Safety in the workplace, Employee rights, Employer reporting, Inspections
Employment Retirement Income Security Act 29 U.S.C. § 441	1974	Disclosure of contributions, investments, loans, Employee vesting, Employee statements
Family and Medical Leave Act 29 U.S.C. § 2601	1993	Protection of job after family leave (for pregnancy, child care, adult illness, elderly care)

Exhibit 18.1
Statutory Scheme for Employee Welfare

WAGES AND HOURS PROTECTION

The Fair Labor Standards Act

Review the Fair labor Standards Act:
http://www.law.cornell.edu/uscode/29/ch8.html

The **Fair Labor Standards Act (FLSA)** is commonly called by workers the "minimum wage law." This act does establish a minimum wage, but it also includes antichild labor provisions, overtime pay requirements, and equal pay provisions. The FLSA was originally introduced in the Senate by Hugo L. Black when he was a senator from Alabama. His 1937 appointment to the U.S. Supreme Court may have helped it pass the high Court's scrutiny. Having been amended several times (with the last major debate in 1996), the FLSA is an enabling statute that sets up various administrative agencies to handle the regulations and necessary enforcement.

Coverage of FLSA

The FLSA applies to all businesses that are engaged in interstate (or foreign) commerce. Some businesses are exempt under the FLSA, but the exemptions are specifically and narrowly defined. Employees working as independent contractors are exempt, as are those in agriculture, commercial fishing, some retail service establishments, and domestic service. Traditional "white-collar" management or professional positions also are not covered if they require the exercise of "discretion and judgment." This "executive, administrative, and professional" exemption covers salespersons, the traditional professions of law and medicine, and the artistic professions (such as ad executives). The management exemption exists because of the belief that these individuals can protect themselves from employer abuses.

C O N S I D E R . . .   **18.1** Would the following employees be covered by the minimum wage and overtime protections of FLSA?

Inmates who are required to work as part of their sentences and perform labor within a state-run correctional facility [*McMaster* v. *Minnesota*, 819 F. Supp. 1429 (D.C. Minn. 1993).]

Manager of Chick-Fil-A mall restaurant who has a capital investment in the restaurant but must follow corporate standards of operation [*Howell* v. *Chick-Fil-A*, 7 FLW Fed.D. 641 (N.D. Fla. 1993).]

Migrant farm workers who harvested pickling cucumbers and are paid regardless of employer's profit on sale [*Cavazos* v. *Foster*, 822 F. Supp. 438 (W.D. Mich. 1993).]

Dancers at an upscale topless nightclub in Dallas who furnish their own costumes but are told when to appear [*Martin* v. *Priba Corp.*, 123 CCH LC 35737 (N.D. Tex. 1992).]

Formerly homeless alcoholic who is working for the Salvation Army under its rehabilitation program and is residing at the Salvation Army facility [*Williams* v. *Strickland*, 837 F. Supp. 1049 (N.D. Cal. 1994).]

Penalties for FLSA Violation

Visit the Department of Labor's Wage and Hour Division: http://www.dol.gov/dol/esa/public/whd_org.htm

The FLSA carries both civil and criminal penalties. Employees have the right to sue civilly to recover from an employer any wages that were not paid or any overtime compensation that was denied, plus reasonable attorney fees required to bring the action to recover. In addition to the employees' rights, the U.S. Department of Labor's Wage and Hour Division has enforcement power for violations. A willful violation of FLSA carries a maximum $10,000 fine and possible imprisonment of up to six months.

To help employees pursue their rights, the FLSA makes it a violation for any employer to fire an employee for filing an FLSA complaint or for participating in any FLSA proceeding.

Liability for FLSA Violation

Employers of course are liable for FLSA violations, but because most employers are corporations, the question arises as to who in the corporation is liable. The answer is that anyone who actively participates in the running of the business is liable under the FLSA. Officers of the corporation can be held individually liable for the corporation's violations. The FLSA imposes fines on both corporations and officers involved in managing employees.

Enforcement of FLSA

Enforcement of the FLSA requirements may begin in several different ways. Employees can initiate the process by filing a complaint with the U.S. Department of Labor. Upon receipt of the complaint, the department begins an investigation that could lead to a finding of no violation, a violation and a settlement with the employer, or a violation and litigation by the employees for collection of back wages.

In some cases, employers make the laws self-enforcing by requesting interpretations from the Labor Department that are then published in the *Code of Federal Regulations*. For example, a 1975 interpretation from the Labor Department prohibited employers from advertising or labeling a job as male or female (waitress; "girl Friday") because such distinctions were violative of the Equal Pay Act. Such interpretations help employers comply with the law.

In a final type of case, the Labor Department initiates its own investigation of a firm for possible violations. The department has broad investigatory authority, including the right to ask for records. In the summer of 1992, when then-Secretary of Labor Lynn Martin initiated a crackdown on child labor violations, for example, department employees entered fast food restaurants and stores to check for violations of statutory maximums of hours worked.

ETHICAL ISSUES

18.1 When rumors concerning the Labor Department's 1992 crackdown on child labor violations began, many national offices of fast food chains began calling their local franchises with instructions to take home the time cards and schedules of employees so that violations would be difficult to prove. If you were a franchise manager, would you take the records home?

FLSA Regulations

MINIMUM WAGES

The original **minimum wage** when the FLSA was passed was 25 cents an hour. That figure has been increased steadily over the years. In 1989, Congress revamped the minimum wage with provisions for annual increases up to $4.25 per hour starting in 1991. A minimum wage increase to $5.15 per hour was approved in 1996 to begin in 1997. Congress has retained a training wage of 80 percent of the minimum wage in effect. The minimum wage can be paid in cash or benefits. Employers who furnish room, board, lodging, or other such benefits can use the value of these as a credit toward the minimum wage. To use these benefits as a credit, however, an employer must be able to show that the benefits were voluntarily taken.

In those businesses in which employees are tipped, the employer can take a tip credit of up to 50 percent. However, the employer must be able to show that the employees, in fact, earn enough to meet this credit. If any employee actually receives less than minimum wage by combining wages and tips, the employer will be liable and will also be required to adjust wages.

E T H I C A L   I S S U E S

18.2 One of the difficult issues in international business involves wage disparities and the employment of children. In many nations, minimum wages are well below U.S. standards, and the employment of very young children is often welcomed as a means of supporting a child's immediate and extended family. A recent edition of the *Harvard Business Review* included a debate among CEOs and ethicists about a firm's decision to employ child labor in those countries in which there are very low wages and neither regulations on employment conditions nor limitations on age eligibility or hours worked. One CEO justified such employment because of the support it provided for children and their families. The rebuttal was that the company was merely taking advantage of the children. Another debater suggested that it would be ethical to employ the children so long as the company made certain the children attended school and provided the schools if necessary. How ethical is the employment of children in other countries when U.S. labor laws prevent or greatly restrict such practices?

HOURS

Employees who are subject to the FLSA work a maximum 40-hour workweek at regular pay. For hours worked in excess of 40, an FLSA employee is entitled to one and one-half times the regular hourly rate. For purposes of this **overtime pay**, each week is separate, and weeks cannot be grouped together to show that the actual total was 40. For example, an employer cannot group a 20-hour week with a 60-hour week to show that an employee's two weeks of work total only 40 hours a week.

If an employee is paid on an hourly basis, the hourly rate is used. If an employee receives a weekly or monthly salary, the "regular hourly rate" is computed by dividing the weekly or monthly salary by the usual number of hours worked. If an employee is paid $400 a week, the regular hourly rate is $400 divided by 40, or $10 an hour.

Bonuses, profit-sharing, and commissions are added to the employee's wages to determine whether overtime compensation is necessary. Travel expenses and vacation benefits, however, cannot be added in to compensate for overtime pay requirements.

The issue of overtime pay is complicated. Many complexities in the law make the "time-and-one-half" rule much more technical than most employees realize. In some cases, employers may not be aware there is a violation.

C O N S I D E R . . .   **18.2** Would the following count as part of hours worked?

Mandatory training time [*Martin* v. *Parker Fire Protection Dist.*, 988 F.2d 1064 (10th Cir. 1993).]

Fire fighters' sleep time while on 24-hour duty [*Alldread* v. *Grenada*, 988 F.2d 1425 (5th Cir. 1993).]

Being on call in case of emergency [*Berry* v. *County of Sonoma*, 30 F.3d 1174 (9th Cir. 1994).]

Time spent by employees at meat slaughter/processing plant waiting in line at knife room to get their knives sharpened [*Reich* v. *IBP, Inc.*, 820 F. Supp. 1315 (D.C. Kan. 1993).]

```
┌─────────────────────────────────────────────────────────────────┐
│                                                                   │
│   ███ E T H I C A L ███  I S S U E S ████                         │
│                                                                   │
│  **18.3**  "Can't live this way. Something should be done about   │
│            payment, work 6 or 7 days                              │
│  a week & no payment & when given after 2 weeks about $5.         │
│  Selling liquor & no                                              │
│  license. Bathrooms are very unhealthy. On Saturday drug dealers  │
│  were around. Very cold                                           │
│  and no chance to wash the blankets & clothing. Got up cold,      │
│  work all day in cold and                                         │
│  come back to cold room. Never warmed up. When ill and could      │
│  not work, would be                                               │
│  cursed and very mad at us."                                      │
│                                                                   │
│      Cleveland Spurlock, a homeless man, wrote these words in     │
│  1992 to describe his                                             │
│  work of 14 weeks on a South Carolina farm crew, often called a   │
│  "wino crew."                                                     │
│                                                                   │
│      Growers search soup kitchens and homeless shelters to round  │
│  up alcoholics and                                                │
│  drug addicts as laborers for harvesting vegetables. They are     │
│  paid $5 to $10 a week,                                           │
│  which they give back to the growers in exchange for drugs or     │
│  alcohol.                                                         │
│                                                                   │
│      The "wino crew" camps are raided each year, and FLSA fines   │
│  are assessed. The                                                │
│  growers maintain that if the homeless men come to work, they     │
│  have it better than                                              │
│  they otherwise would, regardless of wages. Is this an ethical    │
│  policy?                                                          │
│                                                                   │
└─────────────────────────────────────────────────────────────────┘
```

CHILD LABOR PROVISIONS

The child labor provisions of the FLSA were created to keep children in school for at least a minimum number of years. The provisions of the act govern particular ages and restrict the types of employment those age groups can hold:

1. *18 years old and older.* This group is not covered as this age is the cutoff for the child labor provisions. Anyone 18 or older can work in any type of job for unlimited hours.
2. *16–17 years old.* This age group can work in any "nonhazardous" job for unlimited hours. Hazardous jobs include mining, logging, roofing, and excavation.
3. *14–15 years old.* This group can work only in nonhazardous, nonmanufacturing, and nonmining jobs and only during nonschool hours. Work hours are limited to 3 per day on school days and 18 per week during school weeks. On nonschool days, this group can work 8 hours and during nonschool weeks a maximum of 40 hours. Even the hours of the day they may work are restricted: not before 7:00 A.M. or after 7:00 P.M. (except during the summer months, when they can work until 9:00 P.M.).

There are exemptions to the laws; young actors and actresses, for example, are exempt. But even here many states require approval of their contracts and also require that some of the earnings be put in trust for use by the child when the child becomes an adult. Other exemptions apply to work-study programs and farm work.

RECORDKEEPING REQUIREMENTS

Employers subject to the FLSA are required to keep records of hours and wages of their employees. There are no particular formats for these records, but failure to keep them can result in a fine.

The Equal Pay Act of 1963

The **Equal Pay Act of 1963** is an amendment to the FLSA that makes it illegal to pay different wages based on gender to men and women who are doing substantially the same work. If the jobs involve equal responsibility, training, or skill, men and women must have equal pay. Merit systems and seniority systems instituted in good faith do

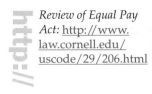

Review of Equal Pay Act: http://www. law.cornell.edu/ uscode/29/206.html

not violate the Equal Pay Act even though they may result in different pay rates for the same jobs. So long as the disparate pay is based on length of employment or a merit-raise system, the disparity is within the act.

It is important to understand that the Equal Pay Act is not an act that requires the application of the doctrine of comparable worth. This doctrine extends the concept of the Equal Pay Act a step further and says men and women should be paid on the same scale, not just for the same jobs but when they are doing different jobs that r quire equal skill, effort, and responsibility. This issue came to light in 1983 when Louise Peterson, a licensed practical nurse at Western State Hospital in Tacoma, Washington, brought suit when she discovered that her salary of $1,462 per month for her supervision of the daily care of 60 men convicted of sex crimes was $192 less per month than that of the hospital groundskeeper and $700 less per month than men doing similar jobs at Washington's state prisons. Although a trial judge found the pay scales to be discriminatory and ordered the state to reimburse its female employees $838 million in back pay, the ruling was later reversed. Nonetheless, there are strong advocates for the comparable worth system, and it is seen by many women as a means for leveling the wage disparities that have developed over the years as women have come and gone from the workforce in their traditionally female job positions. Others are strongly opposed because of the costs of both evaluation under the doctrine and its implementation. Presently, federal standards do not require comparable-worth pay scales.

E T H I C A L   I S S U E S

18.4 The American Association of University Women (AAUW) has found that salaries in fields dominated by women (teaching, nursing, secretarial) are at wage levels that are one-half to two-thirds those of male-dominated jobs that often require less training (construction) or are comparable in terms of number of years required for an undergraduate degree (engineering, accounting).

The AAUW has supported comparable worth. An alternative proposal is that women enter the male-dominated fields. The AAUW response is that women should not be forced to enter fields they do not enjoy and that such a response only perpetuates the devaluation of traditionally female professions. Do you agree with the AAUW?

When comparable worth was implemented for city employees in Seattle, men whose jobs underwent pay reductions left for the private sector, where wages were still market-driven. Is a market system for establishing wages best?

WORKPLACE SAFETY

Occupational Safety and Health Act

One of the worker welfare concerns of Congress has been safety in the workplace. In the past the economic concerns of employers often overshadowed their concern for proper safety precautions. To ensure worker safety, Congress passed the **Occupational Safety and Health Act** of 1970. Its application was broad, protecting virtually every employee in the country. It was an enabling statute that created three agencies responsible for worker safety standards: the **Occupational Safety and Health Administration (OSHA)**, the Occupational Safety and Health Review Commission

*Review the
Occupational Safety
and Health Act:*
http://www.law.
cornell.edu/uscode/
29/651.html
Visit OSHA: http://
www.osha.gov/

(OSHRC), and the National Institute for Occupational Health and Safety (NIOSH). OSHA is the agency responsible for the promulgation and enforcement of workplace safety standards. OSHA's enforcement powers include investigations, record-keeping requirements, and research. The stated purpose of the act is to "assure so far as possible every working man and woman in the nation safe and healthful working conditions and to preserve our human resources." OSHA is an active agency, as the statistics in Exhibit 18.2 indicate. A 1996 survey by the *National Law Journal* revealed that compliance with OSHA is the most expensive regulatory cost of a business.

Anatomy of OSHA

Number of inspections since its 1972 creation:	1,400,000
Number of violations found:	2,400,000
Number of willful or repeat violations:	700,000
Amount of funding over 20 years:	$4.5 billion

Exhibit 18.2
Anatomy of OSHA

*Visit the National
Institute for
Occupational Safety
and Health* http://
www.cdc.gov/
niosh/homepage.
html

The Occupational Safety and Health Act gives the secretary of labor responsibility for administration. OSHA is within the Department of Labor and its function is to develop safety standards and enforce them through inspections, citations, and court actions. OSHA has created the Occupational Safety and Health Review Commission (OSHRC), whose role is to review OSHA citations and is the administrative court of appeal for OSHA violators. It consists of three members who are appointed by the president for staggered six-year terms.

The National Institute for Occupational Safety and Health (NIOSH), often undertakes studies of workplace safety issues. Issues that have been a focus of NIOSH study have included long-term exposure hazards. While OSHA and OSHRC have focused on the traditional issues of equipment use and protective gear, NIOSH has studied the effects of long-term exposure to chemicals and particles.

C O N S I D E R . . . **18.3** Late in 1995, OSHRC reviewed OSHA's policy of multiplying a fine by the number of workers exposed to a hazard. For example, Hartford Roofing Co., a Glastonbury, Connecticut, roofing contractor was found to be in violation of the OSHA requirement that safety railing be used on a roof while workers were there. The fine was $35,000, but because six workers were involved, OSHA increased the fine to $210,000. The U.S. Chamber of Commerce had appealed to the commission, referring to the multiplier factor as "legalized blackmail to get small companies to settle these cases."

OSHA complained that elimination of the multiplier factor would produce "pitifully small fines" for severe violations, but OSHRC ruled to eliminate the multiplier factor.

Do you think the multiplier factor is a necessary enforcement tool? Why or why not?

OSHA COVERAGE AND DUTIES

OSHA coverage is broad: Every employer with one or more employees who is in a business affecting commerce is covered by OSHA. Several other federal acts regulate safety for particular industries, including the Coal Mine and Safety Act and the Railway Safety Act.

The basic responsibilities of employers are to know and follow OSHA's rules, inspect for hazards and correct them, inform employees of their rights, keep statutorily mandated records, and post citations given by OSHA.

OSHA Responsibilities

Search the Federal Register for proposed OSHA rules: http://ssdc.ucsd.edu/gpo/

PROMULGATING RULES AND SAFETY STANDARDS

OSHA is responsible for promulgating rules and regulations for safety standards and procedures. The rules are adopted by the standard administrative process of notice in the *Federal Register*, public input, and final decision (see Chapter 6).

AWARDING VARIANCES

Once a safety standard is set, employers can still apply for a temporary or permanent variance, which exempts them from compliance with an OSHA regulation. Temporary variances are granted when an employer needs time to comply—for example, to obtain safety equipment or to change the structure or rearrange the workplace. Permanent variances are granted when an employer is able to demonstrate that even with the variance, the workplace is just as safe.

INSPECTIONS

OSHA inspections are the administration's enforcement tool. Inspectors can enter the workplace "without delay and at a reasonable time" to inspect. They can check the workplace and the records and can question employees. OSHA's inspection power is limited by numbers, however. There are about 70 million workers, 5 million businesses, and 1,000 OSHA inspectors. Because of OSHA's limited staff, the regulations provide for an order of priority on inspections:

1. Hazards or conditions that could cause death
2. Investigations of fatal accident sites
3. Employee complaints
4. Particularly hazardous industries
5. Random inspections incorporating an emphasis on certain types of industries (roofing, lumbering, meat packing, transportation [car, truck] manufacturing, and longshoring.)

The inspections themselves are regulated as to the procedures that must be followed. An OSHA inspector appears at a workplace and upon showing identification asks permission for an inspection. If the employer allows it, the employer or an agent of the employer can accompany the OSHA inspector. After the inspection, the inspector and employer meet to discuss violations, and the problems are often worked out on the spot and the violations remedied immediately.

If an inspection is the result of an employee complaint, the employer cannot take any retaliatory action against that employee. Because of OSHA's limited staff, there is reliance on those in the workplace to bring violations to its attention. If workers fear retaliation, the violations will remain unreported. An employee who is fired, demoted, or discriminated against for registering an OSHA complaint can file a complaint, and the Department of Labor can pursue the employee's rights in federal district court. The following is a landmark case on the issue of employer retaliatory conduct.

Whirlpool Corp. v. *Marshall*
445 U.S. 1 (1980)

YOU CAN'T MAKE ME GO BACK TO WORK IF I'LL GET HURT

FACTS

Whirlpool is a manufacturer of household appliances. In its plant in Marion, Ohio, Whirlpool uses a system of overhead conveyor belts to send a constant stream of parts to employees on the line throughout the plant. Beneath the conveyor belt is mesh screen to catch any parts or other objects that might fall from the conveyor belt.

Some items did fall to the mesh screen, located some 20 feet above the plant floor. Maintenance employees had the responsibility for removing the parts and other debris from the screen. They usually stood on the iron frames of the mesh screen, but occasionally they found it necessary to go onto the screen itself. While one maintenance employee was standing on the mesh, it broke and he fell the 20 feet to his death on the floor below. After this fatal accident, maintenance employees were prohibited from standing on the mesh screen or the iron frames. A mobile platform and long hooks were used to remove objects.

Two maintenance employees, Virgil Deemer and Thomas Cornwell, complained about the screen and its safety problems. When the plant foreman refused to make corrections, Mr. Deemer and Mr. Cornwell asked for the name of an OSHA inspector, and Mr. Deemer contacted an OSHA official on July 7, 1974.

On July 8, 1974, Mr. Deemer and Mr. Cornwell reported for work and were told to do their maintenance work on the screen in the usual manner. Both refused on safety grounds, so the plant foreman sent them to the personnel office. They were then forced to punch out and were not paid for the six hours left on their shift.

On behalf of Mr. Deemer and Mr. Cornwell, the secretary of labor brought suit against Whirlpool for the lost six hours of pay and to have the written reprimands for the incident removed from the files of the employees. The

trial court found for Whirlpool, and the secretary appealed. The court of appeals found for the secretary, and Whirlpool appealed.

JUDICIAL OPINION
STEWART, Justice

. . . The Secretary is obviously correct when he acknowledges in his regulation that, "as a general matter, there is no right afforded by the Act which would entitle employees to walk off the job because of potential unsafe conditions at the workplace." By providing for prompt notice to the employer of an inspector's intention to seek an injunction against an imminently dangerous condition, the legislation obviously contemplates that the employer will normally respond by voluntarily and speedily eliminating the danger. And in the few instances where this does not occur, the legislative provisions authorizing prompt judicial action are designed to give employees full protection in most situations from the risk of injury or death resulting from an imminently dangerous condition at the worksite.

As this case illustrates, however, circumstances may sometimes exist in which the employee justifiably believes that the express statutory arrangement does not sufficiently protect him from death or serious injury. Such circumstances will probably not often occur, but such a situation may arise when (1) the employee is ordered by his employer to work under conditions that the employee reasonably believes pose an imminent risk of death or serious bodily injury, and (2) the employee has reason to believe that there is not sufficient time or opportunity either to seek effective redress from his employer or to apprise OSHA of the danger.

Nothing in the Act suggests that those few employees who have to face this dilemma must rely exclusively on the remedies expressly set forth in the Act at the risk of their own safety. But

Continued

nothing in the Act explicitly provides otherwise. Against this background of legislative silence, the Secretary has exercised his rulemaking power . . . and has determined that, when an employee in good faith finds himself in such a predicament, he may refuse to expose himself to the dangerous condition, without being subjected to "subsequent discrimination" by the employer.

The question before us is whether this interpretative regulation constitutes a permissible gloss on the Act by the Secretary.

The regulation clearly conforms to the fundamental objective of the Act—to prevent occupational deaths and serious injuries. The Act, in its preamble, declares that its purpose and policy is "to assure so far as possible every working man and woman in the Nation safe and healthful working conditions and to preserve our human resources. . . ."

To accomplish this basic purpose, the legislation's remedial orientation is prophylactic in nature. The Act does not wait for an employee to die or become injured. It authorizes the promulgation of health and safety standards and the issuance of citations in the hope that these will act to prevent deaths or injuries from ever occurring. It would seem anomalous to construe an Act so directed and constructed as prohibiting an employee, with no other reasonable alternative, the freedom to withdraw from a workplace environment that he reasonably believes is highly dangerous.

Moreover, the Secretary's regulation can be viewed as an appropriate aid to the full effectuation of the Act's "general duty" clause. That clause provides that "[e]ach employer . . . shall furnish to each of his employees employment and a place of employment which are free from recognized hazards that are causing or are likely to cause death or serious physical harm to his employees." . . . Since OSHA inspectors cannot be present around the clock in every workplace, the Secretary's regulation ensures that employees will in all circumstances enjoy the rights afforded them by the "general duty" clause.

The regulation thus on its face appears to further the overriding purpose of the Act, and rationally to complement its remedial scheme. . . . [T]he Secretary's regulation must, therefore, be upheld, particularly when it is remembered that safety legislation is to be liberally construed to effectuate the congressional purpose.

CASE QUESTIONS

1. What workplace hazard was at issue?
2. What type of remedy does the secretary of labor (acting on behalf of OSHA) want?
3. Is this remedy provided by statute?
4. Is this remedy provided by regulation?
5. Does the decision allow employees to walk off the job when there is a workplace hazard?

E T H I C A L   I S S U E S

18.5 Does a firm have an obligation to disclose the long-term health hazards that may exist in its working environment? For example, what types of disclosures should be made to employees who operate nuclear power plants? Or to employees who are X-ray technicians? What lessons were learned from the asbestos litigation by former asbestos users and plant workers? Current studies link cancer in utility workers to electromagnetic fields; should employers take action?

OSHA SEARCH WARRANT REQUIREMENTS

Although most businesses voluntarily permit OSHA inspections, on some occasions employers have refused access. In *Marshall v. Barlows, Inc.*, 436 U.S. 307 (1978), the U.S. Supreme Court ruled that OSHA inspectors must obtain warrants if employers refused access.

Business Planning Tip

Often referred to as the sick building syndrome, there are numerous indoor-air pollutants that affect office employees, causing the following: headaches; eye, nose, and throat irritation; and dry, tight facial skin.

The EPA lists the following indoor pollutants:
Computer terminals—Electromagnetic fields
Volatile organic compounds (VOCs)

Fax machines—VOCs
Copy machines—Hydrocarbons
Particulates (toner)
Ink/bubble jet printers—Hydrocarbons
Laser printers—Hydrocarbons
To improve conditions and decrease these pollutants:
Improve air circulation
Inexpensive: open the windows
Expensive: air filtration systems
Building design for circulation
Placement of equipment

West Bend Mutual Insurance Company of West Bend, Wisconsin, installed an air flow and air filter system for $150,000. Absenteeism is down and productivity is up 8-16 percent.

OSHA PENALTIES

There are five types of OSHA violations, each of which carries a different range of penalties. Exhibit 18.3 is a summary of OSHA penalties.

After an inspection, OSHA can issue a citation, which begins the penalty process. Although some employers enter into a consent decree and settle the matter with OSHA, any citation can be challenged by an employer, who must give notice of challenge within 15 days of receiving the citation. A hearing will then be conducted by an administrative law judge (ALJ). The ALJ makes a recommendation to the OSHRC, which decides what action to take. Once the OSHRC decision is made, the employer has 60 days to seek review of the decision by a U.S. court of appeals.

Exhibit 18.3
OSHA Penalties

Type of offense	Description	Penalty
Willful	Employer aware of danger or a repeat violator	Up to $70,000 (not less than $5,000) and/or six months imprisonment
Serious	Violation is a threat to life or could cause serious injury	$7,000
Nonserious	No threat of serious injury	Up to $7,000
De minimis	Failure to post rights	Up to $7,000 per violation
Failure to correct	Citation not followed	$7,000 per day

State OSHA Programs

Most federal regulatory laws preempt state laws, but OSHA is unique. State OSHA laws are not generally preempted, and the states share responsibility for workplace safety with the federal government. Also, state criminal laws may be used to prosecute officers and companies already sanctioned by OSHA .

For a state to assume responsibility for an OSHA program, it must submit a plan for approval by the secretary of labor. The plan must include an enforcement agency, appropriate safety standards, and the authority of the state agency to inspect randomly, as OSHA does. The secretary must be assured that the state plan will be as effective as federal OSHA would be. Also, OSHA is in charge of the Complaints Against State Program Administration, which permits those affected and interested in safety to file complaints with OSHA regarding state performance. OSHA can then investigate and, if necessary, eliminate state approval.

Business Planning Tip

Most businesses are unaware of its availability, but OSHA funds a program administered by the states that offers free consulting services to small businesses in order to assist them in complying with OSHA rules. The program has 42 full-time consultants. If a consultant finds a problem in a business, no citation is issued, but the business is given 30 days to bring its plant into compliance.

Employee Impairment and Testing Issues

One safety problem in the workplace is the presence of impaired co-workers. An employee operating equipment, whether a drill press or a delivery van, while under the influence of drugs or alcohol presents a substantial safety concern for any business. Current estimates are that between 14 and 20 percent of the U.S. workforce is impaired on the job. Employees who use drugs are almost four times more likely to be involved in workplace accidents. Further, the cost in reduced productivity attributable to impaired workers is $100 billion. In 1989, the U.S. Supreme Court issued two decisions, *Skinner v. Railway Labor Executives' Association.*, 489 U.S. 602 (1989), and *National Treasury Employees Union* v. *Von Raab*, 489 U.S. 656 (1984), that upheld the right of government employers to conduct drug screening of federal employees without a warrant and without probable cause if those employees were in "safety sensitive" positions. These two particular cases involved railway employees and customs officers.

In the area of drug and alcohol screening, the interests of employee privacy collide with safety and business issues. Courts at the state and federal level have adopted a near uniform position of holding safety concerns above employees' right of privacy. Their decisions have upheld the right of employer testing even in the private sector, especially in work situations where safety is a concern.

Business Planning Tip

When implementing drug testing:
1. Disclose in advance the company's policy.
2. Provide justification.
   Safety
   Productivity
   Insurance costs
   Personal well-being of employees
3. Ensure fairness of your program.
   Reliability of lab
   Randomness of selection
   Offer of two-lab testing
   Offer of independent choice
4. Protect privacy and dignity of employees.
   Privacy of giving sample
   Privacy of results
5. Offer rehabilitation where appropriate—
   counseling, retesting.
6. Adhere to disciplinary measures.
   Termination only option in many cases

C O N S I D E R . . .

18.4 Evaluate the following employee positions and determine whether you would permit random, warrantless, suspicionless searches of employees holding these jobs:

Department of Education motor vehicle operators [*American Federation of Gov't Employees* v. *Cavazos*, 721 F. Supp. 1361 (D.D.C. 1989).]

Employees with security clearance in the Office of the President [*Hartness* v. *Bush*, 919 F.2d 170 (D.C. Cir. 1990).]

Gas and hazardous liquids pipeline industry workers [*International Brotherhood of Elec. Workers* v. *Skinner*, 913 F.2d 1454 (9th Cir. 1990).]

Civilian employees at a chemical weapons research lab [*Thomson* v. *Marsh*, 884 F.2d 113 (4th Cir. 1989).]

Drug enforcement police officers [*Guiney* v. *Roache*, 686 F. Supp. 956 (D. Mass. 1988).]

Hospital staff with direct patient-care duties [*Kemp* v. *Clairborne County Hosp.*, 763 F. Supp. 1362 (S.D. Miss. 1991).]

Police officers [*Brown* v. *City of Detroit*, 715 F. Supp. 832 (E.D. Mich. 1989).]

Coast Guard crew members [*Transportation Inst.* v. *U.S. Coast Guard*, 727 F. Supp. 648 (D.D.C. 1989).]

Account executive driving company car [*Webster* v. *Motorola, Inc.*, 418 Mass. 425 (1994).]

Drilling rig employee [*Luedtke* v. *Nabors Alaska Drilling, Inc.*, 768 P.2d 1123 (Alaska 1989).]

EMPLOYEE PENSIONS, RETIREMENT, AND SOCIAL SECURITY

One of the concerns of workers is what happens to them when they retire: Will they have an income? Other concerns are whether they will have a source of income in the event of disability, or whether their survivors will have income in the event of their death. Finally, what if no work is available? What income will they have until they find another job? These issues are the social issues of employment law—providing for those who, because of age, disability, or unemployment, are unable to provide for themselves.

Social Security

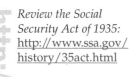

Review the Social Security Act of 1935:
http://www.ssa.gov/history/35act.html

The **Social Security Act of 1935** was a key component of the massive reforms in federal government during Franklin Roosevelt's presidency.

The idea of the Social Security system was to have those who could work shoulder the social burden of providing for those who could not. Every employer and employee is required to contribute to the Social Security programs under the Federal Insurance Contributions Act (FICA). The amount employees contribute is based upon their annual wage, but there is a maximum amount that can be taken.

The benefits paid to the retired and disabled are based on formulas. The amount depends on how long an individual worked and his or her salary range.

Likewise, dependent children whose parents predecease them are entitled to certain benefits based on their parents' work history.

Private Retirement Plans

Review the Employee Retirement Income Security Act of 1974: http://www.law. cornell.edu/uscode/ 29/1001.html

For many, Social Security retirement benefits do not provide enough security, and at present there is no assurance that those employed today will be able to collect their Social Security benefits upon retirement. For these reasons, many employees have invested in their own private retirement plans.

Many retirement and pension plans are set up by employers, who enjoy tax benefits from some plans. However, when there were indications that employees' funds in plans were being misused, not invested wisely, and in some cases embezzled, Congress enacted the **Employee Retirement Income Security Act of 1974 (ERISA)**.

COVERAGE OF ERISA

ERISA applies to any employer engaged in or affecting interstate commerce and to any organization (such as a union) representing employees in interstate commerce. ERISA covers any medical, retirement, or deferral-of-income plan.

REQUIREMENTS OF ERISA PLANS

Covered employers and organizations must give participants an annual report on the insurance or retirement fund that must include a financial statement and an actuarial statement. The annual report must also list any loans made from the fund, including amounts and to whom they were made. The cost of reporting and fiduciary duties under ERISA have caused many employers to drop pension plans. ERISA does not require employer pension plans—it only regulates those who have them.

E T H I C A L   I S S U E S

18.6 Several developers have approached the officials of a national union for a $9 million loan from the union's pension fund. The developers will pay market interest, and the payback term is three years. The developers have offered the officials a $900,000 bonus for approving the loan. The pension's earnings on its portfolio have been only 3 percent over the past five years. This loan will earn them 18 percent. The loan is approved and the officials split the $900,000. Are they justified in their actions?

ERISA EMPLOYEE RIGHTS

ERISA employees are entitled to receive an annual statement showing both their total benefits in any of the covered plans and the amount that is vested or that is nonforfeitable should they leave the job. In addition, ERISA provides minimum vesting requirements or sets standards for when employees will have rights in their retirement, pension, or annuity plans.

Visit the Financial Accounting Standards Board: http://www. rutgers.edu/ Accounting/raw/ fasb/faf.htm

FASB 106 RETIREES AND PENSIONS

In 1995 a new rule of the Financial Accounting Standards Board (FASB) took effect that required companies to reflect as a current expense the costs of benefits for retired employees. This accounting rule will continue to affect earnings as the population ages and benefit costs increase.

E T H I C A L   I S S U E S

18.7 Varity Corporation cut off health benefits for retirees, pointing to language in its official health plan: "The company hereby reserves the right, by action of the board, to amend or terminate the plan or trust at any time." Retirees stress the company's upbeat Project Sunshine campaign (which was used to induce employees to transfer from Varity to Massy Combines Corporation (a Varity spinoff)), which included a letter saying: "When you accept employment with Massey Combines Corp. . . . benefit programs will remain unchanged." "We are all very optimistic that our new company has a bright future." Is it ethical for a firm to have such inconsistent language in its benefit programs? Is there any liability for eliminating such benefits?

Unemployment Compensation

BENEFITS PROVIDED

State laws provide for the amount of **unemployment compensation** that will be paid. The amount is tied to the average amount earned by an individual during the months preceding employment termination. The benefits are usually paid on a weekly or biweekly basis. Most states also have a minimum and maximum amount that can be collected regardless of average earnings during the base period. Further, benefit payments in most states are limited to 26 weeks.

QUALIFYING FOR BENEFITS

Each state has its own standards for payment of benefits. Generally, eligibility requirements demand that an individual be (1) involuntarily terminated from his or her job, (2) able and available for work, and (3) involved in seeking employment.

The payment of unemployment benefits raises many social issues regarding its effects. For example, many opponents of such benefits maintain that awarding them encourages unemployment. In addition, unemployment compensation has created some conflicts in federal labor legislation. In the following case, the U.S. Supreme Court dealt with the conflicting federal rights for labor, management, and unemployment compensation

---

Wimberly v. Labor and Indus. Relations Comm'n of Missouri
479 U.S. 511 (1987)

IF I HAVE A BABY, AM I UNEMPLOYED?

FACTS

After the birth of her child on November 5, 1980, Linda Wimberly (petitioner) was on pregnancy leave from her job at J. C. Penney. Under Penney policy, she could return to work only if a position was available. A position was not available when Mrs. Wimberly tried to return and she then filed a claim for unemployment benefits with the Missouri Division of Employment Security. She was denied the claim because she had left "work

Continued

voluntarily without good cause attributable to [her] work or [her] employer," a provision of a Missouri statute.

Mrs. Wimberly filed suit, and the trial court held that the Missouri statute was inconsistent with the Federal Unemployment Tax Act that prohibits denying compensation "solely on the basis of pregnancy or termination of pregnancy." The court of appeals affirmed, but the Missouri Supreme Court reversed. Mrs. Wimberly appealed to the U.S. Supreme Court.

JUDICIAL OPINION

O'CONNOR, Justice

The Federal Unemployment Tax Act (Act), 26 U.S.C. §§ 3301 et seq., enacted originally as Title IX of the Social Security Act in 1935, 49 Stat. 639, envisions a cooperative federal-state program of benefits to unemployed workers. The standard at issue in this case, § 3304(a)(12), mandates that "no person shall be denied compensation under such State law solely on the basis of pregnancy or termination of pregnancy."

Apart from the minimum standards reflected in § 3304(a), the Act leaves to state discretion the rules governing the administration of unemployment compensation programs.

The treatment of pregnancy-related terminations is a matter of considerable disparity among the States. Most States regard leave on account of pregnancy as a voluntary termination for good cause. Some of these States have specific statutory provisions enumerating pregnancy motivated termination as good cause for leaving a job, while others, by judicial or administrative decision, treat pregnancy as encompassed within larger categories of good cause such as illness or compelling personal reasons. A few states, however, like Missouri, have chosen to define "leaving for good cause" narrowly. In these states, all persons who leave their jobs are disqualified from receiving benefits unless they leave for reasons directly attributable to the work or to the employer.

Petitioner does not dispute that the Missouri scheme treats pregnant women the same as all other persons who leave for reasons not causally connected to their work or their employer, including those suffering from other types of temporary disabilities. She contends, however, that § 3304(a)(12) is not simply an antidiscrimination statute, but rather that it mandates preferential treatment for women who leave work because of pregnancy. According to petitioner, § 3304(a)(12) affirmatively requires states to provide unemployment benefits to women who leave work because of pregnancy when they are next available and able to work, regardless of the state's treatment of other similarly situated claimants.

Contrary to petitioner's assertions, the plain import of the language of § 3304(a)(12) is that Congress intended to prohibit states from singling out pregnancy for unfavorable treatment. The text of the statute provides that compensation shall not be denied under state law "solely on the basis of pregnancy." The focus of this language is on the basis for the state's decision, not the claimant's reason for leaving her job. Thus, a state could not decide to deny benefits to pregnant women while at the same time allowing benefits to persons who are in other respects similarly situated: The "sole basis" for such a decision would be on account of pregnancy. On the other hand, if a state adopts a neutral rule that incidentally disqualifies pregnant or formerly pregnant claimants as part of a larger group, the neutral application of that rule cannot readily be characterized as a decision made "solely on the basis of pregnancy."

Even petitioner concedes that § 3304(a)(12) does not prohibit states from denying benefits to pregnant or formerly pregnant women who fail to satisfy neutral eligibility requirements such as ability to work and availability for work. Missouri does not have a "policy" specifically relating to pregnancy: It neutrally disqualifies workers who leave their jobs for reasons unrelated to their employment.

In *Turner* v. *Department of Employment Security*, this Court struck down on due process grounds a Utah statute providing that a woman was disqualified for 12 weeks before the expected date of childbirth and for 6 weeks after childbirth, even if she left work for reasons unrelated to pregnancy. The Senate Report used the provision at issue in *Turner* as

Continued

representative of the kind of rule that § 3304 (a)(12) was intended to prohibit.

In a number of states, an individual whose unemployment is related to pregnancy is barred from receiving any unemployment benefits. In 1975 the Supreme Court found a provision of this type in the Utah unemployment compensation statute to be unconstitutional. . . . A number of other states have similar provisions although most appear to involve somewhat shorter periods of disqualification. S. Rep. No. 94-1265, at 19, 21, U.S. Code Cong. & Admin. News 1976, pp. 6031, 6015.

In short, petitioner can point to nothing in the Committee Reports, or elsewhere in the statute's legislative history, that evidences congressional intent to mandate preferential treatment for women on account of pregnancy. There is no hint that Congress disapproved of, much less intended to prohibit, a neutral rule such as Missouri's. Indeed, the legislative history shows that Congress was focused only on the issue addressed by the plain language of § 3304(a)(12): prohibiting rules that single out pregnant women or formerly pregnant women for disadvantageous treatment.

Because § 3304(a)(12) does not require states to afford preferential treatment to women on account of pregnancy, the judgment of the Missouri Supreme Court is affirmed.

CASE QUESTIONS

1. Why was Mrs. Wimberly denied unemployment compensation?
2. Was the pregnancy given as a reason?
3. What is the difference between the Utah statute mentioned in the Court's opinion and the Missouri statute?
4. Is the Missouri statute valid?
5. What implications does the decision carry for maternity leaves?

C O N S I D E R . . . **18.5** Alfred Smith and Galen Black were fired by a private drug rehabilitation center because they ingested peyote for sacramental purposes at a ceremony of the Native American Church, of which both are members. When Messrs. Smith and Black applied for unemployment compensation from the state of Oregon, their requests were denied because they were fired for "misconduct." They challenged the decision as a violation of their religious freedom. Are Messrs. Smith and Black correct? [*Employment Div., Dep't of Human Resources of Oregon* v. *Smith*, 496 U.S. 913 (1990).]

WHO PAYS FOR UNEMPLOYMENT BENEFITS?

Although the idea and mandate for unemployment compensation came from the federal government, the states actually administer their own programs. Employers in each state are taxed based on the number of workers they employ and their wages. Those taxes are collected by the states on a quarterly basis. These funds are deposited with the federal government, which maintains an unemployment insurance program with the funds. Each state has an account in the federal fund on which it can draw. Employers effectively pay the costs of the unemployment compensation system.

WORKERS' COMPENSATION LAWS

*For an example of
a state workers'
compensation
law, review
Wisconsin's Workers'
Compensation Act:*
http://badger.state.
wi.us/agencies/
dilhr/wc/chap102.
html

The purpose of **workers' compensation** laws is to provide wage benefits and medical care to victims of work-related injuries. Although each state has its own system of workers' compensation, several general principles remain consistent throughout the states:

1. An employee who is injured in the scope of employment is automatically entitled to certain benefits (a discussion of work-related injuries and the scope of employment follows).
2. Fault is immaterial. An employee's contributory negligence does not lessen his or her right to compensation. Employers' care and precaution do not lessen their responsibility.
3. Coverage is limited to employees and does not extend to independent contractors.
4. Benefits include partial wages, hospital and medical expenses, and death benefits.
5. In exchange for these benefits, employees, their families, and dependents give up their common law right to sue an employer for damages.
6. If third parties (equipment manufacturers, for example) are responsible for an accident, recovery from the third party goes first to the employer for reimbursement.
7. Each state has some administrative agency responsible for administration of workers' compensation.
8. Every employer who is subject to workers' compensation regulation is required to provide some security for liability (such as insurance).

Employee Injuries

As they originated, workers' compensation systems were created to provide benefits for accidental workplace injuries. Over the years, however, the term *accident* has been interpreted broadly. Most injuries are those that result suddenly, such as broken arms, injured backs caused by falls, burns, and lacerations. But workers' compensation has been extended to cover injuries that develop over time. For example, workers involved in lifting heavy objects might eventually develop back problems. Even such medical problems as high blood pressure, heart attacks, and nervous breakdowns have in some cases been classified as work-related and compensable.

The standard for recovery under the workers' compensation system is that the injury originate in the workplace, be caused by the workplace, or develop over time in the workplace. Even stress, when shown to be caused or originated by employment, is a compensable injury.

Workers' compensation issues have become more complex, and many of the hearings involve the issue of determining whether a disability originated on the job or would have existed independently of the job. The following case deals with this type of issue and provides an answer for the chapter's opening "Judgment."

Gacioch v. Stroh Brewery Co.
396 N.W.2d 1 (Mich. 1990)

THE DISABILITY THAT CAME FROM PRODUCTION: ALCOHOLISM AMONG BREWERY WORKERS

FACTS

Casimer Gacioch (plaintiff) began working for Stroh Brewery on February 24, 1947. When he began his work for Stroh, he was predisposed to alcoholism, but he had not yet become an uncontrolled alcoholic.

Beer was provided free at the brewery and was available to all employees on the job at "designated relief areas." This availability had been negotiated through a collective bargaining agreement. Employees could drink beer during their breaks and at lunch with no limit on the amount.

Mr. Gacioch did not drink at home during the week but drank 3 or 4 bottles of beer on the weekend. At work he drank 12 bottles a day. He was not a test taster; he ran a machine that fed cases of beer to a soaker.

In 1973, Stroh Brewery noticed Mr. Gacioch's drinking problem and required him to sign an agreement stating that he could no longer drink on the job. He continued to drink, and seven months after the first agreement he signed a second agreement not to drink on the job. He again continued to drink, was intoxicated on the job, and could not perform his work. He was fired on August 30, 1974.

From April 1976 until September 1978, Mr. Gacioch worked part-time as a church custodian. He pursued a workers' compensation claim against Stroh, alleging he was disabled because of alcoholism. He was denied recovery and appealed to the Workers' Compensation Appeal Board (WCAB), which found that alcoholism is a disease, that the free-beer policy accelerated the problem, and that Stroh should pay compensation. Stroh appealed.

JUDICIAL OPINION

ARCHER, Justice

This case involves a claim for workers' compensation benefits for the chronic alcoholism suffered by plaintiff. We must determine whether, under the circumstances extant in this case, chronic alcoholism suffered by plaintiff who, during breaks drank beer provided free by Stroh Brewery pursuant to a collectively bargained contract provision negotiated by the union is compensable under the Workers' Disability Compensation Act as a personal injury which arose out of and in the course of plaintiff's employment.

The statute in effect on the last day of plaintiff's employment at Stroh Brewery read:

An employee, who receives a personal injury arising out of and in the course of his employment by an employer who is subject to the provisions of this act, at the time of such injury, shall be paid compensation in the manner and to the extent provided in this act, or in case of his death resulting from such injuries the compensation shall be paid to his dependents as defined in this act. Time of injury or date of injury as used in this act in the case of a disease or in the case of an injury not attributable to a single event shall be the last day of work in the employment in which the employee was last subjected to the conditions resulting in disability or death.

"Personal injury" shall include a disease or disability which is due to causes and conditions which are characteristic of and peculiar to the business of the employer and which arises out of and in the course of the employment. Ordinary diseases of life to which the public is generally exposed outside of the employment shall not be compensable.

Defendants contend that alcoholism is not a disease, but, rather, a "social aberration." All three experts testifying in this case, Drs. Smith and Tanay, plaintiff's experts, and Dr. Rauch, defendants' expert, referred to alcoholism as a disease. Dr. Smith described alcoholism as a "lifelong metabolic disease, much like diabetes." Dr. Tanay testified that alcoholism is associated with particular personality disorders which begin during a person's childhood. The WCAB treated plaintiff's chronic alcoholism as a disease. Our review of the professional literature on

Continued

the subject indicates that various organizations representing health care professionals have officially pronounced alcoholism as a disease. Hence, plaintiff's chronic alcoholism is a disease for purposes of the above statute.

Plaintiff asserts that his chronic alcoholism was an occupational disease. We disagree. A review of the record indicates that the WCAB also did not conclude that plaintiff's alcoholic condition was an occupational disease. The board treated plaintiff's alcoholism as an ordinary disease of life. The proper inquiry in this case, therefore, is whether plaintiff's chronic alcoholism was a disease or disability which was due to causes and conditions which are characteristic of and peculiar to the business of Stroh and which arose out of and in the course of employment. In reaching the question concerning whether chronic alcoholism is a disease which is due to causes and conditions which are characteristic of and peculiar to the business of Stroh and which arose out of and in the course of plaintiff's employment, we must be careful not to equate "circumstance" of employment with "out of and in the course" of employment. If chronic alcoholism can be categorized as an ordinary disease of life to which the public is generally exposed outside of the employment, plaintiff is not entitled to a workers' compensation award. The pertinent question then is whether the board made specific findings as to whether brewery workers are more prone to develop chronic alcoholism than is the general public.

We are unable to discern from the opinion of the board whether it found as fact that brewery workers are more prone to suffer from chronic

alcoholism (an ordinary disease of life) than is the general public. We note that none of the experts testifying in this case stated that plaintiff's alcoholism was due to the inherent characteristics and peculiarities of his employment in the brewery industry as a production worker responsible for running a machine. Dr. Smith, for example, testified that "Mr. Gacioch would have most likely become an alcoholic anyway and his drinking outside of work eventually [was] far greater than during work." Dr. Rauch opined that individuals who are predisposed to alcoholism, like plaintiff herein, are likely to become an alcoholic no matter where they work.

We are unable to determine from the opinion of the WCAB whether it understood the applicable legal standard and what facts it specifically relied upon in reaching its conclusion that plaintiff's alcoholism was compensable under the Workers' Disability Compensation Act.

We therefore remand this case to the WCAB for its statement of the law and the specific facts relied upon to support its conclusion.

CASE QUESTIONS

1. What was Stroh's free-beer policy?
2. Who negotiated the policy?
3. Was Mr. Gacioch predisposed to alcoholism?
4. Is alcoholism a disease?
5. Is alcoholism a disease that originated in the workplace in this case?
6. What additional factual information is needed to resolve the case?
7. How do you feel about the no-limit beer policy? Can you foresee other issues of liability for Stroh beyond workers' compensation?

In some situations, an employee is injured by a co-worker. A question that may arise in these situations is whether the injury by the fellow employee arose out of the course of employment. For example, in *Tolbert* v. *Martin-Marietta Corp.*, 621 F. Supp. 1099 (Colo. 1985), a secretary was raped by a janitor as she was leaving her office for lunch. Cases such as this are not covered under workers' compensation; however, employees may sue an employer for failure to screen carefully. The court in *Tolbert* noted:

Adopting this position has the additional advantage of providing employers an incentive to make reasonable efforts to screen prospective employees so as to avoid hiring rapists or those having the identifiable characteristics of potential rapists. Tort law does not impose strict liability—far from it; the plaintiff has the burden of showing negligence, causation, and damages. Women in the workplace are surely entitled to at least the protection of reasonable care where a prospective employee's available past record indicates a substantial foreseeable risk that, if employed, he may rape some woman he encounters on the employer's premises.

The potential for harm and resulting liability in these types of cases requires employers to screen employees carefully.

CONSIDER... **18.6** Walt Disney Company hired Victor Salva in 1994 to direct the movie, *Powder*. He had been convicted in 1988 of molesting a 12-year-old boy and served 15 months of a three-year sentence, completing his parole in 1992. The criminal acts occurred while Mr. Salva was directing a short horror film, *Clownhouse*. *Powder* was a film about high school children, but Disney indicates it did not know of Mr. Salva's background. What liability did Disney have had Mr. Salva molested an actor?

Fault Is Immaterial

The fact that an injury occurs in the workplace is enough for recovery. Employee negligence, employer precautions, contributory negligence, and assumption of risk are not issues in workers' compensation cases.

Employees versus Independent Contractors

Workers' compensation applies to employees but not to independent contractors. Employees are those who are present at the workplace on a regular basis, paid a wage, and supervised. **Independent contractors** are those who work on a job basis, work irregular hours, and are not supervised by the employer. A backhoe operator working daily from 5 A.M. to 1 P.M. for a plumbing company and paid a weekly wage is an employee. A backhoe operator hired and paid on a per-job basis is an independent contractor. A more complete discussion of employee versus independent contractor status can be found in Chapter 17.

Benefits

Workers' benefits can be grouped into three different categories: medical, disability, and death. Medical benefits include typical insurance-covered costs such as hospital costs, physician and nursing fees, therapy fees, and rental costs for equipment needed for recovery.

Disability benefits are payments made to compensate employees for wages lost because of a disability injury. The amount of benefits is based on state statutory figures. Most states base disability benefits on an employee's average monthly wage and they also specify a maximum amount. State statutes also generally have a list of **scheduled injuries**, which will carry a percentage disability figure. For example, loss of a body part is a typical injury. In Arizona, the disability amount for a lost thumb is 55 percent of the average monthly wage for 15 months. (Ariz. Rev. Stat. § 23-1044). For a lost foot, the amount is 55 percent of the average monthly wage for 50 months. Total disability is also defined by statute. Workers who have total disability are generally entitled to two-thirds of their average monthly salary for the period of the disability. Total disability usually includes the loss of both eyes or both hands or complete paralysis.

Some injuries suffered by workers are not listed in statutes. Those not specifically described in statutes are called **unscheduled injuries**. The amount allowed for unscheduled injuries is discretionary and an area of frequent litigation.

Death benefits are paid to the family of a deceased employee and generally include burial expenses. In addition, survivors who were economically dependent on an employee are also paid benefits. The amount of death benefits is generally some percentage of the average monthly salary; for example, a surviving spouse might be entitled to a 35 percent benefit.

Forfeiture of the Right of Suit

The majority of states require employees to forfeit all other lawsuit rights in exchange for workers' compensation benefits. Employees receive automatic benefits but lose the right to sue their employers. Some states even prohibit employees from suing their co-workers, but their states allow suits against negligent co-workers for damages. In addition, some states allow family members to sue employers for direct injury to themselves. In those states, a spouse could bring a lawsuit against an employer for loss of consortium (marital companionship).

Third-Party Suits

If an employee is injured by a machine malfunction while on the job, the employee will be covered by workers' compensation. However, there is an issue of product liability in the accident. If suit is brought against the machine's manufacturer for product liability, any recovery will go first to the employer to compensate for the cost of the employee's benefits. In other words, third-party recovery is first used to reimburse the employer.

Administrative Agency

Every state has some administrative agency responsible for the administration of claims, hearings, and benefits. In most states this agency holds hearings for claims, and its decision is appealable in the same manner as any other agency decision.

The procedure for compensation requires employees to file claims with the agency along with medical documentation for the claim. Most claims are paid without contest. But when there is a challenge to a decision, a hearing with evidence and testimony is held.

Insurance

All states with workers' compensation systems require employers to be financially responsible for benefits under their systems. Employers can show financial responsibility by (1) maintaining an insurance policy, (2) obtaining a policy through the state agency, or (3) offering evidence of sufficient assets and resources to cover potential claims and benefits.

Problems in Workers' Compensation Systems

Increasingly, states and employers are experimenting with reforms to workers' compensation systems. Concerns focus on fraud that stems from incentives in the system. For example, medical benefits in workers' compensation are better than most medical plans. Because nearly all disability payments are tax-free, employees may be living on close to 90 percent of what they lived on (after taxes) before their disability.

Some doubts exist about the legitimacy of many complaints. A janitor moonlighting for HGO, Inc., hurt his little finger while on the job. He collected $16,800 in disability payments over the next three years, even though he was able to continue his regular day job as a police officer.

Suggested reforms have included the elimination of certain claims, as in California, where attempts are being made to eliminate "mental stress" from workers' compensation coverage. Georgia no longer makes lifetime disability payments but instead limits their duration to eight years. Other states have hired more investigators to detect fraud. Companies are also attempting to cut costs by using staff doctors or by returning employees to other jobs that can be done despite an injury.

The nature of work in the United States has changed and continues to change rapidly. The workers' compensation systems were established during the Industrial Revolution, when the injuries sustained were primarily the types of factory and machinery accidents we traditionally associate with workers' compensation claims. However, the majority of jobs in the United States are now in service industries, and the nature of work-related injuries has changed from sudden-accident types to ongoing, progressive problems that are more expensive to treat and correct. For example, the repetitive hand and arm motions of computer keyboard operators cause an injury, often called carpal tunnel syndrome, to word processors, journalists, reservationists, and cashiers. This injury requires expensive surgery and results in many lost work days, if not new job assignments. Such injuries, often called repetitive stress injuries (RSIs), are the basis of 244 pending lawsuits by workers against keyboard and equipment manufacturers.

The office environment itself is presenting new and difficult-to-control health-related problems for workers. Ergonomics is a rapidly growing field that examines the design of work areas and office equipment to minimize such worker injuries as back problems. Architects and engineers are working together to design buildings that eliminate the so-called sick building syndrome in which poor air quality or the lack of fresh air circulation increases the incidence of illness and causes other symptoms in office workers.

Explore the Americans with Disabilities Act: http://janweb.icdi. wvu.edu/kinder/

A final issue in workers' compensation is the relationship between the state systems and the Americans with Disabilities Act (see Chapter 19), which prohibits discrimination against employees with disabilities and requires accommodation of employer facilities to permit disabled persons to work. Traditionally, when an accident caused disability, an employee collected payment in lieu of being rehired. An issue that arises as the systems of laws interact is whether an employer is required to rehire a disabled employee.

LABOR UNIONS

History and Development of Labor Legislation

When workers first began organized efforts to improve their employment situations, the courts were particularly harsh. In early eighteenth-century England, participants in organized labor were prosecuted for criminal conspiracy, which is the crime of organizing with others for the commission of another crime. The first case in the United States (*Commonwealth v. Pullis* (1806)) also charged organized laborers with criminal conspiracy that resulted in a criminal conviction for laborers participating in a strike.

Many employers tried to stifle the labor union movement by requiring their employees to sign **yellow-dog contracts**, which prohibited employees from joining unions. With these attempts came the beginning of protective labor legislation.

THE RAILWAY LABOR ACT OF 1926

Review the Railway Labor Act: http://www.law.cornell.edu/uscode/45/151.html

The **Railway Labor Act** was the first federal legislation to address union issues specifically, but its application was limited to labor relations in the railroad industry. However, the act did establish some basic rights for railway employees that would later carry over to general labor statutes. Railway employees were given the right to form and join unions without employer interference. The employees were also given the right to bargain collectively with their employers. The underlying purpose of the act was to promote peaceful labor-management relations. This act is still effective today and was expanded to cover airline employees in 1936.

THE NORRIS-LAGUARDIA ACT OF 1932

Review the Norris-LaGuardia Act: http://www.law.cornell.edu/uscode/29/101.html

In addressing the problem of courts issuing injunctions to stop union strikes, the **Norris-LaGuardia Act** prohibited the injunction as a remedy in labor disputes and eliminated the common law application of the use of government to control employer-employee relations. Under the act, the government (including the courts) became a neutral force in labor-management disputes.

There were some exceptions to the anti-injunction rule. Violent strikes could be enjoined, provided that it was clear there would be or had been violence and that public officers could not control the violence and any resulting damage. Even in these cases, a hearing allowing all parties to attend was required before a violent strike could be enjoined.

THE WAGNER ACT

Review the National Labor Relations Act: http://www.law.cornell.edu/uscode/29/151.html
Visit the NLBR: http://www.doc.gov/nlrb/homepg.html
Review the Taft-Hartley Act: http://www.law.cornell.edu/uscode/29/141.html

This act, also known as the **National Labor Relations Act of 1935 (NLRA)**, gave employees the right to organize and choose representatives to bargain collectively with their employers. Further, it established the **National Labor Relations Board (NLRB)**, which had two functions: to conduct union elections and to investigate and remedy unfair labor practices.

THE TAFT-HARTLEY ACT—THE LABOR-MANAGEMENT RELATIONS ACT OF 1947

Over President Truman's veto, Congress passed the **Taft-Hartley Act**, which was a response to the public's concern about too many strikes, secondary boycotts, and the unrestrained power of union officials. The act amended the Wagner Act by applying the principle of unfair labor practices to unions as well as employers. Strikes to force employers to discharge nonunion employees, secondary boycotts, and strikes over work assignments were prohibited as unfair labor practices. Employees were also given the right to remove a union they no longer wanted as their representative. The act also contains provisions that allow the president to invoke a **cooling-off period** of bargaining before a strike that threatens to imperil the public health and safety can begin. This power has been used by presidents in transportation and coal strikes.

THE LANDRUM-GRIFFIN ACT—THE LABOR-MANAGEMENT REPORTING AND DISCLOSURE ACT OF 1959

Review the Landrum-Griffin Act: http://www.law.cornell.edu/uscode/29/ch11.html
Visit the AFL-CIO: http://www.aflcio.org/

As unions grew, evidence of corruption and undemocratic procedures within them came to light. The **Landrum-Griffin Act** was passed to ensure employee protection within union organizations. The act gave union members a bill of rights, required certain procedures for election of officers, prescribed financial reporting requirements for union funds, and established criminal and civil penalties for union misconduct.

Today there are nearly 450 active unions in the United States, from the Screen Actors Guild to the Airline Pilots Association. However, over 75 percent of these unions are affiliated with the AFL-CIO (the American Federation of Labor and Congress of Industrial Organizations), the giant that resulted from the merger of the two original labor unions in 1955. These unions, however, make up only 15.5 percent of today's workforce.

Union Organizing Efforts

Employees make the decision of whether a union will represent them and which will serve as their representative. This process is called selecting a bargaining representative, and the NLRB has strict procedures for such selection. The NLRB carefully chooses how employees will be grouped together so that they share common interests.

The courts have decided many questions about union organization efforts. The focus of these cases is often how the union goes about organizing employees. In the following case, the U.S. Supreme Court offered protection for union organizers.

NLRB v. *Town & Country Electric, Inc.*
116 S. Ct. 450 (1995)

"SALTING" THE WORKFORCE: HIRE ME TO UNIONIZE

FACTS

Town & Country Electric, Inc., a nonunion electrical contractor, wanted to hire several licensed Minnesota electricians for construction work in that state. Through an employment agency, Town & Country advertised for job applicants but refused to interview 10 of 11 union applicants. One union applicant was hired, but he was fired by Town & Country after only a few days on the job.

Members of the International Brotherhood of Electrical Workers filed a complaint with the NLRB. An ALJ found for the union, the NLRB affirmed, and the court of appeals reversed. The union appealed.

JUDICIAL OPINION

BREYER, Justice

Can a worker be a company's "employee," within the terms of the National Labor Relations Act, 29 U.S.C. § 151 et seq., if, at the same time, a union pays that worker to help the union organize the company? We agree with the National Labor Relations Board that the answer is "yes."

The National Labor Relations Act seeks to improve labor relations in large part by granting specific sets of rights to employers and to employees. This case grows out of a controversy about rights that the Act grants to "employees," namely, rights "to self-organization,

Continued

to form, join, or assist labor organizations, to bargain collectively . . . and to engage in other concerted activities for the purpose of collective bargaining or other mutual aid or protection."

The relevant statutory language is the following:

The term 'employee' shall include any employee, and shall not be limited to the employees of a particular employer, unless this subchapter explicitly states otherwise, and shall include any individual whose work has ceased as a consequence of, or in connection with, any current labor dispute or because of any unfair labor practice, and who has not obtained any other regular and substantially equivalent employment, but shall not include any individual employed as an agricultural laborer, or in the domestic service of any family or person at his home, or any individual employed by his parent or spouse, or any individual having the status of an independent contractor.

We must specifically decide whether the Board may lawfully interpret this language to include company workers who are also paid union organizers.

Several strong general arguments favor the Board's position. For one thing, the Board's decision is consistent with the broad language of the Act itself—language that is broad enough to include those company workers whom a union also pays for organizing. The ordinary dictionary definition of "employee" includes any "person who works for another in return for financial or other compensation."

For another thing, the Board's broad, literal interpretation of the word "employee" is consistent with several of the Act's purposes, such as protecting "the right of employees to organize for mutual aid without employer interference," and "encouraging and protecting the collective-bargaining process." And, insofar as one can infer purpose from congressional Reports and floor statements, those sources too are consistent with the Board's broad interpretation of the word. It is fairly easy to find statements to the effect that an "employee" simply "means someone who works for another for hire."

Finally, at least one other provision of the 1947 Labor Management Relations Act seems specifically to contemplate the possibility that a company's employee might also work for a union. This provision forbids an employer (say, the company) from making payments to a person employed by a union, but simultaneously exempts from that ban wages paid by the company to "any . . . employee of a labor organization, who is also an employee" of the company.

Town & Country goes on to argue that application of common-law agency principles requires an interpretation of "employee" that excludes paid union organizers. It points to a section of the Restatement (Second) of Agency (dealing with respondent superior liability for torts), which says: "Since . . . the relation of master and servant is dependent upon the right of the master to control the conduct of the servant in the performance of the service, giving service to two masters at the same time normally involves a breach of duty by the servant to one or both of them. . . . [A person] cannot be a servant of two masters in doing an act as to which an intent to serve one necessarily excludes an intent to serve the other." It argues that, when the paid union organizer serves the union—at least at certain times in certain ways—the organizer is acting adversely to the company. Indeed, it says, the organizer may stand ready to desert the company upon request by the union, in which case, the union, not the company, would have "the right . . . to control the conduct of the servant."

Town & Country's common-law argument fails, quite simply, because, in our view, the Board correctly found that it lacks sufficient support in common law. The Restatement's hornbook rule (to which the quoted commentary is appended) says that a "person may be the servant of two masters . . . at one time as to one act, if the service to one does not involve abandonment of the service to the other." The Board, in quoting this rule, concluded that service to the union for pay does not "involve abandonment of . . . service" to the company.

And, that conclusion seems correct. Common sense suggests that as a worker goes about

Continued

his ordinary tasks during a working day, say, wiring sockets or laying cable, he or she is subject to the control of the company employer, whether or not the union also pays the worker. The company, the worker, the union, all would expect that to be so. And, that being so, that union and company interests or control might sometimes differ should make no difference.

Neither are we convinced by the practical considerations that Town & Country adds to its agency law argument. The company refers to a Union resolution permitting members to work for nonunion firms, which, the company says, reflects a union effort to "salt" nonunion companies with union members seeking to organize them. Supported by amici curiae, it argues that "salts" might try to harm the company, perhaps quitting when the company needs them, perhaps disparaging the company to others, perhaps even sabotaging the firm or its products. Therefore, the company concludes, Congress could not have meant paid union organizers to have been included as "employees" under the Act.

This practical argument suffers from several serious problems. For one thing, nothing in this record suggests that such acts of disloyalty were present, in kind or degree, to the point where the company might lose control over the worker's normal workplace tasks. Certainly the Union's resolution contains nothing that suggests, requires, encouraged, or condones impermissible or unlawful activity. For another thing, the argument proves too much. If a paid union organizer might quit, leaving a company employer in the lurch, so too might an unpaid organizer, or a worker who has found a better job, or one whose family wants to move elsewhere. And if an overly zealous union organizer might hurt the company through unlawful acts, so might

another unpaid zealot (who may know less about the law), or a dissatisfied worker (who may lack an outlet for his grievances). This does not mean they are not "employees."

Further, the law offers alternative remedies for Town & Country's concerns, short of excluding paid or unpaid union organizers from all protection under the Act. For example, a company disturbed by legal but undesirable activity, such as quitting without notice, can offer its employees fixed-term contracts, rather than hiring them "at will" as in the case before us; or it can negotiate with its workers for a notice period. A company faced with unlawful (or possibly unlawful) activity can discipline or dismiss the worker, file a complaint with the Board, or notify law enforcement authorities.

This is not to say that the law treats paid union organizers like other company employees in every labor law context. For instance, the Board states that, at least sometimes, a paid organizer may not share a sufficient "community of interest" with other employees (as to wages, hours, and working conditions) to warrant inclusion in the same bargaining unit. We hold only that the Board's construction of the word "employee" is lawful; that term does not exclude paid union organizers.

For these reasons the judgment of the court of appeals is vacated.

CASE QUESTIONS
1. Why is the *Restatement of Agency* important in this case?
2. What does the term "salt" refer to?
3. Do you see a conflict of interest in a union organizer working in a nonunion plant or facility?
4. What remedies will Town & Country have for disloyalty?

THE COLLECTIVE BARGAINING UNIT

The first step in union organization is the establishment of a collective bargaining unit. The **collective bargaining unit** is a group of employees recognized by the NLRB as appropriate for exclusive representation of all employees in that group. Collective bargaining units are determined by a commonality of interest. Because all employees will be represented by a union voted in by the majority, the NLRB requires the unit to consist of homogeneous employees. A union petitioning for representation must carefully define its bargaining unit because a petition will be dismissed if the NLRB determines that the bargaining unit is inappropriate. For example, some bargaining units consist of entire plants of workers, whereas others are specialized units within a plant, such as the maintenance staff or the line workers in an assembly plant. For some national companies, the bargaining unit is all employees, whereas for other national firms the bargaining unit is one particular plant or store. Obviously, defining the bargaining unit is crucial, for it can control whether the union will gain enough votes. A union might not have enough votes in a particular plant, but it could have enough votes if the unit were company-wide; in such cases the union will want the larger bargaining unit.

In determining the appropriateness of a collective bargaining unit, the nlrb considers the following factors:

1. The type of union and its history of bargaining—types of employees and types of industries
2. The duties, wages, and skills of the employees
3. How the bargaining unit fits in an employer's structure
4. The wishes of the employees

CONSIDER... 18.7 Trump Taj Mahal Associates (Trump), a limited partnership, operates the Trump Taj Mahal Casino Resort in Atlantic City, New Jersey. The entertainment department at the Taj includes stage technicians, convention lounge technicians, and entertainment event technicians.

Trump maintains a list of approximately 40 on-call or "casual" employees who perform technical functions and who are called upon on an intermittent basis to perform the same functions as regular technical employees when there are not enough regular employees to perform the work. Trump maintains this casual list because the casino industry is regulated by the New Jersey Casino Control Commission, which requires employees to be "badged" or licensed. Casual employees are also required to be badged. The lists and prequalifications enable Trump to draw from a pool of technicians who have already met certain procedural and technical requirements in order to satisfy short-term labor needs.

During the first 11 months of operation at the Taj Mahal Casino, Trump operated its entertainment department with three full-time stage technicians and five full-time convention lounge technicians, and did not employ any part-time technicians. About March 1, 1991, Trump increased its staff to 28 full-time technicians and 10 regular part-time technicians by hiring from the casual list. Trump selected those employees from the casual list who had worked the most hours at the Taj and had the necessary skills for the particular job. A number of casuals who had worked a considerable number of hours in the past remained on the casual list.

Continued

The 1990 list of casual employees entitled "entertainment technicians" shows that those employees worked from 30 to 952 hours during that year. The regional director found that during 1990 the casuals worked an average of 379 hours during the year, or approximately 7 hours a week, and during early 1991 the casuals worked an average of 119 hours, or approximately 17 hours a week.

The employees sought to have their collective bargaining unit expanded to include both the full-time technicians and the on-call (i.e., casual) employees.

Is this a proper bargaining unit? [*Trump Taj Mahal Associates Ltd.* v. *International Alliance of Theatrical Stage Employees,* 306 N.L.R.B. No. 57 (1992).]

The Petition, Cards, and Vote Once the collective bargaining unit is set, the union, employees, or employers can file a petition for exclusive representation of employees within a unit. The petition is filed with the NLRB and must be supported by at least 30 percent of the members of the bargaining unit. The 30 percent support is shown by signed and dated **authorization cards** filled out by employees. These authorization cards must be signed willingly, and the employee must understand the effect of the cards.

Once the cards are filed, an employer has two choices. First, the employer can voluntarily recognize the union. If the union has obtained authorization cards from a majority of the employees, such recognition is wise unless the employer knows of some illegal conduct used to obtain the cards. If there was illegal conduct, the employer can always file a charge with the NLRB, which will conduct an investigation.

If the authorization cards do not amount to a majority of employees in the bargaining unit, the employer can insist on a formal election. In an election the employees vote for or against the union that petitions for representation, and has the right to campaign and distribute literature before an upcoming election. However, employers can prohibit oral campaigning during work hours and can restrict literature distribution both during and, to a degree, before and after work hours. Employer restrictions cannot be made with the intent of eliminating the possibility of the union. The restrictions must be reasonable and serve some purpose, such as controlling litter and requiring employees to do their work during their work hours.

The election is conducted by secret ballot by the NLRB. A simple majority of the employees must vote in favor of the union for certification to occur.

CONSIDER... **18.8** The Republic Aviation Plant in Suffolk County, New York, was holding a union certification election. The plant had adopted, well before any union activity, a rule against soliciting that provided: "Soliciting of any type cannot be permitted in the factory or offices."

An employee who had been reminded of the rule persisted in passing out cards to fellow employees during his lunch hour. Three other employees wore UAW-CIO union buttons to work and were asked to remove them, but they refused. All four employees were discharged. The four filed a complaint with the NLRB on grounds they had been denied the right to distribute information about the union. Did the plant rule violate the employees' right to distribute information? [*Republic* v. *NLRB,* 324 U.S. 793 (1945).]

Certification Once **certification** of a union has taken place, either because of the employer's consent or a valid election, that union has the exclusive right to represent the employees in all contract negotiations. An employer who refuses to deal with the certified union can be forced to by an injunction obtained by the NLRB.

After a union has been certified, an election for a new union cannot be held for 12 months from the time of certification. If the union signs a collective bargaining agreement, no union certification election can be held until the collective bargaining agreement expires. These limitations on elections and certifications prevent chaos in the workplace that would result from constant changeovers in union representation. Exhibit 18.4 summarizes the steps in the union certification process.

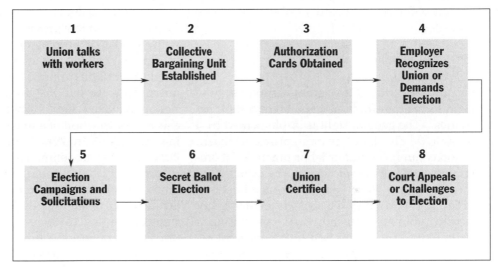

Exhibit 18.4
Union Certification

Nonunion Members in the Certified Workplace Although the NLRA gave unions the right to exist, it also gave workers the right to a choice. Workers are not required to join unions and cannot be coerced into supporting union action. Attempts by a union to force its members to participate in strikes and other union activities are considered unfair labor practices. The following case is a recent interpretation of whether a union coerced employees into participating in a strike.

Pattern Makers' League of N. Am., AFL-CIO v. NLRB
473 U.S. 95 (1985)

YOU CAN'T MAKE ME STRIKE IF I WANT TO WORK

FACTS
The Pattern Makers' League of North America, AFL-CIO, provides in its constitution that union members may not resign during a strike or when a strike is imminent. The league fined ten

of its members who, in violation of this provision, resigned during a strike and returned to work. The NLRB held that the union rule violated section 8(b) of the NLRA, which provides: "It shall be an unfair labor practice for a labor
Continued

organization or its agents—(1) to restrain or coerce (A) employees in the exercise of rights guaranteed herein. . . ."

The union rule (League Law 13) provides: "No resignation or withdrawal from an Association or from the League shall be accepted during a strike or lockout, or at a time when a strike or lockout appears imminent."

The U. S. court of appeals for the Seventh Circuit enforced the board's order. The league appealed.

JUDICIAL OPINION
POWELL, Justice
Section 7 of (the NLRA) grants employees the right to "refrain from any or all (concerted) activities." The general right is implemented by § 8(b)(a)(A). The latter section provides that a union commits an unfair labor practice if it "restrains or coerces employees in the exercise" of their § 7 rights. When employee members of a union refuse to support a strike (whether or not a rule prohibits returning to work during a strike), they are refraining from "concerted activity." Therefore, imposing fines on these employees for returning to work "restrains" the exercise of their § 7 rights. Indeed, if the terms "refrain" and "restrain or coerce" are interpreted literally, fining employees to enforce compliance with any union rule or policy would violate the Act.

Language and reasoning from other opinions of this Court confirm that the Board's construction of § 8(b)(1)(A) is reasonable. In *Scofield v. NLRB*, 394 U.S. 423 (1969), the Court upheld a union rule setting a ceiling on the daily wages that members working on an incentive basis could earn. The union members' freedom to resign was critical to the Court's decision that the union rule did not "restrain or coerce" the employees within the meaning of § 8(b)(1)(A).

The decision in *NLRB v. Textile Workers*, 409 U.S. 213 (1972) also supports the Board's view that prohibits unions from punishing members not free to resign. There, thirty-one employees resigned their union membership and resumed working during a strike. We held that fining

these former members "restrained or coerced" them. In reaching this conclusion, we said "the vitality of Section 7 requires that the member be free to refrain in November from the actions he endorsed in May."

League Law 13 curtails (the) freedom to resign from full union membership. Nevertheless, the petitioners (League) contend that League Law 13 does not contravene the policy of voluntary unionism imbedded in the Act. They assert that this provision does not interfere with workers' employment rights because offending members are not discharged, but only fined. We find this argument unpersuasive, for a union has not left a "worker's employment rights inviolate when it exacts (his entire) paycheck in satisfaction of a fine imposed for working." Congress in 1947 (with the Taft-Hartley Act) sought to eliminate completely any requirement that the employee maintain full union membership. Therefore, the Board was justified in concluding that by restricting the right of employees to resign, League Law 13 impairs the policy of voluntary unionism.

Petitioners . . . argue that the proviso to § 8(b)(1)(A) expressly allows unions to place restrictions on the right to resign.

Neither the Board nor this Court has ever interpreted the proviso as allowing unions to make rules restricting the right to resign. Rather, the Court has assumed that "rules with respect to the . . . retention of membership" are those that provide for expulsion of employees from the union. Accordingly, we find no basis for refusing to defer to the Board's conclusion that League Law 13 is not a "rule with respect to the retention of membership" within the meaning of the proviso.

The petitioners next argue that the legislative history of the Taft-Hartley Act shows that Congress made a considered decision not to protect union members' right to resign.

The legislative history does not support this contention. The "right to resign" apparently was included in the original House bill to protect workers unable to resign because of "closed shop" agreements. Union

Continued

constitutions limiting the right to resign were uncommon in 1947.

The Board has the primary responsibility for applying "the general provisions of the Act to the complexities of industrial life." Where the Board's construction of the Act is reasonable, it should not be rejected. . . . [T]he Board has consistently construed § 8(b)(1)(A) as prohibiting the imposition of fines on employees who have tendered resignations invalid under a union constitution. Therefore we conclude that the Board's decision here is entitled to our deference.

Affirmed.

CASE QUESTIONS
1. What union rule is at issue?
2. Does the rule affect union membership?
3. Can the union enforce the rule?
4. What is the purpose of § 8(b)(1)(A)?
5. Does the legislative history support a prohibition of the union rule?

Union Contract Negotiations

Once a union is certified as the employees' representative, one of its major roles is to obtain a contract or **collective bargaining agreement** between employer and employees. This section discusses the roles of the parties in obtaining that agreement.

GOOD-FAITH BARGAINING

Section 8(d) of the NLRA defines **good-faith bargaining** as a mutual obligation of employer and union to meet at reasonable times, confer in good faith on employment issues, and execute a written agreement reflecting their oral agreement. Both parties must bargain with an open mind and the sincere intent of reaching an agreement.

Whether there has been good-faith bargaining on the part of the parties depends on each situation and on various factors, such as the reasonableness of the position taken, repeated failures to show up at bargaining sessions or to be available for them, and holding steadfast to a predetermined position during the course of bargaining. Most of the cases dealing with the problem of failure to bargain in good faith are the result of employer conduct.

SUBJECT MATTER OF GOOD-FAITH BARGAINING

Two types of subject matters can be discussed during bargaining: (1) mandatory or compulsory subject matter and (2) permissive subject matter. As to the former, the NLRA describes **mandatory bargaining terms** as those dealing with "wages, hours, and other terms and conditions of employment." Obviously, the amount to be paid as wages is included, but so also are related issues, such as merit pay, vacations, overtime, work hours, leaves, and pay days. Exhibit 18.5 (pg. 648) lists the usual topics covered in a collective bargaining agreement.

One of the issues that has been a subject of good-faith bargaining is the two-tier wage structure. In the past, unions have agreed to two-tier wage structures in order to help financially struggling firms survive. Now, however, many corporations are raising the issue in bargaining in order to control wage increases. For example, in the airline industry, pilots with the greatest seniority work under a wage structure that affords them very high pay levels now. But more pilots are available now than before, and some new pilots are willing to enter employment under a different wage and age scale. Although there are many management and labor concerns about a two-tier structure, it appears to be a good-faith bargaining topic that will remain an issue for both groups.

Usual Topics for a Collective Bargaining Agreement

Recognition of the Union	Employee grievances
Wages	Length of agreement/expiration date
Work hours	Incentive plans
Vacations	Union announcements (bulletin board rights)
Sick leave	Definition of terms
Seniority	Leaves of absence
Insurance	Drug testing
Pension/retirement plans	

Exhibit 18.5
Usual Topics for a Collective Bargaining Agreement

Permissive subject matters, in contrast with compulsory subject matters, would be those the parties are required to negotiate but on which they need not reach an agreement. A strike vote of employees before a strike starts is an example of a permissive subject. Any topic that does not directly concern employer-employee relations is a permissive subject. A refusal to bargain on a permissive subject is not, however, an unfair labor practice; a refusal to bargain on mandatory subject matter *is* an unfair labor practice.

Some subjects are "unbargainable." Employers and employees cannot bargain to give away statutory rights—for example, the procedures for certifying a union. Nor can they bargain about having a **closed shop**, which requires employees to be union members before they can be hired. Such shops are illegal under the Taft-Hartley Act.

C O N S I D E R . . .   **18.9** Determine whether the following subjects are mandatory, permissive, or nonbargainable.

- Insurance plans
- Maternity leaves
- Plant rules
- Subcontracting procedures
- Strikes
- Layoffs
- Union bookkeeping procedures
- Meal periods

FAILURE TO BARGAIN IN GOOD FAITH

Failure to bargain on mandatory subject matter is an **unfair labor practice**, which is conduct prohibited by statute or NLRB decision. If there is a failure to bargain on a mandatory topic, a charge can be brought and the NLRB can proceed with a complaint.

C O N S I D E R . . . **18.10** E. I. Du Pont de Nemours & Company is renegotiating its contract with the International Brotherhood of Du Pont Workers. Two issues have arisen during the course of bargaining. The union has asked Du Pont to release a map that was developed as a result of a Du Pont study on its toxic waste locations. The second issue was Du Pont's implementation of its business ethics policy and its application to union members without its being a subject of bargaining. Must the map be released? Is this a mandatory subject? Must the application of the ethics policy be negotiated? [*Du Pont* v. *International Bhd. of Du Pont Workers*, 301 N.L.R.B. No. 14 (1991).]

E T H I C A L   I S S U E S

18.8 During the past decade or so the effects of union strikes have changed dramatically. For example, in 1981 striking air traffic controllers were replaced permanently by other controllers. The same happened in strikes against Greyhound, Continental Airlines, Phelps Dodge, and Danly Machine. These companies were able to survive by hiring permanent replacements during union strikes. The Supreme Court has long held that employers can find permanent replacements for striking workers, but some employers have promised permanent jobs to replacements and then fired them after the strike was over. Discuss the problems with this approach. Does the "permanent replacement" rule undermine the purpose of the NLRA? Is this rule a way for employers to avoid worker pay and benefits issues? Are there practical limits, and should there be legal limits?

Union "Concerted Activities"—Economic Pressure

One of the protections given to workers under the NLRA is the right to engage in **concerted activities**. These activities include a host of economic weapons unions may use to gain bargaining power in reaching an agreement with employers. This section covers these economic weapons.

PICKETING

The term **picketing** is not defined in the NLRA, but various administrative and judicial decisions have defined it as the presence of union members outside the entrances of an employer's place of business. Picketing does have some limitations under federal law, which are discussed on page 652.

BOYCOTTS

A boycott is a refusal to work for, buy from, or handle the products of an employer. A boycott by an employee or union against an employer is a **primary boycott**. A boycott against those who deal with the employer is a **secondary boycott**. Restrictions on boycotting are discussed on page 652.

HOT CARGO AGREEMENTS

A clause in a collective bargaining agreement in which an employer agrees not to use, handle, or sell certain products, or use the services of an unfair employer is a **hot cargo agreement**. In some cases the agreement prohibits an employer from

14

handling the products of a nonunion company. Because these types of agreements are rarely voluntary, they have been prohibited with some exceptions for the clothing and construction industries.

THE SLOWDOWN

A **slowdown** is an economic tool that interrupts the employer's business but falls short of a stoppage or strike. Slowdowns usually occur when employees refuse to perform work or use certain equipment that is in violation of their collective bargaining agreement with the employer.

THE STRIKE

The strike is the best-known and most widely used economic weapon of unions. A strike is a work stoppage because employees no longer report to work. As a result of replacement threats and downsizing, strikes in 1995 are at a level one-half of that in 1985. In 1995, there were only 32 strikes involving 1,000 or more workers. Insecurity and fear about their jobs and companies' ability to continue operation during a strike have curbed the use of this economic weapon by union members.

THE SHAREHOLDERS

In recent years, unions have developed a new economic tool—contacting institutional shareholders and board members to put public pressure on corporate officers to work with unions. These public-attention tactics have been effective.

FOR THE MANAGER'S DESK

FISHY CAMPAIGN TARGETS NONUNION GROCER

Newly elected AFL-CIO President John J. Sweeney promises to use "abrasive and confrontational" tactics to reverse the devastating decline in private-sector union membership to about 10 percent today from about 30 percent in the 1950s. A strategy that is sure to become more widespread is the so-called corporate campaign, whereby unions target nonunion employers with propaganda designed to scare away customers, increase the companies' costs and prices, get them in trouble with regulators, or drive them into bankruptcy.

A good example of what companies can increasingly expect to see from unions is the continuing campaign against the nonunion Food Lion grocery chain conducted by the United Food and Commercial Workers Union (UFCW). Food Lion is attempting to compete in the Maryland, Virginia, and Washington, D.C., markets, which are currently dominated by the unionized Giant Foods, Safeway, and Magruder's chains.

The first successful element of the campaign was to persuade ABC News to air a story in 1992 that promoted the union claim that Food Lion stores routinely sold rotten meat and fish, covering up the smell by bathing the food in

Clorox. The UFCW gave an "undercover" ABC reporter minimal training and a phony letter of recommendation, after which he obtained a job at a Food Lion store.

Anyone who has ever opened a bottle of Clorox would doubt that consumers could not detect the smell if their food was bathed in it. Food Lion denies the claim and is suing ABC, arguing that much of its $174 million decline in earnings from 1992 to 1993 was due to the broadcast. Food Lion's earnings fell 55 percent in the fourth quarter of 1992; its net income declined 42 percent in the second quarter of 1993 compared with the same quarter of 1992; it closed 88 stores

Continued

in 1994 and laid off 1,300 full-time and 2,200 part-time workers.

The UFCW's next tactic was to set up a front organization, Consumers United With Employees (CUE), to fool the public into believing that the union's attacks on Food Lion were motivated by self-less, public spirited "consumer activists."

CUE's letterhead lists several unions and left-of-center political organizations, such as the National Consumers League, Consumer Federation of America, and the American Civil Liberties Union. Interestingly, a board member of the National Consumers League is Odonna Mathews, who is vice president for consumer affairs at unionized Giant Foods, and former Consumer Federation of America board member Carol Tucker Foreman is married to a UFCW vice president. CUE's phone number is the same as the Food and Allied Services Trades, an AFL-CIO subsidiary funded by the UFCW.

CUE issued a series of press releases beginning in February 1994 claiming that a "study" of Food Lion stores had "discovered" that the chain routinely sold out-dated infant formula and other products. Robert Harbrant, president of the Food and Allied Service Trades Department of the AFL-CIO, urged CUE members to "contact your Congressional representatives" and "your state and local representatives also" and "urge them to investigate this matter."

A spokesman for the Food and Drug Administration tried to calm mothers by explaining that "outdated baby formula doesn't pose a health hazard," but his explanation received little publicity. CUE was forced to admit this when questioned, but did not issue a public recantation.

When CUE was asked by reporters why it had not compared Food Lion with other grocery chains, including unionized ones, CUE spokesman Sean Cunniff pleaded poverty: "It's very difficult in terms of resources." CUE targeted stores in Virginia in its "study," but a spokeswoman for the Virginia Department of Agriculture announced that "in Virginia, Food Lion's overall compliance rate with state-inspection requirements is among the highest in the state." "The whole episode is foolish," said Bob Gordon of the North Carolina Department of Agriculture, for "any consumer can pick up a can or bottle and see the expiration date."

In my own analysis (using the same raw data that CUE used) of *all* grocery store chains in Virginia, Maryland and the District of Columbia, I found that, in each instance, Food Lion ranked first, with the least number of out-of-date products per store. In Maryland for the period March 1993 to April 1994—the period of the CUE "study"—Safeway, Giant, Magruder's and Food Lion performed virtually identically in terms of incidence of out-of-date meat, dairy or grocery products. But in the categories of distressed food, unsanitary equipment and vermin problems—data gathered by Maryland's counties—the incidence of problems per store was six times higher at Giant Foods than at Food Lion; eight times higher at Safeway, and 22 times higher at Magruder's.

Food Lion's performance was slightly more favorable than the unionized chains in Virginia and Washington, D.C., as well, but no such comparisons were even attempted in the CUE study. Apparently, CUE would have the public believe that the only problems with out-of-date grocery products are in nonunion stores.

Nonunion companies that suddenly find themselves the targets of regulatory investigations might blame their fate on corporate campaigning. An AFL-CIO organizers' manual notes that "businesses are regulated by a virtual alphabet soup of federal, state, and local agencies," and urges union organizers to "use the regulators to their advantage." If the companies are not in compliance with all relevant regulations—a virtual certainty for any business in America, given the volume of regulation—union organizers are urged to demand a regulatory crackdown on the nonunion "offenders."

AFL-CIO executives have labeled corporate campaigns the wave of the future. Corporate campaigns are designed to extort union contracts from nonunion employers without ever giving the employees a voice in the decision. With corporate campaigns, the union movement's focus is no longer on employees' rights, but on the survival of the union organization itself and, most important, the highly paid positions held by union executives.

SECONDARY BOYCOTTS

If the primary boycott is a protected economic weapon of unions, the concept of a secondary boycott is a complex and difficult one. Nonetheless, asking a third party not to handle an employer's goods appears to be unfair only if there is coercion involved. Further, the request cannot be one to stop work—it simply must be a request that the third party cease doing business with the employer.

C O N S I D E R . . . **18.11** Local 760 of the Teamsters Union called a strike against fruit packers and warehouses doing business in Yakima, Washington. The firms sold their apples to the Safeway chain of retail grocery stores. Local 760 began a consumer boycott against the firms, with union members picketing outside the 46 Safeway stores in Seattle. The pickets wore placards that read: "To the Consumer: Non-Union Washington State apples are being sold at this store. Please do not purchase such apples. Thank you. Teamsters Local 760, Yakima, Washington."

The pickets distributed handbills outside the stores and to the public generally. A typical handbill read:

DON'T BUY WASHINGTON STATE APPLES

The 1960 Crop of Washington State Apples is being Packed by Non-Union Firms. Included in this non-union operation are twenty-six firms in the Yakima Valley with which there is a labor dispute. These firms are charged with being

UNFAIR

by their employees who, with their union, are on strike and have been *replaced by non-union strikebreaking workers* employed under substandard wage scales and working conditions.

In justice to these striking union workers who are attempting to protect their living standards and their right to engage in good-faith collective bargaining, we request that you

DON'T BUY WASHINGTON STATE APPLES

Teamsters Union Local 760
Yakima, Washington

This is not a strike against any store or market.

Is the action taken by Local 760 an unfair labor practice, or is it a proper secondary boycott? [*NLRB* v. *Fruit Packers*, 377 U.S. 58 (1964).]

FEATHERBEDDING

Featherbedding is payment for work not actually performed. It is an unfair labor practice for a union to negotiate an agreement that requires an employer to pay for work that was not actually performed. For example, some bricklayers' unions at one time required payment for a minimum number of bricks even though the work might not have actually involved that many bricks. Other examples include paying workers for tasks completed by someone else. An agreement requiring payment for the task of pressing in a clothing manufacturing firm would be unfair if the clothing was sometimes shipped unpressed.

Employer Rights

FREEDOM OF SPEECH

Employers have the right to give information to employees about unions and the results of union organization. The speech of employers cannot be controlled by the NLRB unless the speech is accompanied by some unlawful conduct, such as a threat of physical force or a promise of benefit. For example, an employer who threatens the loss of jobs if employees join the union is not protected by the free speech rule. An employer who tells employees that he or she will not negotiate with a union is also not protected by the free speech rule. These types of statements are considered unfair labor practices, as is the promise of temporary benefits.

RIGHT-TO-WORK LAWS

Section 14(b) of the Taft-Hartley Act is in some ways a protection for employers as well as for employees. This section outlaws the closed shop, which, as discussed earlier, is a business that requires union membership before an employee can be hired. Based on this section of Taft-Hartley, states can pass **right-to-work laws** that give persons the right to work without having to join a union. About half the states have right-to-work statutes.

Exhibit 18.6 is a summary of management do's and don'ts when faced with an upcoming union election.

Exhibit 18.6
Management Do's and Don'ts in the Unionization Process

Do	Don't
1. Tell employees about current wages and benefits and how they compare to other firms.	1. Promise employees pay increases or promotions if they vote against the union.
2. Tell employees you will use all legal means to oppose unionization.	2. Threaten employees with termination or discriminate when disciplining employees.
3. Tell employees the disadvantages of having a union (especially cost of dues, assessments, and requirements of membership).	3. Threaten to close down or move the company if a union is voted in.
4. Show employees articles about unions and negative experiences others have had elsewhere.	4. Spy or have someone spy on union meetings.
5. Explain the unionization process to your employees accurately.	5. Make a speech to employees or groups at work within twenty-four hours of the election (before that, it is allowed).
6. Forbid distribution of union literature during work hours in work areas.	6. Ask employees how they plan to vote or if they have signed authorization cards.
7. Enforce in a consistent and fair manner disciplinary policies and rules.	7. Urge local employees to persuade others to vote against the union (such a vote must be initiated solely by the employee).

RIGHT TO AN ENFORCEABLE COLLECTIVE BARGAINING AGREEMENT

Once a union is certified and agrees to the terms of a collective bargaining agreement, an employer has the right to expect that the terms of that agreement will be honored. So long as the employer abides by its terms, the union and other employees cannot stage a strike during the period of its effectiveness. Neither can the agreement be abandoned by employees during this period.

Economic Weapons of Employers

Employers have economic weapons that can be used in response to employee economic weapons.

PLANT AND BUSINESS CLOSINGS

In response to union certifications and strikes, some employers have opted to close the affected plants. In some cases, employers have abandoned the business altogether. It is clear that these shutdowns and closures are strong economic weapons, and their legality under the federal labor law scheme has some restrictions. In *Textile Workers Union* v. *Darlington Manufacturing Co.*, 380 U.S. 263 (1965), the Supreme Court ruled that an employer has the right to terminate his or her entire business for any reason. If the reason for the closing is vindictiveness toward the union, neither the NLRB nor the courts can require an employer to stay in business. However, the closing of part of a business (such as a particular plant or one store) is subject to review as a possible unfair labor practice.

Employers cannot use a temporary closing with a promise of reopening after a union is defeated in an election. Further, employers cannot stage a **runaway shop**, which is when work is transferred to another plant or a new plant is opened to carry the workload of the old plant.

The concern of the NLRB in the closing of one plant is that employees in other plants, fearful that their plant will be closed, will fail to exercise their rights to unionize. For a plant closure to be an unfair labor practice, the evidence must show that the closure was done with the intent of curbing unionization in that and other plants owned by the employer. The "purpose and effect" of the closing must have been foreclosure of union activity.

Although the NLRB and courts have recognized the legitimate right of a business to close a particular store or plant, there are many concerns about plant closings. Plant-closing legislation has been proposed since the early 1970s, and Congress, some states, and even some cities have enacted such legislation. The purpose of plant-closing legislation is to take the sting out of an employer's closing of a plant by a variety of mechanisms, such as requiring that employees and community and state officials be given 30 days' notice of the closing, requiring employee severance packages to provide for employees during the time they need to find other employment, or requiring the employer to be partially responsible for the workers' unemployment compensation.

Federal plant-closing legislation is called the **Worker Adjustment and Retraining Notification Act of 1988**. Under this act, employers with one hundred or more workers are required to give workers 60 days' advance notice of plant

http://
Review the Worker Adjustment and Retraining Notification Act:
http://www.law.
cornell.edu/uscode/
29/2101.html

shutdowns that would affect at least 50 workers and of layoffs that would last more than six months and affect one-third of the workers at the site. There are some exceptions to the 60-day notice requirement, such as unforeseeable circumstances and seasonal, agricultural, and construction businesses. Penalties for violations include back pay and benefits for employees for each day of violation and up to $500 per day for each day notice was not given.

E T H I C A L   I S S U E S

18.9 Bleeding from losses of $4.45 billion for 1991, General Motors Corporation (GM) announced on February 24, 1992, that it would close 21 plants over the next few years and named 12 plants it would close in 1992, affecting over 16,300 workers.

GM is the nation's largest manufacturer, and the $4.45 billion loss was the largest ever in U.S. corporate history. Robert C. Stempel, GM's then-chairman, said the United States was in an unusually deep automotive slump: "The rate of change during the past year was unprecedented. And no one was immune to the extraordinary events which affected our lives and the way in which we do business."[1]

More than 3,400 workers at GM's North Tarrytown, New York, plant were laid off by 1995. The Tarrytown plant manufactured GM's minivans: the Chevrolet Lumina, the Pontiac Trans Sport, and the Oldsmobile Silhouette. The minivan, originally designed in the United States, was executed by GM with a wide stance and a sloping, futuristic nose. Projections were that 150,000–200,000 of the vans would be sold annually. Instead, sales reached only 100,000 per year, which represented one-half of the Tarrytown plant's capacity. Dealers maintained that the shape of the van was too avant-garde for significant sales. "It looks like a Dustbuster," noted a GM manager anonymously.[2]

GM executives acknowledged that building one model per plant was a sloppy and expensive way to do business.

Tarrytown United Auto Workers had negotiated with GM in 1987 to get the minivan plant. The union members voted for innovative and cooperative work rules to replace expensive union practices. Also, state and local governments contributed job training funds, gave tax breaks, and began reconstruction of railroad bridges to win the minivan production plant.

When unions (workers) and governments make payments in exchange for promises from a manufacturer to locate a plant in a particular area, should the plant owner have an obligation to continue operations? Did GM just make a business decision to stop losses? Should workers and governments absorb business risks such as a poor-selling minivan?

Some businesses voluntarily provide for the workers at a closed plant by giving them hiring priority at their other plant locations, but unions often argue that the ability to close a plant gives employers too much power at the bargaining table and that employers can coerce communities into giving them special tax treatment or additional services by threatening to close a facility. On the other hand, employers often argue that plant-closing laws unfairly restrict their ability to manage their resources and can force a business to continue operating an unprofitable unit rather than face the costs of closing.

Methuen, Massachusetts, is a small city not unlike the Bedford Falls of *It's a Wonderful Life*. Over the years, the working-class town on the border of New Hampshire and Massachusetts has come to rely on the good heart of one man. While Aaron Feuerstein may not look much like Jimmy Stewart, he is the protagonist of a Christmas story every bit as warming as the Frank Capra movie—or the Polartec fabric made at his Malden Mills.

On the night of December 11, just as Feuerstein was being thrown a surprise 70th birthday party, a boiler at Malden Mills exploded setting off a fire that injured 27 people and destroyed three of the factory's century-old buildings. Because Malden Mills employs 2,400 people in an economically depressed area, the news was as devastating as the fire. According to Paul Coorey, the president of Local 311 of the Union of Needletrades, Industrial and Textile Employees, "I was standing there seeing the mill burn with my son, who also works there, and he looked at me and said, 'Dad, we just lost our jobs.' Years of our lives seemed gone."

When Feuerstein arrived to assess the damage to a business his grandfather had started 90 years ago, he kept himself from crying by thinking back to the passage from

Aaron Feuerstein

King Lear in which Lear promises not to weep even though his heart would "break into a thousand flaws." "I was telling myself I have to be creative," Feuerstein later told the *New York Times*. "Maybe there's some way to get out of it." Feuerstein, who reads from both his beloved Shakespeare and the Talmund almost every night, has never been one to run away. When many other textile manufacturers in New England fled to the South and to foreign countries, Malden Mills stayed put. When a reliance on fake fur bankrupted the company for a brief period in the early '80s, Feuerstein sought out alternatives.

What brought Malden Mills out of bankruptcy was its research-and-development team, which came up with a revolutionary fabric that was extremely warm, extremely light, quick to dry and easy to dye. Polartec is also ecologically correct because it is made from recycled plastic bottles. Clothing made with Polartec or a fraternal brand name, Synchilla, is sold by such major outdoor clothiers as L.L. Bean, Patagonia,

Eastern Mountain Sports and Eddie Bauer, and it accounts for half of Malden's $400 million-plus in 1995 sales.

Even though the stock of a rival textile manufacturer in Tennessee, the Dyersburg Corp., rose sharply the day after the fire, L.L. Bean and many of Malden's other customers pledged their support. Another apparel company, Dakotah, sent Feuerstein a $30,000 check. The Bank of Boston sent $50,000, the union $100,000, the Chamber of Commerce in the surrounding Merrimack Valley $150,000. "The money is not for Malden Mills," says Feuerstein. "It is for the Malden Mills employees. It makes me feel wonderful. I have hundreds of letters at home from ordinary people, beautiful letters with dollars bills, $10 bills."

The money was nothing to the workers compared to what Feuerstein gave them three days later. On the night of December 14, more than 1,000 employees gathered at the gym of Central Catholic High School to learn the fate of their jobs. Feuerstein entered the gym from the back, and as he shook the snow off his coat, the murmurs turned to cheers. The factory owner, who had already given out $275 Christmas bonuses and pledged to rebuild, walked to the podium. "I will get right to my announcement," he said. "For the next 30 days—and it might be more—all our employees will be paid their full salaries." What followed, after a moment of awe, was a scene of hugging and cheering that would have trumped the cinematic celebration for *Wonderful Life's* George Bailey.

True to his word, Feuerstein has continued to pay his employees in full, at a cost of some $1.5 million a week and at an average of $12.50 an hour—already one of the highest textile wages in the world. "I really haven't done anything," says Feuerstein. "I don't deserve credit. Corporate America has made it so that when you behave the way I did, it's abnormal."

Source: Steve Wulf, "The Glow From a Fire," *Time,* January 8, 1996, p. 49. © 1996 Time Inc. Reprinted by permission.

Issues

1. Why did Mr. Feuerstein choose to continue paying his employees?
2. How has his company survived when his wages are the highest in the world?

NOTE: On January 29, 1996, Mr. Feuerstein extended the pay guarantee for another 30 days as he continued the process of rebuilding the plant. He continued the employees' medical benefits for 90 days.

PLANT FLIGHT

One result of the increased globalization of business is the increasing availability of lower-cost labor pools outside the United States. When union demands increase business costs beyond what management feels will allow a firm to remain competitive, plants are closed and work is transferred to plants outside the United States. The global marketplace provides management with a bargaining tool that becomes difficult for unions to address. Demands for wage increases, more benefits, and better working conditions are often met with a plant closing in the United States and a plant opening in another country where the labor pool is large and the wages very small.

THE LOCKOUT

A **lockout** is an employer's economic weapon in which the employer refuses to allow employees to work. Lockouts have been recognized by the U.S. Supreme Court as a legitimate measure to help an employer avoid a strike at an economically damaging time. The reason for an employer's lockout must be economic. A lockout to discourage union membership, therefore, is an unfair labor practice.

CONFERRING BENEFITS

Employers can use benefits as economic weapons; the only restriction is the timing of those benefits. Offering them too close to an election can be an unfair labor practice. Conferring benefits on a temporary basis to gain an advantage (precluding the union) is also an unfair labor practice.

BANKRUPTCY

Bankruptcy has become a solution for many business problems, labor problems among them. When strikes extend for long periods of time, the financial well-being of the firms affected can deteriorate, often to the degree that some firms declare bankruptcy. The type of bankruptcy proceedings that are initiated will determine the fate of labor contracts. In a reorganization, the contracts remain in force. In a straight bankruptcy, the workers stand in line (although with some priority) to collect any wages due and any contributions made to the firm's retirement plan. Bankruptcy can be an escape for a firm, but the bankruptcy laws themselves limit the availability of this economic weapon. The firm must still meet the tests for declaring bankruptcy, so the weapon is not entirely optional.

Exhibit 18.7 (pg. 659) provides a summary of labor weapons, rights, and unfair practices.

C O N S I D E R . . . **18.12** Ideal Macaroni Company required all line employees to wear a smock with buttons to cover their street clothes. The dress code required the smocks to be fully buttoned, but the rule had not been enforced.

Ideal employees were attempting to organize a union, and during this period some employees began wearing union T-shirts. Supervisors were requiring these employees to comply with the dress code and button their smocks. Does this selective enforcement interfere with the employees' unionization rights? [*Ideal Macaroni Co.* v. *Teamsters Local No. 8-CA-19186* (1991) 407,301 NLRB No. 73.]

Economic weapons	Rights	Unfair labor practices

Employer
1. Business closing
    Plant closings
2. Lockouts
3. Right to confer benefits
    (timing)
	1. Freedom of speech
	2. Demand election (30%)
		1. Refusal to bargain in good faith
		2. Refusal to bargain on a mandatory issue
		3. Yellow-dog contracts
		4. Violation of collective bargaining agreement
		5. Interference with joining union
		6. Timing of benefits
		7. Observation of union activities
		8. Domination of labor union
		9. Discrimination in promotion of union members
		10. Blacklisting

Employee 1. Strike 2. Slowdown, refusals to work overtime 3. Picketing 4. Secondary boycotts	1. Freedom of speech 2. Right to union representation upon investigation 3. Right to join union 4. Right of members to adequate representation 5. Right to union office	1. Violation of collective bargaining agreement 2. Secondary boycotts 3. Payment for union cards 4. Coercion or discrimination in union membership 5. Causing an employer to pay excessive wages — featherbedding 6. Hot cargo agreements

Exhibit 18.7
Union Disputes—Economic Weapons and Rights of Employers and Employees

FOR THE MANAGER'S DESK

BASEBALL CAN THROW A FAST ECONOMIC WEAPON

In 1912, Ty Cobb climbed into the stands during a game to hit a fan. The American League suspended Mr. Cobb, and the Detroit Tigers staged the first baseball strike. The Tigers refused to play their game with the Philadelphia Athletics, but Connie Mack, the Athletics' manager, helped the Tigers avoid their $500 fine for a no-show by creating a Detroit Tigers team that consisted of coaches, sandlot players and a Roman Catholic priest. The "Tigers" lost 24–2.

A threatened 1947 strike by the St. Louis Cardinals was based on the team's refusal to play the Brooklyn Dodgers because the Dodgers had signed Jackie Robinson, a black player. Ford Trick, the National League president, threatened to suspend all players who refused to show

Continued

up for the game. The Cardinals played the Dodgers.

A pension dispute in 1972 resulted in a 13-day strike that year which resulted in the cancellation of the first 86 games of the 1972 season.

In 1980, there was an 8-day strike during preseason play that resulted in the cancellation of the last 82 games of the pre-season.

The players returned for the 1980 season with several issues still being negotiated. When an agreement could not be reached, a strike began on June 3, 1981. There was a two-month strike that saw 580 games canceled.

The club owners locked out the players in 1976 and 1990 over salary issues. On March 18, 1990, a 32-day lockout was settled but spring training was delayed.

In 1994, the season began as negotiations dragged on. By August 12, 1994, no agreement was reached, and the players began a strike. After 34 days, the season was officially canceled. It was the first time since 1871 a season ended without a World Series.

President Clinton used the Taft-Hartley Act to mediate, but was unsuccessful, and he could not establish that the baseball strike endangered national health or safety.

On March 31, 1995, via court order, the strike was settled. Opening day was postponed from April 2, 1995 to April 26, 1995. It was a 7 1/2 month strike.

Issues

1. The average annual compensation for a major league baseball player is in excess of $1 million. Is the union here too powerful?
2. Consider the following quote:

The trade-off for the union's agreeing that management retain some form of the reserve clause has been

players' demands for higher pay and a veritable endless rise in salaries, the average annual compensation being in excess of $1 million. This geometric increase in players' pay had likely tilted the balance of power in their favor until this most recent dispute. The owners' resolve during the 1994–95 stoppage, the longest in sports' history, may have eroded this union stronghold so that neither party is now dominant.

The culmination of this labor battle in the business which baseball has become is still undecided at least with respect to the impact of the work stoppage upon public interest. It may well be that the interest and zeal of the fans who constitute the sport's customers has decreased in direct proportion to the increase in the perceived greed of the principals involved. Such persistent disregard of a business's consumers is surely not a cardinal rule of good business practices, nor a recommendation of how to run a commercial concern profitably.

Did the union hurt the players, the business, and the sport?

Source: Carol Daugherty Rasnic, "When Labor Balked and Management Clutched: Legal Issues Surrounding the 1994–95 Major League Baseball Strike," 28 *Business Law Review* 85 (1995). Reprinted with permission.

NEW DIRECTIONS IN LABOR LAW—
THE INTERNATIONAL THREAT

Today's labor market is considerably different from the market that existed at the time of the enactment of federal labor legislation. Today's management is also different from the management in power at the time the labor laws were passed. From true adversaries always looking for a way to "win," labor and management

```
 ┌─────────────────────────────────────────────────────────────┐
 │   E T H I C A L          I S S U E S                         │
 └─────────────────────────────────────────────────────────────┘
```

18.10 In 1982, Gilmore Steel, located in Oregon, was a company suffering losses. Management tried to get concessions from the union for pay reductions, and a year-long strike resulted. Gilmore hired replacement workers and then developed a plan for a management-led buyout. The Employee Share Ownership Plan offered the newly hired employees 100 percent ownership in what would become Oregon Steel. Top management in the firm would own less than 5 percent, and employees as shareholders would receive 20 percent of the company's pretax earnings in profit sharing. Management perks and time clocks were eliminated, and shop-floor workers were placed on the same compensation system as the top executives.

The initial years were tough; it looked like the buyout was a failure. By 1988 the company had gone public. The employees' shares that were once worth only pennies climbed to $38 a share. Oregon Steel's profits per ton are now the best in the industry. It has no debt, and productivity is double the steel industry average. Average pay for workers is $50,000, which is 25 percent above the industry average, and many of the employees are millionaires.

Did the union do the right thing with the strike? Are employees better off without union representation? What if the gamble the employees took had not worked?

Review the Labor Management Cooperation Act: http://www.law.cornell.edu/uscode/29/171.html

have grown to realize the importance of a working relationship that seeks to avoid confrontation and the use of economic weapons. In 1978, Congress passed the **Labor Management Cooperation Act** (29 U.S.C. § 171), which was designed to use the Federal Mediation and Conciliation Service (set up in 1947) to encourage alternative solutions to labor disputes. The act allocated funds for the study of ways to increase communication and encourage the use of collective bargaining as a means for resolving disputes.

Companies today are using more conciliatory methods to balance the economic interests of management and labor. Labor law is moving from the strike to arbitration in advance of disputes.

Solutions to labor issues have been occurring outside the statutory protections and rights given in the massive union legislation of earlier decades. Employees have turned to an individual posture and have sought the protection of individual rights, such as employment at will (see Chapter 17 for a discussion of these individual rights).

Many employers have reorganized their companies around teams of employees to empower them and use their knowledge and ideas. Motorola and Ford are among team companies that let workers make key decisions. A concern raised by unions is that the mixing of labor and management violates the Wagner Act. For example, teams of workers at Electromation, Inc., in Elkhart, Indiana, determined that a wage hike should be skipped because of heavy losses and instead developed programs for absenteeism.

The global marketplace is taking its toll on unions, particularly those for unskilled laborers. The percentage of union members for wage earners in private, nonagricultural industries is down from 17 percent in 1983 to 12 percent in 1991.

Foreign competition has made it difficult for unions to organize and for laborers to command more than minimum wage. Mexican laborers earn 70 cents an hour, and Chinese workers 8 cents. During the 1980s, 500,000 of the 1.2 million U.S. manufacturing jobs that were sent abroad were apparel and textile jobs.

St. John's Knits—Made in the U.S.A.

Marie St. John, a Los Angeles model, purchased a knitting loom and made her own clothes; soon friends asked her to make her trademark knit skirts and short-sleeved tops for them. Miss. St. John's fiancé, Robert Gray, a salesman, marketed the clothes and in 1962 the company earned $18,500 on sales of $92,000.

Mr. Gray and Miss St. John decided to sell only four lines each year with 20 items in each line. Their slow growth allowed them to avoid a public offering. Sales in 1969 were $1 million and $10 million by 1980.

Mr. Gray and Miss St. John also decided to manufacture only in the United States:

- Only U.S. workers and U.S. factories are used in production.
- The wool for the clothing comes from Australia but is twisted to yarn in California.
- All buttons and buckles for its clothing are made in the United States.
- All accessories, including bracelets, earrings, and necklaces are made in the United States.
- Company employees handle nearly 100 percent of all company production.

St. John knits cost $1,300 for a suit and $800 for pants. Sales for 1994 were $128 million with profits of $15 million. Earnings for 1995 were $160 million with $19 million profit.

Issues

1. Is St. John losing to the competition because it refused to use cheap international labor?
2. Is it ethical to ship production overseas?
3. How has the non-shipment of work overseas affected price?
4. Compare St. John's policies with those of Jessica McClintock, who designs and produces Victorian "romance-like" bridal and party dresses. McClintock dresses are sewn under a subcontractor arrangement in factories that are referred to as Asian sweatshops, located primarily in the San Francisco area. The sweatshops pay by the piece so that the unskilled and elderly, who must proceed slowly, have a difficult time earning minimum wage. McClintock is engaged in a very public battle that involves full-page newspaper ads with the group, Asian Immigrant Women Advocates (AIWA). AIWA's ad in the *New York Times* began "Let them Eat Lace." Does St. John's approach, although more costly, constitute a good business decision?

*Review the
International
Covenant on
Economic, Social, and
Cultural Rights:*
http://www.umn.
edu/humanrts/
instree/b2esc.htm
*Visit the International
Labor Organization:*
http://gatekeeper.
unicc.org/ilo/

The United Nations Commission on Human Rights has developed the International Covenant on Economic, Social and Cultural Rights. This covenant includes the right to work; join trade unions; enjoy leisure; earn a decent living; and receive education, medical care, and social security. Although this international covenant would carry with it the protections outlined in this chapter for U.S. workers, there is no enforcement of the covenant. Its real strength comes through documentation and disclosure of its violation.

One of the most successful organs of the United Nations is the International Labor Organization (ILO). This commission, founded in 1920, continues to work to develop such principles as the right to work, to join trade unions, and to have a safe work environment. Member nations submit reports on their nation's status and compliance with the standards of the ILO agreement.

Some nations have individual legislation for their workers. For example, Germany has its own OSHA-like agency for the administration of worker safety issues. Germany's agency has existed longer than OSHA and tends to experience more self-reporting by employers.

E T H I C A L   I S S U E S

18.11 One garment manufacturer notes that he could start a factory in China, where workers would work 15-hour days, 6 days a week, for $29 a month. What ethical dilemmas are presented by this opportunity?

FOR THE MANAGER'S DESK

U.S. SWEATSHOPS

Look Who's Sweating Now

After federal agents raided an El Monte (Calif.) sweatshop last August that had enslaved 72 Thai immigrants, Labor Secretary Robert B. Reich wasted no time. He ran straight to the media with the names of several large retailers whose names had been found on boxes in the dingy shop. Angry and embarrassed, Sears, Montgomery Ward, and Dayton Hudson agreed to meet Reich in New York

in mid-September to discuss ways to combat the use of sweatshops. Even though the chains aren't liable if they unknowingly sell illegally made goods, they promised to adopt a statement of principles calling on their suppliers to adhere to federal labor laws. Retailers fervently hoped that this would end the public-relations debacle and get that pesky Reich off their backs.

No such luck. In recent weeks, Reich has drawn up plans for a media blitz against retailers. His aim: to get

stores to crack down on sweatshops by policing the 20,000 tiny U.S. garment makers that supply the half of the country's clothing that isn't imported. He fired the latest broadside during an Oct. 2 appearance on *The Phil Donahue Show*, where he showed a videotape of the Thai workers who had been held behind barbed wire and paid less than $1 an hour. The largely blue-collar audience cheered when one of them said: "Nobody can live on even $4 and change an hour. We're all being exploited."

Continued

Reich isn't stopping there. He's planning more sweatshop raids and promises to name more stores that sell sweatshop-made goods in a full-scale campaign beginning the week after Thanksgiving. That's the start of the four-week Christmas buying season, when stores rake in 20% of their annual sales. Although it's unclear just how responsive consumers will be, "Reich could hurt the industry," warns Robert C. Blattberg, director of the Center for Retail Management at Northwestern University. Even "a small percentage change in sales can mean a big change in profits."

There's not much doubt that garment sweatshops, once considered a turn-of-the-century problem, have resurfaced in a big way under the pressures of a global economy. It's partly because of the way the apparel industry works. At the top, large retailers sell clothes to the public and negotiate prices with large manufacturers. The manufacturers, from Guess jeans to Ralph Lauren, design garments and rely on some 20,000 subcontractors to sew the clothes. While the industry employs 800,000 people in the U.S., most shops are tiny, with 5 to 50 workers, and they go in and out of business at the drop of a pin. The workforce: mostly female immigrants from Latin America and Asia who earn an average of $7.34 an hour—just over the federal poverty level.

The apparel industry has been under fierce pressure from imports in the past 20 years, largely because the work is so labor-intensive. The com-

petition has held down wages in the U.S. and fostered the spread of sweatshops. A 1989 report by the General Accounting Office found that some two-thirds of the 7,000 garment shops in New York City were sweatshops. Last year, a Labor Dept. spot check of 69 garment shops in Southern California found a stunning 93% had health and safety violations.

BUYING POWER
The Labor Dept. has had a tough time keeping up. Cutbacks under Presidents Reagan and Bush slashed the number of investigators to 816 from 970 in 1989. And congressional Republicans' current budget-cutting efforts have targeted an additional 12% reduction for investigators, who must police all 6.5 million employers covered by federal labor laws.

Now Reich wants the retail industry to take up the enforcement slack. Last year, he mounted a series of raids against garment manufacturers, invoking a little-used 50-year-old law to hold them liable for their suppliers' illegal actions. The law doesn't cover retailers, however.

So the Labor Secretary is turning to public pressure. His goal is to get retailers to use their immense buying power to make sure that subcontractors comply with labor laws. Mainly, he wants them to mount spot checks of their own. Retailers should hire inspectors to visit shops randomly and without warning, he says. "We need to enlist retailers as adjunct policemen," says Reich. "At a time when business says to government, 'Get off our back. We can do

it ourselves,' we're giving them the opportunity."

The retailers say such demands are unfair. The logistics would be enormous, for one thing. A large department store such as Sears, Roebuck & Co. has up to 10,000 direct suppliers, which in turn farm work out to even more subcontractors. Nor do stores have the expertise to detect violations in the government's "very complex" wage and hour laws, says the general counsel at one large retailer. "We can go into a location, but that doesn't mean we would know what we're looking for," he says.

Just making the connections between supplier and retailer isn't always easy. Sears and Mervyn's, a division of Minneapolis-based Dayton Hudson Corp., which were identified as receiving goods from the El Monte shop, still haven't been able to confirm the charge after two months of investigating. Montgomery Ward did confirm a connection and has filed a federal lawsuit against its supplier, New Boys Inc., which subcontracted with El Monte.

Retailers also argue that their contracts don't say anything about spot checks. "We don't have the legal authority or the manpower to do that," says Tracy Mullin, director of the National Retail federation, a trade group. "The Labor Dept. is trying to get us to do their work for them."

LEVERAGE
Reich retorts that retailers are just ducking the issue. They can afford to hire a few inspectors with labor law expertise, he says. The giant companies also have plenty
Continued

of leverage to force both manufacturers and minuscule shops to accept new contracts allowing random spot checks. And while the task may be daunting, any added enforcement is better than doing nothing as the Labor Dept.'s resources dwindle.

Still, it's possible that Reich's campaign won't move price-conscious consumers,

says Northwestern marketing professor Mohanbir Sawhney. After all, union campaigns against companies that make sweatshop goods here and abroad have had relatively little impact.

But image-sensitive retailers may not want to run the risk. They're suffering through a fourth tough year of lackluster apparel sales

and need a home run at year-end. "We didn't know" isn't much of a rallying cry, concedes Robert L. Mettler, Sears' president of apparel, who wants fellow retailers to find ways to address the issue. Retailers aren't directly responsible for sweatshops. But if Reich has his way, they'll have a lot more responsibility in the future.

Source: Bill Vlasic, Kathleen Kerwin, Keith Naughton, David Woodruff, "Look Who's Sweating Now," *Business Week*, Oct. 16, 1995, p. 96. Reprinted from the Oct. 16, 1995 issue of *Business Week* by special permission, copyright © 1995 by The McGraw-Hill Companies.

CONSIDER... **18.13** Monroe Manufacturing is a producer of baby bottles, bibs, pacifiers, and infant clothes. Workers are paid $4.25 an hour, and unions have tried to organize the plant several times. Each time an organizational effort is made, Edward Hakim, the president of Monroe, reminds the employees of foreign competition: "Listen, if I can't compete in America with American workers, I'll take your jobs overseas where we can be competitive."

Do Mr. Hakim's statements constitute an unfair labor practice?

SUMMARY

What wage and hour protections exist for employees?
- Fair Labor Standards Act—federal law that regulates minimum wage and overtime pay
- Minimum wage—federal minimum hourly rate of pay
- Overtime pay—rate of $1^1/_2$ times the hourly rate for hours over 40-per-week worked
- Equal Pay Act—equal wages for equal work regardless of gender
- Child labor standards—restrictions on hours and types of work for children under the age of 18

What protections exist for safety in the workplace?
- Occupational Safety and Health Act—federal law setting and enforcing workplace safety standards
- Occupational Safety and Health Administration—federal agency responsible for safety in the workplace
- Drug testing—screening of employees for impairment

What happens when a worker is injured in the workplace?

- Workers' compensation—state-by-state system of employer strict liability for injuries of workers on the job; the few exceptions to recovery include self-inflicted injuries

What is the Social Security system and what benefits does it provide?

- Social Security Act—federal law establishing disability, beneficiary, and retirement benefits
- Federal Insurance Contributions Act (FICA)—statute establishing system for withholding contributions for social security benefits

Are workers entitled to pensions and are they regulated?

- Employment Retirement Income Security Act (ERISA)—federal law regulating employer-sponsored pension plans
- FASB 106—accounting disclosure for a company's employee retirement obligations

What rights do unemployed workers have?

- Unemployment compensation—federal program handled by states to provide temporary support for displaced workers
- Workers' compensation—system of no-fault liability for employees injured on the job

How are labor unions formed and what is their relationship with employees?

- Railway Labor Act—first federal law providing union protections
- Norris-LaGuardia Act—federal law prohibiting injunctions to halt strikes
- National Labor Relations Act (Wagner Act)—federal law authorizing employee unionization
- Labor Management Relations Act (Taft-Hartley Act)—federal law limiting union economic weapons
- Labor-Management Reporting and Disclosure Act (Landrum-Griffin Act)—federal law regulating union membership and organizations
- NLRB—National Labor Relations Board, federal agency responsible for enforcing labor laws
- Collective bargaining unit—group of employees recognized as appropriate to have an exclusive bargaining agent
- Authorization cards—employee-signed support for election
- Certification—recognition of union as exclusive bargaining agent
- Collective bargaining agreement—exclusive rights agreement between employer and employee in a collective bargaining unit
- Good-faith bargaining—requirement that parties negotiate terms in earnest
- Unfair labor practice—conduct by labor or management prohibited by statute
- Concerted activities—union-sponsored activities
- Picketing—public appearance of striking union members
- Boycotts—refusal to work for or to buy from or handle products of an employer
- Slowdown—workers report to job but don't operate at full speed
- Right-to-work laws—right to work at a company without being required to join a union

- Worker Adjustment and Retraining Notification Act (WARN)—federal law requiring employers to give 60 days' notice of plant shutdowns
- Lockout—employer closes plant or business so workers can't work
- Runaway shop—employer transfers work to nonunion plants

QUESTIONS AND PROBLEMS

1. Ruth Saludes is a Harvard University graduate with a master's degree in linguistics and education. She had worked for several years in various counseling and teaching positions. Feeling "burned out," Ms. Saludes decided she wanted to be a carpenter and left her position at the Free Clinic of Tucson, although she had no skill or experience in construction or carpentry. She filed for unemployment compensation but refused to take counseling jobs and insisted on a carpentry job. Her unemployment was cut off when she refused to take a counseling job. Ms. Saludes brought suit. Is she entitled to compensation? [*Saludes* v. *Department of Employment Security*, 628 P.2d 63 (Ariz. 1981).]

2. H. M. Wilson hired H. J. High as the general contractor for the construction of one of its stores in a shopping center in Tampa, Florida. The shopping center was owned and operated by Edward. J. DeBartelo Corporation and had 85 tenants. The tenants paid a minimum rent plus a percentage of gross sales for maintenance of the common areas in the shopping center.

   H. J. High's workers went on strike, posted themselves at the four entrances to the shopping center, and distributed handbills to customers. The handbills asked customers not to shop at any of the 85 stores until their dispute with High was settled. Is this an unlawful secondary boycott? [*Edward J. DeBartelo Corp.* v. *NLRB*, 463 U.S. 147 (1983).]

3. Joe Ortiz was discharged from Magma Copper Co. for absenteeism. He missed the last shift of work before he was fired because he was temporarily in custody following an arrest for a criminal offense. He filed for unemployment but was denied. Mr. Ortiz said he notified Magma that he was missing because of being detained in jail. The unemployment compensation agency says Mr. Ortiz is disqualified for benefits because he was fired for misconduct. Who is right? [*Magma Copper* v. *Department of Employment Security*, 625 P.2d 935 (Ariz. 1981).]

4. Donald Thompson worked as a machine operator for Hughes Aircraft for 13 years. During that time, his skin (hands) was exposed to Wynn's 331, a coolant oil. In 1978, while working with machines and using Wynn's 331 oil, Mr. Thompson developed an active scaly eruption. He required medical attention but continued to work. The scaly eruption stopped only when Mr. Thompson was off work for medical treatment. He was certified to return to work but only if he avoided contact with Wynn's 331 oil. Hughes refused to rehire him, and Mr. Thompson filed for a permanent unscheduled disability. Does he qualify? [*Hughes Aircraft* v. *Industrial Comm'n*, 606 P.2d 819 (Ariz. 1981).]

5. Janice W. Craig was employed by Drenberg and Associates, an insurance agency. She had approximately 15 years' experience when she started to work at Drenberg in August 1974 and was initially assigned underwriting duties in the personal and commercial lines of insurance. About the time she started to work, Drenberg began a year of explosive growth. Under normal conditions, an agency with 400,000 accounts could expect to acquire approximately 40,000 new accounts in the period of a year.

Drenberg grew from 400,000 to 1,200,000 in just over one year. To keep pace with this growth, the agency's employees worked many overtime hours. Yet, in spite of their best efforts, the agency remained 30 days behind in its accounts.

Mrs. Craig was a conscientious employee and a perfectionist. In addition to her duties for personal and commercial lines, she took over a part of what is described as the commercial desk, handling correspondence, renewals, and changes. Her working conditions created an atmosphere in which she was under constant pressure.

On or about April 1, 1975, Drenberg purchased an agency from Earl Woodland, thereby acquiring 500 new accounts and an additional employee. Mrs. Craig was given responsibility for both supervising the new employee and for merging the books of the two agencies. The additional responsibility and mounting pressure began to affect her. She began to feel frustrated and ineffective. She experienced difficulty relating to her co-workers and on occasions had heated exchanges with customers. On September 25, 1975, she engaged in a particularly emotional telephone conversation with one of the agency's customers, after which she eventually left the office in tears. That night she took a slight overdose of sleeping pills. The following day she sought help at the Tri-City Mental Hospital and was subsequently admitted to Camelback Hospital, where her condition was diagnosed as neurotic depression, or a mental breakdown.

Mrs. Craig filed a claim with the Industrial Commission wherein she related facts establishing that she was suffering from a disabling mental condition brought on by the gradual buildup of the stress and strain of her employment.

In addition to Mrs. Craig's difficulties at the office, she was experiencing domestic disharmony. She and her husband argued frequently concerning his drinking habits. She encountered difficulties in relating to her daughters, and her mother's death caused additional internal pressures. It was on the evening of September 25, 1975, that the Craigs again argued, following which she took the overdose of medication. Should Mrs. Craig receive workers' compensation? [*Fireman's Fund Ins. Co.* v. *Industrial Comm'n*, 579 P.2d 555 (Ariz. 1979).]

6. Harry Connelly was an embalmer's helper. When he cut his hand during the preparation of a corpse, germs from the gangrenous corpse got into his cut, caused blood poisoning, and he eventually died. Would Mr. Connelly's survivors be entitled to workers' compensation? [*Connelly* v. *Hunt Furniture*, 147 N.E. 366 (N.Y. 1925).]

7. Beth Israel Hospital had a rule prohibiting solicitation and distribution of literature in all areas of the hospital except the employee locker rooms. The union challenged the rule as unfair because employees could not be approached in the hospital cafeteria or coffee shop. Can an employer restrict literature distribution? Is this rule too restrictive? [*Beth Israel Hosp.*v. *NLRB*, 437 U.S. 483 (1978).]

8. OSHA requires vehicles with an obstructed rear view to be equipped with a reverse signal alarm. Knight, an independent contractor working for Clarkson Construction, operated a dump truck that had no warning signal but had an obstructed rear view. If an injury resulted to a pedestrian when Mr. Knight backed onto the highway, what liability would there be? What could OSHA do? What could the pedestrian do? What effect does Mr. Knight's being an independent contractor have? If Mr. Knight were also injured, could he recover? [*Clarkson Constr. Co.* v. OSHA, 531 F.2d 451 (10th Cir. 1980).]

9. Earl Webster was a 39-year-old construction worker in good health. While shoveling sand into a wheelbarrow on a Texas road crew in 97-degree heat, he complained to fellow workers that he was sick. He stopped to have a drink of water, pushed two more wheelbarrows, lost consciousness, and was taken unconscious in the car to the company offices. He died a short time later of heat prostration. Is his spouse entitled to death benefits under workers' compensation? Would it make a difference if the water given to him to drink was bad? [*American General Ins.* v. *Webster*, 118 S.W. 2d 1082 (Tex. 1938).]

10. Suppose an employer decided to spin off a particular plant or part of its business to avoid either unionization or the recognition of a collective bargaining agreement. Would the spin-off work, or is this an unfair labor practice? [*International Union, UAW* v. *NLRB*, 470 F.2d 422 (D.C. 1972).]

NOTES

1 Doran P. Levin, "GM Picks 12 Plants to Be Shut as It Reports a Record U.S. Loss," *New York Times*, Feb. 25, 1992, p. Al.

2 Doran R. Levin, "Vehicle's Design Doomed Van Plant," *New York Times*, Feb. 26, 1992, p. C4.

Judgment

Ann Hopkins was a senior manager in the Government Services division of the Washington, D.C., office of Price Waterhouse, a national CPA firm, when she was under consideration for a partnership in 1982. Of the 662 partners in the firm at that time, 7 were women. Of the 88 proposed partners in 1982, Hopkins was the only woman. During the course of her work in the Washington office, Hopkins had secured a $25 million contract with the Department of State. One senior partner noted that "none of the other partnership candidates at Price Waterhouse that year had a comparable record in terms of successfully securing major contracts for the partnership." She was denied a partnership. Comments from evaluating senior partners included words and phrases such as: "macho"; needed a "course in charm school"; "a lady using foul language"; and needed to "walk more femininely, talk more femininely, dress more femininely, wear makeup, have her hair styled, and wear jewelry." Hopkins filed suit under Title VII alleging sex discrimination in the decision to deny her a partnership. Will Ms. Hopkins win?

CHAPTER 19

Employment discrimination has been one of the

fastest-growing

Employment Discrimination

legal issues of the

past decade. There has been a dramatic increase in the

number of suits for discrimination and reverse

discrimination and of cases in matters of unequal pay,

sexual harassment, seniority, and maternity leave.

Few employers have remained unaffected by the

impact of antidiscrimination laws and cases.

In this chapter the following questions are

answered: What laws governing employment discrimi-

nation exist? What types of discrimination exist? Are

there any defenses to discrimination? What penalties or

damages can be imposed for violations?

> *"I have a dream that one day this nation will rise up and live out the true meaning of its creed: 'We hold these truths to be self-evident; that all men are created equal.' I have a dream . . . I have a dream that my four little children will one day live in a nation where they will not be judged by the color of their skin but by the content of their character, I have a dream . . . "*
> **Dr. Martin Luther King, Jr.**
>
> *"Now our generation of Americans has been called on to continue the unending search for justice within our own borders."*
> **President Lyndon B. Johnson**
> upon signing the Civil Rights Act of 1964

HISTORY OF EMPLOYMENT DISCRIMINATION LAW

Protections against employment discrimination are strictly statutory. Common law afforded employees no protection against discrimination. Indeed, common law viewed the entire employment relationship as a private contractual matter in which there should be no judicial interference.

Notwithstanding the **Civil Rights Acts of 1866 and 1870**, the first effective antidiscrimination employment statute was a long time in coming. The first federal legislation to deal directly with the issue of discrimination was the **Equal Pay Act of 1963** (see Chapter 18 for more details). The statutory right to equality was expanded beyond the issue of pay less than a year later by **Title VII** of the **Civil Rights Act of 1964**. Title VII is the basis for discrimination law and judicial decisions in such matters. Although it has been amended many times, its basic purpose is to prohibit discrimination in employment on the basis of race, color, religion, sex, or national origin.

Title VII was first amended by the **Equal Employment Opportunity Act of 1972**. This amendment gave the act's enforcer, the **Equal Employment Opportunity Commission (EEOC)**, greater powers—for example, the right to file suits in federal district court. In 1975, Title VII was again amended with the **Pregnancy Discrimination Act**, which defined "sex" discrimination to include discrimination on the basis of pregnancy and childbirth.

Laws have also been enacted to protect against discrimination because of age or handicap. Discrimination on the basis of age was prohibited by the **Age Discrimination in Employment Act of 1967** (discussed later in this chapter). Under the **Rehabilitation Act of 1973** federal contractors are prohibited from discriminating against certain employees in performing their contracts. With the **Americans with Disabilities Act**, passed in 1990, employers of 25 or more employees (progressed to include employers of 15 or more employees in 1994) are prohibited from discriminating against employees with disabilities and are required to make reasonable accommodations for qualified employees with disabilities. In 1991, the Civil Rights Act of 1991 was passed. Although the substance of the existing antidiscrimination laws remains, this act made significant changes in procedural aspects of Title VII litigation. Exhibit 19.1 (pg. 673) provides a summary of federal antidiscrimination legislation to date.

In 1993, Congress passed the **Family and Medical Leave Act**. This new federal law provides employees with the right to take 12 weeks of leave for childbirth, adoption, or family illness.

In addition to this legislation, several executive orders that apply to administrative agencies (see Chapter 6) have been issued. These orders require federal government contractors to institute, among other things, affirmative action programs in their labor forces.

EMPLOYMENT DISCRIMINATION— TITLE VII OF THE CIVIL RIGHTS ACT

As mentioned earlier, Title VII of the Civil Rights Act of 1964 (also known as the **Fair Employment Practices Act**), as amended in 1991, prohibits discrimination in all areas of employment on the basis of race, color, religion, national origin, and sex (including pregnancy, childbirth, or abortion). Other acts prohibit discrimination based on physical disability or age.

Statute	Date	Provisions
Civil Rights Acts of 1866 and 1870 42 U.S.C. § 1981	1866 1870	Prohibited intentional discrimination based on race, color, national origin, or ethnicity; permit lawsuits
Equal Pay Act 29 U.S.C. § 206	1963	Prohibits paying workers of one sex different wages from the other when the jobs involve substantially similar skill, effort, and responsibility; Wage and Hour Division of Department of Labor enforces; private lawsuits permitted; double damage recovery for up to three years' wages plus attorney fees
Civil Rights Act of 1964 42 U.S.C. § 1981	1964	Outlaws all employment discrimination on the basis of race, color, religion, sex, or national origin; applies to hiring, pay, work conditions, promotions, discipline, and discharge; EEOC enforces; private law suits permitted; costs and attorney fees recoverable
Age Discrimination in Employment Act 42 U.S.C. § 6101	1967	Prohibits employment discrimination because of age against employees over 40 and mandatory retirement restrictions; EEOC enforces; private lawsuits permitted; attorney fees and costs recoverable
Equal Employment Opportunity Act 42 U.S.C. § 2000	1972	Expanded enforcement power of EEOC
Rehabilitation Act 29 U.S.C. § 701	1973	Prohibits employment discrimination on the basis of handicaps
Pregnancy Discrimination Act 42 U.S.C. § 2000e	1975	Prohibits discrimination on the basis of pregnancy and childbirth
Americans with Disabilities Act 42 U.S.C. § 12101	1990	Prohibits discrimination against the handicapped
Civil Rights Act of 1991 42 U.S.C. § 1981	1991	Clarifies disparate impact suit requirements; clarifies the meaning of "business necessity" and "job related"; changes some Supreme Court decisions (*Wards Cove*); punitive damage recovery
Glass Ceiling Act 42 U.S.C. § 2000e	1991	Creates commission to study barriers to women entering management and decision-making positions
Family and Medical Leave Act 29 U.S.C. § 2601	1993	Establishes 12 weeks of leave for medical or family reasons

Exhibit 19.1
Employment Discrimination Statutory Scheme

Application of Title VII

GROUPS COVERED

Title VII does not apply to all employers but is limited to the following groups:

1. Employers with at least 15 workers during each working day in each of 20 or more calendar weeks in the current or preceding year.
2. Labor unions that have 15 members or more or operate a hiring hall that refers workers to covered employers.

3. Employment agencies that procure workers for an employer who is covered by the law.
4. Any labor union or employment agency, provided it has 15 or more employees.
5. State and local agencies.

NONCOVERED EMPLOYERS

Certain employers and employment situations that are not subject to Title VII are listed below:

1. Employment of aliens outside the United States is exempt.
2. Religious corporations, associations, educational institutions, or societies are exempt when the employment of individuals of a particular religion is connected with the activities of such corporations, associations, educational institutions, or societies.
3. Congress is exempt from the Civil Rights Act of 1964 (including Title VII).
4. The federal government and corporations owned by the federal government are exempt from Title VII, but have the same prohibitions against discrimination from other statutes.
5. American Indian peoples and departments or agencies in the District of Columbia subject to the procedures of the civil service are exempt.

EMPLOYMENT PROCEDURES COVERED

Every step in the employment process is covered by Title VII. Hiring, compensation, training programs, promotion, demotion, transfer, fringe benefits, employer rules, working conditions, and dismissals are all covered. In the case of an employment agency, the system for the agency's job referrals is also covered.

THEORIES OF DISCRIMINATION UNDER TITLE VII

There are three basic, but not mutually exclusive, theories of discrimination under Title VII: **disparate treatment, disparate impact,** and **pattern or practice of discrimination**. Often, disparate treatment and disparate impact claims are combined in the same case.

Disparate Treatment

The most common form of discrimination at the time Title VII was passed was treating employees of one race or sex differently from employees of another race or sex. This different, or disparate, treatment results in unlawful discrimination when an individual is treated less favorably than other employees because of race, color, religion, national origin, or sex. The U.S. Supreme Court established the elements required to be shown to establish disparate treatment under Title VII in *McDonnell Douglas Corp.* v. *Green,* 411 U.S. 792 (1973). The case involved the rights of a black mechanic who had been laid off during a general work force reduction and then not rehired. McDonnell claimed Mr. Green was not rehired because of his participation in a lock-in at the plant to protest racial inequality. Mr. Green brought suit for a Title VII violation, and the Supreme Court established the following elements as a prima facie case for discrimination:

1. Plaintiff belongs to a racial minority.
2. Plaintiff applied for and was qualified for a job with the employee.

3. Plaintiff, despite job qualifications, was rejected.
4. After plaintiff's rejection, the job remained open and the employer continued to seek applicants.

It is the employer's burden of proof to show that there was a nondiscriminatory reason for the employment decision. That burden arises when the employee-plaintiff establishes the four elements established in *Green*. The following case deals with the issue of how much proof the defendant-employer must offer as to the reason for the employment decision.

Chescheir v. Liberty Mutual Ins. Co.
713 F.2d 1142 (5th Cir. 1983)

HOW COME HE CAN GO TO LAW SCHOOL BUT I CAN'T: THE CASE OF THE LAW STUDENT CLAIMS ADJUSTER

FACTS

Liberty Mutual Insurance Company has a rule prohibiting its adjustors and first-year supervisors from attending law school. This "law school rule" was proposed and implemented on a national basis by Edmund Carr, a vice president and general claims manager, in November 1972.

Joan Chescheir (plaintiff) was hired by Liberty Mutual's Dallas office in March 1973 as a claims adjustor. In January 1975, she voluntarily resigned but in June of that year was hired in Liberty's Houston office as a claims adjustor.

In August 1976, Wyatt Trainer, the claims manager at the Houston office, received an anonymous letter informing him that Ms. Chescheir was attending law school. After consulting with his assistants and superior, Mr. Trainer fired her after she admitted she was attending law school.

Charity O'Connell also worked in the Houston office as a claims adjustor during the same period Ms. Chescheir did. During a coffee break with a new employee, Timothy Schwirtz (also an adjustor), Ms. O'Connell relayed the story of Ms. Chescheir's firing. Mr. Schwirtz then said, "Oh, that's strange, because when I was hired, when Wells (Southwest Division claims manager) interviewed me, he told me that I could go to law school and in fact if I came down to the Houston office, there were law schools in Houston." Ms. O'Connell then went to her supervisor and told him she also was attending

law school. She refused to quit law school and was fired.

William McCarthy, Liberty's house counsel in its Houston office, attended law school while working as an adjustor and was retained as house counsel upon his graduation. The trial court found that Mr. McCarthy's supervisors were aware of his contemporaneous law school career. Alvin Dwayne White was employed as an adjustor in Liberty's Fort Worth office and asked for a transfer to Houston so he could attend law school. He was given the transfer and attended law school in Houston. James Ballard worked as an adjustor in Houston, attended law school; and was promoted to supervisor while in law school. Supervisors and employees were aware of his law school attendance, but the law school rule was not enforced against him. In short, none of the male employees known to have been attending law school was fired.

Ms. Chescheir and Ms. O'Connell both filed complaints with the EEOC, were given right of suit letters, and filed suit in federal district court. After a lengthy trial, the court found that Liberty Mutual had violated Title VII. Both women were given back pay.

JUDICIAL OPINION

GOLDBERG, Circuit Judge

Title VII applies . . . not only to the more blatant forms of discrimination, but also to subtler forms, such as discriminatory enforcement of work rules.

Continued

The four part test for demonstrating a prima facie case for discriminatory discharge due to unequal imposition of discipline [is]:

1. That plaintiff was a member of a protected group;
2. That there was a company policy or practice concerning the activity for which he or she was discharged;
3. That nonminority employees either were given the benefit of a lenient company practice or were not held to compliance with a strict company policy; and
4. That the minority employee was disciplined either without the application of a lenient policy, or in conformity with the strict one.

Of course, if an employee is unaware that a nonminority employee is in violation of company policy, the absence of discipline does not demonstrate a more lenient policy. It follows from this that if an employer applies a rule differently to people it believes are differently situated, no discriminatory intent has been shown.

The district court made multitudinous findings of subsidiary facts and concluded in a finding of ultimate fact: "The defendant applied its law school rule differently to male and female employees." The subsidiary facts detail a plethora of individual instances that each tend to suggest discrimination.

It is clear that the plaintiffs are members of a protected group and that there was a company policy or practice concerning the activity for which the plaintiffs were discharged; thus the first two elements of the test are met. It is also clear that minority employees were disciplined without the application of a lenient policy, and in conformity with a strict policy. All women known to violate the law school rule were immediately discharged. Furthermore, even potential violations of the rule by women were investigated promptly. An anonymous letter was sufficient to trigger an investigation of Chescheir, and the fact that Chescheir was attending law school moved the company to interrogate another woman.

The only remaining element of the prima facie case is a finding that male employees either were given the benefit of a lenient company practice or were not held to compliance with a strict company policy. This is the element upon which Liberty Mutual focuses its attack. Recasting Liberty Mutual's argument slightly, it claims that other males were strictly disciplined in accord with the law school rule, and that Liberty Mutual never knew that McCarthy, White, and Ballard were attending law school. Thus, claims Liberty Mutual, the third element was not met.

We are not persuaded. First, our review of the record does not disclose any males in the Southwest Division who were discharged because of the law school rule. Second, even were we to accept Liberty Mutual's contention that it did not actually know McCarthy, White, and Ballard were attending law school, we would still affirm the judgment. The operative question is merely whether Liberty Mutual applied a more liberal standard to male employees. The district court found that there were widespread rumors that McCarthy and Ballard were attending law school. Also, THE EEOC notified Liberty Mutual that a male adjustor was attending law school (Ballard) and requested an explanation. Key managerial employees, at a minimum, suspected McCarthy was attending law school but preferred not to ask and confirm their suspicions. One male adjustor was told when he was hired that he could attend law school. In contrast to Liberty Mutual's energetic investigation of women it believed might be attending law school, Liberty Mutual never investigated any of these allegations, suspicions, or rumors about male adjustors. The case of Mr. White is even more dramatic. After he expressed a desire to transfer to Houston in order to attend law school, that transfer was granted and he was never told he could not attend law school.

The preceding facts are more than enough to support the third leg [of the test]. Males at Liberty Mutual were subject to lenient enforcement of the law school rule. The district court's ultimate finding of fact that Liberty Mutual

Continued

applied its law school rule discriminatorily finds firm support in the record; all four elements of the prima facie case are present.

Once Chescheir and O'Connell established a prima facie case of discrimination, the burden shifted to Liberty Mutual to present a justification. The district court found that Liberty Mutual offered no justification. Accordingly, the judgment of the district court is affirmed.

CASE QUESTIONS
1. What employer rule is at issue?
2. How were the plaintiffs fired using the rule?
3. Had any male employees ever been fired under the rule?
4. Were there examples of disparate use of the rule?
5. Is there a prima facie case?
6. What damages were awarded?

C O N S I D E R . . . **19.1** Patricia Jackson, a black female, applied for a server position at Jackie McCleod's Gift Horse restaurant in Foley, Alabama. Ms. McCleod interviewed Ms. Jackson on a Friday afternoon and verbally agreed to hire her as a part-time server beginning Monday morning. Ms. Jackson spent two days of orientation in the kitchen (Saturday and Sunday). When she arrived for work on Monday, she was again scheduled for kitchen work. Ms. McCleod hired a white female server later that day and told Ms. Jackson she couldn't be a server. Is there discrimination? [*Jackson* v. *McCleod*, 748 F. Supp 831 (S.D. Ala. 1990).]

Disparate Impact

Many employment hiring, promoting, and firing practices are not intentionally discriminatory. In fact, the basis for such decisions may be quite rational. Even so, the effect or impact of many employment standards is to discriminate against particular races or on the basis of sex.

In one case, the Alabama prison system had a minimum height requirement of 5′2″ and a minimum weight requirement of 120 pounds for all of its "correctional counselors" (prison guards). The impact of the rule was to exclude many females and very few males [*Dothard* v. *Rawlinson*, 433 U.S. 321 (1977)]. Although the rule had a purpose other than one of discrimination, namely, making sure guards were large enough to perform their jobs, the effect of the rule was to exclude women from the job position.

Disparate impact cases do not require the four steps of proof outlined in the *Green* case. Rather, the proof required in disparate impact cases is a statistical showing of the impact of an employment practice.

In the landmark case of *Wards Cove Packing, Inc.* v. *Atonio*, 490 U.S. 642 (1989), the Supreme Court established standards for employer liability in cases in which there was no intentionally discriminating act or policy (as in the *Liberty Mutual* case). The Court held that the plaintiff always had the burden of showing the impact. The plaintiff was required to show which employment practice had a disparate or disproportionate impact and then demonstrate that the employment practice was actually responsible for the disparate impact. The Court also allowed businesses to demonstrate a business justification; the plaintiff then had to disprove that justification or show a means of accomplishing the business goals through some other means.

The 1991 amendments to the Civil Rights Act changed the *Wards Cove* ruling. All a plaintiff need establish is that a practice or practices have a disparate impact on a protected class. The burden then shifts to the employer to show "business necessity" for the practice. The employer must show that the practice is "job related for the position in question and consistent with business necessity." Many viewed this as the law prior to the *Wards Cove* decision.

The ruling in *Wards Cove* that statistical comparisons must be made between qualified minorities in the labor market and the persons holding the jobs in question is appropriate and still stands. The 1991 Act did not change that ruling in the case. Disparate impact cases thus cannot be based on an analysis of only the demographics of the labor market; the proper comparison is between the skilled labor force (as defined by the position in question) and those actually holding the position.

Also, the 1991 amendments require the plaintiff to show causation between the practice of the employer and the disparate impact. For example, in one case that immediately preceded the 1991 amendments, the Seventh Circuit found that a company's low percentage of blacks in its workforce was due to its location in a Hispanic neighborhood and not because of its practice of hiring by word of mouth. [*EEOC* v. *Chicago Miniature Lamp Works,* 1991 947 F. 2d 292 (7th Cir. 1991).]

Review the 1991 amendments to the Civil Rights Act: http://www.law. cornell.edu/uscode/ 42/1981.html

Pattern or Practice of Discrimination

The "pattern or practice" theory does not involve discrimination against one person but rather against a group or class of persons (for example, women or blacks). Generally, a party bringing suit seeks to show that a particular minority group is underrepresented in an employer's workforce as compared with that group's representation in the population base. Circumstantial evidence and statistics are used to establish a pattern or practice of discrimination. For example, percentages are often compared. An employer's workforce may consist of 6 percent blacks, whereas the city's population consists of 30 percent blacks.

The standards for establishing a pattern or practice of discrimination are affected by the 1991 amendments to the Civil Rights Act; the burdens of proof are those discussed under disparate impact, with a "reasonable justification" defense for employers. In pattern or practice cases, the initial burden of proof of discrimination is upon the plaintiff or the EEOC.

CONSIDER... **19.2** Local 28 of the Sheet Metal Workers' Union had excluded blacks from its membership prior to 1964. In 1964, the New York State Commission for Human Rights ordered the exclusion stopped on the basis of its finding that the union had never had a black member. Local 28 then ceased taking new members into the union or apprenticeship program. Was there a pattern or practice of discrimination? Has the union continued that pattern or practice with its nonmembership policy? [*Local 28* v. *EEOC,* 478 U.S. 42 (1986).]

E T H I C A L   I S S U E S

19.1 Consider the following circumstances and decide whether there has been a violation of Title VII.

1. An employee must be dismissed. There are two women, one white and the other black, who have been with a company for the same amount of time and who have the same rate of absenteeism. Their performance evaluations are about the same. Can the black employee be dismissed without violating Title VII?

2. Company B has had a significant problem with absenteeism, tardiness, and failure to follow through on job assignments among the employees who are of a certain race. The personnel director is concerned about company productivity, the costs of training, and the costs of constant turnover. The personnel director is also aware of the constraints of Title VII. The director instructs those staffing the front office to tell members of that particular race who apply for a job that the company is not accepting applications. The director's theory is that his applicant pool will be prescreened and he will not have to make discriminatory hiring decisions. Is the director correct?

SPECIFIC APPLICATIONS OF TITLE VII

The various theories of Title VII discrimination apply to specific types of discrimination. The following sections cover these types of discrimination and Title VII's application to them.

Sex Discrimination

Although Title VII included sex discrimination in its prohibitions, its presence and effects were not as obviously in existence as the more blatant racial discrimination. Many of the initial discrimination suits were brought in response to "protective legislation," which consisted of state statutes that prohibited women from working in certain fields and occupations for safety reasons. The reasons for such prohibitions were that the jobs were too strenuous, too dangerous, or too stressful. Because the effect of the statutes was to keep women from certain higher-paying occupations and men from certain female-dominated jobs, the EEOC issued guidelines providing that employers guilty of discrimination could not use these statutory cloaks. As a result, in *Dothard* v. *Rawlinson*, 433 U.S. 321 (1977), the Supreme Court held that an Alabama Board of Corrections administrative regulation establishing minimum height and weight requirements was violative of Title VII.

A prima facie case of sex discrimination by an employer requires proof of the same elements established in the *Green* case. The only difference is that the issue of rejection, firing, or demotion is based on sex rather than race.

Other more subtle hints of discrimination have slowly been eliminated from every area of employment. Even job listings in classified ads cannot carry any sexual preference. For example, an employer cannot advertise for just a "waitress"; the ad must be for a "waiter/waitress." Further, state laws and company policies that prohibit women from working during certain hours if they have school-age children are violations of Title VII.

The issue of sex discrimination has flourished in the blue-collar setting, but the *Price Waterhouse* v. *Hopkins* decision in a sex discrimination suit filed by an accountant against a CPA firm indicates the professional world is not exempt from Title VII and provides a result for the chapter's opening "Judgment."

Judgment

Price Waterhouse v. Hopkins
490 U.S. 228 (1989)

THE LESS-THAN-CHARMING ACCOUNTANT: CAN SHE BE A PARTNER?

FACTS

Ann Hopkins (respondent) had worked at Price Waterhouse's (petitioner) Office of Government Services in Washington, D.C., for five years when the partners in that office began to consider her as a candidate for partnership in 1982. At that time, there were 662 partners in the firm; 7 were women. Of the 88 candidates for partner in 1982, Ms. Hopkins was the only woman. Forty-seven of the candidates were admitted to partnership, 21 were rejected, and 20—including Ms. Hopkins—were "held" for reconsideration the following year.

Thirteen of the 32 partners who submitted comments on Ms. Hopkins supported her partnership. Eight stated they did not have an informed opinion about her, and eight recommended that she be denied partnership.

Ms. Hopkins had procured a $25 million State Department contract for Price Waterhouse. One partner commented that "none of the other partnership candidates at Price Waterhouse that year had a comparable record in terms of successfully procuring major contracts for the partnership." Clients described her as "extremely competent, intelligent" and "strong and forthright, very productive, energetic and creative." A high-ranking State Department official described Hopkins at trial as a "stimulating conversationalist" and praised her for her decisiveness, broad-mindedness, and "intellectual clarity."

Both supporters and opponents of her partnership candidacy indicated she was "sometimes overly aggressive, unduly harsh, difficult to work with, and impatient with staff." One partner described her as "macho"; another suggested that she "overcompensated for being a woman"; a third advised her to take "a course at charm school"; others objected to her swearing only "because it's a lady using foul language"; and one partner advised that Hopkins should "walk more femininely, talk more femininely, dress more femininely, wear makeup, have her hair styled, and wear jewelry."

Hopkins brought suit under Title VII for sexual discrimination in the partnership decision. A social psychologist testified that the partnership selection process at Price Waterhouse was likely influenced by sex stereotyping. The lower court found that Price Waterhouse's decision was based in part on the proper behavior of women and therefore that it had unlawfully discriminated against Hopkins. The Court of Appeals affirmed, and Price Waterhouse appealed.

JUDICIAL OPINION

BRENNAN, Justice

According to Price Waterhouse, an employer violates Title VII only if it gives decisive consideration to an employee's gender, race, national origin, or religion in making a decision that affects that employee. On Price Waterhouse's theory, even if a plaintiff shows that her gender played a part in an employment decision, it is still her burden to show that the decision would have been different if the employer had not discriminated. In Hopkins' view, on the other hand, an employer violates the statute

Continued

whenever it allows one of these attributes to play any part in an employment decision. Once a plaintiff shows that this occurred, according to Hopkins, the employer's proof that it would have made the same decision in the absence of discrimination can serve to limit equitable relief but not to avoid a finding of liability. We conclude that, as often happens, the truth lies somewhere in between.

Congress' intent to forbid employers to take gender into account in making employment decisions appears on the face of the statute. In now-familiar language, the statute forbids an employer to "fail or refuse to hire or to discharge any individual, or otherwise to discriminate with respect to his compensation, terms, conditions, or privileges of employment," or to "limit, segregate, or classify his employees or applicants for employment in any way which would deprive or tend to deprive any individual of employment opportunities or otherwise adversely affect his status as an employee, *because of* such individual's . . . sex." 42 U.S.C. §§ 2000e-2(a)(1), (2) (emphasis added). We take these words to mean that gender must be irrelevant to employment decisions. To construe the words "because of" as colloquial shorthand for "but-for causation," as does Price Waterhouse, is to misunderstand them. The critical inquiry is whether gender was a factor in the employment decision *at the moment it was made.* Moreover, since we know that the words "because of" do not mean "solely because of" we also know that Title VII meant to condemn even those decisions based on a mixture of legitimate and illegitimate considerations. When, therefore, an employer considers both gender and legitimate factors at the time of making a decision, that decision was "because of" sex and the other, legitimate considerations—even if we may say later, in the context of litigation, that the decision would have been the same if gender had not been taken into account.

We need not leave our common sense at the doorstep when we interpret a statute. It is difficult for us to imagine that, in the simple words "because of," Congress meant to obligate a plaintiff to identify the precise causal role

played by legitimate and illegitimate motivations in the employment decision she challenges. We conclude, instead, that Congress meant to obligate her to prove that the employer relied upon sex-based considerations in coming to its decision.

The central point is this: while an employer may not take gender into account in making an employment decision (except in those very narrow circumstances in which gender is a BFOQ [bona fide occupational qualification], it is free to decide against a woman for other reasons. We think these principles require that, once a plaintiff in a Title VII case shows that gender played a motivating part in an employment decision, the defendant may avoid a finding of liability only by proving that it would have made the same decision even if it had not allowed gender to play such a role. This balance of burdens is the direct result of Title VII's balance of rights.

We have not in the past required women whose gender has proved relevant to an employment decision to establish the negative proposition that they would not have been subject to that decision had they been men, and we do not do so today.

We have, in short, been here before. Each time, we have concluded that the plaintiff who shows that an impermissible motive played a motivating part in an adverse employment decision has thereby placed upon the defendant the burden to show that it would have made the same decision in the absence of the unlawful motive. Our decision today treads this well-worn path.

As for the legal relevance of sex stereotyping, we are beyond the day when an employer could evaluate employees by assuming or insisting that they matched the stereotype associated with their group, for "'[i]n forbidding employers to discriminate against individuals because of their sex, Congress intended to strike at the entire spectrum of disparate treatment of men and women resulting from sex stereotypes.'" An employer who objects to aggressiveness in women but whose positions require this trait places women in an intolerable and impermissible Catch-22: Out of a job if they

Continued

behave aggressively and out of a job if they don't. Title VII lifts women out of this bind.

Hopkins proved that Price Waterhouse invited partners to submit comments; that some of the comments stemmed from sex stereotypes; that an important part of the Policy Board's decision on Hopkins was an assessment of the submitted comments; and that Price Waterhouse in no way disclaimed reliance on the sex-linked evaluations. This is not, as Price Waterhouse suggests, "discrimination in the air"; rather, it is, as Hopkins put it, "discrimination brought to ground and visited upon" an employee.

In finding that some of the partners' comments reflected sex stereotyping, the District Court relied in part on Dr. Fiske's expert testimony. Without directly impugning Dr. Fiske's credentials or qualifications, Price Waterhouse insinuates that a social psychologist is unable to identify sex stereotyping in evaluations without investigating whether those evaluations have a basis in reality. This argument comes too late. At trial, counsel for Price Waterhouse twice assured the court that he did not question Dr. Fiske's expertise and failed to challenge the legitimacy of her discipline. Without contradiction from Price Waterhouse, Fiske testified that she discerned sex stereotyping in the partners' evaluations of Hopkins and she further explained that it was part of her business to identify stereotyping in written documents. We are not inclined to accept petitioner's belated and unsubstantiated characterization of Dr. Fiske's testimony as "gossamer evidence" based only on "intuitive hunches" and of her detection of sex stereotyping as "intuitively divined." Nor are we disposed to adopt the dissent's dismissive attitude toward Dr. Fiske's field of study and toward her own professional integrity.

Indeed, we are tempted to say that Dr. Fiske's expert testimony was merely icing on Hopkins' cake. It takes no special training to discern sex stereotyping in a description of an aggressive female employee as requiring "a course at charm school." Nor, turning to Thomas Beyer's memorable advice to Hopkins,

does it require expertise in psychology to know that, if an employee's flawed "interpersonal skills" can be corrected by a soft-hued suit or a new shade of lipstick, perhaps it is the employee's sex and not her interpersonal skills that has drawn the criticism.

Certainly a plausible—and, one might say, inevitable—conclusion to draw from this set of circumstances is that the Policy Board in making its decision did in fact take into account all of the partners' comments, including the comments that were motivated by stereotypical notions about women's proper deportment.

We hold that when a plaintiff in a Title VII case proves that her gender played a motivating part in an employment decision, the defendant may avoid a finding of liability only by proving by a preponderance of the evidence that it would have made the same decision even if it had not taken the plaintiff's gender into account. Because the courts below erred by deciding that the defendant must make this proof by clear and convincing evidence, we reverse the Court of Appeals' judgment against Price Waterhouse on liability and remand the case to that court for further proceedings.

Remanded.

CASE QUESTIONS

1. What reasons were offered by the partners in denying Ms. Hopkins her partnership?
2. What argument did Price Waterhouse make with respect to "but for" causation on the discrimination issue?
3. Who has the burden of establishing that a decision was based on sex?
4. Can sex be a factor in the decision-making process?
5. Why is the issue of whether the decision would have been the same regardless of sex crucial in the case?
6. Does "sex stereotyping" provide a basis for recovery under Title VII?

Aftermath: Ms. Hopkins was eventually awarded $350,000 and her partnership as damages. She works in the Washington, D.C., office of Price Waterhouse.

Review the Glass Ceiling Act:
http://www.law.
cornell.edu/uscode/
42/2000e.html

The *Price Waterhouse* v. *Hopkins* case has been referred to as a "mixed motive" case — that is, one in which race, national origin, religion, or sex are "motivating factors" for the case. Under the Court's ruling in *Hopkins,* if an employer can show that it would have made the same decision without a discriminatory motive, there would be no violation. The 1991 amendments overruled *Price Waterhouse*'s position and provided that once a plaintiff shows that race, national origin, religion, or sex was in fact a motivating factor, a violation is established. Also in 1991, Congress passed the Glass Ceiling Act, which created a commission to study barriers that exist for women trying to enter management and decision-making positions.

SEXUAL HARASSMENT

Sexual harassment has been a very public topic since the Senate confirmation hearings for Justice Clarence Thomas, at which Professor Anita Hill raised allegations of sexual harassment, which is a violation of Title VII of the Civil Rights Act. Company policies on this issue should attempt to make it clear that an environment of harassment is not appropriate for any employee. Companies should also enforce policies uniformly.

In a series of decisions from state and federal courts, the judicial response to sexual harassment has evolved. Employers have been held liable for allowing sexual harassment to occur; firing employees for their failure to accept sexual advances has allowed fired employees to collect damages for wrongful termination. In *Ford* v. *Revlon,* 734 P.2d 580 (Ariz. 1987), an employer was found to have committed the tort of intentional infliction of emotional distress for not remedying a sexual harassment situation made known to it.

The following sexual harassment case is the most recent U.S. Supreme Court case on this issue.

Harris v. *Forklift Systems, Inc.*
114 S. Ct. 367 (1993)

"SWEETCAKES" AND OTHER NAMES: SEXUAL HARASSMENT?

FACTS

Teresa Harris worked as a manager at Forklift Systems, Inc., an equipment rental company, from April 1985 until October 1987. Charles Hardy was Forklift's president.

A magistrate found that, throughout Ms. Harris's time at Forklift, Mr. Hardy often insulted her because of her gender and often made her the target of unwanted sexual innuendos. He told Ms. Harris on several occasions, in the presence of other employees, "You're a woman, what do you know" and "We need a man as the rental manager"; at least once, he told her she was "a dumb ass woman." Again in front of others, he suggested that the two of

them "go to the Holiday Inn to negotiate [Ms. Harris's] raise." Mr. Hardy occasionally asked Ms. Harris and other female employees to get coins from his front pants pocket. He threw objects on the ground in front of Ms. Harris and other women, and asked them to pick the objects up. He made sexual innuendos about Ms. Harris's and other women's clothing.

In mid-August 1987, Ms. Harris complained to Mr. Hardy about his conduct. He said he was surprised she was offended, claimed he was only joking, and apologized. He also promised he would stop, and based on this assurance Ms. Harris stayed on the job. But in early September, Mr. Hardy began anew: While Ms. Harris

Continued

was arranging a deal with one of Forklift's customers, he asked her, again in front of other employees, "What did you do, promise the guy . . . some [sex] Saturday night?" On October 1, Ms. Harris collected her paycheck and quit.

Ms. Harris then sued Forklift, claiming that Mr. Hardy's conduct had created an abusive work environment for her because of her gender. The U.S. District Court for the Middle District of Tennessee, adopting the report and recommendation of the magistrate, found this to be "a close case," but held that Mr. Hardy's conduct did not create an abusive environment.

The court of appeals affirmed the decision and Ms. Harris appealed.

JUDICIAL OPINION
O'CONNOR, Justice

We granted certiorari, to resolve a conflict among the Circuits on whether conduct, to be actionable as "abusive work environment" harassment (no quid pro quo harassment issue is present here), must "seriously affect [an employee's] psychological well-being" or lead the plaintiff to "suffe[r] injury."

Title VII of the Civil Rights Act of 1964 makes it "an unlawful employment practice for an employer . . . to discriminate against any individual with respect to his compensation, terms, conditions, or privileges of employment, because of such individual's race, color, religion, sex, or national origin." As we made clear in *Meritor Savings Bank* v. *Vinson*, 477 U.S. 57 (1986), this language "is not limited to 'economic' or 'tangible' discrimination. The phrase 'terms, conditions, or privileges of employment' evinces a congressional intent 'to strike at the entire spectrum of disparate treatment of men and women' in employment," which includes requiring people to work in a discriminatorily hostile or abusive environment.

This standard, which we reaffirm today, takes a middle path between making actionable any conduct that is merely offensive and requiring the conduct to cause a tangible psychological injury. As we pointed out in *Meritor*, "mere utterance of an . . . epithet which engenders offensive feelings in an employee," does not sufficiently affect the conditions of employment to implicate Title VII. Conduct that is not severe or pervasive enough to create an objectively hostile or abusive work environment—an environment that a reasonable person would find hostile or abusive— is beyond Title VII's purview. Likewise, if the victim does not subjectively perceive the environment to be abusive, the conduct has not actually altered the conditions of the victim's employment, and there is no Title VII violation.

But Title VII comes into play before the harassing conduct leads to a nervous breakdown. A discriminatorily abusive work environment, even one that does not seriously affect employees' psychological well-being, can and often will detract from employees' job performance, discourage employees from remaining on the job, or keep them from advancing in their careers. Moreover, even without regard to these tangible effects, the very fact that the discriminatory conduct was so severe or pervasive that it created a work environment abusive to employees because of their race, gender, religion, or national origin offends Title VII's broad rule of workplace equality. The appalling conduct alleged in *Meritor*, and the reference in that case to environments "'so heavily polluted with discrimination as to destroy completely the emotional and psychological stability of minority group workers,'" merely present some especially egregious examples of harassment. They do not mark the boundary of what is actionable.

We therefore believe the District Court erred in relying on whether the conduct "seriously affect[ed] plaintiff's psychological well-being" or led her to "suffe[r] injury." So long as the environment would reasonably be perceived, and is perceived, as hostile or abusive, there is no need for it also to be psychologically injurious.

This is not, and by its nature cannot be, a mathematically precise test. We need not answer today all the potential questions it raises, nor specifically address the EEOC's new regulations on this subject. But we can say that whether an environment is "hostile" or "abusive" can be determined only by looking at all the circumstances. These may include the frequency of the discriminatory conduct; its

Continued

severity; whether it is physically threatening or humiliating, or a mere offensive utterance; and whether it unreasonably interferes with an employee's work performance. The effect on the employee's psychological well-being is, of course, relevant to determining whether the plaintiff actually found the environment abusive. But while psychological harm, like any other relevant factor, may be taken into account, no single factor is required.

We therefore reverse the judgment of the Court of Appeals.

CASE QUESTIONS

1. What is the difference between a quid pro quo case of sexual harassment and an atmosphere of harassment?
2. Must a plaintiff claiming sexual harassment establish psychological or other injury in order to establish his or her case?
3. What factors would be considered in determining whether there was an atmosphere of harassment?
4. Is any single factor required to be established to recover for sexual harassment?

C O N S I D E R . . .

19.3 Kerry Ellison worked as a revenue agent for the Internal Revenue Service in San Mateo, California. During her initial training in 1984 she met Sterling Gray, another trainee, who was also assigned to the San Mateo office. The two co-workers never became friends, and they did not work closely together.

Mr. Gray's desk was 20 feet from Ms. Ellison's desk, two rows behind and one row over. Revenue agents in the San Mateo office often went to lunch in groups. In June 1986, when no one else was in the office, Mr. Gray asked Ms. Ellison to lunch and she accepted. Mr. Gray had to pick up his son's forgotten lunch, so they stopped by his house and he gave Ms. Ellison a tour of his house.

After the June lunch Mr. Gray started to pester Ms. Ellison with unnecessary questions and to hang around her desk. On October 22, 1986, Mr. Gray handed Ms. Ellison a note he had written on a telephone message slip, which read: "I cried over you last night and I'm totally drained today. I have never been in such constant term oil [*sic*]. Thank you for talking with me. I could not stand to feel your hatred for another day." When Ms. Ellison realized that Mr. Gray had written the note, she became shocked and frightened and left the room.

Ms. Ellison later showed the note to Bonnie Miller, who supervised both her and Mr. Gray. Ms. Miller said, "This is sexual harassment." Ms. Ellison asked Ms. Miller not to do anything about it as she wanted to try to handle it herself. She asked a male co-worker to talk to Mr. Gray, to tell him that she was not interested in him and to leave her alone.

Mr. Gray, undaunted, mailed Ms. Ellison a card and a typed, single-spaced, three-page letter. He wrote, in part:

I know that you are worth knowing with or without sex. . . . Leaving aside the hassles and disasters of recent weeks. I have enjoyed you so much over these past few months. Watching you. Experiencing you from O so far away. Admiring your style and elan. . . . Don't you think it odd that two people who have never even talked together, alone, are striking off such intense sparks? . . . I will [write] another letter in the near future.

Continued

Ms. Ellison then requested that Ms. Miller transfer either Mr. Gray or her because she would not be comfortable working in the same office with him. Ms. Miller asked Ms. Ellison to send a copy of the card and letter to the San Mateo office.

Ms. Miller apprised the labor relations department of the situation and also reminded Mr. Gray many times over the next few weeks that he must not contact Ms. Ellison in any way. He subsequently transferred to San Francisco in November. Ms. Ellison returned from training in St. Louis in late November and did not discuss the matter further with Ms. Miller.

Mr. Gray filed union grievances requesting a return to the San Mateo office. The IRS and the union settled the grievances in Mr. Gray's favor, agreeing to allow him to transfer back to the San Mateo office provided that he spend four more months in San Francisco and promise not to bother Ms. Ellison. She first learned of his request in a letter from Ms. Miller.

After receiving the letter, Ms. Ellison was "frantic." On January 30, 1987, she filed with the IRS a formal complaint alleging sexual harassment. She also obtained permission to transfer to San Francisco temporarily when Mr. Gray returned.

The IRS employee investigating her allegation agreed with Ms. Ellison's supervisor that Mr. Gray's conduct constituted sexual harassment. In its final decision, however, the Treasury Department rejected her complaint because it believed that it did not describe a pattern or practice of sexual harassment covered by the EEOC regulations. After an appeal, the EEOC affirmed the Treasury Department's decision and concluded that the agency took adequate action to prevent the repetition of Mr. Gray's conduct.

In September 1987, Ms. Ellison filed a complaint in federal district court.

Has there been sexual harassment? [*Ellison* v. *Brady*, 924 F.2d 872 (9th Cir. 1991).]

SEX DISCRIMINATION AND PENSIONS

Another area of sex discrimination in employment involves the statistical fact that women live longer than men. It costs more for a female employee to have a

E T H I C A L   I S S U E S

19.2 Known as Tailhook, the U.S. Navy's annual Las Vegas gathering for fighter pilots in the fall of 1991 was the beginning of a cultural change for the Navy.

In a series of suites on a floor of the Las Vegas Hilton, a group of Navy officers had unlimited access to alcohol and pornographic movies. After extended participation, the level of conduct among the group deteriorated.

When several women left the elevator and stepped out among the aviators, they found themselves facing a gauntlet of intoxicated men who fondled them and offered verbal harassment. Some of the women were members of the Navy.

A complaint was lodged, but the investigation was delayed, and no one was willing to tell who was present in the gauntlet. The incident and its aftermath cost the secretary of the Navy and several admirals their positions.

Why didn't anyone help the women? Why wasn't anyone willing to identify the participants? Do you agree with one admiral's assessment: "What do you expect when you go to a party with drunken sailors?"

FOR THE MANAGER'S DESK

THE PIZZA MAN WHO WOULDN'T DELIVER

David Papa, 25, worked as a Domino's Pizza shop manager in Port Richey, Florida. His supervisor, Beth Carrier, told him not to bend over because it "turns me on," and she also grabbed his behind. The harassment continued throughout 1988. When Papa asked Ms. Carrier to stop, he was fired.

He took his case to the EEOC and the agency took it to trial; it was the first time the EEOC took to trial a case of a woman harassing a man. Mr. Papa was awarded $237,000 in damages.

Papa, in an interview with the Associated Press stated, "My friends were like, 'Why didn't you just sleep with her? You had a woman coming on to you.'

But this was about my career."

Other sexual harassment cases involving male victims are pending and the EEOC has indicated it will pursue female harasser cases with the same level of commitment and resources that it devotes to cases involving male harassers. The EEOC has not yet taken to trial a same-sex harassment case.

Business Planning Tip

Office Romances
New York lawyer Sidney Siller, who defends sexual harassment suits, offers this advice for office etiquette to avoid litigation:

1. *Leave your office door open during meetings;*
2. *Don't go out to lunch with opposite sex co-workers;*
3. *Don't offer rides home (even in inclement weather); and*
4. *Avoid physical contact in the office.*

Some companies have adopted a policy of no-fraternization among employees.

pension than a male employee because she will live longer after retirement. In *City of Los Angeles Department of Water v. Manhart*, 435 U.S. 702 (1978), the Supreme Court held that employers could not require female employees to contribute more to their pension plans than males. The additional contributions for the female employees were required by the employer because the pension planner had statistical evidence that longevity of female employees exceeded that of male employees. If the Supreme Court had sanctioned the disparity in pension plan payments, the higher cost of having female employees could have been cited by employers as the reason for their hiring practices. Insurers and employers are required to treat employees as a group and not to break them down by their age, sex, or other characteristics.

SEX DISCRIMINATION AND PREGNANCY ISSUES

Review the Pregnancy Discrimination Act:
http://www.law.cornell.edu/uscode/29/621.html

The Pregnancy Discrimination Act was added to Title VII in 1974. Prior to this act, women were forced to take maternity leaves at certain times and for certain lengths of time solely because of their pregnancies. Many women who returned to work after their pregnancies discovered that their pay had been cut or that they had been demoted. Even employees' insurance coverage treated

Business Planning Tip

Because of the potential Title VII liability, many employers require their employees who hold supervisory positions to attend training sessions on discrimination and sexual harassment. Many employers also have annual psychological evaluations of supervisory employees to determine their well-being and fitness for their positions.

pregnancy differently from other medical ailments, and pregnancy was not treated as an illness by most employers in terms of sick leave.

This act revolutionized maternity issues in the employment world. The specific acts prohibited under this statute are as follows:

1. Forcing a resignation
2. Demoting or limiting an employee's job upon her return to work
3. Refusing to allow a mother to return to work after pregnancy
4. Providing different sick leave rules for pregnancy and other medical ailments
5. Providing different medical insurance benefits or disability leave for pregnancy and other ailments
6. Refusing to hire or promote on the basis of pregnancy or family plans

The following landmark case focuses on new issues in sex discrimination.

International Union v. *Johnson Controls, Inc.*
499 U.S. 187 (1991)

THE ACID TEST FOR WOMEN: THE RIGHT TO CHOOSE HIGH-RISK JOBS

FACTS

Johnson Controls, Inc. (respondent), manufactures batteries. In the manufacturing process, the element lead is a primary ingredient. Occupational exposure to lead entails health risks, including the risk of harm to any fetus carried by a female employee.

Before the Civil Rights Act of 1964 became law, Johnson Controls did not employ any woman in a battery-manufacturing job. In June 1977, however, it announced its first official policy concerning its employment of women in jobs with lead exposure risk:

[P]rotection of the health of the unborn child is the immediate and direct responsibility of the prospective parents. While the medical profession and the company can support them in the exercise of this responsibility, it cannot assume it for them without simultaneously infringing their rights as persons. . . .

Since not all women who can become mothers wish to become mothers (or will become mothers), it would appear to be illegal discrimination to treat all who are capable of pregnancy as though they will become pregnant.

Consistent with that view, Johnson Controls "stopped short of excluding women capable of bearing children from lead exposure" but emphasized that a woman who expected to have a child should not choose a job in which she would have such exposure. The company also required a woman who wished to be considered for employment to sign a statement indicating that she had been advised of the risk of having a child while she was exposed to lead. The statement informed the woman that although there was evidence "that women exposed to lead have a higher rate of abortion," this evidence was "not as clear . . . as the relationship between cigarette smoking and cancer," but that it was, "medically speaking, just good sense not to run that risk if you want children and do not want to expose the unborn child to risk, however small. . . ."

In 1982, Johnson Controls shifted from a policy of warning to a policy of exclusion. Between 1979 and 1983, eight employees became pregnant while maintaining lead levels in excess of 30 micrograms per decaliter of blood. The company responded by announcing a broad exclusion of women from jobs that exposed them to lead:

[I]t is [Johnson Controls'] policy that women who are pregnant or who are capable of bearing children will not be placed into jobs involving lead exposure or which could expose them to lead through the exercise of job bidding, bumping, transfer or promotion rights. (App. 85-86)

Continued

The policy defined "women . . . capable of bearing children" as "[a]ll women except those whose inability to bear children is medically documented."

Several employees (petitioners) and their unions filed suit alleging that Johnson Controls's fetal protection policy violated Title VII of the Civil Rights Act. Included in the group were:

Mary Craig	sterilized to avoid losing her job
Elsie Nason	50-year-old divorcee who lost compensation when transferred out of lead exposure job
Donald Penney	denied request for leave of absence to lower his lead level before becoming a father

The district court entered summary judgment for Johnson Controls. The court of appeals affirmed, and the employees appealed.

JUDICIAL OPINION
BLACKMUN, Justice

The bias in Johnson Controls' policy is obvious. Fertile men, but not fertile women, are given a choice as to whether they wish to risk their reproductive health for a particular job. Section 703(a) of the Civil Rights Act of 1964, 78 Stat. 255, as amended, 42 U.S.C. § 2000e-2(a), prohibits sex-based classifications in terms and conditions of employment, in hiring and discharging decisions, and in other employment decisions that adversely affect an employee's status. Respondent's fetal-protection policy explicitly discriminates against women on the basis of their sex. The policy excludes women with childbearing capacity from lead-exposed jobs and so creates a facial classification based on gender. Respondent assumes as much in its brief before this Court.

Nevertheless, the Court of Appeals assumed, as did the two appellate courts who already had confronted this issue, that sex specific fetal-protection policies do not involve facial discrimination. These courts analyzed the policies as though they were facially neutral, and had only a discriminatory effect upon the employment opportunities of women. Consequently, the courts looked to see if each employer in question had established that its policy was justified

as a business necessity. The business necessity standard is more lenient for the employer than the statutory BFOQ [Bona Fide Occupational Qualification] defense. The court assumed that because the asserted reason for the sex-based exclusion (protecting women's unconceived offspring) was ostensibly benign, the policy was not sex-based discrimination. That assumption, however, was incorrect.

First, Johnson Controls' policy classifies on the basis of gender and childbearing capacity, rather than fertility alone. Respondent does not seek to protect the unconceived children of all its employees. Despite evidence in the record about the debilitating effect of lead exposure on the male reproductive system, Johnson Controls is concerned only with the harms that may befall the unborn offspring of its female employees.

Our conclusion is bolstered by the Pregnancy Discrimination Act of 1978, 42 U.S.C. § 2000e(k), in which Congress explicitly provided that, for purposes of Title VII, discrimination "on the basis of sex" includes discrimination "because of or on the basis of pregnancy, childbirth, or related medical conditions." "The Pregnancy Discrimination Act has now made clear that, for all Title VII purposes, discrimination based on a woman's pregnancy is, on its face, discrimination because of her sex." In its use of the words "capable of bearing children" in the 1982 policy statement as the criterion for exclusion, Johnson Controls explicitly classifies on the basis of potential for pregnancy. Under the PDA, such a classification must be regarded, for Title VII purposes, in the same light as explicit sex discrimination. Respondent has chosen to treat all its female employees as potentially pregnant; that choice evinces discrimination on the basis of sex.

We concluded above that Johnson Controls' policy is not neutral because it does not apply to the reproductive capacity of the company's male employees in the same way as it applies to that of the females. Moreover, the absence of a malevolent motive does not convert a facially discriminatory policy into a neutral policy with a discriminatory effect. Whether an employment practice involves disparate treatment through

Continued

explicit facial discrimination does not depend on why the employer discriminates but rather on the explicit terms of the discrimination.

In sum, Johnson Controls' policy "does not pass the simple test of whether the evidence shows 'treatment of a person in a manner which but for that person's sex would be different.'"

We therefore turn to the question whether Johnson Controls' fetal-protection policy is one of those "certain instances" that come within the BFOQ exception.

Johnson Controls argues that its fetal-protection policy falls within the so-called safety exception to the BFOQ. Our cases have stressed that discrimination on the basis of sex because of safety concerns is allowed only in narrow circumstances. In *Dothard* v. *Rawlinson,* 433 U.S. 321 (1977), this Court indicated that the danger to a woman herself does not justify discrimination. We there allowed the employer to hire only male guards in contact areas of maximum-security male penitentiaries only because more was at stake than the "individual woman's decision to weigh and accept the risks of employment." *Ibid*. We found sex to be a BFOQ inasmuch as the employment of a female guard would create real risks of safety to others if violence broke out because the guard was a woman. Sex discrimination was tolerated because sex was related to the guard's ability to do the job—maintaining prison security. We also required in *Dothard* a high correlation between sex and ability to perform job functions and refused to allow employers to use sex as a proxy for strength although it might be a fairly accurate one.

Similarly, some courts have approved airlines' layoffs of pregnant flight attendants at different points during the first five months of pregnancy on the ground that the employer's policy was necessary to ensure the safety of passengers.

The unconceived fetuses of Johnson Controls' female employees, however, are neither customers nor third parties whose safety is essential to the business of battery manufacturing. No one can disregard the possibility of injury to future children; the BFOQ, however, is not so broad that it transforms this deep social concern into an essential aspect of battery making.

Our case law makes clear that the safety exception is limited to instances in which sex or pregnancy actually interferes with the employee's ability to perform the job. This approach is consistent with the language of the BFOQ provision itself, for it suggests that permissible distinctions based on sex must relate to ability to perform the duties of the job. Johnson Controls suggests, however, that we expand the exception to allow fetal-protection policies that mandate particular standards for pregnant or fertile women. We decline to do so. Such an expansion contradicts not only the language of the BFOQ and the narrowness of its exception but the plain language and history of the Pregnancy Discrimination Act.

A word about tort liability and the increased cost of fertile women in the workplace is perhaps necessary. One of the dissenting judges in this case expressed concern about an employer's tort liability and concluded that liability for a potential injury to a fetus is a social cost that Title VII does not require a company to ignore. It is correct to say that Title VII does not prevent the employer from having a conscience. The statute, however, does prevent sex-specific fetal-protection policies. These two aspects of Title VII do not conflict.

More than 40 States currently recognize a right to recover for a prenatal injury based either on negligence or on wrongful death. According to Johnson Controls, however, the company complies with the lead standard developed by OSHA and warns its female employees about the damaging effects of lead. It is worth noting that OSHA gave the problem of lead lengthy consideration and concluded that "there is no basis whatsoever for the claim that women of childbearing age should be excluded from the workplace in order to protect the fetus or the course of pregnancy." Instead, OSHA established a series of mandatory protections which, taken together, "should effectively minimize any risk to the fetus and newborn child." Without negligence, it would be difficult for a court to find liability on the part of the

Continued

employer. If, under general tort principles, Title VII bans sex-specific fetal-protection policies, the employer fully informs the woman of the risk, and the employer has not acted negligently, the basis for holding an employer liable seems remote at best.

Although the issue is not before us, the concurrence observes that "it is far from clear that compliance with Title VII will preempt state tort liability."

Our holding today that Title VII, as so amended, forbids sex-specific fetal-protection policies is neither remarkable nor unprecedented. Concern for a woman's existing or potential offspring historically has been the excuse for denying women equal employment opportunities.

It is no more appropriate for the courts than it is for individual employers to decide whether a woman's reproductive role is more important to herself and her family than her economic role. Congress has left this choice to the woman as hers to make.

The judgment of the Court of Appeals is reversed and the case is remanded for further proceedings consistent with this opinion.

CASE QUESTIONS
1. Describe Johnson Controls's evolving policy on lead exposure.
2. Describe the plaintiffs who brought suit in the case.
3. Are circumstances given when sex is a BFOQ?
4. What problem is presented by the exclusion of men?
5. What is the court's position on tort liability of the company with respect to the fetus?

C O N S I D E R . . . **19.4** Diane McCourtney was employed at Imprimis as a full-time accounts payable clerk. On September 30, 1989, Mrs. McCourtney gave birth to an infant with multiple illnesses, and the baby's father and Mrs. McCourtney's family were unable to assist her with child care. Because of the baby's illnesses, Mrs. McCourtney, who had been an excellent employee until the baby's birth, was frequently absent from work. Her absenteeism rates were as follows:

January 1–February 25	Absent 71 percent of the time
February 25–March 11	Absent 31 percent of the time
March 12–March 25	Absent 13 percent of the time

Ninety-nine percent of the absences were for her baby's illness. She was excused each time but was always given a warning. In April she missed four straight days, was suspended, and was eventually discharged for excessive absenteeism. Mrs. McCourtney applied for unemployment benefits but was refused on grounds that she brought about her termination. Do you agree with this decision?

C O N S I D E R . . . **19.5** Scientists have discovered a genetic marker that could identify workers who run the highest risk of developing a chronic lung disease linked to exposure to beryllium. Beryllium is used in industries ranging from high-tech ceramics to nuclear weapons. A blood test of these workers would reveal the genetic markers. Can employers exclude workers on the basis of the presence of these genetic markers?

Religious Discrimination

Employers are required to make reasonable efforts to accommodate an employee's religious practices, holidays, and observances. Not all religious or church activities, however, are protected; for example, the observance of a religion's Sabbath is a protected activity, but taking time to prepare for a church bake sale or pageant is an unprotected activity. The 1972 amendments to Title VII defined religion to include "all aspects of religious observance and practice, as well as belief." The accommodation of religion thus defined is required unless an employer is able to establish that allowing the employee such an accommodation would result in "undue hardship on the conduct of the employer's business."

In *Trans World Airlines Inc.* v. *Hardison*, 432 U.S. 63 (1977), the Supreme Court confirmed the clear language of the 1972 act that requires an employer to demonstrate inability to accommodate employee's religious needs. As a member of a church that worshiped on Saturdays, Larry G. Hardison expressed a desire not to work that day. TWA worked through several alternatives to afford Mr. Hardison the opportunity for Saturdays off, including asking the union to waive a seniority rule that limited substitutes for him and looking for an alternative job that would not require Saturday work. The union would not waive its rule, and no managers were available to take the shift. When Mr. Hardison refused to work on Saturdays, he was dismissed and filed suit, but the Court found for TWA because of its extensive efforts and the constraints that prevented shifting of workers without substantial interference in TWA's operations.

Title VII requires only reasonable accommodation. Employees are not necessarily entitled to the accommodation they desire. For example, in *American Postal Workers Union* v. *Postmaster General*, 781 F.2d 772 (9th Cir. 1986), several postal employees refused to work at a window in the post office where draft registration forms were handled. They asked to be able to direct draft registrants to the windows of employees who did not have religious objections to the draft. The Postal Service transferred the employees to non-window jobs, which was supported by the court as a reasonable accommodation.

Further, employees are expected to cooperate with their employers in making an accommodation, such as finding a fellow employee to take a shift. In *TWA* v. *Hardison,* the Court noted, "The statute is not to be construed to require an employer to discriminate against some employees in order for others to observe their Sabbath."

Race Discrimination

When Title VII was first enacted, its clear intent was to prevent discrimination against the minority workforce. After Title VII had been in effect for several years, an unanticipated problem arose: Does Title VII's protection extend to all races? Are white employees entitled to the same protection Title VII affords other races?

In 1976, the Supreme Court provided the answer in *McDonald* v. *Santa Fe Trail Transportation Co.*, 427 U.S. 273 (1976). Here, some black employees had been reinstated after committing the same offense as a group of white employees who were not reinstated. The Court held that Title VII prohibited such racial discrimination.

In *Patterson* v. *McClean Credit Union,* 491 U.S. 164 (1989), the U.S. Supreme Court was faced with reprehensible conduct by an employer in the consideration of a black female for promotion. The Court held that there was no violation of the Civil Rights Act because a promotion was not part of a contract as required to establish race discrimination under Section 1981, a nineteenth-century antidiscrimination statute.

FOR THE MANAGER'S DESK

RELIGIOUS DISCRIMINATION SUITS INCREASING

The number of religious discrimination suits filed in 1994 was 2,900, up from 2,651 in 1993 and 2,200 in 1990. Wal-Mart Inc. recently settled a case with the EEOC and Scott Hamby. Mr. Hamby was a theology student who was also working at Wal-Mart. Because he refused to work on

Sunday, his Sabbath, he was fired. In a settlement of the charges of religious discrimination with Mr. Hamby, Wal-Mart agreed to provide company wide training for its managers on religious discrimination and pay Mr. Hamby a sum that was not disclosed.

The EEOC attributes the increase in the number of religious discrimination cases to repeals in the

Midwest and South of the traditional Sunday closing laws. These laws, called blue laws, required stores to remain closed on Sundays. The laws have been subject to constitutional challenges and have not withstood scrutiny by the courts. The result has been more stores open on Sunday and more conflicts with employees' religious convictions with respect to work on their Sabbaths.

The effect of the case was changed by the 1991 Civil Rights Act, which permits victims of race or ethnic discrimination to recover unrestricted compensatory and punitive damages without regard to the technical issue of whether the terms of employment fit within the Court's narrow construction of a contract.

ANTIDISCRIMINATION LAWS AND AFFIRMATIVE ACTION

Some employers, either voluntarily or through the EEOC, have instituted **affirmative action** programs. Nothing prohibits such programs under Title VII, and the Supreme Court has sanctioned them as methods for remedying all the past years of discrimination. Although Title VII does not mandate such programs, employers may legally institute them.

Affirmative action has been described by some as the tool necessary to put all races and the sexes on an equal footing after years of discrimination. Others, however, have described it as an unfair system that discriminates against whites and males and often serves to reduce the self-esteem of those who benefit from it because of their feelings about being hired or promoted solely because of their race or sex. Others have argued that affirmative action encourages inefficiency because it prevents the most qualified or the most deserving from earning a promotion or being hired in the first instance.

What Is Affirmative Action?

Although Title VII prohibits discrimination against any group, there is well-established judicial and legislative support for the establishment of affirmative action programs. Affirmative action is a remedial step taken to ensure that those who have been victims of discrimination in the past are given the opportunity to work in positions they would have attained had there not been discrimination.

Affirmative action programs are used to improve job opportunities for African Americans, Hispanics, Native Americans, Asians, women, persons with disabilities, and Vietnam veterans.

FOR THE MANAGER'S DESK

GARY BECKER ON HOW IS AFFIRMATIVE ACTION LIKE CROP SUBSIDIES?

Many conservative intellectuals are passionately opposed to quotas and other parts of affirmative-action programs, while liberals just as fervently advocate them. Yet the depth of emotion on this issue seems misplaced when affirmative action is recognized for what it is: a federal regulation that probably causes less harm than many other programs but does hurt some individuals, as it caters to minorities with political clout.

I don't like group quotas and other aspects of affirmative-action programs, but I am puzzled by the handwriting and anger of those who are opposed, especially some intellectuals. Although no one has even rough estimates of the social costs and benefits of these programs, I strongly suspect that certain other subsidies and regulations do more damage. Examples include tax and other breaks to the housing industry, the declines in labor-force participation of elderly persons induced by the tax on Social Security benefits, and higher consumer prices due to quotas on imported cars, textiles, computer chips, and, until recently, steel.

Opposition to affirmative-action programs may be strong because their effects can be so visible: for example, when such programs are used to admit students with weak records to law schools, medical schools, and premier universities or to help promote minority members into high-level jobs, while people who are more qualified are passed over. The harm from most other programs is indirect or hidden from view.

Ethical Appeals. Some opponents argue that affirmative-action regulations are worse than other government programs because the criteria are inborn characteristics: race, gender, national origin, and the like. But other programs that have nothing to do with inherited characteristics often in reality help only a small group. For example, hardly anyone not brought up on a farm ever becomes a commercial farmer. Thus, subsidies to agriculture are in a sense unavailable to people who grow up in cities.

Supporters of affirmative action deny that it is the result simply of political power. They argue that justice demands compensation for the horrors of past discrimination. Opponents argue just as strongly that quotas violate our culture's principle of equal treatment for equal skills, and they reject the notion that the

present generation can be held responsible for discrimination in the past.

Both sides in this debate make valid points, but arguments about benefits are usually couched in terms of moral and ethical justifications, partly to gain the support of other voters. When was the last time you heard anyone defend a government program simply on the grounds that the person wanted to have the benefits? Although Republican opposition to quotas has helped the party make political in-roads at the national level among white male blue-collar workers who traditionally voted for Democrats, clearly affirmative-action programs would not be politically viable if they had the support only of those blacks, women, and others who benefit.

Shadow of Doubt. Most other government programs could not have been implemented without support from persons not much affected by them one way or the other. Surely, management and employees at Chrysler Corp. did not have enough clout by themselves to get the large federal bailout a decade ago. Alone, the small number of sugar growers in the U.S. would not have had much chance of getting the restrictive quotas on sugar imports that have been in effect for the past 70 years. This need

Continued

to inflate self-interest into a broader moral and ethical point is why no business executive pleads for government subsidies by explaining that otherwise he might lose his job or have to take a big cut in pay. Instead, he complains about unfair competition from abroad or frightens voters with tales of defense vulnerabilities or the loss of jobs and stockholder equity if help is not forthcoming.

Opponents make much of how affirmative action detracts from the achievements of the most qualified members of minority groups. These able people suffer psychologically from skepticism about whether they deserve their success. Stephen L. Carter, a black professor at Yale Law School, in his book *Reflections of an Affirmative Action Baby*, poignantly describes his experiences with this attitude.

Of course, the doubt cast on the qualifications of successful minority members is unfortunate. But every government program hurts someone—often even some members of the groups that benefit. Studies have documented, for example, that programs involving acreage restrictions on agricultural crops benefit rich farmers sometimes at the expense of poor farmers, who do not get their fair share of the allotments.

Recognizing that affirmative-action programs are government regulations with a complicated incidence of costs and benefits does not resolve the dispute over whether or not they are desirable. But it may help focus the debate on the real question: Do they cause as much harm or do as much good as other government programs that generate very little debate?

Source: Gary S. Becker, "How Is Affirmative Action Like Crop Subsidies?" *Business Week*, April 27, 1992, p. 18. Reprinted from the April 27, 1992 issue of *Business Week* by special permission, copyright © 1992 by The McGraw-Hill Companies.

Who Is Required to Have Affirmative Action Programs?

Some federal funding laws, such as those for education and state and local governments, mandate affirmative action programs.

Some employers have an obligation to take steps to equalize the representation of minorities and women in their labor forces. This equalization of representation in the labor force is the process of affirmative action. Those employers who are obligated to undertake affirmative action programs are:

1. Employers who, pursuant to consent decree or court order, must implement plans to compensate for past wrongs
2. State and local agencies and colleges and universities that receive federal funds
3. Government contractors
4. Businesses that work on federal projects (Ten percent of their subcontract work must employ minority businesses.)

Affirmative action plans cannot simply be **quotas**; a quota program is an unlawful infringement of the rights of a majority group of employees. Rather, affirmative action programs set goals—for example, a certain number of minorities employed by a certain date. If the goal is not met, a business has not violated the law so long as it has made a good-faith effort to recruit and hire minorities. That good-faith effort can be established by a showing of internal and external advertising, monitoring of the program's progress, and changes and improvements in the program's development.

Preparing an Affirmative Action Program

An employer should begin with an equal employment opportunity statement, which says simply that decisions on recruiting, hiring, training, and promotion will be made without regard to race, color, religion, sex, national origin, veteran status, or disability. The statement should be displayed at the place of business, made evident in all recruiting materials, and reaffirmed each year to reestablish commitment to it. The firm should also appoint an affirmative action or equal employment opportunity officer. The role of this employee is to identify problems and propose solutions.

A business should then conduct an initial audit and maintain good records regarding its hiring, promotion, and recruiting of employees. In such an audit, the employer examines job titles and determines key areas in which women and minorities are underrepresented. If the audit finds that these groups are underrepresented with respect to their availability in the workforce, then a system of goals and timetables should be established for each underrepresented job title. The employer then monitors the data to see whether the goal's are met. If goals are not met, further steps should be taken, such as more aggressive recruiting.

Affirmative Action Backlash

Currently there are legislative movements and grass roots referenda that mandate the elimination of affirmative action programs. The University of California system eliminated affirmative action programs in 1995, but the programs were reinstated by a court after the elimination was challenged. The issues of fairness, extent, and need of affirmative action continue to be debated.

In *Adarand Constructors, Inc. v. Pena*, 115 S. Ct. 2097 (1995), the U.S. Supreme Court was faced with the issue of affirmative action programs in a case brought by a contractor that challenged the federal government's program granting socially and economically disadvantaged contractors and subcontractors preferences in the awarding of government contracts. The case was remanded for trial after a ruling by the Court that such programs were subject to a standard of review known as "strict scrutiny." The Court held that all racial classifications, and the government's set-aside program offering preferences to minority-owned businesses, was a racial classification. To survive the strict scrutiny test, which is derived from the Equal Protection Clause of the U.S. Constitution (see Chapter 5), the federal government must be able to show, when a case goes to trial, that the contractor preferences serve a compelling government interest.

> **Business Planning Tip**
>
> Subtle Discrimination
> An employer can't say "Don't send me any blacks" because it would be an obvious violation of Title VII protections. The EEOC uncovered the following code at Interplace, a Los Angeles employment agency:
>
> | | |
> |---|---|
> | "Talk to Maria." | Prefer Hispanics |
> | "See me." | No minorities |
> | "Talk to Mary." | Prefer Caucasians |
> | "No Z." | No blacks |
> | "Talk to Adam." | Prefer male |
> | "Young environment." | No older workers |
> | "Talk to MaryAnne." | Prefer blacks |
> | "Reply to Suite 20-30." | Prefer people in their 20s |
>
> Interplace was fined $2,000,000.

19.6 In 1978, the Santa Clara County Transit District Board of Supervisors adopted an affirmative action plan for the County Transportation Agency. The agency plan allows, in making promotions within a traditionally segregated job category in which women have been underrepresented, the consideration of sex as one factor. The plan recognized that even though women constituted 36.4 percent of the area's workforce, they constituted only 22.4 percent of Agency employees. The plan was intended to achieve "a statistical measurable yearly improvement in hiring, training, and promotion of minorities and women throughout the agency in all major job classifications where they are underrepresented."

On December 12, 1979, the agency announced a vacancy for the promotional position of road dispatcher. Dispatchers assign road crews, equipment, and materials and maintain records on road maintenance jobs. The position requires at least four years of dispatch or road maintenance work for Santa Clara County.

Twelve employees applied for the position, including Diane Joyce and Paul Johnson (petitioner). Ms. Joyce had worked for the agency since 1970, first as an account clerk until 1975, and then as a road maintenance worker (the first woman to hold such a position). Mr. Johnson began work with the agency in 1967 and had experience as a clerk, dispatcher, and road maintenance worker.

Nine of the applicants were interviewed for the position; and seven of the nine scored above 70 on a rating scale used by the interview board. Mr. Johnson scored 75 and Ms. Joyce scored 73. The agency coordinator decided to hire Ms. Joyce. Mr. Johnson filed a complaint with the EEOC and eventually filed suit in federal district court.

Does the affirmative action plan violate Title VII? [*Johnson* v. *Santa Clara County*, 480 U.S. 616 (1987).]

E T H I C A L   I S S U E S

19.3 "How is it not discrimination? It's just not right," muttered Alex Rayburn when he learned that nearly one-third of the companies coming to recruit graduates of State University's College of Business were interviewing only women and minorities. "I guess no white males need apply," he told his business law professor. Can companies exclude a group in this manner? Is it discrimination? Is it fair? Is this method the intent of an affirmative action program?

THE DEFENSES TO A TITLE VII CHARGE

Title VII is not a strict liability statute. Some defenses are provided in the act that employers can use to defend a charge of discrimination.

Bona Fide Occupational Qualification (BFOQ)

A **BFOQ** is a job qualification based on sex, religion, or national origin that is necessary for the operation of business. A particular religious belief is a BFOQ for a pastor of a church. Similarly, an actor, to qualify for a role, may need to be a certain sex for purposes of realism and thus sex is a BFOQ for such employment.

The BFOQ exception has been applied narrowly, however. For a discriminatory qualification for employment to fall within the BFOQ exception, the employer must be able to establish that the job qualification is carefully formulated to respond to public safety, privacy, or other public needs. And the formulation of the policy must not be broader than is reasonably necessary to preserve the safety or privacy of individuals involved. For example, a restriction on hiring male employees for work in a nursing home occupied by women is excessive if male employees can work in jobs not involved with the personal care of the residents. Nor is personal preference a justification for a BFOQ; for example, many airlines have argued that there is a customer preference for female as opposed to male flight attendants. But customer preference is not a basis for a BFOQ; it is not a business necessity.

C O N S I D E R . . . **19.7** The EEOC began investigating Hooters Restaurant chain in 1991. Hooters serves casual food and employs what the company refers to as Hooters Girls as waitresses. The Hooters Girls dress in shorts and T-shirts. In 1995, the EEOC charged Hooters with discrimination, finding that its policy of hiring only female waitresses amounts to sex discrimination. Hooters was fined and ordered to hire male waiters.

Mike McNeil, a vice president of Hooters, responded that federal law does allow some gender-based hiring, and he cited the Playboy organization, which is permitted to hire women only as Bunnies.

Marcia Greenberger, co-president of the National Women's Law Center, said Hooters is violating the law (just as airlines did in the past) when they hired only thin, beautiful women as waitresses. Ms. Greenberger also said Hooters is "stereotyping women in a way that does them no favors. Why would someone put up with this?"

Meghan O'Malley-Barnard, a Hooters bartender in Boca Raton, Florida, feels that the EEOC's "political correctness" could cost her her job. Ms. O'Malley-Barnard led a Hooters Girl march at the White House. She said at the march, "We're here to send one clear message to the EEOC—get a grip."

The EEOC has over 100,000 pending cases involving charges of discrimination. Is the case against Hooters an effective use of government resources? Do you feel Hooters has violated the law?

Seniority or Merit Systems

The goals and objectives of Title VII are often inconsistent with labor union rules of operation. Although matters of discrimination and union supervision are both covered by federal law, there are some conflicts between the two statutory schemes. Which controls the other: the remedial effect of Title VII or the long-standing history of seniority and other union rules? Although the exception for seniority and merit systems has always been a part of Title VII, early decisions made Title VII goals superior and invalidated many of the seniority and merit systems.

The criteria to be used in determining whether a seniority or merit system is valid are as follows:

1. The system must apply to all employees.
2. Whatever divisions or units are used for the system must follow the industry custom or pattern; that is, the divisions cannot be set up so as to discriminate against particular races or groups.
3. The origins of the system cannot lie in racial discrimination.
4. The system must be maintained for seniority and merit purposes and not to perpetuate racial discrimination.

Aptitude and Other Tests

Any employer charged with Title VII discrimination because of employee aptitude testing must be able to show that the tests used are valid. Validity means the tests are related to successful job performance and that a test does not have the effect of eliminating certain races from the employment market.

An employer can validate a test in any of several different ways. Test scores of applicants can later be compared with the applicants' eventual job performance to validate the test. An employer can also give the test to current employees and use the correlation between their scores and job performance as a means for validating the test. Some tests can be validated by their content. For example, requiring potential police officers to complete a driving course, a physical fitness test, and a marksmanship test is valid because the tests are based on the things police officers actually do.

Misconduct

For many years, an absolute defense to discrimination was employee misconduct. If an employee violated company rules, there was no discrimination case. The defense was so broad that even evidence the employer acquired *after* the termination and charge of discrimination could be used as a defense. In the following case, the Supreme Court limited this defense.

McKennon v. Nashville Banner Publishing Co.
115 S. Ct. 879 (1995)

LYING IS NOT A DEFENSE FOR DISCRIMINATION

FACTS

For 30 years, Christine McKennon (petitioner) worked for Nashville Banner Publishing Company (respondent), but was terminated as part of a work reduction plan. She was 62 years old at the time of her termination.

Ms. McKennon filed suit alleging her termination was a violation of the Age Discrimination in Employment Act (ADEA).

In preparation of the case, the Banner took McKennon's deposition. She testified that during her final year of employment, she had copied several confidential documents bearing upon the company's financial condition. She had access to these records as secretary to the Banner's comptroller. Ms. McKennon took the copies home and showed them to her husband. Her motivation, she averred, was apprehension that she was about to be fired because of her age. When she became concerned about her job, she removed and copied the documents for "insurance" and "protection." A few days after

Continued

these deposition disclosures, the Banner sent Ms. McKennon a letter declaring that removal and copying of the records was in violation of her job responsibilities and advising her (again) that she was terminated. The Banner's letter also recited that had it known of Ms. McKennon's misconduct, it would have discharged her at once for that reason.

Nashville Banner conceded its discrimination in district court, which granted summary judgment for Banner on grounds that Ms. McKennon's misconduct was a defense. The court of appeals affirmed and Ms. McKennon appealed.

JUDICIAL OPINION

KENNEDY, Justice

We shall assume that the sole reason for McKennon's initial discharge was her age, a discharge violative of the ADEA. Our further premise is that the misconduct revealed by the deposition was so grave that McKennon's immediate discharge would have followed its disclosure in any event. We do question the legal conclusion reached by those courts that after-acquired evidence of wrongdoing which would have resulted in discharge bars employees from any relief under the ADEA. That ruling is incorrect.

The ADEA, enacted in 1967 as part of an ongoing congressional effort to eradicate discrimination in the workplace, reflects a societal condemnation of invidious bias in employment decisions. The ADEA is but part of a wider statutory scheme to protect employees in the workplace nationwide.

The ADEA and Title VII share common substantive features and also a common purpose: "the elimination of discrimination in the workplace." Congress designed the remedial measures in these statutes to serve as a "spur or catalyst" to cause employers "to self-examine and to self-evaluate their employment practices and to endeavor to eliminate, so far as possible, the last vestiges" of discrimination. The ADEA in keeping with these purposes, contains a vital element found in both Title VII and the Fair Labor Standards Act: it grants an injured employee a right of action to obtain the authorized relief.

The objectives of the ADEA are furthered when even a single employee establishes that an employer has discriminated against him or her. The disclosure through litigation of incidents or practices which violate national policies respecting nondiscrimination in the work force is itself important, for the occurrence of violations may disclose patterns of noncompliance resulting from a misappreciation of the Act's operation or entrenched resistance to its commands, either of which can be of industry-wide significance. The efficacy of its enforcement mechanisms becomes one measure of the success of the Act.

As we have said, the case comes to us on the express assumption that an unlawful motive was the sole basis for the firing. McKennon's misconduct was not discovered until after she had been fired. The employer could not have been motivated by knowledge it did not have and it cannot now claim that the employee was fired for the nondiscriminatory reason. Mixed motive cases are inapposite here, except to the important extent they underscore the necessity of determining the employer's motives in ordering the discharge, an essential element in determining whether the employer violated the federal antidiscrimination law. As we have observed, "proving that the same decision would have been justified . . . is not the same as proving that the same decision would have been made."

The ADEA, like Title VII, is not a general regulation of the workplace but a law which prohibits discrimination. The statute does not constrain employers from exercising significant other prerogatives and discretions in the course of the hiring, promoting, and discharging of their employees. In determining appropriate remedial action, the employee's wrongdoing becomes relevant not to punish the employee, or out of concern "for the relative moral worth of the parties," but to take due account of the lawful prerogatives of the employer in the usual course of its business and the corresponding equities that it has arising from the employee's wrongdoing.

Continued

The proper boundaries of remedial relief in the general class of cases where, after termination, it is discovered that the employee has engaged in wrongdoing must be addressed by the judicial system in the ordinary course of further decisions, for the factual permutations and the equitable considerations they raise will vary from case to case. We do conclude that here, and as a general rule in cases of this type, neither reinstatement nor front pay is an appropriate remedy. It would be both inequitable and pointless to order the reinstatement of someone the employer would have terminated, and will terminate, in any event and upon lawful grounds.

The object of compensation is to restore the employee to the position he or she would have been in absent the discrimination, but that principle is difficult to apply with precision where there is after-acquired evidence of wrongdoing that would have led to termination on legitimate grounds had the employer known about it.

Where an employer seeks to rely upon after-acquired evidence of wrongdoing, it must first establish that the wrongdoing was of such severity that the employee in fact would have been terminated on those grounds alone if the employer had known of it at the time of the discharge. The concern that employers might as a routine matter undertake extensive discovery into an employee's background or performance on the job to resist claims under the Act is not an insubstantial one, but we think the authority of the courts to award attorney's fees, mandated under the statute, 29 U.S.C. §§ 216(b), 626(b), and in appropriate cases to invoke the provisions of Rule 11 of the Federal Rules of Civil Procedure will deter most abuses.

The judgment is reversed.

CASE QUESTIONS
1. Why is the timing of the misconduct disclosure important?
2. Does Banner deny discriminatory intent?
3. Why are "mixed motive" cases not relevant in this analysis?
4. Is reinstatement a remedy?

ENFORCEMENT OF TITLE VII

Title VII is an enabling act that created the Equal Employment Opportunity Commission for the purpose of administration and enforcement. The EEOC is a five-member commission whose members are appointed by the president with the approval of the Senate. As with all other federal commissions, no more than three members can belong to the same political party.

The EEOC was given very broad powers under Title VII. In addition to its rule-making and charging powers, the EEOC has very broad investigatory authority, including the authority to subpoena documents and testimony.

Steps in an EEOC Case

THE COMPLAINT

An EEOC complaint can be filed by an employee or by the EEOC. An employee has 180 days (in some cases, up to 300 days) from the time of the alleged violation to file a complaint. The EEOC does not have such a statute of limitations.

The complaint is filed with either the EEOC or the state administrative agency set up for employment discrimination issues. For the state agency to continue handling the complaint, it must be an EEOC-approved program. If it is not, the EEOC handles the complaint. The EEOC has special forms that can be filled out by any employee wishing to file such a complaint.

NOTIFICATION TO THE EMPLOYER

Once a complaint has been filed, the EEOC has 10 days to notify the employer of the charges. Employers are prohibited from the time of notification from taking any retaliatory action against the charging employee.

EEOC ACTION

After the complaint is filed, the EEOC has 180 days from that time to take action in the case before the complaining party can file suit on the matter. During this time the EEOC can use its investigatory powers to explore the merits of the charges. In the case of *University of Pennsylvania* v. *EEOC*, 493 U.S. 182 (1990), the Supreme Court ruled that the EEOC could have access to all information in an employee's file—even evaluation letters in which evaluators were promised confidentiality. This is also a conciliation period during which the EEOC may try to work out a settlement between the employer and the employee.

THE RIGHT-TO-SUE LETTER

If the EEOC has not settled its complaint within 180 days from the time of its filing, the employee has the right to demand a **right-to-sue letter** from the EEOC, which is a certification that the employee has exhausted his or her administrative remedies. If a state agency is involved, the time for its settlement of the matter must also expire before the employee can take the matter to court.

The employee has the right to this letter regardless of the EEOC's findings. Even if the EEOC has investigated and determined that there are no merits to the charges, the employee can still pursue the case in court.

Remedies Available under Title VII

Remedies available under Title VII include injunctions, back pay, punitive damages, and attorney' fees. If a court finds a violation, it may order that corrective or affirmative action be taken to compensate for past wrongs. An injunction usually requires the employer to stop the illegal discrimination and then institute a plan to hire or promote minorities. Back-pay awards are limited to two years under Title VII. Section 706(b) of the act permits successful parties to recover "reasonable attorneys' fees."

An employer cannot take retaliatory action against employees who file charges or who are successful in a suit; Title VII makes such action unlawful.

Title VII originally allowed damages for back pay for all forms of discrimination. Punitive and compensatory damages were permitted in race and ethnic discrimination cases. The 1991 amendments extend the recovery of punitive and compensatory damages to cases involving sex, religion, or disability. The following caps are placed on compensatory and punitive damages in sex, religion, and disability cases:

Size of Employer	Cap
15–100 employees	$ 50,000
101–200 employees	$100,000
201–500 employees	$200,000
Over 500 employees	$300,000

The limits do not include back pay or medical bills and do not apply to racial or ethnic discrimination cases.

OTHER ANTIDISCRIMINATION LAWS

Age Discrimination in Employment Act of 1967

Review the Age Discrimination in Employment Act:
http://www.law.cornell.edu/uscode/29/621.html

Title VII does not cover the very real problem of age discrimination, which generally involves companies' hiring preference for younger people. To correct this loophole, the Age Discrimination in Employment Act (ADEA) was passed in 1967, and the EEOC was given responsibility for its enforcement. The act covers all employers with 20 or more employees and prohibits age discrimination in the hiring, firing, and compensation of employees. All employment agencies are covered. Those protected under the act are workforce members above age 40.

CONSIDER...

19.8 Edward Ackerman was an employee of Diamond Shamrock Corporation and its predecessor corporations for 23 years. In 1978, he held the title of director of corporate communications. On August 31, 1978, at a meeting with his superior, he was informed that his job was to be eliminated during corporate reorganization and that his duties were to be divided between two employees who had been reporting to him.

Because Mr. Ackerman's job was to be eliminated, his superior suggested that he take early retirement. He was handed a packet of papers that contained a document labeled "Internal Communication" listing organizational changes "which are effective immediately." The documented changes were that Mr. Ackerman had "elected to take early retirement effective January 1, 1979" and that in the interim he was assigned to "corporate communications projects." The document went on to list the assignments of two of Mr. Ackerman's former subordinates. These men were reassigned to different departments of the corporation, and their responsibilities included all the duties formerly performed by Mr. Ackerman. At that time one of these men was in his late thirties and the other was in his early fifties. Mr. Ackerman was 59.

Another document in the packet was a memorandum detailing the terms of Mr. Ackerman's retirement. The retirement agreement would give him much more than the benefits to which he would be entitled if his employment simply were terminated. Under the terms of the proposed agreement, he was to receive approximately $100,000 more than the amount provided under Diamond's normal separation policies. The agreement also contained other miscellaneous benefits.

Mr. Ackerman eventually filed suit under Title VII.

Was there age discrimination? [*Ackerman* v. *Diamond Shamrock Corp.*, 670 F.2d 66 (6th Cir. 1982).]

CONSIDER...

19.9 When firms undergo a process of "trimming the fat" from their organizations, they often turn to older employees and offer them a buyout in exchange for early retirement. Does the ADEA present any problems with such tactics? What if the firm had buyouts for younger employees? Is there any force associated with such offers? Does the force element affect the application of ADEA?

C O N S I D E R . . .

19.10

On October 29, 1982, Preview Subscription Television, Inc., a subsidiary of Time, Inc., hired Thomas Taggart as a print production manager for Preview's magazine guide. Taggart was 58 years old at the time and had over 30 years experience in the printing industry.

In May 1983, Time notified Mr. Taggart that Preview would be dissolved, and that Preview employees would receive special consideration for all Time positions.

Mr. Taggart applied for 32 positions in various divisions at Time and its subsidiaries, including *Sports Illustrated, People, Life, Money,* HBO, and *Cinemax Guide*. He was interviewed but never hired. The reason given was that he was "overqualified."

Mr. Taggart filed suit alleging age discrimination. Time responded by saying he performed poorly at interviews, his letters and résumés for jobs contained numerous typographical errors, and he was argumentative with management and counselors.

Time hired less-qualified younger applicants for all the jobs. Has there been age discrimination? [*Taggart* v. *Time, Inc.*, 924 F. 2d 43 (2nd Cir. 1991).]

Equal Pay Act of 1963

Review the Equal Pay Act: http:// www.law.cornell. edu/uscode/29/ 206.html

The Equal Pay Act of 1963 is an amendment to the Fair Labor Standards Act. (The details of its coverage are outlined in Chapter 18.) The basic purpose of the act is to ensure that equal pay is given for jobs with equal content regardless of sex. Its application is limited to sex-based discrimination. Most of these kinds of cases deal with the issue of whether two jobs are "equal" in their content and whether the employees are thus entitled to equal pay.

Communicable Diseases in the Workplace

Whether employees can be fired because they may carry a communicable disease has recently become a crucial issue. Court decisions on the treatment of infected employees have varied, but a recent Supreme Court decision, *School Board of Nassau County* v. *Arline,* 480 U.S. 273 (1987), has been touted as a protectionist measure as a result of its finding that a school board could not discriminate against a teacher because she had tuberculosis (a contagious disease). The Americans with Disabilities Act (pg. 705) will provide new issues and remedies with regard to communicable diseases.

Rehabilitation Act of 1973

Review the Rehabilation Act: http://www.law. cornell.edu/uscode/ 29/701.html

Congress enacted the Rehabilitation Act to prohibit discrimination in employment against handicapped persons by persons and organizations that receive federal contracts or assistance. Section 504 of the act provides:

No otherwise qualified handicapped individual in the United States . . . shall, solely by reason of his handicap, be excluded from the participation in, be denied the benefits of, or be subject to discrimination under any program or activity receiving Federal financial assistance.

The Labor Department is responsible for enforcement of the act.

COVERED EMPLOYERS

Covered employers include contractors with federal contracts in excess of $2,500. These employers are required to take "affirmative action" to hire handicapped employees. States and municipalities are also covered by the act.

COVERED HANDICAPPED EMPLOYEES

A "handicapped individual" is defined under the act as any person who has a physical or mental impairment that "substantially limits one or more of such person's major life activities." Employees with diabetes, epilepsy, heart disease, cancer, retardation, blindness, or deafness are covered by the act. Individuals with a history of alcoholism and drug abuse are also considered "handicapped" under the provisions of the act.

Under the Rehabilitation Act employers are not required to hire unqualified applicants for job positions, but are required to hire only those handicapped persons who can perform the job after "reasonable accommodation" for their handicaps. Employers are not required to hire job applicants with histories of alcohol or drug abuse whenever such addiction or abuse would prevent successful job performance.

Americans with Disabilities Act

Review the Americans with Disabilities Act:
http://gopher.usdoj.gov/crt/ada/ada-home.html

The intent of the Americans with Disabilities Act (ADA) was to eliminate discrimination against individuals with disabilities. The ADA has been called the "Emancipation Proclamation" for disabled U.S. citizens.

The ADA is divided into five sections. Title I governs employment issues; Title II covers public services; Title III covers public accommodations and services; Title IV covers telecommunications relay services; and Title V has miscellaneous provisions.

The ADA was signed on July 26, 1990. It became effective on July 26, 1992, for employers with 25 or more employees and went into effect on July 26, 1994, for employers with 15 or more employees. The employment provisions (Title I) apply to private businesses and to state and local government agencies, but not to the federal government.

Section 102, the heart of Title I of the ADA, provides that

[n]o covered entity *shall discriminate against a* qualified individual *with a* disability *because of the disability of such individual in regard to job application procedures, the hiring, advancement, or discharge of employees, employee compensation, job training, and other terms, conditions, and privileges of employment.*

Employers cannot discriminate against a "qualified individual with a disability." "Qualified" means that the individual, with reasonable accommodation, can perform all "essential functions" of the job. Impairments such as gambling, kleptomania, pyromania, illegal drugs, and sexual disorders are excluded from protection.

Discrimination against qualified individuals includes hiring, promotion, and selection criteria. (Exams or tests must be job related.)

Employers may not discriminate under the ADA if a person cannot perform essential functions. Whereas a delivery job requires a driver's license, a computer programmer position does not.

Employers must make "reasonable accommodations" for disabled individuals to enable them to perform essential functions. Included in reasonable accommodations are providing employee facilities that are readily accessible to and usable by disabled individuals, job restructuring, allowing part-time or modified work schedules, reassigning disabled individuals to vacant positions, acquiring or modifying equipment, and providing qualified readers or interpreters.

Employers are not required to make accommodations that would result in "undue hardship," as determined by examining four factors:

1. The nature and *cost* of the accommodation
2. The size, workforce, and resources of the specific facility involved
3. The size, workforce, and resources of the covered entity
4. The nature of the covered entity's entire operation

Preemployment medical examinations are prohibited under the ADA, as are specific questions about a protected individual's disabilities. However, an employer may inquire about the ability of the applicant to perform job-related functions. "Can you carry 50 pounds of mail?" is an appropriate question; "Do you have the use of both arms?" is not.

Employers can refuse employment if an ADA-protected individual cannot perform necessary job functions. Also, employers can refuse to hire individuals who pose a direct threat to the health and safety of others in the workplace (assuming the risk cannot be minimized through accommodation).

The ADA is enforced through the EEOC and carries the same rights and remedies provided under Title VII. Exhibit 19.2 provides a list of items to help employers comply with ADA. Exhibit 19.3 (pg. 707) examines proper and improper questions for job interviews under ADA.

Exhibit 19.2
Compliance Tips for ADA

Minimizing an Employer's ADA Risks

1. Post notices describing the provisions of the ADA in your workplace.

2. Review job requirements to ensure that they bear a direct relationship to the ability to perform the essential functions of the job in question.

3. Identify, in writing, the "essential functions" of a job before advertising for or interviewing potential candidates.

4. Before rejecting an otherwise qualified applicant or terminating an employee on the basis of a disability, first determine that (a) the individual cannot perform the essential duties of the position, or (b) the individual cannot perform the essential duties of the position without imminent and substantial risk of injury to self or others, and (c) the employer cannot reasonably accommodate the disability.

5. Articulate factors, other than an individual's disability, that are the basis of an adverse employment decision. Document your findings and the tangible evidence on which a decision

to reject or terminate was based; make notes of accommodations considered.

6. Ask the disabled individual for advice on accommodations. This shows the employer's good faith and a willingness to consider such proposals.

7. Institute programs of benefits and consultation to assist disabled employees in effectively managing health, leave, and other benefits.

8. Check with insurance carriers regarding coverage of disabled employees and attempt (within economic reason) to maintain provided coverage or arrange for separate coverage.

9. Keep disabled individuals in mind when making structural alterations or purchasing office furniture and equipment.

10. Document all adverse employment actions, including reasons for the employment action with respect to disabled employees; focus on the employee's inability to do the job effectively rather than any relation to the employee's disability.

Legal	Illegal
1. Do you have 20/20 corrected vision?	What is your corrected vision?
2. How well can you handle stress?	Does stress ever affect your ability to be productive?
3. Can you perform this function with or without reasonable accommodation?	Would you need reasonable accommodation in this job?
4. How many days were you absent from work last year?	How many days were you sick last year?
5. Are you currently illegally using drugs?	What medications are you currently taking?
6. Do you regularly eat three meals per day?	Do you need to eat a number of small snacks at regular intervals throughout the day in order to maintain your energy level?
7. Do you drink alcohol?	How much alcohol do you drink per week?

Source: EEOC's "Enforcement Guidance on Pre-Employment Disability-related Inquiries," May 12, 1994.

Exhibit 19.3
Legal and Illegal Versions of Similar Job Interview Questions

FOR THE MANAGER'S DESK

AIDS AND THE WORKPLACE

Extract from statement by the World Health Organization in association with the International Labor Office.

Components of workplace policy

Persons in employment

1. HIV/AIDS screening: HIV/AIDS screening, whether direct (HIV testing), indirect (assessment of risk behaviors), or asking questions about tests already taken, should not be required.
2. Confidentiality: Confidentiality regarding all medical information, including HIV/AIDS status, must be maintained.
3. Informing the employer: There should be no obligation of the employee to inform the employer regarding his or her HIV/AIDS status.
4. Protection of employee: Persons in the workplace affected by, or perceived to be affected by HIV/AIDS, must be protected from stigmatization and discrimination by co-workers, unions, employers or clients. Information and education are essential to maintain the climate of mutual understanding necessary to ensure this protection.
5. Access to services for employees: Employees and their families should have access to information and educational programmes on HIV/AIDS, as well as to relevant counseling and appropriate referral.
6. Benefits: HIV-infected employees should not be discriminated against, including access to and receipt of benefits from statutory social security programmes and occupationally related schemes.

Continued

7. Reasonable changes in working arrangements: HIV infection by itself is not associated with any limitation in fitness to work. If fitness to work is impaired by HIV-related illness, reasonable alternative working arrangements should be made.

8. Continuation of employment relationship: HIV infection is not a cause for termination of employment. As with many other illnesses, persons with HIV-related illnesses should be able to work as long as medically fit for available appropriate work.

9. First aid: In any situation requiring first aid in the workplace, precautions need to be taken to reduce the risk of transmitting blood-borne infections, including hepatitis B. These standard precautions will be equally effective against HIV transmission.

E T H I C A L   I S S U E S

19.4 Walt Disney Company extended health insurance coverage to partners of gay and lesbian employees. The *Village Voice* was the first company to offer such benefits and did so in 1982. Other companies, such as Time Warner, Lotus Development, Microsoft, Nynex, Levi Strauss, Coors, and Ben & Jerry's, followed.

Upon Disney's announcement, 15 Florida legislators signed and sent a letter of protest to Disney's CEO, Michael Eisner. The letter stated that "family-friendly" Disney was "belittling the sanctity of marriage" and forcing all 65,000 Disney employees and its customers to pick up the tab for AIDS patients. Disney, Levi Strauss, and Coors responded that they have conducted research and that the additional cost is minimal.

Representative Rob Brooks, a physician and the legislator who initiated the letter to Disney, explains that he treats AIDS patients and that the cost is $150,000 or more. Mr. Brooks added, "I see the tragedy of young people dying from AIDS on a regular basis. I feel this policy is headed in the wrong direction. In the long run, it will result in an increased number of AIDS cases."

Coors indicated that it received 90 calls when it implemented its coverage, two-thirds voicing objection. The callers stated "they would not drink our product anymore."

What are the ethical issues involved in this choice of extending coverage? Are shareholders affected? Are employees affected? Is there a right decision?

The Family and Medical Leave Act

Review the Family and Medical Leave Act: http://www.law. cornell.edu/uscode/ 29/2601.html

Passed in 1993, this federal law requires companies with 50 or more employees to provide 12 weeks' leave each year for medical or family reasons, including the birth or adoption of a child or the illness of a spouse, parent, or child. Although pay is not required during the leave, medical benefits of the employee must continue, and the same or equivalent job must be available for the employee upon his or her return.

Realities of Climbing the Corporate Ladder: Permanent Family Leave

Jeffrey E. Stiefler, Harvard MBA 1970, was described by his classmates as not being a scholar but intensely competitive. He was hired by Boise-Cascade after graduation and then moved to a marketing position at Citicorp. In 1983, he left to serve as a senior VP at IDS Financial Services, which was acquired a few months later by American Express. Harvey Golub was hired to head IDS, and he and Stiefler turned it into a steady producer for American Express. He was described as moving about the office at a half-run. In 1985, Mr. Stiefler left to become president of Philadelphia Saving Fund Society, a troubled thrift. Mr. Golub, now head of American Express, asked Mr. Stiefler to return. He did and IDS continued to perform well. In 1993, Mr. Golub asked that Mr. Stiefler be made president.

Jeffrey E. Stiefler, Former President, American Express

Jeffery E. Stiefler

Mr. Stiefler announced in November 1995 that he was leaving his position as president of American Express to "work at a less intense pace and spend more time with his family."

The 49-year-old executive earned $4 million in 1994 and enjoyed the usual executive perks such as use of the company's four jets for personal and business travel. A "workaholic who gets results," he enjoyed a rapid climb to the top position at American Express. Why would Mr. Stiefler leave?

The death of Mr. Stiefler's father caused him to reflect on his personal life. Mr. Stiefler has had four marriages, two of them to the same woman. He has four sons and notes, "To do this job right is an all-encompassing proposition. I felt I wasn't doing as good a job with the kids as I wanted. I needed to have a better balance between work and my family, and have some time left over for me."

Mr. Stiefler's third wife says, "He's had the corporate success he wanted as a fairly young man, his health is great, he has the resources to do whatever he wants. Why not? He's going to watch his sons grow up. How many presidents of Fortune 500 companies get to do that?"

Issues

1. Is a work/family conflict inevitable?
2. Are there statutory protections to prevent it?
3. How can corporations retain talented executives with these concerns?

THE GLOBAL WORKFORCE

Currently two thousand U.S. companies have 21,000 subsidiary operations in 21 countries throughout the world. With the free trade agreements (see Chapter 7), those numbers will increase, as will the sizes of the global operations. One of the many employment issues that arise with respect to employees in the subsidiary operations is whether the protections of Title VII apply to workers in these foreign operations. In *EEOC* v. *Arabian American Oil Co.*, 499 U.S. 244 (1991), the U.S. Supreme Court was faced with the issue of whether U.S. companies could engage in employment discrimination against U.S. citizens when they are working in countries outside the United States. The Court held that the companies are governed by the employment laws of the country of operations and not the provisions of U.S. legislation.

FOR THE MANAGER'S DESK

OVERSEAS JOB? SEND A WOMAN

Gender fears unfounded in most countries

The management-develoment exercise seemed simple enough.

A group of five executives had to pick someone to head a mining operation in Latin America. After a review of the job requirements and resumes clearly pointed to one person, it seemed even easier.

Until one manager pointed out his biggest concern: The candidate was a woman.

It's not an uncommon reaction. The number of women in plum overseas jobs has grown in recent years, as international business opportunities have exploded, but women still face hurdles.

Some commonly held myths identified by Nancy Adler, a management professor at McGill University and co-editor of *Competitive Frontiers: Women Managers*

in a Global Economy (Blackwell, $29.95):

- Women don't want to work abroad.
- Companies shouldn't risk sending them.
- Business women aren't accepted in foreign countries.

Women actually have far more trouble snagging overseas assignments from North American employers than doing a good job once they get there, Adler says.

Reluctance to place women in global jobs is still a big issue, says Geraldine Barry, manager of Latin American

marketing and business development for General Electric's Medical Systems division.

Barry has worked for GE Medical Systems for almost 20 years. More often than not, she has held overseas jobs, including a four-year stint in Australia as national sales manager.

Culture, not gender

When she started, few women held international posts, especially in such a technical field.

Barry cites "almost an overprotective attitude—'If we put a woman in this position and she fails, then we're set back 20 years.'

"It's improved, but . . . the attitude exists."

Her experiences suggest that competence and cultural sensitivity, not gender, make for successful performance abroad.

"When you go into an international environment, whether you are male or female, people look at you and say, 'What can you do for me'" Barry says.

Continued

"What made the difference for me is that I had instant credibility, because I knew the products. I had something that they needed."

In Japan, she says, "I wasn't there as a woman trying to run Japan" but as a business woman providing essential services, products and information.

Any American on foreign turf with a "We do it better in the United States" approach or a "take no prisoners" attitude is asking for trouble.

"An overaggressive male will have the same problems as an overaggressive female," says Barry, who markets diagnostic-imaging equipment.

Seen in 'a different class'
Female professionals working overseas typically are seen as Americans first, females second, regardless of how the country treats native women.

"Through their work, women must become less gender-typed. They become 'a senior executive,'" says Marlene Rossman, a New York consultant and author of *The International Businesswoman of the 1990s* (Praeger, $19.95).

"Gender becomes a lot less important due to the quality of their work," Rossman says.

It's a phenomenon familiar to Anne Underwood, Corning's marketing manager for Latin America.

"If you are foreign and well-educated, you fit into a different class," she says. "They don't look at you as, say, a Venezuelan woman."

Underwood, based in Corning's Latin American headquarters in Miami, spends about 60 percent of her time traveling between Brazil, Chile and Colombia. She had expected more resistance from businessmen in the region, but found that proper introductions by her management set her up as an "expert" from the start. That's not to say everything is rosy.

Any executive going overseas will encounter stereotypes of Americans as loud and overbearing. And they must adapt to alien cultural norms. Women are no exception.

Off-duty 'family' helpful
In Latin America, for example, Underwood found it wasn't considered appropriate for a single woman to go sightseeing alone. So she made an effort to meet people outside work, looking up friends of friends or making contacts through her Cornell University alumni network.

That's the very strategy advocated by Rossman, who trains executives in multicultural sensitivity. A woman working in cultures where social life revolves around families can help herself by building her own "extended family" outside work.

Rossman advises women not to get caught up by the little hurdles they will encounter, but to build power bases around their positions, job knowledge and understanding of foreign customs.

Rossman learned those lessons in the early 1980s, as a marketing consultant working with agricultural businesses in the Dominican Republic.

"What they saw was a blond, blue-eyed 'dolly' in her early 30s," she says. "I had to spend a great deal of time . . . to shift their mind-set."

Today, the sheer force of numbers—more women traveling to cut international deals and, in some cases, climbing the management ranks in their home countries—may have made it easier.

"In the Pacific Rim, Latin America and Europe, I have seen women succeed wildly," Rossman says.

It's a message more corporate executives should pay attention to, particularly as international business experience becomes a hot ticket to senior management.

"With an open mind," Barry says, "any woman could do it."

Source: Susan Barciela, "Overseas Job? Send a Woman," *Arizona Republic,* May 1, 1994, p. D2. Reprinted with permission.

Congress responded to the Supreme Court's ruling in *Arabian American Oil* by adding a section to the Civil Rights Act of 1991 addressing the issue of foreign operations. The statutory provision on foreign operations and civil rights protections is neither universal nor automatic. The amendment provides basically that if there is a conflict between U.S. employment discrimination laws and those of a host country, a company should follow the laws of the host country. An example would be a law in the host country that prohibits the employment of women in management. The company would be required to follow that prohibition for operations located in the host country. If the host country has no laws on employment discrimination, the company is then required to follow all U.S. antidiscrimination laws.

Several multilateral treaties govern the rights of workers. In 1948 the United Nations adopted its Universal Declaration of Human Rights. The declaration supports, among other things, equality of pay and nondiscriminatory employment policies. Also, the Helsinki Final Act of 1973 supports nondiscriminatory employment policies. In 1977, the International Labor Office issued its Tripartite Declaration of Principles Concerning Multinational Enterprises, which supports equal pay and nondiscriminatory payment policies. The EU has adopted all of these treaties and policies for their implementation.

Review the Universal Declaration of Human Rights: http://www. un.org/Overview/ rights.html

SUMMARY

What laws governing employment discrimination exist?

- Civil Rights Act 1866, 1964—federal statutes prohibiting discrimination in various aspects of life (employment, voting)
- Equal Pay Act—equal pay for the same work regardless of gender
- Equal Employment Opportunity Act—antidiscrimination employment amendment to Civil Rights Act
- Pregnancy Discrimination Act—prohibits refusing to hire or promote or firing because of pregnancy
- Age Discrimination Act—prohibits hiring, firing, promotion, benefits, raises based on age
- Rehabilitation Act of 1973—federal statute prohibiting discrimination on basis of disability by federal agencies and contractors
- Americans with Disabilities Act—federal law prohibiting discrimination on basis of disability by certain employees
- Family Medical Leave Act—federal law providing for 12 weeks of leave for childbirth, adoption, or family illness

What types of discrimination exist?

- Disparate treatment—form of discrimination in which members of different races/sexes are treated differently
- Disparate impact—test or screening device that affects one group more than another
- Pattern or practice of discrimination—theory for establishing discrimination that compares population percentages with workplace percentages
- Sexual harassment—form of discrimination that involves a quid pro quo related to sexual favors or an atmosphere of harassment

Are there any defenses to discrimination?

- BFOQ—job qualification based on sex, religion, or national origin that is necessary for the operation of a business, such as religious affiliation for the pastor of a church
- Affirmative action—programs created to remedy past wrongs that permit choices on the basis of race, sex, or national origin

QUESTIONS AND PROBLEMS

1. Patricia Lorance is an hourly wage employee at the Montgomery Works AT&T electronics products plant. She had been employed there since the early 1970s and under union rules accrued seniority through her years of service at the plant. In 1979 the union entered into a new collective bargaining agreement providing that seniority would be determined by department and not on a plant-wide basis. The effect of the change was to put Ms. Lorance at the bottom of the seniority ladder in the testing area despite her longevity in the plant. When layoffs became necessary, she and the other female testers were laid off because of the new seniority rule. Without the new rule, Ms. Lorance and the other women would not have been victims of the cutbacks. Does the seniority system violate Title VII? [*Lorance v. AT&T Technologies, Inc.*, 490 U.S. 900 (1989).]

2. Wayne Metz is a 54-year-old plant manager for Transit Mix, Inc., earning $15.75 an hour. Transit, which was experiencing a financial setback, discharged Mr. Metz and replaced him with Donald Burzloff, a 43-year-old assistant manager earning $8.05 an hour. A lower court found that age was a factor in the decision to discharge Mr. Metz because of his higher salary resulting from increases for each year of employment, but that economic factors were the prime motivation for the discharge. Mr. Metz has argued that if economic factors were the reason for his discharge, there were other ways to avoid his termination. Is his employer required to explore other options under ADEA? What other options would Transit and Mr. Metz have? [*Metz v. Transit Mix, Inc.*, 828 F.2d 1202 (7th Cir. 1987).]

3. Lois Robinson is a welder at a ship repair yard in Jacksonville, Florida. Her male co-workers had pictures of nude and partially nude women in their work area. Ms. Robinson complained the pictures constituted sexual harassment. Is she right? [*Robinson v. Jackson Shipyards*, 760 F. Supp. 1486 (M.D. Fla. 1991).]

4. On August 11, 1980, Shelby Memorial Hospital hired Sylvia Hayes, a certified X-ray technician, to work the 3–11 P.M. shift in the hospital's radiology department. Two months later, she was fired after she informed her supervisor that she was pregnant. The supervisor fired Ms. Hayes because Dr. Cecil Eiland, the hospital's radiology director and director of radiation safety, recommended that Ms. Hayes be removed from all areas using ionizing radiation and the hospital could not find alternative work for her. After her dismissal, Ms. Hayes filed suit for violation of the Pregnancy Discrimination Act and Title VII. Should she recover? [*Hayes v. Shelby Memorial Hosp.*, 726 F.2d 1543 (11th Cir. 1984).]

5. The Masonic nursing home has mostly female, but some male, occupants and hires fewer male attendants than female ones. The administration of the home maintains that the female occupants (for privacy reasons) would not consent to intimate personal care by males and would, in fact, leave the home. A substantial portion of the women at the home are "total care" patients who require assistance in performing virtually all activities, including bathing, dressing, and using toilets, catheters, and bedpans. In a suit brought by a male nurse's aide who was denied employment, who would win? [*Fessel v. Masonic Home*, 17 FEP Cases 330 (Del. 1978).]

6. Woolworth Victor Davis applied for a position as a firefighter with the city of Philadelphia in 1977. When he reported for his physical exam, the physician noticed a scar; and Mr. Davis explained that he had used amphetamines in 1972 but had not engaged in drug use since then. He was told he could not be hired because the city would not employ anyone with a drug history. Mr. Davis filed suit under the Rehabilitation Act of 1973. What will be the outcome? Will the ADA protect him? [*Davis v. Butcher*, 451 F. Supp. 791 (E.D. Pa. 1978).]

7. Audra Sommers (aka Timothy Cornesh) a self-claimed "female with the anatomical body of a male," was hired by Budget Marketing on April 22, 1980. She was fired on April 24, 1980, because the female workers at Budget refused to allow her in the women's restroom and threatened to quit if she/he were allowed in. Ms. Sommers

brought suit for a violation of Title VII alleging discrimination on the basis that she was a transsexual. Does Title VII apply? [*Sommers* v. *Budget Marketing, Inc.*, 667 F.2d 748 (8th Cir. 1982).]

8. Winnie Teal was a black employee of Connecticut's Department of Income Maintenance. To be promoted to supervisor, Ms. Teal was required to obtain a passing score on a written exam. Of the 324 candidates taking the exam, 48 were black. Of these, 54.17 percent passed, whereas 80 percent of the white candidates passed. Ms. Teal failed and was excluded from consideration for the supervisor's position. She filed a Title VII suit alleging the test was not job related and excluded blacks in disproportionate numbers. What will be the outcome? [*Connecticut* v. *Winnie Teal*, 457 U.S. 440 (1982).]

9. American Airlines passed a grooming rule that prohibited a "corn row" hairstyle on all employees. Renee Rogers, a black woman, brought a Title VII suit alleging that the denial of her right to wear the hairstyle intruded upon her rights and discriminated against her. What will be the result? [*Rogers* v. *American Airlines, Inc.*, 527 F. Supp. 229 (S.D.N.Y. 1981).]

10. American Airlines has a policy of not hiring flight officers over the age of 40. The reason for their policy is that it takes 10 to 15 years for a flight officer to become a co-pilot and then another 10 to 15 years for a co-pilot to become a captain. Because the FAA requires retirement at age 60, service would be limited. Edward L. Murnane, age 43, was denied employment on the basis of age and filed an age discrimination suit. Is age a BFOQ for the job? [*Murnane* v. *American Airlines, Inc.*, 667 F.2d 98 (D.C. 1981).]

Problem 1

America West Airlines, a Phoenix-based airline, recently emerged from Chapter 11 bankruptcy. Competition in the airline industry continues to be intense. America West, along with Southwest and a few other low-fare airlines has not been unionized.

In 1994, several applicants for America West mechanic positions seemed to be "job jumpers." Their employment histories demonstrated a pattern of very short times in jobs at various locations around the country. The supervisor responsible for hiring suspects the mechanics are union salts and he refuses to hire them.

In examining the America West workforce, a local think tank releases information that indicates the America West employees are largely under age 40.

In early December 1995, America West told five hundred mechanics not to report for work hours before their shift was to begin. Some of the mechanics did not receive the message and were told of the layoff as they reported for work and were turned away.

On the evening following the layoffs, some mechanics picketed outside the America West Arena, home of the Phoenix Suns, where the Phoenix Suns were playing a basketball game. One of the mechanics said in a TV interview, "How can I get through Christmas now?"

In early 1996, the America West mechanics voted in favor of unionization.

DISCUSS THE FOLLOWING:
a. The legality of refusing to hire the "job jumpers"
b. Any problems with the age composition of the airlines
c. The legality of the layoff
d. The legality of the picketing
e. The eligibility of the laid-off mechanics for unemployment
f. The nature of the collective bargaining unit.

Problem 2

Jean Bertrum is an auditor with the Denver public accounting firm of Knox, Gilliam and Pugh. Ms. Bertrum has been assigned the audit of the University of Colorado at Boulder. While en route to Boulder one morning to conduct on-site work, Ms. Bertrum dozed at the wheel, veered to the left, and collided with a passing car. Both Ms. Bertrum and the driver of the other car, Carl Davis, were injured. Carl Davis is an employee of the University of Colorado, who was returning to Boulder after a Denver dinner meeting the previous evening and an alumni breakfast that morning.

When Alec Knox, the managing partner of Knox, Gilliam and Pugh, heard of the accident, he said, "It happened because she's up every night with that baby. You can't have it all. Motherhood and public accounting don't mix. I'm not going to support her next promotion."

DISCUSS THE FOLLOWING:
a. Whether Jean Bertrum has any liability for the accident
b. Whether Knox, Gilliam and Pugh has any liability for the accident
c. Suppose Davis's speed at the time of the collision was 90 mph. Would he have any liability? Would the University of Colorado have any liability?
d. Are either Bertrum or Davis covered by workers' compensation?
e. Evaluate the legal issues surrounding Alec Knox's remark about the accident and Ms. Bertrum.

Problem 3

A female manager at a Saks Fifth Avenue retail store was raped by a store security guard on February 3, 1994. She was too traumatized to report the rape. The security guard had told her he wanted to have sexual relations with her and she had refused. The rape occurred shortly thereafter. Five days after the first attack, the same security guard attacked and raped the manager again. She experienced a complete emotional breakdown and went to the police. After the second sexual assault, the guard was charged with rape and sexual abuse. He entered a guilty plea for sexual abuse and is now in prison.

During the course of the police department investigation of the case, the Saks manager learned that the guard had been convicted of violent sexual assault before Saks hired him as a security guard.

A background check was not done on him before he was hired. There was also a pending complaint against him by another female employee for sexual harassment.

The manager filed suit against Saks for negligence. Saks has asked that the manager's suit be dismissed because her injuries are covered by workers' compensation and the damages under these statutes are her sole and exclusive remedy.

In Saks correct? Is workers' compensation the manager's only remedy? Is this fair? What if an employer fails to take action when there is a sexual harassment complaint? Should the employer be held liable for a subsequent sexual assault? Is workers' compensation the only remedy for sexual harassment victims?

This portion of the book covers legal issues in forming and financing a business. The structure of a business determines its owners' rights and liabilities.

Part Five

Different business forms afford varying levels of flexibility for operations. In addition, the type of business structure creates opportunities for both initial financing of the business and its expansion.

Some forms of business financing require compliance with state and federal laws for sales of such business interests

Business Forms and Capitalization

as securities and bonds. These laws include disclosure requirements for sales and provide remedies for investors and impose liabilities on businesses when disclosures made about the nature of the interest and the business are incomplete or inaccurate.

Some businesses combine or merge in order to compete better in the evolving global economy. State and federal laws afford disclosure and protections for merging businesses and their owners and investors.

Judgment

After her husband's death, Dormilee Morton was left with her husband's construction business to run. Although she wanted input, she did not feel she had the time to be involved in overseeing day-to-day operations. She asked her son to handle the business operations with the idea that she would have some say if her son's work drifted too far from her husband's plans. She referred to herself as a "silent" or "limited" partner in the business. Wage taxes for the construction business were not paid, and the IRS tried to collect them from Mrs. Morton. She objected, saying she could not be held personally liable because she was a limited partner only. Is she correct?

CHAPTER 20

It is very often the case that businesses are not formed by

one person alone. The sole proprietorship is a popular

form of doing # *Forms of Doing Business*

business, but the largest businesses and the greatest

amount of income derive from businesses formed by more

than one person. The partnership, limited partner–

ship, and corporation are all multi-individual forms

of doing business. This chapter answers the

following questions: How are various business entities

formed? What are the advantages and disadvantages

of various entities? What are the rights, responsibilities,

and liabilities of the individuals involved?

Each of the forms of doing business is examined

by reviewing its formation, sources of funding, the

personal liability of owners, tax consequences, man-

agement and control, and the ease of transferring

interest. A summary overview of business forms is found

in Exhibit 20.1 (pg. 720).

> *Please accept my resignation. I don't want to belong to any organization that will accept me as a member.*
>
> **Groucho Marx**

Form	Formation	Funding	Management
Sole proprietorship	No formal requirements	Individual provides funds	Individual
Partnership	Articles of partnership	Capital contributions of partners	All partners or delegated to one
Limited partnership	Filing of articles of partnership	Capital contributions of general and limited partners	General partner
Corporation	Formal filing of articles of incorporation	Debt (bonds)/equity (shareholders)	Board of directors, officers and/or executive committee
S corporation or Subchapter S	Same as above (special IRS filings)	Same as above	Same as above
Limited liability company (LLC)	Formal filing—articles of organization	Capital contributions of members	No centralized management; all members manage or delegate to one member

Form	Transfer control	Taxes	Termination	Liability
Sole proprietorship	No transfer	Individual pays on individual return	Death; voluntary	Individual
Partnership	Transfer interest but not partner status	Partner takes profits and losses on individual return	Dissolution upon death; withdrawal of partner	Partners are personally liable
Limited partnership	Same as partnership (except RULPA)	Same as partnership	Same as partnership	General partner is personally liable; limited partners liable to extent of contribution
Corporation	Shares (with reasonable restrictions) are easily transferred	Corporation pays taxes; shareholders pay taxes on dividends	Dissolved only if limited in duration or shareholders vote to dissolve	No shareholder personal liability unless (1) watered or (2) corporate veil
S corporation or Subchapter S	Restrictions on transfer to comply with S corporation	Shareholders pay taxes on profits; take losses	Same as above	Same as above
Limited liability company (LLC)	No transfer without consent of the majority	Pass-through treatment	Dissolved upon death, bankruptcy	Limited liability — only liable to extent of capital contribution

Exhibit 20.1
Comparison of Forms of Conducting Business

THE SOLE PROPRIETORSHIP

Formation

A **sole proprietorship** is not a true business entity because it consists of only an individual operating a business. Often, a sole proprietorship is evidenced by the following language: "Homer Lane d/b/a Green Grower's Grocery"; d/b/a is an acronym for "doing business as."

Because a sole proprietorship comprises but one individual and no separate organization exists, there are no formal requirements for formation. The individual simply begins doing business. In some states, "d/b/a" businesspeople are required to publish and file the fictitious names under which they will be doing business.

Sources of Funding

Visit the Small Business Association: http://www. sbaonline.sba.gov/

Most sole proprietorships are small businesses, and initially their business capital needs are small. Their financing usually comes from loans, either direct loans from banks or loans through such government agencies as the Small Business Administration (SBA).

Some sole proprietorships are started with financial backing from other people, usually in the form of a personal loan. In such cases the sole proprietor may have the skills or clients for a successful business but not the funds necessary to begin.

Liability

Because financing for a sole proprietorship is based on the sole proprietor's credit rating and assets, the proprietor is personally liable for the business loan, and his or her assets are subject to attachment should there be a default. To get financing, a sole proprietor takes personal financial risk.

Tax Consequences

The positive side of unlimited personal liability of a sole proprietor is the right to claim all tax losses associated with the business. The income of the business is the income of the sole proprietor and is reported on the sole proprietor's income tax return. There is no separate filing requirement for the business itself. Moreover, although sole proprietors owe all the taxes, they also get the benefit of all business deductions.

Management and Control

The proprietor is the management of the business. In many businesses, the sole proprietor is both management and employee. The proprietor makes all decisions. This form of business operation is truly centralized management.

Transferability of Interest

Because the business in many ways is the owner, the business can be transferred only if the owner allows it. When a sole proprietor's business is transferred, the transfer consists of the property, inventory, and goodwill of the business. The sole proprietor is generally required to sign a non-competition agreement so that the goodwill that is paid for is preserved (see Chapter 11 for more details).

In addition, upon the owner's death the heirs or devisees of the owner would inherit the property involved in the business. They could choose to operate the business, but the business usually ends upon the death of the sole proprietor.

THE PARTNERSHIP

Review Indiana's Uniform Partnership Act: http://www.law.indiana.edu/codes/in/23/ch-23-4-1.html

Partnerships are governed by some version of the **Uniform Partnership Act (UPA)**, which has been adopted in 49 states. The UPA and similar uniform acts are the work of the National Conference of Commissioners on Uniform State Laws, which is a group of lawyers, judges, and professors who develop model laws in the interest of uniformity among the states. In 1994, a new final version of the UPA was adopted by the commissioners. Nine states have adopted the **Revised Uniform Partnership Act (RUPA)**, but some did not repeal the UPA. The UPA defines a partnership as an "association of two or more persons to carry on as co-owners, a business for profit." "Persons" can include corporations, known as "artificial" persons, and natural persons.

Formation

A partnership can be formed voluntarily by direct action of the parties, or its formation can be implied by the ongoing conduct of the parties.

VOLUNTARY FORMATION

The most desirable way to form a partnership (at least in terms of protecting partners' rights and liabilities) is to have the partners execute a partnership agreement,

Exhibit 20.2
Information Included in Articles of Partnership

Minimum requirements	Suggested provisions
1. Names of the partners	1. Disability issues
2. Name of the partnership	2. Insurance coverage
3. Nature of the partnership's business	3. Sale of interest
4. The time frame of operation	4. Divorce of one of the partners
5. Amount of each partner's capital contribution	5. Indemnity agreements
6. Managerial powers of partners	6. Noncompetition agreements
7. Rights and duties of partners	7. Leaves of absence
8. Accounting procedures for partnership books and records	
9. Methods for sharing profits and losses	
10. Salaries (if any) of the partners	
11. Causes and methods of dissolution	
12. Distribution of property if the partnership is terminated	

or draw up **articles of partnership**. The articles should include certain information, which is summarized in Exhibit 20.2 (pg. 722).

INVOLUNTARY FORMATION: PARTNERSHIPS BY IMPLICATION

A partnership can arise even though there is no express agreement and the parties do not call themselves partners. In certain circumstances, courts infer that a partnership exists even if the persons involved say they are not partners.

Simply owning property together does not result in a **partnership by implication**. But courts examine a number of factors in determining whether a partnership exists by implication. Section 7 of the UPA provides that if two or more parties share the profits of a business, it is prima facie evidence that a partnership exists. (Prima facie evidence means there is a presumption that a partnership exists.) However, the presumption of partnership by profit sharing can be overcome if someone received profits for any of the following reasons:

1. Profits paid to repay debts
2. Profits paid as wages or rent
3. Profits paid to a widow or estate representative
4. Profits paid for the sale of business goodwill

Many shopping center leases, for example, provide for the payment of both a fixed amount of rent and a percentage of net profits. The owners of the shopping center thus profit as the stores do, but they profit as landlords, not as partners with the shopping center businesses.

The following case addresses the question of whether a partnership exists.

Shaw v. Delta Airlines, Inc.
798 F. Supp. 1453 (D. Nev. 1992)

THE SKY IS BIG ENOUGH FOR THE TWO OF US

FACTS

Delta Airlines, Inc. (defendant), operates under a contractual arrangement with SkyWest Airlines, Inc., to serve as its ticketing and marketing agent. Delta is a large airline serving large cities, and SkyWest is a commuter airline shuttling passengers from large cities to outlying small towns.

Samuel Shaw took a Delta flight to Salt Lake City and then took a flight on SkyWest from Salt Lake City to Elko, Nevada. The SkyWest flight crashed just miles from the Elko airport and Shaw suffered serious personal injuries as a result. He and his wife, Lola (plaintiffs), brought suit against Delta as a partner of SkyWest seeking damages for his injuries. Delta moved for summary judgment on grounds that SkyWest was solely liable.

JUDICIAL OPINION

REED, Senior District Judge

Plaintiffs concede that SkyWest is not a subsidiary or division of Delta. However, Plaintiffs' argue that certain facts sustain the conclusion that SkyWest was Delta's agent for the purposes of carrying passengers on less-traveled "commuter" routes that Delta does not itself fly. They present evidence that indicates that SkyWest uses Delta trademarks and insignia, the two companies are often mentioned together by Delta in national print advertisements and airline industry schedules, and that Delta has control over SkyWest routes and timetables. Thus, Plaintiffs claim that Delta presents the image to the public that SkyWest is part of Delta, or at the least Delta's agent. As such, Plaintiffs argue, a jury could hold Delta liable on an apparent authority theory.

Continued

The court can only conceive of three legal relationships that might give rise to vicarious liability under facts such as the ones involved in this case. If Delta is liable to Plaintiffs, it must be because Delta was SkyWest's general partner, Delta was SkyWest's joint venturer, or because SkyWest was Delta's agent with apparent authority to carry passengers on behalf of Delta.

Since Delta and SkyWest were parties to a contract under which both would presumably make a profit from their combined efforts, one might argue that these two parties were engaged in a partnership. The position of the vast majority of states is that if two or more parties intend for their relationship to result in a partnership, the law will treat the relationship as a partnership, regardless of whether the parties themselves call the relationship a partnership or intend the legal consequences that flow from that label.

However, the authorities also clearly indicate that there is no specific test to determine the existence of a partnership. An express written agreement to form a partnership is not required. The trier of fact must look to the conduct of the parties and all the circumstances surrounding their relationship and transactions. The key factor is not the subjective intent of the parties to form a partnership, but instead the intent of the parties to do the things that the law will consider a partnership. It is immaterial that the parties do not call their relationship, or believe it to be, a partnership, especially where the rights of third parties are concerned.

The law provides a laundry list of factors to look at in deciding whether or not parties intended to form a partnership. Nevada has adopted the Uniform Partnership Act ("UPA") "Rules for determining existence of partnership." According to this section, "receipt by a person of a share of profits of a business is prima facie evidence that he is a partner in the business. . . . "

On its face, this section might seem to imply that any contractual agreement under which both parties receive profits is a partnership. However, most jurisdictions find that mere participation in profits does not create a partnership unless the partners also share losses. Also, most authorities require that each partner have some degree and right of control over the business. "Although the sharing of profits and losses is prima facie evidence of a partnership, the issue of control is the more important criterion in determining the existence of a partnership."

In the instant case, the agreement between Delta and SkyWest does not indicate any desire to engage in a business as risk-sharing partners with joint-control over the enterprise. It is true that both parties expected to make a profit from the enterprise; however, a person "who has no proprietary interest in a business except to share profits as compensation for services is not a partner or joint venturer." Even where one party exercises some degree of control over the other, and their joint fortunes depend upon the same business factors, a partnership does not necessarily exist.

In this case, SkyWest certainly did not have joint control over the operations of Delta. Nor did SkyWest directly participate in the profits or losses of the Delta corporation. The "Delta Connection" agreement might be characterized as simply a business referral arrangement whereby Delta benefits through its ability to issue tickets to connecting passengers and SkyWest benefits through the payments it receives on the tickets of passengers that Delta has sent to it. The court concludes that, under the above legal standards, no reasonable jury could conclude that Delta and SkyWest were general partners.

In Nevada, "[a] joint venture is a contractual relationship in the nature of an informal partnership wherein two or more persons conduct some business or enterprise, agreeing to share jointly, or in proportion to capital contributed, in profits and losses." It is usually entered into for a limited business objective and typically for a brief period of time.

The label "joint venture" clearly does not apply in this case. Delta and SkyWest did not agree to a short-term business deal in which they proposed to jointly share in profits or

Continued

losses. Nor did either party invest capital in a joint business deal. The court's reasoning from its partnership analysis applies equally as well here: Delta and SkyWest are contract parties to a business referral agreement. There is no joint venture under Nevada law.

Plaintiffs' major argument is that SkyWest was the agent of Delta for purposes of carrying passengers like Mr. Shaw. Delta argues that although it may be SkyWest's agent for ticketing, marketing, and scheduling, SkyWest is not *its* agent for any purpose. Since there is no explicit agency agreement, Plaintiffs argue instead that the law may deem SkyWest the agent of Delta on an apparent authority theory. They claim that Delta has used advertising and marketing strategies aimed at creating the impression in the minds of the traveling public that SkyWest is somehow a part of Delta.

Delta makes much of the fact that the Delta Connection agreement expressly states that no employee, independent contractor, or agent of either company shall be deemed to be an employee, independent contractor, or agent of the other. However, it is clear that a clause negating agency in a written contract is not controlling.

A principal is bound by the acts of its agent while acting in the course of his or her employment, and a principal is liable for those acts within the scope of the agent's authority. An agent's authority may be express, implied, or apparent. In Nevada, "apparent authority" is that authority which a principal holds its agent out as possessing, or permits the agent to exercise or to represent him- or herself as possessing, under such circumstances as to estop the principal from denying its existence. The existence or non-existence of an agency relationship is a question of fact for the jury.

First, the jury must decide whether or not there existed *any* principal-agent relationship between Delta and SkyWest. Second, if the answer to the first question is yes, the jury must next determine if SkyWest had the apparent authority to carry passengers for Delta. The answer to this second question will depend upon whether or not Delta created the impression in the minds of travelers like Mr. Shaw that SkyWest was its carrier-agent, not whether or not Delta and/or SkyWest actually intended such a relationship to exist or intended passengers to receive such an impression.

As to the first question, taking all the evidence in the light most favorable to the Plaintiffs, a reasonable jury could conclude that SkyWest was a Delta agent of some kind. If the jury were to find as a matter of fact that Delta fostered the impression in travelers' minds that SkyWest was its agent (or subsidiary or partner) then that would be enough to support the conclusion that there was a principal-agent relationship between the two airlines, whether or not Delta intended an actual legal agency. Under such an analysis, the first question collapses into the second and the only remaining relevant inquiry focuses on the apparent authority issue.

Also, this first question of whether an agency exists may be satisfied by *any* finding of agency. Once an agency is found to exist, the important question is actually one of scope. For example, a principal-agent relationship exists between a home seller and his or her real estate agent. However, if the agent took the initiative of selling the home owner's car, the agent would likely be exceeding the scope of the agent's authority, be it express, implied, or apparent. In this case, the jury could easily find that SkyWest was Delta's agent for *something*, for example, a ticketing agent, a booking agent, etc. Almost all contractual relationships will create agencies of one kind or another between the parties, no matter how small or limited in scope. Once the trier of fact has made that determination, the true issue in any agency case becomes the scope of the agent's authority.

After deciding either that the questions of agency and its scope are one and the same, or that an agency of some kind exists, the jury would then consider the apparent authority issue. Put in simple terms, the question here will be whether Delta represented to passengers that SkyWest possessed more authority to act as its agent than SkyWest actually did possess.

Continued

Plaintiffs present uncontroverted evidence that Delta has some measure of control over its relationship with SkyWest. Delta possesses the right to control the printing and distribution of SkyWest time-tables as SkyWest's marketing agent. Delta decides where and how this information gets published and may print SkyWest flight information as Delta connecting flights in appropriate airline guides. Delta also has the power to assign the flight numbers to SkyWest flights.

Plaintiffs also present evidence that tends to show that Delta's actions have effectively managed to equate SkyWest with Delta in the minds of the traveling public. Delta publishes SkyWest flight information in Delta timetables and refers to SkyWest's service as the "Delta Connection." The two names (Delta and SkyWest) appear together in national advertising materials along with the same trademark the "Delta Connection." The agreement between Delta and SkyWest provides for the use of Delta slogans and insignia "reflect the Delta Connection and the relationship between SkyWest and Delta." Advertising materials depict the Delta trademark (a red, white, and blue triangle) close by

the SkyWest name and Delta includes SkyWest destination cities in its own list of destinations. Delta issues SkyWest tickets on Delta ticket stock and provides its ticket stock to SkyWest for some of its ticketing needs.

The jury must decide if SkyWest was the agent of Delta with the apparent authority to carry passengers for Delta.

It is, therefore, hereby ordered that Defendant Delta's motion for summary judgment is denied.

CASE QUESTIONS

1. Why is the sharing of profits not enough to create a partnership between SkyWest and Delta?

2. Is the use of Delta's logo by SkyWest important to the case?

3. What two questions must be decided by the jury?

4. Do you believe Delta created the impression that SkyWest and Delta were one and the same?

5. Why do you think Mr. Shaw wishes to have Delta held liable?

C O N S I D E R . . .

20.1 Richard Chaiken entered into agreements with both Mr. Strazella and Mr. Spitzer to operate a barber shop. Mr. Chaiken was to provide barber chairs, supplies, and licenses. Messrs. Strazella and Spitzer were to bring their tools, and the agreements included work hours and holidays for them. The Delaware Employment Security Commission determined that Messrs. Strazella and Spitzer were employees, not partners, and sought to collect unemployment compensation for the two barbers. Mr. Chaiken maintains that they are partners and not employees. Who is correct? [*Chaiken* v. *Employment Security Comm'n*, 274 A.2d 707 (Del. 1971).]

INVOLUNTARY FORMATION: PARTNERSHIP BY ESTOPPEL

There are times when someone can be held to be a partner because he or she acted like a partner. Some court decisions have held that anyone who helps a new business obtain a loan is holding himself or herself out as a partner. Section 16 of the UPA provides as follows:

> When a person by words spoken or written or by conduct, represents himself, or consents to another representing him to anyone as a partner in an existing partnership or with one or more persons not actual partners, he is liable to any party to whom such representation has been made.

In other words, if the conduct of two or more parties leads others to believe a partnership exists, that partnership may be found to exist legally under the notion of **partnership by estoppel**. Partnerships by estoppel arise when others are led to believe there is a partnership. The *Shaw* case also involved this issue.

C O N S I D E R . . . **20.2** Triangle Chemical Company supplied $671.10 worth of fertilizer and chemicals to France Mathis to produce a cabbage crop. When Mr. Mathis first asked for credit, he was denied. He then told Triangle that he had a new partner, Emory Pope. The company president called Mr. Pope, who said he was backing Mr. Mathis. Mr. Pope had loaned Mr. Mathis money to produce the crop, and Mr. Mathis said Mr. Pope would pay the bills. Mr. Pope said, "We're growing the crop together and I am more or less handling the money." When Mr. Mathis could not pay, Triangle wanted to hold Mr. Pope personally liable. Mr. Pope said his promise to pay another's debt would have to have been in writing. Triangle claimed Mr. Pope was a partner and personally liable. Is he? [*Pope v. Triangle Chemical Co.*, 277 S.E.2d 758 (Ga. 1981).]

C O N S I D E R . . . **20.3** Louise W. Veal, LaWanda W. Davis, and Lynn W. Martin, sisters, agreed to purchase and operate a farm. They bought 124.76 acres of land in Crisp County, Georgia, but did not live on the farm or work it themselves. The sisters had other jobs and agreed to split the profits from the farm. There is no partnership agreement. Do the sisters have a partnership? [*In re LLL Farms*, 111 B.R. 1016 (Bankr. M.D. Ga. 1990).]

Sources of Funding

Funding for a partnership comes from the partners who initially contribute property, cash, or services to the partnership accounts. These contributions are the capital of the partnership. Not only are these contributions put at the risk of the business, but so also are each of the partners' personal assets: Partners are personally liable for the full amount of partnership obligations.

Management and Control

PARTNER LIABILITY

Each partner is both a principal and an agent to the other partners and is liable both for the acts of others and to the others for individual acts. If one partner enters into a contract for partnership business supplies, all the partners are liable. Similarly, if one partner has a motor vehicle accident while on a partnership delivery, all the partners are liable. Under the RUPA, partners are jointly and severally liable for all obligations.

If partnership assets are exhausted, each partner is individually liable. Creditors can satisfy their claims by looking to the assets of the individual partners after the partnership assets are exhausted.

The following case deals with an issue of partnership liability.

Vrabel v. Acri
103 N.E.2d 564 (Ohio 1952)

SHOT DOWN IN A MA & PA CAFE: IS MA LIABLE WHEN PA GOES TO JAIL?

FACTS

On February 17, 1947, Stephen Vrabel and a companion went into the Acri Cafe in Youngstown, Ohio, to buy alcoholic drinks. While Mr. Vrabel and his companion were sitting at the bar drinking, Michael Acri, without provocation, drew a .38-caliber gun, shot and killed Mr. Vrabel's companion, and shot and seriously injured Mr. Vrabel. Michael Acri was convicted of murder and sentenced to a life term in the state prison.

Florence and Michael Acri, as partners, had owned and operated the Acri Cafe since 1933. From the time of his marriage to Florence Acri in 1931 until 1946, Michael Acri had been in and out of hospitals, clinics, and sanitariums for the treatment of mental disorders and nervousness. Although he beat Mrs. Acri when they had marital difficulties, he had not attacked, abused, or mistreated anyone else. The Acris separated in September 1946, and Mrs. Acri sued her husband for divorce soon afterward. Before their separation, Mrs. Acri had operated and managed the cafe primarily only when Mr. Acri was ill. Following the marital separation and until the time he shot Mr. Vrabel, Mr. Acri was in exclusive control of the management of the cafe.

Mr. Vrabel brought suit against Florence Acri to recover damages for his injuries on the grounds that, as Mr. Acri's partner, she was liable for his tort. The trial court ordered her to pay Mr. Vrabel damages of $7,500. Mrs. Acri appealed.

JUDICIAL OPINION
ZIMMERMAN, Judge

The authorities are in agreement that whether a tort is committed by a partner or a joint adventurer, the principles of law governing the situation are the same. So, where a partnership or a joint enterprise is shown to exist, each member of such project acts both as principal and agent of the others as to those things done within the apparent scope of the business of the project and for its benefit.

Section 13 of the Uniform Partnership Act provides: "Where, by any wrongful act or omission of any partner acting in the ordinary course of business of the partnership or with the authority of his copartners, loss or injury is caused to any person, not being a partner in the partnership, or any penalty is incurred, the partnership is liable therefor to the same extent as the partner so acting or omitting to act."

However, it is equally true that where one member of a partnership or joint enterprise commits a wrongful and malicious tort not within the actual or apparent scope of the agency, or the common business of the particular venture, to which the other members have not assented, and which has not been concurred in or ratified by them, they are not liable for the harm thereby caused.

Because at the time of Vrabel's injuries and for a long time prior thereto Florence had been excluded from the Acri Cafe and had no voice or control in its management, and because Florence did not know or have good reason to know that Michael was a dangerous individual prone to assault cafe patrons, the theory of negligence urged by Vrabel is hardly tenable.

We cannot escape the conclusion, therefore, that the above rules, relating to the nonliability of a partner or joint adventurer for wrongful and malicious torts committed by an associate outside the purposes and scope of the business, must be applied in the instant case. The willful and malicious attack by Michael Acri upon Vrabel in the Acri Cafe cannot reasonably be said to have come within the scope of the business of operating the cafe, so as to have rendered the absent Florence accountable.

Since the liability of a partner for the acts of his associates is founded upon the principles of agency, the statement is in point that an intentional and willful attack committed

Continued

by an agent or employee, to vent his own spleen or malevolence against the injured person, is a clear departure from his employment and his principal or employer is not responsible therefor.

Judgment reversed.

CASE QUESTIONS
1. What was the nature of the business?
2. What type of injury occurred, and who caused it?
3. Why wasn't Mr. Acri a defendant?
4. Is Mrs. Acri liable for the injuries?

PARTNERSHIP CONTROL

Unless agreed otherwise, each partner has a duty to contribute time to manage the partnership. Each partner has an equal management say, and each has a right to use partnership property for partnership purposes. No one partner controls the property, funds, or management of the firm (unless the partners so agree).

The partners may agree to delegate day-to-day management responsibilities to one or more of the partners. However, the agency rules of express, implied, and apparent authority (see Chapter 17) apply to partnerships. Each partner is an agent of the other partners, and each has express authority given by the UPA and any partnership agreement, the implied authority relating to those powers, and apparent authority as is customary in their business.

Some management matters are simply a matter of a vote; a majority of the partners makes the decision. The unanimous consent of the partners is required for some decisions, however, such as confessing a judgment (settling a lawsuit), transferring all the partnership's assets, or selling its goodwill. Basically, unusual transactions in which no apparent authority could be claimed require all the partners' approval.

The partners generally are not entitled to compensation for their management of the partnership's business. However, under the UPA, a partner who winds up a dissolved partnership's business can be compensated.

FIDUCIARY DUTIES

Because each partner is an agent for the partnership and the other partners as well, he or she owes the partnership and the other partners the same fiduciary duties an agent owes a principal. A fiduciary duty requires the partners to act in the best interests of the partnership and not to make secret profits. Fiduciaries act for each other's mutual benefit.

Unless there is an agreement to the contrary, a partner cannot engage in any independent activities that involve partnership time, property, or assets. A partner's first duty is to the partnership.

PARTNERSHIP PROPERTY

Partnership property is defined as property contributed to the firm as a capital contribution or property purchased with partnership funds. Partners are co-owners of partnership property in a form of ownership called tenancy in partnership. Tenants in partnership have equal rights in the use and possession of the property for partnership purposes. On the death of one of the partners, rights in the property are transferred to the surviving partner or partners. The partnership interest in the property remains, and the property or a share of the property is not transferred to the estate of the deceased partner.

PARTNER INTERESTS

Partners' interests in the partnership are different from partnership property. A partner's interest is a personal property interest that belongs to the partner. It can be sold (transferred) or pledged as collateral to a creditor. Creditors (personal) can attach a partner's interests to collect a debt.

There are several effects on the partnership of a transfer of a partner's interest. The transfer does not result in the transferee becoming a new partner because no person can become a partner without the consent of all the existing partners. Further, the transfer does not relieve the transferring partner of personal liability. A transfer of interest will not eliminate individual liability to existing creditors.

Some partnership agreements place restrictions on transfer. For example, there may be a provision that allows the partnership the right to buy out a partner before the partner has the authority to transfer his or her interest.

Tax Issues in Partnerships

A partnership does not pay taxes. It simply files an informational return. Each partner, however, must report his or her share of partnership income (or losses) and deductions and must pay taxes on the reported share.

Dissolution and Termination of the Partnership

Dissolution is not necessarily termination. The UPA defines dissolution as one partner's ceasing to be associated with carrying on the business. The RUPA refers to "dissociation" of partners which may or may not lead to dissolution. When a partner leaves, retires, or dies, the partnership is dissolved, though not terminated. Dissolution is basically a change in the structure of the partnership. Dissolution may have no effect on the business: The partnership will be reorganized and will continue business without the partner who is leaving.

Dissolution *can* lead, however, to termination of the partnership. Termination means all business stops, the assets of the firm are liquidated, and the proceeds are distributed to creditors and partners to repay capital contributions and to distribute profits (if any). There are several grounds for dissolution.

DISSOLUTION BY AGREEMENT

The partnership agreement itself may limit the partnership's time of existence. Once that time expires, the partnership is dissolved. If the agreement does not specify the time or there is no partnership agreement, the partners can (by unanimous consent) agree to dissolve the partnership.

DISSOLUTION BY OPERATION OF LAW

Another way a partnership is dissolved is by operation of law. This means that certain events require the dissolution of the partnership. When one partner dies, the partnership is automatically dissolved. The business could go on, but the partnership as it once existed ends and the deceased partner's estate must be paid for his or her interest. Also, if the partnership or an individual partner becomes bankrupt, the partnership is dissolved by law.

DISSOLUTION BY COURT ORDER

The third method for dissolution of a partnership is by court order. Sometimes partners just cannot work together any longer. In such circumstances they can petition a court for dissolution in the interest of preserving their investments.

LIMITED PARTNERSHIPS

A **limited partnership** is a partnership with a slight variation in the liability of those involved. There are two types of partners in a limited partnership: at least one **general partner** and one **limited partner**. General partners have the same obligations as partners in general partnerships—full liability and full responsibility for the management of the business. Limited partners have liability limited to the amount of their contribution to the partnership, and they cannot be involved in the management of the firm. General partners run the limited partnership, and the limited partners are the investors.

The Uniform Limited Partnership Act (ULPA) was drafted in 1916. At that time there were very few limited partnerships, and most of them were quite small. The limited partnership, however, has become a significant part of business structure, particularly over the past 20 years. It has been the predominant form of business organization for oil exploration and real estate development because of the significant tax advantages available through limited partnerships. The attractiveness of limited liability combined with tax advantages has resulted in an increase in the numbers and sizes of limited partnerships.

Review Virginia's Revised Uniform Limited Partnership Act: http://www. state.va.us/dlas/ ses19951/fulltext/ hb1887.htm

Because of this increased use, the ULPA proved to be inadequate for governing the creation, structure, and ongoing operations of limited partnerships. In 1976, the National Conference of Commissioners on Uniform State Laws developed the **Revised Uniform Limited Partnership Act (RULPA)**. The act was designed to update limited partnership law to address the ways limited partnerships were doing business. The RULPA was revised in 1985 and has been adopted in nearly every state.

Formation

As discussed earlier, a valid general partnership can be created through the conduct of the parties and without a formal partnership agreement. A limited partnership, however, is a statutory creature and requires compliance with certain procedures in order to exist. If these procedures are not followed, it is possible that the limited partners could lose their limited liability protection.

To properly form a limited partnership, a certificate of limited partnership is filed with the secretary of state in the state where the partnership will have its principal office. That certificate must include the following items:

1. Name of the limited partnership
2. General character of the partnership business
3. Name and address of a statutory agent
4. Names and addresses of the partners, listing general and limited partners separately
5. Amount of cash, property, services, or promissory notes contributed by each partner
6. Dates or conditions for additional contributions by partners
7. Powers of assignment for limited partners
8. Events that allow partners to withdraw
9. Rights of limited partners to distributions of property
10. Rights to receive return on capital contributions
11. Time for or events causing dissolution.

The RULPA modified these complex requirements and requires only the following information:

1. Name of the limited partnership (It cannot be deceptively similar to another corporation's or partnership's name and must contain the words "limited partnership"; no abbreviations are permitted.)
2. Address of its principal office
3. Name and address of statutory agent
4. Business address of the general partner
5. Latest date for dissolution of the partnership

Under the RULPA, the limited partners need not be named in the certificate, nor are they all required to sign the certificate. These changes resulted from recognition of the size of limited partnerships and the tremendous paperwork burden created by the RULPA.

If an error is made in formation, the partnership could be deemed a general partnership and the limited partners could lose the protection of their limited liability. However, under RULPA, limited partners are permitted to file an amendment correcting the problem or withdraw from the business altogether. A limited partner would still be liable to any third parties for liabilities incurred by the general partnership prior to the time the correction is made.

The certificate of limited partnership is simply public disclosure of the formation and existence of the limited partnership; it does not deal with the many more rights and obligations that the partners may agree on among themselves. Those issues are generally addressed in a much longer document called a **limited partnership agreement** or the **articles of limited partnership**.

Judgment

Failure to comply with the limited partnership filing requirements can result in full liability, just as if the partners were general partners. The following case illustrates this liability (despite assertions to the contrary). This case also addresses the issue posed in the chapter's opening "Judgment."

United States v. *Morton*
682 F. Supp. 999 (E.D. Mo. 1988)

MIXING BUSINESS AND FAMILY:
WHEN IS A SILENT PARTNER NOT SILENT ENOUGH?

FACTS

Until his death in 1980, Cody Morton, husband of Dormilee Morton, operated a construction business from his home in Salem, Missouri. Upon Mr. Morton's intestate death, Mrs. Morton succeeded to her husband's ownership interest in the business, including ownership of supplies, materials, and construction equipment. Steve Morton, their son, took over the operation and management of the construction company with Mrs. Morton contributing the capital assets of business, which consisted of the construction equipment.

From time to time Mrs. Morton would sign bank notes and supporting documents granting security interests in the equipment, designating the borrower as "Dormilee Morton and Steven Morton d/b/a Morton Construction Company." In addition, she also provided funds for the operation of the business. The telephone for the business was situated in Mrs. Morton's home, where she also received the business's mail.

Continued

Between 1980 and 1984, Morton Construction Company employed laborers and other persons to construct commercial and residential buildings and was required to withhold federal income and Federal Insurance Contributions Act (FICA) taxes from the wages paid to its employees. For the taxable quarters between 1980 and 1984, quarterly federal tax returns and an annual federal unemployment tax return for Morton Construction Company were filed with the IRS in the names of Dormilee Morton and Steven D. Morton, partners, by Steven D. Morton.

As a result of business conditions and difficulties, Morton Construction Company failed to make the required deposits of federal withholding and FICA taxes or otherwise pay the amounts of these taxes to the United States.

The IRS imposed assessments against Dormilee Morton, Steven Morton, and Morton Construction for $44,460.52. Tax liens were filed.

Dormilee Morton asserts that she should not be liable for taxes as she was not a general partner in the business but, at most, a limited partner. In support of this contention she cites Steven Morton's notation on the appropriate tax forms that Morton Construction Company was a limited partnership and he was the general partner.

Dormilee Morton was the owner of 92.1 acres of farmland in Dent County, Missouri, on which she lived. On March 19, 1984, five months after the IRS demanded that she pay the delinquent taxes of Morton Construction Company, Dormilee Morton conveyed all of this land to her children and their spouses by separate warranty deeds. Each transfer was made without any consideration, and each deed contained a clause as follows: "Except that as long as Dormilee Morton cares to, shall live in the house, and shall have full and unrestricted control of the lands and buildings described above, and shall receive all benefits thereof."

After the transfers, Dormilee Morton continued to occupy her home on the farm and to receive from unrelated persons the rents and profits from the property. She continued to pay real estate taxes assessed against a portion of the property.

The IRS filed suit, contending that the conveyances of property were fraudulent and designed to avoid payment of delinquent taxes.

JUDICIAL OPINION

GUNN, District Judge

Defendant Dormilee Morton suggests to the Court that she is only a limited partner in the Morton Construction Company and is thereby exempt from tax assessments against the business.

State law is not controlling on the question of whether a partnership exists for federal income tax purposes. But it is essential that a limited partnership be validly organized and conducted under state law before it will be recognized as such for tax purposes.

The record here belies the existence of a limited partnership. Section 359.020, R.S. Mo. 1986, sets forth in substantial detail the requirements for the formation of a limited partnership. None of the statutory requirements has been fulfilled.

Rather, it is apparent from the credible evidence before the Court that Dormilee Morton and Steven Morton were general partners or, at a minimum, joint venturers, in the business, sharing joint liability for the taxes due. *Bank of St. Louis* v. *Morrissey*, 442 F. Supp. 527, 529 (E.D. Mo. 1978), *aff'd*, 597 F.2d 1131 (8th Cir. 1979), appertains to the issues of this case, for in *Morrissey* the Court concluded that a limited partnership was never formed because the limited partnership agreement was not signed, recorded or published. The same situation exists in this case.

Moreover, there is no evidence which suggests the existence of a limited partnership other than Steven Morton's designation of the partnership as such on the tax returns for the business in 1980 and 1982 and Dormilee Morton's 1981 individual return containing a notation to indicate that she was a "silent partner" in the business. All other evidence establishes Mrs. Morton's participation in the business as a general partner, or, at least, a member of a joint venture and, hence, her responsibility for taxes owed.

Continued

Mrs. Morton contributed all the capital assets to Morton Construction Company, granted the Bank of Salem, as lender of money, a security interest in the machinery and equipment of the business, paid the assessed penalty for failure to file a partnership return for the period ending the year 1980 and acknowledged that she owed the taxes assessed for the business in 1981 and 1982. She also took advantage of the 50 percent distribution share of the 1984 business loss on her 1984 individual return.

Although tax returns filed for the years 1980–82 are marked as being for a limited partnership, based on the foregoing actions and participation of Mrs. Morton, the Court concludes that she was not, in fact, a limited partner. The business was a general partnership or, at least, a joint venture. The mere marking on the tax returns of "limited partner" has no effect when it is clear that no limited partnership, either *de facto* or *de jure,* exists.

Thus, the reasons are twofold for denying Mrs. Morton's assertions that she was a limited partner in Morton Construction Company: (1) utter failure to comply with the Missouri statutory requirements for establishing a limited partnership, and (2) her general involvement in the business.

Dormilee Morton must, therefore, be held accountable for the taxes assessed for the years involved despite the fact she may not have had a direct role in the various construction projects of Morton Construction Company.

The Court must conclude that the conveyance of 92.1 acres of farmland from Dormilee Morton to her children and their spouses was fraudulent and designed to elude payment of taxes.

It is the judgment of the Court that defendant Dormilee Morton is liable for the federal tax assessments of $44,680.52 plus statutory additions to tax according to law.

It is also the judgment of the Court that the transfers of real property referred to in this judgment are determined to be fraudulent under § 428.020, R.S. Mo. (1986), and are hereby set aside to be subject to foreclosure sale by the government on the basis of tax liens filed against said real property. Proceeds of the sale of said property shall be paid in order as follows: costs of the action, including costs of sale; to the United States to the extent of federal tax liens plus any statutory additions to tax; the remainder, if any, to Dormilee Morton.

CASE QUESTIONS
1. Describe the business and its operations.
2. Was Dormilee Morton a limited partner?
3. Was she liable for the wage tax?
4. What happens to the conveyances to her children?

Sources of Funding

Capital contributions supply the initial funding for a limited partnership. Both the general and limited partners make contributions upon entering the partnership. Under the RULPA, the contribution can be in the form of cash, property, services already performed, or a promissory note or other obligation to pay money or property. The RULPA requires that limited partners' promises to contribute must be in writing to be enforceable. The limited partners are always personally liable for the difference between what has actually been contributed and the amount promised to be contributed.

Some partners make **advances** or loans to the partnership. The partnership can also borrow money from third parties. However, only the general partner has any personal liability for repayment of the loan to the third party.

Liability

The principal advantage of a limited partnership is that it places on limited partners only limited liability. For limited liability to work, several requirements must be met. First, as discussed above, a certificate of limited partnership must be filed, indicating the limited liability status of the limited partners. Second, there must be at least one general partner. The general partner can be a corporation, but the general partner must also have some personal assets to bear the burden of full liability. Third, the limited partners cannot be involved in the management of the business because such involvement would give the appearance of general partner status. Finally, limited partners cannot use their names in the name of the partnership, which would give the wrong impression to outside parties and create an estoppel type of relationship (discussed on page 726).

Business Planning Tip

During 1992, lawyers and accountants had a total of $1 billion in judgments against them for professional liability. Many of them had a partnership structure for their businesses, making their personal assets subject to attachment by business creditors. Because of this personal liability exposure, 10 percent of all partnerships have changed their structure and incorporated.

Partnerships offer a full share of profits—but also a full share of liability.

Under the RULPA, the liability of limited partners for participation in the business has been largely eliminated. A limited partner who participates in the management of the firm in the same way the general partner does is liable only to those persons who are led to believe by the limited partner's conduct that the limited partner is a general partner. The RULPA has also provided a list of activities that can be engaged in by limited partners without losing their limited liability status. Those activities include:

1. being employed by the general partnership as an employee or contractor;
2. consulting with or advising the general partner;
3. acting as a surety or guarantor for the limited partnership; and/or
4. voting on amendments, dissolution, sale of property, or assumption of debt.

If limited partners comply with the rules for limited liability, their liability is limited to the amount of their capital contribution. If they have pledged to pay a certain amount as capital over a period of time, they are liable for the full amount. For example, some real estate syndications that are limited partnerships allow the limited partners to make their investment in installment payments over two to four years. Limited partners in these types of arrangements are liable for the full amount pledged whenever an obligation to a creditor is not paid.

Partner Relationships

PROFITS AND DISTRIBUTIONS

A general partner has absolute authority to decide not only when distributions are made but if they will be made; the general partner, for example, might decide not to distribute funds but to put them back into the business.

Profits and losses are allocated on the basis of capital contributions. Under the RULPA, the agreement for sharing of profits and losses must be in writing.

PARTNER AUTHORITY

The authority of the general partner in a limited partnership is the same as the authority of the partners in a general partnership. These powers can be restricted by agreement. There are, however, some general activities the general partner cannot perform without the consent of the limited partners. These include:

1. Admitting a new general partner
2. Admitting a new limited partner unless the partnership agreement allows it
3. Extraordinary transactions, such as selling all the partnership assets

Limited partners can monitor the general partner's activity with the same rights provided to partners in general partnerships: the right to inspect the books and records and the right to an accounting.

TRANSFERABILITY OF INTERESTS

Although the assignment of limited partnership interests is not prohibited by the RULPA, a limited partnership agreement may provide for significant restraints on assignment. There are two reasons for transfer restrictions on limited partners' interests. First, limited partnership interests may have been sold without registration as exemptions to the federal securities law (see Chapter 21 for more details on securities registrations). If those exempt interests are readily transferable, the exemption could be lost. Second, for the limited partners to enjoy the tax benefits of limited partner status, the ease of transferability is a critical issue. The more easily an interest can be transferred, the more likely the limited partnership is to be treated (for tax purposes) as a corporation.

The assignment of a partnership interest does not terminate a limited partnership. The assignee is entitled to receive only the distributions and profits the partner is entitled to. The assignee does not become a partner without the consent of the other partners. Under the RULPA, a limited partnership can agree that the assigning limited partner will have the authority to make the assignee a limited partner. The effect of the RULPA provision is to simplify transfers and allow limited partners to decide whether they want to transfer their interest or their limited partner status.

Tax Consequences

Limited partnerships are taxed the same way as general partnerships. The general and limited partners actually report the income and losses on their individual returns and pay the appropriate taxes. A limited partnership files an information return but does not itself pay any taxes. The Tax Reform Act of 1986 made significant changes in the tax shelter benefits of limited partnerships; for example, passive losses (from interest and income) are limited.

One of the benefits of limited partnership status is the combination of limited liability with direct tax benefits. In this sense a limited partnership is the best of both worlds. Because of this ideal situation, limited partnership interests are closely scrutinized by the IRS to determine whether they are, in reality, corporations as opposed to true limited partnerships. Some of the factors examined in determining whether an organization is a corporation or a limited partnership are (1) the transferability of the interests, (2) the assets of the general partners, and (3) the net worth of the general partners. From the perspective of the IRS, organization as a limited partnership is no assurance of treatment as such for tax purposes.

Dissolution and Termination of a Limited Partnership

A limited partnership can be dissolved in one of the following ways:

1. Expiration of the time period in the agreement or the occurrence of an event causing dissolution, as specified in the agreement
2. Unanimous written consent of all partners
3. Withdrawal of a general partner
4. Court order after application by one of the partners.

Upon dissolution, a partnership can continue (assuming a general partner remains). But the partnership can also be terminated after dissolution. If termination occurs, all assets of the partnership are liquidated. The RULPA specifies that the money from the sale of the assets be used to pay partnership obligations in the following order of priority:

1. Creditors (including partners, but not with respect to distributions)
2. Partners and former partners, for distributions owed to them
3. Return of capital contributions
4. Remainder split according to distribution agreement

CORPORATIONS

Corporations have the following characteristics: unlimited duration, free transferability of interest, limited liability, continuity, and centralized management. Corporations are legal entities in and of themselves. Because they are treated as persons under the law, they can hold title to property, they can sue or be sued in the corporate name, and they are taxed separately. The latest U.S. census figures indicate that there are 1.6 million partnerships in the United States but 3.6 million corporations. Corporations earn nearly 90 percent of all business profits.

Types of Corporations

There are diverse types of corporations, each of which can be described by one or more adjectives. For example, there are **profit corporations** (those seeking to earn a return for investors) and **nonprofit corporations**. There are **domestic corporations** and **foreign corporations**. A corporation is a domestic corporation in the state in which it is incorporated and a foreign corporation in every other state. Further, corporations organized by government agencies that exist to achieve a social goal are called **government corporations**. **Professional corporations** are corporations that are organized by physicians, dentists, attorneys, and accountants; they exist by statute in most states. Professional corporation shareholders have no personal liability for any corporate debts, as in any other corporation, except for professional malpractice claims. The **corporate shield** or veil (explained later) will not give them immunity for professional negligence. **Close corporations** are the opposite of **publicly held corporations**; that is, they are corporations with very few shareholders. Close corporations and publicly held corporations are created in the same way, but most states then have a separate statute governing the operation of close corporations. Close corporation owners are generally given more discretion in their internal operations, and the degree of formality required for publicly held corporations is not required.

One of the most popular forms of corporations is the **S corporation** (sometimes called subchapter S or sub S corporation). This type of corporation is formed no differently than any other corporation, but it must meet the IRS requirements for an S corporation and must file a special election form with the IRS indicating it wishes to be treated as an S corporation. The benefit of an S corporation is that shareholders' income and losses are treated like those of partners, but the shareholders enjoy the protection of limited liability behind a corporate veil. The income earned and losses incurred by an S corporation are reported on the shareholders' individual returns, but the shareholders' personal assets are protected from creditors of the business. For tax purposes, the S corporation is like a partnership, and the shareholders avoid the double taxation of having the corporation pay tax on its earnings and their paying tax on the dividends distributed to them.

The Law of Corporations

Examine Arizona's Corporation Laws: http://www.azleg. state.az.us/ars/10/ title10.htm
Examine New York's Corporation Laws: http://www.law. cornell.edu/ny/ statutes/buscorp. htm

The **Model Business Corporation Act (MBCA)** as drafted and revised (1984) by the Corporate, Banking and Business Section of the American Bar Association is the uniform law on corporations. The provisions of the MBCA are quite liberal and give management great latitude in operations. The MBCA is not adopted as widely as the UPA or the Uniform Commercial Code (UCC). Even those states adopting the MBCA have made significant changes in their adopted versions. As a result, each state's law on corporations is quite different. The following sections cover the revised MBCA rules, but each state may have its own variations.

Formation

A corporation is a statutory entity. Formal public filing is required to form a corporation. The following procedures for corporate formation are those of the MBCA.

WHERE TO INCORPORATE

The factors to be considered in determining in which state to incorporate are as follows:

1. The status of the state's corporation laws (Some states are oriented more toward management than to shareholders.)
2. State tax laws
3. The ability to attract employees to the state
4. Incentives states offer to attract the business (new freeways, office space, attractive urban renewal)

THE FORMATION DOCUMENT

All states require **articles of incorporation** to be filed in order to create a corporation. These articles give the structure and basic information about the corporation. Under the MBCA, the articles of incorporation must include the following information:

1. The name of the corporation
2. The names and addresses of all incorporators (In addition, each incorporator must sign the articles of incorporation.)
3. The share structure of the corporation: (a) common and preferred classes, (b) which shares vote, (c) rights of shareholders—preemptive rights
4. The statutory agent (the party who will be served with any lawsuits against the corporation)

WHO IS INCORPORATING

The **incorporators** (required to be listed in the articles of incorporation) are the parties forming the corporation. Under the MBCA, only one incorporator is required, and that person may be a natural person, a corporation, a partnership, a limited partnership, or an association.

Incorporators are personally liable for any contracts entered into or actions taken during the pre-incorporation stage. Until the corporation exists, incorporators are acting as individuals. After incorporation, the corporation could agree to assume liability through a **novation** of the incorporators' acts.

For example, if an incorporator of a lumberyard entered into a contract for the purchase of lumber and the corporate board (after formation) agreed that the contract was a good one, the corporation could ratify it or enter into a novation to assume liability. In novation, the lumberyard agrees to substitute the corporation as the contracting party. In a **ratification**, the corporation assumes primary liability for payment, but the incorporator still remains liable.

Incorporators generally are paid for their efforts in shares of the corporation's stock. They may also be the contributors of initial corporate assets and may be paid in shares for their contributions.

POST-FORMATION

Review the articles of incorporation and bylaws for Educom (Interuniversity Communications Council, Inc), a not-for-profit corporation: http://educom.edu/web/admin.html

After the paperwork of incorporating is complete, a corporation must begin its day-to-day operations with an **initial meeting**. At this meeting, the officers of the corporation are elected and **bylaws** are adopted to govern corporate procedures. The bylaws define the authority of each of the officers, prescribe procedures for announcing and conducting meetings (such as quorum numbers and voting numbers), and set the terms of officers and directors and who is eligible to serve in such offices. Articles of incorporation give an overview of a corporate entity; the bylaws constitute the operational rules.

Capital and Sources of Corporate Funds

A corporation has three basic sources of funds. One source is called "short-term financing" and is the form of financing turned to by most small businesses and individuals. Short-term financing consists of loans from banks. The problems with short-term financing are higher interest rates and shorter payback periods. The other two forms of financing—debt and equity—are the ones used most frequently by corporations.

DEBT FINANCING—THE BOND MARKET

Long-term debt financing is available to corporations when they issue bonds. Bonds are, in effect, long-term promissory notes from a corporation to the bond buyers. The corporation pays the holders interest on the bonds until the maturity date, which is when the bonds are due or must be paid. The interest is fixed and is a fixed-payment responsibility regardless of the corporation's profitability. The benefits to debt financing are the tax deductibility of interest as an expense. Further, bondholders have the benefit of first rights in corporate assets in the event of insolvency. However, a corporation cannot maintain a sound financial policy or rating with debt financing only.

EQUITY FINANCING—SHAREHOLDERS

Equity financing comes through the sale of stock in a corporation. It provides a means of raising capital up front with the exchange of proportionate corporate ownership and the promise of proportionate profits. Shareholders are given shares of stock in exchange for their money. Along with those shares of stock come certain promises of future performance from the corporation. The rights of shareholders will depend upon the type of stock purchased. The various types of stock are discussed below.

COMMON STOCK

Common stock is the typical stock in a corporation and is usually the most voluminous in terms of the number of shares. Common stock generally carries voting rights so that common shareholders have a voice in the election of directors, the amendment of the articles and bylaws, and other major corporate matters. Common stock generally does not have a fixed dividend rate and does not carry with it any right to have a dividend declared. Thus, common stock dividends are dependent on both profitability and decisions of the board of directors. If a corporation is dissolved, the common shareholders have a right to a proportionate share of the assets (after creditors and preferred stockholders have been paid).

PREFERRED STOCK

Preferred stock is appropriately named because its owners enjoy preferred status over holders of a corporation's common stock. For example, preferred stockholders have priority in the payment of dividends. Some preferred dividends are even at a fixed rate, and some types of preferred stock guarantee the payment of a dividend so that if a dividend is not paid one year, the holder's right to be paid carries over until funds are available. This type of stock is **cumulative preferred stock**. Preferred shareholders also have priority over common shareholders in the event the corporation is dissolved and the assets distributed.

THE COSTS OF FINANCING

Corporate financing through public sales seems attractive: Many people each invest a little money to get the corporation the capital it needs. However, the public offering and listing of stock add additional costs to the financing. First, a public offering of stock (with some exceptions for small offerings) must be registered at federal and state levels (see Chapter 21). Second, the corporation is required to pay the dealers who underwrite the issuance of the stock. Further, there are the additional costs of publishing reports, advertising, and compliance with government regulations on publicly held corporations.

Liability Issues

Limited liability is one of the advantages of corporate organization. However, two groups in the corporation have the burden of potential liability: the owners (or shareholders) and the managers (or the directors and officers).

SHAREHOLDER LIABILITY

Shareholders' liability is limited to the amount of their investment in the corporation. The personal assets of shareholders are not subject to the claims of corporate creditors. In some circumstances, however, a shareholder is liable for more than the amount of investment. For example, if a shareholder has not paid for his or her shares or has paid for them with overvalued property, creditors could turn to the shareholder's personal assets for satisfaction of their debt, but only to the extent of the amount due on the shares.

In other more serious circumstances, shareholders can be held liable for the full amount of corporate debts. This happens if a creditor successfully pierces the corporate veil, which means that the creditor overcomes the shield of limited liability protecting shareholders from having to accept personal liability for corporate debts.

One reason for piercing the corporate veil is the **alter ego theory**, which applies when a corporation is not regarded as an entity separate from an individual involved. In such cases no meetings are held and funds are freely transferred back and forth between personal and corporate accounts without explanation or authorization. Personal and corporate property are mixed together and used for both personal and corporate use. The corporation in such circumstances has no separate existence.

The corporate veil can also be pierced on the grounds of **inadequate capitalization**. The owners of a corporation are required to place as much capital at risk in the corporation as is necessary to cover reasonably anticipated expenses of the business. The purpose of this requirement is to ensure that someone does not use the corporation to avoid liability without actually transferring to the corporation some assets for the payment of corporate liabilities.

C O N S I D E R . . . **20.4** Max Rupe was the sole shareholder of Updike Oil Company, a corporation. There was no transfer of shares to Rupe. No records of any meetings or financial records existed. Updike had $56,328 in liabilities and $100 in capital stock. A creditor is seeking to pierce the corporate veil. Is success likely? [*U.S. National Bank of Omaha* v. *Rupe*, 296 N.W.2d 474 (Neb. 1980).]

A final circumstance in which a shareholder's personal assets are subject to attachment by corporate creditors is the case of **watered shares**. Such a circumstance results when a shareholder is issued shares that have a greater value than the amount paid or the property contributed. For example, if a shareholder paid $500 for shares worth $1,000, the shareholder would be personally liable for the $500 difference.

DIRECTOR LIABILITY

Officers and directors are fiduciaries of the corporation which means they are to act in the best interests of the corporation and profit at the corporation's expense. Fiduciaries have an obligation to perform their duties in good faith and with reasonable prudence. They are subject to the **business judgment rule**, a standard of corporate behavior under which, it is understood that officers and directors can make mistakes, but they are required to show that their decisions were made after careful study and discussion. In those decisions, they may consult experts such as attorneys, accountants, and financial analysts; but again they need to show that these experts were well-chosen and reliable individuals.

CONSIDER . . . **20.5** William Shlensky was a minority shareholder of Chicago National League Ball Club Inc. (the Cubs). In 1966, he brought suit against the directors of the Cubs for violation of the business judgment rule because at the time of the suit the Cubs did not play night games at Wrigley Field, their home field. All of the other 19 teams in the major leagues had some night games with substantially all of their weekday and non-holiday games scheduled under the lights. Between 1961 and 1965, the Cubs had sustained operating losses. Mr. Shlensky filed a derivative suit (a suit on behalf of shareholders) against the Cubs' directors for negligence and mismanagement.

Mr. Shlensky's suit maintained that the Cubs would continue to lose money unless night games were played. The directors' response was that baseball was a "daytime" sport and that holding night games would have a "deteriorating effect upon the surrounding neighborhood."

Why does Mr. Shlensky believe the directors did not use good judgment? Is there a difference between negligence and differing business opinions? Does the business judgment rule allow directors to make mistakes? [*Shlensky* v. *Wrigley*, 237 N.W. 2d 776 (Ill. 1968).]

ETHICAL ISSUES

20.1 Many companies have outside directors on their boards who are also paid as consultants to the company. For example, Dr. Henry A. Kissinger, the former secretary of state, has been a member of the American Express Board for a number of years. Dr. Kissinger receives a $64,000 annual retainer, a $30,000 pension, free life insurance, and the right to have the company make a $500,000 charitable gift at the time of his death as part of his director compensation. He also receives $350,000 a year in consulting fees from the company.

W. R. Grace & Co. had five outside directors who also earned $1.5 million in consulting fees from the company.

Shareholder advocacy groups have proposed resolutions to reduce director compensation because such high payments mean they may not represent the interests of the shareholders.

The National Association of Corporate Directors released a report in June 1995 condemning the consultant-director dual role as a conflict of interest.

The American Express Board voted to halt the practice as a "bad idea" that "just confuses roles." Do you agree? Are there conflicts when directors also work for the corporation in exchange for large fees?

Another doctrine officers and directors are bound to follow is the **corporate opportunity doctrine**, under which officers and directors may not take an opportunity for themselves that the corporation might be interested in taking. For example, a director of a lumber company who discovers a deal on timberland would be required to present that opportunity to the corporation before he or she could take it. If the director does not first present the idea to the corporation, a constructive trust is put on the profits the director makes, and the corporation is the beneficiary of that trust. If, however, the director presents the opportunity and the corporation is unable or unwilling to take it, the director may go ahead with the opportunity without the problem of a constructive trust. The *Gailey* case (pg. 744) deals with the problem of a breach of corporate opportunity.

E T H I C A L   I S S U E S

20.2 Exxon Corporation paid some $59 million in corporate funds as bribes or political payments to Italian political parties between 1963 and 1974 in order to secure special political favors. Gall, a shareholder in Exxon, filed suit for violation of the business judgment rule.

The matters complained of by Gall center around the activities of Dr. Vincenzo Cazzaniga, who was president and managing director of Esso Italiana, a wholly owned subsidiary of Exxon. Exxon's investigation revealed that in 1964 and 1965, and again in 1971, Dr. Cazzaniga secretly (and apparently without authorization by Exxon) entered into certain side agreements in the name of Esso Italiana in connection with a transaction between Esso International (another Exxon subsidiary) and SNAM, a gas pipeline subsidiary of the Italian State petroleum company, ENI. In 1971, presumably pursuant to these side agreements, Dr. Cazzaniga made several unauthorized payments out of Esso Italiana funds to SNAM. The payments were in excess of $10 million.

Exxon's investigation further revealed that during the period 1963–1972, Dr. Cazzaniga had made other unauthorized payments of approximately $19 million. The $10 million of unauthorized payments to SNAM and approximately $19 million of other unauthorized payments were largely made from approximately 40 secret bank accounts not recorded on the books of Esso Italiana and known only to Dr. Cazzaniga and, in part, his personal assistants. There also flowed through these secret bank accounts approximately $13.5 million, purportedly expended on authorized political contributions but which the investigation revealed had been recycled into the secret accounts. The 40 bank accounts were also funded by rebates and bank overdrafts totaling approximately $19 million outstanding at the time of their discovery in 1972. The total amount that flowed through the secret accounts was approximately $39 million, including bank interest and commission charges of approximately $3 million.

The investigation also revealed that political contributions by Esso Italiana to various Italian political parties during the nine-year period from 1963 through 1971 totaled $27.9 million. The amounts per year were as follows:

Year	$ millions
1963	0.8
1964	1.1
1965	1.0
1966	2.5
1967	3.8
1968	5.8
1969	5.7
1970	3.5
1971	3.7
	$ 27.9

Of this amount, $13.5 million was recycled into one or more of the 40 secret bank accounts. All political contributions by Esso Italiana were ended in 1972.

It is clear that several Exxon directors were aware of the existence of the political payments in Italy prior to their termination in 1972.

Did the directors violate the business judgement rule by allowing these activities to continue? Were any laws broken by the payments?

In re Gailey, Inc.
119 B.R. 504 (Bankr. W.D. Pa. 1990)

HAVING MY DAY JOB AND MY OWN COMPANY ALL IN ONE PLACE

FACTS

Gailey, Inc. (debtor), incorporated in 1980, removed asbestos and mechanical insulation on contract jobs that required union labor. Richard Gailey had been the president, controlling shareholder, and director of Gailey, Inc., from its inception.

Universal Labs, Inc., was incorporated by Richard Gailey in March 1984 to analyze asbestos samples and air samples and to perform general laboratory work. Mr. Gailey was the sole shareholder of Universal Labs, Inc.

As president and director of Gailey, Inc., Mr. Gailey directed Gailey, Inc., to pay certain debts of Universal Labs. Subsequent to that, $14,500 was provided by Gailey, Inc., to Universal Labs to pay for the latter's start-up expenses and costs.

Gailey, Inc., filed a voluntary petition pursuant to Chapter 11 of the Bankruptcy Code on January 28, 1985. The case was converted to a Chapter 7 proceeding on September 30, 1985.

The trustee in bankruptcy filed suit alleging that Mr. Gailey usurped a corporate business opportunity belonging to Gailey, Inc., when he incorporated Universal Labs.

JUDICIAL OPINION
MARKOVITZ, Bankruptcy Judge

Richard Gailey, by virtue of his position as President and director of Gailey, Inc., stood in a fiduciary relationship to Gailey, Inc. As a consequence, he was required to discharge the duties of his position in good faith.

In general, officers and directors of a corporation are required to devote themselves to the affairs of the corporation with a view of promoting its interests rather than their own. They may not utilize their position in the corporation to obtain any personal profit or advantage beyond that enjoyed by its shareholders.

An officer or director is required to provide the corporation his undivided loyalty. If a business opportunity which lies within the scope of the corporation's business activities and which is of potential advantage to it is presented, an officer or director is not permitted to avail himself of that opportunity and to seize it for himself.

There is no "bright line test" for determining when a particular business opportunity is a corporate opportunity. It is a question of fact to be determined from the totality of the circumstances present at the time when it arose.

As is the case with virtually every legal principle, there are exceptions to this one. An officer may take personal advantage of a corporate business opportunity if the shareholders consent after full disclosure and it is not detrimental to creditors of the corporation. Also, an officer or director may seize a corporate business opportunity if the corporation is incapable of taking advantage of the opportunity for itself.

The totality of the circumstances presented in this case compel the conclusion that Richard Gailey utilized debtor's assets to pay his personal debts. In addition, he usurped a business opportunity belonging to Gailey, Inc. when he incorporated Universal Labs and placed ownership thereof in his name as opposed to that of debtor.

As has been indicated, the corporate purposes of Gailey, Inc. and Universal Labs, although generally interrelated, were somewhat different. Gailey, Inc. was in the business of removing asbestos and mechanical insulation on jobs that required union labor. Universal Labs was in the business of analyzing asbestos and air samples and of providing general laboratory work.

This admitted difference does not, however, compel the conclusion that Richard Gailey did not usurp a business opportunity belonging to Gailey, Inc. when he incorporated Universal Labs. There was nothing to indicate that Gailey, Inc. was incapable of expanding the scope of its activities so as to include analyzing asbestos and air samples. This could have been done as easily as forming a separate corporation to perform such functions.

Continued

Moreover, Richard Gailey's decision to incorporate Universal Labs to perform these functions instead of enlarging the scope of Gailey, Inc.'s activities was never formally approved by the shareholders of Gailey, Inc. His dominion over the affairs of Gailey, Inc. was so absolute that Richard Gailey readily accepted the benefits of the corporate fiction while refusing to comply with its requirements.

Additionally, his decision to incorporate Universal Labs was detrimental to Gailey, Inc. and its creditors. It was detrimental to Gailey, Inc. in that it expended its own funds on behalf of Universal Labs without receiving any obvious benefit in return. The decision was detrimental to Gailey, Inc.'s creditors for much the same reason.

If an officer or director has usurped a corporate business opportunity, the aggrieved corporation may recover all damages suffered by it as a result thereof. Debtor sustained proved damages in the amount of $14,500.00 when it paid Universal's start-up costs and expenses. The trustee therefore is entitled to recover this amount from Richard Gailey.

CASE QUESTIONS
1. What was Gailey, Inc.'s business?
2. What business did Richard Gailey start?
3. Did he usurp a corporate opportunity?
4. Did the two corporations have different purposes?
5. What were the damages to Gailey, Inc.?

C O N S I D E R . . .   **20.6** Governor J. Fife Symington of Arizona was, during the 1980s, a director of Southwest Savings & Loan, a federal thrift headquartered in Phoenix. Mr. Symington was also a developer who constructed two major commercial projects in Phoenix with Southwest Savings & Loan providing the loans for development. Southwest was a victim of the 1980s downturn and was taken over by the Resolution Trust Corporation (RTC). The RTC brought suit against Mr. Symington alleging he took advantage of his board position to obtain the loans. Mr. Symington said he was required to present the projects to the Southwest Board as part of the corporate opportunity doctrine and Southwest took the investment. Who is correct?

OFFICER LIABILITY

Recent prosecutions have demonstrated an increased effort to hold corporate officers criminally responsible for the acts of the corporation. In environmental law, changes in the law and aggressive prosecutions have brought about convictions of officers, particularly concerning the disposal of hazardous waste. The issues of officer liability are covered in Chapters 8 and 17.

Corporate Management and Control

ELECTION OF DIRECTORS

A corporation might be owned by a million shareholders, but its operation will be controlled by the hands of a few, the **board of directors**. The shareholders elect these directors, who serve as the corporate policy makers. The directors also have responsibility for management of the corporation. To that end, the directors usually set up an **executive committee** composed of three board members to handle the more routine matters of running the corporation so that board meetings are not required as frequently.

Directors also elect the officers of the corporation as well as decide the salaries for these officers and themselves.

Michael Monus and David S. Shapira co-founded Phar-Mor, Inc., a discount drug store, in 1982. Mr. Shapira's family owned Giant Eagle, a private grocery store chain. Phar-Mor was based in Youngstown, Ohio, and, within 10 years, had grown to 310 stores and $3 billion in sales.

Phar-Mor and Michael Monus

Mr. Monus ("Mickey") began the World Basketball League (WBL), a league for "short people"—6'7" or less. He spent money lavishly on the teams, the coaches, the managers, and games. Mr. Monus was asked to serve as chairman of Youngstown State University's board of trustees.

Based on an anonymous tip that indicated $100,000 of Phar-Mor property had been transferred to the WBL, Phar-Mor began an investigation through Coopers & Lybrand, its outside auditor.

The investigation discovered that Mr. Monus had funneled about $10 million in Phar-Mor assets to the WBL. In addition, the auditors discovered that earnings had been overstated through a conspiracy of Mr. Monus, CFO, Patrick Finn, and two accounting employees.

Phar-Mor president David Shapira announced that Phar-Mor would take a $350 million write-off that quarter. Further, Phar-Mor was forced to file a Chapter 11 bankruptcy.

Sales at Phar-Mor declined 15 percent and 55 stores were closed with a proposal to close 31 more. Employees were fired, reducing the workforce from 24,500 to 19,800.

The FBI was brought in to investigate the case and litigation is pending as to whether Coopers & Lybrand, Phar-Mor's auditor, has any responsibility for the financial improprieties.

Mr. Monus was convicted of 109 felony counts in May 1995, following his second trial. The first trial ended with a hung jury and following an investigation for jury tampering, both a juror on Mr. Monus's first case and a friend of Mr. Monus's were charged with tampering.

In December 1995, Mr. Monus was sentenced to 20 years in prison, fined $1 million, and given 5 years probation. At his sentencing Monus offered the following:

In the 10 years I was at Phar-Mor, Phar-Mor grew to 300 stores in some 35 states and 20,000 employees. The important thing is not the numbers to me . . . but the employees—all those dedicated, loyal, and highly motivated people. I want them to know the sorrow and regret that I have. The sorrow and regret will live with me for the rest of my life.

Phar-Mor emerged from Chapter 11 in late 1995 under new ownership.

Michael Monus

Issues
1. Why did others beside Mr. Monus participate in the scheme?
2. How did the "cooking of the books" escape the auditors?
3. Was Mr. Monus's sentence appropriate?

FOR THE MANAGER'S DESK

PHAR-MOR— A LESSON IN FRAUD

The examiner's report in the Phar-Mor Inc. bankruptcy case, filed Jan. 19 in Youngstown, Ohio, exposed a compelling tale of fraud and corruption. In my role as attorney for Jay Alix, examiner in the case, I had a bird's-eye view of one of the largest cases of financial fraud in U.S. Bankruptcy Court history. It led not only to Phar-Mor's bankruptcy but ultimately resulted in a $1 billion equity loss to Phar-Mor's shareholders. Phar-Mor, the Midwestern discount retailer, was forced to lay off thousands of employees and close nearly half of its 300 stores.

The price tag in the Phar-Mor case brought it into the spotlight. But many less dramatic cases of corporate fraud never make it into the headlines. In a 1993 KPMP Peat Marwick survey of the nation's top companies, 76 percent of the respondents said they had experienced fraud during the past year. Nearly a fourth of the respondents claimed losses of at least $1 million, and almost two-thirds reported actual or potential losses of more than $100,000. Even more striking was the revelation that nearly half of the companies surveyed conceded that the fraud could have been discovered earlier if warning signs had not been ignored.

Fraud comes in many guises, among them financial statement manipulation, misappropriation of funds, check forgery, false invoices, theft, purchases for personal use, kickbacks, credit card misuse and manipulation of checks, expense accounts and accounts receivable. Annual audits rarely expose such fraudulent activities— in part because audits are not designed for that purpose, but also because the perpetrators of fraud anticipate audits and cover their tracks accordingly.

Here are some preventive measures recommended by the examiner in the Phar-Mor case and respondents to the Peat Marwick survey:

- *Train all employees to detect fraud.* Directors, officers, managers and others must all assume responsibility for understanding how fraud occurs and be able to identify the warning signs. Some "red flags" include: failure of certain departments to pay bills when due; diminishing income or sales; growing inventories, accounts receivable and accounts payable that are inconsistent with the business's revenue, size and direction; and late or incomplete monthly financial reporting.

  Declining profits or cash-flow problems, particularly as compared with past results or competitors' results, could also indicate problems; in some cases, they may even trigger fraud. This was the case at Phar-Mor, where fraud originated with attempts by certain officers to match the company's actual results with targeted results. As actual results deteriorated compared with targeted results, the magnitude of the fraud increased.

- *Establish and maintain an appropriate management information system (MIS).* Appropriate MIS systems are not only critical to the efficient management of a company, but also serve as a deterrent to generating false or misleading information. According to the examiner's report, Phar-Mor's MIS was inadequate on many levels, including warehouse management and inventory control, purchasing, accounting and human resource management. At one point, a Phar-Mor vice president raised concerns about the company's MIS systems and organized a committee to address the problem. However, senior officials involved in the scheme to defraud Phar-Mor dismissed the vice president's concerns and ordered the committee disbanded.

- *Establish appropriate internal controls for all accounting procedures.* Avoid an accounting system that allows for the circumventing of the normal accounts payable auditing and approval system. Phar-Mor's accounting department bypassed the system in

Continued

numerous ways, including through its maintenance of a supply of blank checks on two bank accounts. Irregular payments were made on typed checks drawn from one of the accounts.

- *Hire an internal auditor.* One effective safeguard against fraud is the use of an internal auditor—an individual who reports to an audit committee of the board, rather than to management. In mid-1991—several years into the fraudulent activities at Phar-Mor—the retailer hired an internal auditor. However, the auditor was required to report to one of the officers involved in the fraudulent activity, who was also a member of the audit committee. According to the examiner's report, efforts on the part of the auditor to perform his job were thwarted by management. However, he did raise questions and may well have been on his way to exposing the fraud when, in July 1992, an anonymous tip triggered the discovery.
- *Recognize warning signals within employee ranks.* Familiarize yourself with your employees' personal goals, such as higher salaries, bonuses and promotions, as well

as their personal problems including drug use and gambling. Ambition and/or financial needs can motivate employees to risk their reputation in exchange for quick cash. Be particularly wary of the employee who works excessively long hours, with little or no time for vacations and very little to show for the extra work time—fraudulent activity can be tedious, requiring diligent monitoring.

Also, be sensitive to changes in the behavior of your employees, including changes in personality and attitude. One way to stay in tune with employee attitudes is to cultivate an open atmosphere and provide a forum for grievances. Employees who perceive that they are being treated unfairly may find it easier to steal from the company.
- *Consider establishing— then publicizing and*

enforcing—a corporate code of ethics. Phar-Mor adopted a business ethics policy in 1989 that recommended that the company maintain a system of internal controls and comply with legal standards and generally accepted accounting principles. However, officers questioned by the examiner said they were not aware of its existence.

If despite taking precautions your company finds itself the victim of fraud, you should react swiftly and leave no doubt as to your intentions. Begin by launching an extensive in-house investigation, followed by the dismissal of the responsible parties, reporting of the fraud to authorities and the institution of civil or criminal actions, if appropriate.

Phar-Mor's bitter lesson should serve as a warning—or, at the very least, a reminder—to individuals involved in corporate management of the destruction that can be wrought by disingenuous, ill-intentioned individuals driven by greed or need. Directors, officers and managers alike would do well to re-examine their own operations for warning signs and to adopt—and enforce—stringent measures to prevent fraud in the workplace.

E T H I C A L   I S S U E S

20.3 One of the concerns raised by institutional and other investors is the high level of executive compensation. (Directors are responsible for setting executive-officer compensation levels.) Listed below are the top 20 highest paid CEOs (1995).

Company	CEO	Pay (for 1994)
Green Tree Financial	Lawrence Coss	$65,580,000
Travelers Group	Sanford Weill	49,840,000
General Electric	John Welch, Jr.	22,062,000
Amgen	Gordon Binder	21,505,000
DSC Communications	James Donald	19,183,000
U.S. Robotics	Casey Cowell	18,569,000
Andrew Corp.	Floyd English	17,666,000
Forest Laboratories	Howard Solomon	17,026,000
Goodyear Tire & Rubber	Stanley Gault	16,550,000
Sears, Roebuck	Edward Brennan	16,350,000
Compaq Computer	Eckhard Pfeiffer	16,118,000
Colgate-Palmolive	Reuben Mark	15,068,000
Walt Disney	Michael Eisner	14,771,000
Oracle	Lawrence Ellison	14,143,000
IBM	Louis Gerstner	13,227,000
Coca-Cola	Roberto C. Goizueta	12,909,000
Applied Materials	James Morgan	12,319,000
Morgan Stanley	Richard Fisher	11,915,000
Bank America	Richard Rosenberg	11,854,000
PepsiCo	Wayne Calloway	11,419,000

Regardless of the levels of earnings, shareholders appear to be concerned about such levels of compensation. Michael S. Kesner, National Director of Compensation and Benefits Consulting for Arthur Andersen Company, notes:

With restructuring, cost-cutting, and consolidation the order of the day, the actual impact of, say, a $5 million CEO pay package on the bottom line of a $2 billion sales company is not clearly the issue. People are now saying, to paraphrase the sound advice of late Illinois Senator Everett Dirksen, "Hey, a percent of a billion here and a percent of a billion there adds up to real money." In light of widespread plant closings, layoffs, and long lines of unemployed workers seeking limited jobs, "pay for performance" has simply taken a backseat to what the general public considers "fair." As a result, the issue has moved from the business arena to the political arena. Corporate compensation levels have become only one target in a growing populist movement against public figures who have been afforded undue privileges. The effect of this should be apparent to all: individuals in both the public and private sectors are now opting to repudiate or reduce those privileges. This self-regulation ought to be encouraged.

Do you agree that compensation should be voluntarily reduced? Should other steps be taken? So long as the officers are doing a good job, is it anyone's business how much they are paid?

VOTER CONTROL—ANNUAL MEETINGS

Shareholders have the opportunity to express their views at the annual meeting by electing directors who represent their interests. Annual meetings also give shareholders the opportunity to vote on critical corporate issues. Under the MBCA, shareholders have a right to seek a court order against the corporation if an annual meeting has not been held in 13 months.

VOTER CONTROL—INSPECTION OF BOOKS AND RECORDS

The MBCA gives the shareholders the absolute right to examine shareholder lists. For other records (minutes, accounting), shareholders must give notice of their request. In addition to this mechanical requirement, some courts also require a **proper purpose**, which means a shareholder has a legitimate interest in reviewing corporate progress, financial status, and fiduciary responsibilities. Improper purposes are those related to use of corporate records to advance the shareholders' moral, religious, or political ideas.

VOTER CONTROL—SHAREHOLDERS POOLING RESOURCES

Although there may be millions of shareholders in a corporation, only a few may control the voting rights of these shareholders. The control or pooling of votes can be done in several different ways.

The Proxy The most familiar method of delegating voting authority is the **proxy**, with which shareholders can transfer their right to vote to someone else. This type of vote assignment is temporary. Under the MBCA, a proxy is good only for 11 months, which allows a shareholder to decide to give a different proxy before the next annual meeting. Many shareholder groups solicit proxies to obtain control (see Chapter 22). Those solicitations are subject to the federal securities laws, and certain disclosures are required (see Chapter 21).

Pooling Agreements Another method of grouping together shareholder votes is the **pooling agreement**. This is a contract among shareholders to vote their shares a certain way or for a certain director. One of the problems with pooling agreements is enforceability: If the agreements are breached, it is really too late to do anything about the breach because the corporation will take the action authorized by the votes or a particular director will take a seat.

Voting Trust One last form of shareholder cooperation is the voting trust. In this form of group voting, shareholders actually turn their shares over to a trustee and are then issued a trust certificate. The shareholders still have the right to dividends and could sell or pledge the certificate. However, the shares remain in the hands of the trustee, and the trustee votes those shares according to the terms of the trust agreement. The shareholders get their shares back only when the trust ends. Most states have specific requirements for the voting trust: A copy must be filed with the corporate offices, and some states have a maximum duration (such as 10 years) for such trusts.

VOTER CONTROL—TRANSFER OF SHARES

Stock shares can have **transfer restrictions**, which are valid so long as the following requirements are met:

Business Planning Tip

Board Structure
The 1994 installment of the annual Korn/Ferry study of boards of directors offers the following information about the structure of corporate boards:

Average size of board	12
Average number of outside directors on board	9
Proportion of boards with women	60%
Proportion of boards with CEO or COO from another firm	81%

When CEOs were asked to identify the qualities for an ideal outside director, they cited the following categories, listed here by decreasing order of frequency:

1. CEOs/COOs of other companies
2. Women
3. Minorities
4. Retired CEOs of other companies
5. Academicians
6. Retired senior executives of other companies
7. Former government officials
8. "Professional" directors

1. The restrictions must be necessary. Valid circumstances include family-owned corporations, employee-owned corporations, and corporations that need restrictions to comply with SEC registration exemptions (see Chapter 21).
2. The restrictions must be reasonable. Requiring that the shares first be offered to the board before they can be sold is reasonable; requiring that the shares be offered to all the other shareholders first may be unreasonable if there are more than 5 to 10 shareholders.
3. The restrictions and their existence must be conspicuously noted on the stock shares.

The Dissolution of a Corporation

A corporation can continue indefinitely unless its articles of incorporation limit its duration. Long before perpetuity, however, a corporation can be dissolved voluntarily or involuntarily.

VOLUNTARY DISSOLUTION

Voluntary dissolution occurs when the shareholders agree to dissolve the corporation. This type of dissolution occurs in smaller corporations when the shareholders no longer get along, the business does not do well, or one of the shareholders is ill or dies.

A voluntary dissolution begins with a resolution by the board of directors, which is then put before the shareholders at a special meeting called for that purpose. Under the MBCA, all shareholders (voting and nonvoting alike) vote on the issue of dissolution because all of them will be affected by it. Once the shareholders pass the resolution (a majority or two-thirds vote in most states), the assets of the corporation are liquidated, and debts and shareholders are paid in the order of their priorities. Each state also has filing and publication requirements for dissolution.

INVOLUNTARY DISSOLUTION

An involuntary dissolution is forced by some state agency, usually the state-level attorney's office. A dissolution can be forced because of fraud or failure to follow state law regarding reporting requirements for corporations.

Business Planning Tip

Board Structure
Long perceived as composed of stodgy people paid for the use of their names, boards are undergoing dramatic changes. In 1992, General Motors' board forced out a CEO and its chairman in response to an earnings slump. Directors should be chosen on the basis of their willingness to represent the shareholders' interests, not for their relationship to the CEO and a willingness to support the CEO. Boards are the policymaking arm of a company, and when management decisions are taking the company in an undesirable direction, it is the board's duty to change that direction and, where necessary, to change management as well. Eli Broad, CEO of Broad, Inc., has noted, "I think there's a greater responsibility on the part of outside directors now to really look at a company's management when there are problems. And I think that's good, and it's long overdue. The days are long over when the chairman's buddies are going to be on the board."

Corporate Tax Issues

THE DOUBLE TAXATION COST OF LIMITED LIABILITY

Although corporations have the benefit of limited liability, they have the detriment of double taxation. This means the corporation not only pays taxes on its earnings but the shareholders must also report their dividend income on their separate returns and pay individual taxes on their dividend income. However, these shareholders pay taxes only if the dividends are paid. Unlike partnerships in which the partners pay taxes on earnings whether they are distributed or not, shareholders pay taxes on corporate earnings only when they are distributed to them.

STATUTORY SOLUTIONS TO DOUBLE TAXATION

There are ways to resolve the problem of the cost of double taxation. The S corporation, discussed on page 738, is one solution.

THE LIMITED LIABILITY COMPANY

Examine a state comparison chart, among other materials, for limited liability laws: http://www.hia.com/llcweb/ll-home.html *Review "An Introduction to New Jersey's Limited Liability Company Act," by Lisa M. Fontoura:* http://www.cfg-lawfirm.com/articles/llc.html

This form of business organization, new to the United States and available in 48 states and the District of Columbia, has actually been in existence for many years in Europe (known as a GMBH) and South America (*limitada*). The limited liability company (LLC) is more of an aggregate form of business organization than an entity such as a corporation. Owners of an LLC are called "members." An LLC provides limited liability (members lose only up to their capital contributions) and "pass-through" tax treatment like a partnership in that there is tax only at the member's level of income and not at the business level.

Formation

An LLC is formed through the filing of a document called the **articles of organization** that is filed with a centralized state agency. The name of the business formed must contain either "limited liability company," "L.L.C." or "LLC."

Business Planning Tip

Getting LLC Tax Status
If an LLC is not created according to both state law and IRS guidelines, the tax benefits can be lost. In December 1994, the IRS issued guidelines on the four characteristics of a LLC entitled to pass-through status. An LLC must have limited liability for members, continuity, free transferability of interests, and no centralized management.

Sources of Funding

Members of an LLC make capital contributions in much the same way as partners make capital contributions.

Liability

Members of an LLC have limited liability; the most they can lose is their capital contributions. Debts belong to the LLC and creditors' rights lie with the LLC's assets, not the personal assets of the members.

Tax Consequences

The LLC enjoys the so-called pass-through treatment: The LLC does not pay taxes; income and losses are passed through to the members to be reported on their individual returns. LLC agreements must be drafted carefully to enjoy pass-through status.

Management and Control

Members of an LLC adopt an Operating Agreement that specifies the voting rights, withdrawal rights and issues, responsibilities of members, and how the LLC is to be managed. The members can agree to manage collectively, delegate authority to one member, or hire an outsider to manage the business.

Transferability of Interest

A member's LLC interest is personal property and it is transferable. However, the transferee does not become a member without approval by the majority of members. Members do not hold title to LLC property; the LLC owns the property and has an interest in the LLC that reflects the property's value.

INTERNATIONAL ISSUES IN BUSINESS STRUCTURE

Global trade has resulted in global business structures, with many companies discovering the benefits of **joint ventures**. A joint venture is a partnership of existing businesses for a limited time or a limited purpose. The existing businesses are then partners for that limited transaction or line of business. The Justice Department has relaxed antitrust merger rules to permit joint ventures so that U.S. firms can compete more effectively internationally. For example, Mobil and Exxon are involved in a joint oil exploration venture in the West Siberian Basin in Russia. The joint venture allows the combination of their experience and financing so that Russian negotiators can be persuaded to contract for the exploration rights.

In an attempt to break into the Japanese toy market, Toys "Я" Us, Inc., entered into a joint venture with McDonald's Co., Ltd, a Japanese toy company with 20 percent of the market.

Nestlé and Coca-Cola have formed a joint venture to market ready-to-drink coffees and teas; Nestlé's expertise is in dry goods (instant coffee) and Coca-Cola is a beverage company, so both plan to take advantage of the other's established reputation.

Business structures vary in other countries. In Germany, for example, a public company has both a board of directors and a shareholder advisory committee, which elects the board of directors. It is quite likely, however, that the shareholder advisory committee is composed of shareholders that are large institutional investors (such as banks) or representatives from labor unions.

Learn how to establish a corporation in Belgium: http://www.ib.be/invest-belgium/legal.html

SUMMARY

What are the various forms of business entities?
- Sole proprietorship—individual ownership and operation of a business
- Partnership—voluntary association of two or more persons as co-owners in a business for profit
- Corporation—an entity formed by statute that has the rights of a legal person along with limited liability for its shareholder owners
- Limited liability company—newer form of business organization in which liability is limited except for conduct that is illegal

Continued

How is a partnership formed and operated?
- Uniform Partnership Act—law on partnerships adopted in 49 states
- Revised Uniform Partnership Act—update of partnership law
- Partnership by implication—creation of a partnership by parties' conduct
- Partnership by estoppel—partnership that arises by perception of third parties of its existence
- Dissolution—partner ceases to be associated with the partnership
- Limited partnership—partnership with two types of partners: general and limited
- General partner—full and personal liability partner
- Limited partner—partner whose personal liability is limited to capital contributions
- Uniform Limited Partnership Act—uniform law adopted in nearly every state
- Revised Uniform Limited Partnership Act—uniform law adopted in nearly every state
- Advances—partners' loans to partnership

How is a corporation formed and operated?
- Corporation—business organization that is a separate entity with limited liability and full transferability
- Domestic corporation—a corporation is domestic in the state in which its incorporation is filed
- Foreign corporation—category or label for corporation in all states except in state in which it is incorporated
- Professional corporation—entity with limited liability except for malpractice/negligence by its owner
- S corporation—IRS category of corporation with flow-through characteristics
- Model Business Corporation Act (MBCA)—uniform law adopted in approximately one-third of the states
- Articles of incorporation—document filed to organize a corporation
- Common stock—generally most voluminous type of corporate shares and usually voting
- Preferred stock—ownership interest with priority over common stock
- Corporate veil—liability shield for corporate owners
- Watered shares—failure to pay par value for shares
- Business judgment rule—standard of liability for directors
- Corporate opportunity doctrine—fiduciary responsibility of directors with respect to investments
- Board of directors—policy-setting body of corporations
- Proxy—right to vote for another
- Pooling agreement—shareholder contract to vote a certain way
- Voting trust—separation of legal and equitable title in shares to ensure voting of shares in one way

How is a limited liability company formed?
- Articles of organization
- Flow-through of income

QUESTIONS AND PROBLEMS

1. A buy-sell agreement entered into by the shareholders of Spencer Community Antenna Systems, Inc., provides as follows:

    > It is agreed by and between the parties hereto that from and after the date of June 1, 1975, any party to this Agreement may negotiate a sale of all of the issued and outstanding shares of stock of Spencer Community Antenna Systems, Inc., subject to the right of first refusal, hereinafter set forth to any individual, partnership, or corporation; said negotiated sale must be bona fide and shall be in writing and may be for any amount, but must be payable in cash at the time of the delivery of the stock, which delivery must be not be later than one hundred and twenty (120) days after the date of Notice and the purchase price may not be payable in installments. For the purposes of this Agreement, the shares of Lloyd J. Farrer and George J. Lyon shall be treated as a unit and as one party and the shares of B. V. Willie shall be treated as a unit and as one party. The party negotiating the sale shall submit a true copy of the proposed sale to the other party not negotiating the sale and the party not negotiating the sale shall have the first option to buy the interest of the other fifty percent (50%) proposing to sell at a price based upon the price the negotiating party would be receiving for his one-half interest in the corporation from the outside purchaser. *The party desiring to exercise this first right to buy referred to above shall notify the negotiating party in writing within sixty (60) days from the date of Notice and by making full payment in cash of the above purchase price within one hundred twenty (120) days from the date the written Notice of the negotiated sale is mailed to or delivered in person to the party or parties not negotiating the sale and if said Party or parties fail to exercise the option, then all stockholders shall endorse their stock and deliver said stock to the Security Savings Bank of Eagle Grove, Iowa, on the part of B. V. Willie and The First National Bank of Mason City, Iowa, on the part of Lloyd J. Farrer and George J. Lyon;* said banks to act as escrow agents. The party negotiating the sale may then sell all of the stock of the corporation at the price and on the terms as proposed. It is further agreed that on delivery of stock and payment thereof, all payments due the stockholders under paragraph four (4) of this Agreement shall be paid to the stockholders forthwith as their interests appear.

    Is the agreement valid? Is it too restrictive? Would it make a difference whether the corporation was closely held or publicly held? [*Lyon v. Willie,* 288 N.W.2d 884 (Iowa 1980).]

2. Aztec Enterprises, Inc., was incorporated in Washington with a capital contribution of $500. Aztec's incorporator and sole stockholder was H. B. Hunting. Aztec operated a gravel-hauling business and was plagued with persistent working capital problems. Carl Olson, a frequent source of loans for Aztec, eventually acquired the firm. Mr. Olson, who had no corporate minutes or tax returns, personally paid Aztec's lease fees but did not pay when he had Aztec deliver gravel to his personal construction sites. Mr. Olson never had stock certificates issued to him. Despite annual gross sales of over $800,000, Aztec was unable to pay its debts. Truckweld Equipment Company, a creditor of Aztec, brought suit to pierce the corporate veil and recover its debt from Mr. Olson. Can it pierce the corporate veil? [*Truckweld Equipment Co. v. Olson,* 618 P.2d 1017 (Wash. 1980).]

3. William J. Martin (a 5 percent shareholder in the parent corporation) demanded inspection of the books of the parent corporation as well as those of eight subsidiaries. The parent owned all shares of seven of the eight subsidiaries. Although the boards of directors for all the corporations were the same, the books and records of all companies were separate. Mr. Martin's concern is that the corporation is engaged in illegal activity.

The corporation claims Mr. Martin will use the information to competitively harm the corporation. Who wins? [*Martin* v. *D.B. Martin Co.*, 88 A. 612 (Del. 1913).]

4. Ranton Brouillette had a home he owned moved to a lot he owned with his brothers as partners. Because of a dispute, one of his brothers deliberately drove a bulldozer into the house and damaged it. Mr. Brouillette's insurer says it is not required to pay because the house became partnership property and should be covered by the partnership's insurance. Who is right? [*Brouillette* v. *Phoenix Assur. Co.*, 340 So.2d 667 (La. 1976).]

5. Allan Jones sold a ski shop franchise to Edward Hamilton. Although Mr. Jones did not contribute equity to the business or share in the profits, he did give Mr. Hamilton advice and share his experience to help him get started. Most of Mr. Hamilton's capital came in the form of a loan from Union Bank. When Mr. Hamilton failed to pay, Union Bank sued Mr. Jones for payment under the theory that Mr. Jones was a partner by implication or estoppel. Was he? [*Union Bank* v. *Jones,* 411 A.2d 1338 (Vt. 1980).]

6. Heritage Hills (a land development firm) was organized on July 2, 1975, as a limited partnership, but the partnership agreement was never properly filed. Heritage Hills went bankrupt, and the bankruptcy trustee has sought to recover the debts owed by the partnership from the limited partners. Can he? [*Heritage Hills* v. *Zion's First Nat'l Bank,* 601 F.2d 1023 (9th Cir. 1979).]

7. In June 1985, Carolyn Boose sought the dental services of Dr. George Blakeslee, who proposed to fill two cavities in her teeth. As part of the procedure he administered nitrous oxide to Ms. Boose. She was rendered semiconscious by the drug and while in this state Dr. Blakeslee lifted her shirt and fondled one of her breasts. He was subsequently charged with, and pled guilty to, the crime of indecent liberties.

   Prior to the incident in question, Dr. Blakeslee had incorporated his dental practice as a professional services corporation. He was the corporation's sole shareholder, officer, and director. The corporation thereafter executed an employment agreement with Dr. Blakeslee, who signed the agreement both as an employee of the corporation and as its president.

   At the time of the incident in question, Dr. Blakeslee and the corporation were together covered by an insurance policy with Standard Fire Insurance Company that provided general and professional liability coverage. The general liability portion of the policy provided coverage for bodily injury or property damage caused by an "occurrence" arising out of the use of the insured premises. The insurance contract defined "occurrence" as "an accident, including continuous or repeated exposure to conditions, which results in bodily injury or property damage *neither expected or intended by the insured."*

   The professional liability portion of the policy limited coverage to damages for "injury . . . arising out of the rendering of or failure to render, during the policy period, professional services by the individual insured, or by any person for whom acts or omissions such insured is legally responsible . . . "

   In November 1985, Ms. Boose commenced an action against Dr. Blakeslee and the professional services corporation for the damages she allegedly sustained as a result of his conduct. Standard subsequently commenced a declaratory judgment action against Ms. Boose and Dr. Blakeslee in order to obtain a declaration of its rights and duties in connection with the lawsuit by Ms. Boose against Dr. Blakeslee and the corporation. All parties moved for summary judgment. The trial court granted judgment to Standard, concluding that it had no duty to defend or indemnify the insured (that is, Dr. Blakeslee and the corporation) against Ms. Boose's claim. Should the corporate veil be pierced to hold Dr. Blakeslee liable? [*Standard Fire Insurance Co.* v. *Blakeslee,* 771 P.2d 1172 (Wash. 1989).]

8. Master Chemical Company of Boston, Massachusetts, manufactured chemicals used primarily in the shoe industry. In 1982, when Master discovered that its underground storage tank filled with toluene was leaking, the two thousand-gallon tank was emptied. In 1984 Master sold its plant, and the tank was removed.

Goldberg-Zoino & Associates, Inc. (GZA), was hired to do the cleanup, and it hired MacDonald & Watson to do the excavation, transportation, and disposal of the toluene contaminated soil in the area where the tank had been.

MacDonald & Watson had a permit for liquid waste disposal but none for solid waste disposal. MacDonald & Watson transported nine 25-yard dump-truck loads and one 20-yard load of toluene-contaminated soil to the disposal lot. The Justice Department brought criminal actions against MacDonald & Watson and three of its officers, including Eugene K. D'Allesandro, its president.

Can Mr. D'Allesandro be convicted? [*United States* v. *MacDonald & Watson Waste Oil Co.*, 933 F.2d 35 (1st Cir. 1991).]

9. Madeline Tucker and her son, Bernard Ferris, were co-owners of a duplex in Fair Oaks, California. The 79-year-old Mrs. Tucker and her son mortgaged the duplex for $105,000. Mr. Ferris used the loan proceeds to purchase a bar with his friends, Bill and Clay Biscoe. The bar failed and Mr. Ferris and the Biscos filed for bankruptcy. Mrs. Tucker retained attorney William Dunbar to represent her in the bankruptcy so that she didn't lose her home. Mr. Dunbar, a partner in the firm of Paulsen, Vodonick & Davis, missed some filing deadlines in 1987. The law firm disbanded in 1988. When Mrs. Tucker discovered the missed deadline, she sued Mr. Dunbar's partners. Are they liable? [*Beane** v. *Paulsen*, 26 Cal. Rptr. 2d 486 (Cal. 1993).]

*Mrs. Dunbar died during litigation. Ms. Beane is her executrix.

10. A. W. Ham, Jr., served on the board of directors for Golden Nugget, Inc., a Nevada corporation. In 1969, while Mr. Ham was a director and legal counsel for Golden Nugget, he obtained a leasehold interest with an option to purchase in the California Club. The California Club is at 101 Fremont Street, Las Vegas, Nevada, and is located next to a series of properties on which Golden Nugget operates its casinos. Mr. Ham leased the property from his former wife. Golden Nugget was looking for property to expand and had, in fact, been expanding onto other lots in the area. Was there a breach of a corporate opportunity? What if Mr. Ham offers to lease the property to Golden Nugget? [*Ham* v. *Golden Nugget, Inc.* 589 P.2d 173 (Nev. 1979).]

Judgment

Philip Schein, CEO of U.S. Bioscience, a pharmaceutical company, told Wall Street analysts in November 1991 that the Food and Drug Administration (FDA) approval of his company's cancer-treatment drug, Ethyol, was imminent.

By January 2, 1992, Bioscience shares were trading at their highest ever: $85 a share. On January 31, 1992, the FDA announced that it was not approving Ethyol. The following trading day, Bioscience shares plunged 46 percent. By mid-1992, the stock was down to $11 a share.

Between January 7 and January 31, 1992, Mr. Schein and other officers sold 1.2 million shares of U.S. Bioscience. Did he and the others violate any security laws?

Securities Law

One of the methods for raising the capital needed for a corporation or partnership is to sell interests in them. Corporations sell shares, and partnerships sell limited partnership interests. Investors provide the capital these businesses need to operate. They give the businesses their money to work with and in return are given an interest in the business. The investors' hope is that the business will give them a profit on their investment (dividends) and that the value of their investment will grow as the business increases in value. The investment arrangement in theory is mutually beneficial. However, because people are so eager to have their money grow and because businesses need money, the interests of business and investors are so often at odds that there seems to be an inherent conflict of interest in the investment relationship. Because of this conflict there are laws regulating investments at both state and federal levels. These laws are called securities laws, and they govern everything from the sale of securities to soliciting proxies from owners of securities. This chapter answers the questions: Why do we have securities laws and what is their history? What are the requirements that affect primary offerings of securities? How do securities laws regulate the secondary market? What are the penalties for violating securities laws?

> *October. This is one of the peculiarly dangerous months to speculate stocks in. The others are July, January, September, April, November, May, March, June, December, August and February.*
>
> **Mark Twain**
> *Pudd'nhead Wilson*

HISTORY OF SECURITIES LAW

Review the Securities Act of 1933 and the Securities Exchange act of 1934: http://www.law.uc.edu/CCL/

Although most people think of the market crash of 1929 as the beginning of securities regulation, regulation actually began nearly 20 years earlier at the state level. Kansas had the first securities law in 1911, which regulated the initial sale of securities to members of the public. Some states followed the lead of Kansas, but until 1929 the field of securities was relatively free of regulation.

There was at that time a great deal of speculation in stocks. Investors traded "on margin," which means they borrowed money to invest in stock and when the stock went up in value, they sold it, paid off the loan, and still made money. On a Friday in 1929, however, stock prices dropped on all the exchanges and continued to drop. Investors defaulted on the margin loans, lenders foreclosed on their properties, and the entire country was thrown into a depression.

Because of the 1929 market crash, Congress perceived a problem with the investment market. As a result, the **Securities Act of 1933** and the **Securities Exchange Act of 1934** were passed, the former to regulate initial sales of stock by businesses and the latter to regulate the secondary trading of stock on the markets. These statutes and their accompanying regulations still govern the regulation of the sale of securities today.

PRIMARY OFFERING REGULATION— THE 1933 SECURITIES ACT

A **primary offering**, or an initial public offering (IPO), is a sale of securities by the business itself. The 1933 act regulates this initial sale of securities.

What Is a Security?

Because the 1933 act applies only to the sale of securities, the term *securities* requires definition. The language of the act itself is very broad and lists approximately 20 items that are considered securities, including: notes; stock; bonds; debentures; warrants; subscriptions; voting-trust certificates; rights to oil, gas, and minerals; and limited partnership interests. Every investment contract that gives the owner evidence of indebtedness or business participation is a security.

In interpreting the application of the 1933 act, the courts have been very liberal. The landmark case on the definition of a security is *SEC* v. *W.J. Howey Co.*, 328 U.S. 293 (1946). In holding that the sale of interests in Florida citrus groves constituted the sale of securities, the U.S. Supreme Court defined a security as "a contract, transaction, or scheme whereby a person invests his money in a common enterprise and is led to expect profits solely from the efforts of a promoter or a third party." With this even broader definition than the actual 1933 act language, known as the *Howey* **test**, courts have been reluctant to impose restrictions on the definition of a security. In recent years, the only type of arrangement the U.S. Supreme Court has excluded from this definition is an employer pension plan in which employees are not required to make contributions. The exclusion of these plans from securities laws is probably based on the fact that there are other statutory protections afforded employees (see Chapter 18 and the discussion of the Employment Retirement Income Security Act).

The following case deals with the issue of whether a security (within the definition of the 1933 act) has been sold.

Reves v. Ernst & Young
494 U.S. 56 (1990)

GASAHOL PLANT INTERESTS: ARE THEY SECURITIES?

FACTS

The Farmer's Cooperative of Arkansas (Co-Op) was an agricultural cooperative that had approximately 23,000 members. In order to raise money to support its general business operations, the Co-Op sold promissory notes payable on demand by the holder. The notes were uncollateralized and uninsured, and paid a variable rate of interest that was adjusted to make it higher than the rate paid by local financial institutions. The notes were offered to members and nonmembers and were marketed as an "investment program." Advertisements for the notes, which appeared in the Co-Op newsletter, read in part: "YOUR CO-OP has more than $11,000,000 in assets to stand behind your investments. The Investment is not Federal [sic] insured but it is . . . Safe."

Despite the assurance, the Co-Op filed for bankruptcy in 1984. At the time of the bankruptcy filing, over 1,600 people held notes worth a total of $10 million.

After the bankruptcy filing, a class of note holders (petitioners) filed suit against Arthur Young & Co. (predecessor to Ernst & Young), alleging that Young had failed to follow generally accepted accounting principles in its audit, specifically with respect to the valuation of the Co-Op's major asset, a gasahol plant. The note holders claimed that if Young had properly treated the plant in its audited financials, they would not have purchased the notes. The petitioners were awarded $6.1 million in damages by the federal district court. The Eighth Circuit Court of Appeals held that the notes were not securities and reversed. The note holders appealed.

JUDICIAL OPINION

MARSHALL, Justice

This case requires us to decide whether the note issued by the Co-Op is a "security" within the meaning of the 1934 Act. Section 3(a)(10) of that Act is our starting point:

The term 'security' means any note, stock, treasury stock, bond, debenture, certificate of interest or participation in any profit-sharing agreement or in any oil, gas, or other mineral royalty or lease, any collateral-trust certificate, preorganization certificate or subscription, transferable share, investment contract, voting-trust certificate, certificate of deposit for a security, any put, call, straddle, option, or privilege on any security, certificate of deposit, or group or index of securities (including any interest therein or based on the value thereof), or any put, call, straddle, option, or privilege entered into on a national securities exchange relating to foreign currency, or in general, any instrument commonly known as a 'security'; or any certificate of interest or participation in, temporary or interim certificate for, receipt for, or warrant or right to subscribe to or purchase any of the foregoing, but shall not include currency or any note, draft, bill of exchange, or banker's acceptance which has a maturity at the time of issuance of not exceeding nine months, exclusive of days of grace, or any renewal thereof the maturity of which is likewise limited.

The fundamental purpose undergirding the Securities Act is to "eliminate serious abuses in a largely unregulated securities market." In defining the scope of the market that it wished to regulate, Congress painted with a broad brush. It recognized the virtually limitless scope of human ingenuity, especially in the creation of "countless and variable schemes devised by those who seek the use of the money of others on the promise of profits," *SEC* v. *W.J. Howey Co.*, 328 U.S. 293 (1946), and determined that the best way to achieve its goal of protecting investors was "to define 'the term "security" in sufficiently broad and general terms so as to include within that definition the many types of instruments that in our commercial world fall within the ordinary concept of a security.'" Congress' purpose in enacting the securities laws was to regulate *investments*, in

Continued

whatever form they are made and by whatever name they are called.

While common stock is the quintessence of a security, and investors therefore justifiably assume that the sale of a stock is covered by the Securities Acts, the same simply cannot be said of notes, which are used in a variety of settings, not all of which involve investments. Thus, the phrase "any note" should not be interpreted to mean literally "any note," but must be understood against the backdrop of what Congress was attempting to accomplish in enacting the Securities Acts.

A majority of the Courts of Appeals that have considered the issue have adopted, in varying forms, "investment versus commercial" approaches that distinguish, on the basis of all circumstances surrounding the transactions, notes issued in an investment context (which are "securities") from notes issued in a commercial or consumer context (which are not).

The Second Circuit's "family resemblance" approach begins with a presumption that *any* note with a term of more than nine months is a "security." Recognizing that not all notes are securities, however, the Second Circuit has devised a list of notes that it has decided are obviously not securities. Accordingly, the "family resemblance" test permits an issuer to rebut the presumption that a note is a security if it can show that the note in question bears a strong "family resemblance" to an item on a judicially crafted list of exceptions or convinces the court to add a new instrument to the list.

In contrast, the Eighth and District of Columbia Circuits apply the test we created in *SEC* v. *W.J. Howey*, to determine whether an instrument is an "investment contract" to the determination whether an instrument is a "note." Under this test, a note is a security only if it evidences: "(1) an investment; (2) in a common enterprise; (3) with reasonable expectation of profits; (4) to be derived from the entrepreneurial or managerial efforts of others."

We reject the approaches of those courts that have applied the *Howey* test to notes; . . .

We conclude, then, that in determining whether an instrument denominated a "note" is a "security," courts are to apply the version of the "family resemblance" test that we have articulated here: a note is presumed to be a "security," and that presumption may be rebutted.

Applying the family resemblance approach to this case, we have little difficulty concluding that the notes at issue here are "securities."

To be sure, the notes were not traded on an exchange. They were, however, offered and sold to a broad segment of the public, and that is all we have held necessary to establish the requisite "common trading" in an instrument.

The advertisements for the notes characterized them as "investments," and there were no countervailing factors that would have led a reasonable person to question this characterization.

Finally, we find no risk-reducing factor to suggest that these instruments are not in fact securities. The notes are uncollateralized and uninsured.

We therefore hold that the notes at issue here are within the term "note" in Section 3(a)(10).

Reversed.

CASE QUESTIONS

1. What type of instrument was sold?
2. How was it sold?
3. What happened to the Co-Op?
4. Why was Ernst & Young sued?
5. What test is adopted for determining whether a note is a security?
6. What differences existed between the circuits regarding the definition of a security prior to this decision?

C O N S I D E R . . . **21.1** Limited liability companies (Chapter 20) are an increasingly popular form of investment. Would limited liability memberships be considered securities?

Regulating Primary Offerings: Registration

Visit the Securities and Exchange Commission: http://www.sec.gov/

The **Securities and Exchange Commission (SEC)** is the administrative agency responsible for regulating the sale of securities under both the 1933 and 1934 acts. The SEC is subject to all of the administrative rules covered in Chapter 6, for it is an administrative agency created in an enabling act of Congress, the 1934 Securities Exchange Act. The SEC can issue injunctions, institute criminal proceedings, enter into consent decrees, handle enforcement, and promulgate rules.

The rules promulgated by the SEC provide the requirements for the registration of securities, financial reporting, and stock exchange operations. The SEC has a complete staff of lawyers, accountants, financial analysts, and other experts to assist in both the review of informational filings and in the enforcement of the securities laws.

Regulating Primary Offerings: Exemptions

Unless an **exemption** applies, anyone selling securities must complete certain filing requirements before the securities can be sold legally. There are two types of exemptions: exempt securities and exempt transactions. These exemptions work only for the 1933 act.

EXEMPT SECURITIES

Certain investments, called **exempt securities**, have been excluded specifically from coverage of the 1933 act. The following is a list of some of the exemptions:

1. Securities (bonds, etc.) issued by federal, state, county, or municipal governments for public purposes
2. Commercial paper (includes notes, checks, and drafts with a maturity date under nine months)
3. Banks, savings and loans, and religious and charitable organizations
4. Insurance policies
5. Annuities
6. Securities of common carriers (those regulated by the Interstate Commerce Commission)
7. Stock dividends and stock splits

EXEMPT TRANSACTIONS

Exempt transactions are more complicated than exempt securities; more details are required to comply with the exempt transaction standards. The following subsections discuss these transaction exemptions, which are summarized in Exhibit 21.1 (pg. 764).

THE INTRASTATE OFFERING EXEMPTION

This exemption exists because the Commerce Clause prohibits the federal government from regulating purely intrastate matters (see Chapter 5 for a full discussion of Commerce Clause issues). To qualify for the intrastate exemption, the investors (offerees) and issuer must all be residents of the same state. (If there is one out-of-state offeree, the exemption will not apply.) Further, the issuer must meet the following requirements:

1. Eighty (80) percent of its assets must be located in the state.
2. Eighty (80) percent of its income must be earned from operations within the state.
3. Eighty (80) percent of the proceeds from the sale must be used on operations within the state.

Name	Size limitation	Offeree/buyer limitation	Resale limitation	Public offering
Intrastate exemption, 15 U.C.C. § 77 (c) (a) (11)	No	Buyers must be residents of state of incorporation; triple 80 percent requirements	Yes, stock transfer restrictions	Yes, in state
Small-offering exemption, 15 U.C.C. § 77D, Regulation A	$1,500,000[a]	Short-form registration required	No	Yes
Rule 504 — small-offering Regulation D	$1,000,000[b] or less (in 12–month period)	None, unlimited accredited and nonaccredited alike	Some	No
Rule 505, Regulation D	Up to $7,500,000	No more than 35, excluding accredited investors	Some	No
Rule 506, Regulation D	No	Unlimited accredited and 35 nonaccredited investors; (nonaccredited must be sophisticated)	Yes, stock restrictions	No

[a] Up to $2,000,000 in certain circumstances.
[b] Only in certain circumstances ($500,000 if no blue sky registration).

Exhibit 21.1
1933 Securities Act Transaction Exemptions

Examine registration form S-1: http://www.law.uc.edu/CCL/33forms/index.html

Under the SEC's Rule 147, there are restrictions on the transfer of exempt intrastate offerings, including a nine-month transfer restriction to state residents only.

SMALL-OFFERING EXEMPTION—REGULATION A
Although it is not a true exemption, Regulation A is a shortcut method of registration. The lengthy, complicated processes of full registration are simplified in that only a short-form (S-1) registration statement is filed. Regulation A applies to issues of $1.5 million or less during any 12-month period. In some cases, the amount can be up to $2 million.

The SEC groups or "integrates" registration. Three registrations of $600,000 each would not qualify if issued within one 12-month period. They would qualify, however, if issued over three years.

SMALL-OFFERING EXEMPTION—REGULATION D

Review Regulations A and D: http://www. law.uc.edu/CCL/ 33ActRls/index. html

Regulation D is the product of the SEC's evaluation of the impact of its rules on the ability of small businesses to raise capital. It was designed to simplify and clarify existing exemptions, expand the availability of exemptions, and achieve uniformity between state and federal exemptions.

Regulation D creates a three-tiered exemption structure that consists of Rules 504, 505, and 506, that permits sales without registration. Sellers are, however, required to file a Form D informational statement about the sale. Rule 501 of Regulation D lists the definitions of various terms used in the three exemptions. For example, the term **accredited investor** includes any investor who at the time of the sale falls into any of the following categories:

1. Any bank
2. Any private business development company
3. Any director, executive officer, or general partner of the issuer
4. Any person who purchases at least $150,000 of the securities being offered
5. Natural persons whose net worth is greater than $1 million
6. Any person whose individual income exceeded $200,000 in the last two years and who expects income greater than $200,000 in the current year

Rule 502 places a number of limitations on the means an issuer can use in offering securities. The securities cannot be sold through general advertising or through seminars initiated through advertising. Further, all of the securities sold must be subject to restrictions to prevent the immediate rollover of the securities involved in these exempt transactions.

The three tiers of Regulation D exemptions are as follows:

The **Rule 504** exemption applies to offerings of $500,000 or less (within any 12-month period). The issuer cannot use advertising or make the offer to the public. Sales of stock to directors, officers, and employees are not counted in the $500,000 limitation. Recent challenges permit the use of the Rule 504 exemption in offerings of up to $1 million provided the offering is registered under a state **blue sky law**.

The **Rule 505** exemption covers sales of up to $7.5 million provided there are no more than 35 nonaccredited investors. Again, issuers qualifying under this exemption cannot engage in public advertising. Also, if the issue is sold to both accredited and nonaccredited investors, the issuer must give all buyers a prospectus.

The **Rule 506** exemption has no dollar limitation, but the number and type of investors is limited. There can be any number of accredited investors, but the number of nonaccredited investors is limited to 35, and these investors must be sophisticated (capable of evaluating the offering and its risk). There cannot be advertising under a 506 exemption, and there must be restrictions on the resale of the shares.

CORPORATE REORGANIZATIONS

If a firm is issuing new shares of stock under a Chapter 11 reorganization supervised by a bankruptcy court, then registration is not necessary provided there is court approval for the issue.

What Must Be Filed: Documents and Information for Registration

If none of the exemptions applies, the offeror of the securities must go through the registration process. The offeror (issuer) must file a **registration statement** and sample **prospectus** with the SEC. A prospectus here means the formal document the SEC requires all shareholders to have. However, for purposes of disclosure and misrepresentation issues, a prospectus is any ad or written materials the offeror provides or places.

There is a filing fee based on the aggregate offering price of the sale. The SEC has 20 days to act on the filing, after which the registration statement automatically becomes effective. The SEC, however, always acts within that time period. It need not actually approve or disapprove the offering within that time limit so long as a **comment (or deficiency) letter** is issued. A new registration, for a first-time offeror, generally takes about six months to get through the SEC.

The SEC's guide in reviewing the registration materials is the **full disclosure standard**. The SEC does not pass on the merits of the offering or the soundness of the investment; rather, it ensures that certain information is disclosed. The information required in the registration statement is as follows:

1. A description of what is being offered, why it is offered, how the securities will fit into the business's existing capital structure, and how the proceeds will be used
2. An audited financial statement
3. A list of corporate assets
4. The nature of the issuer's business
5. A list of those in management and their shares of ownership in the firm
6. Other relevant and material information such as pending lawsuits

Before the registration statement is filed, the issuer is very much restricted in what can be done to sell the securities. And even after the registration is filed but is not yet effective, the issuer is restricted.

However, the issuer can run a **tombstone ad,** shown in Exhibit 21.2 (pg. 767), which simply announces that securities will be sold and who will have information but clearly indicates that the ad is not an offer. Also, before the registration statement becomes effective, the issuer can send out a **red herring prospectus**, which has printed in red at the top that the registration is not yet effective. These red herrings are a way to get out information while waiting for SEC approval.

During this interval between filing and the effective date, there can be no sales and no general advertising. Activity is limited until the date the registration gets SEC approval and becomes effective. Exhibit 21.3 (pg. 768) is a diagram of federal securities registration and exemptions.

The SEC permits firms to complete *shelf registrations*. Under this process, a firm completes all the registration requirements and is then free to issue the securities any time within a two-year period, generally when market conditions are most favorable. The company's quarterly and annual filings (pg. 774) serve to update the shelf registration. This means of filing was permitted to facilitate the raising of capital by corporations.

Violations of the 1933 Act

SECTION 11 VIOLATIONS

Section 11 of the 1933 act imposes civil liability on those who do not comply with the act's requirements regarding the submission of a registration statement.

This Announcement is neither an offer to sell nor a solicitation of an offer to buy these securities.
The offer is made only by the Prospectus Supplement and the related Prospectus.

New Issue / December 11, 1991

$150,000,000

Arizona Public Service Company

First Mortgage Bonds, 9% Series due 2021

Price 98.875% and accrued interest from December 15, 1991

Copies of the Prospectus Supplement and the related Prospectus may be obtained
in any State in which this announcement is circulated only from such of the
undersigned as may legally offer these securities in such State.

Salomon Brothers Inc

The First Boston Corporation

Goldman, Sachs & Co.

J.P. Morgan Securities Inc.

Exhibit 21.2
Sample of a Tombstone Ad

Section 11 is used when full disclosure has not been made in the registration statement or if any of the information in that registration statement is false. Section 11 is a statutory fraud section that applies to security registrations.

WHAT IS REQUIRED FOR A VIOLATION?
For an investor to recover under Section 11, the following elements must be proved:

1. The investor purchased a security that was required to have a registration statement.
2. The registration statement contains a material misstatement or omission.
3. The investor need not show reliance unless the purchase was made over a year after the effective date.
4. The investor experienced a loss.

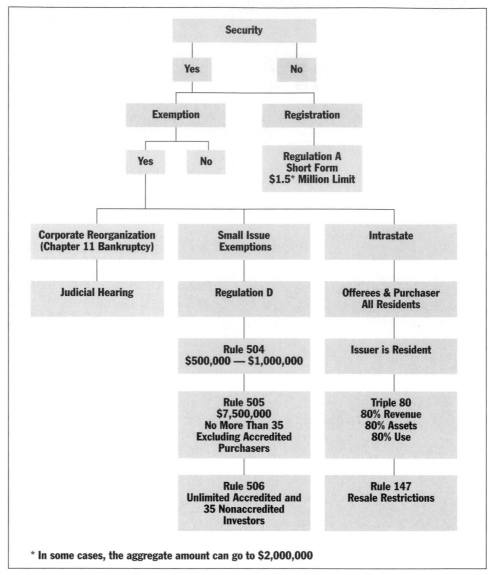

Exhibit 21.3
Federal Securities Registration and Exemptions

WHO IS LIABLE?

Liability under Section 11 attaches to all individuals who signed the registration statement—each director and officer of the issuing corporation, and every accountant, engineer, appraiser, attorney, geologist, or other expert whose input was used in the preparation of the statement. Underwriters are also included as potential defendants. Experts (such as accountants, engineers, appraisers, lawyers) are liable only for the information they provided. Directors and officers are jointly and severally liable under Section 11.

DEFENSES FOR SECTION 11 VIOLATIONS

Several defenses are available to defendants. Proof of these defenses is the burden of the defendants.

1. *Immateriality.* Because proving that a **material misstatement** or omission was made is part of the investor's case, proving that the statement or omission was immaterial is a valid defense. The standards for what is or is not material are basically the same standards used in contract misrepresentation cases.
2. *Investor Knowledge.* If the investor knew of the misstatement or omission and purchased the stock anyway, there is no Section 11 liability. Section 11 defendants can offer proof of knowledge to establish a defense.
3. *Due Diligence.* The **due diligence** defense is one that allows defendants to show that they were acting reasonably in preparing and signing the registration statement. The experts are required to show that they acted within the standards of their profession in preparing their portions of the registration statement. Officers and directors are required to show that they had no reason to suspect or knowledge of an omission or misstatement.

The following case is the leading case on Section 11 liability. It involves a variety of defendants and discusses the defense of due diligence.

Escott v. BarChris Constr. Corp.
283 F. Supp. 643 (S.D.N.Y. 1958)

BOWLING FOR FRAUD: RIGHT UP OUR ALLEY

FACTS

BarChris was a bowling alley company established in 1946. There was rapid growth in the bowling industry when automatic pin resetters went on the market in the mid-1950s. BarChris began a program of rapid expansion and in 1960 was responsible for the construction of over 3 percent of all bowling alleys in the United States. BarChris used two methods of financing the construction of these alleys, both of which substantially drained their cash flow.

In 1959 BarChris sold approximately one-half million shares of common stock. By 1960, its cash flow picture was still troublesome, and it sold debentures. The debenture issue was registered with the SEC, approved, and sold. In spite of the cash boost from the sale, BarChris was still experiencing financial difficulties and declared bankruptcy in October 1962. The debenture holders were not paid their interest; BarChris defaulted.

The purchasers of the BarChris debentures brought suit under Section 11 of the 1933 act. They claimed that the registration statement filed by BarChris contained false information and failed to disclose certain material information. Their suit, which centered around the audited financial statements prepared by a CPA firm, claimed that the statements were inaccurate and full of omissions. The following chart summarizes the problems with the financial statements submitted with the registration statements:

1. *1960 Earnings*
   (a) *Sales*

Per prospectus	$9,165,320
Correct figure	8,511,420
Overstatement	$ 653,900

   (b) *Net Operating Income*

Per prospectus	$1,742,801
Correct figure	1,496,196
Overstatement	$ 246,605

   (c) *Earnings per Share*

Per prospectus	$ .75
Correct figure	.65
Overstatement	$ .10

2. *1960 Balance Sheet*
   Current Assets

Per prospectus	$4,524,021
Correct figure	3,914,332
Overstatement	$ 609,689

Continued

3. *Contingent Liabilities as of December 31, 1960, on Alternative Method of Financing*

Per prospectus	$ 750,000
Correct figure	1,125,795
Understatement	$ 375,795
Capitol Lanes should have been shown as a direct liability	$ 325,000

4. *Contingent Liabilities as of April 30, 1961*

Per prospectus	$ 825,000
Correct figure	1,443,853
Understatement	$ 618,853
Capitol Lanes should have been shown as a direct liability	$ 314,166

5. *Earnings Figures for Quarter Ending March 31, 1961*
   (a) *Sales*

Per prospectus	$2,138,455
Correct figure	1,618,645
Overstatement	$ 519,810

   (b) *Gross Profit*

Per prospectus	$ 483,121
Correct figure	252,366
Overstatement	$ 230,755

6. *Backlog as of March 31, 1961*

Per prospectus	$ 6,905,000
Correct figure	2,415,000
Overstatement	$ 4,490,000

7. *Failure to Disclose Officers' Loans Outstanding and Unpaid on May 16, 1961* $386,615

8. *Failure to Disclose Use of Proceeds in Manner Not Revealed in Prospectus: Approx.* $ 1,160,000

9. *Failure to Disclose Customers' Delinquencies in May 1961 and BarChris's Potential Liability with Respect Thereto: Over* $ 1,350,000

10. *Failure to Disclose the Fact that BarChris Was Already Engaged and Was About to Be More Heavily Engaged in the Operation of Bowling Alleys*

The federal district court reviewed all of the exhibits and statements included in the prospectus and dealt with each defendant individually in issuing its decisions. The defendants consisted of those officers and directors who signed the registration statement, the underwriters of the debenture offering, the auditors (Peat, Marwick, Mitchell & Co.), and BarChris's attorneys and directors.

JUDICIAL OPINION
McLEAN, District Judge

Russo. Russo was, to all intents and purposes, the chief executive officer of BarChris. He was a member of the executive committee. He was familiar with all aspects of the business. He was personally in charge of dealings with the factors. He acted on BarChris's behalf in making the financing agreement with Talcott and he handled the negotiations with Talcott in the spring of 1961. He talked with customers about their delinquencies.

Russo prepared the list of jobs which went into the backlog figure. He knew the status of those jobs.

It was Russo who arranged for the temporary increase in BarChris's cash in banks on December 31, 1960, a transaction which borders on the fraudulent. He was thoroughly aware of BarChris's stringent financial condition in May 1961. He had personally advanced large sums to BarChris of which $175,000 remained unpaid as of May 16.

In short, Russo knew all the relevant facts. He could not have believed that there were no untrue statements or material omissions in the prospectus. Russo has no due diligence defenses.

Vitolo and Pugliese. They were the founders of the business who stuck with it to the end. Vitolo was president and Pugliese was vice president. Despite their titles, their field of responsibility in the administration of BarChris's affairs during the period in question seems to have been less all-embracing than Russo's. Pugliese in particular appears to have limited his activities to supervising the actual construction work.

Continued

Vitolo and Pugliese are each men of limited education. It is not hard to believe that for them the prospectus was difficult reading, if indeed they read it at all.

But whether it was or not is irrelevant. The liability of a director who signs a registration statement does not depend upon whether or not he read it or, if he did, whether or not he understood what he was reading.

And in any case, Vitolo and Pugliese were not as naive as they claim to be. They were members of BarChris's executive committee. At meetings of that committee BarChris's affairs were discussed at length. They must have known what was going on. Certainly they knew of the inadequacy of cash in 1961. They knew of their own large advances to the company which remained unpaid. They knew that they had agreed not to deposit their checks until the financing proceeds were received. They knew and intended that part of the proceeds were to be used to pay their own loans.

All in all, the position of Vitolo and Pugliese is not significantly different, for present purposes, from Russo's. They could not have believed that the registration statement was wholly true and that no material facts had been omitted. And in any case, there is nothing to show that they made any investigation of anything which they may not have known about or understood. They have not proved their due diligence defenses.

Kircher. Kircher was treasurer of BarChris and its chief financial officer. He is a certified public accountant and an intelligent man. He was thoroughly familiar with BarChris's financial affairs. He knew the terms of BarChris's agreements with Talcott. He knew of the customers' delinquency problems. He participated actively with Russo in May 1961 in the successful effort to hold Talcott off until the financing proceeds came in. He knew how the financing proceeds were to be applied and he saw to it that they were so applied. He arranged the officers' loans and he knew all the facts concerning them.

Moreover, as a member of the executive committee, Kircher was kept informed as to those branches of the business of which he did not have direct charge. He knew about the operation of alleys, present and prospective. In brief, Kircher knew all the relevant facts.

Knowing the facts, Kircher had reason to believe that the expertised portion of the prospectus, i.e., the 1960 figures, was in part incorrect. He could not shut his eyes to the facts and rely on Peat, Marwick for that portion.

As to the rest of the prospectus, knowing the facts, he did not have a reasonable ground to believe it to be true. On the contrary, he must have known that in part it was untrue. Under these circumstances, he was not entitled to sit back and place the blame on the lawyers for not advising him about it. Kircher has not proved his due diligence defenses.

Trilling. Trilling's position is somewhat different from Kircher's. He was BarChris's controller. He signed the registration statement in that capacity, although he was not a director.

Trilling entered BarChris's employ in October 1960. He was Kircher's subordinate. When Kircher asked him for information, he furnished it. On at least one occasion he got it wrong.

Trilling may well have been unaware of several of the inaccuracies in the prospectus. But he must have known of some of them. As a financial officer, he was familiar with BarChris's finances and with its books of account. He knew that part of the cash on deposit on December 31, 1960, had been procured temporarily by Russo for window dressing purposes. He should have known, although perhaps through carelessness he did not know at the time, that BarChris's contingent liability was greater than the prospectus stated. In the light of these facts, I cannot find that Trilling believed the entire prospectus to be true.

But even if he did, he still did not establish his due diligence defenses. He did not prove that as to the parts of the prospectus expertised by Peat, Marwick he had no reasonable ground to believe that it was untrue. He also failed to prove, as to the parts of the prospectus not expertised by Peat, Marwick, that he made a reasonable investigation which afforded him

Continued

a reasonable ground to believe that it was true. As far as appears, he made no investigation. As a signer, he could not avoid responsibility by leaving it up to others to make it accurate. Trilling did not sustain the burden of proving his due diligence defenses.

Birnbaum. Birnbaum was a young lawyer, admitted to the bar in 1957, who, after brief periods of employment by two different law firms and an equally brief period of practicing in his own firm, was employed by BarChris as house counsel and assistant secretary in October 1960. Unfortunately for him, he became secretary and director of BarChris on April 17, 1961, after the first version of the registration statement had been filed with the Securities and Exchange Commission. He signed the later amendments, thereby becoming responsible for the accuracy of the prospectus in its final form.

It seems probable that Birnbaum did not know of many of the inaccuracies in the prospectus. He must, however, have appreciated some of them. In any case, he made no investigation and relied on the others to get it right. Unlike Trilling, he was entitled to rely upon Peat, Marwick for the 1960 figures, for as far as appears, he had no personal knowledge of the company's books of account or financial transactions. As a lawyer, he should have known his obligations under the statute. He should have known that he was required to make a reasonable investigation of the truth of all the statements in the unexpertised portion of the document which he signed. Having failed to make such an investigation, he did not have reasonable ground to believe that all these statements were true. Birnbaum has not established his due diligence defenses except as to the audited 1960 exhibits.

Auslander. Auslander was an "outside" director, i.e., one who was not an officer of BarChris. He was chairman of the board of Valley Stream National Bank in Valley Stream, Long Island. In February 1961 Vitolo asked him to become a director of BarChris. As an inducement, Vitolo said that when BarChris received the proceeds of a forthcoming issue of securities, it would deposit $1 million in Auslander's bank.

Auslander was elected a director on April 17, 1961. The registration statement in its original form had already been filed, of course without his signature. On May 10, 1961, he signed a signature page for the first amendment to the registration statement which was filed on May 11, 1961. This was a separate sheet without any document attached. Auslander did not know that it was a signature page for a registration statement. He vaguely understood that it was something "for the SEC."

Auslander attended a meeting of BarChris's directors on May 15, 1961. At that meeting he, along with the other directors, signed the signature sheet for the second amendment which constituted the registration statement in its final form. Again, this was only a separate sheet without any document attached.

Auslander never saw a copy of the registration statement in its final form. It is true that Auslander became a director on the eve of the financing. He had little opportunity to familiarize himself with the company's affairs.

Section 11 imposes liability in the first instance upon a director, no matter how new he is.

Peat, Marwick. Peat, Marwick's work was in general charge of a member of the firm, Cummings, and more immediately in charge of Peat, Marwick's manager, Logan. Most of the actual work was performed by a senior accountant, Berardi, who had junior assistants, one of whom was Kennedy.

Berardi was then about thirty years old. He was not yet a cpa. He had had no previous experience with the bowling industry. This was his first job as a senior accountant. He could hardly have been given a more difficult assignment.

After obtaining a little background information on BarChris by talking to Logan and reviewing Peat, Marwick's work papers on its 1959 audit, Berardi examined the results of test checks of BarChris's accounting procedures which one of the junior accountants had made, and he prepared an "internal control questionnaire" and an "audit program." Thereafter, for a few days subsequent to December 30, 1960, he inspected BarChris's inventories and examined certain alley construction. Finally, on

Continued

January 13, 1961, he began his auditing work which he carried on substantially continuously until it was completed on February 24, 1961. Toward the close of the work, Logan reviewed it and made various comments and suggestions to Berardi.

It is unnecessary to recount everything that Berardi did in the course of the audit. We are concerned only with the evidence relating to what Berardi did or did not do with respect to those items found to have been incorrectly reported in the 1960 figures in the prospectus.

Accountants should not be held to a standard higher than that recognized in their profession. I do not do so here. Berardi's review did not come up to that standard. He did not take some of the steps which Peat, Marwick's written program prescribed. He did not spend an adequate amount of time on a task of this magnitude. Most important of all, he was too easily satisfied with glib answers to his inquiries.

This is not to say that he should have made a complete audit. But there were enough danger signals in the materials which he did examine to require some further investigation on his part. Generally accepted accounting standards required such further investigation under these circumstances. It is not always sufficient merely to ask questions.

CASE QUESTIONS

1. How much time transpired between the sale of the debentures and BarChris's bankruptcy?
2. Did BarChris disclose the amount of delinquent debts?
3. Who was sued under Section 11?
4. Were all of the misstatements or omissions material?
5. Who was held liable?

Business Planning Tip

1933 Act Exposure
The date of the BarChris case is deceptive because it seems to be a very old case. However, few cases on section 11 liability are reported beyond BarChris. Most defendants named in section 11 lawsuits from public accounting firms through geologists to lawyers settle their suits because they are generally large class actions with potentially destructive results.

The number of suits has led to what is called the "Shareholder Suit Bill." The bill, passed in 1995, will prevent so-called strike suits, or class action suits brought against a company's management when share prices drop. Managers would typically settle these cases rather than face litigation. The bill has liability limitations as well as a provision for company recovery of legal fees if the suit is determined to be frivolous.

PENALTIES FOR VIOLATIONS OF SECTION 11

Violations of Section 11 carry maximum penalties of $10,000 and/or five years imprisonment. In addition, the SEC has the authority to bring suit seeking an injunction to stop sales that are based on false or omitted information in the registration statement. Those purchasers who are harmed by the false or omitted statements have a right of civil suit in federal district court for recovery of their losses and other damages.

Section 11's standards had resulted in a state of near strict liability for accountants, underwriters, lawyers, banks, and board members to shareholders who brought suit. Also, the nature of the levels of damages and the certainty of recovery of awards led to large numbers of sizeable class action suits under Section 11. In 1995, Congress passed, over a presidential veto, the Securities Litigation Reform Act of 1995, which is the first major change to the 1933 Securities Act since its enactment. This detailed act contains provisions that limit attorneys' fees to a reasonable percentage of the amount recovered or the agreed-upon settlement amount. The problem of "professional plaintiffs" is also addressed through a section that prevents a plaintiff from being named in more than five class-action securities lawsuits in a three-year period. One final portion of Section 11 reform under the act is the so-called "safe-harbor" protection. With certain precautions and qualifications, companies can now make forward-looking predictions for company performance in materials given to investors without the automatic liability that resulted formerly if future events were even addressed.

SECTION 12 VIOLATIONS

Section 12 carries the same criminal penalties as Section 11 and covers the following offenses:

1. Selling securities without registration and without an exemption
2. Selling securities before the effective date of the registration statement
3. Selling securities using false information in the prospectus (In this case, prospectus includes not only the formal document but all ads, circulars, and so on used in the sale of securities.)

The SEC also has injunctive remedies here, and buyers also have the right of civil suit. The same defenses as those for Section 11 are applicable to Section 12.

THE SECURITIES EXCHANGE ACT OF 1934

The 1934 act steps in to regulate securities and their issuers once they are on the market. Securities sales, brokers, dealers, and exchanges are all regulated under the 1934 act. In addition, the act requires public disclosure of financial information for certain corporations. In effect, the 1934 act is responsible for the regulation of the securities marketplace. The SEC accomplishes its goal of regulating undesirable market practices in several ways, which are discussed in the following sections.

Securities Registration

Under the 1934 act, all securities traded on a national stock exchange must be registered. In addition, any issuer with over $5 million in assets and 750 or more shareholders must register its equity stock (not bonds) under the 1934 act if those shares are traded in interstate commerce. This registration is in addition to all the filing requirements for issuing discussed under the 1933 act.

Periodic Filing

Search the SEC's EDGAR (Electronic Data Gathering, Analysis, and Retrevial) database for corporate 10-Q, 10-K, and 8-K filings: http:// www.sec.gov/ edgarhp.htm

In addition to the one-time registration required under the 1934 act, those same companies (national stock exchange companies or those with 750 or more shareholders and $5 million in assets) must comply with the periodic reporting requirements imposed by the SEC. Each quarter these firms must file a **10-Q** form, which is basically a quarterly financial report. An annual report, the **10-K** form, must be filed by the company at the end of its fiscal year. Any unusual events—bankruptcies, spinoffs, takeovers, and other changes in company control—must be reported on the **8-K** form.

The Antifraud Provision

Review the Rules Promulgated under the Securities Exchange Act of 1934: http:// www.law.uc.edu/ CCL/34ActRls/ index.html

In addition to regulating the reporting of information, the 1934 act regulates the propriety of sales in the marketplace. **Section 10(b)** and **Rule 10b-5** are the antifraud provisions of the 1934 act. These sections are statutory versions of common law fraud. If the idea of the free market is to work, all buyers and sellers must have access to the same information. To withhold information is to commit fraud and is a violation of 10(b). The language of Rule 10b-5 follows:

It shall be unlawful for any person, directly or indirectly, by use of any means or instrumentality of interstate commerce, or of the mails, or of any facility of any national securities exchange,

(1) to employ any device, scheme, or artifice to defraud,

(2) to make any untrue statement of a material fact or to omit to state a material fact necessary in order to make the statement made, in the light of the circumstances under which they were made, not misleading, or

(3) to engage in any act, practice, or course of business which operates or would operate as a fraud or deceit upon any person, in connection with the purchase or sale of any security.

APPLICATION OF 10(B)

Of all the provisions of the 1934 act, section 10(b) has the broadest application. It applies to all sales of securities: exempt, stock exchange-listed, over-the-counter, public, private, small, or large. The only prerequisite for 10(b) application is that interstate commerce be involved in the sales transaction. As Chapter 5 indicates, it is not difficult to find an interstate commerce connection; for example, if the mails or phones were used in the transaction, 10(b) applies. The practical effect is that 10(b) applies to all sales of securities.

PROOF OF 10(B) VIOLATION

The language of 10(b) does not really specify what constitutes an offense of misrepresentation. Determination of 10(b) violations has been left to the SEC and the courts, which have shown that violations of 10(b) can take a variety of forms. For example, if a corporation releases false information about dividends, company growth, or earnings, purchasers and sellers of the corporate stock would have a 109(b) action against corporate management and directors. If an owner of shares gives a buyer false or misleading information, the owner-seller is liable under 10(b). Market manipulations in which brokers buy and sell stock in wash or cover sales in an effort to create the appearance of activity is also covered under 10(b).

One of the most famous 10(b) cases is SEC v. *Texas Gulf Sulphur Co.*, 401 F.2d 833 (2d Cir. 1968). In that case, Texas Gulf Sulphur was involved in test-drilling operations in Canada. Early tests indicated that the company would make a substantial strike. Press releases did not indicate the richness of the strike. Corporate officers, geologists, and relatives bought stock before the richness of the find was finally disclosed, and the price of the stock soared. The court found that the overly pessimistic press release was misleading under 10(b) and held the purchasers liable. The chapter's opening "Judgment" involves a similar problem.

COVERAGE OF 10(b)

Anyone who has access to information not readily available to the public is covered under 10(b). Officers, directors, and large shareholders are included in this group. However, 10(b) also applies to people who get information from these corporate **insiders**. These people are called **tippees**. For example, relatives of officers and directors would be considered tippees if they were given nonpublic information. Who is covered under section 10(b) has been a critical question during the past few years. The Supreme Court has made a distinction between true insiders and those who misappropriate information. While outsiders may obtain an unfair advantage, their unfair advantage is not necessarily fraud for purposes of 10(b), as the following case indicates.

Chiarella v. *United States*
445 U.S. 222 (1980)

READING BETWEEN THE LINES: THE PRINTER WITH ADVANCE INFORMATION

FACTS

Vincent Chiarella was employed as a printer in a financial printing firm that handled the printing for takeover bids. Although the firm names were left out of the financial materials and inserted at the last moment, Mr. Chiarella was able to deduce who was being taken over and by whom from other information in the reports being printed. Using this information, Mr. Chiarella was able to dabble in the stock market over a 14-month period for a net gain of $30,000. After an SEC investigation, he signed a consent decree that required him to return all of his profits to the sellers he purchased from during that 14-month period. He was then indicted for violation of 10(b) of the 1934 act and the SEC's Rule 10b-5. At the federal district court level, he was convicted on all 17 counts of the charges. The court of appeals affirmed, and Mr. Chiarella appealed to the U.S. Supreme Court.

JUDICIAL OPINION

POWELL, Justice

Section 10(b) of the 1934 Act, 15 U.S.C. § 78j, prohibits the use "in connection with the purchase or sale of any security . . . [of] any manipulative or deceptive device or contrivance in contravention of such rules and regulations as the Commission may prescribe."

This case concerns the legal effect of the petitioner's silence. The District Court's charge permitted the jury to convict the petitioner if it found that he willfully failed to inform sellers of target company securities that he knew of a forthcoming takeover bid that would make their shares more valuable.

[S]ilence in connection with the purchase or sale of securities may operate as a fraud actionable under Section 10(b) despite the absence of statutory language or legislative history specifically addressing the legality of nondisclosure. But such liability is premised upon a duty to disclose arising from a relationship of trust and confidence between parties to a transaction. Application of a duty to disclose prior to trading guarantees that corporate insiders, who have an obligation to place the shareholder's welfare before their own, will not benefit personally through fraudulent use of material nonpublic information.

In this case, the petitioner was convicted of violating Sec. 10(b) although he was not a corporate insider and he received no confidential information from the target company. Moreover, the "market information" upon which he relied did not concern the earning power or operations of the target company, but only the plans of the acquiring company. Petitioner's use of that information was not a fraud under Sec. 10(b) unless he was subject to an affirmative duty to disclose it before trading.

The Court of Appeals, like the trial court, failed to identify a relationship between a petitioner and the sellers that could give rise to a duty. Its decision thus rested solely upon its belief that the federal securities laws have "created a system providing equal access to information necessary for reasoned and intelligent investment decisions." The use by anyone of material information not generally available is fraudulent, this theory suggests, because such information gives certain buyers or sellers an unfair advantage over less informed buyers and sellers.

This reasoning suffers from two defects. First, not every instance of financial unfairness constitutes fraudulent activity under Sec. 10(b). Second, the element required to make silence fraudulent—a duty to disclose—is absent in this case. No duty could arise from petitioner's relationship with the sellers of the target company's securities, for petitioner had no prior dealings with them. He was not their agent, he was not a fiduciary, he was not a person in which the sellers had placed their trust and confidence. He was, in fact, a complete stranger

Continued

who dealt with the sellers only through impersonal market transactions.

Reversed.

CASE QUESTIONS
1. What was Mr. Chiarella's job?
2. Did Mr. Chiarella have the names of target companies?
3. Did Mr. Chiarella deal in the stock of the companies? Did he make money?
4. What were the terms of his consent decree?
5. Could he be convicted of a violation of 10(b)?

WHAT MUST BE DISCLOSED

Any material item must be disclosed. To determine whether an item is material, the question to be answered is, "Is this the type of information that would affect the buying or selling decision?" Examples of items that have been held to be material are:

1. Pending takeovers
2. Drops in quarterly earnings
3. Pending declaration of a large dividend
4. Possible lawsuit on product line

Business Planning Tip

Firms must use caution in selecting both employees and independent contractors. Some precautions may be necessary concerning the production of financial data, such as the use of pseudonyms (false names) until the final release.

CONSIDER . . . **21.2** In August 1994, Mervyn Cooper, a psychotherapist, was providing marriage counseling to a Lockheed executive. The executive had been assigned to conduct the due diligence (review of the accuracy of the books and records) of Martin Marietta, a company with which Lockheed was going to merge.

At his August 22, 1994 session with Mr. Cooper, the executive revealed to him the pending, but nonpublic merger. Following his session with the executive, Mr. Cooper contacted a friend, Kenneth Rottenberg, and told him about the pending merger. They agreed that Mr. Rottenberg would open a brokerage account, they would buy Lockheed call options and common stocks, and share in the profits.

When Mr. Rottenberg went to some brokerage offices to set up an account, he was warned by a broker there about the risks of call options. He told the broker that Lockheed would announce a major business combination shortly and that he would not lose his money.

Did Messrs. Rottenberg and Cooper violate section 10(b)? What about the broker? [*SEC* v. *Mervyn Cooper and Kenneth E. Rottenberg*, No.95-8535 (C.D. Cal. 1995).]

One aspect of 10(b) that is overlooked because of focus on individual acts is the obligation of a corporation to offer candid and timely disclosures of corporate status and changes. A merger announcement should be made publicly if too many leaks are resulting in share activity. The disclosure of environmental liability in terms of possible Superfund site cleanup costs should also be made in a timely fashion.

Business Planning Tip

Annual reports and 10K's have become a critical part of disclosure for companies. Most companies disclose all environmental cleanup sites and note that it is impossible to predict future cleanup locations or costs. This disclosure is nearly universal for firms.

WHEN DISCLOSURE MUST BE MADE

Once information becomes public knowledge, insiders and tippees are free to buy and sell the shares affected. However, the time of "public knowledge" is not always easy to determine. In *SEC* v. *Texas Gulf Sulphur*, 401 F.2d 833 (2d Cir. 1968), some of the insiders and tippees waited to buy Texas Gulf Sulphur stock until after a press conference announcement had been made regarding a major mineral find. However, the information released at the press conference had not yet made its way out of the press conference room; there was not enough dissemination for it to be public knowledge. Those who bought by phone immediately following the announcement were found to be in violation of 10(b).

The application and enforcement of section 10(b) have become two of the most significant issues affecting Wall Street. In the following case, the Supreme Court addressed a new set of circumstances in the sale of securities and application of 10(b).

Dirks v. *SEC*
463 U.S. 646 (1983)

NO EQUITY AT EQUITY FUNDING: WHOM CAN I TURN TO?

FACTS

Raymond Dirks was an officer in a Wall Street brokerage house. He was told by Ronald Secrist, a former officer of the Equity Funding of America Company, that Equity Funding had significantly overstated its assets by writing phony insurance policies. Mr. Secrist urged Mr. Dirks to investigate and expose the fraudulent practices. Mr. Dirks checked with Equity Funding management and received denials from them, but he received affirmations from employees.

Mr. Dirks discussed the issue with clients, and they "dumped" nearly $6 million in Equity Funding stock, but Mr. Dirks and his firm did not trade the stock. The price of the stock fell from $26 to $15 during Mr. Dirks' investigation. He contacted the *Wall Street Journal* bureau chief about the problem, but the bureau chief declined to get involved.

The SEC charged Mr. Dirks with violations of 10b-5 for his assistance to his clients. He was censured by the SEC, and he appealed. The D.C. Circuit Court of Appeals entered judgment against him, and he appealed to the U.S. Supreme Court.

JUDICIAL OPINION

POWELL, Justice

We were explicit in *Chiarella* in saying that there can be no duty to disclose where the person who has traded on inside information "was not [the corporation's] agent . . . was not a fiduciary, [or] was not a person in whom the sellers [of the securities] had placed their trust and confidence." Not to require such a fiduciary relationship, we recognized, would "depar[t] radically from the established doctrine that duty arises from a specific relationship between two parties" and would amount to "recognizing a general duty between all participants in market transactions to forgo actions based on material, nonpublic information." This requirement of a specific relationship between the shareholders and the individual trading on inside information has created analytical difficulties for the SEC and courts in policing tippees who trade on inside information. Unlike insiders who have independent fiduciary duties to both the corporation and its shareholders, the typical tippee has no such relationships.

Imposing a duty to disclose or abstain solely because a person knowingly receives

Continued

material nonpublic information from an insider and trades on it could have an inhibiting influence on the role of market analysts, which the SEC itself recognizes is necessary to the preservation of a healthy market. It is commonplace for analysts to "ferret out and analyze information," and this often is done by meeting with and questioning corporate officers and others who are insiders. And information that the analysts obtain normally may be the basis for judgments as to the market worth of a corporation's securities. The analyst's judgment in this respect is made available in market letters or otherwise to clients of the firm. It is the nature of this type of information, and indeed of the markets themselves, that such information cannot be made simultaneously available to all of the corporation's stockholders or the public generally.

The conclusion that recipients of inside information do not invariably acquire a duty to disclose or abstain does not mean that such tippees always are free to trade on the information. The need for a ban on some tippee trading is clear. Not only are insiders forbidden by their fiduciary relationship from personally using undisclosed corporate information to their advantage, but they may not give such information to an outsider for the same improper purpose of exploiting the information for their personal gain. Similarly, the transactions of those who knowingly participate with the fiduciary in such a breach are "as forbidden" as transactions "on behalf of the trustee himself." [A] contrary rule "would open up opportunities for devious dealings in the name of the others that the trustee could not conduct on his own." Thus, the tippee's duty to disclose or abstain is derivative from that of the insider's duty. . . . As we noted in *Chiarella*, "[t]he tippee's obligation has been viewed as arising from his role as a participant after the fact in the insider's breach of a fiduciary duty."

Thus, some tippees must assume an insider's duty to the shareholders not because they receive inside information, but rather because it has been made available to them improperly. Thus, a tippee assumes a fiduciary duty to the shareholders of a corporation not to trade on material nonpublic information only when the insider has breached his fiduciary duty to the shareholders by disclosing the information to the tippee and the tippee knows or should know that there has been a breach. As Commissioner Smith perceptively observed in *In re Investors Management Co.*, 44 S.E.C. 633 (1971), "[T]ippee responsibility must be related back to insider responsibility by a necessary finding that the tippee knew the information was given to him in breach of a duty by a person having a special relationship to the issuer not to disclose the information. . . ."

In determining whether a tippee is under an obligation to disclose or abstain, it thus is necessary to determine whether the insider's "tip" constituted a breach of the insider's fiduciary duty. All disclosures of confidential corporate information are not inconsistent with the duty insiders owe to shareholders.

In some situations, the insider will act consistently with his fiduciary duty to shareholders, and yet release of the information may affect the market. For example, it may not be clear—either to the corporate insider or to the recipient analyst—whether the information will be viewed as material nonpublic information. Corporate officials may mistakenly think the information already has been disclosed or that it is not material enough to affect the market. Whether disclosure is a breach of duty therefore depends in large part on the purpose of the disclosure.

Thus, the test is whether the insider personally will benefit, directly or indirectly, from his disclosure. Absent some personal gain, there has been no breach of duty to stockholders. And absent a breach by the insider, there is no derivative breach.

The SEC argues that, if inside-trading liability does not exist when the information is transmitted for a proper purpose but is used for trading, it would be a rare situation when the parties could not fabricate some ostensibly legitimate business justification for transmitting the information. We think the SEC is unduly concerned. . . .

Continued

Determining whether an insider personally benefits from a particular disclosure, a question of fact, will not always be easy for courts. But it is essential, we think, to have a guiding principle for those whose daily activities must be limited and instructed by the SEC's inside-trading rules, and we believe that there must be a breach of the insider's fiduciary duty before the tippee inherits the duty to disclose or abstain. In contrast, the rule adopted by the SEC in this case would have no limiting principle.

Under the inside-trading and tipping rules set forth above, we find that there was no actionable violation by Dirks. It is undisputed that Dirks himself was a stranger to Equity Funding, with no preexisting fiduciary duty to its shareholders. He took no action, directly or indirectly, that induced the shareholders or officers of Equity Funding to repose trust or confidence in him. There was no expectation by Dirks' sources that he would keep their information in confidence. Nor did Dirks misappropriate or illegally obtain the information about Equity Funding.

It is clear that neither Secrist nor the other Equity Funding employees violated their duty to shareholders by providing information to Dirks. The tippers received no monetary or personal benefit for revealing Equity Funding's secrets, nor was their purpose to make a gift of valuable information to Dirks. As the facts of this case clearly indicate, the tippers were motivated by a desire to expose the fraud. In the absence of a breach of duty to shareholders by the insiders, there was no derivative breach by Dirks. Dirks therefore could not have been "a participant after the fact in [an] insider's breach of a fiduciary duty."

We conclude that Dirks, in the circumstances of this case, had no duty to abstain from use of the inside information that he obtained. The judgment of the Court of Appeals therefore is reversed.

CASE QUESTIONS
1. Who disclosed what and to whom?
2. How was the information used?
3. Is it always a breach of an insider's duty to disclose information to outsiders?
4. What distinguishes *Dirks* and *Chiarella*?
5. If Mr. Dirks had used the information to sell his own stock, would the result have been different?
6. If the information from Secrist was that Equity Funding's assets were *understated*, would the result have been different?

E T H I C A L   I S S U E S

21.1 Dan Dorfman, a former *Wall Street Journal* reporter, is a commentator for CNBC television and *USA Today*. During 1994, Mr. Dorfman recommended several stocks of J.W. Charles Securities of Boca Raton, Florida that performed very poorly.

Douglas A. Kass is the chief of research and institutional trading at J.W. Charles. He is a Wharton School alumnus who has had a series of tax liens on his property and has been censured by the National Association of Securities Dealers. Mr. Kass and Mr. Dorfman have been good friends since the 1970s. Mr. Dorfman has been a speaker at J.W. Charles's top producer weekends. He was not paid a speaker's fee, but his room and travel for himself and his girlfriend were paid for by J.W. Charles.

The SEC is currently investigating Mr. Dorfman and Donald Kessler, a stock promoter, whose clients have told the SEC they paid large sums of money for Mr. Kessler to arrange meetings with Mr. Dorfman. CNBC has suspended Mr. Dorfman.

What ethical breaches do you see in the conduct of Messrs. Dorfman, Kass, and Kessler?

FOR THE MANAGER'S DESK

PSS'T . . . WANT TO MAKE A BUNDLE? WHAT'S ETHICAL IN INSIDER TRADING?

Suppose you hear something that you think will make a stock move. When is it legal to take advantage of the information? The law on insider trading is confusing, even to the experts. See how well you know the subject.

1. The woman you live with, vice-president of a large company, wants to take you out to celebrate. She's not supposed to tell anybody, but she lets you know that her company just landed a big government contract. Can you call your broker before the deal is announced?
__Yes __No __Law unclear

2. You're in the theater lobby at intermission. You overhear a conversation between two men you know are top executives of a big company. "Our stock should really jump when we announce those earnings tomorrow," says one. Can you buy call options now?
__Yes __No __Law unclear

3. A small textile company calls you in as a marketing consultant. Its president shows you samples of a new fabric that sheds dirt and never wears out. You're bowled over—but too busy to take on the account. Can you buy stock in the company?
__Yes __No __Law unclear

4. You're a personnel executive at Mammoth Oil. You learn that the company has just hit a gusher. Can you buy before the news becomes public?
__Yes __No __Law unclear

5. Your broker has an uncanny knack for picking takeover targets. Either he's very smart—or he's getting inside information. He just called to recommend Maximove, an obscure over-the-counter company. Should you buy?
__Yes __No __Law unclear

6. You own stock in the company you work for, and you've been selling 25 shares each month to make payments on your Ferrari. You learn that the next quarterly report will show a huge, unexpected loss. Can you make your regular sale before the bad news hits?
__Yes __No __Law unclear

7. You are a scientist at a research institute. Tomorrow you are going on television to release a study showing that a major fast-food chain's hamburgers cause baldness—and a Wall Street reaction is likely. Can you sell the chain's stock short now?
__Yes __No __Law unclear

Here are the "correct" responses, compiled with the help of securities experts at Kirkpatrick & Lockhart and Gibson, Dunn & Crutcher:

1. **No.** A person who gets a tip from an insider can't trade if he knows the insider revealed the news improperly and if the insider gets some benefit from passing the tip. The SEC says that when there is a "private personal relationship," there is enough of a "personal benefit" to make the trade illegal.

2. **Yes.** The men probably didn't intend to give you the information, and they didn't get anything themselves for doing so. There is no securities fraud under these conditions.

3. **Law unclear.** There is no violation of the law unless there is some obligation to keep information confidential. A court might, however, say that the company president had a reasonable expectation that you would keep the discussion under your hat.

4. **No.** All employees are covered by the insider-trading rules. You can't take advantage of shareholders by trading because of significant information you pick up at work.

5. **Yes.** He and his source may be breaking the law. But as long as you don't know that—or don't have reason to know—you are safe.

6. **Law unclear.** This is a murky area, but some experts say it is illegal only if you make a trade motivated by inside information. The SEC would be likely to argue that simply trading while in possession of the information is enough to make the trade illegal.

Continued

7. **Law unclear**. It is not illegal simply to trade on information that will move markets. But prosecutors and the SEC have successfully alleged that someone who "misappropriates" his employer's information can be guilty of securities fraud.

If you answered all the questions correctly, you should be giving lectures on the subject. A score of three to six means you're as knowledgeable as most judges. Suppose you did worse? You clearly aren't inhibited by legal theory—and you may have piled up enough trading profits to mount a top-notch defense.

Source: "Pss't . . . Want to Make a Bundle?" *Business Week*, April 29, 1985, p. 85. Reprinted from April 29, 1985 issue of *Business Week* by special permission, copyright © 1985 by the McGraw-Hill Companies.

FOR THE MANAGER'S DESK

THE ETHICS OF DERIVATIVES

Derivatives are contracts between two parties that have a value derived from some underlying assets, such as currencies, equities, or commodities. Derivative investment instruments vary in complexity and risk. Some of the more popular derivative investments are interest-rate "swaps." The following example illustrates:

Jake has a $100,000 fixed rate 8 percent mortgage.

June has a $100,000 mortgage with an interest rate tied to Treasury bills. Rate is currently 8 percent.

June worries that interest rates are going up. Jake believes interest rates are going down. The two "swap" interest positions. If interest rates fall, Jake benefits when the two settle up each quarter. If interest rates rise, June benefits.

In a word, these derivative instruments are sophisticated gambling on whether interest rates, currency rates, or the market will go up or down. They are a high-risk investment, particularly if the money in swaps is borrowed.

Consider the following events related to derivatives:

MILESTONES OF THE YEAR:

1994 March—CS First Boston, 'fesses up to having reimbursed a money market client for unauthorized derivatives trades in its account. Two other reimbursements follow. Total cost to the firm: about $40 million.

April—Gibson Greetings reports that it has suffered $20 million of losses on a derivatives contract.

April—Procter & Gamble announced $157 million of losses on leveraged derivatives.

July—Federal Paper Board says it has switched to market-to-market accounting for certain leveraged derivatives, and taken a second-quarter $11 million charge. Subsequently it restated and lowered earnings for several accounting periods.

August—Filing a quarterly report, Air Products & Chemicals discloses it had recently absorbed $122 million in derivatives losses.

October—In connection with a tender for $4.8 billion of debt, Eastman Kodak unwinds numerous swaps and options at a cost of $220 million.

December—Orange County, California, facing billion-dollar losses from leveraged investments in derivatives, goes bankrupt.

December—Bankers Trust is fined and censured by its regulators for defrauding Gibson Greetings in derivatives transactions.

1995 January—Chemical Bank discloses that unauthorized Mexican peso trades by one of its employees cost it $70 million.

February—Sued because of derivatives losses in a government-securities mutual fund it ran, Piper Jaffray settles for $70 million.

March—Barings Bank collapses due to derivative exposure. Leveraged forms of swaps brought down Barings bank.

At the time of all of the investments and losses listed above, there were no regulations on disclosure of derivative exposure.

Should shareholders have been told of these derivative investments?

Source: Adapted from *Fortune* magazine.

E T H I C A L   I S S U E S

21.2 In taped conversations between Bankers Trust salesman Kevin Hudson and his fiancê, Allison Bernhard, during the time Mr. Hudson was handling Procter & Gamble's derivative accounts, some disturbing information is revealed.

On one trade, Bankers Trust made $7.6 million but Procter & Gamble is not told:

Miss Bernhard: They would never know. They would never be able to know how much money was taken out of that.

Mr. Hudson: Never. No way, no way. That's the beauty of Bankers Trust.

After Mr. Hudson obtained an extension from Procter & Gamble on a contract, he called Miss Bernhard to tell her he had an additional two weeks and was "comfortable" with market conditions:

Miss Bernhard: How much is two weeks worth?

Mr. Hudson: A million to them; two million to me.

Miss Bernhard: You're headed for trouble . . . It's going to blow up on you. You're not going to (have) customers to make money with if (you) do stuff like that all the time, you're gonna blow 'em up. You're getting greedier as the days roll by.

Evaluate Mr. Hudson's ethics. Evaluate Miss Bernhard's ethics. Is Procter & Gamble at fault?

C O N S I D E R . . .

21.3 In November 1989, the Food and Drug Administration (FDA), after conducting a long inspection of an Abbott Laboratories facility, issued a report containing 56 observations of activities contrary to good manufacturing procedures, says plaintiffs' attorney Bruce C. Howard.

When Abbott received this report, Mr. Howard says, "they did not disclose this to the public." Instead, Mr. Howard says, a financial analyst with the Chicago Corporation obtained a copy of the report, using the Freedom of Information Act, and made the report public on December 7, 1989. The next day, Abbott stock dropped $1.25 a share.

Abbott downplayed the importance of the report, Mr. Howard says. But on March 14, 1990, the company received a more formal letter from the FDA, which is often a precursor of sanctions. "Abbott did not disclose this either," says Mr. Howard. A few days later, however, the same analyst released the information. On that day, Abbott's stock dropped $1.

Abbott shareholders sued the company, charging fraud and claiming up to $55 million in damages. Abbott denied wrongdoing or damages to the shareholders.

Judg Did Abbott violate § 10(b)? [*Morse* v. *Abbott Laboratories*, 756 F. Supp. 1108 (N.D. Ill. 1991).]

Source: The National Law Journal, April 4, 1994, A11. Reprinted with the permission of The National Law Journal, © 1994, The New York Law Publishing Company.

C O N S I D E R . . .

21.4 Did Philip Schein in the chapter's opening "Judgment" violate the law? Why or why not?

STANDING TO SUE UNDER 10(b)

To be able to recover under section 10(b), a party suing must have standing. **Standing** in theses cases has been defined by the U.S. Supreme Court as the actual sale or

ETHICAL ISSUES

21.3 Edward R. Downe, Jr., age 62 and married to Charlotte Ford, lives in a mansion in South Hampton, Long Island. He was responsible for the development of such magazines as *True Confessions* and *Ladies Home Journal*. He was a member of the board of Bear Sterns Company and through his position there had access to information not generally available to the public. Mr. Downe shared this information with his poker buddies and other friends. Phone documents were used to establish various trades through offshore companies. Did Mr. Downe violate 10(b)? In light of the fact that he was a wealthy man, why was there a need for insider trading? Was it easier to engage in the trades because "everyone does it"?

purchase of stock in reliance upon the information or lack of information given. For example, persons who would have purchased stock had they known the truth could not recover for damages under 10(b). Likewise, they cannot recover damages because they would have sold their stock had they known the truth. There must be an actual sale or purchase for a plaintiff to satisfy the standing requirements of 10(b). In *Blue Chip Stamp* v. *Manor Drug Store*, 421 U.S. 723 (1975), the U.S. Supreme Court held that a pessimistic statement of income and potential was not a 10(b) violation because a potentially interested buyer who did not buy because of the pessimism did not have actual damages and, hence, no standing.

In a recent decision, the U.S. Supreme Court held that shareholders cannot immediately bring suit under 10(b) against their brokers if their brokerage contracts contain an arbitration provision. Standing now requires an exhaustion of arbitration methods. [*Shearson/American Express, Inc.* v. *McMahon*, 482 U.S. 220 (1987).]

THE REQUIREMENT OF SCIENTER UNDER 10(b)

A conviction under 10(b) cannot be based on negligence—that is, the failure to discover financial information. Because 10(b) is a criminal statute, there must be some intent to defraud or knowledge of wrongdoing, or scienter on the part of the violator. Convictions are only for knowing the financial information but failing to disclose it.

In *Ernst & Ernst* v. *Hochfelder*, 425 U.S. 185 (1978), the Supreme Court held that an accounting firm that had negligently performed an audit of a business based on a fraud could not be held liable under 10(b) because, although the accounting firm made a mistake, it had no intent to defraud.

PENALTIES FOR 10(b) VIOLATIONS

Review the Insider Trading and Securities Fraud Enforcement Act of 1988: http://www.law.uc.edu/CCL/34Act/sec21A.html

Under the **Insider Trading and Securities Fraud Enforcement Act of 1988**, an amendment to the 1934 act, violations of Section 10(b) can carry a fine of up to $100,000 and up to five years in prison. Corporate officers face fines of up to the greater of either $1 million or three times the amount of profit gained or loss avoided as a result of the violation by the company or any employee under the officers' control. In addition, the officers can be required to return profits made on the inside information. These penalties are imposed only if an officer knew of the acts leading to the violation or acted with reckless disregard for such action. In addition, there is civil liability because those harmed by the insider trading are permitted to bring suit. The 1988 amendments also provided the SEC with

E T H I C A L ☰ I S S U E S

21.4 Safecard is a public company engaged in mass mail-order marketing of a loss notification service for credit cards. The chief benefit of its service is that a subscriber whose cards are missing need call only the notification service instead of calling each card issuer.

Credit Card Services Corporation (CCSC) also runs a credit card loss notification service. Ferry is their chairman of the board and Hurney their vice president of sales. Messrs. Ferry and Hurney had an agent steal a copy of a Safecard marketing proposal and began to stir up government investigatory agencies by notifying the FTC of Safecard's operation.

Messrs. Ferry and Hurney then enlisted the aid of Abelson and Anreder, two Dow Jones writers who wrote "Up and Down Wall Street" in Barron's. They wrote several articles (with information supplied by Messrs. Ferry and Hurney) that questioned the value of Safecard's stock, impugned its accounting techniques, reported government investigations, and commented on its marketing techniques.

Safecard maintains the articles contain untrue statements of material facts and created a false impression. Further, Safecard claims the statements were made to bring the market for Safecard's stock down so that CCSC could exercise options to purchase Safecard stock at a low price—in other words, market manipulation. Is there a 10(b) violation? Is the conduct of Messrs. Ferry and Hurney in reporting the Safecard plan to the FTC ethical? Was it ethical to enlist the aid of the writers? Refer back to the chapter's opening judgment. Did the officers violate § 10(b)? [*Safecard Services Inc.* v. *Dow Jones & Co. Inc.*, 537 F. Supp. 1137 (E.D. Va. 1982).]

additional funds and staff for investigation and enforcement. The amendments impose stricter regulations on brokers and dealers and permit the SEC to bring court actions to impose civil penalties on all violators. Finally, Congress authorized the SEC to pay bounties of up to 10 percent of the amount recovered to informants who report violations.

Insider Trading and Short-Swing Profits

In addition to the application of Section 10(b) and Rule 10b-5 to trading on inside information, the 1934 act also has a form of a strict liability statute for insider trading. Officers, directors, and 10-percent or more shareholders have greater access to inside information. They are involved in setting a corporation's policy and directions, in dividend decisions, in product decisions, and in expansion decisions. They will always have access to information that is not yet available to the public. **Section 16** of the 1934 act is a **per se** liability section designed to deal with stock trading by corporate insiders, who are defined as officers, directors, and 10-percent shareholders of those companies required to be registered under the 1934 act.

Under 16(a), officers, directors, and 10-percent shareholders (10 percent of any class of stock) are required to file reports declaring their holdings. In addition, they must file updated reports within 20 days after any change in ownership (purchase, sale, or transfer).

Under 16(b), officers, directors, and 10-percent shareholders are required to give to the corporation any short-swing profits—that is, profits earned on the sale and purchase or purchase and sale of stock during any six-month period. For example, suppose Director Cadigan of a New York Stock Exchange company engaged in the following transactions:

April 11, 1993—Ms. Cadigan buys 200 shares of her corporation's stock at $50 each.
April 30, 1993—Ms. Cadigan sells 200 shares at $30 each.
May 15, 1993—Ms. Cadigan buys 200 shares at $20 each.

The SEC will match the highest sale with the lowest purchase. Director Cadigan has a profit of $10 per share even though she has a net loss. This profit must be returned to the corporation. It is irrelevant whether the officer, director, or 10-percent shareholder actually used inside information: The presumption under 16(b) for short-swing trades is that the officer, director, or 10-percent shareholder had access to inside information.

In a recent rule change, corporate officers can now exercise stock options and sell shares immediately. The requirement of a six-month waiting period between the option exercise and sale is eliminated.

Regulating Voting Information

There was once a time when shareholders could give their proxies to the company just by endorsing the backs of their dividend checks; proxies then were obtained easily and without much disclosure. The 1934 act changed the way proxies were solicited. With the same philosophy used for registration, the SEC required full disclosure to be the goal of all **proxy solicitations**. To achieve that goal, the SEC now requires prior filing and adequate representation of shareholder interests.

THE PROXY STATEMENT

Under Section 14 of the 1934 act, all companies required to register under the act must file their proxy materials with the SEC at least 10 days before those materials are to be sent. Proxy materials include the proxy statement and all other solicitation materials that will be sent to shareholders. The proxy statement required by the SEC must contain the following details:

1. Who is soliciting the proxy
2. How the materials will be sent
3. Who is paying for the costs of soliciting
4. How much has been spent to date on the solicitation
5. How much is expected to be spent on the solicitation
6. Why the proxy is being solicited—annual meeting elections, special meeting on a merger, and so on

Exhibit 21.4 (pg. 787) is a sample proxy.

SHAREHOLDER PROPOSALS

Because the purpose of Section 14 is full disclosure, the representation of views other than those of corporate management is important in proxy solicitations. Shareholders can submit proposals to be included in proxy solicitation materials. If the company does not oppose what is being proposed, the proposition is included as part of the proxy materials. If management is opposed, the proposing shareholder has the right of a two-hundred-word statement on the proposal in the materials. These proposals are not permitted along with their two-hundred-word statements unless they propose conduct that is legal and related to business operations, as opposed to social, moral, religious, and political views. During the Vietnam era, many shareholders wanted to include proposals in proxy materials for companies that were war suppliers. Their proposals centered around the political opposition to the war and not the business practices of the company.

P　　**ARIZONA PUBLIC SERVICE COMPANY**　　　　　　　　　**PROXY CARD**
　　　　P.O. Box 53999
　　　　Phoenix, Arizona 85072-3999

R　　**THIS PROXY IS SOLICITED ON BEHALF OF THE BOARD OF DIRECTORS FOR THE ANNUAL MEETING ON MAY 21, 1996.**

O　　The undersigned hereby appoints O. Mark DeMichele and Nancy C. Loftin, and each of them, proxies for the undersigned, each with full power of substitution, to attend the annual meeting of shareholders of Arizona Public Service Company to be held May 21, 1996, at 10:00a.m., Phoenix time, and at any adjournment thereof, and to vote as specified in this Proxy all the shares of stock of the company which the undersigned would be entitled to vote if personally present.

X

Voting with respect to the election of directors and the proposals may be indicated on the reverse of this card. Nominees for director are: O. Mark Demichele, Martha O. Hesse, Marianne Moody Jennings, Robert G. Matlock, Jaron B. Norberg, John R. Norton III, William J. Post, Donald M. Riley, Henry B.

Y　　Sargent, Wilma W. Schwada, Richard Snell, Dianne C. Walker, Ben F. Williams Jr., and Thomas G. Woods, Jr.

**Your vote is important! Please sign, date, and mail promptly
in the enclosed postage-paid envelope.**

This proxy, when properly executed, will be voted in the manner directed herein. If no direction is made, it will be voted FOR the election of directors and FOR the proposals.

The board of Directors recommends a vote FOR the election of directors.	The board of Directors recommends a vote FOR the proposal to amend Article Sixth of the Company's Articles of Incorporation.	The board of Directors recommends a vote FOR the proposal to amend Article Fifth of the Company's Articles of Incorporation.
1. Election of Directors (see other side)	2. Proposal to amend Article Sixth of the Company's Articles of Incorporation.	3. Proposal to amend article Fifth of the Company's Articles of Incorporation.
FOR*　　**WITHHELD**　□　　　□　　*For all nominees, except withhold vote for the following:* _____	**FOR**　**AGAINST**　**ABSTAIN**　□　　□　　□	**FOR**　**AGAINST**　**ABSTAIN**　□　　□　　□

4.　　In their discretion, the proxies are to vote upon such other business as may properly come before the meeting.

　　　　　　　　　　　_____　　　_____
　　　　　　　　　　　Signature　　　　　　　　　　date

　　　　　　　　　　　_____　　　_____
　　　　　　　　　　　Signature　　　　　　　　　　date
　　　　　　　　　　　Please sign as your name(s) appear to the left. Joint owners should both sign.
　　　　　　　　　　　Fiduciaries, attorneys, corporate officers, etc., should state their capacities.

Source: Reprinted with permission of the Arizona Public Service Company.

Exhibit 21.4
Sample Proxy

CONSIDER... **21.5** A shareholder for Cracker Barrel Cheese has submitted for SEC approval a proposal that would require the company not to discriminate against employees who are homosexuals. Should the SEC allow the proposal?

Joseph Jett fulfilled all requirements for a Harvard MBA in 1987, but he did not receive his degree because he still owed a balance on his tuition bill that he did not pay until 1994.

Joseph Jett: The Rogue Trader

Joseph Jett

After completing his Harvard course work, Mr. Jett was hired by CS First Boston. He was dismissed from that job and hired by Morgan Stanley. At Morgan Stanley he became a victim of downsizing, was laid off, but was then hired by Kidder Peabody & Company as a trader in 1991. Based on his initial performance, which was somewhat negative, Kidder had doubts as to whether he should have been hired.

A former trader said, "I don't think he knew the market. He made mistakes a rookie would make." However, despite the doubts of colleagues, Mr. Jett's profit record was climbing. Several colleagues who tracked his trades found they were unprofitable, and his continual increases were not in sync with the fluctuations in the government bond market, the area in which Mr. Jett traded. Some co-workers raised concerns with supervisors and one spoke with Mr. Jett himself. They were fired quite rapidly after asking questions. Mr. Jett was promoted to managing director of Kidder's bond trading desk. The bond portion of Kidder's operation was 20 percent of its fixed income division.

Mr. Jett performed so well in his trades in 1993 that he earned a $9 million bonus. By April 1994, however, Kidder announced that their star trader had created $350 million in phony pretax profits. Mr. Jett had engaged in two years of phantom trading. General Electric, Kidder's parent, reduced its first-quarter earnings for 1994 by $210 million.

The SEC began an investigation of Kidder, Peabody and Mr. Jett. Kidder's board refused to advance to Mr. Jett funds for the federal investigation, citing evidence of "bad faith" on Mr. Jett's part had been established. Mr. Jett's assets were frozen, but he did manage to pay his Harvard bill after the story of his lack of a degree was publicized. Of the 36-year-old Mr. Jett, CEO of GE, Jack Welch, said, "It's a pity that this ever happened. He could have made $2 or $3 million honestly."

By the end of 1995, Mr. Jett was under investigation by the U.S. attorney, the SEC, and the New York Stock Exchange. Possible criminal charges are pending.

Kidder fired Edward Cerullo, Mr. Jett's boss and the head of Kidder's fixed income area; Mr. Melvin Mullin, who hired Mr. Jett, was also fired. The CEO of Kidder, Michael Carpenter, resigned under pressure, and David Bernstein, Mr. Cerullo's assistant, was demoted.

A report issued by Gary Lynch, former director of enforcement at the SEC, concluded that Mr. Jett acted on his own. Mr. Jett maintains Mr. Cerullo told him to make the trades. Mr. Lynch stated in his report, "The obvious motive for this effort was to achieve a degree of recognition and compensation that had previously eluded Jett in his professional career."

In October 1994, GE sold Kidder to Paine Webber at a $500 million loss. Half of Kidder's employees were laid off after Paine Webber took over the firm.

In February 1996, the SEC announced that because of inexplicable earnings increases, that Mr. Jett's supervisors were lax in their oversight. Civil charges were filed against Jett and his supervisors. Mr. Cerullo settled the charges for a fine of $50,000 and a one-year suspension from brokering. Mr. Mullin and Mr. Jett will litigate the charges.

Issues

1. List all the people affected by Mr. Jett's activities.
2. Describe his moral fiber.
3. Did Mr. Jett's supervisors not want to know the truth? Consider this rap song made up by Kidder employees:

> Big Boss and Joe went skiing in the snow:
> He said, Joe, what you're doing, don't wanna know;
> But, keep on doing it, doing it though,
> 'Cause I am the Main Man at Kidder P Blow.
> . . . Then one month Kidder P took a double blow;
> Joe's profits were phony, the man said so;
> And the Fed jacked rates so the economy'd slow;
> April was the cruelest month at Kidder P Blow.
> . . . GE aimed all the blame at Ed Cerullo
> He was the man who'd let the boys go.
> To Joe and the V-Man he never said no.
> 'Twas the worst of times at Kidder P Blow.

E T H I C A L   I S S U E S

21.5 Iroquois Brands, Ltd., is a food company that imports French foie gras, a pâté made from the enlarged livers of force-fed geese. There is a French practice in raising the geese of funneling corn down the geese's throats and gagging them with rubber bands to keep them from regurgitating. A shareholder wishes to include a proposal in the proxy materials that proposes that the company study the practice as an unethical business practice (cruelty to animals). Should the proposal be included? Does Section 14 require that it be included? [*Lovenheim* v. *Iroquois Brands*, *Ltd.*, 618 F. Supp. 554 (D.C. 1985).]

SHAREHOLDERS AND EXECUTIVE COMPENSATION

In 1992, the SEC approved 43 shareholder proposals on executive compensation. The interest generated by shareholders and the public in these compensation levels resulted in the SEC's promulgation of new proxy disclosure rules on executive compensation. A series of charts summarizing executive pay (top five officers in the company) over the previous three years are required, as are other charts on the firm's financial performance. The disclosures and reports on compensation must be prepared by the compensation committee of the board of directors, which must be composed of independent (outside) directors.

REMEDIES FOR VIOLATIONS OF SECTION 14

If proxies are solicited without following the Section 14 guidelines, the proxies are invalid. They must then be resolicited, and if the meeting has been held in which the invalid proxies were used, the action taken at the meeting can be set aside.

THE FOREIGN CORRUPT PRACTICES ACT

Review the Foreign Corrupt Practices Act: http://www.law.cornell.edu/uscode/15/78dd-2.html

In the early 1970s, the nation, Congress, and other officials learned that U.S. companies doing business in other countries were bribing foreign officials for various reasons. Furthermore, these bribes were not disclosed anywhere and in fact were secret payments concealed by internal accounting procedures. As a result, the **Foreign Corrupt Practices Act (FCPA)** was passed in 1977 as an amendment to the 1934 Securities Exchange Act. See Chapter 8 for more details.

STATE SECURITIES LAWS

Today all states have their own securities laws. In addition to federal laws, all issuers are required to follow state **blue sky laws** in all states in which their securities are sold. There are two types of state securities laws for registration purposes. There are those that follow the SEC standards for full disclosure: A filing is required, and so long as all the required information is there, the offering will be approved for public sale. Other states follow a **merit review** standard: The regulatory agency responsible for securities enforcement can actually examine a filed offering for its merits as to adequate capitalization, excessive stock ownership by the promoters, and penny-stock problems. These agencies apply a general standard that the offering be "fair, just, and equitable." This general standard gives them great latitude in deciding which issues will be approved.

Many companies do not register their offerings in states where there is merit review. They sell in the other states to avoid the problems of being denied registration.

As on the federal level, all states have their own exemptions from registration. Most SEC exemptions also work at the state level, the only requirement being that the issuer file a notice of sale with the state agency.

In addition to regulating securities offerings, these state agencies also control the licensing of brokers and agents of securities within the state. The licensing process consists of an application and a background check conducted by the agency to identify possible criminal problems.

Exhibit 21.5 provides a summary of securities regulation under state and federal law.

Exhibit 21.5
State and Federal Securities Law

1933 Act	1934 Act	Blue sky
S1—Registration statement Financial information Officers/directors Prospectus 20-day effective date, deficiency letter	*Section 14* Proxy registration Compensation disclosure	State securities registration
		Merit vs. disclosure standards
	Penalties $100,000 and/or ten years	Federally exempt securities may still need to register at state level
Section 11—Filing false registration statement Liability: Anyone named in prospectus or offering expert materials for it Material, false statement; privity not required unless longer than one year Defenses: due diligence; buyer's knowledge	500 or more shareholders with $5 million or more in assets or listed on national exchange *10K* Annual reports *10Q* Quarterly report	
Section 12—Failure to file; selling before effective date; False prospectus Material; false statement; privity required Defenses: due diligence; buyer's knowledge	*Foreign Corrupt Practices Act* Financial reports Internal controls Applies to 1933 and 1934 act registrants	
Penalties $10,000 and/or five years (criminal/civil suit)	*Section 16A* Officers, directors, 10% shareholders Sales registration	

INTERNATIONAL ISSUES IN SECURITIES LAWS

The following policy statement from the State Department summarizes the nature of international capital markets today: "The United States Government is committed to an international system which provides for a high degree of freedom in the movement of trade and investment flows." There is free flow of money across borders, and although the United States does restrict foreign investments in atomic energy, air transport, hydroelectric power, and fishing, there is much international investment in U.S. projects.

Visit stock exchanges around the world: http://nettvik.no/finansen/oslobors/engelsk/exchanen.htm

The United States has 10 stock exchanges, Germany 8, France 7, and Switzerland 7; the United Kingdom, Japan, Canada, the Netherlands, Belgium, Luxembourg, Norway, Kuwait, Australia, and many others have at least 1 stock exchange each.

A directive from the European Union has developed uniform requirements for disclosure in primary offering. Often called a "listing of particulars" instead of a "prospectus," shareholders are given uniform information prior to their purchases. One difficulty that must be resolved is that accounting practices outside the United States are not uniform. Often these practices create different financial pictures for investors.

Insider trading has been prosecuted vigorously in the United States for the past 30 years, European enforcement has been limited but is undergoing a stage of development and change. Before the 1980s, countries such as Great Britain, Germany, Luxembourg, France, and the Netherlands were the only countries with insider trading restrictions, and their restrictions took the form of codes of ethics imposed on their exchange members.

Beginning with the aggressive U.S. posture on insider trading in the 1980s, Great Britain, Sweden, Norway, Switzerland, Greece, Spain, the Netherlands, Belgium, Ireland, and Portugal adopted insider trading legislation. Enforcement in Europe has become as active as the enforcement efforts in the United States during the 1980s. In 1994, Great Britain amended its insider trading rules with increased scope of coverage and penalties.

The United States is the only country with proxy disclosure requirements. Although Japan regulates solicitations, Germany requires only advance notice of meetings.

SUMMARY

Why do we have securities laws and what is their history?
- Securities Act of 1933—federal law regulating initial sales of securities
- Securities Act of 1934—federal law regulating securities and companies in the secondary market

What are the requirements that affect primary offerings?
- Primary offering—sale of securities by the business in which interests are offered
- Security—investment in a common enterprise with profits to come from efforts of others
- *Howey* test—Supreme Court definition of security (see above)
- SEC—federal agency responsible for enforcing federal securities laws
- Exemption—security not required to be registered
- Exempt transaction—offering not required to be registered
- Regulation D—small-offering exemption rules

- Accredited investor—investor who meets threshhold standards for assets and income
- Rules 504, 505, 506—portion of Regulation D affording exemptions for variously structured offerings
- Registration statement—disclosure statement filed by the offeror with the SEC
- Prospectus—formal document explaining offering or any ad or written materials describing offering
- Comment letter—request by SEC for more information
- Deficiency letter—request by SEC for more information
- Full disclosure standard—review for information, not a review on the merits
- Tombstone ad—ad announcing offering that can be run prior to effective date of registration statement
- Red herring prospectus—redlined prospectus that can be given to potential purchasers prior to effective date of registration statement
- Shelf registrations—SEC approval process that allows approval and then waiting period for market conditions
- Material misstatement—false information that would affect the decision to buy or sell
- Section 11—portion of 1933 act that provides for liability for false statements or omissions in registration statements
- Due diligence—defense of good faith and full effort to Section 11 charges
- Section 12—portion of 1933 act that provides for liability for selling without registration or exemption before effective date or with a false prospectus

How do securities laws regulate the secondary market?
- 10-Q—periodic reporting forms required of 1934 act companies
- 10-K—periodic reporting forms required of 1934 act companies
- 8-K—periodic reporting forms required of 1934 act companies
- Section 10 (b)—antifraud provision of Securities Exchange Act
- Rule 10b-5—SEC regulation on antifraud provision of Securities Exchange Act
- Insider—person with access to nonpublic information about company
- Tippee—person who gains nonpublic information from an insider
- Insider Trading and Securities Fraud Enforcement Act of 1988—federal law increasing penalties for insider trading violations
- Section 16—portion of 1934 act regulating short-swing profits by officers, directors, or 10-percent shareholders
- Short-swing profits—gain on sale and purchase or purchase and sale of securities
- Proxy solicitations—formal paperwork requesting authority to vote on behalf of another
- Blue sky laws—state securities registration regulations
- Merit review—regulation of merits of an offering as opposed to disclosure

QUESTIONS AND PROBLEMS

1. Hector is a North Dakota grain farmer and Wiens owns a feedlot operation in Montana. The two entered into an agreement whereby Mr. Wiens was to buy, feed, and sell cattle and hogs for Mr. Hector. The bank financed the livestock purchases. Mr. Hector was to provide the grain for feeding the animals, the cost of which was deducted from feedlot

costs. The bank loans were to be repaid from the proceeds of selling the animals. The livestock were sold without Mr. Hector's or the bank's knowing of or getting the proceeds. Mr. Hector has sued for fraud under the 1933 act. Mr. Wiens claims no security was involved. Who is right? [*Hector* v. *Wiens*, 533 F.2d 429 (9th Cir. 1976).]

2. Time, Inc., acquired all stock of Warner Communications, Inc., at $70 a share in 1989. Time, which became Time Warner, Inc., was saddled with over $10 billion in debt as a result of the purchase.

   The company embarked on a highly publicized campaign to find an international "strategic partner" who would infuse billions of dollars of capital into the company and who would help the company realize its dream of becoming a dominant world-wide entertainment conglomerate. Ultimately, Time Warner formed only two strategic partnerships, each on a much smaller scale than had been hoped for. Faced with a multibillion dollar balloon payment on the debt, the company was forced to seek an alternative method of raising capital—a new stock offering that substantially diluted the rights of the existing shareholders. The company first proposed a variable price offering on June 6, 1991. This proposal was rejected by the SEC, but it approved a second proposal announced on July 12, 1991. Announcement of the two offering proposals caused a substantial decline in the price of Time Warner stock. From June 5 to June 12, the share price fell from $117 to $94. By July 12, the price had fallen to $89.75.

   A group of shareholders that purchased Time Warner stock between December 12, 1990, and June 7, 1991, brought suit under section 10(b) alleging that Time Warner made materially misleading statements and misrepresented the status of its strategic partnership discussions.

   Did Time Warner violate section 10(b)? [*Time Warner, Inc.* v. *Ross*, 9 F.3d 259 (3d Cir. 1993).]

3. Enok Pedersen had developed a plan to construct prefabricated housing in Margarita Island off the coast of Venezuela. Slevin invested $25,000 with Mr. Pedersen in exchange for a one-third profit. No stock certificate or even a written agreement was executed. The two men agreed that they did not anticipate having Mr. Slevin contribute additional money, services, or labor. However, he became involved in the management of the project after he lost his job. The housing was never completed, and Mr. Slevin sued for fraud under the 1933 act. Did Mr. Slevin buy a security? [*Slevin* v. *Pedersen Assoc., Inc.*, 540 F. Supp. 437 (S.D.N.Y. 1982).]

4. On March 24, 1977, Anschutz Corporation purchased from Kay Corporation a 50 percent interest in Metal Traders, Inc. (MTI). MTI trades in metal ores and concentrates, and it operates a Bolivian antimony mine. In its financial statement, Kay showed that MTI had just declared a $2 million cash dividend. It did not disclose that to declare the dividend, it had to use a substantial portion of an unsecured line of credit, making it unlikely that MTI could continue its operations. When MTI went bankrupt, Anschutz filed suit under Section 11 of the 1933 act. Will Anschutz win? [*Anschutz Corp.* v. *Kay Corp.*, 507 F. Supp. 72 (S.D.N.Y. 1981).]

5. Beginning in March 1981, R. Foster Winans was a *Wall Street Journal* reporter and one of the writers of the "Heard on the Street" column (the "Heard" column), a widely read and influential column in the *Journal*. David Carpenter worked as a news clerk at the *Journal* from December 1981 through May 1983. Kenneth Felis, who was a stockbroker at the brokerage house of Kidder Peabody, had been brought to that firm by another Kidder Peabody stockbroker, Peter Brant, Felis's longtime friend who later became the government's key witness in this case.

   Since February 2, 1981, it was the practice of Dow Jones, the parent company of the *Wall Street Journal*, to distribute to all new employees "The Insider Story," a 40-page manual with 7 pages devoted to the company's conflicts-of-interest policy. Mr. Winans and Mr. Carpenter knew that company policy deemed all news material gleaned by an employee during the course of employment to be company property and that company policy required employees to treat nonpublic information learned on the job as confidential.

Not withstanding company policy, Mr. Winans participated in a scheme with Mr. Brant and later Mr. Felis and Mr. Carpenter in which he agreed to provide the two stockbrokers (Messrs. Brant and Felis) with securities-related information that was scheduled to appear in "Heard" columns; based on this advance information, the two brokers would buy or sell the subject securities. Mr. Carpenter, who was involved in a private, personal, nonbusiness relationship with Mr. Winans, served primarily as a messenger for the conspirators. Trading accounts were established in the names of Kenneth Felis, David Carpenter, R. Foster Winans, Peter Brant, David Clark, Western Hemisphere, and Stephen Spratt. During 1983 and early 1984, these defendants made prepublication trades on the basis of their advance knowledge of approximately 27 *Wall Street Journal* "Heard" columns, although not all of those columns were written by Mr. Winans. Generally, he would inform Mr. Brant of an article's subject the day before its scheduled publication, usually by calls from a pay phone and often using a fictitious name. The net profits from the scheme approached $690,000. Was this scheme a 10(b) violation? [*United States* v. *Carpenter*, 791 F.2d 1024 (2d Cir. 1986); *affirmed, Carpenter* v. *United States*, 484 U.S. 19 (1987).]

6. Who of the following would be tippees?
   a. Parents of a CEO
   b. A printer of financial reports
   c. Ph.D. financial analyst
   d. A geologist doing a mineral analysis for an ore mining firm

7. The president's letter in Rockwood Computer Corporation's annual report stated that most of their inventory consisted of their old computer series. The letter suggested that their new series would cost more money for all users. However, the letter did not disclose, although evidence had indicated, that the new system might be less expensive for those who needed greater performance and capacity. Walter Beissinger (who sold his shares based on the information) brought suit under 10(b). Rockwood claims the statements were based on opinions of sales and were not statements of fact. Who should win? [*Beissinger* v. *Rockwood Computer Corp.*, 529 F. Supp. 770 (E.D. Pa. 1981).]

8. William H. Sullivan, Jr., gained control of the New England Patriots Football Club (Patriots) by forming a separate corporation (New Patriots) and merging it with the old one. Plaintiffs are a class of stockholders who voted to accept New Patriots' offer of $15 a share for their common stock in the Patriots's corporation. They now claim that they were induced to accept this offer by a misleading proxy statement drafted under the direction of Mr. Sullivan, who owned a controlling share in the voting stock of the Patriots at the time of the merger. The proxy statement, plaintiffs claim, contained various misrepresentations designed to paint a gloomy picture of the financial position and prospects of the Patriots, so that the shareholders undervalued their stock. They seek to rescind the merger or to receive a higher price per share for the stock they sold. Does the court have the authority to rescind under Section 14? [*Pavlidis* v. *New England Patriots Football Club*, 737 F.2d 1227 (1st Cir. 1984).]

9. The National Bank of Yugoslavia placed $71 million with Drexel Burnham Lambert, Inc., for short-term investment just months before Drexel's bankruptcy. In effect, the bank made a time deposit. Would the bank be able to proceed under a theory of securities laws violations? Would these time deposits be considered securities? [*National Bank of Yugoslavia* v. *Drexel Burnham Lambert, Inc.*, 768 F.Supp. 1010 (S.D.N.Y 1991).]

10. Joseph Fox, David Ball, Joanne Ball, and Carl J. Fleece were employees of Texas Instruments (TI), working in the Consumer Group of Lubbock, Texas, which was responsible for monthly sales forecasts. Prior to June 10, 1983, these four employees purchased puts or option contracts in TI stock. On June 10, 1983, TI announced cutbacks in its home computer market and was predicting a large loss for that unit. The four defendants were able to profit after the announcement. Did the employees engage in insider trading? [*SEC* v. *Fox*, 654 F. Supp. 781 (N.D. Tex. 1986).]

Judgment

Amanda Zeiss is a shareholder in the Mayflower Corporation, a profitable, but small, firm. Management in the company consists of employees who have been promoted from within. Mrs. Zeiss is personally acquainted with many of Mayflower's officers and feels that her investment is protected and nurtured by them. Mayflower's outstanding financial performance has attracted many offers for purchase, but the officers and board of Mayflower have turned down the offers because of their conviction that its outstanding performance and unique qualities would be lost. Last week, Ligsin, a large multinational corporation, announced that it wants to "take over" Mayflower, but no offer was presented to Mayflower. Mrs. Zeiss is unsure about the term takeover, management's position, and what is happening to Mayflower. Where should she turn? Does she have any rights or protections?

The motivations for takeovers, mergers, and consolidations vary. A takeover can result because the assets of a company are greater than

Business Combinations

the value of its stock. A merger may be the result of a need to acquire the skill or goodwill of a company. A consolidation may be entered into for the purpose of eliminating a competitor. In recent years, takeovers have had profit motives; just the threat of a takeover has caused many companies to buy out those shareholders attempting the takeover.

Regardless of the economic benefits of a merger or consolidation, all the legal aspects of the combination must be followed carefully. Protection of shareholder rights is critical. This chapter considers these legal aspects of business combinations and answers the following questions: What are the types of business combinations? What are the legal rights of shareholders in each? What legal restrictions are imposed on these combinations?

Wall Street has only two emotions:

Fear and greed.

Bill McGowan,
CEO of MCI

TYPES OF BUSINESS COMBINATIONS

Mergers

A **merger** is a combination of two or more corporations, after which only one corporation continues to exist. If Hubbard Company and Inez Corporation decide to merge, then the newly merged corporation must be either Hubbard Company or Inez Corporation. One of the corporations ceases to exist, and the two continue under one name. If Hubbard and Inez decide to merge into Inez Corporation, then Inez will own all of Hubbard's assets and will assume all of Hubbard's liabilities. There are three types of mergers: horizontal, vertical, and conglomerate.

HORIZONTAL MERGERS

Review the Clayton Antitrust Act: http://www.stolaf.edu/people/becker/antitrust/statutes.html

When two competitors merge, there is a **horizontal merger**, which results in fewer competitors and more concentrated power in that industry. Horizontal mergers are carefully scrutinized by the Justice Department under antitrust laws, specifically the Clayton Act (see Chapter 13 for a full discussion).

VERTICAL MERGERS

A **vertical merger** is a merger between companies located at different levels along an industry's chain of distribution. For example, a merger between a manufacturer of appliances and a retailer of appliances is a vertical merger. Although there is not as much concentration of power in a vertical merger as in one that is horizontal, a vertical merger gives both the retailer and the manufacturer more power than either type of firm operating alone. Vertical mergers are also subject to the constraints of the Clayton Act.

CONGLOMERATE MERGERS

A **conglomerate merger** is one neither between competitors nor one along the chain of distribution but rather one between two companies in unrelated fields. One of the motivations for a conglomerate merger is the desire to diversify product line. Another motivation may be a firm's undervalued assets in relation to its stock value.

Consolidations

In a **consolidation**, two or more companies combine into one new company, and none of the old companies continues to exist. Instead of Hubbard Company and Inez Corporation becoming Inez Corporation, under a consolidation Hubbard and Inez become Jasmine Corporation. Each company involved in the consolidation gives all its rights and liabilities to the new company, which holds all assets of the consolidating companies and assumes all their liabilities. Exhibit 22.1 (pg. 799) is an illustration of the difference between a merger and a consolidation.

Tender Offers

A **tender offer** is not a business combination; it is a method for achieving a business combination. An offer that is publicly advertised to shareholders for the purchase of their stock is a tender offer. The offering price for the stock is usually higher than the market price of the shares, which makes the tender offer attractive to the shareholders.

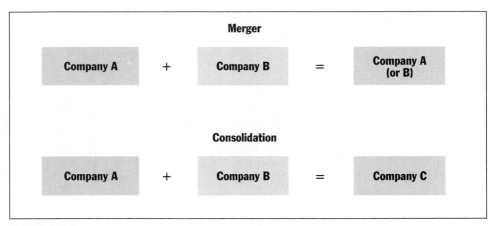

Exhibit 22.1
Mergers and Consolidations

Originally the tender offer was used as a means for a corporation to reacquire its shares. However, it has become a tool of business combinations of every sort, sometimes friendly and sometimes hostile.

Takeovers

Takeovers are accomplished through the use of tender offers and can be either friendly or hostile. A **friendly takeover** is one the management of a firm favors, whereas a **hostile takeover** is one the management of a firm opposes. Restrictions on the use of tender offers and procedures for accomplishing a takeover are discussed later in the chapter.

ASSET ACQUISITIONS

The acquisition of another firm's assets is either a means of expanding or a way of eliminating a creditor; **asset acquisition**, however, is different from the other business combinations. Because the corporate structure does not change, shareholder approval is not required for an asset acquisition. However, asset acquisitions are subject to the constraints of the Clayton Act.

THE STATUS OF MERGERS, CONSOLIDATIONS, AND TAKEOVERS TODAY

In the 1980s takeovers were popular as a means of acquiring assets or tax credits. Today, takeovers occur more for strategic reasons as in the 1993 multimedia battle for Paramount, Inc., between Viacom and QVC or in the recent combinations of Disney, Inc., with ABC/Capital Cities Television or Time Warner with Turner Broadcasting. Price Club and Costco's merger saved operating expenses and enabled it to compete with Sam's Club. Recently, shareholder activity and dissatisfaction with performance led to takeovers or dissolutions such as the disbanding of the Price Club/Costco firm. Exhibit 22.2 (pg. 800) summarizes the biggest problems in mergers.

1. There is no reason for the merger:
   Is the merger for strategy/expansion?
   Cost savings?
   Better ability to compete?
2. The merging firms don't understand each other:
   Scovill, Inc., a brass manufacturer, acquired Hamilton Beach, a change in focus for Scovill, but Hamilton Beach had been a customer for 56 years
3. The acquiring firm pays too much for the target:
   Debt saddles the new firm
4. There are conflicting corporate cultures:
   The Price Club/Costco merger did not work because of different cultures and managers
   Price Club culture: Pop culture and strip-mall-type hired managers
   Costco: Grocery store managers who had worked their way up through Costco
5. There was a failure to check company's financials:
   The acquiring firm must perform its due diligence: verify income, expenses, sales
6. The merger process is too slow:
   Paramount and Time Warner merger failed because it dragged on too long

Exhibit 22.2
Why Mergers Don't Work

FINANCING MERGERS AND TAKEOVERS

In the past, **junk bonds** were used as a takeover financing method. They were high-yield, high-risk bonds that investors purchased to help finance a target offer. Junk bonds, in effect, have the target company's assets as their collateral. Trends in the 1990s have focused on using an offeror's stock for buying out shareholders of a target company.

Business Planning Tip

Boards of directors must handle takeover issues carefully. Shareholders may have profits at stake, and deliberations must be conducted carefully, with full information, and with the advice of experts.

Financing methods can create problems for shareholders. The **two-tier offer** is a takeover mechanism that forces minority shareholders out. In this process, the offeror makes a tender offer that is very attractive and, through its attractive price, acquires a controlling interest. After the offeror obtains control, it then merges the target company into one of its subsidiaries. Minority shareholders usually can do nothing to stop the merger, are paid less for their merger rights, and are thus eliminated at a lower price. Although the fiduciary duty to these shareholders seems to have been breached, one court has held the two-tier bid as valid [*Radal* v. *Thomas*, 772 F.2d 244 (6th Cir. 1985)]. In this case, U.S. Steel made a $125 per share tender offer to Marathon Oil and acquired control, and in the subsequent merger gave remaining Marathon shareholders U.S. Steel stock worth $16 per share. Questions of fairness still remain about these forms of takeovers.

FOR THE MANAGER'S DESK

A CONSOLIDATION TO SOLVE A DESIGNER'S DILEMMA

Tommy Hilfiger began his fashion career with his own clothing store in Elmira, New York. He had to declare bankruptcy. He then went to work as a designer for Murjani International. When it became clear that Murjani was in financial difficulty, Hilfiger terminated Murjani's license to use his name and ventured out to create his own line of clothing.

At the time Hilfiger launched his new lines, Ralph Lauren was dominating the market. Hilfiger's line had brighter colors, looser fit and lower prices. Hilfiger began to make a dent in the market and Ralph Lauren's sales.

But Hilfiger did not have the business experience to expand his company.

On the other side of the globe, Silas Kei Fong Chou, a member of one of Hong Kong's oldest textile and apparel families, was facing a different problem. Chou's family owns Novel Enterprises which manufactures clothing for the Gap and the Limited. However, these companies and others were phasing out Novel because factories with workers who were paid much lower wages were available in India, China, and Vietnam. Chou was looking for a brand name clothing line to acquire exclusive rights.

Hilfiger heard of Chou, Chou noted Hilfiger's line, and the two met. The usual practice in the industry is for the designer to license his name and designs to a manufacturer. But both Hilfiger and Chou were concerned because this licensing approach resulted in both parties trying to skirt the contract and make additional money without having to share with the partner.

Hilfiger and Chou formed a new company that brought together Hilfiger's designs and license and Novel's manufacturing facilities. In other words, Hilfiger and Chou consolidated their firms in order to avoid the problems of conflicts between designer and manufacturer. They both own equal shares in a new company that owns the designs and the name and does all the manufacturing.

Source: Adapted from Justin Doebele, "A Brand is Born," *FORBES,* February 26, 1996, p.65.

E T H I C A L   I S S U E S

22.1 Although takeovers can be profitable, the effect on the target company can be devastating. Much of the target company's energy is put into fighting the takeover, and the result is that corporate progress and development are thwarted. For example, when Gulf Corporation was threatened with a takeover, it cut back research and development. The result was that its research institute was sold and many of its scientists and engineers were laid off. Gulf survived one attempted takeover and then lost another. Clearly, the firm was substantially affected by the battles. Are takeovers for the sake of profit a harm to business? Do these takeover battles divert energy and resources from progress and development? Are takeover profits at the expense of future development?

RIGHTS OF SHAREHOLDERS IN COMBINATIONS

Because shareholder interests are involved, corporations are not free to combine at will. All states have procedures for obtaining shareholder approval for business combinations. The procedures covered here are those of the MBCA (see Chapter 20).

Born in 1946 in Los Angeles, California, Mr. Michael Milken received a bachelor's degree from the University of California in 1968. Following several years of work for Drexel, Burnham and Lambert, a Wall Street brokerage firm and underwriter, Mr. Milken returned to school and earned his MBA from the Wharton School in 1978.

The Rogue of Wall Street— Michael Milken

Michael Milken

Business during the 1980s was characterized by what some referred to as merger mania. Companies were acquiring other firms and mergers occurred on a regular basis. There were negotiated takeovers as well as hostile takeovers. When he returned from Wharton, Mr. Milken developed what came to be known as "junk bond financing." Mr. Milken created bond offerings that were high risk securities, but the securities also carried high yields. These bond offerings were structured and sold for companies that had difficulty obtaining traditional forms of financing and also to finance leveraged buyouts of other companies. Often in takeovers, those who make the offer do not have the cash on hand to purchase the target company. Milken's bond sales provided the cash for the purchases, and the collateral for the bonds sold for these takeovers financings was the assets from the yet-to-be acquired company.

When the bond deals and takeovers were announced, stock prices in the companies involved would soar. Mr. Milken was tied into a network of Wall Street financiers who were exchanging information about forthcoming deals. The disclosure of the information about a takeover, for example, could easily lead to $1,000,000 in profits if stock was purchased in advance of the takeover announcement.

Mr. Ivan Boesky was a part of the network of traders connected to Milken. The Securities Exchange Commission (SEC; see Chapter 21) tracked Mr. Boesky's trades and charged him with insider trading, with documentation that he had earned $12.6 million illegally.

When the SEC first confronted Boesky with its evidence of insider trading, Boesky agreed, in exchange for a reduced sentence of three years, to be wired in order to tape record Mr. Milken and others in the network to establish their insider trading activity.

Through the Boesky tapes, Mr. Milken was charged in 1989 by the SEC on six felony counts including mail fraud, securities fraud, conspiracy, and assisting in the filing of a false income tax return.

Mr. Milken entered a guilty plea. In 1990, he was sentenced to 10 years in prison with the understanding that his sentence would be reduced if he cooperated and helped bring in others from the network.

Mr. Milken did cooperate while he was in jail and four other individuals were indicted from the friends' Wall Street network as a result of his cooperation. His sentence was reduced and he was paroled in March 1993. As part of his sentence, Mr. Milken was barred from the securities industry, Shortly after being released from prison, Mr. Milken was diagnosed with cancer. He was able to force the cancer back into remission. Mr. Milken teaches a business school course on ethics at UCLA.

Issues

1. What was wrong with junk bond financing?
2. Does the phrase, "there is no honor among thieves" have any meaning in this case?

The Procedure

For all mergers, consolidations, and sales of assets (other than in the ordinary course of business), there must be shareholder approval. Further, that approval must be obtained in a manner prescribed by the MBCA.

BOARD RESOLUTION

The process of obtaining shareholder approval begins with the board of directors: They must adopt and approve a resolution favoring the merger, consolidation, or asset sale.

NOTICE TO SHAREHOLDERS

Once the resolution is adopted, it must be sent to the shareholders along with a notice of a meeting for the purpose of taking action on the resolution. A notice is sent to each shareholder regardless of whether he or she is entitled to vote under the corporation's articles.

SHAREHOLDER APPROVAL

The shareholders must then vote to approve the resolution at the announced meeting. In the cases of mergers and consolidations, all shareholders are entitled to vote whether they own voting or nonvoting shares because their interests are affected by the results. The number of votes needed to approve a merger under the MBCA is a majority. However, the articles of incorporation or the bylaws may require more.

Shareholder approval is not required for a short-form merger, which is one between a subsidiary and a parent that owns at least 90 percent of the stock of the subsidiary. In the absence of these narrow requirements, the long-form merger provisions of resolution and voting must be followed.

DISSENTING SHAREHOLDER RIGHTS

Not all shareholders vote in favor of a merger or a consolidation. Under the MBCA and most state statutes, these **dissenting shareholders** are entitled to their appraisal rights. **Appraisal rights** allow shareholders to demand the value of their shares. Under the MBCA, a dissenting shareholder must file a written objection to the merger or consolidation before the meeting to vote on either is held.

If the merger or consolidation is approved, the corporation must notify dissenting shareholders and offer them the fair value of the shares. Fair value is determined as of the *day before* the action is taken on the merger or consolidation because the action taken will affect the value of the shares. If the dissenting shareholders do not believe the corporation's offer is fair, they can bring suit against the corporation for establishing fair value. However, if the value the corporation offered is found to be fair and the dissenting shareholders' rejection arbitrary, they will be required to pay the corporation's costs of the lawsuit.

Dissenting Shareholder and Appraisal Rights

Some corporations have experienced a **freeze-out**, which is a merger undertaken to get rid of the minority shareholders in a corporation. Although these minority shareholders have their dissenting rights, it is expensive to pursue a court action for a determination of fair value. The majority shareholders are thus able to buy out, at a low price, the minority shareholders, who are left without a remedy and usually with a loss. For this reason, many courts now impose on majority stockholders a fiduciary duty to the minority stockholders and will prevent a merger without a business purpose from freezing out minority shareholders. Courts, and some state laws (corporate constituency statutes), also require a showing that a merger or consolidation is fair to the minority shareholders. These general terms of "business purpose" and "fairness" are defined on a case-by-case basis.

LEGAL RESTRICTIONS ON BUSINESS COMBINATIONS

Apart from the corporate processes discussed above, mergers, consolidations, takeovers, tender offers, and asset acquisitions are all subject to state and federal laws that have the effect of containing business combinations.

Federal Securities Restrictions

In all of these business combinations (except asset acquisitions), someone is buying enough stock to own a company. That much buying and selling has long had the attention of the SEC. The Williams amendment to the Securities Exchange Act of 1934 regulates these offers to buy stock or tender offers, and the **Williams Act** was passed in 1968 to apply to all offers to buy more than 5 percent of a corporation's securities.

FILING REQUIREMENTS UNDER THE WILLIAMS ACT

Any offeror subject to the Williams Act is required to file a tender offer statement with both the SEC and the target company. The offeror must also send or publish for shareholders of the target company all the information and details about the offer. If the target company is opposing the takeover (that is, if it is hostile), the target must also file its materials with the SEC.

A registration statement for a tender offer must include the name of the offeror, its source of funding for the offer, its plans for the company if its attempted takeover is successful, and the number of shares now owned.

Shareholders have 7 days after a tender offer to withdraw their shares. This 7-day period is to prevent shareholders from being forced into a "now or never" transaction. The actual purchase of the shares cannot take place until at least 15 days after the tender offer began. If the offeror changes the tender offer terms, shareholders must be notified; and if a better price is offered, all shareholders must be given 10 days to tender their shares at that price (even those who have already tendered their shares at the lower price).

WHEN IS A TENDER OFFER A TENDER OFFER?

The term *tender offer* is not defined in the Williams Act. Even the SEC's definition is unclear, and the courts have responsibility of determining what is or is not a tender offer. Someone who has put out offers to buy stock might not be planning a takeover. Most of the judicial decisions follow a philosophy of intent: Was the offer to buy part of a takeover attempt? The following case is one in which the definition of tender offer was at issue.

Kennecott Copper Corp. v. Curtiss-Wright Corp.
584 F.2d 1195 (2d Cir. 1978)

COPPER CONTROL: WILLIAMS ACT DISCLOSURES

FACTS

Curtiss-Wright was trying to gain control of Kennecott Copper by acquiring a minority interest in Kennecott and then waging a proxy battle. In acquiring the 9.9 percent interest in shares, Curtiss-Wright's brokers solicited both on and off the exchange floor. Those sellers off the exchange were offered market price. There was no deadline, but the sellers were not told of Curtiss-Wright's plans. Kennecott brought suit for violation of the Williams Act. The trial court held that the off-the-exchange solicitations did not constitute tender offers.

JUDICIAL OPINION

VAN GRAAFEILAND, Circuit Judge

Section 3(d) of the Williams Act prohibits the making of a tender offer for any class of a registered stock if, after consummation thereof, the offeror would own more than five percent of the class, unless a Schedule 13D form is first filed with the SEC. If ownership of more than five percent is obtained through more customary modes of stock acquisition, the Schedule 13D form must be filed within ten days after the five percent figure is reached. Curtiss-Wright filed its Schedule 13D on March 17, 1978, which was within ten days of the time it had acquired five percent of Kennecott's stock. Accordingly, unless it had acquired this stock by means of a tender offer, it was not in violation of Section 78n(d).

The trial court rejected Kennecott's contention that Curtiss-Wright's acquisition had been made by means of a tender offer. The district judge found that Curtiss-Wright had purchased substantially all of the stock on national exchanges; that although one of Curtiss-Wright's brokers had solicited fifty Kennecott shareholders off the floor of the exchange, the sales were consummated on the floor. He also found that another broker had solicited approximately a dozen institutional holders of Kennecott, consummating an unspecified number of sales off the floor of the exchange. He

found that the potential sellers were merely asked whether they wanted to sell. They were offered no premium over the market price and were given no deadline by which to make their decision. He also found that the off-market purchases were made largely from sophisticated institutional shareholders who were unlikely to be forced into uninformed, ill-considered decisions. He concluded that Curtiss-Wright had not made a tender offer prior to the filing of its Schedule 13D.

Although the Williams Act does not define the term "tender offer," the characteristics of a typical offer are well recognized. They are described in the House Report of the Committee on Interstate and Foreign Commerce, which held hearings on the proposed Act. The offer normally consists of a bid by an individual or group to buy shares of a company—usually at a price above the current market price. Those accepting the offer are said to tender their stock for purchase. The person making the offer obligates himself to purchase all or a specified portion of the tendered shares if certain specified conditions are met. H.R. Rep. No. 1711, 90th Cong., 2d Sess., reprinted in [1968] U.S. Code Cong. & Admin. News.

This definition of a conventional tender offer has received general recognition in the courts. . . . Several courts and commentators have taken the position, however, that other unique methods of stock acquisition which exert pressure on shareholders to make uninformed, ill-considered decisions to sell, as is possible in the case of tender offers should be treated as tender offers for purposes of the statute.

Although broad and remedial interpretations of the Act may create no problems insofar as the antifraud provisions of Subsection (e) of Section 78n are concerned, this may not be true with regard to Subsections (d)(5)-(d)(7). Subsection (d)(5) provides that securities deposited pursuant to a tender offer may be withdrawn

Continued

within seven days of the publication or delivery to shareholders of the tender offer or at any time after sixty days from the date of the original tender offer. Subsection (d)(6) requires offerors to purchase securities on a pro rata basis where more are tendered than the offeror is bound or willing to take. Subsection (d)(7) provides that where the offeror increases the offering price before the expiration of his tender offer, those tenderers whose stock has already been taken up are entitled to be paid the higher price. It seems unlikely that Congress intended "tender offer" to be so broadly interpreted as to make these provisions unworkable.

In any event, we know of no court that has adopted the extremely broad interpretation Kennecott urges upon us in this case. Kennecott's contention, as we understand it, is that whenever a purchaser of stock intends through its purchase to obtain and exercise control of a company, it should immediately file a Schedule 13D.

Kennecott conceded in the trial court that no pressure was exerted on sellers other than the normal pressure of the marketplace and argued there and here that the absence of pressure is not a relevant factor. Kennecott also conceded in the trial court that no cases supported its argument and that it was asking the court to "make new ground." The district court did not err in refusing to do so.

If this court is to opt for an interpretation of "tender offer" that differs from its conventional meaning, this is not the case in which to do it.

CASE QUESTIONS
1. Which corporation was seeking control?
2. How much Kennecott stock did Curtiss-Wright acquire?
3. How were the shares acquired?
4. What were the terms of the purchase?
5. Were these purchases governed by the regulations of the Williams Act?

WILLIAMS ACT PENALTIES FOR VIOLATIONS

The Williams amendments provide for both civil and criminal penalties for violations of the act's procedures. The penalties are based on the same type of language used for 10(b) violations. Criminal and civil penalties are imposed for "fraudulent, deceptive or manipulative" practices used in making a tender offer. There are also penalties for omissions or misstatements of material facts in the tender offer materials.

PROPOSED CHANGES

As the number of takeover bids has increased, concern over the adequacy of regulation has also increased. Both Congress and the SEC have proposed changes to tighten regulation of tender offers. For example, some proposals would require the tender offeror to disclose its financial situation and plans for the acquired company.

SPECIAL PROTECTIONS FOR THE HOSTILE TAKEOVER

In a noncontested takeover, the target company (within 10 days after the date the tender offer commenced) must declare to its shareholders one of the following:

1. That it recommends acceptance or rejection of the offer;
2. That it has no opinion and remains neutral; and
3. That it is unable to take a position.
     The target company must also justify its position.

In those cases in which the target company does not want to be taken over, both the target company and the offeror develop strategies for stopping the other. Some of the tactics used by a target company to fight takeovers are:

1. Persuading shareholders that the tender offer is not in their best interests
2. Filing legal suits or complaints on the grounds that the takeover violates provisions of the antitrust laws
3. Matching the buy-out with a target company offer
4. Soliciting a "white knight" merger or a merger from a friendly party

Exhibit 22.3 reproduces a tender offer document used by Mesa Petroleum (T. Boone Pickens) in a bid for General American Oil Co.

Competing takeover bids often are hostile affairs marked by a great deal of publicity. The *Martin-Marietta* case was highly publicized and involved the use of antitakeover tactics.

Exhibit 22.3
Sample Tender Offer Document

Offer to Purchase for Cash
13,000,000 Shares of Common Stock
of
General American Oil Company of Texas
at
$40 Net Per Share
by
Mesa Petroleum Co.

The proration period expires at
12:00 Midnight, New York City time, on Wednesday, December 29, 1990.
The withdrawal deadline is
12:00 Midnight, New York City time, on Tuesday, January 11, 1991.
The offer expires at
12:00 Midnight, New York City time, on Tuesday, January 18, 1991,
unless extended.

THE OFFER IS NOT CONDITIONED UPON ANY MINIMUM NUMBER OF SHARES
BEING TENDERED

Any shareholder desiring to tender an or any portion of his Shares should either (1) complete and sign the Letter of Transmittal or a facsimile copy in accordance with the instructions in the Letter of Transmittal and mail or deliver it with his stock certificate(s) and any other required documents to the Depository or (2) request his broker, dealer, commercial bank, trust company or other nominee to effect the transaction for him. A shareholder having Shares registered in the name of a broker, dealer, commercial bank trust company or other nominee must contact such broker, dealer, commercial bank, trust; company or other nominee if he desires to tender such Shares.

A shareholder who desires to tender Shares and whose certificates for such Shares are not immediately available may tender such Shares by following the procedure for guaranteed delivery as set forth in Section 5.

Questions and requests for assistance may be directed to the Dealer Manager or the Information Agent at their respective addresses and telephone numbers set forth on the back cover of this Offer to Purchase. Requests for additional copies of this Offer to Purchase and the Letter of Transmittal may be directed to the Dealer Manager or the Information Agent or to brokers, dealers, commercial banks or trust companies.

The Dealer Manager for the Offer is:
MORGAN STANLEY & CO.
Incorporated

December 20, 1990

Martin-Marietta Corp. v. Bendix Corp.
547 F. Supp. 533 (D. Md. 1982)

WHO'S ON FIRST: THE UT, BENDIX, MARTIN-MARIETTA WALTZ

FACTS

Bendix Corporation made a tender offer for approximately 44.5 percent of Martin-Marietta's common stock at a price of $43 per share; the offer was later increased to $48 per share for 55 percent of the stock. This tender offer was followed by a Martin-Marietta offer for Bendix stock, followed by a United Technologies Corporation offer for Bendix stock. Martin-Marietta brought suit alleging that misleading statements were made in the tender offer materials.

JUDICIAL OPINION

YOUNG, District Judge

On August 25, 1982, Bendix announced a tender offer for approximately 44.5 percent of Martin-Marietta's common stock at a price of $43 per share. On September 7, Bendix increased its offer to $48 per share, and on September 10, Bendix stated that it would purchase approximately 55 percent of Martin-Marietta's common stock. If Bendix succeeds with its tender offer, it intends to acquire all of the remaining Martin-Marietta shares through a squeeze-out merger. The withdrawal deadline for Bendix's offer is midnight September 16—i.e., at that time Martin-Marietta's shareholders who tendered their stock may no longer take back their stock and Bendix may proceed to purchase the stock tendered to it.

On August 30, five days after Bendix announced its tender offer, Martin-Marietta countered with a tender offer for approximately 50.3 percent of Bendix's common stock at a price of $75 per share. The withdrawal deadline for Martin-Marietta's offer is midnight September 22.

United Technologies Corporation jumped into the fray on September 7 with its tender offer for approximately 50.3 percent of Bendix' common stock at a price of $75 per share. On September 15, United Technologies increased its offer to $85 per share. The withdrawal deadline for United Technologies' offer is midnight September 28.

All three tender offers can be aptly, if somewhat understatedly, described as "hostile." . . . In addition to the litigation in this court, the three corporations have battled each other in other federal and state courts, on Wall Street and through the media.

In its Offer to Purchase, sent to all Martin-Marietta shareholders pursuant to Securities and Exchange Commission Rule 14d-6, Bendix stated:

[T]he Purchaser [Bendix] has conducted studies, on the basis of publicly available information, of alternative business strategies that it might consider under varying economic and market conditions in the event it acquires all or substantially all of the equity interest in the Company [Martin-Marietta]. In this regard, the Purchaser has analyzed the possibility of divesting one or more of the non-aerospace divisions of the Company, but the Purchaser has made no determination to pursue any such transaction and has no plan or proposal with respect thereto.

Similarly, on August 27, Bendix issued a press release stating that "it had no plans to divest any of Martin-Marietta's operations following a merger of the two companies" and that "press reports to the contrary were erroneous."

Martin-Marietta alleges that the above statements by Bendix are false and were calculated to mislead Martin-Marietta's shareholders and the investing public. Martin-Marietta claims that, contrary to Bendix' statements, Bendix does have post-acquisition plans or proposals to divest Martin-Marietta's non-aerospace divisions and, therefore, Bendix made misrepresentations and omissions in violation of Sections 14(d) and 14(e).

In support of its allegations that Bendix does have plans and proposals to divest Martin-Marietta non-aerospace divisions, Martin-Marietta marshaled the following evidence that it obtained during ten days of expedited discovery:

(1) Statements made by Bendix Chairman William Agee in January, 1981, that the "companies we will be looking at will have a good

Continued

technological fit," that Bendix "will not go into anything that is very far afield from what Bendix currently does," and that Bendix "would undertake a rationalization process" if it acquired a company that had some businesses that fit with Bendix and others that did not.

(2) An unsigned handwritten internal Bendix document, dated September 17, 1981, stating that if Bendix acquires Martin-Marietta, it will "Probably spin out aluminum, aggregates at right time."

Bendix, on the other hand, submitted the following materials and arguments in support of its position that it does not have any plans or proposals to divest Martin-Marietta's non-aerospace divisions:

(1) Statements by Bendix' top management that diversification is one of the principal elements of Bendix' acquisition strategy. In Bendix' 1981 Annual Report, Chairman Agee stated that Bendix' acquisition program "is directed toward major businesses which could provide additional dimensions to the company."

The public interest requires that a probable legal tender offer such as Bendix' offer be permitted to proceed without intervention by the courts. As the Supreme Court noted in *Edgar* v. *MITE Corp.*, 457 U.S. 624 (1982), the effects of blocking a nationwide tender offer are substantial.

In conclusion, the Court finds that Bendix would be more seriously harmed by the issuance of an injunction than Martin-Marietta would be harmed by its non-issuance. Moreover, Martin-Marietta has failed to make a strong showing that it is likely to prevail on the merits. Lastly, the public interest argues against the issuance of an injunction.

CASE QUESTIONS
1. Which corporation was making the original tender offer?
2. What were the terms of the original tender offer? The modifications?
3. What was the counter-tender offer?
4. What third party became involved? Terms?
5. What counteraction did Martin-Marietta take?

E T H I C A L   I S S U E S

22.2 In a nontakeover environment, managers can make long-term decisions on capital investment and research and development expenditures based on the expectation of an ongoing firm. Those long-term decisions can temporarily decrease profits and make the company attractive for a takeover. Is the profit of a few takeovers destroying long-term corporate growth? Or are takeover bidders a motivator for managers?

State Laws Affecting Tender Offers

For an example of a state law governing takeovers, review the Control Share Acquisitions Chapter of the Indiana Business Corporation Law:
http://www.law.indiana.edu/codes/in/23/ch-23-1-42.html

Today over 40 states have passed laws regarding takeovers. Initially these laws were Williams Act provisions at the state level. However, upon review of these types of statutes, the U.S. Supreme Court held that they were a violation of the Supremacy Clause (see Chapter 5) in that Congress had preempted the field by establishing a full regulatory scheme for takeovers under the Williams Act [*Edgar* v. *MITE Corp.*, 457 U.S. 624 (1982)]. Following the *MITE* case, the states have developed a new type of anti-takeover statute that permits shareholders to have some say in whether a corporation should be taken over. This new breed of state law focuses on corporate governance and not securities regulation, and hence it avoids the preemption issues raised by the earlier statutes. However, these statutes are still subject to judicial review. The following case deals with the validity of state corporate governance statutes on takeovers.

CTS Corp. v. Dynamics Corp. of Am.
481 U.S. 69 (1987)

NOT IN INDIANA YOU DON'T: ANTITAKEOVER LAWS

FACTS

On March 4, 1986, the state of Indiana revised its Indiana Business Corporation Law to include the Control Share Acquisitions Chapter (Indiana act, or act). The act applies to corporations incorporated in Indiana and corporations that have

(1) one hundred or more shareholders;

(2) its principal place of business, its principal office, or substantial assets within Indiana; and

(3) either:
   (A) more than 10 percent of its shareholders resident in Indiana;
   (B) more than 10 percent of its shares owned by Indiana residents; or
   (C) 10 thousand shareholders resident in Indiana.

The act focuses on the acquisition of "control shares" whenever an individual entity acquires shares that, but for the operation of the act, would bring its voting power in the corporation to or above any of three thresholds: 20 percent, 33⅓ percent, or 50 percent. An entity that acquires control shares does not necessarily acquire voting rights. Rather, it gains those rights only "to the extent granted by resolution approved by the shareholders of the issuing public corporation." Section 9 requires a majority vote of all disinterested shareholders holding each class of stock if such a resolution is to pass (§ 23-1-42-9(b)). The practical effect of this requirement is to condition acquisition of control of a corporation on approval of a majority of the preexisting disinterested shareholders.

On March 10, 1986, appellee Dynamics Corporation of America owned 9.6 percent of the common stock of appellant CTS Corporation, an Indiana corporation. On that day, six days after the act went into effect, Dynamics announced a tender offer for another million shares in CTS; purchase of those shares would have brought Dynamic's ownership interest in CTS to 27.5 percent. Also on March 10, Dynamics filed suit in the U.S. District Court for the Northern District of Illinois, alleging that CTS had violated the federal securities laws in a number of respects no longer relevant to these proceedings. On March 27, the board of directors of CTS elected to be governed by the provisions of the Indiana act.

Four days later, on March 31, Dynamics moved for leave to amend its complaint to allege that the act was preempted by the Williams Act and violated the Commerce Clause.

On April 9, 1986, the district court ruled that the Williams Act preempted the Indiana act and cited the case of *Edgar* v. *MITE Corp.* 457 U.S. 624 (1982). One week later, the district court held that the act also violated the Commerce Clause. The Seventh Circuit affirmed the decision, and the state of Indiana and CTS appealed.

JUDICIAL OPINION
POWELL, Justice

As the plurality opinion in *MITE* did not represent the views of a majority of the Court, we are not bound by its reasoning. We need not question that reasoning, however, because we believe the Indiana Act passes muster even under the broad interpretation of the Williams Act articulated by Justice White in *MITE*. As is apparent from our summary of its reasoning, the overriding concern of the *MITE* plurality was that the Illinois statute considered in that case operated to favor management against offerors, to the detriment of shareholders. By contrast, the statute now before the Court protects the independent shareholder against both of the contending parties. Thus, the Act furthers a basic purpose of the Williams Act, "'plac[ing] investors on an equal footing with the takeover bidder.'"

The Indiana Act operates on the assumption, implicit in the Williams Act, that independent shareholders faced with tender offers often are at a disadvantage. By allowing such shareholders to vote as a group, the Act protects them

Continued

from the coercive aspects of some tender offers. If, for example, shareholders believe that a successful tender offer will be followed by a purchase of nontendering shares at a depressed price, individual shareholders may tender their shares—even if they doubt the tender offer is in the corporation's best interest—to protect themselves from being forced to sell their shares at a depressed price. As the SEC explains: "The alternative of not accepting the tender offer is virtual assurance that, if the offer is successful, the shares will have to be sold in the lower priced, second step." The desire of the Indiana Legislature to protect shareholders of Indiana corporations from this type of coercive offer does not conflict with the Williams Act. Rather, it furthers the federal policy of investor protection.

In implementing its goal, the Indiana Act avoids the problems the plurality discussed in *MITE*. Unlike the *MITE* statute, the Indiana Act does not give either management or the offeror an advantage in communicating with the shareholders about the impending offer. The Act also does not impose an indefinite delay on tender offers. Nothing in the Act prohibits an offeror from consummating an offer on the 20th business day, the earliest day permitted under applicable federal regulations. Nor does the Act allow the state government to interpose its views of fairness between willing buyers and sellers of shares of the target company. Rather, the Act allows *shareholders* to evaluate the fairness of the offer collectively.

As an alternative basis for its decision, the Court of Appeals held that the Act violates the Commerce Clause of the Federal Constitution. We now address this holding. On its face, the Commerce Clause is nothing more than a grant to Congress of the power "[t]o regulate Commerce . . . among the several States . . . ," Art. 1, § 8, cl. 3. But it has been settled for more than a century that the Clause prohibits States from taking certain actions respecting interstate commerce even absent congressional action.

The principal objects of dormant Commerce Clause scrutiny are statutes that discriminate against interstate commerce. The Indiana Act is not such a statute. It has the same effects on tender offers whether or not the offeror is a domiciliary or resident of Indiana. Thus, it "visits its effects equally upon both interstate and local business."

Dynamics nevertheless contends that the statute is discriminatory because it will apply most often to out-of-state entities. This argument rests on the contention that, as a practical matter, most hostile tender offers are launched by offerors outside Indiana. But this argument avails Dynamics little. "The fact that the burden of a state regulation falls on some interstate companies does not, by itself, establish a claim of discrimination against interstate commerce." Because nothing in the Indiana Act imposes a greater burden on out-of-state offerors than it does on similarly situated Indiana offerors, we reject the contention that the Act discriminates against interstate commerce.

The Court of Appeals did not find the Act unconstitutional for either of these threshold reasons. Rather, its decision rested on its view of the Act's potential to hinder tender offers. We think the Court of Appeals failed to appreciate the significance for Commerce Clause analysis of the fact that state regulation of corporate governance is regulation of entities whose very existence and attributes are a product of state law.

Dynamic's argument that the Act is unconstitutional ultimately rests on its contention that the Act will limit the number of successful tender offers. There is little evidence that this will occur. But even if true, this result would not substantially affect our Commerce Clause analysis. We reiterate that this Act does not prohibit any entity—resident or nonresident—from offering to purchase, or from purchasing, shares in Indiana corporations, or from attempting thereby to gain control. It only provides regulatory procedures designed for the better protection of the corporations' shareholders. We have rejected the "notion that the Commerce Clause protects the particular structure or methods of operation in a . . . market." The very commodity that is traded in the securities market is one whose characteristics are

Continued

defined by state law. Similarly, the very commodity that is traded in the "market for corporate control"—the corporation—is one that owes its existence and attributes to state law. Indiana need not define these commodities as other States do; it need only provide that residents and nonresidents have equal access to them. This Indiana has done. Accordingly, even if the Act should decrease the number of successful tender offers for Indiana corporations, this would not offend the Commerce Clause.

On its face, the Indiana Control Share Acquisitions Chapter evenhandedly determines the voting rights of shares of Indiana corporations. The Act does not conflict with the provisions or purposes of the Williams Act. To the limited extent that the Act affects interstate commerce, this is justified by the State's interests in defining the attributes of shares in its corporations and in protecting shareholders.

Congress has never questioned the need for state regulation of these matters. Nor do we think such regulation offends the Constitution. Accordingly, we reverse the judgment of the Court of Appeals.

CASE QUESTIONS
1. What did the new Indiana statute require?
2. How much time elapsed between the enactment of the Indiana law and its first challenge?
3. Name the two theories used to challenge the validity of the Indiana law.
4. Does the Court distinguish its previous *MITE* decision?
5. Does the Indiana act create an unfair disadvantage for non-Indiana corporations?
6. Does the Williams Act preempt the Indiana statute?

ETHICAL ISSUES

22.3 Joseph Horne Company, a department store in Pennsylvania, entered into an agreement to have Dillard's (a national retail chain) take it over. Dillard's performed its due diligence—the process of getting internal access to computers and records to verify financial statements. During due diligence, Dillard's assumed responsibility for ordering and shipping merchandise. Employees in Horne's management were told that they would no longer have jobs, and nearly five hundred employees left Horne. Horne's Christmas merchandise was delayed and was often wrong, and the merger fell through. Horne says that Dillard's went too far. Dillard's says that due diligence is part of a takeover, that Horne's financial statements were inaccurate, and that Horne could have stopped the ordering and shipping at any time. One of the officers at Horne's bank says a Dillard's official told him that Dillard's would just wait until the company was in Chapter 11 and pick it up cheaply. Evaluate the ethics of both parties.

The Future for State Antitakeover Statutes

State antitakeover statutes are often classified into three generations. The first generation was the Illinois statute invalidated in *MITE* as preempted by the Williams Act. The second-generation statute is the Indiana statute upheld as valid in *CTS* as part of corporate governance regulation. There is now a third generation of antitakeover statutes, which require bidders to wait three years

*Review Wisconsin's
takeover statute
(Chapter 180, Business
Corporations):* http://
badger.state.wi.us/
agencies/wilis/
Statutes.html

before taking over a company unless the board of the target company agrees to such a takeover. These statutes were enacted after the *CTS* decision and further extend the control of shareholders and the entrenchment of existing management. The effect is to make a takeover very unattractive because of the delay. Wisconsin's three-year, third-generation statute was upheld by the Seventh Circuit Court of Appeals in *Amanda Acquisition Corp.* v. *Universal Foods Corp.*, 877 F.2d 496 (7th Cir. 1989), and the U.S. Supreme Court denied certiorari for the review, giving an implicit validation to these more restrictive state statutes. The Court noted in its review of the Wisconsin statute:

> *If our views of the wisdom of state law mattered, Wisconsin's takeover statute would not survive. Like our colleagues who decided* MITE *and* CTS, *we believe that antitakeover legislation injures shareholders . . . . Skepticism about the wisdom of a state's law does not lead to the conclusion that the law is beyond the state's power. We have not been elected custodians of investors' wealth. States need not treat investors' welfare as their summum bonum. Perhaps they choose to protect managers' welfare instead . . . . Unless a federal statute or the Constitution bars the way, Wisconsin's choice must be respected.*

Since the time of the Wisconsin statute's passage and its declared judicial validity, other states have passed even more protective legislation for companies within their state borders. These statutes, for example, permit corporations to prevent 100 percent acquisition of their stock unless the takeover is done over a three-year period. Other statutes permit corporations to dilute the interest of an offeror by issuing new shares to existing shareholders once a takeover begins.

C O N S I D E R . . . **22.1** In early January 1994, Don Tyson, chairman of Tyson Foods, Inc., met with Jim Keeler, the president of WLR Foods, Inc., a Virginia corporation, to propose Tyson's acquisition of WLR. Mr. Keeler presented Tyson's offer to WLR's board and the board voted to remain independent. When Mr. Keeler informed Tyson of the rejection of the takeover offer, Tyson made a tender offer, on January 24, 1994, to acquire WLR stock for $30 a share, a 56 percent premium over the market price of WLR stock at the time—$19.25.

On January 28, 1994, the WLR board met to obtain advice from its legal and investment advisors. The board adjourned and met again on February 4, 1994, at which time it voted to reject the Tyson tender offer. At that same meeting the WLR board adopted severance packages for officers and employees in the event of a change of control and a "poison pill" that provided for the issuance of shares to existing shareholders in the event Tyson's tender offer was successful. The effect would be that Tyson's newly acquired interest would be diluted.

Tyson filed suit challenging the WLR board's action. WLR's board had taken their actions based on newly passed Virginia antitakeover protections for Virginia corporations. Tyson challenged the Virginia legislation as being preempted by federal law and the Willams Act. Is Tyson correct? Did the WLR board act properly? Why did the WLR board meet so many times to make a decision? Why did they have advisors come to their January 28, 1994 meeting? [*WLR Foods Inc.* v. *Tyson Foods Inc.*, 869 F. Supp. 419 (W.D. Va. 1994); 65 F.3d 1172 (4th Cir. 1995).]

Proxy Regulations and Tender Offers

Once some shares are acquired, a firm poised for a takeover wages a proxy battle, which means it solicits proxies in order to be able to command the number of votes needed to gain control of the board. Even though these proxy solicitations originate outside the company, the proxy statement and solicitation materials must be filed with the SEC.

Failure to file these materials makes the proxies invalid, and any action taken at a meeting using the proxies can be set aside. Mergers voted on with invalid proxies can be "unwound." Either the SEC or shareholders are entitled to bring an action to prevent the use or undo the use of invalid proxies. If a shareholder successfully brings an action seeking a remedy for a violation of the SEC proxy solicitation rules outlined in Section 14, the offeror must fully reimburse the shareholder for all costs of the court action.

Proxies obtained using misleading information or by not disclosing material information are also invalid. Again, either the SEC or individual shareholders can bring suit to stop the use of these proxies or set aside action taken with them.

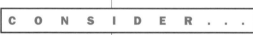

Proxy contests are expensive. Who pays for their costs? If management wins, they can be reimbursed for reasonable costs. However, some courts limit this reimbursement right to battles waged over corporate policy and not over personality conflicts. If the new group wins, they can vote to reimburse for reasonable expenses, but many states require shareholders to ratify such reimbursement.

C O N S I D E R . . .   **22.2** Can you now advise Mrs. Zeiss, from the chapter's opening "Judgment," on her rights in the Ligsin takeover?

ANTITRUST REGULATION OF BUSINESS COMBINATIONS

Review the Hart-Scott-Rodino Antitrust Improvements Act of 1976: http://www. law.cornell.edu/ uscode/15/18a.html

Apart from all the securities and corporate aspects of business combinations are the antitrust issues involved whenever two businesses combine their efforts. Mergers and their legality are governed by both the **Sherman Act** and the **Clayton Act**. The Sherman Act prohibits those mergers and combinations that restrain competition. However, the Sherman Act requires some proof of monopoly power before a combination can be restrained, and so the Clayton Act is the most frequently used antimerger device.

Under the Hart-Scott-Rodino amendments to antitrust laws on mergers, an offeror must file a notice of acquisition or merger with the Justice Department prior to making the offer if the assets of the company to be acquired exceed $15 million.

Justice Department Guidelines

Since 1968, the Justice Department has had its own guidelines for determining the validity of mergers. The guidelines in effect now were adopted in 1982, and the courts have used them in deciding cases.

The overall tone of the guidelines is that mergers should not be permitted to create or enhance market power or to enable the exercise of market power. In determining market power, the guidelines examine such issues as defining the product market, determining product substitutability (elasticity of demand), finding the geographic market and its effect in the merger, and calculating the effects of price increases in both markets.

C O N S I D E R . . . **22.3** Sara Lee Corporation acquired Griffin, Inc., a British shoe-polish manufacturer for $25.8 million in 1991. Sara Lee already owned its own shoe-polish line, Kiwi, which holds about 90 percent of the U.S. drugstore, grocery, and mass-merchandise market sales of shoe polish.

Prior to its acquisition, Sara Lee placed the value of Griffin's assets at less than $15 million. A Justice Department investigation of the merger revealed that cash-flow projections placed the value of Griffin at $17.2 million. The investigation began in 1994 after the Federal Trade Commission (FTC) ordered Sara Lee to divest itself of the Esquire brand shoe-polish company that it had acquired in June 1994 without prior notification of the proposed merger.

Did Sara Lee violate antitrust laws with its Griffin merger? Do you think the Justice Department would have approved the merger had Sara Lee filed notice of the acquisition in advance? What percentage of the market do you think Sara Lee held in 1994 after it acquired Esquire?

What Types of Mergers Are Prohibited?

Those mergers (and other combinations) that involve the asset or stock acquisition of another corporation engaged in commerce "where the effect may be to substantially lessen competition in any line of commerce in any section of the country" are prohibited. Judicial opinions have provided the meaning for the terms used in the Clayton Act. In examining mergers, the courts look for a "reasonable likelihood" that competition will be lessened; absolute proof is not required.

Review Department of Justice and Federal Trade Commission horizontal merger guidelines: http://www.vanderbilt.edu/Owen/froeb/antitrust/law/mg.html

Horizontal mergers receive the greatest scrutiny since competitors are joining. One of the new factors the Justice Department examines in horizontal mergers is the impact the merger will have on innovation. The Justice Department cites the breakup of the telecommunications industry as proof of the technological and product innovations that can result when competition operates freely in an industry. In the proposed merger of Microsoft Inc. with Intuit Inc., another software manufacturer, technological innovation was cited as the greatest concern of regulators. Specifically, Justice Department officials pointed to the domination the merged firms would have held in the market for consumer home banking. Had the merger occurred, Microsoft would have controlled 90 percent of the personal financial computer software market.

Vertical mergers are between firms that have a buyer-seller relationship. For example, if a sandwich-meat manufacturer merged with its meat supplier, there would be a vertical merger. In determining whether a vertical merger violates the Clayton Act, the courts determine the relevant geographic and product markets and then determine whether the effect of the merger will be to foreclose or lessen competition.

If the merger will prevent entry of competitors into any level of the vertical chain, it will be prohibited. For example, if a meat manufacturer acquired a supplier and then a wholesaler, it would become difficult for any firm to enter the market at those levels if the meat manufacturer had a substantial portion of the market.

Similarly, if the merger will prevent other suppliers from selling to the manufacturer and the manufacturer is a large customer in that market, the merger will be illegal.

There is a failing-firm defense to vertical mergers, but the parties must be able to show that there were no other offers to buy and that the company could not be successfully organized under Chapter 11 bankruptcy.

The Clayton Act applies to all types of mergers: horizontal, vertical, and conglomerate. The use of the term **line of commerce** allows the Justice Department this flexibility in enforcement. For example, a merger of a can company with a jar company is a horizontal merger in violation of the Clayton Act because their line of commerce is containers, and the resulting large share of the market can give too much control to the merged firm and would unduly lessen competition. Likewise, the merger of a local grocery chain with the only produce distributor in a particular area would be a violation of the Clayton Act as a vertical merger resulting in too much power to control the market. The following case focuses on a horizontal merger.

United States v. *Gillette*
828 F. Supp. 78 (D.D.C. 1993)

HOW MANY FOUNTAIN PENS CAN YOU FIT IN A MERGER?

FACTS
Pursuant to an Offer Arrangements Agreement dated September 10, 1992, Gillette Company posted a tender offer on March 23, 1993, to purchase all outstanding stock and options of the co-defendant in this action, Parker Pen Holdings, Ltd. Between the date of the agreement and the posting of the offer, the two defendants were in communication with the Antitrust Division of the Department of Justice (plaintiff) concerning a potential violation of Section 7 of the Clayton Act (15 U.S.C. § 18).

The Justice Department's interest in this acquisition focused on the premium fountain pen market in the United States. Based on 1991 sales, Gillette (through its Waterman brand) controls approximately 21 percent of the U.S. premium fountain pen market; Parker has a 19-percent share. Plaintiff's concern is that the effect of the combination of Gillette and Parker "may be substantially to lessen competition" in the premium fountain pen market.

Unable to reach an agreement with the defendants, the Justice Department brought this suit on March 22, 1993, seeking a declaration that the proposed acquisition is in violation of Section 7 as well as a temporary restraining order, a preliminary injunction, and a permanent injunction barring any combination of the two defendants.

JUDICIAL OPINION
LAMBERTH, District Judge
This case is before the court on plaintiff's motion for a preliminary injunction. Often in Clayton Act cases, the suit is brought by the Federal Trade Commission (FTC) pursuant to 15 U.S.C. § 53(b). In those cases, the standard for a preliminary injunction is the statutory "public interest" test: whether "[u]pon a proper showing that, weighing the equities and considering the Commission's likelihood of ultimate success, such action would be in the public interest."

Before a preliminary injunction may be issued, plaintiff must establish that it has demonstrated a likelihood of success on the merits. In a Section 7 case, plaintiff effectively must meet two criteria: (1) it must demonstrate that a proposed combination will affect a "line of commerce," (the determination of which includes the demonstration of a relevant product market

Continued

and a relevant geographic market); and (2) it must demonstrate that the combination "may be substantially to lessen competition."

The first step in any Section 7 case is to determine the relevant product market. To this end, plaintiff alleges that the relevant "line of commerce" is premium fountain pens, which it defines as "high quality refillable fountain pens that have an established premium image among consumers." (A more practical definition, given plaintiff's evidence and arguments, is "refillable fountain pens with a SRP (Suggested Retail Price) of between $50 and $400.") The relevant geographic market, plaintiff asserts, is the United States.

Defendants object to both aspects of this definition. First, defendants assert that a market for fountain pens may not be segregated out from what is a continuum of prices; in other words, the government cannot exclude pens with SRPs of less than $50 or more than $400 in its definition of the relevant product market. Second, defendants claim that the definition would be expanded to include other highline writing instruments. Third, defendants contend that plaintiff's market statistics are incomplete, inconclusive, and unreliable. Finally, addressing the geographic market, defendants assert that the relevant geographic market is Planet Earth.

Defendants' first argument is that a relevant product market cannot be defined by reference to a narrow price range along a broader continuum of prices. In support of this argument, defendants cite several cases in which courts held that so-called "premium" products fell into the same market as so-called "non-premium" products. These cases, defendants contend, preclude plaintiff's segregation of a narrowly drawn $50 to $400 market.

However, the court finds that plaintiff has met its burden and demonstrates that a separate market for fountain pens in the $50 to $400 range exists. The determination of what constitutes the relevant product market hinges on a determination of those products to which consumers will turn given reasonable variations in price. Therefore, the definition must exclude those items to which "only a limited number of buyers will turn; in technical terms, products whose 'cross-elasticities of demand' are small."

[. . . sub-markets *[are] appropriate* in certain circumstances, and [there are] several criteria for courts to consider in determining whether a sub-market exists. Those criteria include some factual circumstances not present here (such as unique production facilities), some partially present (specialized vendors), and some that clearly demonstrate that $50–$400 premium fountain pens are a sub-market of the fountain pen industry (industry or public recognition of the sub-market as a separate economic entity, distinct customers, and sensitivity to price changes).

The court finds that plaintiff has provided ample evidence that fountain pens in the $50 to $400 range effectively do not compete with fountain pens either below or above that range. Plaintiff therefore has met its Clayton Act burden. In contrast to fountain pens with SRPs below $50, the fountain pens here at issue afford their users (as well as those who merely put them in their breast pockets) image, prestige, and status. In accordance with this prestige, manufacturers, retailers, and purchasers of the pens recognize that there is a distinction between these pens, which several of plaintiff's affidavits suggest are priced at approximately $50 and up, and those pens which are priced below this threshold. The evidence suggests that, should the price of a fountain pen costing, for example, $60 be increased in a non-trivial, non-transitory fashion, consumers will nonetheless purchase the now-costlier pen rather than substitute a less expensive, less prestigious model. In other words, there is a low cross-elasticity of demand between these pens and those priced below $50.

Similarly, fountain pens priced above $400 also are not interchangeable with pens costing less than $400. Again, there is a threshold beyond which the pens become mere collectors items or "jewelry" pieces, and the evidence suggests that consumers will not substitute the $400-and-up pens if prices were to be raised on premium fountain pens.

Continued

Although, . . . there indeed is a continuum of fountain pen prices (from less than $10 to more than $10,000), plaintiff has nonetheless demonstrated that—unlike those cases—the fountain pen market may be divided into three sub-markets: for lack of better terms, "base" fountain pens (less than $50); "premium" fountain pens ($50 to $400); and "jewelry" fountain pens ($400 and up).

. . . [t]he evidence [cited by defendants] in five [previous] cases either (1) established that products along the continuum competed with each other; or (2) failed to establish that there were distinct sub-markets.

Defendants—inevitably—claim that, even if the court finds that there might be a distinct sub-market, other factors make the $50 to $400 market definition insupportable. Each of these objections, however, lacks merit. For instance, the claim that some sellers discount their wares to their customers does not preclude a definition based on suggested retail price. A second objection, that the market may start at $40 or $70 rather than $50 (and comparable imprecision at the upper end of the range) is similarly unhelpful to defendants. First, there is sufficient evidence to support each end point. In addition, defendants have failed to demonstrate that a minor modification up or down would have any effect on the market share statistics proffered by plaintiff. Based on the exhibits appended to the affidavit of defendants' expert witness, the court determines that these modifications would not have any material effect.

Therefore, the court finds that plaintiff has met its burden of demonstrating that a sub-market with a price range of $50 to $400 may be segregated out of the larger fountain pen market for Clayton Act purposes.

Defendants' second objection to plaintiff's proposed definition is that other writing modes—ballpoint pens, rollerball pens, and pencils—should also be included. In effect, defendants assert that the relevant product market should be all "highline" writing instruments (with a "highline" instrument being defined as one with an SRP of more than $10). Plaintiff demonstrates that there is a sub-

set of fountain pen consumers who are dedicated to premium fountain pens; these customers will not substitute another mode of writing (be it ballpoint pens, rollerball pens, or mechanical pencils) when faced with a non-trivial, non-transitory increase in price. For this group (and this group only), therefore, the relevant market definition would be the one proffered by plaintiff: refillable fountain pens with SRPs of $50 to $400. Plaintiff has demonstrated that this is a highly-concentrated market (both before and after Gillette acquires Parker); and, if this were the end of the discussion, plaintiff's assertions regarding anti-competitive effects (for instance, unilateral effects such as higher prices, reduced innovations, and fewer products) likely would prevail.

The court therefore holds that the product market proposed by plaintiff is far too narrow. As discussed above, the court finds that the appropriate product market is significantly broader: all premium writing instruments. As to this market, plaintiff has failed to meet its prima facie case.

Even if the court had adopted the proposed market definition proffered by plaintiff, however, the court still would have found that plaintiff had failed to meet its burden. In that market, plaintiff does demonstrate that there is a highly-concentrated market which will become even more concentrated should the proposed merger take place. The court will therefore assume that plaintiff enjoys the presumptions that the merger will create anti-competitive results.

The court finds that the evidence in this case, particularly the evidence derived from the larger market, clearly shows that the anti-competitive effects plaintiff fears are not likely to occur, even in plaintiff's sub-market. Plaintiff does not counter successfully defendants' evidence.

Several factors lead the court to this conclusion. *First*, there is ample evidence that the merged company will not be able to increase prices on premium fountain pens unilaterally:

- There is ample evidence that fountain pens compete with other modes of writing.

Continued

Given the overlap of prices (several fountain pens are priced less than ballpoint pens and rollerball pens), an increase in one type of pen will make it relatively less attractive than other types of pen.

- In addition, many of the manufacturers create "families" of pens; each family may include a fountain pen, a rollerball pen, a mechanical pencil, and a ballpoint pen. If, as the government contends, much of the cachet of these premium instruments is their "image," at least some customers are going to view the fountain pen and the other modes within a family as in competition with each other. Therefore, if Gillette were to increase prices on its fountain pens, it would likely lose customers to its other pens in the same family (if not to other manufacturers).

- And, there is ample evidence that the mechanics of fountain pen design are readily available, thus leaving no technological barriers to entry into the market. There are also no legal or regulatory barriers which would preclude competitors from designing and selling premium fountain pens.

Although it may take a significant investment of time and money to build market share, the record demonstrates that there are new entrants into the fountain pen market which are able to check increases in price. In addition, given the competition between fountain pens and other modes of writing and the ease with which manufacturers may enter this wider market, Gillette will not be able to raise prices unilaterally on its premium fountain pens.

Second, there is ample evidence to indicate that the merger will not create a decrease in available or new products and innovations:

- The evidence demonstrates that innovation (particularly in design) is crucial to maintaining market share; therefore, if Gillette desires to remain competitive in the fountain pen market, it must compete with other companies' innovations in fountain pens and in other modes or writing.

- Again, other companies are free to enter the market as well (and there is much evidence that companies large and small have introduced a multitude of new products over the past few years; there is also evidence that many companies plan on introducing new models in the next few years).

Third, there is no evidence that there will be any collusion in this market between Gillette and Richmont (Montblanc), the current top seller of premium fountain pens.

In sum, the court finds that the merger of Gillette and Parker is not likely substantially to lessen competition and that plaintiff has not demonstrated that it is likely to prevail on the merits should this case proceed to trial.

CASE QUESTIONS
1. What is the submarket the court defines?
2. What is the elasticity of demand with respect to fountain pens?
3. Will this merger substantially lessen competition?
4. Will the merger go forward?

C O N S I D E R . . .

22.4

Christian Schmidt Brewing and Stroh Brewery Company wish to enjoin the merger of G. Heileman Brewing Company and Pabst Brewing Company.

Stroh, Schmidt, Heileman, and Pabst are all brewers selling beer in the Upper Midwest. Heileman sought to acquire Pabst, and on December 6, 1984, those two brewers entered into a Transaction Agreement under which Heileman would make a tender offer, with the support of Pabst, for all of Pabst's outstanding shares of stock. Upon completion of the tender offer, Pabst would then be merged into Heileman. Heileman also entered a separate Disposition Agreement with S&P Company by

Continued

which Heileman would sell certain assets (the Western Assets) owned by Pabst to S&P. These assets include Pabst's Tumwater, Washington brewery and Pabst's Olympia, Hamms, and Olde English 800 brands. After selling the Western Assets to S&P, Heileman would retain the Pabst "family" of brands.

Stroh and Schmidt compete with Heileman and Pabst in the Upper Midwest. They argue that the effect of the proposed merger may be substantially to lessen competition, and therefore Heileman's acquisition of Pabst would violate Section 7 of the Clayton Act, 15 U.S.C. § 18 (1982).

In 1983, the Upper Midwest beer market was divided as follows: Miller— 22.4 percent; Anheuser-Busch—21.1 percent; Heileman—20.4 percent; Stroh— 14.7 percent and Pabst—12.8 percent. The remaining 8.6 percent of the market was divided among a number of small breweries. If Heileman were to acquire Pabst, the resulting firm would be the largest brewer in the region with a 20.7 percent market share (after Heileman disposed of the Western Assets), and would sell nearly 50 percent more beer than its closest competitor.

The four largest firms control 78.6 percent of the market. If the proposed merger were completed, the four-firm concentration ratio would increase to 88.9 percent.

Should the merger be enjoined? [*Christian Schmidt Brewing* v. *G. Heileman Brewing*, 600 F. Supp. 1326 (1985).]

EXEMPTIONS FROM THE CLAYTON ACT

Some types of mergers are not prevented by the Clayton Act. Indeed, some types of mergers actually help competition. One such exemption is the **failing-company doctrine**, which allows the merger of one firm with a failing firm in order to preserve the business, its creditors, and buyers. However, the doctrine is strictly applied, and it must be shown that there were no alternatives for the failing company.

A second exemption is the **small-company doctrine**. This doctrine allows two smaller firms to merge so that they can compete more effectively in a market dominated by larger forces. This doctrine is also narrowly applied: The market must be dominated by others, and the merger of the two firms cannot give them a larger share of the market than any existing firms.

PENALTIES FOR VIOLATIONS

The Clayton Act does not carry criminal penalties for violations. However, both shareholders and the government have the power to seek the equitable remedies of injunction and rescission. Shareholders and companies damaged by a merger have the right to sue for **treble damages**.

GLOBAL CONSOLIDATION

Through stock purchases by companies from other countries, many firms in the United States are now owned by shareholders headquartered outside the United States. Many entertainment conglomerates and real estate syndications have been purchased by Japanese firms. Mergers and consolidations are facilitated by the infusion of capital from outside the United States. Foreign firms acquiring U.S. firms are still subject to Williams Act procedures, as well as to state laws concerning procedures and protection of minority shareholder interests.

The Justice Department has rewritten its guidelines for merger and joint ventures of U.S. firms in foreign and international markets. These joinders are subject to less scrutiny since, in theory, competition should increase as a result.

SUMMARY

What are the types of business combinations?
- Merger—a combination of two or more companies into one
- Horizontal merger—a combination of two or more companies in the same line of business into one
- Vertical merger—a combination of two or more companies in the distribution chain into one
- Conglomerate merger—a combination of two or more companies in different chain industries into one
- Consolidation—combination of two companies into a new firm
- Tender offer—stock acquisition as a means of achieving a business combination
- Takeovers—use of tender offer to achieve a business combination
- Junk bond—financing tool that has as its security the assets of the eventually-to-be-acquired firm
- Group bids—pooled takeovers
- Asset acquisition—buying a firm's property as opposed to its shares in order to acquire control

What are the legal rights of shareholders in combinations?
- Dissenting shareholder—shareholder who objects to merger
- Appraisal rights—value of shares immediately before merger that is paid to dissenting shareholder
- Freeze-out—merger designed to eliminate minority shareholders by buying them out prior to merger action

What legal restrictions are imposed on these combinations?
- Williams Act—federal law regulating tender offers
- Antitakeover statutes—state laws regulating means and requirements for takeovers
- Failing company doctrine—exceptions to antitrust regulations that permit acquisition because competition will increase
- Small company doctrine—exceptions to antitrust regulations that permit acquisition because competition will increase
- Treble damages—recovery of three times actual damages for Clayton Act violations

QUESTIONS AND PROBLEMS

1. Chris-Craft Industries, Inc., made a tender offer to the shareholders of Piper common stock. The tender offer failed because of the actions of Bangor Punta Corporation and Piper. Bangor Punta gained control, and Chris-Craft brought suit for violation of section 14(e) on grounds that Bangor Punta had used misrepresentation to gain control. Can a tender offeror like Chris-Craft recover damages under the Williams Act? [*Piper* v. *Chris-Craft Indus., Inc.*, 430 U.S. 1 (1977).]
2. Mobil Corporation made a tender offer for a minimum of 30 million shares of common stock of Marathon Oil Company for $85 a share in cash. Marathon directors voted to find a white knight and also filed suit alleging that the merger between Marathon and

Mobil would violate Section 7 of the Clayton Act. The federal court issued a preliminary injunction. U.S. Steel became the white knight and made an offer of $125 a share for the 30 million shares. Marathon directors voted to recommend U.S. Steel's offer.

The U.S. Steel offer required an option on 10 million Marathon shares for $90 a share and an option to purchase Marathon's Yates Field mineral rights. These terms were not disclosed, and Mobil filed suit under Section 14(e), alleging a misrepresentation. Was Mobil correct in its claim? [*Mobil Corp.* v. *Marathon Oil Co.*, 669 F.2d 366 (6th Cir. 1981).]

3. International General Industries (IGI) owned 81 percent of Kliklok's outstanding common stock. IGI formed KLK Corporation to acquire by merger all of Kliklok's common stock. Kliklok shareholders were offered $11 a share. Michael and Deborah Tanzer (shareholders in Kliklok) filed suit alleging that the merger was solely for the benefit of the parent and impermissible. What should be the result? [*Tanzer* v. *International General Indus.*, 379 A.2d 1121 (Del. 1977).]

4. Marshall Field & Co., a Delaware corporation with its principal office in Chicago, has operated retail department stores since 1852 and is the eighth largest department store chain in the United States, with 31 stores. CHH (Carter Hawley Hale), a California corporation that owned Neiman-Marcus, attempted several times to merge or take over Field's. During this time, Field's also received merger offers from Federated Department Stores and Dayton-Hudson. Still another retailer—Gamble-Skogmo— offered to acquire a 20 percent block of Field's stock to prevent a takeover. Field's turned down all offers. CHH finally offered a last-effort deal that Field's refused. CHH then began an unfriendly takeover.

In its information to shareholders, Field's suggested that independence was best, growth would continue, and stock prices would increase. These statements were doubtful, but shareholders rejected the takeover offer. CHH withdrew, and Field's stock declined dramatically. A Field's shareholder has sued for misrepresentation. Can he win? [*Panter* v. *Marshall Field & Co.*, 646 F.2d 271 (7th Cir. 1981).]

5. CKH Corporation is a wholly owned subsidiary of the LTV Corporation. LTV attempted through a massive buying program to acquire more than 50 percent of Grumman Corporation stock. No tender offer materials were filed with the SEC. Grumman, in response to LTV, through its employees' pension fund purchased 35 percent of Grumman stock. Grumman did not file any materials. Have there been any violations? [*LTV Corp.* v. *Grumman Corp.*, 526 F. Supp. 106 (E.D.N.Y. 1981).]

6. On August 9, 1977, MCA, Inc., through its wholly owned subsidiary MCA Enterprises, Inc., began to purchase on the open market common stock of CCLA through its stockbroker, Sloate, Weisman, Murray & Company (Sloate). Sloate opened a numbered account for MCA with Bear Stearns, a brokerage house. Bear Stearns was not aware that MCA was Sloate's customer.

Sloate informed Bear Stearns that its unnamed client (MCA) was interested in purchasing three thousand shares of CCLA common stock. Bear Stearns did not have enough CCLA shares to meet this request; thus, it purchased some of the requested shares from Goldman Sachs and Company, another broker. Subsequently, Goldman Sachs, on its own initiative, offered to sell Bear Stearns a number of CCLA convertible preferred shares. Bear Stearns purchased these shares from Goldman Sachs and resold them to MCA through Sloate. Thereafter, Goldman Sachs, again on its own initiative, informed Bear Stearns that more shares of CCLA convertible preferred stock were available for sale. These shares were also purchased by Bear Stearns and resold to MCA. Goldman Sachs had purchased these CCLA convertible preferred stocks from appellees. Neither MCA nor Sloate dealt directly with either Goldman Sachs or appellees.

On October 7, 1977, MCA publicly announced the CCLA stock tender offer. A few days later, on October 11, MCA publicly announced the terms of the tender offer and that it would pay $30.00 a share for CCLA common stock and $58.50 for CCLA convertible preferred stock. MCA's tender offer prices presented, respectively, a 30 percent and 34 percent premium above then-prevailing market prices for these stocks.

On October 19, 1977, Northwest Industries, Inc., made public a competing tender offer for CCLA common and convertible preferred stock at prices of $40 and $78, respectively. According to MCA, it was unaware prior to October 19, 1977, that Northwest would be making this tender offer. MCA did not attempt to outbid the Northwest tender offer for CCLA stock, and on November 3, 1977, MCA tendered all its previously acquired CCLA stock to Northwest. Polinsky sued for violation of the SEC's tender offer regulation. Will he win? [*Polinsky* v. *MCA,* 680 F.2d 1286 (9th Cir. 1982).]

7. Would the Williams Act cover concerted activity among boards of directors to ensure a takeover? What if the nature of their relationship was not disclosed? [*Camelot Indus. Corp.* v. *Vista Resources, Inc.,* 535 F. Supp. 1174 (S.D.N.Y. 1982).]

8. Would a new director acquiring 25 percent of his company's stock be a tender offeror? What if the director were an agent for another corporation? [*Treadway Co., Inc.* v. *Care Corp.,* 490 F. Supp. 668 (S.D.N.Y. 1980).]

9. The state of Ohio has just passed an antitakeover law that applies only to businesses organized outside the United States; that is, only foreign businesses are subject to the Ohio regulatory provisions on takeovers. At the time the statute was passed, a Toronto-based firm, Campeau Corporation, was embroiled in a takeover battle with Federated Department Stores. Does the statute create any constitutional issues?

10. T. Boone Pickens and Mesa Partners announced their intention to acquire Phillips Petroleum on December 4, 1984. At that time, they issued a statement saying they would "not sell any Phillips shares owned by it back to Phillips except on an equal basis with all shareholders." The statement was also made in the disclosure statements filed with the SEC. On December 23, 1984, the group dropped their planned takeover when Phillips agreed to restructure its finances and buy the group's shares at a $10-per-share premium. The group had a pretax profit of $89 million. On Monday, December 24, 1984, the price of Phillips's shares dropped from $54 to $45 each. Would the shareholders have any right of suit under the Williams Act? [*In re Phillips Petroleum Securities Litigation,* 881 F.2d 1236 (3d Cir. 1989).]

Problem 1

Simon & Simon, Inc. (SSI), is a Fortune 500 company primarily involved in publishing magazines and fiction and nonfiction popular press. Like other publishing firms, SSI has been interested in expansion through the acquisition of publishing firms or companies with a multi-media focus. Its shares are listed on the New York Stock Exchange.

SSI has been approached by University Press (UP), a small but successful publishing house with a focus on academic and research-oriented books that would like to sell its assets (physical as well as titles (copyrights)) to SSI. UP is a national company that markets largely through direct mailings and whose stock is sold on the over-the-counter market.

SSI has its own bookstores in malls, downtown city centers, and a few strip malls. It releases approximately 30 major fiction titles (excluding its romance novel line) and 20 major nonfiction titles each year. Other releases include children's books, cookbooks, "how to" books, coffee table (art) books, and several college and test-preparation guides. These types of releases total one hundred a year. UP releases 25 new books each year, but it is in the unique position of having some of its titles continue selling long after the usual six-month hard-cover life of popular press books.

UP's board authorized its CEO to approach SSI. SSI's board heard the proposal for the first time yesterday. SSI's CEO told them, "We should act quickly. The price is right." Another board member asked, "Aren't there some legal issues here? Can we act this quickly?"

Prepare a memorandum for the SSI board and also for the UP board outlining all the legal issues, including corporate, antitrust, and securities issues.

Appendix A

THE UNITED STATES CONSTITUTION

We the People of the United States, in Order to form a more perfect Union, establish Justice, insure domestic Tranquility, provide for the common defence, promote the general Welfare, and secure the Blessings of Liberty to ourselves and our Posterity, do ordain and establish this Constitution for the United States of America.

Article I

Section I

All legislative Powers herein granted shall be vested in a Congress of the United States, which shall consist of a Senate and House of Representatives.

Section 2

The House of Representatives shall be composed of Members chosen every second Year by the People of the several States, and the Electors in each State shall have the Qualifications requisite for Electors of the most numerous Branch of the State Legislature.

No Person shall be a Representative who shall not have attained to the Age of twenty five Years, and been seven Years a Citizen of the United States, and who shall not, when elected, be an Inhabitant of that State in which he shall be chosen.

Representatives and direct Taxes shall be apportioned among the several States which may be included within this Union, according to their respective Numbers, which shall be determined by adding to the whole Number of free Persons, including those bound to Service for a Term of Years, and excluding Indians not taxed, three fifths of all other Persons. The actual Enumeration shall be made within three Years after the first Meeting of the Congress of the United States, and within every subsequent Term of ten Years, in which Manner as they shall by Law direct. The Number of Representatives shall not exceed one for every thirty Thousand, but each State shall have at Least one Representative; and until such enumeration shall be made, the State of New Hampshire shall be entitled to choose three, Massachusetts eight, Rhode Island and Providence Plantations one, Connecticut five, New York six, New Jersey four, Pennsylvania eight, Delaware one, Maryland six, Virginia ten, North Carolina five, South Carolina five, and Georgia three.

When vacancies happen in the Representation from any State, the Executive Authority thereof shall issue Writs of Election to fill such Vacancies.

The House of Representatives shall chuse their Speaker and other Officers; and shall have the sole Power of Impeachment.

Section 3

The Senate of the United States shall be composed of two Senators from each State, chosen by the Legislature thereof, for six Years; and each Senator shall have one Vote.

Immediately after they shall be assembled in Consequence of the first Election, they shall be divided as equally as may be into three Classes. The Seats of the Senators of the first Class shall be vacated at the Expiration of the second Year, of the second Class at the Expiration of the fourth Year, and of the third Class at the Expiration of the sixth Year, so that one third may be chosen every second Year; and if Vacancies happen by Resignation, or otherwise, during the Recess of the Legislature of any State, the Executive thereof may make temporary Appointments until the next Meeting of the Legislature, which shall then fill such Vacancies

No Person shall be a Senator who shall not have attained to the Age of thirty Years, and been nine Years a Citizen of the United States, and who shall not, when elected, be an Inhabitant of that State for which he shall be chosen.

The Vice President of the United States shall be President of the Senate, but shall have no Vote, unless they be equally divided.

The Senate shall chuse their other Officers, and also a President pro tempore, in the Absence of the Vice President, or when he shall exercise the Office of President of the United States.

The Senate shall have the sole Power to try all Impeachments. When sitting for that Purpose, they shall be on Oath or Affirmation. When the President of the United States is tried the Chief Justice shall preside: And no Person shall be convicted without the Concurrence of two thirds of the Members present.

Judgment in Cases of Impeachment shall not extend further than to removal from Office, and disqualification to hold and enjoy any Office of honor, Trust or Profit under the United States: but the Party convicted shall nevertheless be liable and subject to Indictment, Trial, Judgment and Punishment, according to Law.

Section 4

The Times, Places and Manner of holding Elections for Senators and Representatives, shall be prescribed in each State by the Legislature thereof; but the Congress may at any time by Law make or alter such Regulations, except as to the Places of chusing Senators.

The Congress shall assemble at Least once in every Year, and such Meeting shall be on the first Monday in December, unless they shall by Law appoint a different Day.

Section 5

Each House shall be the Judge of the Elections, Returns and Qualifications of its own Members, and a Majority of each shall constitute a Quorum to do Business; but a smaller Number may adjourn from day to day, and may be authorized to compel the Attendance of absent Members, in such Manner, and under such Penalties as each House may provide.

Each House may determine the Rules in its Proceedings, punish its Members for disorderly Behaviour, and, with the Concurrence of two thirds, expel a Member.

Each House shall keep a Journal of its Proceedings, and from time to time publish the same, excepting such Parts as may in their Judgment require Secrecy; and the Yeas and Nays of the Members of either House on any question shall, at the Desire of one fifth of those Present, be entered on the Journal.

Neither House, during the Session of Congress, shall, without the Consent of the other, adjourn for more than three days, nor to any other Place than that in which the two Houses shall be sitting.

Section 6

The Senators and Representatives shall receive a Compensation for their Services, to be ascertained by Law, and paid out of the Treasury of the United States. They shall in all Cases, except Treason, Felony and Breach of the Peace, be privileged from Arrest during their Attendance at the Session of their respective Houses, and in going to and returning from the same; and for any Speech or Debate in either House, they shall not be questioned in any other Place.

No Senator or Representative shall, during the Time for which he was elected, be appointed to any civil Office under the Authority of the United States, which shall have been created, or the Emoluments whereof shall have been encreased during such time; and no Person holding any Office under the United States, shall be a Member of either House during his Continuance in Office.

Section 7

All Bills for raising Revenue shall originate in the House of Representatives; but the Senate may propose or concur with amendments as on other Bills.

Every Bill which shall have passed the House of Representatives and the Senate, shall, before it become a Law, be presented to the President of the United States; If he approve he shall sign it, but if not he shall return it, with his Objections to that House in which it shall have originated, who shall enter the Objections at large on their Journal, and proceed to reconsider it. If after such Reconsideration two thirds of that House shall agree to pass the Bill, it shall be sent, together with the Objections, to the other House, by which it shall like wise be reconsidered, and if approved by two thirds of that House, it shall become a Law. But in all such Cases the Votes of both Houses shall be determined by Yeas and Nays, and the names of the Persons voting for and against the Bill shall be entered on the Journal of each House respectively. If any Bill shall not be returned by the President within ten Days (Sundays excepted) after it shall have been presented to him, the Same shall be a Law, in like Manner as if he had signed it, unless the Congress by their Adjournment prevent its Return, in which Case it shall not be a Law.

Every Order, Resolution, or Vote to which the Concurrence of the Senate and House of Representatives may be necessary (except on a question of Adjournment) shall be presented to the President of the United States; and before the Same shall take Effect, shall be approved by him, or being disapproved by him, shall be repassed by two thirds of the Senate and House of Representatives, according to the Rules and Limitations prescribed in the Case of a Bill.

Section 8

The Congress shall have Power To lay and collect Taxes, Duties, Imposts and Excises, to pay the Debts and provide for the common Defense and general Welfare of the United States; but all Duties, Imposts and Excises shall be uniform throughout the United States;

To borrow Money on the credit of the United States;

To regulate Commerce with foreign Nations, and among the several States, and with the Indian Tribes;

To establish an uniform Rule of Naturalization, and uniform Laws on the subject of Bankruptcies throughout the United States;

To coin Money, regulate the Value thereof, and of foreign Coin, and fix the Standard of Weights and Measures;

To provide for the Punishment of counterfeiting the Securities and current Coin of the United States;

To establish Post Offices and post Roads;

To promote the Progress of Science and useful Arts, by securing for limited Times to Authors and Inventors the exclusive Right to their respective Writings and Discoveries;

To constitute Tribunals inferior to the supreme Court;

To define and punish Piracies and Felonies committed on the high Seas, and Offenses against the Law of Nations;

To declare War, grant Letters of Marque and Reprisal, and make Rules concerning Captures on Land and Water;

To raise and support Armies, but no Appropriation of Money to that Use shall be for a longer Term than two Years;

To provide and maintain a Navy;

To make Rules for the Government and Regulation of the land and naval Forces;

To provide for calling forth the Militia to execute the Laws of the Union, suppress Insurrections and repel Invasions;

To provide for organizing, arming, and disciplining, the Militia, and for governing such Part of them as may be employed in the Service of the United States, reserving to the States respectively, the Appointment of the Officers, and the Authority of training the Militia according to the discipline prescribed by Congress;

To exercise exclusive Legislation in all Cases whatsoever, over such District (not exceeding ten Miles square) as may, by Cession of particular

States, and the Acceptance of Congress, become the Seat of the Government of the United States, and to exercise like Authority over all Places purchased by the Consent of the Legislature of the State in which the Same shall be, for the Erection of Forts, Magazines, Arsenals, dock-Yards, and other needful Buildings;—And

To make all Laws which shall be necessary and proper for carrying into Execution the foregoing Powers, and all other Powers vested by this Constitution in the Government of the United States, or in any Department or Officer thereof.

Section 9

The Migration or Importation of such Persons as any of the States now existing shall think proper to admit, shall not be prohibited by the Congress prior to the Year one thousand eight hundred and eight, but a Tax or duty may be imposed on such Importation, not exceeding ten dollars for each Person.

The Privilege of the Writ of Habeas Corpus shall not be suspended, unless when in Cases of Rebellion or Invasion the public Safety may require it.

No Bill of Attainder or ex post facto Law shall be passed.

No Capitation, or other direct, Tax shall be laid, unless in Proportion to the Census or Enumeration herein before directed to be taken.

No Tax or Duty shall be laid on Articles exported from any State.

No Preference shall be given to any Regulation of Commerce or Revenue to the Ports of one State over those of another; nor shall Vessels bound to, or from, one State, be obliged to enter, clear or pay Duties in another.

No Money shall be drawn from the Treasury, but in Consequence of Appropriations made by Law; and a regular Statement and Account of the Receipts and Expenditures of all public Money shall be published from time to time.

No Title of Nobility shall be granted by the United States: And no Person holding any Office of Profit or Trust under them, shall, without the Consent of the Congress, accept of any present, Emolument, Office, or Title, of any kind whatever, from any King, Prince or foreign State.

Section 10

No State shall enter into any Treaty, Alliance, or Confederation; grant Letters of Marque and Reprisal; coin Money; emit Bills of Credit; make any Thing but gold and silver Coin a Tender in Payment of Debts; pass any Bill of Attainder, ex post facto Law impairing the Obligation of Contracts, or grant any Title of Nobility.

No State shall, without the Consent of the Congress, lay any Imposts or Duties on Imports or Exports, except what may be absolutely necessary for executing its inspection Laws: and the net Produce of all Duties and Imposts, laid by any State on Imports or Exports, shall be for the Use of the Treasury of the United States; and all such Laws shall be subject to the Revision and Control of the Congress.

No State shall, without the Consent of Congress, lay any Duty on Tonnage, keep Troops, or Ships of War in time of Peace, enter into any Agreement or Compact with another State, or with a foreign Power, or engage in War, unless actually invaded, or in such imminent Danger as will not admit of delay.

Article II

Section I

The executive Power shall be vested in a President of the United States of America. He shall hold his Office during the Term of four Years, and, together with the Vice President, chosen for the same Term, be elected, as follows:

Each State shall appoint, in such Manner as the Legislature thereof may direct, a Number of Electors, equal to the whole Number of Senators and Representatives to which the State may be entitled in the Congress: but no Senator or Representative, or Person holding an Office of Trust or Profit under the United States, shall be appointed an Elector.

The Electors shall meet in their respective States, and vote by Ballot for two Persons, of whom one at least shall not be an Inhabitant of the same State with themselves. And they shall make a List of all the Persons voted for, and of the Number of Votes for each; which List they shall sign and certify, and transmit sealed to the

Seat of the Government of the United States, directed to the President of the Senate. The President of the Senate shall, in the Presence of the Senate and House of Representatives, open all the Certificates, and the Votes shall then be counted. The Person having the greatest Number of Votes shall be the President, if such Number be a Majority of the whole Number of Electors appointed; and if there be more than one who have such Majority, and have an equal Number of Votes, then the House of Representatives shall immediately chuse by Ballot one of them for President; and if no Person have a Majority, then from the five highest on the List the said House shall in like Manner chuse the President. But in chusing the President, the Votes shall be taken by States, the Representation from each State having one Vote; a quorum for this Purpose shall consist of a Member or Members from two thirds of the States, and a Majority of all the States shall be necessary to a Choice. In every Case, after the Choice of the President, the Person having the greatest Number of Votes of the Electors shall be the Vice President. But if there should remain two or more who have equal Votes, the Senate shall chuse from them by Ballot the Vice President.

The Congress may determine the Time of chusing the Electors, and the Day on which they shall give their Votes; which Day shall be the same throughout the United States.

No Person except a natural born Citizen, or a Citizen of the United States, at the time of the Adoption of this Constitution, shall be eligible to the Office of President; neither shall any Person be eligible to that Office who shall not have attained to the Age of thirty five Years, and been fourteen years a Resident within the United States.

In Case of the Removal of the President from Office, or of his Death, Resignation, or Inability to discharge the Powers and Duties of the said Office, the Same shall devolve on the Vice President, and the Congress may by Law provide for the Case of Removal, Death, Resignation, or Inability, both of the President and Vice President, declaring what Officer shall then act as President, and such Officer shall act accordingly, until the Disability be removed, or a President shall be elected.

The President shall, at stated Times, receive for his Services, a Compensation, which shall neither be encreased nor diminished during the Period for which he shall have been elected, and he shall not receive within that Period any other Emolument from the United States, or any of them.

Before he enter on the Execution of his Office, he shall take the following Oath or Affirmation:—"I do solemnly swear (or affirm) that I will faithfully execute the Office of President of the United States, and will to the best of my Ability, preserve, protect, and defend the Constitution of the United States."

Section 2

The President shall be Commander in Chief of the Army and Navy of the United States, and of the Militia of the several States, when called into the actual Service of the United States; he may require the Opinion, in writing, of the principal Officer in each of the executive Departments, upon any Subject relating to the Duties of their respective Offices, and he shall have Power to grant Reprieves and Pardons for Offenses against the United States, except in Cases of Impeachment.

He shall have Power, by and with the Advice and Consent of the Senate, to make Treaties, provided two thirds of the Senators present concur; and he shall nominate, and by and with the Advice and Consent of the Senate, shall appoint Ambassadors, other public Ministers and Consuls, Judges of the supreme Court, and all other Officers of the United States, whose Appointments are not herein otherwise provided for, and which shall be established by Law: but the Congress may by Law vest the Appointment of such inferior Officers, as they think proper, in the President alone, in the Courts of Law, or in the Heads of Departments.

The President shall have Power to fill up all Vacancies that may happen during the Recess of the Senate, by granting Commissions which shall expire at the End of their next Session.

Section 3

He shall from time to time give to the Congress Information of the State of the Union, and recommend to their Consideration such Measures as he shall judge necessary and expedient; he may, on extraordinary Occasions, convene both Houses, or either of them, and in Case of Disagreement between them, with Respect to the Time of Adjournment, he may adjourn them to such Time as he shall think proper; he shall receive Ambassadors and other public Ministers; he shall take Care that the Laws be faithfully executed, and shall Commission all the Officers of the United States.

Section 4

The President, Vice President and all Civil Officers of the United States, shall be removed from Office on Impeachment for, and Conviction of, Treason, Bribery, or other high Crimes and Misdemeanors.

Article III

Section 1

The judicial Power of the United States, shall be vested in one supreme Court, and in such inferior Courts as the Congress may from time to time ordain and establish. The Judges, both of the supreme and inferior Courts, shall hold their Offices during good Behaviour, and shall, at stated Times, receive for their Services, a Compensation, which shall not be diminished during their Continuance in Office.

Section 2

The judicial Power shall extend to all Cases, in Law and Equity, arising under this Constitution, the Laws of the United States, and Treaties made, or which shall be made, under their Authority;—to all Cases affecting Ambassadors, other public Ministers and Consuls;—to all Cases of admiralty and maritime Jurisdiction;—to Controversies to which the United States shall be a Party;—to Controversies between two or more States;—between a State and Citizens of another State;—between Citizens of different States,—between Citizens of the same State claiming Lands under Grants of different States, and between a State, or the Citizens thereof, and foreign States, Citizens or Subjects.

In all Cases affecting Ambassadors, other public Ministers and Consuls, and those in which a State shall be Party, the Supreme Court shall have original Jurisdiction. In all the other Cases before mentioned, the supreme Court shall have appellate Jurisdiction, both as to Law and Fact, with such Exceptions, and under such Regulations as the Congress shall make.

The Trial of all Crimes, except in Cases of Impeachment, shall be by Jury; and such Trial shall be held in the State where the said Crimes shall have been committed; but when not committed within any State, the Trial shall be at such Place or Places as the Congress may by Law have directed.

Section 3

Treason against the United States, shall consist only in levying War against them, or in adhering to their Enemies, giving them Aid and Comfort. No Person shall be convicted of Treason unless on the Testimony of two Witnesses to the same overt Act, or on Confession in open Court.

The Congress shall have Power to declare the Punishment of Treason, but no Attainder of Treason shall work Corruption of Blood, or Forfeiture except during the Life of the Person attainted.

Article IV

Section 1

Full Faith and Credit shall be given in each State to the public Arts, Records, and judicial Proceedings of every other State. And the Congress may by general Laws prescribe the Manner in which such Acts, Records and Proceedings shall be proved, and the Effect thereof.

Section 2

The Citizens of each State shall be entitled to all Privileges and Immunities of Citizens in the several States.

A Person charged in any State with Treason, Felony, or other Crime, who shall flee from Justice, and be found in another State, shall on Demand of the executive Authority of the State from which he fled, be delivered up, to be removed to the State having Jurisdiction of the Crime.

No Person held to Service or Labour in one State, under the Laws thereof, escaping into another, shall, in Consequence of any Law or Regulation therein, be discharged from such Service or Labour, but shall be delivered up on Claim of the Party to whom such Service or Labour may be due.

Section 3

New States may be admitted by the Congress into this Union; but no new State shall be formed or erected within the Jurisdiction of any other State; nor any State be formed by the Junction of two or more States, or Parts of States, without the Consent of the Legislatures of the States concerned as well as of the Congress.

The Congress shall have Power to dispose of and make all needful Rules and Regulations respecting the Territory or other Property belonging to the United States; and nothing in this Constitution shall be so construed as to Prejudice any Claims of the United States, or of any particular State.

Section 4

The United States shall guarantee to every State in this Union a Republican Form of Government, and shall protect each of them against Invasion; and on Application of the Legislature, or of the Executive (when the Legislature cannot be convened) against domestic Violence.

Article V

The Congress, whenever two thirds of both Houses shall deem it necessary, shall propose Amendments to this Constitution, or, on the Application of the Legislatures of two thirds of the several States, shall call a Convention for proposing Amendments, which, in either Case, shall be valid to all Intents and Purposes, as Part of this Constitution, when ratified by the Legislatures of three fourths of the several States, or by Conventions in three fourths thereof, as the one or the other Mode of Ratification may be proposed by the Congress; Provided that no Amendment which may be made prior to the Year One thousand eight hundred and eight shall in any Manner affect the first and fourth Clauses in the Ninth Section of the first Article; and that no State, without its Consent, shall be deprived of its equal Suffrage in the Senate.

Article VI

All Debts contracted and Engagements entered into, before the Adoption of this Constitution, shall be as valid against the United States under this Constitution, as under the Confederation.

This Constitution, and the Laws of the United States which shall be made in Pursuance thereof; and all Treaties made, or which shall be made, under the Authority of the United States, shall be the supreme Law of the Land; and the judges in every State shall be bound thereby, any Thing in the Constitution or Laws of any State to the Contrary notwithstanding.

The Senators and Representatives before mentioned, and the Members of the several State Legislatures, and all executive and judicial Officers, both of the United States and of the several States, shall be bound by Oath or Affirmation, to support this Constitution; but no religious Test shall ever be required as a Qualification to any Office or public Trust under the United States.

Article VII

The Ratification of the Conventions of nine States, shall be sufficient for the Establishment of this Constitution between the States so ratifying the Same.

Amendment I (1791)

Congress shall make no law respecting an establishment of religion, or prohibiting the free exercise thereof; or abridging the freedom of speech, or of the press; or the right of the people peaceably to assemble, and to petition the Government for a redress of grievances.

Amendment II (1791)

A well regulated Militia, being necessary to the security of a free State, the right of the people to keep and bear Arms, shall not be infringed.

Amendment III (1791)

No Soldier shall, in time of peace be quartered in any house, without the consent of the Owner, nor in time of war, but in a manner to be prescribed by law.

Amendment IV (1791)

The right of the people to be secure in their persons, houses, papers, and effects, against unreasonable searches and seizures, shall not be violated, and no Warrants shall issue, but upon probable cause, supported by Oath or affirmation, and particularly describing the place to be searched, and the persons or things to be seized.

Amendment V (1791)

No person shall be held to answer for a capital or otherwise infamous crime, unless on a presentment or indictment of a Grand Jury, except in cases arising in the land or naval forces, or in the Militia, when in actual service in time of War or public danger; nor shall any person be subject for the same offense to be twice put in jeopardy of life or limb; nor shall be compelled in any criminal case to be a witness against himself, nor be deprived of life, liberty, or property, without due process of law; nor shall private property be taken for public use, with out just compensation.

Amendment Vl (1791)

In all criminal prosecutions, the accused shall enjoy the right to a speedy and public trial, by an impartial jury of the State and district wherein the crime shall have been committed, which district shall have been previously ascertained by law, and to be informed of the nature and cause of the accusation; to be confronted with the witnesses against him; to have compulsory process for obtaining Witnesses in his favor, and to have the Assistance of Counsel for his defense.

Amendment VII (1791)

In Suits at common law, where the value in controversy shall exceed twenty dollars, the right of trial by jury shall be preserved, and no fact tried by a jury, shall be otherwise reexamined in any Court of the United States, than according to the rules of the common law.

Amendment VIII (1791)

Excessive bail shall not be required nor excessive fines imposed, nor cruel and unusual punishments inflicted.

Amendment IX (1791)

The enumeration in the Constitution, of certain rights, shall not be construed to deny or disparage others retained by the people.

Amendment X (1791)

The powers not delegated to the United States by the Constitution, nor prohibited by it to the States, are reserved to the States respectively, or to the people.

Amendment XI (1798)

The Judicial power of the United States shall not be construed to extend to any suit in law or equity, commenced or prosecuted against one of the United States by Citizens of another State, or by Citizens or Subjects of any Foreign State.

Amendment XII (1804)

The Electors shall meet in their respective states and vote by ballot for President and Vice President, one of whom, at least, shall not be an inhabitant of the same state with themselves; they shall name in their ballots the person voted for as President, and in distinct ballots the person voted for as Vice-President, and they shall make distinct lists of all persons voted for as President, and of all persons voted for as Vice-President, and of the number of votes for each, which lists they shall sign and certify, and transmit sealed to the seat of the government of the United States, directed to the President of the Senate;—The President of the Senate shall, in the presence of the Senate and House of Representatives, open all the certificates and the votes shall then be counted;— The person having the greatest number of votes for President, shall be the President, if such number be a majority of the whole number of Electors appointed; and if no person have such majority, then from the persons having the highest numbers not exceeding three on the list of those voted for as President, the House of Representatives shall choose immediately, by ballot, the President. But in choosing the President, the votes shall be taken by states, the representation from each state having one vote; a quorum for this purpose shall consist of a member or members from two-thirds of the states, and a majority of all the states shall be necessary to a choice. And if the House of Representatives shall not choose a President whenever the right of choice shall devolve upon them, before the fourth day of March next following, then the Vice-President shall act as President, as in the case of the death or other constitutional disability of the President—The person having the greatest number of votes as Vice-President, shall be the Vice-President, if such number be a majority of the whole number of Electors appointed, and if no person have a majority, then from the two highest numbers on the list, the Senate shall choose the Vice-President; a quorum for the purpose shall consist of two-thirds of the whole numbers of Senators, and a majority of the whole number shall be necessary to a choice. But no person constitutionally ineligible to the office of President shall be eligible to that of Vice President of the United States.

Amendment XIII (1865)

Section I

Neither slavery nor involuntary servitude, except as a punishment for crime whereof the party shall have been duly convicted, shall exist within the United States, or any place subject to their jurisdiction.

Section 2

Congress shall have power to enforce this article by appropriate legislation.

Amendment XIV (1868)

Section 1

All persons born or naturalized in the United States and subject to the jurisdiction thereof, are citizens of the United States and of the State wherein they reside. No State shall make or enforce any law which shall abridge the privileges or immunities of citizens of the United States; nor shall any State deprive any person of life, liberty, or property, without due process of law; nor deny to any person within its jurisdiction the equal protection of the laws.

Section 2

Representatives shall be apportioned among the several States according to their respective numbers, counting the whole number of persons in each State, excluding Indians not taxed. But when the right to vote at any election for the choice of electors for President and Vice President of the United States, Representatives in Congress, the Executive and Judicial officers of a State, or the members of the Legislature thereof, is denied to any of the male inhabitants of such State, being twenty-one years of age, and citizens of the United States, or in any way abridged, except for participation in rebellion, or other crime, the basis of representation therein shall be reduced in the proportion which the number of such male citizens shall bear to the whole number of male citizens twenty-one years of age in such State.

Section 3

No person shall be a Senator or Representative in Congress, or elector of President and Vice President, or hold any office, civil or military, under the United States, or under any State, who, having previously taken an oath, as a member of Congress, or as an officer of the United States, or as a member of any State legislature, or as an executive or judicial officer of any State, to support the Constitution of the United States, shall have engaged in insurrection or rebellion against the same, or given aid or comfort to the enemies thereof. But Congress may by a vote of two-thirds of each House, remove such disability.

Section 4

The validity of the public debt of the United States, authorized by law, including debts incurred for payment of pensions and bounties for services in suppressing insurrection or rebellion, shall not be questioned. But neither the United States nor any State shall assume or pay any debt or obligation incurred in aid of insurrection or rebellion against the United States, or any claim for the loss or emancipation of any slave; but all such debts, obligations and claims shall be held illegal and void.

Section 5

The Congress shall have power to enforce, by appropriate legislation, the provisions of this article.

Amendment XV (1870)

Section I

The right of citizens of the United States to vote shall not be denied or abridged by the United States or by any State on account of race, color, or previous condition of servitude.

Section 2

The Congress shall have power to enforce this article by appropriate legislation.

Amendment XVI (1913)

The Congress shall have power to lay and collect taxes on incomes, from whatever source derived, without apportionment among the several States, and without regard to any census or enumeration.

Amendment XVII (1913)

The Senate of the United States shall be composed of two Senators from each State, elected by the people thereof, for six years; and each Senator shall have one vote. The electors in each State shall have the qualifications requisite for electors of the most numerous branch of the State legislatures.

When vacancies happen in the representation of any State in the Senate, the executive authority of such State shall issue writs of election to fill such vacancies: *Provided,* That the legislature of any State may empower the executive thereof to make temporary appointments until the people fill the vacancies by election as the legislature may direct.

This amendment shall not be so construed as to affect the election or term of any Senator chosen before it becomes valid as part of the Constitution.

Amendment XVIII (1919)

Section I

After one year from the ratification of this article the manufacture, sale, or transportation of intoxicating liquors within, the importation thereof into, or the exportation thereof from the United States and all territory subject to the jurisdiction thereof for beverage purposes is hereby prohibited.

Section 2

The Congress and the several States shall have concurrent power to enforce this article by appropriate legislation.

Section 3

This article shall be inoperative unless it shall have been ratified as an amendment to the Constitution by the legislatures of the several States, as provided in the Constitution, within seven years from the date of the submission hereof to the States by the Congress.

Amendment XlX (1920)

The right of citizens of the United States to vote shall not be denied or abridged by the United States or by any State on account of sex.

Congress shall have power to enforce this article by appropriate legislation.

Amendment XX (1933)

Section I

The terms of the President and Vice President shall end at noon on the 20th day of January, and the terms of Senators and Representatives at noon on the 3d day of January, of the years in which such terms would have ended if this article had not been ratified; and the terms of their successors shall then begin.

Section 2

The Congress shall assemble at least once in every year, and such meeting shall begin at noon on the 3d day of January, unless they shall by law appoint a different day.

Section 3

If, at the time fixed for the beginning of the term of the President, the President elect shall have died, the Vice President elect shall be come President. If a President shall not have been chosen before the time fixed for the beginning of his term, or if the President elect shall have failed to qualify, then the Vice President elect shall act as President until a President shall have qualified; and the Congress may by law provide for the case wherein neither a President elect nor a Vice President elect shall have qualified, declaring who shall then act as President, or the manner in which one who is to act shall be selected, and such person shall act accordingly until a President or Vice President shall have qualified.

Section 4

The Congress may by law provide for the case of the death of any of the persons from whom the House of Representatives may choose a President whenever the right of choice shall have devolved upon them, and for the case of the death of any of the persons from whom the Senate may choose a Vice President whenever the right of choice shall have devolved upon them.

Section 5

Sections 1 and 2 shall take effect on the 15th day of October following the ratification of this article.

Section 6

This article shall be inoperative unless it shall have been ratified as an amendment to the Constitution by the legislatures of three fourths of the several States within seven years from the date of its submission.

Amendment XXI (1933)

Section I

The eighteenth article of amendment to the Constitution of the United States is hereby repealed.

Section 2

The transportation or importation into any State, Territory, or possession of the United States for delivery or use therein of intoxicating liquors, in violation of the laws thereof, is hereby prohibited.

Section 3

This article shall be inoperative unless it shall have been ratified as an amendment to the Constitution by conventions in the several States, as provided in the Constitution, within seven years from the date of the submission hereof to the States by the Congress.

Amendment XXII (1951)

Section I

No person shall be elected to the office of the President more than twice, and no person, who has held the office of President, or acted as President, for more than two years of a term to which some other person was elected President shall be elected to the Office of the President more than once. But this Article shall not apply to any person holding the office of President when this Article was proposed by the Congress, and shall not prevent any person who may be holding the office of President, or acting as President, during the term within which this Article becomes operative from holding the Office of President or acting as President during the remainder of such term.

Section 2

This article shall be inoperative unless it shall have been ratified as an amendment to the Constitution by the legislatures of three fourths of the several States within seven years from the date of its submission to the States by the Congress.

Amendment XXIII (1961)

Section 1

The District constituting the seat of Government of the United States shall appoint in such manner as the Congress may direct:

A number of electors of President and Vice President equal to the whole number of Senators and Representatives in Congress to which the District would be entitled if it were a State, but in no event more than the least populous State; they shall be in addition to those appointed by the States, but they shall be considered, for the purposes of the election of President and Vice President, to be electors appointed by a State; and they shall meet in the District and perform such duties as provided by the twelfth article of amendment.

Section 2

The Congress shall have power to enforce this article by appropriate legislation.

Amendment XXIV (1964)

Section I

The right of citizens of the United States to vote in any primary or other election for President or Vice President, for electors for President or Vice President, or for Senator or Representative in Congress, shall not be denied or abridged by the United States or any State by reason of failure to pay any poll tax or other tax.

Section 2

The Congress shall have power to enforce this article by appropriate legislation.

Amendment XXV (1967)

Section I

In case of the removal of the President from office or of his death or resignation, the Vice President shall become President.

Section 2

Whenever there is a vacancy in the office of the Vice President, the President shall nominate a Vice President who shall take office upon confirmation by a majority vote of both Houses of Congress.

Section 3

Whenever the President transmits to the President pro tempore of the Senate and the Speaker of the House of Representatives his written declaration that he is unable to discharge the powers and duties of his office, and until he transmits to them a written declaration to the contrary, such powers and duties shall be discharged by the Vice President as Acting President.

Section 4

Whenever the Vice President and a majority of either the principal officers of the executive departments or of such other body as Congress may by law provide, transmit to the President pro tempore of the Senate and the Speaker of the House of Representatives their written declaration that the President is unable to discharge the powers and duties of his office, the Vice President shall immediately assume the powers and duties of the office as Acting President.

Thereafter, when the President transmits to the President pro tempore of the Senate and the Speaker of the House of Representatives his written declaration that no inability exists, he shall resume the powers and duties of his Office unless the Vice President and a majority of either the principal officers of the executive department or of such other body as Congress may by law provide, transmit within four days to the President pro tempore of the Senate and the Speaker of the House of Representatives their written declaration that the President is unable to discharge the powers and duties of his office. Thereupon Congress shall decide the issue, assembling within forty-eight hours for that purpose if not in session. If the Congress, within twenty-one days after receipt of the latter written declaration, or, if Congress is not in session, within twenty-one days after Congress is required to assemble, determines by two-thirds vote of both Houses that the President is unable to discharge the powers and duties of his office, the Vice President shall continue to discharge the same as Acting President; otherwise, the President shall resume the powers and duties of his office.

Amendment XXVI (1971)

Section 1

The right of citizens of the United States, who are eighteen years of age or older, to vote shall not be denied or abridged by the United States or by any State on account of age.

Section 2

The Congress shall have power to enforce this article by appropriate legislation.

Amendment XXVII (1992)

No law varying the compensation for services of the Senators and Representatives shall take effect until an election of representatives shall have intervened.

ADMINISTRATIVE PROCEDURES ACT (EXCERPTS)

Section 552. Public Information; Agency Rules, Opinions, Orders, Records, and Proceedings (the Freedom of Information Act)

(a) Each agency shall make available to the public information as follows:

(1) Each agency shall separately state and currently publish in the Federal Register for the guidance of the public—

(A) descriptions of its central and field organization and the established places at which, the employees (and in the case of a uniformed service, the members) from whom, and the methods whereby, the public may obtain information, make submittals or requests, or obtain decisions;

(B) statements of the general course and method by which its functions are channeled and determined, including the nature and requirements of all formal and informal procedures available;

(C) rules of procedure, descriptions of forms available or the places at which forms may be obtained, and instructions as to the scope and contents of all papers, reports, or examinations;

(D) substantive rules of general applicability adopted as authorized by law, and statements of general policy or interpretations of general applicability formulated and adopted by the agency; and

(E) each amendment, revision, or repeal of the foregoing.

Section 552b. Open Meetings ("Sunshine Law")

(a) For purposes of this section—

(1) the term "agency" means any agency, as defined in section 552 (e) of this title, headed by a collegial body composed of two or more individual members, a majority of whom are appointed to such position by the President with the advice and consent of the Senate, and any subdivision thereof authorized to act on behalf of the agency;

(2) the term "meeting" means the deliberations of at least the number of individual agency members required to take action on behalf of the agency where such deliberations determine or result in the joint conduct or disposition of official agency business, but does not include deliberations required or permitted by subsection (d) or (e); and

(3) the term "member" means an individual who belongs to a collegial body heading an agency.

(b) Members shall not jointly conduct or dispose of agency business other than in accordance with this section.

Section 553. Rule Making

(c) After notice required by this section, the agency shall give interested persons an opportunity to participate in the rule making through submission of written data, views, or arguments with or without opportunity for oral presentation. After consideration of the relevant matter presented, the agency shall incorporate in the rules adopted a concise general statement of their basis and purpose. When rules are required by statute to be made on the record after opportunity for an agency hearing, sections 556 and 557 of this title apply instead of this subsection.

(d) The required publication or service of a substantive rule shall be made not less than 30 days before its effective date, except—

(1) a substantive rule which grants or recognizes an exemption or relieves a restriction;

(2) interpretive rules and statements of policy; or

(3) as otherwise provided by the agency for good cause found and published with the rule.

(e) Each agency shall give an interested person the right to petition for the issuance, amendment, or repeal of a rule.

Section 603. Initial Regulatory Flexibility Analysis

(a) Whenever an agency is required by section 553 of this title, or any other law, to publish general notice of proposed rulemaking for any proposed rule, the agency shall prepare and make available for public comment an initial regulatory flexibility analysis. Such analysis shall describe the impact of the proposed rule on small entities. The initial regulatory flexibility analysis or a summary shall be published in the Federal Register at the time of the publication of general notice of proposed rulemaking for the rule. The agency shall transmit a copy of the initial regulatory flexibility analysis to the Chief Counsel for Advocacy of the Small Business Administration.

(b) Each initial regulatory flexibility analysis required under this section shall contain—

(1) a description of the reasons why action by the agency is being considered;

(2) a succinct statement of the objectives of, the legal basis for, the proposed rule;

(3) a description of and, where feasible, an estimate of the number of small entities to which the proposed rule will apply;

(4) a description of the projected reporting, recordkeeping and other compliance requirements of the proposed rule, including an estimate of the classes of small entities which will be subject to the requirement and the type of professional skills necessary for preparation of the report or record;

(5) an identification, to the extent practicable, of all relevant Federal rules which may duplicate, overlap or conflict with the proposed rule.

(c) Each initial regulatory flexibility analysis shall also contain a description of any significant alternatives to the proposed rule which accomplish the stated objectives of applicable statutes and which minimize any significant economic impact of the proposed rule on small entities. Consistent with the stated objectives of applicable statutes, the analysis shall discuss significant alternatives such as—

(1) the establishment of differing compliance or reporting requirements or timetables that take into account the resources available to small entities;

(2) the clarification, consolidation, or simplification of compliance and reporting requirements under the rule for such small entities;

(3) the use of performance rather than design standards; and

(4) the exemption from coverage of the rule, or any part thereof, for such small entities.

Appendix C

TITLE VII OF THE CIVIL RIGHTS ACT OF 1964 (EXCERPTS)

Section 703. Unlawful Employment Practices

Employer Practices

(a) It shall be an unlawful employment practice for an employer—

(1) to fail or refuse to hire or to discharge any individual, or otherwise to discriminate against any individual with respect to his compensation, terms, conditions, or privileges of employment, because of such individual's race, color, religion, sex, or national origin; or

(2) to limit, segregate, or classify his employees or applicants for employment in any way which would deprive or tend to deprive any individual of employment opportunities or otherwise adversely affect his status as an employee, because of such individual's race, color, religion, sex, or national origin.

Employment Agency Practices

(b) It shall be an unlawful employment practice for an employment agency to fail or refuse to refer for employment, or otherwise to discriminate against, any individual because of his race, color, religion, sex, or national origin, or to classify or refer for employment any individual on the basis of his race, color, religion, sex, or national origin.

Labor Organization Practices

(c) It shall be an unlawful employment practice for a labor organization—

(1) to exclude or to expel from its membership, or otherwise to discriminate against, any individual because of his race, color, religion, sex, or national origin;

(2) to limit, segregate, or classify its membership or applicants for membership, or to classify or fail or refuse to refer to employment any individual, in any way which would deprive or tend to deprive any individual of employment opportunities, or would limit such employment opportunities or otherwise adversely affect his status as an employee or as an applicant for employment, because of such individual's race, color, religion, sex, or national origin; or

(3) to cause or attempt to cause an employer to discriminate against an individual in violation of this section.

Training Programs

(d) It shall be an unlawful employment practice for any employer, labor organization, or joint labor-management committee, controlling apprenticeship or other training or retraining, including on-the-job training programs to discriminate against any individual because of his race, color, religion, sex, or national origin in admission to, or employment in, any program established to provide apprenticeship or other training.

Businesses or Enterprises with Personnel Qualified on Basis of Religion, Sex, or National Origin; Educational Institutions with Personnel of Particular Religion

(e) Notwithstanding any other provision of this subchapter, (1) it shall not be an unlawful employment practice for an employer to hire and employ employees, for an employment agency to classify or refer for employment any individual, for a labor organization to classify its membership or to classify or refer for employment any individual, or for an employer, labor organization, or joint labor-management committee controlling apprenticeship or other training or retraining programs to admit or employ any individual in any such program, on the basis of his religion, sex, or national origin in those certain instances where religion, sex, or national origin is a bona fide occupational qualification reasonably necessary to the normal operation of that particular business or enterprise, and (2) it shall not be an unlawful employment practice for a school, college, university, or other educational institution or institution of learning to hire and employ employees of a particular religion if such school, college, university, or other educational institution or institution of learning is, in whole or in substantial part, owned, supported, controlled, or managed by a particular religion or by a particular religious corporation, association, or society, or if the curriculum of such school, college, university, or other educational institution or institution of learning is directed toward the propagation of a particular religion.

Seniority or Merit System; Quantity or Quality of Production, Ability Tests; Compensation Based on Sex and Authorized by Minimum Wage Provisions

(h) Notwithstanding any other provisions of this subchapter, it shall not be an unlawful employment practice for an employer to apply different standards of compensation, or different terms, conditions, or privileges of employment pursuant to a bona fide seniority or merit system, or a system which measures earnings by quantity or quality of production or to employees who work in different locations, provided that such differences are not the result of an intention to discriminate because of race, color, religion, sex, or national origin, nor shall it be an unlawful employment practice for an employer to give and to act upon the

results of any professionally developed ability test provided that such test, its administration or action upon the results is not designed, intended or used to discriminate because of race, color, religion, sex, or national origin. It shall not be an unlawful employment practice under this subchapter for any employer to differentiate upon the basis of sex in determining the amount of the wages or compensation paid or to be paid to employees of such employer if such differentiation is authorized by the provisions of section 206(d)) of Title 29.

Section 704. Other Unlawful Employment Practices

Discrimination for Making Charges, Testifying, Assisting, or Participating in Enforcement Proceedings

(a) It shall be an unlawful employment practice for an employer to discriminate against any of his employees or applicants for employment, for an employment agency, or joint labor-management committee controlling apprenticeship or other training or retraining, including on-the-job training programs to discriminate against any individual, or for a labor organization to discriminate against any member thereof or applicant for membership, because he has opposed any practice, made an unlawful employment practice by this subchapter, or because he has made a charge, testified, assisted, or participated in any manner in an investigation, proceeding, or hearing under this subchapter.

Printing or Publication of Notices or Advertisements Indicating Prohibited Preference, Limitation, Specification, or Discrimination; Occupational Qualification Exception

(b) It shall be an unlawful employment practice for an employer, labor organization, employment agency, or joint labor-management committee controlling apprenticeship or other training or retraining, including on-the-job training programs, to print or publish or cause to be printed or published any notice or advertisement relating to employment by such an employer or membership in or any classification or referral for employment by such a labor organization, or relating to any classification or referral for employment by such an employment agency, or relating to admission to, or employment in, any program established to provide apprenticeship or other training by such a joint labor-management committee, indicating any preference, limitation, specification, or discrimination, based on race, color, religion, sex, or national origin, except that such a notice or advertisement may indicate a preference, limitation, specification, or discrimination based on religion, sex, or national origin when religion, sex, or national origin is a bona fide occupational qualification for employment.

Appendix D

CIVIL RIGHTS ACT
OF 1991
(EXCERPTS)

§ 1981. Equal rights under the law

(a) All persons within the jurisdiction of the United States shall have the same right in every State and Territory to make and enforce contracts, to sue, be parties, give evidence, and to the full and equal benefit of all laws and proceedings for the security of persons and property as is enjoyed by white citizens, and shall be subject to like punishment, pains, penalties, taxes, licenses, and exactions of every kind, and to no other.

(b) For purposes of this section, the term "make and enforce contracts" includes the making, performance, modification, and termination of contracts, and the enjoyment of all benefits, privileges, terms, and conditions of the contractual relationship.

(c) The rights protected by this section are protected against impairment by nongovernmental discrimination and impairment under color of State law.

§ 1981a. Damages in cases of intentional discrimination in employment

(a) Right of recovery. (1) Cell rights. In an action brought by a complaining party under section 706 or 717 of the Civil Rights Act of 1964 (42 U.S.C. § 2000e-5 [or 2000e-16]) against a respondent who engaged in unlawful intentional discrimination (not an employment practice that is unlawful because of its disparate impact) prohibited under section 703, 704, or 717 of the Act (42 U.S.C. § 2000e-2 or 2000e-3 [or 2000e-16), and provided that the complaining party cannot recover under section 1977 of the Revised Statutes (42 U.S.C. § 1981), the complaining party may recover compensatory and punitive damages as allowed in subsection (b), in addition to any relief authorized by section 706(g)) of the Civil Rights Act of 1964 [42 USCS § 2000e-5(g)], from the respondent.

(2) Disability. In an action brought by a complaining party under the powers, remedies, and

procedures set forth in section 706 or 717 of the Civil Rights Act of 1964 [42 USCS § 2000e-5(g)] (as provided in section 107(a)) of the Americans with Disabilities Act of 1990 (42 U.S.C. § 12117(a)), and section 505(a) (1) of the Rehabilitation Act of 1973 (29 U.S.C. § 794a(a) (1)), respectively) against a respondent who engaged in unlawful intentional discrimination (not an employment practice that is unlawful because of its disparate impact) under section 501 of the Rehabilitation Act of 1973 (29 U.S.C. § 791) and the regulations implementing section 501 [29 USCS § 791], or who violated the requirements of section 501 of the Act [29 USCS § 791] or the regulations implementing section 501 [29 USCS § 791] concerning the provision of a reasonable accommodation, or section 102 of the Americans with Disabilities Act of 1990 (42 U.S.C. § 12112), or committed a violation of section 102(b) (5) of the Act [42 USCS § 12112(b) (5)], against an individual, the complaining party may recover compensatory and punitive damages as allowed in subsection (b), in addition to any relief authorized by section 706 (g) of the Civil Rights Act of 1964 [42 U.S.C. § 2000e-5(g)], from the respondent.

(3) Reasonable accommodation and good faith effort. In cases where a discriminatory practice involves the provision of a reasonable accommodation pursuant to section 102 (b) (5) of the Americans with Disabilities Act of 1990 [42 USCS § 12112 (b) (5)] or regulations implementing section 501 of the Rehabilitation Act of 1973 [29 USCS § 791], damages may not be awarded under this section where the covered entity demonstrates good faith efforts in consultation with the person with the disability who has informed the covered entity that accommodation is needed, to identify and make a reasonable accommodation that would provide such individual with an equally effective opportunity and would not cause an undue hardship on the operation of the business.

(b) Compensatory and punitive damages.

(1) Determination of punitive damages. A complaining party may recover punitive damages under this section against a respondent (other than a government, government agency or political subdivision) if the complaining party demonstrates that the respondent engaged in a discriminatory practice or discriminatory practices with malice or with reckless indifference to the federally protected rights of an aggrieved individual.

(2) Exclusions from compensatory damages. Compensatory damages awarded under this section shall not include backpay, interest on backpay, or any other type of relief authorized under section 706(g) of the Civil Rights Act of 1964 [42 USCS § 2000e-5(g)].

(3) Limitations. The sum of the amount of compensatory damages awarded under this section for future pecuniary losses, emotional pain, suffering, inconvenience, mental anguish, loss of enjoyment of life, and other nonpecuniary losses, and the amount of punitive damages awarded under this section, shall not exceed, for each complaining party—

(A) in the case of a respondent who has more than 14 and fewer than 101 employees in each of 20 or more calendar weeks in the current or preceding calendar year, $50,000;

(B) in the case of a respondent who has more than 100 and fewer than 201 employees in each of 20 or more calendar weeks in the current or preceding calendar year, $100,000; and

(C) in the case of a respondent who has more than 200 and fewer than 501 employees in each of 20 or more calendar weeks in the current or preceding calendar year, $200,000; and

(D) in the case of a respondent who has more than 500 employees in each of 20 or more calendar weeks in the current or preceding calendar year, $300,000.

(4) Construction. Nothing in this section shall be construed to limit the scope of, or the relief available under, section 1977 of the Revised Statutes (42 U.S.C. § 1981).

(c) Jury trial. If a complaining party seeks compensatory or punitive damages under this section—

(1) any party may demand a trial by jury; and

(2) the court shall not inform the jury of the limitations described in subsection (b) (3).

(d) Definitions. As used in this section:

(1) Complaining party. The term "complaining party" means—

(A) in the case of a person seeking to bring an action under subsection (a) (1), the Equal

Employment Opportunity Commission, the Attorney General, or a person who may bring an action or proceeding under title VII of the Civil Rights Act of 1964 (42 U.S.C. §§ 2000e et seq.); or

(B) in the case of a person seeking to bring an action under subsection (a) (2), the Equal Employment Opportunity Commission, the Attorney General, a person who may bring an action or proceeding under section 505 (a) (1) of the Rehabilitation Act of 1973 (29 U.S.C. § 794a (a) (1)), or a person who may bring an action or proceeding under title I of the Americans with Disabilities Act of 1990 (42 U.S.C. §§ 12101 et seq.).

(2) Discriminatory practice. The term "discriminatory practice" means the discrimination described in paragraph (1), or the discrimination or the violation described in paragraph (2), of subsection (a).

Appendix E

AMERICANS WITH DISABILITIES ACT OF 1990 (EXCERPTS)

Title I—Employment

Sec. 101. Definitions.

As used in this title: . . .

(8) **Qualified individual with a disability.—** The term "qualified individual with a disability" means an individual with a disability who, with or without reasonable accommodation, can perform the essential functions of the employment position that such individual holds or desires. For the purposes of this title, consideration shall be given to the employer's judgment as to what functions of a job are essential, and if an employer has prepared a written description before advertising or interviewing applicants for the job, this description shall be considered evidence of the essential functions of the job.

(9) **Reasonable accommodation.—**The term "reasonable accommodation" may include—

(A) making existing facilities used by employees readily accessible to and usable by individuals with disabilities; and

(B) job restructuring, part-time or modified work schedules, reassignment to a vacant position, acquisition or modification of equipment or devices, appropriate adjustment or modifications of examinations, training materials or policies, the provision of qualified readers or interpreters, and other similar accommodations for individuals with disabilities.

(10) **Undue Hardship.—**

(A) **In general.—**The term "undue hardship" means an action requiring significant difficulty or expense, when considered in light of the factors set forth in subparagraph (B).

(B) **Factors to be considered.—**In determining whether an accommodation would impose an undue hardship on a covered entity, factors to be considered include—

(i) the nature and cost of accommodation needed under this Act;

(ii) the overall financial resources of the facility or facilities involved in the provision of the reasonable accommodation; the number of persons employed at such facility; the effect on expenses and resources, or the impact otherwise of such accommodation upon the operation of the facility;

(iii) the overall financial resources of the covered entity; the overall size of the business of a covered entity with respect to the number of its employees; the number, type, and location of its facilities; and

(iv) the type of operation or operations of the covered entity, including the composition, structure, and functions of the workforce of such entity; the geographic separateness, administrative, or fiscal relationship of the facility or facilities in question to the covered entity.

Sec. 102. Discrimination.

(a) **General Rule.**—No covered entity shall discriminate against a qualified individual with a disability because of the disability of such individual in regard to job application procedures, the hiring, advancement, or discharge of employees, employee compensation, job training, and other terms, conditions, and privileges of employment.

(b) **Construction.**—As used in subsection (a), the term "discriminate" includes—

(1) limiting, segregating, or classifying a job applicant or employee in a way that adversely affects the opportunities or status of such applicant or employee because of the disability of such applicant or employee;

(2) participating in a contractual or other arrangement or relationship that has the effect of subjecting a covered entity's qualified applicant or employee with a disability to the discrimination prohibited by this title (such relationship includes a relationship with an employment or referral agency, labor union, an organization providing fringe benefits to an employee of the covered entity, or an organization providing training and apprenticeship programs);

(3) utilizing standards, criteria, or methods of administration—

(A) that have the effect of discrimination on the basis of disability; or

(B) that perpetuate the discrimination of others who are subject to common administrative control;

(4) excluding or otherwise denying equal jobs or benefits to a qualified individual because of the known disability of an individual with whom the qualified individual is known to have a relationship or association;

(5) (A) not making reasonable accommodations to the known physical or mental limitations of an otherwise qualified individual with a disability who is an applicant or employee, unless such covered entity can demonstrate that the accommodation would impose an undue hardship on the operation of the business of such covered entity; or

(B) denying employment opportunities to a job applicant or employee who is an otherwise qualified individual with a disability, if such denial is based on the need of such covered entity to make reasonable accommodation to the physical or mental impairments of the employee or applicant;

(6) using qualification standards, employment tests or other selection criteria that screen out or tend to screen out an individual with a disability or a class of individuals with disabilities unless the standard, test or other selection criteria, as used by the covered entity, is shown to be job- related for the position in question and is consistent with business necessity; and

(7) failing to select and administer tests concerning employment in the most effective manner to ensure that, when such test is administered to a job applicant or employee who has a disability that impairs sensory, manual, or speaking skills, such test results accurately reflect the skills, aptitude, or whatever other factor of such applicant or employee that such test purports to measure, rather than reflecting the impaired sensory, manual, or speaking skills of such employee or applicant (except where such skills are the factors that the test purports to measure). . . .

Sec. 104. Illegal Use of Drugs and Alcohol. . . .

(b) **Rules of Construction.**—Nothing in subsection (a) shall be construed to exclude as a qualified individual with a disability an individual who—

(1) has successfully completed a supervised drug rehabilitation program and is no longer engaging in the illegal use of drugs, or has otherwise been rehabilitated successfully and is no longer engaging in such use;

(2) is participating in a supervised rehabilitation program and is no longer engaging in such use; or

(3) is erroneously regarded as engaging in such use, but is not engaging in such use; except that it shall not be a violation of this Act for a covered entity to adopt or administer reasonable policies or procedures, including but not limited to drug testing, designed to ensure that an individual described in paragraph (1) or (2) is no longer engaging in the illegal use of drugs. . . .

Appendix F

FAMILY AND MEDICAL LEAVE ACT

29 U.S.C. § 2601 *et seq.*
§ 2601. Findings and purposes

(a) Findings

Congress finds that —

(1) the number of single-parent households and two-parent households in which the single parent or both parents work is increasing significantly;

(2) it is important for the development of children and the family unit that fathers and mothers be able to participate in early childrearing and the care of family members who have serious health conditions;

(3) the lack of employment policies to accommodate working parents can force individuals to choose between job security and parenting;

(4) there is inadequate job security for employees who have serious health conditions that prevent them from working for temporary periods;

(5) due to the nature of the roles of men and women in our society, the primary responsibility for family caretaking often falls on women, and such responsibility affects the working lives of women more than it affects the working lives of men; and

(6) employment standards that apply to one gender only have serious potential for encouraging employers to discriminate against employees and applicants for employment who are of that gender.

(b) Purposes

It is the purpose of this Act —

(1) to balance the demands of the workplace with the needs of families, to promote the stability and economic security of families, and to promote national interests in preserving family integrity;

(2) to entitle employees to take reasonable leave for medical reasons, for the birth or adoption of a child, and for the care of a child, spouse, or parent who has a serious health condition;

(3) to accomplish the purposes described in paragraphs (1) and (2) in a manner that accommodates the legitimate interests of employers;

(4) to accomplish the purposes described in paragraphs (1) and (2) in a manner that, consistent with the Equal Protection Clause of the Fourteenth Amendment, minimizes the potential for employment discrimination on the basis of sex by ensuring generally that leave is available for eligible medical reasons (including maternity-related disability) and for compelling family reasons, on a gender-neutral basis; and

(5) to promote the goal of equal employment opportunity for women and men, pursuant to such clause.

§ 2611. Definitions

(2) Eligible employee

(A) In general
The term "eligible employee" means an employee who has been employed—

(i) for at least 12 months by the employer with respect to whom leave is requested under section 2612 of this title; and

(ii) for at least 1,250 hours of service with such employer during the previous 12-month period.

(B) Exclusions
The term "eligible employee" does not include—

(i) any Federal officer or employee covered under subchapter V of chapter 63 of Title 5; or

(ii) any employee of an employer who is employed at a worksite at which such employer employs less than 50 employees if the total number of employees employed by that employer within 75 miles of that worksite is less than 50.

§ 2612. Leave requirement

(a) In general

(1) Entitlement to leave
Subject to section 2613 of this title, an eligible employee shall be entitled to a total of 12 workweeks of leave during any 12-month period for one or more of the following:

(A) Because of the birth of a son or daughter of the employee and in order to care for such son or daughter.

(B) Because of the placement of a son or daughter with the employee for adoption or foster care.

(C) In order to care for the spouse, or a son, daughter, or parent, of the employee, if such spouse, son, daughter, or parent has a serious health condition.

(D) Because of a serious health condition that makes the employee unable to perform the functions of the position of such employee.

(2) Expiration of entitlement
The entitlement to leave under subparagraphs (A) and (B) of paragraph (1) for a birth or placement of a son or daughter shall expire at the end of the 12-month period beginning on the date of such birth or placement.

(b) Leave taken intermittently or on a reduced leave schedule

(1) In general
Leave under subparagraph (A) or (B) of subsection (a)(1) of this section shall not be taken by an employee intermittently or on a reduced leave schedule unless the employee and the employer of the employee agree otherwise. Subject to paragraph (2), subsection (e)(2) of this section, and section 2613(b)(5) of this title, leave under subparagraph (C) or (D) of subsection (a)(1) of this section may be taken intermittently or on a reduced leave schedule when medically necessary. The taking of leave intermittently or on a reduced leave schedule pursuant to this paragraph shall not result in a reduction in the total amount of leave to which the employee is entitled under subsection (a) of this section beyond the amount of leave actually taken.

(2) Alternative position
If an employee requests intermittent leave, or leave on a reduced leave schedule, under subparagraph (C) or (D) of subsection (a)(1) of this section, that is foreseeable based on planned medical treatment, the employer may require such employee to transfer temporarily to an available alternative position offered by the employer for which the employee is qualified and that —

(A) has equivalent pay and benefits; and

(B) better accommodates recurring periods of leave than the regular employment position of the employee.

(c) Unpaid leave permitted

Except as provided in subsection (d) of this section, leave granted under subsection (a) of this section may consist of unpaid leave. Where an employee is otherwise exempt under regulations issued by the Secretary pursuant to section 213(a)(1) of this title, the compliance of an employer with this subchapter by providing unpaid leave shall not affect the exempt status of the employee under such section.

(d) Relationship to paid leave

(1) Unpaid leave
If an employer provides paid leave for fewer than 12 workweeks, the additional weeks of leave nec-

essary to attain the 12 workweeks of leave required under this subchapter may be provided without compensation.

(2) Substitution of paid leave
(A) In general
An eligible employee may elect, or an employer may require the employee, to substitute any of the accrued paid vacation leave, personal leave, or family leave of the employee for leave provided under subparagraph (A), (B), or (C) of subsection (a)(1) of this section for any part of the 12-week period of such leave under such subsection.
(B) Serious health condition
An eligible employee may elect, or an employer may require the employee, to substitute any of the accrued paid vacation leave, personal leave, or medical or sick leave of the employee for leave provided under subparagraph (C) or (D) of subsection (a)(1) of this section for any part of the 12-week period of such leave under such subsection, except that nothing in this subchapter shall require an employer to provide paid sick leave or paid medical leave in any situation in which such employer would not normally provide any such paid leave.

§ 2614. Employment and benefits protection

(a) Restoration to position

(1) In general
Except as provided in subsection (b) of this section, any eligible employee who takes leave under section 2612 of this title for the intended purpose of the leave shall be entitled, on return from such leave —
(A) to be restored by the employer to the position of employment held by the employee when the leave commenced; or
(B) to be restored to an equivalent position with equivalent employment benefits, pay, and other terms and conditions of employment.

(2) Loss of benefits
The taking of leave under section 2612 of this title shall not result in the loss of any employment benefit accrued prior to the date on which the leave commenced.

(3) Limitations
Nothing to this section shall be construed to entitle any restored employee to —
(A) the accrual of any seniority or employment benefits during any period of leave; or
(B) any right, benefit, or position of employment other than any right, benefit, or position to which the employee would have been entitled had the employee not taken the leave.

§ 2617. Enforcement

(a) Civil action by employees

(1) Liability
Any employer who violates section 2615 of this title shall be liable to any eligible employee affected —
(A) for damages equal to —
(i) the amount of —
(I) any wages, salary, employment benefits, or other compensation denied or lost to such employee by reason of the violation; or
(II) in a case in which wages, salary, employment benefits, or other compensation have not been denied or lost to the employee, any actual monetary losses sustained by the employee as a direct result of the violation, such as the cost of providing care, up to a sum equal to 12 weeks of wages or salary for the employee;
(ii) the interest on the amount described in clause (I) calculated at the prevailing rate; and
(iii) an additional amount as liquidated damages equal to the sum of the amount described in clause (I) and the interest described in clause (ii), except that if an employer who has violated section 2615 of this title proves to the satisfaction of the court that the act or omission which violated section 2615 of this title was in good faith and that the employer had reasonable grounds for believing that the act or omission was not a violation of section 2615 of this title, such court may, in the discretion of the court, reduce the amount of the liability to the amount and interest determined under clauses (i)and (ii), respectively; and
(B) for such equitable relief as may be appropriate, including employment reinstatement, and promotion.

Appendix G

THE UNIFORM COMMERCIAL CODE (EXCERPTS)

ARTICLE I GENERAL PROVISIONS

Part 1 Short Title, Construction, Application and Subject Matter of the Act

Section I—203. Obligation of Good Faith

Every contract or duty within this Act imposes an obligation of good faith in its performance or enforcement.

Section 1—205. Course of Dealing and Usage of Trade

(1) A course of dealing is a sequence of previous conduct between the parties to a particular transaction which is fairly to be regarded as establishing a common basis of understanding for interpreting their expressions and other conduct.

(2) A usage of trade is any practice or method of dealing having such regularity of observance in a place, vocation or trade as to justify an expectation that it will be observed with respect to the transaction in question. The existence and scope of such a usage are to be proved as facts. If it is established that such a usage is embodied in a written trade code or similar writing the interpretation of the writing is for the court.

(3) A course of dealing between parties and any usage of trade in the vocation or trade in which they are engaged or of which they are or should be aware give particular meaning to and supplement or qualify terms of an agreement.

(4) The express terms of an agreement and an applicable course of dealing or usage of trade shall be construed wherever reasonable as consistent with each other; but when such construction is unreasonable express terms control both course of dealing and usage of trade and course of dealing controls usage of trade.

(5) An applicable usage of trade in the place where any part of performance is to occur shall be used in interpreting the agreement as to that part of the performance.

(6) Evidence of a relevant usage of trade offered by one party is not admissible unless and until he has given the other party such notice as the court finds sufficient to prevent unfair surprise to the latter.

Section 1—206. Statute of Frauds for Kinds of Personal Property Not Otherwise Covered

(1) Except in the cases described in subsection (2) of this section a contract for the sale of personal property is not enforceable by way of action or defense beyond five thousand dollars in amount or value of remedy unless there is some writing which indicates that a contract for sale has been made between the parties at a defined or stated price, reasonably identifies the subject matter, and is signed by the party against whom

enforcement is sought or by his authorized agent.

(2) Subsection (1) of this section does not apply to contracts for the sale of goods (Section 2—201) nor of securities (Section 8—319) nor to security agreements (Section 9—203).

ARTICLE II SALES

Part 1 Short Title, General Construction and Subject Matter

Section 2—102. Scope; Certain Security and Other Transactions Excluded from this Article

Unless the context otherwise requires, this Article applies to transactions in goods; it does not apply to any transaction which although in the form of an unconditional contract to sell or present sale is intended to operate only as a security transaction nor does this Article impair or repeal any statute regulating sales to consumers, farmers or other specified classes of buyers.

Part 2 Form, Formation and Readjustment of Contract

Section 2—201. Formal Requirements; Statute of Frauds

(1) Except as otherwise provided in this section a contract for the sale of goods for the price of $500 or more is not enforceable by way of action or defense unless there is some writing sufficient to indicate that a contract for sale has been made between the parties and signed by the party against whom enforcement is sought or by his authorized agent or broker. A writing is not insufficient because it omits or incorrectly states a term agreed upon but the contract is not enforceable under this paragraph beyond the quantity of goods shown in such writing.

(2) Between merchants if within a reasonable time a writing in confirmation of the contract and sufficient against the sender is received and the party receiving it has reason to know its contents, it satisfies the requirements of subsection (1) against such party unless written notice of objection to its contents is given within 10 days after it is received.

(3) A contract which does not satisfy the requirements of subsection (1) but which is valid in other respects is enforceable

(a) if the goods are to be specially manufactured for the buyer and are not suitable for sale to others in the ordinary course of the seller's business and the seller, before notice of repudiation is received and under circumstances which reasonably indicate that the goods are for the buyer, has made either a substantial beginning of their manufacture or commitments for their procurement; or

(b.) if the party against whom enforcement is sought admits in his pleading, testimony or otherwise in court that a contract for sale was made, but the contract is not enforceable under the provision beyond the quantity of goods admitted; or

(c) with respect to goods for which payment has been made and accepted or which have been received and accepted (Sec. 2—606).

Section 2—202. Final Written Expression: Parol or Extrinsic Evidence

Terms with respect to which the confirmatory memoranda of the parties agree or which are otherwise set forth in a writing intended by the parties as a final expression of their agreement with respect to such terms as are included therein may not be contradicted by evidence of any prior agreement or of a contemporaneous oral agreement but may be explained or supplemented

(a) by course of dealing or usage of trade (Section 1—205) or by course of performance (Section 2—208); and

(b) by evidence of consistent additional terms unless the court finds the writing to have been intended also as a complete and exclusive statement of the terms of the agreement.

Section 2—204. Formation in General

(1) A contract for sale of goods may be made in any manner sufficient to show agreement, including conduct by both parties which recognizes the existence of such a contract.

(2) An agreement sufficient to constitute a contract for sale may be found even though the moment of its making is undetermined.

(3) Even though one or more terms are left open a contract for sale does not fail for

indefiniteness if the parties have intended to make a contract and there is a reasonably certain basis for giving an appropriate remedy.

Section 2—205. Firm Offers

An offer by a merchant to buy or sell goods in a signed writing which by its terms gives assurance that it will be held open is not revocable, for lack of consideration, during the time stated or if no time is stated for a reasonable time, but in no event may such period of irrevocability exceed three months; but any such term of assurance on a form supplied by the offeree must be separately signed by the offeror.

Section 2—206. Offer and Acceptance in Formation of Contract

(1) Unless otherwise unambiguously indicated by the language or circumstances

(a) an offer to make a contract shall be construed as inviting acceptance in any manner and by any medium reasonable in the circumstances;

(b) an order or other offer to buy goods for prompt or current shipment shall be construed as inviting acceptance either by a prompt promise to ship or by the prompt or current shipment of conforming or non-conforming goods, but such a shipment of non-conforming goods does not constitute an acceptance if the seller seasonably notifies the buyer that the shipment is offered only as an accommodation to the buyer.

(2) Where the beginning of a requested performance is a reasonable mode of acceptance an offeror who is not notified of acceptance within a reasonable time may treat the offer as having lapsed before acceptance.

Section 2—207. Additional Terms in Acceptance or Confirmation

(1) A definite and seasonable expression of acceptance or a written confirmation which is sent within a reasonable time operates as an acceptance even though it states terms additional to or different from those offered or agreed upon, unless acceptance is expressly made conditional on assent to the additional or different terms.

(2) The additional terms are to be construed as proposals for addition to the contract. Be-

tween merchants such terms become part of the contract unless:

(a) the offer expressly limits acceptance to the terms of the offer;

(b) they materially alter it; or

(c) notification of objection to them has already been given or is given within a reasonable time after notice of them is received.

(3) Conduct by both parties which recognizes the existence of a contract is sufficient to establish a contract for sale although the writings of the parties do not otherwise establish a contract. In such case the terms of the particular contract consist of those terms on which the writings of the parties agree, together with any supplementary terms incorporated under any other provisions of this Act.

Section 2—208. Course of Performance or Practical Construction

(1) Where the contract for sale involves repeated occasions for performance by either party with knowledge of the nature of the performance and opportunity for objection to it by the other, any course of performance accepted or acquiesced in without objection shall be relevant to determine the meaning of the agreement.

(2) The express terms of the agreement and any such course of performance, as well as any course of dealing and usage of trade, shall be construed whenever reasonable as consistent with each other; but when such construction is unreasonable, express terms shall control course of performance and course of performance shall control both course of dealing and usage of trade (Section 1—205).

(3) Subject to the provisions of the next section on modification and waiver, such course of performance shall be relevant to show a waiver or modification of any term inconsistent with such course of performance.

Part 3 General Obligation and Construction of Contract

Section 2—302. Unconscionable Contract or Clause

(1) If the court as a matter of law finds the contract or any clause of the contract to have been

unconscionable at the time it was made the court may refuse to enforce the contract or it may enforce the remainder of the contract without the unconscionable clause, or it may so limit the application of any unconscionable clause as to avoid any unconscionable result.

(2) When it is claimed or appears to the court that the contract or any clause thereof may be unconscionable the parties shall be afforded a reasonable opportunity to present evidence as to its commercial setting, purpose and effect to aid the court in making the determination.

Section 2—312. Warranty of Title and Against Infringement; Buyer's Obligation Against Infringement

(1) Subject to subsection (2) there is in a contract for sale a warranty by the seller that

(a) the title conveyed shall be good, and its transfer rightful; and

(b) the goods shall be delivered free from any security interest or other lien or encumbrance of which the buyer at the time of contracting has no knowledge.

(2) A warranty under subsection (1) will be excluded or modified only by specific language or by circumstances which give the buyer reason to know that the person selling does not claim title in himself or that he is purporting to sell only such right or title as he or a third person may have.

(3) Unless otherwise agreed a seller who is a merchant regularly dealing in goods of the kind warrants that the goods shall be delivered free of the rightful claim of any third person by way of infringement or the like but a buyer who furnishes specifications to the seller must hold the seller harmless against any such claim which arises out of compliance with the specifications.

Section 2—313. Express Warranties by Affirmation, Promise, Description, Sample

(1) Express warranties by the seller are created as follows:

(a) Any affirmation of fact or promise made by the seller to the buyer which relates to the goods and becomes part of the basis of the bargain creates an express warranty that the goods shall conform to the affirmation or promise.

(b) Any description of the goods which is made part of the basis of the bargain creates an express warranty that the goods shall conform to the description.

(c) Any sample or model which is made part of the basis of the bargain creates an express warranty that the whole of the goods shall conform to the sample or model.

(2) It is not necessary to the creation of an express warranty that the seller use formal words such as "warrant" or "guarantee" or that he have a specific intention to make a warranty, but an affirmation merely of the value of the goods or a statement purporting to be merely the seller's opinion or commendation of the goods does not create a warranty.

Section 2—314. Implied Warranty: Merchantability; Usage of Trade

(1) Unless excluded or modified (Section 2—316), a warranty that the goods shall be merchantable is implied in a contract for their sale if the seller is a merchant with respect to goods of that kind. Under this section the serving for value of food or drink to be consumed either on the premises or elsewhere is a sale.

(2) Goods to be merchantable must be at least such as

(a) pass without objection in the trade under the contract description; and

(b) in the case of fungible goods, are of fair average quality within the description; and

(c) are fit for the ordinary purposes for which such goods are used; and

(d) run, within the variations permitted by the agreement, of even kind, quality and quantity within each unit and among all units involved; and

(e) are adequately contained, packaged, and labeled as the agreement may require; and

(f) conform to the promises or affirmation of fact made on the container or label if any.

(3) Unless excluded or modified (Section 2—316) other implied warranties may arise from course of dealing or usage of trade.

Section 2—315. Implied Warranty: Fitness for Particular Purpose

Where the seller at the time of contracting has reason to know any particular purpose for which the goods are required and that the buyer is relying on the seller's skill or judgment to select or furnish suitable goods, there is unless excluded or modified under the next section an implied warranty that the goods shall be fit for such purpose.

Section 2—316. Exclusion or Modification of Warranties

(1) Words or conduct relevant to the creation of an express warranty and words or conduct tending to negate or limit warranty shall be construed wherever reasonable as consistent with each other; but subject to the provisions of this Article on parol or extrinsic evidence (Section 2—202) negation or limitation is inoperative to the extent that such construction is unreasonable.

(2) Subject to subsection (3), to exclude or modify the implied warranty of merchantability or any part of it the language must mention merchantability and in case of a writing must be conspicuous, and to exclude or modify any implied warranty of fitness the exclusion must be by a writing and conspicuous. Language to exclude all implied warranties of fitness is sufficient if it states, for example, that "There are no warranties which extend beyond the description of the face hereof."

(3) Notwithstanding subsection (2)

(a) unless the circumstances indicate otherwise, all implied warranties are excluded by expressions like "as is," "with all faults" or other language which in common understanding calls the buyer's attention to the exclusion of warranties and makes plain that there is no implied warranty; and

(b) when the buyer before entering into the contract has examined the goods or the sample or model as fully as he desired or has refused to examine the goods there is no implied warranty with regard to defects which an examination ought in the circumstances to have revealed to him; and

(c) an implied warranty can also be excluded or modified by course of dealing or course of performance or usage of trade.

(4) Remedies for breach of warranty can be limited in accordance with the provisions of this Article on liquidation or limitation of damages and on contractual modification of remedy (Sections 2—718 and 2—719).

Section 2—318. Third Party beneficiaries of Warranties Express or Implied

Note: If this Act is introduced in the Congress of the United States this section should be omitted. (States to select one alternative.)

Alternative A

A seller's warranty whether express or implied extends to any natural person who is in the family or household of his buyer or who is a guest in his home if it is reasonable to expect that such person may use, consume or be affected by the goods and who is injured in person by breach of the warranty. A seller may not exclude or limit the operation of this section.

Alternative B

A seller's warranty whether express or implied extends to any natural person who may reasonably be expected to use, consume or be affected by the goods and who is injured in person by breach of the warranty. A seller may not exclude or limit the operation of this section.

Alternative C

A seller's warranty whether express or implied extends to any person who may reasonably be expected to use, consume or be affected by the goods and who is injured by breach of the warranty. A seller may not exclude or limit the operation of this section with respect to injury to the person of an individual to whom the warranty extends. As amended 1966.

Section 2—615. Excuse by Failure of Presupposed Conditions

Except so far as a seller may have assumed a greater obligation and subject to the preceding section on substituted performance:

(a) Delay in delivery or non-delivery in whole or in part by a seller who complies with paragraphs (b) and (c) is not a breach of his duty under a contract for sale if performance as agreed has been made impracticable by the occurrence of a contingency the nonoccurrence of which was a basic assumption on which the contract was made or by compliance in good faith with any applicable foreign or domestic governmental regulation or order whether or not it later proves to be invalid.

(b) Where the causes mentioned in paragraph (a) affect only a part of the seller's capacity to perform, he must allocate production and deliveries among his customers but may at his option include regular customers not then under contract as well as his own requirements for further manufacture. He may so allocate in any manner which is fair and reasonable.

(c) The seller must notify the buyer seasonably that there will be delay or non-delivery and, when allocation is required under paragraph (b), of the estimated quota thus made available for the buyer.

Appendix H

THE 1933 AND 1934 SECURITIES ACTS (EXCERPTS)

Securities Act of 1933

Civil Liabilities on Account of False Registration Statement

SECTION 1 1. (a) In case any part of the registration statement, when such part became effective, contained an untrue statement of a material fact or omitted to state a material fact required to be stated therein or necessary to make the statements therein not misleading, any person acquiring such security (unless it is proved that at the time of such acquisition he knew of such untruth or omission) may, either at law or in equity, in any court of competent jurisdiction, sue—

(1) every person who signed the registration statement;

(2) every person who was a director of (or person performing similar functions) or partner in, the issuer at the time of the filing of the part of the registration statement with respect to which his liability is asserted;

(3) every person who, with his consent, is named in the registration statement as being or about to become a director, person performing similar functions, or partner;

(4) every accountant, engineer, or appraiser, or any person whose profession gives authority to a statement made by him, who has with his consent been named as having prepared or certified any part of the registration statement, or as

having prepared or certified any report or valuation which is used in connection with the registration statement, with respect to the statement in such registration statement, report, or valuation, which purports to have been prepared or certified by him;

(5) every underwriter with respect to such security.

If such person acquired the security after the issuer has made generally available to its security holders an earning statement covering a period of at least twelve months beginning after the effective date of the registration statement, then the right of recovery under this subsection shall be conditioned on proof that such person acquired the security relying upon such untrue statement in the registration statement or relying upon the registration statement and not knowing of such omission, but such reliance may be established without proof of the reading of the registration statement by such person.

(b) Notwithstanding the provisions of subsection (a) no person, other than the issuer, shall be liable as provided therein who shall sustain the burden of proof—

(1) that before the effective date of the part of the registration statement with respect to which his liability is asserted (A) he had resigned from or had taken such steps as are permitted by law to resign from, or ceased or refused to act in, every office, capacity, or relationship in which he was described in the registration statement as acting or agreeing to act, and (B) he had advised the Commission and the issuer in writing that he had taken such action and that he would not be responsible for such part of the registration statement; or

(2) that if such part of the registration statement became effective without his knowledge, upon becoming aware of such fact he forthwith acted and advised the Commission, in accordance with paragraph (1), and, in addition, gave reasonable public notice that such part of the registration statement had become effective without his knowledge; or

(3) that (A) as regards any part of the registration statement not purporting to be made on the authority of an expert, and not purporting to be a copy of or extract from a report or valuation of an expert, and not purporting to be made on the authority of a public of official document or state-

ment, he had, after reasonable investigation, reasonable ground to believe and did believe, at the time such part of the registration statement became effective, that the statements therein were true and that there was no omission to state a material fact required to be stated therein or necessary to make the statements therein not misleading; and (B) as regards any part of the registration statement purporting to be made upon his authority as an expert or purporting to be a copy of or extract from a report or valuation of himself as an expert, (i) he had, after reasonable investigation, reasonable ground to believe and did believe, at the time such part of the registration statement became effective, that the statements therein were true and that there was no omission to state a material fact required to be stated therein or necessary to make the statements therein not misleading, or (ii) such part of the registration statement did not fairly represent his statement as an expert or was not a fair copy of or extract from his report or valuation as an expert; and (C) as regards any part of the registration statement purporting to be made on the authority of an expert (other than himself) or purporting to be a copy of or extract from a report or valuation of an expert (other than himself), he had no reasonable ground to believe and did not believe, at the time such part of the registration statement became effective, that the statements therein were untrue or that there was an omission to state a material fact required to be stated therein or necessary to make the statements therein not misleading, or that such part of the registration statement did not fairly represent the statement of the expert or was not a fair copy of or extract from the report or valuation of the expert; and (D) as regards any part of the registration statement purporting to be a statement made by an of official person or purporting to be a copy of or extract from a public of official document, he had no reasonable ground to believe and did not believe, at the time such part of the registration statement became effective, that the statements therein were untrue, or that there was an omission to state a material fact required to be stated therein or necessary to make the statements therein not misleading, or that such part of the registration statement did not fairly represent the statement made by the of official person or was not a fair copy of or extract from the public official document.

(c) In determining, for the purpose of paragraph (3) of subsection (b) of this section, what constitutes reasonable investigation and reasonable ground for belief, the standard of reasonableness shall be that required of a prudent man in the management of his own property.

Civil Liabilities Arising in Connection with Prospectuses and Communications

SECTION 12. Any person who—(1) offers or sells a security in violation of section 5, or

(2) offers or sells a security (whether or not exempted by the provisions of section 3, other than paragraph (2) of subsection (a) thereof), by the use of any means or instruments of transportation or communication in interstate commerce or of the mails, by means of a prospectus or oral communication, which includes an untrue statement of a material fact or omits to state a material fact necessary in order to make the statements, in the light of the circumstances under which they were made, not misleading (the purchaser not knowing of such untruth or omission), and who shall not sustain the burden of proof that he did not know, and in the exercise of reasonable care could not have known, of such untruth or omission, shall be liable to the person purchasing such security from him, who may sue either at law or in equity in any court of competent jurisdiction, to recover the consideration paid for such security with interest thereon, less the amount of any income received thereon, upon the tender of such security, or for damages if he no longer owns the security.

Penalties

SECTION 24. Any person who willfully violates any of the provisions of this title, or the rules and regulations promulgated by the Commission under authority thereof, or any person who willfully, in a registration statement filed under this title, makes any untrue statement of a material fact or omits to state any material fact required to be stated therein or necessary to make the statements therein not misleading, shall upon conviction be fined not more than $10,000 or imprisoned not more than five years, or both.

Securities Exchange Act of 1934

Regulation of the Use of Manipulative and Deceptive Devices

SECTION 10. It shall be unlawful for any person, directly or indirectly, by the use of any means or instrumentality of interstate commerce or of the mails, or of any facility of any national securities exchange—

(a) To effect a short sale, or to use or employ any stop-loss order in connection with the purchase or sale, of any security registered on a national securities exchange, in contravention of such rules and regulations as the Commission may prescribe as necessary or appropriate in the public interest or for the protection of investors.

(b) To use or employ, in connection with the purchase or sale of any security registered on a national securities exchange or any security not so registered, any manipulative or deceptive device or contrivance in contravention of such rules and regulations as the Commission may prescribe as necessary or appropriate in the public interest or for the protection of investors.

Proxies

SECTION 14. (a) It shall be unlawful for any person, by the use of the mails or by any means or instrumentality of interstate commerce or of any facility of a national securities exchange or otherwise, in contravention of such rules and regulations as the Commission may prescribe as necessary or appropriate in the public interest or for the protection of investors, to solicit or to permit the use of his name to solicit any proxy or consent or authorization in respect of any security (other than an exempted security) registered pursuant to section 12 of (781) this title.

Directors, Officers, and Principal Stockholders

SECTION 16. (a) Every person who is directly or indirectly the beneficial owner of more than 10 per centum of any class of any equity security (other than an exempted security) which is registered pursuant to section 12 of this title, or who is a director or an officer of the issuer of such security, shall file, at the time of the registration of such security on a national securities exchange or by the effective date of a registration statement filed pursuant to section 12 (g) of this title, or within ten days after he becomes such beneficial owner, director, or officer, a statement with the Commission (and, if such security is registered on a national securities exchange, also with the exchange) of the amount of all equity securities of such issuer of which he is the beneficial owner, and within ten days after the close of each calendar month thereafter, if there has been a change in such ownership during such month, shall file with the Commission (and if such security is registered on a national securities exchange, shall also file with the exchange) a statement indicating his ownership at the close of the calendar month and such changes in his ownership as have occurred during such calendar month.

(b) For the purpose of preventing the unfair use of information which may have been obtained by such beneficial owner, director, or officer by reason of his relationship to the issuer, any profit realized by him from any purchase and sale, or any sale and purchase, of any equity security of such issuer (other than an exempted security) within any period of less than six months, unless such security was acquired in good faith in connection with a debt previously contracted, shall inure to and be recoverable by the issuer, irrespective of any intention on the part of such beneficial owner, director, or officer in entering into such transaction of holding the security purchased or of not repurchasing the security sold for a period exceeding six months. Suit to recover such profit may be instituted at law or in equity in any court of competent jurisdiction by the issuer, or by the owner of any security of the issuer in the name and in behalf of the issuer if the issuer shall fail or refuse to bring such suit within sixty days after request or shall fail diligently to prosecute the same thereafter; but no such suit shall be brought more than two years after the date such profit was realized. This subsection shall not be construed to cover any transaction where such beneficial owner was not such both at the time of the purchase and sale, or the sale and purchase, of the security involved, or any transaction or transactions which the Commission by rules and regulations may exempt as not comprehended within the purpose of this subsection.

(c) It shall be unlawful for any such beneficial owner, director, or officer, directly or indirectly, to sell any equity security of such issuer (other than an exempted security), if the person selling the security or his principal (1) does not own the security sold, or (2) if owning the security, does not deliver it against such sale within twenty days thereafter, or does not within five days after such sale deposit it in the mails or other usual channels of transportation; but no person shall be deemed to have violated this subsection if he proves that notwithstanding the exercise of good faith he was unable to make such delivery or deposit within such time, or that to do so would cause undue inconvenience or expense.

(d) Wherever communicating, or purchasing or selling a security while in possession of, material nonpublic information would violate, or result in liability to any purchaser or seller of the security under any provision of this title, or any rule or regulation thereunder, such conduct in connection with a purchase or sale of a put, call, straddle, option, or privilege with respect to such security or with respect to a group or index of securities including such security, shall also violate and result in comparable liability to any purchaser or seller of that security under such provision, rule, or regulation.

Liability for Misleading Statements

SECTION 18. (a) Any person who shall make or cause to be made any statement in any application, report, or document filed pursuant to this title or any rule or regulation thereunder or any undertaking contained in a registration statement as provided in subsection (d) of section 15 of this title, which statement was at the time and in the light of the circumstances under which it was made false or misleading with respect to any material fact, shall be liable to any person (not knowing that such statement was false or misleading) who, in reliance upon such statement, shall have purchased or sold a security at a price which was affected by such statement, for damages caused by such reliance, unless the person sued shall prove that he acted in good faith and had no knowledge that such statement was false or misleading. A person seeking to enforce such liability may sue at law or in equity in any court of competent jurisdiction. In any such suit the court may, in its discretion, require an undertaking for the payment of the costs of such suit, and assess reasonable costs, including reasonable attorneys' fees, against either party litigant.

(b) Every person who becomes liable to make payment under this section may recover contribution as in cases of contact from any person who, if joined in the original suit, would have been liable to make the same payment.

(c) No action shall be maintained to enforce any liability created under this section unless brought within one year after the discovery of the facts constituting the cause of action and within three years after such cause of action accrued.

Appendix I

THE COPYRIGHT ACT OF 1990 (EXCERPTS)

Section 102. Subject matter of copyright: In general

(a) Copyright protection subsists, in accordance with this title, in original works of authorship fixed in any tangible medium of expression, now known or later developed, from which they can be perceived, reproduced, or otherwise communicated, either directly or with the aid of a machine or device. Works of authorship include the following categories:

(1) literary works;

(2) musical works, including any accompanying words;

(3) dramatic works, including any accompanying music;

(4) pantomimes and choreographic works;

(5) pictorial, graphic, and sculptural works;

(6) motion pictures and other audiovisual works;

(7) sound recordings; and

(8) architectural works.

(b) In no case does copyright protection for an original work of authorship extend to any idea, procedure, process, system, method of operation, concept, principle, or discovery, regardless of the form in which it is described, explained, illustrated, or embodied in such work.

Section 106. Exclusive rights in copyrighted works

Subject to sections 107 through 120, the owner of copyright under this title has the exclusive rights to do and to authorize any of the following:

(1) to reproduce the copyrighted work in copies or phonorecords;

(2) to prepare derivative works based upon the copyrighted work;

(3) to distribute copies or phonorecords of the copyrighted work to the public by sale or other transfer of ownership, or by rental, lease, or lending;

(4) in the case of literary, musical, dramatic, and choreographic works, pantomimes, and motion pictures and other audiovisual works, to perform the copyrighted work publicly; and

(5) in the case of literary, musical, dramatic, and choreographic works, pantomimes, and pictorial, graphic, or sculptural works, including the individual images of a motion picture or other audiovisual work, to display the copyrighted work publicly.

Section 107. Limitations on exclusive rights: Fair use

Notwithstanding the provisions of sections 106 and 106A, the fair use of a copyrighted work, including such use by reproduction in copies or phonorecords or by any other means specified by that section, for purposes such as criticism, comment, news reporting, teaching (including multiple copies for classroom use), scholarship, or research, is not an infringement of copyright. In determining whether the use made of a work in any particular case is a fair use the factors to be considered shall include—

(1) the purpose and character of the use, including whether such use is of a commercial nature or is for nonprofit educational purposes;

(2) the nature of the copyrighted work;

(3) the amount and substantiality of the portion used in relation to the copyrighted work as a whole; and

(4) the effect of the use upon the potential market for or value of the copyrighted work.

Section 406. Copyright registration in general

(a) Registration Permissive.—At any time during the subsistence of copyright in any published or unpublished work, the owner of copyright or of any exclusive right in the work may obtain registration of the copyright claim by delivering to the Copyright Office the deposit specified by this section, together with the application and fee specified by sections 409 and 708. Such registration is not a condition of copyright protection.

Section 591. Infringement of copyright

(a) Anyone who violates any of the exclusive rights of the copyright owner as provided by sections 106 through 118 or of the author as provided in section 106A(a), or who imports copies or phonorecords into the United States in violation of section 602, is an infringer of the copyright or right of the author, as the case may be. For purposes of this chapter (other than section 506), any reference to copyright shall be deemed to include the rights conferred by section 106(a). As used in this subsection the term "anyone" includes any State, any instrumentality of a State, and any officer or employee of a State or instrumentality of a State acting in his or her official capacity. Any State, and any such instrumentality, officer, or

employee, shall be subject to the provisions of this title in the same manner and to the same extent as any nongovernmental entity.

(b) The legal or beneficial owner of an exclusive right under a copyright is entitled, subject to the requirements of section 411, to institute an action for any infringement of that particular right committed while he or she is the owner of it. The court may require such owner to serve written notice of the action with a copy of the complaint upon any person shown, by the records of the Copyright Office or otherwise, to have or claim an interest in the copyright, and shall require that such notice be served upon any person whose interest is likely to be affected by a decision in the case. The court may require the joinder, and shall permit the intervention, of any person having or claiming an interest in the copyright.

Remedies for Infringement: Damages and Profits

SECTION 504. (a) In General. Except as otherwise provided by this title, an infringer of copyright is liable for either—
1. the copyright owner's actual damages and any additional profits of the infringer, as provided by subsection (b); or
    2. statutory damages, as provided by subsection (c).

(b) Actual Damages and Profits.—The copyright owner is entitled to recover the actual damages suffered by him or her as a result of the infringement, and any profits of the infringer that are attributable to the infringement and are not taken into account in computing the actual damages. In establishing the infringer's profits, the copyright owner is required to present proof only of the infringer's gross revenue, and the infringer is required to prove his or her deductible expenses and the elements of profit attributable to factors other than the copyrighted work.

(c) Statutory Damages—(1) Except as provided by clause (2) of this subsection, the copyright owner may elect, at any time before final judgment is rendered, to recover, instead of actual damages and profits, an award of statutory damages for all infringements involved in the action, with respect to any one work, for which any one infringer is liable individually, or for which any two or more infringers are liable jointly and severally, in a sum of not less than $500 or more than $20,000 as the court considers just. For the purposes of this subsection, all the parts of a compilation or derivative work constitute one work.

(2) In a case where the copyright owner sustains the burden of proving, and the court finds, that infringement was committed willfully, the court in its discretion may increase the award of statutory damages to a sum of not more than $100,000. In a case where the infringer sustains the burden of proving, and the court finds, that such infringer was not aware and had no reason to believe that his or her acts constituted an infringement of copyright, the court in its discretion may reduce the award of statutory damages to a sum of not less than $200. The court shall remit statutory damages in any case where an infringer believed and had reasonable grounds for believing that his or her use of the copyrighted work was a fair use

under section 107, if the infringer was: (i) an employee or agent of a nonprofit educational institution, library, or archives acting within the scope of his or her employment who, or such institution, library, or archives itself, which infringed by reproducing the work in copies or phonorecords; or (ii) a public broadcasting entity which or a person who, as a regular part of the nonprofit activities of a public broadcasting entity (as defined in subsection (g) of section 118) infringed by performing a published nondramatic literary work or by reproducing a transmission program embodying a performance of such a work.

Section 506. Criminal offenses

(a) Criminal infringement—Any person who infringes a copyright willfully and for purposes of commercial advantage or private financial gain shall be punished as provided in section 2319 of title 18.

Appendix J

THE FOREIGN CORRUPT PRACTICES ACT (EXCERPTS)

Section 78dd-2. Prohibited foreign trade practices by domestic concerns

(a) Prohibition. It shall be unlawful for any domestic concern, other than an issuer which is subject to section 30A of the Securities Exchange Act of 1934 [15 USCS § 78dd-1]. or for any officer, director, employee, or agent of such domestic concern or any stockholder thereof acting on behalf of such domestic concern, to make use of the mails or any means or instrumentality of interstate commerce corruptly in furtherance of an offer, payment, promise to pay, or authorization of the payment of any money, or offer, gift, promise to give, or authorization of the giving of anything of value to—

(1) any foreign official for purposes of—

(A) (i) influencing any act or decision of such foreign official in his official capacity, or

(ii) inducing such foreign official to do or omit to do any act in violation of the lawful duty of such official, or

(B) inducing such foreign official to use his influence with a foreign government or instrumentality thereof to affect or influence any act or decision of such government or instrumentality, in order to assist such domestic concern in obtaining or retaining business for or with, or directing business to, any person;

(2) any foreign political party or official thereof or any candidate for foreign political office for purposes of—

(A) (i) influencing any act or decision of such party, official, or candidate in its or his official capacity, or (ii) inducing such party, official, or candidate to do or omit to do an act in violation of the lawful duty of such party, official, or candidate,

(B) inducing such party, official, or candidate to use its or his influence with a foreign government or instrumentality thereof to affect or influence any act or decision of such government or instrumentality, in order to assist such domestic concern in obtaining or retaining business for or with, or directing business to, any person; or

(3) any person, while knowing that all or a portion of such money or thing of value will be offered, given, or promised, directly or indirectly, to any foreign official, to any foreign political party or official thereof, or to any candidate for foreign political office, for purposes of—

(A) (i) influencing any act or decision of such foreign official, political party, party official, or candidate in his or in its official capacity, or (ii) inducing such foreign official, political party, party official, or candidate to do or omit to do any act in violation of the lawful duty of such foreign official, political party, party official, or candidate, or

(B) inducing such foreign official, political party, party official, or candidate to use his or its influence with a foreign government or instrumentality thereof to affect or influence any act or decision of such government or instrumentality, in order to assist such issuer in obtaining or retaining business for or with, or directing business to, any person.

(b) Exceptions for routine governmental action. Subsection (a) shall not apply to any facilitating or expediting payment to a foreign official, political party, or party official the purpose of which is to expedite or to secure the performance of a routine governmental action by a foreign official, political party, or party official.

(c) Affirmative defenses. It shall be an affirmative defense to actions under subsection (a) that—

(1) the payment, gift, offer, or promise of anything of value that was made, was lawful under the written laws and regulations of the foreign official's, political party's, party official's, or candidate's country; or

(2) the payment, gift, offer, or promise of anything of value that was made, was a reasonable and bona fide expenditure, such as travel and lodging expenses, incurred by or on behalf of a foreign official, party, party official, or candidate and was directly related to

(A) the promotion, demonstration, or explanation of products or services; or

(B) the execution or performance of a contract with a foreign government or agency thereof.

(B) Any domestic concern that violates subsection (a) shall be subject to a civil penalty of not more than $10,000 imposed in an action brought by the Attorney General.

(2) (A) Any officer or director of a domestic concern, or stockholder acting on behalf of such domestic concern, who willfully violates subsection (a) shall be fined not more than $100,000, or imprisoned not more than 5 years, or both.

(B) Any employee or agent of a domestic concern who is a United States citizen, national, or resident or is otherwise subject to the jurisdiction of the United States (other than an officer, director, or stockholder acting on behalf of such domestic concern), and who willfully violates subsection (a), shall be fined not more than $100,000, or imprisoned not more than 5 years, or both.

(C) Any officer, director, employee, or agent of a domestic concern, or stockholder acting on behalf of such domestic concern, who violates subsection (a) shall be subject to a civil penalty of not more than $10,000 imposed in an action brought by the Attorney General.

(3) Whenever a fine is imposed under paragraph (2) upon any officer, director, employee, agent, or stockholder of a domestic concern, such fine may not be paid, directly or indirectly, by such domestic concern.

Appendix K

SECTIONS 402A AND 402B OF THE RESTATEMENT (SECOND) OF TORTS

Section 402A. Special Liability of Seller of Product for Physical Harm to User or Consumer

(1) One who sells any product in a defective condition unreasonably dangerous to the user or consumer or to his property is subject to liability for physical harm thereby caused to the ultimate user or consumer, or to his property, if

(a) the seller is engaged in the business of selling such a product, and

(b) it is expected to and does reach the user or consumer without substantial change in the condition in which it is sold.

(2) The rule stated in Subsection (1) applies although

(a) the seller has exercised all possible care in the preparation and sale of his product, and

(b) the user or consumer has not bought the product from or entered into any contractual relation with the seller.

Section 402B. Misrepresentation by Seller of Chattels to Consumer

One engaged in the business of selling chattels who, by advertising, labels, or otherwise, makes to the public a misrepresentation of a material fact concerning the character or quality of a chattel sold by him is subject to liability for physical harm to a consumer of the chattel caused by justifiable reliance upon the misrepresentation, even though

(a) it is not made fraudulently or negligently, and

(b) the consumer has not bought the chattel from or entered into any contractual relation with the seller.

Appendix L

THE FEDERAL TRADE COMMISSION ACT (EXCERPTS)

Section 5. Unfair Methods of Competition Unlawful; Prevention by Commission— Declaration of Unlawfulness; Power to Prohibit Unfair Practices

(a) (1) Unfair methods of competition in or affecting commerce, and unfair or deceptive acts or practices in or affecting commerce, are declared unlawful.

Penalty for Violation of Order; Injunctions and Other Appropriate Equitable Relief

(1) Any person, partnership, or corporation who violates an order of the Commission after it has become final, and while such order is in effect, shall forfeit and pay to the United States a civil penalty of not more than $10,000 for each violation, which shall accrue to the United States and may be recovered in a civil action brought by the Attorney General of the United States. Each separate violation of such an order shall be a separate offense, except that in the case of a violation through continuing failure to obey or neglect to obey a final order of the Commission, each day of continuance of such failure or neglect shall be deemed a separate offense. In such actions, the United States district courts are empowered to grant mandatory injunctions and such other and further equitable relief as they deem appropriate in the enforcement of such final orders of the Commission.

Appendix M

THE CLAYTON
ACT (EXCERPTS)

Section 7. Acquisition by One Corporation of Stock of Another

No corporation engaged in commerce shall acquire, directly or indirectly, the whole or any part of the stock; or other share capital and no corporation subject to the jurisdiction of the Federal Trade Commission shall acquire the whole or any part of the assets of another corporation in any section of the country, the effect of such acquisition may be substantially to lessen competition, or to tend to create a monopoly.

No corporation shall acquire, directly or indirectly, the whole or any part of the stock or other share capital and no corporation subject to the jurisdiction of the Federal Trade Commission shall acquire the whole or any part of the assets of one or more corporations engaged in commerce, where in any line of commerce in any section of the country, the effect of such acquisition, of such stocks or assets, or of the use of such stock by the voting or granting of proxies or otherwise, may be substantially to lessen competition, or to tend to create a monopoly.

Section 8. Interlocking Directorates and Officers

No private banker or director, officer, or employee of any member bank of the Federal Reserve System or any branch thereof shall be at the same time a director, officer, or employee of any other bank, banking association, savings bank, or trust company organized under the National Bank Act or organized under the laws of any State or of the District of Columbia, or any branch thereof, except that the Board of Governors of the Federal Reserve System may by regulation permit such service as a director, officer, or employee of not more than one other such institution or branch thereof; . . .

Appendix N

THE SHERMAN ACT (EXCERPTS)

Section 1. Trusts, etc., in Restraint of Trade Illegal; Penalty

Every contract, combination in the form of trust or otherwise, or conspiracy, in restraint of trade or commerce among the several States, or with foreign nations, is declared to be illegal. Every person who shall make any contract or engage in any combination or conspiracy hereby declared to be illegal shall be deemed guilty of a felony, and, on conviction thereof, shall be punished by fine not exceeding one million dollars if a corporation, or, if any other person, one hundred thousand dollars or by imprisonment not exceeding three years, or by both said punishments, in the discretion of the court.

Section 2. Monopolization; Penalty

Every person who shall monopolize, or attempt to monopolize, or combine or conspire with any other person or persons, to monopolize any part of the trade or commerce among the several States, or with foreign nations, shall be deemed guilty of a felony, and, on conviction thereof, shall be punished by fine not exceeding $10,000,000 if a corporation, or, if any other person, $350,000 or by imprisonment not exceeding three years, or by both said punishments, in the discretion of the court.

Appendix O

THE ROBINSON - PATMAN ACT (EXCERPTS)

Section 2. Discrimination in Price, Services, or Facilities—Price; Selection of Customers

(a) It shall be unlawful for any person engaged in commerce, in the course of such commerce, either directly or indirectly, to discriminate in price between different purchasers of commodities of like grade and quality, where either or any of the purchases involved in such discrimination are in commerce, where such commodities are sold for use, consumption, or resale within the United States or any Territory thereof or the District of Columbia or any insular possession or other place under the jurisdiction of the United States, and where the effect of such discrimination may be substantially to lessen competition or tend to create a monopoly in any line of commerce, or to injure, destroy, or prevent competition with any person who either grants or knowingly receives the benefit of such discrimination, or with customers of either of them; *Provided*, That nothing herein contained shall prevent differentials which make only due allowance for differences in the cost of manufacture, sale, or delivery resulting from the differing methods or quantities in which such commodities are to such purchasers sold or delivered: *Provided, however*, That the Federal Trade Commission may, after due investigation and hearing to all interested parties, fix and establish quantity limits, and revise the same as it finds necessary, as to particular commodities or classes of commodities, where it finds that available purchasers in greater quantities are so few as to render differentials on account thereof unjustly discriminatory or promotive of monopoly in any line of commerce; and the foregoing shall then not be construed to permit differentials based on differences in quantities greater than those so fixed and established: *And provided further*, That nothing herein contained shall prevent persons engaged in selling goods, wares, or merchandise in commerce from selecting their own customers in bona fide transactions and not in restraint of trade: *And provided further*, That nothing herein contained shall prevent price changes from time to time where in response to changing conditions affecting the market for or the marketability of the goods concerned, such as but not limited to actual or imminent deterioration of perishable goods, obsolescence of seasonal goods, distress sales under court process, or sales in good faith in discontinuance of business in the goods concerned.

Section 3. Discrimination in Rebates, Discounts, or Advertising Service Charges; Underselling in Particular Localities; Penalties

It shall be unlawful for any person engaged in commerce, in the course of such commerce, to be a party to, or assist in, any transaction of sale, or contract to sell, which discriminates to his knowledge against competitors of the purchaser, in that, any discount, rebate, allowance, or advertising service charge is granted to the purchaser over and above any discount, rebate, allowance, or advertising service charge available at the time of such transaction to said competitors in respect of a sale of goods of like grade, quality, and quantity; to sell, or contract to sell, goods in any part of the United States at prices lower than those exacted by said person elsewhere in the United States for the purpose of destroying competition, or eliminating a competitor in such part of the United States; or, to sell, or contract to sell, goods at unreasonably low prices for the purpose of destroying competition or eliminating a competitor.

Any person violating any of the provisions of this section shall, upon conviction thereof, be fined not more than $5,000 or imprisoned not more than one year, or both.

THE NATIONAL LABOR RELATIONS ACT (EXCERPTS)

Unfair Labor Practices

Section 8

(a) It shall be an unfair labor practice for an employer—

(1) to interfere with, restrain, or coerce employees in the exercise of the rights guaranteed in section 7;

(2) to dominate or interfere with the formation or administration of any labor organization or contribute financial or other support to it: *Provided,* That subject to rules and regulations made and published by the Board pursuant to section 6, an employer shall not be prohibited from permitting employees to confer with him during work hours without loss of time or pay;

(3) by discrimination in regard to hire or tenure of employment of any term or condition of employment to encourage or discourage membership in any labor organization:

(4) to discharge or otherwise discriminate against an employee because he has filed charges or given testimony under this Act;

(5) to refuse to bargain collectively with the representatives of his employees, subject to the provisions of section 9(a).

(b) It shall be an unfair labor practice for a labor organization or its agents—

(1) to restrain or coerce (A) employees in the exercise of the rights guaranteed in section 7:

Provided, That this paragraph shall not impair the right of a labor organization to prescribe its own rules with respect to the acquisition or retention of membership therein; or (B) an employer in the selection of his representatives for the purpose of collective bargaining or the adjustment of grievances;

(2) to cause or attempt to cause an employer to discriminate against an employee in violation of subsection (a) (3) or to discriminate against an employee with respect to whom membership in such organization has been denied or terminated on some ground other than his failure to tender the periodic dues and the initiation fees uniformly required as a condition of acquiring or retaining membership;

(3) to refuse to bargain collectively with an employer, provided it is the representative of his employees subject to the provisions of section 9(a);

(4) (i) to engage in, or to induce or encourage any individual employed by any person engaged in commerce or in an industry affecting commerce to engage in, a strike or a refusal in the course of his employment to use, manufacture, process, transport, or otherwise handle or work on any goods, articles, materials, or commodities or to perform any services; or (ii) to threaten, coerce, or restrain any person engaged in commerce or in an industry affecting commerce, . . .

(5) to require of employees covered by an agreement authorized under subsection (a) (3)

the payment, as a condition precedent to becoming a member of such organization, of a fee in an amount which the Board finds excessive or discriminatory under all the circumstances. In making such a finding, the Board shall consider, among other relevant factors, the practices and customs of labor organizations in the particular industry, and the wages currently paid to the employees affected;

(6) to cause or attempt to cause an employer to pay or deliver or agree to pay or deliver money or other thing of value, in the nature of an exaction, for services which are not performed or not to be performed; and

(7) to picket or cause to be picketed, or threaten to picket or cause to be picketed, any employer where an object thereof is forcing or requiring an employer to recognize or bargain with a labor organization as the representative of his employees, or forcing or requiring the employees of an employer to accept or select such labor organization as their collective bargaining representative, unless such labor organization is currently certified as the representative of such employees.

Glossary

A

Absolute privilege A defense to defamation; a protection given to legislators and courtroom participants for statements made relating to the proceedings; encourages people to come forward and speak without fear of liability.

Acceptance Offeree's positive response to offeror's proposed contract.

Accord and satisfaction An agreement to pay a debt and full satisfaction of that agreement by payment.

Accredited investor For purposes of Regulation D, an investor with certain financial stability who is not counted in number of purchaser limitations for Rules 505 and 506.

Acid rain Environmental phenomenon caused when acid from coal smoke enters the atmosphere and then appears in precipitation in large areas, sometimes quite far from the coal-burning area.

Act of State Doctrine In international law, a theory that each country's governmental actions are autonomous and not subject to judicial review by the courts in other countries.

Actual notice Private or individual notice sent directly to affected parties; this type of notice is effective only if the party actually receives it, as compared to constructive notice, for which publication is sufficient.

Actus reus Latin term for the criminal act or conduct required for proof of a crime.

Administrative agency Governmental unit created by the legislative body for the purposes of administering and enforcing the laws.

Administrative law judge (ALJ) Special category of judicial official who presides over agency enforcement hearings.

Administrative Procedures Act (APA) Basic federal law governing the creation, operation, and reporting of federal administrative agencies.

Advances In partnerships, loans by the partners to the partnership; makes the partner a creditor of the partnership.

Adverse possession Acquisition of land title through use for the required statutory period.

Affirm Action taken by an appellate court on an appealed case; the effect is that the court upholds the lower court's decision.

Affirmative action Label given to employment processes and programs designed to help underrepresented groups obtain jobs and promotion.

Age Discrimination in Employment Act of 1967 Federal law that prohibits job discrimination on the basis of age; prohibits the consideration of age in an employment decision.

Agency by estoppel Theory for creation of an agency relationship that holds the principle liable because the principal has allowed the agent to represent him or her as his or her principal.

Agent One who acts on behalf of another and at his or her direction.

Air Pollution Control Act (1955) The first federal legislation to deal with air pollution.

Air Quality Act (1967) Federal law that designated HEW to oversee state plans for controlling pollution.

Air rights Ownership rights of surface owner to air above land surface.

Alter ego theory Theory used for disregarding the corporate protection of limited liability for shareholders. It results when individuals treat the corporation's properties and accounts as their own and fail to follow corporate formalities.

Americans with Disabilities Act A 1991 federal law that prohibits discrimination in the workplace against persons with disabilities and requires employers to make reasonable accommodations for employees with disabilities who are otherwise qualified to perform a job.

Answer Pleading filed by the defendant in a lawsuit; contains the defendant's version of the basis of the suit, counterclaims, and denials.

Apparent authority Authority of an agent to act on behalf of a principal that results from the appearance of the agent's authority to third parties.

Appellant The name on appeal for the party who appeals a lower court's decision.

Appellate Adjective that describes courts and processes above the trial level; management of the appeals after trial court procedures.

Appellate court A court of appeals or a court of review; a court whose function is to review the decision and actions of a trial court; does not hear witnesses; only reviews the transcript and studies the arguments and briefs of the parties.

Appellee The name on appeal for the party who won a lower court's decision—that is, the party who does not appeal the lower court decision.

Appraisal rights Rights of dissenting shareholders after a merger or takeover to be paid the value of their shares before the takeover or merger.

Appropriation In international law, the taking of private property by a government; also known as expropriation; in torts, use of the name, likeness or image of another for commercial purposes.

APR Annual percentage rate; a financing term representing the annual debt cost and a required disclosure under Regulation Z.

Arbitrary and capricious Standard for challenging administrative agency rules; used to show decisions or rules were not based on sufficient facts.

Arbitration Alternative form of dispute resolution in which parties submit evidence to a third party who is a member of the American Arbitration Association and who makes a decision after listening to the case.

Area standards picketing Picketing that notifies the public that an employer's standards are lower than other firms in the area.

Arraignment Hearing in criminal procedure held after an indictment or information is returned; trial date is set and plea is entered.

Articles of incorporation Organizational papers of a corporation; lists the company's structure, capitalization, board structure, and so on.

Articles of limited partnership Contract governing the rights and relations of limited partners.

Articles of partnership Organizational papers of a partnership; often called the partnership agreement; lists rights of partners, profit/loss arrangements, and so on.

Asbestos Hazard Emergency Response Act (AHERA) Federal environmental legislation that requires removal of asbestos from public schools and other facilities where exposure is particularly dangerous (where young children are present).

Asset acquisition Form of takeover in which another firm buys all the assets of a firm and gains control through control of the firm's property.

Assignment In contract law, the transfer of the benefits under a contract to a third party; the third party has a right to benefits but is subject to any contract defenses.

Assumption of risk Defense in negligence cases that prevents an injured party from recovering if it can be established that the injured party realized the risk and engaged in the conduct anyway.

Attorney-client privilege Protection of client's disclosures to his or her attorney; attorney cannot disclose information client offers (with some exceptions, such as the client telling the attorney he is going to commit a crime); the confession of a crime already committed cannot be disclosed by the lawyer.

Authorization cards Cards signed by employees and required to establish the 30 percent support necessary to hold an election for a union as exclusive bargaining agent for the collective bargaining unit.

B

Bailee Party who has temporary possession of the property of another.

Bailment Temporary transfer of possession of personal property.

Bailor Party who owns property and surrenders possession.

Bait and switch Term given to advertising technique in which a low-price product is advertised and then the customer is told that the product is unavailable or is talked into a higher-priced product; prohibited by the FTC.

Bargain and sale deed A special warranty deed.

Bargained for exchange The mutual exchange of detriment as the consideration element in a contract.

Basis of the bargain Information the buyer relies on in making the decision to.

Battle of the forms Term used to describe the problem of merchants using their purchase orders and invoices with conflicting terms as their contractual understanding; problem is remedied by § 2-207 of the UCC.

Berne Convention Implementation Act of 1988 Federal law that changed U.S. copyright law to comply with international agreement at Berne Convention.

Best available treatment (BAT) In environmental law, the most advanced and effective technology for preventing pollution; a higher standard than the best conventional treatment.

Best conventional treatment (BCT) Requirement imposed by EPA on point source pollution that requires the firm to use the best existing treatments for water pollution.

BFOQ Bonafide occupational qualification; a justification for discrimination on the basis of sex if it can be established that gender is a requirement for a job. Also applies to discrimination on the basis of religion, national origin, and so on.

Bilateral contract Contract in which both parties make promises to perform.

Bilateral treaty In international law, a treaty between two nations.

Bill of lading Receipt for goods issued by a carrier; used as a means of transferring title in exchange for payment or a draw on a line of credit.

Bill of sale Informal document or contract that serves to prove and transfer title to tangible personal property.

Bill of Rights Portion of the U.S. Constitution that consists of the first ten amendments and includes such rights as freedom of speech, right to privacy, the protections afforded in criminal procedures under the Fourth Amendment search and seizure, and the Fifth Amendment protections against self-incrimination.

Blacklisting Tactic used by employers to prevent employees involved with unions from getting work elsewhere; an exchange of employees' names to prevent unionism.

Blue sky laws State laws regulating the sale of securities.

Board of directors Policy-setting governing group of a corporation.

Brief Document prepared by lawyers on the appeal of a case to provide the appellate court with a summary of the case and the issues involved.

Bubble concept Tactic employed by the EPA in determining levels of air pollution that determines appropriate levels of release by assuming all the pollution in an area comes from one source.

Burden of proof The responsibility of the party for proving the facts needed to recover in a lawsuit.

Business ethics *See* Ethics.

Business judgment rule Duty of care imposed upon members of corporate boards that requires adequate review of issues and information, devotion of adequate time to deliberations, and hiring of outside consultants as necessary for making decisions; the standard does not require foolproof judgment, only reasonable care in making the judgment.

"But for" test In negligence, the standard used for determining whether the defendant's negligence caused the plaintiff's injury; "but for" the fact that the defendant was negligent, the plaintiff would not have been injured.

Bylaws Operating rules of a corporation and its board; usually describes the officers and their roles and authority along with meeting procedures and notices.

C

Capacity Legal term for the ability to enter legally into a contract; for example, age capacity (minors do not have capacity).

Causation In negligence, an element that requires the plaintiff to show that the defendant's lack of care caused the plaintiff's injury.

Caveat emptor Latin term for "let the buyer beware"; summarizes an attitude that once prevailed in contract law of a lack of protection for a buyer of defective goods.

Celebrity endorsements Public figures advertising products on the basis of their personal use.

Celler-Kefauver Act Act that amended Section 7 of the Clayton Act and closed the loophole of merger through asset acquisition by regulating asset acquisitions.

Certification Process of authorizing a union to represent exclusively a group of workers.

Certiorari Latin term meaning "to become informed." A court agrees to hear a case when it grants certiorari.

Charge Complaint to NLRB brought by a private party.

Charitable subscription A promise to make payment to a charitable organization; a pledge; it is enforceable even though the charity gives nothing in exchange.

Chattel mortgage Lien on personal property.

Checks and balances Term describing our tripartite system of government in which each branch has some check mechanism to control abuses of powers by the other branches.

Citation Name given to abbreviated description of a court case or statute; for example, 355 F. Supp. 291.

Cite *See* Citation.

Civil law Laws affecting the private rights of individuals.

Civil Rights Act of 1866 and 1870 Initial act of Congress to help curb discrimination in employment; little was done with it once it was passed.

Civil Rights Act of 1964 Cornerstone of the antidiscrimination statutes. The original statute passed to prevent discrimination in housing, education, and employment.

Class action suit In civil law, a suit by a group of plaintiffs with the same claims; generally used in antitrust and securities lawsuits.

Clayton Act One of the major antitrust laws; governs the control of business through mergers, acquisitions, and interlocking directorates.

Clean Air Act The first effective anti-air-pollution act and the cornerstone of air pollution legislation.

Clean Air Act Amendments of 1990 These first major changes to federal environmental laws on air pollution since 1977 impose additional requirements on industrial emissions controls, auto emissions, and other types of chemical emissions that affect the ozone layer.

Clean Water Act The first effective anti-water-pollution act and the cornerstone of water pollution legislation.

Close corporation A type of corporation created by statute that allows limited liability with direct tax benefits.

Closed-end transaction Term used in Regulation Z to describe credit transactions with definite times for and amounts of repayment that are not ongoing; for example, retail installment contracts.

Closed shop A place of employment restricting hirees to union members only.

Closing argument The summary attorneys give to the jury before it deliberates and after all the evidence has been presented.

Code of ethics A set of rules adopted by a company to establish acceptable behavior standards for its employees.

Code of Federal Regulations (C.F.R.) Series of volumes carrying the enactments of all federal agencies.

Collateral Property subject to a lien, security interest or chattel mortgage.

Collective bargaining agreement Contract between management and labor represented by one union for a collective bargaining unit.

Collective bargaining unit NLRB term for a group of employees represented by one bargaining agent and agreement; can be a plant, a national group, or a subpart of a plant.

Comment letter SEC response to registration filing; requires additional information or clarification on proposed offering.

Commerce Clause Provision in the U.S. Constitution controlling the regulation of intrastate, interstate, and foreign commerce and delineating authority for such regulation.

Commercial impracticability Contract defense for nonperformance under the UCC that excuses a party when performance has become impossible or will involve much more than what was anticipated in the contract negotiations.

Commercial speech The speech of business in the form of advertising, political endorsements, or comments on social issues.

Common law Originally the law of England made uniform after William the Conqueror; today, the nonstatutory law and the law found in judicial precedent.

Common stock Type of shares in a corporation; the voting shares of the corporation and generally the bulk of ownership.

Community Right-to-Know Substance Under federal environmental laws, a toxin used by a business or an operation that must be publicly disclosed; EPA filing is required.

Comparative negligence In negligence, a defense that allocates responsibility for an accident between the plaintiff and defendant when both were negligent and determines liability accordingly.

Compensatory damages Damages to put nonbreaching party in the same position he or she would have been in had the breach not occurred.

Complaint The first pleading in a lawsuit; the document that outlines the plaintiff's allegations against the defendant and specifies the remedies sought; with respect to federal agencies, can also be a formal charge of rules or statutory violations by a company or individual.

Comprehensive Environmental Response Compensation and Liability Act (CERCLA) Federal law that authorized federal funds to clean up hazardous waste disposal.

Concerted activities Organized economic weapons of union.

Condition precedent In contracts, an event or action that must take place before a contract is required to be performed; for example, qualifying for financing is a condition precedent for a lender's performance on a mortgage loan.

Conditions Events that must occur before contract performance is due.

Conditions concurrent (conditions contemporaneous) In contracts, the conditions that must occur simultaneously for contract performance to be required; for example, in an escrow closing in real property, an agent collects title, insurance, funds, and other documents and sees that all the exchanges under the contract occur at the same time; the parties perform their part of the agreement at the same time.

Confidential relationship A relationship of trust and reliance; necessary to establish the defense of undue influence.

Confiscation In international law, the taking of private property by a government.

Conglomerate merger A merger between two firms in different lines of business.

Consent decree For administrative agencies, a type of plea bargain; a settlement document for an administrative agency's charges.

Consequential damages Damages resulting from a contract breach such as penalties or lost profits.

Consideration In contracts, what each party gives to the other as his or her part of the contract performance.

Consolidation A form of merger in which two firms unite and become known by a new name.

Constitution Document that contains the basic rights in a society and the structure of its government; cannot be changed without the approval of the society's members.

Constructive notice Notice given in a public place or published notice, as opposed to actual notice.

Consumer Credit Protection Act Act that provides disclosure requirements for lenders and protections for debtors; more commonly referred to as the Truth-in-Lending Act.

Consumer debt Debt entered into for the purpose of purchasing goods or services for personal or household use.

Consumer Leasing Act Act that provides for disclosure protection for consumers who are leasing goods.

Consumer Product Safety Commission Federal agency that establishes safety standards for consumer goods.

Contentious jurisdiction Consensual jurisdiction of a court that is consented to when the parties have a dispute; for example, U.N. courts.

Contract Binding agreement between two parties for the exchange of goods, real estate, or services.

Contract defense Situation, term, or event that makes an otherwise valid contract invalid.

Contract interference Tort involving a third party's actions resulting in a valid contract being lost or invalidated; an unfair method of competition.

Contributory negligence Negligence defense that results when the injured party acted in a negligent way and contributed to his or her own injuries.

Conventional pollutant EPA classification of water pollutant that must be treated prior to its release into waterways.

Cooling-off period Under the Taft-Hartley Act, a provision that can be invoked by the president to require laborers threatening to strike in an industry that affects the health and safety of the nation to continue to work during a negotiation period.

Copyright Under federal law, a right given to protect the exclusive use of books, music, and other creative works.

Corporate opportunity A business proposition or investment opportunity that a corporation would have an interest in pursuing; precludes directors from taking a profit opportunity when the corporation would have an interest.

Corporate political speech *See* Political speech.

Corporate veil The personal liability shield; the corporate protection that entitles shareholders, directors, and officers to limited liability; can be pierced for improper conduct of business or fraud.

Corporation Business entity created by statute that provides limited liability for its owners.

Corrective advertising Potential FTC remedy required when ads run by a firm have been deceptive; requires company to run ads explaining previous ads or run a new statement in future ads.

Council on Environmental Quality (CEQ) Agency under Executive Branch created in 1966 to formulate environmental policy and make recommendations for legislation.

Counterclaim Pleading in a lawsuit in which the defendant makes allegations against the plaintiff in his or her response to the plaintiff's complaint.

Counteroffer Response by offeree to offer or when offeree changes terms of offer.

County courts Lesser trial courts that hear smaller disputes and misdemeanor cases; like justice of the peace courts in many states.

Course of dealing Pattern of a relationship between two parties who have contracted previously.

Court of Justice of European Communities The court of dispute settlement for the twelve nations in the European Community.

Covenants not to compete Promises to protect employers and buyers from loss of goodwill through employee or seller competition.

Crime A wrong against society that carries penalties of imprisonment and/or fines.

Criminal fraud A crime in which the victim is defrauded by an intentional act of the perpetrator.

Criminal law As opposed to civil law, the law on wrongs against society.

Cross-elasticity Economic term describing the willingness of customers to substitute various goods; for example, waxed paper for plastic wrap.

Cross examination Questioning by opposing parties of a witness in court; that is, defendant cross examines plaintiff's witnesses and plaintiff cross examines defendant's witnesses.

Cumulative preferred stock Type of ownership in a corporation that gives the stock owners preference in the distribution of dividends and also guarantees earnings each year; in the event those earnings are not paid, they are carried over or accumulate until they can be paid.

Customer and territorial restrictions Manufacturer's restrictions on retail sales locations and customers.

D

Deed of trust Alternative form of creditor security in land purchases.

Defamation Tort of making untrue statements about another that cause damage to his or her reputation or character.

Default Judgment entered when the defendant fails to file an answer in a lawsuit.

Defendant The party who is alleged to have committed a wrong in a civil lawsuit; the charged party in a criminal prosecution.

Deficiency letter *See* Comment letter.

Del credere agency Agent who sells principal's goods to a buyer on credit and agrees to pay the principal if the buyer does not pay for the goods.

Delegation Transfer of obligations under a contract; generally accompanied by assignment of benefits.

De minimis Latin term meaning small or minimal.

De novo Latin term for starting over or anew; a trial de novo is a special form of appeal of a trial decision that allows the case to be retried in a different forum.

Deposition Form of discovery in which witnesses or parties can be questioned under oath in recorded testimony outside the courtroom.

Derivative Type of investment that derives its earnings from a contractual agreement based on other obligations.

Dicta In a judicial opinion, the explanation for the decision; not the actual rule of law but the reasoning for the ruling.

Directed verdict Verdict entered by judge upon motion of a party after the presentation of either side's case; can be entered if the plaintiff has not met his or her burden of proof or if the defendant fails to rebut the plaintiff's case.

Direct examination Term that describes a party's questioning of his or her own witness.

Disclaimer A provision in a contract that eliminates liability such as a warranty disclaimer or a disclaimer of tort liability.

Discovery Process occurring before a trial that involves each side's investigation of the case, the evidence, and the witnesses; consists of depositions, interrogatories, requests for admissions and productions, and so on.

Disparagement Form of unfair competition in which a business, its trademark, or its name is maligned; business defamation.

Disparate impact Theory for establishing discrimination; involves using statistical analysis to demonstrate that a particular practice or an employer's hiring practices have a greater impact on protected classes.

Disparate treatment In discrimination law, the application of different rules or standards to people of different races, genders, or national origins.

Dissenting opinion In an appellate court's review of a case, an opinion written by a judge who disagrees with the decision of the majority of the court.

Dissenting shareholder Shareholder who has objected to a merger or consolidation and votes against it; is entitled to receive the value of his or her shares before the merger or consolidation.

Dissolution In partnerships, occurs when one partner ceases to be associated with the business; in corporations, the termination of the corporate existence.

Diversity of citizenship A term referring to a requirement for federal court jurisdiction that plaintiff and defendant must be citizens of different states.

Documents of title Formal legal document that serves to prove and transfer title to tangible personal property.

Domestic corporation A term used to describe a corporation in the state in which it is incorporated.

Double jeopardy In criminal law, a constitutional prohibition against being tried twice for the same crime.

Due diligence Under the Securities Act of 1933, a defense for filing a false registration statement that requires proof that the individuals involved did all they could to uncover the truth and could not have discovered the false statements despite their "due diligence."

Due process Constitutional protection ensuring notice and a fair trial or hearing in all judicial proceedings.

Duress In contract law, a defense that permits nonperformance of a contract if the party can show that physical or mental force was used to obtain the agreement to enter into the contract.

E

Easement Right or privilege in the land of another.

EEOC complaint Complaint against an employer filed by either an employee or the EEOC; initiates an investigation by the EEOC.

Effluent guidelines In environmental law, the standards for release of nonnatural substances into natural waters.

8-K form A filing required by the SEC under the 1934 Securities Act; an 8-K is filed by a registered company within ten days of a significant or material event affecting the company (for example, a dividend being suspended).

Elements The requirements for proof of a crime.

Embezzlement Name for the crime of an employee stealing funds, property, or services from his or her employer.

Eminent domain In constitutional law, the taking of private property by a government entity for a public purpose with compensation paid to the owner.

Emissions offset policy EPA procedure for approval of new facilities in nonattainment areas.

Employment at will Doctrine that gives the employer the right to fire an employee at any time with or without cause; the doctrine and its protection for employers has been eroded by judicial decisions over recent years.

Employment Retirement Income Security Act of 1974 (ERISA) Congressional act establishing requirements for disclosure and other procedures with relation to employees' retirement plans.

Enabling act Act of a legislative body establishing an administrative agency and providing it with guidelines and authority for the enforcement of the law.

En banc Latin term for the full bench; refers to an appellate hearing in which the full court, as opposed to a panel of three judges, hears a case on review.

Endangered Species Act (ESA) Federal environmental law that requires federal agencies to disclose the impact of proposed projects on species listed as protected under the act.

Environmental impact statement (EIS) Report required to be filed when a federal agency is taking action that will affect land, water, or air; an analysis of the effect of a project on the environment.

Environmental Protection Agency (EPA) The main federal agency responsible for the enforcement of all the federal environmental laws.

Equal Credit Opportunity Act (ECOA) Federal law that prohibits discrimination on the basis of race, sex, national origin, marital status, or ethnicity in the decision to extend credit.

Equal Employment Opportunity Act of 1972 Congressional act that established the EEOC and provided strong enforcement powers for Title VII provisions.

Equal Employment Opportunity Commission (EEOC) Federal agency responsible for the enforcement of Title VII and other federal antidiscrimination laws.

Equal Pay Act of 1963 Act prohibiting wage discrimination on the basis of age, race, sex, ethnicity, and so on.

Equal protection Constitutional right of all citizens to be treated in the same manner and afforded the same rights under law regardless of sex, race, color, or national origin.

Equitable remedy A remedy other than money damages, such as specific performance, injunction, and so on.

Equity That portion of the law that originated to afford remedies when money damages were not appropriate; currently, remedies of law and equity have merged and courts can award either or both.

Estoppel Doctrine of reliance; prevents parties from backing out of an obligation they have created; for example, a partner by estoppel has allowed others to use his or her name in connection with a partnership and is estopped from denying liability to third parties who have relied on that representation.

Ethics Moral behavior constraints.

European Court of Human Rights A noncommercial court dealing with disputes over the treatment of a country's citizens.

Exclusionary conduct Monopolistic behavior that attempts to prevent market entry and exclude competition.

Exclusive dealing Antitrust term for contract arrangements in which the seller sells to only one buyer in an area.

Exclusive distributorship *See* Sole outlet.

Exculpatory clause Clause that attempts to hold a party harmless in the event of damage or injury to another's property.

Executed person or contracts Contracts in which performance has been completed.

Executive branch That portion of the federal government that consists of the president and the administrative agencies; often referred to as the enforcement branch.

Executive committee A working board of directors' committee that usually includes company officers and makes day-to-day decisions in between regular board meetings; manages ongoing operations.

Executive order Law of the executive branch; sets policies for administrative workers and contracts.

Executory contracts Contracts that have been entered into but not yet performed.

Exemptions Under the Securities Act of 1933, the securities and transactions that need not be registered with the SEC.

Exempt securities Securities not required to be registered with the SEC under the 1933 Act.

Exempt transactions Under the 1933 Securities Act, sales of securities not required to be registered, such as shares issued under a Chapter 11 bankruptcy court reorganization.

Ex parte contacts Latin term for contacts with a judicial figure or hearing officer outside the presence of the opposing side.

Express authority In agency law, the authority given either in writing or orally to the agent for his or her conduct.

Express contract Contract orally agreed to or in writing.

Express warranty Expressed promise by seller as to the quality, abilities, or performance of a product.

Expropriation The taking of private property by a government for government use, also known as appropriation.

F

Failing company doctrine Under the Clayton Act, a justification for a generally illegal merger on the basis that the firm being merged is in financial difficulty and would not survive alone.

Fair Credit Billing Act Federal law governing credit card bills and requiring monthly statements, disclosure of dispute rights, and so on.

Fair Credit Card Disclosure Act of 1988 Amendment to TILA that requires disclosure of terms in credit card solicitations.

Fair Credit Reporting Act Federal law governing the disclosure of credit information to consumers and the content of those credit reports.

Fair Debt Collections Practices Act Federal law controlling the methods debt collectors may use in collecting consumer debts and also requiring disclosures to consumers when the debt collection process begins.

Fair Labor Standards Act (FLSA) Federal law on minimum wages, maximum hours, overtime, and compensatory time.

Fair trade contracts Agreements requiring retailers not to sell products below a certain price; permitted in some states.

Fair use One of the exceptions to copyright protection; permits limited use of copyright material; for example, an excerpt from a poem.

False imprisonment The intentional tort of retaining someone against his or her will.

Featherbedding Union unfair labor practice of requiring payment for work not actually performed; for example, requiring payment for a minimum number of bricks even though the job does not involve that many bricks.

Federal circuits Geographic groupings of the federal district courts for purposes of appellate jurisdiction.

Federal Consumer Product Warranty Law of 1975 The Magnuson-Moss Act; governs the definitions of limited and full warranties; requires disclosure of warranty terms.

Federal district court The trial court of the federal system.

Federal Environmental Pesticide Control Act Federal law that requires registration of all pesticides with the EPA.

Federal implementation plan (FIP) Under the Clean Air Act, requirements established by the EPA (in the absence of state action) regarding the control of emissions by plants and autos.

Federal Insurance Contributions Act (FICA) Federal law that requires the joint contribution by employers and employees of the funds used for the social security system.

Federal Privacy Act Federal law that prohibits exchange of information about individuals among agencies without request and notification, unless for law enforcement purposes.

Federal Register The federal newspaper that reports the day-to-day actions of administrative agencies.

Federal Register Act Federal law that establishes all the publications and reporting mechanisms for federal administrative law, such as the *Federal Register* and the Code of Federal Regulations.

Federal Register System Part of the federal government responsible for the publication of government notices and rules.

Federal Reporter Series of volumes reporting the decisions of the U.S. Court of Appeals.

Federal Supplement Series of volumes reporting the decisions of the federal district courts.

Federal Trade Commission (FTC) Federal agency responsible for regulation of unfair and deceptive trade practices, including deceptive advertisements.

Federal Trade Commission Act Federal law establishing the FTC and its regulatory role.

Federal Water Pollution Control Act of 1972 Federal law that set goals of swimmable and fishable waters by 1983 and zero pollution discharge by 1985.

Federal Water Pollution Control Administration (FWPCA) Separate federal agency established to monitor water quality standards.

Fee simple Highest degree of land ownership; full rights of mortgage and transferability.

Fiduciary Position of trust and confidence.

Fifth Amendment Portion of the Bill of Rights of the U.S. Constitution providing protection against self-incrimination and ensuring due process.

Finance charges For credit cards, the interest paid each month on outstanding balances.

Financing statement Publicly-filed document reflecting security interest.

First Amendment Portion of the Bill of Rights of the U.S. Constitution providing protection for freedom of speech and religious freedom.

Fixtures Property that was once personal in nature that is affixed to real property and becomes a part of it.

FOIA request Request to a government agency for information retained in that agency's files.

Force majeure Clause in a contract that excuses performance in the event of wars, embargo, and other generally unforeseeable events.

Foreclosure Process of creditor acquiring mortgaged land for resale.

Foreign corporation A corporation in any state except the state in which it is incorporated.

Foreign Corrupt Practices Act (FCPA) Federal law prohibiting bribes in foreign countries and requiring the maintenance of internal controls on accounting for firms registered under the 1934 Securities Exchange Act.

Formal rulemaking Process for developing rules in an administrative agency; involves hearings and public comment period.

Fourteenth Amendment Provision of the U.S. Constitution that provides for equal protection and due process.

Fourth Amendment Part of the Bill of Rights of the U.S. Constitution that provides protection and assurance of privacy; the search and seizure amendment.

Fraud Term for deception or intentional misrepresentation in contract negotiation.

Freedom of Information Act (FOIA) Federal law that permits access to information held by federal administrative agencies.

Freeze-out Merger undertaken with the objective of eliminating minority shareholders.

Friendly takeover A takeover of one firm by another firm when the target firm solicits or agrees to the takeover.

Frolic or detour In agency law, set of rules used to determine when an agent is in the scope of employment; a frolic is a major deviation from duty and eliminates the principal's liability; a detour is a slight deviation such as lunch for a salesperson who makes calls all day.

FTC Improvements Act of 1980 Federal act that provided change in the role of the FTC and placed some limitations on its authority after the FTC's attempt to regulate children's television advertising.

Full disclosure standard SEC standard for registration; materiality disclosure requirements; not a merit standard.

G

Garnishment Judicial process of taking funds or wages for satisfaction of a judgment.

General partner Partner in a general or limited partnership whose personal assets are subject to partnership creditors in the event of nonpayment of partnership debts.

Geographic market Relevant geographic location for a firm's market; used as a basis for determining monopoly power and market share.

Good-faith bargaining Mutual obligation of employer and union to meet at reasonable times, confer in good faith on employment issues, and execute a written agreement.

Government corporation Corporation created by a government agency to achieve a social goal.

Government in the Sunshine Act Federal law that requires advance notice and open meetings of agency heads.

Grand jury Special group of jurors established as a review board for potential criminal prosecutions; generally established for a year to eighteen months.

Gratuitous agency Agency relationship in which the agent has the authority to act for the principal but will not be compensated.

Gray market Market in which trade name goods are sold through unauthorized dealers or without authorization from the owner of the trade name.

Group bids Takeover offer by more than one offeror acting in concert.

Group boycotts A practice prohibited by federal antitrust laws in which several firms agree not to sell or buy from one or several other firms.

H

Hart-Scott-Rodino Antitrust Improvements Act 1976 act that gave the Justice Department greater investigative authority in antitrust violations and established premerger notification requirements.

Hazardous Substance Response Trust Fund Fund set up by CERCLA for waste site cleanup that is funded by the responsible company.

Hearing examiner Quasi-judicial figure for agency hearings.

Hearing officer Quasi-judicial figure for agency hearings.

Hearsay Testimony about the statements of another; often inadmissible evidence in a trial.

Home Equity Loan Consumer Protection Act of 1988 Amendment to TILA that requires disclosures in home equity loan documents, including the possibility of foreclosure, and allows three-day rescission period for home equity loans.

Home solicitation sales Sales originated in the home of the buyer.

Horizontal merger A merger between two competitors.

Horizontal restraint of trade Anticompetitive activity among competitors; for example, price-fixing among competitors.

Hostile takeover A takeover not solicited or approved by the target's management.

Hot cargo agreements Union economic weapon in which others agree not to handle the products of the struck employer.

Howey **test** U.S. Supreme Court definition of a security; investment in a common enterprise with profits to come from the efforts of others.

Hung jury Term used to describe a jury unable to come to a verdict.

Hybrid rulemaking Process by which agency promulgates rules with some hearings but relies mostly on public comments.

I

Implied authority Authority of an agent that exists because of business custom in the principal's operation and in industry.

Implied contract A contract that arises from circumstances and is not expressed by the parties.

Implied-in-law contract *See* Quasi contract.

Implied warranty of fitness for a particular purpose Warranty given by seller to buyer that promises goods will meet the buyer's specified needs.

Implied warranty of merchantability Under the Uniform Commercial Code, Article 2, Sales, (a warranty that the goods are of average quality) that is given in every sale of goods by a merchant.

Impossibility Contract defense that excuses performance when there is no objective way to complete the contract.

Inadequate capitalization In corporation law, the lack of sufficient funds to cover the anticipated debts and obligations of a corporation.

Incidental damages Damages suffered by the nonbreaching party to a contract as a result of the breach; for example, late performance fees on a buyer's contract because the seller failed to deliver on time.

Incorporators Individuals who sign the incorporation papers for a newly formed corporation.

Independent contractor Person who works for another but is not controlled in his or her day-to-day conduct.

Indictment Formal criminal charges issued by the grand jury.

Infant A minor; a person below the age of majority, in most states below the age of eighteen.

Informal rulemaking Process by which an agency promulgates rules without formal public hearings.

Information Formal criminal charges issued by a judge after a preliminary hearing.

Infringement The use of a copyright, patent, or trademark or trade name without permission.

Inherently dangerous activities In agency law, those activities that carry a high risk and for which the party hiring an independent contractor cannot disclaim liability; for example, dynamiting a building to demolish it.

Initial appearance In criminal procedure, the first appearance of the accused before a judicial figure; must take place shortly after arrest.

Initial meeting First meeting of a corporation's organizers after the state provides certification that the corporation exists.

Injunction Equitable remedy in which courts order or enjoin a particular activity.

In personam jurisdiction Jurisdiction over the person; type of jurisdiction court must have to require a party to appear before it.

In rem jurisdiction Jurisdiction over the thing; a method whereby a court obtains jurisdiction by having property or money located within its geographic jurisdiction.

Insider A corporate officer or director or other executive with access to corporate information not available to the public.

Insider Trading and Securities Fraud Enforcement Act of 1988 Act increasing 1934 Act penalties for insider trading.

Instructions Explanation of the law applicable in a case given to the jury at the end of the case.

Intentional infliction of emotional distress Intentional tort in which the defendant engages in outrageous conduct that is psychologically damaging to the plaintiff.

Intentional torts Civil wrongs against individuals that are committed with a requisite state of mind and intention to harm; includes defamation, false imprisonment, battery, assault, and intentional infliction of emotional distress.

Inter-American Court of Human Rights In international law, the court for resolution of noncommercial issues or the violation of human rights by a particular nation in North or South America.

Interbrand competition Competition among like products; for example, competition between Pepsi and Coke.

Interlocking directorates In antitrust law, the presence of the same directors on the boards of various companies that occupy positions in the same chain of distribution or are competitors; concern is the concentration of power.

International Court of Justice Voluntary court in the international system of law; nonbinding decisions.

Interrogatories Method of discovery in which parties send written questions to each other, with responses required to be given under oath.

Intervenors Interested parties who are permitted to participate in agency hearings even though they are not parties to the case.

Intrabrand competition Competition among products made by the same manufacturer; for example, competition between Coke and Diet Coke.

J

Joint venture A partnership for one activity or business venture.

Judge Elected or appointed government official responsible for supervising trials, hearing appeals, and ruling on motions.

Judgment The final decision of a court; formal entry of the decision or verdict.

Judgment on the pleadings A dismissal of a suit by a court for the failure of the plaintiff to state a case in the complaint.

Judgment NOV Judgment non obstante veredicto; a judgment notwithstanding the verdict; a judgment issued by the judge after the jury has rendered a verdict; a trial court's reversal of a jury's decision on the grounds that the verdict was against the weight of the evidence.

Judicial branch One of three branches of the federal government that consists of all levels of federal courts.

Judicial review Review by appellate court of decisions and actions of a lower court to determine whether reversible errors in procedure or law were made.

Junk bond Method for financing takeovers in which buyers have as their security the assets of the target firm; such security is only as good as the takeover is successful.

Jurisdiction The concept of authority of a court to settle disputes.

Jurisprudence The philosophy of law.

Jury instructions Explanation to the jury of the law applicable in the case.

Just compensation Principle in eminent domain that requires the government entity taking private property to pay the owner a fair amount.

Justice of the peace courts Lower courts generally handling traffic citations and other lesser civil matters.

K

Knock-off goods Goods manufactured by someone other than the trademark or trade name holder without authorization and not according to the standards of the owner.

L

Labor Management Cooperation Act Federal law providing funding for the study of alternative solutions to labor disputes.

Labor-Management Relations Act The Taft-Hartley Act; governs management conduct in its relationships with unions.

Landrum-Griffin Act Labor-Management Reporting and Disclosure Act; legislation passed to regulate unions and their governance.

Lanham Act Federal law dealing with trademark and trade name protection.

Lawyer's Edition Private publisher's series of volumes reporting U.S. Supreme Court decisions; contains summaries of the cases and the briefs of counsel.

Lease Temporary possession and use of real property, or right of use and possession or personal property.

Legal remedy At common law a legal remedy consisted of money damages vs. equitable remedies of injunctions and specific performance; different courts afforded different remedies in common law England but the distinction has disappeared today, and all courts have authority to award legal and equitable remedies.

Legislative branch One of the three branches of government; at the federal level, consists of the Congress (the Senate and the House of Representatives) and is the branch responsible for making laws.

Letter of credit Generally used in international transactions, an assurance by a bank of the seller's right to draw on a line of credit established for the buyer.

Libel Written defamation; defamation in a newspaper or magazine or, in some states, on television.

License Right of access; generally oral; personal right that is not transferrable.

Lien An interest in property used to secure repayment of a debt; entitles creditor to foreclosure rights in the event the debt is not repaid. Creditor's right in property to secure debt.

Life estate Right to use and occupy property for life.

Like grade or quality Under Robinson-Patman Act, this means that there are no differences in the physical product.

Limited jurisdiction Specialty courts that have only limited authority over certain types of cases with distinct subject matter; probate courts have limited jurisdiction over probate matters only.

Limited partner Partner in a limited partnership who has no personal liability and can only lose his or her investment in the partnership; must be formed according to statutory requirements; cannot use name in partnership name and cannot participate in the firm's management.

Limited partnership Type of partnership in which some partners have unlimited liability (general partners) and other partners have only their investments at the risk of the business (limited partners); must follow statutory procedures to create properly a limited partnership.

Limited partnership agreement Contract governing the rights and relations of limited partners.

Line of commerce Area of business; determination used by the Justice Department in evaluating mergers.

Lingering apparent authority Type of authority an agent has when the principal fails to announce that the agent is no longer associated with him or her.

Liquidated damages Damages agreed to in advance and provided for in the contract; usually appropriate when it is difficult to know how much the damages will be.

Lockout Economic weapon of employer in which employees are not permitted to work; shop is closed down to avoid a strike.

Long-arm statutes Statutes in each state that allow the state courts to bring in defendants from outside the state so long as they have some "minimum contact" with the state.

M

Madrid Agreement In international law, 1891 multilateral treaty for protection of trademarks that permits registration and protection through a centralized registrar in Geneva.

Mailbox rule Timing rule in contract acceptances that provides that acceptance is effective upon mailing if properly done.

Mandatory bargaining terms In collective bargaining, the terms both sides are required to discuss such as wages, hours, and so on.

Market power The ability of a firm to control prices and product demand.

Master-servant relationship Type of agency relationship in which the principal directly controls the agent; for example, principal controls hours and supervises work directly.

Material fact (or misstatement) A statement of fact that would influence an individual's decision to buy or sell.

Maximum achievable control technology (MACT) Under the 1990 Clean Air Act, the standard required for factories in controlling air emissions; replaced the old, less stringent standard of Best Available Technology (BAT).

Mediation Alternative dispute resolution mechanism in which a third party is brought in to find a common ground between two disputing parties.

Meeting the competition Defense to price discrimination that allows the defense of price reduction when competition in the area dictates that price.

Mens rea Mental intent or state of mind necessary for the commission of a crime.

Merchant's firm offer Under § 2-205 of the UCC, an offer required to be held open if made in writing by a merchant, even though no consideration is given.

Merchant's confirmation memoranda Memos between merchants, signed by one of them, that will satisfy the statute of frauds requirements and create an enforceable contract against both parties.

Merger Process of combining firms so that one firm becomes a part of the other and only one firm's name is retained.

Merit review Process at the state level of reviewing securities registrations for their merit as opposed to the federal review for full disclosure.

Mineral rights Ownership rights to materials beneath the land surface.

Minimum contacts Standard used for determining in personam jurisdiction over residents outside the state of the court of litigation; nonresident defendants must have some contact with the state to justify a court taking jurisdiction.

Minimum wage Part of the FLSA that requires all employees to be paid a minimum wage.

Mini-trial Alternative dispute resolution method in which the officers of two firms in a dispute listen to the key evidence in a case to see if a settlement can be determined.

Minor An infant; an individual under the age of majority; generally someone under the age of eighteen.

Miranda warnings Statement required to be given to individuals when taken into custody to alert them to their right to remain silent, the fact that statements can be used against them, their right to an attorney, and the right to an appointed attorney if they cannot afford one.

Misappropriation Intentional tort of using someone's name, likeness, voice, or image without permission.

Misrepresentation In contract formation, misstatements of material facts.

Misuse In product liability, a defense based on the plaintiff's failure to follow instructions or use of a product for improper purposes.

Model Business Corporation Act (MBCA) Uniform law on corporations.

Modify An option for an appellate court in its review of a lower court case; it is an action that is something less than reversing a decision, but something more than simply affirming it. For example, an appellate court could agree with the verdict but modify the judgment amount or the remedy.

Monopolizing Controlling a product or geographic market.

Monopoly power The ability to control prices and exclude competition.

Mortgage Lien on real property.

Motion A party's request to the court for action .

Motion for judgment on the pleadings A motion made to dismiss a suit for failure by the plaintiff to establish a cause of action in the pleadings.

Motion for summary judgment A motion made for final disposition of a case in which there is no dispute of facts and only a dispute of law and its application.

Motion to dismiss A motion made after the presentation of the plaintiff's case or the defendant's case for failure to establish a prima facie case (in the case of the plaintiff) or failure to rebut the presumption (in the case of the defendant).

Multilateral treaty A treaty agreed to by several nations.

N

National Environmental Policy Act (NEPA) The federal legislation on environmental impact statements.

Nationalization The taking of private property by a government for governmental use.

National Labor Relations Act (Wagner Act 1935) First universal federal legislation that gave employees the right to organize and choose representatives for collective bargaining.

National Labor Relations Board (NLRB) Federal agency charged with supervising union elections and handling unfair labor practice complaints.

National Pollution Discharge Elimination System (NPDES) A system established by the EPA that requires those who discharge pollutants to obtain a permit, the granting of which is based on limits and pretreatments.

Necessaries With regard to minors, items for which minors can be held responsible.

Negligence Tort of accidental wrong committed by oversight or failure to take precautions or corrective action.

Nexus Connection; a term used in constitutional analysis of the authority to tax; there must be a sufficient connection between the business and the taxing state.

NLRB National Labor Relations Board.

Noerr-Pennington **doctrine** An exception to the antitrust laws that allows business to lobby against competitors before legislative and administrative bodies even though the effect may be anticompetitive.

Noise Control Act Federal statute controlling noise levels and requiring product labels.

Nolo contendere A "no contest" plea; the charges are neither denied nor admitted.

Nonattainment area In federal air pollution regulation, an area unable to meet federal clean air goals and guidelines.

Nonconventional pollutant EPA classification of pollutant that requires the highest level of treatment prior to release into waterways.

Nonprofit corporations Those corporations performing a function that covers cost but does not provide a return on investment.

Norris-LaGuardia Act The anti-injunction act; one of the first federal labor acts passed to prevent courts from issuing injunctions to stop labor strikes except in dangerous or emergency situations.

Novation Process of reworking a contract to substitute parties or terms so that the old contract is abandoned and the new contract becomes the only valid contract.

Nuisance Civil wrong of creating a situation (noise, dust, smell) that interferes with others' ability to enjoy the use of their properties.

O

Occupational Safety and Health Act Worker safety statute passed by Congress in 1970 that established OSHA and directs the development of safety standards in the workplace as well as systems for record keeping and compliance.

Offer Indication of present intent to contract; the first step in making a contract.

Offeree In contract negotiations, the person to whom the offer is made.

Offeror In contract negotiations, the person who makes the offer.

Oil Pollution Act (OPA) Federal law providing penalties for oil spills and authorizing federal cleanup when private companies' cleanup efforts fail; also authorizes federal government to collect for costs of cleanup when firm or firms responsible for the spill fail to do so.

Omnibus hearing In criminal procedure, a hearing held before trial to determine the admissibility of evidence.

Open-end credit transaction Under Regulation Z, credit transactions without a definite beginning and ending balance; for example, credit cards.

Opening statement In a trial, each side's overview of the case and the evidence that will be presented.

Open meeting law Law (at either state or federal level) requiring that notice be given of meetings of agency heads and that they be open to the public.

Opposition proceedings In non-U.S. countries, the patent process that allows third parties to appear and object to a patent application.

Option A contract for time on an offer; an agreement to hold an offer open for a period of time in exchange for consideration.

Oral argument Upon appeal of a case, the attorneys' presentation of their points on appeal to the panel of appellate judges.

Ordinances Laws at the city, town, or county level.

Ordinary and reasonably prudent person In negligence, standard used for determining the level of care required in any given situation.

Original jurisdiction Jurisdiction of trial courts; jurisdiction of courts where a case begins.

OSHA Occupational Safety and Health Administration; federal agency responsible for the enforcement of federal health and safety standards in business and industry.

Overtime pay Pay rate required for work beyond the maximum forty-hour work week.

P

Palming off Unfair trade practice of passing off mock goods as the goods of another.

Pan American Convention A 1929 treaty offering trademark protection to member countries.

Parol evidence Extrinsic evidence regarding a contract.

Partnership Voluntary association of two or more persons, co-owners in a business for profit.

Partnership by estoppel *See* Estoppel.

Partnership by implication A partnership that exists because of the conduct of the parties rather than by agreement.

Party autonomy The right of parties to determine privately their choice of law.

Patent Government license or protection for a process, product, or service.

Pattern or practice of discrimination In employment discrimination, a theory for establishing discrimination based on a pattern of dealing with minorities, women, and certain ethnic groups.

Per curiam A judicial opinion of the full court with no judge or justice claiming authorship.

Peremptory challenge Right to strike jurors with or without cause; lawyer's discretionary tool in selecting a jury; number of peremptory challenges is usually limited.

Periodic tenancy Lease that runs from period to period such as month-to-month.

Per se "On its face"; "without further proof."

Petition Often the first document in a case.

Petitioner Party filing a petition; or in the case of an appeal, the party filing the appeal of a lower court decision.

Picketing Economic weapon of labor unions; right to demonstrate in front of employer's place of business to display grievances publicly.

Plaintiff Party filing suit who is alleging a wrong committed by the defendant.

Plain view exception Under the Fourth Amendment, an exception to the warrant requirement that applies when what is seen is in the "plain view" of the law enforcement official.

Plea bargain A negotiated settlement of a criminal case prior to trial.

Pleadings The complaint, answer, and counterclaim filed in a lawsuit.

Point sources In environmental law, direct discharges of effluents.

Police power Constitutional term describing the authority given to the states to regulate the health, safety, and welfare of their citizens.

Political speech Term given to speech of businesses related to political candidates or issues; given First Amendment protection.

Pooling agreement Agreement among shareholders to vote their stock a certain way.

Precedent Prior judicial decisions; the law as it exists; *see also* Stare decisis.

Predatory pricing Discount pricing below cost for a short period of time in an attempt to drive new competition out of the market.

Preemption Constitutional term from the Supremacy Clause, which provides that the federal government preempts state law where such preemption was intended or where the federal regulation is so pervasive that it prevents state regulation.

Preferred stock Nonvoting shares of a corporation entitling its holders to dividend preference above the common shareholders.

Pregnancy Discrimination Act Federal law prohibiting discrimination in hiring or promotion decisions on the basis of pregnancy or plans for pregnancy.

Preliminary hearing In criminal procedure, the hearing in which the prosecution establishes there is sufficient evidence to bind the defendant over for trial.

Pretrial conference Meeting among lawyers and court to narrow issues, stipulate to evidence, and determine method of jury selection.

Prevention of significant deterioration (PSD) areas Clean air areas given special protection by the EPA regarding the maintenance of air quality.

Price discrimination Charging a different price for different customers on a basis other than different marginal costs.

Price-fixing Agreement among horizontal competitors to charge a uniform price.

Prima facie case A case establishing all the necessary elements; without rebuttal evidence from the defendant, entitles the plaintiff to a verdict.

Primary boycott Boycott by an employee or union against the employer.

Primary offering In securities, the initial offering of the security for sale.

Principal The employer or master in the principal-agent relationship.

Private law The law of contracts and the intrabusiness laws such as personnel rules.

Privity Direct contractual relationship.

Probable cause Sufficient cause or grounds for the issuance of a search warrant.

Probate courts Specialized courts set up to handle the probate of wills and estates and, generally, issues of guardianships and conservatorships.

Procedural due process Constitutional protection that gives litigants in civil cases and defendants in criminal cases the right to notice in all steps in the process and the right of participation.

Procedural laws Laws that provide the means for enforcing rights.

Process servers Individuals licensed by a state to deliver summonses and subpoenas to individuals.

Product liability Generic term used to describe the various contract and tort theories for holding parties liable for defective products.

Product market Relevant product market for a firm; used as a basis for determining monopoly power.

Professional corporation A statutory entity that permits professionals such as lawyers and doctors to incorporate and enjoy limited personal liability on all debts except for those arising from malpractice.

Profit corporations Those corporations seeking to earn a return for their investors.

Promissory estoppel A promise that causes another to act in reliance upon it; if the reliance is substantial, the promise is enforceable.

Promulgation The process of passing administrative agency rules.

Proper purpose A shareholder's legitimate interest in accessing a corporation's books and records.

Prospectus A formal document describing the nature of securities and the company offering them; an ad or other description of securities.

Proxy Right (given in written form) to vote another's shares.

Proxy solicitation The process of seeking voting rights from shareholders.

Public comment period In administrative rulemaking, the period during which any member of the public can comment on the rule, its content, and potential efficacy.

Public law Laws passed by some governmental agency.

Publicly held corporation A corporation owned by shareholders outside the officers and employees of the firm.

Puffing Offering opinions about the quality of goods and products; not a basis for misrepresentation; not a material statement of fact.

Q

Qualified privilege A defense to defamation available to the media that permits retraction and no liability so long as the information is not printed or given with malice or with reckless disregard for whether it is true.

Quasi contract A theory used to prevent unjust enrichment when no contract is formed; the court acts as if a contract had been formed and awards damages accordingly.

Quitclaim deed Transfer of title with no warranties.

Quotas Affirmative action plans that dictate a specific number of minority or female applicants be accepted for jobs, graduate school, and so on. Outlawed by U.S. Supreme Court; can only have affirmative action goals, not specific quotas.

R

Railway Labor Act The first federal labor legislation that controlled strikes by transportation employees.

Ratification A principal's recognition of a contract entered into by an unauthorized agent.

Recording Public filing of land documents.

Red herring prospectus A prospectus issued in advance of the effective date of a securities registration statement; permissible to release these before the registration statement is effective so long as a disclaimer that it is not an offer to sell securities is noted in red on the prospectus.

Re-direct examination Plaintiff's questioning of his or her own witness after defendant's cross examination is complete; or vice versa when defendant's witness is involved.

Regional reporter Series of volumes reporting the appeals and supreme court decisions of state courts; grouped by geographic region; for example, Pacific Reporter for the western states.

Registration statement Requirement under the Securities Act of 1933; a filing with the SEC that discloses all the necessary information about a securities offering and the offeror.

Regulation D A regulation of the SEC governing the small offering exemptions under the 1933 Act.

Regulation Z The Federal Reserve Board's regulation for the Truth-in Lending Act; specifies disclosure requirements and offers examples of required forms.

Regulatory Flexibility Act Reform act for federal agency rules promulgation; requires publication of proposed rules in trade magazines so that industries and individuals affected can properly respond during the public comment period.

Rehabilitation Act of 1973 Federal law prohibiting discrimination by federal contractors on the basis of a handicapping condition.

Relevant market Term used to describe the market studied to determine whether a particular seller has a monopoly.

Reliance In misrepresentation, the element that establishes that the buyer placed some importance on the statement.

Remainderman Interest in a third party following the death of the life tenant in a life estate.

Remand Term used to describe the action an appellate court takes when a case is sent down to a lower court for a retrial or other proceedings on the basis of the appellate court decision.

Rent-a-judge Means of alternative dispute resolution in which the parties hire a former judge and a private hearing room and have the judge determine liability.

Request for admissions Discovery tool in which one side asks the other to admit certain facts as proven in a case.

Request for production Discovery tool in which one side asks the other side to produce documents relevant to the case.

Requirements contract Contract in which the buyer agrees to buy all requirements for his or her business from one seller.

Resale price maintenance Practice of manufacturer attempting to control the price at which a product is sold at retail level.

Rescission Process of rescinding a contract.

Resource Conservation and Recovery Act Federal law governing the transportation of hazardous materials; requires a permit for such transportation; also encourages environmental cleanup.

Resource Recovery Act Federal law that gave aid to state and local governments with recycling programs.

Respondent On appeal of a case, the party who is not appealing; in a petition for a divorce, the party against whom the petition is filed.

Restatement A summary of existing common law on a particular topic; for example, Restatement of Contracts.

Restatement of Agency A summary of the majority view of the states of the law of agency followed by courts in resolving agency issues and disputes.

Restatement of Contracts, Second General summary of the nature of common law contracts in the United States.

Restatement § 402A Portion of the Restatement of Torts that deals with product liability.

Reverse Action of an appellate court in changing the decision of a lower court because a reversible error has been made.

Reversible error Mistake made in lower court proceedings that is ruled as improper by an appellate court and that requires a reversal of the case and possible retrials.

Revised Uniform Limited Partnership Act (RULPA) New version of the Uniform Limited Partnership Act that includes changes in the rights of limited partners and distributions on liquidation.

Revocation In contract law, the retraction by the offer or of an outstanding offer.

RICO Racketeer Influenced and Corrupt Organizations Act; federal statute regulating enterprises involved in gambling and other businesses that tend to attract organized crime figures.

Right-to-sue letter Letter issued by the EEOC to a complainant after all necessary administrative steps have been taken in the case; permits the complainant to pursue court action.

Right-to-work laws State laws providing employees with the right to work even though they are not union members.

Rivers and Harbors Act of 1899 A federal law revitalized during the 1960s and 1970s (prior to the enactment of specific federal legislation controlling emissions) to control water pollution.

Robinson-Patman Act Federal law that prohibits price discrimination.

Rule of reason Standard for evaluation of antitrust activity that allows the court to consider various factors and does not require an automatic finding of a violation of antitrust laws.

Rules 504, 505, and 506 *See* Regulation D; the rules governing small offering exemptions under the Securities Act of 1933.

Rule 10b-5 SEC antifraud rule.

Runaway shop Employer economic weapon in which work is transferred to an other plant to avoid the impact of a strike.

S

Safe Drinking Water Act 1986 federal law that sets standards for drinking water systems and requires states to enforce them.

Scheduled injuries Under workers' compensation systems, listed injury for which certain payments are to be made to the injured worker.

Scienter Mental intent; under 10(b) of the 1934 Securities Exchange Act, a requirement of intent to defraud as opposed to a standard of negligence.

Scope of employment Phrase used to describe the liability limits of the principal for the agent; an act must be committed within this scope for the imposition of liability on the principal.

Search warrant Judicially authorized document allowing the search of individuals' or businesses' premises,

Secondary boycott Union economic weapon in which others are asked not to deal with the struck employer.

Section 10(b) Antifraud provision of the 1934 Securities Act.

Securities Investments in a common enterprise with profits to come largely from the efforts of others.

Securities Act of 1933 The federal law governing the initial issuance and sale of securities to the public.

Securities and Exchange Commission (SEC) Federal agency responsible for enforcement of federal securities laws.

Securities Exchange Act of 1934 The federal law governing secondary sales of securities, the markets, and the firms dealing with securities.

Security agreement Contract that creates a security interest.

Security interest Lien in personal property; created under Article IX of the UCC.

Self-incrimination Protection provided under the Fifth Amendment of not being required to be a witness against oneself.

Separation of powers Principle of U.S. Constitution that divides authority for various government functions among the three branches of government.

Sexual harassment Unlawful suggestions, contact, or other advances in the workplace; prohibited under federal law.

Sherman Act Original federal antitrust law; prohibits monopolization and horizontal trade restraints such as price-fixing and boycotts.

Shopkeeper's privilege A defense to the tort of false imprisonment for store owners; allows reasonable detention of shoppers upon reasonable suspicion of shoplifting.

Short-swing profits Profits made by corporate insiders during a period of less than six months between purchase and sale.

SIPs State implementation plans; state plans for attaining federal air quality standards.

Sixth Amendment Amendment to U.S. Constitution that guarantees the right to a jury trial in criminal cases.

Slander Tort of oral defamation.

Slander of title Slander of business.

Slowdown Economic weapon that interrupts the employer's business but falls short of a stoppage or strike.

Small claims court Specialized court designed to allow the hearing of claims of limited monetary amounts without the complexities of litigation and without attorneys.

Small company doctrine Exemption from merger prohibitions that permits two smaller firms to merge in order to compete better against other larger firms in the market.

Social Security Act Federal legislation that provides for the benefits of social security and the payment mechanisms through FICA deductions.

Sole outlet Manufacturer's only designated seller in a particular area.

Sole proprietorship Method of business ownership; one person owns business, receives all profits, and is personally liable for all debts.

Solid Waste Disposal Act Federal law that provided money to state and local governments for research in solid waste disposal.

Security interest UCC lien on personal property.

Special warranty deed Deed that offers title protection only for grantor's period of ownership.

Specific performance Equitable remedy in which party asks for performance of the contract as damages.

Standing Right to bring suit; party who has experienced damages.

Stare decisis Latin term for "let the decision stand"; the doctrine of following or distinguishing case precedent.

State codes State laws passed by legislatures.

Statute of frauds Generic term referring to statutes requiring certain contracts to be in writing.

Statute of limitations Generic term referring to various state statutes controlling the time periods in which suits must be brought by plaintiffs; time varies according to the nature of the suit; for example, contract statutes of limitations are generally four years.

Statutory law Law codified and written; passed by some governmental entity.

Stipulated means In contracts, a method of acceptance specified or stipulated in the offer; if followed by the offeree, the mailbox rule applies for the timing of the acceptance.

Stock restrictions Restrictions on the transfer of stock in a corporation; must be noted on the shares to be valid.

Strict liability Degree of liability for conduct; an absolute standard of liability.

Strict tort liability Standard established under the Restatement of Torts that holds product manufacturers and sellers liable for injuries resulting from their products regardless of whether they knew of the danger that caused the injury.

Strike Economic weapon of employees; refusal to work for a given period of time.

Subchapter S corporation or S corporation A form of corporation for tax purposes that permits the direct flow-through of income and losses to the shareholders.

Subject matter jurisdiction The right of a court to hear disputes involving certain areas of law and/or amounts.

Subliminal persuasion A method of advertising using subtle and undetected means to persuade consumers to make purchases.

Submarket In antitrust law, a segment of a market examined for purposes of determining either the impact on competition of a merger or the market strength of a competitor (for example, tennis court shoes as a submarket of the tennis shoe market).

Substantial evidence test Basis for challenging the actions of an administrative agency on the grounds that the rule promulgated was not based on enough evidence.

Substantial performance Contract defense for performing a contract slightly differently than what was agreed upon; justification for substitute but equal performance; generally applicable in construction contracts.

Substantive due process Constitutional protection that requires laws to apply equally to all and not to deny property or rights without prior notice.

Substantive laws Laws that give rights and responsibilities to individuals.

Summary judgment Method for terminating a case at the trial court level when there are no issues of fact and only a decision on the application of law needs to be made.

Summons Court document issued to the defendant in a lawsuit that explains the requirement of filing an answer and the time period in which it must be done.

Sunset law Law that places an ending date on an administrative agency; if not renewed, an agency terminates at sunset on a particular date; the sun sets on the agency.

Superfund Federal fund used to clean up toxic waste disposal areas.

Superfund Amendment and Reauthorization Act Federal legislation extending CERCLA's authority and the liability of property owners and waste handlers for the cleanup of polluted lands.

Superior skill, foresight, and industry Defense to monopolization based on "building a better mousetrap" and customers flocking to your door.

Supremacy Clause Constitutional provision allowing federal laws to preempt state laws where Congress intended or where the regulation is pervasive.

Supreme Court Reporter Series of volumes reporting the decisions of the U.S. Supreme Court.

Surface Mining & Reclamation Act of 1977 Federal law that requires restoration of surface coal mining land.

T

Taft-Hartley Act Labor-Management Relations Act; federal law governing management in union relations.

Takeover Process of one firm taking over another firm.

Target firm The firm to be taken over in a takeover.

10-K form Annual report filed with the SEC; required of all 1934 Act firms.

10-Q form Quarterly report filed with the SEC; required of all 1934 Act firms.

Tender offer Offer to more than 10 percent of the shareholders of a firm for the purchase of their shares; generally part of a takeover effort.

Theft Crime of taking property away from another permanently.

Three-day cooling-off period Under Regulation Z, the period a buyer has to change his or her mind about a transaction initiated in the home.

Tippee Party who is privy to inside information about a corporation or its securities and uses the information to trade securities profitably.

Title insurance Insurance purchased for buyer's benefit; insures the land title from recorded defects.

Title VII Portion of the Civil Rights Act of 1964 prohibiting employment discrimination.

Tombstone ad Ad run in newspapers announcing an upcoming securities offering; permissible after the registration statement is filed but not yet effective; must indicate it is not an offer for sale.

Tort Private intentional or negligent wrong against an individual.

Toxic pollutant EPA classification of pollutant that requires the highest level of treatment prior to release.

Toxic Substances Control Act Federal statute governing the control of the release of toxic substances into the environment.

Trade fixtures Personal property used in a trade or business that is attached to real property but is considered personal property.

Trade libel Libel of a business.

Trademark The symbol of a firm; entitled to federal protection for exclusive use.

Trade name Name of a firm or product; entitled to federal protection for exclusive use.

Trade restraints Obstacles to free and open competition.

Trade secret A protected method for doing business or an item crucial to a business's success (such as a customer list).

Traffic court Lesser trial court in which traffic cases and violation of other city ordinances are tried.

Transfer restrictions Limitations on the resale of shares of a corporation.

Treaty In international law, an agreement between two or more nations.

Treble damages In antitrust law and securities law, a civil remedy that permits successful claimants to recover three times the amount of their actual damages.

Trial Process in a court of presenting evidence for a determination of guilt, innocence, or liability.

Trial court First stop in the judicial system when a suit is filed; the court where the case is presented and witnesses testify.

Trial de novo Latin for "trial again" or "trial anew."

Trusteeship National union's action of taking control of a local union's treasury (through a trustee) and suspending all democratic union processes.

Truth-in-Lending Act (TILA) The Consumer Credit Protection Act; affords disclosure protection for consumer debt.

Two-tier offer Takeover strategy in which minority shareholders are squeezed out after a tender offer is successful and the target firm is merged into a subsidiary.

Tying Anticompetitive behavior requiring the purchase of another product in order to get the product actually needed.

U

U.S. Constitution The cornerstone of the federal government's structure and the basis of private citizens' rights and protections.

U.S. Court of Appeals The appellate court of the federal system; hears appeals from lower federal courts.

U.S. Government Manual Book published by the U.S. government that includes descriptions and organizational charts for all federal agencies.

U.S. Supreme Court The highest appellate court in the federal system and also the highest appellate court for state appeals.

Ultra vires Action taken beyond the scope of authority; with federal agencies, action taken that is beyond the Congressional authority given in the enabling statute.

Unauthorized appropriation The use of someone's name, likeness, or voice without permission and for commercial advantage.

Unconscionable Term used to describe contracts that are grossly unfair to one side in the contract; a defense to an otherwise valid contract.

Underwriter In securities transactions, the brokerage house offering the shares in a company to the public.

Undue influence Contract defense based on one party taking advantage of a relationship of trust and confidence.

Unemployment compensation Funds paid to individuals who are without a job while they attempt to find new employment; a federal program administered by the states.

Unenforceable contract A contract that cannot be enforced because of a procedural error.

Unfair labor practice An economic weapon used by an employer or employee that is prohibited under the federal labor laws.

Uniform Commercial Code (UCC) Uniform law adopted in 49 states governing sales contracts for goods, commercial paper, security interests, documents of title, and securities transfers.

Uniform laws Series of laws drafted by groups of business people, law professors, and lawyers; adopted and codified by states to help attain a more uniform commercial environment for transactions.

Uniform Partnership Act (UPA) Uniform law adopted in forty-eight states governing the creation, operation, and termination of general partnerships.

Unilateral contract Contract in which one party promises to perform in exchange for the performance of the other party.

Unincorporated association A group of individuals that acts as an entity but has no legal existence.

Union shop A plant or business controlled by a union.

United Nations Convention on Contracts for the International Sale of Goods (CISG) U.N. version of Article II on sales of goods for international transactions.

United States Code (U.S.C.) Statutory volumes of congressional enactments.

United States Reports Official U.S. government reporter for Supreme Court decisions.

Universal treaty A treaty accepted and recognized by all countries; for example, the Warsaw Convention on air travel.

UPA Uniform Partnership Act.

Usury Charging interest above the statutory maximum.

V

Venue Geographic location of a trial.

Verdict The outcome or decision in a trial.

Vertical merger Merger between a manufacturer and a retailer; a merger between two companies in the chain of vertical distribution.

Vertical trade restraint Trade restraints among firms in the distribution system.

Void contract In contracts, a contract that neither side is required to perform; for example, an illegal contract is void.

Voidable contract In contracts, a contract one side can choose not to perform; for example, a minor can choose not to perform his or her contract.

Voir dire Process of questioning jurors to screen for bias and determine whether a lawyer wishes to exercise his or her peremptory challenge.

Voting trust Arrangement among shareholders to gain uniform voting and some power by signing over voting rights on shares to a trustee; shareholders still get dividends but trustee votes the shares; must be in writing and recorded with the corporation.

W

Wagner Act National Labor Relations Act; federal law governing the rights of unions and establishing the NLRB.

Warrant Court document authorizing an arrest or a search.

Warranty A promise of performance or guarantee of quality on a good or service.

Warranty deed Highest level of title protection in real property transfer; greatest number of warranties.

Warranty of merchantability Warranty given in all sales by merchants that provides that goods are of average quality, are packaged properly, and will perform normally.

Warsaw Convention Agreement among various nations on the liability of air carriers for injuries, accidents, loss of luggage, and so on; an international agreement.

Watered shares Shares for which par value was not paid; shareholder is liable for the difference between what was paid and the par value per share.

Water Pollution Control Act of 1948 First federal law directed at water pollution; authorized the Surgeon General to study the problem.

Water Quality Act (1965) First federal law to set water quality standards.

Wheeler-Lea Act Amendment to the FTC Act that permits prosecution under Section 5 if a consumer is injured, even though there is no injury to a competitor.

Whistle-blowing Act of an employee of a company disclosing to a regulatory agency or the press any violations of laws by his or her employer.

Williams Act Federal law governing the tender offer process.

Worker Adjustment and Retraining Notification Act of 1988 Federal plant-closing law requiring advance notice of plant closures and layoffs.

Work product An attorney's thoughts, research, and strategy in a case, nondiscoverable.

Workers' compensation State system of providing for payment for workers injured on the job to avoid having liability suits by employees against employers.

Working requirements Non-U.S. countries' patent requirement that the process or product be placed on the market within a certain time after the patent is granted, or the patent protection is lost.

Writ of certiorari Order of the U.S. Supreme Court for hearing a case. *See* Certiorari.

Y

Yellow-dog contract Agreement by employee with employer whereby employee will not join union.

Z

Zero-base budgeting Process of agency budgeting in which the budget starts with a figure of zero rather than at the level of the previous year's budget; effect is to require an agency to justify its functions and expenditures for each budget period.

Table of Cases

*Cases with an asterisk were actually presented in the text.

N

Table of Products, People, and Companies

Index

A

http://infomanage.com/~icr/abd/ — **Asian Business Daily** Asian Business Daily, maintained by International Competitive Research, provides current Asian business information.

http://www.asia1.com.sg/ — **AsiaOne** AsiaOne provides a gateway to Asia for business, news, entertainment and education.

http://www.backgroundbriefing.com/ — **Background Briefing** Background Briefing provides background information and context for dozens of major news stories.

http://www.businessweek.com/ — **Business Week** Review stories and features from the current edition of *Business Week*.

http://cnn.com — **CNN Interactive** CNN Interactive offers news briefs, comprehensive examinations of major issues and events, special features, and more in a constantly-updated site.

http://www.cnnfn.com/ — **CNNfn, the financial network** CNNfn, the financial network, offers news stories and commentary, as produced by CNN, tailored to business professionals.

http://www.eo.net/ — **Europe Online** Europe Online offers up-to-date news and information, business assistance, online games, and the latest CD charts.

http://www.fortune.com — **Fortune** Review stories and features from the current edition of *Fortune*.

http://www.ft-television.com/ — **FT Television** European business and economics headlines, updated throughout the day, from Financial Times Television.

http://www.hoovers.com/ — **Hoover's Online** Hoover's Online offers a comprehensive business database, frequent news updates, and a powerful search engine.

http://www.vmedia.com/vvc/onlcomp/business/ — **Internet Business Online** A hypertext version of *Internet Business* Online, the Ventana Press guide covering the complete range of business topics on the Web.

http://www.interquote.com/ — **InterQuote** InterQuote provides information on stocks, options, indices, funds, and futures from most U.S. and Canadian exchanges.

http://www.irin.com/ — **Investor Relations Information Network** Corporate Document Systems has created a centralized location --the Investor Relations Information Network--for access to company annual reports.

http://www.leadstory.com/ — **LeadStory** Lead Story, part of the AT&T Business Network, examines timely news topics, providing complete analysis, opinion, and background from a wide variety of sources on the Web.

http://www.prnewswire.com/ — **PR Newswire** PR Newswire specializes in the global electronic distribution of company news releases to the media and the financial community.

http://www.switchboard.com/ — **Switchboard** Switchboard is a free nationwide residential and business directory.